AMERICAN URBAN HISTORY

AMERICAN URBAN HISTORY

An Interpretive Reader with Commentaries
SECOND EDITION

EDITED BY

ALEXANDER B. CALLOW, Jr.
UNIVERSITY OF CALIFORNIA, SANTA BARBARA

NEW YORK
OXFORD UNIVERSITY PRESS
LONDON   1973   TORONTO

4-4-73

To my mother and father

1759756

Preface to Second Edition

I have performed massive surgery upon the old edition to bring out this re- vised second edition. Over a third of the essays were replaced with more up- to-date works. Newness is not necessarily a virtue, as any winetaster knows, so my criterion of selection remains the same as it was for the 1969 edition: Are the essays interpretive, analytical, thoughtful, well-written, and do they make contribution to the field? I have also extensively revised older commentaries and chopped out two chapter and replaced them with "The City in Politics," and "The City in the Life of the Newcomer." I have retained the reference footnotes for each essay because I have found after teaching American urban history for a number of years that they are helpful to students who are writ- ing research papers or who wish to pursue a topic further. Via the footnote, I have also tried to up-date and amplify the bibliographical material, especially those books and articles which have appeared since the first edition. And, finally, I have stayed with the interpretive interdisciplinary approach, for I still am firmly convinced that it is the best way to understand something as challenging and complex as the American city.

I would like to acknowledge my appreciation for the suggestions from friends and colleagues. They make the notion of a community of scholars shine. My thanks to Professors Melvin G. Holli, Joel Arthur Tarr, Humbert S. Nelli, Dwight Hoover, William Bullough, and Bayrd Still. For their ideas and criti- cisms, I would like to acknowledge and thank some of my graduate students who are scrambling for their Third Degrees, and will soon become urban his- torians: Robert Mullins (who was a resourceful and imaginative with the second edition as he was with the first), Raymond Tracy, Peter Costillo, Donald Drake, and William Bennett Peters.

ALEXANDER B. CALLOW, JR.

Santa Barbara, California
June 21, 1972

Contents

Introduction

This is a book about what O. Henry called "a ragged purple dream, the wonderful, cruel, enchanting, bewildering, fatal, great city." It is an attempt to achieve a perspective on a phenomenon that in the past was a critical unifying force in our history and in the present has been described as our No. 1 problem—the American city.

American Urban History is neither a narrative textbook, a collection of primary documents, nor a combination of "conflicting" interpretations. It is an attempt to bring together, chronologically and topically, widely scattered interpretative essays that illuminate important themes and problems in American urban history and encourage an analytical approach to the study of the city. Some selections are broad in scope; others tackle specific topics; none are definitive, but most are provocative and well written. This is, then, largely a book of ideas, introducing what Daniel Boorstin calls "organizing ideas," concepts that fashion the bony, intellectual anatomy of American urban history and give shape to the countless "facts" about the American city.

Each of the nine chapters is preceded by a commentary that introduces the major ideas of the readings, correlates them with the central historical theme of the chapter, underscores notions of particular analytical interest, and raises further questions suggested (or ignored) by the selected essays, in the hope they will not only serve as guidelines but also that they and the selections will be the hors d'oeuvres to a larger feast if the student is excited to plunge deeper, through independent reading and research. Taken together, the commentaries and the selections themselves—especially the excellent survey of the literature of American urban history by Dwight Hoover in the Epilogue—will suggest ideas and sources for research papers, joint research projects, critical book reviews, and themes for class discussions.

This book is predicated upon the proposition that urban history should have an inter-disciplinary approach. Consequently, the selections include some of our best American urban historians as well as some of our ablest students of other phases of urban affairs, sociologists like Herbert Gans and Robert Merton, political scientists like Scott Greer, and city planners like Charles Abrams—men who have something to say, say it well, and, importantly, have an historical orientation.

This book is also based upon a few underlying principles that I feel should characterize the study of the American city. Broadly defined, there are two schools of thought concerning the best way to approach and to understand the history of the American city. One group sees the city as a reflection of national history—indeed, as one of the main currents in the mainstream of American history. Its members seek to reveal the impact of the city upon American history and the impact of history upon the city. The other group stresses the importance of the city as a singularly important phenomenon in itself. To this group the city has coherence, unity, muscles, and sinews of its own. They avoid stitching urban history into the conventional periodization of American history, such as the City and Jacksonian Democracy, the City and the Civil War, the City and the New Deal, insisting that such an approach is archaic and myopic for at least two reasons: the characteristics of urban developments do not always coincide with developments in national history, and such an approach obscures developments that we urgently need to know more about, namely, the various processes of urbanization. I occupy a middle position between these two approaches, not unmindful of both the smugness that moderation implies and the fact that one can get run over in the middle of the road. It seems to me that the two views are not necessarily contradictory and that a better perspective is achieved by trying to balance the two, and I have made my selections accordingly. In a day when we still do not have consensus on what the city is, as well as what we really mean by *urban,* the door should be open to all kinds of approaches. Our future depends upon it.

AMERICAN URBAN HISTORY

I THE CITY IN HISTORY

It has been said that the history of civilization "from Memphis, Egypt, to Memphis, Tennessee," is written in the rise and fall of cities. Perhaps, paradoxically, the city in history has been both inseparable from the course of human history yet a separate historical phenomenon of its own. It has mirrored some of the major tensions of the human condition—rich *vs.* poor, greed *vs.* compassion, change *vs.* tradition, the individual *vs.* the mass, ideology *vs.* ideology. It has reflected the best and worst in man—the hospital and the tenement, the clearinghouse of ideas, music, and the arts, and the refuge of filth, disease, and misery. Indeed, few of man's other creations have been so bewilderingly complex, so infinitely diverse, so compounded by extremes and contradictions.

There is no better example of this than the American city, until recently the scene of unprecedented rapid urbanization. In comparison with the European urban heritage, which stretches back roughly 5500 years, the American transformation from village to city was achieved in a dazzlingly short space of time. From the eighteenth century on, Americans experienced the painful yet rewarding metamorphosis of an agrarian nation becoming an urban-industrial giant that left few of her political, economic, and social institutions untouched, be they the farm, the factory, or the family. In 1790, for example, only a little over 4 per cent of the American population lived in cities; today 70 per cent of Americans live in urban areas. Richard Hofstadter summed it up well: "The United States was born in the country and has moved to the city."

, All of this, of course, begs several questions. How do we account for the rise of the city? What historical forces, what processes of urbanization played determining roles? What was the impact of the rise of the city upon American society? It is the purpose of this chapter to grapple with these questions by showing that behind the maze of complexities, were patterns—political, economic, social, technological—in as well as outside the city, that shaped the rise of urban America and gave its history some coherence.

We begin with three essays, each broad in scope, each analytical and synthetical in nature, each bristling with organizing ideas that illuminate successively the rise of the city, major themes in American urban history, and the internal generating forces behind the city itself. We begin, then, with generalizations, hoping to sketch guidelines which from the very beginning may help one to steer a course through the sea of "facts" about American urban history.

Gideon Sjoberg sets the course by mapping, as it were, the embarkation port, man's first urban creation—the preindustrial city. While this is not *American* urban history, it does provide an expansive historical background making American urban history more meaningful. After all, urbanization was a world-wide phenomenon. American cities were not popped out of a vacuum; hence, the more insights we can get about our antecedents the better comprehension we will have of our own experience. European scholars have chided American historians for their narrow provincialism which often neglects the critical fact that historically we are a part of Western civilization.

In a remarkably compact and well-organized essay, Sjoberg gallops through the centuries, pinning his discussion upon two major questions: what forces account for the origin of cities, and what stages did cities pass through before reaching modern times? Both answers depend upon the technological, economic, social, and political patterns of three levels of human development: the preurban or "folk" society, the preindustrial or "feudal" society, and the modern or "industrial" society. It was in the preindustrial period that the world's first cities emerged, mainly because of the interrelationship of several important factors: a surplus of food, the development of a class structure which provided leadership and harnessed manpower, the appearance of writing which permitted a written tradition, and a technology which exploited new sources of energy. Contingent upon these elements were two other necessities of urbanization: 1) a social system of fulltime specialists, who could handle the food surplus and build the public buildings, city walls and irrigation systems, 2) a favorable environment that yielded an agricultural and water supply to sustain the urban dwellers.

Sjoberg traces the evolution of cities over time, from the Near East and the Orient to the Mesoamerica cities of the New World. He relates the rise and fall of empires to urbanization, and concludes with a discussion of the emergence of the first modern cities of England. Implicit throughout Sjoberg's analysis is that each period of urbanization builds upon the other in a pattern of evolution. This thesis sets the stage for a major argument among urbanists regarding the development of the modern city—was the process evolution or revolution?

In the next selection, Oscar Handlin provides a historical background, without which the history of the American city is incomprehensible. For the American city was heir to a clutch of forces that generated one of the main turning points in world history: the conversion of the medieval pre-industrial city into the sprawling, creative, and disruptive modern city. His thesis is that this transformation constituted not a simple process of evolution, but a drastic break from the past. The continuity of history was ruptured by the emergence of something singularly new, the modern city. Handlin sees the catalysts of this remarkable phenomenon as the rise of the centralized nation-state, technological innovations, the novel developments in production and capital constituting the rise of modern industry, and the subsequent explosion in the urban population. If one major characteristic of the emerging modern city must be underscored, however, it is the change and disruption of the heart of the medieval pre-industrial social system—the traditional, corporate, communal organization of households, at once a social and economic institution.[1]

The American city, then, was born and grew into adolescence during the transitional stage between the pre-industrial and modern industrial city. In a pioneer essay Arthur Schlesinger, Sr., evaluates the evolution of over two hundred years of the American urban experience. This essay is to American urban history what Frederick Jackson Turner's essay was to American western history. It is a sweeping synthesis that provokes attention to a neglected field, and it is a reassessment of American history. It has the strengths and weaknesses of the Turner essay—imaginative insights and a tendency toward exaggeration, perhaps an occupational hazard for pioneer historians. It is, in fact, anti-Turnerian in character, an attempt to balance Turner's thesis that the national character and American institutions were created out of the successive frontiers of the westward movement. "The city," Schlesinger declares, "no less than the frontier, has been a major factor in American civilization. Without an appreciation of the role of both the story is only half told." Essentially, Schlesinger is saying that the city was a frontier as important and dynamic as that of the western wilderness.

The essay is particularly valuable as an introduction to some of the main organizing ideas of American urban history. With the finesse of the gifted generalizer, Schlesinger isolates some of the critical themes that accounted for the rise and particularly the impact of the city upon American history, such as urban rivalry, urban imperialism, a sense of collective responsibility, and the

1. For interesting, and conflicting, interpretations of the city in history, see Henri Pirenne, *Medieval Cities* (Princeton: Princeton University Press, 1925); Max Weber, *The City* (Glencoe, Ill.: The Free Press of Glencoe, 1958); Lewis Mumford, *The City in History* (New York: Harcourt, Brace and World, 1961); and especially, Gideon Sjoberg, *The Preindustrial City* (New York: The Free Press, 1960); and Jane Jacobs, *The Economy of Cities* (New York: Random House, 1969).

city's contributions to American cultural and economic life. Schlesinger may have underplayed the darker sidé of urban history, overstated the rift between farm and city, and elevated city dwellers at the expense of agrarians, but he has exposed some of the anatomy of the American city in history.[2]

2. For a more detailed criticism of the Schlesinger essay, see William Diamond, "On the Dangers of an Urban Interpretation of History," in Eric F. Goldman (ed.), *Historiography and Urbanization* (Baltimore: The Johns Hopkins Press, 1941), pp. 67-108.

Other broad approaches to the American city include W. Stull Holt, "Some Consequences of the Urban Movement in American History," *Pacific Historical Review*, Vol. XXII (November 1953), pp. 337-51; Emrys Jones, *Towns and Cities* (London and New York: Oxford, 1966), Leo F. Schnore, "The City as a Social Organism," *Urban Affairs Quarterly*, Vol I, No. 3 (March 1966), pp. 58-69. See also Philip M. Hauser and Leo F. Schnore (eds.), *The Study of Urbanization* (New York: John Wiley, 1965), for a series of valuable essays by a number of social scientists, discussing the methods and literature of their respective disciplines.

The Origin and Evolution of Cities

GIDEON SJOBERG

Men began to live in cities some 5,500 years ago . . . however, the proportion of the human population concentrated in cities did not begin to increase significantly until about 100 years ago. These facts raise two questions that this chapter proposes to answer. First, what factors brought about the origin of cities? Second, through what evolutionary stages did cities pass before the modern epoch of urbanization? The answers to these questions are intimately related to three major levels of human organization, each of which is characterized by its own technological, economic, social and political patterns. The least complex of the three—the "folk society"—is preurban and even preliterate; it consists typically of small numbers of people, gathered in self-sufficient homogeneous groups, with their energies wholly (or almost wholly) absorbed by the quest for food. Under such conditions there is little or no surplus of food; consequently the folk society permits little or no specialization of labor or distinction of class.

Although some folk societies still exist today, similar human groups began the slow process of evolving into more complex societies millenniums ago, through settlement in villages and through advances in technology and organizational structure. This gave rise to the second level of organization: civilized preindustrial, or "feudal," society. Here there is a surplus of food because of the selective cultivation of grains—

From *Scientific American*, Vol. 213, No. 3 (September 1965), pp. 54-62. Reprinted by permission of the publisher. Gideon Sjoberg is Professor of Sociology at the University of Texas.

high in yield, rich in biological energy and suited to long-term storage—and often also because of the practice of animal husbandry. The food surplus permits both the specialization of labor and the kind of class structure that can, for instance, provide the leadership and command the manpower to develop and maintain extensive irrigation systems (which in turn make possible further increases in the food supply). Most preindustrial societies possess metallurgy, the plow and the wheel—devices, or the means of creating devices, that multiply both the production and the distribution of agricultural surpluses.

Two other elements of prime importance characterize the civilized preindustrial stage of organization. One is writing: not only the simple keeping of accounts but also the recording of historical events, law, literature and religious beliefs. Literacy, however, is usually confined to a leisured elite. The other element is that this stage of organization has only a few sources of energy other than the muscles of men and livestock; the later preindustrial societies harnessed the force of the wind to sail the seas and grind grain and also made use of water power.

It was in the context of this second type of society that the world's first cities developed. Although preindustrial cities still survive, the modern industrial city is associated with a third level of complexity in human organization, a level characterized by mass literacy, a fluid class system and, most important, the tremendous technological breakthrough to new sources of inanimate energy that produced and still sustains the industrial revolution. Viewed against the background of this three-tiered structure, the first emergence of cities at the level of civilized preindustrial society can be more easily understood.

Two factors in addition to technological advance beyond the folk-society level were needed for cities to emerge. One was a special type of social organization by means of which the agricultural surplus produced by technological advance could be collected, stored, and distributed. The same apparatus could also organize the labor force needed for large-scale construction, such as public buildings, city walls and irrigation systems. A social organization of this kind requires a variety of full-time specialists directed by a ruling elite. The latter, although few in number, must command sufficient political power—reinforced by an ideology, usually religious in character—to ensure that the peasantry periodically relinquishes a substantial part of the agricultural yield in order to support the city dwellers. The second factor required was a favorable environment, providing not only fertile soil for the peasants but also a water supply adequate for both agriculture and urban consumption. Such conditions exist in geologically mature and mid-latitude river valleys, and it was in such broad alluvial regions that the world's earliest cities arose.

What is a city? It is a community of substantial size and population density that shelters a variety of nonagricultural specialists, including a literate elite. I emphasize the role of literacy as an ingredient of urban life for good reasons. Even though writing systems took centuries to evolve, their presence or absence serves as a convenient means for distinguishing between genuinely urban communities and others that in spite of their large size and dense population must be considered quasi-urban or nonurban. This is because once a community achieves or otherwise acquires the technological advance we call writing, a major transformation in the social order occurs; with a written tradition rather than an oral one it is possible to create more complex administrative and legal systems and more rigorous systems of thought. Writing is indispensable to the development of mathematics, astronomy and the other sciences; its existence thus implies the emergence of a number of significant specializations within the social order.

As far as is known, the world's first cities took shape around 3500 B.C. in the Fertile Crescent, the eastern segment of which includes Mesopotamia: the valleys of the Tigris and the Euphrates. Not only were the soil and water supply there suitable; the region was a crossroads that facilitated repeated contacts among peoples of divergent cultures for thousands of years. The resulting mixture of alien and indigenous crafts and skills must have made its own contribution to the evolution of the first true cities out of the village settlements in lower Mesopotamia. These were primarily in Sumer but also to some extent in Akkad, a little to the north. Some—such as Eridu, Erech, Lagash and Kish—are more familiar to archaeologists than to others; Ur, a later city, is more widely known.

These early cities were much alike; for one thing, they had a similar technological base. Wheat and barley were the cereal crops, bronze was the metal, oxen pulled plows and there were wheeled vehicles. Moreover, the city's leader was both king and high priest; the peasants' tribute to the city god was stored in the temple granaries. Luxury goods recovered from royal tombs and temples attest the existence of skilled artisans, and the importation of precious metals and gems from well beyond the borders of Mesopotamia bespeaks a class of merchant-traders. Pop-

ulation sizes can only be guessed in the face of such unknowns as the average number of residents per household and the extent of each city's zone of influence. The excavator of Ur, Sir Leonard Woolley, estimates that soon after 2000 B.C. the city proper housed 34,000 people; in my opinion, however, it seems unlikely that, at least in the earlier periods, even the larger of these cities contained more than 5,000 to 10,000 people, including part-time farmers on the cities' outskirts.

The valley of the Nile, not too far from Mesopotamia, was also a region of early urbanization. To judge from Egyptian writings of a later time, there may have been urban communities in the Nile delta by 3100 B.C. Whether the Egyptian concept of city living had "diffused" from Mesopotamia or was independently invented (and perhaps even earlier than in Mesopotamia) is a matter of scholarly debate; in any case the initial stages of Egyptian urban life may yet be discovered deep in the silt of the delta, where scientific excavation is only now being undertaken.

Urban communities—diffused or independently invented—spread widely during the third and second millenniums B.C. By about 2500 B.C. the cities of Mohenjo-Daro and Harappa were flourishing in the valley of the Indus River in what is now Pakistan. Within another 1,000 years at the most the middle reaches of the Yellow River in China supported urban settlements. A capital city of the Shang Dynasty (about 1500 B.C.) was uncovered near Anyang before World War II; current archaeological investigations by the Chinese may well prove that city life was actually established in ancient China several centuries earlier.

The probability that the first cities of

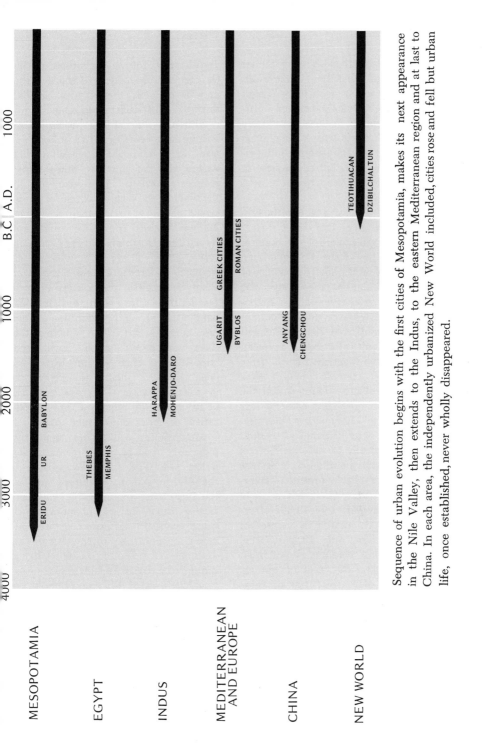

Sequence of urban evolution begins with the first cities of Mesopotamia, makes its next appearance in the Nile Valley, then extends to the Indus, to the eastern Mediterranean region and at last to China. In each area, the independently urbanized New World included, cities rose and fell but urban life, once established, never wholly disappeared.

Egypt were later than those of Sumer and the certainty that those of the Indus and Yellow rivers are later lends weight to the argument that the concept of urban living diffused to these areas from Mesopotamia. Be this as it may, none will deny that in each case the indigenous population contributed uniquely to the development of the cities in its own area.

In contrast to the situation in the Old World, it appears certain that diffusion played an insignificant role or none at all in the creation of the pre-Columbian cities of the New World. The peoples of Mesoamerica—notably the Maya, the Zapotecs, the Mixtecs and the Aztecs —evidently developed urban communities on a major scale, the exact extent of which is only now being revealed by current investigations. Until quite recently, for example, many New World archaeologists doubted that the Maya had ever possessed cities; it was the fashion to characterize their impressive ruins as ceremonial centers visited periodically by the members of a scattered rural population. It is now clear, however, that many such centers were genuine cities. At the Maya site of Tikal in Guatemala some 3,000 structures have been located in an area of 6.2 square miles; only 10 percent of them are major ceremonial buildings. Extrapolating on the basis of test excavations of more than 100 of these lesser structures, about two-thirds of them appear to have been dwellings. If only half the present-day average household figure for the region (5.6 members) is applied to Tikal, its population would have been more than 5,000. At another major Maya site— Dzibilchaltun in Yucatán—a survey of less than half of the total area has revealed more than 8,500 structures.

Teotihuacán, the largest urban site in the region of modern Mexico City, may have had a population of 100,000 during the first millennium A.D.

Although only a few examples of writing have been identified at Teotihuacán, it is reasonable to assume that writing was known; there were literate peoples elsewhere in Mesoamerica at the time. By the same token, the achievements of the Maya in such realms as mathematics and astronomy would have forced the conclusion that they were an urban people even in the absence of supporting archaeological evidence. Their invention of the concept of zero (evidently earlier than the Hindus' parallel feat) and their remarkably precise calculation of the length of the solar year would surely have been impossible if their literate elite had been scattered about the countryside in villages rather than concentrated in urban centers where a cross-fertilization of ideas could take place.

Mesoamerica was by no means the only area of large, dense communities in the New World; they also existed in the Andean region. A culture such as the Inca, however, cannot be classified as truly urban. In spite of—perhaps because of—their possession of a mnemonic means of keeping inventories (an assemblage of knotted cords called a quipu) the Incas lacked any conventionalized set of graphic symbols for representing speech or any concepts other than numbers and certain broad classes of items. As a result they were denied such key structural elements of an urban community as a literate elite and a written heritage of law, religion and history. Although the Incas could claim major military, architectural and engineering triumphs and apparently were on the verge of achieving a civilized order, they were still quasi-urban at the time of the European conquest, much like the Dahomey, Ashanti and Yoruba peoples of Africa.

The New World teaches us two lessons. In Mesoamerica cities were created without animal husbandry, the wheel and an extensive alluvial setting. One reason for this is maize, a superior grain crop that produced a substantial food surplus with relatively little effort and thus compensated for the limited tools and nonriverine environment. In the Andean region imposing feats of engineering and an extensive division of labor were not enough, in the absence of writing, to give rise to a truly urban society.

In spite of considerable cultural diversity among the inhabitants of the Near East, the Orient and the New World, the early cities in all these regions had a number of organizational forms in common. The dominant pattern was theocracy—the king and the high priest were one. The elite had their chief residences in the city; moreover, they and their retainers and servants congregated mainly in the city's center. This center was the prestige area, where the most imposing religious and government buildings were located. Such a concentration had dual value: in an era when communications and transport were rudimentary, propinquity enhanced interaction among the elite; at the same time it gave the ruling class maximum protection from external attack.

At a greater distance from this urban nucleus were the shops and dwellings of artisans—masons, carpenters, smiths, jewelers, potters—many of whom served the elite. The division of labor into crafts, apparent in the earliest cities, became more complex with the passage of time. Artisan groups, some of which even in early times may have belonged to specific ethnic minorities, tended to establish themselves in special quarters or streets. Such has been characteristic of preindustrial cities in all cultural settings, from the earliest times to the present day. The poorest urbanites lived on the outskirts of the city, as did part-time or full-time farmers; their scattered dwellings finally blended into open countryside.

From its inception the city, as a residence of specialists, has been a continuing source of innovation. Indeed, the very emergence of cities greatly accelerated social and cultural change; to borrow a term from the late British archaeologist V. Gordon Childe, we can properly regard the "urban revolution" as being equal in significance to the agricultural revolution that preceded it and the industrial revolution that followed it. The city acted as a promoter of change in several ways. Many of the early cities arose on major transportation routes; new ideas and inventions flowed into them quite naturally. The mere fact that a large number of specialists were concentrated in a small area encouraged innovation, not only in technology but also in religious, philosophical and scientific thought. At the same time cities could be strong bulwarks of tradition. Some—for example Jerusalem and Benares—have become sacred in the eyes of the populace; in spite of repeated destruction Jerusalem has retained this status for more than two millenniums.

The course of urban evolution can be correctly interpreted only in relation to the parallel evolution of technology and social organization (especially political organization); these are not just prerequisites to urban life but the basis for its development. As centers of innovation cities provided a fertile setting for continued technological advances; these gains made possible the further expansion of cities. Advanced technology in turn depended on the increasingly complex division of labor, particularly in the political sphere. As an example, the early urban communities of Sumer were mere city-states with restricted hinterlands, but eventually trade and commerce extended over a much broader area, enabling these cities to draw on the human and material resources of a far wider and more diverse region and even bringing about the birth of new cities. The early empires of the Iron Age—for instance the Achaemenid Empire of Persia, established early in the sixth century B.C., and the Han Empire of China, established in the third century B.C.—far surpassed in scope any of the Bronze Age. And as empires became larger the size and grandeur of their cities increased. In fact, as Childe has observed, urbanization spread more rapidly during the first five centuries of the Iron Age than it had in all 15 centuries of the Bronze Age.

In the sixth and fifth centuries B.C. the Persians expanded their empire into western Turkestan and created a number of cities, often by building on existing villages. In this expansion Toprakkala, Merv and Marakanda (part of which was later the site of Samarkand) moved toward urban status. So too in India, at the close of the fourth century B.C., the Mauryas in the north spread their empire to the previously nonurban south and into Ceylon, giving impetus to the birth of cities such as Ajanta and Kanchi. Under the Ch'in and Han dynasties, between the third century B.C. and the third century A.D.,

city life took hold in most of what was then China and beyond, particularly to the south and west. The "Great Silk Road" extending from China to Turkestan became studded with such oasis cities as Suchow, Khotan and Kashgar; Nanking and Canton seem to have attained urban status at this time, as did the settlement that was eventually to become Peking.

At the other end of the Eurasian land mass the Phoenicians began toward the end of the second millennium B.C. to spread westward and to revive or establish urban life along the northern coast of Africa and in Spain. These coastal traders had by then developed a considerable knowledge of shipbuilding; this, combined with their far-reaching commercial ties and power of arms, made the Phoenicians lords of the Mediterranean for a time. Some centuries later the Greeks followed a rather similar course. Their city-states—actually in a sense small empires—created or rebuilt numerous urban outposts along the Mediterranean shore from Asia Minor to Spain and France, and eastward to the most distant coast of the Black Sea. The empire that did the most to diffuse city life into the previously nonurban regions of the West—France, Britain, the Low Countries, Germany west of the Rhine, central and even eastern Europe—was of course Rome.

Empires are effective disseminators of urban forms because they have to build cities with which to maintain military supremacy in conquered regions. The city strongholds, in turn, require an administrative apparatus in order to tap the resources of the conquered area and encourage the commerce needed both to support the military garrison and to enhance the wealth of the homeland. Even when a new city began as a purely commerical outpost, as was the case under the Phoenicians, some military and administrative support was necessary if it was to survive and function effectively in alien territory.

There is a significant relation between the rise and fall of empires and the rise and fall of cities; in a real sense history is the study of urban graveyards. The capitals of many former empires are today little more than ghostly outlines that only hint at a glorious past. Such was the fate of Babylon and Nineveh, Susa in Persia, Seleucia in Mesopotamia and Vijayanagar in India. Yet there are exceptions. Some cities have managed to survive over long periods of time by attaching themselves first to one empire and then to another. Athens, for example, did not decline after the collapse of Greek power; it was able to attach itself to the Roman Empire, which subsidized Athens as a center of learning. Once Rome fell, however, both the population and the prestige of Athens dwindled steadily; it was little more than a town until the rise of modern Greece in the 19th century. On the other hand, nearby Byzantium, a city-state of minor importance under Roman rule, not only became the capital of the Eastern Roman Empire and its successor, the Ottoman Empire, but as Istanbul remains a major city to this day.

In the light of the recurrent rise and decline of cities in so many areas of the world, one may ask just how urban life has been able to persist and why the skills of technology and social organization required for city-building were not lost. The answer is that the knowledge was maintained within the framework of empires—by means of written records and oral transmission by various specialists. Moreover, all empires have added to their store of skills relating to urban development as a result of diffusion—including the migration of specialists—from other civilized areas. At the same time various civilized or uncivilized subjects within empires have either been purposely educated by their conquerors or have otherwise gained access to the body of urban lore. The result on occasion is that the subjects challenge the power of the dominant ruling group.

The rise and fall of the Roman Empire provides a highly instructive case study that illuminates several relations between the life-span of cities and the formation and decline of empires. The Romans themselves took many elements of their civilization from the Etruscans, the Greeks and other civilized peoples who came under their sway. After Rome's northward expansion in western Europe and the proliferation of Roman cities in regions inhabited by so-called "barbarians"—in this instance preliterate, or "noncivilized," peoples—the Roman leaders were simply unable to staff all the bureaucratic posts with their own citizens. Some of the preliterates had to be trained to occupy such posts both in their own homelands and in the cities on the frontier. This process made it possible for the Romans to exploit the wealth of conquered regions and may have pacified the subjugated groups for a time, but in the long run it engendered serious conflicts. Eventually the Ostrogoths, Vandals, Burgundians and others—having been partially urbanized, having developed a literate elite of their own and having acquired many Roman technological and administrative skills—turned against the imperial power structure and engineered the collapse of Rome and its empire. Nor is this a unique case in history; analogies can be perceived in the modern independence movements of such European colonies as those in Africa.

With the breakup of the Roman Empire, not only did the city of Rome (which at its largest may have had more than 300,000 inhabitants) decline markedly but many borderland cities disappeared or shrank to small towns or villages. The decline was dramatic, but it is too often assumed that after the fall of Rome cities totally disappeared from western Europe. The historian E. Ewig has recently shown that many cities continued to function, particularly in Italy and southern France. Here, as in all civilized societies, the surviving cities were the chief residences and centers of activity for the political and religious elite who commanded the positions of power and privilege that persisted during the so-called Dark Ages.

In spite of Rome's decline many of the techniques and concepts associated with literate traditions in such fields as medicine and astronomy were kept alive; this was done both in the smaller surviving urban communities of Europe and in the eastern regions that had been ruled by the Romans—notably in the cities of the succeeding Eastern Roman Empire. Some of the technology and learning associated with Rome also became the basis for city life in the Arab empires that arose later in the Near East, North Africa, Spain and even central Asia. Indeed, the Byzantine and Arab empires—which had such major intellectual centers as Constantinople, Antioch, Damascus, Cairo and Baghdad—advanced beyond the knowledge inherited from antiquity. The Arabs, for example, took from the Hindus the concept of zero and the decimal system of numerals; by utilizing these concepts in both theory and practice they achieved significant advances over the knowledge that had evolved in the West. Eventually much of the new learning was passed on to Europe, where it helped to build the foundations for the industrial revolution.

In time Europe reestablished extensive commercial contact with the Byzantine and Arab empires; the interchange that followed played a significant role in the resurgence of urban life in southern Europe. The revitalization of trade was closely associated with the formation of several prosperous Italian city-states in the 10th and 11th centuries A.D. Venice and other cities eventually were transformed into small-scale empires whose colonies were scattered over the Mediterranean region—a hinterland from which the home cities were able to extract not only many of their necessities but also luxury items. By A.D. 1000 Venice had forged commercial links with Constantinople and other cities of the Eastern Roman Empire, partly as a result of the activities of the Greek colony in Venice. The Venetians were able to draw both on the knowledge of these resident Greeks and on the practical experience of sea captains and other specialists among them. Such examples make it clear that the Italian city-states were not merely local creations but rather products of a multiplicity of cultural forces.

Beginning at the turn of the 11th century A.D. many European cities managed to win a kind of independence from the rulers of the various principalities and petty kingdoms that surrounded them. Particularly in northern Italy urban communities came to enjoy considerable political autonomy. This provided an even more favorable atmosphere for commerce and encouraged the growth of such urban institutions as craft guilds. The European pattern is quite different from that in most of Asia (for instance in India and China), where the city was never able to attain a measure of autonomy within the broader political structure. At the same time the extent of self-rule enjoyed by the medieval European cities can be exaggerated and often is; by the close of the Middle Ages urban self-rule was already beginning to be lost. It is therefore evident that the political autonomy of medieval cities was only indirectly related to the eventual evolution of the industrial city.

It was the industrial revolution that brought about truly far-reaching changes in city life. In some nations today . . . the vast majority of the inhabitants are city dwellers; nearly 80 percent of the people in the United Kingdom live in cities, as do nearly 70 percent of the people of the U.S. Contrast this with the preindustrial civilized world, in which only a small, socially dominant minority lived in cities. The industrial revolution has also led to fundamental changes in the city's social geography and social organization; the industrial city is marked by a greater fluidity in the class system, the appearance of mass education and mass communications and the shift of some of the elite from the center of the city to its suburban outskirts.

Although there are still insufficient data on the rise of the industrial city— an event that took place sometime between 1750 and 1850—and although scholars disagree over certain steps in the process, the major forces at work in the two or three centuries before the industrial city emerged can be perceived clearly enough. Viewed in the light of Europe's preindustrial urban era, two factors are evident: the expansion of European power into other continents and the development of technology based on inanimate rather than animate sources of energy. The extension of European trade and exploration (which was to culminate in European colonialism) not only induced the growth of cities in Asia, in parts of non-urban Africa and in the Americas but also helped to raise the standard of living of Europeans themselves and made possible the support of more specialists. Notable among the last was a new occupational group—the scientists. The expansion abroad had helped to shatter the former world view of European scholars; they were now forced to cope with divergent ideas and customs. The discoveries reported by the far-ranging European explorers thus gave added impetus to the advance of science.

The knowledge gained through the application of the scientific method is the one factor above all others that made the modern city possible. This active experimental approach has enabled man to control the forces of nature to an extent undreamed of in the preindustrial era. It is true that in the course of several millenniums the literate elite of the preindustrial cities added significantly to man's store of knowledge in such fields as medicine, astronomy and mathematics, but these scholars generally scorned mundane activities and avoided contact with those whose work was on the practical level. This meant that the scholars' theories were rarely tested and applied in the everyday realm. Moreover, in accordance with prevailing religious thought, man was not to tamper with the natural order or to seek to control it, in either its physical or its social aspect. For example, medical scholars in Greek and Roman cities did not dissect human cadavers; not until the 16th century in Europe did a physician—Andreas Vesalius of Brussels—actually use findings obtained from dissection to revise ancient medical theories.

In the field of engineering, as late as the 17th century most advances were made by artisans who worked more or less on a trial-and-error basis. With the development of the experimental method, however, the learning of the elite became linked with the practical knowledge of the artisan, the barber-surgeon and the like; the result was a dramatic upsurge of knowledge and a fundamental revision of method that has been termed the scientific revolution. Such was the basis of the industrial revolution and the industrial city.

That the first industrial cities appeared in England is hardly fortuitous; England's social structure lacked the rigidity that characterized most of Europe and the rest of the civilized world. The Puritan tradition in England—an ethical system that supports utilitarianism and empiricism—did much to alter earlier views concerning man's place in nature. In England scholars could communicate with artisans more readily than elsewhere in Europe.

The advent of industrialism brought vast improvements in agricultural implements, farming techniques and food preservation, as well as in transportation and communication. Improved water supplies and more effective methods of sewage disposal allowed more people to congregate in cities. Perhaps the key invention was the steam engine, which provided a new and much more bountiful source of energy. Before that time, except for power from wind and water, man had no energy resources other than human and animal muscle. Now the factory system, with its mass production of goods and mechanization of activity, began to take hold. With it emerged a new kind of occupational structure: a structure that depends on highly specialized knowledge and that functions effectively only when the activities of the component occupations are synchronized. This process of industrialization has not only continued unabated to the present day but has actually accelerated with the rise of self-controlling machines.

The evolution of the industrial city was not an unmixed blessing. Historians have argued through many volumes the question of whether the new working class, including many migrants from the countryside, lost or gained economically and socially as the factory system destroyed older social patterns. Today, as industrialization moves inexorably across the globe, it continues to create social problems. Many surviving traditional cities evince in various ways the conflict between their preindustrial past and their industrial future. Nonetheless, the trend is clear: barring nuclear war, the industrial city will become the dominant urban form throughout the world, replacing forever the preindustrial city that was man's first urban creation.

The Modern City as a Field of Historical Study

Seen from above, the modern city edges imperceptibly out of its setting. There are no clear boundaries. Just now the white trace of the superhighway passed through cultivated fields; now it is lost in an aspha!t maze of streets and buildings. As one drives in from the airport or looks out from the train window, clumps of suburban housing, industrial complexes, and occasional green spaces flash by; it is hard to tell where city begins and country ends. Our difficulties with nomenclature reflect the indeterminacy of these limits; we reach for some vague concept of metropolis to describe the release of urban potential from its recognized ambit.

Contrast this visual image with that of the ancient or medieval city. It is still possible, coming up the Rhone, to see Sion in the Valais much as it looked four hundred years ago. From a long way off, one can make out its twin castles jutting into the sky. But the vineyards and orchards, the open fields and clumps of woodland, reach along the roadside to the edge of town. There, we cross a boundary to enter another universe, one which is whole and entire to itself. The record of sieges that lasted for months on end confirms the impression of self-containment. It is much so that Paris must once have been, and Athens.

The cities of the past were, of course,

vulnerable to external assault and to disruptive changes that emanated from without. Wars, shifts in patterns of production and trade, and cultural innovations gathered force outside their walls and yet decisively altered their history. But even when they held agricultural lands and even when some residents tilled the soil, those earlier communities possessed an individual life of their own in a sense that their modern successors do not. The ancient world had been a world of cities, but each had been a world unto itself. The towns of the Middle Ages and the Renaissance, even those of the eighteenth century, were self-contained entities walled off from their surroundings, with which they had only precisely defined contacts. They provided a marketplace for the products of rural craftsmen and husbandmen; but the main lines of their trade ran to distant, often overseas, places. They were centers of administration. But the governmental and ecclesiastical functionaries existed apart in detachment. The distance between London and Westminster, between Paris and Versailles, even between Milan and the castle of the Sforzas, was more than symbolic; it measured the genuine isolation of the life of the bourgeois.[1]

On the map today London and Paris and Milan occupy the same sites as did the places which bore those names three

From Oscar Handlin and John Burchard (eds.), *The Historian and the City* (Cambridge: The M.I.T. Press, 1963), pp. 1-26. Copyright © 1963 by the Massachusetts Institute of Technology and the President and Fellows of Harvard College. Reprinted by permission of The M.I.T. Press, Cambridge, Massachusetts. Oscar Handlin is Winthrop Professor of History at Harvard University. John Burchard is Emeritus Dean of the School of Humanities and Social Sciences of the Massachusetts Institute of Technology.

hundred years ago; and subtle institutional and cultural ties run across the centuries. But it would be a mistake to regard the later communities as merely, or even primarily, the descendants of the earlier ones. The modern city is essentially different from its predecessors, and the core of the difference lies in the fact that its life is not that "of an organism, but of an organ." It has become "the heart, the brain, perhaps only the digestive stem, of that great leviathan, the modern state." Its history cannot be understood apart from that of the more comprehensive communities of which it is a part.[2]

The distinctive feature of the great modern city is its unique pattern of relations to the world within which it is situated. Large enough to have a character of its own, the modern city is yet inextricably linked to, dependent upon, the society outside it; and growth in size has increased rather than diminished the force of that dependence. Out of that relationship spring the central problems of urban history—those of the organization of space within the city, of the creation of order among its people, and of the adjustment to its new conditions by the human personality.

It is, of course, perfectly possible to approach the history of these communities in a purely descriptive fashion—to prepare useful accounts of municipalities, markets and cultural centers on an empirical basis. But such efforts will certainly be more rewarding if they are related to large questions of a common and comparative nature. These introductory remarks aim to define some of those questions.

The forces that made the modern city what it is took form outside its own limits. Hence the increases were always unexpected and unanticipated. In the sixteenth and seventeenth centuries London, the first truly modern city, was repeatedly forbidden to grow; men who knew it as it was could not conceive what it would become. For the same reason, projections of future trends—whether prophetic or scientific—almost without fail fell far short of actuality, even in the most optimistic cultures. It was rare indeed that the facilities of a community anticipated its later needs, as those of Los Angeles did. The direction and rate of expansion were not foreseen because the generative impulses were not contained within the older urban society of merchants, artisans, and functionaries. They sprang from three profound and interrelated changes in the society external to them —the development of the centralized national state, the transformation of the economy from a traditional, household, to a rational, capital-using basis, and the technological destruction of distance.[3]

The political changes were first to show themselves; here the medieval cities were at their weakest. Few of them had ever disposed of substantial military force. Venice and Ragusa were unusual in this respect, perhaps because of their relation to the sea. Most other towns, at best, found protection from a stadtholder, or at worst, remained the victims of *condottieri* or feuding barons. Often they welcomed the security of monarchical authority, but they had no illusions about the extent to which that would increase their own power. In the face of any assertion of royal or national will, they could only acquiesce.[4]

That dependent situation has persisted to this day. Despite their wealth and their critical economic position, the great cities do not control themselves;

indeed most of them remain underrepresented in their ability to influence state policy. Their subordination in the polity has decisively shaped many aspects of their development.

The economic metamorphosis from which the modern city emerged is conventionally referred to as industrialization—an inappropriate designation because factory production was only slowly, and late, incorporated into the urban economy and was, in any case, only one aspect of a more general development. The eye of the change occurred outside the city rather than within it. First in agriculture and then in industry, old household-oriented modes of production gave way to large-scale rationalized forms, ultimately mechanized, that immensely increased output. The need to distribute the products to territorially wide, rather than to local, markets directly implicated the city.

The influence of technological change upon communications needs little comment. The evidences are all about us; and the development that led from the early roads and canals to the railroad, the telephone, the wireless, and the airplane permitted the speedy concentration of goods, messages, and persons at the focal points of ever wider areas. The simultaneous acceleration in managerial skills that permitted the organized deployment of great numbers of men and materials was equally impressive. The pace of innovation was particularly rapid in the half century after 1875 when the character of the modern city was most precisely defined. Why there should have been so striking an outburst of creativity in those years is as elusive a question as why there should have been so striking a failure of creativity thereafter.

The centralized national state, the new productive system, and vastly improved communications created the modern city. Together they increased its population, they endowed it with novel economic functions, and they imposed upon its way of life a fresh conception of order.

The initial manifestation of the change was a rapid growth in urban population. The centralizing tendencies of the emerging states of the sixteenth and seventeenth centuries brought significant groups of newcomers to the capitals and to regional subcenters. Operations, formerly dispersed in particular units of administration, were now concentrated; and the steady growth of state power created many additional places. Numerous functionaries carried on the expanded volume of government business and brought with them their families and retainers. Moreover many noblemen found it necessary to live close to the focus of authority, either through choice to be near the source of favors as in Bourbon France, or through compulsion to be subject to control as in Tokugawa Japan. Ancillary educational and religious institutions gravitated in the same direction. All the people thus drawn to the city created a market for trade, crafts, and services which swelled the economy of their place of residence.[5]

These developments had subtle, long-term effects. Channels of communication with the rest of the country were established that deepened through use and that conditioned the routes of later railroad and telephone lines. In some places the extensive fiscal transactions of the central government laid a basis for subsequent banking developments. As important, the seat of power acquired a symbolic value that later acted as a magnet for other detached elements in the society; and national citizenship facilitated their free entry.

Urban population expanded preponderantly by immigration. Cataclysms of many types outside the city borders precipitously swelled the streams that flowed into it. A stroke of fortune such as the discovery of gold near San Francisco and Johannesburg, or population pressure in the hinterland, or a disaster such as the migrations into Bombay and Calcutta after partition quickly raised the number of residents. Colonial trade contributed to the same effect in London and Amsterdam. Most important of all, structural changes in agriculture and industry involved a total reorganization of the labor force and effectively displaced great numbers of human beings for whom the city was the only refuge.[6]

From these sources was derived the rapid increase in numbers characteristic of the metropolis. Through the nineteenth century the pace accelerated, with the very largest places growing more rapidly than the smaller ones. In 1800 the twenty-one European cities with a population of 100,000 or more held, in all, somewhat more than four and a half million souls, one thirty-fifth of the total. In 1900 there were 147 such places with a population of 40,-000,000 or one-tenth of the total; and thirteen and one-fourth million lived within the narrowly defined political limits of the six largest cities. Were there means of estimating the true size of the urban districts involved, the number would be larger still. The same cities in 1960 had a population of about 24,000,000—again a gross underestimation of their genuine numbers. Meanwhile places of comparable dimension had appeared in America and Asia. In 1961 well over 85,000,000 persons lived

in the world's twenty largest cities, each of which contained 2,500,000 or more residents. And the process was not yet over.[7]

Mere accretions of population, however, changed the fundamental character of the city but slightly. New people came in, but their presence in itself called for few radical accommodations on the part of the old residents who generally prospered from the increased demand for their services. The city spread through the addition of new areas to its living space. But the organization of life for some time remained much what it had been earlier. Growth to great size was a necessary precondition, but did not in itself bring the modern city into being. Edo (Tokyo) in 1868 is said to have had a population of about a million, London in 1660 held more than one-half million people; yet these places were but extended towns which functioned according to patterns set long before. Their nobility, mercantile pursuits, and artisans' handicrafts formed larger aggregates than before, but they were aggregates of units that were essentially unchanged. Characteristically, in such places the building trades occupied a large part of the total labor force, and they altered but little with the passage of time. Other pursuits remained much as they had been earlier. The number of smiths and tailors, or drapers and merchants grew; but the mere multiplication of stalls and shops did not change the character of the bazaar, of the lane or of the exchange.[8]

Nor did the new needs thrust upon the city by the transformation of agriculture and industry after the eighteenth century alone give it its modern identity. Viewed simply on the economic plane, there was nothing inherently novel in the relationship of the city to these changes. It had long been accustomed to receiving the placeless men who sought its shelter and it had always provided a market for the products of the countryside. What was new was the desire, and the ability, to impose a rational order upon the relations created by the new productive system. The evolution of that order not only brought the city into intimate dependence upon the surrounding society; it also entailed a thoroughgoing transformation in the urban way of life.

Earlier markets had been dominated by the characteristics of the fair; buyers and sellers had approached in the expectation that they might meet one another, but the actual encounters had been shot through with chance. Monopolies and other political controls, various systems of correspondence and intelligence, and numerous other devices had aimed to impart some regularity to these transactions, particularly in the exchange of the great staples—wine, wool, and later, spices, tea, tobacco, and sugar. But distance and the vagaries of household production had limited the utility of these efforts. In effect, the movement of goods came to a halt, started and stopped, within the city, and that discontinuity gave the entrepôt a considerable degree of autonomy.

That situation ceased to be tolerable after the eighteenth century. The new techniques resulted in a large and growing capacity for production far beyond local need; they involved heavy capital investments and considerable risk; and they entailed difficult administrative problems. The success of any enterprise hinged upon the ability to anticipate with some precision a favorable relationship between cost of production and selling price. It could only survive by

planning, however primitive the means by later standards; and planning required dependability and predictability in access both to markets and to supplies.

The city supplied the essential mechanism: from it radiated the communications network—increasingly more extensive and more rapid—and within it were situated the facilities for transshipping, storing, and processing commodities on their way from producer to consumer. Here, too, was the apparatus of accounting and credit that made the movement of goods possible. The task of the city was that of speedy transmission. The more sensitive communications became, the more thoroughly the city was entangled in a mesh of relations that deprived it of autonomy and integrated it into a larger economic and social whole.[9]

The new role had profound consequences for the internal life of the city. Its effectiveness in the productive system of which it was a part depended upon its ability to create an appropriately functioning order within its own boundaries. The pressures toward doing so were critical in its development.

One can discover premature efforts to create such novel economic relationships in the role of Milan in Lombardy and in the experience of other Renaissance cities with their hinterlands. Such developments were abortive, not only because of their restricted territorial scope and because of technological limitations, but also because the corporate life inherited from the middle ages survived, indeed grew stronger; and that life significantly inhibited further changes. The seventeenth-century syndics who sat for Rembrandt's corporation portraits were custodians of communal organizations which resisted untoward changes. The destruction of their way of life was the necessary preliminary to the creation of a new urban order more in accord with the developing productive system.[10] Where that corporate life was weak or nonexistent to begin with, as in the United States, the process was all the faster.

Destruction of the older way of life was achieved through a convergence of political and economic forces. The national state eroded traditional elements of control and created new loci of power that dominated the city from outside it. The local aristocracy dwindled in importance; the old corporations were drained of influence; privileges were reshuffled; and new people rose to prominence. More generally, the national state undermined all traditional affiliations. It recognized only the indiscriminate relationship of citizenship. In its eyes there were only individuals, not members of clans, guilds, or even of households.

The changes in the productive system redistributed wealth to the advantage of men who could cast aside inherited modes of action to capitalize on fresh opportunities. The new economy encouraged the pursuit of individual profit rather than of status within a defined community; and the city housed a pack of people seeking after gain:

> Where every man is for himself
> And no man for all.[11]

The result was a new concept of orderly city life, one that no longer rested on a corporate organization of households, but instead depended upon a complex and impersonal arrangement of individuals. The process was already at work in the sixteenth century in England; it was immensely stimulated by the American and the French revolutions and was complete by the end of the nineteenth century.

We shall better be able to understand the character of the inner order of the modern city by regarding some of its specific manifestations.

An entirely new pattern for disposing of space appeared. The layout of the old city was altogether inappropriate. The population had already spread beyond the encircling walls and waters but it was inefficiently organized by a cumbersome and anachronistic plan. Churches, palaces, and other monumental structures occupied central places; squares and plazas pockmarked the limited area; and the streets ran but the short distances between nearby termini.

There was no reason why they should do more, for men had little need to travel since the household was both residence and place of work. Various districts were differentiated by occupational, class, or religious distinctions. But in each case, the basic unit was a self-contained familial entity that had a precisely defined place in the corporate life of the city. An increase in numbers was accommodated by multiplying the units, not by altering their character. In those unusual situations, as in the ghettoes, where space was constricted, the buildings rose upward and expansion was vertical. More frequently, where room was available, new clusters of settlement split off from the old and expansion was lateral. But until well into the nineteenth century growth in most places had simply multiplied the number of clusters; it had not altered their essential character.[12]

Reconstruction of the city plan depended upon the differentiation of living and working quarters. Such specialized use of space, reflecting the growing impersonality of business and its separation from the household, became prevalent everywhere except in professions like medicine, and in the service crafts where a personal relationship survived. Elsewhere, the dispersal of the population went hand in hand with the destruction of the household and was eased by the engulfment of suburb after suburb. The father and mother and children lived together but their life was detached from work. The categories of experience they shared in the home were unrelated to those of the job. Each individual left after breakfast to take up a separate task in the counting house or the shop or on the scaffold, to return in the evening to his residence some distance away, for each was an integer subject to a separate reckoning in the accounting of the productive system.[13]

The division of function was economical. Every productive or distributive operation became more efficient when it selected the individual employee according to his talents or cost apart from considerations of kin and clan, of family or ethnic grouping. Of course, no society fully realized the ideal of total fluidity that permitted its population to be sorted out in this manner; but the separation of work from residence encouraged an approach in that direction. The fact that single men and women always constituted a large proportion of the migrants into the city stimulated the trend as did related alterations in the behavior of settled families.

As a result space was released from all sorts of traditional expenses. The enterprise no longer had to bear the charge on land of high value, of wasteful drawing rooms and gardens. Precious urban acreage was withdrawn from farming. And the distribution of population by income levels permitted a rational valuation of space in terms of an abstract, calculated, rent. Speculation was the incidental by-product, rather than the cause, of this development.[14]

Specialization required and facilitated the construction of an entirely new urban plant, a good part of which was built with the aid of a remarkable burst of innovation that began shortly after 1820 and which reached its peak between 1875 and 1925. Space was reallocated with an eye toward its most profitable use; and buildings directed toward a single function—trade, industry, or residence—went up with ruthless efficiency. The process of differentiation created demands for services which theretofore had been unneeded or had been supplied within the household, for fresh foods, milk, water, waste disposal, light, transportation, and recreation. In the frenzy of construction, the city was entirely recast and its ties to the past obliterated. Even topography ceased to be an obstacle; hills were razed, marshes and lakes filled in, and shore lines extended to make way for the limitless grid. Goethe could still make out medieval Frankfurt in place names, markets, buildings, fairs, and topography. By 1870, hardly more than a few of these monuments and ceremonies survived.[15]

Now begins the time of travel, at first on foot. Dickens' characters still walk across London, and at about the same time a resident of Tokyo thinks nothing of tramping five miles to and five miles from his destination every day. Even in twentieth century Rio or Tokyo an inefficient transport system compels workers to spend six hours a day between home and job.[16] But in cost-conscious societies speed is an important consideration; in its interest new streets are driven through the city, straight and wide to carry an ever heavier stream of vehicles—at first horse drawn, later, motor propelled. The wheels roll above and below as well as on the ground and inconvenient rivers are bridged over and tunneled under. The critical breakthrough comes with the appearance of the common carrier. At the beginning of the nineteenth century, every conveyance still bears the appearance of the personal or family carriage or litter —even the long distance stages that take fare-paying passengers. It is not at all clear, when the first railroads are built, that they will follow a different line of development. But the carriages are thrown open for all to enter; mass travel becomes possible; and the meanest laborer moves on wheels.

The pace and ingenuity of this work were impressive by any standard. That the subways of London, Paris, New York, and Boston were built faster than those of Moscow, Stockholm, or Rome fifty years later must mean something, although it would be hazardous to try to make the meaning precise. Any such comparison is to some degree arbitrary and perhaps far-fetched. Yet the standard of achievement certainly was not lower a half century ago than now, if we take into account the presumed improvement in technology since then. Travelers to New York today are aware that it will take seven years (1957-1964) to reconstruct La Guardia Airport and that Idlewild has been more than a decade in the building. Their predecessors fifty years ago were likely to reach the city through one of the largest buildings ever theretofore constructed at one time, one covering eight acres of ground, with exterior walls of one half a mile. They could enter through two tunnels under the Hudson River and

four under the East River extending more than eighteen miles from Harrison, New Jersey, to Jamaica, Long Island. Work on this project began in June 1903; the Hudson tunnels were finished in three years, the East River tunnels in less than five and the Pennsylvania station in less than six. In September, 1910, the whole complex was in operation.[17]

The modern city demanded an immense number and variety of new buildings. Already in the eighteenth century architects like Claude-Nicholas Ledoux were compelled to devise new shapes for warehouses, for banks, for other commercial structures, and for dwellings appropriate to various classes of residents. Considerations of cost compelled them to adhere to the rule of geometry, and to stress functionalism and the rational organization of materials and space. In doing so they struggled against counterpressures toward tradition and individualism, against counterpulls toward exoticism and a romanticized view of nature. By the second half of the nineteenth century, they had begun to work out the styles that accommodated the life of the modern city.[18]

Certainly the New York tenement block of 1900 was an unlovely object. Having dispensed with the old central court, it could pile its residents up in suffocating density. The reformers of the period were altogether right to attack overcrowding there and elsewhere and to complain that the cities had not adequately met their housing needs. Only, one must remember that overcrowding and need are relative concepts; and few later efforts have been notably more successful.[19] Comparison with the experience of Moscow in the 1930's, to say nothing of Calcutta in the

1950's, puts the achievements of a half-century ago in better perspective.[20]

The altered situation of the city called also for a new conception of time. In the rural past, years, months, days, and hours had been less meaningful than seasons, than the related succession of religious occasions, than the rising and setting of the sun. Small communities had their own flexible conceptions of chronology. Such habits had extended to the city as well. Each household had a large margin within which to set its own pace, for the tempo of all activities was leisurely. An analysis of the course of an eighteenth-century merchant's day, for instance, revealed long disposable intervals so that even when he was busy, it was upon terms he could shape for himself.[21]

The complex interrelationships of life in the modern city, however, called for unprecedented precision. The arrival of all those integers who worked together, from whatever part of the city they inhabited, had to be coordinated to the moment. There was no natural span for such labor; arbitrary beginnings and ends had to be set, made uniform and adhered to. The dictatorship of the clock and the schedule became absolute.[22]

No earlier human experience had made such demands. The army camp, plantation labor, and the ship's crew which came closest to it were coherent, closed societies, the members of which lived close together and in isolation from outsiders; the tasks involved had a rhythm of their own that regulated their budgets of time. But the modern city could not function except under the rule of a precise and arbitrary chronological order which alone could coordinate the activities of thousands of individuals whose necessary encounters with one another were totally impersonal. By the same token, literacy or some alternative code of signals was essential to the coexistence of people who did not know one another.

The new uses of space and time were indicative of what order meant in the modern city. Its complex life demanded myriad daily contacts of such sensitivity that it could not depend, as earlier, upon well-established and static connections among the stable households and the fixed corporate groups in which its population had been distributed. Instead it required its residents to behave individually and impersonally in terms of their function, and it assured regularity of contacts by rigid allocations of space and time.

That order made it possible to bring manufacturing, like other large-scale activities, into the cities. The planners of the early great factories thought of the only models of disciplined activity familiar to them, the barrack and the army camp; their sites—visionary or actual—were therefore invariably in the countryside, where the tolling bell from the clock tower of the mill replaced that of the village church. The similarity in design of factories and prisons was by no means coincidental.[23]

The urban factory was conceivable only well in the nineteenth century when it was possible to imagine that a labor force would come to work regularly and dependably. The process of transition in actuality took a number of forms. Some factory centers, like Manchester, grew into cities. In other cases, as in Pittsburgh or Zurich, a commercial center expanded to engulf nearby industrial communities. Elsewhere industry was drawn in by the attractions of superior transportation facilities, or by the presence of an abundant labor supply, as in Berlin, or Chicago; or the shift was a product of conscious government decisions as in Moscow after 1928. But whatever the immediate impulse, the necessary condition was the order that permitted the factory to function.[24]

The way of life of the modern city created grave social and personal problems. Any increase of size had always complicated the police of the community. But so long as the family, the clan, or the guild remained accountable for the behavior of its members, so long as the normal ambit of activities was restricted to a familiar quarter, the primary danger of deviant behavior came from strangers. When the decay of the household weakened the sense of collective security, the initial response was to control or exclude outsiders, to arrive at some accommodation with violent elements, and to maintain the isolation of the district within which its residents felt safe. At the end of the eighteenth century, as large a place as London had not moved beyond this point.

But these expedients were not long useful. The modern city was no *colluvies gentium*—a fortuitous accumulation of unfused populaces—as were ancient Rome, or Alexandria. Extended travel and promiscuous contacts were essential to it; and the frequent mingling of men unknown to each other generated the need for holding each individual responsible for his behavior. The ultimate goal was some sort of total index that would precisely identify and infallibly locate each person so that he could be called to account for his obligations and punished for his delinquencies. The steady development of governmental power, the contrivance of numerous devices for registration, and the appearance of a professional corps of administrators were steps toward an approximation of that goal.

More was involved than the containment of criminality. The urban resident had positive as well as negative responsibilities. He had not merely to refrain from such actions as were injurious to others; he was expected, in ways that were difficult to define explicitly, also to contribute to the total well-being of the community by civic actions. The collective tasks of the old household and guild could not be left in abeyance. Someone had to provide care for dependent persons, education for children, facilities for worship, media for cultural and sociable expression, and commemorative monuments and objects of awe and beauty. The police of a city thus included a wide range of functions connected with its health and security. The state assumed some of these obligations, but the scope of its activity varied widely from country to country. Although we cannot yet explain convincingly the differences in the depth of its involvement, it is clear that it nowhere preempted the field entirely. Much remained to be done through other forms.[25]

It was not possible, although men often longed to do so, to revive the old corporate institutions or the solidary rural communities from which so many residents had migrated. The modern city contained too many disparate elements, too often thrown together, and in too fluid a pattern of relations to permit such regressions. Instead, where abstinence by the state left a vacuum, the characteristic device of a voluntary association, directed toward the specific function, met the need. The rapid proliferation of such organizations drew together memberships united by common interests, common antecedents, or common point of view. The wide expanse of the city and the continuing migration which peopled it, shaped such groupings. In some places the effective modes of organization fell within territorial, neighborhood lines; the *quartier*, ward, *ku,* or *favela* was the matrix within which associations formed. Elsewhere cultural or ethnic affiliations supplied the determining limits of cooperative action.[26]

For a long time, the cost of this adjustment was recurrent, overt conflict. Leadership was effective only within limited circles, and there were few means of resolving the frequent crises that led easily into outbreaks of violence. Bread riots in the West and rice riots in the East expressed the desperation of the uncared-for elements in the community; and racial or social antipathies, smoldering beneath the surface, erupted at the least disturbance.[27]

By the end of the nineteenth century, the instruments for controlling such dangerous disorders were at least available, if not always effectively used. The reconstruction of the great cities permitted a strategic disposition of power to contain the mob. The maintenance of an armed police force deterred overt lawbreakers. Moreover, by then a complex of philanthropic, religious, educational, and cultural institutions had begun to elicit the acquiescence of the urban masses through persuasion. Thereafter conflicts took more negotiable forms, in the bargaining of labor unions and employers, and in politics which was less a partisan contest for power than an instrument of group accommodation. Disputes were increasingly subject to conciliable resolution through the mediating efforts of recog-

nized leaders. However, the issues which could be confronted on the municipal level were limited and concrete; and the deeper economic and emotional grievances of the population were likely to be displaced into other channels.[28]

The life of the modern city created subtle personal problems. Here were distilled many of the general effects of change in the past two centuries: the break with tradition and the dissolution of inherited beliefs, the impact of science and technology, and the transformation of the family and of the productive system. In the city, as elsewhere, such decisive innovations were a source of both release and tension in the human spirit. Only, concentrated as they were in their urban form, these new impulses were far more volatile than elsewhere. Furthermore, the man of the city passed through experiences unique to his setting. The number and variety and speed of his contacts, the products of an original conception of space and time, the separation from nature, the impersonality and individuality of work all were novel to the human situation.

Evidence of the negative consequences was painfully abundant. On the Bowery or in Brigittenau drifted the uprooted masses who had lost personality, identity, and norms and who now were trapped in every form of disorder. The deterioration of man to bum was all too familiar in every modern city. Even the less desperate were heedless of the restraints of church and family; in London, Berlin, and New York of the third quarter of the nineteenth century, a majority of marriages and burials were unsolemnized by the clergy. The most prosperous tore at each other in vicious competition except when they indulged in fierce and expensive debauchery. High rates of mortality, suicide, alcoholism, insanity, and other forms of delinquency showed that men reared in one environment could not simply shift to another without substantial damage to themselves.[29]

At the high point of change, in the half century after 1875, there were two distinct, although not contradictory, interpretations of the effects of the modern city upon the human personality. Those who focused their attention upon institutional developments, like Georg Simmel, Emile Durkheim, and, to some extent, Max Weber, took particular note of the decay of old forms which left the individual unsheltered, unprotected, and isolated, and therefore prone to deterioration. The later exaggerations of Spengler and Mumford distend these insights into a vision of imminent catastrophe.[30]

Exaggeration was easy because personal disorders were more visible in the city than in the country. But these observers were also limited by a fixed preference for what the city had been, a total systematic unit comprehending a defined order of institutions that no longer existed. It is significant that their views mirrored somber predictions, made long before. Rousseau and others had already warned of the inevitable results of urban detachment from nature before the process had even taken form. "Of all animals man is least capable of living in flocks. Penned up like sheep, men soon lose all. The breath of man is fatal to his fellows. . . . Cities are the burial pit of the human species."[31]

The personal hardships of adjustment to city life were genuine but they were distorted when examined in the perspective of the corporate, rural past. Other observers, whose gaze was fastened on the residents as human beings, made out a somewhat different pattern. "What can ever be more stately and admirable to me," asked Whitman, "than mast-hemm'd Manhattan?" Observing the curious procession of the ferry riders leaving work behind for their thousands of homes, he felt and expressed the wonder of their each being a person.[32] This was often the response of compassionate onlookers. At first regard, the city was totally inhuman; jungle, wilderness, hive, machine—these were the terms of the metaphors that sprang spontaneously to mind. But those sensitive enough to look more deeply found marvelous assertions of the human spirit even under these unpropitious circumstances. Here life was real and hard, and tested the human heart and mind so that emotions were deeper and reason more acute than elsewhere. Social scientists influenced by Darwinian conception of the survival of the fittest readily assumed that the city was the new environment within which a new, superior man would develop. And some who began half to understand the character of that life were tempted to idealize and romanticize even its least lovely aspects, the slums, the ruthless competition, and the grinding order.[33]

The two responses were not irreconcilable; indeed, in retrospect, they seem almost complementary, or perhaps, they were but different ways of describing the identical process. The decay of familiar institutions was another way of saying the release from traditional restraints; the unsheltered individual was also the liberated individual. The breakdown of the household and the attenuation of all the relationships formerly centered in it were the conditions of the liberation of modern man to all his painful tensions, all his creative opportunities. The hard stone of the city streets provided the stage for this drama; and it is the task of historical scholarship to explain its triumphs, its defeats, and its conflicts.

The modern city provided the scene for great outbursts of cultural creativity. Georgian London, Paris in the first decades of the Third Republic, Vienna toward the end of the reign of Franz Joseph, and Berlin of the 1920's were the settings of great achievements of the human spirit, in literature, in art, in music, and in science. Yet these were also, and at the same time, the scenes of bitter struggles for existence, of acute hardships suffered by hundreds of thousands of ill-prepared newcomers beaten down by insoluble problems. John Gay and William Hogarth, Anatole France and Honoré Daumier, Robert Musil and Berthold Brecht, and Charlie Chaplin and René Clair compiled a record of personal disasters, of moral disintegration, of human costs so high it could only be contemplated under the palliative gloss of humor. The laughter of their audiences did not conceal, it recognized the harsh truth. Yet the withering away of traditional guides to life, so debilitating in many ways, also set the individual free, left room for spontaneity and discovery, brought together selective new combinations of people, ideas, and forms, that permitted man to catch unsuspected glimpses of an unknown universe and an unfamiliar self.

Every aspect of the development of the modern city generated conflicts not resolvable within its own boundaries; that was a condition of its intimate relations with the society beyond its borders. The urban residents were divided among themselves, and they had to reckon with outsiders in their midst and beyond the walls, whose interests were intimately bound up with their own. Disputes of great importance were the result.

The city plan was therefore never simply the realization of an abstract design. Even in places created entirely afresh, as in Washington or St. Petersburg, it was the product of inescapable compromises. Within the city, the primary interest of the entrepreneurial groups and of the laboring population was to economize on the use of space. They wanted low rents, an efficient, functional allocation of the resources, and speedy interior transportation.

Such people met the determined, and sometimes effective, resistance of other elements, whose conceptions were still dominated by the static images of the rural landscape. The aristocracy—genuine and putative—wished to bring with them the commodious features of their landed estates. They expected the city to provide them with elegant squares to set off their homes, with picturesque monuments, and with parks and boulevards that would supply a back drop for the May Corso, for the Spring Parade, for the *ausflug* or Sunday excursion, for the gentleman on horseback and the lady in her carriage. Public transportation concerned them not at all.[34]

Immigrants who prospered to a lesser degree clung to the rural village as the model of home; they built wasteful villas in the sprawling suburbs and sought a restricted transport system that would take them conveniently to their desks and counters, yet prevent the city from engulfing them. Often their dogged struggles for autonomy hopelessly complicated any effort at urban reorganization, a problem as troublesome in Vienna, Leipzig, Manchester, and Liverpool in 1890 as in Boston and Nashville in 1960.[35]

The persistence of the rural model prevented these people from thinking of the city as a whole and as it was. From Robert Owen, Fourier, and the utopian socialists, to Ebenezer Howard, Frank Lloyd Wright, and Lewis Mumford, a good-hearted but illusory plea went forth for the rebuilding of urban life in garden cities or multiplied suburbs, where adults would not be tempted to squander their resources in the pub or music hall, nor children theirs in the sweetshop; and all would have access to the salubrious and moral air of the countryside.[36]

To such pressures were added those of agriculturists and industrialists in the hinterland concerned only with lowering the cost of transshipment, and of the state, increasingly preoccupied with security against insurrection or lesser threats to order. The great planners, like Baron Haussmann in Paris, found room for maneuver in the play of these forces against one another. But rarely did they find the city material they could mold into a unified and coherent whole.[37]

Urban elements were at a disadvantage in the determination of both municipal and national policies. The level of tariffs in the 1880's and 1890's, the routes of canals and railroads, and the character of the banking system vitally affected all cities. Yet their influence was perilously weak, underrepresented in the councils of state and divided, while the rural interests were monolithic and well entrenched. Paris, Rio, Rome did not govern themselves; and voices from the Platteland or Upstate were more likely to command than

those from Johannesburg or New York. The political power of the country generally outweighed the economic power of the city.[38]

The clash of interests took its most subtle and most significant form in the contact of the diverse cultures that converged on the modern city. The folk traditions of the old bourgeois did not survive the disintegration of the corporate bodies in which it had been embedded; it was totally disrupted by the pressure from both above and below of alien elements.

The aristocracy surrendered its isolation and shifted some of its activities to the city. Still stabilized by its landed estates, it also drew support from new wealth and, in the nineteenth century, began the quest for a uniform, hierarchical culture at the peak of which it could stand. It wished more than indulgence in a lavish style of life; it wished also general acquiescence in its position. Indeed, to some extent it flouted the conventions of inferiors precisely in order to demonstrate its superiority. Legally recognized rank as in England and Prussia, the pretense of ancient lineage as in Austria and France, or arbitrary registers of inclusion as in the United States, asserted its claims to pre-eminence. In addition, it transformed the theater, the opera and the museum into institutions to display its dominance. The aristocracy turned music into classics, art into old masters, and literature into rare books, possessions symbolic of its status.[39]

The problems of other migrants into the city were of quite another order. The mass of displaced peasants were eager to transplant their inherited culture but the soil was inhospitable. Folk wisdom, inappropriate to the new conditions, took on the appearance of superstition; and folk art, detached from its communal setting, lost much of its authenticity. However these people fared, they were driven by anxiety—to retain the rewards of success, to avoid the penalties of failure. Some escaped through alcohol; others found moments of relief in the excitement of the yellow press, the music hall, and the popular theater.[40]

Above all, they needed to interpret their lives by seeing themselves as actors in a meaningful drama, and since it was inconceivable that they should be conquering heroes, they most readily visualized themselves as victims.

Of whom? Rarely of the aristocrat. Peasant and gentleman had a long history of accommodation; and their roles in city life engendered few direct conflicts. The lowly felt no compulsion to ape the high born, and gaped at the splendor of the carriages on the way to the opera without envy.

More often the villains were the capitalists, big business, whose wealth was abstract, was located in no communal context, and was attached to no responsibilities of position. Or sometimes, the enemy was the stranger—the Slav or the Jew or the Catholic or the Protestant Masons or the barbaric foreigner—who could be blamed for the ills of the city. Inhuman materialism, disregard of traditional faith, sensuality and obscenity were crimes against man; and for crimes, criminals were responsible; and they who came were guilty so that we who left home were but the innocent victims.[41]

The factory workers and craftsmen who held places in disciplined organizations found belief in socialism; the class struggle explained their present situation and offered them the hope of an acceptable future. But millions of place-less men could not so readily tear themselves away from the past. The shopkeepers and clerks, the casual laborers, the chaotic mass of men without function did not want the future; they wanted the security of the homes and families and blood communities they had never had or had lost in migration. That is, they wanted a miracle; and in their eagerness they became the gullible victims of nationalistic, racist, religious and quasi-religious fantasies of every sort. There is a particular interest, in Europe, in the ease with which these people allied themselves with some sectors of the aristocracy under the banner of a universal faith—Ultramontane Catholicism, pan-Germanism, pan-Slavism. Drumont and the royalist officer corps in France, Luëger and Prince Alois Liechtenstein in Austria, illustrated the attractiveness of tradition and authority for the demagogue and his mob. Perhaps analogous elements were involved in the revival of Shinto in Japan after 1868; they were certainly present in the history of fascism.[42]

The true miracle, however, was the emergence of a sense of civic consciousness connected with the old burgher traditions but responsive to the new character of the modern city. Its characteristics were tolerance to the point of latitudinarianism, rationalism, cosmopolitanism, pragmatism, and receptivity to change. It attracted the settled middle-class elements of the city, the leaders of organized labor and even demagogues suddenly charged with responsibility, as Luëger was in Vienna and La Guardia in New York; its essence was a creative reaction to the problems of the place; its achievement was the monumental building of the city to which I earlier referred.

Some decades ago—and I am deliberately vague about the date—a significant change appeared. The immediate local causes seemed to be the two wars, the depression, and new shifts in technology and population. However, these may be but manifestations of some larger turning in the history of the society of which the modern city is a part.

The differences between city and country have been attenuated almost to the vanishing point. The movement of people, goods, and messages has become so rapid and has extended over such a long period as to create a new situation. To put it bluntly, the urbanization of the whole society may be in process of destroying the distinctive role of the modern city. It is symptomatic of this change that, in western societies, most migrations now originate, as well as terminate, in the modern metropolis.

This change may be related to a general slackening of urban spirit. The worldwide movement to the suburbs is not in itself new; this was always one of the ways in which the city expanded. What is new is the effective motivation—the insistence upon constructing small, uniform, coherent communities, and the surrender of the adventure of life in the larger units with all the hazards and opportunities of unpredictable contacts. Increasingly the men who now people the metropolis long for the security of isolation from the life about them. They strive to locate their families in space, with a minimum of connections to the hazards of the external world.[43]

Finally, there has been a perceptible decline in urban creativity. The regression to private transportation is indicative of what has been happening in other spheres as well. Despite other advances in technology and despite refinements in methods, the last thirty or forty years have witnessed no innovations to match those of the thirty or forty years earlier. We have done little more than elaborate upon the inherited plant; nowhere has there been an adequate response to the challenge of new conditions.

We console ourselves with the calculation that if the modern city has ceased to grow, the metropolitan region continues to expand. What difference that will make remains to be seen. In any case, it seems likely that we stand at the beginnings of a transformation as consequential as that which, two hundred years ago, brought the modern city into being.

Therein lies the historian's opportunity to throw light on the problems of those involved with today's city, either as practitioners or as participants. His task is not to predict, but to order the past from which the present grows in a comprehensible manner. He can illuminate the growth of the modern city from the eighteenth to the twentieth centuries to make clear what was permanent and what transient, what essential and what incidental, in its development.

Such an account as this essay has presented has perforce touched upon a few themes abstracted from a large number of cases. Yet the historian must deal with particulars, not with generalities. Certainly the stress, laid here upon the connections between the modern city and the surrounding society points to the decisive role of political, cultural, and economic variants, widely different from place to place.

Comparisons crowd immediately to mind. Did the differences between

Washington and St. Petersburg in 1900, new capitals of expanding nations, emanate from the hundred-year disparity in their ages or from discernible differences between the United States and Russia? Did Shanghai and Singapore become what they did because they were perched on the edge of Oriental societies or because they were colonial enclaves? Did a tropical situation set the experiences of Rio and Havana apart from those of cities in the temperate zone; did their European population distinguish them from other tropical cities? Why did some cities fail to grow as others did, why were some more successful than others in resolving their problems?

No amount of theorizing about the nature of the city will answer questions such as these. We need fewer studies of the city in history than of the history of cities. However useful a general theory of the city may be, only the detailed tracing of an immense range of variables, in context, will illuminate the dynamics of the processes here outlined.[44] We can readily enough associate such gross phenomena as the growth of population and the rise of the centralized state, as technological change and the development of modern industry, as the disruption of the traditional household and the decline of corporate life. But *how* these developments unfolded, what was the causal nexus among them, we shall only learn when we make out the interplay among them by focusing upon *a* city specifically in all its uniqueness.

In the modern city, the contest between the human will and nature assumed a special form. Here man, crowded in upon himself and yet alone, discovered his potentialities for good and evil, for weakness and strength.

Compelled to act within a framework of impersonal institutions, he was forced to probe the meaning of his own personality.

In the balance for two centuries now has lain the issue of whether he will master, or be mastered by, the awesome instruments he has created. The record of that issue deserves the best energies of the historian.

NOTES

1. Max Weber, *The City* (Translated and edited by Don Martindale and Gertrud Neuwirth; Glencoe, [1958]), 70 ff.; Raffaele d'Ambrosio, *Alle Origini della città le prime esperienze urbane* (Napoli, 1956); A. Temple Patterson, *Radical Leicester* (Leicester, 1954), 3, 165.
2. George Unwin, *Studies in Economic History* (London, 1927), 49.
3. Norman G. Brett-James, *Growth of Stuart London* (London, [1935]), 67 ff., 105 ff., 296 ff.; Walter Besant, *London in the Time of the Tudors* (London, 1904), 83; Boyle Workman, *The City that Grew* (Caroline Walker, ed., Los Angeles, 1935), 266 ff.
4. William A. Robson, *Great Cities of the World: Their Government, Politics and Planning* (New York, [1955]), 78 ff.; Société Jean Bodin, *Recueils*, VI (1954), 265 ff., 367 ff., 434 ff., 541 ff., 612.
5. See, e.g., Franklin L. Ford, *Strasbourg in Transition 1648-1789* (Cambridge, 1958), 159 ff.; Lewis Mumford, *The City in History. Its Origins, Its Transformations, and Its Prospects* (New York, [1961]), 386 ff.; *Golden Ages of the Great Cities* (London, 1952), 192.
6. Adna F. Weber, *The Growth of Cities in the Nineteenth Century* (New York, 1899), 230 ff.; Besant, *London in the Time of the Tudors*, 226 ff.; Walter Besant, *London in the Eighteenth Century* (London, 1903), 213 ff.; Percy E. Schramm, ed., *Kaufleute zu Haus und über See Hamburgische Zeugnisse des 17., 18., und 19. Jahrhunderts* (Hamburg, 1949), pt. II; Emile Vandervelde, *L'Exode rural et le retour aux champs* (Paris, 1903), 39 ff.; Robson, *Great Cities*, 112 ff., 141, 683.
7. *Information Please Almanac, 1961*, 658; Edmund J. James, "The Growth of Great Cities," *Annals of the American Academy of Political and Social Science*, XIII (1899), 1 ff.; Weber, *Growth of Cities*, 20 ff., gives extensive nineteenth-century statistics. See also for more recent data, International Urban Research, *The World's Metropolitan Areas* (Berkeley, 1959); Kingsley Davis, "The Origin and Growth of Urbanization in the World," *American Journal of Sociology*, LX

(1955), 429 ff.; Norton S. Ginsburg, "The Great City in Southeast Asia," *ibid.*, LX, 455 ff.; Robert I. Crane, "Urbanism in India," *ibid.*, LX, 463 ff.; Donald J. Bogue, "Urbanism in the United States, 1950," *ibid.*, LX, 471 ff.; Irene B. Taeuber, *Population of Japan* (Princeton, 1958), 25 ff., 45 ff., 96 ff., 126 ff., 148 ff.; Kingsley Davis, *Population of India and Pakistan* (Princeton, 1951), 127 ff.; Vandervelde, *L'Exode rural*, 16 ff.; Edmond Nicolaï, *La Dépopulation des campagnes et l'accroissement de la population des villes* (Bruxelles, 1903); R. Price-Williams, "The Population of London, 1801-81," *Journal of the Statistical Society*, XLVIII (1885), 349 ff.
8. For the population of earlier European cities, see Roger Mols, *Introduction à la démographie historique des villes d'Europe* (Louvain, 1955), II, 502 ff. See also M. Dorothy George, *London Life in the XVIIIth Century* (London, 1925), 155 ff.
9. Robert M. Fisher, ed., *The Metropolis in Modern Life* (Garden City, 1955), 85 ff.; Weber, *Growth of Cities*, 170 ff. For earlier market relations see, "La Foire," Société Jean Bodin, *Receuils*, V (1953), *passim*.
10. See Douglas F. Dowd, "Economic Expansion of Lombardy," *Journal of Economic History*, XXI (1961), 143 ff.; *Storia di Milano* (Milan, 1957-1960), VIII, 337 ff., XIV, 835 ff.; Jakob Rosenberg, *Rembrandt* (Cambridge, 1948), I, 70 ff.; Weber, *The City*, 91 ff.; Mumford, *City in History*, 269 ff., 281 ff.; Société Jean Bodin, *Receuils*, VII (1955), 567 ff.; Schramm, *Kaufleute*, 185 ff.
11. Robert Crowley, quoted in Mumford, *City in History*, 343.
12. Gideon Sjoberg, *The Preindustrial City Past and Present* (Glencoe, [1960]), 100 ff.; Martin S. Briggs, "Town-Planning," Charles Singer, *et al.*, eds., *History of Technology* (New York, 1957), III, 269 ff.; *Golden Ages*, 31-34, 67, 230; Mumford, *City in History*, 299 ff.
13. See Otis D. and Beverly Duncan, "Residential Distribution and Occupational Stratification," *American Journal of Sociology*, LX (1955), 493 ff.; R. P. Dore, *City Life in Japan. A Study of a Tokyo Ward* (Berkeley, 1958), 91 ff.
14. Mumford, *City in History*, 421 ff.; Fisher, *Metropolis in Modern Life*, 125 ff.; Weber, *Growth of Cities*, 322 ff.
15. *The Auto-Biography of Goethe. Truth and Poetry: From My Own Life* (John Oxenford, transl., London, 1948), 3, 4, 7-10, 12 ff.
16. Fukuzawa Yukichi, *Autobiography* (transl. by Eiichi Kiyooka, Tokyo, [1948]); Robson, *Great Cities*, 510; Brett-James, *Stuart London*, 420 ff.
17. Pennsylvania Railroad Company, *The New York Improvement and Tunnel Extension of the Pennsylvania Railroad* (Philadelphia, 1910).
18. Emil Kaufmann, "Three Revolutionary Architects," *Transactions of the American Philosophical Society*, XLII (1952), 494 ff.; Helen Rosenau, *The Ideal City in Its Architectural Evolution* (London, [1959]), 79 ff.
19. Mumford, *City in History*, 465 ff.; Dore, *City Life in Japan*, 40 ff.; Reinhard E. Petermann,

Wien im Zeitalter Kaiser Franz Joseph I (Vienna, 1908), 128 ff.
20. Alec Nove, ed., *The Soviet Seven Year Plan* (London, [1960]), 75 ff.; Harry Schwartz, *Russia's Soviet Economy* (2 ed., New York, 1954), 453 ff.; Robson, *Great Cities*, 384 ff.
21. Arthur H. Cole, "The Tempo of Mercantile Life in Colonial America," *Business History Review*, XXXIII (1959), 277 ff.; *Golden Ages*, 44, 45.
22. On the problem of time, see Pitirim A. Sorokin and Robert K. Merton, "Social Time: A Methodological and Functional Analysis," *American Journal of Sociology*, XLII (1937), 615 ff.
23. Kaufmann, "Three Revolutionary Architects," 509 ff.; Rosenau, *Ideal City*, 121, 133.
24. See, e.g., Catherine E. Reiser, *Pittsburgh's Commercial Development 1800-1850* (Harrisburg, 1951), 28, 191 ff.
25. Louis Wirth, "Urbanism as a Way of Life," *American Journal of Sociology*, XLIV (1938), 20 ff.; Patterson, *Radical Leicester*, 222 ff.; Dore, *City Life in Japan*, 71 ff.
26. See, in general, Lloyd Rodwin, ed., *The Future Metropolis* (New York, 1961), 23 ff. For specific illustrations see Louis Chevalier, "La Formation de la population parisienne au XIXe Siècle," Institut National d'Etudes Démographiques, *Travaux et Documents*, X (1950); Alphonse Daudet, *Numa Roumestan—Moeurs parisiennes* (Paris, 1881), ch. iii; Dore, *City Life in Japan*, 255 f.; Alexander Campbell, *The Heart of Japan* (New York, 1961), 3 ff.; William A. Jenks, *Vienna and the Young Hitler* (New York, 1960), 4.
27. Société Jean Bodin, *Receuils*, VII (1955), 398 ff.; J. B. Sansom, *The Western World and Japan* (New York, 1958), 242; J. D. Chambers, *Nottinghamshire in the Eighteenth Century* (London, 1932), 40 ff.; Besant, *London in the Eighteenth Century*, 475 ff.; George Rudé, *The Crowd in the French Revolution* (Oxford, 1959), 232 ff.
28. Robson, *Great Cities*, 210 ff.
29. See Petermann, *Wien*, 331 ff.; Jenks, *Vienna and the Young Hitler*, 11; George, *London Life*, 21 ff.; Besant, *London in the Eighteenth Century*, 140 ff., 263 ff.; Fisher, *Metropolis in Modern Life*, 18 ff.
30. Georg Simmel, "Die Grosstädte und das Geistesleben," *Jahrbuch der Gehe-Stiftung zu Dresden*, IX (1903), 187 ff.; Kurt H. Wolff, ed., *Georg Simmel, 1858-1918*, (Columbus, Ohio, [1959]), 100 ff., 221 ff.; Emile Durkheim, *De la Division du travail social* (5 ed., Paris, 1926), *passim*, but especially the preface to the second edition; Oswald Spengler, *The Decline of the West* (New York, 1950), II, 92 ff.; Mumford, *City in History*, *passim*. See also Wirth, "Urbanism as a Way of Life," *loc. cit.*, 20 ff.
31. J[ean]. J[acques]. Rousseau, *Emile ou de l'éducation* (Paris, 1854), Book I, p. 36; Robert A. Kann, *A Study in Austrian Intellectual History* (New York, 1960), 63; see also the point of view

implicit in such novels as E. M. Forster, *Howard's End* (London, 1910).

32. Walt Whitman, *Complete Writings* (New York, 1902), I, 196.

33. See also Weber, *Growth of Cities*, 368 ff., 441 ff.

34. See Percy E. Schramm, *Hamburg, Deutschland und die Welt* (Hamburg, [1952]), 350 ff.; Mumford, *City in History*, 395 ff.

35. Robson, *Great Cities*, 30 ff., 60 ff., 75 ff.; Sam B. Warner, *Street Car Suburbs* (Cambridge, 1962); Weber, *Growth of Cities*, 469 ff.; H. J. Dyos, *Victorian Suburbs* (Leicester, 1961).

36. Rosenau, *Ideal City*, 130 ff.; Robert Owen, *Book of the New Moral World* (London, 1842), II, 16; Ralph Neville, *Garden Cities* (Manchester, 1904); G. Montague Harris, *The Garden City Movement* (London, 1906); Mumford, *City in History*, 514 ff.

37. David H. Pinkney, *Napoleon III and the Rebuilding of Paris* (Princeton, 1958), 25 ff.

38. Robson, *Great Cities*, 685; Schramm, *Hamburg*, 187 ff.

39. Oscar Handlin, *John Dewey's Challenge to Education* (New York, [1959]), 33 ff., George D. Painter, *Proust; the Early Years* (Boston, 1959), Robert Musil, *The Man Without Qualities* (London, 1953); Hans Rosenberg, *Bureaucracy, Aristocracy and Autocracy* (Cambridge, 1958), 182 ff.; Hannah Arendt, *The Origins of Totalitarianism* (New York, [1951]), 54 ff.; Norman Jacobs, ed., *Culture for the Millions?* (Princeton, 1961), 43 ff.; Kann, *Austrian Intellectual History*, 146 ff.

40. Jacobs, *Culture for Millions?* 64 ff.

41. Oscar Handlin, *Adventure in Freedom* (New York, 1954), 174 ff.; Kann, *Austrian Intellectual History*, 109 ff.

42. Dore, *City Life in Japan*, 291 ff.; Arendt, *Origins of Totalitarianism*, 301 ff.; Jenks, *Vienna and the Young Hitler*, 40 ff., 74 ff., 126 ff.

43. Mumford, *City in History*, 511 ff.; Louis Wirth, *Community Life and Social Policy* (Chicago, [1956]), 206 ff.

44. Weber, *The City*, 11 ff.; Wirth, "Urbanism," 8 ff.; Sjoberg, *Preindustrial City*, 4 ff., 321 ff.

The City in American Civilization

ARTHUR M. SCHLESINGER

"The true point of view in the history of this nation is not the Atlantic Coast," declared Frederick Jackson Turner in his famous essay of 1893, "it is the Great West." Professor Turner, writing in Wisconsin, had formed his ideas in an atmosphere of profound agrarian unrest, and the announcement of the Superintendent of the Census in 1890 that the frontier line could no longer be traced impelled him to the conclusion that "the first period of American history" had closed. His brilliant paper occasioned a fundamental reappraisal of the mainsprings of national development.

Today, however, it seems clear that in the zeal to correct older notions he overlooked another order of society which, rivaling the frontier even in the earliest days, eventually became the major force. The city marched westward with the outposts of settlement, always injecting exotic elements into pioneer existence, while in the older sections it steadily extended its dominion over politics, economics and all the other interests of life. The time came, in 1925, when Turner himself confessed the need of "an urban reinterpretation of our history." A true understanding of America's past demands this balanced

From Arthur M. Schlesinger, *Paths to the Present* (New York: Macmillan, 1949), pp. 210-33. Copyright 1949 by The Macmillan Company. Reprinted by permission of the publisher. The late Arthur M. Schlesinger was Francis Lee Higginson Professor of History at Harvard University.

view—an appreciation of the significance of both frontier and city. The broad outlines of the particular role of the city are here suggested.

I

The Atlantic shore constituted the original frontier. Though the great bulk of colonists took up farming, the immediate object of the first settlers was to found a village or town, partly for mutual protection and partly as a base for peopling the near-by country. Other advantages presently gave these places more lasting reasons for existence. There persons could enjoy friendly intercourse with their neighbors as in Europe and there, too, ply a variety of occupations. These communities, besides taking in farm produce for consumption and export, developed local manufactures, arts and crafts and carried on fisheries and an active overseas trade. Without the articles so provided—hardware, firearms, medicine, books and the like—the colonial standard of living would have greatly suffered.

In time the coastline became beaded with towns, many of them so well situated with respect to geographic and trading advantages as to grow into the great cities of today. The establishment of settlements like Albany, New York, and Lancaster, Pennsylvania, moreover, foreshadowed the rise of urban communities inland. If colonial towns seem small by modern standards, it is well to remember that this was also true of contemporary English provincial towns, for industrialization had not yet concentrated populations in the homeland. Philadelphia with thirty thousand people on the eve of Independence was one of the metropolises of the British Empire.

From the outset townsfolk were plagued with what would today be called urban problems. There were disadvantages as well as advantages in living closely together, and as these disadvantages became flagrant, the citizens were moved to action. Though they seldom assumed community responsibilities willingly, their record compares favorably with that of provincial cities in the mother country. To combat the increase of crime the public-spirited in some places maintained night watches out of their own purses, while in others the city fathers required persons to take turns guarding the streets by night on pain of fines. Sooner or later, however, the taxpayers accepted such policing as a normal municipal charge. The fire hazard early prodded the authorities to regulate the construction of chimneys, license chimney sweeps and oblige householders to keep water buckets; and when these measures fell short of the requirements in the eighteenth century, the people formed volunteer companies which, long after the colonial period, continued to be the chief agency of fire fighting. The removal of garbage generally devolved upon roving swine and goats, while drainage remained pretty much an unsolved problem, though occasional individuals laid private sewers. The pressure of urban needs also fertilized American inventiveness, producing Franklin's lightning rod and the fireplace stove.

Thanks to the special conditions of town life, the inhabitants developed a sense of collective responsibility in their daily concerns that increasingly distinguished them from the individualistic denizens of the farm and frontier. Other circumstances served to widen the distance. As cities grew in size and substance, they engaged in economic rivalry with one another which tended to ignore the interests of the intervening countryside. Boston, New England's metropolis, possessed special mercantile advantages which enabled her for nearly a century to maintain a position of primacy in British America, with New York, Philadelphia and lesser centers hardly more than commercial satellites. These other ports, however, contended as best they could for their share of ocean-borne traffic and briskly cultivated their local trading areas.

New Yorkers, for example, successfully fought the proposal of the East New Jersey authorities to erect a competing port at Perth Amboy, and for a time prevailed upon the provincial legislature to tax and otherwise hinder Boston's commerce with eastern Long Island. The fur trade with the Iroquois brought Manhattan and Albany businessmen immense profits, but watchful of every advantage, the New Yorkers contested with Philadelphia for the trade of the Susquehanna region. Farther to the south, Charleston and Virginia merchants staged a similar struggle for the deerskins of the back country, with the South Carolinians emerging victorious. An unpremeditated result of this fierce competition for pelts was a notable stimulus to westward exploration and settlement.

As the eighteenth century advanced, Boston's rivals came to stand securely on their own feet, aided by their rapidly developing hinterlands. New York now completed its sway over western Connecticut and eastern New Jersey, while Philadelphia merchants annexed western Jersey, Delaware and northern Maryland. So eager was the pursuit of business that the chambers of commerce of New York and Charleston, formed respectively in 1768 and 1774,

antedated all others in English-speaking lands. Meanwhile, in the tributary areas, these early indications of urban imperialism bred jealousies and resentments which were to reach critical intensity in later times. The metropolis of a given region became a symbol of deception and greed. "A Connecticut Farmer," venting his spleen against New York in the *New-London Gazette*, August 17, 1770, expressed the fervent hope that "the plumes of that domineering city may yet feather the nests of those whom they have long plucked."

Happily for America's future independence, Britain's new revenue policy after 1763 struck deeply at the roots of urban prosperity. The business classes rallied promptly to the defense of their interests and, heedless of the dangers of playing with fire, secured the backing of the artisan and mechanic groups. Throughout the decade of controversy the seaports set the pace of resistance, supplying most of the militant leaders, conducting turbulent demonstrations at every crisis, and mobilizing farmer support when possible. Even in rural commonwealths like Virginia and Maryland the most effective steps of opposition were taken when the colonists consulted together at the provincial capitals while attending legislative sessions. Boston's foremost position in the proceedings may well have arisen from the fact that, having recently fallen behind Philadelphia and New York in the commercial race, she was resolved at any cost to stay the throttling hand of Parliament. With the assembling of the First Continental Congress the direction of the movement shifted to Philadelphia, the principal city, presently to become first capital of the new Republic.

The colonial town, however, was more than an embodiment of political and economic energies or a means of gratifying the gregarious instinct. Cities, then as now, were places where one found a whole gamut of satisfactions. Ports of entry for European settlers and goods, they were also ports of entry for European thought and standards of taste. At the same time their monopoly of printing presses, newspapers, bookstores and circulating libraries exposed the residents to a constant barrage of mental stimuli. Hence the spirit of innovation expressed itself quite as much in intellectual as in commercial undertakings. It was townsfolk who led in founding schools and colleges. The protracted battle to establish inoculation as a preventive against smallpox was fought out in the cities. The first great victory for freedom of the press was won by a Philadelphia lawyer defending a New York editor. Besides, mere numbers of people made it possible for the professions to become more clearly differentiated, so that a merchant need no longer plead cases before the courts nor a clergyman practice medicine. Before the colonial period ended, bar associations and medical societies were flourishing in New York, Boston and elsewhere, and medical schools were drawing students to Philadelphia and New York.

The man whom a biographer has called the "first civilized American" was the scion of not one but many cities. Boston, Philadelphia, London and Paris, all contributed to Benjamin Franklin's intellectual growth and social understanding. Few elements of American culture but are indebted to his fostering care: printing, publishing, journalism, belles-lettres, education, the postal service, theoretical and applied science. All these achievements rested in final analysis on that interest, encouragement and

financial support which a populous community alone could provide. How diligently Franklin utilized these advantages appears in his autobiography, which reveals, for instance, how he set about arousing his fellow Philadelphians to the need of such projects as a lending library, a hospital and the American Philosophical Society.

Yet Franklin with all his many-sidedness was less "civilized" than urban society as a whole: his ambit of interests did not embrace the theater, architecture or an active concern with art. In all these lines the pre-Revolutionary town, with the steady increase of wealth and leisure, showed a growing maturity. Cities, for example, vied with one another for the services of outstanding portraitists. Robert Feke, a Newport artist, painted also in Boston, New York and Philadelphia. John Singleton Copley of Boston found on a visit to New York "so many that are impatient to sit that I am never at a loss to fill up all my time." Like the Philadelphian Benjamin West, however, Copley eventually removed to London.

The city, both in its internal life and external relations, deeply affected colonial society politically, economically and culturally. Though in 1776 only about one in twenty-five Americans dwelt in places of eight thousand or more, the urban influence, thanks to its concentrated character, carried far greater weight than its fractional representation in the population indicated. Moreover, city residents evolved a pattern of life which not only diverged from, but increasingly challenged, that of countryside and frontier. These restless, aspiring urban communities foreshadowed the large role that cities would play in the years ahead.

II

That role townsfolk began to assume in the struggle for a strong central government following the Revolution. As a contemporary newspaper observed, "The citizens in the seaport towns . . . live compact; their interests are one; there is a constant connection and intercourse between them; they can, on any occasion, centre their votes where they please." Faced by interstate trade restrictions, stay laws and growing social turmoil, the urban business and cerditor classes feared for their future welfare and the sanctity of property rights. The framing and ratification of the Constitution represented in considerable degree their triumph over the debtor groups and small farmers of the interior. In the circumstances the first Congress under the new instrument was greeted with petitions from Philadelphia, New York, Boston and Baltimore for a tariff to protect American manufactures.

The underlying strife between city and country led also to the formation of the first national parties under the Constitution. Hamilton's famous financial plan, intended to benefit urban capitalists and thus indirectly the nation, formed the rallying point of the Federalists, while Jefferson, imbued with physiocratic notions, organized the Republican opposition. The Virginia planter, unlike the New York lawyer, dreaded the growth of a powerful moneyed class, and in the spread of cities he foresaw a repetition of the social miseries typical of the Old World. "For the general operation of manufacture," he declared, "let our work-shops remain in Europe." He could even regard calmly the destructive yellow-fever epidemics in Philadelphia and other ports in the 1790's, since the pestilence might teach people to avoid populous centers.

The contrasting social ideals and economic motives reflected in this early alignment of parties evoked differing views of constitutional interpretation and of particular measures. From that day to this the chief business of American politics has been to reconcile these interests in furtherance of the national welfare. True, the relative purity of the original groupings gradually became diluted. With the multiplication of urban voters through the years, Jefferson's political progeny, confident of the agricultural South, sought also to appeal to city wage earners. By the same token, the opposition party tended to be a coalition of city businessmen and Northern farmers. Hence each party came in time to constitute a battleground of contending urban and rural elements within its own ranks, a situation which continues to characterize American politics.

III

The westward surge of population beginning shortly after the Revolution has obscured the fact that the leading Atlantic cities, though hard hit by the war, soon resumed their growth, and that with the coming of the nineteenth century the rate of urban development in the nation at large far surpassed that of rural development. Between 1800 and 1860 the number of townsfolk increased twenty-four times while the rural population merely quadrupled. By 1810 one out of every twenty Americans lived in communities of eight thousand or more, by 1840 one out of every twelve, and by 1860 nearly one in every six.

Paradoxically enough, westward migration itself helped to bring this about, for the transappalachian region bred its own urban localities. Serving at first chiefly as distributing centers for commodities from the seaboard, these raw settlements quickly developed into marts where local manufacturer and farm dweller exchanged products. Pittsburgh early began to make glass, shoes, iron castings, nails and textiles, and already in 1814 the *Pittsburgh Gazette* was complaining of the sooty atmosphere. By that time Cincinnati, farther down the river, boasted of two woolen mills and a cotton factory, and its meatpacking business was winning it the sobriquet of Porkopolis. Emboldened by such achievements, apparently every cluster of log huts dreamed of equal or greater eminence. The Indiana pioneers, for example, hopefully named their forest hamlets Columbia City, Fountain City, Saline City, Oakland City and Union City or, setting their sights still higher, called them New Philadelphia, New Paris, Rome City and even New Pekin.

Meanwhile, in the East, scores of cities sprang into being, generally at the fall line of the rivers, where water power was available for manufacturing. As the budding industrialists looked about for new worlds to conquer, they, together with the Eastern merchants and bankers, perceived their El Dorado in the settling West. Soon New York, Philadelphia and Baltimore were racing for the trade of the transappalachian country. This clash of urban imperialisms appeared most strikingly perhaps in the rivalry for transportation routes to the interior. The Baltimoreans led off by building a turnpike to tap the eastern terminus of the Cumberland Road, which the federal government by 1818 had completed as far as Wheeling on the Ohio. In order to counter this move, Pennsylvania promoted Philadelphia's wagon trade with the West by subsidizing a chain of roads to Pittsburgh. New York City, utilizing her natural advantages, now secured state backing for an all-water artery through upstate New York from the Hudson to Lake Erie.

The instant success of the Erie Canal, opened in 1825, forced a change of strategy on Manhattan's competitors. Philadelphia with legislative help promptly instituted a part-water, part-land route through the mountains, while Baltimore pushed the project of a Chesapeake and Ohio canal. Other citizens in the Maryland metropolis, however, conceived a bolder plan. Just as the canal had bested the turnpike, why should not the newly invented railroad best the canal? The construction of the Baltimore and Ohio Railroad, begun in 1828, once more altered the major weapons in the contest. In the next quarter of a century Baltimore and Philadelphia completed their rail connections with the West, New York acquired two lines, and Boston, which had lagged behind during the turnpike and canal eras, recovered some of the lost ground with a railroad linking up with the eastern extremity of the Erie Canal.

Middle Western towns, following the Eastern example, meanwhile entered upon a somewhat similar struggle, each seeking to carve out its own economic dependencies and spheres of influence and to profit from the new ties with the seaboard. By 1840 a network of artificial waterways joined Cleveland and Toledo on Lake Erie with Portsmouth, Cincinnati and Evansville on the Ohio. As in the East, however, the arrival of the steam locomotive changed the situation. Now every up-and-coming municipality strove by hook or crook to become a railroad center, sometimes plunging heavily in debt for the purpose. And looking to the commercial possibilities of the remoter West, Chicago, St. Louis, Memphis and New Orleans concocted rival plans for a Pacific railroad—a maneuvering for position that had political repercussions in Congress and contributed to the passage of the Kansas-Nebraska Act in 1854, which it was thought would facilitate the building of a transcontinental line from St. Louis. This law, by authorizing slavery by "popular sovereignty" in a region hitherto closed to it, helped to set the stage for the Civil War.

The progress in transportation facilities, confined largely to the North, spurred urban development throughout that part of the country. The Erie Canal, reinforced by the rail arteries to the West and the magnificent harbor at the mouth of the Hudson, established conclusively New York's pre-eminence on the seaboard and in the nation. From only sixty thousand inhabitants in 1800 its population (not counting Brooklyn) climbed to eight hundred thousand by 1860, outdistancing Philadelphia and placing it next to London and Paris in size, while Philadelphia with more than half a million was in 1860 larger than Berlin. Brooklyn, Baltimore and Boston came next in size. Indicative of the westward movement of the urban frontier was the fact that at the latter date all the other places of over a hundred thousand—New Orleans, Cincinnati, St. Louis and Chicago—were in the heart of the country. Chicago, though the smallest of these cities in 1860, had already gathered the economic sinews which would make it New York's chief rival before the century closed. Anthony Trollope, observing the Midwest in 1861, remarked that except for a few river and lake sites "settlers can hardly be said to have chosen their own localities. These have been chosen for them by the originators of the different lines of railway." Urban communities greatly augmented the demand for farm products, accelerated the invention of labor-saving implements like the steel plow and the reaper and thus furthered commercial agriculture, which in turn speeded city growth.

To master the new complexities of urban living demanded something more than the easygoing ways of colonial towns. Enlarged populations called for enlarged measures for the community safety and welfare, whether by government or otherwise. As might be expected, the bigger cities set the pace. After the lethal yellow-fever visitations of the 1790's frightened Philadelphia into installing a public water works, other places fell into line, so that more than a hundred systems came into existence before the Civil War. Unfortunately, ignorance of the yet to be discovered germ theory of disease fastened attention on clear water instead of pure water, thus leaving the public health still inadequately protected. To cope with the growing lawlessness the leading cities now supplemented night watches with day police. In 1822 Boston instituted gas lighting and in 1823 set the example of a municipally owned sewerage system. About the same time regular omnibus service was started on the streets of New York, to be followed in the next decade by horsecars running on tracks.

Fire fighting, however, continued generally in the hands of volunteer companies. Though Boston organized a paid municipal department in 1837 and Cincinnati and other Western towns greatly improved the apparatus by introducing steam fire engines in the 1850's, New York and Philadelphia, thanks to the political pull of volunteer brigades, resisted changes in equipment and waited respectively till 1865 and 1871 to municipalize their systems. The cities did nothing at all to combat the evil of slums, an unexpected development due to the great inrush of foreign immigrants into the Atlantic ports in the forties and fifties. Even more serious for the ordinary citizen was the growth of political machines, rooted in the tenement-house population, the fire companies and the criminal classes, and trafficking in franchises for the new public utilities. Appointments to government office for partisan services, first practiced in Eastern cities, preceded and led directly to the introduction of the spoils system into state and national politics.

The "diversities of extreme poverty and extreme wealth," which Edwin H. Chapin etched so sharply in *Humanity in the City* (1854), distressed the tenderhearted and gave rise to most of the reform crusades of the pre-Civil War generation. Compact living facilitated the banding together of such folk and also the collection of funds. Never before had America known so great an outpouring of effort to befriend the poor and the handicapped. Under urban stimulus arose the movement for free schools, for public libraries, for married women's property rights, for universal peace, for prison reform, for a better deal for the insane. The new conditions of city life begot a social conscience on the part of townsfolk which would be lasting of effect and which increasingly differentiated them from their brethren on the farm and frontier.

In these crowded centers, too, the labor movement took form, for the vaunted safety valve of the frontier failed to work for the mass of the wage earners. "The wilderness has receded," declared Orestes A. Brownson in 1840, "and already the new lands are beyond the reach of the mere laborer, and the employer has him at his mercy." Early in the preceding decade trade-unions began to appear, first along the seaboard, then at such inland points as Buffalo, Pittsburgh, Cincinnati and St. Louis; and for a short time a national federation flourished. But the long economic slump following the Panic of 1837 shattered most of the organizations and turned the thoughts of men like George Henry Evans, a New York labor editor, to plans for siphoning excess urban inhabitants into the federal domain by means of free farms. During the discussions over the homestead bill of 1852, even an Alabama member urged Congress "to help the cities to disgorge their cellars and their garrets of a starving, haggard, and useless population." But the House measure failed in the Senate, and until the Civil War further attempts went awry because of Southern fears that anti-slavery Northerners would fill up the Western territories. In any event the farm population would have been the chief beneficiaries, for it is unlikely that urban workingmen could have been enticed to exchange known ills for the hazards and uncertainties of pioneering.

Besides, along with the known ills went cultural opportunities and advantages absent from the countryside. The fast-growing cities afforded the largest public America had yet known for the appreciation and patronage of letters and the arts, and greatly increased the chances for the discovery and recruitment of talent in all fields. Townsfolk, moreover, were the first to feel the bracing impact of new currents of European thought. A varied and vital intellectual life resulted which directly or indirectly affected all members of the community, including the children, for whom municipal authorities now began to provide free high schools.

Newspapers and magazines proliferated. The first modern publishing houses sprang up. The theater became firmly established, native players like Charlotte Cushman and Edwin Booth winning additional laurels in England. Artists multiplied, being at last assured of adequate support at home, and the founding of the National Academy of Design in 1826 raised New York to the position of the country's chief art center. In literature also this richly creative period demonstrated urban superiority, with Boston, Cambridge and Concord largely responsible for the "flowering of New England," and New York and Philadelphia, even Cincinnati and St. Louis, making their own bids for fame. Only in architecture did the city botch the possibilities, for the mushroom growth of population forced new construction at a pace that ignored aesthetic considerations. The typical city, even in its wealthy residential sections, exhibited a fantastic patchwork of styles.

Whatever the attractions of town life, the elevenfold leap in urban population between 1820 and 1860 aroused increasing dismay and foreboding among rural folk who saw their own sons and daughters succumbing to the lure. "Adam and Eve were created and placed in a garden. Cities are the results of the fall," cried Joseph H. Ingraham, a popular religious novelist. Country preachers joined in denouncing these human agglomerations "cursed with immense accumulations of ignorance and error, vice and crime," while

farm journals implored the young not to sacrifice their manly independence in order "to fetch and carry" and "cringe and flatter" for a miserable pittance. Political attitudes further mirrored the deepening distrust. Western opposition to the Second United States Bank sprang largely from alarm at the control of credit facilities by the "great cities of the Northeast, which," according to Missouri's Senator Thomas Hart Benton, "have been for forty years, and that by force of federal legislation, the lion's den of Southern and Western money— that den into which all the tracks point inward; from which the returning track of a solitary dollar has never yet been seen."

Since, however, the West was growing its own towns and cities, it was becoming steadily more like the Northeast, whereas the South, chained by Negro slavery to agriculture, contained few sizable cities and those mostly at its edges. The widening breach between North and South was in no small part due to these divergent tendencies. Every year sharpened the contrast between the urban spirit of progress animating the one section and the static, rural life of the other. Few important industries existed below the Mason and Dixon line. Though illiteracy prevailed among the mass of whites as well as blacks, little or nothing was done to further free schools, and the North's humanitarian crusades were derided as Yankee fanaticism. Moreover, the Southerners, lacking the nerve centers for creative cultural achievement, fell behind in arts, letters and science. "It would have been surprising had they not desired secession," remarked Anthony Trollope, in America shortly after Fort Sumter. "Secession of one kind, a very practical secession, had already been forced upon them by circumstances. They had become a separate people, dissevered from the North by habits, morals, institutions, pursuits and every conceivable difference in their modes of thought and action." Beyond the tie of language, he went on, "they had no bond but that of a meagre political union in their Congress at Washington."

In addition, their economic life lay under thrall to the Northern business community. "It is a hopeless task," affirmed the South Carolinian William Gregg, "to undertake to even approximate to the vast sums of wealth which have been transferred from the South to the North by allowing the Northern cities to import and export for us." For twenty years before the war, Southern commercial conventions sought ways and means to escape this bondage, but the hope of creating their own trading and financial centers was vain so long as lands and Negroes held a superior attraction for capital. It was no mere coincidence that Charleston, dropping rapidly behind the Northern ports, initiated every disunionist movement in the entire South from Jackson's time onward; and the *Charleston Mercury's* bitter comment in 1858 that "Norfolk, Charleston, Savannah, Mobile, are suburbs of New York" suggests that other places shared the bitterness.

Withdrawal from the Union coupled with free trade with England seemed the answer, since then, it was believed, "Charleston in the course of ten years will become a New York"; and other localities nursed similar hopes. Under the circumstances the leading towns and cities strongly supported the movement for separation. Even New Orleans, despite its large infusion of Northerners and foreign-born, chose twenty secessionists and only four unionists to the state convention summoned to take action. Not surprisingly, the Confederate authorities on assuming power invalidated the private indebtedness—estimated variously at forty to four hundred millions—owing to Northern merchants, bankers and manufacturers. But the North's industrial might and greater man power overwhelmed the South in war as well as in peace.

IV

In the generation following the Civil War the city took supreme command. Between 1860 and 1900 the urban population again quadrupled while the rural merely doubled. With one out of every six people inhabiting communities of eight thousand or over in the earlier year, the proportion rose to nearly one out of four in 1880 and to one out of three in 1900. Considerably more than half of the urban-moving throng gravitated to places of twenty-five thousand and upwards. Since every town dweller added to his effectiveness by association with his fellows, even these figures understate the city's new role in the nation. Nevertheless the sheer growth of particular localities is amazing. By 1890 New York (including Brooklyn) had about caught up with Paris, while Chicago and Philadelphia, with over a million each as compared with New York's two and a half million, then outranked all but five cities in Europe. In the Far West, Los Angeles jumped from fewer than 5000 in 1860 to more than 100,000 in 1900, and Denver from nothing at all to 134,000, while in the postwar South, Memphis with a bare 23,000 in the former year surpassed 100,000 in the latter. "The youngest of the nations," wrote Samuel L. Loomis in 1887, "has already more large cities than any except Great Britain and Germany." Thanks to the progress of settlement in the West and the burgeoning of industry in a South emancipated from slavery, the city had at last become a national instead of a sectional institution.

As urban centers grew in size and wealth, they cast an ever stronger spell over the American mind. Walt Whitman, returning to Greater New York in September, 1870, after a short absence, gloried in the "splendor, picturesqueness, and oceanic amplitude of these great cities." Conceding that Nature excelled in her mountains, forests and seas, he rated man's achievement equally great "in these ingenuities, streets, goods, houses, ships—these hurrying, feverish, electric crowds of men." (More tersely, Dr. Oliver Wendell Holmes, weary of hearing Cowper's line, "God made the country and man made the town," retorted, "God made the *cavern* and man made the *house!*") Little wonder that the young and the ambitious yielded to the temptation. "We cannot all live in cities, yet nearly all seem determined to do so," commented Horace Greeley, adding that with "millions of acres" awaiting cultivation "hundreds of thousands reject this and rush into the cities."

The exodus from the older countryside was especially striking. While the cities of Maine, Vermont, Massachusetts, Rhode Island, New York, Maryland and Illinois gained two and a half million people between 1880 and 1890, the rural districts of these states lost two hundred thousand. The drain of humanity from backwoods New England left mute witnesses in deserted hill villages and abandoned farms. In the nation as a whole, 10,063 townships out of 25,746 in thirty-nine states and territories shrank in population during the decade. Some of the rural decline was due to the shifting of agriculturists from older regions to the free unworked lands of the trans-Mississippi West, but the phenomenon was so widespread—and, indeed, as characteristic of Europe during these years as of America—as to evidence the more potent and pervasive influence of the city. True, the 1880's merely climaxed a historic trend. In the century from 1790 to 1890 the total population had grown 16-fold while the urban segment grew 139-fold. Hence the celebrated announcement of the Superintendent of the Census in 1890 that a frontier line no longer existed can hardly be said to have marked the close of "the first period of American history." Rather it was a tardy admission that the second period was already under way.

The lusty urban growth created problems which taxed human resourcefulness to the utmost. Though European precedent helped solve some of the difficulties, American ingenuity in most respects outdistanced that of Old World cities. The record is extraordinary. Hardly had New York in 1870 opened the first elevated railway than San Francisco contrived the cable car, and hardly had the cable car begun to spread over the country than Richmond demonstrated the superiority of the electric trolley system, and Boston at the end of the century added the subway. The need for better lighting prompted the invention of Brush's outdoor arc lamp and Edison's incandescent bulb for indoors, and in another application of electric power the telephone brought townsfolk into instant communication. By means of the apartment house and the department store cities simplified problems of housing and shopping, while by means of the steel-framed skyscraper they saved further ground space by building their business districts upward. Density of population also led to more effective protection of the public health by turning to account the principles of the germ theory of disease just being discovered abroad. Before the century's close nearly every municipality of ten thousand or over had one or more officials charged with the duty of charting and checking communicable maladies. The bigger cities had become healthier places to live than many rural sections.

These civic advances, however, came at a price already beginning to be evident before the Civil War. Americans had developed their political institutions under simple rural conditions; they had yet to learn how to govern cramped populations. Preyed upon by unscrupulous men eager to exploit the expanding public utilities, municipal politics became a byword for venality. As Francis Parkman wrote, "Where the carcass is, the vultures gather together." New York's notorious Tweed Ring denoted a sickness that racked Philadelphia, Chicago, St. Louis, Minneapolis and San Francisco as well. "With very few exceptions," declared Andrew D. White, "the city governments of the United States are the worst in Christendom—the most expensive, the most inefficient, and the most corrupt."

Though an irate citizenry succeeded now and then in "turning the rascals out," the boss and the machine soon recovered control. Nevertheless, the good-government campaigns ventilated the abuses of municipal misrule and aroused the humane to the worsening plight of the urban poor. Under reform prodding, the New York legislature

from 1865 onward adopted a series of laws to combat the slum evil in America's metropolis, though with disappointing results. More fruitful were the steps taken by private groups in Manhattan and elsewhere to establish social settlements and playgrounds and to replace the indiscriminate almsgiving of earlier times with a more rational administration of charity. Religion, awakening to the social gospel, helped out with slum missions and institutional churches. In the city, too, trade-unions made a new start, organizing the swelling army of urban workers on a nation-wide basis, joining with the reformers in securing factory legislation and gradually winning concessions from the employing class. Occasional voices with a foreign accent advocated socialism or anarchism as the remedy for the city's gross disparities of wealth and want, while Edward Bellamy in *Looking Backward* offered a home-grown version of communism in his fanciful account of Boston as it would be in the year 2000.

The increasing tension of living was evidenced in a variety of ways. Masses of people reared in a rustic environment had suddenly to adapt themselves to the frantic urban pace. One outcome was a startling growth of neurasthenia, a word coined by Dr. George M. Beard of New York in his work *American Nervousness* (1881), which traced the malady to the hurry and scurry, the din of the streets, the frenzied struggle for existence, the mental excitements and endless distractions. From the ranks of the high-strung, Mary Baker Eddy gathered most of her converts to the new religion of Christian Science, and for much the same reason townsfolk now gave enthusiastic support to organized sports. Flabby muscles unfitted most persons for direct participation, but they compromised by paying professional contestants to take their exercise for them. If, as a magazine writer said, nervousness had become the "national disease of America," baseball, partly as an antidote, became America's national game.

The stress of existence seemed only to enhance creative powers, however. The cities, re-enacting their role of the "fireplaces of civilization"—Theodore Parker's phrase—provided compelling incentives to cultural achievement, multiplying colleges, public libraries and publishing houses and founding art museums, art schools and conservatories of music. A Henry James might still find Europe an intellectually more congenial milieu, but William Dean Howells, Mark Twain and Joel Chandler Harris discovered the needed stimulus at home; and the same held true of all or nearly all the leading painters, sculptors, architects, composers, playwrights and scholars. A statistical study showed that localities of eight thousand and more gave birth to almost twice as many men of note as their proportionate share, and that in fields like science, engineering, art and literature the ratio was far greater. But even such computations do less than justice to the city, for there, too, gifted newcomers from the countryside and foreign shores entered their Promised Land. Civic pride prompted the holding of two great expositions, one at Philadelphia in 1876 and the other at Chicago in 1893. That the second and grander took place in an inland metropolis revealed how decisively urbanization had altered the face of traditional America.

The new age of the city rested upon an application of business enterprise to the exploitation of natural resources such as mankind had never known. The city, as insatiable as an octopus, tended to draw all nutriment to itself. Railroads, industrial combinations, investment capital, legislative favors, comprised the means. There arose a complex of urban imperialisms, each striving for dominion, each battling with rivals and each perforce yielding tribute to the lord of them all. "Every produce market, every share market," observed James Bryce, "vibrates to the Produce Exchange and Stock Exchange of New York."

As the city forged ahead, imposing its fiat on less developed regions, the rift between country and town widened portentously. Historians speak of a new sectionalism aligning West and South against East in these years, but Charles B. Spahr in *The Distribution of Wealth in the United States* (1896) pointed out more acutely that the antagonism "only exists in so far as the East is the section of the cities, while the South and West are the sections containing the great body of the farmers." Everywhere rural life was in chains: "The people on the farms and in the villages in the East have shared no more in the advancing wealth of the past quarter of a century than the people on the farms and villages of the South and West." He estimated that city families possessed on the average almost three times as much as country families.

The passage of years heightened the husbandman's conviction of being a second-class citizen, of losing out in the technological and cultural progress that dowered townsfolk. He lacked the telephone, electric lights, central heating, plumbing, sewerage, street cars, recreational facilities. Herbert Quick in after years remembered the women as "pining for neighbors, for domestic help, for pretty clothes, for schools, music, art, and the many things tasted when the magazines came in." The drift of youth to the cities emphasized the shortcomings, embittering those who stayed behind, even though they loved the land and would not have left if they could. The farmer, moreover, accepted too readily the urban estimate of his calling. Once acclaimed by orators as the "embodiment of economic independence," now, remarked a magazine writer, he was the butt of humorists: "The 'sturdy yeoman' has become the 'hayseed.'"

This feeling of rural inferiority, this growing sense of frustration, underlay the political eruptions in the farming regions: the Granger movement in the 1870's, the Farmers' Alliances of the eighties and the Populist conflagration in the nineties. Each time specific economic grievances like steep freight rates, high interest charges and low crop prices stirred the smoldering embers into blaze. These were tangible hardships which the farmers demanded the government remove by such measures as railroad regulation and silver inflation. It fell to the greatest of the agrarian champions, addressing the Democratic national convention in 1896, to hurl the ultimate challenge at urban imperialism. "Burn down your cities and leave our farms, and your cities will spring up again as if by magic," cried William Jennings Bryan of Nebraska in a speech that won him the nomination, "but destroy our farms and the grass will grow in the streets of every city in the country." In the election that followed, the big cities of the East and Midwest, including New York which for the first time went Republican, responded by casting decisive majorities against the Democrats and free silver.

V

No one in 1900 could have foreseen the transformation which the twentieth century was to effect in both town and country. In the cities the reformers made steady progress in bridling the predatory forces which, in James Bryce's familiar phrase, had made municipal government "the one conspicuous failure of the United States." Early in the century a crusading type of mayor rode into power—men like "Golden Rule" Jones and Brand Whitlock in Toledo, Tom Johnson in Cleveland and Emil Seidel in Milwaukee—who aroused the citizens from their apathy and showed that elected officials could zealously promote the public good. Even more important was the introduction of the commission-manager plan of government, which by 1948 came to prevail in nearly eight hundred places. A radical departure from the clumsy older form, which imitated the checks and balances of state governments, the new system copied the streamlined structure of business corporations, with the commission corresponding to the board of directors and the city manager resembling the president or general manager named by the board to conduct detailed affairs. In nearly every case the reform quickly justified itself, though eternal vigilance by the voters continued to be the price of ensuring the best results.

Alongside these improvements occurred the first sustained attempts at city planning. Instead of letting urban communities evolve in hit-and-miss fashion, the endeavor now was to guide their growth in the interests of sightliness and the people's convenience, safety and health. By an extensive use of zoning ordinances, appropriate locations were mapped for business and factory districts, residential neighborhoods, recreational facilities; and the New York legislature's adoption of an effective tenement-house code in 1901 inspired other states and municipalities to a vigorous attack on the slum evil, though it was not till the 1930's that the federal authorities took a hand in the matter. Already by 1922 a hundred and eighty-five towns and cities had set up official bodies to chart over-all programs of development, and by 1940 the number had risen to well over a thousand. City planning, moreover, stimulated interest in county planning and state planning and helped create the atmosphere for the New Deal's ventures in regional and national planning.

These advances went hand in hand with a further piling up of townsfolk. By 1930 approximately half the nation dwelt in localities of eight thousand or more and nearly a third in centers of one hundred thousand or more. Urban dominance was further enhanced by the emergence of great metropolitan districts or regions. These "city states" had begun to form in the nineteenth century as swifter means of transportation and communication flung the inhabitants outward into the suburbs, but it was the coming of the automobile and motor truck and the extension of electricity and other conveniences into the surrounding territory that gave these supercommunities their unprecedented size and importance.

Each consisted of one or more core cities with satellite towns and dependent rural areas, the whole knit together by economic, social and cultural ties. The hundred and thirty-three metropolitan regions in 1930 grew to a hundred

and forty by 1940, when they contained almost half the total population. New York's region overlapped four states, an irregular tract twice the area of Rhode Island with 272 incorporated communities and intervening farm lands. Chicago's embraced 115 incorporated places, and San Francisco's 38. Subdivided into independent municipalities, the people faced enormous difficulties in looking after such common governmental concerns as policing, sewage disposal, public health and schooling. Some students, despairing of any other solution, proposed separate statehood for the larger metropolitan regions. New and unanticipated strains have been placed on a federal system framed in the eighteenth century for a simple agrarian economy.

Of all the new trends in urban development, however, none had such profound effects as the altered relationship of country and city. Historians generally attribute the decline of the free-silver movement in the late nineties to the discovery of fresh sources of gold supply and an uptrend of crop prices, but probably the more fundamental cause was the amelioration of many of the social and psychological drawbacks of farm existence. The introduction of rural free delivery of mail after 1896, the extension of good roads due to the bicycle craze, the expanding network of interurban trolleys, the spread of party-line neighborhood telephones after the basic Bell patents expired in 1893, the increase of country schools—all these, coming shortly before 1900, helped dispel the aching isolation and loneliness, thereby making rustic life pleasanter.

Yet these mitigations seem trifling compared with the marvels which the twentieth century wrought. The automobile brought farm families within easy reach of each other and of the city; the motorbus facilitated the establishment of consolidated schools with vastly improved instruction and equipment; while the radio introduced new interests and pleasures into the homes themselves, shedding its benefits impartially on country and town. At the same time the mechanical energy used in agriculture grew eightfold between 1900 and 1935, thus lightening the husbandman's toil and adding to his opportunities for leisure. Moreover, the state and national governments increasingly employed their powers to improve the farmer's economic and social status. The Smith-Lever Act, passed by Congress in 1914, provided for agricultural-extension work in rural communities through county agents; the Federal Farm Loan Board, created in 1916, offered long-term loans at relatively low rates of interest; and the Smith-Hughes Act of 1917 appropriated public funds for teaching vocational agriculture and home economics in country high schools. Such enactments reached a climax in the 1930's when the New Deal embarked upon far-reaching programs of rural betterment like the Tennessee Valley and Columbia River developments, the Triple-A, government-aided electrification and measures to boost farm tenants up the ladder to ownership. Though inequalities remained, the tiller of the soil had come to share many of the comforts and refinements once belonging only to townsfolk. He had attained a position in American society of which his Populist forebears could hardly have dreamed.

Just as rural life became more urbanized, so urban life became more ruralized. Wooded parks, tree-shaded boulevards, beautified waterfronts, mu-nicipal golf courses, athletic fields and children's playgrounds multiplied, while an increasing army of white-collar workers and wage earners piled into motorcars and buses each night to go farther and farther into the suburbs. Within the metropolitan regions population actually grew faster in the rustic outskirts between 1930 and 1940 than in the central cities. Retail trade too felt the centrifugal tug, and even factories showed a tendency to move into outlying villages where taxes, rent and food cost less. The extension of giant power will doubtless speed the trend, affording more and more townsfolk a chance to live and work and bring up their children in country surroundings. The dread specter of atomic-bomb attacks may operate to the same end in the interests of national military security.

Thus the twentieth century has been spinning a web in which city and country, no longer separate entities, have been brought ever closer together. When the city encroaches sufficiently on the country and the country on the city, America may hope to arrive at a way of life which will blend the best features of both the traditional ways. The people will have within grasp the realization of Plato's vision of a society in which "youth shall dwell in a land of health amid fair sights and sounds and imbibe good from every quarter; and beauty, the emanation of noble works, will flow into the eye and ear like an invigorating breeze from a purer region and imperceptibly woo the soul from infancy into harmony and sympathy with the beauty of reason."

From humble beginnings in the early seventeenth century the city thus traced a varied course. In Europe the modern urban community emerged by gradual stages out of the simple town economy of the Middle Ages; by comparison, the American city leaped into being with breath-taking speed. At first servant to an agricultural order, then a jealous contestant, then an oppressor, it now gives evidence of becoming a comrade and co-operator in a new national synthesis. Its economic function has been hardly more important than its cultural mission or its transforming influence upon rural conceptions of democracy. The city, no less than the frontier, has been a major factor in American civilization. Without an appreciation of the role of both the story is only half told.

II THE CITY IN COLONIAL AMERICA

American urban history began with the small town—five villages hacked out of the wilderness. Each of these villages was geographically endowed to profit from seaborne commerce; each an "upstart" town with no past, an uncertain future, and a host of confounding and novel problems; each faced with survival from fire, disease, and war, and with the mightiest of problems when men gang together, living and acting together with tolerance and responsibility.

From their first rude beginnings in the 1600's to the American Revolution, five towns became five cities, five cities in the wilderness became five cities in revolt. The rise of New York, Boston, Newport, Philadelphia, and Charlestown underscored one major theme in the history of the American city: size is disproportionate to influence. In its first 150 years, this was a profoundly agrarian country with only a small portion of the population living in the five major cities, yet the influence, the power, the vitality of the cities transcended their size. By the end of the colonial period the cities imperially dominated their own immediate hinterland; each had grown economically mature as distributing, producing, marketing centers that helped pierce the backcountry with a transportation system that forged new towns and cities; each acted as a magnet luring the native farmer and the foreign immigrant alike by its opportunities and amenities. The cities had become the intellectual and cultural centers of a new nation, the frontiers of social change. Above all, they were symbols of one underlying cause of the American Revolution: the growth of an embryo nation into political, economic, and social maturity that demanded its own identity.

This is the thesis of Carl Bridenbaugh, whose books have thrust the city into the mainstream of American colonial history. In the first selection in this chapter, Bridenbaugh analyzes the growing pains of the major cities-in-the-making as they struggled into puberty confronted with problems strikingly contemporary—housing, health, sanitation, crime, poverty—all demanding public municipal services that reflected a fundamental necessity for urban living:

53

the will for collective responsibility. Indeed, Bridenbaugh sees this as the theme that singularly sets the city apart from other forms of human settlement, such as those experienced by the frontiersman and the farmer. It suggests that many historians who have assessed the national character have overemphasized the characteristics of agrarian self-reliance and individualism and must balance them with the drive for collective action so pronounced in the achievement and failure in the history of the city, from the colonial period to the present.

Today when we are so concerned about the idea and need for community, Darrett Rutman gives us an analysis of one of the first attempts at collective action in John Winthrop's search for community on the eve of the founding of Boston. With compassion, a touch of irony, a sense of tragedy, Rutman explores the aspirations of the Puritan leader's search for an ideal community, "a Citty upon a hill."

Winthrop, an enormously complex man, like his ship the *Arbella,* was on a voyage between two worlds, the old and the new, the premodern and the modern. As a man of the seventeenth century, he felt the need to reconcile the key concepts of his time, status, property, and God. As a leader of a blind thrust into the wilderness, a flank attack upon the corruptions of Christendom, he felt the need to go beyond his own time to create a secular heaven on earth. For with all the rhetoric about "a city of God" he was a "Puritan" in only a limited way, and his mission, according to Rutman, was religious only in the simplest sense. His errand to the new world was a lay movement, founded on earthly social ideals. Its essence a "secular monestary" geared to the all-encompassing ideal of community—a sense of collective responsibility. Winthrop demanded a literal application of "love thy neighbor as thyself." Status, property, and God were seen in the light of brotherhood. Commerce was corrupt and must be balanced by charity and mercy. Men must blend their aspirations and restrain their greed to the benefit of both the welfare of his fellow man and the good of the community.

Utoptianism is fragile, for all its nobility. The opportunities of the new world broke the spine of the ideal community. They excited the acquisitive urges of Englishmen, they nourished the seed of individualism, which shattered the notion of collective responsibility. The inherent contradictions of the seventeenth-century mind helped create the bickering that destroyed the unity that Winthrop sought. Institutions slipped away from the communal ideal and shaped themselves instead to the nature of the new world. In one sense the failure of the "Citty upon a hill" was inevitable (hindsight being twenty-twenty). It was doomed by its own impracticalities. Can the idea of the brotherhood of man survive in an acquisitive community? Thus Winthrop's ideal can be seen as a casuality of modernity in America. As Professor Rutman makes clear, it can also be seen as a tragedy, the failure of a majestic idea.

The next selection is from *The Private City,* which won the Beveridge Prize in 1969. In this book Sam Bass Warner measures the present against the past and asks what went wrong. In the last fifty years, an era of extraordinary change, European countries initiated programs and devised institutions that have far outstripped American efforts to cope with urban problems. When confronted with problems of poverty, racial integration, decent housing, adequate medical care, effective schools, urban amenities such as recreational areas, Americans have staggered and failed. Why? What went wrong? Warner finds his answer not in some peculiar consequence of the urbanization process, nor in the breakdown of the political system, a symptom but not a cause. He finds it in an attitude, a value system, an ideological committment which more than anything shaped the form, the character, and the flaws of the American city. He calls it privatism. And he finds its origins in colonial Philadelphia, which in his view is the prototype of the American city.

The essence of privatism

lay in its concentration upon the individual and the individual's search for wealth. Psychologically, privatism meant that the individual should seek happiness in personal independence and in the search for wealth; socially, privatism meant that the individual should see his first loyalty as his immediate family, and that a community should be a union of such money-making, accumulating families; politically, privatism meant that the community should keep the peace among individual money-makers, and, if possible, help to create an open and thriving setting where each citizen would have some substantial opportunity to prosper.

While he argues that privatism does not illuminate the whole of the American character and does in fact exist in other cultures, it is nonetheless "the most important element" for understanding how our cities have become what they are. The privatism of realtors, speculators, and investors shaped the physical contours of the city. Economic enterprise, not community action, accounts for the welfare of the people. Political decisions were made according to the aspirations of the business community.

Warner develops his thesis by examining three conditions of eighteenth-century Philadelphia that nourished the phenomenon of privatism: its individualized structure of work, its broad prosperity, and its open society and economy. He gives us vivid portraits of family life, working conditions, the bustle of the market place, the activity of (or lack of) municipal government, and a sense of that vital center of communications, the institution of the tavern.

Privatism is a most interesting thesis and will no doubt influence the thinking of many students of the American city. From others, nervous about its all-encompassing application, it might invite questions to ponder. Is it over-stated? Are there other forces of urbanization equally important but neglected? Can one sniff economic if not cultural determinism? Indeed, *is* Philadelphia representative historically of all other American cities?

One thing is sure, there could not have been cities without the small town. Aside from some pious nostalgia about the small town, historians have been little concerned until recently with this critical aspect of urban history.

After all, cities of whatever size began as small towns. And it is an intriguing question why some grew into cities, some did not, and many withered away. Until recently, it has been the tendency of some historians and sociologists to make too sharp a distinction between rural and urban, and it has led to black-and-white oversimplifications. We have sometimes forgotten that the small town was an in-between station, a filtering maze between farm and city. The small town is also important in understanding American attitudes toward the city, for thousands of small towners moved to the city and took their attitudes with them. Thus the small town has influenced the so-called urban spirit, just as the city has to some extent urbanized the small town. And, finally, the small town is a superb comparative device to understand the city better.

Page Smith provides an analysis of what he calls the "covenanted community," the first and classic model of the small town in America, the New England town. Not merely a haphazard collection of individuals, it had a remarkable internal unity and an intensity of spirit that reflected the dedication of Puritan ideals and aspirations. Like the city, its influence far exceeded its modest size. And where urban historians point to the city in arguing that we must go beyond our preoccupation with the farmer and the frontiersman in seeking a more balanced understanding of American development, Smith goes one step further in dramatizing the role of the small town. His thesis is that the covenanted community was the genesis for a new kind of community settlement which produced and reproduced a host of communities in the American march to the Pacific. In a word, it was the "cutting edge" of the westward movement. He does not give us an altogether balanced picture of the impact of the small town, failing to treat the southern and western towns, with their Baptist and Methodist influences, which also played a significant role in small-town America.[1] Nonetheless, this is one of the best interpretations of the pervasive effect of the New England town.

No romantic chronicler of cozy, small-town America, Professor Smith is particularly effective in exploding the myth that the small town, at least the New England type, was a generator of individualism, liberal attitudes, and progressive change. The town was the bastion of rigid conservatism; the liberal pioneer was in the city.

1. For comparison, see Lewis Atherton, *Main Street on the Middle Border* (Bloomington: Indiana University Press, 1954), Duane A. Smith, *Rocky Mountain Mining Camps* (Bloomington: Indiana University Press, 1967), and Robert R. Dykstra, *The Cattle Towns* (New York: Knopf, 1968).

One Hundred Years of Urban Growth

CARL BRIDENBAUGH

The first hundred years of town history on the American continent witnessed the foundation and gradual development of a truly urban society. The story of American life is customarily regarded as a compound of sectional histories, and in the early colonial period two sections are commonly considered,—the tidewater and the frontier. Yet the tidewater was itself divided, and if we consider the sections as social and psychological rather than as purely geographical entities, it is possible to distinguish three of them,—the rural, agricultural society of the countryside; the restless, advancing society of the frontier; and the urban, commercial society of the larger seaports. Beginning as small specks in the wilderness, the five communities grew from tiny villages into towns, and finally attained the status of small cities. With other village communities of similar interests and outlook which multiplied and grew in the eighteenth century, they emerged as a social and economic "section" extending the length of the Atlantic seaboard, and exhibiting definite urban characteristics in striking contrast to rural farming districts and wilder regions of the frontier. Life in urban areas produced its own peculiar problems to be faced, and the urban viewpoint, based upon continuous close contacts with Europe, derived less from agriculture than from trade. Commercially minded town society looked to the East rather than the West, and was destined from the first to serve as the connecting link between colonial America and its Old World parents.

The future of the colonial towns became immediately evident from the conditions surrounding their birth. Designed as trading communities, they were established on sites most favorable for the pursuit of commerce. They were the western outposts of European commercial expansion in the seventeenth century. City-dwellers from the Old World formed the larger proportion of early town populations, and from the start commercial relations with England or Holland were maintained. Most significantly, the founding process occurred at a time when western Europe, under Dutch and English leadership, was gradually outgrowing and casting off the limitations of medieval feudal economy. Colonial towns grew to maturity in the era of world expansion attending the emergence of modern capitalism, and being new communities, with few irrevocably established customs or traditions, they frequently adapted themselves to the economic drift with more ease and readiness than did the older cities of England. Moreover, the colonizing movement was itself an expression of early capitalistic activity. It called forth organized rather than individual efforts and resources, created new and wider markets for economic development, and opened up seemingly unlimited territories for imperialistic exploitation. It thus produced a marked effect upon Old World economy, accelerating the breakdown of local units of business, and facilitating the formation of larger and more complex organizations of commerce and finance.

The problems which confronted town-dwellers in America were not only those of urban communities, but of a pioneer society as well. Urban development depends largely upon community wealth, and upon the willingness of the group to devote portions of it to projects for civic betterment, or to consent to taxation for this purpose. To a considerable extent the nature of town governments and the extent of authority vested in them conditioned the expenditure of town wealth for community enterprises. Here the colonists were hampered by the traditional nature of the charters of medieval English municipal corporations, whose limitations ill accorded with circumstances in seventeenth and eighteenth century America, especially with the imperious demands for expansion and immediate activity in the New World. In New England towns a new political organization, the town meeting, developed, which exhibited considerable efficiency in the handling of urban problems. This institution was more immediately susceptible to social wants and requirements than were the aristocratic, self-perpetuating corporations founded in America after the example of English municipal governments. Its greater powers of local taxation, and the fact that it placed the spending of public moneys and the enactment of civic ordinances in the hands of those directly affected by these operations, made it a far more effective form of government for dealing with community problems. These problems were the greater, because in the first century of their history the five colonial seaports enjoyed a much more rapid physical growth than did the cities of contemporary Europe. The individual enterprise of American town-dwellers, and the commercial expansion and prosperity they achieved, aided in the solution of these problems of town living, but much of the efficiency and success which attended their efforts may be attributed to the emergence in the New World of a relatively high sense of civic responsibility in the early eighteenth century, at a time when public consciousness in Europe had receded to an extremely low ebb.

The towns were primarily commercial communities seeking treasure by foreign trade, and their economic vitality and commercial demands led to their early breaking the narrow bonds of medieval economic practice to forge ahead on uncharted but highly profitable commercial adventures. All five, during their first century, developed from simple manorial organizations, completely dependent upon European connections, into full-fledged commercial centers, only partially tied to England, and in many cases competing with British cities for a share of imperial traffic. Boston entered early into the West Indian provision trade, thereby setting an example for other American commercial communities. Soon Massachusetts mariners were seeking to monopolize the colonial carrying traffic in ships of their own building, and the profits of carrier and middleman became the basis of the Bay town's prosperity. Her priority in this field gave her an advantage which other seaports did not begin to overcome until the fourth decade of the eighteenth century. A further foundation for urban economic prosperity lay in the existence of an expanding frontier society with its great need for manufactured products. This made possible an earlier development of the towns as distributing centers for a wide hinterland than was the case with English cities like Bristol, Norwich and Exeter, and became in this first century as important a factor in the economic growth of New York, Philadelphia and Charles Town as in that of the New England metropolis. As a producer of staple goods for exchange in trade, Boston, with its limited back country was at a disadvantage. More fortunate were New York with its flour and furs, Philadelphia, with its great staples of wheat, meat and lumber, and Charles Town, which after 1710 found prosperity in the important South Carolina crops of rice and indigo. Eventually the communities enjoying this sound economic backing rose to threaten the supremacy of Boston in colonial trade, while Newport and Philadelphia cut heavily into the Bay town's West India commerce. In the eighteenth century also Newport attained importance in shipbuilding and the slave trade. By 1742 Boston merchants were facing a period of relative decline, while their competitors in other colonial towns found the volume and profits of their traffic steadily mounting.

Continual increase in the volume of colonial trade and enlargement of the territory served by the towns led to greater complexity in commercial relations. In the early years merchants performed all types of business, but toward 1700 their functions began to be more specialized. Retail merchandising having definitely emerged by 1700, the great merchant now dealt chiefly with larger operations of exporting, import-

ing and wholesaling, leaving much of the small trade to the shopkeeper. Demands of trade had by 1710 necessitated the issuance of paper currency in most of the colonies, and the establishment of the colonial post office to serve intercolonial communication. Growing business further led to the creation of insurance offices and some extension of credit facilities. Profits from trade, originally completely absorbed in shipbuilding ventures and industries subsidiary to shipping, now began to create a surplus which sought investment in land, or, in some communities, in the development of certain forms of manufacturing.

Economic prosperity thus made possible the rise of colonial cities. It led to physical expansion of town boundaries, and facilitated dealing with urban problems by corporate effort. Wealth wrung from trade, more than any other single factor, determined the growth of a town society, in which urban amusements and a colonial culture might thrive. This is not, however, to force the history of urban America within the narrow bounds of an exclusively economic interpretation. Social and intellectual development are dependent upon and conditioned by economic progress, but they are not its necessary and inevitable result. They are altered, encouraged or stifled by the action and influence of material forces, but they are not necessarily caused or even initiated solely by economic factors.

When we consider American urban society, apart from its economic aspects, we find it characterized by certain problems affecting it as a unit, and with which as a unit it had to deal. Such problems in general, or collective attempts for their control and regulation, are either absent from or unimportant in rural or frontier societies, but in the case of our urban section they are present, in rudimentary form at least, from its inception. They persist and grow with the maturing of that section, and the means taken for dealing with them further differentiate the urban from other types of society.

Logically, the first of these problems to appear are the physical, and of these the most immediate was housing. As in rural regions this remained for the most part an individual problem, and there are only a few cases on record where even indirectly, by sale or subdivision of land or by encouragement of artisans, the community stepped in to relieve a housing shortage. On the other hand, the laying out and maintaining of a highway system constituted a problem, perhaps the first, which transcended private initiative. Not that the community at any time scorned the assistance of private enterprise; a favorite device, at Boston and elsewhere, throughout the colonial era, was by remission of taxes or grant of other privileges to encourage individuals to open up streets and undertake paving operations for public use at their own charge. But from the beginning public authorities indicated the location of roads, supervised the opening up of new ones, ordered their clearing or partial paving by abutters, and strove to prevent encroachments upon them. At Philadelphia and Charles Town, where some prior power had surveyed and planned the thoroughfares, the first task of local authorities was light; it was more arduous in other communities, where there was no preliminary plan, and where the design had constantly to be expanded and altered to keep pace with town growth. The problems accompanying the mere existence of a

highway system,—paving, cleaning and upkeep,—called for full exercise of municipal authority. Sometimes the community exacted from each inhabitant a yearly amount of labor on the streets; in other cases it hired this labor and paid for it outright. In either case it had to levy special taxes, for materials or labor or both. To insure some cleanliness in the streets, it passed mandatory ordinances restricting the conduct of townsmen, impressed the services of carters, and employed public funds for the hire of scavengers. Further to protect the public ways, it restricted and regulated the traffic upon them, especially the weight of cart loads and the width of their wheels. Less necessary but desirable improvements in the highways, like the construction of drains, first came about through private demand and initiative, but as the civic power matured and public funds became available, these too became public functions and responsibilities. In either the municipal or the individual approach to highway problems the towns had good precedent in the Mother Country. In actual execution, especially with regard to refinements like paving and drainage, they seem in some cases to have gone beyond contemporary English cities. With a few exceptions, this generalization does not apply to the corporation governed towns, or to the unfortunately ungoverned metropolis of South Carolina.

Highways may be said to constitute the most rudimentary of public utilities, but there were others,—bridges, wharves, and engineering projects,—of which colonial townsfolk almost immediately felt the need. In the beginning, while municipal authority was politically and financially feeble, these were almost solely the product of private enterprise, but with the gradual tendency of town development they became increasingly matters of public concern. Following Old World precedent, bridges were conceived as parts of the highway system, and hence undoubtedly under public control, but they were usually constructed and operated by private persons or companies, under grant from local or provincial authorities. As the century progressed, in a few cases, notably at Philadelphia and Boston, town governments directly managed the operation and upkeep of bridges. Land reclamation projects, and harbor facilities like lighthouses, pursued a similar history. In the case of wharves, they were either a municipal or a private concern. Most towns maintained a minimum of public docking facilities, while more ambitious wharf projects, like the Long Wharves of Boston and Newport, were only within the capacity of private capital. At Philadelphia public docking facilities were so excellent as to discourage employment of private capital in their erection; at New York, so poor as to require it. Toward the end of the era, when the demands of trade began to make regular transportation between communities desirable, stage and freight routes, too, were operated by private capital, under license, usually from the provincial government.

Fire constitutes a threat especially dangerous to urban communities, and as buildings in colonial towns were from the beginning placed close together, its imminence was immediately felt. The combatting and prevention of fire called forth more than individual efforts from the start. Municipal ordinances required the keeping of fire fighting equipment by all townsmen, regulated their chimneys, forbade bonfires, fire-

works, and the housing of explosives in crowded areas. Public authorities had also to make direct outlays for fire fighting equipment of their own, and hire companies for its care and operation. In Boston, Philadelphia and Newport private societies for the protection of property during fires were organized to supplement public agencies. Similarly, water supply for fire uses was a matter of public concern and regulation. Boston, with its crowded streets and buildings of inflammable construction, and its willingness to spend public money and enegry for public welfare, was in general far in the forefront with regard to its fire defenses, but by the end of the first century all towns possessed fire engines of the latest European model, and fire fighting regulations equal or superior to those of the average English town.

A distinctive urban function grew in part out of the fire hazards of crowded sections,—the enactment of building regulations. Only public authority could specify the nature of legal building materials as did Boston after the fire of 1679 and the South Carolina Assembly after the Charles Town fire of 1740. Exercise of municipal powers was also necessary to prevent imperfect construction and dangerous neglect of town chimneys and hearths. In addition, conditions of urban congestion led to party-wall regulations like those of Boston and Philadelphia.

Another, more subtle class of problems, those which involved the personal relationships of inhabitants, affected town society from its inception. Intensified by the peculiar conditions of urban life, they required collective rather than individual efforts and powers for their control. Old World experience had taught town-dwellers the immediate need for means of preserving the public peace in settled communities, and the early appearance of constables in all towns supplied the traditional response to that need. For their security after nightfall the towns appointed bellmen or watchmen of varying degrees of efficiency. New York, after developing a highly effective nocturnal police in the seventeenth century, allowed this institution to languish from unwillingness to devote the necessary public funds thereto; other towns were slower in supplying the need, though somewhat more successful by the end of the first century. Efficiency of the watch was in direct ratio to the availability of public funds for its support,—impressment of a citizen's watch having revealed its inadequacy by the turn of the century,—and here the New England towns, with their powers of local taxation, were at a distinct advantage. There are numerous instances, during periods of unusual danger or disturbance like wars or epidemics, when the towns entirely failed in their efforts to preserve nocturnal peace, and their functions had to be taken over by the military arm of the provincial government.

Existence of crime and disorder early became a community concern in urban settlements. Here invitations to lawbreaking existed in the inequalities of wealth and opportunity, and materials for its perpetration in the diverse and unruly elements of town and seaport society. The concentration of people, many of them hardworked and underprivileged, also made for mob disorders, which increased in violence and frequency with the growth of the towns. Presence of sailors, blacks, foreigners, paupers, unpopular religious sects, interlopers in trade, profiteers, and rival

political factions, all provided increasing incentives for disorder and violence as the period progressed. Town society clearly soon passed beyond the stage where individual efforts or the force of public opinion could deal with this problem; rather it required the sanctions of the law. Provincial governments passed legislation, and municipal authorities enacted ordinances outlawing offenses against society. Riot acts were drawn up by colonial assemblies, and the local constabulary did its best to round up and confine the perpetrators of disorder and violence. In general, the towns could do little to remove the causes of criminality, and the solution of this peculiarly vexing problem of city life remained as remote in the seventeenth centuries as today.

For punishments, colonial authorities followed a number of Old World precedents, favoring especially the speediest and least expensive methods,—fines, floggings, public humiliation, restitution of stolen goods, and, occasionally, mutilation. In general, their criminal codes were less brutal than those of contemporary Europe. Efforts to make the whole community a partner in the work of law enforcement appeared in the division with informers of the proceeds from fines. Prisons were still generally places of detention for those awaiting trial, though imprisonment as punishment for crime seems to have become more widespread as the period advanced, and save in the case of debtors was probably somewhat more in use in the colonies than in the Old World. The frequency of jail breaks indicates the inefficiency of all colonial prisons, and their inadequacy suggests the absence of more vicious criminal types that troubled older societies. Yet colonial prisons were probably no more inadequate than those of contemporary England, and certainly far less squalid and brutal. Save in the case of Philadelphia in the eighteenth century, the rudimentary penology of the times made no distinction between various classes of offenders, and absence of prison facilities led to frequent misuse of alms and workhouses, wherein pauper and lawbreaker were housed together.

Offenses against the moral and ethical standards which society imposes appear more flagrant in the comparative populousness and congestion of urban environments, and early forced themselves upon the attention of colonial communities. In addition, the psychology of the times made many aspects of the regulation of conduct, manners and dress a legitimate province for the public authority. Early appearance of prostitution in the towns shocked authorities into decreeing harsh penalties for it and similar offenses. With its increasing prevalence in a society which included growingly diverse and uncontrollable elements, they seem everywhere to have become less concerned with the actual offense than with the fear lest the illegitimate offspring become charges to the community. Drunkenness was a prevailing vice, and in all towns the authorities and the better elements fought to eradicate it. Excellent tavern legislation in several of the towns reduced this offense to a minimum, but illegal sale of liquor, and misuse of the legitimate product, continued to baffle municipal authority throughout the period. Sabbath legislation in every town,—as strict in the Anglican South as in Puritan New England,—attempted to insure the sacred character of the Lord's Day. Gambling, card-playing, idleness, extravagance in dress and behavior, and evidence of frivolity came

under the ban of public regulation, either through colony or municipal authority, or as at Philadelphia through the dominant religious group. Especially at Boston and Philadelphia many seemingly innocent amusements suffered from the disapproval of a stern and narrow religion, which served as a powerful and useful supplement to the civic power.

The existence and effects of crime and immorality are intensified in urban communities; so, too, the problem of pauperism. Reports of travelers as to the absence of poverty from colonial towns can only be regarded as comparatively true, for in each town numbers of those unable to care for themselves soon constituted a problem of which the community had to take cognizance. The generally excellent methods with which the towns met this problem indicate a considerable sense of civic maturity and responsibility. New York and Charles Town favored the out-relief method through most of the period, but Boston and Philadelphia had by the end of the century well-regulated and practically self-supporting workhouses, and Newport maintained an adequate almshouse. Considerable direct relief had to be granted, especially at Boston, and in all towns save New York private or religious organizations supplemented the public work of poor relief. Methods to forestall the growth of poverty were devised, such as compulsory apprenticeship of poor children, exclusion of strangers without obvious means of livelihood, and, especially in the New England towns, restriction of immigration. In times of particular stress special devices had to be resorted to, as the distribution of corn or firewood, or a temporary embargo on export of necessary commodities. At Boston, where the problem of poverty became acute in the 1670's and was never thereafter absent, careful registration of all aliens and dependents prevailed, and a public granary was maintained.

The general health, which in rural regions may be privately cared for, early became in urban communities a matter for public concern, and municipal ordinances soon restricted the conduct of inhabitants in matters which might affect the general well-being. Location of wells and privies, and of slaughterhouses and tan pits which might become public nuisances, removal of dumps and disposal of refuse were all subjects of municipal regulation. Similarly, public authorities directed inhabitants in their behavior during epidemics, and enacted quarantine regulations in an attempt to prevent visitations of infectious disease. Toward the end of the century excellent isolation hospitals appeared in several of the towns, erected and operated by the municipality. Despite failure in this period of all attempts to regulate the practice of medicine by town or colony, the medical profession in the towns attained a relatively high development for the times.

In their approach to the physical and social problems of urban life the towns were imitators, not originators. The townsmen came to America with a fund of European experience from which they seldom deviated, and new methods as they employed them had usually first to cross the Atlantic. Poor relief and tavern legislation were directly imported from Great Britain, and the towns might conceivably have done better with their police problem had not Old World precedent served them so exclusively as a guide. Yet it may be said that in several cases there are distinct improvements in the thoroughness with which old methods were employed, and which may usually be traced to the individual civic pride of townsmen, reflected in their municipal governments. This is especially true of communities which enjoyed the town meeting form of government, where, as we have seen, the direct demands of townspeople could effect greater thoroughness and efficiency in dealing with town business, but even in the corporation governments of America there is less indifference to the public welfare than may be noted in contemporary England or Europe. Visitors were impressed with the excellence of poor relief at Boston and Philadelphia, and with Philadelphia's model prison. Fire defences in the towns were a combination of English and Dutch examples, and, especially at Boston, probably unsurpassed for their time. Solution of urban problems in colonial towns was continually hampered by lack of public funds or of necessary authority for obtaining them,—the sad decline of New York's excellent watch is an illustration, —but it was assisted, where public power failed, either politically or financially, by an encouraging growth of civic consciousness among private individuals and non-political organizations. Establishment of private agencies for charity, education, fire protection, improvement of morals, and the like, and the appearance of individual benefactors to the public welfare of the community, in an age not distinguished for civic virtue or interest, is a remarkable and significant accomplishment of town society in colonial America.

Having as they all did a common model and experience, colonial towns exhibit a remarkable similarity in the solution of their urban problems. There are many instances of the failure of a community to provide the usual and accepted necessary solution, but, with the possible exception of Philadelphia's eighteenth century prison, hardly a single example of the development by one town of a unique institution. By the time that local divergences from the original plan might have been expected to appear, communication had sufficiently improved to permit of one town's borrowing from the successful experience of another. The same holds true for privately initiated supplements of municipal endeavor. The Scot's Charitable Society and the Fire Society appear in Boston, copied from European models, and at a later date are further copied by other American towns. In the eighteenth century, because of its long experience in dealing with urban problems, the greater efficiency of its form of government, and its willingness to spend public money for the public good, Boston became the great example, with respect to municipal institutions, for other towns on the continent, but it enjoyed no monopoly of this function. New Yorkers had the fire defences of Philadelphia held up to them as a model, Bostonians were shamed by the excellence of Philadelphia's market, while Charlestonians tried to fashion their city government after the example of the corporation of New York. By the end of the period under review this inter-city exchange of experience had resulted in a striking similarity in municipal institutions, as well as a fairly uniform level of their development. Boston, for the reasons enumerated above, was probably still somewhat in advance in matters of social and material concern, though with its humanitarian agencies Philadelphia

was running a close second. Charles Town, within the limits of its governmental incapacity, dealt in fairly efficient fashion with its problems; at Newport, a lesser development of these problems had not yet necessitated any great display of urban consciousness. Even at New York, where political factionalism, a selfish corporation, and the difficulty of amalgamating two languages and nationalities prevented a consistent and devoted attempt to solve the problems of urban living, a comparison of its municipal life with that of older provincial cities of the British Empire would not have resulted in discredit to the former.

The accumulation of economic resources and their concentration in urban units, their direction in commercial ventures which attracted and supported large populations within these units, and the problems of providing for the physical and social well-being of those who thus became city-dwellers, all these aspects of urban development succeeded in bringing forth in America a distinctive society. In constitution, spiritual life, recreational activities, and intellectual pursuits it differed from types of society to be found in other sections of the continent. In respect neither to national origins nor to economic status of their inhabitants did the towns long remain homogeneous. Settled originally by people of the same nation, usually of the same locality, they soon came to include children of other European countries and of another race. Early in their history there could be found small groups of Scots in Boston, French Huguenots in Boston, New York and Charles Town, Welsh in Philadelphia, and a few Jews in every town. Many Germans settled in the 1680's in the environs of Philadelphia, and New York from the time of the first English occupation presented the problem of two peoples, each with their own language, schools and churches, living side by side under government by the numerically weaker group. This incipient cosmopolitanism flowered with the renewed immigration of the early eighteenth century, when all towns received numbers of Scotch-Irish, and the middle and southern cities, especially Philadelphia, large accessions of German exiles. For the most part these strangers were allowed to settle peaceably in colonial towns, whose economic expansion enabled them easily to absorb the newcomers, and though recent arrivals seldom attained social recognition or overcame the barrier of language where it existed, still there was little nativism and small emphasis on the superior advantages of Anglo-Saxon nativity. Such bountiful immigration did, however, lead to many restrictions, especially in the north, where the labor market was well supplied and the poor rates overburdened, to establishment of special churches and social organizations, and in Philadelphia, at least, to common use of the German language in business transactions. By far the greater problem was created by the presence of African Negroes in all towns. In Boston and Newport, where they were used mainly as house servants, and where many of them were free, the problem was negligible. They were subject to various discriminatory rules, such as those which required them to work out their obligations to the community in menial labor rather than by watch or militia duty. But at New York and Charles Town their greater numbers kept constantly present the fear of servile insurrection. At the former town they were the unfortunate objects of such waves of hysteria as the Negro Conspiracy of 1741, and at Charles Town, where they at times equalled the white population in numbers, a severe slave code kept them in subjection.

Social stratification further differentiated urban society from the easy democracy of the back country, where any man might own land and all must work with their hands. Distinctions between the well-to-do and the not-so-rich were perhaps relatively unimportant in the beginning, when society was still so fluid that luck or diligence might elevate a man above his fellows in a short time, but with the accumulation of wealth and economic power in the hands of a few, and the coming in of numbers of artisans, indentured servants and immigrant laborers, class lines tightened and society crystallized into easily recognizable categories of better, middling, and poorer sorts. In all towns native aristocracies were commercial in origin, even at Charles Town where they later sought land as a basis for social distinction. They consolidated their position by means of wealth from successful trading ventures, collecting thereby social prestige and political influence. They lived grandly, dressed gaily, kept horses and coaches, and employed the labor of the less fortunate. The commercial, political and social leadership of the towns was in their hands. Later, as urban life became more sophisticated, they contributed to the development of secular amusements and to the relaxation of earlier strict moral codes. They gained further brilliance by alliance with representatives of British officialdom in America. Below them the middle class, professional people, tradesmen and artisans, lived comfortably but more plainly, enjoying in prosperous times many of the good things of life, but in hard times feeling the pinch far more than did their wealthy neighbors. Steady laborers might know periods of prosperity, but many of them could be squeezed out by the vicissitudes of the economic cycle. They performed the menial labor of the towns, enlisted as common seamen, and constituted a group from which much urban poverty and disorder were recruited. Negro and Indian slaves, mere unprivileged pieces of property, rounded out the caste system as it developed itself in metropolitan America.

Save Newport, each of the towns had originally been dedicated to a dominant Protestant religious organization, but after a century of growth diversity, indifference and actual unbelief came to characterize the religious scene. The complexities of town society were in large measure responsible for this development, for different national or social groups soon evolved their favored sects and denominations. When the ministry could no longer speak with one voice to all elements of town populations, it lost much of its influence, both social and clerical, and the appearance of agnosticism and irreverence was rapid. In general, at the end of the first century, Anglicanism was in all towns the religion of officials and aristocrats; Quakerism and Congregationalism, which had once in their own localities enjoyed this favored position, had joined the ranks of middle class religions, which further included Baptists and Presbyterians; while for the common man a religious refuge was just appearing in the enthusiastic, emotional revivalism of Whitefield. Absence of devotion penetrated all classes; the poorer sort were largely indifferent to the attractions of religion, freethinking characterized such middle class groups as Franklin's Junto, and aristocrats indulged a fashionable Deism. In contrast, a stern and uniform religious fundamentalism for a much longer time characterized the rural communities of the countryside.

Much of their power the quasi-established churches had attained in an age when religious concerns so dominated men's thoughts as to exclude many other aspects of life. But the commercial success of colonial towns altered this singleness of outlook by acquainting townsmen with the delights of secular grandeurs and providing money for their enjoyment. As the age advanced the church step by step gave way before the institution of more attractive secular recreations. Most successful of these, appearing very early and appealing to all classes, was the tavern. Instituted originally as a necessary convenience for strangers and travelers, it soon showed itself to be the resort of all classes of townsmen, the place where much of their social life was passed. In the eighteenth century coffee houses became as in England the rendezvous of business men and the scene of many commercial transactions. Taverns served not only as places of casual conviviality, but as headquarters for the multifarious clubs into which town social life gradually organized itself. They also offered opportunities for cards, billiards and games of chance, and housed the many traveling shows and exhibitions which the better transportation of the eighteenth century made possible.

Games, contests, tavern recreations, and public celebration of holidays constituted the entertainment of the common man, but for the aristocrats mounting wealth and sophistication were creating more elaborate forms of amusement. To the hearty private dinners and occasional excursions of early days succeeded great public banquets, dances and balls, musical entertainments, and finally, in two of the towns, dramatic presentations. Gradually the commercial aristocracy of the towns, combining with royal officials, evolved a society whose entertainments were artificial, costly, sophisticated and exclusive. But for aristocrat or common man, the vicarious amusements that money could buy, and their variety and attractiveness, differentiated town society from that of the countryside with its simpler, spontaneous pleasures, and tended to draw town-dwellers away from a strict and narrow conception of life as a duty and a task. Copied as they were from the recreations of English society, they also tended to make social life in the towns more like that of the metropolis.

A final characteristic of town society was that it offered to its members a wider intellectual opportunity and challenge than was possible to the man whose life was bounded by his fields or by the hard necessity of clearing away the forest. From earliest childhood opportunities for education, free or otherwise, were open to the town-dweller. Especially was this true of the poor, whose educational needs were largely cared for by religious societies, charity schools, or compulsory apprenticeship. This last system enabled youth of the poorer classes to equip themselves for a trade. In other strata of society young men might fit themselves for business at private vocational schools, for a place in society with private masters, or for higher education for a learned profession at public or private Latin schools or with a private tutor. Young women,

too, in the towns might purchase instruction in various fields of learning or merely in the polite arts of feminine society. Also, in the northern English towns, Boston, Newport and Philadelphia, there was from the start a tradition of scholarliness and of respect for intellectual achievement. It followed that a society so trained, constantly in contact by ship with Europe, was alive and ready to adopt the intellectual fashions of the age. Hence, in this first century of American life, most of the intellectual activity, in science, literature and the arts, and what intellectual progress there was, took place in the towns. Only there were there material and opportunity for such activity. And rather than regard the results of that progress with condescension, we should, with James Franklin's subscriber, wonder at the contrary. In comparison with the Augustan Age of eighteenth century London, intellectual and social life in the colonies may seem bare and sterile, but in comparison with the intellectual barrenness of provincial life in England itself, its cultivation and sophistication appear revealed. Urban culture in the eighteenth century was provincial culture at its best, nourished during this period of faltering imitation, which had to precede that of native accomplishment, by constant contact with the vital intellectual currents of England and Europe.

In these various ways the developments of a hundred years of life under relatively urban conditions created a society at once distinct from that of rural regions, whether tidewater or back country, and even further removed from that of the westward reaching frontier. The communal attitude toward the solution of the physical and social problems of diversified populations dwelling together in close propinquity, and the constantly widening outlook which material progress, commercial expansion, and contact with the larger world of affairs made possible, were its distinguishing characteristics. In general, this society was more cooperative and social, less individualistic in its outlook toward problems of daily life, far more susceptible to outside influences and examples, less aggressively independent than the society of frontier America. At the same time it was more polished, urbane, and sophisticated, more aware of fashion and change, more sure of itself and proud of its achievements, more able to meet representatives from the outside world as equals without bluster or apology than the rural society of the colonial back country. Because its outlook was eastward rather than westward, it was more nearly a European society in an American setting. It had appropriated various points on the American continent and transformed them as nearly as possible into likenesses of what it had known at home. It was itself less transformed in the process than might have been expected, because the contact with the homeland never ceased, but rather increased with the passage of years. Its importance to American life as a whole was therefore great. Here were centers of the transit of civilization from Old World to New,—five points at the least through which currents of world thought and endeavor might enter, to be like other commodities assimilated and redistributed throughout the countryside. It was well for the future of national America that its society should not remain completely rural and agricultural, isolated and self-sufficient, ignorant of outside developments and distrustful of new ideas from abroad, as it might well have done had there been no cities. Instead, the five towns provided the nucleus for a wider and more gracious living in the New World.

Boston: "A Citty upon a Hill"

DARRETT B. RUTMAN

The mind of any period or people of the past is an indescribable thing, for it is a conglomerate of the ever-changing desires, prejudices, and standards of the incoherent many as well as of the vociferous few. The writings of the leading figures will echo basic assumptions which, at the given moment, guide to a degree the conduct of the generality; but the compilation of assumptions does not constitute a description of the mind. What is written or said in one place at one time may not reflect another place or another time, although the difference be only a year or a score of miles. Certainly this is true with re-

From *Winthrop's Boston: Portrait of a Puritan Town* (Chapel Hill: University of North Carolina Press, 1965), pp. 3-22. Reprinted by permission of the publisher. Darrett B. Rutman is Professor of History at the University of New Hampshire.

gard to the mind of the people called Puritans who sailed from England in 1630 intending to settle somewhere in the area of Massachusetts Bay. What the laymen and ministers who led them wrote before or after their migration will tell the present little about the total movement, for it was only the great who wrote, and even their thoughts were subject to change as their condition changed, first from old England to New, then as time progressed.

The mind of one man at one place and time is clear to us, however: that of John Winthrop, lawyer, manor lord of Groton in Suffolk, England, first governor of the Massachusetts Bay commonwealth, he whom the "Chiefe undertakers" of the migration would not do without, "the welfare of the Plantation" depending "upon his goeinge" with them to the New World.[1] En route across the Atlantic on the *Arbella*, the flagship of the 1630 migration— poised, as it were, between two worlds —Winthrop prepared a lay sermon, "A Modell of Christian Charity," which he delivered to his fellow passengers. In one phrase of the peroration he summed up his thought: "Wee shall be as a Citty upon a Hill."[2]

Winthrop's expression was much more than a literary conceit borrowed from the Gospel of Matthew. It reflected the core of his thinking about the society he and his fellows intended to establish. It would be a "city," first, in the literal, physical sense, for the leaders of the Winthrop fleet—eleven ships carrying some seven hundred passengers—anticipated settling in one centralized community.[3] Within the community each settler would have his house and garden; beyond it would be the fields which the generality would cultivate and on which they would graze their cattle, and the larger farms granted to the more wealthy and prominent as their due, or for services rendered the group, or in return for their investment in the enterprise—large enclaves in the wilderness worked by servants. But the community would be the center, the seat of the church, the place of government, a fortified refuge should the Indians prove hostile or foreign enemies make an appearance.

It would be a city, secondly, in the sense of a "city of God." Man would serve God here in all the ways that God demanded He be served. A meetinghouse where God's word in all its purity could be heard would bulk large, and men would worship God as He would have them worship. But far more: Men would serve their fellow men in this city as God would have them serve; men would fit into a society of men in such a way that the society would redound to God's credit, add luster to His crown.

The idea of a godly society predominated in Winthrop's thoughts as he crossed the Atlantic, his *Arbella* discourse being devoted to it rather than to other aspects of the city. And this was natural. For while Winthrop and his fellows of 1630 were coming from a society where ideas of Christian brotherhood and right conduct were expounded from every pulpit, where "the whole society of man" was constantly being claimed for God,[4] it was nevertheless a crass, cruel society marked by fundamental social, political, and particularly economic changes in which emerging individualism, having disrupted the social unity of the past, was proceeding to extol and enrich the greater individual at the expense of the lesser. Some men during the century antedating Winthrop had already come to the conclusion that change at the expense of brotherhood was wrong. The commonweal movement had risen, eschewing the idea that a man could seek his profit without thought of others or limitations by church or state: "If the possessioners would consider themselves to be but stewards and not lords over their possessions," Robert Crowley had written in the mid-sixteenth century, "this oppression would soon be redressed. But so long as this persuasion sticketh in their minds: It is mine own, who should warn me to do with mine own as myself listeth? it shall not be possible to have any redress at all."[5] During the years between Crowley and Winthrop the state had intervened with a succession of statutes regulating the economy and providing for the impotent poor; the church had preached of morals and conscience and the cause of the community above private gain. But the laws remained, to 1629, largely ineffectual; the pulpit was too often ignored. "Conscience," a contemporary wrote, "is a pretty thing to carry to church but he that useth it in a fair market or shop may die a beggar."[6]

To Winthrop, England in 1622 had been "this sinfull lande."[7] And the sin he wrote of was social in nature. Two years later, in a list of "common grevances groaninge for reformation" drawn up in consultation with others, he had listed some of the causes of his dissatisfaction. Among them were those referring to the condition of the church— "the daylye encrease of the multitudes of papistes," "scandalous and dombe ministers," the "suspension and silenceing of many painfull learned ministers for not conformitie in some poynts of ceremonies." But most of Winthrop's complaints referred to lay affairs: "the common scarcitie of woode and tym-

ber," the necessity of reforming the system for "mendinge of hie wayes," "horse stealeinge," inequitable taxation, "the greate delayes in swetes of lawe" and "the undoeinge of many poor familyes" through the actions of "the multitude of Atturnies in the Courtes" and the "multitude and lewdnesse of Baylyfs," "the pittifull complainte of the orphanes fatherlesse and many poore creditors," the "intollerably burdened" farmer subjected to abuses by the "clerke of the market."[8]

Subsequently, as he prepared to leave England in 1629, he was more pointed. God, he wrote, had given "the sons of men" the whole earth that it might "be tilld and improved by them"; he had commanded them "to encrease and multiply and replenish the earth and subdue it . . . that man may enjoye the fruit of the earth, and God may have his due glory from the Creature." But pointing to the vagrants and beggars of England's countryside and cities, the malpractices of the market, the ponderous legal machinery with which he was so familiar, the extremes of rich and poor, he asked where "is the happiness we should rest in?" "In the civill state"? "What means then the bleating of so many oppressed with wronge, that drink wormwood, for righteousness? why doe so many seely sheep that seeke shelter at the judgment seates returne without their fleeces? why meet we so many wandering ghostes in shape of men, so many spectacles of misery in all our streetes, our houses full of victuals, and our entryes of hunger-starved Christians? our shoppes full of riche wares, and under our stalles lye our own fleshe in nakednesse." "Our people perish for want of sustenance and imployment," he went on; "many others live miserably and not to the honor of so bountifull a housekeeper as the lord of heaven and earth is . . .: all our townes complain of the burden of poore people and strive by all menes to ridde any such as they have, and to keepe of[f] such as would come to them." To him, commerce was corrupt. He could not cite a single case "wherein a man may looke for recompence sutable to his expence of tyme and industrye, except falsehood be admitted to equall the ballance." Agriculture in England was uneconomic: "If we should imploye our children in that waye now, their worke would soon eate up their stocks." Redress? It "might be had in these thinges by the magistrate, [but it] dothe not conclude that it shalbe."[9]

Winthrop himself was not personally oppressed in this society. Indeed, he was a comparatively well-to-do member of the English gentry. But his sensibilities were moved by the England about him. He dreamed of a better society, and sought the New World to make it a reality. The "Modell of Christian Charity" was his exposition of the nature of the new society he wished to establish in New England.[10]

In common with Christianity from its inception, Winthrop had of necessity to reconcile status, property, and God. He was too much a part of the seventeenth century to abandon any one of the three. God was, to him, the supreme, omnipotent, and omnipresent Prince of Heaven, the creator of all for His own purposes; God it was who had sent His son to live among men, humbly and without riches, appealing more to the poor in possessions and heart than to the wealthy and vain and promising in effect that the lowest on earth should be the highest in heaven.

Yet society, as it existed, was distinguished by its divisions into rich and poor, high and low; property existed, and the divisions of society rested largely upon its possession or lack. The mental image of God the creator and Christ who preached of rich men and eyes of needles had to be reconciled to the very real picture of property and status. Hence Winthrop began his discourse by establishing the God-ordained nature of social stratification and the ownership of property: "God Almightie in his most holy and wise providence hath soe disposed of the Condition of mankinde, as in all times some must be rich some poore, some highe and eminent in power and dignitie; others meane and in subjeccion." He had done so for a number of reasons: because His glory is made manifest in the creation of variety; because He can display His power over the wicked rich by restraining them from eating up the poor, and over the wicked poor by preventing them from rising up against their superiors; because He would have a setting in which His saints could display themselves, the sainted rich by their love, mercy, gentleness, the sainted poor by their faith, patience, obedience; and finally, He had arranged mankind in orders so that all men might have need for one another. The conclusion Winthrop desired was easily and logically drawn from such a godly and purposeful arrangement: No man is made more honorable or rich out of respect of himself, but for the purposes of God; God therefore has a first call upon his property.

Yet all too obviously there was a misuse of property and position in Winthrop's England and in the world at large, for the rich regularly ate the sustenance of the poor and, on occasion, the poor rose up against the rich. In the lore of Christianity and the Protestant theology of the churches of England, Winthrop found the solution. Man, living in the light of God, would have that perfect love toward God and mankind which would result in a godly use of property. Adam, before the fall, had such love, but Adam had wrenched himself and his posterity from his creator. As a consequence, love for one's brother was corrupted: "Every man is borne with this principle in him, to love and seeke himselfe onely." In this condition he would remain "till Christ comes and takes possession of the soule," gathering together the scattered bones of "perfect old man Adam" and infusing a new principle, "Love to God and our brother."

Looking out over the passengers aboard the *Arbella*, seeing in his mind's eye the men and women aboard the *Ambrose, Talbot, William and Francis*, and the other vessels of the fleet—men and women gathered together through the efforts of himself and his friends— Winthrop thought of the settlers as either actually or potentially infused with this regenerating principle. "Wee are a Company professing our selves fellow members of Christ," he wrote; before, in England, we were scattered, "absent from eache other many miles, and had our imploymentes as farre distant." But having embarked on this voyage "wee ought to account our selves knitt together by this bond of love, and live in the exercise of it." Status and property would then assume their proper position as godly gifts, given for God's purposes. Specifically, Winthrop asked charity of the settlers— the giving of one's abundance in ordinary times, and the giving even beyond one's means on extraordinary occasions. He would have them temper the spirit of commerce with mercy, giv-

ing where it was necessary, lending only where feasible in terms of the capability of the recipient to repay, forgiving a debt when the debtor could not pay.

Winthrop's vision of Christian "love" involved more than mere mercy and charity, however. It embodied his desire for form, unity, and stability in society. Without Christian love, he wrote, society could never be perfect. Men would strive after their own good without thought of the well-being either of their fellows in the society or of the society as a whole. The community resulting from such individuality would be no more than an association of independent objects "as disportionate and as much disordering as soe many contrary quallities or elements." On the other hand, Christian love pervading the society would serve as the "ligament" binding the individual members to the one body. Individuality would remain, but "all the partes of this body being thus united" would be "soe contiguous in a speciall relacion as they must needes partake of each others strength and infirmity, joy, and sorrowe, weale and woe." "This sensiblenes and Sympathy of each others Conditions will necessarily infuse into each parte a native desire and endeavour, to defend preserve and comfort the other." Implicitly, each member of the body would have its place and duty in the total structure, some to serve, others to be served, some to rule, others to be ruled, all happily accepting their place and work for the benefit of all. Winthrop's simile was man's mouth, which "is at all the paines to receive, and mince the foode which serves for the nourishment of all the other partes of the body, yet it hath noe cause to complaine; for . . . the other partes send

backe by secret passages a due propor-
cion of the same nourishment in a better forme for the strengthening and
comforteing the mouthe."

"Goe forth, every man that goeth,
with a publick spirit, looking not on
your owne things onely," John Cotton,
the eminent minister of Boston, England, had exhorted the *Arbella's* passengers in his farewell sermon.[11] Winthrop, describing the individual's duty
in the model society, echoed him: "The
care of the publique must oversway all
private respects." "Wee must love brotherly without dissimulation, wee must
love one another with a pure heart
fervently wee must beare one anothers
burthens, wee must not looke onely on
our owne things, but allsoe on the
things of our brethren." Conscience tells
us this, Winthrop preached, but so too
does necessity, for recall that we are
going to a strange, forbidding land
where dangers and difficulties will constantly beset us. "Wee must be knitt
together in this work as one man, wee
must entertaine each other in brotherly
affeccion, wee must be willing to
abridge our selves of superfluities, for
the supply of others necessities, wee
must uphold a familiar Commerce together in all meekness, gentlenes, patience and liberallitie, we must delight
in each other, make others Conditions
our owne[,] rejoyce together, mourne
together, labour, and suffer together."
And, finally, the settlers were to do
these things not by command of the
magistrate (the law having proved futile in England when it sought to impose itself on the spirit) but by virtue
of the godly nature of that love which
joined them together. Whatever coer-
cion Winthrop would invoke would not
be man's, but God's. We have a covenant with Him, he said; we have ac-

cepted the obligation to live in such a
way that ourselves and our posterity
might be better preserved from the
common corruptions of the world; if we
should fail and embrace this present
world, pursue carnal intentions, the
Lord will break out in wrath against us.

In his discourse, Winthrop did not
deal with the nature of government
and church, though perhaps these subjects had been contemplated to some
extent by the leaders while still in England.[12] Yet his view of the nature of
government is implicit both in his discussion of men rich and poor, "highe
and eminent in power and dignitie;
others meane and in subjection," and
in his comment about the covenant
binding the settlers with God. The first
thought took cognizance of the natural
disparity between men which Winthrop, as the master of Groton, could
not help accepting and which the English pulpit constantly pronounced as
God's will, minister William Perkins,
for example, writing that "God hath
appointed that in every societie one
person should be above or under another; not making all equall, as though
the bodie should be all head and nothing else."[13] Reacting against conditions
in England, however, Winthrop could
not allow natural disparities to go un-
tempered: Power was not a right of the
mighty but a godly duty to deal in
"love mercy, gentlenes, temperance"
with those in subjection.

The second thought pertaining to
government in the "Modell" reflected
the pervasive contemporary view of the
nature of the state which held that man
in society selected the forms and personnel of government by way of a compact, and then bound himself to that
government. In the western world, this
idea of contract—or compact, or cove-

nant—was ancient, but it was particularly relevant for the religious polemicists of the sixteenth and seventeenth centuries. The French *Vindiciae Contra Tyrannos*, establishing a philosophic basis for Protestants to rebel against a Catholic king, argued for the sovereignty of the people and the contracts which a people, as a people of God, made with God that "it will remain the people of God" and with its ruler "to obey the king truly while he rules truly."[14] Protestant England wrote of the "covenant and bargaine" inherent in the coronation of the king by which "the people is bound and sworne to doe their allegance to their Kings, so the Kings are also solemnly sworne to maintaine and defend true Religion, the estate of Justice, the peace and tranquility of their subjects, and the right and priviledges (which are nothing but the Lawes) of the Realme."[15] Richard Hooker, in his *Ecclesiastical Polity*, would have kings hold "their right to the power of dominion, with dependency upon the whole entire body politic over which they rule as kings," though he attempted to avoid the tendency toward revolutionary doctrine by confirming the divine nature of kings once established. "God creating mankind did endue it naturally with full power to guide itselv, in what kind of societies soever it should choose to live," yet those on whom power "is bestowed even at men's discretion, they likewise do hold it by divine right," for "albeit God do neither appoint the thing nor assign the person; nevertheless when men have established both, who doth doubt but that sundry duties and offices depending thereupon are prescribed in the world of God." Therefore, Hooker concluded, "we by the law of God stand bound meekly to

acknowledge them for God's lieutenants."[16]

From the aura of his times and from the Gospel—for he cited only the Gospels as his authority—Winthrop derived his own idea of the covenant. He spoke of the settlers having "entered into Covenant" with the Lord by virtue of their having committed themselves to His protection on the voyage and in the land where they were going. The covenant, though, was in the simplest of terms: their agreement to be God's people, to live in a godly fashion—that fashion which Winthrop had already outlined in terms of Christian love—in return for which "the Lord will be our God and delight to dwell among us." Having said this, he needed to say nothing more about government, for the divisions of rich and poor, rulers and ruled, were ordained by God. Consequently, in his city, the natural leaders —the wealthy, the gentlemen—would rule in the interest of the people, seeking "their welfare in all things,"[17] and the people would accept the government of these natural leaders out of their own God-ordained duty to "faithe patience, obedience."

Only subsequently would Winthrop elaborate on the covenant between the rulers and ruled. Fifteen years later, to the Massachusetts General Court and through it to the populace, he was to define the covenant in terms of "the oath you have taken of us"—the oath of fidelity required of all inhabitants by that time—"which is to this purpose, that we shall govern you and judge your causes by the rules of God's laws and our own, according to our best skill." But the governors were not self-appointed; they were, rather, God-appointed through the people. "It is yourselves," he said, "who have called us to this office, and being called by you, we have our authority from God, in a way of ordinance, such as hath the image of God eminently stamped upon it, the contempt and violation whereof hath been vindicated with examples of divine vengeance."[18]

In contemplating the nature of the church, Winthrop also undoubtedly derived his ideas from the aura of his times, most notably from the assumptions of the churches of England. His terminology in the "Modell of Christian Charity" was that of English Calvinism. He saw the effects of the difficult economic and social adjustment in England in terms of the depravity of man. His own social attitudes and those he would have the settlers adopt were phrased in terms of the regeneration of man. He reflected faithfully the utter dependence of man upon God in effecting this regeneration, quoting the Apostle John in describing his Christian love, the ligament of the new society. "Love cometh of god and every one that loveth is borne of god, soe that this love is the fruite of the new birthe, and none can have it but the new Creature."

Yet Winthrop expressed social ideas in theological terms only because there were no other terms available to him, not because they formed the basis of his thought. He was not bound by the logic of the theology he expressed; indeed, he regularly violated that logic. His equating of Christian love with "new birthe," for example, echoed basic Calvinism and its relegation of man to the status of "an empty vessel" awaiting God's pleasure in filling it, a mute, inactive recipient of God's free grace. But there is no indication that Winthrop in his *Arbella* discourse was directing his words to a particular

body of love-infused saints within the total number of settlers, nor was there a thought in the "Modell" or elsewhere in Winthrop's writings of the impossibility of creating a society bound by Christian love when the persons embarked on the attempt included (as they must have included) regenerates and reprobates, saints and sinners. There is, then, the paradox in the "Modell" of anticipating a society of saints and sinners held together by a quality available only to the saints.

The paradox, though it does not disappear, becomes at least explicable on realizing the confused, chaotic, and contradictory thought of the English churches from which Winthrop was emerging. There was the England of the Thirty-Nine Articles of Faith, a reiteration of basic Calvinism, but there was also the England which had drifted away from Calvin to pronounce that "despite the fact that man cannot will himself into salvation [or into Winthrop's Christian love], nonetheless he does possess the capacity to cooperate with and consent to God's will to save him."[19] There was the England, too, which had gone even further, exceeding the limitations on ministerial activity inherent in Calvinism by actively soliciting conversion, as when Hugh Peter prayed for the Queen that "the light of Goshen might shine into her soul, and that she might not perish in the day of Christ" or reported his activity at St. Sepulchre in London: "There was six or seven thousand Hearers, and the circumstances fit for such good work" that "above an hundred every week were persuaded from sin to Christ."[20] As one modern study expresses it, "the very activities of an intensely proselytizing and evangelical church, as early [English] Protestantism was, are directly contradictory, in terms of simple logic, to strict predestinarian doctrine. Indeed, the whole literature of English Protestantism is a product of ministerial enthusiasm which seems constantly to be overstepping the limits which logically it has set for itself."[21] In this climate, is it too much to expect that Winthrop should pay homage to God's free grace and proceed illogically to the optimistic view of man's ability to rise above his depraved nature by himself and form a godly society on earth? For in the last analysis, the "Modell of Christian Charity" is an optimistic document. All the men and women of the migration were considered to be capable of that Christian love for brothers and for the community necessary to the creation of a godly city. Christians all, the settlers were "to worke upon their heartes, by prayer meditacion continuall exercise . . . till Christ be formed in them and they in him all in eache other knitt together by this bond of love."

In still another area—that of church polity—English thought was confused. On the one hand, the religious establishment constituted a national church embracing the total population of England; it was, too, an authoritarian church, pyramidally organized from the peak of earthly authority (the king) downward through archbishops, bishops, and priests to the lowly communicant. On the other hand, however, theory held that original authority rested in the individual congregations within the church and was merely delegated upward. Richard Hooker, in constructing a philosophic basis for the episcopal hierarchy, had written of "the whole body of the Church being the first original subject of all mandatory and coercive power within itself." That

the churches in England had granted power to a higher body and even a single man (as had the people of England with regard to the state) did not diminish the validity of the concept of original power residing at the bottom, and Hooker could even envision the congregations drawing power back to themselves in extreme cases. Theory also held that there were in reality two churches, one visible, one invisible. Hooker, concerned as he was with the visible institutional church of all Englishmen, nevertheless recognized the true saints of the invisible church as well, "that Church of Christ, which we properly term his body mystical" and which resides within the body of the institutional church but cannot be "sensibly discerned by any man," only by God. William Perkins, too, spoke of the church as a "mixt . . . companie of men . . . true beleevers and hypocrites mingled together," the believers being the invisible church known to God, the totality being the visible church of man. James Ussher, on the other side of many doctrinal fences from Perkins, similarly acknowledged the outer church but stressed that true membership was confined to those who "are by the Spirit and Faith secretly and inseparably conjoyned unto Christ their head." And along with some other English Protestants, he strained the logical barrier— that God, not man, identifies His saints —to advise the godly to shun the ungodly, "to renounce all fellowship with sin and sinners" and keep company with "one another in faith and love . . . in the society of the Saints."[22] The espousal of the communion of the elect was the antithesis of the principle of a national church.

As Winthrop and his companions sailed, English religious thought was—

as it had been for long, and would be for longer yet—in the throes of a reconciliation of its innate contradictions. Orthodox Anglicanism was being hammered out, and with it dissent. The process was agonizing, the intellectual air electric with clashing doctrines, the disputations of the clerics in print and pulpit a thunderous discord. The forms and practices of worship were in constant dispute as many, frequently the most ardent and zealous of the churchmen, called for a wiping away of the last vestiges of Catholicism and a return to the verities of the primitive church of the first centuries after Christ. The mingling of godly and ungodly within the church, at times under the spiritual care of ministers who were themselves ungodly, was for some churchmen a most heinous error. Such clerics stressed the communion of the elect at the expense of the national church and sought, by excluding the palpably ungodly, to form a rough correlation between the visible and invisible churches. They tended, moreover, to accent the congregational nature of the churches. Finding in their studies of the New Testament and the "fathers" of the church that the primitive church had been congregationally organized, they considered the hierarchy of prelates found in England an aberration from Christ's pure structure and, going beyond Hooker's theoretic congregationalism, they argued for a return of actual authority to the English congregations. Here and there extremists renounced the English churches entirely, declared them "false and counterfeit," and set about establishing separatist congregations, voluntarily covenanting together to live as a people of God under ministers of their own choosing (rather than ministers set over them

by a bishop), free to discipline their own membership, and admitting to communion and to the baptism of their children only those who, "so far as men in charity could judge," were "justified, sanctified, and entitled to the promises of salvation, and life eternal."[23] Their course was a dangerous one, for separation was anathema to the English mind and such "schismatics" were subject to persecution. But their number was small. More normally the dissenting ministers remained within the national church as nonconformists, accepting the establishment with all its errors in the hopes of an ultimate reformation, all the while using casuistry and taking advantage of the relative laxness of the hierarchy prior to the late 1620's and early 1630's to purify their services and, in some cases, profess in varying degrees and ways a vague and ill-defined congregationalism devoid of separatist connotations.

Winthrop and the leaders of the 1630 migration emerged from that area of England most affected by the dissenting zeal—London and the eastern counties from Kent to Lincoln; they were themselves zealous in their desire to cleave to God and undoubtedly familiar to an extent with the various arguments put forth by their ardent ministers. But as a group they do not appear as advocates of any precise synthesis.[24] They sailed as English Protestants and went out of their way to say so in *The Humble Request* to the congregations of England written and published as they departed. Belief was not leading them to separate from the English church, they wrote; the church was, rather, "our deare Mother," and they drew a parallel between themselves sailing to the New

World to establish another church and the primitive church of Philippi "which was a colonie from Rome."[25] Winthrop's own writings reflect not that he had chosen between the contradictions in English religious thought, but the contradictions themselves. The very act of leaving sinful England to found a godly city was an expression of the idea of the communion of the elect; but the joining together of the godly and ungodly in the attempt (even with undertones of the ungodly being capable of conversion from sin to the good life) implied the idea of a universal church. The contradiction between the two went unresolved.

In the New World, however, resolution would be forced upon Winthrop and his followers. There they would be faced with the necessity of forming churches as centers for new communities without an existing prelacy to which the congregations could delegate power; they would find churches at Plymouth and Salem composed of the professedly godly and organized on a congregational basis. There, too, the newcomers would drift into the same practices, drawing upon the knowledge of congregational theory which they brought from England and using Salem and Plymouth as models. Yet the drift was not without difficulties, indicating that the practices they were to adopt were not implicit in Winthrop's "Citty upon a Hill." Indeed, Winthrop's initial contact with the congregational practices of Salem was seemingly something of a surprise. On first landing, he and some of his companions appeared at the Salem church seeking communion for themselves and the baptism of a child born at sea. They came, as they would to any church in England, to take advantage of the facilities held out to all. But Salem refused to accept them inasmuch as the church there had come to hold that the seals of the church (baptism and communion) should be offered only to covenanted members and those recommended by a similarly organized congregation. One or more of the Winthrop group was disturbed enough by the incident to report it to the Reverend John Cotton in England, prompting that worthy divine to write a critical letter to the Salem minister about the church's practices.[26]

Subsequently the leaders and ministers among the settlers found themselves divided over church polity. Samuel Fuller, who, together with others from Plymouth and Salem, was free with his advice as to the form of church organization which the newcomers should adopt, wrote of holding long wearisome conferences with the ministers and lay leaders of the Bay. "Opposers" of the Plymouth-Salem way "there is not wanting, and satan is busy," he reported to Governor William Bradford at Plymouth. The Reverend John Warham argued for a church organization in line with contemporary English practice, a universal church consisting "of a mixed people,—godly, and openly ungodly." Some of the leaders of the Winthrop fleet apparently insisted that the Reverend George Phillips should minister to them by virtue of his English ordination rather than a congregational call, for Phillips told Fuller during a private conference "that if they will have him stand minister, by that calling which he received from the prelates in England, he will leave them." (Years later Cotton Mather was to write that Phillips was, from the standpoint of what would become New England orthodoxy, "better acquainted with the true *church-discipline* than most of the ministers that came with him into the country.") The Reverend John Wilson, on the other hand, seemed more amenable in this regard, for he was to accept the call of the church gathered at Charlestown "with this protestation by all, that it was only as a sign of election and confirmation, not of any intent that [he] should renounce his ministery he received in England."[27]

That Winthrop and his compatriots sailed without a precise idea of the nature of the church they were to erect should not be surprising. The Winthrop migration was a lay movement, not clerical. "Able and sufficient Ministers" were sought after to journey with the settlers, for religion was an integral part of life.[28] But notably few ministers were willing to hazard themselves in the venture in 1629 and 1630. Only later would they come, and then eagerly, seeking sanctuary from Archbishop William Laud's attempt to create a Church of England out of the diverse churches of England.

As a lay movement, the ideals of 1630 were lay ideals, social, rather than religious, though to the extent that the church was a part of the social organization, it too would be reformed. Winthrop quite obviously did not subscribe to all the practices of the English church. His 1964 catalogue of "common grevances groaninge for reformation" included criticisms of the establishment, particularly the conduct of that part of the ministry which was corrupted by impoverishment and intent upon the pursuit of security in this world rather than the next; he preferred a simplicity of religious service, yet he conformed to the forms and practices of England, considering

that "ceremonyes ar by our ch[urch] of England holden to be put thinges indifferent."[29] His great peculiarity, however, was his intensity, his literal application to society of the Biblical injunction to "love thy neighbor as thyself." Time after time this intensity—and its origin in the pulpit pronouncements and polemic literature of Protestant England—appears in his writings. As to "the estate of our Churche and Com[mon]w[ealth]," he wrote just prior to the migration, "let the grones and fears of Godes people give a silent answer: If our condition be good, why doe his Embassadours [the ministers] turne their messages into complaintes and threateninges? why doe they so constantly denounce wrathe and judgment against us? why doe they pray so muche for healinge if we be not sicke?"[30] And on the *Arbella*, summing up the duties of the citizen in the godly society, he preached, "Whatsoever wee did or ought to have done when wee lived in England, the same must wee doe and more allsoe where wee goe: That which the most in theire Churches maineteine as a truthe in profession onely, wee must bring into familiar and constant practise."

One can call Winthrop a "Puritan," but not in the sense of his holding to a logical edifice of theology and polity. He was a Puritan only in the most limited of senses—that of Perry Miller when he writes of "the Augustinian strain of piety" which leads men to that futile search for a road to bring them face to face with truth, God; of Alan Simpson and James F. Maclear when they write of Puritanism as a "blind thrust," an "unbelievable intensity" of feeling toward God and fellow man, "deep emotional longings for personal encounter and direct communion with God"; and of William

Perkins when he described "Puritans and Presitions" as "those that most indeavour to get and keepe the puritie of heart in a good conscience."[31] Similarly, one can term Winthrop's errand to the New World "religious" in but the simplest sense of the word. His was a blind thrust into the wilderness, undertaken precipitously—there is no evidence of his preparing to remove prior to 1629—and without elaborate planning. Fear lay behind the movement to America, fear of the successes of Catholicism in the Counter Reformation then in progress. But more important as a motivating factor was what can be termed Winthrop's "social conscience"—his concern for the generality of an England which to him was growing "wearye of her Inhabitantes, so as man which is the most pretious of all Creatures, is heere more vile and base, then the earthe they treade upon"—and his vision of a new society, perhaps one which in God's good time the rest of the world would emulate, a setting in which salvation would be more readily obtainable for himself and all who desired to live in Christ's shadow.[32] In the broadest sense of the word, too, one can call Winthrop a "utopian" as he crossed the Atlantic aboard the *Arbella*, a dreamer of heaven on earth; he would have Christian love pervade the new society, while holding that "to love and live beloved is the soules paradice, both heare and in heaven."

Ironically, however, Winthrop was doomed to failure, in large measure by the very land he chose for his venture. Reacting to the contemporary English scene, he envisioned a society in which men would subordinate themselves to their brothers' and the community's good, but he sought to erect that society in a land where opportunity for individual profit lay ready to every hand. And Winthrop's optimism that man could overcome his own nature—so illogical in view of his apparent Calvinism—was to prove sadly misplaced. Speaking aboard the *Arbella*, his was but one small voice, one mind, among hundreds; his dream was not necessarily that of the whole number of settlers, nor of those who would arrive in the commonwealth in the years ahead. On the contrary, to judge by actions in the New World, his was the exceptional mind. In America, the acquisitive instincts of the contemporary Englishman would rush to the surface, overwhelming Winthrop's communal ideal; conflicting minds would fragment the society which Winthrop would have perfectly united in thought, speech, judgment, and, above all, God's holy love. Institutions—defined as the various postures the community assumes in undertaking specific functions—would initially display the marks of Winthrop's ideal, but their evolution would reflect other minds and the new land. The process of disruption would begin immediately upon landing. Within two months a stunned Winthrop would write of Satan bending "his forces against us . . . so that I thinke heere are some persons who never shewed so much wickednesse in England as they have doone heer." Within five years another would comment that in leaving England men of pure hearts had "made an ill change, even from the snare to the pitt."[33] Within twenty years, Winthrop—who had rejected the vision of modern man he had seen in England and sought the refuge of a secular monastery (for that is what this "Citty upon a Hill" sums up to)—would be dead, and his commonwealth would be distinctly modern.

NOTES

1. "Perticular Considerations in the case of J:W: [1629]," in Massachusetts Historical Society, *Winthrop Papers*, 5 vols. (Boston, 1929-47), II, 133, hereafter cited as *Winthrop Papers*.

2. Matt. 5:14; "A Modell of Christian Charity," *Winthrop Papers*, II, 282-95. Except where otherwise noted, all quotations in this chapter are from the "Modell."

3. In the absence of a direct statement, the intent of the leadership to settle a single community must be assumed from the evidence of what happened. For elaboration, see Appendix I.

4. Charles H. and Katherine George, *The Protestant Mind of the English Reformation, 1570-1640* (Princeton, 1961), 183.

5. Quoted in Stanley T. Bindoff, *Tudor England* (Harmondsworth, Eng., 1950), 131.

6. Quoted in Wallace Notestein, *The English People on the Eve of Colonization, 1603-1630* (New York, 1954), 22.

7. Winthrop to Thomas Fones, Jan. 29, 1621/22, *Winthrop Papers*, I, 268.

8. Winthrop, "Common Grevances Groaninge for Reformation," *ca.* Feb-Mar., 1623/24, *ibid.*, 295 ff.

9. Winthrop, "General Observations [For the Plantation of New England, 1629]," and Winthrop to [?], 1629, *ibid.*, II, 115, 122-23.

10. In the absence of a major modern work on Winthrop, his own writings constitute his best biography; hence, because it is so replete with quotations, Robert C. Winthrop's *Life and Letters of John Winthrop* . . . , 2 vols. (Boston, 1864-67), is the most adequate. Highly suggestive, however, is Edmund S. Morgan, *The Puritan Dilemma: The Story of John Winthrop* (Boston and Toronto, 1958). Winthrop's political and to a lesser extent social thought have been the subject of occasional commentary, most notably by Stanley Gray, "The Political Thought of John Winthrop," *New England Quarterly*, 3 (1930), 681-705, aนd George L. Mosse, *The Holy Pretence: A Study in Christianity and Reasons of State from William Perkins to John Winthrop* (Oxford, 1957), chap. 6.

11. John Cotton, *Gods Promise to His Plantation* . . . (London, 1630), 19.

12. Arthur Tyndal to Winthrop, Nov. 10, 1629, *Winthrop Papers*, II, 166.

13. Williams Perkins, *The Works of That Famous and Worthie Minister of Christ*, 3 vols. (London, 1612-13), I, 755.

14. Quoted in Sir Ernest Barker, *Church, State and Education* (Ann Arbor, 1957), 87-88. On the impact of the *Vindiciae* in England see J. H. Salmon, *The French Religious Wars in England Political Thought* (Oxford, 1959), *passim*.

15. Thomas Beard, *The Theatre of God's Judgements* . . . , 3rd ed. (London, 1648), 10.

16. Richard Hooker, *Of the Laws of Ecclesiastical Polity*, Bk. VIII [1648], chap. 2, par. 5-6, 9, as reprinted in *The Works of* . . . *Mr. Richard Hooker*, 7th ed. (Oxford, 1887).

17. Thomas Hutchinson, comp., *A Collection of Original Papers Relative to the History of the Colony of Massachusetts-Bay* (Boston, 1769), 100.

18. James Kendall Hosmer, ed., *[John] Winthrop's Journal "History of New England," 1630-1649*, 2 vols. (N.Y., 1908), II, 237-39; hereafter cited as *Winthrop's Journal*.

19. George and George, *Protestant Mind of the English Reformation*, 64-65, quoting Bishop Lancelot Andrewes.

20. Quoted in Raymond Phineas Stearns, *The Strenuous Puritan: Hugh Peter, 1598-1660* (Urbana, 1954), 36, 44.

21. George and George, *Protestant Mind of the English Reformation*, 58.

22. Hooker, *Ecclesiastical Polity*, Bk. VIII, chap. 6, par. 3; Bk. III [1594], chap. 1, par. 2; Perkins, *Works*, III, 16; James Ussher, *A Body of Divinitie or The Summe and Substance of Christian Religion* . . . , 5th ed. (London, 1658), 188, 191.

23. *A True Confession of the Faith, and Humble Acknowledgment of the Alegeance, Which Wee Hir Majesties Subjects, Falsely Called Brownists, Doo Hould [towards] God, and Yield to Hir Majestie* (n.p., 1596), as reprinted in Williston Walker, ed., *The Creeds and Platforms of Congregationalism*, Pilgrim Press ed. (Boston, 1960), 51; John Robinson, quoted in Edmund S. Morgan, *Visible Saints: The History of a Puritan Idea* (N. Y., 1963), 57.

24. See below, chap. 3, pp. 47-48, and Appendix II.

25. *The Humble Request of His Majesties Loyall Subjects, the Governour and the Company Late Gone for New England; to the Rest of Their Brethren in and of the Church of England* (London, 1630), as reprinted in *Winthrop Papers*, II, 232.

26. The child was William Coddingtons. *A Sermon Preached by the Reverend, Mr. John Cotton, Teacher of the First Church in Boston in New England. Deliver'd at Salem, [June] 1636* . . . (Boston, 1713), 1-2; John Cotton to Samuel Skelton, Oct. 2, 1630, in Thaddeus Mason Harris, *Memorials of the First Church in Dorchester* (Boston, 1830), 53-57.

27. Samuel Fuller to William Bradford, June 28, 1630, Mass. Hist. Soc., *Collections*, 1st Ser., 3 (1794), 75; Cotton Mather, *Magnalia Christi Americana; or, the Ecclesiastical History of New-England* . . . , 2 vols. (Hartford, 1853), I, 377; *Winthrop's Journal*, I, 51.

28. John Winthrop and others to [?], Oct. 27, 1629, *Winthrop Papers*, II, 163-64.

29. "Common Grevances," *ibid.*, I, 295 ff, 305;

Christopher Hill, *Economic Problems of the Church: From Archbishop Whitgift to the Long Parliament* (Oxford, 1956), chap. 9.

30. Winthrop to [?], 1629, *Winthrop Papers*, II, 121.

31. Perry Miller, *The New England Mind: The Seventeenth Century*, Beacon Press ed. (Boston, 1961), 3 ff; Alan Simpson, *Puritanism in Old and New England* (Chicago, 1955), 21, and pas-

sim; James Fulton Maclear, " 'The Heart of New England Rent': The Mystical Element in Early Puritan History," *Mississippi Valley Historical Review*, 42 (1956), 623; Perkins, *Works*, III, 15.

32. "General Observations," *Winthrop Papers*, II, 114.

33. Winthrop to Margaret Winthrop, July 23, 1630, and Nathaniel Ward to John Winthrop, Jr., Dec. 24, [1635], *ibid.*, 303, III, 216.

Philadelphia: The Private City

SAM BASS WARNER

American cities have grown with the general culture of the nation, not apart from it. Late eighteenth-century Philadelphia was no exception. Its citizens, formerly the first wave of a Holy Experiment, had been swept up in the tide of secularization and borne on by steady prosperity to a modern view of the world. Like the Puritans of Massachusetts and Connecticut, the Quakers of Pennsylvania had proved unable to sustain the primacy of religion against the solvents of cheap land and private opportunity. Quaker, Anglican, Presbyterian, Methodist, Pietist—each label had its social and political implications—but all congregations shared in the general American secular culture of privatism.[1]

Already by the time of the Revolution privatism had become the American tradition. Its essence lay in its concentration upon the individual and the individual's search for wealth. Psychologically, privatism meant that the

individual should seek happiness in personal independence and in the search for wealth; socially, privatism meant that the individual should see his first loyalty as his immediate family, and that a community should be a union of such money-making, accumulating families; politically, privatism meant that the community should keep the peace among individual money-makers, and, if possible, help to create an open and thriving setting where each citizen would have some substantial opportunity to prosper.

To describe the American tradition of privatism is not to summarize the entire American cultural tradition. Privatism lies at the core of many modern cultures; privatism alone will not distinguish the experience of America from that of other nations. The tradition of privatism is, however, the most important element of our culture for understanding the development of cities. The tradition of privatism has al-

From *The Private City: Philadelphia in Three Periods of Its Growth* (Philadelphia: University of Pennsylvania Press, 1968), pp. 3-11; 14-21. Reprinted by permission of the publisher. Sam Bass Warner is William Edwards Huntington Professor of History and Social Science, Boston University.

ways meant that the cities of the United States depended for their wages, employment, and general prosperity upon the aggregate successes and failures of thousands of individual enterprises, not upon community action. It has also meant that the physical forms of American cities, their lots, houses, factories, and streets have been the outcome of a real estate market of profit-seeking builders, land speculators, and large investors. Finally, the tradition of privatism has meant that the local politics of American cities have depended for their actors, and for a good deal of their subject matter, on the changing focus of men's private economic activities.[2]

In the eighteenth century the tradition of privatism and the social and economic environment of colonial towns nicely complemented each other. Later as towns grew to big cities, and big cities grew to metropolises, the tradition became more and more ill-suited to the realities of urban life. The tradition assumed that there would be no major conflict between private interest, honestly and liberally viewed, and the public welfare. The modes of eighteenth-century town life encouraged this expectation that if each man would look to his own prosperity the entire town would prosper. And so it had.

Founded in 1682 under William Penn's liberal instructions, and settled first with Quaker artisans and a few Quaker merchants, the town had since prospered as the capital of a thriving colony.[3] By 1720 Philadelphia was said to have 10,000 inhabitants; by 1775 it had more than doubled to 23,700.[4] The townsite bordered the Delaware and Schuylkill rivers, both of which tapped rich forests and excellent farm lands. The line of north-south

trade ran nearby, and Philadelphia also lay within reach of the Susquehanna and Potomac rivers openings to the west. Philadelphia, thus, soon excelled in most of the staples of colonial trade, exporting furs, lumber, staves, iron, wheat, and flour, and importing rum, sugar, wine, and English manufactures.

Conditions outside the colony encouraged a heavy immigration of new settlers. Because Pennsylvania had been founded late, by comparison to other Atlantic colonies, west-bound space abounded on ships sailing from Great Britain and the Low Countries. Quakers, of course, fleeing persecution in England came to the colony in large numbers, but by the early eighteenth century their group came to be rivaled by Scotch-Irish and German immigrants. The Act of Union joining Scotland to England opened up the entire British Empire to poor Scots, while Irish wars and famines, and rack-renting landlords drove their fellow Presbyterians from Ulster. On the continent west German peasants fled the destruction of Louis XIV's repeated wars. Finally, in America the Indian control of upstate New York deflected the flow of westward settlers south to Pennsylvania. The result of all these outside events was a boom in the colony and the town; Pennsylvania and Philadelphia had everything, settlers, natural resources, capital, religious freedom, and comparatively little government.[5]

Within the town three conditions confirmed its privatism—its individualized structure of work, its general prosperity, and its open society and economy. When eighteenth-century Philadelphians spoke of the individual and his search for wealth as the goal of government they were simply basing their political arguments on the common place facts of town life. The core element of the town economy was the one-man shop. Most Philadelphians labored alone, some with a helper or two. A storekeeper tended his shop by himself or with the aid of his family or a servant. Craftsmen often worked with an apprentice, or more rarely with another skilled man.[6]

More than at later times, this Philadelphia was a town of entrepreneurs. Artisans sewed shoes, made wagons, boiled soap, or laid bricks for customers who had already placed an order. Workers did not labor under the close price and time disciplines of manufacture for large-scale inventories or big speculative wholesale markets. Most Philadelphians were either independent contractors hiring out on a job-by-job basis, or they were artisan shopkeepers retailing the products of their work. Even the establishment of a large merchant more resembled a small store than a modern wholesale house. Such a merchant frequently had a partner and the two partners carried on the business with the aid of a full-time clerk and an apprentice or servant to help with errands.[7] When a cargo arrived at the pier the partners would hire some laborers to unload the goods and move them to the storehouse. Thus, a very large proportion of the town's men—artisans, shopkeepers, and merchants—shared the common experience of the individual entrepreneur.

In later years the work groups of factories, offices, stores, and constructions crews would have enormous significance for the discipline, acculturation, and education of Philadelphia's residents. Such groups were almost entirely absent from the eighteenth-century town, Shipyard, ropewalk, and distillery workers labored in groups of five and even ten, but theirs were exceptionally large urban production units. In the colonial era the plantation, whether for agriculture or manufacture, was the characteristic place of large work gangs.[8] In 1775, associated with Philadelphia's general run of family enterprises were only about 900 indentured servants, 600 slaves, and perhaps 200 hired servants who lived with their employers.[9] These helpers shared the discipline of family life and work; they did not live by the modes of the work gang. Taken all together the eighteenth-century exceptions to the entrepreneurial role had but little significance for the functioning of the town's society.

A German visitor of 1750 wrote: "Pennsylvania is heaven for farmers, paradise for artisans, and hell for officials and preachers."[10] By the same token, Philadelphia on the eve of the Revolution was a town of freedom and abundance for the common man. For young persons there was a great demand for apprentices in all lines of work. An unskilled laborer without connections could find work with board and wages to begin accumulating a little money for tools. An artisan who wanted to carry a few shopkeeping goods in his shop, or a storekeeper with a good reputation, could get his stock from the merchant and settle for his advance a year later.

The ordinary artisan or shopkeeper, if his health was good, could be assured of a comfortable, if frugal, living. To be sure, houses were small and rents high, and furnishings were spare compared to later levels of living: no carpets, no upholstered furniture, a sand-scrubbed floor, and whitewashed walls. Stoves and fireplaces only partially heated drafty rooms, and in severe winters the cost of firewood or imported coal was a major item of family expense. Nevertheless, at the city's markets food was cheap and plentiful. The earnings of the ordinary artisan and shopkeeper could support a wife and children without their having to take outside employment. The rapid growth of the town and its trade meant regular work and good earnings for artisans and easy business, if not wealth, for shopkeepers.[11]

Although the customary hours of work were long, sunrise to sunset, the pace of work was often easy and varied with the season. Those who worked outside their homes, like men in the building trades, took an hour for breakfast, a break in the middle of the day, and an hour for dinner in the afternoon. Coopers, shoemakers, smiths, and men who practiced their craft in their own houses and yards must have stopped work as customers and friends came in, and a trip or two to the local tavern must also have been usual. Although there were no formal vacations, the traditional English holidays and frequent *ad hoc* town celebrations provided about twenty days off each year.

Franklin's *Autobiography* abounds with injunctions for regular habits, and the reputation for diligence he established by staying at his bench for the entire formal working day suggests that his was an extraordinary pace. For most workers rush seasons of hard work and long hours alternated with slack times. These variations meant days for fishing or spare moments for gossip on the streets and visits to the tavern.

Such a commonplace prosperity, generous at least by eighteenth-century standards, confirmed the privatism of the town and its age. As important

a confirmation came from the openness of its economy and society. The failure of the craft guilds to control the trades of the town gave newcomers and resident artisans alike an occupational freedom unknown in Europe. Shopkeepers and artisans—and often one man was both—could take up any craft or open any line of business they wished. Although Philadelphia had inherited English regulations favoring the "freemen" of the town, established artisans could not maintain their control of the town's businesses against newcomers. The carpenters and cordwainers managed to form associations to set prices for their work, but failed when they attempted to close the membership of their trades. In Philadelphia men added trades and lines of goods as they thought demand justified. Although this freedom undoubtedly produced a great deal of incompetent craftsmanship, the importance to the individual artisan or shopkeeper of open trades and plentiful work cannot be overestimated. It meant for the common man that there was always a chance for a fresh start. This chance for a new beginning was the urban equivalent of the contemporary farmer's chance to pick up and try again in the West.[12]

Already in these years the American pattern of social mobility by property obtained. No invidious distinction between land and trade favored some occupations over others. As eighteenth-century Philadelphians grew rich they kept their original occupations, whether they were carpenters, distillers, printers, or lawyers. Whatever a man's occupation, there were only a few channels for investment open to the rising man. Since there were no banks, private money lending was the most important investment opportunity in the town. Houses and land were also a favorite way of using savings both among the rich and those with a little capital. Only 19 percent of the families of Philadelphia owned their houses and therefore home rentals offered a safe investment. Other opportunities were shares in voyages, marine insurance, and, of course, land and farms outside the town.[13]

The prosperity and abundant opportunity of the town should not be confused with an even distribution of wealth. According to the published tax list for 1774 the upper tenth of the taxpaying households owned 89 percent of the taxable property. In this respect late eighteenth-century Philadelphia resembled the later Philadelphias—it was a pyramid of wealth in which about five hundred men guided the town's economic life. Its unique quality lay in the general prosperity of the common artisan and shopkeeper and the widely shared entrepreneurial experience and goals of the artisan, shopkeeper, and merchant.[14]

The wealthy presided over a municipal regime of little government. Both in form and function the town's government advertised the lack of concern for public management of the community. The municipal corporation of Philadelphia, copied from the forms of an old English borough, counted for little. Its only important functions in the late eighteenth-century were the management of the markets and the holding of the Recorder's Court. A closed corporation, choosing its members by co-option, it had become a club of wealthy merchants, without much purse, power, or popularity.

By modern standards the town was hardly governed at all. The constable in each ward and a few watchmen provided an ineffective police, the safety of the house and shop being secured by citizens' helping each other to drive away intruders or pursue thieves.[15] Most streets went unpaved, the public wharves little repaired. There were no public schools, no public water, and at best thin charity.

The enduring contribution of the colonial era to Philadelphia government lay in its inauguration of the committee system of municipal government. This system, if system it may be called in the eighteenth century, consisted of placing the administration of specific tasks in the hands of independent committees, or commissions. The Pennsylvania Provincial Assembly, lacking faith in the municipal corporation, created a number of commissions. First came the Board of Assessors established to raise money to pay the debts of the corporation and to require that wharves and streets be repaired and a workhouse erected. Then came separate street commissioners, next the City Wardens to manage the night watch and the lighting of the streets, and, still later, a Board of Overseers of the Poor. None of these commissions' performance would satisfy modern municipal standards. The commissioners were elected officials, chosen under the colonial fifty-pound, freehold qualification by the voters of Philadelphia. Like the town's fire companies, lending libraries, and tavern clubs these commissions helped train Philadelphians to the habits of committee government, a form of management they would have to call upon when creating a new independent government during the Revolution. Like many of the laws and forms of the colonial era which passed into the usage of the subsequent Commonwealth of Pennsylvania, the committee system of government was the legacy of colonial municipal life to later Philadelphias.[16]

The real secret of the peace and order of the eighteenth-century town lay not in its government but in the informal structure of its community. Unlike later and larger Philadelphias, the eighteenth-century town was a community. Graded by wealth and divided by distinctions of class though it was, it functioned as a single community. The community had been created out of a remarkably inclusive network of business and economic relationships and it was maintained by the daily interactions of trade and sociability. Because it was small and because every rank and occupation lived jumbled together in a narrow compass the town suffered none of the communications problems of later Philadelphias.

At most, 23,700 people lived in Philadelphia on the eve of the Revolution, 16,500 in the city proper, 7,000 in the adjacent districts of Northern Liberties and Southwark. The town crowded next to its shore. Its wharves and warehouses stretched a mile and a half along the Delaware river, but the built-up blocks of houses at their deepest point, along Market street, reached back from the river at most half a mile to about Seventh Street.[17]

The settlement pattern of the town combined two opposing social tendencies. The clustering of marine trades and merchants next to the Delaware suggested the beginnings of the specialized industrial quarters then characteristic of European cities. On the other hand, the rummage of classes and occupations found in many Philadelphia blocks continued the old tradition of mixed work and residence characteristic of American and English country towns.

＊　＊　＊

One can get some idea of the quality of urban life imposed by this settlement pattern by looking at one ward in a little detail. The Constable in making his enumeration of the residents of the Middle Ward left notes on his list showing when the turned the corner of a street. This record, plus some material from tax ledgers make it possible to reconstruct the settlement pattern of this ward in 1774.

As its name suggests, the Middle Ward lay in the center of town bounded on the north by Market Street, then the highway connecting Philadelphia to Chester and the south and to Lancaster and the west. The ward also was next to the market traffic. The sheds of the farmers' market in these years stretched up Market Street from the Delaware River only as far as Fourth Street. The Middle Ward was not a crowded dockside ward, but began just behind the dockside wards at Second Street. Its well-filled section covered five blocks to Seventh Street, Market to Chestnut. Beyond these blocks of houses the farms of the ward extended all the way west to the Schuylkill River.

Many famous Philadelphians lived within the ward. The old-fashioned Quaker radical, Anthony Benezet, the Proprietors John and Richard Penn, two opponents of the British who later turned Tory, Joseph Galloway, and James Allen, and the steadfast revolutionaries Benjamin Franklin and Daniel Clymer all lived in the center of the ward. The State House Yard (now Independence Square) stood across Chestnut Street between Fifth and Sixth streets. Such distinction, however, did not create the solid blocks of *haut bourgeois* fashion that they would to-day; rather it embroidered the com-manplace fabric which was the revo-lutionary town. In 1774 the Middle Ward was the home of at least 1,401 men, women, and children of every degree and condition from Proprietor to slave (Table 1).

The physical arrangements of the ward reflected the high cost of eight-eenth-century housing and the crowd-ing of Philadelphians near their port. Each of the Middle Ward's five settled blocks contained slightly less than five acres of land. On the first block of the ward (between Second and Third streets, the area nearest the Delaware River) there stood 137 dwellings, on the next 65, on the next 67, on the next 29, and on westernmost 39. To accommodate so many families in so little space some of the blocks of the ward had been cut by alleys so that little houses might be crowded onto the back lots of the houses facing the main streets. Strawberry Alley and El-bow Lane cut through the first block, Petty's Alley divided the third block,

and Benjamin Franklin had begun the alley process with his house lot off Market Street in the second block of the ward. He had built a row of three houses on Market Street, thereby turn-ing his home yard into an interior lot. His son-in-law Richard Bache, a mer-chant, rented one of the new row houses, Eden Haydock, plumber, rented another, and Frederick Stonemetz, a cooper, took the third. In the early nineteenth century Franklin's home parcel became Franklin Court, an alley lot which opened up the interior of the block.[18]

Such density of housing and such methods of land division had by 1774 destroyed the hopes of Penn and his surveyor for a "Green Town."[19] The practice of subdividing blocks with al-leys and jamming tiny houses on vacant rear yards continued strongly for the next ninety years. By 1860 the density of population in Philadelphia's inner wards reached its all-time peak.[20] Then, in the second half of the nineteenth century the street railway opened up vast tracts of cheap suburban land and thereby destroyed the market for new

Table 1

The Middle Ward of Philadelphia, April 8, 1774

Free Adults (346 households x 2 for wives)	692
Children	469
Negro Slaves	78
Bound Servants in Residence	65
Hired Servants in Residence	17
Inmates (other free adults living in households)	80
Population	1,401
Homeowners	80
Houserenters	266
Taxpayers living with other families	102
Total Taxpayers	448

alley construction. The old alleys with their dark and cramped houses, however, did not disappear at once. Rather they remained standing for years, giving discomfort to Philadelphia's poor for many generations, and the history of some alleys is not yet closed.

Already in the 1770's the crowding of the land exceeded the sanitary capabilities of the town. The streets and alleys reeked of garbage, manure, and night soil, and some private and public wells must have been dangerously polluted. Every few years an epidemic swept through the town. In the 1790's the city would pay a terrible price in deaths from recurring yellow fever.[21]

Though dangerous to health the eighteenth-century pattern of settlement guaranteed every citizen a knowledge of town life. At such density and small scale no generation could be raised ignorant of the other side of town, of the ways of life of the working class, or of the manners of the *haut bourgeois*. Within the Middle Ward at least 346 families with 469 children, 17 hired servants, 65 indentured servants, 78 Negro slaves, and 80 tenants share the settled 25 acres (Table 1). Those who left a record carried on seventy different occupations.[22]

Although merchants and shopkeepers, hatters, innkeepers, and tavernkeepers concentrated more heavily in this ward than in most others, variety best characterizes the occupational structure of the ward as it did all the other wards of the first Philadelphia. The Proprietors, the merchants, and the doctors shared the narrow compass of the Middle Ward with such ungenteel occupations as laborer, porter, carter, skinner, watchman, crier, paver, grazier, and even goatkeeper. The outer three blocks of the ward also housed several breweries and a distillery, and every one of the five blocks contained one or more of those notorious enemies of sweet residential air—the stable.[23]

One cannot, at this late date, reconstruct in detail the communications patterns of eighteenth-century Philadelphia, but the crowded living of the age encouraged a street and tavern life which more resembled the social habits of the later nineteenth and early twentieth-century immigrant ghettos than the isolated private family life of today's working class and middle class.

The high cost of building kept houses small, cramped, and in short supply. The common artisan's or shopkeeper's house was a narrow structure, about seventeen feet wide and twenty-five feet deep. A story-and-a-half high, it offered about eight hundred square feet of floor space on its ground floor and attic. Most often the owner plied his trade in the largest front room. The Middle Ward records show that although some families had five to seven children, most had few. The average number of children per household was 1.3, and counting servants and slaves the average household was four persons. The small houses, thus, were cramped but not severely crowded. If the artisan or shopkeeper prospered he would add a kitchen ell or more likely move to a house of similar proportion with a kitchen ell at the rear. The house of an ordinary merchant or even a craftsman who had grown rich, would be like the artisan's house with the ell, but would be two and one-half stories instead of one and one-half. Such houses of the prosperous also possessed deep lots for gardens, a shed for a cow and some chickens, and perhaps a horse.[24]

A town of small houses, where most houses also served as stores, offices and workshops, encouraged people to live out upon the streets. Moreover, the pace of work, most of it governed by the seasons or advance orders from customers, was irregular, what one would call today a rural pace. Both the physical structure of the town and the pace of its work thus encouraged a more public, gossipy style of life than could later be sustained when a steady pace of work, and larger interiors drove people into sharply defined spaces for work and residence.

The ordinary housewife shopped daily, going to the baker's for her bread, and taking her meat and pies to the baker's oven to be cooked. Street peddlers called her out for fish, eggs, and produce, and twice a week the farmers of Philadelphia County held a full market at the public stalls. As in the nineteenth century with its dark tenements and crowded row houses, sunlight must have been a great source of pleasure for women sewing and spinning and many must have worked at these and other household chores out on their doorsteps, as their tenement sisters did years later.

For the husband the eighteenth-century custom of men's gossip at the tavern provided the first Philadelphia's basic cells of community life. Every ward in the city had its inns and taverns. The 1774 tax list recorded 93 tavernkeeprs and 72 innkeepers in the city of Philadelphia, Southwark, and the Northern Liberties, approximately one neighborhood drinking place for every 140 persons in the city (23,000/ 165). The Middle Ward, alone, held 18 inns and taverns. Some must have served purely a neighborhood custom; others, like the London Coffee House or the City Tavern serves as central communications nodes for the entire city.

Then, as now, each one had its own crowd of regulars and thus each constituted an informal community cell of the city. Out of the meetings of the regulars at the neighborhood tavern or inn came much of the commonplace community development which preceded the Revolution and proved later to be essential to the governance of the city and the management of the ward. Regular meetings of friends, or men of common occupations, led to clubs of all kinds and of every degree of formality from regular billiard sessions to fire companies and political juntos. Benjamin Franklin and the many community innovations of his junto showed the potential of these informal tavern groups. They provided the underlying social fabric of the town and when the Revolution began made it possible to quickly gather militia companies, to form effective committees of correspondence and of inspection, and to organize and to manage mass towns meetings.

At the center of the town's communications system stood the merchants' coffee houses. On the eve of the Revolution Philadelphia had two such major meeting places—the old London Coffee House (established 1754), run by William Bradford, the newspaper publisher, and the new City Tavern (established 1773), just founded by a syndicate of merchants. The London Coffee House, located at Front and Market streets, adjacent to the town's principal market stalls and overlooking the Delaware, had been for many years the place where merchants gathered every noon to read incoming newspapers, to discuss prices, and to arrange for cargoes and marine insurance. These noon meetings in time ripened into the specialized institutions of exchanges, banks, and insurance companies. As yet, Philadelphia had but one insurance company and its merchants' business depended on the variety of functions of these daily tavern gatherings. For many years ship captains and travelers first stopped at the London Coffee House when they arrived in town, messages were left, auction notices posted and auctions held. Frequently on market days, after a parade through the streets, horses were auctioned in front of the tavern doors. Slaves and indentured servants stood before the same block.

As the town grew the importing merchants no longer had a need to be near the market dealers. The merchant community split into at least two parts. The new City Tavern surpassed the old London Coffee House as a place of fashion with the importing merchants, though its function remained that of its competitor. On May 19, 1774, Paul Revere brought his news of the closing of the Port of Boston to the City Tavern, and here numerous Revolutionary committees gathered. The still extant Philadelphia Assemblies were held at this new tavern, as was the endless series of banquets and balls which served the town with high entertainment.[25]

Because the merchants' tavern was a public place in a small town it escaped the limitations of later Philadelphia merchant centers—the exchanges, the Chamber of Commerce, and the gentlemen's clubs. These later gatherings were either meeting places of specialists and thereby encouraged only the brokers' or downtown merchants' view of the city, or they were

closed organizations which directed their members' attention inward toward the sociability of the group. The eighteenth-century tavern, however, opened out to all the life of the street and it did not shield the leaders of the town from contact with the life that surrounded them.[26]

It was the unity of everyday life, from tavern, to street, to workplace, to housing, which held the town and its leaders together in the eighteenth century. This unity made it possible for the minority of Revolutionary merchants, artisans, and shopkeepers to hold together, run the town, and manage a share of the war against England, even in the face of Quaker neutrality and Tory opposition.

NOTES

1. Quaker historians agree that the Holy Experiment died from materialism and secularization during the eighteenth century, Frederick B. Tolles, *Meeting House and Counting House* (Chapel Hill, 1948), 240-243; Sydney V. James, *A People among Peoples* (Cambridge, 1963), 37-43, 211-215; and see the charges against his contemporaries in John Woolman, *The Journal of John Woolman* (F. B. Holles, Introduction, New York, 1961).

2. Howard Mumford Jones, *O Strange New World* (New York, 1964), 194-272, treats with this tradition as a blend of Christian and classical ideas.

3. Tolles, *Meeting House*, 41.

4. Carl Bridenbaugh, *Cities in the Wilderness* (N.Y. 1938), 303; and see notes to Table I. Also, James T. Lemon, "Urbanization of the Development of Eighteenth Century Southeastern Pennsylvania," *William and Mary Quarterly*, XXIV (Oct., 1967), 502-542; Hannah B. Roach, "The Planning of Philadelphia," *Pennsylvania Magazine*, XCII (January and April, 1968).

5. Marcus L. Hansen, *Atlantic Migration* (Cambridge, 1940), Ch. II.

6. Comments suggesting an individualized or family work structure, Carl Bridenbaugh, *The Colonial Craftsman* (New York, 1950), 126-129, 136-139, 141-143.

7. Harry D. Berg, "The Organization of Business in Colonial Philadelphia," *Pennsylvania History,* X (July, 1943), 157-177; Arthur H. Cole, "The Tempo of Mercantile Life in Colonial America," *Business History Review,* XXXIII (Autumn, 1959), 277-299.

8. Richard B. Morris, *Government and Labor in Early America* (New York, 1946), 38-40.

9. . . . The reconstruction of the Middle Ward as of April 8, 1773 showed seventeen hired servants in residence there. On this basis two hundred servants were guessed for the city.

10. Gottlieb Mittelberger, *Journey to Pennsylvania* (Oscar Handlin and John Clive, eds., Cambridge, 1960), 48.

11. Jackson Turner Main, *The Social Structure of Revolutionary America* (Princeton, 1965), 74-83, 115-163; Chapter IV; Mittelberger, *Journey,* 48-51, 74-75.

12. Morris, *Government and Labor in Early America,* 2-3, 141-143; the American jack-of-all-trades tradition, Mittelberger, *Journey,* 42-43; artisans' associations, Bridenbaugh, *Colonial Craftsman,* 141-143.

13. Wilbur C. Plummer, "Consumer Credit in Colonial Philadelphia," *Pennsylvania Magazine,* LXVI (October, 1942), 385-409. The homeownership percentage was calculated from the number of homeowners and renters listed in the manuscript version of the Seventeenth Eighteenth Penny Provincial Tax of April 8, 1774 (in possession of the Pennsylvania Historical and Museum Commission, Harrisburg). A reconstruction of the Middle Ward as of April 8, 1774 shows holdings of land and houses in small lots, and pairs of structures, not big tracts. Rich men, like Israel Pemeberton, and men of few investments, both participated in the housing market.

14. The published version of the Seventeenth Eighteen Penny Provincial Tax, *Pennsylvania Archives, 3rd Series,* XIV (Harrisburg, 1897), 223-445, was used for a quick calculation of the distribution of taxable wealth. The taxpayers on this published list were arranged in order of the size of their published "assessment." The top ten percent, or 498 names, accounted for 89 percent of the 86,100 pounds of assessment given for Philadelphia, the Northern Liberties, and Southwark. This published list is not a sufficient guide to the distribution of wealth since the tax was largely a real property tax to which a head tax and a few personalty items were added. The very important property of stock-in-trade and money-on-loan went untaxed and hence unlisted. Also, the compilers of the published list mixed in many cases the taxes-paid entries with the assessment entries thereby distorting even the assessment distribution.

15. There are charming accounts of private policing in Henry D. Biddle, ed., *Extracts from the Journal of Elizabeth Drinker* (Philadelphia,

1889), robbery in her alley, Dec. 15, 1777; insane soldier wanders into the house June 30, 1778; "saucy Ann" and her soldier, Nov. 25, 26, Dec. 2, 1777, Jan. 4, 1778. A call for more considerate treatment of the town watchmen, Advertisement, *Pennsylvania Gazette,* Jan. 20, 1779.

16. For a description of the colonial government of Philadelphia, Judith M. Diamondstone, "Philadelphia's Municipal Corporation, 1701-1776," *Pennsylvania Magazine,* XC (April, 1966), 183-201; Edward P. Allinson & Boise Penrose, "The City Government of Philadelphia," *Johns Hopkins Studies in Historical and Political Science,* V (Baltimore, 1887), 14-33.

17. The tax records and constables' returns of 1774 and 1775 show dense settlement to end and Seventh Street with but a few families living on scattered farms west from this point to the Schuylkill river. A map made by John Reed of the City and Liberties of Philadelphia, supposed to have been made in 1774 (now in the possession of the American Philosophical Society) was shaded to show dense settlement to Tenth street.

18. Edward M. Riley, "Franklin's Home," *Historic Philadelphia* (American Philosophical Society, *Transactions,* XLIII, 1953), 148-160.

19. Anthony N. B. Garvan, "Proprietary Philadelphia as Artifact," *The Historian and the City* (Oscar Handlin and John Burchard, ed., Cambridge, 1964). 177-201.

20. Philadelphia City Planning Commission Map, "Year of Population Peak, Philadelphia, by Wards," dated August, 1949.

21. Bad conditions in alley "huts" of the poor, presumably one-story houses with a sleeping attic reached by a ladder as in the typical rural one-room cabin, Benjamin Rush," *Autobiography of Benjamin Rush* (American Philosophical Society, *Memoirs,* XXV, 1948), 83-84; cellar of a drunken, perhaps insane woman oyster seller, *Journal of Elizabeth Drinker,* Sept. 2, 1793; eighteenth century epidemics, small pox, yellow fever, dysentery or typhoid, John Duffy, *Epidemics in Colonial America* (Baton Rouge, 1953), 78-100, 142-161, 220-230, and Struthers Burt, *Philadelphia Holy Experiment* (New York, 1946), 159.

22. No authority tells to what extent eighteenth century artisans worked at home as opposed to working outside. With the exception of the building and marine trades most artisans are supposed to have worked at home. This supposition gets some indirect confirmation from the general agreement that most men labored alone and that most businesses in the city were family businesses. Neither Bridenbaugh in his *Colonial Craftsman* nor Morris in his *Government and Labor* tell of many urban establishments which might have employed many workers outside of their own homes.

23. A good sense of what the mixed settlement pattern of the city meant is given by Alexander

Graydon, *Memoirs of a Life, Chiefly Passed in Pennsylvania* (Harrisburg, 1811), 34-35.

24. The tax records of 1774 give evidence of a colonial housing shortage, for the ratio of occupied to unoccupied dwellings did not exceed two percent that year. Artisans' houses, Grant M. Simon, "Houses and Early Life in Philadelphia," *Historic Philadelphia*, 282-3; typical house for the prosperous, Advertisement, *Pennsylvania Gazette*, March 17, 1779.

25. The name "coffee house," which had been imported from England, merely designated a genteel tavern. Coffee, tea, lemonade, and beer were served, but the customers favored wines and liquors, Robert E. Graham, "The Taverns of Colonial Philadelphia," *Historic Philadelphia*, 318-323.

26. Graydon tells an amusing story of the confrontation of Benjamin Chew, lawyer for the Penns and then Recorder of the town and an alderman with two drunken British officers, *Memoirs*, 43-44; an excellent review of travellers and visitor's accounts mentions the importance to the social structure of the town of immigrant societies life St. David's and St. Tammany, Whitfield J. Bell, Jr., "Some Aspects of the Social History of Pennsylvania, 1760-1790," *Pennsylvania Magazine*, LXII (July, 1938), 301.

The Expansion of New England

PAGE SMITH

"The Expansion of New England" was the title chosen by Lois Kimball Mathews for her turn-of-the-century study of the spread of New England settlement and institutions to the Mississippi. Miss Mathew's book, published in 1909, marks a kind of watershed in American historiography. Most of the prominent historians of nineteenth-century America were New Englanders, bred and trained in a tradition-bound society and dedicated to the proposition that Old England had given birth to the greater part of what was estimable in the world and that New England had brought it to fruition.

The phrase "Anglo-Saxon" was often on the tongues of these historians, and through their genial monopoly of American history they spread the impression across the country that the finest flowers of our society had been nurtured in New England soil. There was, moreover, a good deal of evidence to back them up, and if they were sometimes inclined to bear heavily on the evidence in order to prove, for instance, that the Puritans were the fathers of American democracy, they were nonetheless high-minded, scholarly, and industrious gentlemen who contributed greatly to, if they did not in fact make up, American historiography in their century.

In the last decades of the nineteenth century a number of young historians rose to challenge what might be called the Anglo-New England interpretation of our past. Frederick Jackson Turner

From Page Smith, *As a City Upon a Hill* (New York: Knopf, 1966), pp. 36-54. Copyright © 1966 by Page Smith. Reprinted by permission of Alfred A. Knopf, Inc. Page Smith is Provost of Cowell College, University of California, Santa Cruz.

was the most effective spokesman of the thesis that it was to uniquely American factors, rather than to our English heritage, that the United States owed its remarkable development. Turner's brilliant essay on the role of the frontier in American history had symbolic as well as scholarly significance. It was received, not as proven fact—it was, as it turned out, not provable—but as revelation. The response that it evoked in the historical profession showed how inadequate the Anglo-New England version of our past had become in a world awakened to new intellectual currents. The hinterland could not forever be brought to worship at a temple whose high priests were Yankee historians. The Turner thesis was, perhaps primarily, the Midwest's declaration of intellectual and moral independence from the East. But there was more to it than that. The social and political attitudes of the older generation of historians had been thoroughly conservative. Their emphasis was on the persistence of tradition and the continuity of institutions; by dwelling on the Old World roots of American culture, they ensured New England's eminence as its preserver and transmitter.

It was hardly to be expected that these claims would go forever undisputed. If a Weaver, a Bryan, or a La Follette appeared to challenge the political hegemony of the Northeast, there must be a Turner to provide the historical rationale for the new claims. But if it was the West that saw in Turner the prophet of intellectual and cultural equality, the East was also ready to embrace him. He preached a national doctrine. The younger generation of historians had been deeply affected by those currents of reform that

manifest themselves in Progressivism. Turner became the preceptor of a generation of historians many of whom came, like their master, from the Middle West and most of whom were passionate crusaders for a wider social democracy. Turner taught them to look skeptically on the old gods and to examine their credentials with a ruthless disregard of the accepted pieties. The study and writing of American history profited enormously thereby. But the new schools inevitably produced their own distortions.

Lois Kimball Mathews stood between the two traditions—that of George Bancroft on the one hand and that of Turner on the other. She gave her scholarly allegiance without question to the exciting new spokesman of the West, but she had strong emotional ties with the Anglo-New England school. As a result the subject on which she chose to write her doctoral dissertation —the expansion of New England—was perfectly suited to elaborate the new dogma while propitiating the old gods. Her book professed to show how important New England had been in the settlement of the West; but at the same time it acknowledged the Turner doctrine by stressing the degree to which the frontier modified the ideas and institutions of the pioneers, and it accepted as a basic tenet that, in every New England town, it was the "radical," "progressive," and "independent" spirits who migrated westward.

Although a product of the new scholarship, Miss Mathews could not free herself of all vestiges of the older tradition. Thus we find frequent references to the marvelous properties of "Anglo-Saxon blood," the same blood that Miss Mathews's predecessors had exalted as having unique propensities for freedom—in the classic phrase "liberty-loving Anglo-Saxon blood"—blood whose individual corpuscles were imbued with zeal for civil rights and popular government. For Miss Mathews, it was also blood containing a "wanderlust" that helped to explain the migratory impulses of those through whose veins it flowed. The mysterious properties of this blood, which it may be feared will continue to evade chemical analysis, was the favorite *deus ex machina* of the earlier New England historians. Whatever was otherwise elusive and inexplicable might at last be traced to this magic fluid.

In Miss Mathews we might therefore discern a historian of New England, ready to join the new champions of the frontier, but on terms which enabled her to preserve a good measure of glory for the auld sod. The story of the frontier, she wrote, in the best Turner tradition, was "a study of institutions transplanted and transformed, the old ones influencing the new ones, the new ones reacting upon the old, making the latter broader and more flexible." Cramped by the conservatism of the New England towns "the more radical spirits began to chafe, and turn to newer sections where they might be unhampered by either tradition or habit." In this way "the spirit of radicalism so conspicuous among the pioneer's motives" had contributed "immeasurably" to the development of the country, since the frontier showed thereby a "tendency to radicalism in all matters."

"The conservative element," by Miss Mathews's reading, remained in the "settled portions of the country" making those sections increasingly stodgy with each passing decade. The forces that influenced the pioneer to start on

his westward trek were his "radicalism," his "sometimes excessive individualism," "the desire for greater material prosperity" and, of course, his wandering Anglo-Saxon blood. The classic pioneer was "a New Englander grown more independent and probably more tolerant under his new environment."

The pioneers were in the terms of the new dogma individuals who longed "for the open, for the free life of an unorganized community." But the fact was that the frontier town settled by New Englanders, far from being "a community where people might do as they pleased," was if anything more highly organized, more rigid and repressive than its parent community, while the forces of change, sparked by an expanding ocean commerce with its attendant prosperity, appeared first, as Carl Bridenbaugh has shown, in the large seacoast towns and cities. If there were any Puritans who founded communities "where people might do as they pleased" they have escaped this historian's notice.

The propositions about the migrating New Englander that are stated so confidently, Miss Mathews does not attempt to prove. They were part of the new dispensation, taken by her and by many of her contemporaries as articles of faith. Yet Miss Mathews, aware that theory is not entirely consistent with fact, reveals her own uneasiness when she notes of the pioneers that "curiously enough . . . when the malcontents found themselves in the majority instead of the minority (as they had been before their removal), they frequently became as intolerant as their comrades had been."[1] The key word in this passage is "curiously." That settlers on the frontier should be as intolerant as their cousins back home (or more so) was only "curious" if the historian saw the pioneer as the forerunner of Progressivism. The idea that the frontier was populated by individuals imbued with the ideals of twentieth-century liberal reform could be dismissed as simply naïve if it had not been accepted by so many historians. The myth of the "liberal" pioneer has been almost as enduring as the older image of the noble Anglo-Saxon, which it replaced.

The story of New England's expansion is far more complex than Miss Mathews suggests. The development of the American frontier has of course been continuous. From the earliest years of colonial settlement the older seacoast towns bred new communities deeper in the wilderness. The spectacular settlement of the West that took place in the nineteenth century had been preceded, and was indeed accompanied by the settlement of northern New England, New York, and Pennsylvania as well as the southern frontier of Kentucky and Tennessee. No radical change occurred in the motives of settlement from the colonial period through the early decades of the nineteenth century. The Puritans who had pushed out from the Massachusetts Bay area had had for the most part the same motives as their descendants who moved into Ohio, Illinois, and Michigan two hundred years later. One of the principal causes of such migration was religious controversy.

Robert East has pointed out that "a distinctive force in the expansion of the New England frontier in the seventeenth century *and later* [italics mine] . . . is a certain explosive character in Calvinistic Puritanism itself. The dynamic church principle inherent in the doctrine of every man his own priest was in constant disharmony with the

severe external authority attempted in practice by the Puritan clergy and elders."

The result was the constant fragmenting of the parent communities, but the secessions were of a group, rather than an individual, type. True, the group generally formed about a person of unusual force of character, but it was as a group that the dissenters departed, not as separate individuals; and a new covenant was invariably the first order of business. Certainly some of "the rag-tag and bobtail element" fled from settled communities to the frontier, but as East states it, "the effective spearhead of expansion was generally in the religiously discontented."

With such a figure as Roger Williams in mind we are inclined to think of these dissenters as being somehow "liberal," but in reality they were often the most rigidly orthodox members of the community, individuals who were alarmed at the softening of Puritan dogmas and who withdrew to the wilderness to recover the purity of the ancient faith. It was often, at least in terms of theology, the liberal elements who achieved dominance in the older towns and cities, precipitating the exodus of the conservatives. In East's words, again, the farther west one traveled "the more 'orthodox' was the Puritanism at work; contrarily, the more liberal and enlightened (or corrupt and defiled, according to one's point of view) did Harvard and Boston appear. . . . The forward-looking, the liberal religious element of the eighteenth century was invariably found in the older settlements of the seaboard and the [Connecticut] valley."[2]

It was, after all, Cotton Mather, the high priest of Boston Puritanism, who favored private examination for church

membership as opposed to the traditional examination by the congregation. It was in Boston, too, that the
Half-Way Covenant got its strongest
backing. The church at Branford, Connecticut, offended by the union of the
colonies of New Haven and Connecticut and at the spread of the Half-Way
Covenant, moved en masse to Newark,
New Jersey; a similar dispute in Strat-
ford led to the founding of Woodbury,
Connecticut. Bennington, Vermont, was
settled from Hardwick, Massachusetts,
by Captain Samuel Robinson who took
twenty-two people with him, all of them
conservatives who wished to preserve
the old faith.

The records of one New England
town after another disclose bitter and
often protracted disputes over theological doctrines and even over the
personalities of particular ministers.
Wethersfield, Connecticut, alone colonized a number of towns as the result
of splittings off from the original
church. It might be argued that quarreling was one of the principal causes of
the expansion of New England. It was
then, as it is today, difficult to repair
the unity of the town once it was shattered; it was generally easier for the
minority to withdraw, and it did so.
The emigrants were, however, no more
radical, tolerant, or independent than
their less mobile neighbors.

In essence, the process was this: as
the original community began to break
down—sometimes because of theological
wrangles, sometimes because of progressive economic and social differentiation, sometimes because of its own inner
tensions—individuals within the community coalesced around aggressive
leaders and then broke off to found
their own communities, hoping thereby
to recapture the classic unity of their
common life.

An example of this is Worthington,
Ohio, formed by settlers from Granby,
Connecticut, who "drew up articles of
association, among which was one
limiting their number to forty, each of
whom must be unanimously chosen by
ballot, a single negative being sufficient
to prevent an election." It would be
difficult to discover in such action any
yearning for independence or any desire to be free of the tyranny of the
community.

Colonization by congregations and
kinship groups, fiercely exclusive in
many instances, refutes the argument
that the pioneers were champions of
"individualism." The settler who wished
to go his own way, free from the scrutiny of his neighbors, stood a better
chance in the older towns than in frontier communities, unless, of course, he
was willing to live the precarious life
of an isolated trapper and hunter. While
it is true that the emigrants often left
their home communities pronouncing
an anathema on them as being sunk in
vice, vain presumption, and worldliness, these strictures were not related to
"radical" or liberal political theories, or
indeed related, in most instances, to
politics at all. They referred to the community's failure to live up to the covenant, and thus they have a better claim
to the title of "conservative" than of
"radical."

The New Englanders who colonized
towns, far from being conscious or unconscious innovators, sought to reproduce the institutions and values of their
home communities. They wished in
Norwalk, Ohio, to create a refined and
purified version of Norwalk, Connecticut. A historian, discussing the founding
of Hudson, Ohio, by colonists from
New Haven, has written that while the
town "might, in many ways, be more
primitive and ruder than New Haven,

yet, in another way, it was the Connecticut original in purer form, undiluted and undistracted by modern worldliness and the change encroaching on the east."[3]

It must be said that many communities did not have their origins in religious dissent and contention. The need for new land was undoubtedly the most persistent motive for emigration, and the strength of the ties between new town and old is suggested by the frequency with which the frontier settlement took the name of its parent community. Richmond, New Hampshire, was named after Richmond, Rhode Island. Lebanon, Lyme, and Plainfield of the Granite State were all offspring of Connecticut towns with the same names, and the list could be extended by the hundreds and indeed thousands.[4]

The settlement of Maine and Vermont was not halted by the Revolution. In 1780 nine new towns were founded in Maine and twelve in Vermont. Almost all the early settlers of Andover, Maine, migrated from Andover, Massachusetts, in protest of the relaxed theology of the Massachusetts town. New Vineyard was peopled from Martha's Vineyard, and Exeter, Maine, was settled from Exeter, New Hampshire. Vermont's Braintree was the offshoot of Massachusetts' Braintree, and Pittsfield and Groton were named after towns in the Bay State.

It was not, however, to northern New England that emigrating Yankees went in largest numbers. New York, Pennsylvania, and Ohio claimed tens of thousands. A Congregational church organized in Poultney, Vermont, moved in a body to East Springfield, New York, and became like many others with similar origins a model New England community. Wherever the settlers went they carried their politics with

them as well as their religion. Luzerne County, New York, was a stronghold of New England Federalism and so it continued for more than a generation.

Hudson, New York, was settled in 1783 by thirty Quaker fishermen and their families from Martha's Vineyard; and from Plymouth, Massachusetts, to Plymouth, Connecticut, to Plymouth, Ohio, we can trace families, civil institutions, and church dogmas in an unbroken line; from Greenwich, Connecticut, to Greenwich, Ohio, and from the New England Deerfield to its western counterparts.

Religious revivals and "awakenings," perhaps more than any other single factor, were responsible for the establishment of colonized towns. The Great Awakening of the 1730's and 1740's led directly to the founding of a number of "New Light" communities and a half dozen colleges. The awakening which swept through Connecticut at the end of the eighteenth century scattered Connecticut towns through New York, Vermont, and Ohio. Hudson, Ohio, was just such a community; it was started by David Hudson, a native of Goshen, Connecticut, who, according to his own testimony, had been a Godless man and then was caught up in a revival, underwent a profound spiritual crisis and, pledging himself to God's service, vowed to found a community in the wilderness which would live according to God's ordinances. In the words of Richard Wohl: "From the very first he determined that his resolve should not be dissipated under the stress of a frontier life with its attendant hardships. He need not have feared. The isolation, the hard work done in common, sustained the original homogeneity of the group and served, indeed, to provide it with added vitality." Having established his covenanted community in the forest,

Hudson went on to help found Western Reserve College.[5]

The story was a typical one. The older towns were like ripe seed pods which when heated by one of the periodic revivals would burst open and scatter seedlings wherever the winds of migration were blowing at the moment.

After the earlier period of migration, the increase in missionary activity—especially by the Congregationalists and Presbyterians—led to the settling of many new communities and to the gathering together of individual farm families into congregations.

When a group from Granville, Massachusetts, decided to move to the Ohio country, a 24-member Congregational church drew up a covenant and a constitution and transplanted pastor, deacons, and church members to Granville, Ohio. The emigrants numbered 176 and their first act upon reaching the new settlement was to hold a service of worship in the forest. One of the little band later wrote of how they wept when they heard their voices echoing among the lonely and forbidding trees; "they wept when they remembered Zion."

Oberlin, in Lorain County, was another classic example of the transplanted New England community. The colonists were asked to subscribe to a covenant which pledged them to "a life of simplicity, to special devotion to church and school, and to earnest labor in the missionary cause."[6]

Illinois and Indiana's earliest settlers were Southerners, many of them from North Carolina, Kentucky, and Tennessee. The great influx of New Englanders into Indiana came in the 1830's and the decades that followed. In Elkhart County, 213 out of 255 settlers in the years between 1828 and 1840 came from New England. Grange, Noble, and La Porte counties were largely settled by families from Massachusetts, Connecticut, and Vermont. A Connecticut colony was established in 1834 at Rockwell, Illinois, and in 1836 three New England colonies were founded, one at Tremont in Tazewell County, one in Knox County, and one at Lyons near Varna. A company from Gilmanton, New Hampshire, settled Hanover in 1835 and settlers from Pittsfield, Massachusetts, established a purified version of their hometown in Pittsfield, Illinois.[7] Wethersfield was founded by a pastor and his congregation from Wethersfield, Connecticut, while a church colony from Benson, Vermont, moved as a group to Du Page County. From Rhode Island in 1836 came forty families, members of the Providence Farmers' and Mechanics' Emigrating Society, who had organized a church and school before their departure.

A colony from Northampton, Massachusetts, was adjacent to one from Norwich, Connecticut. The so-called Hampshire colony organized its own church and academy and planted a town in Bureau County. By 1840 Illinois could count at least twenty-two colonies in northern or central Illinois, all of which had their origin in New England or New York. There was, to be sure, a great number of people who came at random into the state and who either joined established towns or formed loosely knit rural communities. But the colonized towns played a role in the history of the state that was out of all proportion to their numbers. In a few years these centers came to dominate the social and political life of Illinois. As a former governor wrote, the Yankee was "the most liberal in contributing to whatever is for the public benefit. Is a schoolhouse, a bridge, or a church to be built, a road to be made, a school or minister to be maintained, or taxes to be paid for the honor or support of the government, the northern man is never found wanting."[8]

The Southerners on the other hand, while more picturesque, were notoriously indolent, a vice which led to many others. "On a bright day," a traveler wrote, "they mount their horses and throng the little towns in the vicinity of their homes, drinking and trading horses until late in the evening." Toward education the Southerner had a humorous hostility. "He 'reckons' they should know how to write their names, and 'allows it's a right smart thing to be able to read when you want to' . . . but he don't 'calculate' that books and the sciences will do as much good for a man in these matters as a handy use of the rifle. . . . As for teaching 'that's one thing he allows the Yankees are just fit for'; he does not hesitate to confess that they are a 'power smarter' at that than the western boys. But they can't hold a rifle nor ride at wolf hunt with 'em; and he reckons, after all, these are the great tests of merit."[9]

Sixty New Englanders came to Romeo, Michigan, in 1827 and gave that town a thoroughly Yankee character. By 1850 almost half of Michigan's population had come from New England by way of New York, and as much as a third or a quarter came directly from New England.

The Union Colony got its start in Poultney and Bennington, Vermont, where the Reverend Sylvester Cochrane recruited ten families, adding three more from Benson and Bellevue, Michigan. Before the Vermonters left home they signed a covenant which began:

Whereas, The enjoyment of the ordinances . . . of the Gospel is in a great measure unknown in . . . the western country, and

Whereas, We believe that a pious and devoted emigration is . . . one of the most efficient means, in the hands of God, in removing the moral darkness which hangs over a great portion of the valley of the Mississippi; and

Whereas, We believe that a removal to the West may be a means of promoting our temporal interest, and we trust [may] be made subservient to the advancement of Christ's kingdom;

We do therefore, form ourselves into . . . a colony with the design of removing into some parts of the western country which shall hereafter be designated, and agree to bind ourselves to . . . the following rules. . . .

The rules covered codes of behavior and, since the town wished to preserve equality among its members, the rules for the distribution of land. No settler was to be allowed to take more than "one farm lot of 160 acres, and one village lot of 10 acres, within the limits of the settlement."

A final injunction to the colonists of Vermontville, as the community came to be called, carried overtones of John Winthrop's "Modell of Christian Charity." "As we must necessarily endure many of those trials and privations which are incident to a settlement in a new country," the statement read, "we agree we will do all in our power to befriend each other; we will esteem it not only a duty, but a privilege to sympathize with each other under all our trials, to do good and lend, hoping for nothing again, and to assist each other on all necessary occasions."[10]

While the tide of colonizing by the purer type of covenanted religious community declined as the nineteenth century wore on, there continued to be many such towns founded. And those such as the temperance and antislavery towns that were established on some substitute version of the covenant were generally deeply imbued with religious feeling.

After the passage of the Kansas-Nebraska Bill in March, 1854, New England emigrants poured into Kansas. New Haven sent a band of seventy settlers known as the Connecticut Colony, a group which included tradesmen, teachers of music, tutors in Yale College, politicians, farmers, and ministers. The community, the forerunner of a number of future colonies, settled on the Wabaunsee River, armed with twenty-five rifles and twenty-five Bibles, gifts from Henry Ward Beecher's Brooklyn congregation.

Amenia, North Dakota, was founded by pioneers from Sharon, Connecticut, who planted their church at once and prided themselves on never having "sought for Eastern sources a single dollar in its support." Down to the end of the century, the Yale Divinity School dispatched its famous "Bands" of young ministers to the Far West and Northwest, and many New Englanders followed them to California, Oregon, and Washington. Moreover town building went on in the unclaimed regions of the older Midwestern states as well as on the frontier, and New England contributed generously to such communities.[11]

As for the Turner-Mathews thesis, while it is undoubtedly true that much individual migration was motivated by a desire to escape from the restraints of organized society, myth has vastly exaggerated their number and importance. Such emigrants were certainly not town builders, though they became in many instances the nucleus for towns. They were the cutting edge of the westward movement (Timothy Dwight called them "foresters"), whose function it was "to cut down trees, build log-houses, lay open forested grounds to cultivation, and prepare the way for those who come after them. These

men," Dwight wrote, "cannot live in regular society. They are too idle; too talkative; too passionate; too prodigal; and too shiftless; to acquire either property or character. They are impatient of the restraints of law, religion, and morality; grumble about the taxes, by which Rulers, Ministers, and Schoolmasters are supported; and complain incessantly, as well as bitterly, of the extortions of mechanics, farmers, merchants, and physicians; to whom they are always indebted."[12]

This is, to be sure, a somewhat jaundiced view of the classic pioneer figure. Nevertheless we know from many other accounts that the description is not far wide of the mark. Such individuals were the restless, the discontent, the psychologically and economically marginal portions of older communities. Yet the myth has associated them with a dream of romantic freedom. We might well recall the words of D. H. Lawrence: "Men are free when they are in a living homeland, not when they are straying and breaking away. Men are free when they are obeying some deep, inward voice of religious belief. Obeying from within. Men are free when they belong to a living, organic, *believing* community, active in fulfilling some unfulfilled, perhaps unrealized purpose."[13]

The lonely, wide-ranging frontiersmen bulk large in historical fiction and in the popular mind, but they counted for little in comparison with the town builders of the covenant.

If New England placed the stamp of its own spirit on the Middle West, it did so by dispatching what were by any reasonable standards its most conservative sons and daughters to fill up the vast empty spaces. The colonized communities of Puritans who occupied the frontier states were composed neither of "radicals," nor "independents," nor "lovers of freedom" as an abstract principle. Far from being "tolerant," they were highly intolerant of cities, of the big business of the day, of alien races and faiths, of drinking, of Sabbath-breaking, and indeed of a host of things. Those who remained in the Eastern towns and cities learned to live with the Irish, the French-Canadians, the Poles, the Italians, "the offscourings of the earth," and often to make profits from them. They learned to tolerate what they could not well evade. But in the iron soul of the Puritan town builder there was little tolerance for those who stood outside of the covenant of grace. These builders were the true believers, nerved by their faith to subdue the heartland of a continent in the name of a Jehovah who, if he was terrible in his wrath, was also wonderfully forgiving.

The transplanting of Eastern "culture" froze rather than liberated it. The new town "clung to traditional institutional forms and social practices; and it hungered after intellectual and social contact and parity with the East. A large part of western opportunity was the opportunity to imitate an older society." Before the West could claim parity, it had to prove that it could successfully emulate its supercilious parent. The frontier towns were thus an enormously conservative force since they clung tenaciously to "forms" and "practices" that were a generation old by city standards.

"Much has been said, and foolishly said, of Western character," wrote the Reverend Rufus Babcock. "Most people in the West formed their characters before they emigrated thither; and they have been slightly or not at all modified by their change of residence."[14] The great majority of those who came to the frontier were conservative to begin with. Their situation on a frontier where they felt that the forms and order of civilized life were threatened made them far more resolute in resisting change than their urban cousins.

NOTES

1. Lois Kimball Mathews: *The Expansion of New England* (Boston: Houghton Mifflin Company; 1909), pp. 4, 5, 6, 73, 72.
2. Robert A. East: "Puritanism and New England Settlement," *New England Quarterly*, XVII (June, 1944), 255, 256-7, 263.
3. Richard Wohl: "Henry Day," in William Miller, ed.: *Men in Business* (Cambridge, Mass.: Harvard University Press; 1952), p. 164.
4. Mathews: *Expansion*, p. 114.
5. Wohl: "Henry Day," p. 162.
6. Henry Howe: *Historical Collections of Ohio* (Cincinnati: Derby, Bradley & Co.; 1848), pp. 296, 297; James H. Fairchild: *Oberlin, the Colony and the College, 1833-1883* (Oberlin, Ohio: E. J. Goodrich; 1883), pp. 9-16.
7. Theodore Calvin Pease: *The Frontier State, 1818-1848* (Springfield, Ill.: Illinois Centennial Commission; 1918), pp. 178-9.
8. Thomas Ford: *A History of Illinois* (New York: Iverson & Phinney; 1854), p. 281; Albert Shaw: *Local Government in Illinois* (Baltimore: Johns Hopkins University; 1838), p. 11; Charles A. Church: *History of Rockford, Illinois, and Winnebago County* (Rockford, Ill.: W. P. Lamb; 1900), pp. 160 ff.; William V. Pooley: "The Settlement of Illinois from 1830 to 1850," *Bulletin* of the University of Wisconsin, no. 220 (1908).
9. Clyde E. Buckingham: "Early Settlers of the Rock River Valley," *Journal of the Illinois State Historical Society*, XXXV (September, 1942), pp. 242, 241 quoting Eliza W. Farnham: *Life in Prairie Land* (New York: Harper & Brothers; 1846).
10. Edward W. Barber: "The Vermontville Colony: Its Genesis and History," *Michigan Pioneer and Historical Collections*, XXVIII (1900); J. Harold Stevens: "The Influence of New England in Michigan," *Michigan Historical Magazine*, XIX (autumn, 1935), pp. 321-53.
11. Lois Kimball Mathews Rosenberry: "Migrations from Connecticut after 1800," *Tercentenary Commission of the State of Connecticut*, LIV (New Haven: Yale University Press, 1936), pp. 18, 19, 20, 29.
12. Dwight: *Travels*, II, 459.
13. D. H. Lawrence: *Studies in Classic American Literature* (London: M. Secker; 1933), p. 12.
14. Earl Pomeroy: "Towards a Reorientation of Western History," *Mississippi Valley Historical Review*, XLI (March, 1955), pp. 597, 593.

III THE CITY IN THE ERA OF MANIFEST DESTINY

The nineteenth century was "the century of cities." From Australia to Europe, urbanization was an international phenomenon, but it was seldom surpassed in the speed and size of its growth than in the United States. The popular conception of urban expansion usually associates it with the rise of the industrial giants in the forty years after the Civil War. But the first sixty years of the century were as dynamic as (and in some ways more dramatic than) the post-Civil War period. Cornfields, trading stations, forts, lake and river ports, construction camps, and whistle stops, developed into towns, small and large, and sometimes sank into ghost towns. It was a period of unprecedented optimism and wild speculation, where the enthusiasm of "manifest destiny" to conquer a continent was also poured into town and city building.

Perhaps never in our history have so many Americans shown such unbridled faith and competitive rivalry about their cities: undoubtedly, Athens, Ohio, would outshine her ancient Greek namesake, Chicago would outgrow New York, St. Louis would dominate the American heartland—all would be bigger and better than their wicked and dirty European counterparts. Never in our history has the United States experienced such rapid urban growth as the four decades preceding the Civil War. From 1820 to 1860 the total population of the country increased by 226 per cent, while the urban population increased by almost 800 per cent. Whereas roughly 6 per cent of Americans lived in cities in 1800, not only were 20 per cent urban dwellers by 1860, but Philadelphia was bigger than Berlin, New York was the third largest city in the world, and Chicago was the most spectacular of them all. A scruffy little village of fifty people in 1830, Chicago survived a panic and depression and, with little more than mud and a prayer, seized upon canal and railroad building to explode by 1853 into a city of 60,000 people with 150 hotels. Old and new cities in the East and South continued to grow, with the South, significantly for the later Civil War period, lagging behind. But nowhere was there more hope, lusty vitality, and bigger dreams in the seventy years after the formation of the new nation than in the urban expansion in the new West.

Whereas Page Smith described the small town as the cutting edge of the wilderness, Richard Wade, in the first selection—a major essay in the literature of American urban history[1]—describes the cities of the trans-Appalachian West from 1790 to 1830 as the "spearheads of the frontier." To the familiar array of such western characters as the hunter and farmer, Wade adds the urbanite, many of whom moved west to settle good towns rather than to cultivate good land. His thesis of the urban frontier is another important revision of the frontier thesis of Frederick Jackson Turner, for Wade shows that the city dweller often preceded the farmer in the westward plunge of the early nineteenth century. Cities like Cincinnati, Lexington, Louisville, St. Louis, and Pittsburgh were not only spearheads of settlement, but spearheads of political, economic, and cultural leaderships as well. Although they worked in mutual dependence with the farm, the cities were more aggressive, more dynamic, and more creative than the farm in giving a frontier wilderness diversity, direction, growth, opportunity, and, above all, maturity. Like Bridenbaugh, Wade sees the cities forging a distinct urban society sharply distinct from the countryside and the farm; like Schlesinger, he concludes that without the role of the cities the story of American development is only half told. Indeed, it is interesting to note the continuity of themes established by previous essays that Wade carries forward into the early nineteenth century.

Whereas Wade is concerned with the history of the interior river and valley cities up to 1830, Bayrd Still analyzes the emergence of Buffalo, Cleveland, Detroit, Chicago, and Milwaukee, the five major cities of the Great Lakes region in the middle years of the nineteenth century. Like Wade, he sees the urban frontier as a major event in facilitating the westward movement; like Bridenbaugh, he sees more similarities than differences among cities. In discussing such patterns of urbanization as urban politics, municipal and cultural services, urban competition, and the transition from commerce to manufacturing, he is fascinated by the striking similarities that bound the lake cities in a common mould. In tackling the reasons for similarity, he demonstrates a delicate handling of the thorny balance between change and continuity.

What Still has done in this important essay is to see the lake cities of the mid-nineteenth century in a transitory, intermediary stage of urban development between the old and the new, although one might want more evidence that they reflect other cities of the same period.

First, there was similarity because the lake cities were facing the same demands and problems that confronted the older coastal cities of fifty or more years before. The response was continuity, an intense imitation of the older

1. His thesis is more fully developed in his book, *The Urban Frontier, 1790-1830* (Cambridge: Harvard University Press, 1957), indispensable for the study of American urban history.

and tested ideas and institutions of the eighteenth-century city, from its charter to its municipal services. Yet, at the same time, the lake cities infused the newer influences of Jacksonian democracy, such as manhood suffrage, to eliminate some older, eighteenth-century restrictions on political authority. Second, the lake cities shared the problem of size, the confounding difficulty of rapid urbanization. The response to size was a burst of civic responsibility centered around voluntary associations. Still makes one of his most insightful points by showing that the response was not, however, one of seizing upon a new philosophy that recognized the novel and changing character of urban settlement, a view which emerged in the late nineteenth and early twentieth centuries. Rather, it was one that was heavily saturated with older village and agrarian attitudes which emphasized private, individual responsibility and the sanctity of private property. It was not what he calls the "municipal consciousness" of the twentieth century, but a "group consciousness . . . still very largely articulated by and pivoted around the individual." The response to older village and agrarian values suggests that the city did not necessarily transform by some uncanny urban magic a former farmer or villager who moved to the city into a complete urbanite. Newcomers could tenaciously cling to their former attitudes and prejudices despite the novel demands of urbanization.

Up to this point, the readings have covered large chunks of time and a multitude of urban themes. The last two essays in this chapter, however, were selected to achieve more depth by pinpointing two critical forces shaping the city, urban rivalry and the urban entrepreneur.

Rivalry is a dynamic theme in American urban history. Like gladiators, cities and towns fought each other for their lives and for a stake in the American bonanza. For the winners, urban rivalry built cities, enriched regions, generated—among other things—a vast transportation network, and contributed to the economic prosperity of the nation as a whole. For the losers, it stunted cities and created bankruptcy, depression, and broken dreams. The two classic cases of rivalry in the nineteenth century were the eastern rivalry over access to western markets, won by New York with her Erie Canal,[2] and the famous battle between Chicago, Milwaukee, and St. Louis for control of the Mississippi Valley. But these were examples of what was going on elsewhere on perhaps a less heroic scale, but of no less significant importance, as Harry N. Scheiber indicates in his essay on urban rivalry in the Old Northwest.

In a vivid account, Scheiber catches the fierce competition, wild hopes, bitter disenchantment, enormous growth, and unbelieveable waste, as the cities and towns of the Old Northwest, by means fair and foul, invested their pride,

2. See Julius Rubin's perceptive, *Canal or Railroad? Imitation and Innovation in the Response to the Erie Canal in Philadelphia, Baltimore, and Boston* (Philadelphia: American Philosophical Society, 1961).

fortune, and future in a furious scramble for dominance over canal and rail-road routes. He traces the tactics, often ruthless, the jockeying for position, often chaotic, the ambitions, sometimes narrowly selfish, the results, often un-anticipated and self-defeating, but in the large, beneficial, in this frantic con-test for security. Above all, he analyzes its significance by showing that both the "transportation revolution" and its result, a burgeoning economic growth, were not merely the outcome of state and national efforts, but that they were also a local and regional phenomenon, urban and regional rivalry. The key factors of private financing, public aid, political and business promotion, were expressly aimed and directed at local needs and ambitions. In a real sense, Scheiber goes beyond linking the city intimately to the canal and railroad age. He demonstrates how local history, if not blighted by provincialism and sen-timentality, can illuminate the larger issues of state and national history.

Cities did not grow as a result of urban rivalry alone, or transportation, or a convenient location, or the impersonal forces of urbanization. They were also the creatures of the men and women who lived in them—their hopes, their energy, their community spirit, their initiative, their adaptability. A railroad could make a city, a fire could break a city, but ultimately whether a city prospered through good luck or survived bad luck depended upon the spirit of its citizens. Daniel Boorstin catches the flamboyant spirit of the human element in urban manifest destiny by examining the roles and impact of three men, William B. Ogden of Chicago, Dr. Daniel Drake of Cincinnati, and William Larimer of Denver, who were representative of countless others in cities everywhere.

These men were a new breed of the promotor extraordinary—the entrepre-neur as the city booster, the dreamer as the city builder. They were "upstart businessmen" who helped build upstart cities. They pinned their hopes and fortunes to cities without a past and with only a future. They constituted a perfect marriage of city booster and self-booster, fusing private interests to community interests. Their energies at first directed to promoting real estate and railroads, spread to building practically every aspect of city life, from municipal services, hospitals, colleges, parks, and, not the least, politics. They in turn reflected an attitude of the general community, the booster spirit—an ethos, a state of mind, often a mystique, the intensity of or lack of which sealed the success or failure of many a city in America.

Urban Life in Western America, 1790-1830

RICHARD C. WADE

The towns were the spearheads of the American frontier. Planted as forts or trading posts far in advance of the line of settlement, they held the West for the approaching population. Indeed, in 1763, when the British drew the Proclamation Line across the Appalachians to stop the flow of migrants, a French merchant company prepared to survey the streets of St. Louis, a thousand miles through the wilderness. Whether as part of French and Spanish activity from New Orleans or part of Anglo-American operations from the Atlantic seaboard, the establishment of towns preceded the breaking of soil in the transmontane West.

In 1764, the year of the founding of St. Louis, settlers made the first plat of Pittsburgh. Twelve years later and four hundred miles down the Ohio, Louisville sprang up at the Falls, and the following decade witnessed the beginnings of Cincinnati and Lexington. Before the century closed, Detroit, Buffalo, and Cleveland were laid out on the Great Lakes. In fact, by 1800 the sites of every major metropolis in the old Northwest except Chicago, Milwaukee, and Indianapolis had been cleared and surveyed.

Furthermore, these urban outposts grew rapidly even in their infant decades. By 1815 Pittsburgh, already a thriving industrial center, had 8,000 inhabitants, giving it a slight margin over Lexington. Cincinnati estimated its population at 4,000 at the end of the war with Great Britain, while farther west Louisville and St. Louis neared half that figure.

The speed and extent of this expansion startled contemporaries. Joseph Charless, the editor of the *Missouri Gazette,* who had made a trip through the new country in 1795, remembered the banks of the Ohio as "a dreary wilderness, the haunt of ruthless savages," yet twenty years later he found them "sprinkled with towns" boasting "spinning and weaving establishments, steam mills, manufactures in various metals, leather, wool, cotton and flax," and "seminaries of learning conducted by excellent teachers."[1] The great transformation moved a Cincinnati bard to a somewhat heroic couplet:

> Here where so late the appalling sound
> Of savage yells, the woods resound
> Now smiling Ceres waves her sheaf
> And cities rise in bold relief.[2]

Not all the towns founded in the trans-Allegheny region in this period fared as well, however. Many never developed much beyond a survey and a newspaper advertisement. Others after promising beginnings, slackened and settled down to slow and unspectacular development. Still others flourished briefly then faded, leaving behind a grim story of deserted mills, broken buildings, and aging people—the West's first harvest of ghost towns. Most of

From *American Historical Review* (October 1958), pp. 14-30. Reprinted by permission of the publisher. Richard C. Wade is Professor of American History at the University of Chicago.

these were mere eddies in the westward flow of urbanism, but at flood tide it was often hard to distinguish the eddies from the main stream. Indeed, at one time Wheeling, Virginia, St. Genevieve, Missouri, New Albany, Indiana, and Zanesville, Ohio, were considered serious challengers to the supremacy of their now more famous neighbors.

Other places, such as Rising Sun, Town of America, or New Athens, were almost wholly speculative ventures. Eastern investors scanned maps looking for likely spots to establish a city, usually at the junction of two rivers, or sometimes at the center of fertile farm districts. They bought up land, laid it out in lots, gave the place a name, and waited for the development of the region to appreciate its value. Looking back over this period one editor called it a "city-making mania," when everyone went about "anticipating flourishing cities in vision, at the mouth of every creek and bayou."[3] This speculation, though extensive, was not always profitable. "Of the vast number of towns which have been founded," James Hall declared, "but a small minority have prospered, nor do we think that, as a general rule, the founders of these have been greatly enriched by their prosperity."[4]

Despite many failures, these abortive attempts to plant towns were significant, for they reveal much about the motives of the people who came West in the early period. Many settlers moved across the mountains in search of promising towns rather than good land, their inducements being urban opportunities rather than fertile soil. Daniel Drake, who was among the earliest urbanites of the frontier, later commented on this process:

It is worthy of remark, that those who made these beginnings of settlement, projected towns, which they anticipated would grow into cities. . . . And we may see in their origins, one of the elements of the prevalent tendency to rear up towns in advance of the country which has ever since characterized Ohio. The followers of the first pioneers, like themselves had a taste for commerce and the mechanic arts which cannot be gratified without the construction of cities.[5]

Proprietors competed for these urban migrants, most of whom came from "those portions of the Union which cherish and build up cities."[6] In fact, the preference of some settlers for towns was so great that in 1787 Lexington petitioned the Virginia legislature for incorporation to be "an inducement to well disposed persons, artizens [sic] and mechanics who from motives and convenience do prefer Town life."[7]

The West's young cities owed their initial success to commerce. All sprang from it, and their growth in the early years of the century stemmed from its expansion. Since the Ohio River was the chief artery of trade and travel, the towns along its banks prospered most. Pittsburgh, where the Allegheny meets the Monongahela, commanded the entire valley; Cincinnati served the rich farm lands of Kentucky and Ohio; Louisville fattened on the transshipment of goods around the Falls; and St. Louis, astride the Mississippi, was the focus of far-flung enterprises, some of which reached to the Pacific Ocean. Even Lexington, landlocked in a country of water highways, grew up as the central mart of Kentucky and Tennessee.

Though these cities were firmly established by the first decade of the century, the coming of the steamboat greatly enhanced their size and influence.[8] By quickening transportation and cutting distances, steam navigation telescoped fifty years' urban development into a single generation. The flow of commerce down river was now supplemented by a northward and eastward movement, giving cities added opportunities for expansion and growth. "The steam engine in five years has enabled us to anticipate a state of things," a Pittsburgher declared enthusiastically, "which in the ordinary course of events, it would have required a century to have produced. The art of printing scarcely surpassed it in beneficial consequences."[9] The "enchanter's wand" not only touched the established towns but created new ones as well. A French observer noted that "in the brief interval of fifteen years, many cities were formed . . . where before there were hardly the dwellings of a small town. . . . A simple mechanical device has made life both possible and comfortable in regions which heretofore have been a wilderness."[10]

As these commercial centers grew, some inhabitants turned to manufacturing. Indeed, this new interest spread so rapidly in Pittsburgh that in 1810 a resident likened the place to "a large workshop," and already travelers complained of the smoke and soot.[11] Between 1803 and 1815 the value of manufactured goods jumped from $350,000 to over $2,600,000, and the city's iron and glass products became known throughout the new country.[12] Watching this remarkable development, the editor of *Niles' Register* exclaimed: "Pittsburgh, sometimes emphatically called the 'Birmingham of America,' will probably become the *greatest manufacturing town in the world*."[13] Lexington also turned increasingly to industry, her ropewalks and textile mills supplying the whole West. Beginnings were more modest in other places, but every city had at least a few ambitious enterprises.

Some of this urban expansion rested on a speculative base, and the depression of 1819 brought a reckoning. Lexington, already suffering from its landlocked position, received fatal wounds, while Pittsburgh, the West's foremost city, was crippled for a decade. Elsewhere, however, the setback proved only momentary and the mid-twenties saw the old pace renewed. Population growth again provides a convenient index of development. Cincinnati quickly overtook its faltering rivals, the number of its residents leaping from 6,000 in 1815 to over 25,000 in 1830. By the latter date the census recorded Pittsburgh's recovery. Though the figure had dropped to 7,000 during the depression, it rose to 13,000 in 1830. Farther west Louisville and St. Louis enjoyed spectacular expansion, the former boasting over 10,000 inhabitants at the end of the period, while the Mississippi entrepôt passed the 6,000 mark. Lexington alone lagged, its population remaining stable for the next two decades.

Even these figures, however, do not convey the real growth. In most places municipal boundaries could no longer contain the new settlers, and many spilled over into the suburbs. For instance, Allegheny, Bayardstown, Birmingham, Lawrenceville, Hayti, and East Liberty added nearly 10,000 to Pittsburgh's population, bringing the total to 22,000.[14] The same was true of Cincinnati where 2,000 people lived in the Eastern and Northern Liberties.[15] In Louisville, Preston's and Campbell's "enlargements" and Shippingport and Portland swelled the city's total to 13,-

000.[16] Ultimately, the urban centers annexed these surrounding clusters, but in the meantime local authorities grappled with early manifestations of the suburban problem.

As the cities grew they staked out extensive commercial claims over the entire West.[17] Timothy Flint calculated that Cincinnati was the central market for over a million people, while a resident asserted that its trade was "co-extensive with steamboat navigation on the western waters."[18] Louisville's economic penetration was scarcely less impressive. As early as 1821, a local editor declared that "the people of the greater part of Indiana, all Kentucky, and portions of Tennessee, Alabama, Illinois, Missouri, now report to this place for dry goods, groceries, hardware and queensware."[19] St. Louis' empire touched Santa Fe on the south, Canada on the north, and the Pacific on the west. "It is doubtful if history affords the example of another city," wrote Hiram M. Chittenden, "which has been the exclusive mart for so vast an area as that which was tributary to St. Louis."[20]

In carving out these extensive dependencies, the young metropolises overwhelmed their smaller neighbors. The rise of St. Louis destroyed the ambitions of Edwardsville across the Mississippi, which once harbored modest hopes of importance. Pittsburgh's recovery in the late twenties condemned Wheeling and Steubenville to minor roles in the upper Ohio region. And Louisville's development swallowed two Kentucky neighbors while reducing Jeffersonville and New Albany on the Indiana side of the river to mere appendages.

Not satisfied with such considerable conquests, the cities reached out for more. Seeking wider opportunities, they built canals and turnpikes and, even before 1830, planned railroads to strengthen their position. Cincinnati, Pittsburgh, and St. Louis tried to tap the increasing trade on the Great Lakes by water links to the North. Pennsylvania's Iron City also hoped to become a major station on the National Road, and for a decade its Washington representatives lobbied to win that commercial bond with the East. Lexington, suffocating in its inland position, frantically strove for better connections with the Ohio River. A turnpike to Maysville was dashed by Jackson's veto, technical difficulties made a canal to the Kentucky River impractical, but some belated hope rose with the possibility of a railroad to Louisville or Cincinnati.

The intensive search for new advantages brought rivalry and conflict. Though the commerce of the whole West lay untouched before them, the cities quarreled over its division. Thus Louisville and Cincinnati fought over a canal around the Falls of the Ohio. The Kentucky town, feeling that its strength depended upon maintaining the break in transportation, obstructed every attempt to circumvent the rapids. Only when Ohio interests threatened to dig on the Indiana side did Louisville move ahead with its own project. Likewise, harsh words flew between Wheeling and Pittsburgh as they contended for the Ohio River terminus of the National Road. Smaller towns, too, joined the struggle. Cleveland and Sandusky, for instance, clashed over the location of the Ohio Canal, the stake being nothing less than control of the mounting trade between the Valley and the lakes. And their instinct to fight was sound, for the outcome shaped the future of both places.

Urban rivalries were often bitter, and

the contestants showed no quarter. In the late twenties when only the success of Transylvania University kept Lexington's economy from complete collapse, Louisville joined the attack which ultimately destroyed the school. In a similar vein Cincinnatians taunted their upriver competitor as it reeled under the impact of the depression of 1819. "Poor Pittsburgh," they exclaimed, "your day is over, the sceptre of influence and wealth is to travel to us; the Cumberland road has done the business."[21] But even the Queen City found her supremacy insecure. "I discovered two ruling passions in Cincinnati," a traveler remarked, "enmity against Pittsburgh, and jealousy of Louisville."[22] This drive for power and primacy, sustained especially by merchants and articulated by editors, was one of the most consistent and striking characteristics of the early history of Western cities.

As they pursued expansive policies, municipalities also ministered to their own growing pains. From the beginning, urban residents had to contend with the problems of living together, and one of their first acts was to petition the territory or state for governing authority to handle them. The legislatures, representing rural interests and generally suspicious of towns, responded with charters bestowing narrow grants of power which barely met current needs and failed to allow for expansion. As localities grew, however, they developed problems which could be met only with wider jurisdiction. Louisville's charter had to be amended twenty-two times before 1815 and Cincinnati's underwent five major changes between 1815 and 1827. Others, though altered less often, were adjusted and remade until finally scrapped for new ones. Reluctantly, and bit by bit, the states turned over to the cities the responsibility of managing their own affairs, though keeping them starved for revenue by strict tax and debt limitations.

Despite inadequate charters and modest incomes, urban governments played a decisive role in the growth of Western cities. Since these were commercial towns, local authorities paid special attention to mercantile requirements. They not only constructed market houses but also extended municipal regulation over a wide variety of trading activity. Ordinances protected the public against adulterated foods, false measurements, and rigged prices. Some municipalities went even farther and assumed responsibility for seeing that "justice is done between buyer and seller."[23] In search of this objective, officials fixed prices on some goods, excluded monopolies from the market, and tried to equalize opportunities for smaller purchasers. To facilitate access to the exchange center, they lavished time and money on the development of wharves and docks and the improvement of streets.

Municipalities also tackled a wide variety of other problems growing out of urban life. Fire protection, at first casually organized, was placed on a more formal basis. Volunteer companies still provided the manpower, but government participation increased markedly. Local councils legislated against many kinds of fire hazards, and public money furnished most of the equipment. Moreover, some places, haunted by the image of Detroit's disaster in 1805, forbade the construction of wooden buildings in the heart of the city, a measure which not only reduced fire risks but also changed the face of downtown areas. The development of adequate police was much slower. By

1830 only Lexington and Louisville had regular patrols, and these were established with the intent more of control of slaves than the general protection of life and property. In other towns law enforcement was lax by day and absent at night, though the introduction of gas lighting in Pittsburgh and Cincinnati in the late twenties made the after-dark hours there less dangerous than before.

Congested living created new health hazards and especially increased the likelihood of epidemics. Every place suffered, but none like Louisville, which earned a grim reputation as the "Graveyard of the West" because of the constant visitations of yellow fever and malaria.[24] Cities took preventive measures, such as draining stagnant ponds and clearing streets and lots, and also appointed boards of health to preside over the problem. Municipal water systems, introduced in Pittsburgh and Cincinnati before 1830, made life healthier and certainly more comfortable, while the discussion of installing underground sewers pointed to still more extensive reform in sanitation.

In meeting urban problems, Western officials drew heavily on Eastern experience. Lacking precedents of their own, and familiar with the techniques of older cities, they frankly patterned their practice on Eastern models. There was little innovation. When confronted by a new question, local authorities responded by adopting tested solutions. This emulation characterized nearly every aspect of development—from the width of streets to housing regulations. No major improvement was launched without a close study of established seaboard practices. St. Louis' council, for example, instructed its water committee to "procure from the cities of Philadelphia and New Orleans such information

as can be obtained on the subject of conveying water and the best manner of clearing it."[25] When Cincinnati discussed introducing underground sewers, an official group was designated to "ascertain from the city authorities of New York, Philadelphia, Baltimore and Boston, how far the sinking of common sewers is approved in those cities."[26] Pittsburgh undertook gas lighting only after exhaustive research and "very full enquiries at New York and Baltimore."[27]

Though the young towns drew upon the experience of all the major Atlantic cities, the special source of municipal wisdom was Philadelphia. Many Western urbanites had lived or visited there; it provided the new country with most of its professional and cultural leadership; it was the model metropolis. "She is the great seat of American affluence of individual riches, and distinguished philanthropy," a Pittsburgh edtiorial declared in 1818. "From her . . . we have everything to look for."[28] Newspapers often referred to it as "our mother city."[29]

From street plans to cultural activity from the shape of market houses to the habits of people, the Philadelphia influence prevailed. Robert Peterson and John Filson, who had a hand in the founding of Louisville, Lexington, and Cincinnati, borrowed the basic grid pattern of the original plats from the Pennsylvania metropolis.[30] Market location and design came from the same source as did techniques for fire fighting and police protection. Western towns also leaned on Philadelphia's leadership in street lighting, waterworks, and wharfing. Even the naming of suburbs—Pittsburgh's Kensington and Cincinnati's Liberties—came from the mother city. The result was a physical likeness which struck many travelers and which Phila delphians themselves recognized. Gideon Burton, for instance, remembered his first impression of Cincinnati in the 1820's: "How beautiful this city is," he remarked, "how much like Philadelphia."[31]

The Quaker City spirit, moreover, went beyond streets, buildings, and improvements, reaching into a wide range of human activity. Businessmen, yearly visitors in the East, brought marketing and promotion techniques from there;[32] young labor movements lifted their platforms from trade union programs in the mother city; employment agencies were conducted "principally on the Philadelphia plan."[33] The same metropolis trained most of the physicians of the West and a large share of the teachers and ministers. Caspar Wistar's famed Sunday evening gatherings of the intelligentsia provided the idea for Daniel Drake's select meetings of Cincinnati's social and cultural elite. Moreover, Philadelphia furnished the model of the perfect urbanite, for the highest praise that Western town dwellers could bestow upon a fellow citizen was to refer to him as their own "Benjamin Franklin."[34] In short, Philadelphia represented the highest stage of urban development, and progress was measured against this ideal.

Such borrowing was a conscious policy. In 1825 Mayor William Carr Lane of St. Louis, the most able urban statesman of the period, provided the justification. "Experience is the best guide . . . ," he told his councilmen. "The records of other towns are a source from which we may expect to derive useful hints. . . . It is therefore incumbent upon us to examine carefully what other communities similarly situated have done."[35] The process, however, was selective, not slavish. Investigation usually revealed a wide variety of possibilities, allowing Western cities to choose the most appropriate technique. Nevertheless, young towns preferred to meet their urban problems by adopting the established ways of the East. The challenge of the new country, far from producing a bold and fresh response, led to greater dependence on the older sections of the Union.

As transmontane cities developed they created societies whose ways and habits contrasted sharply with those of the countryside. Not only was their physical environment distinct, but their interests, activities, and pace of life also differed greatly. In 1811 a farmer near Lexington expressed the conflict as contemporaries saw it in a dialogue between "Rusticus" and "Urbanus." The latter referred to the "rude, gross appearance" of his neighbor, adding: "How strong you smell of your ploughed ground and corn fields. How dismal, how gloomy your green woods. What a miserable clash your whistling woodland birds are continually making." "Rusticus" replied with the rural image of the town dweller. "What a fine smooth complexion you have Urbanus: you look like a weed that has grown up in the shade. Can you walk your streets without inhaling the noxious fumes with which your town is pregnant? . . . Can you engage in calm contemplation, when hammers are ringing in every direction—when there is as great a *rattling* as in a storm when the hail descends on our house tops?"[36]

One of the most conspicuous differences was in social structure. The stratification of urban societies was in marked contrast with the boisterous equality of the countryside. Social lines developed very quickly in the city. Though not as tightly drawn as in the East, they represented the meaningful distinctions in Western communities. The groupings were basically economic, though professional people were set apart by their interest and training, and Negroes by their color. No rigid boundaries divided the classes, and movement between them was constant. Yet differences did exist; people felt them and contemporaries thought them significant. It is suggestive in this regard that the first great literary product of the West, *Modern Chivalry*, satirized the notion of equality, and the author, Hugh Henry Brackenridge, was one of Pittsburgh's leading citizens.

These divisions deepened in the postwar years. As the cities grew the sense of neighborliness and intimacy diminished, giving way to the impersonality characteristic of urban living. To old-timers the changing social configuration bred a deep nostalgia and raised the image of happier, simpler days. "We cannot help looking back with sorrowful heart, in that time of unaffected content and gaiety," a Pennsylvanian lamented, "when the unambitious people . . . in the village of 'Fort Pitt' in the yet unchartered town of Pittsburgh, were ignorant and careless of all invidious distinctions, which distract and divide the inhabitants of overgrown cities. Then all was peaceful heartfelt felicity, undisturbed by the rankling thorns of envy; and equality . . . was a tie that united all ranks and conditions in our community."[37] Town life in the West had never been that idyllic, but the distortion of the vision was itself a measure of the rapid change. "We have our castes of society, graduated and divided with as much regard to rank and dignity as the most scrupulous Hindoos maintain in defense of their religious prejudices," the same source admitted

in 1826. Moreover, social distances were great. "Between the . . . classes . . . there are lines of demarcation drawn wide, distinct and not to be violated with impunity."[38] Nor was this stratification surprising. Having come from places where differences mattered, early city dwellers tried to re-create them in a new setting. The urge for status was stronger than the appeal of equality, and as the towns expanded cleavages deepened.

Urban ways were further distinguished from rural habits by the collective approach to many problems. City living created issues which could not always be solved by the highly individualistic methods of agrarian society. Local governments assumed an ever wider responsibility for the conduct of community affairs, and voluntary associations handled a large variety of other questions. Merchants formed chambers of commerce to facilitate cooperation on common problems; professional people organized societies to raise the standards of their colleagues and keep out the untrained. Working people, too, banded together in unions, seeking not only greater economic strength but also fraternity and self-improvement. Religious and philanthropic clubs managed most charity and relief work, while immigrants combined to help new arrivals. In addition, other associations grew up to promote literature and music, encourage debating, advocate social innovations, support public causes, and conduct the welter of amusements which larger cities required. Just as conditions in the countryside placed greatest emphasis on individual effort, so the urban situation made cooperative action seem more appropriate.

Rural and metropolitan West were also separated by distinctive social and cultural developments. The towns very quickly produced a surprisingly rich and diversified life, offering opportunities in many fields similar to those of Eastern cities but lacking on the farm or frontier.[39] They enjoyed a virtual monopoly of printing presses, newspapers, bookstores, and circulating libraries. Theaters sprang up to encourage local players and traveling troupes, while in larger places museums brought the curious and the scientific to the townfolks.[40] In addition, every week brought numerous lectures and debates on all kinds of topics, keeping urban residents abreast of the latest discoveries and developments in every field. By 1815 these amenities had already lost their novelty. Indeed, some thought the civilizing process was getting out of hand. "Twenty sermons a week—," a Cincinnatian wearily counted, "Sunday evening Discourses on Theology—Private assemblies—state Cotillon parties —Saturday Night Clubs, and chemical lectures— . . . like the fever and the ague, return every day with distressing regularity."[41]

Of course, the whole transmontane region matured culturally in this period, but the towns played a strategic role. "Cities have arisen in the very wilderness . . . ," a St. Louis editor noticed in 1821, "and form in their respective states the *foci* of art and science, of wealth and information."[42] A Cincinnatian made a similar observation. "This *city*, in its growth and cultural improvements has anticipated the western country in general."[43] The hinterland, already bound to urban communities by trade, readily admitted its dependence. The *Pittsburgh Gazette* merely stated the obvious when it remarked in 1819 that the surrounding region "looks up to Pittsburgh not only as a medium through which to receive the comforts and luxuries of foreign commodities, but also a channel from which it can most naturally expect a supply of intellectual wealth."[44] Thus while the cities' merchants staked out markets in the countryside, their civic leaders spread a cultural influence into the same area.

This leadership extended into almost every field. For example, the educational opportunities of town children greatly exceeded those of their rural neighbors. Every municipality developed a complex of private tuition schools topped by an academy and, in every place except Louisville, a college. Moreover, the cities organized the movement of public schooling. Ohio's experience is illustrative. The movement for state legislation started in Cincinnati, received its major impetus from the local press, and was carried in the Assembly through the efforts of representatives from Hamilton county. It is also significant that the first superintendent of common schools in Ohio was Samuel Lewis of Cincinnati. Nor was this urban leadership surprising. The cities, as the great population centers, felt the educational pressure first and most acutely. In addition, they alone had the wealth needed to launch ambitious projects for large numbers of children. Hence the towns were ready for comprehensive public programs long before the countryside.

The most striking illustration of the cultural supremacy of the cities, however, was Lexington's unique reign as the "Athens of the West."[45] The area's largest town until 1810, it was early celebrated for its polish and sophistication and was generally conceded to be the region's capital of arts and science. But the coming of the steamboat and the depression of 1819 combined to undermine its economic position. To offset this commercial and industrial decline, Lexington's civic leaders inaugurated a policy of vigorous cultural expansion.[46] They built schools, subsidized Transylvania University, and advertised the many opportunities for advancement in learning and letters in the metropolis. Throughout the twenties this campaign was a spectacular success. The town became the resort of the most talented men of the new country. Educators, scientists, painters, lawyers, architects, musicians, and their patrons all flocked there. Transylvania University attained national eminence, attracting most of its faculty from the East and drawing students from better than a dozen states. Like a renaissance city of old Italy, Lexington provided the creative atmosphere for a unique flowering that for a decade astonished travelers and stimulated the best minds of the West.

In its golden age the town boasted the most distinguished collection of intellectuals the new country had ever seen in a single city. The central figure in this awakening was Horace Holley, a Unitarian minister from Boston and the president of Transylvania. Though not an accomplished scholar himself, he recruited a remarkable faculty and raised the institution from a small denominational college to a university of the first rank. The medical department achieved a special distinction. Its dean was Charles Caldwell, one of Benjamin Rush's favorite pupils, who turned down important posts in New York, Philadelphia, and Baltimore to join the Kentucky experiment. Members of the staff included the botanist, Charles Wilkins Short, Daniel Drake, later the author of a pioneering study of diseases in the Mississippi Valley, and the surgeon,

Benjamin Winslow Dudley. Among them, too, was the furtive and erratic, yet highly talented, Turkish-born naturalist, Constantine Rafinesque, whose most fruitful years were spent in Lexington.[47]

The graduating class of the medical school in 1826 demonstrated the extent of the university's reputation and influence. With sixty-seven degrees granted in that year, twenty-eight of the recipients came from Kentucky, ten from Tennessee, five each from Virginia, South Carolina, and Alabama, three from Ohio, two each from Mississippi, Illinois, and Louisiana, and one each from North Carolina and Georgia. During the twenties the college trained many of the West's most distinguished people. In politics alone it turned out at least seventeen congressmen, three governors, six United States senators, and the president of the Confederacy. In the same decade the school produced scores of lawyers, clergymen, and physicians, who did much to raise professional standards in the new country. Few universities have left such a clear mark on a generation; in its heyday Transylvania fully deserved its title of the "Harvard of the West."[48]

The college was the center of this wilderness renaissance, but around it moved other figures—artists, architects, musicians, and poets—who gave added luster to the movement. In Matthew Jouett the city had the West's most famous painter. A student of Gilbert Stuart and a portraitist of considerable gifts, he made his studio the exciting headquarters for a group of promising young artists. Gideon Shryock provided Lexington with an architect equal to its enlightenment. After studying with William Strickland in Philadelphia, he brought the Greek revival across the mountains. His work, especially the state capitol at Frankfort and Morrison College at Transylvania, brought him immediate fame and has led a modern critic to assert that he "was almost a decade ahead of his time even when judged by sophisticated eastern standards."[49] Music shared the upsurge, and in 1817 townsfolk heard Anthony Phillip Hennrich conduct the first performance of a Beethoven symphony in the United States.

The glitter of this city drew young people from all over the transmontane region, including many from the countryside. In doing so, it provoked a familiar lament from the rural areas whose children succumbed to the bewitchment of Lexington. "We want our sons to be practical men," wrote a Kentucky farmer, "whose minds will not be filled with those light notions of refinement and taste, which will induce them to believe that they are of a different order of beings, or that will elevate them above their equals."[50] Later, agrarian representatives in the legislature joined the attack on Transylvania by voting to cut off state financial assistance.

No less striking than cultural cleavages were the differences in rural and urban religious development. Progress in the cities was steadier and more substantial—though less spectacular—than in the back country. Traveling ministers might refer to Pittsburgh as "a young hell, a second Sodom,"[51] and Francis Asbury might complain in 1803 that he felt "the power of Satan in those little, wicked western trading towns,"[52] but both churches and membership multiplied rapidly in urban centers. Furthermore, the growth owed nothing to the sporadic revivals which burned across the countryside at the beginning of the

century. These movements were essentially rural, having their roots in the isolation of agricultural living and the spiritual starvation of people unattended by regular services. The city situation, with its constant contacts and settled church organizations, involved neither of these elements. Instead, religious societies proliferated, sects took on such additional functions as charity and missionary work, and congregations sent money back East to aid their seminaries. Far from being sinks of corruption, Western cities quickly became religious centers, supplying Bibles to the frontier, assisting foreign missions, and, in the twenties, building theological schools to provide priests and ministers for the whole region.

Political life also reflected the growing rural-urban division. Though the rhetoric of the period often obscured them, differences existed from the very beginning. Suspicion of the towns led states to avoid economic and cultural centers when locating their capitals. Nearly all these cities sought the prize, but none was successful. The *Missouri Gazette* candidly stated the issue in 1820. "It has been said that St. Louis is obnoxious to our Legislature—that its growth and influence . . . are looked on with a jealous eye, and its pretensions . . . ought to be discouraged."[53] The same clash had earlier occurred in Kentucky, where state leaders virtually invented Frankfort to keep the capital away from Louisville or Lexington.

As the region developed, however, the conflict became increasingly apparent, though it was still expressed cautiously. "We must be permitted to say," an editor asserted in 1829, "that in Cincinnati we have separate interests" from the countryside.[54] Likewise, a Pittsburgher prefaced a strong attack on the neighboring areas by declaring that "we think it wrong to stir up a jealousy between city and county."⁵⁵ Nevertheless, the split represented one of the fundamental facts of Western politics.

Of course, farm dwellers easily outnumbered urbanites, but the latter wielded disproportionate power. The case of Jefferson and Oldham counties in Kentucky was illustrative. In the mid-twenties the combined vote reached 3,-200, Louisville residents casting roughly a quarter of them. Yet the state senator and both representatives came from the city. In 1829 when a third assemblyman was added, the rural interests pleaded with Louisville leaders to name someone from the surrounding area. "It may seem strange," wrote an observer, "that it would be necessary thus to ask for the liberality of 800 voters in favor of 2,400. . . . Nevertheless, the concentrated energies of 800 do entirely outweigh the scattered influence of the 2,400—that all past experience teaches."⁵⁶ The situation was the same elsewhere. At one time all of Missouri's representatives in Washington—two senators and one congressman—as well as its governor came from St. Louis.

The cities' political influence rested on their ability to produce leadership. As the economic and intellectual centers of transmontane life they attracted the talented and ambitious in all fields. Politics was no exception. Nearly all the great spokesmen of the West had important urban connections and their activity often reflected the demands of their town constituents. Henry Clay was one of Lexington's most prominent lawyers when he went to the United States Senate in 1806. Thomas Hart Benton held local offices in St. Louis before moving on to the national scene,

and William Henry Harrison, though he lived in nearby North Bend, had deep roots in Cincinnati affairs through most of his long public life. Moreover, all were alive to the interests of their city. Benton's successful attack on government factories in the Indian territory culminated a long and intense campaign by St. Louis merchants to break federal trade control on the Missouri. Clay's enthusiasm for an ample tariff on hemp derived at least as much from the pressure of Lexington's manufactures as from that of the growers of the Blue Grass. And Harrison, as state senator, led the campaign for public schools in Ohio largely at the behest of his Cincinnati supporters. These were not isolated cases; an examination of the careers of these men demonstrates the importance of their urban connections.

By 1830, then, the West had produced two types of society—one rural and one urban. Each developed its own institutions, habits, and living patterns. The countryside claimed much the larger population and often gave to transmontane affairs an agrarian flavor. But broadcloth was catching up with buckskin. The census of 1830 revealed the disproportionate rate of city growth. While the state of Ohio had four times as many inhabitants as it counted in 1810, Cincinnati's increase was twelve-fold. The story was the same elsewhere. Louisville's figure showed a growth of 650 per cent compared with Kentucky's 50 per cent, and Pittsburgh tripled in size while Pennsylvania did not quite double its population. By 1830 the rise of these cities had driven a broad wedge of urbanism into Western life.

Though town and country developed along different paths, clashes were still infrequent. The West was large enough to contain both movements comfortably.

Indeed, each supported the other. The rural regions supplied the cities with raw materials for their mills and packinghouses and offered an expanding market to their shops and factories. In turn, urban centers served the surrounding areas by providing both the necessities and comforts of life as well as new opportunity for ambitious farm youths. Yet the cities represented the more aggressive and dynamic force. By spreading their economic power over the entire section, by bringing the fruits of civilization across the mountains, and by insinuating their ways into the countryside, they speeded up the transformation of the West from a gloomy wilderness to a richly diversified region. Any historical view which omits this aspect of Western life tells but part of the story.

NOTES

1. *Missouri Gazette* (St. Louis), July 13, 1816.
2. *Liberty Hall* (Cincinnati), June 11, 1815.
3. *Missouri Republican* (St. Louis), Aug. 29, 1825.
4. Hall, *The West: Its Commerce and Navigation* (Cincinnati, 1848), p. 227.
5. Drake, "Dr. Drake's Memoir of the Miami County, 1779-1794," Beverley Bond, Jr., ed., Historical and Philosophical Society of Ohio, *Quarterly Publications*, XVIII (1923), 58.
6. *Ibid.*
7. James R. Robertson, ed., *Petitions of the Early Inhabitants of Kentucky to the General Assembly of Virginia, 1769-1792* (Louisville, Ky., 1914), p. 106.
8. Louis C. Hunter, *Steamboats on the Western Rivers, An Economic and Technological History* (Cambridge, Mass., 1949), pp. 27-32.
9. Morgan Neville, "The Last of the Boatman," *The Western Souvenir for 1829* (Cincinnati, Ohio, n.d.), p. 108.
10. [Jean Baptiste] Marestier, *Mémoire sur les Bateaux à vapeur des États-Unis d' Amérique* (Paris, 1824), pp. 9-10.
11. Zadock Cramer, *Pittsburgh Almanack for the Year of Our Lord 1810* (Pittsburgh, Pa., 1810), p. 52.
12. Pittsburgh's industrial foundations are discussed in Catherine Elizabeth Reiser, *Pittsburgh's Commercial Development, 1800-1850* (Harrisburg, Pa., 1951), pp. 12-21.

13. *Niles' Register*, May 28, 1814.
14. *Pittsburgh Gazette*, Nov. 16, 1830.
15. *Cincinnati Advertiser*, Aug. 18, 1830.
16. United States *Census*, 1830, pp. 114-15.
17. For an appreciation of the economic importance of the cities in the growth of the West, see Frederick Jackson Turner, *Rise of the New West, 1819-1829* in *The American Nation: A History*, A. B. Hart, ed., XIV (New York, 1906), 96-98.
18. Flint, "Thoughts Respecting the Establishment of a Porcelain Manufactory at Cincinnati," *Western Monthly Review*, III (1830), 512; Benjamin Drake and Edward W. Mansfield, *Cincinnati in 1826* (Cincinnati, Ohio, 1827), p. 71.
19. *Louisville Public Advertiser*, Oct. 17, 1829.
20. Chittenden, *The American Fur Trade of the Far West* (2 vols. New York, 1902), I, 99.
21. *Pittsburgh Gazette*, Dec. 18, 1818.
22. *Pittsburgh Gazette*, Feb. 5, 1819.
23. *Pittsburgh Gazette*, Mar. 9, 1810.
24. Benjamin Casseday, *The History of Louisville from Its Earliest Settlement till the Year 1852* (Louisville, Ky., 1852), p. 49.
25. St. Louis City Council, Minutes, Court House, St. Louis, June 12, 1829.
26. Cincinnati City Council, Minutes, City Hall, Cincinnati, Oct. 6, 1827.
27. Pittsburgh City Council, City Council Papers, City Hall, Pittsburgh, May 10, 1827. The extent of Western urban indebtedness to the East is perhaps best illustrated in the establishment of the high school in Louisville. The building was "mainly after the plan of the High School of New York, united with the Public School Rooms of Philadelphia." Most of the teachers came from the East, while the curriculum and even reading assignments derived from "the High School of New York and some of the Boston establishments." *An Account of the Louisville City School, Together With the Ordinances of the City Council, and the Regulations of the Board of Trustees for the Government of the Institution* (Louisville, Ky., 1830), pp. 5 ff.
28. *Pittsburgh Gazette*, Oct. 27, 1818.
29. For example, see *Pittsburgh Gazette*, June 23, 1818.
30. For example, see Rufus King, *Ohio First Fruits of the Ordinance of 1787* (Boston, 1888), p. 209.
31. Burton, *Reminiscences of Gideon Burton* (Cincinnati, Ohio, 1895). The strategic location of Western cities in the life of the new country reminded some visitors of the regional supremacy of Philadelphia. Lewis Condict, for example, referred to Lexington as "the Philadelphia of Kentucky." "Journal of a Trip to Kentucky in 1795," *Proceedings of the New Jersey Historical Society*, n.s., IV (1919), 120.
32. *Cincinnati Enquirer*, Apr. 22, 1923.
33. *Pittsburgh Mercury*, Aug. 7, 1827.
34. The phrase was constantly used in characterizing John Bradford of Lexington and Daniel Drake of Cincinnati, but it was applied to others as well.
35. St. Louis City Council, Minutes, Court House, St. Louis, Apr. 25, 1825.
36. *Kentucky Reporter* (Lexington), July 2, 1811.

37. Samuel Jones, *Pittsburgh in 1826* (Pittsburgh, Pa., 1826), p. 43.

38. *Ibid.*

39. For a day-to-day account of the cultural offerings of a Western city between 1820 and 1830 see the highly informative but unpublished diary of William Stanley Merrill in the library of the Historical and Philosophical Society of Ohio (Cincinnati).

40. The development of the theater in Western cities is outlined in Ralph Leslie Rush, *The Literature of the Middle Western Frontier* (New York, 1925), I, 352-400. For a detailed study of a single town see William G. B. Carson, *The Theatre on the Frontier, The Early Years of the St. Louis Stage* (Chicago, 1932), pp. 1-134.

41. *Liberty Hall* (Cincinnati), Dec. 9, 1816.

42. *Missouri Gazette* (St. Louis), Dec. 20, 1820.

43. *Liberty Hall* (Cincinnati), June 29, 1819.

44. *Pittsburgh Gazette,* Apr. 30, 1819.

45. For Lexington's growth and brief supremacy see Bernard Mayo, "Lexington, Frontier Metropolis," in *Historiography and Urbanization,* Eric F. Goldman, ed. (Baltimore, Md., 1941), pp. 21-42.

46. See, for example, *Kentucky Reporter,* Oct. 4, 1820.

47. Transylvania's "golden age" is treated in detail in Walter William Jennings, *Transylvania, Pioneer University of the West* (New York, 1955), pp. 99-124, and Niels Henry Sonne, *Liberal Kentucky, 1780-1828* (New York, 1939), pp. 160-242.

48. The reputation of Lexington in Cincinnati is charmingly portrayed in the letters of young Ohioans attending Transylvania University to their friends back home. See especially the William Lytle Collection in the library of the Historical and Philosophical Society of Ohio (Cincinnati).

49. Talbot Hamlin, *Greek Revival Architecture in America: Being an Account of Important Trends in American Architecture and American Life prior to the War between the States* (New York, 1944), p. 244.

50. *Kentucky Reporter* (Lexington), Feb. 16, 1824.

51. *Pittsburgh Gazette,* Sept. 23, 1803.

52. Francis Asbury, *Journal of Rev. Francis Asbury, Bishop of Methodist Episcopal Church* (n.p., 1821), III, 127.

53. *Missouri Gazette* (St. Louis), Dec. 6, 1820.

54. *Cincinnati Advertiser,* Sept. 16, 1829.

55. *Pittsburgh Statesman,* Aug. 26, 1823.

56. *Louisville Public Advertiser,* July 28, 1824.

Patterns of Mid-Nineteenth Century Urbanization in the Middle West

BAYRD STILL

Until recently a persistent preoccupation with the agrarian aspects of the westward march of American settlement has to some extent obscured the fact that the prospect of future towns and cities as well as the promise of broad and fertile acres lured settlers to the "sunset regions." On many a frontier the town builder was as conspicuous as the farmer pioneer; the western city, through the efforts of its founders to extend its economic hinterland, actually facilitated the agrarian development of the West; and the opportunities attending city growth as well as those afforded by cheap farm lands contributed to the dynamic sense of economic abundance felt by Americans of the mid-nineteenth century. As early as 1845 one middle western editor identified this urban growth with the rapid development of the West when he wrote:

From *Mississippi Valley Historical Review* (September 1941), pp. 187-206. Reprinted by permission of the publisher. Bayrd Still is Head of the Department of History at New York University.

The tide of emigration to the West seems to increase daily. . . . What an enterprising spirit characterizes the American people. . . . This . . . activity and enterprise . . . are the result of free institutions, which give an impetus to the human mind. In no other country have towns and villages sprung up so suddenly as in this. Everything seems to go ahead with railroad velocity. Well might Marryat remark that cities grow up here to more importance in ten years than they do in Europe in a century.[1]

The growth of cities is admittedly a significant aspect of the history of the West. But any precise estimate of the bearing either of urbanization upon the expansion of the American frontier or of the westward movement of population upon city growth in the United States awaits a more adequate exposition of urban development in specific sections of the country than has as yet been set forth.[2]

The migrants who poured into the Mississippi Valley in the middle of the nineteenth century built cities as well as cultivated farms. By the seventies, when the American people were first becoming conscious of the drift of population to the city, the Middle West showed a spectacular urban growth. It could then boast seven cities of more than a hundred thousand people,[3] whereas thirty years before only New Orleans had achieved that size. To be sure, the total population of the ten major midwestern cities in 1870 still fell slightly short of the more than 1,800,000 city dwellers then living in New York, Philadelphia, and Boston; but in the rate of their growth the former were putting to shame the cities of the Atlantic coast. Among these mushroom metropolises of the West, the lake cities—Buffalo, Cleveland, Detroit, Chicago, and Milwaukee—rather than the valley cities—Pittsburgh, Cincin-

nati, Louisville, Nashville, and St. Louis—showed the greatest proportional increase in numbers.[4] By 1870 the five lake cities had attained a combined population of more than sixteen times their total of 1840, although the population of the states in which they were located had barely tripled.[5]

Because of their rapid and parallel growth, a comparative analysis of these five lake cities provides a useful means of studying the nature of the emerging city in the Middle West. With striking similarity, they all limited themselves to those duties of the urban community which were common to eighteenth century cities. They all responded to the democratic movement by extending popular participation in municipal government and then by broadening the authority of the executive or administrative commission. Not only did they rely upon the individual to provide most of the services which are demanded today of the city itself but they also expected him to promote the city's growth—a promotion which in every case involved substituting the encouragement of manufacturing for an earlier emphasis on trade. And with equal uniformity they imitated the experience of one another in ordering the details of their municipal life. While it is never too wise to try to compress the variety of human behavior into patterns, the common responses of the five cities suggest the conclusion that these at least are qualities which may well be characteristic of mid-nineteenth century urbanization in the upper Middle West.

A comparative study of the charters under which the Great Lakes cities were governed between 1830 and 1870 discloses the imitation of form and limitation of function in which the powers of the urban community were at that time conceived. These charters were cut from an almost identical constitutional pattern, laid down in the spirit of eighteenth century America. Admittedly the creature of the legislative will of the state, each city nevertheless resorted frequently to the public meeting for the purpose of proposing charter changes and civic improvement.[6] With the advance to city status the meagre functions of the village period—protection against fire, opening and repairing streets, regulating markets, licensing shows, and sinking public wells—were considerably expanded. These functions were enlarged by a uniform extension of regulatory powers, services, and guarantees—additions which were, however, more boldly granted than enforced if one judges from the charges of non-enforcement levied against the city administration by the Milwaukee press.

The first city charters of Buffalo (1832), Cleveland (1836), and Chicago (1837) were strikingly similar in form. The Chicago charter is almost an identical copy of the Buffalo document save for certain local references. In the more than thirty clauses enumerating the powers of the council, the wording of the Chicago charter is different from that of Buffalo in less than half a dozen instances. The Chicago charter added provisions with respect to street lamps and ferries, but lacked the provision for the assize of bread that is found in the Buffalo framework of government. Significantly, the contemporaneous government of Milwaukee, organized at virtually the same time (1836), was still confined to the restricted duties of a village. Ten years later, however, when it emerged as a city, its citizens sought, and the state legislature granted, an expansion of powers quite similar to those of its sister cities of the Great Lakes. The Chicago consolidation act of 1851 found an echo in a like measure for Milwaukee in 1852 and in a revision of Buffalo's charter in 1853. These charters elaborated rather than expanded the powers of the municipality in ways dictated by closer acquaintance with the problems of city government. Again the customary parallelism in form stands out both in the general pattern of the documents and in the many identical clauses, such as those setting up the fire department and compelling the removal of ill-smelling nuisances.[7]

The advance from village to city brought an extension of municipal responsibilities, but only to an extent normally resulting, especially in America, from the crowding of people into small compass. These new powers were limited in general to the protection of life and property, although the results of each extension of authority were recognized as having a bearing on the promotion of trade and hence on the prosperity of the municipality. Concern for securing property against the chronic fire hazard of the western city made possible the enactment of building restrictions and encouraged the organization of fire-fighting facilities. Concern for health prompted the authorities to establish pesthouses, to quarantine immigrants coming through the lake ports, and to abate such nuisances as stagnant pools, foul-smelling substances, and slaughter houses—reforms stimulated not so much by aesthetic considerations as by the prevailing conviction that urban filth and the spread of cholera went hand in hand. While thus exhorting cleanliness, the authorities at the same time, perhaps paradoxically, laid restrictions on wasting water and prohibited bathing in the rivers from which the city water supply was drawn.

In the interests of urban order, the city councils were empowered to provide watchmen and police; to suppress disorderly houses; to impound animals running at large; to prevent immoderate driving, rolling hoops or playing ball in the streets, and the cluttering of sidewalks with snow, dirt, firewood, awnings, or cigar store Indians; to restrain "runners" for boats and stages; and to curtail city noises. Nor were these idle grants of authority. The Cleveland council, as one of its first acts, passed an ordinance on May 9, 1836, which provided that the streets were to be swept semi-monthly on Friday mornings by the owners or occupants of property; that horses should not be fastened so as to obstruct passage in the streets nor be driven on the sidewalks; and that the huge wooden replicas of boots, saddles, and kettles with which merchants advertised their wares were not to project over three feet into the street. In addition to providing for quarantine and hospitalization of the sick poor, the health ordinances of Milwaukee required that physicians report cases of contagious diseases and that records of burials show the cause of death lest criminal or dangerous causes be left unknown; decreed a fine of ten dollars for refusal to be vaccinated on the request of a physician employed by the city council; set up barriers to the immigration of the diseased, going so far as to empower constables to call upon the aid of bystanders in forcibly keeping immigrants from landing; and banned slaughter houses within the city limits. The Buffalo council prohibited interment within certain limits and ordered that graves be not less than five feet deep. Anti-noise ordinances in Buffalo and Milwaukee prevented the playing of musical instruments on docks or wharves on Sunday, and in Milwaukee the ringing of bells or loud outcries at public sales were forbidden.

In providing for markets and the regulation of traffic in necessary commodities, these western cities followed practices by which frontier and colonial communities had attempted to protect an often insufficient food supply, prevent monopolistic practices detrimental to the public health and security, avoid the competition of foreign vendors and hucksters, and at the same time force competition upon the licensed merchants.[8] In 1849 Chicago had three markets for the retailing of perishable foods. Butchers were forced to hold stalls there until an act of 1851 permitted the establishment of meat shops outside the market.[9] City markets and strict market ordinances were justified as a means of supplying large cities with fresh and wholesome provisions, because leniency in this respect, it was felt, might encourage disease. Vendors of fresh meat, poultry, eggs, butter, lard, fruit, and vegetables were forced to sell their goods at the market during the market hours unless licensed to sell at some other place or in some other way. To guarantee the wholesomeness of the products, cleanliness of the stalls, and orderliness of the market, prohibitions were set up against pitching quoits, the presence of dogs, and the use of obscene and profane language in the vicinity of the market place. Purchasing goods at the markets for resale elsewhere or forestalling country producers for the purpose of buying their produce for resale was prohibited.[10]

Similar regulations for supervising weights and measures affected the purchase of boards, brick, coal, firewood, casks, hay, flour, tobacco, potash, and salted provisions such as fish. According to a Cleveland ordinance of May 8, 1839, vendors of hay without a certificate of weight were subject to a fine of twenty-five dollars. In 1859 Milwaukee farmers opposed as an inequitable tax the weighing charge of five cents per load of wood and twenty-five cents per load of hay—a concession sold by the city to the highest bidder.[11] The assize of bread, customary in the colonial city charter and in early charters in the West, was apparently abandoned in Chicago and for a while in Cleveland, though provided for elsewhere.[12] In these young urban communities, commerce in such necessary commodities as food, fodder, and firewood was of sufficient public interest to warrant close regulation. Other pursuits related to the public welfare were also restricted. For instance, ordinances regulating the fees of hackmen and carters were not unusual. Chapter XIII of the Buffalo ordinances of 1855 stipulated that a hackman might be fined for refusing to carry a passenger or for going by other than the shortest route. Interest in attracting immigrants prompted a Milwaukee ordinance of May 3, 1849, which fixed a maximum charge of ten cents per article on the goods of immigrants and other passengers landed on the piers of the city.

These principal activities of the mid-nineteenth century city were laid down at the inception of cityhood and were based upon the regulations commonly existing during the colonial period. Later amendments elaborated these functions of municipal government as specific problems arose, and occasionally a measure was passed which suggested an expanding concept of city government, as in the Chicago provision of 1851 with respect to planting and preserving ornamental trees along the streets and in the public grounds of the city. In general, however, the close of this middle period saw only a limited expansion of urban responsibilities beyond those assumed with the grant of the original charter. Nor did these differ in any marked way from the eighteenth century pattern of powers granted the government of New York City at the close of the colonial period.

However, in defining the political authority underlying municipal management, these cities, developing in the current of nineteenth century democracy, left eighteenth century limitations far behind. Here again is a striking uniformity of behavior in the five lake cities. Each began its career as a city with a property qualification, in addition to a residence requirement of varying length, for at least one class of voters—whites, aliens, or negroes. Detroit in 1824 required its electors to be freemen who had paid a city tax. Buffalo extended the suffrage to United States citizens but required negro voters to have a freehold estate of $250 on which taxes had been actually rated and paid. A tax qualification was prerequisite to voting in Cleveland in 1836, and Chicago in 1837 expected its voters to be householders or to have paid a city tax of not less than three dollars within the year. As late as 1846 Milwaukee exacted payment of a property tax or required highway or fire duty of male aliens who had declared their intention of becoming citizens. At the outset of cityhood in Chicago, Detroit, and Buffalo, only those owning a freehold estate were eligible for the major elective posts; Milwaukee, having demanded a similar qualification of her village trustees, abandoned this provision upon becoming a city in 1846. Chicago took the lead in a democratic movement which brought by the early fifties the abolition of property qualifications for suffrage and office holding. Milwaukeeans called a proposal to restrict the suffrage to United States citizens an "odious and anti-republican" attempt to deprive "one-half of the citizens of Milwaukee, who will be taxed for the support of the city government, of their right to a voice in electing their officers or making their laws."[13] Like the framers of the state constitutions of the middle period, these mid-western city dwellers believed in representative government closely responsive to the popular will. A proposal to allow aldermen to hold their offices for three years was opposed in Milwaukee as "placing them beyond the reach of public opinion for a time almost equal to an age in older communities."[14] Consequently, annually-elected councils were endowed with wide authority and the power of the executive office was greatly curtailed. In Buffalo the mayor was the creature of the council, and in the other cities little more than a figurehead. Chicagoans in 1840 openly resented the fact that their mayor was given a salary and pointed to Detroit and Buffalo where, they said, the mayors "in fact received nothing."[15] Adherence to the democratic principle of passing jobs around was the practice if not the provision. In Cleveland between 1836 and 1870 only five mayors succeeded themselves in office, and of the twelve available council positions the yearly average of councilmen who were reëlected was two. A study of the situation in Chicago and Milwaukee shows a similar rotation in office. In Detroit it became necessary to force men by threat or danger of fine to serve once they had been elected, although they were spe-

cifically exempted from holding the same office two years in succession. The municipal legislators served without salary, but this did not prevent many of them from amassing fortunes, especially when they held the office of street commissioner.[16] To judge from an analysis of the trades and occupations of those who were councilmen in Cleveland and Milwaukee in the first twenty years of their cityhood, commission merchants, grocers, joiners, builders, masons, and attorneys took a predominantly active part in the government of these young western cities.

Charter changes both in the early fifties and after the financial crisis of 1857 brought some decrease in the amateur management of these governments and a consequent strengthening of the executive arm. In 1852 Milwaukee was provided with an appointed comptroller, soon made elective, to manage city finances. In 1858 the state legislature devised a bicameral council for the city in the hope of retarding hasty legislation. The mayor was granted the veto power in Chicago in 1851 and in Milwaukee in 1859, a negative that was strengthened in the latter city in 1861 and in the former in 1872 by requiring two-thirds rather than a majority of the elected councilmen to override it. The major development in all the Great Lakes cities at the close of the period under discussion was in the direction of establishing boards and commissions as a means of divorcing city management from amateur direction and political interference. This trend, realized in the late sixties and early seventies, was motivated, according to the Milwaukee *Sentinel*, by a feeling that it was inefficient and costly to commit the complicated problems of street improvements and urban services to elected councilmen. It would be better, said the editor, to trust the outlay of great sums of the people's money to "three capable, honest, experienced business men . . . with a moderate compensation for their services, than take the chances under the elective principle of having men of doubtful qualities . . . without compensation . . . under the constant imputation of petty frauds and speculations upon the ward funds."[17] Vesting in the mayor the power of appointing the members of these boards and commissions is an index of the increased prestige of the executive and the decreasing influence of the legislative branch of city government at the opening of the seventies. The Great Lakes cities, growing to maturity in the environment of nineteenth century democracy, thus broadened the base of urban politics but narrowed the administration of municipal affairs.

These major cities of the Middle West did not "just grow." The promotional activities of the original speculator-founders were only the beginning of a long-time program in which newspaper editors, merchants, and citizens at large combined their efforts to attract settlers and business to a given city and away from its neighboring rivals.[18] The promoters of the embryo village on the east side of the Milwaukee river expended nearly $100,000 laying out streets and effecting other improvements designed to attract the settler. By the exertion of political influence and the donation of land they secured the county courthouse for their growing community. Across the river, the promoters of the "west side" were spending similar sums upon improvements, filling the columns of the Milwaukee *Advertiser* with glowing reports of their city's promise, and, by employ-

ing a river boat to meet the lake steamers that touched Milwaukee harbor, preëmpting immigrants possibly destined for their rivals' village. Subsequently many a subterfuge was devised by Chicago and Milwaukee in an attempt to discredit the other in the eyes of European immigrants and eastern capitalists. Only the combination of geography and the railroad left Milwaukee a tired but still confident second in the race. "Forcing" immigrants was accomplished through the use of representatives and promotional advertising in eastern cities. For example, propaganda concerning deaths from cholera, or the absence of them, figured prominently in such campaigns.[19]

The promotion of business in these cities followed a common pattern. A predominant concern for trade and commerce gave way in the middle sixties to the encouragement of manufacturing. Economic developments in Milwaukee and Cleveland substantiate this interpretation. The early interest in trade was reflected by the editor of the Milwaukee *Daily Sentinel and Gazette* in 1846: "It is . . . clearly to the interest of our merchants, millers, forwarders, and business men generally to unite upon some plan for extending and improving roads leading to Milwaukee"[20] Even before this, popular contributions had subsidized a bridge that promised to facilitate the trade of neighboring farmers with the village merchants. Plank roads and railroads were heralded as a means of tapping the markets of the hinterland. Connections by rail with the Columbia River, with the Mississippi River (completed by 1857), and with the Minnesota country, and routes eastward by steam ferry across Lake Michigan and by the Detroit and Michigan railroad were only a few of the projects. They were supported by city funds, by loans of city credit, and by popular subscription—contributions often appealed for and given as a matter of civic duty.[21] Clevelanders were equally convinced of the importance of roads and railways for prosperity. The editor of the Cleveland *Daily True Democrat* wrote in 1849: "Let us, like the wise Cincinnati merchants, spend liberally for these [plank] roads and do all to arouse our farmers and everybody to the importance of increasing our facilities for trade and travel and thus make Cleveland the center of a large region."[22] By 1856 it was asserted in the Cleveland *Leader* that railroads were responsible for the city's growth. The establishment of Boards of Trade in Buffalo (1844), Detroit (1847), Cleveland and Chicago (1848), and Milwaukee (1849); the organization and promotional excursions of merchants; the contesting of disputed trade areas through the use of runners and drummers—these activities suggest the early emphasis on trade and commerce as the key to civic prosperity. In 1857, Milwaukee merchants were urged to compete for trade in Iowa and Minnesota where

already Chicago, St. Louis, Dubuque, Galena, Cincinnati even, have their runners, posters, and advertisements scattered broadcast . . . offering tempting inducements to merchants to come and buy. . . . Now is the time for our merchants, manufacturers, and traders to . . . scatter their cards, handbills, circulars, and advertisements up and down the Mississippi. Let them dispatch some of their shrewdest clerks to La Crosse, Winona, Prescott, Hudson, St. Paul . . . and canvass thoroughly for orders.[23]

By 1855, however, Cleveland editors were sounding a warning note. Business men were blinded, they said, "by the belief that commerce alone" would make the city great. The *Leader* asserted in 1856 that "no thinking man with capital will stop here when we have only commerce to sustain us. A manufacturing town gives a man full scope for his ambitions."[24] That newspaper encouraged popular subscriptions to factory enterprises, urged the reduction of real estate prices as an inducement to capital, and agitated for the protection and consumption of home manufactures.[25] An appeal to civic duty attended this promotion as it had the earlier agitation for railroad connections. By the late sixties when Cleveland had become a manufacturing center, earlier arguments used there were being echoed in Milwaukee. Vigorous newspaper agitation, together with the organization of the Milwaukee Manufacturers Association in January 1863, excited industrial ambitions. "Commerce alone can never give us a permanent prosperity," counselled a Milwaukee editor in 1866.[26] By 1872, as a result, one-third to one-half of the working population of Milwaukee was engaged in manufacturing goods valued at $20,000,000.[27] Stimulated by the economic developments of the Civil War period, pressed by the expansion of population into areas farther west of them, and in a sense taking a cue each from the economic experiences of the other, the lake cities had turned by 1870 from an almost exclusive interest in commerce to endorse sentiments to the effect that "a thousand dollars put into manufacturing does more to gather population than a million dollars put into trade."[28]

A major source of the urban services of these young communities developed from the sense of individual responsibility which prompted thousands of city dwellers to invest their savings in the railroads and factories that were supposed to bring prosperity to the urban center. The mid-nineteenth century saw the Great Lakes cities in what might be called the "subscription period" of their municipal growth. Two to three days' work on the streets, for which money payments could be substituted, was expected of all able-bodied men.[29] Street and sidewalk improvements as well as the eradication of nuisances were to be taken care of individually or charged against the property benefited. For protection against theft and riot Milwaukeeans had to rely upon occasional watchmen, volunteer firemen, and members of free military companies until a night watch and a police force were organized in 1852. As late as 1855 men carried weapons for their own protection, and an ordinance of that year compelled all citizens to aid the police when called upon to do so. In 1837 the Cleveland *Herald and Gazette* referred to the "Mutual Protecting Society," and in 1839 a number of the citizens "with commendable spirit formed themselves into companies for a city watch." In 1859 the merchants of Detroit, where as early as 1825 volunteer watchmen had been mobilized by passing around a subscription paper, subscribed to the support of a patrol for the business district, and the Milwaukee Board of Trade offered a bonus for additional protection in 1860.[30] By the late fifties and early sixties police service was generally provided at city expense, and the management of the police by a commission was agitated or passed in Milwaukee (1864), Detroit (1865), and Cleveland (1866).

Fire protection came also in a major degree from individual contributions of time and money. In the middle thirties Clevelanders were fined when they refused to serve in the bucket line at fires. Local editors appealed to property owners to contribute their share of volunteer firemen and in 1840 congratulated Phoenix Company Number Four for having won the premiums offered annually by the insurance companies to stimulate competitive-minded fire fighters to efficiency and accomplishment. Milwaukeeans from all levels of society were members of the organized volunteer firemen, who met a portion of the costs of their own equipment and whose service exempted them from highway or militia duty. Donations, benefit concerts, and dinners raised $2,500 in 1851 to swell the funds by which the Ocean, Neptune, and Cataract companies of volunteer firemen carried on their work. Despite the pleas of property owners for more efficient service than unpaid volunteers could give, it was not until the appearance of the steam fire engine in the sixties that professional fire fighters were generally maintained from public funds.[31]

Aside from a meagre and inadequate tax to support almshouses and to furnish medical care for the sick poor, urban relief, too, was provided by individual donation. Invariably the cessation of navigation in the winter season brought demands from the unemployed of the city. Out of public meetings came plans for raising money and organizations for dispensing relief. Mayor D. A. J. Upham of Milwaukee expressed a general opinion in 1849 when he held that private enterprise was best equipped to meet the problem. The Cleveland *Daily True Democrat* said the poor could not be taken care of "unless individual activity and associated effort act."[32] Women's organizations, such as the Martha Washington Society of Cleveland and the Ladies

Benevolent Society of Milwaukee, were soon supplanted by more systematically managed relief groups, like the Milwaukee Provident Association and the Cleveland Relief Association. The Milwaukee group advertised its cause as a community responsibility, raised over $20,000 in the five years ending in 1867, and distributed fuel and provisions only after careful investigation of the needy. Private contributions were the chief means of support of the Chicago Relief and Aid Society, incorporated in 1857. Soup kitchens were also subsidized by private gifts and meal tickets were sold to those citizens who wished to offer them to the poor. The Milwaukee women who managed these enterprises trusted "to the benevolence of our citizens . . . for the food to be supplied."[33]

To a large extent the cultural services of the city, beyond the provision for public schools, were the result of support by subscription. Forerunners of the public libraries of the seventies were the membership libraries of such organizations as the Young Men's Associations in Chicago and Milwaukee and the Reading Room Association in Cleveland.[34] Imitating Chicago's example, and realizing that the lack of private libraries compelled "voluntary association," several Milwaukeeans organized to promote a library in 1847.[35] In canvassing for funds and members they did not neglect to stress community obligation and the example of other cities. The promotional value of good libraries to the city was "a pretty safe index of the mental advancement . . . of a city." They also emphasized the "gallantry of the Association [which] admits even ladies to a full participation of the advantages of membership, with the exception, we think, of voting."[36] Char-

tered in 1848, the Cleveland Library Association issued stock certificates and charged yearly dues. Soliciting subscriptions in 1851 for a reading room, the editor of the Cleveland *Daily True Democrat* was convinced that "nothing . . . adds so much to the reputation of a city as a good Reading Room and Library."[37]

Many other cultural activities were fostered by subscription. Local musicians and actors volunteered their services in aid of the fire department, orphan asylum, and other causes. The Milwaukee Musical Society when soliciting members in 1857 advised the public that its monthly dues of forty cents plus a two dollar initiation fee were "but a moderate tax to pay towards the support of an organization which ministers so largely to the enjoyment of our citizens and which reflects such credit upon our city."[38] The founders of academies and colleges in asking for endowments also appealed to civic duty.[39] By 1870 the beginning of public libraries[40] and the agitation for parks—following New York's example with Central Park—were slight but indicative signs of the rôle that the urban government was ultimately to play in providing aesthetic satisfaction and social and cultural benefits to its citizens.[41] A Cleveland editor went so far as to start a crusade in 1870 against city noises— "an evil rapidly becoming unendurable." He wrote: "While suppressing so rigorously all offences to the sight and smell, and punishing in general all disturbances of the peace, it would be only consistent to include in the proscription the still greater plague of noise." Yet he concluded a year later that the cure for city noises still lay in the field of individual responsibility: "We have not yet reached that point where the law will guard the nerves of the aged, the tender, and infirm from unnecessary torture."[42] Such a concept of city function did not square with the "subscription period" of city growth.

These striking parallels in the institutional history of the five major cities of the Great Lakes are to be explained in part by the contemporaneous character of their growth, by the common sources from which their population sprang, and by the similarity of the economic forces influencing their behavior. In all five cities, the foreign born provided about half the population, with natives of Germany, Ireland, and Great Britain distributing themselves in early uniform proportions, except in Milwaukee where European immigrants were more predominantly German. In the sectional origins of native Americans these cities were also similar. New York, Massachusetts, and Pennsylvania contributed most abundantly to each of the five cities save Chicago, which drew a large number from neighboring Michigan. The census of 1870 showed as well a remarkable uniformity in the percentages of people engaged in various occupational pursuits. But it was not simply a matter of similar social ingredients, for this municipal development of the Great Lakes area was apparently following a pattern or process not unusual to urban evolution elsewhere. As they grew to comparable size of the coastal cities half a century earlier. For example, after a generation of city growth the expanded powers of the lake cities in 1870, like those of the seaboard cities in 1800, represented a response more to the problems of size than to any changed philosophy of the functions of urban communities for which a difference in environment or personality

might have been responsible. By 1870 each of these lake cities was a more conscious "municipal entity" than in its village period. Commercial regulations for the common good, cooperation through taxes and subscriptions for the promotion and improvement of the city, and the recognition of some of the social responsibilities presented by the interdependence of city life certainly had fostered a group consciousness—a group attitude, however, still very largely articulated by and pivoting around the individual. The "municipal consciousness," twentieth century pattern, was more than a generation in the future. Its full development awaited the flow of population, new economic needs, and changing social philosophy of the late nineteenth and early twentieth centuries.

In these urban centers of the Middle West in the mid-nineteenth century, the houses, to one traveller's surprise, were not "wigwamified," the dress and ornament not "wampumized."[43] As Anthony Trollope said, the "general level of . . . material and intellectual wellbeing—of beef . . . and book learning" was "no doubt infinitely higher than in a European town."[44] These cities sprang from beginnings closely associated in practice and attitude with the westward expansion of the American people. As they grew, their concern for popular management and their emphasis upon the intrinsic rôle of the individual in the promotion of the physical and cultural growth of the city reveal attitudes often observed by students of the agrarian frontier. At the same time, they showed a willing dependence upon eastern sources in the transmission of culture, a studied imitation of tested forms of municipal practice and urban service, and an expanding assumption of community responsibility. Such influences suggest that in the rise of the large city in the West, as elsewhere, one sees another—perhaps equally important if less explored—side of American social history in the nineteenth century.

NOTES

1. Milwaukee *Daily Sentinel*, May 26, 1845.

2. The following are the most useful titles for making comparative studies of urban development in the Mississippi Valley. Buffalo: Robert W. Bingham, *The Cradle of the Queen City: A History of Buffalo to the Incorporation of the City* (Buffalo, 1931); Henry W. Hill, ed., *Municipality of Buffalo, New York; A History, 1720-1923* (4 vols., New York, 1923); Josephus N. Larned, *A History of Buffalo, Delineating the Evolution of the City* (2 vols., New York, 1911). Cleveland: Elroy M. Avery, *A History of Cleveland and its Environs* (3 vols., Chicago, 1918); William R. Coates, *A History of Cuyahoga County and the City of Cleveland* (3 vols., Chicago, 1924); Samuel P. Orth, *A History of Cleveland, Ohio* (3 vols., Chicago, 1910). Detroit: George B. Catlin, *The Story of Detroit* (Detroit, 1923); Clarence M. Burton, ed., *The City of Detroit, Michigan, 1701-1922* (4 vols., Chicago, 1922); Silas Farmer, *History of Detroit and Michigan* (Detroit, 1884); Arthur Pound, *Detroit, Dynamic City* (New York, 1940); Robert B. Ross and George B. Catlin, *Landmarks of Detroit* (Detroit, 1898). Milwaukee: William G. Bruce, *History of Milwaukee City and County* (3 vols., Milwaukee, 1922); John G. Gregory, *History of Milwaukee, Wisconsin* (4 vols., Chicago, 1931); Bayrd Still, "The Growth of Milwaukee as Recorded by Contemporaries," *Wisconsin Magazine of History* (Madison), XXI, 1938, pp. 262-292, and "Milwaukee, 1870-1900: the Emergence of a Metropolis," *loc. cit.*, XXIII, 1939, pp. 138-162. Chicago: Alfred T. Andreas, *History of Chicago, 1670-1885* (3 vols., Chicago, 1884-1886); J. Seymour Currey, *Chicago: Its History and Its Builders* (3 vols., Chicago, 1912); Bessie L. Pierce, *A History of Chicago* (2 vols., New

York, 1937, 1940), and *As Others See Chicago* (Chicago, 1933). Pittsburgh: Leland D. Baldwin, *Pittsburgh, the Story of a City* (Pittsburgh, 1937); George T. Fleming, *History of Pittsburgh and Environs* (5 vols., New York, 1922); Frank C. Harper, *Pittsburgh of Today, Its Resources and People* (4 vols., New York, 1931); Sarah H. Killikelly; *The History of Pittsburgh, Its Rise and Progress* (Pittsburgh, 1906). Cincinnati: Clara Chambrun, *Cincinnati: Story of the Queen City* (New York, 1939); Henry A. and Kate B. Ford, *History of Cincinnati, Ohio* (Cleveland, 1881); Charles T. Greve, *Centennial History of Cincinnati and Representative Citizens* (2 vols., Chicago, 1904). Louisville: Reuben T. Durrett, *The Centenary of Louisville* (*Filson Club Publications*, no. 8, Louisville, 1893); L. A. Williams and Co., eds., *History of the Ohio Falls Cities and their Counties* (Cleveland, 1882); J. Stoddard Johnston, ed., *Memorial History of Louisville from its first Settlement to the Year 1896* (2 vols., Chicago, n. d.). Minneapolis: Norman S. B. Gras, "The Significance of the Twin Cities for Minnesota History," *Minnesota History* (St. Paul), VII, 1926, pp. 3-17; Mildred L. Hartsough, *The Twin Cities as a Metropolitan Market: a Regional Study of the Economic Development of Minneapolis and St. Paul* (Minneapolis, 1925); Calvin F. Schmid, *Social Saga of Two Cities: An Ecological and Statistical Study of Social Trends in Minneapolis and St. Paul* (Minneapolis, 1937). St. Louis: John T. Scharf, *History of St. Louis City and County, from the Earliest Periods to the Present Day* (2 vols., Philadelphia, 1883); Walter B. Stevens, *St. Louis, the Fourth City, 1764-1911* (2 vols., St. Louis, 1911). Memphis: Gerald M. Capers, Jr., *The Biography of a River Town; Memphis: Its Heroic Age* (Chapel Hill, 1939). New Orleans: Henry Rightor, ed., *Standard History of New Orleans, Louisiana* (Chicago, 1900).

3. St. Louis, 310,864; Chicago, 298,977; Cincinnati, 216,239; New Orleans, 191,418; Pittsburgh, 139,256; Buffalo, 117,714; Louisville, 100,753. *Fifteenth Census of the United States, 1930, Population*, I, 18-19.

4. Between 1860 and 1870 the total population of the lake cities increased over 100 per cent; that of the valley cities, 60 per cent; that of New York, Philadelphia, and Boston, 20 per cent; that of the United States, 22.6 per cent. *Ibid.*, 12 *et passim*.

5. Comparative population of the Great Lakes cities:[*]

	1820	1830	1840	1850	1860	1870
Buffalo	2,095	8,668	18,213	42,261	81,129	117,714
Cleveland	606	1,076	6,071	17,034	43,417	92,829
Detroit	1,422	2,222	9,102	21,019	45,619	79,577
Chicago			4,470	29,963	109,260	298,977
Milwaukee			1,712	20,061	45,246	71,440

[*] *Ibid.*, 19. The total population of the East North Central States increased during 1840 to 1870 from 2,924,728 to 9,124,517. *Ibid.*, 11.

6. Chicago's first charter was the result of popular agitation. It was submitted to a mass meeting for popular approval, there slightly altered, and sent

to the legislature. Edmund J. James calls it a self-proposed charter, "a practical recognition of local self-government on a large scale." Edmund J. James, *The Charters of the City of Chicago* (Chicago, 1898), 23. Such local participation did not prevent imitation in selecting the form of the charter.

7. For an example of identical clauses in these city charters see *Laws of the State of New York, 1853* (Albany, 1853), p. 461; *Laws of Wisconsin, 1852* (Madison, 1852), p. 81; and *Statutes of Illinois, Private Laws, 1851* (Springfield, 1851), p. 143.

8. For colonial legislation on this subject consult Henry W. Farnam, *Chapters in the History of Social Legislation in the United States to 1860* (Washington, 1938), 92-115.

9. Bessie L. Pierce, *A History of Chicago* (New York, 1937-), II, 461, note.

10. As an example of this type of early municipal regulation see "An Ordinance Relating to the First Ward Market, and to License and regulate Butcher's Stalls, Shops and Stands for the sale of Butcher's Meat, Poultry, Game, and Fresh Fish," in *Charters and Ordinances of the City of Milwaukee* (Milwaukee, 1857), 464-465. Of similar nature is a Buffalo ordinance of April 23, 1855, and one in Cleveland, June 3, 1851.

11. Milwaukee *Sentinel*, January 4, 1859.

12. An act regulating the "Assize of Bread" seems to have been in force in Detroit as late as 1820. The price of bread was fixed according to a sliding scale based on the price of flour. George N. Fuller, *Economic and Social Beginnings in Michigan, 1805-1837* (Lansing, 1916), 126. A Massachusetts regulation, based on the price of grain plus a a reasonable allowance for labor, was abandoned in 1801. Farnam, *Social Legislation to 1860*, 110. The Milwaukee ordinance regulating the manufacture and sale of bread (July 13, 1836) required registration of the baker's place of business, the use of wholesome flour, and the marking of loaves with the weight of the loaf and the initials of the baker. This was virtually the same bread legislation as that of New York in 1839 and of Boston as late as 1834. A similar provision is found in Chapter XXXVII of the Cleveland ordinances as codified in 1877.

13. Milwaukee *Courier*, January 27, 1845, quoted in Milwaukee *Evening Wisconsin*, October 15, 1895.

14. *Ibid.*

15. Pierce, *Chicago*, I, 328, note.

16. Laurence M. Larson, *A Financial and Administrative History of Milwaukee* (Bulletin of the University of Wisconsin, no. 242, *Economics and Political Science Series*, Vol. IV, no. 2, Madison, 1908), 27-28; Milwaukee *Sentinel*, June 27, 1857.

17. Milwaukee *Sentinel*, April 5, 1869. See also *ibid.*, March 11, 1852, and March 23, 1864; John G. Gregory, *History of Milwaukee, Wsiconsin* (Chicago, 1931), I, 253.

18. The Cincinnati *Gazette*, quoted in the Milwaukee *Sentinel* of June 10, 1859, asserted that a newspaper served the founders of towns by acting as a kind of credential to the reality of the inchoate city, and as a light to direct the pioneer to a new home and to direct business and emigration into new channels.

19. The Boston *Chronotype*, as quoted in the Milwaukee *Daily Sentinel and Gazette*, August 29, 1846, referred to the "forcing process" as circulating "numberless libels in handbills" in the East. Milwaukeeans claimed that Chicago newspapers were libeling their health record, and Cleveland papers labored during the thirties to deny that the village was sickly.

20. Milwaukee *Daily Sentinel and Gazette*, March 11, 1846. In his inaugural address, Mayor D. A. J. Upham averred that "the improvements we most need . . . are the roads and facilities of securing trade from the country." *Ibid.*, April 12, 1849.

21. The city of Milwaukee soon substituted the issuance of bonds as loans to railroad companies for the earlier practice of buying railroad stock. Substantial security and a popular vote of authorization were required. This popular support was freely given, and by 1858 the loans to railroad companies totaled $1,614,000, all of which was ultimately repaid except two issues of $100,000 each. Larson, *Financial History of Milwaukee*, 74-75. By contrast the city of Chicago had made no railroad investments by 1870, and individual Chicagoans had not found it necessary to invest much in enterprises that eastern capitalists were eager to finance. Pierce, *Chicago*, II, 75.

22. Cleveland *Daily True Democrat*, June 1, 1849.

23. Milwaukee *Sentinel*, March 17, 1857.

24. Cleveland *Leader*, October 31, 1855, and March 10, 1856.

25. *Ibid.*, March 30, 1858.

26. Milwaukee *Sentinel*, October 20, 1866. See also *ibid.*, April 16, 1869, for an assertion by manufacturers that Milwaukeeans were still putting all their eggs in one basket.

27. Frederick Merk, *Economic History of Wisconsin During the Civil War Decade* (Madison, 1916), 127.

28. Cleveland *Leader*, April 10, 1873.

29. Chicago in 1847 required males between the ages of twenty-one and sixty to work on the streets three days each year, with commutation at the rate of fifty cents per day. Milwaukee in 1846 required two days' work with commutation at seventy-five cents per day.

30. Cleveland *Herald and Gazette*, June 28, 1837; Gregory, *Milwaukee*, II, 1123; Milwaukee *Daily Sentinel and Gazette*, April 16, May 20, 1847, and February 6, 1850; Milwaukee *Sentinel*, August 16, 1855, and January 14, 1860; Cleveland *Herald*, November 28, 1839; Clarence M. Burton, ed., *The City of Detroit, Michigan* (Detroit, 1922), I, 406.

31. Cleveland *Herald and Gazette*, December 22, 1837; Cleveland *Herald*, June 24, 1840; Cleveland *Leader*, November 25, 1862, and April 14, 1863; Milwaukee *Sentinel*, January 22, 1852, March 4, 1861, and March 4, 1862; Gregory, *Milwaukee*, II, 795 ff.; Burton, *Detroit*, I, 402.

32. Cleveland *Daily True Democrat*, December 20, 1850.

33. Milwaukee *Sentinel*, November 30, 1857. See also *ibid.*, November 23, 1857, November 12, 1866, and December 20, 1867; Milwaukee *Daily Sentinel and Gazette*, April 12, 1849; Pierce, *Chicago*, II, 445-446.

34. The Young Men's Association organized in Chicago in 1841 was modeled after a similar organization in Albany. Members were asked to donate books to the library and non-members might use the reading room at a charge of fifty cents a month. By 1847 the library had a thousand volumes, plus current newspapers. Pierce, *Chicago*, I, 286-288. The Cleveland Reading Room Association was supported by voluntary subscriptions. Elroy M. Avery, *A History of Cleveland and Its Environs* (Chicago, 1918), I, 188. Judging from an advertisement in the Cleveland *Herald*, November 30, 1836, dues were five dollars a year.

35. The charge for life members was twenty-five dollars. Regular members paid an entrance fee of two dollars and fifty cents quarterly thereafter. The sum of $1,513 was collected in the first two months. The association had 810 books at the end of the first year. The librarian donated his services, and the library was open two afternoons a week. By 1867 the association had three thousand members and more than ten thousand volumes. Gregory, *Milwaukee*, II, 1077-1078.

36. Milwaukee *Sentinel*, December 2, 1857.

37. Cleveland *Daily True Democrat*, January 29, 1851. "Lucy Ann," having come to Cleveland from the East, wrote to the editor of the Cleveland *Herald*, July 14, 1845, bemoaning the lack of a Young Men's Association or a Reading Room Association. "There are enough young men here to support a . . . library, but . . . they are more fond of riding . . . in buggies, eating ice cream,

and smoking cigars . . . than they are of obtaining worth of mind."

38. Milwaukee *Sentinel*, December 7, 1857.

39. *Ibid.*, March 4, 1852, November 26, 1853, and August 3, 1855.

40. The nucleus of Cleveland's public library was a collection of books provided under the school library law of 1853. A free public library was authorized by an act of 1867 and realized in 1869. According to the Cleveland *Leader*, March 16, 1869, "A free library is proof of the enlightened liberality in a community and of the intellectual culture and refinement thereof." Detroit's public library was formally opened in 1865. Burton, *Detroit*, I, 838. The library of the Young Men's Association of Milwaukee was transferred to the city of Milwaukee in 1878. Gregory, *Milwaukee*, II, 1078.

41. Public parks, according to the press, would counteract "the downward tendencies of city life" (Milwaukee *Daily Sentinel and Gazette*, April 24, 1845); enhance the value of property (Cleveland *Herald*, December 31, 1840); and offset urban congestion as a consequence of which "few grounds around the city remain occupied" (Milwaukee *Sentinel*, December 18, 1865). Detroit was agitating for an extensive park and Cleveland for three of them in 1865. The park question was discussed in a desultory way in Chicago during the fifties and sixties, but not until the late sixties was much accomplished. Pierce, *Chicago*, II, 339-341.

42. Cleveland *Leader*, September 3, October 18, 1870, and May 9, 1871. See also *ibid.*, May 7, 1869.

43. A narrative of Nathaniel P. Willis of 1860, quoted in Gregory, *Milwaukee*, II, 1320.

44. Anthony Trollope, *North America* (New York, 1862), I, 182.

Urban Rivalry and Internal Improvements in the Old Northwest, 1820-1860

HARRY N. SCHEIBER

At the very beginning of settlement in the Old Northwest urban communities developed in response to the commercial needs of the surrounding country. And almost as soon as they appeared, there was "urban rivalry," that is, competition among them for advantages that would promote their growth and

From *Ohio History* (October 1962), pp. 227-39, 290-92. Reprinted by permission of The Ohio Historical Society. Harry N. Scheiber is Professor of History at Dartmouth College.

enhance their attractiveness to emigrants and investors.[1] The earliest rivalries usually involved competition for advantages that government might bestow. Designation as the county seat or as the territorial or state capital marked the beginning of growth for many a rude village in the West, and the pursuit of these choice prizes was inevitably marked by keen political struggles. The presence of federal land offices, colleges and academies, or government installations such as arsenals and prisons was for many towns the only factor that permitted them to outdistance less favored rivals with equivalent natural or geographic endowments.[2]

Sustained urban growth and economic viability were in most cases dependent upon more than initial advantages that this sort of government patronage could provide. Probably the most important single requirement for urban growth and commercial development was adequate transportation. Without reliable transport facilities connecting a town with an expanding hinterland and with outside markets, there were oppressive limitations upon growth. The struggle for internal improvements therefore became the cause of the most vigorous and persistent rivalries among western urban communities—rivalries marked by intense ambitions, deeply rooted fear of failure, and ingenious employment of the instruments of political and economic leverage at the disposal of urban leaders.[3]

The period of early urban growth in the Old Northwest coincided with the period of canal construction by the states. How, then, did urban rivalries influence state transport policy in the canal era, 1820-45? How did continued rivalry affect the planning and construction of western railroads when private promotion supplanted state enterprise, from the mid-forties to 1860? Before dealing with these questions, it must be noted that self-interested urban activities and urban consciousness cannot be strictly separated from the more embracing force of which they were manifestations, that is, from "localism," a collective consciousness and sense of common interests among the people of a given locality. The definition of common objectives and self-interest might find expression at many levels, and often urban aims and objectives were merely an intense reflection of regional aims.[4] Towns frequently spoke in state politics for the trade areas with which they were associated; yet within intrastate regions (as within interstate sections) cities might compete for hegemony. New transport facilities and redirection of trade—or even the prospect of such change—might alter drastically the regional identification of given urban centers.

The interplay of regional and local rivalries at the state level is illustrated in the history of Ohio's improvements policy. The movement for construction of a canal between Lake Erie and the Ohio River, which, it was hoped, would open eastern markets to Ohio farmers and merchants, began to gather strength about 1820 in response to construction of the Erie Canal in New York. In 1822 the Ohio legislature assigned to a special commission the task of planning such a canal. The canal commissioners soon recognized that their problem was as much one of politics as of engineering. As long as the project remained a subject of discussion in general terms, optimistic business and political leaders throughout the state gave it their support. But once the project took precise form and the commission recommended specific routes, the virtue of vagueness was lost, and the towns and regions that would be bypassed united immediately in opposition to the proposal. Spokesmen for the disappointed communities evoked the specter of oppressive taxation, argued in principle against state intervention in the economy, and denounced the commissioners for alleged corruption. Yet some of the same men had earlier been among the most outspoken advocates of a state canal project.[5]

In 1825 the Ohio canal commission recommended, and the legislature adopted, a canal program that represented a fusion of several important regional interests within the state. Two canals were authorized, rather than the single work originally contemplated. One, the Miami Canal, satisfied Cincinnati's mercantile community and southwest Ohio; it was to run sixty-seven miles from the Queen City north through the Miami Valley to Dayton, with the understanding that it would later be extended northward to the Maumee Valley and Lake Erie. The second canal, the Ohio Canal, followed a wide-sweeping reverse-S-shaped route from the Ohio River to the lake, passing first up the heavily settled Scioto Valley, then arching eastward to the headwaters of the Muskingum, there turning northward again to its terminus on the lake shore at Cleveland.[6]

This canal program gave new focus to urban and regional ambitions, which adjusted quickly to take account of inter-regional connections and new trade relationships that the canals would create. In the first place, within regions through which the canals passed, there was an intensified struggle for positions on the projected works. Everywhere along the canal routes there was speculation in new town-sites. A Tuscarawas County promoter expressed the thoughts of hundreds like himself when he wrote to one of the canal commissioners: "I expect a new town will spring up [along the canal], which, from the great trade which must center there, from the country between us and the Ohio, must be a flourishing one. But *where* the spot is, I want *you* to tell *me*."[7] Sensitive to the potential threat to their own interests, established market towns in the interior petitioned for construction of feeder canals that would connect them with the main works. In many instances the townspeople offered to pay a portion of the cost. Several towns organized private canal companies to build feeder lines, not in expectation of direct profits, but rather to protect their commercial position.[8]

Events in the Scioto Valley, the southern route of the Ohio Canal, indicated the extremes to which localism might run. Piketon and Chillicothe had joined with other towns in the valley to support the canal bill of 1825 in the legislature. But as soon as it became necessary for the commission to set the exact canal location, each town advanced its own cause and all sense of regional unity dissolved. The Chillicothe interests were determined to obtain a canal connection. They forced through the legislature a resolution ordering the canal commission to build the canal through Chillicothe, even if it was necessary to build a dam or aqueduct across the river in order to bring the canal through the town. The canal commission complied, crossing the river to place the route through Chillicothe. To avoid further expenditure the commission decided not to re-cross the Scioto below Chillicothe. Piketon and other communities on the opposite bank downriver opposed this action bitterly, since it would prevent them from achieving a canal connection, but they were unsuccessful in their protests.[9] Ironically, the state's accommodation of Chillicothe quieted the clamor there for only a few months. Once actual construction had begun, neighborhoods within the town vied with one another in what may be termed "neighborhood rivalry," various factions demanding that a particular street or section of town be designated as the canal route. Passions ran high for several months, and the mayor finally had to hold a referendum on "the *naked* and *abstract* question" of the canal route.[10]

State officials systematically exploited such local rivalries. Where the canal might be located on either side of a river, the Ohio commissioners solicited donations of land or cash from townspeople and landowners on opposite sides of the stream, indicating that the more generous communities would be favored when the canal was located. This practice often stimulated unreasonable expectations and resulted in bitter disillusionment.[11]

Once the initial canal undertaking was approved, the "disappointed" communities—those entirely outside the region of the canals—did not give up their quest for improved transportation. On the contrary, they proposed a multitude of new projects, many of them reflecting an effort by ambitious towns to overcome the lead of commercial rivals that had obtained places on the canals. "Shall narrow views and sectional feelings withhold our assistance from a work of such evident public utility?" the promoters of one new project asked the general assembly. "Shall we, palsied by untimely fears, stop mid-way in the career of public improvement, to calculate the cost, before our fellow citizens in other parts of the State participate in their advantages?"[12]

Such new improvements schemes disrupted older regional alliances and introduced new forces into state politics. Sandusky's railroad project is a case in point. Only a few years after their town had lost to Cleveland in the struggle for designation as the lake-shore terminus of the Ohio Canal, a group of Sandusky promoters requested state aid for the Mad River and Lake Erie Railroad. The Mad River Railroad was planned in 1831 to run from Sandusky southwest to Dayton, which was then head of navigation on the Miami Canal, and ultimately to Cincinnati. When the first canal program had been debated in the legislature, six years earlier, the Miami Canal proposal had been supported by the western counties located north of Dayton—but only because of the understanding that the canal would be extended northward as soon as finances permitted. Having enjoyed the benefits of its position as head of navigation on the Miami Canal, Dayton now shifted its allegiance, and the town's representatives decided to support state aid for the Mad River Railroad instead of for extension of the canal.[13] This move threatened to strand the area to the north, and the towns in that region (especially Piqua) resented what they regarded as Dayton's treachery. "The Canal *must* be extended," Piqua's newspaper editor declared, despite "the selfish policy of those, who at a former period made such professions of friendship to us; but who, since *their* views have been accomplished, *forget* their obligations."[14]

The projects that blossomed forth in every part of the state also came into conflict with one another in the effort to secure the patronage of the legislature, which at this time commanded only limited funds. If logrolling was an important feature of the legislative process, so too was the log jam. The Ohio General Assembly was virtually stalemated for several years in the early 1830's because of conflicting demands for internal improvements.[15] The jam began to break when extension of the Miami Canal and construction of the Wabash and Erie Canal were authorized—but only because the federal government had provided land-grant aid for these projects. Finally, the pressure of local ambitions became too great to resist further. In 1836-37 the legislature approved a comprehensive system of new canals and state aid to railroad and turnpike companies, a program that within five years would bring Ohio to the verge of default on its enlarged debt. Every region had to be satisfied, it seemed; every little community able to advance half the cost was to receive state assistance in the construction of turnpikes or railways.[16]

With adoption of the enlarged improvements program, urban and regional ambitions adjusted rapidly to the new transportation developments. Many of the patterns of localism and rivalries witnessed a decade earlier now reappeared. In the Muskingum Valley, where a project to improve the river for steamboat traffic was undertaken, Zanesville and Dresden fought over which town should be the head of navigation, just as Dayton and Piqua had struggled for headship on the Miami Canal. Meanwhile, Marietta, situated at the mouth of the Muskingum, protested that the size of the locks was too limited. The vision of every town in the valley appeared to be one of infinite

optimism and boundless growth. "We look forward," a petition of Marietta merchants declared glowingly,

and [we] see our situation placed on the thoroughfare, between the Atlantic & the Mederterranean [sic] of the North, the Mississippi & the St. Lawrence. We look forward to the arrival of the Ohio & Chesapeake Canal and the Baltimore & Ohio Rail Road. . . . We look & expect to see the Ohio made slackwater by Locks & dams, from Marietta to Pittsburgh . . . & Lastly we expect to see the Locks, on the Muskingum Improvement, increased. . . . We wish to convince you, that the discriminating principle, attending the small locks, is derogatory to social Commerce, & has been discarded by all civilized nations.[17]

In the Maumee Valley, then sparsely settled, the people of several small towns—Toledo, Maumee, Perrysburg, and Manhattan—and the absentee proprietors of the towns (including several of the most prominent Ohio political leaders), all had favored construction of the Wabash and Erie Canal, a project designed to continue Indiana's Wabash and Erie Canal from the state line through the Maumee Valley to the lake. But once the Ohio legislature had decided to undertake the project, these villages competed bitterly with one another for designation as the terminus.[18] Among the instruments of rivalry employed were court injunctions, petitions to the legislature and to congress, and pressure on the United States General Land Office to limit the extent of the federal land grant by designating one of the competing towns as head of lake navigation. State officials finally decided to satisfy all the major competing points by extending the canal to the mouth of the river, with terminal locks and basins at Manhattan, Toledo, and Maumee. To equalize the conditions of rivalry the state agreed also to open all the terminal locks simultaneously.[19] Thus even after a major improvement had been authorized, the competition of rival communities could serve to increase the costs of construction.

Roughly the same patterns of localism characterized the evolution of public transport policy in the other states of the Old Northwest. During the early promotional phase of internal improvements, when state officials or private pressure groups were agitating for projects in general terms, there tended to be divisions between the great trade regions of each state. In Indiana, for example, the southern river counties viewed with suspicion the proposal for the Wabash and Erie Canal, and they coalesced to press for roads and railways from the interior to the Ohio River.[20] In Illinois, too, the region tributary to the Mississippi River and southern markets adamantly opposed state aid exclusively for the proposed canal to Chicago. The towns on the eastern lake shore in Wisconsin (still a territory) all sought canal or railroad connections with the interior; but they were prevented from realizing their objectives because of opposition in the northern region, which demanded priority for the Fox and Wisconsin river improvement project, and in the western river towns.[21]

Once specific projects had been formulated, broad regional divisions gave way under pressure for more localized objectives. "Most of the members [of the legislature] vote for nothing which does not pass through their own county," the Indiana state engineer complained in 1835. Indiana's Michigan Road, supported in a general way by all the Ohio River counties, became an object of sharp urban rivalry when designation of the southern terminus had to be made. Similarly, the program that the state's engineers submitted to the legislature in 1835 was not rendered acceptable until it had been expanded elaborately, "to buy votes," a year later.[22] In Michigan all the lake shore towns demanded connections with the interior, yet no policy could command adequate support until one embracing the objectives of every competing town had been formulated. And so Indiana, Illinois, and Michigan all adopted comprehensive state programs that overextended their resources. In both Illinois and Indiana the political strength of localism was further manifested in provisions of the law requiring simultaneous starts on all projects; in addition, each of the states' settled regions was granted representation on the boards of public works.[23] Once construction had begun, moreover, scores of proposals were put forward in each state for branch lines, feeder canals, and turnpike and railroad connections designed to satisfy the needs of towns outside the immediate areas of the main improvements.[24]

Still another feature of urban and regional rivalry as it affected state policy concerned canal tolls. Toll schedules were commonly established by state authorities on a protectionist basis. The states maintained two toll lists—one for "domestic," or in-state, manufactures and a higher schedule of tolls for "foreign," or out-of-state, commodities. In Ohio, for example, manufacturers of glassware, iron, salt, crockery, and other products were the beneficiaries of protectionist tolls.[25] As long as canals remained the sole means of cheap transport to the interior, manufacturers located inland from Lake Erie or the Ohio River enjoyed a form of tariff protection from out-of-state competition. Merchants at the terminal cities on the lake and the Ohio River condemned the protectionist policy as one which imposed artificial restrictions upon the canal commerce that was their economic lifeblood. The conflict between terminal cities and inland towns was expressed in the 1840's in a debate over wheat and flour tolls. The millers of the interior demanded tolls on unprocessed grain that were proportionally higher than tolls on flour. This, they argued, would encourage Ohio's milling industry and reduce the flow of Ohio grain to New York State mills. Merchants and millers at terminal cities opposed such action; they favored equivalent tolls on grain and flour (or even discrimination against flour) as a means of fostering the milling industry of their cities or the export of increasing quantities of grain.[26]

Similarly, merchants at Cleveland, then gateway for import of salt from the East, fought discrimination in salt tolls that protected Ohio producers in the central portion of the state. Thus within the state there was a conflict between mercantile and manufacturing interests, comparable to the division in national politics over tariff policy. The issue of canal tolls cut across party lines, and special regional alignments were fostered by this important question. State officials were forced to mediate such conflicts, with no resolution possible that could fully satisfy all contending interests.[27]

In the period of canal construction, urban and regional ambitions were directed largely toward manipulation and control of state policy. The panic of 1837 and the post-1839 depression marked the end of the era of state canals in the Old Northwest. As the depression came to an end in the mid-forties a new internal-improvements movement gathered momentum, with a new set of conditions shaping the character of the movement. In the first place, there had been a revulsion against further large-scale construction by state government, the result of scandals in management of the public works, intolerable indebtedness, and default on their debt by several states in the depression period.[28] In the second place, the advantages of the railroad over the canal had been demonstrated. Construction of railways to meet local needs was a task that many communities believed they could undertake independently of state aid, particularly if municipal, township, or county governments extended assistance to private companies.[29] This enthusiasm for railroads was heightened by another force: the infusion of eastern capital into western railroad construction and reorganization after 1845-46. Foreign investors, too (particularly the English), showed renewed interest after 1852 in purchasing railroad bonds or local-government securities issued for railroad aid.[30] Moreover, in the canal states the railroad promised to liberate urban centers and regions that had formerly been at the mercy of geographic conditions. Limitations of terrain that had characterized canal planning were no longer relevant, a change that urban leadership was quick to comprehend. The new railroad technology reopened the critical question of which city would dominate trade in each region of the Old Northwest. As Chicago, Milwaukee, and St. Louis battled for control of the Mississippi Valley trade in the most spectacular western urban rivalry, so too in every area of the West towns competed for positions on the new railroads and for hegemony in local trade areas.[31]

Most of the projected western railroads were designed at first to serve primarily local needs and objectives. This fact explains the enthusiasm with which communities, small and large, supported private railroad companies with public aid.[32] Among the arguments of railroad promoters seeking local subscriptions and public assistance were many that had become familiar in the canal era. Multiple market outlets were a major objective of many communities, and numerous railroad schemes were designed to free towns from "monopoly" conditions, under which they were tributary to a single market; in the same way, the state canal programs had been designed to open alternate markets to western producers formerly dependent upon the New Orleans outlet. Established metropolitan centers, such as Cleveland and Cincinnati, extended municipal aid to railroads in an effort to multiply and extend their transport radii or to obtain all-rail connections with the East. Some railroad promoters even advertised their projects as potential links in transcontinental systems that would carry the trade of Asia and the Far West through a particular town or village. And by the early fifties there had emerged the well-known competition among major cities for designation as the eastern terminus of a land-grant transcontinental railway.[33] Less pretentious communities sought places on the new railroad lines merely to survive, or else to overcome advantages enjoyed by rival towns on canals or rivers.[34]

Indicative of the emphasis upon local objectives in railroad promotion was the ambivalent western attitude toward eastern influence. The western railroad promoter was usually quite willing to accept financial assistance from established railroad companies, and he eagerly solicited eastern investment in bonds or stock. But he generally had to rely in the first instance upon local resources, public and private; and the prospect that outsiders might control the enterprise could hinder seriously his efforts to raise funds locally. One Ohio railroad organizer, for example, argued with his fellow promoters in 1851 that it was inadvisable to employ an engineer from the East to locate the line. Local people would, he said, suspect "that this Eastern man would come here with Eastern habits, feelings, associations and *interests,* the effect of which must be, to give everything an Eastern aspect."[35] In the same vein, the president of the New Albany and Salem Railroad in Indiana wrote in 1852 that because most of the stockholders lived along the route, the company was protected from "the prejudice that exists in the public mind in many places against [railroads], where they are looked upon as monopolies owned and managed by persons having no interests or sympathies in common with them."[36] Yet two of the strongest arguments employed by western railroad promoters to secure local support were that their roads might one day merge with others to form a large integrated system or that they might bring an eastern main line to the sponsoring communities.[37]

Western railroad entrepreneurs skillfully induced and exploited local rivalries, as state canal authorities had once done, by soliciting subscriptions or donations from communities on alternative routes. One may trace the routes of many early western railroads by naming the towns and counties (seldom on a straight line!) that extended public aid. Similarly, the major eastern trunk lines—notably the Pennsylvania and the Baltimore and Ohio—gave financial support to several parallel-running western railroads, thereby stimulating competition among rival communities on all the routes thus aided.[38]

Private financing and public aid at the local level were critical determinants of the pace and character of western railroad expansion. Urban rivalry continued to find expression, however, in the arena of the state legislatures. Debate over charters often involved bitter conflict over routes; and in some cases railroad interests would block altogether the chartering of rival companies.[39]

Opposition to local aid was scattered, and not until 1851 in Ohio and long afterward in other western states was it effective. Urban leaders did occasionally divide over the question of priority in allocation of funds among several companies competing for a town's patronage. A few opponents of aid took an ideological position, condemning public assistance of any kind. There were also some instances of urban-rural conflict, with farming areas opposing county aid to railroads which, they averred, would merely enhance the wealth of already affluent market towns. The farm-mortgage railroad subscriptions notorious in Wisconsin—and to a lesser extent in Illinois—testify eloquently, however, to the fact that rural opposition to railroads was by no means universal. Finally, there were some instances of rivalry involving towns within counties, with several vying for connections on the route of a railroad seeking county aid.[40]

The results of generous public and private support of western railroads were highly uneven. Whether or not their railroad stock paid dividends, many communities were amply rewarded by commercial advantages conferred by the new transport lines.[41] But precisely because the objectives of western railway promotion had been defined within a context of local ambitions, the reaction was severe when these ambitions were frustrated. Throughout the Old Northwest the people resisted payment on bonds and subscriptions that aided railroads never built or which once built had fallen victim to bankrupt reorganization. Sometimes there was violence, as in Athens, Ohio, where townspeople tore up the tracks of the Marietta and Cincinnati Railroad, which had bypassed the town even though its citizens had voted for county aid to the company.[42] In the 1850's there appeared anti-railroad sentiment that presaged the Granger movement, a sentiment stimulated by resentment against emergent eastern dominance over railroads built initially with local aid; the outsiders often imposed rates unfavorable to the western communities that had helped build the roads.[43]

Whether or not the objectives of westerners who supported early railroads were later frustrated, the debates over transportation heightened urban community consciousness and sharpened local pride in many western towns. The issues concerning internal improvements that dominated town politics over many years constantly forced farmers and urban residents alike to re-examine their local interests, needs, and hopes in a period of rapid change in the West.

What occurred in the Old Northwest in the period 1820-60 also characterized development of the national transportation system in the pre-Civil War years: localism and regionalism were so strong that they rendered impossible any comprehensive, rational planning of a system of internal improvements.[44] A . . . transport map of the West in 1860 . . . [would reveal] the gross absurdities of parallel lines and over-dense construction in many areas. The highly rational response of western leaders to their communities' transport needs had led to a highly irrational result. But the western transport network included many lines of communication, built mainly with the resources of state and local government, that were vital in the development of a national economy. And the growth of this transport network had been influenced significantly by the effects of urban and regional rivalry.

NOTES

1. Richard C. Wade, *The Urban Frontier: The Rise of Western Cities, 1790-1830* (Cambridge, Mass., 1959), *passim*, especially 322-336. It was a signal feature of western urban rivalry in the early nineteenth century that it often mattered little whether competing towns were populated or not. Given the nature of frontier politics and town-site speculation, the "paper village" might have great political strength in the territorial or state legislature, or even at Washington.
2. See Francis P. Weisenburger, "The Urbanization of the Middle West: Town and Village in the Pioneer Period," *Indiana Magazine of History*, XLI (1945), 19-30.
3. Wade, *The Urban Frontier*, 336.
4. For useful discussions of regionalism, see Louis Hartz, *Economic Policy and Democratic Thought: Pennsylvania, 1776-1860* (Cambridge, Mass., 1948), 14-21, and Louis Wirth, *Community Life and Social Policy: Selected Papers*, edited by E. W. Marvick and A. J. Reiss, Jr. (Chicago, 1956), *passim*, especially 160-161, 166-169. See also Harvey S. Perloff and others, *Regions, Resources, and Economic Growth* (Baltimore, 1960). Two seminal studies are Frederick Jackson Turner, *The United States, 1830-1850* (New York, 1935), and Arthur M. Schlesinger, "The City in American History," *Mississippi Valley Historical Review*, XXVII (1940), 43-66.
5. Harry N. Scheiber, "The Ohio Canal Movement, 1820-1825," *Ohio Historical Quarterly*, LXIX (1960), 231-256.
6. *Ibid.*, 249-250. The Portsmouth-Cleveland canal was named the Ohio Canal in 1825; in 1849 the designation Ohio and Erie Canal became official.
7. Jacob Blickensderfer to Micajah T. Williams, June 23, 1825. Micajah T. Williams Papers, Ohio

State Library, Columbus. See also *Senate Journal*, 31 Ohio General Assembly, 1 sess., 340.
8. Among the side cuts aided by private contributions were the Granville Feeder and the Dresden Feeder. The Lancaster Lateral Canal, a twelve-mile feeder from Lancaster to the Ohio and Erie Canal, was constructed by a private company. There is evidence in the Lancaster Lateral Canal Company minutes that direct profits were not expected. Lancaster Lateral Canal Company Records, John T. Brasee Papers, Ohio Historical Society.
9. *House Journal*, 24 Ohio General Assembly, 1 sess., 280-281; John C. Parish, *Robert Lucas* (Iowa City, Iowa, 1907), 91; Ebenezer Buckingham to E. A. Brown, July 21, 1828, Ethan Allen Brown Papers, Ohio State Library.
10. William Steele to Canal Commission, January 16, 1830, Micajah T. Williams to Mayor of Chillicothe, April 5, 1830, Jesse Fulton to Alfred Kelley, April 15, 1830, and correspondence of 1829-30, *passim*, in Canal Commission Papers, State Archives, Ohio Historical Society. For a later neighborhood rivalry, albeit of a somewhat different nature, see H. J. Stratton, "The Northern Cross Railroad," *Journal of the Illinois State Historical Society*, XXVIII (1935), 17-19.
11. Scheiber, "Ohio Canal Movement," 254; B. M. Atherton and others to Alfred Kelley, May 17, 1826, Canal Commission Papers.
12. See the report of the select committee on a Sandusky-Dayton railroad charter in *Senate Journal*, 29 Ohio General Assembly, 1 sess., 364ff. See also Ohio Auditor of State, *Annual Report, 1835*, 16; E. L. Bogart, *Internal Improvements and State Debt in Ohio* (New York, 1924), 47ff.; and C. P. McClelland and C. C. Huntington, *History of the Ohio Canals* (Columbus, 1905), 38ff.
13. "The Dayton people are opposed to the extension of 'their Canal,' " a federal land officer reported in 1832. Thomas Van Horne to Peyton Symmes, August 23, 1832, Miscellaneous Letters File, Ohio Auditor's Office, Records Room. See also Charles Anthony and Simpson Mason to Commissioners of Canal Fund, a broadside dated March 1833, in the same place. The regional voting pattern on the issue of canal extension versus state aid to the railroad is confirmed by a vote of March 1, 1831, in *House Journal*, 29 Ohio General Assembly, 1 sess., 600-601. For the Mad River Railroad, see Leola Stewart, "Sandusky: Pionner Link Between Sail and Rail," *Ohio State Archaeological and Historical Quarterly*, LVII (1948), 227-236.
14. *Piqua Gazette*, March 2, 1831. The entire controversy may be traced in the *Gazette* from February 1831 to December 1833.
15. So reported by a member of the legislature. Leicester King to Simon Perkins, February 11, 1835. Simon Perkins Papers, Western Reserve Historical Society, Cleveland.
16. Bogart, *Internal Improvements and State Debt in Ohio*, 47ff. See also Carter Goodrich, *Government Promotion of American Canals and Railroads* (New York, 1960), 134-138.

17. Joseph Barker and others to Canal Commission, August 14, 1838. Canal Commission Papers. On the Dresden-Zanesville conflict, see petition of July 31, 1838, in the same place, and Ohio Canal Commission, *15th Annual Report* (Columbus, 1839), 17-19.

18. H. S. Knapp, *History of the Maumee Valley* (Toledo, 1876), 557-558; John W. Weatherford, "The Short Life of Manhattan, Ohio," *Ohio Historical Quarterly*, LXV (1956), 381-382.

19. *Ibid.*; Micajah T. Williams to E. A. Brown, September 2, 1836, Brown Papers; Williams to Leander Ransom, August 1, 1840, Williams Papers.

20. Indiana Canal Commission to Benjamin Tappan, June 16, 1835, Canal Commission Papers; Logan Esarey, *Internal Improvements in Early Indiana* (Indiana Historical Society, *Publications*, V, No. 2, Indianapolis, 1912), 87-98.

21. I. A. Lapham, *Wisconsin: Its Geography and Topography* (Milwaukee, 1846), 46. Theodore Calvin Pease, *The Frontier State, 1818-1848* (C. W. Alvord, ed., *The Centennial History of Illinois*, II, Chicago, 1922), Chap. 10; John H. Krenkel, *Illinois Internal Improvements, 1818-1848* (Cedar Rapids, Iowa, 1958), 34ff.

22. Jesse Williams to Micajah T. Williams, January 12, 23, 1835. Micajah T. Williams Papers. See also John D. Barnhart and D. F. Carmony, *Indiana: From Frontier to Industrial Commonwealth* (New York, 1954), I, 291-292.

23. R. Carlyle Buley, *The Old Northwest: Pioneer Period, 1815-1840* (Bloomington, Ind., 1954), II, 299-300; Goodrich, *Government Promotion of Canals and Railroads*, 138-147; Esarey, *Internal Improvements in Early Indiana*, 105-106; Pease, *The Frontier State*, 216-217.

24. For the manner in which projects promoted in response to initial undertakings of the states helped produce the "long swing" characteristic of canal construction, see Carter Goodrich and others, *Canals and American Economic Development* (New York, 1962), 176-179.

25. Ohio Board of Public Works, *Special Report . . . Relative to the Toll Charged on Salt . . . January 29, 1848* (Columbus, 1948), 5. For a full discussion of this problem, see Harry N. Scheiber, "The Rate-Making Power of the State in the Canal Era: A Case Study," *Political Science Quarterly*, LXXVII (1962), 397-413.

26. Atkins & Blair to Board of Public Works, December 9, 1843; Cincinnati Chamber of Commerce petition, June 20, 1845; Collins Brown & Co. and others petition, January 1, 1848; G. W. Addams to John Waddle, February 19, 1859. Board of Public Works Papers, State Archives, Ohio Historical Society.

27. Ohio Board of Public Works, *Special Report . . . January 29, 1848*, 7; correspondence with Ohio salt manufacturers, 1840-49, *passim*, Board of Public Works Papers. See also Cleveland petition, October 2, 1858, in the same place.

28. Carter Goodrich, "The Revulsion Against Internal Improvements," *Journal of Economic History*, X (1950), 145-151.

29. For example, Alphonso Taft, *A Lecture on Cincinnati and Her Rail-Roads* (Cincinnati, 1850), 12. See also Carter Goodrich, "Local Planning of Internal Improvements," *Political Science Quarterly*, LXVI (1951), 431ff.

30. Alfred D. Chandler, Jr., "Patterns of American Railroad Finance, 1830-1850," *Business History Review*, XXVIII (1954), 258-259; Ralph W. Hidy and Muriel E. Hidy, "Anglo-American Merchant Bankers and the Railroads of the Old Northwest, 1848-1860," *ibid.*, XXXIV (1960), 154ff.

31. The St. Louis-Chicago-Milwaukee rivalry is discussed in W. W. Belcher, *The Economic Rivalry Between St. Louis and Chicago, 1850-1880* (New York, 1947), and Bayrd Still, *Milwaukee: The History of a City* (Madison, Wis., 1948). For a discussion of Cincinnati and her railroads in the 1850's, see Sherry Hessler, " 'The Great Disturbing Cause' and the Decline of the Queen City," *Historical and Philosophical Society of Ohio, Bulletin*, XX (1962), 169-185.

32. This was a national, not merely a western phenomenon. See George R. Taylor and Irene Neu, *The American Railroad Network* (Cambridge, Mass., 1956), 3-6, and Goodrich, "Local Planning of Internal Improvements," 437ff.

33. Goodrich, "Local Planning of Internal Improvements," 437-438; Herbert W. Rice, "Early Rivalry Among Wisconsin Cities for Railroads," *Wisconsin Magazine of History*, XXXV (1951), 10-15; Carrie Cropley, "When the Railroads Came to Kenosha," *ibid.*, XXXIII (1949), 189-191; Dwight L. Agnew, "Beginning of the Rock Island Lines," *Journal of the Illinois State Historical Society*, XLVI (1953), 413-415; Wylie J. Daniels, *The Village at the End of the Road* (Indianapolis, 1938), 57-58; O. Morrow and F. W. Bashore, *Historical Atlas of Paulding County, Ohio* (Madison, Wis., 1892), 24-25.

34. For an example, see Thomas D. Brock, "Paw Paw Versus the Railroads," *Michigan History*, XXXIX (1955), 129-131.

35. Samuel Carpenter to John T. Brasee, May 17, 1851. Brasee Papers.

36. Quoted in Frank F. Hargrave, *A Pioneer Indiana Railroad: The Origin and Development of the Monon* (Indianapolis, 1932), 33-34.

37. Daniel Kilgore to Thomas Swan, December 26, 1849, Kilgore Papers, Ohio Historical Society; Cleveland and Mahoning Railroad, *Annual Report, 1852* (Cleveland, 1853), 27; Fayette B. Shaw, "Transportation in the Development of Joliet and Will County," *Journal of the Illinois State Historical Society*, XXX (1937), 119ff.

38. Hargrave, *A Pioneer Indiana Railroad*, 37ff.; Walter R. Marvin, "The Steubenville and Indiana Railroad," *Ohio Historical Quarterly*, LXVI (1957), 17; William P. Smith, *The Book of the Great Railway Celebrations of 1857* (New York, 1858), *passim*; H. W. Schotter, *Growth and Development of the Pennsylvania Railroad Company* (Philadelphia, 1927), 36-38; Ohio Commissioner of Railroads, *Report, 1870*, I, 477-492; Alice E. Smith, ed., "Wisconsin's First Railroad: Linsey

Letters, 1852," *Wisconsin Magazine of History*, XXX (1947), 349.

39. Paul W. Gates, *The Illinois Central Railroad and Its Colonization Work* (Cambridge, Mass., 1934), Chap. 3; Agnew, "Beginning of the Rock Island Lines," 411; Daniels, *Village at the End of the Road*, 65-68; Victor M. Bogle, "New Albany," *Indiana Magazine of History*, L (1954), 160.

40. Kathleen B. Jacklin, "Local Aid to Railroads in Illinois, 1848-1870" (unpublished M.A. thesis, Cornell University, 1958), 68ff.; Luther M. Feeger, *The History of Transportation in Wayne County, Indiana* (reprinted from *Richmond* [Indiana] *Palladium-Item*, 1953-54), installment of September 3, 1953; Frederick Merk, *Economic History of Wisconsin During the Civil War Decade* (Madison, Wis., 1916), 238-270.

41. The citizens of Mansfield, Ohio, subscribed about $500,000 to railroad stock; nearly all of it was lost by 1870, yet a county official declared they were "unanimous in the opinion that it is money well spent." Ohio Railroad Commissioner, *Report, 1870*, II, 322.

42. Thomas W. Lewis, *History of Southeastern Ohio* (Chicago, 1928), I, 612-613. See also Ohio Railroad Commissioner, *Report, 1870*, II, 321. Estimates of the amounts of local aid extended to railroads in the Old Northwest appear in Goodrich, *Government Promotion of Canals and Railroads*, 137-148.

43. Thus the Cincinnati Chamber of Commerce complained of "the manner in which the great [railroads] discriminate against the city which helped to build them, on the ground they would help to build up her interests." William Smith, *Annual Statement of the Trade and Commerce of Cincinnati, 1860* (Cincinnati, 1860), 25. See also *Kalida* (Ohio) *Venture*, March 3, 1854, and Ohio General Assembly, Senate, *Report of the Standing Committee on Railroads* (n.p., [1861]), 2.

44. See unsigned review (by Charles Francis Adams) in *North American Review*, LI (1840), 320-321, and Goodrich, *Government Promotion of Canals and Railroads*, 45.

The Businessman as City Booster

DANIEL J. BOORSTIN

The American businessman—a product (and a maker) of the upstart cities of the American West between the Revolution and the Civil War—was not an American version of the enterprising European city banker or merchant or manufacturer. Not an American Fugger or Medici or Rothschild or Arkwright, he was something quite different. His career and his ideals are an allegory of an American idea of community, for he was born and bred in the dynamic American urbanism in the period of our greatest growth.

The changing meaning of his very name, "businessman," gives us a clue. In 18th-century England to say someone was a "man of business" was primarily to say he engaged in public affairs. Thus David Hume in 1752 described Pericles as "a man of business." Before the end of the 18th century the expression had begun to lose this, its once primary meaning, and instead to describe a person engaged in mercantile transactions; it became a loose synonym for "merchant." But our now common word "businessman" seems to have been American in origin. It came into use around 1830 in the very period

From Daniel J. Boorstin, *The Americans: The National Experience* (New York: Random House, 1965), pp. 115-23. Copyright © 1965 by Daniel J. Boorstin. Reprinted by permission of Random House, Inc. Daniel J. Boorstin is Preston and Sterling Morton Professor of American History at the University of Chicago.

when the new Western cities were founded and were growing most rapidly. Even a casual look at this early American businessman, who he was, what he was doing, and how he thought of his work, will show how inaccurate it would be to describe him as simply a man engaged in mercantile transactions. We might better characterize him as a peculiarly American type of community maker and community leader. His starting belief was in the interfusing of public and private prosperity. Born of a social vagueness unknown in the Old World, he was a distinctive product of the New.

The new fast-growing city, where nothing had been before, a city with no history and unbounded hopes, was the American businessman's first natural habitat. In the period when he first appeared, his primary commodity was land and his secondary commodity transportation. This transformation of land rights and transport rights from political symbols and heirlooms into mere commodities was also an American phenomenon.

The businessman's characteristics would appear in the story of any one of the thousands who made their fortunes in the early 19th century. "I was born close by a saw-mill," boasted William B. Ogden (1805-77), "was early left an orphan, was cradled in a sugar-trough, christened in a mill-pond, graduated at a log-school-house, and at fourteen fancied I could do any thing I turned my hand to, and that nothing was impossible, and ever since, madame, I have been trying to prove it, and with some success." He was destined to be an upstart businessman on a heroic scale. Born into a leading local family in a small town in the Catskills in New York, he was actively dealing in real

estate before he was fifteen. Before thirty he was elected to the New York Legislature on a program to construct the New York & Erie Railroad with State aid. He was a great booster for his State, to whose growth he called the new railroad essential. "Otherwise," he argued "the sceptre will depart from Judah. The Empire State will no longer be New York. . . . Philadelphia is your great rival, and, if New York is idle, will gather in the trade of the great west."

But Ogden's enthusiasm for New York was not immovable. In 1835, the very year when the money was appropriated for the New York & Erie Railroad, he met some Eastern investors who had formed the American Land Company. They had already shown the foresight to invest heavily in Chicago real estate. One of these was Charles Butler, a politically and philanthropically minded lawyer of Albany, who married Ogden's sister. Butler himself (once a clerk in the law office of Martin Van Buren) was an energetic promoter of real estate and railroads. A man of wide public interests, he was a founder of Hobart College and of Union Theological Seminary, and an early supporter of New York University, among his other community works. He asked Ogden to go to Chicago to manage his interests. Ogden then joined in the purchase of considerable tracts there.

William B. Ogden arrived in Chicago in June, 1835. The town census showed a population of 3265, almost all of whom had come since 1832 (when the settlement had numbered under a hundred). Quickly Ogden transferred his extravagant hopes from the Empire State to the City of Chicago. In 1837, when Chicago was incorporated, Ogden was elected its first mayor, and the city census counted 4170—an increase of almost thirty per cent in two years.

"He could not forget," one of Ogden's fellow businessmen observed, "that everything which benefitted Chicago, or built up the great West, benefitted him. Why should he?" His commodity was land, whose value rose with the population. And Chicago now grew as few cities had ever grown before. The population approximately trebled, decade after decade: from 29,963 in 1850, to 109,260 in 1860, and to 298,977 in 1870. Chicago held over half a million people in 1880 and over a million by 1890, when it was already the second city on the continent. Meanwhile, real-estate values, especially in choice locations such as those Ogden was shrewd enough to buy, rose even more spectacularly. Men like Ogden proudly recorded their business success as the best evidence of their faith in their city. "In 1844," Ogden recalled, "I purchased for $8000, what 8 years thereafter, sold for 3 millions of dollars, and these cases could be extended almost indefinitely." Property he had bought in 1845 for $15,000 only twenty years later was worth ten million dollars. Successes were so common and so sudden, it was hard to know where fact ended and where fable began. Some of this purchasing was, of course, sheer speculative mania. The Chicago *American* (April 23, 1836) boasted of a piece of city property sold for $96,700 which, in romanticized arithmetic, they said had "risen in value at the rate of *one hundred per cent per* DAY, on the original cost ever since [1830], embracing a period of *five years* and a half."

Not to boost your city showed both a lack of community spirit and a lack of business sense. "Perhaps, the most striking trait of his character," a con-

temporary remembered of Ogden, "was his absolute faith in Chicago. He saw in 1836, not only the Chicago of today, but in the future the great City of the continent. From that early day, his faith never wavered. Come good times—come bad times—come prosperity or adversity —Chicago booming, or Chicago in ashes, its great future was to him a fixed fact." Quite naturally Ogden became a leader in community affairs, and within a few years Chicagoans called him their "representative man."

There was hardly a public improvement in which he did not play a leading role. He built the first drawbridge across the Chicago river, laid out and opened many miles of streets in the north and west parts of the city, promoted the Illinois and Michigan Canal and advocated laws for its construction and enlargement, projected and built thousands of miles of railroads serving Chicago, and did a great deal to develop Chicago's water supply, sewage system, and parks. More than a hundred miles of streets and hundreds of bridges were built at the private expense of Ogden and his real-estate clients. He helped introduce the McCormick reaping and mowing machines into the West, and helped build the first large factory for their manufacture. He was the first president of Rush Medical College (the first institution of its kind in Chicago), a charter member of the Chicago Historical Society, president of the Board of Trustees of the first "University of Chicago," and one of the first directors of the Merchants Loan and Trust Company (1857). He was elected to the Illinois Senate by the Republicans in 1860. He supported the Theological Seminary of the Northwest, the Academy of Sciences, and the Astronomical Society. The French historian Guizot only slightly exaggerated when he said Ogden had built and owned Chicago.

Characteristic also was Ogden's interest in improving transportation. An upstart community, a community of boosters measuring itself by its rate of growth, depended on transportation in a new way. Settled communities of the Old World—Bordeaux, Lyon, Manchester, or Birmingham—especially when, as in the early 19th century, they were fast becoming industrial towns, needed transportation to feed raw materials and labor to their factories and to take away finished products. But Chicago and the other upstart cities of the American West needed it for their very lifeblood. In the Old World a city might grow or decline, prosper or languish, depending on its transportation, among other facilities. But here, without transportation there was no city at all.

An American city had to "attract" people. The primary community service was to make it easier, cheaper, and pleasanter for people to join your community. In all this, too, William B. Ogden was a paragon, for he pioneered the railroads. One of the first to run out of Chicago was the Galena & Chicago Union Railroad, built to connect Chicago with the great Mississippi River traffic. Chicago businessmen bought a controlling interest in 1846, and tried to raise money from local citizens to complete the railroad. Ogden worked hard to obtain numerous individual subscriptions in small amounts. This, its first railroad, opened a new era in the life and expansion of Chicago. Citizens subscribed its stock "as a public duty, and not as an investment." "Railroads," one of Ogden's collaborators later boasted, "were built as public enterprises, and not as money-making speculations. They were regarded as great highways con-

structed by the people, either at the expense of the government or by means of private capital, to accommodate the public, and not for the especial benefit of the stockholders." In April, 1849, the first locomotive started west from Chicago on the Galena line.

Ogden took the lead in promoting many more railroads for Chicago. In 1853 he was a director of the Pittsburg, Ft. Wayne & Chicago Railroad; in 1857, president of the Chicago, St. Paul & Fond-du-Lac Railroad which later became part of the Chicago & Northwestern Railroad, of which he was also president (1859-68). A transcontinental railroad with Chicago as the great junction was, of course, his dream. In 1850 he presided over the National Railway Convention and, on the organization of the Union Pacific Company in 1862, its first president was William B. Ogden.

The Ogden story was re-enacted a thousand times all over America—wherever there were upstart cities. Scenes were different, stakes smaller, and dimensions less heroic, but the plot everywhere was much the same. Here was a new breed: the community builder in a mushrooming city where personal and public growth, personal and public prosperity intermingled.

Another example was Dr. Daniel Drake (1785-1852), born in New Jersey, and raised in Kentucky, whose family sent him when he was only fifteen to study in the offices of a leading physician of the small town of Ft. Washington (later called Cincinnati). Within a few years he himself became the town's most prominent practitioner. He opened a drug store where, in 1816, he pioneered in the sale of artificial mineral water; soon he was also running a general store. His *Picture of Cincinnati in 1815*, with its full statistics, and its vivid account of the archaeology, topography, climate, and promise of the city, was translated and circulated widely abroad. Drake, in his own way, was as much a booster as Ogden; using subtler techniques of precise and calculated understatement, he produced the first detailed account of an upstart city. Many believed him when he concluded that small towns like Cincinnati were "destined, before the termination of the present century, to attain the rank of populous and magnificent cities." Drake had established himself in the high noon of Cincinnati prosperity, before the Panic of 1819.

Drake's boosterism was as energetic as Ogden's. Hoping to make Cincinnati a great medical center in 1819, he founded the Ohio Medical College (later the Medical College of the University of Cincinnati). He did a great deal to promote all kinds of community enterprises: the Commercial Hospital and Lunatic Asylum, the eye infirmary, the circulating library, the teacher's college. He helped plan and develop canals and he promoted railroads leading toward the South, which included the successful municipal line, the Cincinnati Southern Railway.

Still another example with a more western habitat was General William Larimer (1809-75). Born and raised in Pennsylvania, he tried many different businesses around Pittsburgh: a general store, a freight service, horse trading, a coal company, a wholesale grocery, his father's hotel, railroads, and banking. When he lost everything in the depression of 1854, Larimer, quickly resolving to start afresh farther west, was in Nebraska the very next spring. There he too became the instantaneous booster of a town which did not yet exist. We have an intimate record in letters he sent east. On May 23, 1855:

I have taken two claims at La Platte, Nebraska Territory . . . and we are laying out a town. I am elected President of the Company, and secured ⅓ of the town. . . . I like this country very much indeed. . . . I think I can make a big raise here in a few years.

Already he claimed a good chance of being elected to Congress from Nebraska. Within a week his optimism had risen still higher: he planned to pay off his creditors with town lots, for he owned a thousand acres within the proposed city.

Now my plan is this: I intend to live in La Platte City. I intend to open up a large farm. I can raise hemp, corn or anything. . . . I will go on with the farm and if the land is ever wanted for a town it is ready. . . . I intend not only to farm simply but I will open a Commission House. I expect to supply the Territory with iron nails, lumber, etc., this will not only be profitable in itself but will be the great means of building up the city. If I go there I can build the city if I do not go only to sell lots as the city may never rise.

Larimer expected the transcontinental railroad to go through La Platte, but this proved a miscalculation. Then, after a heavy winter, the town suffered deep spring floods. "We were not long in coming to the conclusion that La Platte was doomed as a town site." The pattern of western hope was all-or-nothing.

From La Platte, Larimer moved on to Omaha. There he lived in a prefabricated house that had actually been framed in Pittsburgh, knocked down and shipped out in 1856. When Omaha, too, looked unpromising (as it did within less than two years) he moved to Leavenworth, Kansas. This was in 1858, just in time for him to learn of the discovery of gold at Cherry Creek by Pike's Peak. Unwilling to wait for the better traveling conditions of the following spring, Larimer and his son immediately made up a party and left that fall. After a forty-seven-day trip, the Larimers were among the first to arrive at the mouth of Cherry Creek, where they found two dozen cabins under construction. This, the first settlement in Colorado, was named Auraria. Larimer's son recorded the events of November 17, 1858:

On our very first night here, my father, without consulting anyone outside of our own Leavenworth Party, packed his blankets and some provisions, left camp and crossed the Creek to pick out a new site. He left instructions for us to get up the oxen and join him, as he believed the east side of the Creek was much the best location for a town and no one in the country laid claim to it, or if so had abandoned it and left the country. . . . When we finally reached the eastern side of Cherry Creek, we found him near the bank with a camp fire awaiting us. He had 4 cottonwood poles crossed, which he called the foundation of his settlement and claimed the site for a town,—for *the* town which has now grown into the one of which Colorado is the proudest.

This time Larimer chose well. He had located on the site of Denver.

At first there was competition between the sites on either side of Cherry Creek. Then the stockholders combined and became a single city named Denver (in honor of the Virginian who had become Governor of the Kansas Territory) in 1860. "I am Denver City," Larimer wrote in a letter in February 1859. And his whole later career proved the extraordinary ability of the American businessmen of these upstart cities to fuse themselves and their destiny with that of their community—at least so long as the community remained prosperous or promising.

At the beginning Larimer had been put in charge of the town and made "Donating Agent," which authorized him to give two city lots to anyone who would build a cabin there measuring at least 16 by 16 feet. He promoted a good hotel and gave valuable shares to men "who were already or could be induced to become interested in the welfare of the city and might be influential in bringing a stage line into the country with Denver as its objective point." He encouraged the founding of drugstores, general stores, sawmills, and newspapers. Complaining that the town lacked the ultimate convenience, he finally helped organize a cemetery.

Examples could be multiplied. But even these three—Ogden, Drake, and Larimer—suggest the variety of opportunities, motives, and attitudes which created the new species *Businessman Americanus*. None of the characteristics of his American habitat was quite unique but their extreme American form and their American combination were.

Cities with no history. The upstart western cities were the rare examples of a dynamic urban environment where almost nothing had been pre-empted by history. Cities were proverbially the centers of institutions, where records were kept and the past was chronicled, hallowed, and enshrined. They were sites of palaces, cathedrals, libraries, archives, and great monuments of all kinds. The American upstart city, by contrast, had no past. At its beginning, it was free of vested interests, monopolies, guilds, skills, and "No Trespassing" signs. Here was the fluidity of the city —the spatial dimension of cosmopolitanism, movement, diversity, and change —but without the historical dimension. There were no ancient walls between classes, occupations, neighborhoods, and nationalities. The American upstart cities began without inherited neighborhood loyalties, without ghettos. "Everything," recalled Larimer, "was open to us."

Quick growth and high hopes. The pace of growth of the upstart cities fired imaginations. A town where nobody was ten years ago, but which today numbered thousands, might be expected to number tens or hundreds of thousands in a few decades. Mankind had required at least a million years to produce its first urban community of a million people; Chicagoans accomplished this feat in less than a century. Within a few days' wagon ride of Drake's Cincinnati, hundreds of towns were laid out, all guaranteed to have unrivalled advantages. Precisely one week after Larimer cut his four cottonwood poles on the future site of Denver, he wrote his wife back east that "we expect a second Sacramento City, at least." In 1834, H. M. Brackenridge noted, his Pittsburgh was changing so fast that anyone returned after ten years felt himself a stranger. He confidently foresaw that the settlement which had grown from village to big city in a quarter-century would very soon reach half a million. He could not be surprised that Cincinnati had grown from a forest to a city in thirteen years. He himself had hopes "of attaining, on the Ohio or Mississippi, distinction and wealth, with the same rapidity, and on the same scale, that those vast regions were expanding into greatness." The centennial history of St. Louis in 1876 called the city's site superior to that of any other in the world, and predicted that, when its railroad network was completed, it would outstrip Chicago and the eastern metropolises. "And yet, when this has been said, we have but commenced to tell of the wonders of a city destined in the future to equal London in its population, Athens in its philosophy, art and culture, Rome in its hotels, cathedrals, churches and grandeur, and to be the central commercial metropolis of a continent."

Community before government. On this landscape too it was normal to find communities before governments. Men in sudden urban proximity, bound together by specific, concrete purposes, first felt their common needs. Afterwards they called governments into being. From force of circumstance, then, government became functional. Early Chicagoans, and their upstart counterparts elsewhere, were not confronted with the problem of evading obsolete regulations or of transmuting time-honored tyrannies. They simply combined to provide their own water, their own sewage system, their own sidewalks, streets, bridges, and parks. They founded medical schools and universities and museums. Eager for these and other services, they created municipal governments and enlisted state and federal government aid. An upstart government had neither the odor of sanctity nor the odium of tyranny. It was a tool serving personal and community prosperity at the same time.

Intense and transferable loyalties. In upstart cities the loyalties of people were in inverse ratio to the antiquity of their communities, even to the point of absurdity. Older towns could point only to the facts of limited actual accomplishment, while the uncertain future was, of course, ever more promising. Ogden removed his enthusiasm from New York to Chicago; Larimer removed his from La Platte to Omaha to Leavenworth to Auraria to Denver. Men could do this in the twinkling of an eye, and without so much as a glance over the shoulder. Promise, not achievement, commanded loyalty and stirred the booster spirit. One was untrue to oneself and to the spirit of expanding

America if one remained enslaved to a vision which had lost its promise. The ghost town and the booster spirit were opposite sides of the same coin.

Competition among communities. The circumstances of American life in the upstart cities of the West produced a lively competitive spirit. But the characteristic and most fertile competition was a competition among communities. We have been misled by slogans of individualism. Just as the competition among colonial seaboard cities helped diffuse American culture and kept it from becoming concentrated in a European-style metropolis, so the competition among western upstart cities helped create the booster spirit. Where there had been no cities before, where all were growing fast, there was no traditional rank among urban centers. If Lexington, Kentucky, could quickly arise by 1800 to be the most populous city of the West, if St. Louis and Cincinnati and Chicago had so suddenly arisen, might not some new Lexington displace them all? Many of each community's institutions had been founded to give it a competitive advantage. Dr. Drake's medical college helped Cincinnati keep ahead of Lexington, just as Ogden's streets and bridges and parks helped Chicago lead Cincinnati. Where individual and community prosperity were so intermingled, competition among individuals was also a competition among communities.

         *   *   *

The emerging businessman of the upstart cities had much in common with the energetic American of an earlier generation. He was the Franklin of the West. He was the undifferentiated man of the colonial period, but in a more expansive setting. The new language of that day called him a "businessman"; the retrospective language of our century calls him the booster. He thrived on growth and expansion. His loyalties were intense, naive, optimistic, and quickly transferable.

Versatility was his hallmark. He usually had neither the advantages nor the disadvantages of specialized skills or monopolistic protection. In Dr. Drake's Cincinnati, physicians became merchants, clergymen became bankers, lawyers became manufacturers. "The young lawyer," H. M. Brackenridge shrewdly advised the Western seeker after fortune (in one of the first recorded uses of the word "businessman") "should think more of picking up his crumbs, than of flying like a balloon. He must be content to become a *business man*, and leave the rest to fortune." For success in this environment, the specialized skills—of lawyer, doctor, financier, or engineer—had a new unimportance. Rewards went to the organizer, the persuader, the discoverer of opportunities, the projector, the risk-taker, and the man able to attach himself quickly and profitably to some group until its promise was tested.

IV THE CITY IN THE AGE OF INDUSTRY

The emergence of the modern city, in the sixty years following the Civil War, parallels the unfolding of the Industrial Revolution in America. As Constance Green has written in her *Rise of Urban America*, "Which came first, the hen of mounting industrial strength or the egg of increasing urban influences, may be arguable, but the fact of profound change remains."

The question is not so much which came first but how they interacted with and buttressed each other. If railroads, heavy industries, and technological inventions helped build cities, urbanization in turn helped accelerate the hallmarks of industrialization: mass production, mass consumption, mass distribution of goods and services. If industrialization produced a more co-ordinated network of economic development, the network of cities became the muscles and sinews of that development—producing, selling, financing, and providing it with a market and a labor force. If industrialization meant increasing specialization, cities specialized: Cleveland with her oil, Pittsburgh with her steel, Milwaukee with her beer, Detroit with her automobiles, and Los Angeles with her sunshine. If the booming factories brought affluence along with shocking working conditions, labor violence, and corruption, the booming cities dramatized the irony of the Industrial Revolution: the collision between progress and poverty—the wealth of Wall Street, State Street, Montgomery Street, and the wretched streets of Cockroach Row, Hell's Kitchen, and the Barbary Coast. Together, the massive forces of industrialization and urbanization wrought a profound change that touched every aspect of American life: the transformation of a land of farms and villages into a nation of cities and towns. The watershed, the point of no return for an old agrarian America, was here by 1920, when the census returns showed that for the first time more than half the population lived in urban areas. Americans had moved to the city.

The city came of age in this period, but it was an era of mixed blessings for the older urban giants. New York became the Empire City, the largest city in the country. It "just growed." Philadelphia and St. Louis, like New York, fed by mass migrations, foreign and domestic, continued to expand, whereas Baltimore, Boston, and New Orleans declined. It was a boom time for the "big-little city," as Kansas City, Omaha, Denver, Birmingham, and San Francisco, began to take a more commanding position on the urban scene. If there was one city that best characterized the age of industry, it was the soaring Chicago. Only the eighth largest city in 1860, devastated by fire in 1871, it rose to become second only to New York in size and power by the last decade of the century. No one has caught the flair and fixed the image of the "City of the Big Shoulders" better than Carl Sandburg:

> Hog Butcher for the World,
> Tool Maker, Stacker of Wheat,
> Player with Railroads and the Nation's
>   Freight Handler;
> Laughing the stormy, husky, brawling
> Laughter of Youth. . . .

The emergence of the industrial city represented another stage of a phenomenon, begun in the colonial period, and extremely vital to us today, one that lies at the heart of American urban history—the city as a revolution in the nature of human settlement. This theme is fundamental to each of the following essays, and its significance and complexity is shaped as each author develops it with a different emphasis.

Blake McKelvey raises this question: how did the basic ingredients of nineteenth- and early twentieth-century industrialization—new sources of energy and raw materials, new supplies of labor and industrial skills, new machines and techniques of production—affect the emergence of the industrial city? He finds that the development was by no means uniform, in fact, there appeared a number of different *kinds* of industrial cities. One city would profit from one aspect of industrialization rather than another, some would flounder, others would blossom. Thus, some prospered as regional centers by controlling their hinterland, absorbing assessory industries, and extending urban economic services, like Pittsburgh. Others would exploit a near-by agricultural resource, as Milwaukee did with hops and beer, or Memphis in converting cotton into cottonseed oil. Many cities profited from cheap immigrant or migrant labor, such as the shoe industry in Philadelphia and New York, or the textile industries in New England and the South. Others used the specialities of skilled immigrant workers to enhance growth—witness Rochester with her clothing, shoe, nursery, brewing, and woodworking industries. Still others rose to urban distinction upon the ingenious inventions of clever men—the telephone, the elevator, the trolley car, the bicycle, built cities. The classic example is the automobile and Detroit. Other cities that could not adopt new industries or save old ones, or were plagued with absentee ownership or by-passed by the railroad, would wither away. At the close of the first decade of the twentieth century, the transition from commerce to industry as the main source of economic growth was completed. The result: urban monuments to industrial America—a leading industrial giant in its own right, now freed from dependence upon foreign factories and foreign investments.

Leon S. Marshall uses the comparative approach, enlarging our scope and decreasing our provincialism, by contrasting the American industrial city with its English counterpart. Although he points out their important similarities, he shatters any tight analogy between the two by underscoring some of their differences. He also stresses the disruptive influences of the city as an agent for the Industrial Revolution. It was not a pretty picture, as Pittsburgh ("hell with the lid off") or Manchester ("this pell-mell of society") posed new problems and enlarged old ones for the family, working conditions, the poor, crime, disease, and immorality. Bleak as life was for many of the nineteenth-century industrial cities, a more balanced view would contrast it to the farm and village of the time, which also offered its share of poverty, drudgery, disease, and immorality.[1]

To understand the industrial city, then, it is not enough for one either to interpret its role as a promotor of social evils—important as it was—or to see it primarily in economic terms as a center for business and industry. It must also be seen, as Ralph Turner suggests, as a center for cultural change. He argues that the industrial city was a "new element" in history because it was an agent of social change, a dynamic force that caused a reorientation of the traditional cultural structure of behavior and thought.

Seeing cultural history as a clash between the old and new in action and thought, an interaction involving dislocation and assimilation, a tension between innovation and clinging to the past, Turner defines the role of the industrial city as a social and psychological force affecting several areas of cultural change, such as nineteenth-century economic thought, modern technology, the decline of localism and tradition, patterns of both conformity and diversity in human behavior, and ideas about private property. His thesis is that the city, a new kind of human settlement, churned such waves of social change that it necessitated "a reëducation of the masses," who in moving to the city brought a traditional, "peasant" mentality not adequate to cope with the changes in the labor market, machine technology, and problems of urban association. Here, then, is a variation on a theme established earlier by Carl Bridenbaugh: the city introduced us to modern times.

1. See Dorothy George's provocative *England in Transition* (London: Penguin Books, 1953). For an excellent book employing the comparative approach to examine urbanization throughout the world, see Sylvia Fleis Faral (ed.), *Urbanism in World Perspective: A Reader* (New York: Thomas Y. Crowell, 1968).

If the foregoing essays suggest there are several ways to look at the emergence and impact of the industrial city, one enduring historical view has remained consistent from the nineteenth century to the present, embraced in varying degrees by both pro-urbanites and anti-urbanites; namely, the direct relationship between the growth of urbanization, industrialization, and the rise of the crime rate. Many a politician has marched to high office to the tune of "crime in the streets," "safety in the streets," not to mention, "law and order." It is an old tune, only the lyrics change. City-dwellers in the nineteenth century were also terrified as newspapers, magazines, books —and politicians—shrilly, sometimes hysterically, announced an ever increasing high tide of crime that might eventually, lacking better law and order, swamp the city. Since 1933, when criminal statistics were collected nationally for the first time, and the Federal Bureau of Investigation published its first annual statistical crime index, rhetoric has been backed by the seemingly irrefutable logic of cold hard statistical fact. Given the rise of organized crime, the turbulent decade of the 1960's with its riots, political assassinations, drug addiction, and the FBI with its "mounting crime waves," there seemed no question that rapid urbanization created a rising crime rate. One could almost expect to hear from the grave of Thomas Jefferson, an old anti-urbanite, a triumphant " 'I-told-you-so.' "

But an increasing number of scholars, including Daniel Bell,[2] Robert M. Cipes,[3] and Fred P. Graham,[4] have questioned both the validity of crime waves and the statistical integrity of the FBI indexes, for any number of reasons, including the notion that "figures never lie, but figurers do." Doubt invites an historical perspective, especially of the nineteenth-century industrial city, the seedbed of modern crime. This is given us in the next essay by Roger Lane, an historian who cut his scholarly teeth on a fine study of the Boston police.[5]

Choosing the state of Massachusetts and the city of Boston, Lane picked his area well. In a time (1822-1885) when reliable national statistics were difficult if not impossible to find, when city records were not conspicuous for their accuracy, state and local officials in Massachusetts had an "enormous appetite" for statistical information of all kinds and kept their records well. Moreover, with one large city and several smaller cities, Massachusetts

2. "The Myth of Crime Waves: The Actual Decline of Crime in United States," *The End of Ideology* (Glencoe: The Free Press, 1961).

3. *The Crime War* (New York: New American Library, 1968).

4. "A Contemporary History of American Crime," in Hugh Davis Graham and Ted Robert Gurr (eds.), *Violence in America*, Vol. 2 (Washington, D.C.: Superintendent of Documents, 1969). See also Fred P. Graham's *The Self-Inflicted Wound* (New York: Macmillan, 1970). Another interesting essay in Vol. 2 of the Graham-Gurr book is Sheldon Hackney's "Southern Violence."

5. *Policing the City: Boston, 1822-1885* (Cambridge: Harvard University Press, 1967).

served as an excellent model of the urban industrial experience. After carefully weighing his evidence, Lane comes to several stunning conclusions: (1) there is not a necessary or inevitable connection between the rise of the city and rising crime rates; (2) from the Civil War to the end of the century, as the cities became more industrialized and more urbanized, crime actually *decreased;* (3) urbanization itself was responsible for the decrease in crime because it was a means of absorbing, adjusting, and accommodating urban dwellers to the life of the city. Urbanism, in short, was a mechanism of socialization; it demanded more cooperative habits necessary for living successfully in the city. Lane leaves us with an insight sharply relevant to our own time. Criminal activity can never be measured with any precision by the degree of public opinion. Indeed, there is a kind of irony of hysteria: the crime rate has often decreased as the public's concern about crime has mounted.[6]

Joel Arthur Tarr looks at the industrial city in another way, asking different questions. He is interested in the spatial dynamics, the ecological and demographic patterns of the city, asking why did the industrial city take the shape it did. His answer: the decisive influence of the urban transportation system—the omnibus, the subway, the elevated railroad, and most especially, the streetcar[7]—which helped create the suburbs, disperse the population, concentrate commercial operations in the inner-city and, compared with the pretransit city, reverse the spatial distribution of the various socio-economic classes.

Today we hear much about the "urban transportation crisis." Automobiles clog the freeways, poison the air, and choke city streets meant for streetcars, and, in the case of Boston, cows. Subways become the survival of the meanest, buses carry only a drop in the bucket, and the cry is for rapid transit. Chicago tinkers with it, Washington thinks about it, Los Angeles avoids it, and San Francisco builds BART. As Tarr shows us in this historical analysis of urban transportation from 1840 to 1910, there is nothing new about either a sense of crisis or the demand for rapid transit. In the mid-nineteenth-century city, cities were still "walking" cities, small enough for a man to easily walk back and forth to work. But with the waves of immigrants from Europe and the migrants from the American hinterland, plus the growing multiplicity of factories, banks, stock-exchanges, hotels, and other enterprises, the crisis was on, it took longer to get to work, human congestion was the order of the day, and the call was for better transportation.

What makes this essay particularly interesting, is Tarr's analysis of the

6. For another phase of nineteenth-century crime, and one long ignored by historians, see Joseph M. Hawes, *Children in Urban Society: Juvenile Delinquency in Nineteenth-Century America* (New York: Oxford University Press, 1971).

7. See Joel A. Tarr, "Urban Pollution—Many Years Ago," *American Heritage* (October 1971).

rationale for better transportation. There were the economic arguments one might expect. Rapid transit would attract manufacturing, enhance real estate values, bulge the pockets of the city's businessmen and contractors. But what gave the argument its urgency, its intensity, its unflinching optimism was the fact that rapid transit was a pair of dice loaded with moral imperatives. Speedy transportation would solve the slum problem. Workingmen and the poor would be relocated from the evil city to the virtuous countryside. Suburbia was morally glamorized as a haven of clean air, bright sunshine, a decent place to live compared with the wicked city. To wit, rapid transit would deliver a solid one-two punch: congestion would be dissolved, a social problem would be solved. Tarr questions the motives of some of the suburbia hucksters as a diversionary tactic from the real problems of the slum, as a means of social control for the unwanted. Given the values of the time, however, rapid transit did alleviate congestion, widen housing opportunities, and give those who wanted it (and who could afford it) suburban amenities. For our own time, Tarr notes that the boosters of the automobile made some of the same promises. The elegant motor car would be the escape from the unheavenly city to the arcadian delights of suburban living. And then there was Los Angeles.

The Emergence of Industrial Cities

BLAKE McKELVEY

So many ambitious towns sprang up in the early days on each frontier that many were threatened with atrophy when the railroads enabled a few to stake out broad hinterlands at the expense of their neighbors. Only through industrial enterprise could most cities hope to prosper. Some enjoyed special opportunities as a result of the timely discovery of mineral resources nearby or at points easily reached by cheap water transport. A few achieved industrial leadership through the exploitation of local water power or by the invention of machinery to process regional products more efficiently. Others escaped a way-station fate because a steady flow of immigrants spurred residents to develop new industries based in part on cheap labor and to produce for a national market. Still others prospered through the manufacture of patented or specialty articles. Several combined these tactics, and all labored to produce a marketable surplus.[1]

The rise or decline of an individual

From *The Urbanization of America, 1860-1915* (New Brunswick, N. J.: Rutgers University Press, 1963), pp. 35-46. Reprinted by the permission of the publisher. Blake McKelvey has been City Historian of Rochester, New York, since 1948.

town was of major concern only to its promoters and its more settled residents; others could and did move elsewhere without loss. But the widespread survival of many threatened communities by means of industrial enterprise was of primary significance. A few such towns became the prototypes of the industrial city and endowed it with special characteristics. Several others pressed the advantages their manufacturing activities brought and did so with such vigor that they achieved metropolitan status; a few of these, notably Minneapolis, acquired regional hegemony. Moreover the emphasis they gave to industry forced their commercial rivals also to accord it increased attention. To promote these efforts, the business leaders of most communities reorganized old boards of trade or established new associations. By the turn of the century the industrial output of American cities had so outstripped that of any foreign country that the character of international trade was transformed, and with it the services performed by the great ports.

The industrialization of America is a separate story, but the impetus given to that development by the rise of the city cannot be overlooked.[2] The impetus given to industrialism by the rapid discovery and exploitation of the country's natural resources is more fully documented and understood, and so also is the effect of the great influx of immigrant workmen in this period.[3] Here, however, we are interested in the converse side of these historic movements—the contributions that new sources of energy and raw materials, new supplies of labor and industrial skills, new machines and techniques of production made to urban growth.

Because of their glamour, the successive gold rushes have long had a place in American history, yet their product never compared in value with that of the silver and copper mines and appeared insignificant when measured against the output of the iron and coal fields. Similar contrasts marked their respective towns. Gold-mining towns such as Virginia City were more pretentious than those based on silver and copper, but their permanence depended on the discovery nearby of "baser" metals. Not even the iron- and copper-mining camps became major cities (Butte, Montana, was a possible exception). Only where abundant supplies of coal or other fuels were found manufacturing encouraged and urban growth maintained.[4]

Even in the coal fields, few mining towns became major cities. In the hard-coal region of Pennsylvania, where the ore deposits extended over several counties, numerous settlements or "patches" sprang up about many colliery shafts, creating a density of as much as 1300 persons per square mile without achieving the integration essential for urban status. By 1900 only Scranton and Wilkes-Barre had exceeded 100,000 and 50,000 respectively, and this chiefly because they were not as exclusively occupied with mining as, for example, neighboring Hazleton, which barely numbered 25,000 a decade later. In fact Scranton, at the turn of the century, had more industrial workers than either miners or tradesmen.[5]

Generally a nearby commercial or industrial city supplied the marketing, banking, and other urban services for mining districts, thus strenghtening its claim to regional leadership. Sometimes a mining town developed a new industry to convert the products of neighboring collieries, as in the coke district around Uniontown and Brownville, only to see its control absorbed in time by a regional capital, in this case Pittsburgh.[6] Most mining communities, victims of absentee ownership and constricted by their specialty, failed to develop the internal leadership necessary to attract competing transport arteries or to tap new sources of credit.[7]

Other fuel strikes brought dubious benefits to communities at their sites, but presented great opportunities to the commercial marts that acquired control. The oil towns of northwestern Pennsylvania, which displayed great vitality during the seventies, were soon checked as monopoly control over refining and marketing siphoned the profits of the industry into the hands of Rockefeller and his colleagues in Cleveland and other processing centers.[8] Natural gas brought a sudden boom to several communities, notably Findlay and Toledo, Ohio, but their fortunes ebbed with the arrival of outside control.[9] Toledo, already an important railroad hub and advantageously situated for lake trade, remained primarily a regional market until civic leaders, reasserting the town's rights to its power resources, enabled industry finally to pull ahead of commerce and boost the city into the 100,000 bracket by the close of the period.[10]

Some cities prospered as processors of regional farm products. Minneapolis, a small neighbor of St. Paul in the seventies, captured leadership in the wheat belt of the Northwest during the eighties by developing mills able to produce a better flour from the spring wheat of that area than St. Louis or other rivals could mill from winter wheat. Kansas City won its independence from St. Louis and Chicago by building up its meat-packing industry. Milwaukee ventured with less success

into each of these fields but achieved its greatest triumph in the brewing industry, likewise based on products of the area. Memphis competed with many other places in lumber milling but excelled in the production of cotton-seed oil. Each of these and several like them strengthened their positions by developing accessory industries and by extending urban economic services to a hinterland which they constantly endeavored to expand. All attained metropolitan status chiefly because of their manufacturing services.[11]

Many cities, even when overshadowed by near neighbors, prospered through the employment of cheap immigrant labor.[12] The shoe industry, in which the introduction of machinery after the mid-century tended to supersede old craft skills, lent itself to this use. Lynn and Haverhill had developed a reputation for shoes in earlier decades, and after the Civil War Cincinnati and Rochester, among others, began to specialize in this field. New York and Philadelphia, because of their large markets and abundant supply of newcomers, became shoe producers, although not as important as the older New England centers, where the earlier craftsmen supervised a new work force of immigrants.[13]

But cheap labor, even when supplied from abroad, did not long remain content in America, and the shoe industry produced some of the most determined union-organizing drives of these decades. Unfortunately, from the viewpoint of the cities involved, when union demands mounted in one town, many firms (except those engaged in quality production) sought new sites, such as Milwaukee, Chicago, or Manchester, New Hampshire, where the organizers had not yet penetrated. The migration of shoe companies, facilitated by the practice of leasing rather than purchasing the machinery, presented a constant threat to cities in this field. It also provided an extreme example of the industrial mobility that contributed to both the diffusion and the fluidity of America's urban development.[14]

The textile industry, too, displayed an intense interest in cheap labor, but the range of its migrations was limited. Originally established at water-power sites in New England, where textiles nurtured several of the country's first factory towns, notably Lowell and Manchester, this industry quickly replaced its early native-born labor from the first influx of Irish and other immigrant groups, thus speeding the urbanization as well as the cosmopolitan transformation of the Yankee homeland. During the post-Civil War expansion, when steam began to supplement water power, Fall River pulled into the lead among textile centers because of its easy access to water-borne coal and its cheap immigrant labor, including that of women and children.[15] Some textile towns added other specialties; Chicopee developed tool shops and began to produce bicycles; Holyoke became a paper city; Lowell ventured into woolens, carpets, knitted products, and other enterprises. Successive waves of new immigrants—Polish, French Canadian, and Portuguese—enabled management to fight off many union demands; yet pressure from the workers and the restraints of labor legislation in America's second most urbanized commonwealth presented Massachusetts textile firms with an increasing disadvantage in competition with the new cotton mills of the South.[16]

The development of the textile industry in the South had a substantial economic basis. The slow spread of cotton factories in North and South Carolina and Georgia during post-Civil War years uncovered a new supply of cheap labor in the poor whites of the Piedmont area and began in the eighties to attract northern capital, some of it from the New England firms themselves. Advances in technology—the Northrop automatic loom and the ring spindle, which eliminated the skilled mule spinners who had formed the backbone of textile unions in the North —enabled the southern mills to employ unskilled labor and to defeat the first effort at organization around 1900. Since many northern firms hesitated to make the fresh investments that new machinery required, New England textile cities saw the greater part of the expanding market after 1890 pass by by default to new towns in the South.[17]

A major reason for the embarrassment of some of the New England towns was the defection of their absentee entrepreneurs and the failure to replace their talents from among the immigrant workers.[18] On the other hand, some cities prospered because of the enterprise and skills that waves of newcomers brought. British and Dutch glassmakers strengthened the economy of Pittsburgh and Toledo and gave economic vitality to Corning, New York, La Salle, Illinois, and many other towns. German brewers helped to build up Cincinatti, St. Louis, Rochester, Chicago, and especially Milwaukee; despite some opposition from local temperance forces, they ultimately won acceptance and influence in each place.[19] Skilled mechanics and technicians from England, Germany, and elsewhere received a more immediate welcome and financial support in developing enterprises ranging in one town from buttons to optical instruments;[20] the classic example of immigrant enterprise, however, was the clothing industry, and many cities fattened upon it.

When the ready-to-wear clothing trade appeared at mid-century its most enterprising leaders were German Jews. Many who had gained a footing as tailors or peddlers or retail merchants now expanded their operations by employing some of their more recently arrived fellow countrymen. Several of these firms, which sprang up in the more populous centers and engaged the talents of vigorous salesmen, installed the newly invented sewing machines, employing women and girls to operate them. As cutting machines were perfected and the specialization of tasks increased, some of the shops blossomed into factories. Others, particularly in New York and Chicago, where the largest influx of a new wave of Eastern European Jews occurred, developed a contract system that enabled the recent comers to work under men of their own group and in neighborhood lofts where they could speak their native tongue.[21]

This activity spread widely and unobtrusively, helping to sustain sizable colonies of Eastern Jews in Boston and Baltimore, in Cleveland, Cincinnati, Rochester, and a dozen smaller places. Every member of the family lent a hand, but it soon became evident that only the contract bosses were prospering. Again a union movement developed and brought long years of bitter strife, with both the owners and the organizers seeking to gain an advantage by playing one city against another in regional lockouts and boycotts. Nevertheless the industry, responding to the rapid urban growth, continued to expand, and the companies, closely dependent on their labor supply, could not migrate freely. Wages remained low, and the wide use of sweatshops helped to foster living standards that were among the worst in America—so wretched, in fact, that the public conscience was pricked. Soon local, state, and federal investigations began to study the problem. New pressure for governmental supervision developed, and a resurgence of union effort occurred among the workers as the period closed.[22]

If the classic example of immigrant enterprise was the clothing industry, that of the native was the commercial bank, though foreign-born bankers increased in number after the seventies. Each new settlement boasted one or more of these institutions, which quickly multiplied as the towns grew. By 1880, 6532 banks with national, state, or private charters—one to every 2000 urban residents—served a variety of functions, among them the promotion of city growth. Although the accumulation and use of private savings was still a minor feature, as was investment banking, the facility these establishments brought to commercial transactions, and the concentration they effected of fluid capital in the sixteen cities designated as redemption centers under the National Banking Act of 1863-64, strengthened the leading marts within their respective regions and tied their economy to the great central reserve capital in New York.[23]

It was not the banks, however, but enterprising men who determined the direction of a city's industrial development. Sometimes an influx of newcomers with special skills transformed a town's activity. Thus at Rochester after the mid-century, when flour milling and canalling had passed their apogee, a host of immigrant craftsmen created the clothing, shoe, nursery, brewing, and woodworking industries that gave it a new burst of growth, placing it in the 100,000 bracket by 1885. The lack of convenient coal, iron, and other natural resources had threatened to blight the "Flower City's" manufacturing prospects, but the new industries depended less on raw materials than on human skills and on the excellence of their products. Such varied and specialized instruments were designed and built that they again transformed Rochester, within three decades, into a center of technical industry. A young bank clerk, George Eastman, discovered that the photographic laboratory he set up in his mother's kitchen held more fascination than a teller's cage, and the city soon shared his rewards.[24]

Enterprise in abundance characterized most cities throughout these decades. Growth itself created a rich market, not only for food and apparel and building materials but also for a variety of new articles that promised urban convenience. Ingenious men perfected the telephone, the elevator, the trolley car, the bicycle, and the automobile—to name only a few that contributed to the ease and speed of communications in cities, thus increasing the momentum of their growth. Energetic promoters extended the use of these products widely through the towns of America and at the same time greatly benefited those where the factories were located.[25]

The widespread technological advance frequently prompted independent inventors to work on similar problems at the same time. Occasionally a city assembled so many skilled craftsmen in a particular industry that it generated innovations and attracted experts from distant places. The Edison shops at Harrison, New Jersey, the Brush Electric Company at Cleveland, and the Thomson-Houston works at Lynn drew proficient electrical workers to these centers; Eastman attracted to Rochester rival photographic and optical companies eager to share its concentration of specialized skills. Although many manufacturers, impelled to acquire patent rights that might obstruct the development of their products, hastened to absorb competitors, the formation of new firms almost in the shadow of the expanding companies often continued unabated. Some of the new concerns developed subsidiary articles which they produced for the major distributors—speed shutters for cameras in Rochester, lamp stems for incandescent globes at Harrison—thus contributing to the integration of major community industries while retaining the enterprise many restless but talented craftsmen desired.[26]

The upsurge of inventiveness flooded the patent office with the applications as the 120,000 registered before 1870 mounted by 1910 to well over a million.[27] Promoters who helped to develop the new mechanical devices generally enlisted support from local capitalists. The limited-dividend corporation, freely available under the general laws of most states, proved especially attractive, and such incorporations, almost nonexistent in manufacturing in 1860, numbered over 40,000 at the close of the century. Although they comprised barely a tenth of all establishments, they produced 60 per cent of the value, and almost completely dominated the metal and technical branches. The flexibility of these economic "persons"—their capacity for expansion or consolidation, for a shift in leadership or a change in product—fitted them admirably for growing cities faced with problems of economic integration.[28]

The most rapid increase among giant corporations occurred at the turn of the century, as they mushroomed from twelve in 1896, each valued at $10 million or more, to fifty that exceeded $50 million by 1903.[29] Even after the move for consolidation began and strong, often monopolistic groups took hold, a rapidly expanding market and more effective sales promotion frequently enabled the trust to keep all its affiliated plants in operation, at least for a time. Sometimes a new factory site was selected, as in the case of the General Electric Company, a consolidation of Edison and rival concerns, but the new beginning it made at Schenectady in 1886 could not absorb all the work in process at Harrison, Lynn, and Cleveland, among other places. Several of the old centers prospered, while Schenectady became an industrial city of high quality.[30]

Numerous towns, though not the majority, enjoyed similar benefits. The typewriter brought life to Ilion, New York, and new vigor to Syracuse; telephone factories clustered for a time at Boston and Chicago, but soon spread out; the cash register placed Dayton on the industrial map. A score of cities manufactured elevators, and many more contributed to the production of trolley cars and their equipment.[31] Bicycle companies sprang up in a host of towns during the early nineties, but shortly after 1899, when the American Bicycle Company absorbed forty-eight of them, production was centered in ten plants at Springfield, Massachusetts, and Hart-

ford, Connecticut, each of which suffered a severe blow when the trust collapsed a few seasons later. Several former cycle factories had meanwhile shifted to the manufacture of automobiles, in which Detroit quickly took the lead. Its surplus of capital from an expiring lumber trade, together with an overabundance of skilled marine-engine mechanics, welcomed the new industry.[32]

So many cities suffered from the migration of old companies and other effects of consolidation that the antitrust forces won general approval. The long battle for the regulation of railroads had spread antimonopoly doctrines, nurturing a strong faith in competition, and prepared the way for the speedy adoption of the Sherman Anti-Trust Act in 1890. Yet its vague provisions left many issues undecided. In the courts, where the rising trusts had much more effective representation than in the legislatures, the legal curbs atrophied and almost disappeared. Protests against government interference with "free enterprise," on which the welfare, particularly of industrial cities, seemed to depend, enlisted support from most business groups and discouraged efforts to halt consolidations. Only the more flagrant invasions of local community interests aroused effective action, such as the Standard Oil Company's stranglehold over the fortunes of Toledo and other Ohio towns in the early nineties, or the Trans-Missouri Freight Association's attempt to control the traffic of the Southwest a few years later. Champions of the efficiency of large-scale enterprise multiplied, and in 1889 New Jersey provided a corporate form for the holding companies that widely superseded the old trusts.[33]

In most cities new firms quickly

replaced those absorbed or otherwise lost, and many small market towns grew into promising industrial centers. The number reporting at least 10,000 factory workers increased from thirty to fifty-four during the last two decades of the century; those listing 5000 or more rose from forty-five to eighty-one. After 1900 many factories migrated to the suburbs, and this presented the parent city with new problems of economic integration. All growing towns felt an increasing need for local leadership.[34]

Boards of trade and chambers of commerce sprang up in city after city as rallying points for their businessmen. Only a few of the thirty or more such organizations formed before the Civil War had survived, notably those of Chicago, Buffalo, Pittsburgh, and New York. Now the extension of the telegraph and the laying of the Atlantic cable in 1866 opened new possibilities for long-distance trade negotiations and stimulated the formation of organizations to conduct local exchanges and disseminate trade information. Most of the new crop of business clubs were, like their predecessors, chiefly concerned with commerce, but in 1869 the Milwaukee Chamber of Commerce raised a fund of $860 "to promote the city's industrial growth." Its list of the town's advantages for trade and industry, published in 1871 and widely circulated, heralded a new, more industrial approach. A few years later, the same body initiated an industrial exposition patterned after the Centennial in Philadelphia. Its building, erected at a cost of $300,000 and opened in 1881, supplied facilities for annual exhibitions during the next two decades and inspired businessmen in St. Louis, Chicago, and Minneapolis to similar efforts.[35]

The most forthright movie in this direction occurred at Philadelphia in 1894, when the city council oganized a Commercial Museum and provided it with a building and equipment to display local industrial products and to promote foreign trade. San Francisco, St. Louis, and Boston established similar museums. Not to be outdone, an Association for the Advancement of Milwaukee urged real-estate men to grant free sites or free rent to new industrial ventures and collected subscriptions from capitalists to back them. The association, which also proposed tax concessions, boasted after two years that its efforts had attracted a score of new industries to the city, helping it to reach fifteenth place by 1900.[36]

Some of the post–Civil War boards of trade declined after a few seasons, but new organizations generally appeared in response to urgent business needs. Several midwestern towns formed promotional bodies similar to Milwaukee's. In 1892 the Cleveland Board of Trade created a committee for the promotion of industry, which led in turn to the reorganization of the board as a Chamber of Commerce a year later, when a full-time secretary was engaged to handle such activities and to develop new civic and welfare functions. Other chambers, too, were seeking competent secretaries, and in 1913 as their activities became standardized the newly established Harvard Business School organized a course for them.

The effort to provide free sites or other subsidies for new industries lost favor in some chambers after concerns of questionable merit accepted such benefits only to move on when a higher bid arrived. But the promotional value of numerous trade conventions, industrial exhibitions, and publications that featured local advantages gained wide acceptance among the several hundred boards and chambers of the early 1900's. If the annual reports often sounded a bit boastful, even to local observers, such growing industrial cities as Milwaukee, Cleveland, Pittsburgh, Detroit, Buffalo, Columbus, and Rochester—not to mention several of the newer towns of the West—all gladly supported active groups.[37]

Although the basic philosophy of most of these chambers involved unfaltering support for "free enterprise," especially after events in the nineties sharpened the issue, some of their committees did try to establish voluntary standards of production and fair dealing. Their resolutions generally opposed state and federal regulations, but many were quick to appeal to the I. C. C. or to an appropriate state authority when a long-haul railroad rate schedule or some other monopoly practice seemed prejudicial to the locality. Their concern for the city's welfare often aligned them against freebooting utility combines and high-handed industrial giants. Leadership in the continuing attack on trusts and corporate monopolies generally came from other sources, but the chambers were exponents of community business interests.[38]

Most growing towns had, of course, developed a sense of the community's interest long before organizations to promote it emerged. An informal leadership, which later sociologists would call the power structure, generally directed important aspects of the development of each city. The promoters of town sites and urban subdivisons, who frequently joined the merchants to support and direct the expansive projects of the commercial centers, seldom

gave effective leadership to the industrial cities. There the initiative more frequently came from ambitious craftsmen, often men with inventive talents, whose struggle to produce and market new products transformed them into captains of industry. They were the most alert developers of each town's external economy. Newcomers from abroad, and others from small towns nearby, rose in this fashion to positions of influence.

Many industrial cities developed specialties based on the skills of their workers or the inventive talents of their technicians. On the other hand the mining towns and some others largely dependent on one industry frequently lost control to absentee owners who opposed the development of independent enterprise. The widespread reaction to, or fear of, that fate strengthened the antimonopoly forces of the commercial centers, plagued by railroad pools, and hastened the triumph of the progressive movement.

The most important contribution of the industrial cities was the mounting output of their factories. Statistics show that the value added by manufacturing doubled between 1859 and 1879 and more than doubled again in the prosperous eighties, and yet again, despite two depressions, by 1909. The value added by manufacturing increased tenfold in the half-century, almost trebling the increased value of farm products. Moreover the portion of the national income derived from manufacturing mounted from 16.6 to 20.8 per cent during the last three decades, while that derived from agriculture held steady and the contributions of both trade and transportation declined.[39]

In this period, at least, industry rather than commerce was the chief source of urban growth. Over nine-tenths of the industrial production occurred in urban factories, and as their output increased a surplus for export developed in some fields. Shipments abroad of manufactured foodstuffs and of finished industrial products mounted steadily after 1876 until, by 1898, even the latter exceeded comparable imports. As American factories progressively crowded European products out of the domestic consumer trade, the American farm was relieved of the burden of balancing foreign payments. The export of foodstuffs, both raw and manufactured, declined after the turn of the century, but the exports of other manufactured products more than took up the slack, maintaining a sufficiently favorable balance of trade to liquidate some of the foreign investments. Thus urban industrial growth freed the national economy not only from dependence on European factories, but also from reliance on foreign banks for new capital. That, however, was only a minor aspect of the industrial city's accomplishment, for the value added to its products exceeded the total value of all imports almost seven to one by 1899, as contrasted with a ratio of five to two, four decades earlier. As foreign trade diminished in relative importance, domestic trade mounted, and the industrial worker produced material goods in sufficient volume to raise the standards of consumption throughout the country.[40]

NOTES

1. Edgar M. Hoover, *The Location of Economic Activity* (New York, 1948). See Edward Ullman, "A Theory of Location for Cities," *American Journal of Sociology*, Vol. 46 (May, 1941), pp. 853-863, for a review of several theories concerning the location of cities.

2. Numerous books recognize this contribution, but few have treated it adequately. See Kirkland, *op. cit.*, pp. 237-261; Harold U. Faulkner, *The Decline of Laissez Faire: 1897-1917* (New York, 1951), pp. 92-114; Hays, *op. cit.*, pp. 48-58. For an early study of urban contributions, see Arthur Shadwell, *Industrial Efficiency* (London, 1909). For an able geographical study of urban economy, see Gunnar Alexandersson, *The Industrial Structure of American Cities* (Lincoln, Nebraska, 1956).

3. Charlotte Erickson, *American Industry and the European Immigrant: 1860-1885* (Cambridge, 1957); Eric E. Lampard in Harvey S. Perloff and associates, *Regions, Resources and Economic Growth* (Baltimore, 1960), pp. 122-221.

4. Kirkland, *op. cit.* (1961), pp. 133-142; Edmund E. Day, "An Index of the Physical Volume of Production," *Review of Economic Statistics*, II (Oct., 1920), p. 294; Ray B. West, Jr., *Rocky Mountain Cities* (New York, 1949), pp. 230-255; Paul H. Landis, *Three Iron Mining Towns* (Ann Arbor, 1938); Alexandersson, *op. cit.*, pp. 27-34. See the bibliography in Caroline Bancroft's fictionalized history of Central City, Colorado, *Gulch of Gold* (Denver, 1958), pp. 365-367.

5. T. A. Rickard, *A History of American Mining* (New York, 1932), pp. 91 and *passim*; U. S. *Census* (1900), Occupations, p. 728; Peter Roberts, *Anthracite Coal Communities* (New York, 1904); Chauncy D. Harris, "A Functional Classification of Cities in the United States." *Geographic Review*, Vol. 33 (Jan., 1930), pp. 86-96. See also Kirkland, *op. cit.* (1961), pp. 137-162.

6. Muriel E. Sheppard, *Cloud by Day* (Chapel Hill, 1947); *Cost of Living in American Towns* (Senate Doc. 22, 1911), pp. 337-339, 344-348. See also Henry L. Hunker, *Industrial Evolution of Columbus, Ohio* (Columbus, 1958), pp. 39-55, for an account of how Columbus absorbed the energies of nearby mining districts.

7. Herman F. Otte, *Industrial Opportunity in the Tennessee Valley of Northwestern Alabama* (New York, 1940), pp. 20-26; Vance and Demerath, *op. cit.*, pp. 10-12; Woodward, *op. cit.*, pp. 314-316.

8. Johnson, *op. cit.*, *passim*; Thomas Greenwood, *A Tour of the States and Canada* (London, 1883), pp. 94-100; Tarbell, *op. cit.*, pp. 74-79; Cochran and Miller, *op. cit.*, pp. 135-146. See also, John P. Herrick, *Empire Oil* (New York, 1949).

9. Chester M. Destler, *American Radicalism: 1856-1901* (New London, 1946), Chapter VII.

10. Randolph C. Downes, *Lake Port* [Lucas County History Series III] (Toledo, 1951), pp. 59-93; U. S. *Census* (1900), Occupations, p. 742; (1910), IX: 996-997.

11. Henrietta Larson, *The Wheat Market and the Farmer in Minnesota, 1858-1900* (New York, 1926); Mildred Hartsough, *The Twin*

Cities (Minneapolis, 1925), pp. 36-46; Henry C. Haskell, Jr., and R. B. Fowler, *City of the Future: A Narrative History of Kansas City, 1850-1950* (Kansas City, 1950); Gerald M. Capers, *River Town, Memphis* (Chapel Hill, 1939), pp. 220-228; Alice Lantherman, "Kansas City as a Grain and Milling Center," *Missouri Historical Review*, XLII (1947), pp. 132-155; *Cost of Living in American Towns* (Senate Doc. 22, 1911), pp. 243-283; Alexandersson, *op. cit.*, pp. 34-35, 86-88.

12. Erickson, *op. cit.*, pp. 65-105; Mary R. Coolidge, *Chinese Immigration*, (New York, 1909), pp. 357-401. Boston's sudden emergence as an industrial city in the fifties has been attributed to cheap immigrant labor—see Oscar Handlin, *Boston's Immigrants: 1790-1865* (Cambridge, 1951), pp. 79-87.

13. George W. Chase, *History of Haverhill* (Haverhill, 1921), pp. 532-536; Edgar M. Hoover, *Location Theory and the Shoe and Leather Industries* (Cambridge, 1937), pp. 219-228.

14. *Ibid.*, pp. 229-255; Horace B. Davis, *Shoes, The Workers and the Industry* (New York, 1940), p. 17 and *passim*; Blake McKelvey, "A History of the Rochester Shoe Industry," *Rochester History*, Apr., 1953, pp. 6-20; U. S. Industrial Commission, *Reports*, VII: 176-180, 369-370; Alexandersson, *op. cit.*, pp. 80-82.

15. Thomas R. Smith, *The Cotton Textile Industry of Fall River, Mass.; A Study of Industrial Localization* (New York, 1944), pp. 40-99; Marcus L. Hansen, *The Immigrant in American History* (Cambridge, 1940), pp. 154-174; Arthur W. Calhoun, *A Social History of the American Family* (Cleveland, 1919), III: 67; *Cost of Living in American Towns* (Senate Doc. 22, 1911), pp. 197-203, 208-214, 231-238; Shadwell, *op. cit.*, pp. 208-230.

16. Vera Shlakman, *Economic History of a Factory Town: A Study of Chicopee, Mass.* [Smith College Studies in History, XX] (Northampton, 1935), pp. 151-225; Margaret T. Parker, *Lowell: A Study of Industrial Development* (New York, 1940), pp. 85, 118-147; Constance M. Green, *Holyoke, Mass.* (New Haven, 1930), pp. 137-251; U. S. Industrial Commission, *Report*, VII (1900), pp. 68-84, 90, 219-226, 343-348; Hansen, *op. cit.*, pp. 160-174, 188-190; Alexandersson, *op. cit.*, pp. 63-70; Faulkner, *op. cit.*, pp. 142-144.

17. Anthony M. Tang, *Economic Development in the Southern Piedmont* (Chapel Hill, 1958), pp. 22-65 ff.; Smith, *op. cit.*, pp. 80-121; Herbert Lahne, *The Cotton Mill Worker* (New York, 1944), pp. 70-84, 175-195; Melvin T. Copeland, *The Cotton Manufacturing Industry of the United States* (Cambridge, 1923), pp. 27-133; F. B. Garver, F. M. Boddy and A. J. Nixon, *The Location of Manufacturers in the United States: 1899-1929* (Minneapolis, 1933), pp. 65-75; Broadus Mitchell and George S. Mitchell, *The In-*

dustrial Revolution in the South (Baltimore, 1930), pp. 126-140; William H. Simpson, *Life in Mill Communities* (Clinton, S. C., 1943), pp. 14-25.

18. Smith, *op. cit.*, pp. 119-121; Parker, *op. cit.*, p. 210 ff. But see also Victor S. Clark, *History of Manufacturers in the United States* (New York, 1929), II. 181-198; Shlakman, *op. cit.*, pp. 196-198; Green, *American Cities*, pp. 82-90.

19. Erickson, *op. cit.*, pp. 139-147; Bayrd Still, *Milwaukee, The History of a City* (Madison, 1948), pp. 329-332 and *passim*; Pierce, *Chicago*, II: 89; Blake McKelvey, *Rochester, The Flower City: 1854-1890* (Cambridge, 1949) [cited below as *Rochester, II*], pp. 106-107, 238-240; Thomas C. Cochran, *Pabst Brewing Company: The History of an American Business* (New York, 1949); *Cost of Living in American Towns* (Senate Doc. 22, 1911), pp. 152-157, 257-265, 373-376.

20. McKelvey, *Rochester, II*: 227, 243, 322, 380; U. S. Industrial Commission *Report*, XV (1901), *passim*; Carl Wittke, *We Who Built America* (New York, 1940), pp. 392-401. See Erickson, *op. cit.*, *passim*.

21. Jesse E. Pope, *The Clothing Industry in New York* [University of Missouri Studies, Vol. I] (St. Louis, 1905), pp. 45 ff.; U. S. Industrial Commission *Report* (1901), pp. xxiv-xxxii, xlvii, 316-384, 449-490; *Cost of Living in American Towns* (U. S. Senate Doc. 22, 1911), pp. 20-21, 23, 137-138; Edward E. Pratt, *Industrial Causes of Congestion of Population in New York City* (New York, 1911), pp. 79-86. See also Moses Rischin, *The Promised City: New York's Jews, 1870-1914* (Cambridge, 1962), pp. 51-68.

22. Mabel A. Magee, *Trends in Location of the Women's Clothing Industry* (Chicago, 1930), pp. 9-11, 133-134; Leonard A. Drake and Carrie Glasser, *Trends in the New York Clothing Industry* (New York, 1942), pp. 39-47; Louis Levine, *The Women's Garment Workers* (New York, 1924), pp. 1-195; Calhoun, *op. cit.*, III: 74-75; *Cost of Living in American Towns* (Senate Doc. 22, 1911), pp. 18-24, 75-78, 105-108, 137-141, 154-156, 162-166, 177-179, 323-324; Charles Hirschfeld, *Baltimore: 1870-1900* [Johns Hopkins Studies in History and Political Science, Series 59, No. 2] (Baltimore, 1941), pp. 41-42, 57-63.

23. *World Almanac* (1889), p. 91; U. S. Census (1880), Compendium, p. 8; Cochran and Miller, *op. cit.*, pp. 135-153; Margaret G. Myers, *The New York Money Market* (New York, 1931), I: 213-233; Pierce, *Chicago*, III: 192-233; Douglas North, "Capital Accumulation in Life Insurance Between the Civil War and 1905," in William Miller, *Men of Business* (Cambridge, 1952), pp. 238-253. See also Kirkland, *op. cit.* (1961), pp. 216-236.

24. McKelvey, *Rochester, II*: 98-126, 200-256.

25. Roger Burlingame, *Engines of Democracy* (New York, 1940), pp. 95-125, *passim*; Herbert

N. Casson, *The History of the Telephone* (Chicago, 1910); Hays, *op. cit.*, pp. 48-58; Kirkland, *op. cit.* (1961), pp. 163-182.
26. Harold C. Passer, *The Electrical Manufacturers, 1875-1900* (Cambridge, 1953); Blake McKelvey, *Rochester, The Quest for Quality* (Cambridge, 1956) [cited below as *Rochester*, III], pp. 256-272; Faulkner, *op. cit.*, pp. 115-134; Alexandersson, *op. cit.*, pp. 48-49, 62-63.
27. Felix Frankfurter, *The Public and Its Government* (New Haven, 1930), pp. 9-10; *Recent Social Trends in the United States* (New York, 1934), pp. 125-127; Edward W. Byrn, *The Progress of Invention in the Nineteenth Century* (New York, 1900).
28. U. S. *Census* (1900), VII: 503-509; Hirschfeld, *op. cit.*, pp. 44-46, 76-82; Kirkland, *op. cit.* (1961), pp. 196-214; Fine, *op. cit.*, pp. 146-151.
29. John Moody, *The Truth About the Trusts* (New York, 1904), pp. 453-476; William Miller, "American History and the Business Elite," *Journal of Economic History*, IX (1949), 184-208; Cochran and Miller, *op. cit.*, pp. 135-153, 181-191; Faulkner, *op. cit.*, 153-164.
30. Abbott P. Usher, *A History of Mechanical Inventions* (Cambridge, 1954), pp. 401-406; Paul W. Keating, *Lamps for a Brighter America* (New York, 1954), pp. 21 ff.; Joel H. Monroe, *Schenectady, Ancient and Modern* (Schenectady, 1914), p. 277-280; Passer, *op. cit.*, pp. 52-57, 100-104, 321-330; Kirkland, *op. cit.* (1961), pp. 195-215.
31. *MacRae's Blue Book* (New York, 1910); Byrn, *op. cit.*, pp. 76-87, 171-182, 459-460; Clark, *op. cit.*, II: 377-387; III: 165-170; Bruce Bliven, *The Wonderful Writing Machine* (New York, 1954); Lee, *op. cit.*, pp. 97-104.
32. Arthur S. Dwing, *Corporate Promotions and Reorganizations* (Cambridge, 1914), pp. 249-268; Lloyd Morris, *Not So Long Ago* (New York, 1949), pp. 229-265; Shlakman, *op. cit.*, pp. 200-205; Merrill Denison, *The Power to Go* (New York, 1956), pp. 92-180; *Cost of Living in American Towns* (Senate Doc. 22, 1911), pp. 172-175; H. H. McCarthy, *Industrial Migration in the United States, 1914-1927* (Iowa

City, Iowa, 1930), p. 10; Ralph C. Epstein, *The Automobile Industry* (New York, 1928), pp. 123, 209, 257-260, 296; Green, *op. cit.*, pp. 199-203; Alexandersson, *op. cit.*, pp. 49-54.
33. Henry R. Seager and C. A. Gulick, Jr., *Trust and Corporation Problems* (New York, 1929), pp. 48-60, 367-398; Destler, *op. cit.*, pp. 105-134; R. H. Bremner, "The Civic Revival in Ohio," *American Journal of Economics and Sociology* (1951), X: 417-429; Fine, *op. cit.*, pp. 126-164; Faulkner, *op. cit.*, pp. 175-186, 202-210.
34. U. S. *Census* (1900), VII: ccxix-ccxxiv; (1910), X: 901-975; Glenn E. McLaughlin, *Growth of American Manufacturing Areas* (Pittsburgh, 1938), pp. 127-132, 186-188.
35. Kenneth Sturges, *American Chambers of Commerce* (New York, 1915), pp. 11-43; Still, *op. cit.*, pp. 345-348.
36. Still, *op. cit.*, pp. 345-348; see also Lloyd Graham and Frank H. Severance, *The First Hundred Years of the Buffalo Chamber of Commerce* (Buffalo, 1945), p. 142 ff.; U. S. Industrial Commission *Report*, VII (1900), pp. 16-17, 990-999; XIV: 439-460; see also Hirschfeld, *op. cit.*, pp. 36-38; Pierce, *Chicago*, III: 80, 93, 475.
37. Sturges, *op. cit.*, pp. 117-166, 231-240; William G. Rose, *Cleveland, The Making of a City* (Cleveland, 1950), pp. 537, 542; George W. Doonan, "Commercial Organizations in Southern and Western Cities," U. S. Bureau of Foreign and Domestic Commerce, *Special Agents Series*, No. 79, 1914; Hunker, *op. cit.*, pp. 53-55.
38. Sturges, *op. cit.*, *passim*; Howard L. Childs, *Labor and Capital in National Politics* (Columbus, 1930); Paul Studenski, "Chambers of Commerce," *Encyclopedia of the Social Sciences*, III: 325-329; Fine, *op. cit.*, pp. 96-125.
39. U. S. Bureau of the Census, *Historical Statistics of the United States: Colonial Times to 1957* (Washington, 1957), pp. 139-140, 283-284; Kirkland, *op. cit.* (1961), pp. 278-305, 399-409.
40. *Historical Statistics of the United States to 1957*, pp. 544-546; Faulkner, *op. cit.*, pp. 52-63.

The English and American Industrial City of the Nineteenth Century*

Leon S. Marshall

Cities throughout history have been the focal points of civilization; and the association of such cities as Babylon with the ancient Oriental empires, Athens with Greece, Rome with the Mediterranean empire of the Caesars and with medieval Christianity, and Venice and Florence with the Renaissance are commonplaces in history and literature. Although trite from frequent repetition, true and significant is the observation that, with all that cities have been, in no previous age has urban society had so complete domination over the life of mankind as at the present. To the student of English or American history, therefore, the rise of the industrial city of the nineteenth century is particularly important, for in that history may be found the origins of many of the critical problems troubling our own disjointed and embittered society.

The supremacy of earlier towns over their neighboring countrysides was due to the domination of commerce over industry: that is, the facilities of the city for the distribution of productions beyond the means and requirements of household and simple agrarian economy stimulated the productive energies of the surrounding population and, in consequence, the economic needs of the city set up the pattern of economic life existing around it. In the present day, however, the economic system created by the industrial city has approached the solution of the problem of production, but has created a new set of problems arising out of that of distributing the wealth produced by this modern industrial system.

In an economic sense, an industrial city is one whose resources are almost wholly devoted or subordinated to the producing of *form* utility—the shaping of raw materials into goods for human use. London, Liverpool, and New York, where manufacturing plants are only incidental to the principal business of the city, are commercial rather than industrial cities since exchange (wholesale, retail, or financial) together with transportation is their chief activity. On the other hand, Manchester, Birmingham, and Pittsburgh, even though they are not now so predominantly characterized by factories and mills, are industrial cities because their wealth, population, and economic activities are largely devoted to the supplying of their factories and those of the surrounding communities with the essentials of industrial life, and their prosperity is dependent upon that of their leading industries.

In the first half of the nineteenth century, Manchester, Birmingham, and other towns in England developed into

From *Western Pennsylvania Historical Magazine* (September 1937), pp. 169-80. Reprinted by permission of the publisher. Leon S. Marshall is Professor of History at Kent State University.

industrial cities according to a pattern which recurred in Cincinnati, Pittsburgh, and other American cities whose leading businesses were transformed by the industrial revolution. The adoption of a series of labor-saving inventions and of improved processes of manufacture led to the concentration in factories of the cotton industry around Manchester, the iron industry around Birmingham and woollen manufacture around Leeds, where facilities for labor, power, and capital were abundant. The increased prosperity and the demand for labor accompanying this concentration of industry brought in a flood of immigrants to these towns. The earlier balance in a town society composed of gentlemen, merchants, and artisans was shaken to its roots by this influx of what soon became an urban proletariat badly housed, subject to extremes of temporary affluence and poverty, and not easily adapted to the discipline of town and factory life. On the other hand, self-made capitalists accumulated fortunes by amazing combinations of luck, foresight, determination, and energy. Recognizing their importance in the community and in the nation, these frequently uncultured and ruthless factory owners seized political leadership from the older dominant interests, and ultimately forced government to protect and foster the system that had enriched them. At the same time, green spaces and quaint old buildings disappeared as land was needed for offices and warehouses, and beyond the new "business districts" grimy factories pushed rows of jerry-built dwellings past the original limits of the town. Disease, poverty, crime, industrial conflict, and social animosities broke down the traditional institutions that had controlled smaller and more orderly popula-tions, while the bewildered and alarmed inhabitants strove to erect new political and social machinery to control and refine the social revolution that was going on around them.

Wherever this pattern of development recurred, its most striking effects appeared in the growth of urban population. By 1860 more than half the people of England lived in cities and factory towns, and by 1920 more than half the population of the United States lived in urban centers. In the first fifty years of the industrial revolution, the American, as had the English cities previously, received the greatest impact of the population movement. Paterson, New Jersey, grew from 7,500 in 1840 to 68,000 in 1890; Philadelphia from less than a hundred thousand to over a million in the same period; and Pittsburgh and Allegheny from 31,000 to a third of a million fifty years later.[1] Chicago, Cincinnati, Milwaukee, Kansas City, and scores of other cities rivaled this growth, and the rise of the automobile industry produced a recurrence of this phenomenon in the twentieth century.

The influx of population was much more rapid than the expansion of housing facilities. Congestion affected all classes, driving first the wealthy and later the middle classes to the suburbs; but for the incoming workers, too poor to afford better, the only accommodations were cheap lodging houses, and run-down tenement buildings from which absentee landlords derived as much rent with as little expense as possible while awaiting the profits of rising real-estate values. Five families living abroad and contributing little to the community in the form of taxes or improvements of their property drew most of the rentals from Pittsburgh's slums, a fact that accounts for much of the great following of Henry George's single-tax program in Pittsburgh.[2]

Until epidemics of cholera, typhoid fever, and smallpox terrified the middle classes of townspeople into attempting sanitary reforms, the disease and death lurking in the dark squalor of the slums was hardly known to the general public. Whether in England or America the discoveries made by sanitary reformers reveal a depressing similarity. Manchester with two hundred thousand inhabitants had scarcely a sewer, irregular scavengers' carts hardly touched the filth that rotted in dumps to make it more marketable as fertilizer, and until the middle of the century the town's water supply was not sufficient for more than one-third its population. Such facts as these explain why in 1841 the average expectation of life at birth in Manchester was only a few months over twenty-four years.[3] In America, a little later, few cities possessed half as many miles of sewers as of streets, and half the latter were unpaved. Fully one-third of the houses in the eighties relied upon private vaults and household utensils for the disposal of human waste. A large part of Philadelphia's million inhabitants drank water from the Delaware River into which had been emptied daily thirteen million gallons of sewage.[4] Typhus, typhoid, and scarlet fever were the natural concomitants of such sanitary inadequacies, and Pittsburgh's share in this ghastly record consisted of the highest mortality rate for typhoid in the world between 1899 and 1907, or 1.30 per thousand.[5]

Public philanthropy tried first to stem this invasion of disease and death by erecting hospitals, of which Pittsburgh added eight between 1882 and 1895.[6]

Street improvements because of the demands of traffic proceeded more rapidly than improvement in sewage, which also involved scientific knowledge as well as expense to property. Although building societies for the erection of model cottages were common in the English towns as the result of experience with congestion, only a few such attempts were made in the United States, and only where industrial corporations erected model "company houses" in the new industrial areas were these successful. Except in the new cities of the West, such as Salt Lake City, the United States lagged far behind England in city planning.

A report on a survey of Pittsburgh in 1908 pointed out as another feature of industrialism "an altogether incredible amount of overwork by everybody, reaching its extreme in the twelve-hour shift for seven days in the week in the steel mills and the railway switchyards."[7] Although the report considered the proportion of women in local industries as "menacing," Pittsburgh's mills were not so adaptable to the labor of women and children as were canning and textile factories, where light though fatiguing routine made possible their employment because of their cheapness and amenableness to discipline. In the single decade of the eighties the number of children employed increased from 1,-000,000 to 1,750,000.[8] In spite of ten-hour laws the usual working day in many industries even where women and children were employed was twelve hours. Although the labor of women and children was not new, the factory and the industrial city created new problems of family disintegration, fatigue, delinquency, and industrial superannuation, and impressed the critical-ness of these problems by the vividness of the industrial scene. The public reaction to these conditions were the factory and public-health movements in England in the thirties and forties, and state agitations in America for ten-hour laws and legislation for sanitary improvements.

Legislative protection for women and children in industry in response to the demands of public opinion was achieved more rapidly in England than in America. Using as an accepted principle Sir Robert Peel's Act of 1819, which attempted to remedy abuses in the employment of children in cotton mills, societies of English humanitarians and factory workers forced Parliament to pass the Factory Act of 1834, the Mines Act of 1842, and the Ten Hours Act of 1847 in spite of the millowners' appeal to the currently accepted theory of laissez-faire in the relations between the state and industry. In America the manufacturing interests entrenched themselves in the state legislatures behind the argument that regulatory legislation would enable industries in those states not having such regulations to ruin the manufacturers of the states where the employment of women and children was limited. In spite of this opposition the National Eight-Hour League succeeded in obtaining such laws in six states. Although the effect of these laws was greatly vitiated by lax enforcement, the enlightened opinion aroused by the agitation, the example of a few states, and the constant pressure of shorter-hours advocates brought a gradual reduction of the hours of labor and an improvement in health conditions in American factories.

The increase in leisure afforded by the shorter-hours movement and the belief that the open air of the country made the agricultural population healthier than the urban produced considerable activity in the founding of parks, and in the census of 1880 the acreage and description of such places received a prominent place in the report for each town. A Boston society in 1880 provided sand gardens for children, and by 1898 thirteen other cities in the East had established children's playgrounds.[9] Philanthropic organizations such as the Women's Christian Temperance Union, the Society for the Prevention of Cruelty to Animals, the Society for the Prevention of Cruelty to Children, the State Charities Aid Association, and the Red Cross were established to deal with other problems of industrial life.

The human animal appeared to be changing his habitat and his manner of living with all the effects known to biology of such changes in animal life. The entire effect upon human physiology of the transition in dwelling place and even in diet (particularly because of the widespread use of factory-made foods) has not even yet been determined, for historians of this period have given their attention principally to the alterations of the industrial environment by which the inhabitants of the city tried to make it a more suitable place for living. That improvements were possible was due in large part to the greater productivity of the new system of manufacture and distribution.

Startling as was the growth of population in the towns of the nineteenth century, it was far exceeded by the increase in productions. In the last half of the century American textile production increased sevenfold, agricultural implements twenty-five, packing fourteen, and iron and steel, ten. In this increased productivity, laborers as well as capitalists shared. If Professor Clapham is correct, industrial wages in England advanced forty per cent and the cost of living decreased seventeen per cent in the sixty years after 1790; Miss Coman has estimated that in the United States wages increased twelve and a half per cent and prices decreased forty between 1867 and 1900;[10] thus there were approximate net gains of seventy and eighty-six per cent for the English and American workingmen, respectively, in the margin between earnings and subsistance as compared with the initial years. While capital gains from this improved position appear in the increase of savings-bank deposits and in insurance, the mass of wage earners did not invest in either of these[11] but spent the difference upon a higher standard of living which the greater variety of manufactures made possible.

From the point of view of the city, the significant fact was that this increased economic productivity and the improved economic position of the mass of its inhabitants with respect to subsistence did not bring economic security. The replacement of skilled laborers by machinery produced a series of crises in various trades. This and the constant lowering of the limit of industrial superannuation added constantly to the number of unemployed. The competition of women and children and of immigrants of low standards of living augmented suffering and discontent. Finally, incapacitation from industrial accidents and disease completed the demoralization of a large section of labor and made poverty a norm of existence even in prosperous times. Commenting on these conditions, a French visitor to Manchester in 1844 thus compared the pov-

erty in the old with that in the new cities, "At Paris, half the population go to the hospitals and almshouses to die. At Manchester, half the births take place in the public charities."[12]

Cyclical depression, which appeared in both England and the United States almost regularly every decade after 1815, demonstrated the failure of the new system to provide economic security to the laboring population. During the depression of 1837 a charitable society in Manchester found forty thousand pawn tickets representing an indebtedness of $27,500 at sixteen per cent in four thousand working-class homes.[13] In the United States nearly half a million were thrown out of work on the railways alone by the panic of 1873, only 400 out of 666 furnaces were in operation in the following spring, bread lines were common in every large city, and wages fell on an average of ten per cent and did not reach their former level until 1890.[14] During the panic of 1907 the surveyors of Pittsburgh reported: "Low wages for the great majority of the laborers employed by the mills, not lower than in other large cities, but low compared with prices,—so low as to be inadequate to the maintenance of a normal American standard of living; wages adjusted to the single man in the lodging house, not to the responsible head of a family."[15] To Englishmen and Americans who remembered that under the domestic system the wage earner had owned a plot of ground to supply him with food in bad times and that in earlier days the West had offered homesteads to oppressed craftsmen, the pre-industrial era appeared as the golden age now replaced by suffering and chaos.

Of Manchester in 1844 Léon Faucher

said: "At the very moment when the engines are stopped . . . moral order . . . disappears in an instant. The rich man spreads his couch amidst the beauties of the surrounding country, and abandons the town to the operatives, publicans, thieves, and prostitutes, merely taking the precaution of leaving behind him a police force whose duty it is to preserve some material order in this pell-mell of society."[16] A visitor described Pittsburgh in the eighties as "hell with the lid off." Pittsburgh, Chicago, Detroit, and Cincinnati were centers of organized crime, and in the nation the homicide rate quadrupled while the population doubled.[17] The failure of the police to cope with this growing disorder was accompanied by a series of embittered industrial disputes which appeared to be the first skirmishes of a social revolt.

Between 1816 and 1850 scarcely a year passed without a great strike in either the cotton industry or the building trades in Manchester, while these conflicts were increasingly supported by unions in other cities. The panic of 1873 produced a long strike in the New England textile mills. A ten per cent cut in wages in 1877 precipitated the first nationwide railway strike marked by battles between soldiers and workmen in Baltimore, Reading, and Pittsburgh. The workers of Baltimore foreshadowed the contemporary sit-down strike when they seized the railway yards and prevented the moving of trains, and in Pittsburgh the defeat of the militia gave control of the town to a lawless mob for two days. The bloody Homestead strike of steel workers in 1892 inaugurated an almost continuous series of strikes and lockouts lasting during the remainder of the century.

To restore order to a society that appeared near self-destruction, the philanthropically-inclined wealthy and other community leaders attempted to strengthen the church, the schools, charitable institutions, and the local government. In England, the distress uncovered during the cholera epidemic led six wealthy Manchester philanthropists to found the first statistical society in the world in 1833 "to assist in promoting the social improvement of the manufacturing population" by "collecting facts concerning the inhabitants."[18] Clergymen, merchants, and manufacturers supported monitorial schools under rival organizations in the twenties; temperance societies, mechanics' institutions, and savings banks in the thirties; and associations to promote public health, factory reform, public parks, and national education in the forties. The leaders of the new British manufacturing communities neglected few opportunities to inculcate what they believed to be the virtues of urban citizenship: knowledge of the "useful arts," temperance, industry, and thrift.

So closely parallel were the problems of the cities within the industrial pattern that the counterpart of each of the foregoing activities might be found in the history of almost any American manufacturing city. Local and national scientific and social associations took up the task of fact-finding. Washington Gladden of Columbus, Ohio, and other clergymen supported the rights of labor in its battle with capital and reorganized their congregations into "institutional churches" with charitable and educational agencies.[19] American advocates of broader educational opportunities were more successful than English in obtaining the assistance of the state to education, and illiteracy dropped from seventeen to eleven per cent in the last twenty years of the century.[20] In adult education the business genius of Redpath and Horner combined with philanthropy and local patriotism in an attempt to raise the general level of culture through the lyceum and the Chautauqua movement.

As philanthropy and mutual assistance proved at best only ameliorative, the pressure of these problems and of the interests affected by them was greatest upon government. In the 1760's the residents of Manchester had congratulated themselves on their lack of a municipal corporation, but in 1790 they began to create a series of new governmental agencies to perform tasks too complex for the traditional institutions. Beginning with watching and poor relief, the local government added before 1850 the regulation of hackney coaches (the traffic and transport problem of the day), street improvement, water supply, gas lighting, fire protection, sewage disposal, and market and public park administration. As in American municipal growth, this progress was accomplished by struggle with vested interests and against corruption: Manchester had a "boss Nadin" sixty years before New York experienced "boss Tweed."

There is not sufficient space within the limits of this article to present details illustrating the expansion of American municipal government, but the facts are sufficiently well known and depart but little from the Manchester pattern. Whether contemporary municipal government has restored the order and security demanded by its citizens is still an open question but not a new one, for the issue has been raised in each town as it has developed into an industrial city and is inherent in its life, as, indeed, are each of the problems that have been suggested as elements in the history of English and American industrial cities in the nineteenth century.

While the conception of a pattern of development is of invaluable assistance in the study of the rise of contemporary society, the student of this history must realize that four points of differentiation between the English and American industrial revolutions make parallels and analogies not only hazardous but if not carefully done very misleading. Briefly these differences are: first, the priority of the industrial revolution in England; second, the existence in England of privileged classes strongly intrenched in government and in social influence; third, the powerful influence of the agricultural West and South in America; and fourth, the enormous proportion of foreign-born population in the United States due to immigration. In these differences, however, lie additional reasons why the American social scientist should be intimately acquainted with the evolution of the English industrial city.

The first great advantage in the study of the English pattern in the nineteenth century is that in their earliest phases the basic processes of a society undergoing industrialization appear in relative simplicity, since the historian has but to consider the impact of a relatively few new developments upon a traditional background. With the passing of the West and the industrialization of the South, those purely American differentiations will be of less importance in analyzing the continuation of the processes at the present time. Finally, the influence of foreign immigration upon the United States may not have exerted so differentiating an effect as might be supposed, and because of the present immigration policy and the rapid Americanization of the descendants of the foreign-born the greater part of this difference in conditions is bound to disappear.

The industrial revolution, it has been said, has been succeeded by a scientific revolution, industrial capitalism by finance capitalism, urbanization by metropolitanization, but the process is not yet complete, and as long as remain the problems created by the industrial revolution—the control of disease, poverty, and crime by urban communities, the raising of cultural standards necessary to urban citizenship, and the removal of economic insecurity—social scientists and historians will be interested in the American and English industrial city of the nineteenth century.

NOTES

° Presented on April 10, 1937, at the eighth annual history conference sponsored by the history department and the extension division of the University of Pittsburgh. Dr. Marshall's article is based upon researches made in the preparation of his doctoral dissertation on "The Development of Public Opinion in Manchester, 1780-1820," presented to the University of Pittsburgh in January, 1937, and of a book he is writing on "The Cul-

tural Evolution of the First Industrial City: Manchester, 1780-1850."

1. *United States Census,* 1880, *Social Statistics,* 18:721, 733, 773, 850.
2. Robert A. Woods, "Pittsburgh: An Interpretation of Its Growth," in *The Pittsburgh District Civic Frontage,* 17 (Paul U. Kellogg, ed., *The Pittsburgh Survey,* vol. 5—New York, 1914).
3. Great Britain, Registrar General, *Seventh Annual Report,* 338 (London, 1841).
4. Allan Nevins, *The Emergence of Modern America, 1865-1878,* 321 (*A History of American Life,* vol. 8—New York, 1927).
5. Frank E. Wing, "Thirty-five Years of Typhoid," in *The Pittsburgh District Civic Frontage,* 66.
6. Sarah H. Killikelly, *The History of Pittsburgh, Its Rise and Progress,* 393-408 (Pittsburgh, 1906).
7. Edward T. Devine, "Pittsburgh the Year of the Survey," in *The Pittsburgh Civic Frontage,* 3.
8. Arthur M. Schlesinger, *The Rise of the City, 1878-1898,* 129 (*A History of American Life,* vol. 10—New York, 1933).
9. Schlesinger, *Rise of the City,* 130.
10. John H. Clapham, *The Early Railway Age, 1820-1850,* 561, 601, 602 (*An Economic History of Modern Britain,* second edition, vol. 1—Cambridge, 1930); Katharine Coman, *The Industrial History of the United States,* 306 (revised edition, New York, 1925).
11. Clapham, *Early Railway Age,* 299, 300.
12. Léon Faucher, *Manchester in 1844: Its Present Condition and Future Prospects,* 145 (London, 1844).
13. Joseph Adshead, *Distress in Manchester,* 41 (London, 1842).
14. Nevins, *Emergence of Modern America,* 299, 300, 301.
15. Devine, in *The Pittsburgh District Civic Frontage,* 3.
16. Faucher, *Manchester in 1844,* 26, 27.
17. Schlesinger, *Rise of the City,* 114.
18. Thomas S. Ashton, *Economic and Social Investigations in Manchester, 1833-1933,* 13 (London, 1934).
19. Schlesinger, *Rise of the City,* 340.
20. Schlesinger, *Rise of the City,* 171.

The Industrial City: Center of Cultural Change

In 1832 the *Manchester Guardian*, commenting on an exposure of bad living conditions among the factory population, offered as an apology for their existence the following observation: "The manufacturing system as it exists in Great Britain, and the inconceivably immense towns under it, are without previous parallel in the history of the world." This recognition of the industrial city as an unprecedented phenomenon was developed, not as an apology for bad living conditions, but as an explanation of the general changes under way in society, by two English observers of early industrialism, namely, William Cooke Taylor and Robert Vaughan, both of whom, it is worth noting, were historians. Taylor wrote a general history of civilization under the title *The Natural History of Society* (1841), besides many textbooks; and Vaughan, before he became president of the Lancashire Independent College at Manchester, was professor of history at the University of London. In a sense, therefore, it may be said that the view of the industrial city as a center of cultural change belongs peculiarly to historians.

Taylor held that the industrial town was a "new element" in society, which could not develop without deranging old institutions and relationships. It exhibited, he said, "a system of social life constructed on a wholly new principle, a principle yet vague and indefinite but developing itself by its own spontaneous force, and daily producing effects which no human foresight had anticipated." Above all, he was impressed by the formation of the urban masses who, developing new habits of thought without external aid or guidance, would ultimately, like the slow rising and gradual swelling of the ocean, "bear all elements of society aloft upon its bosom." But, although these masses lacked guidance, they were, in his opinion, no worse off than their superiors who, however educated, found little in past human experience of use in understanding the unforeseen innovations of the factory towns. The Greek verse, said Taylor, meant nothing in Manchester, and philosophy knew no circumstances like those which prevailed there.

Vaughan, who pointed out the fact, none too well recognized even today, that rural and urban populations have played different roles in the growth of civilization, argued that in the "unavoidable intercourse" of the new towns there was occurring an education of the people that would stimulate science, advance self-government, improve the arts and literature, and raise the general level of popular life. "Such, indeed, is often the astuteness acquired in the exercise of this greatest of free schools," he said, "that the smith of Sheffield, or the weaver of Manchester, would frequently prove, on any common ground,

From Carolin F. Ware, *The Cultural Approach to History* (New York: Columbia University Press, 1940), pp. 228-42. Reprinted by permission of the publisher. The late Ralph E Turner was Professor of History at Yale University.

more than a match for a college graduate." Vaughan saw the new industrial towns as centers of "vast experiments" like those which had occurred in the cities of other lands and ages.

For us who live today in the midst of what is a chaos understood badly if at all, the views of Taylor and Vaughan may provide a point of departure for a consideration of the prevailing confusion. At least, it is clear that, if the English industrial city of the 1840's was a scene of "vast experiments," today, with similar cities having become the dominant type of community in all industrial nations, "vast experiments" have probably been carried further than they had gone in the early nineteenth century. Similarly, if, as Taylor said, the urban masses will ultimately bear all society aloft, it is probable that the tendency of this bearing is more clear today than when he noted it.

An examination of the industrial city as a center of cultural change may indicate something of these "vast experiments," may possibly show the general direction the urban masses are tending. It is the purpose of this paper to sketch the outlines of such an examination.

The postulates of the examination are to be found in the concept of culture, as developed in recent social thought, especially by anthropologists and sociologists. According to their views, "a culture" is a socially organized and transmitted structure of behavior and thought. The structure is integrated functionally, that is, its elements provide more of a unity than of a conflict of services to life and have coherence psychologically in terms of a relatively clearly focused outlook on life. The basis of this integration is a process of social interaction, through which individual interests and needs are organized into collective forms or patterns. In the growth of culture, the social process impels individuals to new modes of action and thought—innovations, they are called—and these new modes, in turn, become organized as enduring patterns, through selection in the social process. The evolution of any structure of human behavior and thought, when viewed in historical perspective, is recognizable as the evolution of a cultural tradition which, from time to time as new social conditions arise, assimilates new elements in what may be called a reorientation of the tradition. The newly assimilated elements, it may be believed, seldom outweigh those persisting from the past.

This conception of the evolution of behavior and thought also predicates that, although cultural development goes forward constantly both by the loss of old elements and by the assimilation of innovations, there may be far-reaching disturbances in a cultural tradition which, disorganizing a long-persisting integration, produces finally a new integration. At the base of such new integration, setting its pattern and tendency of growth, is the social process through which individual behavior and thought are originally organized and finally assimilated into transmitted materials. In the words of A. A. Goldenweiser,

In its constituent elements culture is psychological and, in the last analysis, comes from the individual. But as an integral entity culture is cumulative, historical, extra-individual. It comes to the individual as part of his objective experience, just as do his experiences with nature, and, like these, it is absorbed by him, thus becoming part of his psychic content.[1]

It is from the point of view of these predications that the industrial city can be seen as having special significance for cultural development. Relative to the life that prevailed in the traditional countryside and the old market and port towns, it is not difficult to understand that the industrial city tends to organize a new structure of behavior and thought. The original patterns of this structure, as they emerged in Manchester, England, have been sketched in another essay in this volume;[2] here it is important to emphasize that the industrial city, as a focus of technological, economic, political, intellectual, and esthetic changes, organized cultural influences from many sources in a social process in which the constantly increasing populations participated. Whatever the influences of industrial cities, these influences move in the social interaction that arises in city populations, as individuals carry on their occupations, pursue their interests, and obtain their satisfactions. In terms of the concept of culture, the industrial city is, then, a milieu which everywhere has the same general elements and everywhere supports the development of a structure of behavior and thought from these elements. Because it is a predication of the concept of culture that both behavior and thought, although individually expressed, are socially organized, this milieu may be conceived as bringing about, through time, the transformation of the various organizations of behavior and thought carried in the traditional culture. Thus, for example, the organizations of behavior and thought characterizing the historic sociocultural types —the peasant, the noble, and the priest— are transformed into new structures of behavior and thought, which, however different for workers, technicians, and entrepreneurs, are nevertheless the common base of their lives.

Some of the aspects of this develop-

ing structure of behavior and thought may be briefly noted. Its primary elements are evident in the intricate division of labor, which, instead of standardizing and routinizing work as commonly supposed, gives it a manifold variety of forms which make the new urban workers not a "uniform mass" but a composite of diversified types. In contrast to the historic peasants, the members of the new industrial working class possess individuality in a great variety of forms. This developing structure of thought and behavior is also evident in new social services, in new amusements, in new intellectual and artistic pursuits, as well as in new technological and economic procedures. Also the new structure of behavior and thought is embodied in new standards of consumption, in new relationships of the sexes and the members of families, in new positions of the several age groups, in new circumstances affecting health, and in new causes of death. For individuals, these aspects are elements of a changing behavior and mentality; for the industrial city milieu, they are attributes fixed upon individuals coming under its influences.

From the point of view of cultural development, it is necessary to conceive of the beginnings of this structure of behavior and thought as appearing in the early industrial cities, of its elements spreading and maturing as industrial cities have grown, and, finally, of these elements becoming integrated through an intellectual outlook upon or a feeling for life shaped in terms of the frame of reference organized in experience as it goes on among the masses who now live in industrial cities. This matter may be stated in another way. If the industrial city, considered as the social milieu of a new structure of behavior and thought, is influencing ever larger parts of national populations, this influence is evident, on the one hand, in the dislocation of old forms of behavior and thought in the several national traditions and, on the other hand, in the appearance and spread of new forms. However, at the moment, because the dislocation of the old forms intensifies the emotional attachments to them, the new ones are not recognized. If at the moment such is the case, the prevailing confusion is understandable in the feeling that, although the old modes of behavior and thought no longer serve life, there is nothing to replace them. In truth, however, the modes of behavior and thought of a *new* culture may be implicit in the industrial city, requiring only recognition and acceptance to become the basis of conscious action. In the words of Robert H. Lowie, the anthropologist, "Culture, it seems, is a matter of exceedingly slow growth until a certain 'threshold' is passed, when it darts forward, gathering momentum at an unexpected rate."[3] The present disturbed situation in western culture, where the industrial city originated and has had its fullest development, may be only the approach to such a "threshold."

Before turning to a consideration of some of the aspects of industrial-city life which may be factors at the "threshold" of a cultural change, it is well to note that no one meant to create the industrial city or, as currently designated in the United States, the "metropolitan urban area." It arose as entrepreneurs pursued their interest—profits—and engineers served that interest by technological ingenuity. But once created, it became something other than a center of business and machine industry, that is, it became a milieu having the power to organize socially a structure of behavior and thought for those coming under its influence. For this reason the industrial city may ultimately react on business and industry, giving them new forms, in spite of the interests of entrepreneurs. It seems that commonly men do two things when they perform an act, first, what they intend to do and, second, what they do not intend to do. And often the second thing is more important than the first. Certainly this seems to be the case with those persons who, while their intentional activities were chiefly concerned with making money, unknowingly created the industrial city, which, as a social milieu, is now the matrix of cultural change.

An examination of the development of industrial cities shows three classes of factors which may be considered as having significance for further cultural development. Although these factors may not have originated completely in the industrial city, their influence in contemporary life is focused in its milieu, so that they must be considered as elements of a complex of urban psychological influences. These three classes of factors may be designated: (1) the paradox of economic liberalism, (2) conditions having origin in machine technology, and (3) conditions of urban association. Each of these classes of psychological factors ramifies through contemporary society, having many manifestations and exciting many comments. However, only in the industrial city or the metropolitan urban milieu can they be viewed objectively.

By the paradox of economic liberalism, the central predications of which are too widely accepted to require statement here, is meant that entrepreneurial activity has created conditions which not only restrict the freedom of individuals but also reveal that the presumptions that universal competition promotes the automatic realization of a constantly advancing well-being are false. The restrictions on individual freedom of action have objective form in the hierarchies of employment which have appeared as technological developments have brought together ever larger units of capital. For individuals employed in these hierarchies, economic advancement is more a matter of rising from grade to grade than a shift from the status "employee" to the status "entrepreneur." Moreover, in these hierarchies economic power is exercised from the top downward. Through the "right to fire," the qualities of behavior that bring advancement become less and less those summed up in the phrase "individual initiative" and more and more those implied in the word "loyalty." Actually "conformity" rather than "initiative" is the quality desired in an ever-increasing body of individuals who occupy the status of employee. It is also important to note that economic power exerted from the top of these hierarchies upon individuals in the lower levels of employment does interfere upon occasions with the exercise of personal liberties in areas of life quite beyond that of the economic functioning of the hierarchies. The effect of this interference is to impose upon more and more individuals a regimentation in terms of private interests. Indeed, in many ways the current assertion of the doctrines of economic liberalism is merely a defense for economic power that functions as private regimentation.

Probably no more concise statement of the contradiction between the theory of economic liberalism and the fact of the private regimentation which prevails among the populations of indus-

trial cities can be cited than the following words from Walter Lippmann's column, "How Liberty Is Lost":

> To have economic independence a man must be in a position to leave one job and go to another; he must have enough savings of some kind to exist for a considerable time without accepting the first job offered. . . . the industrial worker who has a choice between working in one factory and not working at all, the white collar intellectuals who compete savagely for the relatively few private positions and for posts in the bureaucracy—these are the people who live too precariously to exercise their liberties or to defend them. They have no savings. They have only their labor to sell, and there are very few buyers of their labor. Therefore, they have only the choice of truckling to the powerful or of perishing heroically but miserably.[4]

Who are the great to whom these workers shall truckle? The private employers or the politicians who promise jobs? The economic and political crises which have already swept away some liberal regimes, and which now threaten the remainder, root in this social soil.

In this connection, it is worth observing that, from the cultural point of view, the mere criticism of a social order cannot be the basis of social reconstruction. Indeed, if a program of social reform or amelioration can be successfully based on a critique of a social order, progress away from the conditions giving rise to the paradox of economic liberalism should have been rapid, since the rise of the early industrial cities, for the eloquence of the writers of those times on these conditions has not been surpassed by writers of the present century. But to be able to point out social evils—even, in fact, to understand their origin—is not to become adequate to deal with them. For they cannot be dealt with in terms of themselves or even in terms of the institutions which give rise to them. In other words, the evils cannot be dealt with merely as problems of distress, unemployment, and the like, or as aspects of a social order retaining the essential characteristics described in the doctrines of economic liberalism; they must be dealt with in terms of the potentialities of cultural change, implicit in the industrial city milieu. To know these potentialities involves not the emotional excitement raised by pointing to the evils, but a technique of analysis of the factors in cultural development. And to the development of this technique few social critics have made contributions.

In turning to a consideration of the two other classes of factors which are elements of the industrial city milieu, namely, conditions having their origin in machine technology and conditions of urban association, it is necessary to point out that the items listed under these headings have been arrived at in a certain way. This way has been an isolation of the repetitive, or recurring elements in industrial urban life, or, in other words, the finding of its continuously pervasive elements. This mode of analysis has been adopted on the ground that a culture, as an integrated and persisting structure of behavior and thought, is constructed psychologically upon a relatively stable order of stimuli, in terms of which patterns of reaction are developed. To such repetitive stimuli the great part of an industrial population react, and the recurring reactions become the determining tendencies of the development of the urban structure of life. Culture, it must be remembered, is both a psychological and a social phenomenon.

This way of analysis is not unfamiliar in American historiography. In fact, the classic essay, *The Significance of the*

Frontier in American History, by Frederick Jackson Turner, which has received the lip, if not the mind service of a generation of students of American history, embodies it. The fundamental postulate of this essay is that a persisting underlying influence gave distinctive patterns to national life and furthermore created an intellectual outlook which unified the national culture. Certainly the following excerpts can be so understood.

The existence of an area of free land, its continuous recession, and the advance of American settlement westward explain American development.
Behind institutions, behind constitutional forms and modifications, lie the vital forces that call these organs into life and shape them to meet changing conditions. . . .
The frontier individualism has from the beginning promoted democracy. . . .
The result is that to the frontier the American intellect owes its striking characteristics. That coarseness and strength combined with acuteness and inquisitiveness, that practical inventive turn of mind, quick to find expedients, that masterful grasp of material things, lacking in the artistic but powerful to effect great ends, that restless, nervous energy, that dominant individualism, working for good and for evil, and withal that buoyancy and exuberance which comes with freedom, these are traits of the frontier, or traits called out elsewhere because of the existence of the frontier.[5]

In terms of the concept of culture, the fact of "free land" may be understood as having established patterns which, as the frontier was pushed westward, were worked into the various phases of national life and, as individual experience and behavior were organized in these patterns, came to embody a pervasive psychological reaction which was the source of the subjective tradition of the national culture. In a sense, therefore, an analysis of current American developments in cultural terms is not greatly different from the mode of thinking which led Turner to his view of national development.

In every culture the integration of man with physical nature, in terms of technology, is significant in the life of the people who carry the culture. From this integration flows the wealth which supports the social order and certain basic judgments on life that have entered always into social attitudes, religious beliefs, and moral practices. There is no need here to discuss these phenomena, as they have long existed in cultures having an agrarian base. From contemporary technology come, it seems, at least three recognizable conditions that may contribute to the shaping of new cultural forms:

First: The sense of human control. Machine technology is operated by energy produced and controlled by man; in fact, it represents the fullest expression of his rationality. He creates power, orders its flow, governs its movement, and determines its resultant. In this circumstance exists ground for the assumption that what man achieves in one field of action, he may also do in another field. As a result of man's triumph in technology, it may be that he feels more able to command his fate socially. The emergence of the concept "planned economy" roots at least partly in this circumstance.

Second: The utility of objective knowledge. That knowledge is power is appreciated by the simplest mechanic; in terms of a special body of knowledge, every machine operator or machine fixer performs his task. This circumstance boldly insists that it is knowledge which functions to give success in every situation, that myth, tradition, and special interest must give way to knowledge—and the knowledge meant is worldly, factual, and utilitarian. By

implication, therefore, machine technology supports the view that social distress exists either because of lack of knowledge or because of the unwillingness to apply what is at hand.

Third: The increasing capacity to produce wealth. With the advent of machinery and applied science in agriculture and industry, man's capacity to produce wealth expanded enormously. For example, between 1920 and 1930 the agricultural population of the United States decreased by 4,000,000 persons, while agricultural production increased by 25 percent; now agricultural economists estimate that the agricultural population, not counting the backlog of persons who would have migrated to cities if jobs had been available, could be decreased by at least 3,000,000 persons without seriously affecting the agricultural production necessary to maintain national consumption at present standards. It has been estimated that since about 1870 the capacity to produce in manufacturing industries has increased 3 percent per year. Especially important is the fact that the increase of productivity has gone on steadily during the present depression decade. This fact is relevant to the present situation, which finds industrial production near the 1929 level without the employment of an equal number of workers.

These three conditions having their origin in contemporary technology—the sense of human control, the utility of objective knowledge, and the increasing capacity to produce wealth—point more and more directly to an economy in which human control, exercised with knowledge rather than with self-interest, may utilize the new capacity, to produce wealth for the support of a more secure life.

In closing this comment on the new

conditions of life that have come with contemporary technology, it should be noted that one does not need to be a philosopher in order to know them, for they run constantly in the experience of all who actually work at the production of real goods. In other words, these conditions are part and parcel of the life of the masses of industrial cities.

The conditions of urban association are certainly no less significant for setting the direction of cultural change than those arising in contemporary technology. In fact, because they have existence in social interaction, they are primary to these influences which, after all, are reactions of men to physical nature and not of men to men. Culture, it may be noted, stands between man and nature, whereas man comes to culture through the social process.

From this point of view four conditions of industrial urban association are significant:

First: The disintegration of localism and tradition. Innumerable social stimuli flow through the contemporary urban population. Newspapers, movies, and radio pour the world into their eyes and ears; from these visual and aural images there is no escape. By the number and impact of these social stimuli, local prejudices and old traditions are disintegrated. By this wearing away, the urban masses are freed to take on views which harmonize with their social environment—the industrial city as a whole, not merely as a place where labor is sold and a profit is made. Indeed, the rise of propaganda, i.e., the organized control of mass opinion, has its origin in this circumstance, for as the masses are released from local and traditional opinions, they become free to move in new directions. Propaganda is organized by special interests in order to determine this direction. In the end,

however, the movement of mass mentality will necessarily be in the direction set by the milieu which exists in the going experience of thousands of individuals.

Second: The cult of uniformity. As social stimuli flow continuously through the urban masses by way of machine-made commodities and routinized social services, manners, customs, and tastes are shaped into a wide conformity. This conformity is the necessary base of the organization of a complex social order among a large population; it makes for frictionless movement among large aggregates of individuals, who can, as a result, move together in actions not possible for them when they were embedded in local communities. Conformity serves the need for orderly coöperation in the intricate processes of urban society.

Third: The diversification of individual behavior. In communities antedating industrial cities, refinement, elegance, and taste were, in the main, attributes of small classes; to belong to these classes meant the possession of an explicit moral code, special forms of dress and manner, and particular intellectual affectations. In some respects these class attributes survive now, but among urban masses individual tastes find release from such controls. Thus there appear among urban populations innumerable groups pursuing self-selected interests, and individuals are permitted wide variations from all norms of conduct. The modern urban milieu is fostering a diversification of intellectual, artistic, and amusemental pursuits, unheard of in earlier types of communities. Individual energies are free to find expression in more ways than ever before. The industrial city well exemplifies the sociological principle that as social organization becomes more complex, individuals necessarily have more opportunity for development.

Fourth: The reorientation of the right of property. From the point of view of the concept of culture, the social rather than the economic factor is decisive in historical development. Thus it need cause no surprise that the social milieu of the industrial city is affecting the right of property—indeed, the whole relationship of men and wealth. The prevailing concept of property was derived from societies mainly agrarian in their economic and social organization. It is a concept developed mainly in terms of tangible goods, for it emphasizes possession on the ground that from possession flow the benefits of ownership. Now it appears that property in this sense has been becoming less and less important in the lives of all urban dwellers. Urban dwellers, even those having great wealth, can own very little of the property upon which their lives continually depend. The rich and the poor alike are dependent upon a continuity of services—water, food, light, heat, protection—which are maintained only through social coöperation. And they demand not ownership of these services, but their continuous functioning, regardless of ownership. Similarly, the owner of tangible property, whatever it may be, can produce little with the property that contributes to real satisfaction. His property probably functions to create any wealth that gives real satisfactions only through a minute division of labor, and such wealth is produced only through the maintenance of this division of labor. Finally, since the individual in the modern urban economy, no matter who he may be, can command few real goods through the possession of real property, he must possess some claim upon wealth

which can be executed in diverse ways; for only by such execution can he acquire the diversity of real goods which supports urban modes of living. Thus it appears that in the modern industrial city the ownership of property is far less important to the support of individual life than the maintenance of certain fundamental economic services and the establishment of some kind of claim on currently produced real goods. In fact, the elaboration of the modes of ownership through various kinds of legal claims—securities, trusts, insurance annuities, and social security claims— is an adjustment to this growing social orientation of the right of property.

However confused and clouded this exposition of the factors in the industrial urban milieu has been, it has made these factors far more clear than they are. Actually they exist today as part of the chaos previously noted. They are vaguely felt impulses, uncertain judgments, and befogged visions; they are neither defined nor oriented. However, they run in the experience of urban masses, as life goes on in terms of the labor market, machine technology, and urban association; and, as combined in a day-by-day routine, they form a frame of reference which for these masses, without conscious effort on their part, becomes the point of departure of feeling and thinking. Thus from this frame of reference issues, in the life of the masses, new attitudes toward their problems, new definitions of their interests, and new concepts of what life ought to be like. More important still in the day-by-day routine of behavior, as organized under the influence of this complex of urban forces, are the elements which may be combined in new patterns of behavior that will constitute the culture which is correlative with the modes of thinking and feeling set in this frame of reference. In other words, the frame of reference, as the subjective content of life shaped by the complex of urban forces, and the day-by-day routines of behavior, as the objective content of life shaped by this complex, together form the psychological basis for the integration of thought and behavior in a new culture.

In the concept of culture, it is postulated that at any time there are a limited number of possible modes of thinking and acting; therefore, as far as the contemporary world is concerned, if the old forms of thought and behavior are to be displaced (as, indeed, they are being displaced), the complex of urban forces which shapes this frame of reference and day-by-day routine of behavior of the urban masses fixes the possibilities for the future. It is pertinent to state here that because this frame of reference and this day-by-day routine of behavior are organized through social interaction, they affect, to some degree, the smaller specialized urban groups as well as the urban masses; for this reason contemporary cultural change is not merely an adjustment to the rise of a new social class. It is, in fact, far more fundamental, for it is touching all classes, compelling those which have been dominant to alter the forms of their control if they are to remain dominant. The twentieth century cannot have just any kind of social order; it must have one oriented in terms of the contemporary industrial urban milieu.

If one seeks a general heading under which to sum up the most significant aspect of the cultural change under way in nations whose chief communities are industrial cities or metropolitan urban areas, it would seem to be the phrase "a reëducation of the masses." Before the rise of industrial cities, the overwhelming proportion of population in all lands consisted of peasants—socially isolated, superstitious, tenacious of the land, and illiterate. As industrial cities grew, the peasant element declined and the urban masses formed. It should be recognized that, as the masses shifted to the cities, they brought with them the mentality of peasants; this has been a primary condition in their reëducation which, even today, the contrivers of propaganda know how to use. But, once in the city, the new circumstances of life—the labor market, machine technology, and urban association—began to affect their behavior and thought. It is not contended that the urban masses have been or are now conscious of this process of reëducation; it is only argued that they necessarily act and think under its effects, and that such action and thought are the elements of the cultural change now under way.

NOTES

1. A. A. Goldenweiser, *History, Psychology, and Culture* (New York, 1933), p. 59.
2. See Chap. X [of C. F. Ware's *The Cultural Approach to History*].
3. Robert H. Lowie, *Culture and Ethnology* (New York, 1917), p. 78.
4. *New York Herald Tribune*, July 16, 1938.
5. "The Significance of the Frontier in American History," *The Early Writings of Frederick Jackson Turner*, compiled by E. E. Edwards (Madison, 1938), pp. 185-229, at pp. 186, 220, 227-28.

Urbanization and Criminal Violence in the Nineteenth Century

ROGER LANE

America is now an urban nation, but Americans are still afraid of cities. There are many dimensions to this fear, but one of them is especially direct, and starkly physical. The current concern with "safety in the streets" echoes a belief, as old as the Republic, that the city is dangerous, the breeding ground of vice and violence. Observers of varying sophistication have pointed out that dark streets hide dark deeds, and that the anonymity and freedom of urban society, its temptations and frenzied pace, all contribute to encourage criminal behavior. From this it is easy to conclude that with metropolitan growth and the multiplication of all these conditions, the rate of violent crime is inexorably multiplied also.

But constant repetition of a myth is no substitute for proof. Under some circumstances it does in fact seem clear that migration to the metropolis has been accompanied by disruption and violence. This does not mean that there is a necessary or inevitable connection between the growth of cities and the growth of crime. In fact the existing historical evidence suggest the very reverse, that over a long-term urbanization has had a settling, literally a civilizing, effect on the population involved.

The statistical evidence for such a long-term trend is necessarily fragmentary and local. But for this purpose local studies may well be more reliable than national. Figures for the United States as a whole, compiled by the Federal Bureau of Investigation, have been available only since 1930. Based on the records of police departments with widely varying standards of accuracy, these have provided a generation of criminologists with material for argument.[1] Analyses of crime rates in individual urban areas, on the other hand, are less complicated by discrepancies in definition and in police practice. While few of these reach back to any period before the FBI's Uniform Crime Reports, these few are significant. None points to any clear proportional increase in serious crime within particular cities. And the more recent suggest, on the contrary, a sometimes striking proportional decrease.[2]

Both the decrease and some of the explanation for it may be demonstrated since it is necessary to choose a single area to represent the whole—by an examination of 19th-century Massachusetts. A stable Eastern state, with one growing metropolis and a number of thriving smaller cities, this Commonwealth had a fairly typical experience with industrial urbanization. As a result of the legislature's enormous appetite for statistical information, its official records, including all those re-

From *The Journal of Social History*, Vol. II, No. 2 (December 1968), pp. 156-63. Reprinted by permission of the publisher. Roger Lane is Associate Professor of history at Haverford College.

lating to criminal behavior, are probably better than any kept elsewhere.[3] And while criminal statistics are notoriously difficult to deal with, and by themselves offer no firm conclusions, the history of the Commonwealth has been abundantly studied, and may be used to help interpret the raw numerical data. Together, the statistics and the social record can illuminate several aspects of the history of criminal violence in America. These include: the changing incidence of disorder itself, the relation of this change to urban growth, the special conditions which may upset this relation, and lastly the problem of public attitudes or concern.

While all criminal statistics are subject to some doubt, the central conclusion about the figures from Massachusetts may be stated with confidence: serious crime in metropolitan Boston has declined sharply between the middle of the 19th century and the middle of the 20th. This often ragged downward trend does not, of course, apply equally to all offenses, but it does to most of the more serious common-law crimes. Three independent studies, by a lawyer, a historian, and a sociologist, confirm this basic direction.[4] While the three cover different periods, and employ somewhat different methods, they do fit together, and all are based essentially on police arrest statistics, the index most widely used by contemporary criminologists.[5] The most comprehensive, covering the years from 1849 to 1951, shows a drop of nearly two-thirds in those crimes which the FBI classifies as "major."[6]

But only half the story, at best, can be told through the figures from the metropolis alone. Our concern is with the whole society. And it has been argued that the difference in crime rates between urban and nonurban areas may be great enough so that a drop in the incidence of criminality in the cities is more than offset by the fact that a continually greater percentage of the population is living in them.[7] It is necessary, to meet this problem, to look at the statistics for Massachusetts as a whole.

For most of the 19th century, the use of police records is neither possible nor desirable on a statewide basis.[8] But other indices of real criminal activity are available. And four of them may be used to establish the changing incidence of "serious" crime, defined as that which involves real injury to persons or loss of property.[9] These four are lower court cases, jail commitments, grand jury cases, and state prison commitments, all involving the major common-law offenses against persons or property. The first date for which two of these indices were published in trustworthy form is 1834; the first year for which all four were compiled is 1860. The figures for these periods, expressed in 3-year averages, may be compared with those for the end of the century in table 1.[10]

The decline in the officially recorded crime rate is unmistakable here. And it is strongly probable that the real decline is greater than the statistics indicate. The key problem in the interpretation of criminal statistics is posed by "the dark figure," representing those illegal activities or incidents which never come to the light of official attention. But since in later years, as will be discussed below, there was both an increasing intolerance of criminal activity and a great growth in the numbers of police and investigative agents, all evidence suggests that this "dark figure" was growing propor-

Table 1

Average yearly incidence of cases per 100,000 population

	1834-36	1860-62	1899-1901
Lower Court Cases		777	707
Jail commitments		333	163
Grand jury cases	89	117	63
Imprisonments	16.8	11.9	5.9

tionately smaller as the century progressed. Thus table 1 considerably understates the real decline.

For purposes of explanation, it is almost equally important to note the pattern of this decline. The table lists offenses in the order of their severity: lower court cases generally involve the least important crimes, jailings the next, indictments next, and imprisonments the most. And with one exception—the relative rise in indictments between the 1830's and the 1860's, which will be considered later—it is especially notable that the recorded drop in the crime rate is directly pro-

tion—not only a fall over time but a fall most marked in the most serious categories.

Meanwhile, however, while the serious crime rate was falling, the total crime rate—or the officially recorded total—was actually rising. This apparent paradox results from the fact that the downward curve described above may be wholly reversed simply by adding a third official category, "Crimes Against Public Order," to the two above. When these offenses are added in—drunkenness is by far the largest of them—the results for the lower courts may be indicated as follows:[12]

Table 2

Yearly incidence of cases per 100,000 population

	1840	1860	1900
Total lower court cases	595	1,869	3,317

portional to the seriousness of the offense. This is generally true also when the four indices used are examined further and broken into subcategories. Thus for example the combined rate of commitments for homicide, rape, armed robbery, and arson in 1860-62 was 6.8 per 100,000; by 1900 it has dropped to 2.9 per 100,000.[11] Most of the other data point in the same direc-

The pattern for these minor crimes is the obverse of that for serious offenses, in that the more trivial the degree of the offense the larger its proportional increase over time. While virtually no indictments or imprisonments resulted from third-class offenses, their addition makes less difference in the case of jailings than of lower court cases:[13]

Table 3

Yearly incidence of cases per 100,000 population

	1841	1860	1900
Total jail commitments	419	548	969

This upward curve in total offenses does not have the same importance as the other, downward curve in the incidence of serious crime. The latter represents the basic statistical conclusion, in that it reflects a real situation, a real decline in the rate of criminal activity. But the former, while it is merely statistical, is nonetheless important. There is a complementary relationship between the two trends, and the nature of this relationship helps account for much that underlies the numbers.

The entire increase in the criminal statistics of Massachusetts, during the period covered, may in fact be attributed wholly to the rise in cases of drunkenness. Indeed this one offense, together with simple assault, its constant companion, may serve as a focus for much more. To understand the reasons for the rise in drunk arrests is to understand much about the social changes occurring in the 19th century, changes which affected all of its criminal patterns.

It is clear, first, that the mounting total of cases fed into the official machinery of justice does not reflect a real increase in the consumption of alcohol. The misuse of drink was throughout the 19th century a problem of enormous dimensions. The continuing debate about the nature of drunkenness, although some of it anticipated the best of current thinking, was on the whole punitive, and tended to blame the use of alcohol for virtually every individual and most social evils.[14] But even the most ardent spirits in the temperance movement did not usually suggest that there was any long-term rise in drunken behavior. They and their opponents generally united in agreeing that the situation, in ragged fashion,

was improving with time.[15] Because much of the alcohol was made and sold illegally, especially in the countryside, it is difficult to investigate this statistically. But certainly in the metropolis and probably elsewhere the evidence does suggest a decline. Early in the century even ministerial ordinations, to say nothing of less grave occasions, were frequently bibulous affairs.[16] By the 1830's a substantial portion of the middle class had renounced the use of hard liquor. The prohibition was extended later to all drinks, and its champions carried on a continuous political and educational campaign against it. In the 1830's, and again in the 1850's, law enforcement officers estimated that 1 in every 65 inhabitants of Boston—men, women, and children —were selling alcohol for a living, in the latter period in defiance of a state law which prohibited all private sales.[17] Certainly neither this proportion nor this widespread evasion of the law was matched later in the century; by about 1880 the ratio was down to 1 seller in 150 and rising fast.[18]

On one level, the rising statistics of drunk arrests simply reflect an increase in the numbers of professional police and in the penal apparatus. It was not until 1837 that Boston organized a squad of full-time professionals, and for many years these were the only ones in the Commonwealth. But by 1860 all of the larger cities had organized forces of varying sizes, and these had grown and spread to the smaller towns well before 1900.[19] The effect of this, and of a proportionate increase in the rest of the agents of justice, is easily demonstrated. In the absence of police, ordinary citizens were expected to make complaints on their own, and to call on constables only to execute warrants already sworn. But while private individuals may make the effort to initiate the processes of justice when directly injured, professionals are required to deal, in number, with those whose merely immoral or distasteful behavior hurts no one in particular. It takes real cops, in short, to make drunk arrests.

Again on this level, the relative shortage of official agents of law enforcement accounts for one of the most striking characteristics of table 12-1 above. The farther back the figures go, as noted, the higher is the relative proportion of serious crimes. The authorities, with limited resources, obviously had to deal with felony first, indictable crime next, and misdemeanor only when resources permitted.

Conversely it is notable that as time advanced and it became easier for injured citizens to complain to a policeman, the tables indicate that proportionately fewer such complaints were being made. In the city of Boston, at least, the result was a progressive decrease in the number of annual arrests made by each patrolman: in 1855, the average was 71 per man, while by 1885 this had dropped to 37.[20]

Drawn as a model, this development may explain the only apparent anomaly in table 1, already referred to. This is the fact that between the 1830's and the 1860's the figures show both a fall in prison commitments and a rise in grand jury indictments. Perhaps—the subject will be investigated further—there is no great paradox at all. District attorneys in the 1830's, faced with a high incidence of truly violent criminal behavior, may have had to concentrate on the more important prisonable offenses, to the neglect of others, even indictable ones. As their resources were increased, and as the real crime rate

fell, they would be able by the 1860's to catch up on lesser indictments.

But there remains a more fundamental level of explanation. To account for the rise in lesser offenses or the drop in more serious crimes simply in terms of the expansion of police, courts, and prosecutors is to misplace the emphasis. The expansion is not cause but symptom. The machinery of justice was increased because of a felt need, a growing intolerance of behavior which had earlier been tolerated, coupled with a belief that the state and not the individual citizen was required to do the necessary job.

This process is most evident in Boston itself. Leading citizens and governmental officials were always proud of their reputation for maintaining a tidy and well-governed "order" in the city. But the definition of what constituted "order" changed considerably with time.

Josiah Quincy, one of Boston's first mayors, was also the first to boast that in no other city "of equal population, are there fewer instances of those crimes, to which all populous places are subject."[21] He had in fact assumed charge, in 1823, of a newly incorporated city of about 45,000 inhabitants, which officially issued some 697 liquor licenses and ignored the existence of a large number of illegal sellers. Relatively little attention was paid to such common offenses as simple drunkenness and assault. The night watch, largely concerned with the danger of fire or arson, was afraid to enter some of the more notorious neighborhoods. No one patrolled anywhere in the daytime. Quincy's several terms of office were marked by frequent battles between rival gangs of firemen, whose hunger for looting threatened the whole institution of fire insurance. When, after one of the city's numerous "riots, routs, and tumultuous assemblies" had spluttered on for a full week during the long hot summer of 1825, Quincy was forced to take personal charge of a posse of citizens to put it down. This was cleary an unusual action, and the mayor refused later opportunities to risk his limbs and authority in physical combat, preferring to let mob violence burn out by itself. Nevertheless, neither he nor the voters were unduly alarmed by the prevailing level of disorder. Citizens were traditionally supposed to take care of themselves, with the help of family, friends, or servants when available. An organized professional police would certainly be expensive and might be a threat to valued freedoms. And Quincy was proud to point out, at the end of his official career, that he had not added a single constable or watchman to Boston's part-time corps of peace officers.

By the 1880's, when an aldermanic committee echoed Mayor Quincy's earlier claim that Boston was the most orderly of America's larger cities, the situation had changed considerably.[22] In 1837, after three major riots in 4 years, the city had acquired a police force.[23] Since then it had been growing steadily, at a rate faster than the population. By the Civil War, the citizens had abandoned their objection to uniforms, with their paramilitary connotations, and the patrolmen had begun to carry guns.[24] By the 1880's the force had acquired most of its familiar modern characteristics and functions.[25] And the demand for more men continued—despite the fact that the crime rate had been dropping for some time, and with it the workload for each man on the force.

The demand for more men, then, reflected not a worsening situation but higher standards, a change in attitude. Really violent crime brought more severe retribution than formerly; the same offenses which had earned 2-year sentences in the 1830's were now punished by 3 to 4 years or more in the state penitentiary, and the average was still going up.[26] While the police stations were still being built for "defensibility," there had been—and would be —no large-scale riot for years.[27] It is impossible to imagine a late-century mayor wrestling with mobs as did Quincy in the twenties and Theodore Lyman in the thirties. All of the city had been brought under more or less effective patrol, and the voters were demanding that the streets be cleared not only of arsonists but of drunks, peddlers, and truants. Traffic problems were settled not by teamsters with their fists but by officers with whistles. The responsibility for individual safety had been decisively shifted to these agents of the law; uniformed men with revolvers were stationed not only in potentially dangerous areas but in the quiet confines of the public library.[28] And the end result, reflected in many arrests for minor breaches of conduct, was a degree of "order" which would have astonished and perhaps dismayed an earlier and rougher generation.

The progressive heightening of standards of propriety, and with it the increasing reliance on official law enforcement, were processes which, while most sharply visible in Boston, were common to the whole society. Traditionally, criminologists have interpreted the zigs and zags of recorded criminal statistics in terms of individual events or situations—war, for example, or depression. But the change in social behavior reflected in the two dominant curves of criminality in Massachusetts is so long term and so widespread as to suggest a connection with the most fundamental of contemporary social processes, that of industrial urbanization itself. The nature of that connection has never been studied in detail, but it may at least be outlined.

Massachusetts in 1835 had a population of some 660,940,81 percent rural, overwhelmingly preindustrial and native born.[29] Its citizens were used to considerable personal freedom. Whether teamsters, farmers, or artisans, they were all accustomed to setting their own schedules, and the nature of their work made them physically independent of each other. None of the more common occupations provided any built-in checks against various kinds of personal excess. Neither fits of violence nor bouts of drunkenness disrupted any vital patterns. Individual problems, sins or even crimes, were not generally cause for wider social concern.

Under these circumstances, while scarcely a frontier, the Commonwealth could afford a fairly high degree of lawlessness. No city in the state boasted a professional police, and the machinery of justice was not equipped to handle many cases. Many of the more common forms of violence or crime were simply not reported to the agents of law, as those affected either shrugged off their injuries or struck back directly.

But the impact of the twin movements to the city and to the factory, both just gathering force in 1835, had a progressive effect on personal behavior throughout the 19th century and into the 20th. The factory demanded regularity of behavior, a life governed by obedience to the rhythms of clock and calendar, the demands of foreman and supervisor. In the city or town, the needs of living in closely packed neigh-borhoods inhibited many actions previously unobjectionable. Both blue- and white-collar employees in larger establishments were mutually dependent on their fellows; as one man's work fit into another's, so one man's business was no longer his own.

The results of the new organization of life and work were apparent by 1900, when some 76 percent of the 2,805,346 inhabitants of Massachusetts were classified as urbanites.[30] Much violent or irregular behavior which had been tolerable in a casual, independent society was no longer acceptable in the more formalized, cooperative atmosphere of the later period. The private, direct response to criminal injury was no longer necessary or approved. All cities and most towns had acquired police forces, constantly expanding to meet greater expectations. Throughout the state, the victims of violence and theft were conditioned to seek official help. The move to the cities had, in short, produced a more tractable, more socialized, more "civilized" generation than its predecessors.[31]

The trend in the direction of higher standards and a lower level of violence may be measured from the early 19th century through much of the 20th. But what is true in the long run is not necessarily evident in the short. While the process or urbanization has helped to raise standards of personal behavior, it may not do so by itself. And there is some indication in the history of 19th-century Massachusetts that under unfavorable conditions migration to the cities may at some times have increased the incidence of violently unsocial behavior. This may well be true, at least, of the long generation between 1835 and 1860.

The existing statistics, alone, are no

sure guide to what was actually happening during these crucial early decades. The Boston arrest figures were not kept until 1849. For the state as a whole, much of the remaining evidence remains ambiguous. As explained above, the two main indices, the rate of grand jury indictments and of imprisonments for felony, point stubbornly in opposite directions. But there is good reason to suspect that the period from the mid-1830's to the Civil War illustrates at least a partial, and important, exception to the general developments previously sketched.

From the war on to the end of the century and beyond, the industrial development of Massachusetts, however painful for those involved, was at least proceeding at a pace and along lines already laid out. The era just before was the one which witnessed the turbulence of transition. No similar timespan in fact encompassed a more rapid increase in the urban population. Between 1835 and 1860, while the total population was growing from 660,940 to 1,231,066, the proportion of city dwellers leaped from 19 to 44 percent of the total.[32] At the same time, too, the major railroad lines were laid in patterns still existing. As steam began to replace waterpower as the major source of industrial energy, the factories, earlier confined to rural sites near waterfalls, began to move into the cities.

Social dislocation, meanwhile, accompanied economic. All through the period, and especially during and after the "hungry forties," heavy Irish immigration exacerbated all of the problems of city living. By 1855, some 68,100 of the 168,031 residents of Boston were natives of Ireland.[33] Uprooted from a rural setting, wholly without skills, the newcomers experienced the kind of culture shock, prejudice, and alienation which would plague other waves of migrants later. Crowded into stinking hovels, some of them underground, their miserable conditions of living strained all of the city's institutions of charity and police. Smallpox, once virtually eliminated, became again a problem, cholera struck hard, and the death rate about the middle of the century climbed to the highest point in the city's recorded history.[34]

In terms of its effect on behavior, all of these rapid and wrenching changes promoted the worst aspects of living in the city without benefit of its compensations. It must be stressed that economic developments were not fully able to keep pace with migration. Between 1837 and 1845, it has been estimated, the amount of large-scale or factory employment did not increase at all.[35] And in the 15 years following, while the total of factory employees grew to something like 25,000 or 30,000, the number of outright paupers in the metropolitan area was increasing at an even faster rate, to reach a peak of nearly 13,000 in 1860.[36] Without the discipline imposed by regular employment, this first large-scale flow of migrants into the city was a kind of mutual disaster. The raw arrivals from the countryside, Yankees as well as Irish, had not yet learned to weave warily through crowds, with their arms held in close. Often radically insecure, in neighborhoods still unstable, they sought release in drink. But to drink with strangers requires different rules, and more restraints, than drinking in more familiar situations. In this era of swinging elbows, bewilderment, and desperate unemployment, it is hard to find evidence that the level of violence was declining.

Indeed it is easy to find the opposite. During this whole period Massachusetts was wracked by political instability, aggravated by one unpopular war and the overhanging threat of another one.[37] The 1850's, in particular, witnessed a resurgence of mob violence as Know-Nothings and Irishmen, opponents and defenders of slavery, all found occasions to take to the streets.[38] These clashes, superimposed on and partly resulting from the already unhealthy social condition of Boston, were deeply disturbing to the inhabitants. If the real incidence of criminal behavior was not actually rising at this time, then surely it was not falling at the rate apparent in the generations following the Civil War.

All evidence points to the long-term drop in criminal activity as normative, and associated with urbanization. But the process was not complete without the accompaniment of rapid industrial development also. It was this which provided the means of absorbing raw migrants, of fitting them into a "system" which socialized and accommodated them into more cooperative habits of life. Without this other process, migration to the city alone, simply by multiplying human contacts, may very well multiply the incidence of criminally violent interaction among inhabitants unsuited to its demands.

Because of its clear connection with ethnic prejudice, and its dangerous political and social implications, the violent state of Boston during the 1850's was the source of considerable public concern. But the relation between concern about violence and violence itself is not always so complicated. Both in the 19th and the 20th centuries, the attitudes of newspapers, scholars, and the public generally have been various and volatile, the product often of special interests or misinformation. This makes such attitudes difficult to measure. But they are nevertheless crucially important to the study of criminal disorder.

In the long run and in the short, popular concern has a direct effect on the shape of criminal statistics. As it was changing public standards which accounted for the rising total of arrests during the 19th century, so police departments still concentrate on those offenses of greatest current interest. Moreover, it is not simply the actual level of criminal activity, but the balance between this and social attitudes, which determines how much violence is a "problem" at any given time.

While public "attitudes" are slippery concepts to compare, it does seem that in the sense above the state of Massachusetts, and the United States in general, had a criminal problem less worrisome in the 19th century than in the 1960's. The citizens of the Commonwealth, still close to their rural antecedents, were indeed afraid of cities, which one legislative committee called "the common sewers of the state."[39] And one major source of this fear was the "poverty, vice, and crime" commonly associated with Boston, in particular.[40] But hostile critics were more interested in the first two than in the last, and reformers endlessly debated the causal relation between them. The charge that the city had lost control of its "dangerous classes" was used in several attempts to limit self-government in Boston, but mob action was the only form of violence which generally figured in these complaints, and "crime" was used typically as a synonym for "vice."[41] It is significant that the laws concerning drink, especially, were subject to constant revision, but except for a reduction in the number of cases involving the death penalty, the general criminal code was not.[42] Legislative action or inaction mirrored public concern in this case. As the sons and daughters of Massachusetts migrated to the metropolis, the image conjured by the fearful was the rake or tempter, not the robber or rapist.

Nevertheless, however overshadowed by other issues, there were periodic outbursts of concern about violence or other crime. Often these occurred in response to some new development, or threat, for which the public or authorities were unprepared. In fact, the history of these threats, and the responses to them, comprises much of the history of criminal law enforcement.[43]

Thus the multiplication of banks and bank notes, through the 1820's, provided golden opportunities for counterfeiters. The nature of the problem, in this case, required a network of private banker's agents to cooperate, across state and even national boundaries, with the appropriate public authorities. Anti-Catholic rioting, in the 1830's, was a principal spur to the development of professional police. During the 1870's, the growing sophistication of professional criminals, dramatized by a spectacular series of bank robberies, led to an overhaul of existing detective methods in many American cities. During the same period, bands of healthy native vagrants, fugitives from the new industrial age, were a subject of great concern to the readers of sensational newspapers, who feared the violent potential in these "wild-eyed" strangers. The response in this case was harsher police

action, and a tightening of the rules governing charity and soup kitchens.

These concerns were at any rate real, and had often lasting effects, although they had little to do with the overall crime rate. Another and more frequent kind of scare resulted not from some genuinely new problem but from sudden attention focused on an old one. Lincoln Steffens, as a cub reporter in New York, learned how easy it was to manufacture a "crime wave," with techniques still familiar.[44] Thus a particularly brutal murder or a series of muggings could touch off a wave of arrests "on suspicion."[45] Often it was simply an investigation or expose of some endemic form of crime which generated a sudden excitement, during which the public was assured that Boston was facing a threat of unprecedented proportions.

But it is impossible, from these brief scares, to get any clear sense of direction. While the definition of the tolerable was altering with time, it was altering slowly and imperceptibly. And there is no evidence that, as the century progressed, the gap between the level of order expected and the level actually obtaining was changing in any constant direction. It is true that the police often felt that they were faced with problems of unprecedented magnitude, and chiefs decades apart warned that the level of juvenile delinquency, and the general breakdown of authority, threatened the very basis of society.[46] Other observers too, perhaps beguiled by the image of a more peaceful golden age in the past, sometimes asserted that crime was growing faster than the population. But this tendency to fear was balanced throughout the century by pride in growth and progress. And the

---

many apocalyptic statements may be countered with an equal number of others, more optimistic. Thus even in the troubled year of 1859, the State's attorney general could declare that "at no time in the history of Massachusetts have life, liberty, and property been more secure than at present."[47]

In short, while it is possible now to discover a long-term drop in the level of violence, contemporaries were simply not aware of this. The degree of public concern has never been, nor is it now, an accurate index of the degree of criminal activity. Indeed the reverse is often true. And it is doubly ironic that a drop in the actual incidence of disorder has been accompanied by—and contributed to—a heightened sensitivity to disorder. Such sensitivity, by leading to a more demanding standard of conduct, has been essential to the functioning of an interdependent urban society. But unless the process is recognized and understood, it may have unsettling effects. There are times when for various reasons the level of violence overbalances current expectations. In such situations the social pressure to maintain and extend high standards, and to enforce them universally, may result in frustration. The frustration may translate into fear. And this fear, in turn, may focus on the very urban process which helped to create those standards, on the growth of cities itself.

NOTES

1. See The Challenge of Crime in a Free Society: A Report by The President's Commission on Law Enforcement and The Administration of Justice (Washington, 1967), p. 29.
2. Four studies are especially germane: Harold A. Phelps, "Frequency of Crime and Punishment," Journal of the American Institute of

Criminal Law and Criminology, vol. XIX, No. 2 (Aug. 1926), p. 165-180, which covers Rhode Island between 1897 and 1927; Sam Bass Warner, Crime and Criminal Statistics in Boston (Boston, 1934), "Crime as a Function of Anomie," Journal of Criminal Law, Criminology, and Police Science (June 1966), covering Buffalo from 1854 to 1956; and Theodore Ferdinand, "The Criminal Patterns of Boston Since 1849," The American Journal of Sociology (July 1967), pp. 84-99, which runs to 1951. These all differ in purpose and sophistication, and none is directly concerned with the long-term decline, which helps to make their results the more striking
3. A survey of many of the official and criminal records of Boston and Massachusetts is contained in Roger Lane, Policing the City: Boston, 1822-1885 (Cambridge, Mass.: Harvard University Press, 1967), pp. 225-229 and 239-241.
4. See the works by Ferdinand, Warner, and Lane, in footnotes 2 and 3, above. There is no attempt, in these or in this paper, to measure the extent of statutory or white-collar crime.
5. Thorsten Sellin and Marvin E. Wolfgang, The Measurement of Delinquency (New York, 1964), p. 31.
6. Ferdinand, "Criminal Patterns of Boston," p. 87. Together with roughly similar results in Powell's study of Buffalo, these figures suggest that the main conclusions of the present paper, which is largely confined to the 19th century, may be projected up to the founding of the Uniform Crime Reports and beyond.
7. Ferdinand, "Criminal Patterns of Boston," p. 99.
8. Statewide arrest figures were not compiled until very late in the 19th century, and comparing those for different cities involves many of the same problems as plague students of the Uniform Crime Reports.
9. In this paper except where specifically noted, no distinction is made between violent crimes—against the person—and other serious offenses. Such terms as "crime" or "disorder" are used to cover both.
10. For references in this table, see Roger Lane "Crime and Criminal Statistics in Nineteenth Century Massachusetts," Journal of Social History (December 1968), footnote 8.
11. For references, see ibid., footnote 8.
12. For references, see ibid., footnote 10. 1840 is the first year for which these figures are available.
13. For references, see ibid., footnote 11. The year 1841 is the first for which these figures are available.
14. Compare The Challenge of Crime, p. 235, and Lane, Policing the City, passim, especially pp. 112-113.
15. For testimony of both reformers and conservatives, see especially Massachusetts House Document No. 415, Reports on the Subject of a

License Law . . . *Together With a Stenographic Report of the Testimony* (Boston, 1867), *passim*.

16. Alice Felt Tyler, *Freedom's Ferment: Phases of American Social History to 1860* (Minneapolis, 1944), ch. 13, especially p. 311.

17. Lane, *Policing the City*, pp. 41 and 71.

18. *Ibid.*, p. 211.

19. Unfortunately, neither the federal nor the state census permits an accurate statewide count of policemen during the 19th century.

20. Lane, *Policing the City*, pp. 230-232. The trend has continued. Modern police, despite the introduction of patrol cars and call wagons, make fewer arrests, in general, than did their predecessors, especially when the whole class of minor auto violations is eliminated.

21. Quoted in *ibid.*, p. 25. For the other information in this paragraph see ch. 2 *passim*.

22. *Ibid.*, p. 204.

23. *Ibid.*, pp. 29-35.

24. *Ibid.*, pp. 104-105.

25. *Ibid.*, p. 224.

26. These are figures for the average sentences to the state penitentiary. The range of offenses listed remained about the same through the century. For references, see Lane, "Crime and Criminal Statistics," footnote 14.

27. *Annual Report of the Commissioners of Police of the City of Boston for* . . . *1885* (Boston, 1885), pp. 28-30.

28. Lane, *Policing the City*, p. 173.

29. Population figures are from *The Census of Massachusetts* . . . *1905* (Boston, 1909), vol. 1, p. xxxi. The urban definition is based on a population of 8,000.

30. *Ibid.*

31. It should be noted that after the 1880's, when Boston already had nearly 2 policemen per 1,000 inhabitants, which is close to the present nationwide average for major cities, it was the smaller places only where the arrest rate continued to climb dramatically. Boston, because of its very small geographical area, was ahead of most American cities in this respect. It was still possible in other places to raise the arrest figures by extending patrol and demanding higher standards in previously neglected areas, such as outlying slums. This process, and the reduction of the "dark figure" which results from better policing in general, may account for many apparent "rises" in crime rates which occur right up to the present.

32. See footnote 29.

33. Oscar Handlin, *Boston's Immigrants: A Study in Acculturation* (rev. ed., Cambridge, 1959), p. 244.

34. *Ibid.*, pp. 114-116.

35. *Ibid.*, p. 74.

36. *Ibid.*, pp. 74 and 256.

37. For political conditions in Massachusetts, see William Gleason Bean, "Party Transformation in Massachusetts, 1848-1860, with Special Reference to the Antecedents of Republicanism" (unpublished Ph.D. dissertation, Harvard University archives, 1922), *passim*.

38. Lane, *Policing the City*, pp. 72-74, 90-91, and 94-95.

39. *Ibid.*, p. 132.

40. First used by Josiah Quincy in his "remarks on some of the Provisions of the Massachusetts Affecting Poverty, Vice, and Crime" (Cambridge, 1822), these last four words became a stock phrase among the Commonwealth's reformers.

41. Lane, *Policing the City*, especially pp. 122-125, 128-134, 142-156, and 213-219.

42. *Ibid.*, *passim*. For the criminal code, summed up in revisions compiled in 1835, 1859, 1881, and 1900, see p. 239.

43. For references in the following paragraph, see *ibid.*, pp. 55-56, 29-35, 142-156, 157-160, and 193-195.

44. Lincoln Steffens, *Autobiography* (New York, 1931), pp. 285-291.

45. In 1865, inspired by a fear of returning veterans much like that following World War II, the police made some 2,532 such arrests. See Lane, *Policing the City*, p. 149.

46. See, e.g., *ibid.*, pp. 68, 137, and 34.

47. *Ibid.*, p. 117.

From City to Suburb: The "Moral" Influence of Transportation Technology

JOEL ARTHUR TARR

Humanity demands that men should have sunlight, fresh air, the sight of grass and trees. It demands these things for the man himself, and it demands them still more urgently for his wife and children. No child has a fair chance in the world who is condemned to grow up in the dirt and confinement, the dreariness, ugliness and vice of the poorer quarters of a great city. . . . There is, then, a permanent conflict between the needs of industry and the needs of humanity. Industry says men must aggregate. Humanity says they must not, or if they must, let it be only during working hours and let the necessity not extend to their wives and children. *It is the office of the city railways to reconcile these conflicting requirements.*
Charles Horton Cooley, 1891

The theme of the evil city and the virtuous countryside has persisted throughout American history. Warnings of the unhealthiness of the urban environment and the threat that the urban masses posed to American ideals emanated from public spokesmen and intellectuals throughout the nineteenth century. Articulators of this point of view, such as Thomas Jefferson, Ralph Waldo Emerson, and Josiah Strong, usually regarded rural life, in contrast to city life, as morally superior and generative of the virtues of health, strength of character, and individualism.[1]

Recently, however, Peter J. Schmitt and Scott Donaldson have expanded the classic urban-rural dichotomy.[2] As Schmitt observes, few of those in the late nineteenth and early twentieth centuries who attacked the city and praised their rural childhoods ever returned to farming. While they looked with nostalgia to the rural virtues, they were unwilling to sacrifice the opportunities for the acquisition of wealth found in the city. Rather than being imbued with the philosophy of "agrarianism," which demanded that man draw his livelihood from the soil, they settled for the "spiritual values" of nature. And these values, which Schmitt calls "arcadian," thrived not only in the distant country, but also on the urban periphery in an area easily reached from the crowded city. In short, the suburb, *rus in urbe,* would enable Americans to pursue wealth and yet retain the amenities and values of rural life.[3]

The suburb, in the view of those who praised it, had certain desirable characteristics that distinguished it from the city. While the city was crowded, dirty, and smoky, the suburb had an abundance of "fresh air and clear sunlight, green foliage and God's blue sky." In the suburbs, which were primarily residential, most people lived in single family dwellings or "cottages" far from the smoke and noise of busi-

The research for this article was carried out with the aid of grants from the National Endowment for the Humanities and the Carnegie-Mellon Transportation Research Institute. Printed by permission of the author. Copyright © 1973 by Joel Arthur Tarr. Joel Arthur Tarr is Associate Professor of History and Urban Affairs at Carnegie-Mellon University.

ness and industry. Serenity and calm rather than hustle and bustle were the hallmarks of the suburbs. Natural surroundings, "cottage" living, and peace and quiet provided ideal conditions for family life and for the raising of children, all within easy commuting distance of offices and factories in the core of the city.[4]

Without transportation technology, however, the suburb as the halfway house between city and country and as the embodiment of the best of these diverse worlds would have been impossible. A number of writers have commented at length on the significance of the concept of technology in American thought, but often they have viewed the machine as opposed to the values of the pastoral or rural ideal.[5] Many influential spokesmen on the urban scene in the late nineteenth and early twentieth centuries, however, viewed technology as putting arcadia within the reach of city dwellers who would otherwise have been denied its moral benefits. If suburbia was the garden that all urbanites should strive to reach, then it was the machine that made it possible to work in the city but live in that garden.

The "machines" in this instance were various forms of urban transit ranging from the omnibus to the electric street railway, subway, and elevated railroad. All of these, theoretically, enabled the busy urbanite who labored in the city and resided in congested and unhealthy districts to continue to work in the city but to live in the suburbs in a superior environment. Statements about the role of transportation technology in permitting people to escape crowded and dirty cities occur throughout the literature on the city, but they appear with special frequency at the time of transit innovation. For, it was then that Americans, concerned with the social dangers posed by urban growth, reaffirmed their faith in technology and saw in transit innovation the means to escape successfully from urban problems.

Public transit developments had their largest impact on urban and suburban patterns roughly from 1840 to 1910. During these years urban population grew at a rapid rate, rising from 1,845,000 or 10.8 of the total population to 44,639,989 or 45.7 per cent. European immigrants, mainly from the rural areas of Ireland, Germany, Austria-Hungary, Italy, Poland, and Russia, accounted for a large part of the new urbanites, a fact which increased the fears of nativists and their spokesmen that the cities threatened American values.[6] At this time, cities also greatly increased their size by annexing contiguous incorporated and unincorporated territory.[7] Within these burgeoning urban areas, public transit systems facilitated the dispersal of population, concentrated commercial activities, and reversed the spatial distribution of socio-economic classes as compared with the patterns of the pre-transit city, thus giving rise to the modern core-oriented metropolitan area.

This transformation of the city's ecological and demographic patterns had its beginnings in the 1840's and 1850's, when many large American cities faced what one historian calls an "urban transportation crisis."[8] Cities in the 1840's and 50's were still primarily walking or pedestrian cities characterized by a "crowded compactness." By 1850 New York had a population density of 135.6 persons per acre in its "fully settled area," Boston 82.7, Philadelphia, 80.0, and Pittsburgh, 68.4.

Most urban residences were two- or three-story wooden or brick buildings. Those occupied by the working class and the poor were often packed with many families and their lodgers.[9] Land uses were not clearly specialized, and middle and upper class residences were interspersed with those of lower income groups and located comparatively close to manufacturing and commercial structures. In contrast to contemporary living patterns, the elite often lived close to the business and governmental center of the city, while the majority of workingmen distributed themselves in the outlying wards. Those workingmen who lived in the urban core packed into narrow alley dwellings, tenements, and cellars. As population pressure increased, already crowded lower class living areas disintegrated into slums.[10]

The growth of manufacturing and business activities accompanied the increased population congestion within cities. Most of the industrial and commercial development was clustered in the older sections of cities, especially near the waterfront seaports and river towns. These central locations offered savings in transportation costs as well as the benefits of agglomeration economies.[11] As the spatial needs of industries and businesses increased, residential population was pushed out of the central business areas. Many workers who were displaced moved into adjacent sections, creating increased problems and overcrowding and housing deterioration. These declining neighborhoods ringing the city center often attracted a large immigrant population who sought low-cost housing near their places of employment.[12]

The absence of a system of public transit exacerbated the problems of urban congestion. Without public trans-portation, persons whose workplace was separated from residence were forced to walk to work unless they could afford the expense of a private horse or carriage. The development of factories, banks, stock exchanges, and other such urban enterprises by the mid-nineteenth century greatly increased the number of persons confronted with a journey to work, often of some considerable distance. While the peripheral areas of cities as well as towns outside of cities grew rapidly in the 1830's, 40's, and 50's, they were not necessarily bedroom communities. Towns close to the central city such as Lawrenceville and Birmingham near Pittsburgh and the Northern Liberties outside of Philadelphia had their own separate economic focus and did not serve as residential sections for a large number of persons employed in the central city.[13]

During the decades before the Civil War, however, several key transportation innovations occurred that eventually made possible a suburban life for many people employed in the central cities. The earliest of these innovations were the omnibus and the commuter railroad, both of which appeared in Boston, New York, and Philadelphia in the 1830's and in Baltimore and Pittsburgh by the early 1850's. The omnibus was usually drawn by two horses and carried about twelve to fifteen passengers over an established route of city streets for a fixed fare. A coachman, mounted on an elevated seat at the front of the vehicle, collected the fares and drove the horses, while the passengers, who entered through a door at the rear of the vehicle, sat on long seats along the side of the omnibus.[14] The steam railway, of course, was not originally intended for city-suburban travel, but was rapidly adapted to that use.

Boston led the way in the development of commuter railroad traffic, followed by New York and Philadelphia. Regulations that prevented the running of steam locomotives on streets, however, restricted the use of commuter trains in the latter cities, as they did in Pittsburgh, for some years.[15]

The transit innovation that had the most significant impact on urban patterns was the streetcar. First introduced in New York City in the early 1850's, it had spread to Boston, Philadelphia, Baltimore, Chicago, Cincinnati, and Pittsburgh by the end of the decade.[16] The running of cars on rails through city streets was a major technological breakthrough. Alexander Easton, the author of *A Practical Treatise on Street or Horse-Power Railways,* published in 1859, called streetcars the "improvement of the age," and in terms of the increased facility of the intra-city transportation of passengers, his enthusiasm was justified. Powered initially by horses and mules, then by cable, and ultimately by electricity, the streetcar dominated urban transit throughout the nation from the Civil War until the 1920's. Because of the much lower average fares of the streetcar as compared to the omnibus or commuter railroad, it had the greatest potential for enabling working people to move to residential areas with suburban characteristics.[17]

Although the electric streetcar, developed during the late 1880's, was often referred to as "rapid transit," this title properly belongs to the elevated train and to the subway, both of which operated on paths separate from street traffic and with trains of cars rather than single cars.[18] An elevated system was first constructed in New York in 1871, with the cars pulled by steam locomotives. Elevated systems with electricity as the motive power were developed in Chicago in 1892, Boston in 1894, and Philadelphia in 1905. Boston built the first subway in 1897, followed by New York in 1904, and Philadelphia in 1909. Elevated and subway trains traveled at a much faster rate of speed than did surface cars, but their high construction costs made them feasible only for larger cities with a high volume of traffic.[19] Public transit, therefore, for most cities, involved streetcar systems.

Without the implementation of these transportation innovations, American cities would have developed in a different spatial pattern. Public transit produced an urbanized area roughly characterized by a central business district (CBD) or downtown surrounded by concentric circles or zones with specialized residential and industrial functions. Traction lines radiated from the core into the residential areas. The CBD became, over time, a section devoted almost entirely to business and commercial uses with a concentration of office buildings, banks, specialized retail outlets, and department stores. The residential areas usually had sharply distinguished socio-economic patterns with the poorer sections near the core and the wealthier neighborhoods toward the fringe. Those areas with suburban characteristics (single-family detached homes and an absence of industry) developed both within and outside the city's boundaries. Many of the residents of those districts worked in the CBD and commuted by public transit; their daily journey-to-work significantly affected the tenor of life in the twentieth century city.[20]

The two-part city, divided between residential and commercial-industrial sections, developed over the last half of the nineteenth century and first decades of the twentieth century in response to public transit expansion. Heavily congested workingclass and immigrant living areas with problems of poor sanitation, high disease rates, and deteriorating housing, however, still persisted in large cities such as New York, Chicago, Boston, Philadelphia, and Pittsburgh. Manhattan's 10th ward, for instance, had a density of 523.6 persons per acre in 1890 and the 13th ward 428.8, with the population jammed into five and six story tenement houses. In Pittsburgh, in the same year, density in the wards surrounding the CBD had advanced to 121.9 persons per acre in a section with few dwellings over two or three stories.[21] Members of the middle and upper classes worried that these congested living conditions, especially among the poor and the alien, posed a danger to "the moral integrity and the unity of the community."[22]

Many commentators on the evils of urban life in the latter half of the nineteenth and the beginning of the twentieth century argued that the solution of the city's problems lay in the further extension of mass transit. They explained that through public transportation systems, men who labored in the city would be able to live and raise their families in the superior suburban environment. This theme was first articulated before the Civil War when omnibus and horsecar lines were begun and was heard with greater frequency toward the end of the nineteenth century as urban population growth and transportation development continued apace.[23] As more and more centrally employed middle class citizens moved to suburbs, urban spokesmen advocated the improvement and cheapen-

ing of mass transit to make possible a suburban life for the workingclass people remaining in the city.[24]

In the 1870's, for instance, Congregationalist minister Charles Loring Brace, in his book *The Dangerous Classes of New York*, warned of the deleterious effect of overcrowding on public morals and advocated the dispersal of population from city slums. Specifically Brace recommended the building of a subway or an elevated railway with cheap fares as the means to enable workers to settle in "pleasant and healthy little suburban villages." In the suburbs each family would have its "own small house and garden," while children would grow up "under far better influences, moral and physical, than they could possibly enjoy in tenement-houses."[25]

Other writers in the 1870's and 80's repeated Brace's arguments about the moral influence of improved transit but also went beyond the social context. William R. Martin in *The North American Review* and L. M. Haupt in *Proceeding of the Engineer's Club of Philadelphia* held that the building of rapid transit would have economic as well as social benefits. Rapid transit, they maintained, would encourage the development of manufacturing within the city, increase real estate values, and stimulate building in open areas. The solution of the city's congestion problems would therefore be accompanied by financial gain for the metropolis's businessmen and builders.[26]

Many cities, however, could not afford the expense of either an elevated rapid transit system or a subway, and their expansion appeared limited by the speed and capacities of the horsecar. The application of cable and electric power to street railways in the 1880's appeared to resolve this problem. During the ten years from 1880 to 1890, the length of street railway track in the United States jumped from 2,050 to 5,783 miles, an advance of 182 per cent at a time when urban population increased 56.7 per cent. Urbanites in 1890 averaged 111 rides per year, with totals over 270 rides per year per inhabitant in Kansas City, New York, and San Francisco.[27] In that year horses and mules still supplied the motive force on 71 per cent of the streetcar trackage, but this total plummeted during the decade. Most significant about the change in motive power was the increased speed of traction service. Streetcars now traveled at approximately 10 miles per hour, just about double the speed of the horsecar, greatly expanding the areas within commuting distance of the downtown core. From 1890 to 1902 track mileage increased from 5,783 to 22,577, almost all of it operated by electricity, and rides per urban inhabitant from 111 to 181. Five years later, in 1907, track mileage had jumped 53.5 per cent to 34,404 and rides per inhabitant to 250, as the use of public transit continued to far out-distance population increase.[28]

These transit developments gave further encouragement to those concerned with urban congestion that technology could solve the city's congestion problems. City boosters held this view as well as "urbanologists." In Pittsburgh, which began electrifying its streetcar system in the late 1880's, publications intended for visitors boasted of how the city's traction system permitted working people to live in "cosy residences" in the suburbs away from the "noise, smoke and dust of a great city." Suburban life, in turn, said one Pittsburgh guidebook, prevented the "breeding of vice and disease" and "elevated in equal proportion the moral tone of the laboring classes."[29]

The 1890 Census included, for the first time, a volume on transportation, with a special section on the "Statistics of Street Railway Transportation" prepared by sociologist Charles H. Cooley.[30] A number of writers on urban trends in the 1890's used this material to demonstrate that the concentration of people in cities, with its deleterious effects, could be mitigated by improved urban transit. Carroll D. Wright, writing in the *Popular Science Monthly*, Thomas C. Clarke in *Scribner's Magazine*, Henry C. Fletcher in the *Forum*, and Cooley himself in his work on *The Theory of Transportation*, all agreed that while the conditions of modern industrial and commercial life necessitated concentration, "humanity" required that men and their families live among "sunlight, fresh air, grass and trees."[31] In the words of United States Commissioner of Labor, Carroll D. Wright, adequate urban transportation was "something more than a question of economics or of business convenience; it is a social and an ethical question as well." For, concluded Wright, only suburbs could supply the "sanitary localities, [the] moral and well-regulated communities, where children can have all the advantages of church and school, of light and air . . ." so necessary to "the improvement of the condition of the masses."[32]

By the turn of the century, however, many commentators on urban congestion had come to question whether improved transit alone would make possible a suburban life for the families that filled the city's tenements. In his seminal work of 1899, *The Growth of Cities in the Nineteenth Century*, Adna Weber argued that the development of suburbs rather than other "palliatives" such as model tenements, building laws, and housing inspection offered the best hope of escaping the evils of city life stemming from overcrowding. But while cheap and rapid transit was essential for suburban development, said Weber, it had to be accompanied by a shorter working day and inexpensive suburban homes if workingmen were to take advantage of an environment that combined "the advantages of both city and country life."[33]

Such sentiments were repeated by other urban reformers during the beginning of the twentieth century. Some, such as Benjamin C. Marsh, secretary of the Committee on Congestion of Population in New York, saw city planning, tax reform, and even municipal land ownership as indispensable accompaniments to improved transit if urban decentralization was to become a reality; others, such as Frederic C. Howe, believed that a single tax upon land values should accompany rapid transit development.[34] Many of the most heated local political battles of the Progressive Period were fought over the issue of municipal regulation or ownership of streetcar lines. Reform mayors such as Hazen Pingree of Detroit, Tom Johnson of Cleveland, and Samuel "Golden Rule" Jones and Brand Whitlock of Toledo advocated better and cheaper traction service as a means to better the lot of urban workingmen; undoubtedly they believed that such improvements would permit residents of crowded inner city districts to move to neighborhoods where they could realize the suburban ideal.[35]

In its *Special Report on Street and Electric Railways* published in 1902, the Bureau of the Census of the Department of Commerce and Labor presented the most comprehensive statement yet on the street railway as a "social factor." The report observed that street railway development had come "in response to an imperative social need," and that urban transit had facilitated the dispersal of population from the city while encouraging the concentration of commercial and manufacturing establishments. Traction companies had also performed an important social service by transporting people from crowded cities to "places of outdoor recreation." But, added the report, because city transit service was often inadequate, it had actually hampered potential suburban growth. The report recommended increased speed, additional cars, and lower fares as one means to deal with transit deficiencies. Satisfactory suburban and interurban transit service in congested great cities, concluded the report, could only be supplied by elevated or subway sysments in coordination with surface lines, but the expense of such systems perhaps precluded a "wholly satisfactory solution of the problem of transportation in great and rapidly growing cities. . . ."[36]

✧   ✧   ✧

By the end of the first decade of the twentieth century, therefore, there existed a large body of literature which viewed urban transit as the means by which men could escape the evils of the crowded city and live in suburbs with the benefits of cottage living, clean air and sunshine, and close communication with nature. Some reformers, however, believed that changes such as tax reform, municipal ownership, and cheap housing had to accompany transit improvements if suburban living for the working-class was to become a reality. In reviewing this material, it is difficult not to conclude that many who advocated urban decentralization were as motivated by considerations of social control as by a desire to enable men to live more comfortable or healthy lives. City slums crowded with immigrants usually had high crime rates and poor sanitary conditions, and middle and upper class citizens worried about the threat of violence and disease posed by congested workingclass areas. Transit systems, by making it possible for working people to leave the unhealthy city for arcadian suburbs, seemingly offered a relatively inexpensive method of curtailing the threat of the slum.[37]

Were the advocates of a technological solution to the problems of the city stemming from congestion, whatever their motivation, misguided? As early as 1866, The Nation editorialized that the time and money required for commuting to suburbs eliminated it as an alternative for many members of the working-class, a conclusion also reached by the leading contemporary student of the beginnings of mass transit.[38] But what of later traction developments? Writing in 1890, journalist and social critic Jacob Riis pessimistically noted that rapid transit in New York had failed to resolve the problems of the tenement house slum. Technology had proved ineffective, he held, when faced by the "system" resulting from a combination of "public neglect and private greed."[39] Even the 1902 Bureau of the Census traction

report, which had praised the impact of the streetcar, noted that most suburbanites were well-to-do and that poverty and long work hours prevented many workers from utilizing public transit to escape the city.[40] And, in his study Streetcar Suburbs, historian Sam Bass Warner, Jr. observes that urban transit provided a "safe, sanitary environment" for only half of the Boston metropolitan population; the remainder were condemned to the crowded city. In addition, says Warner, the emphasis on a system of individualistic capitalism that promised a suburban life for those who could pay the price meant that the society neglected the immense social and housing needs of the workingclass and immigrant poor.[41]

Some of this criticism is justified. Many members of the working-class could afford neither the time nor the money required to commute to suburbs. Moreover, the stress on facilitating the movement of people from city to suburb via urban transit undoubtedly did divert attention from the housing and recreational needs of the poor who remained in the city. But this emphasis suited the American value system—a value system that combined a strong belief in the capacity of technology to solve social ills, a belief in the moral superiority of a suburban to a city existence, and a commitment to a system of private capitalism and decision-making which theoretically allowed each person to make his own choice of residence according to his income and preference.[42]

Given this set of values, the streetcar did not "fail" in its promise. Urban transit systems did enable many citizens to leave the congested areas of central cities for living areas with more amenities. Housing vacated by these groups in turn provided more housing choice for those remaining.[43] That areas of some cities like New York and Philadelphia grew more rather than less congested during the streetcar era resulted as much from the constant influx of new urban residents as from deficiencies in the transit system. Given this rush into the cities, the ability of many of these newcomers to leave city congested areas as quickly as they did is perhaps more astonishing than the fact that congestion remained high in some wards.

Today the private automobile has replaced public transit as the chief means by which Americans commute between suburban residences and city jobs. Not surprisingly, many early auto boosters predicted that it would serve the same function that gave mass transit such an appeal generations earlier—the motor car would open a suburban existence for those who wanted to escape the crowded and unpleasant city.[44] The automobile has been largely successful in this role, and the flow of people leaving central cities for suburban amenities continues year after year. As the 1970 census revealed, more people live today in the suburban rings around central cities than in the cities themselves. The poor and the minorities, however, as during the streetcar era, still seem condemned to the central cities.[45] The "garden" continues to beckon, but obviously it will take more than transportation improvements alone to make possible a suburban life for all those who desire it.

NOTES

1. For discussions of this literature, see David R. Weimer (ed.), *City and Country in America*

(New York: Appleton-Century-Crofts, 1962), Morton and Lucia White, *The Intellectual versus the City* (Cambridge: Harvard University Press, 1962), and Anselm Strauss, *Images of the American City* (Glencoe: Free Press, 1961).
2. Scott Donaldson, *The Suburban Myth* (New York: Columbia University Press, 1969); Peter J. Schmitt, *Back to Nature: The Arcadian Myth in Urban America* (New York: Oxford University Press, 1969).
3. Donaldson, pp. 24-25; Schmitt, pp. xvii-xviii.
4. See, for example, Edward E. Hale, "The Congestion of Cities," *Forum* (1888) IV, pp. 532-33; Adna F. Weber, "Suburban Annexations," *North American Review* (May, 1898) CLXVI, p. 616; Donaldson, pp. 24-27; Sam Bass Warner, Jr., *Streetcar Suburbs: The Process of Growth in Boston, 1870-1900* (Cambridge: Harvard University Press and the M.I.T. Press, 1962), pp. 11-14.
5. Leo Marx, *The Machine in the Garden* (New York: Oxford University Press, 1964); Marvin Fisher, *Workshops in the Wilderness* (New York: Oxford University Press, 1967); and Hugo A. Meier, "American Technology and the Nineteenth-Century World," *American Quarterly* (1958) X, pp. 116-130.
6. Charles N. Glaab and A. Theodore Brown, *A History of Urban America* (New York: Macmillan Co., 1967), pp. 25-27, 93-95, 107-111, 138-142.
7. Kenneth T. Jackson, "Metropolitan Government Versus Suburban Autonomy: Politics on the Crabgrass Frontier," in Kenneth T. Jackson and Stanley K. Schultz (eds.), *Cities in American History* (New York: Alfred A. Knopf, 1972), pp. 442-452.
8. George Rogers Taylor, "The Beginnings of Mass Transportation in Urban America: Part I," *The Smithsonian Journal of History* (Summer, 1966) I, p. 37.
9. *Ibid.*, pp. 37-38; Sam Bass Warner, Jr., *The Private City: Philadelphia in Three Periods of Its Growth* (Philadelphia: University of Pennsylvania Press, 1968), pp. 49-62; Warner, *Streetcar Suburbs*, pp. 15-21; Peter G. Goheen, *Victorian Toronto 1850-1900* (Chicago: University of Chicago Department of Geography Research Paper No. 127, 1970), pp. 8-9; Joel A. Tarr, "Transportation Innovation and Changing Spatial Patterns in Pittsburgh, 1850-1910," (Pittsburgh: Carnegie-Mellon University Transportation Research Institute, 1971) pp. 2-5.
10. *Ibid.*, pp. 3-5; Goheen, pp. 8-9; Allan R. Pred, *The Spatial Dynamics of U.S. Urban-Industrial Growth, 1800-1914* (Cambridge: M.I.T. Press, 1966), pp. 196-197; David Ward, *Cities and Immigrants* (New York: Oxford University Press, 1971), pp. 105-109.
11. Taylor, p. 39; Ward, p. 86; Pred, pp. 148-152, 167-177.
12. Ward, pp. 85-109.
13. Taylor, p. 37; Kenneth T. Jackson, "The Suburban Trend Before the Civil War" (un-

published paper delivered at American Historical Convention, Washington, D.C. Dec. 30, 1969), pp. 10-11; Bernard J. Sauers, "A Political Process of Urban Growth: Consolidation of the South Side with the City of Pittsburgh, 1872," (unpublished seminar paper, Department of History, Carnegie-Mellon University, 1972), pp. 3-10.

14. Taylor, pp. 40-44.

15. Taylor, "The Beginnings of Mass Transportation in Urban America, Part II," *The Smithsonian Journal of History* (Autumn, 1966) I, pp. 31-38; Pittsburgh *Post*, Nov. 3, 1860. For railroad commuter traffic in 1890, see John S. Billings (comp.), *Report on the Social Statistics of Cities, Eleventh Census* (Washington: Government Printing Office, 1895), p. 50.

16. Taylor, "Beginnings of Mass Transportation: Part II," pp. 39-50.

17. Ward, pp. 125-143; George M. Smerk, "The Streetcar: Shaper of American Cities," *Traffic Quarterly* (Oct., 1967) XXI, pp. 569-584.

18. James Blaine Walker, *Fifty Years of Rapid Transit 1864-1917* (New York: Arno Press, 1970, reprint of 1918 edition), p. i.

19. Blake McKelvey, *The Urbanization of America 1860-1915* (New Brunswick: Rutgers University Press, 1963), pp. 76-85.

20. Smerk, pp. 569-584; Warner, *The Private City*, pp. 177-200; Warner, *Streetcar Suburbs, passim*; Ward, pp. 125-143. Cities obviously diverged in their patterns of development according to topographical factors and the individual locational decisions of businessmen and householders. I have not meant to endorse any particular theory of urban development but rather to point out that traction increased the tendency towards specialized residential and commercial districts. Some businesses and industries remained scattered throughout the city at the height of the streetcar period. See Raymond L. Fales and Leon N. Moses, "Thünen, Weber and the Spatial Structure of the Nineteenth Century City," to be published in Charles Leven (ed.), *Essays in Honor of Edgar M. Hoover.*

21. Roy Lubove, *The Progressives and the Slums* (Pittsburgh: University of Pittsburgh Press, 1962), p. 94; Adna F. Weber, *The Growth of Cities in the Nineteenth Century* (Ithaca: Cornell University Press, 1967, reprint of 1899 edition), pp. 460-464; Pittsburgh data from U.S. Department of Commerce and Labor, Bureau of the Census, *Vital and Social Statistics, Part II: Cities of 100,000 Inhabitants, Eleventh Census* (Washington: Government Printing Office, 1895) XXI, pp. 293-311.

22. Lubove, pp. 10, 82.

23. For articulation of this theme in regard to the omnibus see Glen E. Holt, "The Changing Perception of Urban Pathology: An Essay on the Development of Mass Transit in the United States," in Jackson and Schultz, pp. 325-326. On the horsecar, see the Pittsburgh *Post*, Dec. 17, 1859. The *Post* editorialized: "The con-

venience of these cars to the citizens cannot be over estimated. The effect upon the health and morals of the city by scattering the population is certain to be beneficial to all classes. Those in moderate circumstances will no longer be compelled to rent houses in narrow courts and alleys. . . . . People can keep themselves and their children out of the temptation and proximity of vice. In the country, people must hunt after occasions for wickedness, in the city they are thrust upon them." See also, Rev. S. C. Aiken, "Moral View of Railroads," *Hunts' Merchants Magazine and Commercial Review* (Nov., 1852) XXVII, pp. 577-584; Warner, *Streetcar Suburbs*, pp. 26-27.

24. Legislation providing for "workingmen's" fares at a lower than usual cost were required for commuter railroads in Massachusetts in 1872 and for streetcars in Detroit in 1893. Parliament required commuter railroads in the London area to run "workmen's trains" with low fares as early as 1860. For American developments see Charles J. Kennedy, "Commuter Services in the Boston Area, 1835-1860," *Business History Review* (Summer, 1962) XXXVI, pp. 169-170 and Melvin G. Holli, *Reform in Detroit: Hazen S. Pingree and Urban Politics* (New York: Oxford University Press, 1969), pp. 47-48; for London, T. C. Barker and Michael Robbins, *A History of London Transport* (London: George Allen & Unwin LTD, 1963) I, pp. 173-174.

25. Charles Loring Brace, *The Dangerous Classes of New York* (New York: Wynkoop and Hallenbeck, 1880, 3rd ed.), pp. 57-60. (The author is indebted for this reference, as well as those cited in note 25, to Clay McShane of the Smithsonian Institution.) For a study of Brace and his attitude toward the city see R. Richard Wohl, "The 'Country Boy' Myth and Its Place in American Urban Culture: The Nineteenth-Century Contribution," ed. by Moses Rischin, *Perspectives in American History* (Cambridge: Harvard University Press, 1969) III, pp. 107-121.

26. William R. Martin, "The Financial Resources of New York," *The North American Review* (Nov.-Dec., 1878) CXXVII, pp. 442-443; L. M. Haupt, "Rapid Transit," *Proceedings of the Engineer's Club of Philadelphia* (Aug., 1884) IV, pp. 135-148.

27. Charles H. Cooley, "Statistics of Street Railway Transportation," in Henry C. Adams (comp.), *Report on the Transportation Business in the United States, Part I, Transportation by Land, Eleventh Census* (Washington: Government Printing Office, 1895) XVIII, pp. 681-684.

28. U. S. Department of Commerce and Labor, Bureau of the Census, *Street and Electric Railways 1907* (Washington: Government Printing Office, 1910), p. 33.

29. *Illustrated Guide and Handbook of Pittsburgh and Allegheny* (Pittsburgh, 1887), p. 50; Consolidating Illustrating Company (comp.), *Pittsburgh of Today* (Pittsburgh: Consolidating Illustrating Co., 1896), p. 69; Knights Templar,

Official Souvenir 27th Triennial Conclave Knights Templar (Pittsburgh, 1898), n.p.

30. Charles H. Cooley, "Statistics of Street Railway Transportation," in Henry C. Adams (comp.), *Report on the Transportation Business in the United States, Part I, Transportation by Land, Eleventh Census* (Washington: Government Printing Office, 1895) XVIII, pp. 681-791.

31. Carroll D. Wright, "Rapid Transit. Lessons from the Census. VI," *Popular Science Monthly* (Apr., 1892) XL, pp. 785-792; Thomas Curtis Clarke, "Rapid Transit in Cities," *Scribners Magazine* (May-June, 1892) XI, pp. 568-578, 743-758; Charles H. Cooley, "The Social Significance of Street Railways," *Publications of the American Economic Association* (1891) VI, pp. 71-73; Cooley, *The Theory of Transportation, Publications of the American Economic Association* (May, 1894) IX, no. 3; Henry J. Fletcher, "The Drift of Population to Cities: Remedies," *Forum* (Aug., 1895) XIX, pp. 737-745.

32. Wright, p. 790.

33. Weber, *The Growth of Cities*, pp. 467-475. See also, Weber, "Suburban Annexations, p. 617, and "Rapid Transit and the Housing Problem," *Municipal Affairs* (Fall, 1902) VI, pp. 409-417.

34. Frederic C. Howe, *The City: The Hope of Democracy* (Seattle: University of Washington Press, 1967, reprint of 1905 edition), pp. 202-206; Lubove, pp. 231-238. See also, Charles M. Robinson, "Improvement in City Life," *Atlantic* (Apr., 1899) LXXXIII, p. 531; Delos F. Wilcox, *Municipal Franchises* (New York: Engineering News Publishing Co., 1911, 2 vols.) II, pp. 6-11; Henry C. Wright, "The Interrelation of Housing and Transit," *American City* (Jan., 1914) X, pp. 51-53; and the summary of the report of the New York City Commission on Congestion of Population in *The Survey* (Mar. 25, 1911) XXV, pp. 1064-1067.

35. See, for example, Holli, pp. 33-55; Hoyt Landon Warner, *Progressivism in Ohio 1897-1917* (Columbus: Ohio State University Press for the Ohio Historical Society, 1964), *passim;* and Tom L. Johnson, *My Story,* ed. by Elizabeth J. Hauser (Seattle: University of Washington Press, 1970), *passim.*

36. U. S. Department of Commerce and Labor, Bureau of the Census, *Street and Electric Railways 1902* (Washington: Government Printing Office, 1905), pp. 26-43.

37. On the theme of social control and urban decentralization see Lubove, pp. 131, 250-251.

38. "The Future of Great Cities," *The Nation* (Feb. 22, 1866) II, p. 232; Taylor, "The Beginnings of Mass Transportation: Part II," pp. 51-52.

39. Jacob A. Riis, *How the Other Half Lives* (New York: Sagamore Press, Inc., 1957, reprint of 1890 edition), p. 2.

40. *Electric Railways 1902*, pp. 31-33. See also, Edward C. Pratt, *Industrial Causes of Congestion of Population in New York City*, (New York: AMS Press, 1968, reprinting of 1911 edition), pp. 191-96.

41. Warner, pp. 160-161. Warner also feels that the suburbs failed to supply the reinforced community life that supposedly was a goal of those who left the city.

42. See *ibid.*, pp. 153-166.

43. Ward, pp. 120-121.

44. See, for example, Harlan Paul Douglass, *The Suburban Trend* (New York: Arno Press, 1970, reprint of 1925 edition); James J. Flink, *America Adopts the Automobile, 1895-1910* (Cambridge: M.I.T. Press, 1970), pp. 108-110; Blain A. Brownell, "A Symbol of Modernity: Attitudes Toward the Automobile in Southern Cities in the 1920's," *American Quarterly* XXIV (March 1972), pp. 25-26.

45. U.S. Department of Commerce, Bureau of the Census, *Trends in Social and Economic Conditions in Metropolitan and Nonmetropolitan Areas* (Washington: Government Printing Office, Sept 3, 1970, Series P-23, No. 33). The current revival of interest in mass transit to connect suburbs with downtown business districts has different roots than the programs and proposals of a century or so ago. Urban transit proposals today are intended to deal with the problems of automobile congestion rather than with people and housing congestion. See John W. Dyckman, "Transportation in Cities," in Scientific American *Cities* (New York: Alfred A. Knopf, 1968), pp 133-155.

V THE CITY IN POLITICS

Behind any topic involving the urbanization process, be it transportation, commercial developments, housing, or the immigrant, looms the omnipresent factor—politics, defined by Edward C. Banfield as "the management of conflict." And one unique phenomenon of urban politics from the Civil War to the Second World War was the rise and decline of that peculiar American urban institution, the city boss and his political machine.

Our heritage of big-city machines is as American as a black derby, a fat cigar and a kind word at Mr. O'Higgins' wake. The city machine is an organization involved in politics as a business, the business of gaining political power by offering services to a number of diverse groups and inducements of power, prestige, and profit to its followers. In his heyday (a generation before World War I), the city boss could "deliver" the votes because the nature of American society permitted him to act as a broker in ethnic, economic, social, and political relations. But when significant social and political changes presented either obstacles or better services and inducements (e.g. the merit system, reforms in voting and registration methods, the rise of the labor union and the welfare state) the machine declined. Whereas the old-fashioned machine of a Richard Crocker in New York or a James Michael Curley in Boston became a thing of the past, some managed to survive by adapting to changing conditions, like the machine of Richard Daley's organization in Chicago and the city machine of Pittsburgh. Others managed to adapt but destroyed themselves through scandal, like the Pendergast machine of Kansas City.[1]

1. For an interesting account of how a city machine survived its nineteenth-century heritage and adapted to modern social change by creating new alliances, see Lyle W. Dorsett, *The Pendergast Machine* (New York: Oxford, 1968). Dorsett also disagrees with the long-accepted view that the New Deal destroyed the city machine, as does Bruce Martin Stave in his "The New Deal, the Last Hurrah, and the Building of an Urban Machine: Pittsburgh Committee Men, A Case Study," *Pennsylvania History* (October 1966). Stave, in fact, argues that for Pittsburgh, at least, the New Deal invigorated and strengthened the political machine.

With perception and skill, Zane L. Miller, *Boss Cox's Cincinnati* (New York: Oxford,

In the first selection of this chapter, Robert Merton demonstrates how sociological insights can enrich the understanding of a historical problem. He asks: How do you account for the rise of the political machine? He answers: By responding to the political needs of a motley clutch of groups whose aspirations and frustrations were not satisfied by the existing agencies of society. Merton sees the machine as an alternative to formal government. Disciplined and centralized in itself, it was an alternative to the decentralized dispersed, overlapping pattern of municipal authority, and, as such, despite its enormous waste and corruption, the city boss and his organization did serve to fulfill important social functions that society would not or could not satisfy. The machine, according to Merton, emerged because it responded especially to three groups: it humanized politics for the "deprived" classes and through patronage, handouts, and personal relationships, it opened one of the few doors to advancement available to them; through alliances with legitimate and illegitimate business, it functioned to serve the interests of the respectable businessman and the racketeer, both of whom wanted order created out of the chaos of unrestrained competition.

The second essay centers on a specific political organization, the Tweed Ring of New York, one of the most notorious city machines in American urban history. It is an analysis of a persistent theme in urban politics, the reformer *vs.* the machine, in this case, the reform movement that sought to destroy Boss Tweed and his machine, and one which culminated in one of the most dramatic elections in New York City's history. The author attempts to show how the crusade against the Tweed Ring reflected the attitudes of the reformers toward reform, the machine, corruption, the poor, and urban political institutions, and how their resounding "victory" was actually an ironic defeat.[2]

1968), correlates the processes of urbanization with the rise of bossism in Cincinnati Another interesting and recent study of urban politics is that of Theodore J. Lowi, *At the Pleasure of the Mayor* (New York: The Free Press, 1964), who argues that the decline of the machine has not necessarily been beneficial for the city. For an excellent study of the changing twentieth-century urban machine which focusses on the emergence of "transitional bosses," a link between the old-fashioned and modern city boss, see Harvey Wheeler, "Yesterday's Robin Hood: The Rise and Fall of Baltimore's Trenton Democratic Club," *American Quarterly* (Winter 1955). See also Joel Arthur Tarr's insightful *A Study in Boss Politics: William Lorimer of Chicago* (Urbana: University of Illinois Press, 1971), Jerome Mushkat, *Tammany: The Evolution of a Political Machine* (Syracuse: Syracuse University Press, 1971), Bruce M. Stave (ed.), *Urban Bosses Machines, and Progressive Reformers* (Lexington: D. C. Heath, 1972). For the modern boss, see Mike Royko, *Boss: Richard J. Daley of Chicago* (New York: E. P. Dutton 1971), David Halberstam, "Daley of Chicago," *Harper's Magazine* (August 1968), and Blanche Blank, "The New Style Boss," *The New Republic* (September 11, 1961). See also Eric L. McKittrick, "The Study of Corruption," *Political Science Quarterly* (December 1957).

2. For a brilliant interpretation of the "liberal" mind of the late nineteenth-century reformer, see John G. Sprout, *"The Best Men": Liberal Reformers in the Gilded Age* (New York: Oxford, 1968).

Today it is almost a truism to say that urban problems are national problems. But many who make this point, especially journalists, politicians, and TV and radio commentators, tend to speak of the impact of the city upon national affairs as a recent phenomenon. Actually, it has a long history and there are innumerable examples in this book alone that show the direct and indirect influences that the city has had upon the national arena, socially, economically, and technologically. Probably the best example is the Progressive Period.

The Progressive Era provoked the first *national* reform movement that reflected the transition of an agrarian nation into an urban-industrialized giant. Of course the Populist movement of the 1890's was also a part of this transition, but its appeal was limited largely to the rural South and parts of the West and Midwest. The Progressive crusade, more than the Populist movement, was relevant to all geographic sections and all social classes, and it provoked a sharper response to the urban, industrial, and technological realities of the late nineteenth and early twentieth centuries. For some reformers it meant the redemption of democracy, for others an opportunity to resurrect an older and more virtuous America, and for still others the chance to transform innovations in business and technology into political action.

The seedtime of Progressivism was the 1890's; its heyday, the decade before the First World War; its impulse, an urban response to a new age. Although today most historians agree the Progressive movement was largely an urban phenomenon, there is considerable disagreement about its meaning, leadership, goals, and success that has thrown up a flurry of paradoxes.[3] For the movement has been seen as liberal and conservative, a triumph and a flop, led by either the working class, the middle class, or the upper class, or a combination of politicians reflecting all classes, who either looked to the future or to the past. This debate, whose fury seems to be increasing, suggests that the Progressive movement has become a battleground for historians to argue the success or failure of the liberal tradition in the United States.

Samuel P. Hays is a good example of one who is leading a flank attack against the bastions of Progressive interpretation. An article published in 1964[4] was both a major interpretation of Progressivism and an opportunity to review other interpretations. Hays's target was a group of revisionist historians, primarily Richard Hofstadter, who sought to revise the interpretation of the Progressive historians who saw the movement as a continuation of Jeffersonian reform—a class struggle of "the people" battling acquisitive businessmen, seeking the democratization of political institutions, fighting for

3. For an excellent bibliographical essay on the Progressive Era, see Robert Wiebe, *The Search for Order* (New York: Hill and Wang, 1967), pp. 303-24.
4. "The Politics of Reform in Municipal Government in the Progressive Era," *Pacific Northwest Quarterly* (October 1964), pp 157–69.

an equalitarian society open to all with special privilege to none. Hofstadter
in his *Age of Reform* (1955) held that the movement was actually led by
reasonably affluent members of the middle class who were tormented with
"status anxieties" and inspired by the values of the Protestant ethic and who
sought to turn back to an older America hardly in tune with the realities of
a modern urban age. Revisionism is an occupational hazard that often
invites the criticism that can convert the victor into the victim. Hence, Hays
attacked Hofstadter and the proponents of the "status revolution" theory
to argue that Progressivism was in fact led by an upper-class group who,
rather than alienated by society, were experts in the techniques of business
management and the newer technological procedures and sought to introduce them into city government.[5] Hays argued that there was a striking
difference between what Progressives said and what they did. They spoke
as champions of the equalitarian society, enemies of special privilege, and
friends of the poor. In practice, however, they destroyed a broad form of
representative government, were agents of a special privileged group, and
were profoundly distrustful of the lower and middle classes. The judgments
come from Hays's study of the two major reforms of municipal government
coming out of the Progressive period: the commission system and the city-
manager plan, reforms that were in fact elitist in nature with definite anti-
democratic overtones. While some historians who favor a more plural approach to Progressivism might argue there was more to the movement than
this, Professor Hays did show that reform does not always advance "progressive" and "liberal" objectives. The voice of the people can also be the
voice of elitism. In the next selection, Melvin G. Holli, one of the growing
army of historians who have probed the motives of the liberal reformers,[6]

5. For an opposing view which stresses the importance of the working class, see
J. Joseph Hutchmacher, "Urban Liberalism and the Age of Reform," *Mississippi Valley
Historical Review* (September 1962). See James Weinstein, *The Corporate Ideal in the
Liberal State, 1900–1918* (Boston: Beacon Press, 1968), especially chapter 4, as well as
the indictments of Lawrence J. R. Herson, "The Lost World of Municipal Government,"
American Political Science Review (June 1957).
6. For those historians who have made a searching and often critical analysis of the
liberal reformer on various governmental levels before the Progressive period, see Geoffry
Blodgett, *The Gentle Reformers: Massachusetts Democrats in the Cleveland Era* (Cam-
bridge: Harvard University Press, 1966), Alexander B. Callow, Jr., *The Tweed Ring*
(New York: Oxford University Press, 1966), Vincent P. De Santis, *Republicans Face the
Southern Question: The Departure Years, 1877–1897* (Baltimore: The Johns Hopkins
University Press, 1959), Ari Hoogenboom, *Outlawing the Spoils: A History of the Civil
Service Reform Movement, 1865-1883* (Urbana: University of Illinois Press, 1961),
James H. McPherson, *The Struggle for Equality: Abolitionists and the Negro in the Civil
War and Reconstruction* (Princeton: Princeton University Press, 1964), David Mont-
gomery, *Beyond Equality: Labor and the Radical Republicans* (New York: Knopf 1967),
Robert P. Sharkey, *Money, Class, and Party: An Economic Study of the Civil War and
Reconstruction* (Baltimore: The Johns Hopkins University Press, 1959), Jack Sproat,
"The Best Men": Liberal Reformers in the Gilded Age (New York: Oxford University

expands some of Hays's ideas, incorporates some of his own, and broadens the panoply of reformers to include another important variety. It is an artful accomplishment in generalization.

Holli examines two broad groups of reformers who differed profoundly on two of the most fundamental questions in politics: what is the proper role of government and whose interests shall it serve? The first group, by far the most numerous, he calls structural reformers, men like Grover Cleveland of Buffalo, Seth Low and John Purroy Mitchel, the "oddly puritanical Catholic," of New York, San Francisco's reform mayor James D. Phelan, and the prototype of structural reformers, William F. Havemeyer of New York. With the battle cry of efficiency, economy, responsibility, clean government, the structural reformers sought to return to office the "respectabilities"—the middle and patrician class—who would transform municipal government into a tight, efficient business-like operation. It was government by businessmen serving the interests of the business community. Reform was considered in structural terms: tinkering with city charters, hacking budgets to the bone, drastically reducing municipal services. Unless forced by scandal, little was done to interfere with vested interests. Outrageous franchise contracts, bloated gas and light rates, services for the working and lower class were ignored, but special tax advantages were pursued with an almost breathless zeal. Mayor Phelan, for example, suspended vital health services, allowed police to protect strikebreakers, and created such a low tax rate that the city withheld teacher's salaries. John Purroy Mitchel attacked economy with the "ledger book ethics of the corporation accountant." Clean government meant moral sanitation as well. The evils of the city were defined as the vices of the working class—drinking, gambling, and prostitution. The saloon was viewed with more moral indignation than the absence of good parks and schools.

Unlike the structural reformers, the social reformers, men like "Golden Rule" Jones, Brand Whitlock, Tom Johnson, Mark Fagan, Newton D. Baker, and the prototype of the group, Hazen S. Pingree of Detroit (1890-97), felt that the business of government was not business but people. Humane and pragmatic, they dismissed legislation regulating morals as something akin to building a howitzer to kill a mouse. They felt this tactic affected only symptoms, not causes; it diverted public attention away from the real sources

---

Press, 1968), Irwin Unger, *The Greenback Era: A Social and Political History of American Finance* (Princeton: Princeton University Press, 1964), and Kermit Vanderbilt, *Charles Eliot Norton* (Cambridge: Belnap Press, 1959).

For a recent assessment of the Progressive reformers, see Otis A. Pease, "Urban Reformers in the Progressive Era: a Reassessment," *Pacific Northwest Quarterly*, Vol. 62 (April 1971).

of corruption. As Brand Whitlock, the social reform mayor of Toledo wrote, "The good people are always insisting upon 'moral issues,' urging us to turn aside from our large immediate purpose, and concentrate our official attention on the 'bad' people—and wreck our movement." The social reformer's immediate purpose was two-pronged. To eliminate graft, they attacked the special privileges of groups which sponsored many of the structural reformers, such as the real estate interests, the utilities firms, the public service corporations. To redress the balance, they attempted to regulate franchises, gas, water, and street railway rates, and equalize the tax rate. The social reformers also sought to improve the quality of urban life by promoting public baths, schools, parks, and public welfare programs.

By the third decade of the twentieth century, it was evident that the champions of efficiency had triumphed over the social reformers. The structural reform movement, was at once radical, since it drastically changed the government of the majority of our cities; conservative, since it was based on the values of the business community. The structural reform movement, as they say, put it all together and reached its peak in the city-commissioner and city-manager movements. It smacked of a thermidor revolution. The reaction against nineteenth-century bossism made the pendulum swing violently to the other extreme: bureaucratic elites replaced the boss, administrative experts replaced the ward leader, "taking politics out of politics" removed the management of conflict, respect for public opinion fell to a profound distrust of popular democracy. Reform government—good, clean, and decent—had won the battle, but at what a price?

Theodore Lowi answers that question by examining the results of Reform government from the 1930's to the decade of the '60's. In his "Machine Politics—Old and New," Lowi compares the old-fashioned machine with its predecessor, the creature of the structural reformer, and in so doing pinpoints the essentials of both. After several decades of Reform government, he asks, "How does it shape up?" It is a tale of fine political ironies. For all the rhetorical huff and puff about cleansing government by taking politics out of politics, politics has not been banished, only its form has been changed. Reform created a balkanized city-state. It was the bureaucratic agencies which became the new bases of power, certainly not impotent but rather powerfully independent and more entrenched than the power bases of the old-time machine. Reform created the ultimate irony, as Lowi puts it, a well-run but ungoverned city. Ungoverned because a powerless mayor is unable to manage the "organized decentralization" of entrenched bureaucratic agencies. "Our modern mayor has been turned into the likes of a French Fourth Republic Premier facing an array of intransigent parties in the National Assembly." The panacea of efficiency has created a bureaucracy of "organized disorganization." The city is efficient and well-run in so far as the agencies remain in their own bailiwicks. But when given tasks outside their

scope, or when their jurisdictions overlap, the city becomes ungovernable
either by stalemate or by a kind of urban elephantiasis. Witness the failure of
the modern machine to cope with such critical problems as welfare, water
pollution, land-use patterns, transportation, or the enforcement of civil
rights. Implicit in this essay is a question which might be mind-stretching
because with all its ramifications, it is not an easy one. Considering the consequences of the new machine, matching them with the defects of the old
machine—its graft and corruption, its enormous waste, its outrageous inefficiency, which machine, old or new, is the "better"?

The political life of the city is by no means limited to local government
alone, but is related to the state legislature, and even more important, especially for the future, to the federal government itself. Many students of
urban affairs are concerned that the burgeoning growth of the large metropolitan areas constitute a new and drastic change in American federalism
as the cities bypass the states to cement a direct federal-city relationship.
Thus the old structure of federalism based on the dual arrangement of
federal-state will become, like Gaul, divided into three parts: federal-
state-city. Fundamental to this view is the assumption that a meaningful federal-city relationship is a fairly recent novelty, beginning in 1933
with the New Deal. In other words, the federal government employed a
laissez-faire policy toward the American city until the New Deal. Daniel J.
Elazar shatters these assumptions, showing: (1) The federal-city relationship is decidedly not new; discussing innumerable urban needs met by
federal engagement, Elazar shows it has a long history reaching back into
the earlier years of the nineteenth century.[7] (2) The new specialized demands of the large cities began not in 1933, but originated some fifteen to
thirty years before the New Deal. If a watershed has to be made it should
be 1913 which, according to Elazar, was the real end of the nineteenth
century.

Certainly the most arresting feature of the federal pattern was the cleavage
caused by the emergence of big cities as special entities, smacking of the city-
state. With their different and specialized needs, they created a cleavage not
only between urban and nonurban areas but within the urban world as well.
For as Elazar points out, many smaller cities with a fifty thousand population
or less still tend to ally themselves with rural areas and often resist, to the
point of rejection, big city ideas. This and other implications that Elazar discusses necessitate a new and deeper examination of the urban impact upon
the federal structure.

7. See also Robert A. Lively, "The American System: A Review Article," *Business
History Review* (March 1955), and Norman Bechman, "Federal System and Development," *Journal of American Institute of Planners*, Vol. 29 (August 1963), pp. 152-167.

Latent Functions of the Machine

ROBERT K. MERTON

. . . [I]n large sectors of the American population, the political machine or the "political racket" are judged as unequivocally "bad" and "undesirable." The grounds for such moral judgment vary somewhat, but they consist substantially in pointing out that political machines violate moral codes: political patronage violates the code of selecting personnel on the basis of impersonal qualifications rather than on grounds of party loyalty or contributions to the party war-chest; bossism violates the code that votes should be based on individual appraisal of the qualifications of candidates and of political issues, and not on abiding loyalty to a feudal leader; bribery, and "honest graft" obviously offend the proprieties of property; "protection" for crime clearly violates the law and the mores; and so on.

In view of the manifold respects in which political machines, in varying degrees, run counter to the mores and at times to the law, it becomes pertinent to inquire how they manage to continue in operation. The familiar "explanations" for the continuance of the political machine are not here in point. To be sure, it may well be that if "respectable citizenry" would live up to their political obligations, if the electorate were to be alert and enlightened; if the number of elective officers were substantially reduced from the dozens, even hundreds, which the average voter is now expected to appraise in the course of town, county, state and national elections; if the electorate were activated by the "wealthy and educated classes without whose participation," as the not-always democratically oriented Bryce put it, "the best-framed government must speedily degenerate";—if these and a plethora of similar changes in political structure were introduced, perhaps the "evils" of the political machine would indeed be exorcized.[1] But it should be noted that these changes are often not introduced, that political machines have had the phoenix-like quality of arising strong and unspoiled from their ashes, that, in short, this structure has exhibited a notable vitality in many areas of American political life.

Proceeding from the functional view, therefore, that we should *ordinarily* (not invariably) expect persistent social patterns and social structures to perform positive functions *which are at the time not adequately fulfilled by other existing patterns and structures*, the thought occurs that perhaps this publicly maligned organization is, *under present conditions*, satisfying basic latent functions.[2] A brief examination of current

From Robert K. Merton, *Social Theory and Social Structure* (New York: The Free Press, 1957), rev. enl. ed., pp. 71-82. Copyright 1949 by the Free Press Collier-Macmillan Canada, Ltd., Toronto, Ontario. Copyright © 1957 by the Free Press, a corporation. Reprinted by permission of the publisher. Robert K. Merton is Professor of Sociology at Columbia University.

analyses of this type of structure may also serve to illustrate additional problems of functional analysis.

SOME FUNCTIONS OF THE POLITICAL MACHINE

Without presuming to enter into the variations of detail marking different political machines—a Tweed, Vare, Crump, Flynn, Hague are by no means identical types of bosses—we can briefly examine the functions more or less common to the political machine, as a generic type of social organization. We neither attempt to itemize all the diverse functions of the political machine nor imply that all these functions are similarly fulfilled by each and every machine.

The key structural function of the Boss is to organize, centralize and maintain in good working condition "the scattered fragments of power" which are at present dispersed through our political organization. By this centralized organization of political power, the boss and his apparatus can satisfy the needs of diverse subgroups in the larger community which are not adequately satisfied by legally devised and culturally approved social structures.

To understand the role of bossism and the machine, therefore, we must look at two types of sociological variables: (1) the *structural context* which makes it difficult, if not impossible, for morally approved structures to fulfill essential social functions, thus leaving the door open for political machines (or their structural equivalents) to fulfill these functions and (2) the subgroups whose distinctive needs are left unsatisfied, except for the latent functions which the machine in fact fulfills.[3]

Structural Context: The constitutional framework of American political organization specifically precludes the legal possibility of highly centralized power and, it has been noted, thus "discourages the growth of effective and responsible leadership. The framers of the Constitution, as Woodrow Wilson observed, set up the check and balance system 'to keep government at a sort of mechanical equipoise by means of a standing amicable contest among its several organic parts.' They distrusted power as dangerous to liberty: and therefore they spread it thin and erected barriers against its concentration." This dispersion of power is found not only at the national level but in local areas as well. "As a consequence," Sait goes on to observe, "when *the people or particular groups* among them demanded positive action, no one had adequate authority to act. The machine provided an antidote."[4]

The constitutional dispersion of power not only makes for difficulty of effective decision and action but when action does occur it is defined and hemmed in by legalistic considerations. In consequence, there developed "a much *more human system* of partisan government, whose chief object soon became the circumvention of government by law. . . . The lawlessness of the extra-official democracy was merely the counterpoise of the legalism of the official democracy. The lawyer having been permitted to subordinate democracy to the Law, the Boss had to be called in to extricate the victim, which he did after a fashion and for a consideration."[5]

Officially, political power is dispersed. Various well-known expedients were devised for this manifest objective. Not only was there the familiar separation of powers among the several branches of the government but, in some measure, tenure in each office was limited, rotation in office approved. And the scope of power inherent in each office was severely circumscribed. Yet, observes Sait in rigorously functional terms, "Leadership is necessary; and *since* it does not develop readily within the constitutional framework, the Boss provides it in a crude and irresponsible form from the outside."[6]

Put in more generalized terms, *the functional deficiencies of the official structure generate an alternative (unofficial) structure to fulfill existing needs somewhat more effectively.* Whatever its specific historical origins, the political machine persists as an apparatus for satisfying otherwise unfulfilled needs of diverse groups in the population. By turning to a few of these subgroups and their characteristic needs, we shall be led at once to a range of latent functions of the political machine.

Functions of the Political Machine for Diverse Subgroups. It is well known that one source of strength of the political machine derives from its roots in the local community and the neighborhood. The political machine does not regard the electorate as an amorphous, undifferentiated mass of voters. With a keen sociological intuition, the machine recognizes that the voter is a person living in a specific neighborhood, with specific personal problems and personal wants. Public issues are abstract and remote; private problems are extremely concrete and immediate. It is not through the generalized appeal to large public concerns that the machine operates, but through the direct, quasi-feudal relationships between local representatives of the machine and voters in their neighborhood. Elections are won in the precinct.

The machine welds its links with ordinary men and women by elaborate networks of personal relations. Politics is transformed into personal ties. The precinct captain "must be a friend to every man, assuming if he does not feel sympathy with the unfortunate, and utilizing in his good works the resources which the boss puts at his disposal."[7] The precinct captain is forever a friend in need. In our prevailingly impersonal society, the machine, through its local agents, fulfills the important social *function of humanizing and personalizing all manner of assistance* to those in need. Foodbaskets and jobs, legal and extra-legal advice, setting to rights minor scrapes with the law, helping the bright poor boy to a political scholarship in a local college, looking after the bereaved —the whole range of crises when a feller needs a friend, and, above all, a friend who knows the score and who can do something about it,—all these find the ever-helpful precinct captain available in the pinch.

To assess this function of the political machine adequately, it is important to note not only that aid *is* provided but *the manner in which it is provided.* After all, other agencies do exist for dispensing such assistance. Welfare agencies, settlement houses, legal aid clinics, medical aid in free hospitals, public relief departments, immigration authorities—these and a multitude of other organizations are available to provide the most varied types of assistance. But in contrast to the professional techniques of the welfare worker which may typically represent in the mind of the recipient the cold, bureaucratic dispensation of limited aid following upon detailed investigation of *legal* claims to aid of the "client" are the unprofessional techniques of the precinct captain who asks no questions, exacts no compliance with legal rules of eligibility and does not "snoop" into private affairs.[8] For many, the loss of "self-respect" is too high a price for legalized assistance. In contrast to the gulf between the settlement house workers who so often come from a different social class, educational background and ethnic group, the precinct worker is "just one of us," who understands what it's all about. The condescending lady bountiful can hardly compete with the understanding friend in need. In *this struggle between alternative structures for fulfilling the nominally same function* of providing aid and support to those who need it, it is clearly the machine politician who is better integrated with the groups which he serves than the impersonal, professionalized, socially distant and legally constrained welfare worker. And since the politician can at times influence and manipulate the official organizations for the dispensation of assistance, whereas the welfare worker has practically no influence on the political machine, this only adds to his greater effectiveness. More colloquially and also, perhaps, more incisively, it was the Boston ward-leader, Martin Lomasny, who described this essential function to the curious Lincoln Steffens: "I think," said Lomasny, "that there's got to be in every ward somebody that any bloke can come to—no matter what he's done—and get help. *Help, you understand; none of your law and justice, but help.*"[9]

The "deprived classes," then, constitute one subgroup for whom the political machine satisfies wants not adequately satisfied in the same fashion by the legitimate social structure. For a second subgroup, that of busi-

ness (primarily "big" business but also "small"), the political boss serves the function of providing those political privileges which entail immediate economic gains. Business corporations, among which the public utilities (railroads, local transportation and electric light companies, communications corporations) are simply the most conspicuous in this regard, seek special political dispensations which will enable them to stabilize their situation and to near their objective of maximizing profits. Interestingly enough, corporations often want to avoid a chaos of uncontrolled competition. They want the greater security of an economic czar who controls, regulates and organizes competition, providing that this czar is not a public official with his decisions subject to public scrutiny and public control. (The latter would be "government control," and hence taboo.) The political boss fulfills these requirements admirably.

Examined for a moment apart from any moral considerations, the political apparatus operated by the Boss is effectively designed to perform these functions with a minimum of inefficiency. Holding the strings of diverse governmental divisions, bureaus and agencies in his competent hands, the Boss rationalizes the relations between public and private business. He serves as the business community's ambassador in the otherwise alien (and sometimes unfriendly) realm of government. And, in strict business-like terms, he is well-paid for his economic services to his respectable business clients. In an article entitled, "An Apology to Graft," Lincoln Steffens suggested that "Our economic system, which held up riches, power and acclaim as prizes to men bold enough and able enough to buy corruptly timber, mines, oil fields and franchises and 'get away with it,' was at fault."[10] And, in a conference with a hundred or so of Los Angeles business leaders, he described a fact well known to all of them: the Boss and his machine were an *integral part* of the organization of the economy. "You cannot build or operate a railroad, or a street railway, gas, water, or power company, develop and operate a mine, or get forests and cut timber on a large scale, or run any privileged business, without corrupting or joining in the corruption of the government. You tell me privately that you must, and here I am telling you semi-publicly that you must. And that is so all over the country. And that means that we have an organization of society in which, *for some reason,* you and your kind, the ablest, most intelligent, most imaginative, daring, and resourceful leaders of society, are and must be against society and its laws and its all-around growth."[11]

Since the demand for the services of special privileges are built into the structure of the society, the Boss fulfills diverse functions for this second subgroup of business-seeking-privilege. These "needs" of business, as presently constituted, are not adequately provided for by conventional and culturally approved social structures; consequently, the extra-legal but more-or-less efficient organization of the political machine comes to provide these services. To adopt an *exclusively* moral attitude toward the "corrupt political machine" is to lose sight of the very structural conditions which generate the "evil" that is so bitterly attacked. To adopt a functional outlook is to provide not an apologia for the political machine but a more solid basis for modifying or eliminating the machine, *providing* specific

structural arrangements are introduced either for eliminating these effective demands of the business community or, if that is the objective, of satisfying these demands through alternative means.

A third set of distinctive functions fulfilled by the political machine for a special subgroup is that of providing alternative channels of social mobility for those otherwise excluded from the more conventional avenues for personal "advancement." Both the sources of this special "need" (for social mobility) and the respect in which the political machine comes to help satisfy this need can be understood by examining the structure of the larger culture and society. As is well known, the American culture lays enormous emphasis on money and power as a "success" goal legitimate for all members of the society. By no means alone in our inventory of cultural goals, it still remains among the most heavily endowed with positive affect and value. However, certain subgroups and certain ecological areas are notable for the relative absence of opportunity for achieving these (monetary and power) types of success. They constitute, in short, sub-populations where "the cultural emphasis upon pecuniary success has been absorbed, but where there is *little access to conventional and legitimate* means for attaining such success. The conventional occupational opportunities of persons in (such areas) are almost completely limited to manual labor. Given our cultural stigmatization of manual labor,[12] and its correlate, the prestige of white-collar work, it is clear that the result is a tendency to achieve these culturally approved objectives *through whatever means are possible.* These people are on the one hand, "asked to orient their conduct toward the prospect of accumulating wealth [and power] and, on the other, they are largely denied effective opportunities to do so institutionally."

It is within the context of social structure that the political machine fulfills the basic function of providing avenues of social mobility for the otherwise disadvantaged. Within this context, even the corrupt political machine and the racket "represent the triumph of amoral intelligence over morally prescribed 'failure' when the channels of vertical mobility are closed or narrowed *in a society which places a high premium on economic affluence, [power] and social ascent for all its members.*"[13] As one sociologist has noted on the basis of several years of close observation in a slum area:

The sociologist who dismisses racket and political organizations as deviations from desirable standards thereby neglects some of the major elements of slum life. . . . He *does not discover the functions they perform for the members* [of the groupings in the slum]. The Irish and later immigrant peoples have had the greatest difficulty in finding places for themselves in our urban social and economic structure. Does anyone believe that the immigrants and their children could have achieved their present degree of social mobility without gaining control of the political organization of some of our largest cities? The same is true of the racket organization. *Politics and the rackets have furnished an important means of social mobility for individuals, who, because of ethnic background and low class position,* are blocked from advancement in the "respectable" channels.[14]

This, then, represents a third type of function performed for a distinctive subgroup. This function, it may be noted in passing, is fulfilled by the *sheer* existence and operation of the political machine, for it is in the machine itself that these individuals and subgroups find

their culturally induced needs more or less satisfied. It refers to the services which the political apparatus provides for its own personnel. But seen in the wider social context we have set forth, it no longer appears as *merely* a means of self-aggrandizement for profit-hungry and power-hungry *individuals,* but as an organized provision for *subgroups* otherwise excluded from or handicapped in the race for "getting ahead."

Just as the political machine performs services for "legitimate" business, so it operates to perform not dissimilar services for "illegitimate" business: vice, crime and rackets. Once again, the basic sociological role of the machine in this respect can be more fully appreciated only if one temporarily abandons attitudes of moral indignation, to examine in all moral innocence the actual workings of the organization. In this light, it at once appears that the subgroup of the professional criminal, racketeer or gambler has basic similarities of organization, demands and operation to the subgroup of the industrialist, man of business or speculator. If there is a Lumber King or an Oil King, there is also a Vice King or a Racket King. If expansive legitimate business organizes administrative and financial syndicates to "rationalize" and to "integrate" diverse areas of production and business enterprise, so expansive rackets and crime organize syndicates to bring order to the otherwise chaotic areas of production of illicit goods and services. If legitimate business regards the proliferation of small business enterprises as wasteful and inefficient, substituting, for example, the giant chain stores for hundreds of corner groceries, so illegitimate business adopts the same businesslike attitude and syndicates crime and vice.

Finally, and in many respects, most important, is the basic similarity, if not near-identity, of the economic role of "legitimate" business and of "illegitimate" business. *Both are in some degree concerned with the provision of goods and services for which there is an economic demand.* Morals aside, they are both business, industrial and professional enterprises, dispensing goods and services which some people want, for which there is a market in which goods and services are transformed into commodities. And, in a prevalently market society, we should expect appropriate enterprises to arise whenever there is a market demand for certain goods or services.

As is well known, vice, crime and the rackets *are* "big business." Consider only that there have been estimated to be about 500,000 professional prostitutes in the United States of 1950, and compare this with the approximately 200,000 physicians and 350,000 professional registered nurses. It is difficult to estimate which have the larger clientele: the professional men and women of medicine or the professional men and women of vice. It is, of course, difficult to estimate the economic assets, income, profits and dividends of illicit gambling in this country and to compare it with the economic assets, income, profits and dividends of, say, the shoe industry, but it is altogether possible that the two industries are about on a par. No precise figures exist on the annual expenditures on illicit narcotics, and it is probable that these are less than the expenditures on candy, but it is also probable that they are larger than the expenditure on books.

It takes but a moment's thought to recognize that, *in strictly economic*

terms, there is no relevant difference between the provision of licit and of illicit goods and services. The liquor traffic illustrates this perfectly. It would be peculiar to argue that prior to 1920 (when the 18th amendment became effective), the provision of liquor constituted an economic service, that from 1920 to 1933, its production and sale no longer constituted an economic service dispensed in a market, and that from 1934 to the present, it once again took on a serviceable aspect. Or, it would be *economically* (not morally) absurd to suggest that the sale of bootlegged liquor in the dry state of Kansas is less a response to a market demand than the sale of publicly manufactured liquor in the neighboring wet state of Missouri. Examples of this sort can of course be multiplied many times over. Can it be held that in European countries, with registered and legalized prostitution, the prostitute contributes an economic service, whereas in this country, lacking legal sanction, the prostitute provides no such service? Or that the professional abortionist is in the economic market where he is legally taboo? Or that gambling satisfies a specific demand for entertainment in Nevada, where it constitutes the largest business enterprise of the larger cities in the state, but that it differs essentially in this respect from motion pictures in the neighboring state of California?[15]

The failure to recognize that these businesses are only *morally* and not *economically* distinguishable from "legitimate" businesses has led to badly scrambled analysis. Once the economic identity of the two is recognized, we may anticipate that if the political machine performs functions for "legitimate big business" it will be all the more likely to perform not dissimilar functions for "illegitimate big business." And, of course, such is often the case.

The distinctive function of the political machine for their criminal, vice and racket clientele is to enable them to operate in satisfying the economic demands of a large market without due interference from the government. Just as big business may contribute funds to the political party war-chest to ensure a minimum of governmental interference, so with big rackets and big crime. In both instances, the political machine can, in varying degrees, provide "protection." In both instances, many features of the structural context are identical: (1) market demands for goods and services; (2) the operators' concern with maximizing gains from their enterprises; (3) the need for partial control of government which might otherwise interfere with these activities of businessmen; (4) the need for an efficient, powerful and centralized agency to provide an effective liaison of "business" with government.

Without assuming that the foregoing pages exhaust either the range of functions or the range of subgroups served by the political machine, we can at least see that *it presently fulfills some functions for these diverse subgroups which are not adequately fulfilled by culturally approved or more conventional structures.*

Several additional implications of the functional analysis of the political machine can be mentioned here only in passing, although they obviously require to be developed at length. First, the foregoing analysis has direct implications for *social engineering*. It helps explain why the periodic efforts at "political reform," "turning the rascals out"

and "cleaning political house" are typically (though not necessarily) short-lived and ineffectual. It exemplifies a basic theorem: *any attempt to eliminate an existing social structure without providing adequate alternative structures for fulfilling the functions previously fulfilled by the abolished organization is doomed to failure.* (Needless to say, this theorem has much wider bearing than the one instance of the political machine.) When "political reform" confines itself to the manifest task of "turning the rascals out," it is engaging in little more than sociological magic. The reform may for a time bring new figures into the political limelight; it may serve the casual social function of re-assuring the electorate that the moral virtues remain intact and will ultimately triumph; it may actually effect a turnover in the personnel of the political machine; it may even, for a time, so curb the activities of the machine as to leave unsatisfied the many needs it has previously fulfilled. But, inevitably, unless the reform also involves a "re-forming" of the social and political structure such that the existing needs are satisfied by alternative structures or unless it involves a change which eliminates these needs altogether, the political machine will return to its integral place in the social scheme of things. *To seek social change, without due recognition of the manifest and latent functions performed by the social organization undergoing change, is to indulge in social ritual rather than social engineering.* The concepts of manifest and latent functions (or their equivalents) are indispensable elements in the theoretic repertoire of the social engineer. In this crucial sense, these concepts are not "merely" theoretical (in the abusive sense of the term), but are eminently practical. In the deliberate enactment of social change, they can be ignored only at the price of considerably heightening the risk of failure.

A second implication of this analysis of the political machine also has a bearing upon areas wider than the one we have considered. The paradox has often been noted that the supporters of the political machine include both the "respectable" business class elements who are, of course, opposed to the criminal or racketeer and the distinctly "unrespectable" elements of the underworld. And, at first appearance, this is cited as an instance of very strange bedfellows. The learned judge is not infrequently called upon to sentence the very racketeer beside whom he sat the night before at an informal dinner of the political bigwigs. The district attorney jostles the exonerated convict on his way to the back room where the Boss has called a meeting. The big business man may complain almost as bitterly as the big racketeer about the "extortionate" contributions to the party fund demanded by the Boss. Social opposites meet—in the smoke-filled room of the successful politician.

In the light of a functional analysis all this of course no longer seems paradoxical. Since the machine serves both the businessman and the criminal man, the two seemingly antipodal groups intersect. This points to a more general theorem: *the social functions of an organization help determine the structure (including the recruitment of personnel involved in the structure), just as the structure helps determine the effectiveness with which the functions are fulfilled.* In terms of social status, the business group and the criminal group are

indeed poles apart. But status does not fully determine behavior and the interrelations between groups. Functions modify these relations. Given their distinctive needs, the several subgroups in the large society are "integrated," whatever their personal desires or intentions, by the centralizing structure which serves these several needs. In a phrase with many implications which require further study, *structure affects function and function affects structure.* . . .

NOTES

1. These "explanations" are "causal" in design. They profess to indicate the social conditions under which political machines come into being. In so far as they are empirically confirmed, these explations of course add to our knowledge concerning the problem: how is it that political machines operate in certain areas and not in others? How do they manage to continue? *But these causal accounts are not sufficient.* The functional consequences of the machine, as we shall see, go far toward supplementing the causal interpretation.
2. I trust it is superfluous to add that this hypothesis is not "in support of the political machine." The question whether the dysfunctions of the machine outweigh its functions, the question whether alternative structures are not available which may fulfill its functions without necessarily entailing its social dysfunctions, still remain to be considered at an appropiate point. We are here concerned with documenting the statement that moral judgments based *entirely* on an appraisal of manifest functions of a social structure are "unrealistic" in the strict sense, *i.e.*, they do not take into account other actual consequences of that structure, consequences which may provide basic social support for the structure. As will be indicated later, "social reforms" or "social engineering" which ignore latent functions do so on pain of suffering acute disappointments and boomerang effects.
3. Again, as with preceding cases, we shall not consider the possible dysfunctions of the political machine.
4. Edward M. Sait, "Machine, Political," *Encyclopedia of the Social Sciences*, IX, 658 b [italics supplied]; *cf.* A. F. Bentley, *The Process of Government* (Chicago, 1908), Chap. 2.
5. Herbert Croly, *Progressive Democracy*, (New York, 1914), p. 254, cited by Sait, *op. cit.*, 658 b.

6. Sait, *op. cit.*, 659 a. [italics supplied].

7. *Ibid.*, 659 a.

8. Much the same contrast with official welfare policy is found in Harry Hopkins' open-handed and non-political distribution of unemployment relief in New York State under the governorship of Franklin Delano Roosevelt. As Sherwood reports: "Hopkins was harshly criticized for these irregular activities by the established welfare agencies, which claimed it was 'unprofessional conduct' to hand out work tickets without thorough investigation of each applicant, his own or his family's financial resources and probably his religious affiliations. 'Harry told the agency to go to hell,' said [Hopkins' associate, Dr. Jacob A.] Goldberg." Robert E. Sherwood, *Roosevelt and Hopkins, An Intimate History,* (New York: Harper, 1948), 30.

9. *The Autobiography of Lincoln Steffens,* (Chautauqua, New York: Chautauqua Press, 1931), 618. Deriving largely from Steffens, as he says, F. Stuart Chapin sets forth these functions of the political machine with great clarity. See his *Contemporary American Institutions* (New York: Harper, 1934), 40-54.

10. *Autobiography of Lincoln Steffens,* 570.

11. *Ibid.*, 572-3 [italics supplied]. This helps explain, as Steffens noted after Police Commissioner Theodore Roosevelt, "the prominence and respectability of the men and women who intercede for crooks" when these have been apprehended in a periodic effort to "clean up the political machine." *Cf.* Steffens, 371, and *passim.*

12. See the National Opinion Research Center survey of evaluation of occupations which firmly documents the general impression that the manual occupations rate very low indeed in the social scale of values, *even among those who are themselves engaged in manual labor.* Consider this latter point in its full implications. In effect, the cultural and social structure exacts the values of pecuniary and power success even among those who find themselves confined to the stigmatized manual occupations. Against this background, consider the powerful motivation for achieving this type of "success" by any means whatsoever. A garbage-collector who joins with other Americans in the view that the garbage-collector is "the lowest of the low" occupations can scarcely have a self-image which is pleasing to him; he is in a "pariah" occupation in the very society where he is assured that "all who have genuine merit can get ahead." Add to this, his occasional recognition that "he

didn't have the same chance as others, no matter what they say," and one perceives the enormous psychological pressure upon him for "evening up the score" by finding some means, whether strictly legal or not, for moving ahead. All this provides the structural and derivatively psychological background for the "socially induced need" in *some* groups to find some accessible avenue for social mobility.

13. Merton, "Social structure and anomie," chapter IV of this volume.

14. William F. Whyte, "Social organization in the slums," *American Sociological Review,* Feb. 1943, 8, 34-39 (italics supplied). Thus, the political machine and the racket represent a special case of the type of organizational adjustment to the conditions described in chapter IV. It represents, note, an *organizational* adjustment: definite structures arise and operate to reduce somewhat the acute tensions and problems of individuals caught up in the described conflict between the "cultural accent on success-for-all" and the "socially structured fact of unequal opportunities for success." As chapter IV indicates, other types of *individual* "adjustment" are possible: lone-wolf crime, psychopathological states, rebellion, retreat by abandoning the culturally approved goals, etc. Likewise, other types of *organizational adjustment* sometimes occur; the racket or the political machine are not *alone* available as organized means for meeting this socially induced problem. Participation in revolutionary organizations, for example, can be seen within this context, as an alternative mode of organizational adjustment. All this bears theoretic notice here, since we might otherwise overlook the basic functional concepts of functional substitutes and functional equivalents, which are to be discussed at length in a subsequent publication.

15. Perhaps the most perceptive statement of this view has been made by Hawkins and Waller. "The prostitute, the pimp, the peddler of dope, the operator of the gambling hall, the vendor of obscene pictures, the bootlegger, the abortionist, all are productive, all produce services or goods which people desire and for which they are willing to pay. It happens that society has put these goods and services under the ban, but people go on producing them and people go on consuming them, and an act of the legislature does not make them any less a part of the economic system." "Critical notes on the cost of crime," *Journal of Criminal Law and Criminology,* 1936, 26, 679-94, at 684.

The Crusade Against the Tweed Ring

ALEXANDER B. CALLOW, JR.

I thank my God the sun and moon
Are both stuck up so high
That no presumptuous hand can stretch
And pluck them from the sky.
If they were not, I do believe
That some reforming ass
Would recommend to take them down
And light the world with gas.

Judge James T. Brady

For five years the Tweed Ring had led a great treasury raid. The power of the Ring, like the tentacles of an octopus, encircled city government, the courts, the police, the underworld, and the State legislature. The command centers of political power from the Governor to the Board of Aldermen were controlled by the Ring and its lieutenants. The Ring ruled over an empire of patronage with thousands of the faithful on the city payrolls. Tammany Hall had been remodeled into an awesome political machine, supported by the immigrant and the native poor, and sustained on election day by a horde of Tammany warriors, repeaters, and corrupt election officials who made a mockery out of the power of the ballot. No wonder Boss Tweed could ask the reformer, "What are you going to do about it?"

Seldom have the forces of "good" government faced such a formidable opponent as they did in July 1871. Yet five months later the Tweed Ring was destroyed. Most accounts of this campaign emphasize the Ring's sensational thefts. But few questions have been raised about the crusade itself; few attempts have been made to understand the anatomy of a reform movement on a local, grass-roots level. For example, how was the crusade conducted? What was the impact of the Tweed Ring upon the reformer's imagination and in what way did the Ring reveal his attitudes toward reform, corruption, and political institutions? If the rascals were such capital rogues, why did it take so long to destroy them?

By the fall of 1871, when damning evidence was being unearthed and New York echoed from the cries of one reform rally after another, most of the press, a multitude of reform groups, and politicians from both parties were noisily scrambling after the scalps of the Tammany Ring braves. Now that the Ring was disintegrating, all vied for the heroic role of redeemer. Samuel Tilden almost reached the Presidency on the claim that he destroyed the Ring. But Tilden was a hero of last moments. A skillful general when the enemy was in retreat, he was the soul of indecision, procrastination, and lost opportunities when the Ring was in power. In those quiet days before the great uprising, only two led the crusade against the Tweed Ring: Thomas Nast of *Harper's Weekly*, and the *New York Times*. *Harper's Weekly* began in 1868 to print Thomas Nast's brilliant political cartoons, and his talent with the poisoned-

From Alexander B. Callow, Jr., *The Tweed Ring* (New York: Oxford, 1966), pp. 253-78, 298-300. Copyright © 1965, 1966 by Alexander B. Callow, Jr. Reprinted by permission of the publisher. Alexander B. Callow, Jr., is Associate Professor of American History at the University of California, Santa Barbara.

pen portrait, which could at once inspire fear and ridicule, had led many to think he was the chief wrecker of the Ring. Tweed himself thoroughly recognized Nast's artistry in making a cartoon a deadly political weapon. "I don't care a straw for your newspaper articles, my constituents don't know how to read, but they can't help seeing them damned pictures."[1] A picture may say a thousand words, but it still took many a thousand words to excite and motivate the indignation of New Yorkers. It was the *New York Times* which published the first evidence of corruption, helped to raise the crusade to the heights of near hysteria, and therefore deserves the mantle of champion opponent of the Tweed Ring. The role played by the *Times* is a kind of case study of the enormous difficulties and stubborn persistence involved in arousing a sometimes confused and often apathetic public.

Prior to September 1870, the fight against corruption was represented by a series of angry but irregular outbursts from reform groups and newspapers. These in turn were thwarted by grand juries vulnerable to the persuasion of hard cash and lack of evidence. The Citizens' Association and the Union League, both eminent bodies of "respectabilities," had long fished in the murky waters of New York politics with only occasional luck.[2] While the reformers suspected that something was desperately wrong, the rub was in proving it. Although the Ring was organized as early as 1866, there was little awareness by reformers of either a centralized city machine or of how politics operated at the level of the ward and precinct. Instead, there was talk of a host of "rings" but uncertainty as to who were the ringleaders.

Apathy, a lack of civic conscience, and fear—which permeated every level of society—also accounted for the reformers' failure to get an audience. An absence of consensus, generated by party partisanship, divided the press and the gentry, the two groups who might have sounded the alarm and carried the fight. While the business community furnished several leaders to the reform groups, other businessmen were either afraid of the retaliatory power of Tammany Hall or they benefited from the Ring's operations, while others, too interested in making money, simply did not care.

The Tweed Ring exploited these conditions and reinforced complacency by giving something to everyone: city advertising to the press, special favors to businessmen, state aid to charitable and religious organizations, jobs and food to the poor. Tweed through his business connections and Hall through his clubs ingratiated themselves in the upper branches of society, while Sweeny and Connolly, seasoned ward leaders, were effective in the rank and file. And then there was the Astor Committee and its whitewash of the Comptroller's records, which contributed as much as any event to creating complacency.

Into this atmosphere, the champion of reform, the *New York Times*, made its "auspicious" beginning in the winter of 1870, by announcing that Messrs. Sweeny, Hall, and Hoffman were busily engaged in bringing good government to New York![3] One delicious irony was topped by another when the *Times* gave its first (and last) cheer for the Boss himself.

Senator Tweed is in a fair way to distinguish himself as a reformer. . . . From beginning to end the Tweed party has not manifested the slightest disposition to evade or prevaricate. . . . As a whole, the appointments of the heads of the various departments of the City Government . . . are far above the average in point of personal fitness, and should be satisfactory.[4]

The *Times*'s course, however, was radically altered by the summer of 1870. Ugly rumors of corruption were once again abroad, and George Jones, the *Times* publisher, apparently feeling hoodwinked and humiliated, angrily turned on the charter and its creators. An Englishman, Louis Jennings, was imported as editor. Jennings's zest for a good fight, his acerbic prose, coupled with Nast's cartoons in *Harper's Weekly*, infused the campaign with a pitch and tempo of almost evangelical fervor. For over a year, from September 20, 1870, on, there was not a day that the *Times* did not, with furious and heroic invective, assault the Tweed Ring, its organization, and allies. The *Times* begged, cajoled, scolded, and demanded that the electorate rout the rascals; nevertheless, the public, including some of the "best people," seemed to sink deeper in its apathy, and the Ring got stronger. What was wrong? Was it entirely public indifference, the usual scapegoat for corruption, or did the trouble lay partly in the nature of the crusade itself?

Two elements are necessary in any successful campaign against civic corruption: moral indignation and facts. Until July 1871, the *Times*'s attack was a grand crusade conducted without fear and without facts; it was long on denunciation, short on documentation. The slack in legal evidence was taken up in an amazing exercise of invective, the central theme of which was the wickedness of the Tweed Ring, a theme with a hundred variations on the words "thief," "rogue," and "scamp." The crusade had persistence. It had gusto. It

had all the subtlety of a sledge hammer. It was literary alchemy using the crudest of alloys. There was none of the humor or painful ridicule of a Nast cartoon, none of the dash of the *New York Herald* or the deft sarcasm of Dana's *Sun* when those two papers finally joined the bandwagon later in 1871. It was just a juggernaut of epithets, taking the edge off the crusade by dulling the reader's senses with a repetitive cry of "wolf." E. L. Godkin of *The Nation*, although admiring the newspaper's spirit, found its denunciation "tiresome."[5] Even the *Times* admitted that its readers were probably bone-tired from the constant accusations.[6] And while the *Times* spewed platitudes about political sin, the elegant Mayor of New York quipped, "Who's going to sue?"[7]

Nor was abuse heaped solely on the Ring, for the public in general, and the rich, the workingman, and the church in particular, came within the *Times*'s range as it sharpened its aim at iniquity. One major strategic device of the crusade was to arouse a feeling of guilt and shame. The public had failed its civic responsibilities. There should be a moment of self-castigation coupled with redeeming political New Year's resolutions to sweep away the apathy that allowed the monstrosities of the Tweed Ring. The rich were scorned for their complacency, hypocrisy, and lack of action.[8] They were "cowardly and effeminate," refusing to leave the comfort of their libraries for the "unpleasant smells" of the political arena.

The policy of the Ring, in fact, was to drive the honest, decent middle class out of the city and leave it to the very rich and the very poor—"the one too lazy to oppose them, and the other too ignorant."[9] If the workingman understood the elementary principles of political economy, he would not be grateful for the jobs the Ring gave him on the streets and in the parks. He should realize that the robbery of the rich was the robbery of the poor. Labor actually took the full brunt of the Ring's adventures in graft through raised rents, increased taxes, and higher priced goods.[10] As for the church, the *Times* said, at most it applauds while others fight. If only the church acted with responsibility, the public conscience would be inflamed, and the sores on the body politic would be burned out, "as if by fire."[11]

With these tactics of shock, blame, and invective, the *Times* seemed to be searching for some way to shatter the complacency of the public. An attempt was made, in a pedestrian Jeffersonian vein, to exploit the chasm between town and country, the fear—and fascination—of the city. The "hay-loft and cheese-press Democrats" were told of the moral quagmire of the Sodom-by-the-Hudson, its city-slicker politicians, its crime, its cancerous effect on the Democratic party.[12] The trouble with that approach was that upstate politicos well knew that the success of the party depended on the city Democrats' delivering a large bloc of votes, and the Tweed Ring had time and again shown it could deliver.

Perhaps an appeal to the citizens' pocketbook would help, for here lay men's hearts—"touch them there and they will wince and exhibit more sensitiveness than they will show to even the strongest appeals made to their sympathies," as the *Times* said.[13] The newspaper became choked with figures demonstrating the Ring's damage to property owners. But most of the electorate did not own real property. Columns

were devoted to an awkward analysis of city finances. But the average voter would have difficulty making sense of them. As the *Times* executed its complicated sums, apathy seemed to increase.

One reason why the crusade raged on for so long amid apparent indifference from the rest of the New York press was that the Democratic press, from the *World* on down—"or rather up, for you cannot get lower than the *World*"—(as the *Times* remarked)—were infuriated over the profound Republican partisanship of Nast and the *Times*. The *Times* was fond of repeating the adage that every Democrat was not a horse-thief, but that every horse-thief was a Democrat. Moreover, according to the *Times*, "all" Democrats were corrupt; the party had "never" undertaken a "genuine" reform.[14] Righteous moral indignation was rudely compromised when the *Times* condemned city Democrats and blithely whitewashed the Grant administration.[15]

Skepticism (and perhaps jealousy) also influenced the press. The *Times* motto should read, said one newspaper, "Print everything you please, without regard to whether it is true or false, but refuse to prove anything."[16] Horace Greeley, who puffed hot and cold throughout the campaign, even suggested that the Ring sue the *Times* for libel.[17] The *New York World*, after a brief flirtation with the Young Democracy, returned to revolve around Tammany Hall; it stoutly defended the Ring, calling the crusade as "stupid and absurd as it is wicked," and designed to introduce "a reign of anarchy."[18] Moreover, both the *Herald* and the *World* liked Oakey Hall. James Gordon Bennett of the *Herald* once said approvingly of Tweed's left-hand man, "He calls a spade a spade and Horace Greeley a humbug."[19]

Thus when Tammany wildly celebrated on July 4, 1871, it seemed that Nast's cartoons and the *Times*'s river of rhetoric had produced a crusade without followers, a cause apparently lost to corruption and apathy. All had not been lost, however, for it prepared New Yorkers for what was to follow. This was made possible not by any renewed moral gusto from Tammany's "unloyal" opposition, but by a quirk of fate and an emotion common in politics—the hankering for revenge.

The first real step in the Ring's fall to disaster came on January 21, 1871, when James Watson, the trusty County Auditor and Ring bookkeeper, was killed in a sleighing accident. The Ring was to learn how indispensable he was, for the door was now open for espionage. Matthew O'Rourke was appointed County Auditor, but was not taken into the Ring's confidence. It was a fatal appointment—"a dirty traitor and a fraud," Tammany's *Leader* cried later. O'Rourke was not a happy man. He once had a claim against the city which the Ring had seen fit not to pay. A disgruntled claim-seeker could be as vicious as a woman scorned. With the patience and accuracy of a good bookkeeper, O'Rourke copied the explosive facts and figures of corruption from the Ring's account books and passed them on to the *Times*.[20]

Acting independently, Jimmy O'Brien, one of the leaders of the rebel Young Democracy, assumed the role of a political Judas. He had managed to ingratiate himself back into the good graces of the Ring, by abandoning the Young Democracy and acting as an enthusiastic trustee for the Tweed monument association. But beneath his ruddy Irish complexion, he smouldered with resentment over the Ring's refusal to pay him $300,000 in claims he collected while Sheriff. O'Brien persuaded Connolly to give one William Copeland a job in the Comptroller's office. Copeland was, in fact, O'Brien's spy, sent to obtain information to use as blackmail to get O'Brien's claims. With Watson dead, Copeland found the voucher records loosely guarded. Lush accounts, such as "County Liabilities," furnished him with a wealth of information, which he copied for O'Brien. Confronted with this political dynamite, Tweed began to pay blackmail. He paid O'Brien over $20,000 with the promise that $130,000 would be forthcoming in mortgages on prime property. O'Brien coolly pocketed the cash and turned his information over to the *Times*.[21]

The breakthrough in the crusade had come. Publisher Jones began his attack with uncommon good sense. He bought up a large block of *Times* stock, fearful the Ring might retaliate by a stock raid. And then on Saturday, July 22, 1871, the *Times* opened up with its first front-page blast: "The Secret Accounts: Proofs of Undoubted Frauds Brought to Light." Slowly and deliciously, as if opening a long-awaited Christmas package, Jones released his figures—on the armories, the courthouse, padded payrolls, judicial indiscretion—topping one horror with another.[22] On the 29th the *Times* printed a special supplement in English and German of statistics on the armory and courthouse swindles; 200,000 copies of the first printing were quickly sold out. It was not only a sensation in New York, but it also attracted immediate national attention. For the next four months Jones never let up; front page and editorial page boiled with journalistic frenzy—and Nast drew his cartoons with even greater venom.

Now as the facts were exposed, New York stirred, rumbled, and awoke—shocked, frightened, angry. It was now time for the reformers to take more decisive action. The massive reform rally on September 4 at Cooper Union, the first of many, registered the impact of the *Times*'s exposures: the temper was explosive, the spirit was that of a backcountry revival meeting. The rally was sponsored by the Committee of Seventy, whose roster bulged with some of the most distinguished names in New York, such as William F. Havemeyer, Judge James Emott, Robert Roosevelt, Charles Richard O'Conor, and Joseph H. Choate, who presented the Committee's resolutions against the Tweed Ring with the battle cry, "This is what *we* are going to do about it!"[23]

A rostrum of distinguished speakers aroused the audience to a passionate fervor: "We shall get at them. The wicked shall not always rule"; "Pitch into the boss, give it to him, he deserves it"; "There is no power like the power of the people armed, aroused, and kindled with the enthusiasm of a righteous wrath"; "What are we going to do about it?"—"Hang them," cried the voices from the audience.[24] The *Times* said afterward that if the Ring had heard the curses, hisses, and denunciations heaped on them they would have felt "too mean to live."[25]

It was evident that New York had awakened from its apathy. The Citizens' Association, the New York Council of Political Reform, and the Union League threw their weight into the crusade, and they were followed by a host of reform groups—the Young Men's Municipal Reform Association, the Apollo Hall Democracy, the Young De-

mocracy, the German Reform Organization, and the Ward Councils of Political Reform. The press joined the chorus. Prominent businessmen and attorneys like R. A. Hunter, George W. Benster, and James Whitten met and considered forming a Vigilance Committee, but cooler heads prevailed. And Samuel Tilden entered on his somewhat gray charger. It was now expedient for him to be a reformer. The crusade reached a new dimension. It was no longer the concern of two but an issue that attracted many New Yorkers.

The impact of the Tweed Ring upon the reformer's imagination once again demonstrated the American capacity to create a morality play out of politics. Here was a drama of good versus evil. The principal characters were so wonderfully wicked that little embellishment seemed necessary. But embellished they were. While the reformers' responses were varied and often contradictory, certain dominant themes emerged.

The beginning theme, which Thomas Nast did more than anyone else to fix, was the image of the city boss, a portrait of evil. Tweed was pictured as gross, vicious, lowborn, colossally corrupt. Sweeny was the man with the black brains; Connolly was dark and oily; and Nast's favorite target, Oakey Hall, was the buffoon. These "beastly rascals" were also seen not as an indigenous product of the American urban political system, but as something sinister and alien. The corruption of the Ring was compared to the treachery of a Judas Iscariot, to the cunning of a Robespierre, the slothful greed of Oriental potentates; in tyranny and insolence they "would put their Roman predecessors to the blush."[26]

But the Boss and his ministers were

only mirrors in larger size and more evil proportions of those who flocked to their support—the Irish-Catholic immigrants. One of the most significant responses to the Tweed Ring, one which rounded out the image of evil by adding fear to it, was the revival of nativism in New York. On July 12, 1871, Protestant and Catholic Irish engaged in a bloody riot which shocked New York and revived the Know-Nothing attitudes of the 1850's and nativist fears of the 1863 draft riots. The Ring was vehemently denounced for trying to prevent the annual parade for the Orangemen, which precipitated the riot, as pacifying the Catholic Irish. When the parade was allowed, the Ring was accused of protecting the Catholic rioters. No other single event so well illustrated the tie between Tammany Hall and the Irish-Catholic voter. The cry for "clean government" now emitted the voice of nativism. There was a papal conspiracy as "Irish Catholic despotism rules the City of New York, the Metropolis of free America."[27] Letters poured into the *Times* office calling for a revival of the Native American party.[28] The Citizens' Association announced that the city had become a "common sewer" for the "dregs" of Europe; an army of ignorance was being led to the polls by the Tweed Ring.[29]

Nativism, in turn, elicited another response. The reformers, for the most part of the middle and upper class— professional men, bankers, merchants, journalists, the "better" politicians—felt a distinct loss of status since their old position of leadership had been captured by the wicked and the mob. Prior to the reign of Fernando Wood, political factions were controlled by men belonging to the upper or middle class, to whom the emoluments of office,

while desirable, were not always essential. From the days of Tweed's Forty Thieves through the Civil War, a change was occurring in New York politics, gradually, not completely, not easy to recognize; like the grin of the Cheshire Cat, sometimes it was seen, sometimes it was not. The old ruling groups, even the august Albany Regency, were being slowly displaced by a group not new, but different in numbers and the ranks from which it came—the lower-middle class, and the bottom of the social heap, the immigrant and native poor. The old ruling groups had to begin to move over and make a place for a new group, the Irish. This change found its source in the city, its growth, the changing composition of its population, the nature of its government. But the old middle- and upper-class elite, especially the reformers, who largely came from these groups, never completely understood this change and felt only bitterness toward the new and not always "respectable" elite. Republican institutions under the Tweed Ring, the reformers declared, were safe only in the "rightful" hands of the educated, the wealthy, and the virtuous. Now power had shifted to those at the bottom of society, their morals decayed, their religion Romanist, their Alma Mater the corner saloon.[30] The *Times* echoed the reformer's fears: We exist over a volcano, a vast, explosive mass of the poor and ignorant—"the dangerous classes," who "care nothing for our liberty and civilization."[31] E. L. Godkin traced the phenomenon back to the excessive democratization of the 1846 New York State Constitution.[32] Others saw it compounded by another insidious development, the rise of a new political breed, the professional politician.

As New York itself grew, politics became more centralized, more disciplined, more professionalized. While the professional politician had long been on the scene in New York politics, the impact of the Tweed Ring seemed to wipe out that memory and fix the emergence and the novelty of the professional as coinciding with the Tweed era. The *Times*, in fact, wrote of the "new profession" as if it were just making its appearance.[33] The reformer gave the professional little credit for skill in handling men or for artful political techniques at the "low" level of the ward or precinct, or for his sometimes masterful sense of organization. The reformer generally was little interested in the rude day-by-day operations of politics. His middle and upper class sensibilities were congenial to ideals and principles, not to the often rough, dreary, but necessary work of the primaries. The professional, in the reformer's eyes, was not a Robin Hood to the needy, but rather a Robin the Hood to the degenerate, wasting the taxpayers' money by giving jobs to the immigrant, bailing the drunkard out of jail, and corrupting the unemployed by giving them food and cigars—a parasite undermining the Protestant ethic of civic responsibility. The New York Council of Political Reform summed it all up. It was a contest between two forces: one made up of ruffians and desperadoes, and the other of "the delicately reared, the moral, humane, and the peace loving."[34]

Thus his sense of lost status, his contempt and fear of the masses, his nativism, his reaction to the city boss as rogue and professional politician—all indicate that the reformer's response to the Tweed Ring was more than simple moralizing about political sin. But if there was one response, a dynamic one

which gave cohesion and direction to his other reactions and provided the most powerful stimulus to reform, it was the fear that civil liberties were in danger, which to a certain degree was true. This response finally gave to the crusade a sense of genuine crisis, its *raison d'être*. The capital crime, then, was not merely the plundering of the treasury, nor the danger to the taxpayer's pocketbook; it was something more sinister than that. It was that a gang of rogues and its vicious brood, an organization alien to American life, was threatening the very bases of republican institutions—the ballot box, the schools, the church, the freedom of speech and press. "This wholesale filching and slaughter of the suffrage is a deadly thrust at the very source and fountain of our liberties . . . [we must] recover our mutilated liberties and vindicate our civil rights," shouted Joseph Choate at Cooper Union.[35] The danger to civil liberties was one of the most persistent themes of the *New York Times*.[36] Judge James Emott, Henry Clinton, Henry G. Stebbins, William Evarts, and others, all repeated the same theme: the Tweed Ring had threatened "the existence of free institutions," republicanism was "poisoned," "the glories of liberty are in danger."[37] The threat was felt even outside New York. "Democratic principles can no more carry this curse of Tammany upon them than virtue can thrive in a brothel," said the *Chicago Times*.[38]

If these fears seem exaggerated, it was because the reformers of the Tweed era were faced with their first city boss and his well-organized machine. There had been corruption in the past, but no precedent of modern city bosses to temper the reformer's idealism and sharpen his realism.

Although there were differences among the reformers, and their schemes often overlapped, there were broadly two schools of thought on how best to cleanse New York City. The largest school believed that the Ring was not a natural product of American municipal government but a political disease alien to New World representative democracy. The cure, therefore, was relatively simple. Rout the rascals, lance the boil on the body politic, and the organism would be healthy again. This prognosis reflected an implicit faith in the efficacy of American institutions. The defeat of the Tweed Ring meant the vindication of republicanism, not the questioning of it. There were, of course, minor wounds to be treated: the charter needed patching up, there were too many appointive offices, and a tight little bureaucracy should replace the Ring's bloated monster. If the Ring discredited any institution, it was the political party. Partisanship, therefore, should be replaced by efficiency, honesty, and the methods of business. "The government of a city," declared the Union League, "is altogether more a matter of business, than of statesmanship." The party system led only to "lawlessness, disorganization, pillage and anarchy."[39]

For these reformers, the cause of corruption could be the cure of corruption. The absence of the "best people" in government had allowed the wicked to rule. Thus the call was for the return to power of men with substantial wealth, education, and virtue. "The Ring could not keep its own for a day in the teeth of a combined and vigorous opposition from the men of large property."[40] New York was choked with foreigners, "many of them not pos-

sessed of virtue and intelligence sufficient for self-government."[41] Therefore, what was needed, said the New York City Council of Political Reform, under the heading of "The Effectual Remedy," was for the "right-minded" to enter "into a covenant with each other . . . and the work is done."[42] If this sounded like the voice of the happy ending, it was also the voice of elitism. By implication, the "right-minded" were always the old ruling elite. It represented government of the people, for the people, *by* the "best people."

The second group of reformers did not share the extravagant optimism of the first. Corruption had forced them to re-examine the efficacy of democratic institutions and in so doing they found them wanting. Patchwork will not answer, wrote James Parton. The ship of state needed an overhaul from keel to taffrail, and perhaps it was necessary to "abandon the vessel and build a new one."[43] There must be some "profound defect," said C. C. P. Clark, in the American system which produced the horrors of the Tweed Ring.[44] The defect these reformers saw was one of the hallowed tenets of the American dream, universal suffrage. The comments of E. L. Godkin best illustrate this position. It was nonsense to talk about the Ring as a novelty to the American scene; it was the inevitable result of a "process of evolution," and other great cities have their "mute, inglorious Tweeds" waiting for their opportunity.[45] The curse of the city, "the great city problem," *is* the "people"—or about half of them who constitute the poor, "that huge body of ignorant and corrupt voters." The poor have no conception of self-government and choose only to live off the rich. The blight of universal suffrage is the secret of the Ring's power because it gave them an army. There can be, then, only two cures: first, suffrage should be limited, because only the propertied class, those who have a stake in society, should rule, for "we must somehow put the government into the hands of men who pay taxes." And second, the municipality should be converted into a business, stripped of political influence.[46] This program did not go far enough for Francis Leiber, James Parton, and Isaac Butts. They wanted to impose a literacy test on all New York voters.[47] It was a fine irony that those who felt their civil liberties in danger should seek to curtail the liberties of others.

From whence had come these dreams for a reformed New York? Not from the reformer's own time, for which he expressed a withering indictment. The reformer turned away from his own era, which spawned chaos and upheaval, looked back over his shoulder and found his solutions in a remembrance of things past—or what he *thought* had passed. He reached back for a lost innocence, the simplicity of an older era, the chaste republican order of a golden yesteryear. When he called for the return of the "best people," he thought of past mighties—James Kent, De Witt Clinton, Edward Livingston. His plan for a small, simplified government was the vision of the clean, honest symmetry of the town meeting, which James Welsh fondly recalled as the "natural school of American statesmanship."[48] The concept of limited suffrage, that ideological dog which had had its day, was an image of Order, a responsible aristocracy balancing a rapacious mob. The warmth of reminiscence, however, was an anesthetic to the re-

former's memory. For him the Tweed era dated the decline of political virtue. Before that ranged the long years of paradise to be found again. Forgotten were the gentlemen rogues, Fernando Wood, the Forty Thieves, and Samuel Swartwout. Nostalgia even led the reformer to tidy up the Albany Regency. Now it was remembered as an organization of "culture, integrity, and character."[49] And Thurlow Weed, an able opponent of the old, honest Regency, apparently with straight face, testified that "formerly the *suspicion* of corruption in a member [of the State legislature] would have put him 'into Coventry.' "[50] As one reform pamphlet said, "Pause here, Reader, sadly to drop a tear on the grave of departed Patriotism."[51]

As the crusade accelerated and unified both reformers and the press by early fall of 1871, the Ring, realizing it was in deep trouble, fought back like a trapped tiger and made some clumsy but typical maneuvers. George Jones was offered a bribe of $500,000 to silence the *Times*. He turned it down saying, "I don't think that the devil will ever bid higher for me than that."[52] Perhaps Thomas Nast needed a rest. He was promised $500,000 if he would leave the country and study art in Europe. "Well, I don't think I'll do it," Nast said. "I made up my mind not long ago to put some of those fellows behind the bars, *and I'm going to put them there!*"[53]

For a while Tweed remained cool and calm. A reporter for the *Missouri Republican* asked him if it were true that he had stolen money. Tweed thought a while and said, "This is not a question one gentleman ought to put to another."[54] George Templeton Strong said: "Tweed's impudent serenity is sublime. Were he not a supreme scoundrel, he would be a great man."[55] Finally, on September 8 he lost his composure and declared to a *Sun* reporter:

The *Times* has been saying all the time I have no brains. Well, I'll show Jones that I have brains. . . . I tell you, sir, if this man Jones had said the things he has said about me, twenty-five years ago, he wouldn't be alive now. But, you see, when a man has a wife and children, he can't do such a thing (clenching his fists). I would have killed him.

Nor did Mayor Hall help matters. He became ensnarled in his own contradictory statements and succeeded only in deepening the Ring's guilt. At first Hall cried innocent. The disclosures of the *Times* were "a tempest of ciphers and calumny . . . a second-hand roar about the accounts of the Supervisors and the salaries of extinct sinecures." Then he admitted some frauds were committed by the "old" Supervisors, but not by the Ring. This was interesting, because Tweed was president of the old Board of Supervisors. He said he never signed the alleged fraudulent warrants, and blamed Watson. He retracted this and admitted signing them, but only as a "ministerial act." He then claimed the signatures were forged; then retracted again and said he had signed but had been "hoodwinked." He tried sonorous prose: "When at last the smoke shall clear away, it will be seen where the political sun will clearly shine, that the proudest flag of them all, waving untorn from the highest staff of the victorious army, is that which shall never cease to be borne by Tammany Hall."[56]

And naturally Hall attempted humor. "We are likely to have what befell

Adam—an early Fall."[57] In an interview with a newspaper, he showed what the *Times* called "cheek."

Reporter: "You are looking very well."
Mayor: "Oh yes, I am always cheerful. You know the true philosophy of life is to take things just as they come. How was the clever definition—let me see, I forget his name—of life? What is mind? No matter. What is matter? Never mind. That's my philosophy."[58]

Once more cupidity came to the aid of the reformers. The Committee of Seventy as well as the Citizens' Committee, composed of private citizens and Aldermen, made plans to examine Comptroller Connelly's books for further proofs of the Ring's misdeeds. On Sunday, September 10, the day before this was to happen, Connolly's office was broken into. From three small cupboards more than 3500 vouchers were stolen. It became a sensation. The Ring had panicked. The *Times* asked sarcastically why the city had spent $404,-347.72 on safes and had not given one to the Comptroller. At the same time news came from Washington that Mrs. Connolly had just put one and a half million dollars into government bonds. No longer could the *World, Sun,* and *Herald* spoof the *Times* on its crusade. Even Horace Greeley overcame his jealousy of the *Times* and admitted that a crusade was in order. The theft only intensified Tilden's efforts—he had now committed himself completely to the crusade—to find more proof, which he did when he investigated the accounts at the Ring's Broadway Bank. So careless was the Ring that duplicates of the stolen vouchers were found by Tilden at the bank.

The Ring at best had been untidy. Now all became a shambles. The pressure of the crusade was more than the

Ring could endure. The thieves who had traveled so far and so long together quarrelled and split into two enemy camps. Hall and Sweeny, joining forces against Tweed and Connolly, saw a chance for survival with the voucher disaster. On September 12, 1871, Hall asked Connolly to resign. Connolly, with some logic, replied to Hall that such a step would be equal to a confession, and added: "My official acts have been supervised and approved by your superior vigilance. So far as my administration is questioned equal responsibility attaches to yourself."[59]

It was now, as George Templeton Strong put it, "skunk vs. rattlesnake." Connolly, caring little for the role of sacrificial skunk, fled to the reformers. Tilden then performed a master stroke. He persuaded Connolly to step aside for four months, naming in his place Andrew Green as Acting Comptroller. Green was a distinguished public servant, and by no coincidence, a member of the Committee of Seventy.[60] Hall had made himself ridiculous by demanding Connolly's resignation, which he had no authority to do; Connolly refused and imported some of his toughs from the lower wards to guard his office. It was now skunk vs. *coiled* rattlesnake. Hall asked former General George McClellan to take Connolly's post, but McClellan, cautious in peace and war, refused. The press hooted that Hall had failed. In an interview, Hall told reporters, "Gentlemen, some of you yesterday said that I had received a severe check, and *in testimonium veritatis*, I have, so as you see, put on a check suit."[61] Connolly did deputize Green, and so one of the principal bastions of the Ring's stronghold, the Comptroller's office, was captured.

In the meantime, treason developed

on the general staff. John Foley, president of one of the ward reform clubs, applied to George Barnard for an injunction to stop the Ring from paying or raising money in any way in the name of or on the credit of the County and City. Barnard, sensing the coming debacle of the Ring, responded with all the agility of a rat leaping from a sinking ship and granted the injunction. The reformers, never expecting this boon, were elated. As Tweed explained it:

So he put the injunction upon us, and in the straitened condition of our credit, which was so extended on every side, it broke us. You see our patronage had become so enormous and so costly that the injunction, which might not have troubled us at any other time, destroyed all our power to raise money from the banks or elsewhere and left us trapped.[62]

Although the injunction was later modified, government was temporarily brought to a standstill. With the city treasury nearly empty, and no recourse to raise money, city employees went for weeks without wages. Tweed gave $50,000 from his own pocket to help laborers and their families, and the *Star*, one of a few remaining journals kind to the Ring, called on the laborers to start a bread riot.[63] New Yorkers, remembering the horror of the draft riots of 1863, and the bloody Orange Parade riot of July 12, 1870, redoubled their efforts to oust the Ring.

The injunction accomplished its purpose. The main arteries of political power, money, and patronage were suddenly dried up. The thieves were fighting among themselves. With Green ruthlessly chopping off sinecure appointments, the shiny hats, stripped of place and status, were losing faith in their chiefs. With an election coming

up, *Harper's* and the *Times* were
joined by the rest of the New York
press, and the crusade reached fever
pitch. The public was daily reminded
of Tweed's arrogant, "What are you
going to do about it?" The Tweed Ring
seemed on the threshold of disaster.
But the reformers underestimated the
talents of the Boss.

For the leaders of the anti-Tammany
Democracy it seemed that victory was
in easy grasp. All that was necessary
was to control the State nominating
convention at Rochester. This did not
appear difficult in light of the disasters
that had befallen Tweed and company.
Then the reformers could elect a reform
platform, reveal the further evidence
compiled by the investigations of the
Committee of Seventy, campaign
against the horrors of the Tweed Ring,
and ride to victory in the November
election. Tilden made elaborate preparations to capture the convention by
sending out 26,000 letters to Democratic politicos asking for support with
a one-two punch: he put the name of
Charles O'Conor in nomination for
the attorney-generalship, and disputed
the right of the regular Tammany delegates to represent the city in the convention. Thus with belated courage,
Tilden arose, rallied the reformers, and
denounced the Ring. He realized the
Ring's only chance of survival lay in
renominating its henchmen for city and
state offices, and helping the election of
Republicans who had worked with it
in past legislatures—but so did the Boss.

The reformers lost some of their confidence when Tweed and his entourage,
gangs of New York toughs, arrived in
Rochester. Threats of violence were
made against anyone who should interfere with the Ring; delegates were
warned that the convention would be
broken up by force if anti-Tammany
delegates were admitted to the floor.
The reformers found themselves reliv-
ing an old story: once again they were
outmaneuvered and outwitted. Crafty
as usual, Tweed moved among the delegates and argued that the recent exposures were merely a local issue and
that an all-out' fight in the convention
would undoubtedly split the party and
allow the Republicans an easy victory
in November. For the sake of party
unity he was willing to compromise. If
the reform representatives were omitted
from the roll of delegates, he would
omit the Tammany representatives.

What appeared as a compromise was
actually a victory. Even with the Tammany delegation missing, Tweed was
able to control the convention, through
lack of opposition from the reformers,
and with the help of friends won by
bribery. Charles O'Conor, who would
never have hesitated to throw the entire machinery of the state against the
Ring, was defeated for the attorney-
generalship by a large majority. A state
ticket bulging with names of the Ring's
minions was nominated. Tweed turned
against the reformers with arrogance.
He called Tilden, Horatio Seymour, and
Francis Kernan "three troublesome old
fools."[64]

Tweed had good reason to gloat. A
few days before the convention he was
re-elected chairman of the Tammany
General Committee, and at the convention he was renominated for State
Senator. He returned to New York in
triumph. At Walton House he took the
platform, removed a little Scotch tweed
cap, and told a boisterous audience:

The newspapers have already indicted,
tried, convicted and sentenced and sentenced (roars of laughter), but I feel perfectly free to appeal to a higher tribunal,

and have no fear of the result (cheers). I do not come to you, my fellow citizens, in a circuitous way, indicative of the possession of the thought of the necessity of caution engendered by fear, but directly, openly, squarely, as a man to men, and without an appeal for your sympathy other than so far as my family have suffered from the cruel indignities that have been heaped upon them for my political actions (sensation). But asking at your hands the justice and fair play that have been denied me by bitter, unrelenting, unscrupulous, prejudiced and ambitious partisan foes (deafening shouts of approval)....[65]

The reformers, who had once gloated, returned to New York shaken and sober. The glitter of their confidence was dulled, but their resolution was firm—even firmer. Tweed's victory at Rochester had robbed them of a valuable tactical weapon, the opportunity to proclaim themselves the regular Democratic organization. The Ring, even though quarrelling among themselves, still commanded a powerful election-day army. But failure only reinforced the reformers' determination. What had seemed after the exposures to be an easy victory was now an uphill fight. The reformers were forced to be a rival of the regular organization, and hence a third-party group, with all the difficulties a third party faced. Many of the reformers' leaders were political prima donnas— O'Conor was known for his irascibility, Tilden could be exasperatingly aloof. If thieves fell out, reformers seemed to delight in dissension and to fragment into splinter groups. If the reformers were going to battle the Tweed Ring, they needed unity, organization, and outside support. But the Republicans were notoriously weak and inept. Then, as now, thousands of eligible voters never bothered to go to the polls. There was the danger that the none-too-reputable

groups, like Mozart Hall and the Young Democracy, posing as reformers now that the Ring was embarrassed, might capture leadership from the reformers.

If the odds were formidable, the reformers were driven to work together if for no other reason than the fact that election day might be the last chance to destroy the Ring. Public indignation could not be sustained at a high pitch forever. Six days before the election, the Committee of Seventy released the evidence they unearthed from the Broadway Bank accounts. Important Republicans were persuaded to unite in a common cause by voting a straight reform ticket and not to present a separate Republican ticket to complicate matters. Young Men's Reform Associations were organized. The students of New York University, to whom Hall had recently lectured with applause, tore down the Mayor's portrait from their walls. The newspapers maintained a heavy barrage, exhorting voters to register, publicizing the facts behind the Ring's schemes, and explaining all the tactics Tammany might use to defraud the public on election day. Huge express wagons, drawn by six horses, stood ready to convey a reserve police force to any scene of disorder. Plans were made to take detected repeaters to the armories for custody to avoid the sure chance of their discharge by the courts. With a burst of excitement and energy, the reformers invaded the lower wards, the central nervous system of Tammany Hall, posting signs, passing out pamphlets, haranguing the native and immigrant poor with sidewalk speeches.

The tempo increased as the clergy of New York, pounding their pulpits, spoke out against the Tweed Ring for the first time. Dr. Henry D. Northrup of the Presbyterian Church echoed a common theme: there were but two parties, he roared, God's and the devil's. Election day "is a time when every citizen should show himself to be a man and not a sneak."[66]

The reformers who now thought they could win, called several rallies to keep things at a white heat. On November 2, a rally was held to receive the report of the Committee of Seventy. The motto over the president's chair read: "What are we going to do about it?" George Templeton Strong, pessimistic as usual, did not think they were going to do anything. "The disease of this community," he wrote in his diary, "lies too deep to be cured by meetings, resolutions, and committees. We the people are a low set, without moral virility. Our rulers, Tweed and Company, are about good enough for us."[67]

But Strong's pessimism seemed to be shared by few. The cadence of protest from the reformers, the press, the clergy, was picked up in the saloons, the restaurants, the clubs. Apathy had vanished. New York was agog with one topic of conversation, not the recent Chicago fire, not the visit of the Grand Duke Alexis, but the chance—the bare chance—that the reformers might beat the Tweed Ring on November 7th. On the eve of election day, New Yorkers waited with apprehension, and prepared themselves for one of the most important and exciting elections ever held in New York City.

Much to their own astonishment, the reformers gave Tammany Hall one of the worst defeats in its history up to that time. The scandals had finally roused New Yorkers into action. There was an unusually large turn-out, and many who previously had been apathetic, went to the polls and registered

their indignation with Tammany. The reformers guarded the polling places well, and were successful in protecting themselves against excessive fraud and repeating. Moreover, several of the repeater gangs sensed the fall of the Ring and withdrew their support. The reformers elected all fifteen Aldermen, thirteen Assistant Aldermen out of twenty-one, and carried fourteen of the twenty Assembly districts. Prominent among the new Assemblymen were ex-Mayor Daniel E. Tiemann and Samuel Tilden. General Franz Siegel effectively wooed the Germans and became State Register. There were impressive upstate gains. The reformers captured four out of five Senatorial seats. The one they failed to win was the sour note. O'Donovan Rossa had once led the Irish against the British but could not do the same against Tweed in New York. The people of the Seventh District stood by the man who had served them so well with patronage and charity, and Tweed won over Rossa by over 10,000 votes. The reformers' broom swept out many of the Ring's important lieutenants. Henry Woltman was defeated by Augustus Weismann, the first German-born man to be elected to the State Senate. Timothy Campbell, Henry Genet, James Irving, and Michael Norton were all defeated. Alexander Frear and Thomas Fields were prevented from taking their seats because of election fraud. The full measure of defeat was revealed a few days later. It was announced that the annual American Club ball was postponed.

Once again the *Times* reported a quiet election day. It was a moot point the newspaper said, whether this resulted from the precautions taken by the reformers or that Tammany was cowed. Of course there were some "altercations and word-combats," and "heads punched in the good old fashion so dear to the Democracy." Compared to the previous year, the reformers had won away from the regular Democrats almost 75,000 votes in the city and state, "one of the most remarkable political revolutions in the history of the country," said a contemporary, with some exaggeration.[68] The *Times* maintained that the election was won by the strong vote of the so-called neutral population, who seldom voted—"the gentlemen and quiet citizens."[69] But while there was a large registration, there were not enough neutrals to decide the election. Ironically, it was the very people the reformers despised the most, the immigrants and the native poor, who, because of their great numbers, put the reformers into office by splitting their vote between Tammany and the men running on the Democratic reform ticket.[70]

The victory over Tammany was seen as the end of a great crusade. There was much excitement. For most it meant the vindication of popular government, the triumph of the people's voice, a moral struggle where good overwhelmed evil. Under a huge headline, "New York Redeemed," the *Times* said:

The victory we have won is priceless, not only from what it gives us now, but because it will revive every man's faith in the ultimate triumph of truth and justice—because it will teach scheming politicians that the voice of the people is supreme, and that immortal principles on which this Government is founded, although they may be momentarily stifled by dishonest factions, will constantly rise triumphant, while the men who assailed them will pass away to everlasting infamy.[71]

The reformer George C. Barrett, a successful candidate, said the victory was an answer to those who had scoffed at the success of a republican form of government.[72] *Harper's Weekly* said it was one of the most significant events in the history of free governments.[73]

Only E. L. Godkin pondered whether the great "uprising" was the final and complete triumph over political corruption, whether routing the rascals was only the beginning of reform—real reform. . . .[74]

What, then, was the final reckoning of the Tweed Ring? Although Judges Barnard and McCunn were impeached, and removed from office, and Cardozo resigned but continued to practice law, none of the three were criminally prosecuted. With two exceptions, none of the Ring and its many partners in graft were ever caught or punished. Only Tweed and Ingersoll went to jail. From 1871 to 1878, Tweed spent less than half of that time in prison. Ingersoll who turned himself in, hoping for a light sentence, was sentenced to five years and seven months, but served only a few months of his term before he was pardoned by Tilden for turning State's evidence and promising to become a witness in any forthcoming Ring trials. At the time of Tweed's death sixteen suits were pending against various members of the Tweed Ring organization.[75] None came to trial. Garvey was granted immunity to appear as a witness at the Tweed and Hall trials. Although a millionaire, he never returned any of the money he made. Woodward was granted immunity for returning $155,000, although he had stolen over a million. John Keyser had the delightful gall to claim that it was the city who owed him, and he was almost successful in being awarded a $33,000 claim based on a fraudulent contract![76] Of the twenty to two hundred million dollars estimated to have been stolen by the Ring, it cost the city

$257,848.34 to recover $894,525.44, most of which came from the estates of two dead men, James Watson and James Sweeny.

The ethos of reform, however, was essentially moralistic and conservative. For some the issue was a total commitment to punishing bad men, not the examination of the institutions and conditions that made it possible for bad men to exist and thrive. To them, the cause of corruption was the work of evil men. Their optimism blinded them to the realities of a rapidly growing society, the massive growth of a great city and the effects it would have on political life. For those who questioned institutions, the answer lay not in adaptation but in a return to the good old days of rule by gentry, suffrage restrictions, tight economy, and a tiny bureaucracy. In the months, years, and decades following the Ring's fall, the reformer, imprisoned by his own social philosophy, continued to alienate the immigrant newcomer. What could have been a source of power for the reformer remained the strength of later city bosses. As the city grew and its problems multiplied, the reformer continued to turn back to that Promised Land of the good old days for his solutions to corruption, patching the charter here, passing a resolution there, always haunted by his failure to restore the profession of politics to the nobility of the Old Republic. Exposure of the Tweed Ring had given him a glimpse into the hard realities of big-city politics. But he continued to be an innocent abroad in the strange land of the professional politician and practical politics, preferring the platitude to the free cigar. He never understood the politicians who made politics their business, their appeal to the masses, their atten-

tion to the plight of the immigrant, nor, indeed, the kind of world they were living in. Thus the rascals were routed, but their supreme achievement, the city machine itself, remained essentially intact, to become a model, a legacy, to be improved upon by succeeding monarchs of New York, the Kellys, the Crokers, and the Murphys.

After all was said and done, the crusade against the Tweed Ring won the battle but lost the war. In a real sense, William Marcy Tweed had the last word, when he asked, "Well, what are you going to do about it?"

NOTES

1. Wingate, "Episode in Municipal Government," July 1875, p. 150.
2. See Citizens' Association, "An Appeal by the Citizens' Association of New York against the Abuses in the Local Government to the Legislature of the State of New York, and to the Public' (New York, 1866); "Items of Abuse in the Government of the City of New York" (New York, 1866); "Report of the Executive Council to the Honorary Council of the Citizens' Association' (New York, 1866); "Wholesale Corruption! Sale of Situations in Fourth Ward Schools" (New York, 1864); Union League Club, "Report on Cities" (New York, 1867); "The Report of the Committee on Municipal Reform" (New York, 1867).
3. Jan. 24-25, Feb. 15, 1870. The *Times* also reported on Mar. 9, 1870, that Richard Connolly was fighting the Ring.
4. Apr. 8, 13, 1870. See also Apr. 6, 12, and May 1, 1870.
5. July 13, 1871, quoted in the *Times*, July 14, 1871.
6. Apr. 3, 1872.
7. J. D. Townsend, *New York in Bondage* (1901) p. 73.
8. Nov. 3, 1870.
9. Ibid.
10. Ibid.; Sept. 16, 1871.
11. Dec. 4, 1870. When the celebrated Henry Ward Beecher said he pitied wicked men because their consciences would surely suffer, the *Time* replied in a blistering attack, saying Beecher's pity was "morbid, unwholesome, sentimental." Oct. 24, 1871.
12. Oct. 3, 1870.
13. Sept. 24, 1870.
14. Feb. 26, May 1, 1871; Oct. 3, 1870.
15. "The great strength of General Grant's Ad

ministration . . . lies in the fact that he is believed to be honest himself, and disposed to enforce honesty and fidelity in all departments of the Government under his control." *New York Times*, Sept. 21, 1871.

16. Unidentified newspaper, *Scrapbooks of Clippings Relating to the Career of A. Oakey Hall* (New York Public Library), Vol. IV, p. 113.

17. *New York Times*, Jan. 25, 1873.

18. July 28, 31, 1871. See also *New York World*, Aug. 2, 7, 10, 1871. The *New York Sun* and *New York Evening Post* also criticized the *Times*. Bowen, *The Elegant Oakey*, p. 99. Moreover, Charles Nordhoff, the managing editor of the *Evening Post*, was fired for attacking Tweed. Lynch, *Boss Tweed*, p. 355.

19. Bowen, *The Elegant Oakey*, p. 106. See also Allan Nevins and Thomas Milton Halsey, *The Diary of George Templeton Strong*, III (4 vols.), pp. 376, 383, 385-6.

20. Genung, *Frauds of New York*, pp. 9-13.

21. *Tweed Investigation*, pp. 50-55; Hirsch, "More Light on Boss Tweed," p. 272.

22. For a compilation of the *Times*'s evidence, see *New York Times*, "How New York is Governed. Frauds of the Tammany Democrats," 1871.

23. Breen, *Thirty Years of New York Politics*, p. 337.

24. *New York Times*, Sept. 5, 1871.

25. Oct. 2, 1871.

26. *New York Times*, Oct. 10, 1870; Jan. 20, Mar. 6, 1871.

27. *New York Times*, July 12, 1871.

28. Ibid. July 16, 1871.

29. "Report of the Executive Council to the Honorary Council of the Citizens' Association" (New York, 1866), p. 21. See also "Civil Rights: A History of the New York Riot of 1871" (1871), p. 20; Nevins and Halsey, *Diary of Strong*, IV, p. 352; Thomas Nast, *Miss Columbia's School, or Will It Blow Over?*, 1871, p. 71, *passim*; *Harper's Weekly*, July 29, 1871. For other examples of the nativist impulse, see *The Nation*, July 20, 1871, p. 36; *New York Times*, Mar. 18, Apr. 7, July 17-18, 21, 24, Aug. 17, 1871; Wingate, "Episode in Municipal Government," Oct. 1874, pp. 378-9; Townsend, *New York in Bondage*, p. 186; Nevins and Halsey, *Diary of Strong*, IV, p. 317.

While nativism was widespread in the reformers' camp, some were anti-nativist. See A. R. Lawrence, "The Government of Cities" (New York, 1868), pp. 4-5, 11.

30. *New York Times*, Sept. 17, 1869; Jan. 7, Nov. 30, 1870; Mar. 19, 26, July 16, Sept. 17, 1871. Otto Kempner, "Boss Croker's Career," p. 6.

31. July 16, 1871. See also Sept. 17, 1869; Oct. 17, 1870; Feb. 2, Mar. 19, 1871.

32. *The Nation*, Nov. 16, 1871, p. 316.

33. Jan. 25, 1871. See also *New York Times*, Jan. 24, 1870; *New York Star*, Mar. 25, 1870; Wingate, "Episode in Municipal Government," CXIX (Oct. 1874), p. 379.

34. "Statement and Plea of the New York City Council of Political Reform," p. 34.

35. *American Addresses*, pp. 61-2, 72; *New York Times*, Sept. 18, 1871; (Anon.) "Why Vote at All in '72," p. 37. Robert Roosevelt declared that the Ring "pulled away the very keystone of the arch of liberty." If the public money is stolen, wrote another reformer, "why not the public liberties too?"

36. Feb. 8, April 3, Oct. 12, 17, Nov. 3-4, 1870; Jan. 24, Feb. 24-25, Apr. 7, May 1, July 16, Sept. 5, 26-27, Oct. 27, Nov. 3, 1871.

37. Jones, *Fisk*, p. 226; *New York Times*, Sept. 4, Nov. 3, 1871. See also Abram Genung, *The Frauds of the New York City Government Exposed*, p. 41; Gustav Lening, *The Dark Side of New York*, p. 694; James Welsh, "The Root of the Municipal Evil," p. 7; Nast, *Miss Columbia's School*, pp. 39, 71; New York Council of Political Reform, "Statement and Plea," p. 40.

38. Sept. 29, 1871.

39. "Report on Municipal Reform," pp. 17-18; see also, "Why Vote at All in '72," p. 72; Welsh, "Root of the Municipal Evil," p. 5.

40. *New York Times*, Jan. 23, 1871.

41. New York City Council of Political Reform, "Report of the New York City Council of Political Reform," p. 3.

42. "Statement and Plea," p. 28. See also "Report of the New York City Council of Political Reform," pp. 4-11; the Citizens' Association, "Report of the Executive Council to the Honorary Council," p. 22; Wilson, *Memorial History*, III, p. 562; Bryce, *American Commonwealth* (1889 ed.), II, p. 353, (1895 ed.), II, pp. 391, 403. For an interesting criticism of the "best people" theory, see *The Nation*, Aug. 24, 1871, p. 125.

43. "The Government of New York," p. 451.

44. "The Commonwealth Reconstructed," p. 26.

45. *The Nation*, Apr. 18, 1878, p. 257; Nov. 9, 1871, p. 300; Nov. 27, 1873, p. 350.

46. Ibid. Nov. 4, 1875, p. 288; Oct. 18, 1877, p. 238; Nov. 27, 1873, p. 350; Apr. 18, 1878, p. 257; Oct. 12, 1871, p. 237; Nov. 4, 1875, p. 289. See also Union League, "Report on Municipal Reform," pp. 19-20, 76-7, 88; Parton, "Government of New York," p. 463.

For an attack on this position, see Charles Nordhoff, "The Mis-Government of New York, a Remedy Suggested," *North American Review*, CCXXXIII (Oct. 1871), pp. 321-43, *passim*.

47. Francis Lieber, "Reflections on the Changes Which May Seem Necessary in the Present Constitution of the State of New York," p. 4; Parton, "Government of New York," p. 460; *Rochester Union and Advertiser*, Oct. 3, 1871.

48. "Root of Municipal Evil," p. 19.

49. *New York Times*, Sept. 11, 1869.

50. Parton, "Government of New York," p. 457.

51. (Anon.), "Why Vote at All in '72," p. 29.

52. Werner, *Tammany Hall*, p. 210.

53. Albert Paine, *Thomas Nast*, 1904, p. 182.

54. *New York Times*, Aug. 24, 1871.

55. Nevins and Halsey, *Diary of Strong*, Vol. IV, p. 394.

56. For Hall's excuses, see *New York Times*, July

12, 29, Aug. 12, Sept. 11, Oct. 10, 13; *The Leader,* Aug. 19, 1871.

57. Flick, *Tilden,* p. 213; see also *New York Times,* Aug. 29, 1871.

58. *New York Times,* Sept. 22, 1871.

59. Ibid. Sept. 17, 1871.

60. Green had served thirteen years on the Park Commission, helped to plan Central Park, suggested Riverside Drive and many of the smaller parks, established the American Scenic and Historic Preservation Society, and did much to effect the merger of the Tilden, Astor, and Lennox foundation in the New York Public Libary.

61. Wingate, "Episode in Municipal Government," Oct. 1876, p. 379.

62. Lynch, *Boss Tweed,* p. 375.

63. Sept. 27, 1871.

64. Flick, *Tilden,* p. 219.

65. *New York Times,* Nov. 5, 1871.

66. Ibid. Nov. 6, 1871.

67. Nevins and Halsey, *Diary of Strong,* Vol. IV, p. 382.

68. Wingate, "Episode in Municipal Government," Oct. 1876, p. 389.

69. Nov. 11, 1871.

70. O'Connor, *Hell's Kitchen,* p. 50; Lynch, *Boss Tweed,* pp. 383-4.

71. Nov. 8, 1871.

72. Ibid.

73. Cited with no date in *New York Times,* July 12, 1872.

74. *The Nation,* Nov. 9, 1871, p. 300.

75. *Tweed Investigation,* pp. 841-5.

76. Ibid. pp. 601-85.

Varieties of Urban Reform

MELVIN G. HOLLI

Pingree's brand of social reform—whose objective was to lower utility rates for the consumer and which attempted to place a larger share of the municipal tax burden on large corporations—was not the prevailing mood of urban reform in late-nineteenth and early-twentieth-century America. Far more prevalent in the programs of large-city mayors who earned the epithet "reformer" was the effort to change the structure of municipal government, to eliminate petty crime and vice, and to introduce the business system of the contemporary corporation into municipal government. Charter tinkering, elaborate audit procedures, and the drive to impose businesslike efficiency upon city government were the stock-in-trade of this type of urban executive. Mayors of this kind of reform persuasion could be found in New York, Brooklyn, Buffalo, San Francisco, and countless other cities.

Although most of these structural reformers did not articulate their positions as eloquently as Seth Low or attempt to install business methods as ruthlessly as John Purroy Mitchel, they all shared a certain style, a number of common assumptions about the cause of municipal misgovernment, and, in some instances, a conviction about which class was best fitted to rule the city. Few of them were as blatantly outspoken in their view of democracy

as Samuel S. McClure, the publisher of the leading muckrake journal. He instructed Lincoln Steffens to prove that popular rule was a failure and that cities should be run by a dictatorship of wise and strong men, such as Samuel S. McClure or Judge Elbert Gary. Similarly New York's former reform mayor, Abram Hewitt asserted in 1901 that "ignorance should be excluded from control, [and] the city business should be carried on by trained experts selected upon some other principle than popular suffrage."[7]

None of the structural reformers had the unqualified faith in the ability of the masses to rule themselves intelligently that social reformers Hazen S. Pingree, Samuel "Golden Rule" Jones, or Tom L. Johnson did. "I have come to lean upon the common people as the real foundation upon which good government must rest," Pingree told the Nineteenth Century Club in 1897. In a statement that represented more than a rhetorical flourish, "Golden Rule" Jones chastised Reverend Josiah Strong for his distrust of the masses and told him that the "voice of the people is the voice of God." Tom Johnson, asserted Brand Whitlock, knew that "the cure for the ills of democracy was not less democracy, as so many people were always preaching, but more democracy." When Johnson was defeated by the Cleveland

From *Reform in Detroit: Hazen S. Pingree and Urban Politics* (New York: Oxford University Press, 1969), pp. 161-81. Copyright © 1969 by Oxford University Press, Inc. Reprinted by permission of the publisher. Melvin G. Holli is Associate Professor of History at the University of Illinois, Chicago Circle.

electorate at the very pinnacle of one of the most productive urban reform careers in the nation, he told Whitlock, "The people are probably right."[8] The structural reform movement was in sharp contrast to the democratic mood of such a statement. It represented instead the first wave of prescriptive municipal government which placed its faith in rule by educated, upper class Americans and, later, by municipal experts rather than the lower classes. The installation in office of men of character, substance, and integrity was an attempt to impose middle class and patrician ideals upon the urban masses. The movement reached its height in the second and third decades of the twentieth century with the city-manager and city-commissioner forms of government, which called for the hiring of non-partisan experts to decide questions hitherto viewed as resolvable only by the political process. Like the structural reform movement of the late-nineteenth-century, the city-manager movement reflected an implicit distrust of popular democracy.[9]

New York's Mayor William F. Havemeyer was a prototype of the twentieth-century structural reformers. Having inherited a substantial fortune, he retired from the sugar refining business at the age of forty and devoted most of his career to public service. Elected mayor in 1872 during the public exposure of the Tweed Ring, Havemeyer was a reformer who championed "clean government," "economy," and the business class point of view. Obsessed with tax cuts and retrenchment, he and his fiscal watchdog, city Treasurer Andrew H. Green, cut wages on public works and demanded elaborate procedures to account for all petty expenditures of public funds. Green's painstaking scrutiny of every claim snarled the payroll so badly that the city's laborers rioted when their pay checks got lost in an administrative tangle.[10]

To practice economy, Havemeyer sacrificed important public services and, in the process, "crippled downtown development." During a three-month period in 1874 the Mayor vetoed more than 250 bills related to street grading, paving, and widening, board of education contracts, and appropriations intended for public charities. In justifying his liquidation of work relief, Havemeyer told the Harvard Association that contributions of private individuals and Christian and charitable associations were generous enough to meet the needs of the poor. According to Seymour Mandelbaum, the lower classes and the promoters of new areas of the city suffered most from Havemeyer's policies.[11]

During his second year in office, the aging Mayor fought with the city council and accomplished nothing of lasting importance. Havemeyer and the New York Council of Political Reform were so obsessed with "honest, efficient and economical government" that they indicted every public improvement as a "job" and labeled every politician who supported such measures as an "exponent of the class against which society is organized to protect itself." The Mayor's death in 1874 mercifully ended the agony of a reform administration which was strangling the city with red tape generated by its own economy programs. Ironically, Havemeyer helped to perpetuate the widespread belief that reformers were meddling, ineffectual reactionaries, or, as George Washington Plun kitt charged, "morning glories" who wilted in the heat of urban politics.[12] Buffalo's "fighting mayor," Grover Cleveland, 1882, was another one of the progenitors of the structural reform tradition. Preoccupied as much as Havemeyer with cutting taxes and municipal expenditures, Cleveland had no positive programs to offer, with one notable exception: he fought and won authorization for a massive interceptor sewer system to diminish the dumping of refuse into the Erie Canal. He made his mark in Buffalo by the veto of a corrupt street cleaning contract, the "most spectacular single event" of his administration in Allan Nevins's view. In addition, Cleveland fought to stop the constant proliferation of city jobs, exercised a Havemeyer type of vigilance over all claims made against the city treasury, and directed city employees to stop closing their offices at 4:00 p.m. and to perform a full day's work. His inflexible drive for economy and efficiency and his contempt for the dishonesty of city machines won him a reputation as a rugged veto and reform mayor.[13]

Seth Low, a wealthy merchant, philanthropist, and university president, was mayor of Brooklyn (1882-85) and later of New York (1902-03). Perhaps more than any other American mayor, he possessed the qualities of a high-minded, nonpartisan structural reformer who attempted to infuse a large dose of businesslike efficiency into municipal government. He was widely recognized by his generation as one of the most prominent practicing reformers on the urban scene, but also built a considerable reputation as a scholar of municipal affairs. In countless addresses, Low argued that

the answer to urban problems was charter reform to bring nonpartisanship and a centralized administration into city government. Reform of this sort would arouse a new civic consciousness and create a cohesive corporate government that could be run along business lines, free from outside influences.[14]

Under the aegis of a silk-stocking Citizens' Committee, Low, with his refined eloquence and business support, had waged an effective campaign against political spoilsmanship and partisanship and won Brooklyn's mayoralty election in 1881. Low disregarded political affiliation and based his appointments on ability and merit. Although his two terms proved to be unspectacular, Low had advanced what he considered the cardinal principles of municipal reform: he had reduced the city's debt, tightened up the tax system, and conducted a vigorous campaign at Albany to stop special state legislation from interfering in Brooklyn's affairs. Such social questions as tenement house reform and aid to the aged, the poor, or workingmen were for Seth Low but special benefits which could not be considered until local partisanship had been wiped out and municipal government had been reorganized along the lines of authority and responsibility. Low's name had become synonymous with efficiency, responsibility, and clean government.[15]

After a particularly flagrant period of municipal corruption under Tammany Hall, a reform-minded Citizens' Union, which counted J. Pierpont Morgan and Elihu Root among its founders, asked Seth Low to enter the lists as an independent candidate for mayor of New York against the Tammany favorite in 1901. Low ran on a platform of home rule and nonpartisanship, avoided the social-welfare planks endorsed by the Citizens' Union, and discussed honesty, economy, and responsibility in his speeches. Low was known to the voters because he had assisted in drafting the first charter for Greater New York, which consolidated hundreds of small towns and three large cities into one unit. Low's victory in 1901 was probably less an endorsement of his brand of reform than a public reaction against the excesses of Tammany.[16]

As New York's mayor, Low brought in experts to operate the various departments, pared away Tammany's payroll padding, and set himself up as the businessman in office. He cut salaries, increased the length of the working day for municipal employees, and reduced the city's annual budget by $1,500,000. In the public transit and utility field, Low saw to it that franchises were carefully drafted to safeguard the city's interests and to provide for additional revenue. He failed to press for lower rates, to agitate for a public rate-making body, or to instruct his district attorney to investigate the corrupt alliances between private business and politicians. He balked at appointing one of the best-qualified housing reformers, Lawrence Veiller, to head the tenement house commission, apparently because Low did not wish to disturb the conservative real estate interests. Low was willing, however, to use the full force of law against Sunday drinking, petty gambling, and prostitution, which were commonly found in the immigrant and lower class sections of the city. The Bureau of Licenses also cracked down on the city's 6,000 pushcart peddlers who were operating without licenses, and the Department of Law prosecuted

residents whose tax payments were delinquent. With similar zeal, the Department of Water raised nearly $1,000,000 in income from overdue water bills.[17]

Low's tinkering with the machinery of government, his charter revision and rewriting, his regularization of tax collections, his enforcement of the city statutes, his appointment of men of merit, and his reduction of city expenditures were laudable actions by almost anybody's test of good government. Unfortunately, these measures bore most severely upon the lower classes. Low's structural reforms were also very impolitic, as his defeat in the election of 1903 demonstrated. Low never seemed to realize that his municipal reform had nothing to offer the voters but sterile, mechanical changes and that fundamental social and economic conditions which pressed upon the vast urban masses of immigrants and poor could not be changed by rewriting charters or enforcing laws.[18]

San Francisco's reform mayor James D. Phelan, a wealthy banker and anti-Bryan Democrat who held office from 1897 to 1902, was also a structural reformer like his model, Seth Low, whom Phelan frequently quoted. Phelan's program for reform included the introduction of efficiency and economy to ensure "scientific, systematic and responsible government," which was also the goal of the San Francisco Merchants' Association. Franchise regulation, lower traction rates, municipal ownership, and equal taxation were not part of Phelan's design for a better San Francisco. The distinguishing mark of the Phelan administration was its sponsorship of a strong mayor, and a short ballot charter that provided rigid fiscal controls over expenditures, city-wide elections for the council, and a merit system. Known as a "watch-dog of the treasury," Mayor Phelan supported a low tax rate that forced the city to withhold schoolteachers' salaries, suspend many of the essential functions of the city health department, subject patients at the city hospital to inadequate care, and turn off the street lights at midnight. Phelan crippled his administration when he permitted the president of the police commissioners (who was also president of the Chamber of Commerce) to protect strikebreakers and club pickets during a teamsters' and a dock-workers' strike against the open shop. Although the 18 unions lost their strike, they retaliated by forming their own political party and defeating the reformers in 1901. In the famous graft prosecutions after 1901, Phelan continued to act like a "member of his class" or, as Fremont Older put it, "a rich man toward a great business in which he is interested."[19] Like Low, Phelan failed to attack what social reformers recognized as the basic problems confronting the city.

Equally ineffectual in his attempt to make New York the best governed city in the nation was Mayor John Purroy Mitchel, who served from 1914 to 1917. He was an "oddly puritanical Catholic" who represented the foibles and virtues of patrician class reform. Mitchel's election in 1913 was the result of voter reaction to a decade of brazen looting by Tammany Hall. Like his reform predecessors, Mitchel was responsible for little of lasting importance and did not generate enthusiasm among the large mass of voters with his structural reforms.[20]

Mitchel's failure was due to his misconception that city government could be conducted by the "ledger book ethics of the corporation accountant." So dedicated was Mitchel to budgetary cutbacks that he adopted the Gary Plan of education, which enabled New York City to cram more children into the existing schools. He decreased appropriations for the city's night schools, thus seriously hampering the entire program; for the summer program, Mitchel asked the teachers to volunteer their services without remuneration. Mitchel also appointed cost-cutting charity agents who began either to return feeble-minded children to their parents or to threaten to charge the often hard-pressed parents if their children were kept in public supported institutions. In addition, he instituted an investigation of the city's religious child care organizations, hoping thus to cut the city subsidy; but this action brought the wrath of the Catholic church down upon him.[21] Mitchel, although well-intentioned, had a kind of King Midas touch in reverse: everything he touched seemed to turn to ashes.

Robert Moses dismissed the Mitchel administration's efficiency drives as "saving rubber bands" and "using both ends of the pencil," but its flaws were much greater. The Mitchel administration and the structural reform movement were not only captives of a modern business mentality but sought to impress middle and upper class social values upon the urban community and to redistribute political power to the patrician class.[22]

Built upon a narrow middle and patrician class base and a business concept of social responsibility, the structural reform movement, with its zeal for efficiency and economy, usually lacked staying power. As George Washington Plunkitt pointed out, such crusaders were usually repudiated by lower class voters after a brief tenure in office. Unlike the social reformers, who were also interested in economy, the structural reformers had a blind spot when it came to weighing the human cost of their programs. They failed to recognize that a dose of something as astringent as wage-cutting and payroll audits had to be counterbalanced with social welfare programs if the public were to be served effectively. Too often they blamed the immigrant for the city's shortcomings or directed much of the force of their administrations to exterminating lower-class vices, which they saw as the underlying causes of municipal problems.[23]

Unlike the structural reformers, social reform mayors such as Hazen S. Pingree (1890-97), "Golden Rule" Jones (1897-1903), Tom Johnson (1901-09), Mark Fagan (1901-07), Brand Whitlock (1906-13), and Newton D. Baker (1912-16) began with a different set of assumptions about the basic causes of misgovernment in the cities. They shared the view, which Lincoln Steffens later publicized, that big business and its quest for preferential treatment and special privileges had corrupted municipal government. The public service corporations, the utilities, the real estate interests, and the large industrial concerns all had vested interests in urban America. They sought special tax advantages, franchises which eliminated competition, and other municipal concessions. They bought aldermen, councilmen, and mayors to protect these interests and, in the process, demoralized urban politics and city government. Mayor Tom Johnson's aide Frederic C. Howe was shocked when he was berated by his upper class friends for opposing a franchise steal; they explained that the public utilities have "millions of dollars invested" and had to "protect their investments." "But I do say emphatically," declared Mayor Pingree in 1895, ". . . better take [the utilities] out of private hands than allow them to stand as the greatest corruptors of public morals that ever blackened the pages of history."[24]

The programs of the social reform mayors aimed at lower gas, light, telephone, and street railway rates for the community and higher taxes for railroads and business corporations. When they were unable to obtain the regulation of public utilities, these mayors fought for municipal ownership, the only technique to redistribute economic power available to them as urban executives. Establishment of free public baths, expansion of parks, schools, and public relief were similarly attempts to distribute the amenities of middle class life to the masses. The social reformers recognized that the fight against crime in its commonly understood sense (i.e. rooting out gambling, drinking, and prostitution) was an attempt to treat the symptoms rather than the disease itself and that such campaigns would burn out the energies of a reform administration and leave the fundamental problems of the urban masses untouched. Pingree, like Jones and Johnson, believed that such binges of "Comstockery" were irrelevant to municipal reform. "The good people are always insisting upon 'moral' issues," asserted Toledo Mayor Brand Whitlock, "urging us to turn aside from our large immediate purpose, and concentrate our official attention on the 'bad' people—and wreck our movement."[25]

The saloons where drinking, gambling, and other vices flourished, Pingree, Jones, and Johnson, agreed, were but poor men's clubs and offered the workers but a few of the comforts that most rich men enjoyed. "The most dangerous enemies to good government are not the saloons, the dives, the dens of iniquity and the criminals," Pingree told the Springfield, Massachusetts, Board of Trade. "Most of our troubles can be traced to the temptations which are offered to city officials when franchises are sought by wealthy corporations, or contracts are to be let for public works." For refusing to divert public attention from the "larger and more complex immoralities" of the "privileged" interests, as Brand Whitlock put it, to the more familiar vices, the social reformers earned the bitter censure of the ministerial and "uplift" groups.[26]

The whole tone of the social reform movement was humanistic and empirical. It did not attempt to prescribe standards of personal morality nor did it attempt to draft social blueprints or city charters which had as their goals the imposition of middle class morality and patrician values upon the masses. Instead, it sought to find the basic causes of municipal misgovernment. Pingree, the first of the broad gauged social reformers, discovered the sources of municipal corruption in his day-to-day battle with the light, gas, telephone, and traction interests, the latter represented at the time by Tom Johnson. Johnson, like Mayor Newton D. Baker, knew from his own experience as a utility magnate why municipal government had been demoralized. Mayor Mark Fagan discovered that Jersey City could neither regulate nor tax the utilities and the railroads because both parties were dominated by these interests.[27]

In attempting to reform the city, Pingree, Jones, Johnson, and Whitlock lost upper class and business support and were forced to rely upon the lower classes for political power. The structural reformers, on the other hand, were frequently members of and sponsored by the very social and economic classes which most vehemently opposed social reform. "If we had to depend upon these classes for reforms," Pingree told the Outlook in 1897, "they could never have been brought about." "It is not so much the undercrust as the upper crust," asserted Professor Edward Bemis, who served as a Pingree aide, "that threatens the interests of the people."[28]

The inability of the structural reformers to pursue positive programs to alter the existing social and economic order was probably a reflection of their own business and class backgrounds. Their high regard for the sacrosanct nature of private property, even if obtained illegally, limited them to treating but one aspect of the municipal malaise, and then only when corruption by urban machines reached an intolerable point. This half-way attempt at urban reform prompted Brand Whitlock to observe in 1914: "The word 'reformer' like the word 'politician' has degenerated, and, in the mind of the common man, come to connotate something very disagreeable. In four terms as mayor I came to know both species pretty well, and, in the latter connotations of the term, I prefer politician. He, at least, is human."[29]

III

The structural reform tradition drew much of its strength from a diverse group of theorists composed of good government people, spokesmen for the business community, civic uplifters, representatives of taxpayers' associations, editors, and college professors. The most prominent and influential spokesmen of this persuasion were the Englishman James Bryce, college professors Frank J. Goodnow and William B. Munro, and the editor and scholar Albert Shaw. These theorists diagnosed problems of the city differently from the social reformers. Of fundamental importance to the models they formulated to bring about better city government was their view of the basic causes of the urban malaise. New York's problems, according to Professor Frank Goodnow, had begun in 1857, when the "middle classes, which had thus far controlled the municipal government, were displaced by an ignorant proletariat, mostly foreign born." Three decades later, James Bryce, who dealt with the problems of the city in one of the most influential books of his age, observed that the same "droves of squalid men, who looked as if they had just emerged from an emigrant ship" were herded by urban bosses before magistrates to be enrolled as voters. Such men, said Bryce, were "not fit for suffrage" and "incompetent to give an intelligent vote." Furthermore, their odious habits and demeanor had driven "cultivated" and "sensitive" men out of political life and discouraged the business classes from assuming their share of civic responsibility. One of the most able students of comparative municipal government, Albert Shaw, agreed with Bryce and Goodnow and concluded that the foreign-born had provided the opportunities for the "corruptionist and the demagogue,"[30] who had demoralized city government and lowered the

tone of civic responsibility. The immigrant was central to the analyses of the theorists: although a few of them admitted other contributing factors, it is doubtful that any of them believed that the quality of civic responsibility, the level of public morality, and the honesty of urban administrations could have sunk as low had not the immigrant been present in overwhelming numbers in American cities.

Unlike the immigration restrictionists, the theorists did not distinguish between the new and old immigrants but lumped them together with the urban lower classes and attacked the political agencies that had facilitated the rise to power of these new groups. Even the newcomers from Northern Europe "know nothing of the institutions of the country, of its statesmen, of its political issues," Bryce argued. "Neither from Germany nor from Holland do they bring much knowledge of the methods of free government." Lower class reresentatives from the wards were not welcome in municipal circles, for presumably the district system produced "inferior men" of "narrowed horizons," or as Alfred Conkling put it, permitted the balance of power to be held by the "worst class of men." "Wards largely controlled by thieves and robbers," Cornell's Andrew D. White warned, ". . . can control the city." Harvard's Professor Munro argued that the ward system elected councils that only wasted time and money in "fruitless debate" and sent to councils men "whose standing in the community is negligible." The ward system of representation was denounced by Professors Goodnow and Munro and Delos F. Wilcox for producing the worst representatives in the city. The National Municipal League's model charter called upon municipalities to abolish local representation. In Goodnow's view there were no local interests worthy of political representation anyway.[31]

In building their case against the ability of a mass urban electorate to rule itself, the theorists also drew upon psychology and history. The "craving for excitement" and the "nervous tension" of the city had a degenerative effect, Delos F. Wilcox argued, for "urban life tends to endanger the popular fitness for political power and responsibility." City populations were "radical rather than conservative," and "impulsive rather than reflective," asserted Goodnow, and far less inclined than rural populations to have "regard for the rights of private property." This was caused in part by the fact, Goodnow continued, that urban residents, unlike rural, had "no historical associations" with the cities in which they lived and thus had a poorly developed "neighborhood feeling." The elective system that depended upon familiar relationships and a cohesive community for its success was thus a failure in the city. Goodnow was also disturbed by his study of the larger contours of Western municipal history which convinced him that when city populations had been permitted to develop free of outside control, they evinced an "almost irresistible tendency to establish oligarchical or despotic government." American cities that were under Boss rule, in his opinion, showed similar tendencies.[32]

The first solutions proposed by many spokesmen of reform were hardly original. Outright disfranchisement had been suggested frequently since the end of the Civil War. Some cities had enacted stiffer registration require-

ments to pare down the vote of the unwashed, and some states had followed the pattern of Michigan, which revoked the alien franchise in 1894. Just as effective, although less direct, was the 1876 recommendation of the New York commissioners for the creation of an upper house with control over money bills in New York City, which was to be elected by propertied voters.[33]

The theorists, however, appear to have been inspired by a contemporary historical event. Drawing upon the Southern experience of disfranchising the Negro, Albert Shaw and Frank Goodnow suggested that such a measure might be applied to Northern cities. The "grandfather clause" apparently convinced Goodnow that the nation was not irrevocably committed to universal suffrage: once the people became convinced that "universal suffrage inevitably must result in inefficient and corrupt government, it will be abandoned," he predicted. The safe guards of suffrage, Fourteenth and Fifteenth Amendments, did not pose insurmountable obstacles, argued Goodnow. He dismissed the Fourteenth Amendment as merely an appeal to Congress, and he pointed out that the Fifteenth left room for educational and property qualifications.[34]

Accepting the Southern solution as reasonable, Shaw argued that the franchise in the North should be "absolutely" restricted to those who could read English, and "in the case of the foreign-born, to those showing positive fitness for participation in our political and governmental life." Furthermore Shaw argued that European immigrants should be directed southward where they would provide competition for Negroes which would result in a beneficial "survival of the fittest." In order to upgrade the quality of the urban electorate, Professor Munro recommended that the literacy test for the franchise should be extended throughout the nation. Universal suffrage was a "sacrifice of common sense to abstract principles," Bryce asserted. "Nobody pretends that such persons [immigrant voters] are fit for civic duty, or will be dangerous if kept for a time in pupilage, but neither party will incur the odium of proposing to exclude them."[35]

Although demands to purge the unfit elements from urban voting lists were often voiced during the 1890's, it became apparent that such a solution was too drastic. Few civic federations and even fewer politicians picked up the suggestion. Despite the prestige and influence of the theorists, it was evident that disfranchisement was unacceptable to the American public as a way to solve its urban problems. Clearly, less abrasive and more refined techniques would have to be found.

The theorists often spoke of installing into office the "better" classes, the "best" citizens and civic patriots. Excluded were labor, ethnic, or lower class representatives. As Goodnow put it, their choice was "men engaged in active business" or professionals, presumably associated with the business community. The theorists did not distinguished between big and small businessmen, or between entrepreneurs and financiers. What they wanted, as Conklin expressed it, was "any business or professional man . . . who has been successful in private life" and who was reasonably honest. As Richard T. Ely observed, the battle cries of the good government crowd in the 1890's had been: "Municipal govern-

ment is business not politics." "Wanted, A municipal administration on purely business principles." If one accepted the premise it followed logically, as Ely noted, that businessmen were the "natural and inevitable directors of local affairs."[36]

The theorists argued that the business of city government was business and not politics. The "purely administrative functions—that is to say business functions—outweighed the political functions nine to one," declared Walter Arndt. They extensively used the modern business corporation as a model in their discussions of city government; some called the citizens "stockholders," and others referred to the council as the "board of directors" and the mayor as the "chairman of the board." They spoke of the pressing need for efficiency, the complexity of urban problems, and favored the use of experts to replace elected amateurs. Goodnow argued that a clear distinction must be drawn between legislative and administrative duties and that municipal departments must be staffed by experts. Munro warned that public opinion was the "worst" enemy of the expert and therefore should be rendered less influential in municipal decision-making. In short, the theorists were arguing that the role of public opinion and political expression should be substantially reduced in governing the modern city.[37]

In urging the reconstruction of city government, the theorists called for far-reaching changes in city charters. They advocated a strong mayor system, which accorded with what most of them knew about New York City politics: at least once during each decade since the end of the Civil War, "reformers" had been able to win the mayoralty, although they repeatedly failed to control the city council. The theorists also recommended that the mayor be given complete authority to appoint members to the various municipal boards. Board members, they argued, should serve without pay since this would remove the mercenary motive that prompted professional politicians to serve and, incidentally, would eliminate most of those without substantial wealth as well. If those who got their "living out of their salaries" could be excluded from municipal office, Goodnow argued, the way would be open for the "business and professional classes" to assume control of the city.[38] At the lower levels of municipal administration, Shaw, Goodnow, and Munro recommended a thoroughgoing application of the civil-service system, which also tended to eliminate ethnic and lower class representatives. A professional civil service at the lower grades, the theorists argued, would create a good technical and supportive staff and, as Goodnow put it, "make it possible for the business and professional classes of the community to assume the care of public business without making too great personal sacrifices."[39]

The recommendations of the theorists aimed at weakening popular control over the legislative arm of government, the city council. Goodnow was convinced that the council system, since it provided so many "incompetent if not corrupt men," should not be a powerful force in municipal government. Goodnow was more favorably impressed by municipal arrangements in Berlin, Germany, where a propertied electorate comprising less than 10 per cent of the voters elected two-thirds of the city council. "This gives

to the wealthier class the directing voice in municipal affairs," commented Professor Leo S. Rowe with approval. Andrew D. White argued that men of property should be represented by a board of control, "without whose permission no franchise should be granted and no expenditure should be made." The English system which in effect disfranchised most lower class slum residents also met with Goodnow's favor. Councils elected by a nonpropertied franchise disturbed Goodnow, for such bodies often prodded cities into "undertakings which are in excess of the city's economic resources." Evidently pessimistic about changing the basis of municipal suffrage to one of property, Goodnow reversed the formula and suggested that to extend the taxpaying obligation to more citizens might produce better councils. That failing, he supported state intervention to limit taxing and spending of municipal governments. "The trouble with leaving our cities to govern themselves, at least along purely democratic lines," argued C. E. Pickard, is "that they are utterly unworthy of trust."[40]

The theorists also argued for fewer elective offices and smaller city councils. "Men of little experience and less capacity have found it easy to get themselves elected to membership in large city councils," asserted Munro. Smaller councils would presumably concentrate responsibility and produce better men. The at-large election was a favorite device of the theorists and one of the most important structural changes they proposed. City-wide elections to the council, in their opinion, could be won only by men of commanding presence and city-wide prominence. Obviously the lower class politician or the ethnic representative who served his ward well would come out second best if pitted against a prominent businessman or professional. Not until late in the Progressive period, after the at-large system began to elect the "better classes" into office, did the theorists return to decentralizing authority and to expanding the powers of councilmen who then would be known as city commissioners. The ideas of the theorists make it difficult to quibble with Frederic C. Howe's observation: "Distrust of democracy has inspired much of the literature on the city."[41]

Agencies to regulate utility rates, to investigate tax inequities, or to foster and advance social reform were not on the drawing boards of the theorists. Few of them focused their wrath and moral indignation upon the corrupting influence of privately owned utilities and the real estate interests on city councils. They were less bothered by the businessman who bribed the city council than by the machine politician who accepted the bribe. Yerkes and Whitney seldom warranted their attention in the way that Tweed did. They chose instead to focus responsibility upon the individuals who sat on councils and the political systems that elected them rather than upon the business interests that sought favorable franchises, tax favoritism, and city services, such as paving, sewers, and water, which enhanced the value of their enterprises.

The ideas of the theorists were not lost upon the practitioners and designers of good city government. The structural reformers began to design new forms of urban organization and to codify the ideas of the theorists into new city charters. Two decades of searching and theorizing produced

the city commissioner and later the city manager systems.

The theorists provided the rationale for the most radical departure the American city took in all its history. The widespread adoption of the commissioner and manager systems late in the Progressive period brought about what one scholar called a "revolution in the theory and practice of city government." Although the commissioner system had its origins in an accident of nature, it and the manager plan soon became the favored devices for achieving what the old political system could not—namely, the large scale movement of businessmen and business-minded representatives into public office. Both systems were patterned after the modern business corporation and rapidly adopted its ideals. Henry Bruère, a director of the New York Bureau of Municipal Research, boasted that commission governments were often made a "part of the progressive programs of 'boosting' commercial organizations." "Money saving and efficiency" were pursued as key objectives under the manager plan. The "Godfather of City Managerism," Richard S. Childs, observed that the city managers at their fourth annual conference could "unblushingly point with pride" to an average savings of 10 per cent in tax levies in the cities under his brain child. The first city manager of the publicized "Dayton Plan," Henry M. Waite, admitted that the "main thing" the nation's fifty manager towns had accomplished up to 1917 was a "financial saving." "Economy, not service," James Weinstein correctly asserted, was the "basic principle" of both the commissioner and manager systems. As Harold A. Stone has suggested, and Weinstein has demonstrated, no important reform movement of the Progressive period was more peculiarly the captive of organized business than the commissioner and manager movements.[42]

Although the commissioner and manager systems achieved their greatest success in middle-sized and smaller cities, they represented the ultimate ideal of the earlier theorists (whose major concern had been large American cities). Commissioner and manager reorganization brought about in its finished form the structural arrangements that facilitated the movement into office of that class of people whom Bryce, Goodnow, Munro, and Shaw believed best fitted and qualified to rule the city. Chambers of commerce and the dominant business groups were the main force behind the movement, and, as James Weinstein and Samuel P. Hays have demonstrated, these new forms facilitated the inflow of the commercial and upper class elements into the centers of municipal power at the price of ethnic and lower class representation.[43] The business model of municipal government would eventually spread to nearly one-half of our cities, and the structural-reform persuasion would dominate the main stream of urban reform thought in the twentieth century.[44] This extension of the instruments and the ideology of the business world would help to return to power men with the temperaments of Havemeyer, Cleveland, and Low and considerably diminish the electoral prospects for men like Pingree, Jones, and Johnson—as well as like Tweed.

The conservative revolution in city government would also help to end the process whereby astute politicians and socially-conscious reformers used the political system to ease the shock of assimilation for newcomers into American life. The political machine may have been one of the most important institutions not only for acknowledging the immigrant's existence but for interpreting a new environment to him and helping him to adjust to a bewildering new society.

By concentrating on the mechanistic and bureaucratic aspects of city government and by throwing the weight of their influence behind the election of businessmen, the theorists grossly oversimplified the problems of the city. Wiping out lower class and foreign-born corruption unfortunately took precedence in their minds over the social needs of the city. The theorists confined themselves to dealing with the plumbing and hardware of city government and finally became narrow administrative reformers. In the process, they deceived themselves and helped to mislead a generation of reformers into thinking that they were dealing with the fundamental problems of the city, when in reality they were retooling the machinery of urban government to fit the needs of the business world.

Characteristically, the manager and commissioner movement, which represented the greatest achievement of the structural-reform tradition, experienced its greatest success during the twilight of the Progressive period and during the nineteen twenties,[45] when great expectations for social reform were withering and receding. This late triumph of good government reform was not an accident of historical timing. It was not a case of cultural lag, nor can it be attributed to a late blooming of the urban Progressive spirit. If anything, new concepts and systems of organization usually appeared sooner at the urban level than at the national. The victory of the manager-commissioner system during the age of Harding and Coolidge was an historical acknowledgement of the basically conservative nature of the structural-reform tradition. The nation had finally tailored the urban political organization and molded reform thought to respond to the most powerful economic forces in the city. In this instance it was not free silver but the chamber of commerce that became the cowbird of reform. This should not be surprising, for the chamber of commerce and its affiliates had also proved to be the greatest obstacle to social reform in Pingree's Detroit.

NOTES

1. Henry Demarest Lloyd to Richard T. Ely, November 16, 1896, Lloyd Papers; Samuel M. Jones to Hazen S. Pingree, August 4, 1899, Jones Papers.
2. Pingree quoted in Detroit Free Press: November 27, 1896 and Detroit Evening News: March 17, 1897, P.S.
3. B. O. Flower to Hazen S. Pingree, February 1, 1896, Pingree Papers; Richard T. Ely to Henry Demarest Lloyd, November 12, 1896; Henry Demarest Lloyd to Samuel M. Jones, May 23, 1897, Lloyd Papers.
4. Richard Hofstadter, The Age of Reform: From Bryan to F.D.R. (New York, 1960), pp. 135-48.
5. Hazen S. Pingree address to Detroit Chamber of Commerce, November 2, 1895, Pingree Papers; Hazen S. Pingree, Facts and Opinions (Detroit, 1895), pp. 85-86; Pingree quoted in New York Journal: December 8, 1896, P.S.
6. Detroit Tribune: May 1, 1899, P.S.
7. Lincoln Steffens, The Autobiography of Lincoln Steffens (New York, 1931), pp. 374-75; Hewitt quoted in Pilgrim, III (December, 1901), 4.
8. Hazen S. Pingree, "Address to the Nineteenth Century Club of New York," November 11, 1897, p. 7; S. M. Jones to Josiah Strong, November 15, 1898, Jones Papers; Brand Whitlock, Forty Years of It (New York, 1914), pp. 172-74.
9. Frederic C. Howe, The City: The Hope of Democracy (New York, 1913), pp. 1, 2. For the elitist views of reformers who overthrew Boss

Tweed, see Alexander B. Callow, Jr., The Tweed Ring (New York, 1966), pp. 69-71, 265-67. Charles R. Adrian, "Some General Characteristics of Nonpartisan Elections," Robert C. Wood, "Nonpartisanship in Suburbia," both in Democracy in Urban America, ed. Oliver P. Williams and Charles Press (Chicago, 1964), pp. 251-66. For an exposition of the views regarding municipal government of one of the most prominent twentieth-century "structural" reformers, see Richard S. Childs, "The Faith of a Civic Reformer," ibid., pp. 222-24. The "elitist commitments" of the city manager system (as prescribed in city government textbooks) can also be seen in Lawrence J. R. Herson, "The Lost World of Municipal Government," American Political Science Review, LI (June, 1957), 330-45.
10. Howard B. Furer, William Frederick Havemeyer: A Political Biography (New York, 1965), pp. 14, 144-54, 160; Seymour J. Mandelbaum, Boss Tweed's New York (New York, 1965), pp. 91, 97, 108, 111; Callow, The Tweed Ring, pp. 253-86.
11. Mandelbaum, Boss Tweed's New York, pp. 98-100, 111; Furer, William F. Havemeyer, pp. 156, 158, 160-61, 169.
12. Ibid., p. 161; Mandelbaum, Boss Tweed's New York, pp. 112-13; William L. Riordin, Plunkitt of Tammany Hall (New York, 1963), p. 17.
13. Allan Nevins, Grover Cleveland, A Study in Courage (New York, 1941), pp. 61-62, 83-94.
14. Harold Coffin Syrett, The City of Brooklyn 1865-1898, A Political History (New York, 1944), p. 134; Steven C. Swett, "The Test of a Reformer: A Study of Seth Low," New York Historical Society Quarterly, XLIV (January, 1960), pp. 8, 9; Lincoln Steffens, The Shame of the Cities (New York, 1966), p. 201.
15. Syrett, Brooklyn, pp. 104-6, 109-19, 134; Swett, "Test of a Reformer," pp. 7-9.
16. Albert Fein, "New York City Politics From 1897-1903; A Study in Political Party Leadership" (M.A. thesis, Columbia University, 1954), pp. 19-20; Swett, "Test of a Reformer," pp. 10-14, 16-18.
17. Ibid., pp. 21-23, 26-31, 35-36; Roy Lubove, The Progressives and the Slums, Tenement House Reform in New York City, 1890-1917 (Pittsburgh, 1962), pp. 153-54.
18. Swett, "Test of a Reformer," pp. 6, 32, 35-36, 38-41; Wallace S. Sayre and Herbert Kaufman, Governing New York City Politics in the Metropolis (New York, 1960), p. 695.
19. James D. Phelan, "Municipal Conditions and the New Charter," Overland Monthly, XXVIII (no. 163, 2nd series), pp. 104-11; Roy Swanstrom, "Reform Administration of James D. Phelan, Mayor of San Francisco, 1897-1902" (M.A. thesis, University of California-Berkeley, 1949), pp. 77-79, 80, 83, 85, 86; Walton Bean, Boss Ruef's San Francisco: The Story of the Union Labor Party, Big Business, and the Graft Prosecu-

tion (Berkeley, 1952), pp. 8, 9, 16, 17, 23; George E. Mowry, *The California Progressives* (Chicago, 1963), pp. 23-25; Fremont Older, *My Own Story* (San Francisco, 1919), pp. 27, 31, 65
20. William E. Leuchtenburg, Preface to Edwin R. Lewinson, *John Purroy Mitchel: The Boy Mayor of New York* (New York, 1965), pp. 11-13; Lewinson, *Boy Mayor*, pp. 93, 95, 100, 102, 117, 124.
21. Leuchtenburg, *ibid.*, p. 12; Lewinson, *ibid.*, pp. 18, 151-69, 175-88.
22. Leuchtenburg, *ibid.*, pp. 11-13; Samuel P. Hayes, "The Politics of Reform in Municipal Government," *Pacific Northwest Quarterly*, LV (October, 1964), pp. 157-69.
23. Lewinson, *Boy Mayor*, pp. 11-13, 18, 93, 95, 102; Riordin, *George Washington Plunkitt*, pp. 17-20; Swett, "Seth Low," pp. 8, 9; Allan Nevins, *Abram S. Hewitt: With Some Account of Peter Cooper* (New York, 1935), pp. 515-16, 529-30; Seth Low, "An American View of Municipal Government in the United States," in James Bryce, *The American Commonwealth* (New York, 1893), I, 651, 665.
24. Hoyt Landon Warner, *Progressivism in Ohio 1897-1917* (Columbus, 1964), pp. 32, 70-72; Whitlock, *Forty Years of It*, pp. 211, 252; Clarence H. Cramer, *Newton D. Baker: A Biography* (Cleveland, 1961), pp. 46-47; Steffens, *Autobiography of Lincoln Steffens*, pp. 477, 492-93; Frederic C. Howe, *The Confessions of a Reformer* (New York, 1925), pp. 98, 102-8; Pingree, *Facts and Opinions*, p. 196. For Mark Fagan, see Lincoln Steffens, *Upbuilders* (New York, 1909), pp. 28, 30, 33, 35, and Ransom E. Noble, Jr., *New Jersey Progressivism before Wilson* (Princeton, 1946), pp. 13-42. St. Louis Circuit Attorney Joseph W. Folk (1901-04), who began his career by investigating and prosecuting franchise "grabs," discovered that the real despoilers of municipal government were not minor city officials but promoters, bankers, and corporation directors who profited by misgovernment. After he became governor he dropped his crime-busting and supported progressive and urban reforms. Louis G. Geiger, *Joseph W. Folk of Missouri* (Columbia, 1953), pp. 32, 41, 81, 88, 93, 99-117. Robert Wiebe's assertion that the "typical business ally of the boss, moreover, was a rather marginal operator, anathema to the chamber of commerce" is at variance with what is known about the political influence wielded in Detroit by urban capitalists such as the Hendries, McMillans and Johnson or for that matter with the role played by Yerkes and Insull in Chicago, Mark Hanna in Cleveland and the Huntington interests in Los Angeles, just to cite a few examples. *The Search for Order, 1877-1920* (New York, 1967), p. 167.
25. Steffens, *Upbuilders*, pp. 3-45; Warner, *Progressivism in Ohio, 1897-1917*, pp. 71, 74; Cramer, *Newton D. Baker*, pp. 50-52; Howe, *Con-*

fessions of a Reformer, pp. 90-93, 108-9; Carl Lorenz, *Tom L. Johnson, Mayor of Cleveland* (New York, 1911), p. 152; Steffens, *Autobiography of Lincoln Steffens*, p. 480; Detroit *Free Press*, March 14, 1896, P.S.; Samuel M. Jones to Henry D. Lloyd, April 16, 1897, Lloyd Papers; Samuel M. Jones to James L. Cowes, April 27, 1897; Tom L. Johnson to S. M. Jones, May 3, 1902, Jones Papers; Harvey S. Ford, "The Life and Times of Golden Rule Jones" (Ph.D. thesis, University of Michigan, 1953), pp. 185, 284-85, 330; Whitlock, *Forty Years of It*, p. 212. William D. Miller has argued that "Boss" Edward H. Crump, who was Memphis mayor from 1910 to 1916, stands with "Golden Rule" Jones and Tom L. Johnson as a typical progressive of the period, but an examination of Miller's book raises serious doubts about that judgment. Although Crump occasionally employed reform rhetoric, established a few milk stations for the poor, and put screens on public school windows, he used most of the energy of his administration to enforce the laws and instill efficiency into the municipal government in the structural-reform tradition. Crump wiped out "policy" playing by Negroes, eliminated loafing by the garbage collectors and street pavers, forced the railroads to construct eleven underpasses, lowered city taxes, reduced waste in municipal government by extending audit procedures even to the purchase of postage stamps, and increased city income by selling empty bottles, feed sacks, and scrap. William D. Miller, *Mr. Crump of Memphis* (Baton Rouge, 1964), pp. 79-113. Brooklyn's Mayor Charles A. Schieren (1894-95), who gained some stature as a reformer by defeating a venal Democratic machine, also followed a well-trodden path of cleaning out "deceit and corruption" and installing "integrity, nonpartisanship, and routine efficiency." Like most of the reform mayors of his period, Schieren failed to advance or support social reform programs, Harold C. Syrett, *The City of Brooklyn, 1865-1898, A Political History* (New York, 1944), pp. 218-32. Geoffrey Blodgett has tried to show that Boston became for "a brief time the cutting edge of urban reform in America" under Mayor Josiah Quincy (1896-1900), who established a publicly owned printing plant and expanded the city's playgrounds. Although the Dover Street Bath House may have been a "monument to municipal socialism" as Blodgett contends, Mayor Quincy stopped his programs short of anything that would have threatened the vested interests in the traction and utility business. Geoffrey Blodgett, *The Gentle Reformers: Massachusetts Democrats in the Cleveland Era* (Cambridge, 1966), pp. 240-61. For Quincy's absurd notion that regular bathing would cause the "filthy tenement house" to disappear, crime and drunkenness to decrease and the death rate to drop, see Josiah Quincy, "Municipal Progress in Boston," *Independent*, LII (February 15, 1900), 424. Henry Demarest Lloyd was critical

of Mayor Quincy's failure to resist the traction interests and referred to the Mayor's public baths as Quincy's "little sops." H. D. Lloyd to Samuel Bowles, December 13, 1898, Lloyd Papers.
26. Ford, "Golden Rule Jones," pp. 151, 166, 339; Samuel M. Jones to Dr. [Graham] Taylor, October 5, 1897; S. M. Jones to L. L. Dagett, April 17, 1899, Jones Papers; Hazen S. Pingree address to Springfield, Massachusetts Board of Trade, March 3, 1894, Ralph Stone Scrapbook; Whitlock, *Forty Years of It*, pp. 252, 254.
27. Robert H. Bremner, "The Civic Revival in Ohio: The Fight Against Privilege in Cleveland and Toledo, 1890-1912" (Ph.D. thesis, Ohio State University, 1943), p. 25; Hazen S. Pingree, "The Problem of Municipal Reform. Contract by Referendum," *Arena*, xvii (April, 1897), 707-10; Cramer, *Newton D. Baker*, p. 46; Steffens, *Upbuilders*, pp. 28-30, 33, 35; Noble, *New Jersey Progressivism before Wilson*, pp. 25-26, 35, 38.
28. Tom L. Johnson, *My Story* (New York, 1911), p. 113; Ford, "Golden Rule Jones," pp. 136-37, 170, 339; Hazen S. Pingree, "Detroit: A Municipal Study," *Outlook*, lv (February 6, 1897), 437; Bemis quoted in Detroit *Evening News:* June 21, 1899, Stone Scrapbook; Whitlock, *Forty Years of It*, p. 221.
29. Whitlock, *Forty Years of It*, p. 221.
30. Frank J. Goodnow, "The Tweed Ring in New York City," in James Bryce's *The American Commonwealth* (London, 1888), ii, 335; Bryce, *ibid.*, p. 67; Bryce, *ibid.*, i, 613; Albert Shaw, *Political Problems of American Development* (New York, 1907), p. 66. According to Edwin L. Godkin, New York City's problems began with the establishment of universal suffrage in 1846 which coincided with the beginning of the great Irish migration. Edwin L. Godkin, *Problems of Modern Democracy*, ed. Morton Keller (New York, 1896, Cambridge, 1966), p. 133.
31. Bryce, *American Commonwealth*, ii, 67; William B. Munro, *The Government of American Cities* (New York, 1913), pp. 308-9, 310, 312; Andrew D. White, "The Government of American Cities," *Forum*, x (December, 1890), 369; Alfred R. Conkling, *City Government in the United States* (New York, 1899), p. 49; Frank J. Goodnow, *Municipal Problems* (New York, 1897), pp. 150-53; Delos F. Wilcox, *The Study of City Government* (New York, 1897), p. 151; "Report of the Committee on Municipal Program," *Proceedings* of the Indianapolis Conference for Good City Government and Fourth Annual Meeting of the National Municipal League (Philadelphia, 1898), p. 11 (hereafter cited *Proceedings for Good City Government*).
32. Wilcox, *The Study of City Government*, pp. 237-38; Frank J. Goodnow, *Municipal Government* (New York, 1910), pp. 39, 149, 378-79; James T. Young, *Proceedings for Good City Government*, 1901, p. 230.
33. *Michigan Legislative Manual and Official Directory 1899-1900* (Lansing, 1899), p. 322;

Report of the Commission to Devise a Plan for the Government of Cities in the State of New York (New York, 1877), pp. 35-36.
34. Goodnow, *Municipal Problems*, pp. 148-49.
35. Shaw, *Political Problems of American Development*, pp. 65-67, 82, 125; Munro, *Government of American Cities*, pp. 120-21; Bryce, *American Commonwealth*, ii, 67.
36. Goodnow, *Municipal Problems*, p. 278; Conkling, *City Government in the United States*, p. 34; Richard T. Ely, *The Coming City* (New York, 1902), p. 29.
37. Walter T. Arndt, *The Emancipation of the American City* (New York, 1917), p. 12; Frank M. Sparks, *Government As a Business* (Chicago, 1916), pp. 1, 7; Goodnow, *Municipal Government*, pp. 150, 381-82; Munro, *Government of American Cities*, p. 306; William H. Tolman, *Municipal Reform Movements in the United States* (New York, 1895), p. 34.
38. Conkling, *City Government in the United States*, pp. 6, 32; Goodnow, *Municipal Problems*, pp. 262-65.
39. *Ibid.*, pp. 204-5, 265; Munro, *Government of American Cities*, pp. 241, 279-80; Albert Shaw, "Civil Service Reform and Municipal Government," in *Civil Service Reform and Municipal Government* (New York, 1897), pp. 3-7.
40. Goodnow, *Municipal Government*, pp. 142-46, 385-86, and *Municipal Problems*, pp. 66-67; Leo S. Rowe, "City Government As It Should Be And May Become," *Proceedings for Good City Government, 1894*, p. 115; White, "The Government of American Cities," p. 370; John Agar, "Shall American Cities Municipalize?" *Municipal Affairs*, iv (March, 1900), 14-20; C. E. Pickard, "Great Cities and Democratic Institutions," *American Journal of Politics*, iv (April, 1894), 385. The Boston mayor Nathan Mathews, Jr., asserted that the proposal to restrict municipal suffrage to the propertied classes was one of the most common remedies for the evils of city government of his age. Nathan Mathews, Jr., *The City Government of Boston* (Boston, 1895), p. 176.
41. Munro, *Government of American Cities*, pp. 294, 308-10; Goodnow, *Municipal Problems*, pp. 150-53; Leo S. Rowe, "American Political Ideas and Institutions in Their Relation to the Problem of the City," *Proceedings for Good City Government, 1897*, p. 77; William Dudley Foulke, *ibid.*, 1898, p. 137; Frederic C. Howe, *The City, The Hope of Democracy* (New York, 1913), p. 1.
42. Henry Bruère, "Efficiency in City Government," *Annals* of the American Academy of Political and Social Science, xli (May, 1912), 19; Richard S. Childs, "Now that We Have the City Manager Plan, What Are We Going to Do With It," *Fourth Yearbook of the City Managers' Association* (Auburn, 1918), pp. 82-83; Henry M. Waite, *ibid.*, pp. 88-89; Harold A. Stone, Don K. Price and Kathryn H. Stone,

City Manager Government in the United States (Chicago, 1940), pp. 25-27; James Weinstein, "Organized Business and the City Commissioner and Manager Movements," *Journal of Southern History*, xxviii (May, 1962), 166, 179.

43. *Ibid.*, p. 173; Samuel P. Hayes, "The Politics of Reform in Municipal Government in the Progressive Era," *Pacific Northwest Quarterly*, lv (October, 1964), 157-69.

44. Edward C. Banfield and James Q. Wilson, *City Politics* (New York, 1963), p. 148.

45. The peak period for the spread of the city commissioner and the city manager system was 1917-27. Leonard D. White, *The City Manager* (Chicago, 1927), p. 317; Harold Zink, *Government of Cities in the United States* (New York, 1939), p. 301.

Machine Politics—Old and New

THEODORE J. LOWI

The political machine is an institution peculiar to American cities. Like the militant party elsewhere, the American machine as a classic type is centralized, integrated, and relatively ruthless. But there the similarity ends.

Machines have been integrated from within, as fraternities; they do not arise out of opposition to the state or to a hostile class. The power of the machine rested upon being integrated in a dispersed, permissive, and unmobilized society. Integrated, however, in a special American way.

The most militant parties of Europe have depended upon homogeneity—enforced if necessary. Machines have developed ingenious techniques for capitalizing upon ethnic and racial heterogeneity. Militant parties have typically been based on common ends at the center, holding the periphery together by fear. The machines were based upon a congeries of people with uncommon ends, held together at the center by logrolling and at the periphery by *fraternité*, *egalité*, and ignorance.

As to the significance of the machine for the development of the American city, the returns are still not in. Typically, it was the European observers who were the first to appreciate this unusual, American phenomenon. Ostrogorski, Bryce, Weber Michels, Schumpeter, and Duverger each in his own way made an outstanding effort to appreciate the peculiarities of urban democracy in America. Harold F. Gosnell, in *Machine Politics: Chicago Model* (1937), was one of the very first Americans to join that distinguished company with anything approaching a systematic treatment of the subject. (By this standard the muckrakers do not count.)

However, Gosnell was limited by the fact that there was in his time, insufficient experience with alternative forms of big cities politics. Too few

From *The Public Interest*, No. 9 (Fall 1967), pp. 83–92. Reprinted by permission of the publisher. Theodore J. Lowi is Professor of Political Science at the University of Chicago.

big cities in the United States had been "reformed" in sufficient degree to provide any basis for comparison. In the 1960's, sufficient time has passed. The machine is nearly dead, and we have experienced lengthy periods of Reform government. We can now see the machine in perspective. How does it shape up?

CHICAGO AND NEW YORK

We can begin to introduce perspective by immediately setting aside Gosnell's claim that the Chicago experience on which his book was based is representative. It is the very uniqueness of Chicago's experience with the machine that gives his study such value. It is New York that is the representative big city, not Chicago. Its representativeness derives from the fact that it has experienced Reform in a way that Chicago has not. In 1967, political power in Chicago still has an extremely strong machine base; political power in New York has an entirely new and different base. As New York was being revolutionized by the New Deal and its successors, the structure of Chicago politics was being reaffirmed. When New York was losing its last machine and entering into a new era of permanent Reform, Chicago's political machine was just beginning to consolidate. New York became a loose, multi-party system with wide-open processes of nomination, election, and participation; Chicago became a tight, one-party system. New York sought to strengthen a weak mayor who already operated under a strong-mayor government; Chicago has had the opposite problem of an already strong mayor in a weak-mayor government.

To evaluate the machine we must ask whether, by surviving, machine

politics in Chicago in any way distorted that city's growth and development. How much change would there have been in Chicago's history if the nationalization of politics had made possible in Chicago, as it did in virtually every other big American city, ways of "licking the ward boss" and altering precinct organization, means of loosening the hold of the county organization on city hall, power for liberating the personnel and policies of the professional agencies of government? We cannot answer these questions for Chicago because the basis of machine strength still exists there, and the conditions for its continuity might well continue through the remainder of the century. However, we may be able to answer them, at least better than before, by looking at Chicago from the vantage point of New York's experience.

POPULISM AND EFFICIENCY

New York city government, like government in almost all large American cities except Chicago, is a product of Reform. It is difficult to understand these cities without understanding the two strains of ideology that guided local Reform movements throughout the past three-quarters of a century. *Populism* and *efficiency,* once the foundation of most local insurgency, are now almost universally triumphant. These two tenets are now the orthodoxy in local practice.

Populism was originally a statement of the evils of every form of bigness in the city, including big business, big churches, big labor, as well as big political organizations. Decentralization was an ultimate goal. In modern form, it has tended to come down to the aim of eliminating political parties, partisanship, and if possible "politics" itself.

Efficiency provided the positive program to replace that which is excised by populist surgery. The doctrine calls essentially for the centralization and rationalization of government activities and services to accompany the decentralization of power. Some Reformers assumed that services do not constitute power. Others assumed the problem away altogether by positing a neutral civil servant who would not abuse centralized government but who could use it professionally to reap the economies effected by rationalization and by specialization. That was the secret of the business system; and, after all, the city is rather like a business. ("There is no Republican or Democratic way to clean a street.")

While there are many inconsistent assumptions and goals between the doctrines of populism and efficiency, they lived well together. Their coexistence was supported by the fact that different wings of the large, progressive movement they generated were responsible for each. Populism was largely the province of the working class, "progressive" wing. Doctrines of efficiency were very much the responsibility of the upper class wing. Populism resided with the politician-activists. Efficiency was developed by the intellectuals, including several distinguished university presidents, such as Seth Low, Andrew Dickson White, Harold Dodd, and, pre-eminently, Woodrow Wilson, who, while still a professor of political science, wrote a classic essay proclaiming the virtues of applying Prussian principles of administration in the United States.

These two great ideas were, by a strange and wonderful chemistry, combined into a movement whose influence forms a major chapter of American history. Charters and laws have been enacted that consistently insulate city government from politics, meaning party politics. It has become increasingly necessary, with each passing decade, to grant each bureaucratic agency autonomy to do the job as each commissioner saw fit, as increasingly appointments were made of professionals in each agency's fields.

On into the 1960's, the merit system extends itself "upward, outward, and downward," to use the Reformers' own rhetoric. Recruitment to the top posts is more and more frequent from the ranks of those who have made careers in their agencies, party backgrounds increasingly being a mark of automatic disqualification. Reform has succeeded in raising public demand for political morality and in making "politics" a dirty word. A "good press" for mayors results from their determination to avoid intervening in the affairs of one department after another. The typical modern mayor is all the more eager to co-operate because this provides an opportunity to delegate responsibility. Absolution-before-the-fact for government agencies has become part of the mayoral swearing-in ceremony.

Reform has triumphed and the cities are better run than ever before. But that is, unfortunately, not the end of the story, nor would it have been the end of the story even had there been no Negro revolution. The triumph of Reform really ends in paradox: *Cities like New York became well-run but ungoverned.*

THE NEW MACHINES

Politics under Reform are not abolished. Only their form is altered. *The legacy of Reform is the bureaucratic city-state.*

Destruction of the party foundation of the mayoralty cleaned up many cities but also destroyed the basis for sustained, central, popularly-based action. This capacity, with all its faults, was replaced by the power of professional agencies. But this has meant creation of new bases of power. Bureaucratic agencies are not neutral; they are only independent.

Modernization and Reform in New York and other cities has meant replacement of Old Machines with New Machines. The bureaucracies—that is, the professionally organized, autonomous career agencies—are the New Machines.

Sociologically, the Old Machine was a combination of rational goals and fraternal loyalty. The cement of the organization was trust and discipline created out of long years of service, probation, and testing, slow promotion through the ranks, and centralized control over the means of reward. Its power in the community was based upon services rendered to the community.

Sociologically, the New Machine is almost exactly the same sort of an organization. But there are also significant differences. The New Machines are more numerous, in any given city. They are functional rather than geographic in their scope. They rely on formal authority rather than upon majority acquiescence. And they probably work with a minimum of graft and corruption. But these differences do not alter their definition; they only help to explain why the New Machine is such a successful form of organization.

The New Machines are machines because they are relatively irresponsible structures of power. That is, each agency shapes important public policies, yet the leadership of each is relatively self-perpetuating and not readily subject to the controls of any higher authority.

The New Machines are machines in that the power of each, while resting ultimately upon services rendered to the community, depends upon its cohesiveness as a small minority in the midst of the vast dispersion of the multitude.

The modern city has become well-run but ungoverned because it has, according to Wallace Sayre and Herbert Kaufman, become comprised of "islands of functional power" before which the modern mayor stands denuded of authority. No mayor of a modern city has predictable means of determining whether the bosses of the New Machines—the bureau chiefs and the career commissioners—will be loyal to anything but their agency, its work, and related professional norms. Our modern mayor has been turned into the likes of a French Fourth Republic Premier facing an array of intransigent parties in the National Assembly. These modern machines, more monolithic by far than their ancient brethren, are entrenched by law, and are supported by tradition, the slavish loyalty of the newspapers, the educated masses, the dedicated civic groups, and, most of all, by the organized clientele groups enjoying access under existing arrangements.

ORGANIZED DECENTRALIZATION

The Reform response to the possibility of an inconsistency between running a city and governing it has been to assume the existence of the Neutral Specialist, the bureaucratic equivalent to law's Rational Man. The assumption is that, if men know their own specialties well enough, they are capable of reasoning out solutions to problems they share with men of equal but different echnical competencies. That is a very shaky assumption indeed. Charles Frankel's analysis of such an assumption in Europe provides an appropriate setting for a closer look at it in modern New York; ". . . different [technical] elites disagree with each other; the questions with which specialists deal spill over into areas where they are *not* specialists, and they must either hazard amateur opinions or ignore such larger issues, which is no better . . ."

During the 1950's, government experts began to recognize that, despite vast increases in efficiency flowing from the defeat of the Old Machine, New York city government was somehow lacking. These concerns culminated in the 1961 Charter, in which the Office of Mayor was strengthened in many impressive ways. But it was quickly discovered that no amount of formal centralization could definitively overcome the real decentralization around the Mayor. It was an organized disorganization, which made a mockery of the new Charter. The following examples, although drawn from New York, are of virtually universal application:

(1) Welfare problems always involve several of any city's largest agencies, including Health, Welfare, Hospitals, etc. Yet during more than 40 years, successive mayors of New York failed to reorient the Department of Health away from a "regulative" toward a "service" concept of organization. And many new aspects of welfare must be set up in new agencies if they are to be set up at all. The new poverty programs were set up very slowly in all the big cities—except Chicago.

(2) Water pollution control has been "shared" by such city agencies as the Departments of Health, Parks, Public Works, Sanitation, Water Supply, and so on. No large city, least of all New York, has an effective program to combat even the local contributions to pollution. The same is true of air pollution control, although for some years New York has had a separate Department for this purpose.

(3) Land-use patterns are influenced one way or another by a large variety of highly professional agencies. It has proven virtually impossible in any city for one of these agencies to impose its criteria on the others. In New York, the opening of Staten Island by the Narrows Bridge, in what may be the last large urban frontier, found the city with no plan for the revolution that is taking place in property values and land uses in that borough.

(4) Transportation is also the province of agencies too numerous to list. Strong mayors throughout the country have been unable to prevent each from going its separate way. To take just one example: New York pursued a vast off-street parking program, at a cost of nearly $4,000 per parking space, at the very moment when local rail lines were going bankrupt.

(5) Enforcement of civil rights is imposed upon almost all city agencies by virtue of Federal, state, and local legislation. But efforts to set up public, then City Council, review of police processes in New York have been successfully opposed by professional police officials. Efforts to try pairing and busing on a very marginal, experimental basis have failed. The police commissioner resigned at the very suggestion that values other than professional police values be imposed upon the Department, even when the imposition came via the respected tradition of "legislative oversight." The

Superintendent of Education, an "outsider," was forced out; he was replaced by a career administrator. One education journalist at that time said: "Often . . . a policy proclaimed by the Board [of Education], without the advice and consent of the professionals, is quickly turned into mere paper policy . . . The veto power through passive resistance by professional administrators is virtually unbeatable. . . ."

The decentralization of city government toward its career bureaucracies has resulted in great efficiency for the activities around which each bureaucracy was organized. The city is indeed well-run. But what of those activities around which bureaucracies are not organized, or those which fall between or among agencies' jurisdictions? For these, as suggested by the cases above, the cities are suffering either stalemate or elephantiasis—an affliction whereby a particular activity, say, urban renewal or parkways, gets pushed to its ultimate "success" totally without regard to its importance compared to the missions of other agencies. In these as well as in other senses, the cities are ungoverned.

THE 1961 ELECTION

Mayors have tried a variety of strategies to cope with these situations. But the 1961 mayoralty election in New York was the ultimate dramatization of the mayor's plight. This election was a confirmation of the New York system, and will some day be seen as one of the most significant in American urban history. For New York, it was the culmination of many long-run developments. For the country, it may be the first of many to usher in the bureaucratic state.

The primary significance of the election can be found in the spectacle of a mayor attempting to establish a base of power for himself in the bureaucracies. The Mayor's running mate for President of the City Council had been Commissioner of Sanitation, a position which culminated virtually a lifetime career of the holder in the Department of Sanitation. He had an impressive following among the sanitation men— who, it should be added, are organized along precinct lines. The Mayor's running mate for Comptroller had been for many years the city Budget Director. As Budget Director, he had survived several Administrations and two vicious primaries that pitted factions of the Democratic Party against one another. Before becoming Director he had served for a number of years as a professional employee in the Bureau. The leaders of the campaign organization included a former, very popular Fire Commissioner who retired from his commissionership to accept campaign leadership and later to serve as Deputy Mayor; and a former Police Commissioner who had enjoyed a strong following among professional cops as well as in the local Reform movement. Added to this was a new and vigorous party, the Brotherhood Party, which was composed in large part of unions with broad bases of membership among city employees. Before the end of the election, most of the larger city bureaucracies had political representation in the inner core of the new Administration.

For the 1961 election, Mayor Wagner had put his ticket and his organization together just as the bosses of old had done. In the old days, the problem was to mobilize all the clubhouses, districts, and counties in the city by putting together a balanced ticket about which all adherents could be enthusiastic. The same seems true for 1961, except that by then the clubhouses and districts had been replaced almost altogether by new types of units.

The main point is that destruction of the machine did not, in New York or elsewhere, eliminate the need for political power. It simply altered what one had to do to get it. In the aftermath of twenty or more years of "modern" government, it is beginning to appear that the lack of power can corrupt city hall almost as much as the possession of power. Bureaucracy is, in the United States, a relatively new basis for collective action. As yet, none of us knows quite how to cope with it.

WHAT IF . . . ?

These observations and cases are not brought forward to indict Reform cities and acquit Chicago. They are intended only to put Chicago in a proper light and to provide some means of assessing the functions of the machine form of collective action.

Review of Reform government shows simply and unfortunately that the problems of cities, and the irrational and ineffectual ways city fathers go about their business, seem to obtain universally, without regard to form of government or type of power base. All cities have traffic congestion, crime, juvenile delinquency, galloping pollution, ghettos, ugliness, deterioration, and degeneracy. All cities seem to be suffering about equally from the quite recent problem of the weakening legitimacy of public institutions, resulting in collective violence and pressures for direct solution to problems. All cities seem equally hemmed in by their suburbs and equally prevented from getting at the roots of many of their most fundamental problems. Nonpartisan approaches, even the approaches of New York's Republican mayor to Republican suburbs and a Republican governor, have failed to prevent rail bankruptcy in the vast Eastern megalopolis, to abate air or water pollution, to reduce automobile pressure, or to ease the pain of the middle-class Negro in search of escape from his ghetto.

The problems of the city seem to go beyond any of the known arrangements for self-government. However, low public morality and lack of what Banfield and Wilson call "public-regardingness" may be a function simply of poor education and ethnic maladjustment. The Old Machine and its abuses may just have been another reflection of the same phenomena. If that is so, then passage of more time, and the mounting of one socio-cultural improvement after another, might have reformed the machines into public-regarding organs, if they had been permitted to survive.

Are there any strong reasons to believe that real reform could have come without paying the price of eliminating the popular base of political action? Intimations can be found in the last of the machine-recruited leaders of Tammany, Carmine DeSapio and Edward Costikyan. Each was progressively more public-regarding than any of his predecessors. Indeed, Costikyan was a model of political responsibility for whom the new New York had no particular use. However, for this question the best answers may lie in looking afresh at Gosnell's Chicago. With a scientific rigor superior to most political analysis of the 1960's, his book goes further than any other single work to capture what political behavior was like under Old Machine conditions. The sum total of his findings, despite Gosnell's own sentiments, does not constitute a very damning indictment of the Chicago machine—if contemporary experience is kept clearly in mind.

CHICAGO IN PERSPECTIVE

Even amidst the most urgent of depression conditions, the machine in Chicago does not seem to have interfered with the modest degree of rationality distributed throughout the United States. Take for instance the case of voting behavior on referendum proposals, the most issue-laden situation an electorate ever faces. Gosnell criticized the referendum as generally subject to fraud and other types of abuse, and most particularly so in Chicago during the 1920's and '30's. But even so, his figures show that the electorate, despite the machine, did not behave indiscriminately. The theory that universal suffrage provides no check against the irresponsible acceptance of financing schemes which pass the real burden on to future generations is simply not borne out in Chicago. Conservative appeals by the propertied were effective. Over a twelve-year period, including six fat years and six lean years, 66 local bond issues were approved and 48 were rejected. Those rejected included some major bond issues offered for agencies whose leaders had become discredited. Other types of issues show responsiveness to appeals other than local precinct or county organizations. As the antiprohibition campaign began to grow, so did the vote on the prohibition repealer. Clear irrationalities tended to be associated primarily with highly technical proposals involving judicial procedure or taxation; but this is true everywhere, and to much the same degree.

In a bold stroke, Gosnell also tried to assess the influence of the newspapers, the best source for rational—at least nonmachine—voting decisions. For this particular purpose Gosnell's data were weak, but fortunately he was not deterred from asking important questions merely for lack of specially designed data. Factor analysis helped Gosnell tease out of census tract data and newspaper subscription patterns a fairly realistic and balanced sense of the role of the local newspapers. Gosnell was led to conclude that the influence of news media is limited, but that this was a limitation imposed far less by the machine than by the extent to which newspapers were regularly read. Newspaper influence on issues was measurably apparent wherever daily readership was widely established—the machine notwithstanding. Here again is suggested the possibility that real machine domination rested upon a level of education and civic training that was, at the very time of Gosnell's research, undergoing a great deal of change.

Taking all the various findings together, and even allowing for abuses that were always more frequent in cities than towns, and probably more frequent in Gosnell's Chicago than other cities, we can come away from Gosnell's analysis with a picture not at all at odds with V. O. Key's notion of the "responsible electorate."

Gosnell felt his book to be an indictment of machine politics. But today, looking at the Chicago experience from the vantage point of New York's, one feels less able to be so sure.

Urban Problems and the Federal Government: A Historical Inquiry*

DANIEL J. ELAZAR

In recent years there has been a growing concern among political scientists and political practitioners alike with the evolution of the relationships between the federal government and the cities. This concern is variously directed toward federal relations with the nation's largest cities in particular toward federal relations with urban concentrations generally, or toward the need for developing a coherent pattern of relationships between the federal government and the nation's burgeoning metropolitan areas. Regardless of its immediate focus, it is based on public recognition of an obviously great increase in the dollar amounts of federal aid to the cities and a proliferation of federal programs specifically directed toward contemporary urban problems.

It is generally assumed that the federal-city relationship that is evolving is radically new in several respects: in its very concern with urban problems as such; in the fact that much of it appears to be a direct relationship, for all intents and purposes, bypassing the states insofar as active implementation of the programs is concerned; and, finally, in its overall impact on American federalism. These assumptions are based on several premises, among them that the federal government ignored the cities until recently, and that meaningful (usually taken to mean direct) federal-city relationships date back no further than

the beginning of the New Deal, prior to which time the cities received such minor federal benefits as were available via the states and then only as political subdivisions of the states. As an outgrowth of these two assumptions, there is a third: that the new federal-city relationship represents a new departure for American federalism by changing the basis of the federal system from a two-level (federal-state) to a three-level (federal-state-city) relationship.[1]

In at least one sense, the foregoing assumptions are well grounded in fact. The cities (and other urban entities) in this country are indeed carving a place for themselves in the scheme of American federalism not quite like any they had before, if only because they bulk so much larger on the American scene than ever before. At the same time, to the extent that the assumptions rest on the idea that the federal-local (substituting the word "local" for "city" so as to encompass urban counties, towns, boroughs, and the like) relationship of today is a radically new one, it is necessary to examine the historical record to see if such is the case before drawing any conclusions about the course of American federalism. Only if the federal-local relationship before 1933 is properly explored and examined in light of our knowledge of the nature of American federalism as it has evolved since the adoption of the Constitution is it

From *Political Science Quarterly*, Vol. LXXXII (December 1967), pp. 505-25. Reprinted by permission of the publisher. Daniel J. Elazar is Professor of Political Science at Temple University.

possible to build an understanding of the evolution of the federal system in light of recent urbanizing trends.

This article will (1) raise some basic questions as to the character of federal-city relations in the period prior to 1933, (2) make a preliminary examination of those relations in light of the historical evidence in an effort to (3) bring the inquiry into the problem of federal-city relations today into proper historical focus and (4) to suggest some lines of further inquiry.

THE EVOLUTION OF DE FACTO ARRANGEMENTS

It would appear that the first step in an inquiry into the evolution of city-federal relationships in the United States is to determine at what point cities, as such, began to make specialized demands on the state and federal governments (past those related to simple incorporation) that differed from the demands of other local governments.

(1) Much is made of the change in city-federal relations since 1933. However, much of the supposed lack of sophisticated relations in the nineteenth century was simply due to a lack of large cities. The dates of the incorporation of today's largest cities provide one indicator of this. Table 1 (all tables follow text) reveals that prior to 1815 only seven of the nation's fifty largest cities of today were incorporated. In point of fact, they represented a majority of the incorporated cities of their time. In 1810, the nation had only forty-six urban places of more than 2,500 population, only eleven of which had more than 10,000 people and none of which reached 100,000.[2]

(2) Even when cities were established, they did not immediately develop specialized governmental needs that could not be handled to their general satisfaction within the existing structure of government. Boston, for example, the country's third largest city in the early nineteenth century, did not even see fit to incorporate until 1822, when its population was already 47,000. Until then it was governed by the same town system used in the most rural areas of New England. Admittedly, Boston was an exception. However, even after the development of incorporated municipalities, the size factor (that is, the smallness of the "cities") placed limits on the need for specialized urban services. As indicated in Tables 2 and 3, before 1840 there were no large cities in the United States and it was not until after 1900 that the medium size and large cities came to contain as much as twenty-five per cent of the nation's total population.

(3) In this regard it is also important to note that the total number of urban places (population 2,500 or more) in the United States did not exceed 1,000 for the first time until 1890 and only in that year did the urban share of the total population reach one third of the national total (Table 4). Not until 1920 did the total population of places over 2,500 exceed the total rural population. That same year the total population in cities of 100,000 and over exceeded the total population in all smaller urban places for the first time (significantly, this was reversed in 1950 as part of the suburbanizing trend).

(4) There is considerable evidence to the effect that even today virtually all cities below 50,000 in population, excepting only a few older suburban cities which face "central city"-type problems, really do not develop a "city" outlook in the political arena. As a rule, they

align themselves with the so-called "rural" areas (really a misnomer in the demographic sense today) against the "big city" in urban-rural conflict situations. Indeed, it is likely that most cities below 150,000 population (again excepting certain older suburban and industrial cities) also reject "city" ideas and align themselves in opposition to the big-city bloc on most issues. Certainly these smaller cities have not been the source of specialized city pressures on the states and demands on Washington because they have not had such demands. If the situation that prevails today can be projected backward to the period between 1790 and 1930, it is probable that widespread specialized "city" demands sufficiently differentiated from those of other local governments to create substantial intrastate urban-rural conflict did not develop until the period of the First World War, except in the cases of the very largest cities, those with present (1960) populations of over 750,000 and which then exceeded 250,000 in population. In 1910, the nineteen cities of 250,000 or more had hardly more than fifteen per cent of the nation's population. Even as late as 1930, they did not encompass a quarter of the nation's people. The big cities' desire to turn to the federal government instead of the states could not have become a national issue until then, if only because there were not enough big cities with specialized demands.

(5) This is not to imply that there were no conflicts between the states and their big cities prior to 1913, but that they were few, not uniquely urban, and not particularly unmanageable within the states until then. In Illinois, for example, the origins of the Chicago-downstate cleavage date back to the post-

Civil War period and no further. Before the Civil War, the basic intrastate conflict was a sectional one between Yankee-settled northern Illinois, including Chicago, and Southern-dominated southern Illinois. The first overt conflict between the mayor of Chicago and the governor of Illinois developed in 1871 in the aftermath of the Chicago Fire, when Mayor Mason turned directly to the federal government for troops to maintain order in the gutted city even though Governor Palmer was prepared to send state militia to Chicago to do the job.[3] Still, until World War I the conflicts were few and minor and were generally resolved to the mutual satisfaction of both sides. In 1904 Chicago even obtained a limited amount of "home rule" through a constitutional amendment ratified state-wide, and in 1912 Edward Dunn, a former mayor of Chicago, was elected governor (the only time this has happened). Though his victory came in a three-way race, it and his very nomination are at least testimony to the fact that it was still considered politically feasible to nominate a Democratic mayor of Chicago for the office of governor, something which would be most unexpected today. Actually, until well after World War I, the partisan cleavage between "Democratic" Chicago and "Republican" downstate did not exist, Chicago being as Republican as the rest of northern and central Illinois.

Similar embryonic big city-outstate conflicts existed in Massachusetts, New York, Maryland, and Missouri, and perhaps elsewhere as well. But, just as in the Chicago-downstate Illinois conflict, most of those states took some steps to alleviate the situation through amendment of their constitutions to grant to their largest cities some measure of home rule of a kind not given to other cities in the same states even today. The metropolitan problems of New York City, for example, were substantially ameliorated through state assistance in the consolidation of the five boroughs in 1898. The creation of city-counties in Baltimore, Denver, Philadelphia, St. Louis, San Francisco, and other large cities at the turn of the century was also indicative of the then still existing ability and willingness of the states to assist the few large cities in meeting their relatively few specialized demands.[4] However, by 1910 or thereabouts, this option appears to have been closed off.

(6) At this point it is wise to add one caveat. Despite relative smallness in *size*, the larger pre-twentieth-century cities functioned in a more complex manner than cities of similar size today because of the magnitude of the social and economic as well as political functions that accrued to them as the largest cities of their time. Insofar as this was the case, there were "big-city" attributes present even in what today would be considered small and medium size cities. This certainly affected the major nineteenth-century cities' needs for outside aid and to some extent influenced their specific demands.

(7) One of these demands, and indeed a basic one, related to the physical growth of the cities themselves. Dynamic small and medium size cities grew to become today's large cities through annexation of adjacent lands to provide a basis for population growth. Until the late nineteenth century, annexation was, under state law and in fact, a commonly used—and an easily used—device which contributed to the internal growth of cities and met such problems of suburbanization as affected them. Annexation was often used uni-

laterally by the cities to meet, directly or indirectly, problems of suburbanization and metropolitanization that today lead cities to turn to the federal and state governments for more active assistance.[5] Examples of the problems attacked by the then relatively simple device of annexation include: (a) the need for a single municipal government to serve all urban residents in a given area; (b) the provision of reasonably uniform area-wide services, few as they may have been; (c) the establishment of such area-wide regulatory standards and codes as were considered appropriate at the time; and (d) the establishment of uniform, if minimal, area-wide tax levies and revenue collections. Given the low level demands for local services in even the larger cities until relatively late in the nineteenth century, simple extension of ordinary municipal powers was usually sufficient to relax all but the most eager municipal reformers.

(8) The rise of the big city as a national entity coincides with the actual (as opposed to the chronological) end of the nineteenth century, which can be placed somewhere between 1913 and 1917. Several landmark events occurred to mark its passing: (a) Woodrow Wilson inaugurated the twentieth-century versions of "big government" and co-operative federalism, though still endowing them with a rural bias; (b) the land frontier, as expressed, for example in the opportunity for homesteading new lands, which actually increased after 1890 for a brief period, finally ceased to exist; and (c) the United States became involved in World War I and its accompanying international entanglements. Consequently, the real line of demarcation in the history of cities demands on the federal government—if one exists—is perhaps better drawn

at 1913 than at 1933. In the Wilson administration, however, the rural biases of the Southern- and Western-dominated Congress strictly limited the aids available to cities under the new programs.[6] Consequently, the latter year is especially significant, because it was only then that the federal government began to respond to the cities' new specialized demands.

LOCAL DEMANDS AND FEDERAL RESPONSES

What was the nature of the general demands of localities that did exist and were relevant to the cities prior to 1913? What was the nature of the responses of the federal and state governments to those demands and to such specialized demands as were then generated by the major cities? In other words, how did the federal system respond to urban needs before 1913?

The major government-oriented demands of localities prior to 1913 centered around:

(1) the development and maintenance of lines of communication with the rest of the country—particularly through the postal service;

(2) the development and maintenance of facilities for commercial intercourse locally and with the rest of the country —particularly through waterways, roads, and railroads;

(3) the development and maintenance of a limited number of local services— particularly schools, rudimentary police and fire services, rudimentary street and sanitation services, and limited welfare services (such as poor relief);

(4) contributions by extra-local governments to the local economic base to ensure prosperity and growth in a variety of specific ways, depending on the particular situation of each locality —these included items as diverse as the maintenance of federal and state institutions (and payrolls) in the locality; benefits from the federal tariff for local manufacturing establishments; state and federal contracts for locally-based businesses and various other governmental services that aided the development of local economies;

(5) outside financial assistance in some form for the support of all the above demands—particularly through grants-in-land, reimbursements of local expenditures, and distributions of the earnings of permanently endowed and earmarked funds.

Despite the considerably lower "velocity of government" (amount of government activity at all levels in relation to the total activity of society) prior to 1913, these demands were not inconsiderable. What is more, they were probably met with nearly as much relative success as the more exacting and varied demands of the twentieth century are met today.

Central to understanding the responses of the federal and state governments is an understanding of the functioning of the federal system prior to 1913. As this writer has demonstrated in *The American Partnership*, what we today call "cooperative federalism" was the dominant form of federalism even prior to the New Deal. The differences in American federalism then and now are primarily differences arising from the increased velocity of government in the twentieth century. Consequently, one may look for an absolute increase in direct federal-city relations since 1913 or 1933, but this does not necessarily imply radically new departures in federal-city relations (though this indeed may be the case in the relations between the great metropolitan centers and the federal government). It may even be that the percentage of formal federal-*local* programs in relation to the overall number of formal intergovernmental programs has not changed appreciably even as it is likely that the percentage of federal-city programs has increased as urbanization has increased. Two illustrations: (1) The direct federal-city relations created by the river and harbor improvement programs in the nineteenth century were possibly as extensive in proportion to the total amount of intergovernmental activity of the time as are direct federal-city relations in contemporary redevelopment programs. These were and are direct relations of the kinds that were later to burgeon in other fields. (2) Quasi-formal federal-county relations were developed in the post-Civil War period to conduct federal surveys of various kinds. These were federal-local relations that were not urban in character because the programs were not urban ones. Non-urban-related federal-local relations are certainly not unexpected in a generally non-urban society.

The federal response before 1913 led to city-federal relations in the following fields:

(1) Postal service was often the first governmental service of any sort demanded by residents of newly-settled local communities. Today, the extension of postal service is often overlooked as an important aspect of federal city relations because it is taken for granted. In the days of the land frontier, it was often a crucial factor influencing the possibilities for local commerce to develop and even the probability of a community's survival by providing it with: (a) a drawing card as a potential center of commerce with which to attract neighboring settlers; (b) a means of communication with the outside world that made commerce possible and lessened isolation in an age when travel was difficult and expensive; (c) cash in the form of postal receipts—often the only more or less steady flow of cash available in a frontier community; and (d) freight and passenger service, which developed from stagecoach and railroad lines established as a result of obtaining mail contracts.

Nor did communities acquire postal service without exerting effort. Their leaders used pressure, political influence, and sheer public relations to gain the services of the post office, the construction of post office buildings, and the expansion of both. Among the best received new programs of Lincoln's administration were the initiation of parcel post, railway mail cars, and free delivery in cities of over fifty thousand population, all vital measures for the growth of American cities. The impact of the post office did not pass with the passing of the community's frontier stage. As the community grew, so did the post office—as a center of communication, as a business attraction, as a source of payrolls, and, most important, as a center of local politics—both as a source of political patronage and as a base of operations for local political leaders.[7]

(2) Since the close of the War 1812, the U.S. Corps of Engineers has been involved in a federal-city partnership in waterway improvement and, later, flood control. Cities actively sought federal aid in this field and were usually responsible for securing federal waterway improvements not only for themselves but for the regions (and states) they served. This was not only a matter of lobbying for federal aid, but often in

volved joint day-to-day efforts, after the congressional appropriations were made, in carrying out projects. These efforts were usually the product of negotiations between local officials and federal administrative personnel, frequently with the assistance of the local representative in Congress. They ranged from the construction of a dredge by the City of Richmond, with federal funds, to be leased to the Army Engineers while the latter were engaged in local projects and then used by the city to maintain the improvements, to the inclusion of federal harbor services personnel on a quasi-formal Board of Harbor Improvement for the City of Boston to advise the city fathers on needed improvements so the latter could lobby for federal funds to pay for them.[8]

Cities also lobbied for and contributed toward (until forbidden to do so in most state constitutions) the construction of roads and railroads to serve their needs. Roads were either constructed by federal agencies directly or through federal land grants to the states. Railroads were constructed through federal land grants to the states or directly to federal-chartered companies. In either case, those cities competed for location of road and railroad routes and often those that lost withered away or ceased to grow. The struggle for transportation facilities involved considerable federal-city contact, collaboration, and conflict.[9]

(3) Normally there was little direct federal aid to local governmental agencies except in the earlier stages of the development of cities west of the Appalachians before the territories in which they were established achieved statehood. In those early stages, however, direct federal aid was often very significant, involving, as it did, direct grants of land for townsites and local institutions, as well as the federal land survey which, as the nation's foremost effort at national planning, provided a basis for all local development in the public land states.[10] After statehood, federal aid for local services was important, but was almost invariably channeled through the states.

After the middle of the nineteenth century a new form of federal-local relations began to develop in the form of contacts between professionals in such diverse fields as education, library science, agriculture, and public welfare. These contacts were made privately and through the professional associations that began to emerge in the eighteen-forties. Over time, they grew to be a significant means of improving government services at both levels and of forging strong, if informal, cooperative lines between Washington and the localities.[11]

(4) Federal contributions to the local economic base through federal institutions, payrolls, tariffs, contracts, and the like have always been an important factor in American history. Again, their relative impact in the years before 1913 was no less than it has been since the great increase in the velocity of government in the twentieth century and may even have been greater. Though they have virtually disappeared from view today as historians have concentrated on more dramatic events of the past, the community leaders of that day were fully aware of their importance.[12] Federal military installations almost invariably were sought as contributors to local prosperity. Marine hospitals, post offices, customs offices, sub-treasuries, mints, and the like were equally sought. Military and civil construction and mail contracts were prized. Tariff concessions on particular items could make or break

particular cities which survived because of particular industries. Nineteenth-century Americans were quite conscious of this, too.

Despite the fact that the cities' demands were not much different from the demands of smaller localities, the larger cities as a general rule almost certainly benefited more than the smaller towns from the aforementioned programs. The exceptions were important because they almost invariably meant that the fortunate town would grow beyond reasonable objective expectations. Thus, in the years between 1827 and 1857 Chicago received more benefits from the federal government than St. Louis, its larger sister to the south. Most of this aid came in the form of land grants earmarked for it though channeled through the State of Illinois or directly transferred to the new city, but mail subsidies and new federal installations were also important, particularly in making the new city a center for federal activities in the Northwest. By 1860 Chicago had surpassed St. Louis in growth, no doubt aided by the extra measure of federal assistance available to the entrepreneurs who used that city as their base.[13] Almost all of these "benefits" contributed greatly to the urbanization of the United States in the long run.

Between 1913 and 1933 all of these responses were extended or modified and some new ones introduced in response to new needs.

(1) Post offices declined in importance as active elements in federal-city relations; their political importance declined, other federal agencies came into the local community, and cities grew less clearly dependent on the postal service as the primary means of communication with the outside world.

However, the establishment of postal savings banks that served the new immigrants who had flocked to the big cities of the Northeast temporarily added a new dimension to the role of the post office in urban affairs.

(2) Waterway improvements continued to be an important source of direct federal-city collaboration. Highway construction was added to the list, though as a federal-state-local program, not as a direct federal-city effort.

(3) The federal government first became involved—though only marginally —with urban housing in the eighteen-nineties when Congress became concerned with slum conditions in the great Eastern cities. Direct federal activity in the field of urban housing developed briefly during World War I, in response to the wartime situation. It lapsed after the end of hostilities.

(4) World War I also had an extraordinary though brief effect on the level of federal contributions to the local economies, urban and rural. While the cities benefited greatly from wartime industrial expansion, the agricultural areas also benefited from wartime agricultural expansion. Before and after the war, a state of "normalcy" may be said to have prevailed in the localities' search for government contributions to their economies and in the federal response, but this was not a "normalcy" of inaction.

THE EMERGENCE OF
SPECIALIZED DEMANDS

In light of all this, what were the new specialized big city demands that developed between 1913 and 1933, and how did they relate to the earlier demands of the cities?

It was in the field of local services

that specialized urban demands really developed in the twentieth century. These demands originated in the late nineteenth century. They continued to develop at an accelerated rate after 1913, so that the explosion in federal-city relations that occurred during the New Deal actually did not spring full-blown from Depression-created needs but was the culmination of demands generated fifteen to thirty years earlier. These demands did not lead the cities to bypass the states for the first time. The cities had been seeking aid from the federal government in fields where pioneering programs were required for generations. Even though new urban needs were leading to new demands, few of the newly created federal programs were designed to favor urban areas over others.

The general categories we have already listed continued to be basic in the demands of both the localities generally and the new big cities after 1913, with some modifications which grew out of the changing needs of a dynamic society.

(1) Promotion of new communications facilities generally ceased to be a direct governmental concern, since post offices were already established in all but the very smallest hamlets, and telephone (like telegraph) services were developed through private enterprise. Government now became concerned with *regulation* of privately-owned communications facilities and *improvement* of postal services. Here big city needs did not appreciably differ from the general needs of all localities even after 1913, until the post-World War II years.

(2) Promotion of inter-city commercial facilities continued to involve river and harbor improvements but was also expanded into a concern for airports and highways. Needs for the former were primarily big city-oriented before World War II (since 1945 even the smaller urban places have been actively competing for navigable channels and harbor facilities) and did contribute to the cities' turning to the federal government, much in the same way that river and harbor improvements have since the War of 1812. The need for highways was more general, but, though big cities sought more federal assistance for intra-city highway connections because of the greater costs of urban highway construction, the states' primary concern with farm-to-market highways in a still half-rural nation led to congressional restrictions on the amount of federal aid which could be used for urban areas. These restrictions were not fully removed until the nineteen-forties.

(3) The need for local services increased generally, but the cities' search for federal assistance in every field (except welfare at the very end of the period under discussion) did not depart from the limited claims of localities generally. Here and there requests for assistance in urban redevelopment were heard.

(4) The demands for contributions to the local economic base were in no way diminished, nor were they specific to the big cities any more than they had been prior to 1913. If anything, the biggest cities ceased to be as dependent upon such contributions as smaller localities because of their more diverse economic bases.

Outside financial assistance, then, was sought in new ways primarily for highways and welfare, both to a limited degree. Otherwise, the previous patterns were maintained with slight modifications.

New and specialized big city demands were generated after 1913 in the fields of metropolitanization and the physical improvement of the urban environment. Both were new fields of interest that first emerged in the eighteen-nineties and were not publicly acknowledged until after 1910, and they were the demands which later evoked a response from the New Deal. Prior to 1933 little was done to meet them other than to make provision for the cities' unilateral action through permissive state legislation. This was primarily because they were expensive demands and, historically, the federal government has had to take the lead in expending large sums for the introduction of new programs managed by any level of government in the United States.

All of this points to the hardly radical conclusion that what really was occurring in the period between 1913 and 1933 was a subtle reshaping of the greater part of the range of government activities to the demands of an increasing urbanized society.

As a consequence of this reshaping of the activities of the federal-state-local partnership, virtually all cities except the largest metropolitan centers received sufficient federal and state assistance and benefits to satisfy most of their demands without leading them to take steps to alter the established patterns of federalism.

This was not the case after 1913 (and particularly after World War I) for the great metropolitan centers. They had grown so big that their needs and problems no longer fit into the same categories as those of their smaller urban sisters or of the nation's local communities, rural or urban. This change was multifaceted: On one hand, the large metropolitan centers had developed unique problems of urbanization and metropolitanization; on the other hand, the great metropolitan centers

had grown so large and socio-economically complex that they had become as self-contained and self-sufficient within the national framework (and as diverse internally) as the states of which they were parts.

Turned inward and possessing their own problems, the residents and leaders of the big metropolitan centers fell out of harmony with their states and the other urban centers within them. This estrangement led cities like New York, Chicago, Philadelphia, Detroit, Los Angeles, and others slightly smaller in population to turn to the federal government, not as constituent elements of their states advocating programs of interests to all localities (or even all cities), but as self-contained civil societies in their own right, seeking aid for their own specialized problems. At the close of the period discussed here, at least one well-known Chicagoan, Charles E. Merriam, was calling for the transformation of the large metropolitan centers into city-states. That this did not come to pass is a tribute to the stability and the flexibility of the federal system. It is also evidence that the basic cleavage in interest was not between urban and non-urban America, but between the great metropolitan centers and the rest of rapidly urbanizing America. The latter continued to appeal directly and indirectly to the federal government for aid and assistance just as they had been doing since the establishment of the Republic, but as constituent elements of their respective states, not as competing civil societies.

SOME UNANSWERED QUESTIONS

If this brief discussion has raised some of the salient questions concerning the development of city-federal relations and has presented some of the evidence and possible conclusions which may be drawn from it, it is obviously far from exhaustive. Among the important questions not discussed or only briefly mentioned are several other points of concern:

(1) *The role of the cities as participants in the political processes of federalism.* Federal aid came to the localities partly because of national necessity and partly as a result of local pressures. The latter were made manifest by the political role of the localities within the non-centralized federal system whereby their leaders and representatives could agitate for aid, mobilize support for their efforts on all levels, adapt acquired aid to local conditions, and even play the state and federal governments off against one another to their advantage.[14]

(2) *Sectional differences in federal-city relations, which seem to be quite significant.* Hints of these differences can be found in the foregoing pages—for example, in the way in which Western cities benefited primarily from federal expenditures locally. The extent of these differences appears to be more widespread, subtle, and important than such hints can indicate, reflecting, as they do, basic differences in the character of cities in the North, South, and West.

(3) *The differences in city-state relations in the several states.* The kinds of demands different cities made of the federal government and the way in which those demands were made depended, even before 1933, on the responses of their states to their special needs.

Nobody can deny that recent federal responses to urban problems have been of unprecedented scope and magnitude. At the same time, there is considerable evidence that they are not unprecedented in their roots and may not even be unprecedented in their impact. The evidence is not all in, but it should be clear that failure to understand the federal-city relationship before 1933 may lead to erroneous conclusions regarding the impact—or the proper management —of the federal-city relationship today. Such conclusions could, in turn, drastically affect the future of the American system as we know it.

Table 1

Incorporation Dates of Fifty Largest U.S. Cities by Historical Period*

I. Pre-1776 (2)	II. 1776-1815 (5)	III. 1816-1848 (22)	IV. 1849-1876 (17)	V. 1877-1912 (5)
New York (1685)	Baltimore (1797)	Atlanta (1847)	Akron (1865)	Honolulu (1909)
Philadelphia (1701)	Dayton (1805)	Boston (1822)	Birmingham (1871)	Long Beach, California (1888)
	New Orleans (1805)	Buffalo (1832)	Dallas (1856)	Miami (1896)
	Richmond (1782)	Chicago (1837)	Denver (1861)	Oklahoma City (1890)
	San Antonio (1809)	Cincinnati (1819)	Fort Worth (1873)	
		Cleveland (1836)	Indianapolis (1874)	
		Columbus (1834)	Jersey City (1855)	
		Detroit (1824)	Kansas City (1850)	
		Houston (1837)	Los Angeles (1850)	
		Jacksonville (1832)	Minneapolis (1867)	
		Louisville (1828)	Oakland (1854)	
		Memphis (1826)	Omaha (1857)	
		Milwaukee (1846)	Portland (1851)	
		Newark (1836)	St. Paul (1853)	
		Norfolk (1845)	San Diego (1850)	
		Pittsburgh (1816)	San Francisco (1850)	
		Providence (1832)	Seattle (1869)	
		Rochester (1834)		
		St. Louis (1822)		
		Syracuse (1848)		
		Toledo (1837)		
		Worcester (1848)		

* Dates are those in which cities were incorporated as cities.

Table 2

Number and Population of U.S. Cities by Category: 1790-1930

Year	Towns (2,500-10,000)		Small Cities (10,000-50,000)		Med.-Size Cities (50,000-250,000)		Large Cities (250,000-1,000,000)		Great Cities (1,000,000+)	
	No.	Total Pop. (000s)	No.	Total Pop. (000s)	No.	Total Pop. (000s)	No.	Total Pop. (000s)	No.	Total Pop. (000s)
1790	19	92	5	110						
1800	27	140	5	122	1	61				
1810	35	186	9	189	2	150				
1820	48	251	10	192	3	250				
1830	67	357	19	346	4	405				
1840	94	500	32	640	4	392	1	313		
1850	174	913	52	1,172	9	943	1	516		
1860	299	1,541	77	1,555	13	1,445	3	1,646		
1870	495	2,364	143	2,640	18	1,758	7	3,140		
1880	716	3,335	188	3,636	27	2,735	7	3,218	1	1,206
1890	994	4,661	296	5,720	47	4,809	8	3,254	3	4,468
1910	1,665	7,946	488	9,572	90	9,019	16	6,961	3	8,501
1920	1,970	9,354	608	12,110	119	11,785	22	10,764	3	10,146
1930	2,183	10,615	791	15,523	154	14,032	32	13,720	5	15,065

Source: *Historical Statistics of the United States, 1957.*

Table 3

Cities' Cumulative Per Cent of Total
Population by Size of Place:
1790-1930

Size of Place	1790	1850	1900	1930
1,000,000 plus			8.5	12.3
250,000 plus		2.2	14.4	23.4
50,000 plus		6.3	22.3	34.9
10,000 plus	2.8	11.3	31.7	47.5
2,500 plus	5.1	15.3	39.7	56.2

Source: 1950 Census of Population, Vol. II,
Characteristics of Population, Part 1.

Table 4

Distribution of U.S. Population According to Size of Place: 1790-1930

	Population Distribution Per Cent				Number of Urban Places by Size		
Year	Total Urban	One Million Plus	100,000 to One Million	Under 100,000	Total Rural	One Million Plus	100,000 to One Million	Under 100,000
1790	5.1	—	—	5.1	94.9	—	—	24
1800	6.1	—	—	6.1	93.9	—	--	33
1810	7.3	—	—	7.3	92.7	—	—	46
1820	7.2	—	1.3	5.9	92.8	—	1	60
1830	8.8	—	1.6	7.2	91.2	—	1	89
1840	10.8	—	3.0	7.8	89.2	—	3	128
1850	15.3	—	5.1	10.2	84.7	—	6	230
1860	19.8	—	8.4	11.4	80.2	—	9	383
1870	25.7	—	10.7	15.0	74.3	—	14	649
1880	28.2	2.4	10.0	15.8	71.8	1	19	919
1890	35.1	5.8	9.6	19.7	64.9	3	25	1,320
1900	39.7	8.5	10.2	21.0	60.3	3	35	1,699
1910	45.7	9.2	12.9	23.6	54.3	3	47	2,212
1920	51.2	9.6	16.3	25.3	48.8	3	65	2,654
1930	56.2	12.3	17.3	26.6	43.8	5	88	3,072

NOTES

° The bulk of the research for this article was made possible through a grant of funds from the University Research Board of the University of Illinois and of time from the Institute of Government and Public Affairs of that university. The initial hypotheses were developed and preliminary data gathered in the course of the author's other studies of nineteenth-century American federalism. See his *The American Partnership* (Chicago, 1962). Aside from the materials cited below, the author has made extensive use of documents in the State Historical Society and State Archives of Colorado, the Burton Historical Collection of the Detroit Public Library, the Barlow Collections in the Henry E. Huntington Library, the Minnesota Historical Society and State Archives of Minnesota, the Virginia State Archives, and the National Archives.

1. This viewpoint is expressed either explicitly or implicitly in recent works on federal-city relations. See, for example, *The Federal Government and the Cities* (Washington, 1962), a collection of lectures delivered at The George Washington University in 1961, of which Roscoe C. Martin's excellent "Washington and the Cities: An Introduction" is most enlightening. Two other important sources of material on the evolving federal-city relationship are Robert H. Connery and Richard H. Leach, *The Federal Government and Metropolitan Areas* (Cambridge, Mass., 1960) and "City-Federal Relations," *Proceedings of the American Municipal Congress, 1958* (Washington, 1958).

2. All statistical data are taken from U. S. Census Bureau, *Historical Statistics of the United States* (Washington, 1957) unless otherwise indicated.

3. The correspondence from that exchange was published by the State of Illinois as *Letters From Governor Palmer Concerning the Chicago Fire* (Chicago, 1873).

4. See Frank J. Goodenow, *Municipal Problems* (New York, 1897).

5. Annexation as a device declined when a sufficient number of suburban communities (including those created as suburbs or, more likely, those previously-settled towns suburbanized in the course of the expansion of the central city) began to desire to retain their "independence" and identities. They became a countervailing power within the state and were generally able to create a stalemate which served their interests. Significantly, most major annexations in recent years have taken place in the South and Southwest (Atlanta, Dallas, Houston, Nashville, Phoenix, San Antonio, Oklahoma City, to mention a few) in areas without established suburban communities to fight them. City-county consolidation and separation cases had similar histories before 1913. The *Municipal Year Book* publishes annexation data for the nation's cities annually.

6. The effects of the rural biases of the Wilson administration on the new federal grant programs are discussed in Austin F. Macdonald, *Federal Aid* (New York, 1928).

7. An abundance of documents on the role of the post office in the nineteenth century can be found in U. S. Congress, *American State Papers*. The political role of the department is discussed in Dorothy G. Fowler, *The Cabinet Politician: The Postmasters General, 1829-1909* (New York, 1943). The economic impact of postal services in cities has not been adequately treated, but Wayne E. Fuller's *RFD: The Changing Face of Rural America* (Bloomington, Ind., 1964) does much to indicate the possibilities even while focusing on rural post offices. Political studies of the extension of postal services can be found in Clyde Kelly, *United States Postal Policy* (New York, 1931) and Daniel C. Roper, *The United States Post Office* (New York, 1917).

8. *American State Papers* contains much documentary material on river and harbor improvements. Though there has been no comprehensive study of the economic impact of river and harbor improvements, there are numerous contemporary and historical studies of specific waterways and ports which deal with the question. See such standard works as E. W. Gould, *Fifty Years on the Mississippi or Gould's History of River Navigation* (St. Louis, 1889); Mildred L. Hartsough, *From Canoe to Steel Barge on the Upper Mississippi* (Minneapolis, 1934); and William E. Lass, *A History of Steamboating on the Upper Missouri River* (Lincoln, Neb., 1962). Lucille M. Kane, *The Waterfall that Built a City* (St. Paul, Minn., 1966), shows the impact of federal improvements on one major city, Minneapolis. For a brief overview of the pre-Civil War period, see Forest G. Hill, *Roads, Rails, and Waterways: The Army Engineers and Early Transportation* (Norman, Okla., 1957). For data on the appropriations and activities in every city in the United States, see U. S. House of Representatives, *Index to the Reports of the Chief of Engineers, U. S. Army, 1866-1912*, I (Rivers and Harbors) Doc. 740, 63rd Congress, 2d Session, 1914. The Richmond case is discussed in Elazar, *The American Partnership*, Chap. 16.

9. For exemplary studies of the local impact of federal aid to roads, see Philip D. Jordan, *The National Road* (Indianapolis, 1948). W. Turrentine Jackson, *Wagon Roads West* (Berkeley, 1952), Hill, Paul W. Gates, *The Illinois Central Railroad and its Colonization Work* (Cambridge, Mass., 1934), and Richard C. Overton, *Burlington West: A Colonizing History of the Burlington Railroad* (Cambridge, Mass., 1941) and undoubtedly the best studies of cities and railroad development. This writer drew extensively on the sources listed in the bibliographies of both. For overviews of federal activity, see Lewis H. Haney, *A Congressional History of Railroads in the United States, 1850-1887* (Madison, 1908, 1910), 2 Vols., and John B. Sanborn, *Congressional Grants of Land in Aid of Railways* (Madison, 1899).

10. The laws and statistics of direct federal grants

to localities are presented in Thomas C. Donaldson, *The Public Domain* (Washington, 1884), and R. M. Robbins, *Our Landed Heritage, The Public Domain, 1776-1936* (Princeton, 1942). See, also, George M. Stephenson, *The Political History of the Public Lands* (Boston, 1917).

11. Elazar, *The American Partnership*, Chap. 15.

12. The documentary evidence of federal-city relations contains many acknowledgments of the importance of these federal aids. Among the easily accessible published materials, see, for example, Thomas Hart Benton, *Thirty Years View* (New York, 1854-56). John G. Van Deusen discusses local reactions to federal expenditures and assembles excellent fiscal data on these expenditures before the Civil War in *Economic Bases of Disunion in South Carolina* (New York, 1928).

13. Bessie L. Pierce, *A History of Chicago* (New York, 1937), 2 Vols., and James W. Putnam, *The Illinois and Michigan Canal* (Chicago, 1918).

14. See the writer's "Local Government in Intergovernmental Perspective," in *Illinois Government* (Urbana, 1961) for a brief delineation of the various roles of the localities in the federal system today, which are reasonably applicable to the period before 1933 as well.

VI THE CITY IN THE LIFE OF THE NEWCOMER

The United States is a nation of immigrants; her cities are populated with newcomers propelled by two forces of urbanization, the waves of European immigrants and the migration of native Americans lured from the farm, the village, and the small town. Beginning with the flood of Catholic Irish and Germans in the 1840's, a major turning point in immigration history, significant changes took place in the nature and number of newcomers who came to the United States. More stayed in the cities, fewer were Protestant and middle class, more were of rural peasant stock, desperately poor and often illiterate, especially between 1880 and 1910 when eighteen million immigrants, mostly Catholics and Jews, poured in from southern and eastern Europe. By 1920, when census reports established that the United States had become an urbanized nation, more than three quarters of the urban population were people either of foreign birth or the sons and daughters of immigrants. The distribution of immigrants was uneven. The South was feeling important affects of urbanization even though it conspicuously lagged behind other regions in attracting newcomers. While cities were booming on the Pacific Slope, they could not compare to the two areas which took the greatest impact of immigration: the North Central States, and that area on the eastern seaboard from the Middle Atlantic to the New England states which absorbed the majority of immigrants, over 70 per cent of the foreign-born population.

Between 1840 and 1920 the immigrant helped to change the character of many American cities: Chicago with her Slavs, Milwaukee with her Germans, San Francisco with her Chinese, New Haven with her Italians, and New York, the most "foreign" city in the world, with her mulligan stew of nationalities. The ethnic clusters of "Little Europes" created an exciting diversity to urban living in language, customs, values, food, entertainment, and the arts. But the city also crystallized the plight of the immigrant: the pain of cutting old ties; the shock of alienation in and adjustment to a strange, new urban world; the hostility, contempt, bigotry, and fear of the "native" American.[1] One result of this cultural collision was the emergence of what often has been called the shame of the city, the ghetto. In the first selection, David Ward asks one of the major questions in American urban history: how do you account for the origins and development of the immigrant ghetto? A large question with a thicket of thorny problems, it is subject to several approaches. One approach, often used by historians, is to stress the common hardships shared by most immigrant groups in housing, income, employment, sanitation, and the like, which helped create urban ghettos. This view highlights the similarities between various ethnic and religious groups. Ward looks at the problem with the cool and detached eye of the urban geographer, examining aspects of the ghetto not always explored by historians, such as the ecology of the inner city, differences in age, sex ratio, the spatial relationship between residences and employment, the selective influences of the central city, the death rate, business expansion, and so on. While careful to point out that he does not intend to minimize the very real difficulties faced by immigrants, he concludes nonetheless that "the internal spatial structure rather than the common deficiencies of immigrant residential districts may well be more revealing of their generic characteristics." Aside from an interpretation of the making of a ghetto, this view gives us a sense of the *differences* between various ethnic groups in the ghetto. For example, why the Irish had a higher death rate than the Russian Jew; why social organization was shattered in one ghetto and remained relatively stable in another; how the quality of sanitation varied from city to city, and how an expanding central city could have any number of effects. In Ward's view the ghetto is not fixed and rigid, but changing, in flux. It further enhances our understanding of the diversity, the rich pluralism of urban immigrant life.

Intimately related to the emergence of the ghetto in urban America, is another major theme of immigration—the difficulties of assimilation to a new culture.

In a chapter from his Pulitzer prize-winning book, *The Uprooted,* Oscar Handlin presents a poignant saga of the immigrant family and its problems of assimilation, which illuminate a larger theme of urban history: the breakdown of the traditional European communal tradition in an American urban environment. According to Handlin, the immigrant brought to the New World a highly structured concept of the family, meaningful for a village community

---

1. For an analysis of both immigration policy and attitudes toward the immigrant, see John Higham's brilliant *Strangers in the Land: Patterns of American Nativism, 1860-1925* (New York: Atheneum, revised ed., 1963), and Barbara Miller Solomon, "The Intellectual Background of the Immigration Restriction Movement in New England," *New England Quarterly* (March 1952).

but irrelevant to the conditions of the American city. The vital cohesion of the family, sealed by the social cement of precise authority, obligations, and responsibilities, was shattered. Poverty, the language barrier, the street gang, American values regarding marriage and individualism, dissolved old familial roles and reversed others. The family roots nourished by the village soil lay scattered on the city streets. Parental authority disintegrated and with it respect; cut by shame, misunderstanding, and the hard realities of American urban life, the European heritage was shredded. The family drifted apart, wife from husband, children from parents. Handlin sums it up when he has his immigrant mother look at her family and ask, "Would the strangeness of the setting make strangers also of these her dear ones?"

Handlin does not suggest that it happened to every family, nor that all immigrants were poor. But enough were poor to make it a bleak and tragic story.[2] It was not always a story, however, with a hideous ending, at least for second and third generation immigrants, many of whom in time were able to flee the ghetto into the larger life of the city. This was true for the Irish and Germans, the dominant groups of the so-called "old" immigration of the mid-nineteenth century. It is part of the interesting story, told by Moses Rischin in the next essay, of the New York Jews, the most numerous group of the "new" immigration from 1880 to 1910.

The Jewish immigration was massive. In 1870 they constituted only 9 per cent (80,000) of the city's population. Forty-five years later there were more Jews than the entire population of New York City in 1870, nearly a million and a half, almost 28 per cent of the population. Professor Rischin gives us a vivid description of the sights, sounds, smells—and tribulations—of one of America's classic ghettos, New York's Lower East Side. This is an essay that seizes the imagination and pulls it back to the narrow, teeming streets of Manhattan, where one can almost *feel* the squalor of immigrant life, the disease, the crime, the poverty, all consummated by tenement life—"a place so dark," the little girl said, "it seemed as if there weren't no sky." Yet, on the other hand, one can sense the enormous vitality, the optimism, the sense of challenge that permeated the Jewish community. For all its misery, the Lower East Side was a better world than the desperate poverty of the towns and villages of Eastern Europe, and the slums of Berditchev, Vilna, Kovno, or Warsaw. It was the triumph of the Jews that they survived their ghetto,

2. Does disorganization mean disaster for the family? Not necessarily, say some sociologists who argue that if the old bonds were broken, new associations arose to replace them. In effect, the family, like other institutions, responded to social change; change does not necessarily mean total disruption. See Herbert J. Gans's perceptive study of a second-generation Italian community in Boston, *The Urban Villagers* (New York: The Free Press, 1962).

thanks largely to strong family ties, certain attitudes toward drink and charity and, above all, hope. By 1910 the Lower East Side began dissolving as a ghetto, its borders melting in with the surrounding city, as a large stream of Jews moved out.

The experience of the Italians was in many ways similar to that of the Jews, in other ways, especially in the popular mind, quite different. In 1953 Daniel Bell, a sociologist, published an important essay in the *Antioch Review* (Summer issue) which emphasized a particular element of immigrant society that has long fascinated the American imagination: the urban gangster and the rise of organized crime in America. In this article Bell destroyed the myth that the Italian-American was the godfather of organized crime. For years Italian-Americans have rightfully winced as the mass media bombarded the American mind with stereotypes of the Italian gangster—pudgy, dark, mean—waging war on city streets. Bell showed that the dominance of the Italian-American in organized crime is but another stage of ethnic succession to leadership. Crime, he argued, is a means of social mobility for submerged immigrant groups. In the last half of the nineteenth century, leadership was controlled by the Irish, who shared it with east European Jews until the decade of the 1920's, when the Italians began to compete effectively for dominance.

According to Bell, organized crime is indigenous to American economic, ethnic, and political life. It exists and thrives, not because of an alien conspiratorial importation of steely-eyed Mafia "bad guys," nor primarily for the motive of gain, but because it serves the function of being a "queer ladder of social mobility" for those who seek status, prestige, and power. Crime is an American way of life because the urban gangster, despite deviant methods, strives for the same goals as "normal" citizens in an achievement-oriented society: "gettin' ahead and goin' places" up the golden ladder to success and respectability. This, then, is the underlying, unifying drive to the forces that account for the rise of organized crime: the mainspring of gambling and its operators and its consumers, the role of various immigrant groups as leaders of organized crime, and the changing needs of the urban political machine.

For all its contributions, Bell's essay has become dated. He busted one myth only to replace it with another: the denial that no nation-wide crime organization exists, call it what you like, the Mob, the Mafia, the Syndicate, or the Cosa Nostra. Today many of those who are knowledgeable about organized crime would vigorously deny Bell's contention that a single nation-wide crime organization is a myth. There has been more evidence to the contrary since his essay appeared. Many of those local, state, and federal law-enforcement officials who were skeptical about the "Syndicate" in the 1950's changed their minds in the 1960's—especially the FBI, largely because of the dynamic leadership of Robert F. Kennedy as Attorney General in the Kennedy administration.[3]

Furthermore, the thesis of ethnic secession has more validity for the years up to the late 'twenties and early 'thirties, than it does for the decades that follow. For more than forty years the Italian-American gangster has not given up leadership to other submerged groups, such as the blacks, the Puerto Ricans, or the Mexican-Americans. This does not mean that every member of that loose confederation of urban and regional groups that make

3. There is a vast literature on crime, varying enormously in quality. Curiously, the professional scholars of the academic community, especially historians, have shown little or no interest in organized crime and its relation to and impact upon American society. They have left the subject largely to journalists and a sprinkling of social scientists and public officials. Perhaps historians feel it is not a "respectable" subject, even though for many years it has been a part of our social, cultural, and political history.

Among the recent studies that would both deny Bell's claim that there is no national crime organization and expand our knowledge about organized crime are: the President's Commission on Law Enforcement and Administration of Justice, *The Cause of Crime in a Free Society* (Washington, D.C.: U.S. Government Printing Office, 1967), and *Task Force Report: Organized Crime, Annotations and Consultants' Papers* (Washington, D.C.: U.S. Government Printing Office, 1967). The best scholarly monograph is by Donald R. Cressey, a distinguished criminologist, *Theft of the Nation: The Structure and Operations of Organized Crime in America* (New York: Harper and Row, 1969). See also Ralph Salerno and John S. Tompkins, *The Crime Confederation* (Garden City, N.Y.: Doubleday and Co., 1969), Peter Mass, *The Valachi Papers* (New York: G. P. Putnam's Sons, 1968), Gay Talese, *Honor Thy Father* (New York: World Publishing, 1971), Nicholas Gage, *The Mafia Is Not an Equal Opportunity Employer* (New York: McGraw-Hill, 1971), Ovid Demaris, *Captive City* (New York: Lyle Stuart, Inc., 1969); the best book on Al Capone is John Kobler, *Capone* (New York: G. P. Putnam's Sons, 1971); Jack McPhaul, *Johnny Torrio* (New Rochelle, N.Y.: Arlington House, 1970), the books of Hank Messick: *Lansky* (New York: G. P. Putnam's Sons, 1971), *Syndicate Abroad* (New York: Macmillan, 1969), *Secret File* (New York: G. P. Putnam's Sons, 1969), *Syndicate Wife* (New York: Macmillan, 1968), *Syndicate in the Sun* (New York: Macmillan, 1968), and *The Silent Syndicate* (New York: Macmillan, 1967); Ed Reid, *The Grim Reapers* (Chicago: Henry Regnery Co., 1969), Alvin Moscow, *Merchants of Heroin* (New York: The Dial Press, 1968); Fred J. Cook, *The Secret Rulers* (New York: Duell, Sloan and Pearce, 1966); Wallace Turner, *Gamblers' Money* (Boston: Houghton Mifflin, 1965); Ed Reid and Ovid Demaris, *The Green Felt Jungle* (New York: Trident Press, 1963); Raymond V. Martin, *Revolt in the Mafia* (New York: Duell, Sloan and Pearce, 1963); Gus Tyler (ed.), *Organized Crime in America* (Ann Arbor: University of Michigan Press, 1962); Robert F. Kennedy, *The Enemy Within* (New York: Harper, 1960); Earl Johnson, Jr., "Organized Crime: Challenge to the American Legal System," *Journal of Criminal Law, Criminology and Police Science* (December 1962, and January 1963); Robert T. Anderson, "From Mafia to Cosa Nostra," *American Journal of Sociology* (November 1965); Daniel P. Moynihan, "The Private Government of Crime," *The Reporter* (July 6, 1961); Michele Pantaleone, *The Mafia and Politics* (New York: Coward-McCann, 1966), John A. Gardiner, *The Politics of Corruption: Organized Crime in an American City* (New York: Russell Sage Foundation, 1970), Joseph L. Albini, *The American Mafia* (New York: Appleton-Century, 1971), Francis A. J. Ianni, "The Mafia and the Web of Kinship," *Public Interest* (Winter 1971), Thomas C. Schelling, "Economics and Criminal Enterprise," *Public Interest* (Spring 1967), and Mark H. Haller's excellent "Organized Crime in Urban Society: Chicago in the Twentieth Century," *Journal of Social History* (Winter 1971-72).

up organized crime is an Italian-American. It does mean that while the Italian-Americans have dominated criminal leadership since the days of Al Capone and Charlie "Lucky" Luciano, they have done so by working closely with other ethnic groups. The long, astonishing career of the Jewish gangster, Meyer Lansky, is a case in point. Also a glance at the roster of the powerful Cleveland Mob of the 1950's, will reveal names of men with a variety of ethnic backgrounds, such as Moe Dalitz, Morris Heinman, Louis Rothkopkf, Charles Polizzi, Sam Tucker, and Tommy McGinty.

The next selection is from one of the best students of the urban Italian community. Humbert S. Nelli is also one of the very few *professional* historians who have seriously studied organized crime in urban America. He could not have picked a better city—Chicago, or a better time—the late nineteenth century through Prohibition, to explore the relation of the Italian community to organized crime. For example, in 1916 Chicago alone had twenty more murders than all of England and Wales together. In 1921 there were only 95 robberies in England. Chicago had 2147.

Nelli establishes three major themes: crime served as a means for immigrants to adjust to a new urban environment; crime was not shaped by Mafia traditions rooted in Sicily, but from the social conditions, the values, the opportunities found in the new world; and, finally, contrary to popular belief, the origins of organized crime in Chicago existed long before Prohibition. Nelli shows that the first major figure in the Chicago underworld, the flamboyant Big Jim Colosimo, was not in fact the creator of organized crime in that city. That dubious honor goes to an Irish gambler, Michael Cassius McDonald, who built the first syndicate back in the 1870's. After clearing the air of misconceptions about the Black Hand Society, a mysterious Italian criminal group which preyed upon the Italian community, Nelli gives us a fascinating analysis of the role of the "Big Fellow," Al Capone, in the rise of big-time crime in the booming, bloody days of Prohibition.

In the next essay, Nathan Glazer and Daniel Moynihan look at assimilation in a different way; indeed, they challenge it as a process and as a reality insofar as it accounts for one of America's favorite concepts of itself—the notion of the melting pot. For years the popular image of the American as a national group has been seen as the result of a kind of ethnic recipe: add a dash of French and Greek, pinches of Poles and Scandinavians, flavor heavily with English, add generous portions of Irish, Jews, and Italians and you produce a marvelous blend, the American, the tasty homogenous mixture of a variety of ethnic, religious, and national groups. This is a myth, argue Glazer and Moynihan: individuals assimilate, but cultural groups do not assimilate to the point where they produce a "seamless national web." If the metaphor of the cauldron must be used, America may be seen more as a boiling pot than a melting pot.

To fortify their argument, Glazer and Moynihan use as a test case the biggest pot of them all, New York City. They examine the recent history of the four most important subcultures that embrace the ethnic and religious pattern of New York—the Jews, Catholics, Negroes, and Puerto Ricans—and conclude that their differences and divisions rather than their melting are increasing. Their thesis is that American nationality is still brewing; it is not yet "done" and the divisive ingredients of religion and race will for the future make the American city very much a boiling pot.

The next selection shows which cities make the pot boil over and why. Gilbert Osofsky charts the making of Harlem, the nation's largest ghetto, a study of internal migration and the failure of assimilation. During the First World War the travels of the Negro from the South to the big cities in the North constituted one of the great folk wanderings in American history. If the foreign newcomer added the spice of diversity to the American city, so did the Negro as he filled the bleak pockets of the ghettos of Philadelphia, New York, Chicago, Cleveland, and Washington. If the slum of the white immigrant changed during the twentieth century, allowing many to scramble upward to the more affluent ranks of middle-class America, the ghetto of the Negro became more and more the inner city of little or no escape, a fixed eyesore of poverty and despair, a striking contradiction to democratic aspirations.

Osofsky shows that the Manhattan ghetto of today was in fact created by the 1920's.[4] It is the ironic tale of how one of New York's most exclusive residential areas became the city's most depressed area, where one of the main industries was the undertaking business. Of particular interest is his discussion of the split within the Negro community—the cultural antagonisms between the native American Negro and the foreign-born West Indian Negro, which sapped the unity that Harlem needed so desperately during the 1920's.

The Negro was but a minority among the native masses who migrated to the city. What about the untold thousands of farm boys who migrated to the city to help shape the rank and file of the urban working class? Did they "make it" in the big city? How did their experiences compare with those of the foreign newcomer? What did the move cost them in terms of the quality of life and the opportunities they left behind?

These are just some of the questions that Stephan Thernstrom raises in his essay, "Urbanization, Migration, and Social Mobility in Late Nineteenth-Century America," where he quite rightfully argues that historians have tended to deal more with foreign immigration than with the equally important thrust of internal migration.

In a provocative attempt to set the balance straight, Thernstrom becomes a resolute revisionist, flogging cherished notions concerning the migrant, the farm vs. the city, the impact of industrialism upon the worker, and the Ameri-

4. For a study of poverty in New York City in the late eighteenth and early nineteenth century, see Raymond A. Mohl, *Poverty in New York, 1783-1825* (New York: Oxford University Press, 1971).

can success story of rags to riches. Thus, the native migrant was no less exploited than the foreign immigrant; the farm was not superior to the city as a way of life nor as a source of opportunity, for the move to the city was "an advance of a kind . . . even the bottom of the urban heap was a step up from the farms they had left behind." Industrialism neither demoralized the urban worker nor made class lines more rigid. And finally, his major thesis: the notion of the wide-open society that permits the humble to become the elite, is largely a myth. In his discussion of three kinds of social mobility, Thernstrom argues that only a precious few entered the tiny room at the top. Those who made it were either the exceptions, like Andrew Carnegie, or the people who began in the room just below, but not in the basement. For most ex-farm urban workers, social mobility meant a rise to the *middle* of the social ladder or a drop to the lower rung. Thernstrom reminds us that mobility is, after all, a movement that can carry you either upward *or downward*, seemingly an obvious point but nonetheless one not always pinpointed by historians. Perhaps Thernstrom's most imaginative insight is his point about the restless, footloose, geographic mobility of the urbanite on the move, especially its effects upon the class consciousness of the urban worker.[5]

5. See also Stephen Thernstrom and Peter R. Knights, "Men in Motion: Some Data and Speculations about Urban Population Mobility in Nineteenth-Century America," *Journal of Interdisciplinary History,* Vol. I, No. 1 (1970).
   The urban worker was not of course the only constant wanderer. For a discussion of Americans as transients, see Daniel Boorstin, *The Americans: The National Experience* (New York: Random House, 1965), pp. 49-112.

The Making of Immigrant Ghettos 1840–1920

DAVID WARD

The central concentration of urban employment after about 1850 strongly influenced the location and characteristics of the residential areas of new immigrants, most of whom sought low-cost housing close to their places of employment. People of foreign birth soon dominated the central residential quarters, and, although there was considerable mixing of ethnic groups, members of each major group usually concentrated in one area, eventually identified as a ghetto. These central concentrations of low-income groups contrasted strikingly with the peripheral location of the poor in pre-industrial cities.[1] Under the conditions of a pedestrian city, the rich lived in central

From *Cities and Immigrants: A Geography of Change in Nineteenth-Century America* (New York: Oxford University Press, 1971), Copyright © 1971 by Oxford University Press, Inc. pp. 105-121. Reprinted by permission of the publisher. David Ward is an Associate Professor of Geography at The University of Wisconsin.

areas—for convenience as well as for the prestige that came with living close to the city's political and religious institutions—and the immigrant poor tended to squat near the edge of town. Before the Industrial Revolution, the very rich often had developed small and exclusive residential sections beyond the city limits. But with the first signs of industrial and commercial development in the center, they accelerated their outward movement. The lack of transportation, however, greatly restricted suburban residence, and only after adequate systems had been developed were middle-income people able to leave central areas for peripheral cites. The vacated residences were then subdivided to provide cramped housing for new immigrants near to the growing sources of employment.

The first major influx of foreign immigrants took place before either urban employment had been centralized or local transportation had been improved; consequently, the residential pattern of the mid-nineteenth-century American city was transitional between pre-industrial and modern. Before the Civil War, Irish and German immigrants concentrated in central locations abandoned by more prosperous residents, but this source of housing served only a small part of the total influx. Others had to seek accommodation and employment in almost every section of the city, and many squatted in peripheral "shanty-towns," which were displaced only after the Civil War when streetcar systems opened new areas to middle-income development. At the same time, businesses also made claims on adjacent residential areas, and, although these areas were expanding outwards, most later immigrant arrivals were housed on the immediate edge of the central business district—by in-

creasing the density of buildings and the number of people in each building.

Indeed, the most frequent theme of past evaluations of immigrant residential districts was the mortal and socially pathological repercussion of congested and unsanitary housing conditions. These districts came to symbolize both material and social failure in urban America and were often erroneously identified with high rates of infant mortality, crime, prostitution, drunkenness, and various other symptoms of social ills. Thus it was assumed that the living conditions endured by immigrants undermined personal health and domestic morality. Furthermore, the tendency of immigrants of similar nationalities and religions to congregate in ghettoes was often regarded as a threat to the "Americanization" or assimilation of the newcomer. Sensitive observers argued that housing reform and the regulation of living conditions would remove the major causes of the social problems, but less optimistic observers were convinced that restricting the entry of the more recent (and apparently less desirable) immigrants would alone solve the basic causes of urban problems. The bulk of the literature on immigrant living conditions, therefore, was strongly influenced by the political polemics of housing reform or immigration restriction, and, although existing records provided detailed and often penetrating evaluations of ghettoes, they rarely isolated the generic from the purely local characteristics of their particular investigation.[2]

THE LOCATION OF IMMIGRANT RESIDENTIAL DISTRICTS

Yet observers were generally able to agree that most immigrants congregated on the edge of the central business district, which provided the largest and most diverse source of unskilled employment. Although local transportation was improved and extended, many immigrants had jobs with long and awkward hours and preferred a short walk to work. Almost all immigrant families depended on the wages of every adult member of the family; consequently, the multiplication of low individual commuter fares inflated transportation costs beyond the means of most low-income families.[3] The tenure of most unskilled occupations was also characteristically uncertain, and daily hiring was the common procedure in general laboring. Immigrants thus faced not only constant changes in the locations of their work,[4] but also frequent spells of unemployment, and under these circumstances convenient access to the central business district was almost a necessity for workers who periodically were forced to search for substitute employment. Suburban industrial districts also attracted many immigrants, and cheap housing was built nearby, but residential areas close to the city center supported far larger numbers of immigrants because of the variety of industrial and commercial employment available there. Only in specialized manufacturing cities, where concentrations of large-scale industrial plants frequently employed more people than the central business district, were substantially fewer immigrants housed in central areas.

The first generation of immigrants to arrive in American cities in large numbers often provided almost the entire labor force in certain activities of the central business district, for the tendency of individual groups to specialize was marked. Irish immigrants found employment in the warehouses and terminal facilities they had helped to build, while German immigrants worked in the sewing machine and consumer supply trades, which were housed in the upper stories of warehouses.[5] New arrivals from Italy in part replaced the Irish as general laborers and were attracted to distributing fresh food from the central wholesale markets.[6] Jewish immigrants, equipped with long experience in the handicraft industries and the local commercial life of Eastern Europe, quickly developed many branches of merchandising at a time when the retail and wholesale segments of marketing were firmly established as distinct and specialized areas in the central business district.[7] Members of this group also rapidly took over the ready-made clothing industry, and, although they diverted production from warehouses to residential premises, the credit and informational needs of the industry still demanded locations with ready access to the central business district. Also, many of the immigrant businesses, which originally provided only for the distinctive material or dietary needs of the immigrant community, eventually expanded to serve far wider urban, regional, and national markets.

The residential fringe of the central business and manufacturing districts also indirectly provided by far the largest supply of cheap housing in most cities, for the threat of commercial and industrial expansion encouraged families whose income and working hours permitted a longer journey to work to abandon central residential areas. Before abandoned dwellings were demolished, the single-family houses were usually converted into multi-family tenements and their rear yards or surrounding grounds were filled with cheap new structures. Apartments rented at rates appropriate to the low incomes of most immigrants, but overcrowding, dilapidated structures, and unsanitary living conditions made even low rents exorbitant. Since the rents for units providing minimum housing needs were far beyond the means of most immigrants, few satisfactory low-rent structures were built.

Yet not all centrally located residential districts were taken over by immigrants immediately after the departure of the previous residents. In particular, spacious houses once belonging to the wealthiest members of the middle class were often utilized as lodging houses for single professional and clerical workers. Generally, these houses were further removed from the edge of the central business district than were the tenement districts, and it was assumed that converting them to lodging houses would not only maintain the status of the area, but would also be less costly than conversion to multi-family units.[8] These dwellings were the only centrally located housing available to black Americans when they arrived in northern cities in large numbers after about 1900.[9] The ratio of plumbing to rooms made the houses unsuitable for multi-family occupancy, but by then all alternative central and low cost housing had been preempted by European immigrants.

Most central residential districts, however, had been vacated on the assumption that demolition and commercial redevelopment would proceed quite rapidly. Thus capital improvements to the dwellings during the period of initial immigrant occupancy were extremely limited. But, there were often unanticipated delays in the expansion of commerce or industry, and, with the continued arrival of large numbers of immigrants, dilapidated tenements were demolished or removed to the rear of the lot and new multi-story structures were built on the vacant space. In older eastern cities, and especially in New York, the complete redevelopment of an entire lot with a five- or six-story structure was common, but in newer cities the relocation of the original building and the construction of two- to six-family tenements in the remaining space was the usual course. In cities with limited amounts of older housing, low-cost dwellings were constructed on newly platted land, and frequently drainage problems and the lack of adequate utilities rather than housing density created the major difficulties. Yet it was the construction of multi-story tenements for large numbers of families that excited the greatest popular concern in the late nineteenth century, and new minimum housing standards were designed, primarily to prevent the overcrowding of lots with tall structures. Because the new standards increased construction costs, rents in the improved buildings were often too expensive for low-income immigrants, and they continued to seek accommodation in older structures.[10]

THE INTERNAL SPATIAL STRUCTURE OF IMMIGRANT DISTRICTS

Living Conditions

Although the common material deficiencies of the immigrant residential districts attracted considerable publicity and legislative activity, living conditions in those areas varied conspicuously both in quality and in the effects they had on the vital rates of the resident populations. Evaluations of conditions at the time emphasized the physically debilitating effects of over-crowded housing; nevertheless, local exceptions to the assumed relationship between mortality or morbidity and congestion aroused great curiosity. Although newly arrived immigrants tended to live in more cramped quarters than more established groups, the overall death rate of the populations of foreign birth were frequently somewhat lower than those of foreign parentage. The age structures of the newer immigrant groups, however, were dominated by vigorous young adults, whereas the earlier groups included large numbers of both very young and old people. Thus, although many earlier groups had moved into less crowded and often better housing, their more balanced age structures exposed them to the inflationary effects of higher death rates among infants and older adults.[11]

Yet age structure alone failed to explain strong contrasts in the death rates of groups with similar proportions of people of foreign birth and parentage. Russian-Jewish and Italian immigrants, for example, often lived alongside each other in extremely congested quarters, and, although the greater prevalence of family immigration among the Jews supposedly made them more vulnerable to infant mortality, such rates among the Russian-Jews were often the lowest in the city, whereas among Italians they were often nearly the highest. Most observers attributed the low death rates to the urban ancestry of Jewish people who, unlike most other immigrant groups, had made their adjustments to slum conditions long before arriving in Amer-

ican cities. In particular, there was an extremely low death rate among Russian Jews from pulmonary tuberculosis, one of the leading causes of death in the crowded areas; this immunity was shared by their co-religionists in European cities.[12] Some authorities attributed the extremely high death rate of Italians to dietary deficiencies and lack of familiarity with the severe American winter.[13] Even longer established immigrant groups also exhibited sharp contrasts in their mortality characteristics. People of Irish birth and parentage were afflicted with unusually high death rates throughout the nineteenth century, and tuberculosis, in particular, was more prevalent than among other immigrants who had arrived during the same period.[14] Finally, mortality rates were frequently high among people of native parentage who lived in immigrant neighborhoods because they were either the oldest or the most impoverished remaining members of the earlier resident group.

In spite of these demographic and ethnic considerations, most authorities rarely identified the spatial implications of the relationship between congested living conditions, high mortality, and large numbers of different ethnic groups and generally assumed that within the city high population density, high death rates, and high proportions of immigrants exhibited identical rather than separate distributions. On the basis of data for New York City and Brooklyn in 1890, it has been possible to demonstrate that high age-standardized death rates and a high population density per built-up acre occurred in quite separate locations which were associated with different ethnic groups.[15] For example, the population of Russian-Jewish parentage was strongly associated with high density and that of Italian parentage with high mortality, although the association was somewhat weaker. Earlier immigrant groups were not clearly connected with either high density or high mortality, and the ethnically more diverse districts occupied by long-established groups probably obscured a frequently publicized association between Irish populations and high mortality.

To summarize, a descriptive model of immigrant districts might show high mortality rates, a high population density, and proportionately large populations of immigrants as circles which occupy largely separate but occasionally overlapping locations within a large city (Fig. 1). Areas which are described by different combinations of more than one of the three most widely publicized characteristics of immigrant quarters indicated above record the effects of distinctive ethnic groups. Area A describes districts with all three characteristics and represents the worst sections of the Italian ghetto; Area B, extremely crowded districts but ones with low death rates—clearly the Russian Jewish ghetto; and Area C, less congested sections with high mortality, representing earlier and frequently Irish immigrant groups. Area D, which combines high mortality and high density, describes remnant and impoverished populations of native parentage.

Quite apart from the different adjustments of ethnic groups to their housing environment, the rapid improvements in sanitation, piped water supply, and building practices changed the quality of the urban environment. At a time when housing reformers

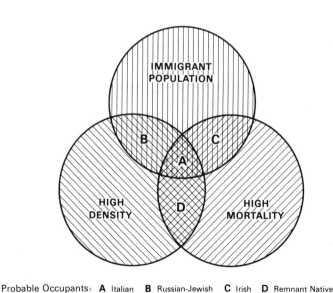

Probable Occupants: **A** Italian **B** Russian-Jewish **C** Irish **D** Remnant Native

Figure 1. Model of the Internal Spatial Structure of Immigrant Residential Districts, 1890

were publicizing the mortal or morbid consequences of congestion, others were popularizing the impact of sanitary engineering on the secular decline in urban death rates.[16] The paradox of declining death rates and increasing congestion could perhaps have been resolved if declining mortality had been confined to the expanding suburban districts, but some of the most spectacular reductions in local death rates took place in overcrowded districts where sanitary conditions had improved. The material rewards of sanitary improvement, however, did not extend to all areas occupied by immigrants, for the arrangement and site conditions of the housing they inherited often defied attempts to improve the surroundings. Districts which originally had been developed as either individual dwellings set in spacious lots or as row houses with substantial front and rear grounds were swamped by cheap new structures in the form of rear tenements or of virtually inaccessible courts. Most sanitary facilities and utilities were confined to the public streets, and little attempt was made to alter this arrangement in the new buildings. The size of the original single-family residences also influenced living conditions, for large houses were frequently subdivided without the addition of new plumbing.

Local site conditions also strongly influenced sanitary improvements. For example, low-lying areas with saturated subsoil remained major centers of unsanitary living conditions. Wherever possible, shallow waterfront locations and local water bodies had been filled to create new land for both commercial and residential developments. Until about the mid-nineteenth century, there were no restrictions on the composition or the subsequent topography of the fill; thus buildings were often constructed on inadequate base material and were associated with threats to public health which could not be removed except by expensive redevelopments of entire localities.[17] Finally, the unsanitary practices of slaughter houses, breweries, and horse stables, which were frequently found side by side with immigrant housing, also influenced local living conditions.

For these reasons, it was possible for cities with neither extremely high-density residential districts nor extensive central concentrations of immigrants to have morbid living conditions. Even among the immigrant districts of the largest cities there was considerable variation in the proportions of high-density dwellings. For example, although more than half of the residential buildings in the immigrant districts of New York City contained more than six dwellings, more than two thirds of the residential buildings in Philadelphia were single-family dwellings . . . .   , In spite of these apparent advantages in housing, however, mortality rates in Philadelphia were among the highest in the nation, largely because of structural defects and the lack of adequate water supply and sewage disposal.[18] Immigrant districts in Chicago and St. Louis were characterized by large proportions of two- and three-family structures, but again structural defects and the neglect of sanitation created debilitating living conditions. Since overcrowded and ill-ventilated rooms, poor water, and lack of sewerage and street-cleaning systems were the common discomforts of most immigrant districts, the selective effects of sanitary improvements within and between cities strongly

Inter-City Contrasts in Immigrant
Housing Characteristics, 1890

Per Cent Deviation of Each Individual City from the Mean for All Six Cities: 1890							
Families per Dwelling:	1	2	3	4	5	6	7-9	9+
Mean Per Cent	27.2	21.9	13.9	9.3	5.5	4.7	7.0	10.4
New York	−13.8	−14.9	−6.7	−2.7	0.0	0.8	8.9	28.5
Boston	−5.8	5.3	12.1	0.5	−0.4	−0.6	−2.6	−8.4
Philadelphia	39.1	−5.8	−6.2	−4.5	−3.3	−3.3	−5.9	−10.1
Chicago	7.5	3.4	1.1	2.8	−0.2	−0.8	−4.1	−9.7
Brooklyn	−9.4	1.0	4.0	2.1	4.5	4.7	2.7	−7.7
St. Louis	4.9	16.1	−2.3	0.9	−2.2	−2.4	−4.4	−8.8

None: Statistics refer only to those wards with more than 70 per cent of their populations of foreign parentage.

influenced the morbid effects of the urban environment.[19]

Social Characteristics

Congested living quarters were frequently regarded as a basic cause of not only high rates of sickness and death but also of social disorganization among immigrants. It was for long assumed that the behavior in many low-income immigrant neighborhoods was socially pathological and directly related to the breakdown of the traditional social organization of rural people in the impersonal and anonymous social environment of the city. Subsequent reevaluations of low-income neighborhoods have suggested that many observers failed to identify the presence of adequate and even elaborate social organization among immigrant populations largely because their behavior and priorities were different from those of suburban or native America.[20] Indeed, most newly arrived immigrants were hardly aware of the society of middle- and high-income native Americans with whom they were apparently expected to assimilate. Instead, their initial exposure was to earlier immigrant groups who had gradually gained control of segments of the political and economic life of many cities. Moreover, once a ghetto was established, it became in part a voluntary association. Most immigrants preferred to spend their early years in the city in a district where their fellow countrymen or coreligionists—often their friends and relatives—lived.[21] Under these circumstances, although few escaped the material and social discomforts of crowded living, some groups were able to avoid severe social disorganization and occasionally to attract laudatory, if often condescending, comments upon the stability and moral orthodoxy of their family and neighborhood life.[22] Although both legitimate and corrupt forms of political patronage excited popular condemnation, residential concentration provided large immigrant groups with proportionate shares of patronage at a time when public welfare was weakly developed.[23]

These social attractions and political advantages, however, were not shared by all immigrant groups nor did they exist in all central districts. Small groups not only lacked the numbers to support their own institutions but also rarely received their share of political patronage or jobs. Young single men living in rooming houses—those who hoped eventually to return home with the profits of American employment—were particularly affected, and their social predicament was often reflected in socially pathological behavior.[24] The age structure, sex ratio, and diverse ethnic characteristics of these quarters clearly distinguish them from those more typical immigrant ghettoes in which one or two large immigrant groups composed largely of families dominated extensive residential sections.[25]

THE EFFECT OF BUSINESS EXPANSION ON IMMIGRANT CONCENTRATION

Even the largest and most stable immigrant groups were unable, however, to establish enduring ghettoes in central fringe areas threatened by the continuous invasion of business premises. Different edges of the central business district expanded at different rates at different times, and this selective expansion of commercial premises was in part responsible for the variations in the living conditions and social characteristics of the central concentrations of immigrants. Early students of urban ecology emphasized the blighting effects of the central business district on adjacent areas and, in keeping with descriptions of these locations, concentrated upon their common material and social deficiencies.[26] Nevertheless, most ecologists acknowledged

that the zone of blight was occasionally interrupted by high-income residences, and, subsequently, a sector arrangement of urban residential types was suggested to accommodate substantial variations in the rent levels.[27] The survival of both high-income districts and well organized ghettoes in central locations has been related to the sentiments and values of the occupants,[28] and, although these perspectives indicate more clearly the range of living conditions and social characteristics, their relationship to the selective and sequential emergence of different segments of the central business district remains obscure.

Both the rate and the extent of the advance of the business district clearly influenced the longevity of adjacent residential quarters and therefore, the material and social conditions of immigrants who settled there.[29] From the discussion of sequential expansion in Chapter 3, it is clear that on some margins of the central business district commercial activities followed so closely after the original inhabitants had left that newcomers had neither the time nor the incentive to establish a stable community (Fig. 2). These districts were occupied most frequently by the smallest or poorest immigrant groups along with the older and often more impoverished members of earlier groups that had moved on to better locations. Manifestations of social disorganization were thus rooted in the insecurity of residential tenure, frequent population turnover, and the failure of any one immigrant group to establish the institutional fabric of the ghetto. In contrast, other margins remained remarkably stable throughout the nineteenth century. . . . Where commercial encroachment was limited, for example,

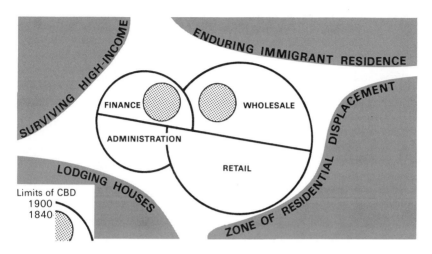

Figure 2. Diagrammatic Representation of the Relative Locations of Different Central Residential Areas

immigrants were able to establish enduring ghettoes and, indeed, areas which had initially been occupied by Irish and German immigrants eventually passed to Italian, Russian Jewish, and other later arrivals toward the turn of the century.

The selective characteristics of business expansion also allowed some residents of adjacent districts to maintain their homes and, consequently, influenced the location of surviving central high-income districts. Although site or historic status were the most frequently publicized advantages of central high-income districts, most large cities had several alternative locations similarly endowed but which had capitulated to immigrant settlement and business encroachment. Yet one segment of the central business district—the financial and administrative—attracted rather than discouraged people of wealth and status . . . , and throughout the nineteenth century many families highly valued living close to the seats of financial and political power. Since this district provided decidedly limited opportunities for unskilled employment, the demand for low-rent housing was much weaker than on margins adjoining the center of unskilled employment. Ecological theory clearly recognized the spatial impact of the central business district on adjacent residential districts, but it should be noted that the impact was selective and, therefore, responsible for the impressive variations in the material and social conditions of this central residential zone.

The term "ghetto" frequently has been applied to concentrations of poverty-stricken immigrants living in congested and segregated areas. It has been suggested that the progressive enlargement and internal spatial differentiation of immigrant areas limited the generic applicability of the term to restricted parts of the city. Because of the limited supply of abandoned housing and the dispersed pattern of urban employment, the Irish and German immigrants who arrived in American cities before the Civil War found housing in almost every section of the city. The largest single immigrant concentrations were in central locations, but many also settled in "shantytowns" beyond the physical limits of the city. The expansions of streetcar systems in the 1870's and their electrification in the 1880's encouraged most middle-income people of native parentage to leave central residential locations. During the same period the concentration of employment opportunities for immigrants in the central business district encouraged a proportionately greater central concentration of new arrivals from southern and eastern Europe, and by about 1900 immigrants of diverse ethnic origins occupied extensive sections of the inner city, while many established immigrants sought new accommodations in the inner suburbs.

Immigrants and their children thus accounted for a large, if not a dominant, proportion of the total populations of many large American cities; consequently, the concentration of particular ethnic groups in well defined districts separated them from other ethnic groups housed under similar circumstances rather than from a homogenous majority group. Moreover, the boundaries of ethnic ghettoes were seldom fixed or well defined and mixed ethnic populations lived in many immigrant districts.[30] Certainly the degrees of concentration of ethnic groups was not closely related to the quality of their living conditions nor was housing congestion closely related to their vital rates. Although ghettoes were frequently identified with the pathological social problems of urban society, certain advantages of residential concentration were also noted. The variable longevity and diversity of central immigrant concentrations, however, depended on the timing, scale, and direction of the expansion of adjacent non-residential land uses and on the appropriateness of the original housing for multi-family occupancy or a higher density of single-families. These conclusions are not intended to depreciate the amount of the discomfort endured by most immigrant families but rather to imply that the internal spatial structure rather than the common deficiencies of immigrant residential districts may well be more revealing of their generic characteristics.

NOTES

1. G. Sjoberg, *The Pre-industrial City*, New York, 1960, pp. 91-105.
2. E. E. Lampard, "American Historians and the Study of Urbanization," *American Historical Review*, 67, 1961, pp. 49-61.
3. F. H. Streightoff, *Standard of Living Among the Industrial People of America*, Boston and New York, 1911, pp. 22-28; United States Senate Document, No. 22, 62nd Congress, 1st Session, Serial 6082, *Cost of Living in American Towns*, Washington, D.C., 1911, pp. iv-v; E. E. Pratt, *Industrial Causes of Congestion of Population in New York City*, New York, 1911, pp. 116-85; H. L. Cargill, "Small Houses for Workingmen," in R. W. DeForest and L. Veiller, eds. *The Tenement House Problem*, Vol. 1, New York, 1903, pp. 331-32.
4. F. W. Streightoff, *op. cit.*, pp. 30-34.
5. R. Ernst, *Immigrant Life in New York City: 1825-1863*, New York, 1949, pp. 61-77; O. Handlin, *Boston's Immigrants*, Cambridge, 1959, pp. 54-87.
6. R. F. Foerster, *The Italian Emigration of Our Times*, Cambridge, 1919, pp. 332-44; E. Lord, et al., *The Italian in America*, New York, 1905, pp. 66-69.
7. S. Joseph, *Jewish Immigration to the United States from 1881 to 1910*, New York, 1914, pp. 42-46; C. S. Bernheimer, ed., *The Russian Jew in the United States*, Philadelphia, 1905, pp. 102-21.

8. A. B. Wolfe, *The Lodging House Problem in Boston*, Cambridge, 1913, pp. 9-14, 39-50.
9. G. Osofsky, *The Making of a Ghetto*, New York, 1967, pp. 105-49; E. F. Frazier, "Negro Harlem: An Ecological Study," *American Journal of Sociology*, 1937, pp. 72-88; A. H. Spear, *Black Chicago: The Making of a Negro Ghetto, 1890-1920*, Chicago, 1967, pp. 11-27.
10. L. Veiller, "Housing Conditions and Tenement Laws in Leading American Cities," in R. W. De Forest and L. Veiller, eds., *op. cit.*, pp. 129-72; E. E. Wood, *The Housing of the Unskilled Wage Earner*, New York, 1919, p. 25; C. Aronovici, "The Cost of a Decent Home," *Forum*, 58, 1914, pp. 111-12; R. Lubove, *The Progressives and the Slums*, Pittsburgh, 1962, pp. 217-56; J. Ford, *Slums and Housing*, Cambridge, 1936, pp. 72-204.
11. W. H. Guilfoy, "The Death Rate of the City of New York as Affected by the Cosmopolitan Character of Its Population," *Quarterly Publications of the American Statistical Association*, 10, 1907, pp. 515-22; F. L. Hoffman, "The General Death Rate of Large American Cities: 1871-1904," *Quarterly Publications of the American Statistical Association*, 10, 1906-7, pp. 1-75.
12. M. Fishberg, "Health and Sanitation of the Immigrant Jewish Population of New York," *The Menorah*, 33, 1902, pp. 37-46, 73-82, 168-180; L. I. Dublin, "The Mortality of Foreign Race Stocks in Pennsylvania and New York: 1910," *Quarterly Publication of the American Statistical Association*, 17, 1920-21, pp. 13-44.
13. Kate H. Claghorn, "Foreign Immigrants in New York City," *Report of the Industrial Commission*, 15, 1901, pp. 449-91; R. Brindisi, "The Italian and Public Health," *Charities*, 12, 1904, pp. 443-504.
14. William H. Guilfoy, *op. cit.*, pp. 515-22; Kate H. Claghorn, *op. cit.*, pp. 460-61.
15. D. Ward, "The Internal Spatial Structure of Immigrant Residential Districts in the Late Nineteenth Century," *Geographical Analysis*, 1, 1969, pp. 337-53.
16. F. L. Hoffman, "American Mortality Progress During the Last Half Century," in Mazyck P. Ravenal, ed., *A Half Century of Public Health*, New York, 1921, pp. 94-117; G. E. Clark, "Sanitary Improvement in New York During the Last Quarter of a Century," *Popular Science Monthly*, 39, 1891, 319-30.
17. J. S. Billings, "Municipal Sanitation: Defects in American Cities," *Forum*, 15, 1893, pp. 304-10.
18. C. F. Wingate, "The City's Health—Sanitary Construction," *Municipal Affairs*, 2, 1898, pp. 261-70.
19. United States Senate Document, No. 338, 61st Congress, 2nd Session, Serial No. 5665, *Report of the Immigration Commission*, 1911, Vol. 66, *Immigrants in Cities*, Washington, 1911, p. 5.
20. W. F. Whyte, *The Street Corner Society*, Chicago, 1943, pp. 94-104, 255-278; H. J. Gans, *The Urban Villagers*, New York, 1962, pp. 3-41.
21. R. E. Park and H. A. Miller, *Old World Traits Transplanted*, New York, 1921, pp. 60-80; C. F. Ware, *Greenwich Village, 1920-30*, Boston, 1935, pp. 3-8, 81-126; W. I. Thomas and F. Znaniecki, *Polish Peasant in Europe and America*, New York, 1927, pp. 1468-1546.
22. W. T. Elsing, "Life in New York Tenement Houses as Seen by a City Missionary," in R. A. Woods, ed., *The Poor in Great Cities*, New York, 1895, pp. 42-85; A. F. Sanborn, "The Anatomy of a Tenement Street," *Forum*, 18, 1894, pp. 554-72.
23. T. J. Lowi, *At the Pleasure of the Mayor: Power and Patronage in New York City: 1898-1958*, New York, 1964.
24. H. W. Zorbaugh, *The Gold Coast and the Slum*, Chicago, 1929, pp. 142-51; R. A. Woods, ed., *The City Wilderness*, Boston, 1898, pp. 33-57; E. Abbott, *The Tenements of Chicago: 1908-1935*, Chicago, 1936, p. 100.
25. G. C. Homans, *The Human Group*, New York, 1950, pp. 334-68; H. W. Zorbaugh, *op. cit.*, p. 129; W. I. Firey, *Land Use in Central Boston*, Cambridge, 1947, pp. 170-97, 290-313.
26. E. W. Burgess, "The Growth of the City," in R. E. Park, ed., *The City*, 1925, pp. 47-62.
27. H. Hoyt, *The Structure and the Growth of Residential Neighborhoods in American Cities*, Washington, D.C., 1939.
28. W. I. Firey, "Sentiment and Symbolism as Ecological Variables," *American Sociological Review*, 10, 1945, pp. 140-48.
29. D. Ward, "The Emergence of Central Immigrant Ghettoes in American Cities: 1840-1920," *Annals of the Association of American Geographers*, 58, 1968, pp. 343-59.
30. *Report of the Immigration Commission, op. cit.*, pp. 6-8.

Generations

OScar Handlin

Sometimes at night she'd wake and turn to feel if he were there. She'd reach the space across to where he lay, sense the reassuring bulk of him. She'd hug the thought. *All else has passed away with our passing from that place. But this will never change. By holy matrimony he has made me wife and mother to his family. That* (fiercely) *we can hold intact.*

In morning's light the certainty was gone. Through the day the fear came that this most intimate part of life would not remain the same. At the stove later she paused while the long spoon in her hand continued its mechanical stirring; she looked in bewilderment at the gathering table. Would the strangeness of the setting make strangers also of these her dear ones? Resolve came back, but confidence not altogether. It would be a desperate battle to hold firm in these relationships, outside the context that had nurtured them.

The difficulty was that formerly the family had not been a thing in itself, but an integral element of the village community. It had been fixed in a framework of numerous links and knots that held each individual within it in his place. As the functioning unit within the economy it was the means through which bread was produced and con-

sumed. No one could live except as the member of a family.

As the medium for holding and transmitting land, its stability had been vital to social order. Every change in its structure affected the whole community. On the quality of a single marriage depended the welfare of all the brothers and sisters and less directly a widening circle of other persons. The connection with the soil had also been an element in extending these affiliations beyond the single household to a broad range of other kin tied together by inheritance, of blood and of possible claims to a common patrimony.

The family had therefore never been isolated. Its concerns were those of the entire village. While each home was expected to be the source of its own discipline, the community stood ready with sanctions of its own to make sure that children were obedient, that parents were good, and that relatives were helpful to each other. The network of mutual rights and obligations had thus the support of both an inner and an outer control.

Emigration took the family out of the village. The mere going was disruptive. The struggles of departure and resettlement subjected the household to a severe strain under most trying and most unusual conditions and at the same time

From Oscar Handlin, *The Uprooted* (Boston: Little, Brown & Co., 1051), pp. 227-58. Copyright © 1951 by Oscar Handlin. Reprinted by permission of Atlantic-Little, Brown & Co. Oscar Handlin is Charles Warren Professor of History at Harvard University.

deprived it of the counsel and assistance upon which it had traditionally depended. When so many new decisions were to be made, they had to be made alone. That alone distinguished the new family from the old.

In America also the economic unity of the common household enterprise disappeared. The minority who found their way to the farms or who, by their labors, maintained little businesses where wife and children could work along with the father, held on to the former ways. Vestiges of the old order also remained in the sweating homework system; as the father brought back the bundles that would be sewn into shirts or twisted into artificial flowers, the gathered group in the tenement room recaptured the sense of common effort familiar in recollection from the Other Side.

These were, however, but byways in the economy. In the characteristic immigrant employment, the individual was hired as an integer. He was one line in the ledger, one pair of hands on the floor, one pay envelope at the window, with no reference to who was there at home. Ultimately this pattern supplanted all others. Would they continue to take his bidding, to toil in the dim room with him, the one to pocket all, when they could go out to be their own wage earners? There was no point to it. Of what inheritance could he deprive them?

Properly speaking the family no longer had an income; there were only the combined incomes of its members. The larger unit was now a source of weakness rather than of strength. Those who could, broke away; it was madness for a man who was capable of supporting himself to maintain the ties of uncle or cousin when those ties would only draw off a share of his earnings. Those who remembered the old obligations, alas, were generally those more likely to consume than to produce—the aged, the weak, the ill. With these the circumstances, and with no outside force to assign the blame, the extensive family of the Old World disintegrated. *So it is now, a brother stabs his brother, a sister drowns her sister, for profit's sake.*

Steadily the relatives dropped away; the husband, wife, and children were left alone. Where need compelled additions to the income of this narrower household, it was better to take in boarders, tenants, on an impersonal, cash-down basis. The more compelling duties of the old extended family were treacherous here; it was safer by avoiding them to transform the relationship into one of mere occasional sociability.

The bonds to those left at home also disintegrated. There was a piece of land, and if he had not gone away it would have been his; but having gone away he ought not ask that it be sold and money set to him in America. Endless quarreling followed. Or the old folks, staying, bitterly resented the departed son who should have been the staff on which they might lean in age. *You went to make money and you forgot that you left parents; may God and your own children care for you as you for us.*

Is it the loss of income they minded, or the sadness of being abandoned? *We cannot know whether we shall yet speak with you, embrace you, at least once before our death.* It does not matter. The demands are too heavy on both emotions and purse. The old ties gradually are loosened. The family steadily tapers down to the conjugal unit, a father, a mother, and their immediate offspring. The New World has separated them from all the others who would have been one with them in the Old.

Perhaps for that reason she wished so intensely to hold together what was left. From mistress in an extensive household she had become mother of a more intimate group; that hard core she would labor to keep intact.

The early experiences of the new family entity fed her hopes. That they were cut off from all else that was familiar led the members to value each other the more. With whom else could they discuss the memories of the past and the problems of the present? Depending upon each other because there was no one else upon whom they could depend, they drew steadily together.

The very process of migration had been shared. Mostly they had come together, together faced the open road and the close quarters of the steerage. In the long lapse of time between departure and arrival, they were deprived of the busying occupations of the farm, of the comradeship of neighbors, and had for company only one another. The occasion was one for deeper understanding; and long after the final settlement, recollections would come back of the joys and tribulations of the way, come back to unite those who had made the journey together.

The warmth of participation in the enterprise of crossing cheered even those later immigrants who divided for the critical steps, husband first to make a start, wife and children after. Such a separation created problems of its own, but it did not of itself lessen the attachment of the partners to it. Though the ocean lay between, they were joined by the gravity of the common effort.

That is why, as the years passed and they thought back to the first exploratory days in America, it seemed to them that the family had been strongest and purest before its exposure to the new life. As strangers they had known no one. Evening brought them always back together. Excited with discoveries or downcast with disappointments, they communicated to one another the freshness of each occurrence. They knew then they were one like the meager loaf from which they would begin each to slice the sustenance of all. It was a tenement room or a sod hut. But it was home; and those who came to it worn out with wandering acquired for home an enduring devotion.

Only soon, the conditions of their being in the United States would break in upon them. The narrow family would not remain alone together. Individually, its members in going out would make each their own adjustments to the society about them, and coming back would be less alike. Man and woman, boy and girl, they would find for themselves new roles and establish for themselves new relationships. It would happen more quickly in the cities than on the farms where a rural environment extended the family's isolation. But ultimately it would happen everywhere. The woman meditating by the stove would resist it. But already as they took their places her heart chilled to the fear of failure.

Across the long table they confronted each other, the two who were now central to all. It was as if daily they felt the need of a fresh view of the familiar features in the light of the new experiences. In the anxious regards were mingled two questions. Is this the same being united to me those many years ago and now still unchanged? How adequate will this union be to the present demands upon it?

Indeed these were no longer the man and woman joined in wedlock at that distant date; they had never then imagined that such questions might ever arise. Their marriage had not been the product of an individual passion, but a social arrangement under the oversight of the community. She had accepted the obligations of her situation, to be obedient and faithful, to further his health and comfort, to be a good and kindly wife, the crown of her husband's life. He had taken on the responsibilities of the efficient provider who would safeguard her from degrading work, keep want away, and mildly satisfy her will. The union upon which fortune smiled was one blessed with the dignified respect of the partners for their rights and duties.

The day they turned their backs upon the old home, the relationship began to change. At the very outset, the course of the crossing led to troubles. In the long suspended period between departure and arrival, neither he nor she had duties or could expect fixed dues. They were then thrown more together than ever before, but as never before found it difficult to judge one another. The intimacy of shared miseries brought them together, but, as it were, only to be the more conscious of each other's deficiencies. A sorry figure he made, lounging about from day to day with nothing to do; while her derelictions of housewifely obligations were served up in the stale biscuits of every meal.

If migration involved a temporary separation as, after 1880, it often did, the results were more disruptive still.

He went away to the sound of the children's crying; and heard it echo through the months apart. In his unaccustomed singleness, he came to miss what before he had taken for granted, the warmth of the woman's presence. *As the fish thirst for water, so I long for you.*

It is hard to know what may happen across that far dividing distance. *Only I beg you write more often.* As the letters fail to appear, for she is not familiar to the pen, worries take their place, and suspicions. Resentful, he asks a friend in the village to inform him of her doings. Does she hold to the home? At the same time the fear will rise lest she be unable to manage. The stock of grain may be too small, the labor in the field too hard. Cautionary advice covers the pages he sends home.

She has the advantage of waiting in a known place in the company of the children. But her double role is burdensome; she cannot be as he was, head of the household. The boys are unruly and, though she gives them some of the broomstick, they are snow to obey. She hires a hand to help in the field, but he is negligent; he has not for her the fear as for a master. Often she thinks of her husband and what a life he must lead there among strangers, his work heavier than a stone, his strength being drained away into a foreign soil. *The day passes in labor but in the evening I long very much and at night I cannot sleep. We can be united in heart and thought but that satisfies me not. Take us or come back; let it be so or so; as it is I exist neither upon ice nor upon water.*

Sometimes the months stretch out and the separateness widens. He sets himself a goal: I will have a thousand rubles and then send for them. But the goal is never attained. Meanwhile he is hardened in his bachelor life and puts off indefinitely the day of reunion. Or she at home grows reluctant. The dread of the new place mounts up in her and feeds off the complaints in his letters. She wishes him back—enough of this America—and when the call comes, procrastinates.

Whatever division, long or short, appeared in the transplantation was not mended in the resettlement. On the farms, the man could resume his place as head of the household enterprise; but the millions who stayed in the cities found their positions drastically altered. She could not think that he was here satisfying his obligations toward the family. No longer the sole or even the main provider, he seemed to her wanting in the most critical duty of all. Why, there were times when she herself ör the children earned more than he, times when he sat home idle while they went out to bring home his bread. When he was taken on, it was not at work she understood or could respect. Away at some menial task, she could not regard him as she had that husbandman who had once managed their tiny plot and had brought up her sons to follow in his steps.

Nor could he be satisfied as to her adequacy for the life of the New World. Deprived of the usual household chores of the garden, the needle, and the loom, she appeared often lethargic; the blood hardly ran in her veins. On the other hand management of the domestic economy under American conditions was frequently beyond her comprehension. When the results were unhappy—disorderly quarters, poor food—it was hard to draw the line between the effects of negligence and the effects of poverty and ignorance. The necessity that drove her to labor for others was the source of resentment, both because it reflected upon his own abilities and because it took her away from her proper job in the home.

Roles once thoroughly defined were now altogether confounded. The two got on under the continual strain of uncertainty as to their place in the family, as to their relationships to each other. And their experience, no longer one for the two, added constantly to that underlying uncertainty.

Sometimes it was he went out to the wide world, learned the language of the country, and grew sophisticated in the ways of the place, while she was confined to the flat and remained ignorant of the rudiments of English. *I at least know where there's an Eighth Street, and a One Hundred and Thirtieth Street with tin works, and an Eighty-fourth Street with a match factory. I know every block around the World Building and the place where the car line stops. But you know no more than if you had just landed.* Sometimes it was she, in service in some other's home, who earlier learned the ways—what food they ate and clothes they wore and how they sat of an evening in the polished sitting room. It was bitter hard to be the satisfying helpmate when one could hardly guess what wants the other had.

As the situation clarified, aspects at first hidden emerged with oppressive distinctness. In the Old World her status had been fixed by a variety of elements —whose daughter she was, what dowry she brought, into what family she married. Let her husband be unfortunate or unskillful or unthrifty, she had still a set place in the village. Here her fate was completely tied up in his success.

What she was or had been mattered nothing, only what he could do. Well, it was galling to see what other, lesser women had, to watch their men push their way ahead. The utter dependence on his efforts put an acrimonious tone in her greetings as he came nightly home no better than before.

Nagging demands he could not meet confirmed his own inner doubts about himself. Was not the whole migration the story of his succession of failures? He had been unable to hold on to the land, to direct the family comfortably across the ocean or to establish it securely on this side. He felt respect ebb away and carried about a gnawing shame at his own lack of capacity. Most of all, he resented his loss of authority. Indeed he became accustomed to request, not to order, but knew it was not right it should be so; and he resented his wife's growing dominance over the household. It was a poor state of affairs when the cow showed the way to the ox.

In the secret night when her stirring waked him he did not move. Fatigue pinned him down. Yet sleep would not return. Instead an angry tension crept into his heart. Her body's presence intruded on his consciousness. Limbs rigid, he pushed the thought away; to this demand too he would not respond, by so much had he now lost his manhood.

Clenched eyelids would not keep the moonlight out. Not a beam came down the narrow airshaft; still his sight tingled to the streaks reflected from a distant meadow where they had walked amidst the long grasses, and had been young, eager for the enjoyment of each other to which marriage had opened the way. There had been no strain then;

what the community had to that day forbidden, it now welcomed; and these two had been carried along by confidence in the rightness of their acts, by certainty they would each be gratified.

It was coming away that had first added wormwood to the taste. They had lost the benevolent oversight of the village which by its insistence on traditional propriety had answered every how and when. Now the deed required ever a decision; it raised ever some question; and it involved ever some clash of wills, his or hers. By leaving they had created doubts they knew not how to resolve.

He remembered the darkness of successive borrowed beds. In the enforced closeness of boardinghouses and shipboard he had stifled the groping desires. Years later, the confined warmth of many bodies would come back to assault his senses, would bring the painful recollection of urges never satisfied. And in this place that was their own it was rare that wish and opportunity coincided. In the cramped quarters they had been never alone and therefore never really together. Often there was the startling chill of interruption—the uneasy stirring of a child, the banging progress of a neighbor through the ill-lit hall. Always there was the uncertainty of when and how. Even the times when, flushed with the cheap certitude of liquor or with the passing exuberance of some new job, he had asserted his passion, there had followed inevitably an aftermath of regret and doubt. What had really been given and what received in these exchanges?

Perhaps he should not have expected more. He himself knew the dull indifference that came with being often tired. He knew too her deep fear of recurrent childbirth. Not that this was a subject of conversation between them; but it took no words to convey her dismay at each discovery of her condition. But the terms must be accepted, the price paid. Worse would follow the attempt to avoid it; often enough she had heard the stories of such a one, desperate at the approach of an eighth or ninth, who had sought the relief of self-abortion and had found only the painful death of blood poisoning.

Vaguely also they suspected that there were ways of forestalling pregnancy. But the old wives' knowledge did not extend that far; in this matter the midwife was not helpful; and, as for doctors—why, if a woman had thought of them, she would have found it difficult even to frame the terms of her inquiry. The husband had once cautiously sounded out an apothecary, but got only a jocular response: *Better sleep out on the fire escape, Joe.* Besides it all smacked of the illicit and the shameful. The law frowned on it; the priest cautioned against it; and deep inner forebodings conjured up the visions of nature's reprisals for interference with her processes.

There was, therefore, not much joy to their desiring; the shadow of the reckoning was too close. There was no blame. Only, sometimes, as she nursed her discontent, the thought came to her that, if only he had managed better, all would be otherwise. And he, reading the accusations in her eyes, felt the pangs of a sudden guilt, the acknowledgment of his own inadequacies. At such times, a sullen anger entered the household, lingered unexpressed for days. The mornings when he went to work, he carried off a pained exasperation. Suspicions might come; the scandal of that other's wife, who with the

boarder shamed her home, might cross his mind. The memory galled his wounds and, returned that night, edged his answers with acerbity. Peace then departed in an exchange of taunting words, then blows, and sad conciliation.

Some men surrendered. Confronted by intolerable burdens they deserted their families, lost themselves alone somewhere and put thus an end to this striving. Then the fatherless home, adrift, was not long from its foundering.

Mostly however they held together, the man and woman. Yes, partly it was the thought of the children that kept the family whole and partly it was the consciousness that in abandoning each other they would sever every last tie with their own past, diminish thereby their own human identity. Yes, often as they lay there, longing for escape to an undefined freedom, there was no move simply because the effort seemed too great, the means far out of reach.

But it was more than that that curbed the passing wish to flee. But it was more than that that drew them at last to each other. The old fixed order of respect between husband and wife had disappeared as the obligations on which it rested became irrelevant in the New World. Without the protective cover of well-defined roles they faced each other as individuals under the most trying conditions. That was difficult. But then as he looked upon this person who shared his bed and recalled the long way she had come, the sufferings she had borne, his heart went out to her. And then as she sensed the turning of his eyes upon her and thought of the little pleasure all his efforts brought, her heart went out to him.

It was not pity that sealed them in this attachment, but the brief glimmers of comprehension that they shared a life as they shared a bed. They were individuals, separate, two, and had been so since they left the village. But they had been two together. In those moments of recognition they knew they had been partners in a common experience and were now involved in a common situation. Only in each other could these beings find the complete understanding that would alone bring what they so desperately wanted, some reaffirmation of their own human dignity. For warmth they moved toward each other, for the warmth that came from the knowledge that here was consolation. Another knew and understood. That was a precious certainty, where all else was insecure.

About the children they can feel no certainty whatever.

This country is full of children. In the morning their clatter down the staircase fills the house. In the afternoon they occupy the streets. In the evening they pour back into the waiting flat which they quickly distend with the clamor of their ceaseless activity.

The immigrants were by no means strange to the idea of full families. The little ones had always made up a sizable part of the village population. But the spot had not been so taken up with their presence. They had had each their places, where they ought to be and where they ought not to be. They had had each their functions, what they ought to do and what they ought not to do. They had not been, therefore, so prominent in the sight of their elders.

Perhaps it was because, in these matters as in so much else, the Old World community had been very specific in its definitions of proper behavior. What a parent owed his offspring was clear. The child was to be fed, clothed, and

housed decently as befitted the status and the resources of his father. The boys and girls were to be properly brought up, taught the skills necessary for their own adulthood and imbued with the beliefs necessary for continued membership in the community. It was their due at maturity to receive the land or dowry that would permit them to take the rank their ancestors had held; and one was not unduly to be favored at the expense of his brothers and sisters.

The obligations of the young were equally plain. They were to obey their elders and particularly him who stood at the head of the family, him whom they were to approach always in fear and with respect as the source of all authority. They were to assist, to the extent they were able, in the labors of the common enterprise; every age had its appropriate tasks. Even those fully grown but without households of their own were still to work for their parents. The unmarried had strictly speaking no property, no possessions of their own; if they went out to toil for strangers they were expected still to hand over their earnings to the father.

The neat balance of rights and duties was enforced by the village as a whole. Parents delinquent in the support or the discipline of their progeny, children remiss in compliance, could expect the swift censure of the organized opinion of their neighbors. There was no breaking the pattern of these relationships without a complete break with the community. But conversely, separation from the community by emigration would altogether disrupt the relationships of parents and children.

They might suppose it was the same as they strolled to worship on a holiday, Papa, Mama, and the boys and girls, covering the paved walk in a pair of uneven rows. They were wrong. Even then they knew the momentary solidarity would disintegrate before the day was over. They no longer cohered as a family and, as individuals, could scarcely say how they stood to one another.

The divisions created by differences of experience were too great. The older ones, sedately in the rear, had been eight or nine or in their teens in the year of the crossing. They had vivid memories of the Old Country, of the troubles that drove them off, and of the hardships of the journey. They spoke their mother's language and their unaccustomed English bore a heavy accent that united them with their past. Trained under the discipline of the household that had been, they were still ready to accept obligations. Necessity had long since heaped responsibilities upon them; no doubt they had been wage earners since soon after their arrival.

There was impatience in their scrutiny of the younger ones. Before them were two to be watched, scrabbling along without regard for appearances. These had been infants or little more when the migration came; their early childhood had passed under the unsettled conditions of the transition. They had never learned the proper ways at home, and a brief attendance at the public school had confused them so they knew not where they stood. They were clumsy in the speech of both the old land and the new; their names came from abroad but had already been corrupted into nicknames here. They were neither one thing nor the other.

At the head of the procession toddled the citizens. These more fortunate ones had been born into their environment. They had never known the Old World;

they had not shared the experience of coming. They were Americans from the start, had lisped the words in English, and often received names appropriated from the older inhabitants.

It was at such times the parents were fullest of their responsibilities. As they led the way on these occasions they became gravely conscious of a disturbing uncertainty. What if the children should cease to follow, should take it into their heads to march off in some altogether strange direction! It was difficult enough to show them the right ways around the corners of the city blocks; it was infinitely more difficult to show them the right ways around the twisting curves of the new way of life.

As they consider the heaviness of their tasks, the mother and father grow somber. They remember the failures. Their minds go to that one who came to them as if on a visit, then sickened and went away. It occurs to them that they cannot possibly meet their obligations to the children. Not only that the food will hardly go around to nurture all, not only that the mended garments pass from one to another, but that by the act of migration, they, the parents, have destroyed the birthright of their sons and daughters. These boys who should be picking berries or hunting nuts, these girls who should be approaching mastery of the stove, have all been robbed and must endure the present, enter the future without their proper due. To each other, the parents acknowledge the guilt: *Yes, dear, and therefore let us sacrifice ourselves and live only for them. If there is any hope in this world, it is not for us but for them.*

It was easier to bend the neck in readiness than to be certain that the yoke would fit. With bewilderment the immigrants learned that to be willing to sacrifice was not enough, that their children must be also willing to accept the sacrifice; and of that there could be no confidence. The initial dissimilarities of experience widened with time as youngsters ventured out from the home and subjected themselves to influences foreign to their elders. The life of school and the life of street completed the separation between the generations.

If it did nothing else to the child, the school introduced into his life a rival source of authority. The day the little boy hesitantly made his way into the classroom, the image of the teacher began to compete with that of the father. The one like the other laid down a rigid code of behavior, demanded absolute obedience, and stood ready to punish infractions with swift severity. The day the youngster came back to criticize his home (*They say in school that . . .*) his parents knew they would have to struggle for his loyalty.

That was an additional reason why the immigrants labored to create educational institutions of their own; they hoped thereby to minimize the contest. But the parochial schools were expensive and spread very slowly; they accommodated at best only a small fraction of the children. The strong-minded and well-to-do could hold out against the pleas of their offspring who wished to go where everyone else went; mostly the newcomers were compelled by circumstances and by the law to depend on public instruction.

The building itself was familiar enough; this was one of the known landmarks of the neighborhood. The idea of attendance was also familiar; this had happened already to older brothers and friends. And as the lad entered the yard, even sight of the fellows playing or waiting in line had the appearance of familiarity; he recognized some from around his own block, the others were much like himself. The public school was universal, but each nevertheless reflected the quality of the homogeneous residential district within which it was situated. In effect it was Irish or Jewish or German or Polish; the first impression it made on the new scholar was that of the altogether familiar and the altogether expected.

The ringing bell broke the continuity of his life; as he walked up the cast-iron staircase he left the narrow orbit of his home and moved into the limitless world. He stood in the stiff lines and sat motionless in the formal rows of seats. He learned silence and passivity who had never before felt restraints on his actions. He came to conform to rules: there were ways of rising and of sitting, ways to come dressed, ways to leave the room on certain occasions, and ways without words to signal the need. This order would now be his life.

Mostly the boys accede, and the girls too. At least the youngest do. There are truancies, some from their stubborn will, some from their shame at the poverty of clothing, some from necessity that keeps them home or sends them out to work. But mostly they give in and come. There is vaguely an understanding that the school will help them get on; and everyone else goes, so they go along. Besides they fear the law, want no trouble.

Only often, as they sat in the torpid classrooms, their attention wandered from the drone of recitations. Through the windows, gray filmed-over, they could see the bustle of purposeful men. By contrast, the school seemed empty of achievements, empty of the possibility of achievement. For what reason were they thus confined? What could they hope to gain from all this?

They did not ask those questions. They had long ago heard the trite answers. They came in order to grow up good and useful citizens. How would the school help them? By teaching them what was in these books.

Idly the boys fingered the battered volumes from which wisdom was to flow. There was no need to open them; the bold type of their pages was familiar enough from constant drilling. THIS IS JACK. THIS IS JACK'S HOUSE. THIS IS JACK'S DADDY. JACK GOES SHOPPING. JACK GOES TO SCHOOL. ON THE WAY HE MEETS A COW. ON THE WAY HE MEETS A SHEEP. JACK COMES HOME. JACK FALLS ASLEEP.

And surely enough, across the top from page to page the brightly colored pictures show it all. Blue-eyed and blond, Jack himself stares out over the nice white collar and the neatly buttoned jacket. Across the green lawn, from the porch of the pretty yellow house, a miraculously slim mother waves. By the side of a road that dips through the fields of corn, the animals wait, each in turn to extend its greeting. There it all is, real as life.

Except that it is all a lie. There is no Jack, no house, no brightly smiling "Mummy." In the whole room there is not a boy with such a name, with such an appearance. One can walk streets without end and there will be never a glimpse of the yellow clapboards, of the close-cropped grass. Who sleeps like Jack alone in the prim room by the window to be wakened by singing birds? *Good morning, Mr. Robin.* The whole book is false because nothing in

it touches on the experience of its readers and no element in their experience creeps into its pages.

Falsity runs through all their books, which all were written to be used by other pupils in other schools; even the arithmetic sets its problems in terms of the rural countryside. Falsity runs through all their education. They learn the songs their mothers never sang. They mouth the words of precepts with no meaning: *A rolling stone gathers no moss. Make hay while the sun shines.* But what stone, what moss, what hay? The time that man appeared to speak from the platform and roused them, he shook with his talk until they cheered the thin line at Bunker Hill, at Plymouth through the snow. *Our fathers' God, to Thee.* . . . Then later they thought, *Whose fathers'?* Again a deception!

They themselves compounded the enormity of the untruth by the inability to give it the lie. From the desk the teacher looked down, a challenge they dared not meet. It was foolhardy of course to question her rightness. What an arsenal was at her command to destroy them! The steel-edged ruler across the knuckles was the least of her weapons. Casually she could twist the knife of ridicule in the soreness of their sensibilities; there was so much in their accent, appearance, and manners that was open to mockery. Without effort she could make them doubt themselves; the contrast of positions was too great. As she snapped shut the closet upon the symbols of her ladyhood within—the white gloves, the rolled-up umbrella, and the sedate hat—she indicated at once the superiority of her own status. There was visible evidence of her correctness in her speech and in her bearing, in her dress, and in the frequent intimations of the quality of her upbringing.

Perhaps a few were touched with sympathy at the condition of their charges. But what these offered was pity, nobler than contempt, but to the children no more acceptable. It was rare indeed to find the dedicated woman whose understanding of her students brought a touch of love into her work. After all, it was not of this they had dreamed in normal school when they had surrendered a part of their girlhood to acquire a profession, that they would devote the rest of their lives to the surveillance of a pack of unwashed ruffians. Mostly the teachers kept their distance, kept flickering the hope that a transfer might take them to a nicer district with nicer pupils from nicer homes. When that hope died, bitterness was born; and there was thereafter more savagery than love in their instruction. To admit the least question of the rightness of what they taught would undermine the whole structure of their self-esteem. So a boy should look and be, so a home, and so a parent. Many a woman, tired with all the years of it, looked out at her "scholars" tumbling into the street, and discovered a hidden crumb of satisfaction in the thought they were not so, nor the homes to which they'd go, nor the parents who'd greet them.

It took no uncommon sagacity to learn it was better not to question the teacher's world. The wise fellow kept his mouth shut and accepted it; he came to believe in a universe, divided as it were into two realms, one for school and one for home, and each with rules and modes of behavior of it own.

Acquiescence was no solution, however. Their lives could not be so divided. As the children of the immigrants grew up, they felt increasingly the compulsion to choose between the one way and the other. For some, the vision of the yellow house was peremptory. The kindness of a teacher, taken with the earnestness of the exceptional good student, may have opened the prospect of attaining it. Or the intense will of the ambitious youngster may have done so. Or the desperate dislike of a repressive home may have made this the only tolerable alternative. In any case, this way involved the complete identification with Jack, and that meant the total rejection of the origins and the background Jack could not have had.

Only a few, however, had the ability or the desire to make the radical break. The much greater number recognized the existence of the world they saw through school, were even willing to acknowledge its superiority, but they were not willing or, perhaps, not able to enter it themselves; their ties with their families were still binding. They developed perforce a kind of life of their own, an intermediary ground from which they could enter when necessary both the life of the school and the life of the home.

The setting generally was the street, where the young were free of oversight and masters of themselves. The boys and girls of an age who played together fell spontaneously into little coteries, for the very acts of play depended upon a sense of community and upon some degree of organization. There could be no games without rules and without subjection to the sanctions that enforced them. The interests of these groups changed as their members matured, from childhood to youth to adolescence to adulthood. But with notable persistence the members held together at least until marriage made them heads of families in their own rights or until they moved out of the neighborhood.

The structure of these organizations was simple, although they were endowed with a certain formality that mirrored the associational forms of the immigrant parents. There was a consciousness of belonging; you were in the gang and that set you off from outsiders. The sense of participation was tied to a specific place, a street or a district that was their own. Within the group each individual had a role which reflected his own capacities and qualities—the leader, the fighter, the buffoon, the clever one. And the whole was held together by a code of loyalty; they were in a common situation, understood one another and felt understood, and found strength in being together. In these matters the young folk followed the behavior and adopted the standards of their elders.

But the boys in the gang had also learned something from the school and from the world it represented. The teacher had told them, and the books, that the end was to get ahead, to make good, to strive so that success might come. They must not repeat the errors of their fathers who had not made good, had not gotten ahead. The consequences of failure were everywhere apparent about them.

They could see the point of such injunctions. Only the hoary aphorisms did not ring true. A penny saved was not in their lives a penny earned; or the best policy. They were not much in demand to fill posts as office boys, so that road to a vice presidency was closed to them; and the runaway carriage of the banker's daughter came rarely into their neighborhood. The atmosphere of the street, where so much of reality was in open view, was not congenial to the ideal of the self-made businessman.

The impulse toward success found expression in terms dictated by the nature of their own group life. In childhood they strove in the competitive play of the alley, games of pursuit and capture, of sides that struggled against each other for a goal. As the boys grew older and their gangs took form, there were fighting forays in the rivalry of block against block; or (and it was not much different), where space permitted, there were savage athletic contests for the winning's sake.

The growth of professionalism gave an enormous impetus to this interest in sports which, after 1880, persisted on through adolescence to adulthood. On the baseball diamond, in the boxing ring, a lad could win fame and fortune. In these arenas, opportunity was free and only ability counted. The tone of one's name, the manners of speech and behavior, antecedents and affiliation were matters of no consequence. The pure capacity to succeed, with no other advantages, would bring the acclaim of the newspapers and wealth beyond the reach of these boys in any other way. The outstanding athletes who actually won such prizes were, of course, few in number. But each had his tremendous following of boys and young men who gained a kind of derivative satisfaction from his achievements and who sought within their own gangs to emulate his exploits. Increasingly the thoughts of the children were preoccupied with the events of the world of sport within which were played out the vivid dramas of American success and failure.

Down by the corner where the older

fellows congregated another kind of game held out the excitement of winning and losing. Watching the parades at campaign time, the youngsters looked forward with anticipation to the age when they too might be old enough to carry a banner. Meanwhile on the outskirts of the crowd around the ladder, they heard the orators' stirring periods and yelled the slogans of their partisanship. Its members were not yet voters when the gang was pressed into service, performing the menial jobs that might nevertheless win it the boss's notice. Here too was the possibility of rewards and of public esteem; and here too they need not labor against the liability of their own background.

The pursuit of success might take still another form. On the same corner, or on another much like it, the same boys or others much like them waited to turn the fight within them to riches. The violence of their childish play would grow up into racketeering; there were opportunities in plenty for such efforts.

For some the chance came through politics itself; perhaps they gained a proper "in" through roughing-up intransigent voters near the polls. For others the knock came in connection with gambling, or boxing, or labor organization, or in illicit liquor dealing. In whatever form, the ability to amass force in the gang, the willingness to defy rules the binding quality of which they did not recognize, and the burning desire by whatever means to elevate themselves above their origins, led such young men into organized criminality.

There were still other ways of rising, the professions, for instance. But sports, of course—the church, the stage, and politics, and the rackets had a larger importance even for the passive mass of

the young who never ventured to be more than followers, who married and reconciled themselves to a stolid family life without the hope for success. For in these three endeavors were the closest approximations to the American standards of achievement open to persons like themselves. In no other way could the children of newcomers readily earn the appreciation of the whole society.

In the face of this whole development the immigrants were helpless. They had neither the will nor the ability to turn their offspring into other directions. The nominal authority of the fathers was only halfheartedly used; they were cruelly torn by the conflicting wishes that their sons be like themselves and yet lead better lives than they. Sensing that the school and street would tear the next generation away, the parents knew not how to counteract those forces without injuring their own flesh and blood.

If there was a serious one favored by the teachers who came home to sneer at the family ways, it was clear enough that when he could he would break away, change names, and drop all old connections. Could or should the father therefore stand in the way of his becoming a doctor?

That the brothers ran about all day with a crowd of wild ones was also disquieting. The worried parents could see no sense in the athletics, the infantile antics of grown men playing at ball. The immigrants had a deep fear of the consequences of the use of force in the rackets and an uneasy distrust of politics. But they could not deny that these were the ways to success, that these were the means of gaining the approval of the American onlookers. Even the older folk indeed derived a kind of satisfaction from the fame of men who bore names like their own, as if John L. Sullivan or Honus Wagner or Benny Leonard, somehow, testified to their own acceptance by American society. How could they then hold the youngsters to the traditional ideals of status and propriety?

In truth, the children were more in this world than they the parents. Often it was necessary for the fathers to turn for enlightenment to their sons. *We also keep a paper, but you have read more and studied in school.* The young wore their nativity like a badge that marked their superiority over their immigrant elders. It was this superiority that gave the second generation its role as mediator between the culture of the home and the culture of the wider society in the United States.

Accepting that role, the immigrants nevertheless resented it. It reversed the proper order of things. They could remember how they themselves had feared and respected the father; and they were embittered by their own failure to evoke the same fear and respect from their children. Beyond the loose behavior at the table and in the streets, these parents sensed the tones of ridicule. In their eyes the young Americans were undisciplined and ungrateful, good only at throwing stones and snow at strangers. When the boys and girls were small, it was still possible to curb their rebelliousness; the swift punishment of the strap held them temporarily in line. But as age increased their power, they were not so amenable to authority. As they grew in knowledge and in craftiness, as their earnings rose above those of the head of the family, they ceased to bow to restraints and would no longer be ordered about.

Adolescence was therefore a time of acute crisis, and particularly for the girls. As infants they had played with their brothers, but already at seven or eight they were excluded from the society of the gang and thereafter had little to do with boys. In girlhood they stayed close to their mothers since the home was to be their place. But even they could not be shut off from the world outside. They went to school or to work, observed the American familiarity of association between men and women, and soon enough revolted against the old restrictions. They learned to dress like others, with petticoats dragging behind to shut out the air and with their waists laced up in corsets so tightly the blood could not flow; and they lost their health—or so it seemed to their elders.

The worry was that they could not be guided by the safe rules of the Old World. They knew too much, boys as well as girls. Coming down Ann Street, they could not help but notice the "jilt shops" open for the dubious satisfaction of the sailors. Sometimes they could earn pennies distributing the cards of the brothels that flourished in their neighborhoods; and it was often years before they got to understand that a hotel could be other than a house of assignation. Why, even at home, through the thin walls, through the open windows, across the narrow courts, came the revealing sights and sounds. It was all familiar enough by the time they were of an age to conduct their own exploratory operations.

Well, such a girl or boy was open to error, by betrayal or by the longing for a withheld joy. Having spent the day in the closeness of the factory, having come back to the dank room where there was no room, it was release they sought and the assertion of themselves as individuals. Everywhere crowds hemmed them in so they had never the feeling of being one, uniquely one and not one of many. And so it might happen once when the sense of inner powers would no longer tolerate constriction, and the still night offered unaccustomed privacy, and there was a yearning for identity—to be a being, to desire and be desired.

Or, it might not happen; and then only the empty wish remained, returning evening after empty evening as the moody hours went by before sleep came.

Here was the ultimate barrier between the generations: they would never understand each other's conception of marriage. Sure, the parents tried to explain the nature of this most crucial step, that this was a means of extending on in time the continuity of the family, that it involved the sacrifice of personality toward some larger end: *From a maiden you will become a married woman, from a free being a slave of your husband and fortune.* The children would not listen. For them, marriage was an act of liberation by which they cast off the family ties and expressed themselves as persons through the power to love.

Nor could the children make their parents understand the longing for individuality. To enter upon such a relationship without consultation with one's elders, to make such decisions on the basis of chance impressions, to undertake this partnership with a stranger of unknown antecedents, was a madness of the reason. To many a saddened father and mother it seemed that their sons and daughters had moved gross passion to the center of marriage and had thereby obscured the true end of the family, perpetuation of the succession of generations.

Often enough, then, the old couple were left alone. Looking back across the years, they realized they had been incapable of controlling the course of events. Out of the village context and without the support of the community, the family as they had known it had been doomed. Though they clung to the vestige of home and urged their children to hold together, they would never recapture the essential solidarity.

Perhaps sometimes it occurred to them how much of these tribulations they would have avoided if only they had been able to find that farm and there to work united together. They need not have grieved over it. Certainly the immigrants in agriculture did not need to guard their boys and girls against the influences of the street; and there, where the father was still effective head of the household, his authority was not readily questioned. But the parents could no more keep America away in the country than in the city. As the young matured and discovered wills of their own in school and in more frequent worldly contacts, they too were rebellious and refused to be bound.

Indeed, the impact of separation, when it came, was more decisive on the farm. Lacking as rich an associational life as was possible in the urban places, the second generation had not so full a function as mediators between the cultures. The sparseness of settlement, moreover, was more likely to encourage marriage with strangers that cut the children completely off from their parents. Only here and there was an occasional township, closely knit, homogeneous, stubbornly resisting all changes in a declared antagonism to America. There the family might survive a generation in its traditional form because there the family could call on the support of communal sanctions analogous to those of the Old World. Nowhere else could it survive with its roots pulled out of the village soil.

Perhaps they never took the time to make a balance sheet of their lives, those two old ones left alone, never stopped to reckon up how much they had gained and how much lost by coming. But certainly they must occasionally have faced the wry irony of their relationships with their offspring. What hope the early seasons of their years had held was hope of efforts for their children's sake. What dreams they had had were dreams of the family transplanted, that generation after generation would bear witness to the achievement of migration.

In the end, all was tinged with vanity, with success as cruel as failure. Whatever lot their sons had drawn in this new contentious world, the family's oneness would not survive it. It was a sad satisfaction to watch the young advance, knowing that every step forward was a step away from home.

The Lower East Side: The Jewish Experience

MOSES RISCHIN

From their homes they come rosy-cheeked and with health and Spring. They have had little fish, little meat, little bread, and it is to get more that they come hither. But they have had air and light. . . . Air and light, and water have been from all time the heritage of man and even of the animals.

Evening Journal (1903)

By the first decade of the twentieth century, the Lower East Side had become an immigrant Jewish cosmopolis. Five major varieties of Jews lived there, "a seething human sea, fed by streams, streamlets, and rills of immigration flowing from all the Yiddish-speaking centers of Europe." Clustered in their separate Jewries, they were set side by side in a pattern suggesting the cultural, if not the physical, geography of the Old World. Hungarians were settled in the northernmost portion above Houston Street, along the numbered streets between Avenue B and the East River, once indisputably *Kleindeutschland.* Galicians lived to the south, between Houston and Broome, east of Clinton, on Attorney, Ridge, Pitt, Willett, and the cross

From *The Promised City: New York's Jews, 1870-1914* (Cambridge, Mass.: Harvard University Press, 1962), pp. 76-94. Reprinted by permission of the publisher. Moses Rischin is Professor of History at the California State University at San Francisco.

31 Labor Temple
32 Rand School
33 Hebrew Charities Building
34 Metropolitan Life Building
35 Madison Square Garden
36 City College

BOUNDARIES OF
SUB-ETHNIC
DISTRICTS
······ Hungarian
—+— Galician
+-○-+ Rumanian
∿∿∿ Levantine
——— Russian

Shaded blocks
indicate Tenth Ward

0   MILE   ¼

THE LOWER EAST SIDE

1 Newspaper Row
2 World Building
3 Chatham Sq. Library
4 Beth Israel Hospital
5 Israel Elchanan Yeshiva
6 Seward Park Library
7 Forward Building on
   Yiddish Newspaper Row
8 Educational Alliance
9 Henry St. Settlement and
   Clinton Hall
10 Machzike Talmud Torah

11 Hebrew Sheltering House
12 Hebrew Technical School
   for Girls
13 Home for Aged
14 Jewish Maternity Hospital
15 Young Men's Benevolent
   Association
16 Camp Huddleston
   Hospital Ship School
17 Beth Hamedrash Hagadol
18 Pro-Cathedral Mission
19 University Settlement

20 Grand Theater
21 Yiddish Rialto
22 Thalia Theater
23 People's Bath
24 Police Headquarters
25 Public School 63
26 Music School Settlement
27 Asch Building
28 Astor Library
29 Cooper Union
30 Hebrew Technical School
   for Boys

streets. To the west lay the most congested Rumanian quarter, "in the very thick of the battle for breath," on Chrystie, Forsyth, Eldridge, and Allen streets, flanked by Houston Street to the north and Grand Street to the south, with the Bowery gridironed by the overhead elevated to the west. After 1907 Levantines, last on the scene and even stranger than the rest, for they were alien to Yiddish, settled between Allen and Chrystie streets among the Rumanians with whom they seemed to have the closest affinity. The remainder of the great Jewish quarter, from Grand Street reaching south to Monroe, was the preserve of the Russians—those from Russian Poland, Lithuania, Byelorussia, and the Ukraine—the most numerous and heterogeneous of the Jewries of Eastern Europe.[1]

The leading streets of the Lower East Side reflected this immigrant transformation. Its most fashionable thoroughfare, East Broadway, bisected the district. To the north lay crammed tenements, business, and industry. To the south lay less crowded quarters where private dwellings, front courtyards, and a scattering of shade trees recalled a time when Henry, Madison, Rutgers, and Jefferson street addresses were stylish.

The Russian intelligentsia, for whom the Lower East Side was New York, fancied East Broadway as New York's Nevsky Prospect, St. Petersburg's grand boulevard. In addition to the physicians and dentists who occupied the comfortable brownstone fronts that lined its shaded curbs, an ever-growing number of public and communal buildings came to endow it with a magisterial air. By the second decade of the twentieth century, the ten-story edifice of the *Jewish Daily Forward*, set off by Seward Park on Yiddish Newspaper Row, loomed commandingly over the two Carnegie-built libraries, the Educational Alliance, the Home for the Aged, the Jewish Maternity Hospital, the Machzike Talmud Torah, the Hebrew Sheltering House, the Young Men's Benevolent Association, and a host of lesser institutions.

Only second to East Broadway was Grand Street. Long a leading traffic artery and a major retail shopping center of lower New York, Grand Street fell into eclipse after the turn of the century with the widening of the Delancey Street approach to the Williamsburg Bridge and the comparative decline in ferry traffic. Grand Street's popular department stores, Lord and Taylor's, Lichtenstein's, and O'Neill's, moved uptown, and Ridley's closed, leaving the way open for conquest by the newcomers. Bustling Delancey Street, lined with naptha-lite stalls crammed with tubs of fish; Hester Street, with its agents on their way to becoming bankers after the example of Jarmulowsky's passage and exchange office; and the Bowery, with the largest savings bank in the world, symbolized the district's new retail character.[2]

Only after 1870 did the Lower East Side begin to acquire an immigrant Jewish cast. In the early years of the century a small colony of Jewish immigrants had lived there. Dutch, German, and Polish Jews had settled on Bayard, Baxter, Mott, and Chatham streets in the 1830's and 1840's. Shortly thereafter, German and Bohemian Jews took up quarters in the Grand Street area to the northeast and subsequently Jews of the great German migration augmented their numbers. Except for highly visible store fronts, Jews made little impress on the dominantly German and Irish neighborhood. But practically all East European immigrants arriving after 1870 initially found their way to the Lower East Side. Virtually penniless upon their arrival in the city, they were directed to the Jewish districts by representatives of the immigrant aid societies, or came at the behest of friends, relatives, or employers.[3]

The changes brought about by the great Jewish migration forced the district's middle-class Germans and Irish, living in predominantly two- and two-and-one-half story dwellings, to retreat to less crowded quarters. By 1890 the Lower East Side bristled with Jews. The tenth ward (loosely coinciding with the Eighth Assembly District), closest to the central factory area was the most crowded with 523.6 inhabitants per acre; the adjacent wards, the thirteenth and seventh, numbered 428.6 and 289.7 persons per acre respectively. Exceeding 700 persons per acre by 1900, the tenth ward was the most densely settled spot in the city; residential block density was even more appalling as factories and shops crowded tenements. In 1896 a private census counted 60 cigar shops, 172 garment shops, 65 factories, and 34 laundries in the tenth ward. In 1906, of fifty-one blocks in the city with over 3000 inhabitants each, thirty-seven were on the Lower East Side. On Rivington Street, Arnold Bennett remarked, "the architecture seemed to sweat humanity at every window and door." Hardy, older, or improvident remnants of the region's earlier Irish residents and a floating seafaring population still clung to the river edges along Cherry and Water streets; at the turn of the century, Italian immigrants crossed the Bowery on Stanton and East Houston streets and crowded into the lower

reaches of East Broadway. But in the second decade of the new century, the Lower East Side, from the Bowery to within a stone's throw of the East River, and from Market Street to 14th Street, had become a mass settlement of Jews, the most densely packed quarter in the city. In 1914 one sixth of the city's population was domiciled below 14th Street upon one eighty-second of the city's land area; most of New York's office buildings, and factories that employed over one half of the city's industrial workers were located in this district.[4]

Once the immigrants had come to rest on the Lower East Side, there was little incentive to venture further. Knowing no English and with few resources, they were dependent upon the apparel industries, the tobacco and cigar trades, and other light industrial employments that sprang up in the area or that were located in the adjacent factory district. Long hours, small wages, seasonal employment, and the complexity of their religious and social needs rooted them to the spot. It was essential to husband energies, earnings, and time. Lodgings of a sort, coffee morning and evening, and laundry service were available to single men for three dollars a month. Bread at two and three cents a pound, milk at four cents a quart, a herring for a penny or two, and apples at from one to five for a cent, depending on quality, were to be had. Accustomed to a slim diet, an immigrant could save much even with meager earnings and still treat himself to a bracing three-course Sabbath dinner (for fifteen cents). Thrift and hard work would, he hoped, enable him in time to search out more congenial and independent employment. Until new sections of the city were developed at the turn of the century only country peddlers were to stray permanently beyond the familiar immigrant quarters.[5]

There was a compelling purpose to the pinched living. Virtually all immigrants saved to purchase steamship tickets for loved ones and many regularly mailed clothing and food parcels to dependent parents, wives, and children overseas. The power of home ties buoyed up the spirits of immigrants wedded to the sweatshop and peddler's pack, whose precious pennies mounted to sums that would unite divided families. Among the early comers women were relatively few, but the imbalance between the sexes soon was remedied. In 1890 an investigation by the Baron de Hirsch Society into the condition of 111,690 of an estimated 135,000 Jews on the Lower East Side counted 60,313 children and 22,647 wage-earners, with 28,730 unspecified, mostly women. Undoubtedly, the proportion of women and children in New York was far greater than it was elsewhere. In 1910 women exceeded men among Hungarians and Rumanians, were equal among Austrians, and made up 47 per cent of the Russians. As non-Jews from these countries were heavily male, Jewish women clearly outnumbered men, accentuating the group's domesticity. Among the major ethnic groups of New York, only the Irish, 58 per cent female, exceeded the Jewish ratio.[6]

A nondescript colony of Jews in the 1870's swelled into a center of Jewish life by the turn of the century, the drama of whose fortunes and passions was closely followed by fellow immigrants throughout the country as well as by those in the lands they left behind. A highly visible knot of Jews "huddled up together" around Baxter and Chatham streets had been engulfed by an influx that saturated the whole region with its flavor and institutions.[7]

THE TENEMENT BOOM

Ever since the 1830's New York's housing problem had been acute. Manhattan's space limitations exacerbated all the evils inherent in overcrowding, and refinements in the use of precious ground only emphasized the triumph of material necessities over human considerations. New York's division of city lots into standard rectangular plots, 25 feet wide by 100 feet deep, made decent human accommodations impossible. In order to secure proper light and ventilation for tenement dwellers twice the space was needed, a prohibitive sacrifice considering real estate values. No opportunity was overlooked to facilitate the most economical and compact housing of the immigrant population. To the improvised tenements that had been carved out of private dwellings were added the front and rear tenements and, finally, the dumbbell-style tenement of 1879.

With the heavy Jewish migration of the early 1890's, the Lower East Side, still relatively undeveloped compared to the Lower West Side, became the special domain of the new dumbbell tenements, so called because of their shape. The six- to seven-story dumbbell usually included four apartments to the floor, two on either side of the separating corridor. The front apartments generally contained four rooms each, the rear apartments three. Only one room in each apartment received direct light and air from the street or from the ten feet of required yard space in the rear. On the ground floor two stores generally were to be found; the living quarters behind each had windows only on

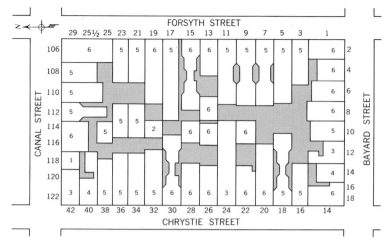

A tenement block: smaller numbers indicate number of stories.

the air shaft. The air shaft, less than five feet in width and from fifty to sixty feet in length, separated the tenement buildings. In the narrow hallways were located that special improvement, common water closets. In 1888 a leading magazine described typical dumbbell tenements on Ridge, Eldridge, and Allen streets.

They are great prison-like structures of brick, with narrow doors and windows, cramped passages and steep rickety stairs. They are built through from one street to the other with a somewhat narrower building connecting them . . . The narrow court-yard . . . in the middle is a damp foul-smelling place, supposed to do duty as an airshaft; had the foul fiend designed these great barracks they could not have been more villainously arranged to avoid any chance of ventilation . . . In case of fire they would be perfect death-traps, for it would be impossible for the occupants of the crowded rooms to escape by the narrow stairways, and the flimsy fire-escapes which the owners of the tenements were compelled to put up a few years ago are so laden with broken furniture, bales and boxes that they would be worse than useless. In the hot summer months . . . these fire-escape balconies are used as sleeping-rooms by the poor wretches who are fortunate enough to have windows opening upon them. The drainage is horrible, and even the Croton as it flows from the tap in the noisome courtyard, seemed to be contaminated by its surroundings and have a fetid smell.

As if the tenement abuses were not degrading enough, the absence of public toilet facilities in so crowded a district added to the wretched sanitation. It was reported that "in the evening every dray or wagon becomes a private and public lavatory, and the odor and stench . . . is perfectly horrible." [8]

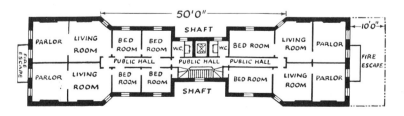

A typical dumbbell tenement

Conditions became almost unendurable in the summer months. Bred in colder and dryer climates, tenement inhabitants writhed in the dull heat. Added to the relentless sun were the emanations from coal stoves, the flat flame gas jets in lamps, and the power-producing steam boilers. Inevitably, roofs, fire escapes, and sidewalks were converted into sleeping quarters, while the grassed enclosure dividing Delancey Street and Seward Park supplied additional dormitory space. Late July and early August of 1896 were especially savage. Between August 5 and 13, 420 New Yorkers perished from the continuous heat, "the absolute stagnation of the air, and the oppressive humidity," noted Daniel Van Pelt, although the temperature averaged 90.7 degrees and never reached 100.

Fire and the possibilities of fire brought added terror to the inhabitants of overcrowded tenements. "Remember that you live in a tenement house," warned insurance agents. In 1903, 15 per cent of the tenements in the district still were without fire escapes. Of 257 fatalities in Manhattan fires between 1902 and 1909, 99 or 38 per cent were on the Lower East Side, all victims of old-law tenements.[9]

Few families could afford the privacy of a three- or four-room flat. Only with the aid of lodgers or boarders could the $10 to $20 monthly rental be sustained. The extent of overcrowding in the tenements, reported a witness before the United States Immigration Commission, was never fully known.

At the hour of retiring, cots or folded beds and in many instances simply mattresses are spread about the floor, resembling very much a lot of bunks in the steerage of an ocean steamer . . . The only way to properly determine the census of one of these tenements, would be by a midnight visit, and should this take place between the months of June and September, the roof of the building should not be omitted.

However trying tenement living proved to be for adults, for children it was stultifying, concluded a settlement worker. "The earlier years of the child are spent in an atmosphere which . . . is best described by a little girl, 'a place so dark it seemed as if there weren't no sky.' "

Evictions for nonpayment of rent and rent strikes were perennial. Uncertainty of employment, nonpayment of wages, unexpected obligations, dependents, and adversities contributed to the high incidence of evictions. In the year 1891 −1892 alone, in two judicial districts of the Lower East Side, 11,550 dispossess warrants were issued by the presiding magistrates. In 1900 the absence of mass evictions was regarded as a mark of unexampled well-being.[10]

Earlier residents of the Lower East Side and hereditary property owners profited from the overcrowding. The rise in real estate values, exorbitant rents, and the low upkeep provided tenement owners with ample returns upon their investments. Even allowing for losses due to nonpayment of rent and an average occupancy of ten months in the year, landlords earned ten per cent. By more studied neglect, a resourceful agent might reap even higher returns. The Lower East Side tenements soon came to be recognized as the most lucrative investment in the city. Nowhere else did the speculator's market in tenement properties flourish as luxuriantly as it did here, where earlier immigrants had learned to exploit the misery of later comers.

In 1901 the further construction of

dumbbell tenements was prohibited. The Tenement House Law of that year set new standards for future housing and attempted to correct the worst abuses in the existing buildings. All new tenements were to have windows that opened at least twelve feet away from those opposite. Toilets and running water in each apartment, unobstructed fire escapes, and solid staircases were required. In the old buildings modern water closets were to be installed in place of the outside privies. Finally, a Tenement House Department was established to supervise and enforce the provisions of the law. While the law never was effectively enforced, its initial achievements proved encouraging.

Many new tenements were quickly built according to the new specifications. In the fiscal year ending July 1, 1903, 43 per cent of New York's new tenements were located on the Lower East Side. Its inhabitants eagerly welcomed the brightly lighted rooms, bathtubs, and other improvements. At first, landlords on the Lower East Side were more prompt to make alterations in old-law tenements than landlords elsewhere in the city, for the heavy pressure of population made even remodeled properties attractive. The years 1905 to 1909 saw an unparalleled boom throughout the city with houses to fit every taste, from tenements to palatial mansions for chance customers, at unprecedented prices ranging up to $500,-000. "It is doubtful if New York City, or in fact any other city in the world, ever before witnessed the expenditure of so many millions of dollars in the construction of tenement houses during a similar period." [11]

While new housing was on the rise, the fast developing clothing trades also were relocating and building. As the heavy settlement of East Europeans decisively affected the housing of the city's earlier residents, so the new growth of the apparel industry, manned by Lower East Side Jews, helped to transform the city's business districts. Once legislation and the advent of electric power combined to reduce Lower East Side sweatshops, thousands of garment shops and factories pushed up the axial thoroughfares of Lower Manhattan. By 1910 the continued march uptown found the garment industry intruding upon once fashionable Madison Square, the site of New York's tallest skyscrapers. Brownstones and brick residences were razed to be displaced by 16- to 20-story steel-girdered loft buildings trimmed with granite and marble and housing scores of clothing shops. In the course of this displacement, the city's central retailing district and its theater and hotel district were forced northward. The main retailing center, at 14th Street in 1880 and at 23rd Street in 1900, became anchored at 34th Street by 1910.[12]

DISEASE AND CRIME

Superficially, East European Jews seemed ill-prepared to contend with the demands that tenement living thrust upon them. "Their average stature is from five feet one inch to five feet three inches, which means that they are the most stunted of the Europeans, with the exception of the Hungarian Magyars." Shortest were the Galicians, tallest and sturdiest, the Rumanians. Undersized and narrow-chested, a high proportion were described as "Physical Wrecks." Centuries of confinement, habituation to mental occupations, chronic undernourishment, and a deprecation of the physical virtues ill-fitted them for heavy labor. Between 1887 and 1890 nearly five thousand immigrants were returned to Europe labeled physically "unfit for work." Seemingly helpless and emaciated, they were to exhibit exceptional capacity for regeneration; traditional moral and religious disciplines were to serve them in good stead.

Despite the trying conditions under which the immigrants lived, they showed a remarkable resistance to disease. With the highest average density of tenants per house in the city, the tenth ward had one of the lowest death rates. Indeed only a business ward and a suburban ward surpassed it in healthfulness. Dr. Annie Daniel, a pioneer in public health, volunteered her interpretation of this before the Tenement House Committee:

> The rules of life which orthodox Hebrews so unflinchingly obey as laid down in the Mosaic code . . . are designed to maintain health. These rules are applied to the daily life of the individuals as no other sanitary laws can be . . . Food must be cooked properly, and hence the avenues through which the germs of disease may enter are destroyed. Meat must be "kosher," and this means that it must be perfectly healthy. Personal cleanliness is at times strictly compelled, and at least one day in the week the habitation must be thoroughly cleaned.

True, only some 8 per cent of Russian Jewish families had baths, according to a study of 1902, and these often without hot water. Yet the proliferation of privately owned bathhouses in the city was attributable largely to the Jewish tenement population. "I cannot get along without a 'sweat' (Russian bath) at least once a week," insisted a newcomer. In 1880, one or two of New York's twenty-two bathhouses were Jewish; by 1897, over half of the city's sixty-two bathhouses (including Russian, Turkish, swimming, vapor, and medi-

cated bathhouses) were Jewish. If standards of cleanliness were not as faithfully maintained as precept required, the strict regimen of orthodoxy, even when weakened, contributed to the immigrant's general well-being.[13]

Nevertheless, close crowding and unsanitary conditions made all communicable diseases potentially contagious. Despite great apprehension between 1892 and 1894, Jewish immigrants did not carry to New York the cholera and typhus epidemics raging at the European ports of embarkation. But in 1899 the United Hebrew Charities became alarmed by the Board of Health's report of the mounting incidence of tuberculosis in the city. That Jewish immigrants might become easy victims of the "White Plague" was hardly to be doubted. "As many as 119 Jewish families have lived in one tenement house on Lewis Street within the past five years." Hundreds of flats had been occupied by fifteen successive families within a brief period. "Many of these houses are known to be hotbeds of the disease, the very walls reeking with it." Increasingly, the dread disease with its cough and crimson spittle took its toll. Ernest Poole, an investigator, frequently heard the plea of the afflicted. "Luft, gibt mir luft— Air, give me air." Especially susceptible were the intellectuals, whose often shattered spirits, overwrought minds, and undernourished bodies fell prey to the killer. Yet so great was the immigrant's concern for health that the mortality rate from tuberculosis was lower on the East Side than in the city's prosperous districts. Venereal diseases, previously almost unknown among Jews in Eastern Europe, became progressively more common among young men, as restraints were weakened by exposure to new temptations.[14]

Alcoholism, a prime contributor to

poverty, ill-health, and mortality among other national groups, was unusual among Jewish immigrants. As Jews replaced the earlier inhabitants, the many saloons of the Lower East Side, trimmed with shields that proclaimed them "the workman's friend," declined. Those that survived drew few clients from a neighborhood addicted to soda water, "the life-giving drink"; they depended on the throng of transients that passed through the district. Jews did not abstain from drink. Yet only upon religious festivals and during the Sabbath ritual when the Kiddush cup was emptied did alcohol appear in the diet of most immigrants. In 1908, $1.50 a year for holiday and ritual wine seemed adequate for a family of six. "The Day of Rejoicing of the Law and the Day of Purim are the only two days in the year when an orthodox Jew may be intoxicated. It is virtuous on these days to drink too much, but the sobriety of the Jew is so great that he sometimes cheats his friends and himself by shamming drunkenness," Hutchins Hapgood noted. Jews habitually imbibed milder beverages. Russians were notorious tea drinkers. Hungarians were addicted to coffee. The less austere Galicians and Rumanians tippled mead and wine respectively. But in the New World all fell victim to the craze for seltzer or soda water with its purported health-giving powers. In his long experience, reported the president of the United Hebrew Charities in 1892, he had known only three chronic Jewish drunkards.[15]

Neurasthenia and hysteria, however, took a heavy toll of victims. Their sickness was the result of a history of continual persecution and insecurity, intensified by the strains of settlement in unfamiliar surroundings. Diabetes, associated with perpetual nervous strain,

was common. Suicide, rarely recorded among the small-town Jews of Eastern Europe, also found its victims in the tenements of New York. Despair, poverty, and the fears generated in the immigration led some immigrants to take their own lives. "Genumen di gez" (took gas) was not an uncommon headline in the Yiddish press. Yet in the late 1880's only the city's Irish showed a lower suicide rate than did Russian Jews.

However desperate the straits in which Jewish immigrants found themselves, confirmed paupers among them were few. The rarity of alcoholism, the pervasiveness of the charitable impulse, the strength of ties to family and *lanslite*, and a deep current of optimism preserved the individual from such degradation.[16]

Prior to the 1880's only the Rubinstein murder case spotted the record of New York's Jews. Upon the testimony of doubtful witnesses, Rubinstein was sentenced to death for the slaying of his girl cousin, but cheated the hangman by taking his own life. The first crime of violence attributed to a Jew in the city's annals, its very novelty gave rise to the popular street song, "My Name is Pesach Rubinstein." So unassailable was the peaceful reputation of the Jewish districts that it was a matter for continual commendation. In 1878 Jews numbered 7 in a workhouse population of 1178; 8 among 485 prison inmates; and 12 among 1110 house-of-correction inmates.

The obloquy attached to the strident Jews of Baxter and Chatham Streets; to the Canal Street clothing shop puller-in and the Division Street millinery shop pulleress; to Michael Kurtz, better known as "Sheeney Mike," reputedly the "champion burgler of America"; and to "Marm" Mandelbaum, unmatched receiver of stolen goods, did not detract from the high repute of the city's Jews. The two dozen Bowery pawnshops were owned by Americans or earlier immigrants who catered to the needs of a heterogeneous population and were not part of the immigrant community.

The major crime and violence in the area did not stem from the immigrants. They were its victims. The Lower East Side had always attracted much of the city's criminal element to its margins. By the last decades of the nineteenth century, it had shed the ferocity of earlier years when the "Bowery B'hoys" and the "Dead Rabbits" terrorized the area. But Mayor Hewitt's reform drive in 1887 inadvertently reinforced the district's frailties by forcing criminals and prostitutes from their accustomed uptown resorts into the less conspicuous tenements of the tenth ward, where they remained, undisturbed even by the Parkhurst crusade. The Raines Law, which provided that only hotels could serve liquor on Sundays, worsened the situation. In 1896, of 236 saloons in the tenth ward, 118 were Raines Law hotels, while 18 were outright houses of prostitution. In the first decade of the twentieth century, crusading District Attorney William Travers Jerome kept open house in his special office on Rutgers Street, at the hub of the Lower East Side, and the most salient features of criminality were forced underground. By 1905 the "peripatetic sisterhood" had been driven from the Bowery, and Captain Godard's Anti-Policy Society's campaign banished gambling from the thoroughfare. But the criminal elements soon returned.[17]

Crime was endemic to the Lower East Side. The close collaboration between police officers, politicians, and criminals, revealed in detail in the Lexow and Mazet investigations of the 1890's, had turned the district into a Klondike that replaced the uptown Tenderloin as a center of graft and illicit business. Invariably the culprits in these activities were not immigrants, but Americanized Jews learned in street-corner ways and shorn of the restraints of the immigrant generation. "It is not until they have become Americanized, have adapted themselves to the environment of the district and adopted its ways and vices, that they become full-fledged wretches," commented Dr. I. L. Nascher. In the early years of the twentieth century the effect of such conditions upon the young deeply disturbed those anxious for the public weal. In 1909 some 3000 Jewish children were brought before Juvenile Court and in the next few years Jewish criminals regularly made newspaper headlines. The appearance of an ungovernable youth after the turn of the century was undeniable and excited apprehension.[18]

The violations of the law that characterized the immigrant community differed from the crimes of the sons of the immigrants. The former were an outgrowth of occupational overcrowding, poverty, and religious habits. Straitened circumstances contributed to the large number of cases of family desertion and nonsupport. Concentrated in marginal commerce and industry, Jews were prone to transgress the codes of commercial law. "The prevalence of a spirit of enterprise out of proportion to the capital of the community" gave rise to a high incidence of felonious larceny, forgery, and failure to pay wages. Peddlers and petty shopkeepers were especially vulnerable to police oppression for evading informal levies as well as formal licensing requirements. Legislation controlling business on Sunday found Jewish immigrants natural victims. In so congested a district, the breaking of corporation ordinances was unavoidable and the slaughtering of chickens in tenements in violation of the sanitary code proved to be a distinctly Jewish infraction.[19]

The Bowery, way-station of derelicts, transients, and unsuspecting immigrants, attracted the less stable and wary of the immigrant girls. The dancing academies that sprang to popularity in the first decade of the twentieth century snared impetuous, friendless young women. Lured by promises of marriage, they soon were trapped by procurers for the notorious Max Hochstim Association and other white slavers who preyed upon the innocent and the unsuspecting. The appearance of prostitution, previously rare among Jewesses, alarmed the East Side.[20]

The Lower East Side, girded by the Bowery with its unsavory establishments and Water Street with its resorts of ill-fame that catered to the seafaring trade, was surrounded by violence. Bearded Jews often were viciously assaulted by young hoodlums, both non-Jews and Jews, the area adjacent to the waterfront being especially dangerous. In 1898 and 1899, the newly organized American Hebrew League of Brooklyn protested a rash of outrages in the wake of the Dreyfus affair. Nevertheless there was only one instance of mass violence: the riot of July 30, 1902 at the funeral of Rabbi Jacob Joseph. This incident, the only one of its kind, can be attributed to the stored-up resentment of the Irish who were being forced out of the area by the incursion of Jews.[21]

Gradually the miseries and trials of adjustment were left behind. For those who had inhabited the hungry villages of Eastern Europe, the hovels of Berditchev, and the crammed purlieus of Vilna and Kovno, the factories and sweatshops of New York provided a livelihood and possible stepping-stone. Despite unsteady and underpaid employment, tenement overcrowding and filth, immigrants felt themselves ineluctably being transformed. The Lower East Side, with its purposeful vitality, found no analogue in the "leprous-looking ghetto familiar in Europe," commented the visiting Abbé Félix Klein. Physical surroundings, however sordid, could be transcended. Optimism and hope engulfed every aspect of immigrant life. For a people who had risen superior to the oppressions of medieval proscriptions, the New York slums acted as a new-found challenge. Each passing year brought improvements that could be measured and appraised. Cramped quarters did not constrict aspirations. "In a large proportion of the tenements of the East Side . . . pianos are to be seen in the dingy rooms." And soon the phonograph was everywhere. "Excepting among the recent arrivals, most of the Jewish tenement dwellers have fair and even good furniture in their homes."[22]

The East Europeans began to venture beyond the boundaries of the Lower East Side into other areas where employment was available on terms compatible with religious habits. Brooklyn's German Williamsburg district, directly across the East River, where Central European Jews had been established for some decades, was settled early. In the late 1880's a few clothing contractors set up sweatshops in the languid Scottish settlement of Brownsville, south and east of Williamsburg. The depression delayed further expansion for a decade despite the extension of the Fulton Street El in 1889. Then the tide could not be stemmed. Between 1899 and 1904 Brownsville's population rose from ten thousand to sixty thousand. Land values soared as immigrants came at the rate of one thousand per week. Lots selling for two hundred dollars in 1899 brought five to ten thousand dollars five years later. As the real estate boom revolutionized land values, many a former tailor was suddenly transformed into a substantial landlord or realtor who disdained all contact with shears and needles of bitter memory.[23]

The mass dispersion of Jews from the Lower East Side to other parts of the city was in full swing in the early 1890's, as the more prosperous pioneers hastened to settle among their German coreligionists in Yorkville between 72nd and 100th streets, east of Lexington Avenue. For many a rising immigrant family in this period of swift change, it was judged to be a ten-year trek from Hester Street to Lexington Avenue.

The unprecedented flow of immigrants into the old central quarter, exorbitant rents, and the demolition of old tenements incidental to the building of parks, schools, and bridge approaches drastically reduced the area's absorptive capacity and spurred the search for new quarters. The construction of the Delancey Street approach to the Williamsburg Bridge in 1903 displaced 10,000 persons alone. The consolidation of the city and the growth and extension of rapid transit facilities connected what were once remote districts with the central downtown business quarters. In the new developments, cheaper land made possible lower rents that compensated for the time and expense of commuting. On Manhattan Island, the construction of underground transit opened to mass settlement the Dyckman tract in Washington Heights and the Harlem flats. The new subway also opened the East Bronx to extensive housing development. In Brooklyn, in addition to the heavy concentrations in Brownsville, Williamsburg, and South Brooklyn, Boro Park with "tropical gardens" and "parks" became increasingly accessible. Even distant Coney Island was brought into range by improved transit facilities.[24]

With 542,061 inhabitants in 1910, the Lower East Side reached peak congestion. Thereafter, a decline set in. By 1916 only 23 per cent of the city's Jews lived in the once primary area of Jewish settlement, compared to 50 per cent in 1903 and 75 per cent in 1892. By the close of the first decade of the twentieth century the Lower East Side had lost much of its picturesqueness. In tone and color, the ghetto was perceptibly merging with the surrounding city. East European Jews had scattered to many sections of the city and were swiftly becoming an integral, if not as yet a fully accepted, element in the life of the community.[25]

In 1870 the Jews of New York were estimated at 80,000, or less than 9 per cent of the city's inhabitants. By 1915 they totaled close to 1,400,000 persons (nearly 28 per cent), a number larger than the city's total population in 1870. Before 1880 the Jews of the city were hardly more than a subject for idle curiosity. But thereafter, the flow of East European Jews quickened the city's industrial life, helped to transform its physical shape, and contributed a varied and malleable people to the metropolis. Despite poverty and great numbers, these immigrants created no new problems. But their presence accentuated New York's shortcomings in the face of unprecedented demands upon its imagination and resources. In the early years of the new century, their voice would be heard. The problems of industrial relations and urban living accentuated on the Lower East Side were to become the focus for major reforms.[26]

NOTES

1. Abraham Cahan, Yekl, A Tale of the Ghetto (New York, 1896), p. 28; United States Immigration Commission, Reports (Washington, 1907-1910), XXVI, 167; Seventeenth Annual Report, University Settlement Society (1903), p. 8; Arbeiter Zeitung, June 20, 1890; Forward, March 23, 24, 1904; February 20, 1906, February 8, 1911; Volksblatt, February 18, May 27, 1910; I. L. Nascher, The Wretches of Povertyville (Chicago, 1909), p. 1 of; Miriam Blaustein, ed., Memoirs of David Blaustein (New York, 1913), pp. 123-124.
2. Gregory Weinstein, The Ardent Eighties (New York, 1928), p. 79; Yiddishes Tageblatt, March 20, 1910; Forward, February 14, 1912; Report, Committee on Manufactures on the Sweating System, 52nd Congress, 2nd Session, H. R. Report no. 2309, 1893, p. 182; Wegweiser in der Amerikaner bizness velt, February 8, 1892; Nascher, The Wretches, p. 12.
3. H. B. Grinstein, The Rise of the Jewish Community of New York, 1654-1860 (New York, 1945), p. 31f; United States Industrial Commission, Reports (Washington, 1900-1902), XV, 476, 478; P. Cowen, Memories of An American Jew (New York, 1932), p. 103; B. Weinstein, Fertsig yor in di idishe arbeter bavegung in amerika (New York, 1924), pp. 21-22.
4. New York Labor Bulletin, 10:314-315, 322 (September 1908); E. E. Pratt, The Industrial Causes of Congestion in New York City (New York: 1911), pp. 19-20; Report of the University Settlement Society (1897), p. 3; Arnold Bennett, Your United States (New York, 1912), p. 187; Harold M. Finley, "New York's Populous and Densest Blocks," Federation, 4:8 (November 1906); H. C. Brearley, The Problem of Greater New York and Its Solution (New York, 1914), p. 28; Report of the University Settlement Society 1896), p. 10.
5. G. M. Price, Di yuden in amerika (Odessa, 1891), p 13; New York Herald, November 25, 1892; Louis Waldman, Labor Lawyer (New York, 1944), pp. 23, 28; Autobiography 45 (MS, YIVO Institute of Jewish Research), p. 153.
6. Z. Szjaikowski, "The Attitude of American Jews to East European Jewish Immigrants, 1881-1893," Publ. Amer. Jew. Hist. Soc.,

40:272-273 (March 1951); Report, Select Committee, H. R. Importation of Contract Laborers, Paupers, Convicts and Other Classes (Washington, 1889), p. 289f; W. T. Elsing, The Poor in Great Cities (New York, 1898), p. 103. The following are the 1910 population figures for East Europeans in New York City:

	Total	Male	Female
Rumania	33,584	16,461	17,123
Hungary	76,625	35,224	41,401
Austria	190,237	95,941	94,296
Russia	484,189	257,418	226,771

Walter Laidlaw, Statistical Sources for Demographic Studies of New York, 1910 (New York, 1912), I, i.
7. W. M. R., "A Sabbath Among Orthodox Jews," Galaxy, 14:379f (September 1872); Report, Committee of the Senate, Relations between Capital and Labor (Washington, 1885), I, 94.
8. C. D. Wright, The Housing of the Working People (Washington, 1895), p. 196; Forty-third Annual Report, New York Association for the Improvement of the Condition of the Poor, 1886, p. 43f; Allen Forman, "Some Adopted Americans," The American Magazine, 9:51-52 (November 1888): Report of the Tenement House Committee of 1894, New York (1895), pp. 8, 12, 104.
9. Daniel Van Pelt, Leslie's History of Greater New York (New York, 1898), I, 544; 21st Annual Report, University Settlement Society, 1907, pp. 27-28; Abendblatt der Arbeiter Zeitung, January 11, 1896; Idisher Zhurnäl, July 14, 1899; Fifth Report, Tenement House Department, City of New York, 1909, pp. 106-107, 112-113.
10. Report of the Year's Work, University Settlement Society, 1900, p. 34; William P. McLoughlin, "Evictions in New York's Tenement Houses," Arena, 7:50-52 (December 1892); Hebrew Standard, August 25, 1893; Samuel Gompers to Henry Goldfogle, September 14, 1893 (Gompers Papers); Yiddishes Tageblatt, January 1, 1901.
11. United States Industrial Commission, Reports, XIV, 87; Frank Moss, The American Metropolis (New York, 1897), III, 205; Joseph Barondess to Charles D. Spivak, June 11, 1908 (Barondess Papers); Report, Tenement House Department, 1902-1903, I, 141; Fifth Report, Tenement House Department, New York, 1909, pp. 19, 103; Ralph D. Paine, "Are Riches Demoralizing American Life?" World's Work, 6:3917f (September 1903).
12. Stephen Jenkins, The Greatest Street in the World (New York, 1911), p. 191; B. J. Hendrick, "The Jewish Invasion of America," McClure's Magazine, 40:134 (March 1913); M. Feinstone and H. Lang, eds., Geverkshaftn (New York, 1938), pp. 100-102; Donald H. Daven-

port, et al., *The Retail Shopping and Financial Districts in New York* (New York, 1927), p. 23; George Filipetti, *The Wholesale Markets in New York* (New York, 1925), p. 46.

13. M. Fishberg, "Health and Sanitation of the Immigrant Jewish Population of New York," *Menorah*, August-September 1902, pp. 4, 14; M. Fishberg, "Materials for the Physical Anthropology of the Eastern European Jews," *Memoirs of the American Anthropological and Ethnological Societies* (June, 1905), vol. I, pt. I, pp. 36-37, 41-42; Szjaikowski, "The Attitude of American Jews," p. 243; *Report of the Tenement House Committee of 1894*, pp. 21-22, 47-48; United States Immigration Commission, *Reports*, XXVI, 165; Joseph Barondess to Mrs. M. A. Davis, March 22, 1902 (Barondess Papers); *Wilson's Business Directory of New York City, 1880-1881*, p. 45; *The Trow Business Directory of New York City, 1897*, pp. 86-87; *Trow Business Directory of Greater New York, 1907*, pp. 102-103.

14. C. E. A. Winslow, *The Life of Hermann M. Biggs* (Philadelphia, 1929), pp. 80, 95-96; *Eighteenth Annual Report, United Hebrew Charities, 1892-1893*, p. 21; United States Industrial Commission, *Reports*, XIV, 87; *Twenty-fifth Annual Report, United Hebrew Charities, 1899*, p. 35; Ernest Poole, *The Plague In Its Stronghold* (New York, 1903), p. 3f; Joseph Barondess to Dr. J. S. Billings, September 9, 1908 (Barondess Papers); M. Fishberg, "Tuberculosis Among Jews," *American Israelite*, October 18, 1908; A. J. Rongy, "Half a Century of Jewish Medical Activities in New York City," *Medical Leaves*, 1:159 (1937). Cf. advertisements by specialists in "men's diseases" like "Old Dr. Grey," *Yiddishes Tageblatt*, January 16, 1899; *Forward*, March 2, 1901.

15. *Abendblatt der Arbeiter Zeitung*, January 13, 1896; *Forward*, February 14, 1912; Ida Van Etten, "Russian Jews as Desirable Immigrants," *Forum*, 15:178 (April 1893); S. Foster, "The Workingman and the Synagogue," *Yearbook, Central Conference of American Rabbis*, 20:482 (1909); Hutchins Hapgood, *The Spirit of the Ghetto* (New York, 1902), p. 14; *Forward*, March 23, 1904; *Report of the Tenement House Committee of 1894*, p. 431.

16. M. Fishberg, *The Jews* (London, 1911), pp. 367, 530-531; *Arbeiter Zeitung*, June 20, 1890; *Forward*, July 26, August 13, 1897, March 25, 1908; M. Osherowitch, "Di geshikhte fun forverts, 1897-1947" (MS, New York Public Library); 17; *Nayer Gayst* (December 1897), p. 133; L. K. Frankel, "Jewish Charities," *The Making of America*, ed. R. M. LaFollette (Chicago, 1906), X, 64; United States Industrial Commission, *Reports*, XIV, 119, 121; K. H. Claghorn, "Jewish Immigration and Pauperism," *Jewish Charity*, 3:31-32 (November 1903); L. K. Frankel to Herbert Parsons, January 12, 1905 (Parsons Papers).

17. Grinstein, *The Rise of the Jewish Community*, p. 16; *Trial of Pesach Rubinstein for the Murder of Sarah Alexander in the Town of New Lots* (New York, 1876), *passim*; Frank Weitenkampf, *Manhattan Kaleidoscope* (New York, 1947), p. 82; prison statistics are cited in Allen Tarshish, "The Rise of American Judaism; A History of American Jewish Life from 1848-1881" (doctoral dissertation, Hebrew Union College, 1938), p. 433; George Walling, *Recollections of a New York Chief of Police* (New York, 1887), pp. 19, 280f; A. E. Costello, *Our Police Protectors* (New York, 1885), p. 324; I. Markens, *Hebrews in America* (New York, 1888), p. 24; Nascher, *The Wretches*, pp. 12, 40, 63, 129-130; Jacob Riis, *How The Other Half Lives*, p. 109; Moss, *The American Metropolis*, II, 366, III, 55, 154; Rupert Hughes, *The Real New York* (New York, 1904), pp. 333-334; *Report, University Settlement Society, 1896*, p. 10; C. C. Regier, *The Era of the Muckrackers* (Chapel Hill, 1932), p. 80.

18. *Arbeiter Zeitung*, January 26, October 12, 1894; *Yearbook, University Settlement Society, 1899*, p. 89; Nascher, *The Wretches*, pp. 10-12, 40; *Forward*, May 15, 1908; United States Industrial Commission, *Reports*, XIV, 124; David Blaustein to Paul Abelson, January 29, 1907 (Abelson Papers); *American Hebrew*, December 17, 1909.

19. *Twenty-Sixth Annual Report, President, Treasurer, and Attorneys, Legal Aid Society, 1901*, p. 18; Joseph Barondess to Desertion Bureau, United Hebrew Charities, May 27, 1908 (Barondess Papers); S. Lowenstein, "Jewish Desertions," *Jewish Charity*, 5:143 (February, 1905); *Yearbook, University Settlement Society, 1900*, pp. 28-29; J. B. Reynolds to Henry C. Potter, October 1, 1900 (Reynolds Papers); *Hebrew Standard*, August 25, 1893; *Twenty-Third Annual Report, United Hebrew Charities, 1896*, p. 45; *Twenty-Eighth Annual Report, Legal Aid Society, 1903*, p. 31.

20. *American Hebrew*, December 17, 1909; *Report of the Tenement House Committee of 1894*, p. 81f; *Importing Women for Immoral Purposes* (New York Senate, Doc. 196, 1909), p. 14; *Jewish International Conference on the Suppression of Traffic in Girls and Women* (London, 1910), *passim; Forward*, January 10, 1901, January 1, 1902.

21. Morris D. Waldman, *Nor By Power* (New York, 1953), p. 298; J. D. Eisenstein, *Otser Zikhronotsay* (New York, 1929), pp. 79, 98, 112; S. Sheinfeld, *Zikhroines fun a shriftzetser* (New York, 1946), p. 33; Rose A. Halpern, "The American Reaction to the Dreyfus Case" (M.A. thesis, Columbia University, 1941), pp. 85-86.

22. Anatole Leroy-Beaulieu, *Les Immigrants Juifs et le Judaisme aux Etats-Unis* (Paris, 1905), pp. 11-12; Felix Klein, *In the Land of the Strenuous Life* (Chicago, 1905), p. 3; Peter

Wiernik, *History of the Jews in America* (New York, 1912), pp. 270-272; Fishberg, *The Jews,* p. 368; C. S. Bernheimer, *The Russian Jew in the United States* (Philadelphia, 1905), p. 112. Cf. ads for Schleicher and Weser pianos; *Abendblatt der Arbeiter Zeitung,* January 11, 1896; *Yiddishes Tageblatt,* January 16, 1899.

23. *New York City Guide* (WPA: New York, 1939), p. 498; *The Menorah,* 27:298 (November 1904); *Weekly Bulletin of the Clothing Trades,* 3:11 (April 29, 1904); H. C. Syrett, *The City of Brooklyn, 1865-1898* (New York, 1944), p. 237.

24. Eisenstein, *Otser,* pp. 70, 124; United States Industrial Commission, *Reports,* XIV, 477; United States Immigration Commission, *Reports,* XLI, 198; *Weekly Bulletin of the Clothing Trades* 3:14 (April 29, 1904); Joseph Barondess to Thompson, November 12, 1907 (Barondess Papers).

25. W. Laidlaw, *Population of the City of New York, 1890-1930* (New York, 1932), pp. 52, 53; Regional Survey, *Population, Land Values, and Government* (New York, 1929), p. 63.

26. W. M. Rosenblatt, "The Jews, What They Are Coming To," *Galaxy,* 13:47 (January, 1872), estimated their number at from 60,000 to 100,000; *The New York Times,* December 18, 1870, estimated 70,000; Z. H. Bernstein, "Dvorim achadim al dvar hayehudim lifnay shloshim v'arba shonim b'New York," *Yalkut Maarabi,* 1:4 (1904), estimated 80,000; Wiernik, *History,* p. 256. The religious census conducted by the Board of Delegates of American Israelites in 1878, by the nature of its method, appeared to err on the side of conservatism; 60,000 Jews for New York City, where the religiously unaffiliated were numerous indeed, seems low. *Statistics of the Jews of the United States* (Philadelphia, 1880), p. 9. In 1885, Carl Schurz estimated that New York's German Jews alone numbered 85,000. Glanz, *Jews in Relation to the Cultural Milieu of the Germans* (New York, 1947), p. 27; the figure 1,400,000 for 1914 is based on estimates for the years 1913 to 1917, *Jewish Communal Register of New York City, 1917-1918* (New York, 1918), p. 89. For a discussion of the problems of Jewish demography see *Jewish Communal Directory* (New York, 1912), p. 1f, and Henry Chalmers, "The Number of Jews in New York City," *Publications of American Statistical Association,* 14:68f (March 1914).

The Italians and Organized Crime

HUMBERT S. NELLI

Americans reacted to crime among Italian newcomers with a frenzy of emotion aroused by no other immigrant activity. Official reports, books, pamphlets, magazine articles, and newspaper stories criticized and analyzed, lamented and decried "Southern" criminalty which, in the period to the 'twenties, invariably meant the Black Hand or Mafia. Some writers argued that Italians naturally possessed criminal inclinations, others blamed slum conditions in American cities, and still others denied the existence of lawbreaking organizations in the United States patterned after the Sicilian Mafia or the Neapolitan Camorra.

Contemporaries emphasized such problems as possible operating procedures of the Black Hand among Italians in America, whether Italian crime represented a reaction to new-world conditions or a carry-over of old-world traditions, and whether Italian criminals

From *Italians in Chicago, 1880-1930: A Study in Ethnic Mobility* (New York: Oxford University Press, 1970), pp. 125-26; 130-40; 147-55; 211-22. Copyright © 1970 by Oxford University Press, Inc. Reprinted by permission of the publisher. Humbert S. Nelli is Associate Professor of History at the University of Kentucky.

worked from centralized headquarters or as independent groups and individuals. Preoccupation with these and similar aspects obscured factors of deeper significance. First, the groundwork of Italian dominance of Chicago's crime after 1920 was laid in the years prior to national prohibition legislation. In addition, Italian lawbreaking in the era before 1920 involved a wide variety of operations, many of them with no Black Hand connections. In those years also—a time of mass immigration from the Italian Kingdom—crime served an important (although not necessarily desirable) function as one method of group adjustment to a new environment. Finally, two separate and relatively distinct levels of criminal activity involving Italians developed during the formative period of Italian crime in Chicago, one entirely within the immigrant quarter and affecting only its residents. The other took place as Italians began to move into "big time" crime, which operated within the larger society. Before January 16, 1920, most "Southern" crime took place only within the colony. Prohibition encouraged many to move into organized crime, which, in Chicago, they eventually came to dominate.

* * *

On October 15, 1890, New Orleans Superintendent of Police David Hennessy was murdered. City residents assumed Sicilians to be responsible, for Hennessy had been engaged in a crackdown on crime in the Italian colony. In a city-wide atmosphere of near hysteria, the police arrested hundreds of Italians for the crime and brought nine to trial. To the consternation of the American community, the jury found six defendants "not guilty" and could reach no verdict on the other three. Rumors of

bribery and intimidation of witnesses filled New Orleans; public officials and city newspapers demanded that "the failure of justice" be remedied. With widespread local support, a mob raged to the parish prison, dragged from it eleven Italian prisoners and lynched them.

The incident quickly grew into a national crisis and an international affair. Italy demanded punishment of the lynch mob and financial compensation for the victims' families. For a short time in 1891, war between Italy and the United States appared to be a distinct possibility. President Harrison eased the situation somewhat when he spoke of the New Orleans Affair in his annual message to Congress (on December 9, 1891) as "a most deplorable and discreditable incident, an offense against law and humanity." Relations between the two countries improved in the following months, and the breach healed rapidly after Harrison offered an indemnity payment.[1]

Chicago's Italian leaders sympathized with the New Orleans Italian community and subscribed money to pay for the defense of the nine accused men. They emphasized the need for group solidarity and cooperation and tended to view the New Orleans Affair as part of a general pattern of anti-Italian attitudes on the part of Irish policemen and English-language newspapers in New Orleans, Chicago, and other American cities. Applauding the Italian government's involvement on behalf of the families of the eleven murdered men, they strongly supported the mother country in its diplomatic exchanges with the United States. They were shocked by Italy's acceptance of the American government's offer to pay what *L'Italia* described on March 19,

1892, as "a small indemnity" without recognizing or suitably condemning American responsibility in the Affair.

Prior to 1890, crime in Chicago's Italian community consisted of illegal activities in employment, child labor, crimes of passion growing out of alcoholic indulgence or presumed insults to female family members, and vendettas from the old country. Outlaws within the community had not organized, and the city's newspapers made little use of the term "Mafia" in connection with Chicago's Italians. The New Orleans Affair marked a complete turning point.

To their horror, Italians in Chicago found themselves objects of open fear and contempt during the course of the Affair. "Mafia" began to appear frequently in Chicago's newspapers, and many tabloids proclaimed the criminal inclinations of all Italians, doubtless as an outgrowth of the popular assumption that the Mafia had effected Hennessy's murder. Americans concluded that the Mafia flourished wherever "Southerners" lived. This belief strongly affected Chicagoans, for by 1891-92 the city contained a sizable and rapidly growing Italian community composed largely of "Southerners." Italian leaders reacted, for personal reasons (in order to gain American acceptance) as well as through ethnic pride, by denying the existence of the Mafia in Chicago. Some, like Durante of L'Italia, insisted that it did not exist even in Italy.[2]

In order to make clear to Americans that old-world criminal patterns and groups did not carry over into immigrant colony crime, shortly after the turn of the century Italian-language newspapers began to use the term "Black Hand" to identify crimes within the immigrant community. "Black Hand"

became favored by both American and immigrant newspapers in the first two decades of the twentieth century. From 1904, for example, "Black Hand" supplanted "Mafia" as the preferred term for crimes committed by Italians against each other, at least so far as L'Italia was concerned, and the replacement remained in use until the 1920's.[3]

Whichever name they used to publicize Italian crimes, foreign-language journals at first denied the existence of organized gangs. In an article printed on August 27, 1904, Durante repeated in L'Italia the belief he had stated in 1892: "The 'Black Hand' does not exist, the crimes must be treated singly as individual events which do not have any relation with organized groups." As time passed, the immigrant press attributed an increasing number of crimes to the Black Hand. Even L'Italia credited a quantity of blackmailings, bombings, and murders to the secret society: "Black Hand in Chicago. Blackmail Letter for $300" (July 14, 1906); "Italians on Trial. 32 Italians Accused as Members of the Black Hand" (April 27, 1907); "Once Again the Black Hand" (June 5, 1909).

In 1910 L'Italia reported the capture of Black Hand leaders: "Chicago police are elated over the arrest of four Italians accused of being leaders of the so-called Black Hand organization of Chicago." As in earlier cases, however, crimes continued even after gang leaders had been caught and their criminal societies smashed.[4]

Oscar Durante admitted in February, 1911, that 'if we continue at the present rate, the Italian colony of Chicago will soon take the lead over that of New York, in the matter of bombings, murder and blackmail." The number of criminal activities in the Italian colony did, in fact, increase as the community grew in population, although few contemporaries recognized the relationship between crime and population growth. The editor blamed Italian-Americans for the fear-ridden situation, for "when they are questioned by the police they become as dumb as fish and answer with the usual shrug of the shoulders"; as a result the criminal element could flourish "until its effect is felt from one end of the city to the other." Displaying his middle-class orientation, he complained that these conditions worked "to the detriment of the better class Italians."[5]

Although in April, 1910, *L'Italia* congratulated the police on their fight against the Black Hand—"This arrest is proof that the forces of law and order in our city are always on the alert"— one year later Durante held local officials responsible for the Black Hand's existence. "There have been 34 murders in the past two years and not one of these murders has been solved by the police. This lack of capacity shown by the police gives criminals the courage to strike again. The police must cooperate with us to clear up this situation." Mastro-Valerio and other community spokesman agreed that corrupt, incompetent police encouraged or permitted widespread criminal activity in the Italian colony. Many Americans reached the same conclusion. The Black Hand, they argued, could not possibly function without police complicity or inability. The Massachusetts Commission on Immigration, for example, identified police corruption, "which takes the form of protection of criminals," as the factor primarily responsible for Black Hand successes in cities outside Massachusetts, including Chicago.[6]

Fear and concern pervaded the Ital-

ian district because of the Black Hand's notoriety. Editor Mastro-Valerio warned in *La Tribuna Italiana Transatlantica* of the all-encompassing menace of the secret society: "Yesterday this one, today that one, tomorrow it may strike even you." Durante felt compelled to publicize the seriousness of the Black Hand problem, which he had for so long denied: "Day after day, week after week, more and more crimes are being committed, the perpetrators of which are invariably Italians . . . ." Admitting that almost every crime involved the name of the Black Hand, he described a typical method of acquiring money. Blackhanders simply demanded cash "from innocent people who work for a living." If the gangsters received nothing, they murdered their victim; should they spare his life, they bombed his home. "Naturally, these frequent crimes give a bad impression of the Italian colony to other nationalities. . . . Italians! We must do something to prevent these crimes."[7]

As more and more "Southerners" flocked to Chicago, they became an increasingly tempting source of money, more readily intimidated by threats because of the reputation of the Mafia in Sicily. After the publicity surrounding the New Orleans Affair, American papers quickly labeled all lawbreaking in the immigrant community as Mafia crimes. The successes or failures of gangs in Chicago's Italian neighborhoods, however, depended less on old-world techniques and personnel than on local conditions and opportunities.[8]

In 1907 and 1908 leaders of the Italian colony cooperated wtih leaders of the press in a concerted effort to combat and eliminate Black Hand crimes. On November 11, 1907, they organized the

White Hand Society, largely through the efforts of Italian consul Guido Sabetta. The *Unione Siciliana* played a leading role in the formation and operation of the White Hand, a significant fact in the light of that society's involvement with criminals in the 1920's and the last years of the preceding decade. The *Unione*'s unfortunate entanglement with criminals in later years should not detract from its sincere concern in 1907 and 1908 over the unfavorable image that Black Hand activities presented of "Southerners" and especially Sicilians, and its efforts to eradicate crime within the immigrant area.

Chicago's Italian-language newspapers, particularly *L'Italia* and *La Tribuna Italiana Transatlantica*, fully supported the new organization, as did the Italian ambassador in Washington and the Italian Minister of Foreign Affairs in Rome. The organizers felt that a glorious era had begun with their "war without truce, war without quarter." Bubbling enthusiasm filled early meetings held to plan action against the enemy.[9]

By the end of November the idea of the White Hand had spread to other cities and the founders conceived the notion of organizing a White Hand "in all the cities which contain large Italian colonies, which suspect the existence of mafiosi or camorristi in their midst." The eventual goal, "the day in which the Italian colonies, free of the festering evil of the Black Hand, will become models among the foreigners," unintentionally publicized the problem of crime among Italians in the United States. Ironically, many of the leaders who formulated this goal had minimized the seriousness of Italian crime or publicly denied the existence of the Black Hand. Some continued to deny its existence

while supporting White Hand activities against it.[10]

The White Hand was legally incorporated in December, 1907. Joyously, the members announced that at last Chicago's *cafoni*, or ignorant "Southern" peasants, too often the victims of Black Hand hoodlums, had "a protector in the White Hand." As stated in the Society's constitution, the White Hand intended "to paralyze and eradicate individual and organized crime which exists in the midst of the Italian colony, forcing it to submit to threats and violence," to eliminate a pervasive atmosphere of "mystery and terror," and to "present to the American public the truth concerning Italy and the Italians, frequently misrepresented by incorrect reports."[11]

In January, 1908, the White Hand called for closer cooperation with various Italian societies in the city and a program to educate *cafoni* (in Chicago and other cities) as to their duties and obligations. The Society also announced its first tangible success, claiming that it had driven ten of Chicago's most dangerous criminals—Italians—out of the city. By February the Society listed additional successes in Chicago and similar achievements in other American cities. *L'Italia* jubilantly announced, "Black Hand in Hot Water. The Arrest of One of the Heads Places the Black Hand in the Hands of the Police." The White Hand's attorney, Stephen Malato, played a major role in this capture.[12]

Never again did the White Hand achieve such glory, although it remained in existence for a number of years. It soon became a dead letter, failing in large part because of inadequate financial support. White Hand leaders lamented as early as 1908 that "so wealthy a colony as that of Chicago should have given such niggardly support to a movement intended to . . . purge it" of the Black Hand menace. The seemingly widespread "Southern" trait of indifference led to this financial distress. Reluctantly, the Society's leaders admitted that they could not gain, much less hold, the support of immigrant-area residents, the American public, or the police. The Society maintained that newcomers believed it planned to use the money collected from impoverished workers "to defend the lives and wealth of the prominent men of the colony." Among upwardly mobile members of the community the conviction had grown that by admitting the gravity of the problem of crime among Italians, the White Hand had "thrown suspicion and discredit upon the Italian name."[13]

More fundamental to rank-and-file immigrants, however, was their sense of self-preservation, which, rather than apathy or desire to protect their Italian good name, determined their behavior. "Southerners" knew that crime pervaded their communities; they knew also that authorities could or would do little to terminate it. They believed the White Hand to be powerless in the face of official corruption or tolerance of corruption, and they had no desire to involve themselves with it.[14]

While this situation existed in Chicago, it did not necessarily operate elsewhere. Domestic factors at work in individual cities strongly influenced and determined the course taken by Black Hand gangs. The Illinois Crime Commission noted that "in some American cities where the law is effectual, the 'black handers' have ceased to operate." According to John Landesco of the Illinois Crime Survey, who observed conditions in Chicago and Milwaukee for a number of years, the Black Hand in

Milwaukee had a much shorter life and "Southerners" adjusted to their new surroundings with a minimal amount of crime and dealings in corrupt politics. John S. Kendall stated that in New Orleans the Sicilian immigrants "under the leadership of the better element of their own nationality, . . . set their faces against the activities of such organizations," with the result that after 1907 the Black Hand disappeared in that city.[15]

The adjustment of Italians in Boston and elsewhere in Massachusetts contrasted even more sharply with the Chicago experience. In a study published in 1902, social worker Robert A. Woods maintained that few murders committed by Italians in the North End of Boston could be attributed to premeditation, for in the majority of cases impulse and passion formed the motivating forces. Furthermore, no murder had been traced "directly or indirectly" to the Mafia. Twelve years later the Massachusetts Commission on Immigration reported that "so-called 'Black Hand' crimes are practically unknown in Massachusetts," although Italians committed criminal violations. As a "very large proportion" of the immigrants came from the "South," the Commission considered the absence of Black Hand crime to be proof that "local American conditions are responsible for those criminal organizations elsewhere."[16]

Even more striking in indicating the impact of local conditions upon crime were differences between Italian colonies in the United States and those in Latin America, specifically Brazil and Argentina, the countries of major Italian immigration. Radicalism rather than crime in the Chicago style constituted the most serious social problem involving Italian immigrants in South America. Argentinians, for example, viewed socialism and anarchism among Italians as grave difficulties, in contrast to the more limited appeal that these doctrines exerted upon "Southerners" in the United States.[17]

While southern Italians committed violent crimes in Latin America, neither Brazil nor Argentina exhibited any indication of the Black Hand or any equivalent of Anthony D'Andrea or Al Capone. The principal reason for this difference was that in the United States, and Chicago in particular, "social and political conditions are so favorable" to the rise and spread of crime for profit.[18]

Many Chicago policemen worked illegally and in close harmony with criminals and politicians. Models of success in the city's immigrant neighborhoods often turned out to be (as Chicago's few but vociferous socialists claimed and the White Hand Society found to its distress) corrupt politicians and lawbreakers who operated under the protection of the guardians of the law. They displayed all the outward signs of economic achievement: expensive clothes and cars, quantities of ready money, food and drink of excellent quality. They also commanded attention, often respect, from the American community and Italian-language newspapers. Socialists blamed the Italian-language press, "with few exceptions," for permtiting itself to be "the main lever for the elevation of these rascals" and "an accessory to all the disgraceful things befalling our colonies."[19]

Socialists might well have had Anthony D'Andrea in mind, for he exhibited characteristics decried by the socialist press as typical of colony leaders. He (and, during the 1920's, other presidents of the Unione Siciliana) commonly associated with criminal friends and businessmen, involved himself in gangland activities and rivalries, and held a criminal record. Before his death, D'Andrea had been not only president of the Unione, but also labor-union president and candidate for political office. He and those like him gained leadership of the Unione and other societies through their own personal power and connections. They aspired to such offices because of the prestige and influence that accompanied these positions, including some measure of political power through control of members' votes on election days. On the other hand, members of societies willingly or knowingly elevated men of questionable reputation to positions of authority, possibly through ethnic pride, hope of reward, or fear of injury.[20]

Many Chicagoans, however, abhorred poverty more than crime. Dishonesty, bribery, and misuse of power simply provided ready methods for overcoming lack of money. Native-born as well as immigrant residents of the city held this view, as concerned Chicagoan Samuel Paynter Wilson observed in 1910. Conditions in Chicago favored many types of lawbreaking, and Black Hand groups flourished in the city for a number of years.[21]

Chicago attracted professional Italian crooks, generally from Sicily, because of opportunities available to extort money from fellow "Southerners," unimpeded by police and under the magic name, "Black Hand." In the Illinois Crime Survey John Landesco reported the results of a study of more than 300 crimes attributed to the Black Hand. He found that these crimes were "limited almost entirely to the Sicilian neighborhoods" of Chicago. Writing in 1909, Arthur Woods, Deputy Police Commissioner of New York City, reported a similar situation. New York police discovered that "in almost every case" Black Hand crimes were committed by men who had been involved in criminal activities in Italy and who had immigrated to New York in order to continue "fattening off the main body of their fellow-countrymen." At this period, such criminals were not, however, members of a tightly organized, highly centralized structure. "The Black Hand is not a cohesive, comprehensive society, working with mysterious signs and passwords," maintained Woods. "Given a number of Italians with money, and two or three ex-convicts, you have all the elements necessary for a first-rate Black Hand campaign." Landesco reached a similar conclusion concerning the Black Hand in Chicago and further insisted, "It is the purest banality to excuse the nefarious, bloody practices and widespread tribute paid by the victims, by the historical explanation that blackmail and the conspiracy of silence are old-world traits transplanted." Rather, the Black Hand's success in Chicago grew out of local conditions that "have favored the rise, spread and persistence of extortion by violence" even among groups "which did not import the pattern" from the old world.[22]

Black Hand activities in Chicago virtually disappeared in the 1920's. At least three factors caused this decline. First, the supply of simple, pliable victims dwindled soon after the termination of immigration in the years after 1914. Action by federal authorities formed a second factor; enforcement of laws prohibiting use of the mails to defraud forced personal delivery of threatening Black Hand notes, potentially a dangerous activity because of possibilities of being recognized.[23]

While the preceding two factors limited opportunities for criminals in the ethnic colony, a vast new city-wide field of endeavor had presented itself because of new federal laws prohibiting the manufacture and sale of alcoholic beverages. American drinking tastes and capacities did not adjust to the new regulations, and enterprising young men found themselves in a position to reap immense profits. Many American robbers, murderers, blackmailers, burglers, and thieves left their former fields of labor for the more lucrative work offered through Prohibition—for which their former professions had provided good training. It is likely that many well-qualified Blackhanders also forsook the less-profitable extortion rackets of the Italian quarter in order to join the liquor-traffic scramble. Thus immigration restriction along with Prohibition marked the end of the Black Hand era and introduced many who had been involved in crime within Italian areas into the mainstream of American gangsterdom.[24]

❊   ❊   ❊

Within the immigrant colony, bankers and *padroni*, Blackhanders and other lawbreakers realized small but important profits by swindling or terrorizing compatriots. Another level of crime involved Italians. Organized crime, business operations reaping vast profits in and from the whole city, offered almost limitless opportunities for promotion within the hierarchy.

Chicago's organized crime originated in the 1870's with the activities of Michael Cassius McDonald. In the years before the Great Fire, gambling dens operated openly with police protection, some of them 24 hours a day. Joseph Medill, elected mayor in 1871 on a "Let's Rebuild Chicago" platform, openly fought gamblers, liquor interests, and the criminal elements of the city. McDonald retaliated by organizing the underworld for political action, and he and his forces succeeded in electing Harvey D. Colvin mayor in 1873.

Gambling interests suffered a temporary setback with the election of Monroe Heath in 1876, but they returned to power in 1879 and except for a brief eclipse during the mayoralty of John A. Roche (1887-89), McDonald controlled city politics until the mid-1890's. Recalling the McDonald era on August 18, 1907 (a few days after his death), the *Chicago Record-Herald* stated that "he never held office, but he ruled the city with an iron hand. He named the men who were to be candidates for election, he elected them, and after they were in office they were merely his puppets." Chicago historian Bessie Louise Pierce described him as "virtually the dictator of the City Hall." With his political power established following Carter Henry Harrison's mayoral success in 1879, "Mike" McDonald turned to organizing the city's first "syndicate," which centered on gambling. During his reign, McDonald, as political party boss and head of the "syndicate," forged the powerful and highly effective coalition of criminals, politicians, and compliant policemen that the Torrio-Capone organization utilized so successfully during the 1920's.[25]

Following the assassination of Mayor Harrison in October, 1893, McDonald's star began to fade, and a number of new independent organizations or "syndicates" formed. By 1907, when "Mike" died, various spheres of interest controlled gambling in Chicago. Mont Tennes gave orders on the North Side, James O'Leary on the South Side, and Alderman Johnny Rogers on the West Side. First Ward political bosses "Hinky Dink" Kenna and "Bathhouse John" Coughlin, early patrons of "Diamond Jim" Colosimo, presided over gambling in the Loop.[26]

After years of gang warfare most of McDonald's former gambling empire centered in the hands of Mont Tennes, who ruled, in turn, until the 1920's when the Torrio-Capone group pushed him aside and seized control of gambling as well as other illegal activities in the Chicago area. Although the real entry of Italians into a big-time crime (and most of their successes therein) came after 1920—that is, during Prohibition—they did make a strong beginning under Colosimo in the first two decades of the twentieth century.

While still a youth, Colosimo left Calabria for the United States. His first employment in this country, and the work that took him to Chicago, was that of waterboy for a railroad section gang. Before the turn of the century Colosimo became a streetsweeper and established his residence in the First Ward at 416 South Clark Street. Rocco De Stefano, who later became "Big Jim's" lawyer, also lived in this tenement. Colosimo organized his fellow street sweepers (or "white wings") of the First Ward into a political bloc that he led as a unit to the polling station at election time in order to vote for candidates supported by the Democratic machine. This action quickly brought him to the attention of aldermen Kenna and Coughlin, who had dominated First Ward politics since 1893. They made "Big Jim" a precinct captain and he delivered the vote so successfully for his patrons that before his death he rivaled Kenna and Coughlin as a political power in the ward.[27]

In the meantime Colosimo and his wife, Victoria Moresco, acquired a string of brothels and saloons, as well as a legitimate business—a nationally known restaurant called "Colosimo's Cafe." (Socially prominent Chicagoans patronized it and dined among theater and opera personages, including George M. Cohan and Enrico Caruso.) By 1914, "Big Jim" and associates had built a "syndicate," the first one organized by Chicago Italians, based on vice operations and gambling. In that year State's Attorney Maclay Hoyne launched a grand jury investigation of vice in Chicago's First Ward and found the existence of three vice rings or "syndicates." The first and largest consisted of the Colosimo-Torrio outfit, headed by "Big Jim" and his chief lieutenant, Johnny Torrio.[28]

Colosimo brought his number two man to Chicago in 1909 to deal with Black Hand extortion threats, since Torrio had effectively arranged for the elimination of bothersome Blackhanders in New York. Within five years, his efficient and ruthless methods advanced Torrio to second-in-command and a power in his own right through his organizing of gambling in the city and some nearby suburbs. (At this time Torrio lived in the same building as "Big Jim," 101 West Twenty-first Street.) In 1919 Henry Barrett Chamberlain, Operating Director of the Chicago Crime Commission, described increasingly efficient "syndicate" crime: "Modern crime, like modern business, is tending toward centralization, organization, and commercialization. Ours is a business nation. Our criminals apply business methods. . . . The men and women of evil have formed trusts.[29]

When the National Prohibition Enforcement Act (The Volstead Act) went into effect on January 16, 1920, the Colosimo-Torrio organization expanded from prostitution and gambling into an even more lucrative business, the manufacture and distribution of liquor. Colosimo did not live long enough to reap the full financial harvest of his bootlegging ventures, for he was murdered on May 11, 1920.

Responsibility for his death was never determined. Some maintained that the murder formed the climax of a struggle for political control of the First Ward, with Kenna and Colosimo allied against Frank Brady, the ward's Republican leader, and Frank Chiaravalotti. The *Chicago Daily News* advanced this possibility the day after Colosimo's death. More people accepted the theory that the shooting grew out of Colosimo's affection for Miss Dale Winter, a hired singer in his restaurant. For love of Dale, "Big Jim" divorced Victoria. A big, crude, gross man with a passion for diamonds (which shone from his belt and suspender buckles, his shirt, vest, fingers, and even his garters), Colosimo won the affection of Miss Winter, described by contemporaries as a lovely girl, gentle and sweet, with a beautiful singing voice. According to this second theory, the first Mrs. Colosimo hired thugs to murder the man who had cast her aside for a younger woman. The fact that Victoria remarried only two weeks after the divorce and some three weeks before "Diamond Jim" married his Dale weakened this argument.[30]

Another popular theory held that John Torrio, tired of being the number two man, lusted for full control of the organization and took steps to achieve this end. After Colosimo's death, Torrio did indeed succeed to the "syndicate" throne, which he occupied until his retirement in 1925. In contrast to his rough and vulgar predecessor, Torrio was quiet, crafty, and businesslike; he shunned alcohol, tobacco, personal violence, and foul language. An able and effective leader, Torrio excelled as a master strategist and organizer and quickly built an empire that far exceeded Colosimo's in wealth, power, and influence. He received invaluable aid from his chief lieutenant, Alphonse Capone. Italian domination of Chicago's organized crime had made a strong beginning indeed.[31]

Several factors facilitated Italian successes in the highly competitive (and deadly) business of organized crime. Some related to old-world backgrounds and characteristics, others to conditions and opportunities in the host society. Mafia-expert Michele Pantaleone has presented a billiant exposé of the Sicilian Mafia in a recent book, *The Mafia and Politics*. His comments on Sicilians in American crime, however, raise more questions than they answer. According to Pantaleone, men schooled in he Sicilian Mafia "founded and organized gangsterdom in America fifty years ago" —that is, in the decade following 1910. These criminals operated in "St. Louis, Chicago, Kansas City, Detroit, New Orleans, New Jersey [sic] and other cities." The list omits, significantly, Boston and Milwaukee. Also pointedly missing are —first—any indication that "organized gangsterdoms" existed in Chicago, New York and other cities long before 1910, and—second—the fact that when an Italian "syndicate" developed after 1910 in competition with organizations composed of members of other ethnic groups, it was not staffed solely by Sicilians or even entirely by Italians, any more than Irish, Jewish, or Polish criminal organizations contained only members of these groups. Thus many alleged

capo mafiosi (leaders) of Chicago's Italian "syndicate" had no Sicilian ancestry, while others born in Sicily emigrated as children and grew to maturity in urban America. James Colosimo for example, was born in mainland Italy (Calabria) and arrived in Chicago as a boy; John Torrio, a native of the province of Naples, immigrated (with his parents) at the age of two and grew up in Brooklyn; Al Capone was born in Brooklyn of Neapolitan parents; while Jake Gusick (or Jack Cusick), the "so-called brains of the Capone organization," was only one of many non-Italian members of the "American Mafia hierarchy."[32]

The ethnic cohesion and group loyalty exhibited by the Italian criminal element in its struggle to dominate Chicago's organized crime formed a more significant factor than the Sicilian origin of some gangsters. The "Southern" background of most of the city's Italians included a deep loyalty to clan traditions held to be sacred from "outside" interference. As some writers on Italian-American criminality have pointed out, these traditions and connections provided a ready-made nucleus for criminal gangs in the new world and ensured a fierce partisanship toward the group's laws and rituals rather than to "outside" rules and regulations.[33]

To a Southern Italian or Sicilian living in the Kingdom, however, the concept of *paese* (homeland) meant locality of origin, rather than the nation. Localism—due to the mountainous character of the country, which isolated communities—operated to the extent that even adjacent areas in Italy developed their own characteristics, customs, speech patterns, and loyalties. "There are Campanians, Abruzzians, Apulians, Calabrians, Lucanians (Lucania being another name for Basilicata), Sicilians and Sardinians, all differing greatly from each other, while inside each region are many varieties of type," as English historian Margaret Carlyle pointed out. "Not only is a Campanian, particularly a Neapolitan, as different from a Calabrian as a Norfolk man from a Cumbrian, but a peasant from one of the primitive agricultural towns of the Ionian side of Calabria is a completely different type from the man who farms a tiny bit of good land on the Tyrrhenian coast."[34] This meaning of *paese* contrasted sharply with the situation in the United States, where Sicilians and mainlanders alike regarded themselves as Italians, and were so regarded by Americans.

In Chicago this expanded sense of loyalty and patriotism manifested itself in celebrations supporting the Italian Kingdom, membership in mutual-aid and fraternal societies based on regional or national groupings, and support of an "Italian" press and Italian Catholic parishes. In the new homeland, therefore, village loyalties grew into national loyalties and members of the ethnic group came to look upon non-Italians, rather than people from outside a particular village in Italy, as foreigners. "American" Italians, who established and operated Chicago's Italian "syndicate," excluded members of other ethnic groups until they had proved themselves to be worthy of acceptance. Since conditions in Chicago offered fertile ground for lawless activities, gangs composed predominantly of other ethnic groups— Irish, German, Scandinavian—operated openly and often under the protection of the law and elected officials long before "Southerners" arrived. This "favorable" situation could not be found in all urban areas to which "Southerners"

migrated, with the significant result that second-generation Italians became prominently involved in criminal organizations in some cities and not in others. Undoubtedly many Sicilian Blackhanders moved into the "syndicate," but "American" Italians provided the leadership. Hence local conditions permitting or even encouraging lawlessness clearly occupied a place of basic importance in Italian successes within Chicago's organized crime.[35]

Chicago's early Italian settlement, largely composed of northern Italians, took little interest in, and avoided contact with, "Southerners." Most of the city's southern Italians, especially those from Sicily, arrived between 1900 and 1914. Children of "Southern" immigrants grew to maturity at a time when educational requirements were increasingly important when qualifying for jobs in public as well as in private employment. The fluid political, social, and financial patterns, which had aided (and in fact had speeded) the assimilation of Germans, Irishmen, Bohemians, Poles, Swedes, and Norwegians in the three decades following 1870, gradually grew more rigid and unyielding as earlier immigrant elements became entrenched. These early arrivals sought to establish barriers to prevent later ones (with other ethnic backgrounds) from challenging their positions.

If at all possible, ethnic group members tried to "look after their own" whether in politics, crime, organized labor, or the professions. Thus Anton J. Cermak, whether in his capacity as alderman, president of the Cook County Board of Commissioners, or mayor, made sure that his fellow Bohemians (Czechs) received patronage jobs and support when they tried for elective office. Early arriving northern Italians, however, did not consider "Southerners" to be "of their own." Lacking established patrons, southern Italians did not make their political presence in the city really felt until the 1920's when, under the leadership and guidance of John Torrio and Al Capone, they found politics and its urban handmaiden, crime, to offer an increasingly important source of money as well as a means of social mobility.[36]

Chicago's Italians enjoyed great success in criminal activities, whether within immigrant areas through Black Hand and other extortion methods or by "syndicate" techniques in the larger, American environment. The Black Hand existed, but as a method of criminal action, a *modus operandi*, and not a formal organization. As the White Hand Society pointed out in 1908, many other Italian-community residents who did not consider themselves Blackhanders—among them bankers, interpreters, labor agents, and small businessmen—worked diligently to extort fellow immigrants. They employed more subtle and refined methods than did the Black Hand thugs, "but they too are means of exacting tribute from the sweat of the Italian working man, who pays because of his ignorance, and because of the absolute lack of any assistance and protection in a foreign land."[37]

Profits gained through Black Hand methods in the immigrant colony seemed small when compared with the lucrative returns won by "syndicate" gangsters from Prohibition law violations, gambling, prostitution, and drug peddling. Italians born or raised in Chicago quickly learned to adapt American business techniques to crime by organizing compatriots (and acceptable "outsiders"), centralizing the chain of command, and controlling and directing the flow of money. In this process of "Americanizing" Italian criminal activities, "American" Italians established the Italian "syndicate."

Crime even facilitated immigrant adjustment. The "syndicate" required the repression of lingering old-world prejudices against fellow members from other provinces or countries, because of the overriding importance of cooperation in the common quest for money, that symbol and substance of success. In the new urban home—cynical, cruel, vulgar, avaricious Chicago—Sicilians and Italians, northern as well as southern, joined together for mutual benefit and profit. Because of its function as a means of economic betterment and social mobility, crime occupied a place in the acculturation of Italians in the United States, along with immigrant-community institutions, education, the padrone system, and politics.

* * *

Italians realized incredible financial success from organized crime. At a time when "American" Italians (those born or raised in the United States) were arriving at maturity only to find economic advancement made difficult—but not impossible—by inadequate education, "undesirable" social and ethnic backgrounds, and lack of political connections, a new field of endeavor appeared, requiring as qualifications only ambition, ruthlessness, and loyalty. With its fast, lush monetary opportunities, prohibition provided a powerful attraction for many qualified young men who felt irresistibly drawn to this novel form of economic enterprise. "Prohibition is a business," maintained "Scarface Al" Capone. "All I do is to supply a public demand. I do it in the best and least harmful way I can." He and others like him undoubtedly convinced themselves that they worked simply as labor and distribution organizers in a strongly competitive field. Criminals could persuade themselves of their value to society and the business world because the liquor trade provided a service that rich and poor alike desperately wanted and willingly paid for. Prohibition "opened up a new criminal occupation, with less risk of punishment, with more certainty of gain, and with less social stigma than the usual forms of crime like robbery, burglary, and larceny."[38]

Under the leadership of John Torrio and his successor, Capone, Italians exerted a powerful economic and political influence in Chicago, and made a spectacular and notorious entrance into the mainstream of city life and consciousness during the 'twenties. Their glittering successes and extravagant excesses, and the extensive publicity accorded their actions by the press, diverted public attention from widespread but less sensational accomplishments of Chicago's law-abiding Italians.

James Colosimo's funeral on May 15, 1920, signified a major turning point in the emergence of Italians in organized crime and indicated the growing influence of gangsters in city politics. The elite of Chicago's officialdom attended the ceremony. Three judges, eight aldermen, an assistant state's attorney, a congressman, and a state representative served as honorary pallbearers, along with gamblers, vice-resort operators, and racketeers. The event proved to be, in the words of Chicago Crime Commission Executive Director Virgil W. Peterson, "a public announcement that the criminal world ruled the city, and political success depended upon the favor of those in control of gambling and vice. The voice of the general public which abhorred such criminal-official alliances was weak and politically insignificant." Chicago had "capitulated to the underworld."[39]

Following Colosimo's burial, John Torrio—also an honorary pallbearer—quickly consolidated his control over the Levee and moved to extend his influence throughout the city as well as South Side and West Side suburbs. The former Colosimo lieutenant established a highly efficient city-wide "syndicate" to operate breweries and convoys of trucks needed for the manufacture and distribution of beer, a product for which Chicagoans exhibited a powerful craving. During the initial period, many pre-prohibition brewery owners apparently formed partnerships with gangsters. Others employed underworld leaders as "fronts" while continuing to operate their companies; these seemed to comply with legislation prohibiting the manufacture of alcoholic beverages for general consumption. In short order the criminal elements established their supremacy, at least partly because of the unwillingness of legitimate owners to continue their involvement when police enforcement became more effective and the prospect of jail terms, consequently, more likely.[40]

Between 1920 and 1923, Torrio brought a measure of peace among warring criminal factions, and elevated himself to a position of dominance by convincing his fellow gangsters of the advantages of cooperation as opposed to competition. He presided over the city's division into spheres of influence, keeping most of the South Side under his personal control. Realizing that violence harmed his business, he avoided conflicts whenever he could. As John Landesco pointed out, however, "when murder must be done, it was done deft-

ly and thoroughly." Torrio acted quickly, for example, to discourage two free-
lance bootleggers, Morrie Keane and
William Egan, who attempted to in-
vade his territory in December 1923.
Their venture ended violently, with two
bullet-ridden bodies sprawled by a
roadside—a lesson not lost on other
overly ambitious hoodlums. Torrio's success, however, rested on more than
strong-arm methods. He provided his
bootlegging associates with protection
from the law, and with lavish outlays of
money purchased the cooperation of local politicians and police officers. "Immunity from punishment," concluded
Landesco, "appears to be an almost indispensable element in maintaining the
prestige and control of a gangster
chief."[41]

The "syndicate" operated quietly, efficiently, and profitably in Chicago under the benign eyes of grafting politicians and police, during the years of the
second Thompson administration. According to newspapermen Lloyd Wendt
and Herman Kogan, "as long as Thompson was in office, despite all his fuss
about driving out the criminals, this
alliance progressed smoothly, in the
business-like way Torrio hoped it
would." In his techniques of organization, Torrio was "not unlike a master
politician, using the powers of patronage and favor when it suited his purpose, punishing when his purpose was
thwarted, breaking and upsetting alliances when an underling sought to defy
him." A United States District Attorney admitted that "as an organizer and
administrator of underworld affairs,
Johnny Torrio is unsurpassed in the annals of American crime; he is probably
the nearest thing to a real mastermind
that this country has yet produced."
Writing at the end of the Capone era,

Walter Noble Burns judged that Torrio
"would have been an outstanding success in any field of endeavor," possessing as he did a remarkable degree of
"poise, sound judgment, finesse, shrewd
diplomacy, common sense, and clear
vision. He was, in his way, a genius."
To Elmer Irey, who succeeded in accumulating enough evidence in the 1930's
to send Torrio to jail (for two and a
half years) for tax violation, "he was
the smartest and, I dare say, the best
of all hoodlums. 'Best' referring to talent, not morals."[42]

The election of William E. Dever as
Mayor in April 1923, upset this harmonious arrangement and resulted in
Torrio's retirement two years later. The
refusal of Dever and his chief of police, Morgan A. Collins, to cooperate
with Torrio destroyed the old system
of official protection and damaged the
prestige and control of the "syndicate"
chief. On May 19, 1924, Chief Collins
directed a secret and highly successful
raid on the Sieben Brewery, which net-
ted, along with the usual small-time
crooks (truck drivers, gunmen, workmen), three major gang leaders including Torrio himself. Torrio's arrest and
indictment proved beyond any doubt
that the "syndicate" did not control the
new city administration, a fact that
encouraged ambitious underlings like
Dion O'Banion and Hymie Weiss to
challenge the established criminal hierarchy.[43]

The relative calm of the corrupt
Thompson era ended abruptly. The
"union of each for the good of all" under the guidance of Torrio gave way to
the "war of each against all," in which
yesterday's ally often became today's
enemy. Between September 1923, and
October 1926, an estimated 215 gangsters murdered each other in the strug-

gle to seize control of local booze and beer businesses. Police accounted for another 160 outlaw deaths. One casualty was former altar boy Dion O'Banion, who bossed the so-called North Side gang at the time of his demise on November 10, 1924. Although the killers were never identified or apprehended, general gossip assumed them to be either members of the Genna clan, which had long feuded with O'Banion, or paid assassins employed by the Torrio-Capone organization. Dion's successor, Polish-American Hymie Weiss (born Wajciechowski), vowed to avenge his Irish friend's murder. On January 12, 1925, unknown assailants tried to kill Capone; later in the month Torrio suffered a near-fatal attempt on his life. In February, a thoroughly shaken Torrio appeared in United States District Court to face charges growing out of his part in the Sieben Brewery affair. Found guilty, he received a sentence of nine months in jail. The former overlord of crime uncomplainingly accepted the temporary safety that prison offered. Following his early release from jail, Torrio hastily departed from Chicago, abandoning the organization that he and Colosimo had taken years to build. The "syndicate" now functioned under the leadership of a new and handpicked director, Al Capone, who assumed control of the empire while he was still in his twenties.[44]

The war for control of Chicago's underworld continued its violent course (in the process damaging the reputation of the city's reform mayor) until the rival factions finally concluded that the prize did not justify the cost. On October 21, 1926, representatives of the major gangs met to negotiate a settlement. This provided for a division of the city among rival organizations and an agreement not to operate outside the allotted territory. While Capone apparently obtained direct rights only to part of the West Side and the western suburbs, he continued to exert great influence on the South Side. The powerful and cohesive organization bequeathed him by Torrio gave him a tremendous advantage over his major rivals, the North Side mob.

Lasting little more than five months, the truce of October 21 ended with the death of Vincent "the Schemer" Drucci at the hands of the police on April 4, 1927. As boss of the O'Banion gang, Drucci had abided by the terms of the October agreement. His successor, George "Bugs" Moran, refused to compromise with the Capone organization, a feeling shared by Moran's allies, Christian P. "Barney" Bertsche, Jack Zuta, and the Aiello brothers. The relative quiet of the interim period ended, and the gang wars progressed toward what newspaperman Denis Tilden Lynch (writing in 1932) termed the underworld's "most gory act of terrorism." On February 14, 1929, four men —two dressed like police officers—entered a garage at 2122 North Clark Street and murdered seven members of the North Side group. This St. Valentine's Day Massacre failed to eliminate Moran, who happened not to stop by the garage that particular morning. He left shortly afterward for the East Coast, and the once-strong North Side organization disintegrated. With all Capone's rivals removed from competition, "Scarface Al" ruled Chicago's underworld at the age of thirty-two, just ten years after his inauspicious arrival in the city.[45]

In appearance, personality, and behavior the "Big Fellow" (as Capone was known to friend and enemy alike) contrasted sharply with his predecessor. The slim, quiet, conservatively attired

Torrio suggested a successful business-man—perhaps a banker—rather than the leader of a criminal gang. His reputation as a man who indulged in no debauchery reinforced this impression, although the organization he directed offered for sale every vice known to man. While his underlings beat, maimed, and murdered countless numbers of victims, Torrio despised violence and proudly boasted that never in his life had he fired a gun. The tall and husky Capone, on the other hand, fitted the gangster stereotype. He was loud, uncouth, and a flashy dresser. He enjoyed alcohol and women, and had a passion for gambling, once losing $500,000 in a day at the racetrack. Nothing in his manner or looks indicated the qualities of mind, the shrewdness, subtlety, and keen intelligence that enabled him to seize and maintain control over Chicago crime while still a young man. The "Big Fellow" also had the ability to withstand the pressures of his work and to face without visible fear the constant threat of violent death. To the underworld and the general public, Torrio's precipitous flight from Chicago after the attempt on his life dimmed the luster of his earlier achievements. In contrast, numerous assassination attempts never deflected Capone from his objectives.[46]

Capone, or "Al Brown," as he called himself at the time of his arrival from Brooklyn, began his career in Chicago as bodyguard for "syndicate" boss James Colosimo. After "Big Jim's" death in 1920, "Scarface Al" quickly moved upward in the organization and two years later emerged as chief lieutenant to Torrio. In 1923 Torrio felt his position threatened by the election of reformer William Dever, the Democratic candidate for mayor, who vowed to prosecute the major prohibition violat-

ors rather than the "small fry" operating in Chicago. Torrio soon found himself confronted with the problem of finding an alternate base of operations for metropolitan-area beer distribution and gambling, a base that could not be touched by the militant new city administration. Cicero offered an ideal location. It lay adjacent to Stickney, where Torrio already operated several houses of prostitution; and of all Chicago suburbs, Cicero was most accessible to the Loop and other core areas of the city. In addition, the suburb itself promised to be a rich market for liquor and beer sales as well as gambling. With a population of 50,000 people (the majority of them of Slavic or German background) Cicero formed the largest urban area in the county (outside Chicago) and the fifth in size in Illinois.[47]

Torrio's forces moved into Cicero in the fall of 1923. Local political-criminal elements led by Eddie Vogel and Eddie Tancl, and Miles and William "Klondike" O'Donnell (whose gang supplied Cicero and Chicago's West Side with beer and other liquors), attempted unsuccessfully to block Torrio. Before the end of the year Torrio had imposed a compromise agreement that assured his gang a monopoly of gambling activities in the greater part of the town. Capone directed "syndicate" activities in the West Side suburb in his first independent "command" assignment. "Scarface Al" proceeded quietly and carefully at first, emphasizing the vital services he provided to the community through his beer-running activities. "It's a shame," he noted disapprovingly, "that a man should be denied a glass of beer after a hard day's work," a line of argument designed to appeal to the residents of the working-class suburb. Cicero's mayoralty election of April 1,

1924, provided an opportunity for Capone to gain control of the entire town. Through fraudulent registration, bribery, ballot-box stuffing, kidnapping, slugging, and shooting, Capone "elected" his candidate over an opposition equally corrupt but less resourceful.[48]

In following years Capone emerged as the "feudal baron of Cicero" (in the words of his biographer Fred D. Pasley). In addition to Cicero, the "syndicate" allegedly controlled Burnham, Chicago Heights, Melrose Park, Stickney, and other nearby towns. Mayor Dever's action in attempting to eliminate crime and corruption in the city drove the Torrio-Capone forces into the suburbs, where they carried on their illegal and highly profitable business openly and without effective opposition from county officials, among them Anton J. Cermak, President of the Cook County Board of Commissioners. The captivity of Cicero continued even after the election of Republican "Big Bill" Thompson as mayor in 1927 prepared the way for Capone's return to Chicago. John Lyle, Judge of the Municipal Court (and a publicity-conscious reformer) recalled in 1960 that "Cicero besmirched and looted, would in the end, have revenge on its prime minister of evil." Evidence captured in raids on Capone-controlled Cicero gambling houses and speakeasies made possible the conviction of the "Big Fellow" for income tax evasion in 1931. During the six years between Torrio's retirement and Capone's conviction, "Scarface Al" directed an organization that exceeded that of his predecessor in extent, influence, power, and wealth.[49]

Capone, Torrio, Drucci, the Aiellos, the Gennas, and other "Southerners" acquired millions of dollars during prohibition years. No accurate measure of

their wealth exists, but estimates of the Capone "syndicate's gross annual income ranged from $100,000,000 to over $300,000,000 by the late 1920's. Beer and other alcoholic beverages accounted for about 60 per cent of each year's intake, with gambling, prostitution, and other activities bringing in smaller but still significant amounts. Thus records seized by United States Bureau of Internal Revenue agents showed net profits in excess of $500,000 for a single Capone-controlled gambling house, The Ship, during an 18-month period in 1925-26. On Chicago's Near West Side the Genna brothers, at the height of their power and glory, employed hundreds of neighborhood "Southerners" to distill alcohol in their own homes. This particular business enterprise resulted in a highly lucrative operation with gross sales of $350,000 a month, and total assets valued at $5,000,000.[50]

For American gangsters and especially second generation "Southerners," prohibition formed a Golden Age, when ambitious youngsters could amass wealth and power beyond their wildest dreams. Practical considerations rather than moral values shaped the attitude of ethnic district youths toward criminal activity, declared John Landesco. On the basis of existensive interviews conducted during the late twenties with youth gang members, Landesco concluded that "where the choice of a young man is between a low paid job as an unskilled laborer and good wages for driving a beer truck, a stigma is soon attached to legitimate employment."[51]

During prohibition, professional criminals—pickpockets, extortionists, safecrackers and others—abandoned their former practices in the Italian community and joined the growing ranks of bootleggers. The last vestiges of the

Black Hand disappeared as members (allegedly among them the Genna brothers) entered the "syndicate." Many legitimate businessmen found the lure of the fast money too powerful to resist. John Landesco noted that the Aiellos, who later became prominent members of the North Side organization, worked initially in business, first appearing in the city's bootlegging activities as suppliers of sugar "on a large scale to wholesalers." To laboring-class "Southerners," the "syndicate's" eagerness to buy the product of home stills offered a quick and easy way to augment family incomes.[52]

Journalistic accounts of Chicago crime in the prohibition era generally ascribed control and direction of the production of bootleg booze in the city's Italian neighborhoods to the *Unione Siciliana* (after 1925 the Italo-American National Union). Before World War I this organization enjoyed a prestigious reputation for its opposition to immigrant colony crime as a supporter of the White Hand Society. By 1929 Fred D. Pasley would write that the Union "comprises some 15,000 Sicilians, disciplined like an army; implacable of purpose; swift and silent of deed; the Mafia of Italy transplanted to the United States." Walter Noble Burns claimed that "its members distilled the greater part of the basic alcohol used in the whisky, brandy, rum, and gin sold in Chicago and held a monopoly on the sale of sugar and yeast used by Sicilian distillers." Rumor held that ample profits led to a tug-of-war between rival criminal elements in 1928 over control of the Union, the two main protagonists being the Aiellos and Capone. A number of murders took place, including those of Antonio Lombardo, Pasqualino Lolardo, Joseph Giunta, and Joseph

Aiello, all presidents of the Italo-American National Union or aspirants to that position. The Capone faction emerged victorious.[53]

In contrast to years before 1920, the greater part of illegally gained cash during prohibition came from outside the ethnic group. Chicagoans decried the violence and bloodshed, the debasement of public officials, the involvement of the *Unione Siciliana,* and the enrichment of social undesirables. At the same time city residents subsidized the "syndicate" by patronizing its establishments (speakeasies, gambling parlors, and houses of prostitution), drinking its booze and glorifying its criminals. Foremost among these antiheroes, of course, was Al Capone.

The general public admired Capone's audacity, respected his power, and envied his wealth. Many people saw the gangster chieftain's life as one of glamour, danger and excitement, far removed from the sweat and drudgery of daily labor. Millions of Americans ignored his crimes and lionized him for "disdaining a law that was becoming increasingly unpopular; they sympathized when he objected to being called a bootlegger and a racketeer" and offered no objection when he described his activities as being those of a harassed businessman. During the days of his glory, Capone received fan letters from all over the world. Foreign authors traveled thousands of miles to interview him and write books and articles about his place in American life. In 1931 Frederick Lewis Allen observed that Capone, by the end of the preceding decade, had grown "as widely renowned as Charles Evans Hughes or Gene Tunney. He had become an American portent."[54]

Significantly, Italian-language newspapers devoted less space to crime during the 1920's (when Italians scaled the heights of criminal success) than they had earlier to Black Hand activities. Any readers who depended solely on *L'Italia* or *La Tribuna Italiana Trans-atlantica* for news during prohibition years remained ignorant of the actions and notoriety of John Torrio and Al Capone. The attempts to murder the "Big Fellow" and Torrio in January, 1925, for example, received no mention in Italian periodicals. While Italian journals did report the St. Valentine's Day killings, they indicated no connection between that event and organized crime. This deliberate policy of silence reflected the middle class aspirations and orientations of newspaper pubilshers and their intention to minimize the sordid and unpleasant aspects of Italian-American life in the city. Chicago's Italians who had departed from the immigrant quarter in search of acceptance and respectability, or who planned to do so, saw in "Scarface Al" and other gangland figures a constant source of chagrin and embarrassment. Giovanni E. Schiavo's paean of praise for Italian-American achievements, *Italians in Chicago,* completely ignored the city's wealthiest and most widely known Italian, although the book appeared in 1928 when Capone had reached the height of his power.[55]

To many ethnic colony residents, Capone appeared to be a benefactor. In Chicago and Cicero he supplied the needy with coal, groceries, clothing, and other necessities. Capone's benevolence, like the criminal organization that he headed (and that provided the cash for his welfare activities) reached beyond his fellow "Southerners." The "Big Fellow" opened his wallet and his "syndicate" to anyone, regardless of race, creed, or color. Novelist Mary Borden,

who in 1930 visited her native Chicago after an absence of twelve years, described Capone as "an ambidextrous giant, who kills with one hand and feeds with the other." The gangster chief's concern for the plight of poor Chicagoans was more than the outpouring of a generous spirit. Along with his multifarious illegal activities, Capone functioned as a political boss and knew that favors lavished on voters and potential voters often paid dividends on election day.[56]

NOTES

1. John E. Coxe, "The New Orleans Mafia Incident," *Louisiana Historical Quarterly,* XX (Oct. 1937), 1067-1110; John S. Kendall, "Who Killa de Chief?" *Louisiana Historical Quarterly,* XXII (Apr. 1939), 492-530; A. Pierantoni, *I Fatti di Nuova Orleans e il Diritto Internazionale* (Rome, 1891).
2. *L'Italia,* Oct. 25, Nov. 1, Dec. 27, 1890; Mar. 7, 21, May 9, July 18, Sept. 12, Dec. 12, 1891; Feb. 6, Mar. 19, Apr. 16, 1892.
3. Several theories have been offered to explain the appearance of the term "Black Hand" to describe certain types of crime within the Italian colony. Perhaps the most acceptable was the one advanced by Gaetano D'Amato, a New York City Italian community leader and friend of police lieutenant Joseph Petrosino of New York's Italian detective squad. In a 1908 article, "The 'Black Hand' Myth," 548, D'Amato stated, "The term 'Black Hand' was first used in this country about ten years ago, probably by some Italian desperado who had heard of the exploits of the Spanish society, and considered the combination of words to be high-sounding and terror-inspiring. One or two crimes committed under the symbol gave it a vogue among the rapacious brotherhood; and, as it looked well and attracted attention in their headlines, the newspapers finally applied it to all crimes committed by the Italian banditti in the United States."
4. *L'Italia,* Apr. 16, 1910; Aug. 10, 1901; *La Tribuna Italiana Transatlantica,* Feb. 8, 1908.
5. *L'Italia,* Feb. 4, 1911.
6. *L'Italia,* Apr. 1, 1911; *La Tribuna Italiana Transatlantica,* Nov. 9, 1907; Commonwealth of Massachusetts, *The Problem of Immigration in Massachusetts. Report of the Commission on Immigration* (Boston, 1914), 105-6.
7. *La Tribuna Italiana Transatlantica,* Nov. 9, 1907; *L'Italia,* Apr. 1, 1911.
8. The Italian "White Hand" Society in Chi-

cago, Illinois, *Studies, Action and Results* (Chicago, 1908), 25-26.

9. *La Tribuna Italiana Transatlantica*, Nov. 16, 23, 1907; *L'Italia*, Nov. 16, 1907.

10. *L'Italia*, Nov. 30, 1907. For the appearance of the White Hand in New Orleans see *La Tribuna Italiana Transatlantica*, Dec. 7, 1907.

11. *La Tribuna Italiana Transatlantica*, Dec. 14, 28, 1907. See Italian "White Hand" Society, *Studies, Action and Results*, 21-22 for the organization's aims.

12. *La Tribuna Italiana Transatlantica*, Jan. 11, Feb. 1, 15, 22, Mar. 7, 1908; *L'Italia*, Feb. 15, Mar. 14, May 23, 1908.

13. Italian "White Hand" Society, *Studies, Action and Results*, 24. Also *Chicago Record-Herald*, Mar. 20, 1911; *La Parola dei Socialisti*, Mar. 28, 1914.

14. Local Community Research Committee, *Chicago Communities*, Vol. VI, "East Side," Document 8. See also Vol. VI, "West Englewood," Document 1a; *La Tribuna Italiana Transatlantica*, Nov. 9, 1907.

15. Landesco, *Organized Crime in Chicago*, 947-48, 953-54; Kendall, "Who Killa de Chief?" 504.

16. Robert A. Woods, ed., *Americans in Process* (Boston, 1902), 207-9; *The Problem of Immigration in Massachusetts*, 105.

17. Robert J. Alexander, *Labor Relations in Argentina, Brazil and Chile* (New York, 1962), 147-49, 162-65, and *Communism in Latin America* (New Brunswick, N.J., 1957), 155; Robert D. Ochs, "A History of Argentine Immigration, 1853-1924," unpublished Ph.D. dissertation, University of Illinois, 1939, 149-57; James Bryce, *South America, Observations and Impressions* (new ed.; New York, 1914), 320.

18. Charley Wagley, *An Introduction to Brazil* (New York, 1963), 181-83; Thomas F. McGann, *Argentina, the United States and the Inter-American System* (Cambridge, Mass., 1957), 193; Italian "White Hand" Society, *Studies, Action and Results*, 26.

19. John Landesco, "Crime and the Failure of Institutions in Chicago's Immigrant Areas," *AICLC*, XXIII (July-Aug. 1932), 244; *La Parola dei Socialisti*, Mar. 28, 1914.

20. *L'Italia*, Oct. 12, 1913; Nov. 2, 1919.

21. Samuel Paynter Wilson, *Chicago and Its Cesspools of Infamy* (11th ed.; Chicago [1910?]), 29.

22. Landesco, *Organized Crime in Chicago*, 937, 947-48; Arthur Woods, "The Problem of the Black Hand," *McClure's Magazine*, XXXIII (May 1909), 40.

23. Landesco, *Organized Crime in Chicago*, 946-47.

24. John Landesco, "Prohibition and Crime," *Annals*, CLXIII (Sept. 1932), 125.

25. Bessie Louise Pierce, *A History of Chicago*, Vol. III. *The Rise of a Modern City, 1871-1893* (New York, 1957), 305; Herbert Asbury, *Gem of the Prairie: An Informal History of*

the Chicago Underworld (New York, 1940), 142 ff.

26. Virgil W. Peterson, *Barbarians in Our Midst: A History of Chicago Crime and Politics* (Boston, 1952), 84-91; Landesco, *Organized Crime in Chicago*, 868-70.

27. Fred D. Pasley, *Al Capone; the Biography of a Self-made Man* (Garden City, N.Y., 1930), 9-14; Emmet Dedmon, *Fabulous Chicago* (New York, 1953), 289-90. Information on Colosimo's residence in 1897 is from *Precinct Lists*, Apr. 1897.

28. Landesco, *Organized Crime in Chicago*, 850-57.

29. Henry Barrett Chamberlain, "Crime as a Business in Chicago," *Bulletin of the Chicago Crime Commission* (Oct. 1, 1919), 1. Information on residence is from *Precinct Lists*, Nov. 1912.

30. *Chicago Daily News*, May 12, 1920; Dedmon, *Fabulous Chicago*, 290-91; Peterson, *Barbarians in Our Midst*, 108-9.

31. Lloyd Wendt and Herman Kogan, *Lords of the Levee: The Story of Bathhouse John and Hinky Dink* (Indianapolis, 1943), 340-41; Virgil W. Peterson, "Chicago: Shades of Capone," *Annals*, CCCXLVII (May 1963), 31-32.

32. Michele Pantaleone, *The Mafia and Politics* (London, 1966), 38-39 (see also the preface to the English edition written by Denis Mack Smith, 17-18); Peterson, *Barbarians in Our Midst*, 135. Denis Mack Smith examines the origins and growth of the Mafia in Sicily in his recent *A History of Sicily: Medieval Sicily: 800-1713* (London, 1968); and *Modern Sicily: After 1713* (London, 1968).

33. Among others, Ed Reid, *Mafia* (rev. ed.; New York, 1964), Chap. II.

34. Margaret Carlyle, *The Awakening of Southern Italy* (London, 1962), 13; also Carlo Sforza, *The Real Italians* (New York, 1942), Chaps. V and IX.

35. Harold Ross, "Crime and the Native Born Sons of European Immigrants," *AICLC*, XXVIII (Mar.-Apr. 1938), 202-9. Significantly, Italian residents of Latin American countries apparently indicated no propensity to indulge in crime for profit.

36. Alex Gottfried, *Boss Cermak of Chicago: A Study of Political Leadership* (Seattle, 1962), 68-70, 86, 268-69.

37. Italian "White Hand" Society, *Studies, Action and Results*, 27.

38. Edward Dean Sullivan, *Chicago Surrenders* (New York, 1930), 205; John Landesco, "Prohibition and Crime," *Annals*, CLXIII (Sept. 1932), 125.

39. *Chicago American*, May 15, 1920; *Chicago Tribune*, May 15, 1920; *Avanti!*, May 22, 1920; Virgil W. Peterson, *Barbarians in Our Midst: A History of Chicago Crime and Politics* (Boston, 1952), 109.

40. John Landesco, "Prohibition and Crime," 120.

41. John Landesco, *Organized Crime in Chicago: Part III of the Illinois Crime Survey* (Chicago, 1929), 910-11, 916-18.
42. Lloyd Wendt and Herman Kogan, *Big Bill of Chicago* (Indianapolis, 1953), 238-39; Alson J. Smith, *Syndicate City: The Chicago Crime Cartel and What to Do About It* (Chicago, 1954), 36-37; Irey and Slocum, *The Tax Dodgers*, 165; Walter Noble Burns, *The One-way Ride: The Red Trail of Chicago Gangland from Prohibition to Jake Lingle* (Garden City, N. Y., 1931), 112.
43. *Chicago Tribune*, May 20, 1924; *Chicago Daily News*, Nov. 17, 1924; National Commission on Law Observance and Enforcement, *Publications, Vol. IV. Report on Prosecution* (Washington, 1931), 372.
44. File of newspaper articles on criminal activities in Chicago during the 1920's, maintained by the Chicago Crime Commission. None of the events discussed in the text received passing mention in the city's Italian-language press.
45. Landesco, *Organized Crime in Chicago*, 929-30; Denis Tilden Lynch, *Criminals and Politicians* (New York, 1932), 120-21; *Al Capone and Chicago's Gang Wars* (Chicago, 1931), 10-36.
46. Fred D. Pasley, *Al Capone; The Biography of a Self-made Man* (New York, 1930); William H. Stuart, *The Twenty Incredible Years* (Chicago, 1935), 193.
47. Pasley, *Al Capone*, 38-40; *This Is Cicero* (Cicero, N.D.), 1-3; Walter Spelman, *The Town of Cicero* (Cicero, 1923), 11-12.
48. John H. Lyle, *The Dry and Lawless Years* (Englewood Cliffs, N.J., 1960), 76-78; *Chicago Tribune*, Apr. 1, 2, 1924.
49. Pasley, *Al Capone*, 62; Lyle, *The Dry and Lawless Years*, 80; Eliot Ness, *The Untouchables* (New York, 1957), 227; Robert Ross, *The Trial of Al Capone* (Chicago, 1933). For a

defense of Cermak's lack of action against Capone see Alex Gottfried, *Boss Cermak of Chicago: A Study of Political Leadership* (Seattle, 1962), 140-43.
50. Frank J. Wilson (as told to Howard Whitman), "How We Caught Al Capone," *Chicago Tribune Sunday Magazine*, June 14, 1959; Herbert Asbury, *Gem of the Prairie: An Informal History of the Chicago Underworld* (New York, 1940), 346-47; *Al Capone and Chicago's Gang Wars*, 1.
51. Landesco, *Organized Crime in Chicago*, 1046.
52. Lloyd Lewis and Henry Justin Smith, *Chicago: The History of Its Reputation* (New York, 1929), 436; Landesco, *Organized Crime in Chicago*, 1077-79. Repeal of the Eighteenth Amendment in 1933 doomed the bootlegging business and removed the major source of "syndicate" income. Years before this, however, the organization had discovered a lucrative new field of criminal exploitation and profit—labor and business racketeering. Gordon L. Hostetter and Thomas Quinn Beesley, *It's a Racket* (Chicago, 1929); Fred D. Pasley, *Muscling In* (New York, 1931).
53. Pasley, *Al Capone*, 59; Burns, *The One-way Ride*, 225; Edward D. Sullivan, *Rattling the Cup on Chicago Crime* (New York, 1929), 175-79.
54. Herbert Asbury, *The Great Illusion: An Informal History of Prohibition* (Garden City, N.Y., 1950), 291; Frederick Lewis Allen, *Only Yesterday: An Informal History of the Nineteen-Twenties* (New York, 1931), 220.
55. Based on examination of Chicago's Italian-language press during the Torrio-Capone era and interview with former *L'Italia* editor Vincent Coco, July 28, 1964.
56. Mary Borden, "Chicago Revisited," *Harper's Magazine*, CLXII (Apr. 1931), 542; Burns, *The One-way Ride*, 32.

Beyond the Melting Pot

NATHAN GLAZER AND DANIEL P. MOYNIHAN

The idea of the melting pot is as old as the Republic. "I could point out to you a family," wrote the naturalized New Yorker, M-G. Jean de Crèvecoeur, in 1782, "whose grandfather was an Englishman, whose wife was Dutch, whose son married a French woman, and whose present four sons have now four wives of different nations. *He* is an American, who leaving behind him all his ancient prejudices and manners, receives new ones from the new mode of life he has embraced. . . . Here individuals of all nations are melted into a new race of men. . . ."[1] It was an idea close to the heart of the American self-image. But as a century passed, and the number of individuals and nations involved grew, the confidence that they could be fused together waned, and so also the conviction that it would be a good thing if they were to be. In 1882 the Chinese were excluded, and the first general immigration law was enacted. In a steady succession thereafter, new and more selective barriers were raised until, by the National Origins Act of 1924, the nation formally adopted the policy of using immigration to reinforce, rather than further to dilute, the racial stock of the early America.

This latter process was well underway, had become in ways inexorable, when Israel Zangwill's play *The Melting Pot* was first performed in 1908. The play (quite a bad one) was an instant success. It ran for months on Broadway; its title was seized upon as a concise evocation of a profoundly significant American fact.

Behold David Quixano, the Russian Jewish immigrant—a "pogrom orphan" —escaped to New York City, exulting in the glory of his new country:

. . . America is God's Crucible, the great Melting Pot where all the races of Europe are melting and reforming! Here you stand, good folk, think I, when I see them at Ellis Island, here you stand in your fifty groups with your fifty languages and histories, and your fifty blood hatreds and rivalries, but you won't be long like that brothers, for these are the fires of God you've come to— these are the fires of God. A fig for your feuds and vendettas! German and Frenchman, Irishman and Englishman, Jews and Russians—into the Crucible with you all! God is making the American.

⁂

. . . The real American has not yet arrived. He is only in the Crucible, I tell you—he

From Nathan Glazer and Daniel P. Moynihan, *Beyond the Melting Pot* (Cambridge: The M.I.T. Press, 1963, paperback edition), pp. 288-315, 346-47. Copyright © 1963 by the Massachusetts Institute of Technology and the President and Fellows of Harvard College. Reprinted by permission of the M.I.T. Press, Cambridge, Massachusetts. Nathan Glazer is Professor of Sociology at the University of California, Berkeley. Daniel P. Moynihan is Director of the Joint Center for Urban Studies of the Massachusetts Institute of Technology and Harvard University.

will be the fusion of all the races, the coming superman.[2]

Yet looking back, it is possible to speculate that the response to *The Melting Pot* was as much one of relief as of affirmation: more a matter of reassurance that what had already taken place would turn out all right, rather than encouragement to carry on in the same direction.

Zangwill's hero throws himself into the amalgam process with the utmost energy; by curtainfall he has written his American symphony and won his Muscovite aristocrat: almost all concerned have been reconciled to the homogeneous future. Yet the play seems but little involved with American reality. It is a drama about Jewish separatism and Russian anti-Semitism, with a German concertmaster and an Irish maid thrown in for comic relief. Both protagonists are New Model Europeans of the time. Free thinkers and revolutionaries, it was doubtless in the power of such to merge. But neither of these doctrines was dominant among the ethnic groups of New York City in the 1900's, and in significant ways this became less so as time passed. Individuals, in very considerable numbers to be sure, broke out of their mold, but the groups remained. The experience of Zangwill's hero and heroine was *not* general. The point about the melting pot is that it did not happen.

Significantly, Zangwill was himself much involved in one of the more significant deterrents to the melting pot process. He was a Zionist. He gave more and more of his energy to this cause as time passed, and retreated from his earlier position on racial and religious mixture. Only eight years after

the opening of *The Melting Pot* he was writing "It was vain for Paul to declare that there should be neither Jew nor Greek. Nature will return even if driven out with a pitchfork, still more if driven out with a dogma."[3]

We may argue whether it was "nature" that returned to frustrate continually the imminent creation of a single American nationality. The fact is that in every generation, throughout the history of the American republic, the merging of the varying streams of population differentiated from one another by origin, religion, outlook has seemed to lie just ahead—a generation, perhaps, in the future. This continual deferral of the final smelting of the different ingredients (or at least the different white ingredients) into a seamless national web as is to be found in the major national states of Europe suggests that we must search for some systematic and general causes for this American pattern of subnationalities; that it is not the temporary upsetting inflow of new and unassimilated immigrants that creates a pattern of ethnic groups within the nation, but rather some central tendency in the national ethos which structures people, whether those coming in afresh or the descendants of those who have been here for generations, into groups of different status and character.

It is striking that in 1963, almost forty years after mass immigration from Europe to this country ended, the ethnic pattern is still so strong in New York City. It is true we can point to specific causes that have served to maintain the pattern. But we know that it was not created by the great new migrations of Southern Negroes and Puerto Ricans into the city; nor by the "new" immigration, which added the great communities of East European Jews and Italians to the city; it was not even created by the great migration of Irish and Germans in the 1840's. Even in the 1830's, while the migration from Europe was still mild, and still consisted for the most part of English-speaking groups, one still finds in the politics of New York State, and of the city, the strong impress of group differentiation. In a fascinating study of the politics of the Jacksonian period in New York State, Lee Benson concludes: "At least since the 1820's, when manhood suffrage became widespread, ethnic and religious differences have tended to be *relatively* the most widespread sources of political differences."[4]

There were ways of making distinctions among Welshmen and Englishmen, Yorkers and New Englanders, long before people speaking strange tongues and practicing strange religions came upon the scene. The group-forming characteristics of American social life—more concretely, the general expectation among those of new and old groups that group membership is significant and formative for opinion and behavior—are as old as the city. The tendency is fixed deep in American life generally; the specific pattern of ethnic differentiation, however, in every generation is created by specific events.

We can distinguish four major events or processes that have structured this pattern in New York during the past generation and whose effects will remain to maintain this pattern for some time to come—to be replaced by others we can scarcely now discern. These four formative events are the following:

First, the shaping of the Jewish community under the impact of the Nazi persecution of the Jews in Europe and the establishment of the state of Israel; second, the parallel, if less marked, shaping of a Catholic community by the reemergence of the Catholic school controversy; third, the migration of Southern Negroes to New York following World War I and continuing through the fifties; fourth, the influx of Puerto Ricans during the fifteen years following World War II.

THE JEWS

Developments within the Jewish community have had the most immediate significance. A fourth of the city is Jewish; very much more than a fourth of its wealth, energy, talent, and style is derived from the Jews. Over the past thirty years this community has undergone profound emotional experiences, centered almost entirely on the fact of Jewishness, has been measurably strengthened by immigration, and has become involved in vast Zionist enterprises, the rationale of which is exclusively Jewish. There are two aspects of these developments as they affect melting pot tendencies, one negative, the other positive.

The negative aspect has prevented a change that might otherwise have occurred. Prior to the 1930's Jews contributed significantly to the ethnic pattern of New York politics by virtue of their radicalism. This kept them apart from the Catholic establishment in the Democratic party and the Protestant regime within the Republican party but did give them a distinct role of their own. At the time of *The Melting Pot* there were, to be sure, a great many Democratic and Republican Jewish merchants and businessmen. Most East

Side Jews probably voted the Tammany ticket. But indigenous Jewish politics, the politics of the *Jewish Daily Forward*, of the Workmen's Circle, and the needle-trades unions were predominantly socialist. The Russian Revolution, in which Russian Jews played a prominent role, had a strong attraction for a small but important number of their kinsmen in New York. It would appear, for example, that during the 1930's most Communist party members in New York City were Jewish.[5] It must be stressed that the vast majority of New York Jews had nothing whatever to do with Communism. Some of the strongest centers of anti-Communist activity were and are to be found within the New York Jewish community. Nonetheless there was an ethnic cast to this form of political radicalism in New York, as there had been to the earlier Socialist movement.

Both Socialism and Communism are now considerably diminished and both have lost almost entirely any ethnic base. But just at the moment when the last distinctly Jewish political activity might have disappeared, a transcendent Jewish political interest was created by the ghastly persecutions of the Nazis, the vast dislocations of World War II, and the establishment of the State of Israel. These were matters that no Jew or Christian could ignore. They were equally matters about which little could be done except through politics. From the beginnings of the Zionist movement a certain number of New York Jews have been involved on that account with the high politics of the nation. Since the mid-1930's, however, this involvement has reached deeper and deeper into the New York Jewish community. They are the one group in the

city (apart from the white Protestant financial establishment) of which it may fairly be said that among the leadership echelons there is a lively, active, and effective interest in who will be the next U.S. Secretary of State but one . . . or two, or three.

In a positive sense, events of the Nazi era and its aftermath have produced an intense group consciousness among New York Jews that binds together persons of widely disparate situations and beliefs. A pronounced religious revival has occurred. Among those without formal religious ties there is a heightened sense of the defensive importance of organized Jewish activity. Among intellectuals, the feeling of Jewishness is never far from the surface.

Now, as in the past, the Jewish community in New York is the one most actively committed to the principles of racial integration and group tolerance. But open housing is something different from the melting pot. There is no reason to think that any considerable portion of the Jewish community of New York ever subscribed to Israel Zangwill's vision of a nonreligious, intermarried, homogeneous population, but it surely does not do so today. To the contrary, much of the visible activity of the community is aimed in directions that will intensify Jewish identity: Jewish elementary and secondary schools, Jewish colleges and universities, Jewish periodicals, Jewish investments in Israel, and the like. In the meantime, Jewish politicians make more (or at least not less) of the "Jewish" vote.

This is not to say the Jewish community of New York has been *created* or *maintained* by these events of the thirties or forties: that would be too narrow a view of Jewish history, and would

ignore the group-making characteristics of American civilization. But the Jewish community was *shaped* by these events. Moving rapidly from working-class to middle-class occupations and styles of life, many alternative courses of development were possible. Within the frame set by these large social movements, the historical drama shaped a community intensely conscious of its Jewishness. Religion plays in many ways the smallest part of the story of American Jews. In New York City in particular the religious definition of the group explains least. Here the formal religious groups are weakest, the degree of affiliation to synagogues and temples smallest. In a city with 2,000,000 Jews, Jews need make no excuses to explain Jewishness and Jewish interests. On the one hand, there is the social and economic structure of the community; on the other, ideologies and emotions molded by the specific history of recent decades. Together they have shaped a community that itself shapes New York and will for generations to come.[6]

THE CATHOLICS

Outwardly, events since World War I have brought Catholics, notably the Irish Catholics, ever closer to the centers of power and doctrine in American life. But following a pattern common in human affairs, the process of closing the gap has heightened resentment, among some at all events, that a gap should exist. Here, as in much else concerning this general subject, it is hardly possible to isolate New York events from those of the nation generally, but because New York tends to be the center of Catholic thinking and publishing, the distinction is not crucial. The great divi-

sion between the Catholic Church and the leftist and liberal groups in the city during the period from the Spanish Civil War to the era of McCarthy has been narrowed, with most elements of city politics converging on center positions. However issues of church-state relations have become considerably more difficult, and the issue of government aid to Catholic schools has become acute.

Controversy over church-state relations is nothing new to the American Catholic Church. What is new, however, and what is increasingly avowed, is the extent to which the current controversy derives from Catholic-Jewish disagreements rather than from traditional Catholic-Protestant differences. Relations between the two latter groups have steadily improved: to the point that after three centuries of separation Catholics in the 1960's began increasingly to talk of the prospects of reestablishing Christian unity. In general (there are, of course, many individual exceptions) the dominant view within Protestant and Catholic circles is that the United States is and ought to be a Christian commonwealth, to the point at very least of proclaiming "In God We Trust" on the currency and celebrating Christmas in the public schools. However, as this *rapprochement* has proceeded, within the Jewish community a contrary view has arisen which asserts that the separation of church and state ought to be even more complete than it has been, and that the "Post-Protestant era" means Post-Christian as well, insofar as government relations with religion are concerned.

The most dramatic episode of this development was the decision of the United States Supreme Court on June

25, 1962, that the recitation of an official prayer in the New York school system was unconstitutional. The case was brought by five parents of children in the public schools of the New York City suburb of New Hyde Park. Two of the parents were Jewish, one a member of the Ethical Culture Society, one a Unitarian, and one a nonbeliever. Before it concluded, however, the principal protagonists of the Catholic-Jewish controversy in New York City were involved. The attorney for the Archdiocese of New York, for example, argued in the Supreme Court for a group of parents who supported the prayer. The response to the decision could hardly have been more diametrical. Cardinal Spellman declared, "I am shocked and frightened. . . ." The New York Board of Rabbis, on the other hand, hailed the decision: "The recitation of prayers in the public schools, which is tantamount to the teaching of prayer, is not in conformity with the spirit of the American concept of the separation of church and state. All the religious groups in this country will best advance their respective faiths by adherence to this principle." The American Jewish Committee, the American Jewish Congress, and the Anti-Defamation League of B'nai B'rith strongly supported the Court. Only among the Orthodox was there mild disagreement with the Supreme Court decision.

Although the argument could certainly be made that the American Catholic Church ought to be the first to object to the spectacle of civil servants composing government prayers, and although many Catholic commentators noted that the decision strengthened the case for private Church-sponsored schools, the general Catholic reaction was most hostile. The Jesuit publication *America*, in an editorial "To our Jewish Friends," declared that Jewish efforts to assert an ever more strict separation of church and state were painting the Jewish community into a corner, where it would be isolated from the rest of Americans.

Significantly, Protestant reaction to the decision was mixed. The Brooklyn *Tablet* took the cue, stating that the crucial question raised by the decision was "What are the Protestants going to do about it? For, although this is a national problem, it is particularly a Protestant problem, given the large Protestant enrollment in the public schools. Catholics have been fighting long—and sometimes alone—against the Church-State extremists. May we count on Protestants to supply more leadership in this case? If so, we pledge our support to join efforts against the common enemy: secularism."[7]

The subject of aid to Catholic schools is only one aspect of the more general issue of church-state relations, and here again the ethnic composition of New York City tends to produce the same alignment of opposing groups. There are elements within the Jewish community, again the Orthodox, that favor public assistance for religious schools, but the dominant view is opposed. In 1961 the New York Republican party at the state level made a tentative move toward the Catholic position by proposing a Constitutional amendment that would have permitted state construction loans to private institutions of higher learning, sectarian as well as secular. Opposition from Jewish (as well as some Protestant) groups was pronounced, and the measure was beaten at the polls.

The situation developing in this area could soberly be termed dangerous. An element of interfaith competition has entered the controversy. As the costs of education mount, it becomes increasingly difficult to maintain the quality of the education provided by private schools deprived of public assistance. It is not uncommon to hear it stated in Catholic circles that the results of national scholarship competitions already point to the weakness of Catholic education in fields such as the physical sciences. The specter is raised that a parochial education will involve sacrifice for the students as well as for their parents.

There is understandably much resentment within Catholic educational circles at the relative crudity of most such observations. At the same time this resentment is often accompanied by an unmistakable withdrawal. In a thoughtful address calling for more meticulous assessment of the qualities of Catholic education, Bishop McEntegart of the Diocese of Brooklyn went on to state that "Judgment on the effectiveness of an educational system should be something more profound and more subtle than counting heads of so-called intellectuals who happen to be named in Who's Who or the 'Social Register.' "[8]

Whether the course of the controversy will lead Catholics further into separatist views of this kind is not clear. But it is abundantly evident that so long as Catholics maintain a separate education system and the rest of the community refuses to help support it by tax funds or tax relief, a basic divisive issue will exist. This will be an ethnic issue in measure that the Catholic community continues to include the bulk of the Irish, Italian, and Polish population in the city, at least the bulk of those affili-

ated with organizations taking a position on the issue. If, as may very well happen, the Catholics abandon elementary and even secondary education to concentrate on their colleges and universities, the larger issue of church-state relations will no doubt subside.

But it is not the single issue of school aid, no matter how important and long-lived it is, that alone shapes the polarization between the Jewish and the emerging Catholic community. There have been other issues in the past—for example, the struggle over the legitimacy of city hospitals giving advice on birth control, which put Jews and liberal Protestants on one side and Catholics on the other. There are the recurrent disputes over government censorship of books and movies and magazines that have become freer and freer in their handling of sex and sexual perversion. This again ranges Jewish and Protestant supporters of the widest possible freedom of speech against Catholics who are more anxious about the impact of such material on young people and family life. One can see emerging such issues as the rigid state laws on divorce and abortion.[9]

Many of these issues involve Catholic *religious* doctrine. But there exists here a situation that is broader than a conflict over doctrines and the degree to which government should recognize them. What is involved is the emergence of two subcultures, two value systems, shaped and defined certainly in part by religious practice and experience and organization but by now supported by the existence of two communities. If the bishops and the rabbis were to disappear tomorrow, the subcultures and subcommunities would remain. One is secular in its attitudes, liberal in its outlook on sexual life and divorce, positive about science and social science. The other is religious in its outlook, resists the growing liberalization in sexual mores and its reflection in cultural and family life, feels strongly the tension between moral values and modern science and technology. The conflict may be seen in many ways—not least in the fact that the new disciplines such as psychoanalysis, particularly in New York, are so largely staffed by Jews.

Thus a Jewish ethos and a Catholic ethos emerge: they are more strongly affected by a specific religious doctrine in the Catholic case than in the Jewish, but neither is purely the expression of the spirit of a religion. Each is the result of the interplay of religion, ethnic group, American setting, and specific issues. The important fact is that the differences in values and attitudes between the two groups do not, in general, become smaller with time. On the contrary: there is probably a wider gap between Jews and Catholics in New York today than in the days of Al Smith.[10]

NEGROES AND PUERTO RICANS

A close examination of Catholic-Jewish relations will reveal some of the tendency of ethnic relations in New York to be a form of class relations as well. However, the tendency is unmistakably clear with regard to the Negroes and Puerto Ricans. Some 22 per cent of the population of the city is now Negro or Puerto Rican, and the proportion will increase. (Thirty-six per cent of the births in 1961 were Negro or Puerto Rican.) To a degree that cannot fail to startle anyone who encounters the re-

ality for the first time, the overwhelming portion of both groups constitutes a submerged, exploited, and very possibly permanent proletariat.

New York is properly regarded as the wealthiest city in the nation. Its more affluent suburbs enjoy some of the highest standards of living on earth. In the city itself white-collar wages are high, and skilled labor through aggressive trade union activity has obtained almost unprecedented standards. Bricklayers earn $5.35 an hour, plus 52¢ for pension, vacation, and insurance benefits. Electricians have a nominal twenty-five hour week and a base pay of $4.96 an hour plus fringe benefits.[11] But amidst such plenty, unbelievable squalor persists: the line of demarcation is a color line in the case of Negroes, a less definite but equally real ethnic line in the case of Puerto Ricans.

The relationship between the rise of the Negro-Puerto Rican labor supply and the decline of industrial wages is unmistakable. In 1950 there were 246,000 Puerto Ricans in the city. By 1960 this number had increased by two and one-half times to 613,000, or 8 per cent. In 1950 the average hourly earnings of manufacturing production workers in New York City ranked tenth in the nation. By 1960 they ranked thirtieth. In the same period comparable wages in Birmingham, Alabama, rose from thirty-third to tenth. In 1959 median family income for Puerto Ricans was $3,811 as against $6,091 for all the city's families (and $8,052 for suburbs of Westchester). In 1962 average weekly earnings of manufacturing production workers were 19 per cent higher in Birmingham than in New York City, 15 per cent higher in New Orleans, and almost 10 per cent higher in the nation as a whole.

These economic conditions vastly reinforce the ethnic distinctions that serve to separate the Negro community and the Puerto Rican community from the rest of the city. The Negro separation is strengthened by the fact that the colored community is on the whole Protestant, and much of its leadership comes from Protestant clergy. Thus the Negroes provide the missing element of the Protestant-Catholic-Jew triad.

Housing segregation, otherwise an intolerable offense to the persons affected, serves nonetheless to ensure the Negroes a share of seats on the City Council and in the State Legislature and Congress. This power, as well as their voting power generally, has brought Negro political leaders to positions of considerable prominence. Following the 1961 mayoralty election, Mayor Wagner appointed the talented Harlem leader, J. Raymond Jones, as a political secretary through whom he would deal with all the Democratic party organizations of the city. Puerto Ricans have only begun to make their influence felt, but they are clearly on the way to doing so.

Their fate gives them an interest in the same issues: the housing of the poor in a city of perpetual housing shortage; the raising of the wages of the poorly paid service semiskilled occupations in which most of them work; the development of new approaches to raising motivation and capacity by means of education and training in the depressed areas of the city. They live adjacent to each other in vast neighborhoods. And they cooperate on many specific issues —for example, in fighting urban renewal programs that would displace them. But there are deeply felt differences between them. The more Americanized group is also more deeply marked by color. The furtive hope of the new

group that it may move ahead as other immigrants have without the barrier of color, and the powerful links of language and culture that mark off the Puerto Ricans, suggest that, despite the fact that the two groups increasingly comprise the proletariat of the city, their history will be distinct.

Thus the cast of major characters for the next decades is complete: the Jews; the Catholics, subdivided at least into Irish and Italian components; the Negroes; the Puerto Ricans; and, of course, the white Anglo-Saxon Protestants. These latter, ranging from the Rockefeller brothers to reform district leaders in the Democratic party are, man for man, among the most influential and powerful persons in the city, and will continue to play a conspicuous and creative role in almost every aspect of the life of the metropolis.

THE ROLE OF POLITICS

The large movements of history and people which tend to reinforce the role of the ethnic groups in the city have been accompanied by new developments in political life which similarly strengthen ethnic identities. This is a complicated matter, but we can point to a number of elements. First, there is some tendency (encouraged by the development of genuine ethnic-class combinations) to substitute ethnic issues in politics for class issues. Second, there has been a decline in the vigor and creativity of politics in New York City, which seems to make New York politicians prefer to deal in terms of premelting pot verities rather than to cope with the chaotic present. Third, the development of public opinion polling would seem to have significantly strengthened the historic tendency of New York political parties to occupy the same middle ground on substantive issues, and indirectly has the effect of strengthening the ethnic component in political campaigns. As competing parties and factions use substantially the same polling techniques, they get substantially the same information about the likes and dislikes of the electorate. Hence they tend to adopt similar positions on political issues. (In much the same way, the development of marketing survey techniques in business has produced standardized commercial products such as cigarettes, automobiles, detergents, and so forth.) For the time being at least, this seems to have increased the importance of racial and ethnic distinctions that, like advertising, can still create distinctions in appearance even if little or none exist in fact. Everything we say in this field is highly speculative, but the impression that the political patterns of the city strengthen the roles of ethnic groups is overwhelming.

It is not easy to illustrate the substitution of ethnic appeals for class appeals. To the extent it occurs, those involved would hope to conceal it, always assuming the practice is deliberate. The basic fact is that for the first half of the twentieth century New York was a center of political radicalism. Faced with fierce opposition, some at least of the left wing discovered that their best tactic was to couch class appeals in ethnic terms. In such manner Vito Marcantonio, a notorious fellow traveler, flourished in the United States Congress as an Italian representative of the Italians and Puerto Ricans of East Harlem. In response to such tactics, the traditional parties have themselves employed the ethnic shorthand to deal with what are essentially class problems. Thus much

was made in terms of its ethnic significance of the appointment of a Puerto Rican as a City Commissioner responsible for the relocation of families affected by urban renewal projects, but behind this significance was the more basic one that the slum-dwelling proletariat of the city was being given some control over its housing. In much the same way the balanced ticket makes it possible to offer a slate of candidates ranging across the social spectrum—rich man, poor man, beggar man, thief—but to do so in terms of the ethnic groups represented rather than the classes. In a democratic culture that has never much liked to identify individuals in terms of social classes, and does so less in the aftermath of the radical 1930's and 1940's, the ethnic shorthand is a considerable advantage.

This is of course possible only because of the splintering of traditional economic classes along ethnic lines, which tends to create class-ethnic combinations that have considerable significance at the present time in New York. The sharp division and increasing conflict between the well-paid Jewish cutters in the International Ladies' Garment Workers' Union and the low-paid Negro and Puerto Rican majority in the union have been widely publicized. One Negro cutter hailed the union before the State Commission for Human Rights and obtained a favorable decision. Similar distinctions between skilled and unskilled workers are common enough throughout the trade unions of the city. At a higher level, not dissimilar patterns can be found among the large law firms and banks, where Protestant-Catholic-Jew distinctions exist and are important even if somewhat less so than in past times.

From time to time the most significant issues of class relations assume ethnic form. Reform movements in New York City politics have invariably been class movements as well. Citing a study of Theodore Lowi, showing that reform in New York City has always meant a change in the class and ethnic background of top city appointees, James Q. Wilson summarized the phenomenon as follows:

The three "reform" mayors preceding Wagner favored upper-middle-class Yankee Protestants six to one over the Irish as appointees. Almost 40 per cent of the appointees of Seth Low were listed in the Social Register. Further, all four reform mayors—Low, Mitchel, La Guardia, and Wagner—have appointed a much larger percentage of Jews to their cabinets than their regular organizations predecessors.

In fact, of course, the problem posed by the amateur Democrats is not simply one of ethnic succession. Militant reform leaders in Manhattan get angry when they hear this "explanation" of their motives, for they reject the idea that ethnicity or religion ought to be considered at all in politics. Although most amateur Democrats are either Jewish or Anglo-Saxon and practically none are Catholic, it is not their entry into politics so much as it is their desire to see a certain political ethic (which middle-class Jews and Yankees happen to share) implemented in local politics.[12]

The 1961 Democratic primary fight, which ended with the defeat of Carmine DeSapio and the regular Democratic organization, was a mixture of class and ethnic conflict that produced the utmost bitterness. In the mayoralty election that followed, the Democratic State Chairman, Michael H. Prendergast, in an unprecedented move, came out in support of an independent candidate, a conservative Italian Catholic, Lawrence E. Gerosa, against Mayor Wagner, who was running for reelection with the support of the middle-

class reform elements within the Democratic party. In a bitter *cri de coeur*, almost inevitably his last statement as an acknowledged political leader, Prendergast lashed out at what he regarded as a leftwing conspiracy to take over the Democratic party and merge it with the Liberal party of David Dubinsky and Alex Rose, in the process excluding the traditional Catholic leadership of the city democracy. He declared:

The New York Post lays the whole plot bare in a signed column entitled "One Big Party?" in its September 27 issue. Every Democrat should read it. "The first prerequisite of the new coalition," James A. Wechsler writes, "is that Mayor Wagner win the election." He goes on to say that the new "troops" which Messrs. Dubinsky and Rose will bring to this alliance will have to fight a "rear-guard action" on the part of "Catholics of Irish descent" who, Mr. Wechsler declares, "take their temporal guidance from Patrick Scanlan and his Brooklyn Tablet propaganda sheet.

*　　*　　*

It's time to call a spade a spade. The party of Al Smith's time was big enough for Democrats of all descent. The Democratic party of today is big enough for Americans of every race, creed, color or national origin.

Although much larger issues were at stake, it was natural enough for a traditionalist in politics such as Prendergast to describe the conflict in ethnic terms. And in justice it must be said that the ethnic elements of the controversy were probably much more significant than Prendergast's opponents would likely admit.

Apart from the reform movement represented by the Committee for Democratic Voters (which has yet to wield any decisive power over city—or statewide political nominations), the level of political creativity in New York politics has not been high over the past several decades. The almost pathetic tendency to follow established patterns has been reinforced by the growing practice of nominating sons and grandsons of prominent public persons. The cast of such men as Roosevelt, Rockefeller, Harriman, Wagner, and Morgenthau seems almost bent on recreating the gaslight era. In this context the balanced ticket and the balanced distribution of patronage along ethnic lines have assumed an almost fervid sanctity—to the point indeed of caricature, as in the 1961 mayoralty contest in which the Republican team of Lefkowitz, Gilhooley, and Fino faced Democrats Wagner, Screvane, and Beame, the latter victors in a primary contest with Levitt, Mackell, and Di Fede. It will be noted that each ticket consisted of a Jew, an Italian Catholic, and an Irish Catholic, or German-Irish Catholic in the case of Wagner.

The development of polling techniques has greatly facilitated the calculations—and perhaps also the illusions—that go into the construction of a balanced ticket. It should be noted that these techniques would apply equally well, or badly, to all manner of social and economic classifications, but that so far it is the ethnic information that has attracted the interest of the political leaders and persons of influence in politics. Here, for example, is the key passage of the poll on the basis of which Robert M. Morgenthau was nominated as the Democratic candidate for governor in 1962:

The optimum way to look at the anatomy of the New York State electorate is to take three symbolic races for Governor and two for the Senate and compare them group by group. The three we will select for Governor are Screvane, Morgenthau, and Burke.* We select these because each represents a different fundamental assumption. Screvane makes sense as a candidate, if the election should be cast in terms of an extension of the Wagner-Rockefeller fight. This could have the advantage of potentially firming up a strong New York City vote, where, in fact, the election must be won by the Democrats. On the other hand, a Rockefeller-Screvane battle would make it more difficult to cast the election in national terms of Rockefeller vs. Kennedy which, as we shall also see, is a critical dimension to pursue.

A Morgenthau-Rockefeller race is run mainly because it represents meeting the Rockefeller-Javits ticket on its own grounds of maximum strength: among Jewish and liberal-minded voters, especially in New York City. Morgenthau is the kind of name that stands with Lehman, and, as we shall see, has undoubted appeal with Jewish voters. The question of running a moderately liberal Jewish candidate for Governor is whether this would in turn lose the Democrats some conservative Catholic voters who are not enchanted with Rockefeller and Javits to begin with, but who might normally vote Republican.

The third tack that might be taken on the Governorship is to put up an outstanding Irish candidate on the assumption that with liberal Republicans Rockefeller and Javits running, the Catholic vote can be moved appreciably over to the Democratic column, especially in view of Rockefeller's divorce as a silent but powerful issue. Here, Court of Appeals Judge Adrian Burke, who so far outstripped the statewide ticket in 1954 might be considered typical of this type of candidate.

Let us then look at each of these alternatives and see how the pattern of the vote varies by each. For it is certain that the key Democratic decision in 1962 must be over the candidate for Governor first, and then followed by the candidate for U.S. Senate. We also include the breakdowns by key

---

* Paul R. Screvane, President of the City Council, an Italian Catholic; Robert M. Morgenthau, United States Attorney for the Southern District of New York, a Jew; Adrian P. Burke, Judge of the Court of Appeals, an Irish Catholic.

	Key Group Breakdowns*				
	Democratic Candidates for Governor Pitted Against Rockefeller			Democratic Candidates for U.S. Senate Against Javits	
	Screvane	Burke	Morgenthau	Bunche	Murrow
	%	%	%	%	%
Statewide	47	43	49	47	46
By Area					
New York City (43%)	61	54	61	57	55
Suburbs (16%)	41	41	43	42	40
Upstate (41%)	35	35	40	40	40
By Occupation					
Business and					
Professional (14%)	35	22	30	57	33
White Collar (19%)	36	44	51	50	44
Sales and Service (8%)	49	49	54	42	42
Labor (34%)	56	53	57	34	52
Small Business,					
Shopkeeper (5%)	38	41	41	42	36
Retired and other (13%)	39	30	39	52	43
By Ethnic Groups					
White USA (29%)	35	37	36	36	40
Irish (9%)	44	49	44	48	36
English-Scotch (7%)	42	26	33	34	34
German (16%)	29	34	39	42	41
Italian (13%)	59	53	53	45	55
By Religion and Race					
White Protestant (37%)	27	27	29	35	32
White Catholic (37%)	51	54	51	42	48
White Jewish (18%)	70	56	82	81	61
Negro (8%)	70	55	68	93	74
Sex by Age					
Men (49%)	47	40	48	47	43
21-34 (15%)	42	39	40	43	34
35-49 (16%)	53	39	54	43	54
50 and over (18%)	48	43	51	55	42
Women (51%)	47	48	50	47	49
21-34 (15%)	56	56	58	55	45
35-49 (18%)	50	52	59	53	58
50 and over (18%)	39	35	36	37	41
By Union Membership					
Union Member (25%)	66	61	65	49	57
Union Family (11%)	56	59	57	52	47
Nonunion (64%)	38	35	42	45	40
By Income Groups					
Upper Middle (22%)	33	20	32	40	27
Lower Middle (64%)	47	47	52	45	48
Low (14%)	63	61	62	66	61

* Each figure gives the percentage of total vote that the proposed candidate received in the specified category. Thus, 35 per cent of the business and professional vote were recorded as saying they would vote for Screvane against Rockefeller.

groups for Bunche and Murrow against Javits.°

Here some fascinating and revealing patterns emerge which point the way sharply toward the kind of choice the Democrats can make optimally in their selection of Gubernatorial and Senatorial candidates for 1962 in New York:

—By area, it appears that the recent Democratic gains in the suburbs are quite solid, and a range of from 40 to 43 per cent of the vote seems wholly obtainable.

—By race and religion, we find equally revealing results. The Protestant vote is as low as it was for Kennedy in 1960, when the religious issue was running strong.

—By contrast, the Catholic vote remains relatively stable, with a slight play for Burke above the rest, and with Bunche and Murrow showing some weaknesses here. (The relative percentages, however, for a James A. Farley† race against Javits show Farley with 30 percent Protestant, a relatively lower standing; 58 percent of the Catholics, a very good showing, but with only 36 percent of the Jewish vote, a very poor result; and 67 percent of the Negro vote, only a fair showing).

The really volatile votes in this election clearly are going to be the Jewish and Negro votes. The Jewish vote ranges from a low of 56 percent (for Burke); 61 percent for Murrow (against Javits); 70 percent for Screvane (against Rockefeller); a very good 71 percent for Bunche (against Javits); and a thumping 82 percent for Morgenthau (against Rockefeller). Here the conclusion is perfectly obvious: by running a Lehman type of Jewish candidate against Rockefeller, the Jewish vote can be anchored well up into the high 70's and even into the 80's. By running an Irish Catholic candidate against Rockefeller, the Jewish vote comes tumbling precipitously down into the 50's. What is more, with Javits on the ticket, with strong appeal among Jews, any weakness among Jews with the Gubernatorial candidate, and the defection of the Jewish vote can be large

† James A. Farley, former Postmaster General, an Irish Catholic.

° Ralph J. Bunche, United Nations official, a Negro; Edward R. Murrow, Director, United States Information Agency, a white Protestant; Jacob K. Javits, United States Senator, a Jew.

enough to reduce the city vote to disastrously low proportions for the Democrats.

The Negro vote is only slightly less volatile. It ranges from a low of 55 percent (for Burke, again); to 68 percent for Morgenthau, not too good (an indication that Negroes will not automatically vote for a Jewish candidate, there being friction between the two groups); 70 percent for Screvane (who carried over some of the strong Wagner appeal among Negroes); 74 percent for Murrow, a good showing; and an incredibly high 93 percent for Bunche.

Observation: The conclusion for Governor seems self-evident from the results. A candidate who would run in the Wagner image, such as Screvane, would poll a powerful New York City vote, but would fade more upstate and would not pull in a full measure of the Jewish swing vote. An Irish Catholic candidate would not do appreciably better than Screvane upstate (a pattern that has been repeated throughout New York's modern political history, with Kennedy the sole exception in 1960), but with good appeal in the suburbs, yet with a disastrous showing among Jews and Negroes in New York City. A Lehman-type Jewish candidate, such as Morgenthau, by contrast, would appeal to a number of Protestants upstate (as, indeed, Lehman always did in his runs), would hold well in the suburbs, and could bring in solidly the pivotal Jewish vote in New York City.

The first choice must be a Jewish candidate for Governor of the highest caliber. (*sic.*)

There are two things to note about this poll. In the first place, the New York Jews did *not* vote solidly for Morgenthau, who lost by half a million votes. A week before the election Morgenthau headquarters received a report that a follow-up poll showed that 50 per cent of New York City Jews who had voted for the Democratic candidate Averell Harriman in 1958 were undecided about voting for Morgenthau four years later. An analysis of the vote cast in predominantly Jewish election districts shows that Rockefeller significantly improved his performance over 1958, when he had run against Averell Harriman, another white Protestant. In important areas such as Long Beach, Rockefeller went from 37.2 per cent in 1958 to 62.7 per cent in 1962, which is sufficient evidence that a Jewish name alone does not pull many votes. It could also confirm the preelection fears of the Democrats that the notoriety of their search for a "Lehman type of Jewish candidate" had produced a strong resentment within the Jewish community. The following are returns from predominantly Jewish districts:

Rockefeller got barely a fifth of the vote in the third Assembly district of Democratic Bronx, while he got almost three-quarters in Harrison in Republican Westchester, but he improved his performance in both areas despite the fact that his 1962 plurality was lower, statewide, than 1948. Similarly, Rockefeller got as little as 8.8 per cent on the vote in the predominantly Negro third ward of Democratic Albany, and as much as 76 per cent in upper-middle-class, Republican Rye in Westchester, but generally speaking, Rockefeller appears to have lost Negro votes in 1962 over 1958.

A second point to note is that while

	Rockefeller			Javits		
	1962	1958	Dif.	1962	1956	Dif.
New York City						
Bronx AD 2, School 90	27.2	20.5	+6.7	41.9	19.2	+22.7
3	21.6	18.7	+2.9	44.0	17.5	+26.5
5	26.4	19.8	+6.6	39.9	21.4	+18.5
Queens AD 7 School 164	43.8	36.5	+7.3	66.5	32.0	+34.5
Suburbs						
Jericho (part)	50.7	34.4	+16.3	60.7	36.1	+24.6
Long Beach (part)	62.7	37.2	+25.5	66.2	34.3	+31.9
Harrison (part)	71.3	69.6	+1.7	71.4	64.6	+6.8
New Rochelle Ward 4	57.8	58.8	−1.0	57.1	55.8	+1.3

These returns, which are typical enough, reveal an important fact about ethnic voting. Class interests and geographical location are the dominant influences in voting behavior, whatever the ethnic group involved. In urban, Democratic Bronx, the great majority of Jews vote Democratic. In suburban, Republican Westchester, the next county, the great majority of Jews vote Republican. But within that over-all pattern a definite ethnic swing does occur. Thus

the poll provided detailed information on the response to the various potential candidates classified by sex, occupational status, and similar characteristics of the persons interviewed, the candidates proposed were all essentially ethnic prototypes, and the responses analyzed in the commentary were those on the ethnic line. These are terms, howsoever misleading, which are familiar to New York politics, and with which New York politicians prefer to deal.

THE FUTURE

We have tried to show how deeply the pattern of ethnicity is impressed on the life of the city. Ethnicity is more than an influence on events; it is commonly the source of events. Social and political institutions do not merely respond to ethnic interests; a great number of institutions exist for the specific purpose of serving ethnic interests. This in turn tends to perpetuate them. In many ways, the atmosphere of New York City is hospitable to ethnic groupings: it recognizes them, and rewards them, and to that extent encourages them.

This is not to say that no individual group will disappear. This, on the contrary, is a recurring phenomenon. The disappearance of the Germans is a particularly revealing case.

In terms of size or the achievements of its members, the Germans ought certainly to be included among the principal ethnic groups of the city. If never quite as numerous as the Irish, they were indisputably the second largest group in the late nineteenth century, accounting for perhaps a third of the population and enjoying the highest reputation. But today, while German influence is to be seen in virtually every aspect of the city's life, the Germans *as a group* are vanished. No appeals are made to the German vote, there are no German politicians in the sense that there are Irish or Italian politicians, there are in fact few Germans in political life and, generally speaking, no German component in the structure of the ethnic interests of the city.

The logical explanation of this development, in terms of the presumed course of American social evolution, is simply that the Germans have been "assimilated" by the Anglo-Saxon cen-

ter. To some extent this has happened. The German immigrants of the nineteenth century were certainly much closer to the old Americans than were the Irish who arrived in the same period. Many were Protestants, many were skilled workers or even members of the professions, and their level of education in general was high. Despite the language difference, they did not seem nearly so alien to the New York mercantile establishment as did the Irish. At the time of their arrival German sympathies were high in New York. (George Templeton Strong was violent in his support of doughty Prussia in its struggle with imperial, tyrannical France.) All of this greatly facilitated German assimilation.

In any event, there were obstacles to the Germans' becoming a distinct ethnic bloc. Each of the five groups we have discussed arrived with a high degree of homogeneity: in matters of education, skills, and religion the members of the group were for the most part alike. This homogeneity, as we have tried to show, invested ethnicity with meaning and importance that it would not otherwise have had. But this was not so with the Germans, who were split between Catholics and Protestants, liberals and conservatives, craftsmen and businessmen and laborers. They reflected, as it were, an entire modern society, not simply an element of one. The only things all had in common were the outward manifestations of German culture: language for a generation or two, and after that a fondness for certain types of food and drink and a consciousness of the German fatherland. This was a powerful enough bond and would very likely be visible today, except for the impact of the World Wars. The Germanophobia of America during the

First World War is, of course, notorious. It had limits in New York where, for instance, German was *not* driven from the public school curriculum, but the attraction of things German was marred. This period was followed, in hardly more than a decade, by the Nazi era, during which German fascism made its appearance in Jewish New York, with what results one can imagine. The German American Bund was never a major force in the city, but it did exist. The revulsion against Nazism extended indiscriminately to things German. Thereafter, German Americans, as shocked by the Nazis as any, were disinclined to make overmuch of their national origins.

Even so, it is not clear that consciousness of German nationality has entirely ceased to exist among German-Americans in the city, or elsewhere. There is evidence that for many it has simply been submerged. In New York City, which ought logically to be producing a series of Italian and Jewish mayors, the political phenomenon of the postwar period has been Robert F. Wagner.

It is even possible that the future will see a certain resurgence of German identity in New York, although we expect it will be mild. The enemy of two world wars has become an increasingly powerful and important ally in the Cold War. Berlin has become a symbol of resistance to totalitarianism; Germany has become an integral part of the New Europe. Significantly, the German Americans of the city have recently begun an annual Steuben Day Parade, adding for the politicians of the city yet another command performance at an ethnic outing.

Despite this mild German resurgence, it is a good general rule that except where color is involved as well the specifically *national* aspect of most ethnic groups rarely survives the third generation in any significant terms. The intermarriage which de Crèvecoeur described continues apace, so that even the strongest national traditions are steadily diluted. The groups do not disappear, however, because of their *religious* aspect which serves as the basis of a subcommunity, and a subculture. Doctrines and practices are modified to some extent to conform to an American norm, but a distinctive set of values is nurtured in the social groupings defined by religious affiliation. This is quite contrary to early expectations. It appeared to de Crèvecoeur, for example, that religious as well as national identity was being melted into one by the process of mixed neighborhoods and marriage:

. . . This mixed neighborhood will exhibit a strange religious medley, that will be neither pure Catholicism nor pure Calvinism. A very perceptible indifference even in the first generation, will become apparent; and it may happen that the daughter of the Catholic will marry the son of the seceder, and settle by themselves at a distance from their parents. What religious education will they give their children? A very imperfect one. If there happens to be in the neighborhood any place of worship, we will suppose a Quaker's meeting; rather than not shew their fine clothes, they will go to it, and some of them may attach themselves to that society. Others will remain in a perfect state of indifference; the children of these zealous parents will not be able to tell what their religious principles are, and their grandchildren still less.

Thus all sects are mixed as well as all nations; thus religious indifference is imperceptibly disseminated from one end of the continent to the other; which is at present one of the strongest characteristics of the Americans.[13]

If this was the case in the late eighteenth century, it is no longer. Religious identities are strongly held by New Yorkers, and Americans generally, and they are for the most part transmitted by blood line from the original immigrant group. A great deal of intermarriage occurs among nationality groups of the three great religious groups, of the kind Ruby Jo Kennedy described in New Haven, Connecticut, under the general term of the Triple Melting Pot,[14] but this does not weaken religious identity. When marriages occur between different religions, often one is dominant, and the result among the children is not indifference, but an increase in the numbers of one of the groups.

Religion and race seem to define the major groups into which American society is evolving as the specifically national aspect of ethnicity declines. In our large American cities, four major groups emerge: Catholics, Jews, white Protestants, and Negroes, each making up the city in different proportions. This evolution is by no means complete. And yet we can discern that the next stage of the evolution of the immigrant groups will involve a Catholic group in which the distinctions between Irish, Italian, Polish, and German Catholic are steadily reduced by intermarriage; a Jewish group, in which the line between East European, German, and Near Eastern Jews is already weak; the Negro group; and a white Protestant group, which adds to its Anglo-Saxon and Dutch old-stock elements German and Scandinavian Protestants, as well as, more typically, the white Protestant immigrants to the city from the interior.

The white Protestants are a distinct ethnic group in New York, one that has probably passed its low point and will now begin to grow in numbers and probably also in influence. It has its special occupations, with the customary freemasonry. This involves the banks, corporation front offices, educational and philanthropic institutions, and the law offices who serve them. It has its own social world (epitomized by, but by no means confined to, the *Social Register*), its own churches, schools, voluntary organizations and all the varied institutions of a New York minority. These are accompanied by the characteristic styles in food, clothing, and drink, special family patterns, special psychological problems and ailments. For a long while political conservatism, as well as social aloofness, tended to keep the white Protestants out of the main stream of New York politics, much in the way that political radicalism tended to isolate the Jews in the early parts of the century. Theodore Roosevelt, when cautioned that none of his friends would touch New York politics, had a point in replying that it must follow that none of his friends were members of the governing classes.

There has been a resurgence of liberalism within the white Protestant group, in part based on its growth through vigorous young migrants from outside the city, who are conspicuous in the communications industry, law firms, and corporation offices of New York. These are the young people that supported Adlai Stevenson and helped lead and staff the Democratic reform movement. The influence of the white Protestant group on this city, it appears, must now grow as its numbers grow.

In this large array of the four major religio-racial groups, where do the Puerto Ricans stand? Ultimately perhaps they are to be absorbed into the

Catholic group. But that is a long time away. The Puerto Ricans are separated from the Catholics as well as the Negroes by color and culture. One cannot even guess how this large element will ultimately relate itself to the other elements of the city; perhaps it will serve, in line with its own nature and genius, to soften the sharp lines that divide them.

Protestants will enjoy immunities in politics even in New York. When the Irish era came to an end in the Brooklyn Democratic party in 1961, Joseph T. Sharkey was succeeded by a troika (as it was called) of an Irish Catholic, a Jew, and a Negro Protestant. The last was a distinguished clergyman, who was at the same time head of the New York City Council of Protestant Churches. It would have been unlikely for a rabbi, unheard of for a priest, to hold such a position.

Religion and race define the next stage in the evolution of the American peoples. But the American nationality is still forming: its processes are mysterious, and the final form, if there is ever to be a final form, is as yet unknown.

NOTES

1. J. Hector St. John Crèvecoeur (Michel-Guillaume Jean de Crèvecoeur), *Letters from an American Farmer*, New York: Fox, Duffield & Co., 1904, pp. 54-55.
2. Israel Zangwill, *The Melting Pot*, New York: Macmillan, 1909, pp. 37-38.
3. Joseph Leftwich, *Israel Zangwill*, New York: Thomas Yoseloff, 1957, p. 255.
4. Lee Benson, *The Concept of Jacksonian Democracy*, Princeton, N.J.: Princeton University Press, 1961, p. 165.
5. See Nathan Glazer, *The Social Basis of American Communism*, New York: Harcourt, Brace & World, 1961, Chap. IV.
6. For the complex interplay of religious, ideological, and socioeconomic factors within the American Jewish community, see *American Judaism* by Nathan Glazer, Chicago: University of Chicago Press, 1957.
7. Quoted in the *New York Herald Tribune*, July 2, 1962.
8. *The Tablet*, February 17, 1962. In an address given in Washington on April 30, 1962, Very Reverend William F. Kelley, S.J., President of Marquette University, implicitly proposed a secondary role for Catholic education. As reported in *The Washington Post*, Father Kelley suggested that Catholic schools leave "research and the exploration for new knowledge" to "research institutes" like Hopkins, Harvard, and M.I.T., it being "perfectly respectable and professionally honorable" to concentrate on the transmission of the knowledge of the past:

> It is an entirely sound plan to be trailing along at a respectable distance with a trained and educated citizenry competent to appreciate and consume the discovery of the successful investigator. Let us remember that if there are no followers, there can be no leader.

9. See *A Tale of Ten Cities*, Albert Vorspan and Eugene Lipman, New York: *Union of American Hebrew Congregations*, 1962, pp. 175 ff.
10. Gerhard Lenski, *The Religious Factor*, New York: Doubleday, 1961, gives a great deal of evidence to the effect that value differences between Catholics and white Protestants and Jews (the latter two often linked, but not always) in Detroit have increased as the groups move from working-class and immigrant generation to middle-class and later generations. Parochial schooling plays some part in these differences. For an interesting evocation of the milieu in which Jewish-Catholic political cooperation flourished, see *Al Smith*, by Oscar Handlin, Boston: Little, Brown, 1958.
11. U. S. Bureau of Labor Statistics data for October, 1962.
12. James Q. Wilson, *The Amateur Democrat*, Chicago: University of Chicago Press, 1962, p. 304.
13. de Crèvecoeur, *op. cit.*, pp. 65-66.
14. Ruby Jo Reeves Kennedy, "Single or Triple Melting Pot: Intermarriage in New Haven," *American Journal of Sociology*, Vol. 58, No. 1, July, 1952, pp. 55-66.

Harlem Tragedy: An Emerging Slum

GILBERT OSOFSKY

"I sit on my stoop on Seventh Avenue and gaze at the sunkissed folks strolling up and down and think that surely Mississippi is here in New York, in Harlem, yes, right on Seventh Avenue."

The Messenger, 1923

"I have been in places where cattle and dogs sleep with masters, but never before have I been in such a filthy house."

Judge William Blau's description of a Harlem tenement, 1922

I

The creation of a Negro community within one large and solid geographic area was unique in city history. New York had never been what realtors call an "open city"—a city in which Negroes lived wherever they chose—but the former Negro sections were traditionally only a few blocks in length, often spread across the island and generally interspersed with residences of white working-class families. Harlem, however, was a Negro world unto itself. A scattered handful of "marooned white families . . . stubbornly remained" in the Negro section, a United States census-taker recorded, but the mid-belly of Harlem was predominantly Negro by 1920.[1]

And the ghetto rapidly expanded. Between the First World War and the Great Depression, Harlem underwent radical changes. When the twenties came to an end Negroes lived as far

south as One Hundred and Tenth Street—the northern boundary of Central Park; practically all the older white residents had moved away; the Russian-Jewish and Italian sections of Harlem, founded a short generation earlier, were rapidly being depopulated; and Negro Harlem, within the space of ten years, became the most "incredible slum" in the entire city. In 1920 James Weldon Johnson was able to predict a glowing future for this Negro community: "Have you ever stopped to think what the future Harlem will be?" he wrote. "It will be the greatest Negro city in the world. . . . And what a fine part of New York City [the Negro] has come into possession of!"[2] By the late 1920's and early 1930's, however, Harlem's former "high-class" homes offered, in the words of a housing expert, "the best laboratory for slum clearance . . . in the entire city." "Harlem conditions," a *New York Times* reporter concluded, are "simply deplorable."[3]

II

The Harlem slum of the twenties was the product of a few major urban developments. One of the most important was the deluge of Negro migration to New York City then. The Negro press, now largely dependent on the migrant community for support, changed its former critical attitude of migration to one openly advocating urban settlement. (The exodus was so large, a Negro minister preached, that it must have been "inspired by Almighty God.")[4] If one is looking for a dramatic turning point in the history of the urbanization of the Negro—"a race changing from farm life to city life"—it was certainly the decade of the twenties. Between 1910 and 1920 the Negro population of the city increased 66 per cent (91,709 to 152,-467); from 1920 to 1930, it expanded 115 per cent (152,467 to 327,706). In the latter year less than 25 per cent of New York City's Negro population (79,-264) was born in New York State. There were more Negroes in the city in 1930 than the combined Negro populations of Birmingham, Memphis and St. Louis. Similar population increases occurred in urban areas throughout the country.[5]

Negro migration in the twenties drew on areas of the South that had previously sent few people to New York City. The seaboard states of the Upper South —especially Virginia and the Carolinas —continued to be the main sources of New York's migrant Negro population, but people from Georgia and Florida and other Deep South states formerly under-represented also came in greater numbers: "Harlem became the symbol of liberty and the Promised Land to Negroes everywhere," the Reverend Dr. Powell wrote. "There was hardly a member of Abyssinian Church who could not count on one or more relatives among the new arrivals."[6] In 1930, some 55,000 foreign-born Negroes added to the growing diversity of the city's Negro population.

The following chart presents an exact description of the geographical origins of Negro migrants to New York City in 1930. I have selected states with 900 or more residents in the city:[7]

Negro In-Migration, New York City, 1930
Born in:

Virginia	44,471
South Carolina	33,765
North Carolina	26,120
Georgia	19,546
Florida	8,249
Maryland	6,656
Pennsylvania	6,226
New Jersey	5,275
District of Columbia	3,358
Alabama	3,205
Massachusetts	2,329
Louisiana	2,182
Ohio	1,721
Tennessee	1,651
Texas	1,592
Kentucky	1,216
Mississippi	969
Foreign-born	54,754

The rapid settlement of a heterogeneous Negro population coincided with another population change—the migration of whites from all sections of Manhattan to other boroughs. For the first time since Dutch settlement Manhattan's population *declined* in the 1920's as first- and second-generation immigrants moved to nicer residential areas in the Bronx, Brooklyn and Queens. Many of the homes they left behind had deteriorated significantly. By 1930 a majority of New York City's foreign-born and second-generation residents lived outside Manhattan.[8] As whites moved out of Manhattan, Negroes moved in. The population of that borough declined 18 per cent in the 1920's as its Negro population increased 106 per cent. By 1930 Negroes represented 12 per cent of Manhattan's population —although they composed only 4.7 per cent of the population of the entire city.[9]

Harlem was the New York neighborhood most radically revamped by the population movements of the 1920's, although the Lower East Side also changed rapidly. Harlem underwent a revolution—what one contemporary accurately called a "stupendous upheaval." Between 1920 and 1930, 118,792 white people left the neighborhood and 87,417 Negroes arrived.[10] Second-generation Italians and Jews were responding to the same conditions of prosperity that promoted mobility in all the immigrant neighborhoods of Manhattan—they were not *only* moving away because Negroes settled near them. Conditions of life which satisfied immigrant parents were often unacceptable to children: "The tenements which housed their parents," immigration expert Edward Corsi wrote in 1930, "are being left behind by the children. . . ." "East Harlem used to have a great deal larger population," a survey of the Mayor's Committee on City Planning during the Great Depression concluded. "Like others of the older residential districts, it has suffered by the exodus of families to newer surroundings. . . ."[11]

The city's newest migrants moved into the Harlem flats vacated by Italians and Jews. Puerto Ricans came to live in East Harlem, created community organizations, and laid the foundations for "El Barrio" of today. By 1930 some 45,000 Puerto Ricans resided in New York City and most were heavily concentrated in East Harlem.[12] Negroes moved north along St. Nicholas Avenue —"On the Heights," they called it— and south into the heart of "Little Russia," the former Jewish section. "Just Opened for Colored" signs were common in the neighborhood. Mount Olivet Baptist Church occupied, and still occupies, the once exclusive Temple Israel of Harlem. Prince Hall Masons bought a building that "was formerly a

home for aged Jews." Graham Court, a magnificent block-length apartment house on One Hundred and Sixteenth Street, with eight separate elevators and apartments of seven to ten rooms, was opened to Negroes in 1928.[13] By 1930, 164,566 Negroes, about 72 per cent of Manhattan's Negro population, lived in Harlem.[14] The Negro ghetto remained and expanded as the other ethnic ghettos disintegrated. The economic and residential mobility permitted white people in the city was, and would continue to be, largely denied Negroes. Most Negroes were "jammed together" in Harlem—even those who could afford to live elsewhere—with little possibility to escape.[15] "One notable difference appears between the immigrant and Negro populations," an important federal study of Negro housing concluded. "In the case of the former, there is the possibility of escape, with improvement in economic status, in the second generation, to more desirable sections of the city. In the case of Negroes, who remain a distinguishable group, the factor of race and certain definite racial attitudes favorable to segregation, interpose difficulties to . . . breaking physical restrictions in residence areas."[16] A rather ponderous paragraph, but a significant truth.

III

The settlement of West Indian Negroes in Harlem in the 1920's added another complicating dimension to the racial problems of this community—one that fostered discord rather than harmony among the city's Negroes. There were ten times as many foreign-born Negroes in New York City as in any other American urban area. In 1930, 54,754 foreign Negroes lived in the city—39,833 of whom resided in Manhattan. Miami, the next largest American city in terms of immigrant Negroes, was settled by only 5,512 people; Boston ranked third with 3,287 West Indians. About 25 per cent of Harlem's population in the twenties was foreign-born. Harlem was America's largest Negro melting pot.[17]

In the era of immigration restriction, West Indian Negroes came to America through what a contemporary called the "side door." The immigration laws of the 1920's seriously restricted the migration of Europeans and totally excluded Orientals but had little effect on peoples of the Caribbean. At first there were no restrictions on West Indian Negroes. After 1924, they could enter the country under quotas set aside for their mother countries. Since these quotas were never filled there was, in reality, a free flow of people from the islands to the United States in the 1920's.[18]

Although American Negroes tended to lump all the migrants together in a uniform image—"There is a general assumption," one migrant wrote, "that there is everything in common among West Indians"—it is important to recognize that Harlem's Negro immigrants represented a diverse group of peoples from dozens of different islands in the Caribbean.[19] Most Negro immigrants felt a strong attachment to their homeland. They demonstrated an "exaggerated" nationalism in America—a buffer against the strangeness of the new culture and the hostility they experienced—which was typical of white immigrant groups. It was common, for example, to find former British subjects at the office of the British consul protesting some difficulty they experienced in America.[20] Nationalistic organizations kept close check on American foreign policy in the

Caribbean and often gave banquets for and listened to addresses by West Indian dignitaries. West Indian Negroes from all countries had the lowest rate of naturalization of all immigrant groups. The people white Americans and American Negroes called "West Indians" were really individuals from Jamaica, Trinidad, Barbados, Martinique, St. Vincent, St. Lucia, Dominica, British Guiana, St. Kitts, Nevis, Montserrat, Antigua, Virgin Islands, Bermuda, the Bahamas, and so on. Although the majority spoke English, some considered French their first tongue; others Spanish; a few Dutch. The fraternal and benevolent associations they founded were not inclusive organizations for all Negro immigrants, but exclusive ones—*landmannschaften*—for people from specific islands. Danish settlers kept pictures of the King of Denmark in their homes; former British subjects held coronation pageants and balls ("Boxes, 12s. 6d.—Loges, 8s. 4d.") and flew the Union Jack in Harlem; Frenchmen had annual Bastille Day dances.[21]

Negro immigrants differed from each other in origin, yet in a broader sense they shared general experiences, desires and mores which set them apart *as a group* from their American brethren. Most came from societies in which class distinctions played a more important role in one's life than the color line—although the latter was certainly significant. Unaccustomed to common American racial slurs, they often refused to accept them without protest. The Pullman Company, for example, hesitated to employ West Indian Negroes, it was said, "because of their refusal to accept insults from passengers quietly."[22] Out of this heightened class consciousness came a small group of political and economic radicals in Harlem—"foreign-born agitators," local Negroes called them.[23] Many of Harlem's street-corner orators in the 1920's, though not all, were West Indian migrants. Hubert H. Harrison, a Virgin Islander, was among the most prominent. Harrison was a socialist, an expert in African history, a militant critic of American society and a proud defender of the "Negro's racial heritage." He conducted formal lectures in what he called the "Harlem School of Social Science," and others from street corners—his "outdoor university." A Harlem church, the Hubert H. Harrison Memorial Church, honors his memory. Others presented talks on "Socialism vs. Capitalism," organized tenants' leagues, published Marxist journals and tried to make Harlemites labor-conscious. Richard B. Moore, Frank R. Crosswaith and the Reverend Ethelred Brown—all Negro immigrants—were prominent local candidates for Board of Aldermen, Assembly and Congress on Socialist and Communist tickets—they usually polled an exceedingly small vote. Some organized rent strikes, "rent parades," lobbied for social legislation at City Hall and Albany and distributed radical literature in Harlem. "There is no West Indian slave, no American slave," the short-lived radical magazine *Challenge* commented. "You are all slaves, base, ignoble slaves."[24]

This concern with "class" led to the emergence of a broader tradition in America. What is striking about the Negro immigrant is the way his response to American conditions, such as his exaggerated sense of nationalism, was similar to the typical reactions of most European immigrants. The Negro immigrant "did not suffer from the local anesthesia of custom"[25] and he tried to create a meaningful economic position

for himself within American society. Menial labor was, among most first-generation Negro immigrants, considered a sign of social degradation and looked upon with "disgust." Most were forced to accept such jobs initially, but were strongly motivated by their traditions to improve themselves. As a group, West Indians became noted for their ambition, thrift and business acumen. They were called "pushy," "the Jews of the race," "crafty," "clannish."[26] Negro journalist George S. Schuyler "admired their enterprise in business, their pushfulness."[27] "The West Indians [are] legendary in Harlem for their frugalness and thrift," one student noted. When a West Indian "got ten cents above a beggar," a common local saying ran, "he opened a business." Contemporary surveys of Negro business in Harlem and Columbus Hill demonstrate that a disproportionate number of small stores—the traditional "Race Enterprise" —were owned by Negro immigrants. Dr. P. M. H. Savory, one of the leading spokesmen of New York's foreign-born Negro community from the 1920's to his death in June 1965, owned and published the *Amsterdam News*. Many others achieved success within the racial barrier.[28]

Another significant distinction between the foreign-born Negro and the American was their attitude toward family life. Slavery initially destroyed the entire concept of family for American Negroes and the slave heritage, bulwarked by economic conditions, continued into the twentieth century to make family instability a common factor in Negro life. This had not been true for most West Indians, and they arrived in America with the orthodox respect for family ties that was traditional of rural people. The West Indian family was patriarchal in structure—contrasted with the typically matriarchal American Negro home. The father, as key worker and wage earner in the islands, ruled the household with a solid hand. It was beneath his dignity to help with domestic chores. (This led American Negroes to brand West Indian men "cruel.")[29] Children were supposed to obey their pa.ents rigidly—American Negroes considered them strait-laced; have long and formal courtships; and receive parental approval before marriage. Illicit sexual relations were considered the worst form of moral evil.[30] These traditions began to change in the second generation, but throughout the 1920's family solidarity was a pervasive force among New York's Negro immigrants.[31]

These differences in style of life were also evident in another important institution—the church. The majority of Harlemites were Baptists and Methodists; the immigrants were predominantly Episcopalian and Catholic.[32] The beautiful St. Martin's Episcopal Church was founded in Harlem in 1928 to minister to the needs of West Indian migrants. Services in immigrant churches were generally staid and quiet; Sunday a day of prayer, rest and visiting—as it had been on the islands. Observers were impressed with the differences between the emotionalism of a typical Harlem religious service and the moderation and restraint shown in churches of the foreign-born. Negro immigrants also objected to the general frivolity and "fast ways" that were part of a typical Sunday in Harlem.[33]

All these factors combined to make Harlem in the 1920's a battleground of intraracial antagonism. American Negro nativism spilled over to taint Harlemites' reactions to the West Indian.

The Negro immigrant was ridiculed; his tropical clothing was mocked; children tossed stones at the people who looked so different; foreigners were taunted with such epithets as "monkey-chaser," "ring-tale," "king Mon," "cockney." "When a monkey-chaser dies/Don't need no undertaker/Just throw him in de Harlem River/He'll float back to Jamaica," was a verse from a Harlem ditty of the twenties. West Indians came to Harlem, ran another common saying, "to teach, open a church, or start trouble." "Bitter resentment grew on both sides." Each group called the other "aggressive." "We have . . . in Harlem," NAACP director Walter White wrote, "this strange mixture of reactions not only to prejudice from without but to equally potent prejudices from within." "If you West Indians don't like how we do things in this country," an American Negro said tersely, "you should go back where you came from. . . ."[34]

The obvious hostility of American Negroes forced Negro immigrants to unite in defense organizations larger than their individual national groups. The West Indian Committee on America, the Foreign-Born Citizens' Alliance and the West Indian Reform Association were founded in the twenties to soften these intraracial tensions and promote "cordial relations between West Indians and colored Americans." Radio programs were devoted to discussions of "Intra-Race Relations in Harlem," and immigrants were urged to become naturalized citizens. American Negroes, in turn, were asked to tone down their "considerable prejudice against West Indians." A semblance of co-operation was achieved as mass meetings were held in Harlem churches. The hatreds of the 1920's did not die, however, until West Indian Negroes stopped migrating to New York. During the Depression more immigrants left New York than entered and intraracial tensions slowly eased. Young Harlemites today, even third-generation descendants of Negro immigrants, are often unaware of these old divisions. The unique type of intraracial hostility so prominent in the twenties has never reappeared. While it lasted, however, it served to weaken a Negro community in great need of unity. A divided Harlem confronted major social problems that desperately called for the co-operation of all.[35]

IV

The most profound change that Harlem experienced in the 1920's was its emergence as a slum. Largely within the space of a single decade Harlem was transformed from a potentially ideal community to a neighborhood with manifold social and economic problems called "deplorable," "unspeakable," "incredible." "The State would not allow cows to live in some of these apartments used by colored people . . . in Harlem," the chairman of a city housing reform committee said in 1927. The Harlem slum of today was created in the 1920's.[36]

The most important factor which led to the rapid deterioration of Harlem housing was the high cost of living in the community. Rents, traditionally high in Harlem, reached astounding proportions in the 1920's—they skyrocketed in response to the unprecedented demand created by heavy Negro migration and settlement within a restricted geographical area. "Crowded in a black ghetto," a sociologist wrote, "the Negro tenant is forced to pay exorbitant rentals because he cannot escape." In 1919 the

average Harlemite paid somewhat above $21 or $22 a month for rent; by 1927 rentals had *doubled* and the "mean average market rent for Negro tenants in a typical block" was $41.77. In 1927 Harlem Negroes paid $8 more than the typical New Yorker for three-room apartments; $10 more for four rooms; and $7 more for five rooms, an Urban League survey noted.[37] Another report concluded that the typical white working-class family in New York City in the late twenties paid $6.67 per room, per month, while Harlem Negroes were charged $9.50.[38]

Realty values which had declined significantly prior to World War I *appreciated* in Harlem in the twenties.[39] Harlem experienced a slum boom. "The volume of business done in the section . . . during the last year is . . . unprecedented," *Harlem Magazine* announced in 1920. "Renting conditions have been very satisfactory to the owners and the demand for space . . . is getting keener every year [due] to the steady increase in the Negro population," a *New York Times* reporter wrote in 1923. There was, in the language of a Harlem businessman, an "unprecedented demand for Harlem real estate."[40] For landlords—Negro and white (Negro tenants continually complained that Negro landlords fleeced them with equal facility as whites)—Harlem became a profitable slum.[41]

High rents and poor salaries necessarily led to congested and unsanitary conditions. The average Negro Harlemite in the 1920's, as in the 1890's, held some menial or unskilled position which paid low wages—work which was customarily "regarded as Negro jobs." There were generally two types of businesses in New York in terms of Negro hiring policy, E. Franklin Frazier wrote: "Those that employ Negroes in menial positions and those that employ no Negroes at all." Macy's, for example, hired Negroes as elevator operators, escalator attendants and cafeteria workers; Gimbel's used none. "We have felt it inadvisable to [hire] colored people," a Metropolitan Life Insurance Company executive explained in 1930, "not because of any prejudice on the part of the company, but because . . . there would be very serious objection on the part of our white employees. . . ."[42] Throughout the city the vast majority of Negro men worked as longshoremen, elevator operators, porters, janitors, teamsters, chauffeurs, waiters and general laborers of all kinds. Negro women continued to work as domestics ("scrub women"), although in the 1920's an increasing number were employed as factory operatives in the garment industry and in laundries. Less than 20 per cent of Harlem's businesses were owned by Negroes.[43] The average Harlem family, according to President Hoover's Conference on Home Building and Home Ownership, earned $1,300 a year in the twenties; the typical white family in the city, $1,570. A variety of social investigations noted that working-class whites expended approximately 20 per cent of their income for rent, considered the proper amount by economists; Harlemites, 33 per cent and more.[44] An Urban League study of 2,160 Harlem families demonstrated that almost half (48 per cent) spent 40 or more per cent of their earnings on rent. A 1928 sample of tenement families found that Harlemites paid 45 per cent of their wages for housing. Similar conclusions were reached in a variety of local community studies.[45] Whatever the exact figure, few Negroes looked to the first of the month with expectancy.

Added to the combination of "high rents and low wages"[46] was the fact that Harlem's apartment houses and brownstones were originally built for people with radically different family structure from that of the new residents. Seventy-five per cent of Harlem's tenements had been constructed before 1900.[47] The Negro community of the twenties, like all working-class peoples in times of great migration, continued to be most heavily populated by young adults—men and women between the ages of 15 and 44. Family life had not yet begun for many Negro Harlemites —as it had for older Americans and earlier immigrants who lived in the community previously. In 1930, 66.5 per cent of Harlem Negroes were between the ages of 15 and 44, contrasted with 56.5 per cent for the general population of Manhattan and 54.4 per cent for New York City at large. Harlemites who were married had few children. In 1930, 17.5 per cent of Harlem's population was under 14; the corresponding figure for New York City was 24.5 per cent. The number of Harlemites under the age of 15 declined 14 per cent between 1920 and 1930, as whites left the neighborhood. There was a corresponding decrease of 19 per cent for those over 45 years of age.[48]

What all these statistics mean is simply that apartments of five, six, and seven rooms were suitable for older white residents with larger families and larger incomes—they obviously did not meet the needs of the Negro community in the 1920's. "The houses in the section of Harlem inhabited by the Negro were not only built for another race," E. Franklin Frazier noted, "but what is more important, for a group of different economic level, and consisting of families and households of an entirely different composition from those which now occupy these dwellings." "Unfortunately," Eugene Kinckle Jones of the Urban League stated, "the houses built before [the Negroes'] arrival were not designed to meet the needs . . . of Negroes." "The class of houses we are occupying today are not suited to our economic needs," John E. Nail said in 1921. Negro Harlemites desperately needed small apartments at low rentals: "One of the community's greatest needs [is] small apartments for small families with a reasonable rent limit. . . ."[49] Few realtors were philanthropic enough to invest their capital in new construction; older homes, properly subdivided, produced sufficient income. Only a handful of new houses were built in Harlem in the 1920's.[50]

A variety of makeshift solutions were found to make ends meet: "What you gonna do when the rent comes 'round," had been an old Negro song. The most common solution was to rent an apartment larger than one's needs and means and make up the difference by renting rooms to lodgers—"commercializing" one's home. In the twenties, approximately one white Manhattan family in nine (11.2 per cent) took in roomers, contrasted with one in four (26 per cent) for Negroes. Most lodgers were strangers people let into their homes because of economic necessity. It was difficult to separate "the respectable" from "the fast." "The most depraved Negroes lived side by side with those who were striving to live respectable lives," a contemporary complained. Urban reformers blamed many of Harlem's social problems on this "lodger evil."[51]

Every conceivable space within a home was utilized to maximum efficiency: "Sometimes even the bathtub is used to sleep on, two individuals taking turns!" Negro educator Roscoe Conkling Bruce wrote. Boardinghouses were established which rented beds by the week, day, night or hour. A large number of brownstones were converted to rooming houses: "Private residences at one time characteristic of this part of the city have been converted into tenements. . . ." One landlord transformed apartments in nine houses into one-room flats, a state commission investigating New York housing reported. Space which formerly grossed $40 a month now brought in $100 to $125. People were said to be living in "coal bins and cellars." In an extreme case, one social investigator discovered seven children sleeping on pallets on the floor of a two-room apartment. More common was the "Repeating" or "Hot Bed System"—as soon as one person awoke and left, his bed was taken over by another.[52]

An additional Harlem method devised to meet the housing crisis of the twenties was the "Rent Party." Tickets of admission were usually printed and sold for a modest price (25¢). All who wanted to come were invited to a party. Here is an example:[53]

> If you're looking for a good time,
>   don't look no more,
> Just ring my bell and I'll answer
>   the door.
> Southern Barbecue
> Given by Charley Johnson and Joe
>   Hotboy, and How hot!

Chitterlings, pigs' feet, coleslaw and potato salad were sold. Money was raised in this way to pay the rent: "The rent party," *The New York Age* editorialized in 1926, "has become a recognized means of meeting the demands of extortionate landlords. . . ." The white world saw rent parties as picturesque affairs—in reality they were a product of economic exploitation and they often degenerated into rowdy, bawdy and violent evenings.[54]

A significant part of the deterioration of the neighborhood was caused by the migrants themselves. Some needed rudimentary training in the simplest processes of good health and sanitation (Booker T. Washington, it will be remembered, preached the "gospel of the toothbrush").[55] E. Franklin Frazier called many Negro Harlemites "ignorant and unsophisticated peasant people without experience [in] urban living. . . ." They often permitted homes and buildings to remain in a state of uncleanliness and disrepair. Landlords complained that apartments were looted and fixtures stolen, that courtyards and hallways were found laden with refuse. Clothes and bedding were hung out of windows; trash sometimes thrown down air shafts; dogs walked on rooftops; profanities shouted across streets; "ragtime" played throughout the night. "Ragtime is a sufficient infliction of itself," one wag complained, "but when it keeps up all night, it becomes unbearable." "Since the so-called 'Negro invasion,'" a colored woman noted, "the streets, the property and the character of everything have undergone a change, and if you are honest, you will frankly acknowledge it has not been for the . . . improvement of the locality. . . . Are we responsible for at least some of the race prejudice which has developed since the entry of Negroes in Harlem?" Negro journals criticized "boisterous" men who laughed "hysterically" and hung around street corners, and those who used "foul language on the streets." An editorial in the *Age*, one of many, attacked "Careless Harlem Tenants": "A great deal might be said about the

necessity for training some of the tenants in the matter of common decency," it suggested. The absence of a sense of social and community responsibility, characteristic of urban life, obviously affected Negro Harlemites.[56]

All these factors combined to lead to the rapid decline of Harlem. The higher the rents, sociologists said, the greater the congestion: "Crowding is more prevalent in high-rent cities than in cities in which rent per room is more reasonable." In 1925, Manhattan's population density was 223 people per acre —in the Negro districts it was 336. Philadelphia, the second most congested Negro city in the country, had 111 Negroes to an acre of land; Chicago ranked third with 67. There were two streets in Harlem that were perhaps the most congested blocks in the entire world.[57]

People were packed together to the point of "indecency."[58] Some landlords, after opening houses to Negro tenants, lost interest in caring for their property and permitted it to run down—halls were left dark and dirty, broken pipes were permitted to rot, steam heat was cut off as heating apparatus wore out, dumb-waiters broke down and were boarded up, homes became vermin-infested. Tenants in one rat-infested building started what they called "a crusade against rats." They argued that the rats in their house were "better fed" and "better housed" than the people. Some common tenant complaints in the 1920's read: "No improvement in ten years"; "Rats, rat holes, and roaches"; "Very very cold"; "Not fit to live in"; "Air shaft smells"; "Ceilings in two rooms have fallen"; "My apartment is overrun with rats"; and so on.[59] There were more disputes between tenants and landlords in Harlem's local district court

–the Seventh District Court–than in any municipal court in the five boroughs. Traditionally, municipal courts were known as "poor-men's courts"; Harlemites called the Seventh District Court the "rent court." Occasionally, socially conscious judges of this court made personal inspections of local tenements that were subjects of litigation. Without exception what they saw horrified them: "Conditions in negro tenements in Harlem are deplorable"; "Found few fit for human habitation"; "Negro tenants are being grossly imposed upon by their landlords"; "On the whole I found a need for great reformation"; were some of their comments. One municipal official accurately called the majority of Harlem's houses "diseased properties."[60]

V

And the disease did not confine itself to houses. To touch most areas of Harlem life in the 1920's is to touch tragedy. This was especially true of the health of the community. Theoretically, a section of the city inhabited by relatively young people should have ranked below the general population in mortality and sickness rates. Just the reverse was true. Undertaking was a most profitable Harlem business.[61]

From 1923 to 1927 an Atlanta University professor made an intensive study of Harlem health. His findings were shocking. During these years Harlem's death rate, for all causes, was 42 per cent in excess of that of the entire city. Twice as many Harlem mothers died in childbirth as did mothers in other districts, and almost twice as many Harlem children "passed" as did infants in the rest of New York. Infant mortality in Harlem, 1923-1927, was 111 per thousand live births; for the city, 64.5 Families wept at the processions of "so many little white caskets." Similar statistics are recorded for deaths from tuberculosis (two and a half to three times the city rate), pneumonia, heart disease, cancer and stillbirths.[62] An astounding number of Harlemites had venereal diseases. Negro children commonly suffered from rickets–a disease of malnutrition. More women than ever reported themselves "widows" to census-takers. Negro deaths by violence increased 60 per cent between 1900 and

Health center districts, 1930	Infant mortality per 1,000 live births	TB mortality per 100,000 population	Pulmonary TB new case rate per 100,000 population	Other infectious diseases, rate per 100,000 population	Venereal disease new case rate per 100,000 population	General mortality rate per 1,000 population
Manhattan						
Central Harlem	98	251	487	987	2826	15.3
Lower East Side	62	116	302	1,160	892	14.0
Kips Bay–Lenox Hill	73	75	184	937	629	12.7
East Harlem	75	137	311	1,326	913	12.0
Lower West Side	83	156	391	1,201	1,318	16.7
Riverside	64	75	196	827	778	12.3
Washington Heights	52	72	203	937	668	10.5
Total	73	122	294	1,049	1,455	13.3

1925.[63] With the single exception of the Lower West Side Health District, which included the old San Juan Hill neighborhood, Harlem was the most disease-ridden community in Manhattan.[64]

Whatever the causes of Harlem's health problems—and medical investigators continue to search for all the answers—a good deal can be laid at the door of slum environment. Urban reformers consistently showed a high correlation between poverty and congestion on the one hand and disease and death on the other. Mortality rates for infants whose mothers worked away from home, for example—and twice as many Negro women as white women in the city did—was higher than for children whose mothers remained at home; working-class families in old-law tenements (pre-1901) died at a higher-rate than those in newer houses; poverty led to the consumption of the cheapest foods, and this in turn fostered diseases of poor diet; working mothers died more readily in childbirth than unemployed women; and so on.[65] Added to all these considerations, however, was a deep strain of peasant ignorance and superstition embedded in the minds of thousands of migrants—foreign-born as well as native—who settled in Harlem. Quackery abounded in the community in the 1920's.[66]

Harlem had the reputation of a "wide-open city." Whatever you wanted, and in whatever quantity, so the impression went, could be bought there. This was certainly true for the variety of "spiritualists," "herb doctors," "African medicine men," "Indian doctors," "dispensers of snake oils," "layers-on-of-hands," "faith healers," "palmists," and phrenologists who performed a twentieth-century brand of necromancy there: "Harlem sick people are flocking to all sorts of Quacksters," an *Age* reporter noted. One man, "Professor Ajapa," sold a "herb juice" guaranteed "to cure consumption, rheumatism, and other troubles that several doctors have failed in." Powders could be purchased to keep one's wife home at night, make women fertile and men sexually appealing. "Black Herman the Magician" and "Sister P. Harreld" held séances and sold "blessed handkerchiefs," "potent powders," love charms, lodestones, amulets and "piles of roots." "Ignorance, cherished superstitions and false knowledge often govern Negroes in illness and hamper recoveries," a colored physician with the Board of Health wrote in 1926. Nine wood lice gathered in a little bag and tied around a baby's neck, some believed, would end teething. An egg fried brown on both sides and placed on a woman's abdomen would hasten labor. If a mother in the course of childbirth kicked a Bible from her bed to the floor, either she or her child would die. People had faith in the medicinal qualities of dried cobwebs, rabbit brains, "dirt-dauber tea," and something called "cockroach rum." In spite of efforts of physicians, health agencies and the Negro press to bring modern-day medical information to the community, quackery "continued to thrive with impunity in Harlem." It aggravated an already tragic situation.[67]

Accompanying the proliferation of healers, and rooted in the same rural consciousness which made quackery possible,[68] was the host of storefront churches founded in Harlem in the twenties. These were places that healed one's soul: "Jesus is the Doctor, Services on Sunday," read a sign which hung over one door. An investigator found 140 Negro churches in a 150-block area of Harlem in 1926. "Harlem is perhaps overchurched," W. E. B. DuBois said modestly. Only about a third—fifty-four —of Harlem's churches were housed in regular church buildings—and these included some of the most magnificent and costly church edifices in New York City. The rest held services in stores and homes and appealed to Harlem's least educated people. "Jack-leg preachers," "cotton-field preachers," as their critics called them, hung out their poorly printed signboards and "preached Jesus" to all who wanted to listen. One self-appointed pastor held meetings in the front room of his home and rented chairs from the local undertaker to seat his small congregation. In Harlem in the twenties one could receive the word of the Lord through such nondenominational sects as: "The Metaphysical Church of the Divine Investigation," "The Temple of the Gospel of the Kingdom," "The Church of the Temple of Love," "Holy Church of the Living God," "Temple of Luxor," "Holy Tabernacle of God," "Royal Fraternity Association," "Knights of the Rose and Cross," "Sons of God," "Sons of Christ," "Sons of Jehovah," "Sanctified Sons of the Holy Ghost," and the "Live-Ever-Die-Never" church. People not only had their worries removed in these places, a Negro clergyman wrote, but "their meager worldly goods as well."[69]

The ministers of these churches preached a fundamentalism which centered around the scheming ways of Satan, who was everywhere, and the terror and joy of divine retribution, with an emphasis on terror. One congregation expelled members who attended the theater or movies. "The devil runs every theatre," its pastor said. "He collects a tax on the souls of men and robs them of their seat in heaven." Services were fervent, loud and boisterous as members felt the spirit of the Lord and shouted and begged for His forgiveness. Tambourines sometimes kept up a rhythmic beat in the background and heightened the emotionalism to a state of frenzy. Neighbors of one storefront church sued the congregation for "conducting a public nuisance." The "weird sounds" which emanated from the building, they complained, seemed like a "jazz orchestra."[70]

Are you ready-ee? Hah!
For that great day, hah!
When the moon shall drape her face in
    mourning, hah!
And the sun drip down in blood, hah!
When the stars, hah!
Shall burst forth from their diamond
    sockets, hah!
And the mountains shall skip like lambs,
    hah!
Havoc will be there, my friends, hah!
With her jaws wide open, hah!
And the sinner-man, hah!
And cry, Oh rocks! Hah!
Hide me! Hah!
Hide me from the face of an angry God,
    hah!
Hide me, Ohhhhhh! . . .
Can't hide, sinner, you can't hide.[71]

Contemporaries were uniformly critical of these evangelists—there were many Harlem "Prophets"—and most of these preachers were probably charlatans in some form. There was at least one exception, however. A new denomination, the Church of Christ, Apostolic Faith, was founded on the streets of Harlem by the Reverend Mr. R. C. Lawson in 1919. The Reverend Mr. Lawson, of New Iberia, Louisiana, "the only real Apostolic—Holy Ghost-Bible Preacher," presented what he called the "Full Gospel" on street corners of Harlem's worst blocks. He decried the lack of emotionalism in the more established urban churches—copying "the white man's style," he said—and offered recent migrants a touch of fire and brimstone and personal Christianity characteristic of religion in the rural South:

> I have found it, I have found it,
> the meaning of life, life in God,
> life flowing through me by the
> Holy Spirit, life abundant, peace,
> joy, life in its fullness.

Lawson started preaching on One Hundred and Thirty-third Street, east of Lenox Avenue. This area "was to Harlem what the Bowery is to the lower East Side," a Negro journalist recorded. From the streets, the Reverend Mr. Lawson moved into a small building and held services for those "fast drifting to a life of eternal darkness" every day and every night of the week. His Refuge Church of Christ became the founding church of the new denomination, and the Reverend Mr. Lawson its first bishop. By 1930 the Apostolic Church had some forty branches throughout the country and ran an orphanage, elementary school and "Bible Supply House"; it continues to prosper today. Annual conventions met in Refuge Church, "the most honored in the sisterhood of the Apostolic Church," and local leaders praised and publicized its good works for Harlem Negroes: "This church has had one of the most remarkable growths of any religious organizations in the country."[72]

Harlem was also a "wide-open city" in terms of vice and gambling.[73] The annual reports of the anti-vice Committee of Fourteen, founded in 1905, showed Harlem as the leading or near-leading prostitution center of Manhattan throughout the twenties. The Committee hired a Negro doctor, Ernest R. Alexander, to do a secret study of Harlem vice in 1928. His report emphasized the "openness of vice conditions in this district." Dr. Alexander personally

found sixty-one houses of prostitution in the neighborhood—more than the combined totals of four other investigators hired at the same time to survey other districts. "There is a larger amount and more open immorality in Harlem than this community has known in years," Negro alderman George W. Harris noted in 1922. "It is a house of assignation . . . this black city," Eric D. Walrond wrote bitterly in the Negro journal *The Messenger*.[74]

> Her dark brown face
> Is like a withered flower
> On a broken stem.
> Those kind come cheap in Harlem,
> So they say.[75]

The Committee of Fourteen also disclosed that more than 90 per cent of these "daughters of joy" institutions were owned and managed by whites. Other evidence verifies this.[76]

Gambling also prevailed in the neighborhood: "Bootleggers, gamblers, and other panderers to vice have found it profitable to ply their vicious trades in this section." The poorest of the poor sought instant riches through the numbers racket. No sum was too small to bet—starting with pennies. "One can bet with plenty of takers on anything from a horse race to a mule race," the *Age* editorialized. Many Harlemites "would rather gamble than eat," it concluded. People selected numbers to coincide with birthdays, dreams, hymns or chapters and verses of Scripture in expectation that they would coincide with the clearing-house figures of the day. The odds were thousands to one against success, yet the smallest hope for a richer life was better than none and Negroes continued to play "policy" avidly. "The chief pastime of Harlem seems to be playing the numbers," George S. Schuyler wrote in 1925.[77]

"Buffet flats," "hooch joints," "barrel houses," and cabarets supplied Harlemites with illegal liquor, and occasionally other things, in the Prohibition era. Drugstores, cigar stores, sweetshops and delicatessens were used as "fronts" for speakeasies. "Harlem can boast of more drugstores than any similar area in the world," one Negro commented. "A plethora of delicatessen stores may be found in the Negro sections of New York, most of which are simply disguised bootlegging stores," a Harlemite concluded in 1924. "And so many confectioners! One never dreamed the Negroes were so much in need of sugar." "Speakeasies downtown are usually carefully camouflaged," a *New York Tribune* reporter noted. "In Harlem they can be spotted a hundred yards off."[78]

Poverty and family instability also led to a high incidence of juvenile delinquency. A community with fewer young teenagers should have shown a proportionally lower juvenile crime rate; as with Negro health, just the reverse was true. "The records of the Children's Court of New York for every year from 1914 to 1927 show a steady increase in the percentage of all crimes committed by Negro boys and girls," Owen R. Lovejoy of the Children's Aid Society reported. In 1914 Negro children represented 2.8 per cent of all cases before the juvenile court of New York City; in 1930 this figure rose to 11.7 per cent.[79]

Working mothers had little time to care for their children. Youngsters "with keys tied around their necks on a ribbon" wandered around the streets until families came home at night. A substantial portion were products of broken homes—families without a male head. One Harlem school principal testified that 699 of his 1,600 pupils came from families whose fathers were not living

at home. Nor did the majority of Harlem schoolchildren ever have time to accustom themselves to the regularity of school life; many families were rootless. Three-fourths of all the Negro pupils registered in one Harlem school, for example, transferred to some other before the end of one school year; some schools actually experienced a 100 per cent turnover. Pupils from the South were seriously deficient in educational training: "They are at times 14 to 15 years of age and have not the schooling of boys of eight," a Harlem principal wrote. "We cannot give a boy back seven years of wasted life. . . ." The typical Harlem school of the twenties had double and sometimes triple sessions. The "usual class size" was forty to fifty and conditions were generally "immensely over-crowded": "The school plant as a whole is old, shabby, and far from modern." In some schools 25 per cent and more of the children were overage or considered retarded.

Negro children in Harlem often led disrupted and harsh lives from the earliest years of their existence: "Testimony has been given before us as to the moral conditions among children, even of tender age," a municipal agency investigating Harlem schools recorded, "which is not to be adequately described by the word 'horrifying.'" These conditions were obviously reflected in high rates of juvenile crime but more subtly, and worst of all, in a loss of respect for oneself and for life in general. Harlem youngsters developed "a sense of subordination, of insecurity, of lack of self-confidence and self-respect, the inability . . . to stand on their own feet and face the world with open eyes and feel that [they have] as good a right as anyone else."[80]

This then was the horror of slum life

—the Harlem tragedy of the 1920's. "Court and police precinct records show," a municipal agency maintained, "that in arrests, convictions, misdemeanants, felons, female police problems and juvenile delinquencies, these areas are in the lead. . . ." It was no wonder that narcotics addiction became a serious problem then and that Harlem became "the center of the retail dope traffic of New York"; nor that local violence and hatred for the police were continually reported in the press.[81] The majority of Harlemites even during normal times lived "close to the subsistence level." Many were "under care" of charitable agencies in the period of relatively full employment. Those who needed money quickly and had no other recourse were forced to turn to loan sharks, Negro and white, who charged 30 to 40 per cent interest: Harlem "has been infested by a lot of loan sharks," a municipal magistrate who dealt with such cases stated. In one form or another the sorrow and economic deprivation of the Depression had come to Harlem in the twenties: "The reason why the Depression didn't have the impact on the Negroes that it had on the whites," George S. Schuyler said, "was that the Negroes had been in the Depression all the time."[82]

NOTES

1. The Mayor's Commission on Conditions in Harlem, "The Negro in Harlem: A Report on Social and Economic Conditions Responsible for the Outbreak of March 19, 1935" (unpublished manuscript in La Guardia Papers, Municipal Archives), p. 53. This important study, prepared under the direction of E. Franklin Frazier, will hereafter be cited as "The Negro in Harlem."
2. "The Future Harlem," The New York Age, January 10, 1920.
3. John E. Nail to James Weldon Johnson, March 12, 1934, Johnson Collection, Yale University; "Harlem Conditions Called Deplorable," The New York Times, September 6, 1927.

4. "Let Them Come," "The New Exodus," The New York Age, March 3, 1923, October 16, 1920, September 14, 1929.
5. Bureau of the Census, Fifteenth Census, 1930: Population (Washington, D.C., 1933), II, 216-218; Walter Laidlaw, Population of the City of New York, 1890-1930 (New York, 1932), p. 51.
6. Reverend Dr. Adam Clayton Powell, Sr., Against the Tide: An Autobiography (New York, 1938), pp. 70-71.
7. Bureau of the Census, Fifteenth Census, 1930: Population (Washington, D.C., 1933), II, 216-218. Note the difference in Chicago's migrant population. In order of greatest numbers Chicago Negroes came from Mississippi, Tennessee, Georgia, Alabama and Louisiana.
8. James Ford, et al., Slums and Housing: With Special Reference to New York City (Cambridge, Mass., 1936), II, 311-315.
9. Ibid., p. 317; Bureau of the Census, Negroes in the United States, 1920-1932 (Washington, D.C., 1935), p. 55.
10. Winfred B. Nathan, Health Conditions in North Harlem, 1923-1927 (New York, 1932), pp. 13-14.
11. Harlem Magazine, XIX (June 1930), 8; Mayor's Commission on City Planning, East Harlem Community Study (typescript in New York Public Library, 1937), p. 16.
12. Slums and Housing, p. 370; Antonio T. Rivera to La Guardia, June 24, 1935, La Guardia Papers; "Harlem Puerto Ricans Unite to Prove Faith," The New York Times, July 2, August 9, 16, 1926; Opportunity, IV (October 1926), 330.
13. The New York Age, August 27, 1927, March 31, 1928, January 11, 1930; The New York Times, October 19, 1924.
14. Slums and Housing, p. 314.
15. The attempt of Negroes to move into Washington Heights, Yonkers and Westchester was opposed in these sections as it had been in Harlem earlier. The Neighborhood Protective Association of Washington Heights urged landlords to sign racially restrictive covenants. Mortgage pressures from financial institutions closed down a Negro housing development in Yonkers. As a result of population pressure, however, another large ghetto was created in the Bedford-Stuyvesant section of Brooklyn in the 1920's. Of the 68,921 Negroes in Brooklyn in 1930, 47,616 lived in what is now called Bedford-Stuyvesant. "Negro Community Near Yonkers Abandoned," The New York Age, July 3, 1926, March 24, August 4, 1928, April 19, 26, 1930; Slums and Housing, p. 314. For a sketch of Brooklyn's Negro community see Ralph Foster Weld, Brooklyn Is America (New York, 1950), pp. 153-173.
16. The President's Conference on Home Building and Home Ownership, Report of the Committee on Negro Housing (Washington, D.C., 1931), p. 5.
17. Bureau of the Census, Fifteenth Census, 1930: Population (Washington, D.C., 1933), II, 70; Ira De Augustine Reid, The Negro Immigrant (New

York, 1938), pp. 248-249; Barrington Dunbar, "Factors in the Cultural Background of the American Southern Negro and the British West Indian Negro that Condition their Adjustment in Harlem" (M.A. thesis, Columbia University, 1935), foreword, p. 4.

18. Reid, *The Negro Immigrant*, pp. 31-35; Reid, "Negro Immigration to the United States," *Social Forces*, XVI (March 1938), 411-417; W. A. Domingo, "Restricted West Indian Immigration and the American Negro," *Opportunity*, II (October 1924), 298-299.

19. W. A. Domingo, "Gift of the Black Tropics," in Alain Locke, ed., *The New Negro: An Interpretation* (New York, 1925), p. 343.

20. *The New York Age*, July 9, 1924, February 4, 1928; Harry Robinson, "The Negro Immigrant in New York" (WPA research paper, Schomburg Collection), p. 9.

21. Garrie Ward Moore, "A Study of a Group of West Indian Negroes in New York City" (M.A. thesis, Columbia University, 1923), pp. 19-20; Reid, *The Negro Immigrant*, pp. 126-128; *The New York Age*, February 28, 1931, July 29, 1933.

22. "The Negro in New York" (unpublished WPA manuscript, Schomburg Collection), pp. 25-27; Gardner N. Jones, "The Pilgrimage to Freedom" (WPA research paper, Schomburg Collection), p. 25.

23. Reid, *The Negro Immigrant*, p. 159.

24. *Ibid.*, p. 123; "Communists in Harlem," *The New York Age*, September 21, 1929, October 2, 9, 1926, December 24, 1927, January 21, May 12, December 8, 1928, September 21, 1929.

25. Domingo, "Gift of the Black Tropics," p. 347.

26. Robinson, "Negro Immigrant in New York," pp. 21-22; Moore, "West Indian Negroes in New York City," p. 26.

27. "The Reminiscences of George S. Schuyler" (Oral History Research Office, Columbia University, 1960), p. 73.

28. Robinson, "Negro Immigrant in New York," p. 9; "The Negro in New York," p. 25; Moore, "West Indian Negroes in New York City," p. 25; Reid, *The Negro Immigrant*, p. 133; *The Messenger*, VII (September 1925), 326; 337-338; *The New York Age*, February 22, 1930; Baltimore *Afro-American*, January 9, 1932.

29. Moore, "West Indian Negroes in New York City," p. 5.

30. Dunbar, "Negro Adjustment in Harlem," pp. 14-25.

31. Reid, *The Negro Immigrant*, *passim*.

32. *Ibid.*, p. 125; Greater New York Federation of Churches, *Negro Churches in Manhattan* (New York, 1930).

33. Reid, *The Negro Immigrant*, p. 174; Moore, "West Indian Negroes in New York City," pp. 20-25; Dunbar, "Negro Adjustment in Harlem," chap. IV, pp. 22-23.

34. Roi Ottley, *'New World A-Coming': Inside Black America* (New York, 1943), pp. 47-48; Gardner Jones, "The Pilgrimage to Freedom"

(WPA research paper, Schomburg Collection), p. 25; Beverly Smith, "Harlem—Negro City," *New York Herald Tribune*, February 14, 1930; Reid, *The Negro Immigrant*, p. 115; *The New York Age*, July 19, 1924, March 17, 1934; Dunbar, "Negro Adjustment in Harlem," chap. III, p. 4; Walter White, "The Paradox of Color," in Alain Locke, ed., *The New Negro: An Interpretation* (New York, 1925), p. 367.

35. *The New York Age*, March 3, 24, April 21, 1928; Domingo, "The Gift of the Black Tropics," p. 344-345; Reid, *The Negro Immigrant*, p. 235.

36. "Harlem Slums," *The Crisis*, XLVIII (December 1941), 378-381; *The New York Age*, January 22, 1927.

37. New York Urban League, "Twenty-four Hundred Negro Families in Harlem: An Interpretation of the Living Conditions of Small Wage Earners" (typescript, Schomburg Collection, 1927), pp. 16-18.

38. *Report of the Committee on Negro Housing*, p. 64.

39. "Appreciation" of prices "came [when owners] remained calm. . . ." T. J. Woofter, *et al.*, *Negro Problems in Cities* (New York, 1928), p. 75. *The New York Times* printed dozens of articles on Harlem's new business prosperity.

40. "Harlem Real Estate Increasing in Value," *Harlem Magazine*, VIII (February 1920), 18b; "Unprecedented Demand for Harlem Real Estate," *ibid.*, X (November 1920), 6; "Revival of Speculative Activity on Harlem's Main Thoroughfare," *The New York Times*, January 18, 1920, July 24, 1921, June 10, 1923, February 13, 1927.

41. "Of all the gouging landlords in Harlem, the colored landlords and agents are the worst, according to the records of the Seventh District Municipal Court." "Race Landlord is Hardest on His Tenants," *The New York Age*, November 20, 1920, June 16, September 22, 1923, May 29, 1926.

42. "The Negro in Harlem," pp. 27-32; *The New York Age*, April 26, 1930.

43. Bureau of the Census, *Fourteenth Census, 1920: Population* (Washington, D.C., 1923), IV, 366-367, 1157-1179; *Fifteenth Census, 1930: Occupations* (Washington, D.C., 1933), 1130-1134; Helen B. Sayre, "Negro Women in Industry," *Opportunity*, II (August 1924), 242-244.

44. *Report of the Committee on Negro Housing*, p. 64; *Negro Problems in Cities*, p. 122.

45. "Twenty-four Hundred Negro Families in Harlem," p. 19; Sidney Axelrad, *Tenements and Tenants: A Study of 1104 Tenement Families* (New York, 1932), p. 15; New York Building and Land Utilization Committee, *Harlem Family Income Survey* (New York, 1935), p. 3; James H. Hubert, "Harlem—Its Social Problems," *Hospital Social Service*, XXI (January 1930), 44.

46. *Report of the Committee on Negro Housing*, p. vii.

47. William Wilson to La Guardia, October 6, 1944, La Guardia Papers.

48. *Health Conditions in North Harlem*, pp. 16-

17; *Fifteenth Census, 1930: Population* (Washington, D.C., 1933), II, 733-734; "The Negro in Harlem," p. 20.

49. ". . . The greatest need is the construction of model tenements. These should consist of one, two, three and four room apartments." "Modern Housing Needs," *The New York Age,* February 12, 1921, January 20, 1923, January 26, 1926, January 29, 1927; "The Negro in Harlem," p. 53; Eugene Kinckle Jones, "Negro Migration in New York State," *Opportunity,* IV (January 1926), 9.

50. Victor R. Daly, "The Housing Crisis in New York City," *The Crisis,* XXXI (December 1920), 61-62.

51. National Urban League, *Housing Conditions Among Negroes, New York City* (New York, 1915), *passim;* Ford, *et al., Slums and Housing,* p. 338.

52. "Very often it is found that there are two shifts." William Wilson to La Guardia, October 6, 1944, La Guardia Papers; *The New York Age,* March 12, 1921, February 26, 1927; "Along Rainbow Row," *The New York Times,* August 15, 1921, January 27, 1922; "Twenty-four Hundred Negro Families in Harlem," *passim;* Roscoe Conkling Bruce, "The Dunbar Apartment House: An Adventure in Community Building," *The Southern Workman,* LX (October 1931), 418.

53. *New York Herald Tribune,* February 12, 13, 1930.

54. "I promoted a weekly party, to get money to pay rent." "Boisterous rent parties, flooded with moonshine, are a quick and sure resource." "The Reminiscences of Benjamin McLaurin" (Oral History Research Office, Columbia University, 1960), p. 155; *The New York Age,* August 11, 1923, June 21, December 11, 1926; Clyde Vernon Kiser, *Sea Island to City* (New York, 1932), pp. 44-45.

55. Booker T. Washington, *Up from Slavery: An Autobiography* (New York 1959), pp. 122-123. Note the following statement of a recent study: "There are many cases in which migratory workers do not understand or properly use ordinary living facilities, such as toilets, showers, bedding, kitchen appliances, and garbage cans. The result has been unnecessary damage to property and needless expense for repairs." 87th Cong., 1st Sess., *Senate Report 1098* (1961), p. 8.

56. *The New York Age,* August 1, 1912, June 5, 1920, September 16, 1922, July 14, 1928; National Urban League, *Housing Conditions Among Negroes,* pp. 9-10; "The Negro in Harlem," p. 113; Eslanda Goode Robeson, *Paul Robeson: Negro* (London, 1930), p. 46.

57. Woofter, *et al., Negro Problems in Cities,* pp. 79, 84; "The Negro in Harlem," p. 53; Ernest W. Burgess, "Residential Segregation in American Cities," *The Annals,* CXL (November 1928), 105-115; Ford, *et al., Slums and Housing,* p. 749.

58. Owen R. Lovejoy, *The Negro Children of New York* (New York, 1932), p. 15.

59. *The New York Age,* October 28, 1922, January 17, 1925; *Housing Conditions Among Negroes, passim;* "Twenty-four Hundred Negro Families in Harlem," *passim.*

60. "I do not think I need to say that our problem of Harlem is one of the most serious we have to face." Langdon W. Post (Chairman of New York City Housing Authority) to La Guardia, April 30, 1936, La Guardia Papers. "The Negro families of the West Harlem section have undoubtedly the most serious housing problem in the City." Ford, *et al., Slums and Housing,* p. 326. *The New York Times,* September 16, 1920, October 17, 23, 1921, April 22, 1922, January 17, June 13, 1925; *The New York Age,* February 28, August 8, 1925, January 9, 1926; "Preliminary Report on the Subject of Housing (1935)," La Guardia Papers.

61. "High Cost of Dying," *The New York Age,* February 25, 1928.

62. *Health Conditions in North Harlem, passim; The Negro Children of New York,* p. 22; "Fighting the Ravages of the White Plague Among New York's Negro Population," *Opportunity,* I (January 1923), 23-24; Dr. Louis R. Wright, "Cancer as It Affects Negroes," *ibid.,* VI (June 1928), 169-170, 187; Louis I. Dublin, "The Effect of Health Education on Negro Mortality," *Proceedings of the National Conference on Social Work, 1924* (Chicago, 1924), 274-279. Hereafter cited as PNCSW.

63. ". . . Syphilitic infection is one of the most fruitful causes of stillbirths, miscarriages, and early death of infants." New York Association for Improving the Condition of the Poor, *Health Work for Mothers and Children in a Colored Community* (New York, 1924), p. 3; "The Negro's Health Progress During the Last Twenty-five Years," *Weekly Bulletin of the Department of Health,* XV (June 12, 1926), 93-96; *Fifteenth Census, 1930: Population* (Washington, D.C., 1933), II, 959; E. K. Jones, "The Negro's Struggle for Health," *PNCSW, 1923* (Chicago, 1923), 68-72.

64. Adapted from Godea J. Drolet and Louis Werner, "Vital Statistics in the Development of Neighborhood Health Centers in New York City," *Journal of Preventive Medicine,* VI (January 1932), 69.

65. In 1920, 30.3 per cent of white women in the city worked, and 57.9 per cent of colored women were employed. *Fourteenth Census, 1920: Population* (Washington, D.C., 1923), IV, 367. Robert Morse Woodbury, *Causal Factors in Infant Mortality* (Washington, D.C., 1925); L. T. Wright, "Factors Controlling Negro Health," *The Crisis,* XLII (September 1935), 264-265, 280, 284; Mildred Jane Watson, "Infant Mortality in New York City, White and Colored, 1929-1936" (M.A. thesis, Columbia University, 1938); Charles Herbert Garvin, "White Plague and Black Folk," *Opportunity,* VIII (August 1930), 232-235.

66. For "voodoo" and "devil worship" among

West Indians see Reid, *The Negro Immigrant,* pp. 48-49, 136-138.

67. ". . . Many [are] bringing with them their simple faith in roots, herbs, home remedies, [and are] imposed upon by unscrupulous venders of worthless . . . remedies," Dr. Peter Marshall Murray, "Harlem's Health," *Hospital Social Service,* XXII (October 1930), 309-313; C. V. Roman, "The Negro's Psychology and His Health," *PNCSW, 1924* (Chicago, 1924), 270-274; *Opportunity,* IV (July 1926), 206-207; *The Crisis,* XLII (August 1935), 243; *The New York Age,* September 23, 1922, February 17, July 21, August 11, 25, 1923, January 6, April 5, 1924, February 21, March 14, 1925, January 18, July 23, 1927.

68. Note the striking similarities between the medical and healing superstitions of urban Negroes in the twentieth century and those of slaves in the early nineteenth century. The following is a description of slave superstition by an ex-slave: "There is much superstition among the slaves. Many of them believe in what they call 'conjuration,' tricking, and witchcraft; and some of them pretend to understand the art, and say that by it they can prevent their masters from exercising their will over their slaves. Such are often applied to by others, to give them power to prevent their masters from flogging them. The remedy is most generally some kind of bitter root; they are directed to chew it and spit toward their masters. . . . At other times they prepare certain kinds of powders, to sprinkle their masters' dwellings." *Narrative of the Life and Adventures of Henry Bibb, An American Slave, Written by Himself* (New York, 1849), pp. 25-31.

69. Beverly Smith, "Harlem—Negro City," *New York Herald Tribune,* February 11, 1930; Ira De Augustine Reid, "Let Us Prey!" *Opportunity* IV (September 1926), 274-278; Reverend James H. Robinson, *Road Without Turning: An Autobiography* (New York, 1950), 231.

70. *The New York Age,* February 19, 1927; *The New York Times,* September 24, 1919.

71. Zora Neale Hurston, *Dust Track on a Road* (Philadelphia, 1942), pp. 279-280.

72. *The New York Age,* January 15, 1927, February 9, 1929, August 23, 1930, August 8, September 19, 1931, July 23, 1932, August 26, 1933, September 1, 1934.

73. "A Wide Open Harlem," *ibid.,* September 2, 1922.

74. Committee of Fourteen, *Annual Reports,* 1914-1930; *The Crisis,* XXXVI (November

1929), 417-418; *The Messenger,* VI (January 1924), 14.

75. Langston Hughes, "Young Prostitute," *The Crisis,* XXVI (August 1923), 162.

76. "Gambling is popular in Harlem, but the big shots of the racket are white." Fiorello La Guardia, "Harlem: Homelike and Hopeful" (unpublished manuscript, La Guardia Papers), p. 9; "A Summary of Vice Conditions in Harlem," Committee of Fourteen, *Annual Report for 1928* (New York, 1929), 31-34; *The New York Times,* February 13, 1922; *The New York Age,* February 28, 1925, May 18, 1929. Although whites seemed to control most of Harlem vice, Virgin Islander Casper Holstein—well-known as a philanthropist and café owner—was reputed to be a head of the numbers racket.

77. "Harlem—The Bettor," *The New York Age,* March 7, 1925, November 6, 20, 1926, June 4, 1927, June 23, 1928; *The New York Times,* June 12, 1922, March 11, 1927; "New York: Utopia Deferred," *The Messenger,* VII (October, November 1925), 344-349, 370.

78. *The New York Age,* September 16, 1922, April 21, 1923; *New York Herald Tribune,* February 13, 1930; *The Messenger,* VI (August 1924) 247, 262.

79. Lovejoy, *The Negro Children of New York,* p. 37; *New York Herald Tribune,* February 12, 1930; Joint Committee on Negro Child Study in New York City, *A Study of Delinquent and Neglected Negro Children Before the New York City Children's Court* (New York, 1927).

80. Jacob Theobald, "Some Facts About P.S. 89, Manhattan," *The New York Age,* January 17, 1920; "Report of Subcommittee on Education," La Guardia Papers; "The Problem of Education and Recreation," *ibid.;* "The Negro in Harlem," p. 73; Lovejoy, *The Negro Children of New York,* p. 22; *The New York Age,* March 12, 1921.

81. "Results of the Crime and Delinquency Study," La Guardia Papers; *The New York Age,* January 6, February 17, June 23, 1923, June 12, 1926, December 3, 1927, July 28, 1928, January 4, 1930. A white Harlem policeman, at a later date, wrote the following: "Every one of [us] is made to feel like a soldier in an army of occupation. He is engulfed by an atmosphere of antagonism." *The Crisis,* LII (January 1945), 16-17.

82. Lovejoy, *The Negro Children of New York,* p. 15; "The Negro in Harlem," p. 110; *The New York Age,* February 9, 1929; "The Reminiscences of George S. Schuyler" (Oral History Research Office, Columbia University, 1960), p. 232.

Urbanization, Migration, and Social Mobility in Late Nineteenth-Century America

STEPHAN THERNSTROM

The United States, it has been said, was born in the country and has moved to the city. It was during the half-century between the Civil War and World War I that the move was made. In 1860, less than a quarter of the American population lived in a city or town; by 1890, the figure had reached a third; by 1910, nearly half. By more sophisticated measures than the mere count of heads, the center of gravity of the society had obviously tilted cityward well before the last date.

If to speak of "the rise of the city" in those years is a text-book cliché, the impact of this great social transformation upon the common people of America has never been sufficiently explored. This essay is intended as a small contribution toward that task. It sketches the process by which ordinary men and women were drawn to the burgeoning cities of post-Civil War America, assesses what little we know about how they were integrated into the urban class structure, and suggests how these matters affected the viability of the political system.

I

The urbanization of late nineteenth-century America took place at a dizzying pace. Chicago, for instance, doubled its population every decade but one between 1850 and 1890, growing from 30,000 to over a million in little more than a generation. And it was not merely the conspicuous metropolitan giants but the Akrons, the Duluths, the Tacomas that were bursting at the seams; no less than 101 American communities grew by 100 percent or more in the 1880s.[1]

Why did Americans flock into these all too often unlovely places? There were some who were not pulled to the city but rather pushed out of their previous habitats and dropped there, more or less by accident. But the overriding fact is that the cities could draw on an enormous reservoir of people who were dissatisfied with their present lot and eager to seize the new opportunities offered by the metropolis.

Who were these people? It is conventional to distinguish two broad types of migrants to the American city: the immigrant from another culture, and the farm lad who moved from a rural to an urban setting within the culture. It is also conventional in historical accounts to overlook the latter type and to focus on the more exotic of the migrants, those who had to undergo the arduous process of becoming Americanized.

This is regrettable. To be sure, immigration from abroad was extremely important in the building of America's cities down to World War I. But the

From Barton J. Bernstein (ed.), *Towards a New Past: Dissenting Essays in American History* (New York: Pantheon, 1968), pp. 158-75. Copyright © 1967, 1968 by Random House, Inc. Reprinted by permission of Pantheon Books, a division of Random House, Inc. Stephan Thernstrom is Professor of History at the University of California, Los Angeles.

most important source of population for the burgeoning cities was not the fields of Ireland and Austria, but those of Vermont and Iowa. The prime cause of population growth in nineteenth-century America, and the main source of urban growth, was simply the high fertility of natives living outside the city.

We tend to neglect internal migration from country to city, partly because the immigrants from abroad seem exotic and thus conspicuous, partly because of the unfortunate legacy left by Frederick Jackson Turner's frontier theory, one element of which was the notion that the open frontier served as a safety valve for urban discontent. When there were hard times in the city, according to Turner, the American worker didn't join a union or vote Socialist; he moved West and grabbed some of that free land. This theory has been subjected to the rather devastating criticism that by 1860 it took something like $1,000 capital to purchase sufficient transportation, seed equipment, livestock, and food (to live on until the first crop) to make a go of it; that it took even more than $1,000 later in the century, and that it was precisely the unemployed workmen who were least likely to have that kind of money at their command. It is estimated that for every industrial worker who became a farmer, twenty farm boys became urban dwellers.[2] There was an urban safety valve for rural discontent, and an extremely important one. The dominant form of population movement was precisely the opposite of that described by Turner.

Since scholarly attention has been focused upon immigrants from abroad, upon Oscar Handlin's "Uprooted," it will be useful to review what is known about their movement to the American city and then to ask how much the same

generalizations might hold for native Americans uprooted from the countryside and plunged into the city.

Immigration is as old as America, but a seismic shift in the character of European immigration to these shores occurred in the nineteenth century, as a consequence of the commercial transformation of traditional European agriculture and the consequent displacement of millions of peasants.[3] Compared to earlier newcomers, these were people who were closer to the land and more tradition-bound, and they generally had fewer resources to bring with them than their predecessors. One shouldn't overwork this; a substantial fraction of the German and Scandinavian immigrants had enough capital to get to the West to pick up land. But some of the Germans and Scandinavians, and most men of other nationalities, had just enough cash to make it to the New World and were stuck for a time at least where they landed—New York, Boston, or wherever. They swelled the population appreciably and the relief rolls dramatically, particularly in the pre-Civil War years, when they entered cities which were basically commercial and had little use for men whose only skill in many cases was that they knew how to dig. Eventually, however, the stimulus of this vast pool of cheap labor and the demands of the growing city itself opened up a good many unskilled jobs—in the construction of roads, houses, and commercial buildings, and in the manufacturing that began to spring up in the cities.

That they were driven off the land in the Old World, that they arrived without resources, immobilized by their poverty, and that they often suffered a great deal before they secured stable employment is true enough. But these harsh facts may lead us to overlook other aspects which were extremely significant.

One is that immigration was a *selective* process. However powerful the pressures to leave, in no case did anyone in a community pull up stakes. This observation may be uncomfortably reminiscent of the popular opinion on this point: that it was the best of the Old World stock that came to the New—the most intelligent, enterprising, courageous. But this should not lead us to neglect the point altogether. The traits that led some men to leave and allowed them to survive the harrowing journey to the port, the trip itself, and the perils of the New World, could be described in somewhat different terms: substitute cunning for intelligence, for example, or ruthlessness for courage. Still, whatever the emphasis, the fact remains: as weighed in the scales of the marketplace, those who came—however driven by cruel circumstance—were better adapted to American life than those who remained in the village or died on the way.

The other main point about the immigrants, and especially those who suffered the most extreme hardships—the Irish in the 1840s and 1850s, the French Canadians in the 1870s, the Italians and various East Europeans after 1880 —is that they appraised their new situations with standards developed in peasant society. Lowell was terrible, with its cramped stinking tenements, and factory workers labored from dawn till dark for what seems a mere pittance. Children were forced to work at a brutally early age; the factories and dwellings were deathtraps. But Lowell was a damn sight better than County Cork, and men who knew from bitter experience what County Cork was like could

not view their life in Lowell with quite the same simple revulsion as the middle-class reformers who judged Lowell by altogether different standards. It is not so much the objectively horrible character of a situation that goads men to action as it is a nagging discrepancy between what *is* and what is *expected*. And what one expects is determined by one's reference group—which can be a class, an ethnic or religious subculture, or some other entity which defines people's horizon of expectation.[4] Immigration provided an ever renewed stream of men who entered the American economy to fill its least attractive and least well rewarded positions, men who happen to have brought with them very low horizons of expectation fixed in peasant Europe.

That those Americans with greatest reason to feel outrageously exploited judged their situation against the dismally low standards of the decaying European village is an important clue to the stunted growth of the labor movement and the failure of American Socialism. Working in the same direction was what might be called the Tower of Babel factor. A firm sense of class solidarity was extremely difficult to develop in communities where people literally didn't speak each other's language. Even in cases where groups of immigrant workers had unusually high expectations and previous familiarity with advanced forms of collective action—such as the English artisans who led the Massachusetts textile strikes in the 1870s—they found it hard to keep the other troops in line; a clever Italian-speaking or Polish-speaking foreman could easily exploit national differences for his own ends, and if necessary there were always the most recent immigrants of all (and the

Negroes) to serve as scabs to replace the dissenters en masse.

A somewhat similar analysis applies to the migrants who left the Kansas farms for Chicago. They were linguistically and culturally set apart from many of their fellow workers; they too had low horizons of expectation fixed in the countryside and brought to the city. The latter point is often missed because of the peculiar American reverence for an idealized agrarian way of life. As we have become a nation of city dwellers, we have come more and more to believe that it is virtuous and beautiful to slave for fourteen hours a day with manure on your boots. Recently that sturdy small farmer from Johnson City, Texas, remarked that "it does not make sense on this great continent which God has blessed to have more than 70 percent of our people crammed into one percent of the land." A national "keep them down on the farm" campaign is therefore in the offing.[5] But it is damnably hard to keep them down on the farm after they've seen New York (or even Indianapolis), and it was just as hard a century ago, for the very good reason that the work is brutal, the profits are often miserably low, and the isolation is psychologically murderous. Virtuous this life may be, especially to people who don't have to live it, but enjoyable it is not—not, at least, to a very substantial fraction of our ever shrinking farm population.

This applies particularly to young men and women growing up on a farm. Their parents had a certain stake in staying where they were, even if it was a rut. And the eldest son, who would inherit the place eventually, was sometimes tempted by that. But the others left in droves, to tend machines, to dig and haul and hammer—or in the case of the girls, to sell underwear in Marshall Field's, to mind someone else's kitchen, or in some instances to follow in the footsteps of Sister Carrie.

There were some large differences between native-born migrants to the cities and immigrants from another land, to be sure. But the familiar argument that native workmen "stood on the shoulders" of the immigrant and was subjected to less severe exploitation is somewhat misleading. The advantages enjoyed by many American-born laborers stemmed more from their urban experience than their birth, and they did not generally accrue to freshly arrived native migrants to the city. The latter were little better off than their immigrant counterparts, but then they too were spiritually prepared to endure a great deal of privation and discomfort because even the bottom of the urban heap was a step up from the farms they had left behind. The two groups were one in this respect, and perceptive employers recognized the fact. In 1875, the Superintendent of one of Andrew Carnegie's steel mills summed up his experience this way: "We must steer clear as far as we can of Englishmen, who are great sticklers for high wages, small production and strikes. My experience has shown that Germans and Irish, Swedes and what I denominate 'Buckwheats'— young American country boys, judiciously mixed, make the most honest and tractable force you can find."[6]

II

The move to the city, therefore, was an advance of a kind for the typical migrant. Were there further opportunities for advancement there, or did he then find himself crushed by circumstance and reduced to the ranks of the permanent proletariat? Did his children, whose expectations were presumably higher, discover correspondingly greater opportunities open to them? Remarkably little serious research has been devoted to these issues. Historians who see American history as a success story have been content to assume, without benefit of data, that the American dream of mobility was true, apparently on the principle that popular ideology is a sure guide to social reality. Dissenting scholars have been more inclined to the view that class barriers were relatively impassable, an assumption based upon generalized skepticism about American mythology rather than upon careful empirical study. Some recent work, however, provides the basis for a tentative reappraisal of the problem.

We know most about mobility into the most rarefied reaches of the social order regarding such elite groups as millionaires, railroad presidents, directors of large corporations, or persons listed in the *Dictionary of American Biography*. What is most impressive about the literature on the American elite is that, in spite of many variations in the way in which the elite is defined, the results of these studies are much the same. It is clear that growing up in rags is not in the least conductive to the attainment of later riches, and that it was no more so a century ago than it is today.[7] There have been spectacular instances of mobility from low down on the social scale to the very top—Andrew Carnegie, for instance. But colorful examples cannot sustain broad generalizations about social phenomena, however often they are impressed into service toward that end. Systematic investigation reveals that even in the days of Andrew Carnegie, there was little room at the top, except for those who started very close to it.

Furthermore, this seems to have been the case throughout most of American history, despite many dramatic alterations in the character of the economy. It seems perfectly plausible to assume, as many historians have on the basis of impressionistic evidence, that the precipitous growth of heavy industry in the latter half of the nineteenth century opened the doors to men with very different talents from the educated merchants who constituted the elite of the preindustrial age, that unlettered, horny-handed types like Thomas Alva Edison and Henry Ford, crude inventors and tinkerers, then came into their own; that the connection between parental wealth and status and the son's career was loosened, so that members of the business elite typically had lower social origins and less education, and were often of immigrant stock. Plausible, yes, but true, no. It helped to go to Harvard in Thomas Jefferson's America, and it seems to have helped just about as much in William McKinley's America. There were the Edisons and Fords, who rose spectacularly from low origins, but there were always a few such. Cases like these were about as exceptional in the late nineteenth century as they were earlier. The image of the great inventor springing from common soil, unspoiled by book-larnin', is a red herring. It is doubtful, to say the least, that the less you know, the more likely you are to build a better mousetrap. And in any event it was not the great inventor who raked in the money, in most cases— Henry Ford never invented anything— but rather the organizer and manipulator, whose talents seem to have been highly valued through all periods of American history.

These conclusions are interesting, but an important caution is in order. It by no means follows that if there was very little room at the top, there was little room anywhere else. It is absurd to judge the openness or lack of openness of an entire social system solely by the extent of recruitment from below into the highest positions of all. One can imagine a society in which all members of the tiny elite are democratically recruited from below, and yet where the social structure as a whole is extremely rigid with that small exception. Conversely, one can imagine a society with a hereditary ruling group at the very top, a group completely closed to aspiring men of talent but lowly birth, and yet with an enormous amount of movement back and forth below that pinnacle. Late nineteenth-century America could have approximated this latter model, with lineage, parental wealth, and education as decisive assets in the race for the very peak, as the business elite studies suggest, and yet with great fluidity at the lower and middle levels of the class structure.

Was this in fact the case? The evidence available today is regrettably scanty, but here are the broad outlines of an answer, insofar as we can generalize from a handful of studies.[8] At the lower and middle ranges of the class structure there was impressive mobility, though often of an unexpected and rather ambiguous kind. I will distinguish three types of mobility: geographical, occupational, and property, and say a little about the extent and significance of each.

First is geographical mobility, physical movement from place to place, which is tied up in an interesting way with movement through the social scale. Americans have long been thought a restless, footloose people, and it has been assumed that the man on the move has been the man on the make; he knows that this little town doesn't provide a grand enough stage for him to display his talents, and so he goes off to the big city to win fame and fortune, or to the open frontier to do likewise. When you examine actual behavior instead of popular beliefs, however, you discover that things are more complicated than that.

It proves to be true that Americans are indeed a footloose people. In my work on Newburyport, a small industrial city, I attempted to find out what fraction of the families present in the community in the initial year of my study—1850—were still living there in the closing year, 1880, one short generation. Less than a fifth of them, it turned out—and this not in a community on the moving frontier, like Merle Curti's Trempealeau County, where you would expect a very high turnover. There the true pioneer types, who liked to clear the land, became nervous when there was another family within a half day's ride of them and sold out to the second wave of settlers (often immigrants who knew better than to try to tame the wilderness without previous experience at it). But to find roughly the same volatility in a city forty miles north of Boston suggests that the whole society was in motion.

The statistics bear out the legend that Americans are a restless people. What of the assertion that movement and success go hand in hand, that physical mobility and upward social mobility are positively correlated? Here the legend seems more questionable. It seems likely that some who pulled up stakes and went elsewhere for a new start did improve their positions; they found better land, or discovered that they possessed talents which were much more highly valued in the big city than in the place they came from. What ever would have happened to Theodore Dreiser in small-town Indiana had there been no Chicago for him to flee to?

But the point to underline, for it is less commonly understood, is that much of this remarkable population turnover was of quite a different kind. As you trace the flow of immigrants into and then out of the cities, you begin to see that a great many of those who departed did so in circumstances which make it exceedingly hard to believe that they were moving on to bigger and better things elsewhere. There is no way to be certain about this, no feasible method of tracing individuals once they disappear from the universe of the community under consideration. These questions can be explored for contemporary America by administering questionnaires to people and collecting life histories which display migration patterns, but dead men tell no tales and fill out no questionnaires, so that part of the past is irrevocably lost. But some plausible inferences can be drawn about the nature of this turnover from the fact that so many ordinary working people on the move owned no property, had no savings accounts, had acquired no special skills, and were most likely to leave when they were unemployed. They were, in short, people who had made the least successful economic adjustment to the community and who were no longer able to hang on there. At the lower reaches of the social order, getting out of town did not ordinarily mean a step up the ladder somewhere else; there is no reason to assume that in their new destinations migrant laborers found anything but more of the

same. When middle-class families, who already had a niche in the world, moved on, it was often in response to greater opportunities elsewhere; for ordinary working people physical movement meant something very different.

That is a less rosy picture than the one usually painted, but I think it is more accurate. And we should notice one very important implication of this argument: namely, that the people who were least successful and who had the greatest grievances are precisely those who never stayed put very long in any one place. Students of labor economics and trade union history have long been aware of the fact that there are certain occupations which are inordinately difficult to organize simply because they have incessant job turnover. When only 5 percent or 1 percent of the men working at a particular job in a given city at the start of the year are still employed twelve months later, as is the case with some occupations in the economic underworld today (short-order cooks or menial hospital workers, for instance), how do you build a stable organization and conduct a successful strike?

An analogous consideration applies not merely to certain selected occupations but to a large fraction of the late nineteenth-century urban working class as a whole. The Marxist model of the conditions which promote proletarian consciousness presumes not only permanency of membership in this class—the absence of upward mobility—but also, I suggest, some continuity of class membership *in one setting* so that workers come to know each other and to develop bonds of solidarity and common opposition to the ruling group above them. This would seem to entail a stable labor force in a single factory; at a minimum it assumes considerable stability in a community. One reason that a permanent proletariat along the lines envisaged by Marx did not develop in the course of American industrialization is perhaps that few Americans have *stayed* in one place, one workplace, or even one city long enough to discover a sense of common identity and common grievance. This may be a vital clue to the divergent political development of America and Western Europe in the industrial age, to the striking weakness of socialism here, as compared to Europe— though we can't be sure because we don't definitely know that the European working-class population was less volatile. I suspect that it was, to some degree, and that America was distinctive in this respect, but this is a question of glaring importance which no one has yet taken the trouble to investigate.

When I first stumbled upon this phenomenon in sifting through manuscript census schedules for nineteenth-century Newburyport, I was very doubtful that the findings could be generalized to apply to the big cities of the period. It seemed reasonable to assume that the laborers who drifted out of Newburyport so quickly after their arrival must have settled down somewhere else, and to think that a great metropolis would have offered a more inviting haven than a small city, where anonymity was impossible and where middle-class institutions of social control intruded into one's daily life with some frequency, as compared to a classic big-city lower-class ghetto, where the down-and-out could perhaps huddle together for protective warmth and be left to their own devices —for instance, those Irish wards of New York where the police made no attempt to enforce law and order until late in the century. Here if anywhere one should be able to find a continuous

lower-class population, a permanent proletariat, and I began my Boston research with great curiosity about this point.

If Boston is any example, in no American city was there a sizable lower class with great continuity of membership. You can identify some more or less continuously lower-class areas, but the crucial point is that *the same people do not stay in them.* If you take a sample of unskilled and semi-skilled laborers in Boston in 1880 and look for them in 1890, you are not much more likely to find them still in the city than was the case in Newburyport.[9]

The bottom layer of the social order in the nineteenth-century American city was thus a group of families who appear to have been permanent transients, buffeted about from place to place, never quite able to sink roots. We know very little about these people, and it is difficult to know how we can learn much about them. You get only occasional glimpses into the part of this iceberg that appears above the surface, in the person of the tramp, who first is perceived as a problem for America in the 1870s and reappears in hard times after that—in the 1890s and in the great depression most notably. But what has been said here at least suggests the significance of the phenomenon.

So much for geographical mobility. What can be said about the people who come to the city and remain there under our microscope so that we can discern what happened to them? I have already anticipated my general line of argument here in my discussion of migration out of the city—which amounted to the claim that the city was a kind of Darwinian jungle in which the fittest survived and the others drifted on to try another place. Those who did stay in the city and make their way there did, in general, succeed in advancing themselves economically and socially. There was very impressive mobility, though not always of the kind we might expect.

In approaching this matter, we must make a distinction which is obscured by applying labels like "open" or "fluid" to entire whole social structures. There are, after all, two sets of escalators in any community; one set goes down. To describe a society as enormously fluid implies that there are lots of people moving down while lots of others are moving up to take their place. This would obviously be a socially explosive situation, for all those men descending against their will would arrive at the bottom, not with low horizons of expectation set in some peasant village, but with expectations established when they were at one of the comfortable top floors of the structure.

Downward mobility is by no means an unknown phenomenon in American history. There have been socially displaced groups, especially if you take into account rather subtle shifts in the relative status of such groups as professionals.[10] But the chief generalization to make is that Americans who started their working life in a middle-class job strongly tended to end up in the middle class; sons reared in middle-class families also attained middle-class occupations in the great majority of cases. Relatively few men born into the middle class fell from there; a good many born into the working class either escaped from it altogether or advanced themselves significantly within the class. There is a well-established tradition of writing about the skilled workman, associated with such names as the Hammonds, the Lynds, Lloyd Warner, and Norman Ware, which holds the con-

trary, to be sure.[11] This tradition still has its defenders, who argue that with industrialization "class lines assumed a new and forbidding rigidity" and that "machines made obsolete many of the skilled trades of the antebellum years, drawing the once self-respecting handicraftsmen into the drudgery and monotony of factory life, where they were called upon to perform only one step in the minutely divided and automatic processes of mass production."[12] Rapid technological change doubtless did displace some skilled artisans, doubtless produced some downward mobility into semiskilled positions. But defenders of this view have built their case upon little more than scattered complaints by labor leaders, and have not conducted systematic research to verify these complaints.

Careful statistical analysis provides a very different perspective on the matter. Two points stand out. One is that as certain traditional skilled callings became obsolete, there was an enormous expansion of *other* skilled trades, and, since many of the craftsmen under pressure from technological change had rather generalized skills, they moved rapidly into these new positions and thus retained their place in the labor aristocracy.[13] Second, it is quite mistaken to assume that the sons of the threatened artisan were commonly driven down into the ranks of the factory operatives; they typically found a place either in the expanding skilled trades or in the even more rapidly expanding white-collar occupations.[14]

As for workers on the lower rungs of the occupational ladder, the unskilled and semiskilled, they had rarely drifted down from a higher beginning point. Characteristically, they were newcomers to the urban world. A substantial minority of them appear to have been able to advance themselves a notch or two occupationally, especially among the second generation; a good many of their sons became clerks, salesmen, and other petty white-collar functionaries. And the the first generation, which had less success occupationally, was commonly experiencing mobility of another kind—property mobility. Despite a pathetically low (but generally rising) wage level, despite heavy unemployment rates, many were able to accumulate significant property holdings and to establish themselves as members of the stable working class, as opposed to the drifting lower class.[15]

It may seem paradoxical to suggest that so many Americans were rising in the world and so few falling; where did the room at the top come from? The paradox is readily resolved. For one thing, our attention has been fastened upon individuals who remained physically situated in one place in which their careers could be traced; an indeterminate but substantial fraction of the population was floating and presumably unsuccessful. By no means everyone at the bottom was upwardly mobile; the point is rather that those who were not were largely invisible. Furthermore, the occupational structure itself was changing in a manner that created disproportionately more positions in the middle and upper ranges, despite the common nineteenth-century belief that industrialization was homogenizing the work force and reducing all manual employees to identical robots. The homogenizing and degrading tendencies that caught the eye of Marx and others were more than offset, it appears, by developments which made for both a more differentiated and a more top-heavy occupational structure. Third, there were

important sources of social mobility that could be attained without changing one's occupation, most notably the property mobility that was stimulated by the increases in real wages that occurred in this period. Finally, there was the so-called "demographic vacuum" created by the differential fertility of the social classes, best illustrated in the gloomy late nineteenth-century estimate that in two hundred years 1,000 Harvard graduates would have only 50 living descendants while 1,000 Italians would have 100,000. The calculation is dubious, but the example nicely clarifies the point that high-status groups failed to reproduce themselves, thus opening up vacancies which had necessarily to be filled by new men from below.

For all the brutality and rapacity which marked the American scene in the years in which the new urban industrial order came into being, what stands out most is the relative absence of collective working-class protest aimed at reshaping capitalist society. The foregoing, while hardly a full explanation, should help to make this more comprehensible. The American working class was drawn into the new society by a process that encouraged accommodation and rendered disciplined protest difficult. Within the urban industrial orbit, most of its members found modest but significant opportunities to feel that they and their children were edging their way upwards. Those who did not find such opportunities were tossed helplessly about from city to city, from state to state, alienated but invisible and impotent.

NOTES

1. C. N. Glaab and A. T. Brown, *A History of Urban America* (New York, 1967), pp. 107-11.

2. Fred Shannon, "A Post Mortem on the Labor-Safety-Valve Theory," *Agricultural History*, XIX (1954), 31-37.

3. For general accounts, see Marcus L. Hansen, *The Atlantic Migration, 1607-1860* (paperback ed.; New York, 1961); Oscar Handlin, *The Uprooted* (Boston, 1951).

4. For discussion of the sociological concepts of reference groups and the theory of relative deprivation, see Robert K. Merton, *Social Theory and Social Structure*, rev. ed. (Glencoe, Ill., 1957) and the literature cited there. The problem of assessing the level of expectations of any particular migratory group in the past is extremely complicated, and it is obvious that there have been important differences between and within groups. But the generalizations offered here seem to me the best starting point for thinking about this issue.

5. *Boston Globe*, February 5, 1967.

6. Quoted in Oscar Handlin, *Immigration as a Factor in American History* (Englewood Cliffs, N.J., 1959), pp. 66-67.

7. For a convenient review of this literature, see Seymour M. Lipset and Reinhard Bendix, *Social Mobility in Industrial Society* (Berkeley, Cal., 1959), Ch. 4.

8. The main sources for the generalizations which follow, unless otherwise indicated, are: Stephan Thernstrom, *Poverty and Progress: Social Mobility in a Nineteenth Century City* (Cambridge, Mass., 1964); Merle E. Curti, *The Making of an American Frontier Community* (Stanford, Cal., 1959); Donald B. Cole, *Immigrant City: Lawrence, Massachusetts, 1845-1921* (Chapel Hill, N.C., 1963) —for my reservations about this work, however, see my review in the *Journal of Economic History*, XXIV (1964), 259-61; Herbert G. Gutman, "Social Status and Social Mobility in 19th Century America: Paterson, N.J., A Case Study," unpublished paper for the 1964 meetings of the American Historical Association; Howard Gitelman, "The Labor Force at Waltham Watch During the Civil War Era," *Journal of Economic History*, XXV (1965), 214-43; David Brody, *Steelworkers in America: The Nonunion Era* (Cambridge, Mass., 1960); Pauline Gordon, "The Chance to Rise Within Industry" (unpublished M.A. thesis, Columbia University); Robert Wheeler, "The Fifth-Ward Irish: Mobility at Mid-Century" (unpublished seminar paper, Brown University, 1967); and the author's research in progress on social mobility in Boston over the past century, in which the career patterns of some 8,000 ordinary residents of the community are traced.

9. Recent work suggesting that even the most recent U.S. Census seriously undernumerated the Negro male population may make the critical reader wonder about the accuracy of the census and city directory canvases upon which I base my analysis. Some elaborate checking has persuaded me that these nineteenth-century sources erred primarily in their coverage—their lack of coverage, rather—of the floating working-class population. For a variety of reasons it seems clear that families which had been in the community long enough to be included in one of these canvases—and hence to be included in a sample drawn from them—were rarely left out of later canvases if they indeed still resident in the same city. A perfect census of every soul in the community on a given day would therefore yield an even higher, not a lower, estimate of population turnover for men at the bottom, which strengthens rather than weakens the argument advanced here.

10. The assumption that discontent stemming from social displacement has been the motive force behind American reform movements has exerted great influence upon American historical writing in recent years. See for instance David Donald, "Toward a Reconsideration of Abolitionists," *Lincoln Recosidered* (New York, 1956), pp. 19-36; Richard Hofstadter, *The Age of Reform: From Bryan to F.D.R.* (New York, 1955). Donald's essay is easily demolished by anyone with the slightest acquaintance with sociological method. Hofstadter's work, while open to a very serious objection, is at least sufficiently suggestive to indicate the potential utility of the idea.

11. J. L. and Barbara Hammond, *The Town Labourer (1760-1832)* (London, 1917); Robert S. and Helen M. Lynd, *Middletown* (New York, 1929), and *Middletown in Transition* (New York, 1937); W. Lloyd Warner and J. O. Low, *The Social System of the Modern Factory* (New Haven, Conn., 1947); Norman J. Ware, *The Industrial Worker, 1840-1860* (Boston, 1924).

12. Leon Litwak, ed., *The American Labor Movement* (Englewood Cliffs, N.J., 1962), p. 3.

13. This is evident from aggregated census data and from my Boston investigation, but we badly need an American counterpart to Eric Hobsbawm's splendid essay on "The Labour Aristocracy in Nineteenth Century Britain," in *Labouring Men: Studies in the History of Labour* (London, 1964), pp. 272-315.

14. So, at least, the evidence from Boston and Indianapolis indicates; for the latter, see Natlic Rogoff, *Recent Trends in Occupational Mobility* (Glencoe, Ill., 1953).

15. The clearest demonstration of this is in Thernstrom, *Poverty and Progress*, Ch. 5. It might be thought, however, that the remarkable property mobility disclosed there depended upon the existence of an abundant stock of cheap single-family housing available for purchase. It could be that where real estate was less readily obtainable, laborers would squander the funds that were accumulated with such sacrifice in places where home ownership was an immediate possibility. It appears from Wheeler's unpublished study of nineteenth-century Providence, however, that the working-class passion for property did not require an immediate, concrete source of satisfaction like a home and a plot of land. The Irish workmen of Providence were just as successful at accumulating property holdings as their Newburyport counterparts; the difference was only that they held personal rather than real property.

VII THE CITY IN THE AMERICAN MIND

The fundamental crisis of the American city, according to one knowledgeable student of urban affairs, is an intellectual crisis involving inherited attitudes and images of the city that are either distorted or no longer applicable to the reality of an urban environment. The heart of every urban problem, be it housing, poverty, transportation, or even air pollution, evokes a judgment, an attitude toward the city itself; indeed,

the action crisis of the metropolis cannot be disengaged from the intellectual crisis, for the very definition of a metropolitan problem is dependent upon one's picture of the city and the kind of life it should contain, as the choice of action to improve or revolutionize is dependent upon one's estimate of the city as an existing entity.[1]

It has been a crisis of long standing, for the intellectual history of the American city has been a battleground of conflicting attitudes of Americans, who have argued about the value of the city and the kind of life it should contain. And for good reason. As a new form of human settlement, the city broke older village and agrarian traditions and forced new adjustments, new problems, new fears, and new hopes. As a dynamic source of social change, it was seen by some as the "Hope of Democracy," by others, many of whom measured it through the lens of agrarian or small-town America, as a corruption of democracy. Thus emerged two dominant attitudes toward the city, anti-urbanism and pro-urbanism—the city as a House of Ill-Fame and as the House of God.

Morton and Lucia White have engagingly capsuled the raft of anti-urban attitudes as:

too big, too noisy, too dusky, too dirty, too smelly, too commercial, too crowded, too full of immigrants, too full of Jews, too full of Irishmen, Italians, Poles, too artificial, destructive of conversation, destructive of communication, too greedy, too capitalis-

1. Scott Greer, *The Emerging City: Myth and Reality* (New York: The Free Press, 1964), p. 21.

411

tic, too full of automobiles, too full of smog, too full of dust, too heartless, too intellectual, too scientific, insufficiently poetic, too lacking in manners, too mechanical, destructive of family, tribal and patriotic feeling.[2]

On the other side of the attitudinal fence, listen to Charles Abrams's ringing eulogy of the city:

From earliest history, the city has been linked with man's freedoms—a refuge in the days of Cain and Joshua, the hub of a vigorous political life in Greece, the impetus to law in Rome. When man's mind roamed free in Utopian dreams, it was the city that was so often closest to his conception of heaven—the "Celestial City," the "Heavenly City," the "New Jerusalem," the "Holy City," and the "City of God." Moreover, it was the city of trade, commerce, and property that helped undermine serfdom and that ushered in other freedoms in the process. . . . For despite its changes and challenges, the city still contains the raw ingredients of freedom. . . . It is still the marketplace for goods and ideas, the locus of a contractual society, the mirror for emulation, the meeting place for diversities, the center of culture.[3]

Perhaps the best examples of the ancient confrontation of anti-urbanism and pro-urbanism are the remark made by the poet William Cowper, "God made the country, man made the town," and the spirited rejoiner of Oliver Wendell Holmes, "God made the cavern and man made the house!"

But the intellectual history of the city is not adequately depicted by the simple symmetry of pro and con. It is muddled and complex because of another dominant attitude toward the city, one of ambivalence, a mixture of attitudes reflecting a wide variety of personal, class, ethnic, and even regional differences. A Southerner, for example, might praise his own city but find New York a Sodom-on-the-Hudson.

This chapter seeks to sketch the shifting currents of thought toward the city, for what men *thought* was just as important as what men *did*. It is a topic vital to understanding not only the course of American urban history but also how that history reflects, at least in part, the American's response to his society as a whole, for the city in many ways concentrates and sharply delineates national characteristics.

Anti-urbanism in all its blatant and subtle forms is the theme of the first essay of this chapter. It is concerned with the views of the most articulate and literate group of society, the philosophers, poets, and writers.

Morton and Lucia White argue that, with few exceptions, the intellectual has been the sharpest critic of the American city.[4] Mustering an imposing intellectual varsity of some of the greatest figures in American thought, from

2. *The Intellectual versus the City* (Cambridge: Harvard and The M.I.T. Press, 1962), p. 222.
3. *Man's Struggle for Shelter in an Urbanizing World* (Cambridge: The M.I.T. Press, 1964), p. 10.
4. Their thesis is more fully developed in *The Intellectual versus the City: From Thomas Jefferson to Frank Lloyd Wright*.

Thomas Jefferson to John Dewey and Frank Lloyd Wright, they analyze the various patterns of urban hostility that distinguished Emerson from Thoreau, and Henry James and Henry Adams from earlier thinkers, such as Melville, Hawthorne, and Poe. The Whites conclude that although the intellectuals differed widely in their response to the city, they did share the basic disenchantment that the city subverted fundamental values prized by Americans throughout their history. The accumulated verdict, then, seems to be that the city was a failure, morally, esthetically, and physically.[5]

The Whites' essay suggest that historically the most dominant attitude toward the city was indeed anti-urbanism. Perhaps it was. But the question is begged: were the attitudes of the intellectual community *typical* of the rest of society? The Whites feel they were. Yet they also suggest the intellectuals were alienated from the rest of their society. But alienated intellectuals can hardly be seen as being representative of a larger society which repels and in many ways rejects them. Thus some urban historians argue that anti-urbanism has been so overstated that it has obscured other important attitudes, such as the affirmations of city-boosterism and the ambivalent attitude of both liking and distrusting the city.[6]

The next essay, in fact, points out that anti-urbanism must share a place with other attitudes that make up the complex web of ideas about the city. In "Urbanism and American Democracy," Francis E. Rourke challenges the assumption of anti-urbanism by showing that the city was more constructive than destructive in the unfolding of democracy. Whereas the other essay has emphasized the moral, esthetic, and physical accents of anti-urban thought, Rourke, finding its origins in the Jeffersonian agrarian tradition, traces anti-urbanism through American political history. He underscores an important aspect of urban thought: the skyscraper may have replaced the barn as the dominant symbol of the American landscape, but the power of agrarian thought continues through the decades of the twentieth century to our own time.[7] He suggests that many Americans still feel today that the agrarian past

5. See Robert Walker's excellent study, *The Poet and the Gilded Age* (Philadelphia: University of Pennsylvania Press, 1963). For an interesting account of how prose writers viewed New York City, see Eugene Arden, "The Evil City in American Fiction," *New York History* (July 1954).
6. Charles N. Glaab and A. Theodore Brown, *A History of Urban America* (New York: Macmillan, paperback edition, 1967), pp. 53-54. For a rejoinder to Glaab and Brown, see Jeffrey K. Hadden, Louis H. Masotti, and Calvin J. Larson (eds.), *Metropolis in Crisis* (Itasca, Ill.: F. E. Peacock Publishers, 1967), pp. 120-21.
For the enormous complexity of attitudes toward one city alone, see Bayrd Still's indispensable study of New York, *Mirror for Gotham* (New York: New York University Press, 1956) and his "The Personality of New York City," *New York Folklore Quarterly* (Summer 1958).
7. He may have overstated the agrarian dominance of the Ku Klux Klan and temperance movement. See Kenneth T. Jackson, *The Ku Klux Klan in the City, 1915-1930* (New York: Oxford, 1967), and James H. Timberlake, *Prohibition and the Progressive Movement: 1900-1920* (Cambridge: Harvard University Press, 1963).

nourished "the roots of Americanism." Some might insist that as far as urban problems are concerned, their solutions will be found not on the prairies but on the pavements.

At this point you might be tempted to tick off the virtues of the city, weigh them against the charges of the anti-urbanists, and try to determine your own position. You might say, however, that it is not that simple and there is more to it than that. And you would be right. Anselm Strauss in his engaging essay on the variety of American attitudes shows why.

Strauss's theme is ambivalence and ambiguity as he develops the elaborate complexity of Americans' attitudes toward their cities. He sees the shifting images arising out of a number of clashes: the values of the city vs. American values in general, regionalism vs. nationalism, the old vs. the new, specialization vs. cosmopolitanism, and ruralism vs. urbanism. He shows that if one city best attests to ambivalent, ambiguous attitudes that are filled with striking contadictions, it is New York. The paradoxical nature of these attitudes is fundamentally a reflection of the ambiguities and controversies about American values themselves. To add to the complexity, he demonstrates how the image of a particular city can be remarkably changed through growth and diversification. The heart of the matter is "the strain between ideal and reality, or ideal and presumed fact [which] runs like a brilliant thread through all our antithetical thinking about America and about our cities."

If Francis Rourke has given us an analysis of agrarian attitudes toward the city, Peter J. Schmitt, with wit and gentle irony, gives us an idea of the attitudes of urbanites toward the countryside, or more precisely, Nature. Struggling with the pressures and tensions of rapid urbanization at the turn of the century, Americans were caught up in a passion for returning to nature. In the years that followed, the back-to-nature movement was powerful enough to affect a variety of institutions, from the national park system, suburbia, the automobile, education, and popular literature to city planning and the Boy Scouts of America. This urge is very much with us today. Witness the widespread ecology movement, heavily loaded with emotion. Witness the cities on a Friday afternoon disgorging its millions of recreational vehicles, equipped with all the urban amenities for surviving in the wilderness, driven by men with soft bellies and shiny shoes itching for the rugged life of camping "outdoors."

In one sense, it was another hug in the long love affair Americans have had with nature. In another sense, it was a reflection of the attitudes of middle- and upper-class urbanites toward both their cities and their hinterland. Indeed, it was the urban response to the Arcadian myth. If small towners brought a village mentality to the city, the city dweller brought the comforts, the pleasures, and the illusion of the city to Nature. The life-style of a dude rancher in a stark Montana setting did not differ markedly from that of a Philadelphia suburbanite. For Schmitt makes it quite clear that urban nature-lovers neither hated nor rejected the city. They might wail at urban problems, but they prefered to live and work in the city.

For all its nostalgia, the back to nature mania was not an attempt to recapture the agrarianism of Thomas Jefferson, nor was it a return to the nineteenth-century Transcendentalism of Ralph Waldo Emerson. As Schmitt points out, "a mythology so full of urbane illusions offered poor support for any naïve primitivism." It was in short an urban view of nature, cast to urban needs and attitudes. As such, it was a myth, a poignant one for it was always just out of reach. For a nature lover who reads this essay, say a hardy backpacker tramping down the John Muir Trail, the freeway of the high Sierra, with his thirty-dollar boots, goose-down sleeping bag, primus stove, aluminum Kelty backpack carrying that triumph of modern technology, dehydrated food, it might make him smile a little—at himself.

Where Morton and Lucia White suggested that the earlier intellectuals anticipated the views of the modern social scientist, Scott Greer, in the final essay of this chapter, examines the ideas and methods of twentieth-century social science and finds them wanting. In a provocative, slashing attack upon political scientists, urban sociologists, and economists, he argues they have been both myth makers and myth mongers whose images of the city assert a validity, relevance, scope, and monolithic understanding not matched with the changing realities of the modern city. He criticizes particularly the theorists of the "mass society"; and he points out the built-in small-town bias which helped to lead to studies emphasizing only the extremes and the "dramatic contrasts" and which illuminated nothing of the "excluded middle" of urban life. The study of the city as a kind of human pathology, as Greer maintains, has sharply contributed to the crisis of the city. It is a crisis of myth *vs.* reality.

The American Intellectual versus the American City[*]

Morton and Lucia White

Although the city has become one of the most absorbing and most intensively studied social problems in America today, and although it is now fashionable for intellectuals to express an almost tender concern for its future, to hope that its decay can be arrested, and to offer plans for its revitalization, this has not always been the attitude of our greatest American thinkers. For a variety of reasons they have expressed different degrees of hostility toward urban life in America, hostility which may be partly responsible for a feeling on the part of today's city planner and urban reformer that he has no mythology or mystique on which he can rest or depend. We have no tradition of romantic attachment to the city in our highbrow literature, nothing that remotely resembles the Greek philosopher's attachment to the *polis* or the French writer's affection for Paris. And this fits very well with the frequently defended thesis that the American writer has been more than usually alienated from the society in which he lives, that he is typically in revolt against it. Throughout the nineteenth century our society was becoming more and more urbanized, but the literary tendency to denigrate the American city hardly declined in proportion. If anything, it increased in intensity.

Faced with this fact about the history of American thought, the contemporary student of the city can take one of two opposing attitudes. He, at his peril, can turn his back on the tradition of Jefferson, Emerson, Thoreau, Hawthorne, Melville, Poe, Henry Adams, Henry James, Louis Sullivan, Frank Lloyd Wright, and John Dewey. In this case he will treat some of the American city's profoundest critics as irresponsible literary men or as idle metaphysicians who fled the city rather than face its problems. Or he can regard this critical tradition as a repository of deep, though troubling, wisdom, one which raises basic questions for any urban reformer, and some of whose premonitions and fears have been more than justified by the passage of time. There is no doubt that the second is the wiser course. He who would improve the American city can only profit by an awareness of what some of our greatest minds have said, felt, and thought about one of the most conspicuous and most troubling features of our national life.

One cannot deny, of course, that there were pro-urban literary voices like Whitman's, or that there were urban sociologists like Robert Park who tried to speak up for the city. But they are voices in "the city wilderness," never comparing in volume with the anti-urban roar in the national literary pantheon. The urbanist must face the fact that the anti-urbanist does not live only in the Kentucky hills, in the Rockies, in the Ozarks, in the Cracker country, or the bayous. He lives in the mind and heart of America as conceived by

From *Daedalus* (Winter 1961), pp. 166-79. Copyright © 1961 by Morton and Lucia White. Reprinted by permission of the authors. Morton White is Professor at the Institute for Advanced Study, Princeton University.

the intellectual historian. The intellect, whose home is the city, according to some sociologists, has been the American city's sharpest critic. Everyone knows that Jefferson once hoped to discourage the development of the city in America, but he was only the first of a long and varied list of critics of the city.

Jefferson despised the manners and principles of the urban "mob" as he knew it in Europe and he hoped to keep it from crossing the Atlantic intact. He certainly did not think of the city as "The Hope of Democracy," as some Progressive theorists did at the turn of the twentieth century. He adopted a conciliatory tone about the city in his old age when he said in 1816 that we could not possibly depend on England for manufactures, as he had originally thought, and therefore we *needed* cities. But this does not show any *love* for the city. The country and its yeomen Jefferson loved all his life; in his old age he grudgingly accepted the manufacturing city as a necessity.

The same War of 1812 which led Jefferson to reassess his views was followed by a great expansion of the American city. It inaugurated a major phase of urban civilization between the Revolution and the Civil War. By 1860 the urban population was eleven times what it had been in 1820. The early decades of the nineteenth century saw the decline of Jefferson's empiricism among American intellectuals, and the emergence of philosophical transcendentalism, but a distaste for the city persisted among American writers.

The growth of the city in the North produced an even sharper reaction in Ralph Waldo Emerson than the European city had produced in Jefferson. Emerson's first philosophical work, *Na-ture,* appeared in 1836, in the middle of that interval which witnessed an eleven-fold increase in our urban population. Its very title was a protest against what he thought was happening. Partly under the influence of English romanticism, Emerson and some of his friends took to deprecating manufacture, art, and civilization, and so it was not long before they took to criticizing the city, the greatest of artifacts. The distaste for the city as an artificial creation was associated in Emerson's mind, as it was in the case of many romantic thinkers, with doubts about the value of science as an avenue to truth. And yet Emerson agreed with the scientifically minded Jefferson about the nasty manners and principles of the city. Whereas Jefferson was given to arguing the defects of the city in common-sense political terms, Emerson sought to buttress his feelings by a metaphysical theory. Hence we may label his period as the metaphysical period of anti-urbanism. To be is to be natural for Emerson. In the wilderness he said he found "something more dear and connate than in streets or villages." The life of the city was "artificial and curtailed"; it destroyed solitude, poetry, and philosophy.

One will find passages in which Emerson extolled the application of science and the virtues of civilization, the need for sociability to educate a man's sympathies, and the advantages of specialization that allow each man to develop his own talents. This suggests a more friendly view of the industrial urban society which was emerging in his own lifetime. But he always harped on the human failings of State Street and commercialism. At times Emerson could celebrate the artifice of pure technology, but he persistently attacked the debasement of moral standards by those who pursued nothing but wealth in the cities as he knew them. One is reminded of Thorstein Veblen's praise of urban industry even as he attacked its financial captains, for it was Veblen who saw the modern industrial city as the *locus classicus* of conspicuous waste.

Thoreau went even farther than Emerson in his distaste for civilization and the city, for Thoreau also attacked the village and the farm. *Walden* is a bible of anti-urbanism, in which Thoreau celebrates the life of the isolated individual, living in Nature and free of *all* social attachments. No wonder that Thoreau refused to visit the Saturday Club, which provided one of the few values of Boston in Emerson's eyes: intellectual conversation. And when Thoreau refused, Perry Miller reminds us, he put his refusal in no uncertain terms: "The only room in Boston which I visit with alacrity is the Gentlemen's Room at the Fitchburg Depot, where I wait for cars, sometimes for two hours, in order to get out of town."[1] No wonder Henry James said that Thoreau "was essentially a sylvan personage."[2]

If Jefferson attacked the city on political grounds, and if Emerson and Thoreau may be represented as criticizing it from the point of view of transcendental metaphysics, what shall we say of Poe, Hawthorne and Melville, all of whom may be added to our list of pre-Civil War critics of the city? They were far from political theorists or metaphysicians but all of them saw the city as the scene of sin and crime. Speaking of them, Harry Levin says: "For our dreamers, America was a garden, an agrarian Eden, which was losing its innocence by becoming citified. Melville had located his City of Woe in London

or Liverpool; Poe had tracked down imaginary crimes in the streets of an imagined Paris; and Hawthorne had exposed sins most luridly among the ruins of Rome."[3] As in Jefferson's case, the urban models of extreme crime and sinfulness were not located in the United States by most of our pre-Civil War anti-urbanists, but they saw dark omens in the streets of American cities which made them fear that they might become like Paris, London, Liverpool or Rome.

The observant de Tocqueville expressed his worry about the American city in 1835, one year before Emerson's essay *Nature* appeared. He said that the fact that America as yet had no dominating metropolis was one of those circumstances which tended to maintain a democratic republic in the United States and to counteract that great danger to which all democracies are subject—the tyranny of the majority. But de Tocqueville thought that the "lower ranks" which inhabited Philadelphia (pop. 161,000) and New York (pop. 202,000) in the 1830's "constitute a rabble even more formidable than the populace of European towns. They consist of freed blacks . . . who are condemned by the laws and by public opinion to a hereditary state of misery and degradation. They also contain a multitude of Europeans who have been driven to the shore of the New World by their misfortunes or their misconduct; and they bring to the United States all our greatest vices, without any of those interests which counteract their baneful influence. As inhabitants of a country where they have no civil rights, they are ready to turn all the passions which agitate the community to their own advantage; thus, within the last few months, serious riots have broken out in Philadelphia and New York."[4] So seriously did de Tocqueville treat this matter that he said: "I look upon the size of certain American cities, and especially on the nature of their population, as a real danger which threatens the future security of the democratic republics of the New World; and I venture to predict that they will perish from this circumstance, unless the government succeeds in creating an armed force which, while it remains under the control of the majority of the nation, will be independent of the town population and able to repress its excesses."[5]

If this could be the conclusion of the most astute foreign observer ever to visit our shores, it is not surprising that some of our great literary figures might have developed less than an admiring view of our urban culture between the Revolution and the Civil War. Optimistic empiricists like Jefferson, optimistic transcendentalists like Emerson, pessimistic believers in original sin like Hawthorne and Melville, all forgot their philosophical differences when they looked upon the American city, even before it developed into the industrial jungle it was to become between the Civil War and the end of the nineteenth century.

Between 1860 and 1900 the urban population quadrupled while the rural population only doubled; and, what is more staggering and significant, between 1790 and 1890, while the total population of the country increased sixteen times, the urban population increased 139 times.[6] The great exodus from the countryside was in full force, and New England became the scene of deserted hill and village farms, while the city's problems became the great social problems of the nation. The city became the home of the elevated railroad, the trolley car, the cable car, the subway, the apartment house, the telephone, and the skyscraper, while it continued to en-

courage what one physician called "American nervousness."

Among the most influential and most fastidious observers of this development were Henry Adams and the younger Henry James. Both were men of literary genius, both were members of cultivated families with wealth in their backgrounds, and for both of them the American city provided a profound spiritual problem. Because Henry Adams and Henry James lived in the age of the city's supremacy, they did not speak of it, as Jefferson had, as a remote future phenomenon or as something existing in Europe alone. And, unlike Thoreau, they did not feel as though they had only the American city and the American wilderness to choose between. Adams and James were both refined, civilized, indeed urban men whose animadversions on the American city are made more significant precisely because they were not opposed to cities in principle. They demonstrate what a hard time the American city had at the hands of nineteenth-century intellectuals. For here at least were two *city* types who also found the American city sadly wanting. Their reaction to the American city is more esthetic, more literary, more psychological than that of their predecessors Jefferson and Emerson.

The two most important documents for an understanding of the views of Adams and James are the former's *Education* and the latter's *The American Scene*. It is significant that the great problem of the *Education of Henry Adams* was to steer a course between the poles of town and country, between the Boston and Quincy of his childhood. "Town," Adam tells us, "was restraint, law, unity. Country, only seven miles away, was liberty, diversity, outlawry, the endless delight of mere sense impressions given by nature for nothing, and breathed by boys without knowing it."[7] Adams also tells us that he spent his life trying to choose between the ways of life they represented, without ever making up his mind. And yet, in a sense, he did make up his mind, or the social forces of America made it up for him. He could not go back to the Quincy house of his grandfather Adams. And, being no Thoreau, he had to live in the American city if he was to live anywhere in America. But what was *the* American city in his mature years? Surely not Boston, but New York. And when Henry Adams looked at the New York of 1868, he tells us in a book which he wrote in 1905 that he felt swept aside by the forces pushing the country in a new direction. "His world," he lamented, "was dead. Not a Polish Jew fresh from Warsaw or Cracow—not a furtive Yaccob or Ysaac still reeking of the Ghetto, snarling a weird Yiddish to the officers of the customs—but had a keener instinct, and intenser energy, and a freer hand than he —American of Americans, with Heaven knew how many Puritans and Patriots behind him, and an education that had cost a civil war."[8] Adams felt like the dispossessed Indian and the buffalo in America after 1865, for it was a banker's, and neither a buffalo's nor a Bostonian's world. To Henry Adams, New York symbolized the spiritual confusion of America at the end of the nineteenth century.

Henry James, as one might expect, also complained about his birthplace, New York, after a period of flirtation with it. James attacked it most explicitly in *The American Scene*, published in 1907 as the report of an expatriate revisiting the country of his birth. He, too, spoke of the city's chaos, and even the New York skyline insulted his very expressively complex sensibilities. He complained of the lack of history and of the lack of time for history in a way that reminds one of his early critical work on Nathaniel Hawthorne. The buildings, he said, "never speak to you, in the manner of the builded majesties of the world . . . towers, or temples, or fortresses or palaces with the authority of things of permanence or even of things of long duration."[9] History had given way to commerce: "The great city is projected into its future as practically, a huge continuous fifty-floored conspiracy against the very idea of the ancient graces."[10] The city lacked order, structure, dignity, history. James speaks of it as "a heaped industrial battlefield" and as a scene of "the universal will to move —to move, move, move, as an end in itself, an appetite at any price."[11] He missed what he called "organic social relations,"[12] and he felt some pleasurable relief when he visited Philadelphia, because it didn't "bristle," and because "it went back."[13] In this spirit he warned: "Let not the unwary . . . visit Ellis Island"[14] as Henry Adams might have warned in *his* snobbish way. James was upset by what he called "that loud primary stage of alienism which New York most offers to sight."[15] And he dreamed "of the luxury of some such close and sweet and *whole* national consciousness as that of the Switzer and the Scot."[16] His final head-shaking conclusion was "that there was no escape from the ubiquitous alien into the future or even into the present; there was no escape but into the past."[17]

Of course, one must not forget that Henry James was a cosmopolite, a lifelong inhabitant of cities, a man who is reputed to have dined out more than any resident of London in his day. One must be mindful of the fact that his novel *The*

Princess Casamassima represents an effort to penetrate the depths of London, as does his famous admiring essay on that city. But James viewed the *American* city in an entirely different way. After his harsh handling of the Boston reformers in *The Bostonians,* the American city did not provide him with any serious material for a full-length novel because he found neither the uptown nor the downtown of the American city sufficiently interesting, as F. O. Mathiessen has pointed out.[18] And even *The Princess Casamassima* shows a greater interest in the bizarre doings of weirdly inspired misfits and aristocrats, whose philanthropic concern with the slums James satirizes, than a sustained interest in the typical life of London. With characteristic delicacy and insight he saw the crushing, oppressive defects of the British metropolis of his day, but he could never bring himself to the same kind of sympathetic concern with the American metropolis that we find in Dreiser, Crane, or Norris.

Although we are primarily concerned with recording the theme of *anti*-urbanism in American writing and thinking, it would be absurd to argue that *every* great writer or thinker in the American pantheon was hostile to urban life. The fact is that at the end of the nineteenth century there emerged a tendency to view the American city in a more friendly manner. By contrast to his brother Henry, William James had very little desire to escape from the American city into the past. His philosophy was one of hope, of optimism, of possibility —indeed, a little bit too much so—and it was this that allowed him to view the urbanization of America in a way that might encourage Americans to do something about urban problems. Unlike Henry, he did not adore the great cities

of Western Europe. For ten days after his arrival in Florence in 1875 he "was so disgusted with the swarming and reeking blackness of the streets and the age of everything, that enjoyment took place under protest."[19] As for London, during his visit of 1889 he wrote his sister that he was "thoroughly sated" with it, and "never cared to see its yellow-brownness and stale spaciousness again."[20]

William James loved the country but his love of nature was tempered by a fondness for sociability, and therefore he was unable to subscribe either to Thoreau's primitivism or to the ultra-civilized sentiments of his brother. With Emerson he looked to the future, but unlike Emerson he did not think that the future excluded the possibility of a decent life in the cities of America. Many of William James's reactions to the buzzing confusion of New York of 1880 and 1900 had been unfavorable because of "the clangor, disorder and permanent earthquake conditions" which he experienced on his customary daylong visits. But in 1907 he spent a longer time there and as he says, "caught the pulse of the machine, took up the rhythm, and vibrated *mit,* and found it simply magnificent."[21] He spoke of it as an "*entirely* new New York, in soul as well as in body, from the old one, which looks like a village in retrospect. The courage, the heaven-scaling audacity of it all, and the *lightness* withal, as if there were nothing that was not easy, and the great pulses and bounds of progress, so many in directions all simultaneous that the coordination is indefinitely future, give a drumming background of life that I have never felt before. I'm sure that one *in* that movement, and at home, all other places would seem insipid."[22] This was written to his brother, of all people, after the appearance of the latter's *The American Scene,* but William had evidently read the manuscript, for he says: "I observe that your book—'The American Scene,'—dear H., is just out. I must get it and devour again the chapters relative to New York." William would not have liked them upon rereading them, and one can imagine how Henry must have winced when William exclaimed, "I'm surprised at you, Henry, not having been more enthusiastic, but perhaps the superbly powerful subway was not opened when you were there!"[23]

William James, like Walt Whitman, saw virtue and promise in the American city. Both William James and Whitman not only accept the city as an inescapable part of America, but they *enjoy* it, as Jefferson most certainly did not. The year of William James's discovery of what he called "the new New York" was 1907, when he delivered his most famous set of lectures, entitled *Pragmatism,* at Columbia. James thought his philosophy would mediate between the views of those whom he called "tenderfoot Bostonians" and those he labeled "Rocky Mountain toughs" in philosophy. It is not too fanciful to suppose that James identified the great future city, along with his pragmatic philosophy, as a blend of, a compromise between, the insipidity of Boston and the craggy brutality of the Rockies. A livable city on earth, one is temped to say, is the social counterpart of James's pragmatism, and therefore he is one of the first great American writers to associate himself with the effort to accept what is good and to root out what is bad in the American city. He does not escape to the country with Emerson and Thoreau, or to the past with his brother and Henry Adams. He revives the wisdom of the older Jefferson after a century of trans-cendentalism, Brook-farming and expatriation, and adds to it a love of the city. In doing so he becomes the herald of a pragmatic phase in urban thinking.

But this pragmatic phase, in which the city was joyfully described by Frederic C. Howe in 1905 as "The Hope of Democracy," did not last very long. Indeed, Howe's book contained within itself the classical argument for the central city's impending destruction. "The open fields about the city are inviting occupancy," Howe said, "and there the homes of the future will surely be. The city proper will not remain the permanent home of the people. Population must be dispersed. The great cities of Australia are spread out into the suburbs in a splendid way. For miles about are broad roads, with small houses, gardens, and an opportunity for touch with the freer, sweeter life which the country offers."[24] Howe calls the city the hope of democracy, but he is, it would appear, a suburban booster rather than a city-lover. He shares the basic inability of greater American intellectuals to go all out in their admiration for the modern American city.

A more striking illustration of the same thing may be found in the writings of John Dewey, the disciple of William James, who sympathized with so much of James's interest in the American city. In his earlier writing Dewey expressed a typically progressive interest in the city. This was part of the political liberalism of the period, with its interest in urban planning, social work, socialism, the single tax, and muck-raking. The city was not regarded as a perfect form of life, but it was seen as having promise. And, to the extent to which it showed promise, it became the concern of all sorts of people who could criticize it in a constructive spirit quite different from that which dominated the work of militant anti-urbanists from Jefferson to Henry James. For a variety of reasons Chicago became the most conspicuous locale of this new way of looking at the city. It was the home of a great university, which had opened its doors in the 'nineties and which became a center of urban sociology and, it might be said, of urban philosophy. One can understand, therefore, why William James looked to Dewey and other Chicago intellectuals as his friends, and why they regarded him as their spiritual leader. For Chicago at the turn of the century was the home of James's pupil, Robert Park, his worshipper, Jane Addams, and his disciple, John Dewey.

As early as 1899 Dewey was urging that the congregation of men into cities was one of the most conspicuous features of the modern world and that no theory of education could possibly disregard the fact of urbanization. Indeed, *the* problem of education, as Dewey saw it in his *School and Society*, was how to adjust the child to life in the city. The earlier kind of rural environment, in which he had been raised as a boy in Vermont, had its virtues, he admitted. It encouraged habits of personal orderliness, industry, and responsibility; it led to a firsthand acquaintance with nature. But, Dewey said in 1899, "it was useless to bemoan the departure of the good old days . . . if we expect merely by bemoaning and by exhortation to bring them back."[25] The problem, as Dewey saw it, was that of retaining some advantages of the older mode of life while training the child to cope with the new urban world. The school, therefore, was to be a miniature urban community, a microcosmic duplication of macrocosmic Chicago, much as Hull House was in Jane Addams' eyes. The essence of so-

ciety, said Dewey—and in this he was joined by Robert Park and other sociologists—was communication—and therefore the school was to encourage and develop this peculiarly social phenomenon, this salient feature of the urban age. Dewey's progressivism in educational theory was defined by his broad conception of communication, his idea that it takes place while children are building blocks, dancing, and cooking, as well as on the more formal level of asserting propositions.

Soon, however, a new and more critical attitude toward the city began to enter Dewey's writing. In *The Public and Its Problems* (1927) he concluded that steam and electricity, the very forces that had created modern society, that had provided it with the means of transportation and communication that made urban concentration possible, were creating a situation in which communication at its most human level was being destroyed. The very forces which brought Bangkok and Chicago closer to each other and which brought people from isolated farms to urban centers had diminished the possibility of "face-to-face" relationships. The primary group, in the phrase of the sociologist, Charles Horton Cooley, was disappearing rapidly. And while Dewey did not use our current jargon, he said, in effect, that modern society was becoming a lonely crowd of organization men.

Dewey warned: "Unless local communal life can be restored, the public cannot adequately resolve its most urgent problem: to find and identify itself."[26] But the local communal unit of which Dewey spoke now was not the enormous city as it was coming to be known in the twentieth century. It was more like the University Elementary School at the University of Chicago, or

Hull House. "Democracy must begin at home," Dewey said, "and its home is the neighborly community."[27] As a result, a curious reversal takes place in Dewey's thinking. Instead of taking the city as the model *for* the progressive school, he almost speaks as though the urban community should be modeled *on* the progressive school. Jefferson wrote at the end of his life: "As Cato concluded every speéch with the words, 'Carthago delenda est,' so do I every opinion with the injunction, 'Divide the counties into wards.'" At the end of his life Dewey seemed to conclude every speech with the words, "Divide the cities into settlement houses."

It is ironic to find the most influential philosopher of the urban age in America reverting to the localism of Jefferson, but no more ironic than the anti-urbanism of Louis Sullivan and Frank Lloyd Wright, our most distinctive architects. For functionalism, like pragmatism, is one of a complex of American ideas that could not exist in a nonurban society, and yet its greatest spokesmen seem to hate the American city. Sullivan's *Autobiography* records his distaste for Boston in his childhood, and in his *Kindergarten Chats* he fulminates against New York and Chicago. "Lieber Meister," as Wright called Sullivan, bequeathed this hostility to his disciple, and the disciple, as everyone knows, added his own powerful spice to the brew of anti-urbanism. John Dewey may have reverted to Jefferson's localism, but Wright was a little more partial to Emerson. Not only are there copious references to Emerson in Wright's books, but he adds as a red-printed appendix to *The Living City* a long excerpt from Emerson's essay, "Farming," which concludes with a typically tran-

scendental warning: "Cities force growth and make men talkative and entertaining, but they make them artificial." And so the great American architect of the twentieth century went back spiritually to Concord, while the great American philosopher retreated to Monticello.

One moral of this tale is the city-loving urban reformers will not find much boosting or sentimental admiration of city life in the writings of those who have been canonized in our national literature and philosophy. A brief flurry of pro-urban sentiment in the late nineteenth and early twentieth century under the encouraging eye of Walt Whitman and William James was swiftly buried by the exploding megalopolis, but after it our most sensitive and gifted intellectuals went on criticizing the American city. Readers who may feel that this story is based on an excessively narrow selection of writers and thinkers should remember that other readers will find in these pages the names of our greatest political thinker, our greatest essayist, our greatest philosopher, our greatest theorist of education, our greatest novelist, our greatest autobiographer, and our greatest architect, all of them throwing up their hands about the most distinctive and most pressing features of our national life. If *their* views should not be typical of the nation's view on this topic, that in itself would be a fact that is worth recording and pondering. Moreover, it is impossible to produce a list of *pro*-urban American thinkers who remotely approach this collection in distinction and intellectual influence.

In spite of the anti-urbanism of our literary and philosophical tradition, the city planner would make a grave mistake if he were to dismiss that tradition, if he were to treat it as a point of view from which nothing could be learned, if he were to forget it and disregard it. Those who must live in today's American city or who like to live in it can profit by taking seriously the urban criticism of our great writers, for it was deep and many-sided. It was not only esthetic but also moral in character. Henry James spoke most persuasively for those who saw the city as a scene of chaos as it presented itself to "the painter's eye." It lacked order, structure, history, and dignity in 1907, and God knows that these virtues have not been miraculously supplied in the age of urban sprawl and suburban slums. But the city, as Robert Park said, is a state of mind as well as an esthetic object, and the profoundest critics of the American city have found other faults with it.

When Jefferson warned of the dangers of what he called the city mob, when Emerson complained of the city's artificiality and conventionalism, when John Dewey lamented the decline of neighborliness, all of them thought of the city as a place in which certain basic human values were being subverted, values which are cherishable today as they were in the eighteenth century of Jefferson, the nineteenth century of Emerson, and the twentieth century of Dewey. And what are these values? Jefferson's worry about the mobs of the city arose from doubt about the American city's capacity to educate its inhabitants in a way that would preserve and extend the democratic process. And when Emerson worried about the growth of artificiality and conventionalism in the city, he was thinking, as were his contemporaries, Kierkegaard and John Stuart Mill, about the increase

in conformity, about the decline of individuality which was proportional to the increase of urbanization in America. Dewey's main concern was with the improvement of human communication within the city; and by communication he did not mean the exchange of information alone. He valued the capacity to share feelings and experiences, the capacity to discuss with, to learn from and intelligently persuade others, and to *live* with them in the profoundest sense.

Who can deny in 1960, then, that the great problem of the American city is to demonstrate at least three things: first, that it can solve the problem of education for the millions of people who are entering its gates, that it can absorb the Puerto Rican, as it has other immigrant groups, into the democratic process; second, that it can foster individuality, the capacity and the right of the human being to develop into a rounded personality who is concerned with more than merely commercial values; and third, that it can be more than a vast prison of unconnected cells in which people of different occupations, color, class, or creed fail to understand one another on the basic human issues of social life, let alone agree with one another.

The moral message of the intellectual critic of the city today is not fundamentally different from what it was in the age of Jefferson, Emerson, and Dewey. For today's serious thinker must also build upon a respect for the fundamental values of education, individuality, and easy communication among men. But, unlike his predecessors, he cannot deceive himself about the *place* in which those values must be realized today. The wilderness, the isolated farm, the plantation, the self-contained New England town, the detached neighborhood are things of the past. All the world's a city now and there is no escaping urbanization, not even in outer space.

NOTES

° The argument of this essay has been developed and documented more fully in Morton and Lucia White, *The Intellectual versus the City: From Thomas Jefferson to Frank Lloyd Wright* (Cambridge: Harvard University Press and The M.I.T. Press, 1962).

1. Perry Miller (editor), *Consciousness in Concord* (Boston, 1958), p. 46.
2. Henry James, *Hawthorne* (New York, 1880), p. 80.
3. Harry Levin, *The Power of Blackness* (New York, 1958), p. 234.
4. Alexis de Tocqueville, *Democracy in America* (New York, 1945), Vol. I, p. 289, note.
5. *Ibid.*
6. Arthur M. Schlesinger, *Paths to the Present* (New York, 1949), pp. 223-225.
7. Henry Adams, *The Education of Henry Adams* (Boston, 1918), pp. 7-8.

8. *Ibid.*, p. 238.
9. Henry James, *The American Scene* (reprint, New York, 1946), p. 77.
10. *Ibid.*, p. 92.
11. *Ibid.*, p. 84.
12. *Ibid.*, p. 279.
13. *Ibid.*, pp. 275, 280.
14. *Ibid.*, p. 85.
15. *Ibid.*, p. 86.
16. *Ibid.*
17. *Ibid.*, p. 115.
18. F. O. Mathiessen, *Introduction to The American Novels and Stories of Henry James* (New York, 1947), p. x.
19. Ralph Barton Perry, *The Thought and Character of William James* (Boston, 1935), Vol. I, p. 351.
20. *Ibid.*, p. 412.
21. Henry James (editor), *The Letters of William James* (Boston, 1920), Vol. II, p. 264.
22. *Ibid.*
23. *Ibid.*
24. Frederic C. Howe, *The City: The Hope of Democracy* (New York, 1905), p. 204.
25. John Dewey, *School and Society* (Chicago, 1899), p. 9.
26. Dewey, *The Public and Its Problems* (reprint edn., Chicago, 1946), p. 216.
27. *Ibid.*, p. 213.

Urbanism and American Democracy*

FRANCIS E. ROURKE

"The United States," writes Richard Hofstadter in his *Age of Reform,* "was born in the country and has moved to the city. From the beginning its political values and ideas were of necessity shaped by country life." Few could disagree with this appraisal. At the time of the first census in 1790, more than nine out of ten Americans lived in rural territory, and as late as 1860 the proportion of the population living outside of cities remained well over 75 per cent.

Thus, from the Revolution to the Civil War, agrarian dominance was a major fact of life in American politics. This was a time when rural ascendancy rested on the solid basis of numerical superiority rather than upon the legislative malapportionment and gerrymandering that have since served to shore up agrarian power against the steady erosion of population in rural areas.

What was most striking about this early system of domination by agrarian

From *Ethics*, LXXIV (July 1964), pp. 255-68. Reprinted by permission of The University of Chicago Press. Francis E. Rourke is Professor of Political Science at The Johns Hopkins University.

interests was the uncontested philosophical justification it received at the hands
of Jefferson and those who followed in
his wake. No such fervent ideological
support was to crown the power of
either of the other major groups who
were in time to lay claim to supremacy
in American politics—the business elite
which came into prominence in the period following the Civil War, or the
popular coalition which has sustained
the broad outlines of the welfare state
since the presidency of Franklin Roosevelt. In the days of agrarian supremacy,
political power and political ideology
were linked together in a neat pattern
of harmony, while since that time they
have often been poles apart.

Easily the most familiar protagonist
of this system of agrarian democracy
was Thomas Jefferson. As Griswold
points out: "No one believed so implicitly as he in a causal connection between the occupation of farming and
the political system of democracy, and
no one, before or since his time, has
given that belief a greater impetus
among his countrymen."[1] Of course the
doctrine of agrarian superiority which
Jefferson espoused—"those who labor in
the earth are the chosen people of God"
—is a very old theme in Western
thought. It was widely prevalent in both
Greek and Roman culture, from Hesiod
to Horace, and this classical view was
adopted and advanced in subsequent
European literature, drawing on Christian as well as pagan sources to support
the comparison it drew between the
virtue and vitality of the countryside
and the vices and decay of urban society.

Much of this pastoral tradition stresses
the physical, economic, and moral advantages of agricultural life; but
throughout it there also runs the persistent theme that farming makes for
better citizens as well as healthier, nobler, and more affluent men. Western
intellectual history provided ample
precedent for Jefferson's view that the
farmer was not only the mainstay of the
economy and the pillar of civil recti-
tude, but the backbone of the state as
well: "The proportion which the aggregate of the other classes of citizens bears
in any State to that of its husbandmen,
is the proportion of its unsound to its
healthy parts."

With the steady advance of urbanization in American society, the passages
in Jefferson which retain the most telling impact today are those in which he
takes specific note of what he considers
to be the ill effects of cities upon the
healthy functioning of a democratic society. For it was Jefferson who set the
style for the treatment the city was to
receive in subsequent political thought.
Few statements in American political
doctrine are as celebrated as his assertion that "the mobs of great cities add
just so much to the support of pure
government as sores do to the strength
of the human body." But the view he
put forward in a letter to Benjamin
Rush was even more extreme. There he
argued that a recent outbreak of yellow
fever in coastal cities, however unfortunate its consequences in terms of human
suffering, might at least have the advantage of discouraging the establishment
of large urban centers in this country.
For such cities, Jefferson declared, are
more "pestilential" than yellow fever
"to the morals, the health and the liberties of man."[2]

It has been suggested—most recently
by Morton and Lucia White in their
study of attitudes toward the city in
American intellectual history—that Jefferson recanted these antiurban senti-

ments after he became president.[3] If so, this retraction was a grudging one, based largely on Jefferson's belated recognition during the Napoleonic Wars that the political independence of this country might ultimately be lost if it remained completely dependent upon the industrial cities of Europe for manufactured goods. Nor was it a permanent conversion, since Jefferson returned to his agrarian outlook in the later years of his life. Certainly there is little in Jefferson's career to support the Whites' description of him as "a great intellectual defender" of the American city.

But it is interesting to note that for a time at least the harsh realities of international politics forced Jefferson to accept some measure of urbanization, even though he regarded this development as altogether undesirable for a democratic society from a purely domestic point of view. For the individual as opposed to the state, Jefferson never lost his conviction that the highest degree of political independence rested upon the economic security provided by ownership of a small farm. But as has often been true in American history, when the requirements of foreign policy required a modification of domestic political doctrine, this modification was quickly forthcoming. The needs of national security soon overcame even Jefferson's antipathy for cities. As he himself put it in a letter to DuPont: "What is practicable must often control what is pure theory."

Jefferson's views on the negative impact of urbanization were not disputed by any of the more influential of his contemporaries. James Madison, for example, faithfully echoed the same sentiment in his own writings. "The life of the husbandman is pre-eminently suited to the comfort and happiness of the individual," he wrote. "The extremes both of want and of waste have other abodes. 'Tis not the country that peoples either the Bridewells or the Bedlams. These mansions of wretchedness are tenanted from the distresses and vices of overgrown cities."

More surprising, perhaps, than the support Jefferson received from a fellow Virginian planter like Madison was the fact that there was no dissent from his adverse judgment regarding cities on the part of leading Federalists of the day. For in principle at least these Federalists were committed to a course of economic development, the encouragement of manufacturing and commerce, which would inevitably promote the growth of urban centers. Alexander Hamilton nowhere attempted to refute the Jeffersonian point of view, however much his "report on manufactures" may have contributed to urbanization, and John Adams affirmed his belief that "agriculture is the most essential interest of America."[4]

Later on, Federalists like Chancellor Kent were even to use Jefferson's attacks on cities to buttress their own aristocratic stand against eliminating suffrage restrictions. In New York, for example, the proposal to extend the franchise stirred prolonged and bitter controversy at the state constitutional convention in 1821, and on that occasion leading Federalist spokesmen sounded warnings against the city that were thoroughly Jeffersonian in tenor:

Elisha Williams, the young Van Buren's brilliant adversary in the courts of Columbia County and chief figure in the haughty Columbia Junto, explicitly dared the Democratic delegates to confront the reasoning of their great god Jefferson on the moral influence of cities. Would Jefferson's disciples spread "the contents of those [urban] sores through the whole political body" and so expose the yeoman interest to the will of "the ring streaked and speckled population of our large towns and cities, comprising people of every kindred and tongue?" "These cities," Williams warned, "are filled with men too rich, or too poor to fraternize with the yeomen of the country." With Kent, he placed the democratic menace in the city and the future.[5]

Not the least of the paradoxical aspects of Jefferson's impact on American politics is thus the fact that his prejudice against cities ultimately became a weapon in the hands of his bitterest political opponents.

THE JEFFERSONIAN HERITAGE

Since Jefferson's antiurban views were in accord with traditional political doctrine and were expressed at a time when the overwhelming majority of all Americans lived outside of cities, these sentiments certainly did not expose him to any substantial political risk. Quite to the contrary, Jefferson's agrarian posture may be said to have served him quite well from the point of view of political advantage. Much more remarkable was the way in which this Jeffersonian attitude was to persist down through American history even into the day when the great majority of Americans had come to live in an urban environment. While Jefferson's agrarian point of view was neither risky nor original, it proved to be an extraordinarily durable part of the American political tradition.

When the Jacksonian Democrats came to power, their political base rested on the support of the labor vote in the eastern cities as well as the farmers of the West. Antagonism toward the "money power" provided the bond of unity between these two divergent

groups. And yet, Jefferson's dislike of cities continued to weave its spell over large sections of the Jacksonian movement, in part perhaps because the hated banking interests were themselves located in the cities. In his study of the Jackson era, Schlesinger points out that Jackson's followers were far from happy over the dependence of their party upon the votes it received in urban areas:

The situation in New York, where the country regularly voted Whig and the city Democratic, very much worried the *Democratic Review*, a fairly pious organ of Jeffersonianism. "As a general rule," the *Review* observed in some perplexity, we are free to confess that we prefer the suffrages of the country to those of the city. . . . The farmer is naturally a Democrat—the citizen may be so, but it is in spite of many obstacles.[6]

Other Jacksonian Democrats attempted to relieve their anxiety over the party's urban support by arguing that great cities need not necessarily be as "great sores" on the American body politic as Jefferson had originally believed.

In the decades immediately preceding the Civil War the Jeffersonian antagonism toward the city was clearly discernible in the arguments put forward by the southern apologists for slavery. This was one of the few occasions in which the proslavery argument had occasion to lean upon Jefferson's support, since Calhoun, Fitzhugh, and the other writers prominent in defense of the southern cause generally found it necessary to spend much of their time refuting Jeffersonian heresies, including the notion of the inherent equality of all mankind as expounded in the Declaration of Independence. But the defense of slavery was based in large measure on the proposition that the condition of the slave on a southern plantation was often a good deal better than the life of the wage earner in northern and European cities. And in this connection southern criticism of the odious characteristics of industrial cities bore a close resemblance to Jefferson's strictures against an urban civilization. "Large cities," wrote George Fitzhugh, "are great curses, because they impoverish a world to enrich a neighborhood."[7]

Since the Civil War hostility toward the city has also found repeated expression in the various movements of political protest which have agitated rural America, from the Grangers in the 1870's to the Farmers' Holiday Association in more recent times. Much of this antiurban sentiment is implicit rather than explicit in the literature of agrarian revolt. It is reflected in the fulsome praise lavished upon the occupation of husbandry, in dogmatic assertions regarding the indispensable role which agriculture plays in the national economy, or in persistent tirades against banking and other urban commercial interests disliked by farmers. But it is praise of agriculture which is at the center of attention rather than overt attacks on the city.

William Jennings Bryan perhaps symbolized more strikingly than any other figure the spirit of agrarian protest in American politics, and Bryan's preference for the country over the city was never left in doubt. It received its most vivid expression in his Cross of Gold speech at the 1896 Democratic national convention: "The great cities rest upon our broad and fertile prairies," said Bryan in his fervent peroration. "Burn down your cities, and leave our farms, and your cities will spring up again as if by magic; but destroy our farms and the grass will grow in the streets of every city in the country." But as a presidential candidate bidding for support

in urban as well as rural constituencies, Bryan could ill afford to reject the city altogether. In setting forth to begin the presidential campaign of 1896 in New York City, he spoke of his trip as one he was taking into the "enemy's country," but this was an area, he hastened to add, "we hope to be our country before this campaign is over."[8] Politicians like Bryan with ambitions which depended for their fulfilment upon urban as well as farm support were compelled to avoid the cruder kinds of assault upon the city in which a purely rural politician could indulge. Some of the lesser Populists were under no such inhibitions.

In its manifestations in the early part of this century, the antagonism toward cities was reinforced by two interdependent developments which exercised a major influence upon the course of American politics, the nativist movement and the drive for national prohibition. Early nativist sentiment was, as John Higham has shown in his *Strangers in the Land,* largely an urban rather than a rural phenomenon. The hostility toward immigrants was initially strongest in the areas where native Americans most frequently rubbed elbows with newcomers from other countries—in the great cities of the East. By the turn of the century, however, the antagonism toward the foreign-born had come to be centered in rural areas, where it blended with and helped to harden the historic agrarian prejudice against the city. The "foreign" character of American cities became one of their major liabilities in rural America—the region most aroused by the wave of nativist sentiment which swept the country in the years following World War I. Speaking of the role of the Ku Klux Klan during this period, Higham writes:

"Significantly, the Klan's home was not in the great cities. Its strength came chiefly from the towns, from the villages, and from the ordinarily tranquil countryside."

The prohibition movement was also predominantly rural in its origins, and like nativism served to sharpen hostility toward cities. The city saloon was in fact the bête noire of the temperance crusade, and the attack upon it was an effort at political as well as moral reform, since the saloon was regarded as the headquarters of, and the sustaining force behind, the system of boss rule in cities. "At the door of the saloon was laid the blame for political corruption. It was represented as the *sine qua non* of such political machines as Tammany Hall and the Cox Machine of Cincinnati, 'none of which could continue in existence for a day but for the liquor traffic.' "⁹ The nativist movement likewise had the purification of city politics as a central goal in its efforts to restrict the influx of immigrants, since the support of the foreign-born was widely looked upon as a major prop upon which the power of the urban political machine rested.

The fusion between the traditional agrarian dislike of cities, nativism, and the prohibition movement came to white heat in the 1920's at both the Democratic national convention in 1924 and during the presidential campaign of 1928. In each case it was the presidential candidacy of Al Smith which triggered this reaction, since Smith was simultaneously a product of the Tammany political machine in New York City, a descendant of urban Catholic immigrants, and a "wet." It would be difficult to conceive of a less prepossessing set of qualifications from the standpoint of rural America, and the campaign against Smith became at times a crusade against the city and all that it had traditionally symbolized in American politics. Witness the viewpoint of even a liberal Republican like William Allen White: "I make no claim . . . that Smith is a Tammany plug-ugly. . . . But the Tammany system goes on to-day, as it went on 100 years ago, and, indeed, as it will go on in our American cities unless Governor Smith and the sinister forces behind him are overthrown. Tammany is indeed Tammany, and Smith is its Major Prophet."¹⁰

Walter Lippmann, himself a Smith supporter, explained the resistance to his candidate in these terms: "Quite apart even from the severe opposition of the prohibitionists, the objection to Tammany, the sectional objection to New York, there is an opposition to Smith which is as authentic, and, it seems to me, as poignant as his support. It is inspired by the feeling that the clamorous life of the city should not be acknowledged as the American ideal. . . . The cities exist, but they are still felt to be alien, and in this uncertainty as to what the cities might yield up, men turn to the old scenes from which the leaders they have always trusted have come."¹¹ And in the wake of Smith's defeat, interpretations of the 1928 election echoed the same theme. An editorial in one midwestern newspaper proclaimed that "America is not yet dominated by its great cities. Control of its destinies still remains in the smaller communities and rural regions, with their traditional conservatism and solid virtues. . . . Main Street is still the principal thoroughfare of the nation."¹²

While the agrarian prejudice against cities has thus been a continuous theme in American politics since pre-Revolutionary days, the precise nature of the danger which urbanism represents to the rural mind has varied considerably over time. During some periods it has been the propertied classes in cities—the merchants, the shippers, and the bankers—whose activities helped mold rural resentment of cities. On other occasions, and particularly in recent times, it has been the submerged proletariat which has been looked upon as the chief source of danger from urban areas—the industrial hirelings, the newly arrived immigrants, the trade union members, and, in today's metropolitan city, the non-white population.

At different times, the city has thus been regarded as a center of entrenched plutocracy and as a hotbed of radical doctrines subversive of the free-enterprise system, and it has been attacked with equal vehemence by opponents of both capitalism and socialism. Perhaps there is some reconciliation of this seeming contradiction in the fact that the farmer has, depending upon his economic circumstances, tended to regard himself both as a member of the "toiling masses" and as an entrepreneur, and these varying conceptions of the agricultural role in the economy are actually embodied in two distinct national farm organizations, the Farmer's Union and the Farm Bureau Federation.

The tendency of the city to become an odious symbol in the dialogue of American politics found its most eloquent expression in the work of Josiah Strong. Strong argued that American civilization in the closing years of the nineteenth century was confronted by a variety of perils, including immigration, Romanism, intemperance, and socialism. But it was the city which Strong identified as the focal point of all these evils. In the city, he contended, "the

dangerous elements of our civilization are each multiplied and all concentered." With Strong as with other writers, the rejection of the city was—quite apart from considerations of religious and ethnic prejudice—a negative response to the industrialization which had spawned large urban centers. For it was industrialism which was regarded as the source of the worst features of urban life, especially the great extremes in wealth—"the rich are richer and the poor are poorer in the city than elsewhere"—which appeared to be so characteristic of an urban economy.[13]

THE IMPACT OF AGRARIAN THOUGHT

There is a sense in which the recurrent note of an antagonism toward the city in American political thought may be regarded as but another illustration of the lack of congruence between political doctrine and the actual course of political events. For even as the city was being treated with such persistent disdain in the formal literature of political philosophy during the nineteenth and early twentieth centuries, the general population was simultaneously voting with its feet for urban life—moving into the city in ever increasing numbers in response to economic and other incentives. The trend toward urbanization was certainly not reversed by the hostility shown the city in the American political tradition. Indeed much of this antagonism may rather be viewed as a peevish reaction against a development that could not be prevented.

And yet it cannot be assumed that the rural assault upon the city was altogether without practical effect. For while its influence cannot be precisely measured, the argument for agrarian superiority has certainly played a useful role in providing an ideological underpinning for the prevailing pattern of underrepresentation of the urban population that has characterized the legislative process in this country at both the state and national levels of government for better than half a century. The identification of farming with democracy may not have prevented the movement of population from rural areas, but it could and did provide rural politicians with a convenient line of defense against the impact this loss of population might otherwise have had upon their own power.

The extent of this urban underrepresentation has been underscored in numerous studies of state legislative apportionment in the United States. To be sure, this inequity has slowly been modified in recent years as a result of the exodus of population from city to suburb that has occurred since World War II. In many parts of the country today it is the suburbs rather than the cities which are most grossly discriminated against in terms of legislative apportionment. The movement of population thus tended to bring representation of urban centers in state legislatures into much closer accord with their proportionate share of the population even before the decision of the Supreme Court in *Baker* v. *Carr*, which provided cities with a judicial remedy against the traditional pattern of discrimination to which they have been subject. However, a statistical analysis of state legislative representation published in 1961 was still able to conclude that "as of 1960, the average value of the vote in the big city was less than half the average value of the vote in the open country, so far as electing members of the state legislature is concerned."[14]

In the debates which have taken place across the country over the reapportionment problem, the Jeffersonian theme of urban inferiority has often been sounded by groups interested in preserving the disproportionate influence of rural areas in state legislatures. One of the oddities of this system of underrepresentation is the fact that it has very often been given impressive support by urban residents themselves. This was the case in Michigan in 1953, where urban as well as rural residents voted in favor of continuing a system of legislative apportionment highly disadvantageous to the cities. Of course the city is far from unified from a political point of view, and there are, in fact, important urban groups which have long had a vested interest in urban underrepresentation. Many of the salient economic interests centered in cities —business concerns and public utilities, for example, have strong grounds for preferring a system of legislative representation which discriminates against cities simply because the pressure for regulatory legislation adverse to their interests may reasonably be expected to originate in urban rather than rural constituencies. In many parts of the country these business interests have been as much the beneficiary of the prevailing practice of underrepresenting cities in state legislatures as the farmers themselves.

However, it is by no means inconceivable that there is an element of honest conviction as well as self-interest in the apparent willingness of urban dwellers to resign themselves to a system of legislative representation in which they are discriminated against politically. In some cases this tolerance may simply reflect the sentimental tie of many urban residents with the rural milieu in which they were raised and which they left in order to seek their fortune in the city. Hofstadter suggests that such an ambivalent orientation was characteristic of earlier periods of American history: "Throughout the nineteenth century hundreds upon hundreds of thousands of farm-born youths . . . sang the praises of agriculture but eschewed farming as a vocation and sought their careers in the towns and cities."[15]

The most confirmed of all supporters of agrarian dominance may thus be the city resident with ancestral roots in the country, just as some of the most ardent support today for the policy of preserving wilderness areas in their primitive simplicity may come from eastern urbanites, transplanted from their native habitat in the West to the alien pavements of New York. And in point of fact the agrarian vision of the city as an infamous creation has always received considerable support from the romantic fascination with nature that has been an enduring tradition in American life. The fact that the city has been so aesthetically unappealing to urban nature lovers has not been the least of the political disadvantages under which it has labored.

REFORMING THE CITY

At its root, the Jeffersonian point of view was characterized by a fundamental antipathy toward cities. If it had been possible, some of the more fervent agrarians would unquestionably have prevented the development of cities altogether, so destructive to democracy did they regard the city as a political force. And in point of fact a great deal of energy was actually expended on efforts to keep people on the farm, or to launch "back-to-the-farm" movements when periods of temporary urban distress gave such proposals hope of success. From Jefferson to Bryan, the note of overt hostility toward cities in agrarian thought is clear and unmistakable.

However, in the decades following the Civil War, a critique of the city began to emerge which was quite different in character from this Jeffersonian point of view. The source of this new criticism was the movement for urban reform which sprang up in the latter part of the nineteenth century and has remained a salient force in municipal politics down to the present time. As a group, the reformers were highly critical of the political development of cities as it was taking place in the Gilded Age. Indeed, if the movement had a text, it was Bryce's celebrated dictum in the *American Commonwealth* that the "government of cities is the one conspicuous failure of the United States." But the reformer's orientation was one of redemption rather than antagonism, the cities were to be saved, to be lifted up, and, hopefully, even to become showcases of American democracy.

The rise of the reform movement was in direct response to the widespread corruption and mismanagement which characterized municipal government in the post-Civil War period. All of Jefferson's worst forebodings regarding the evil effects which cities would eventually have upon American democracy seemed amply justified by the exposures of the Tweed Ring in New York and the other scandals which plagued municipal governments in the nineteenth and early part of the twentieth centuries. As a matter of fact it would have been much easier for Jefferson to obtain evidence to support his condemnation of cities in the decades following the Civil War than it was during his own life time, when American cities were on the whole comparatively well governed.

The typical urban reformer did not, however, share Jefferson's pessimism regarding the city. From the reformer's point of view, there was no necessary reason why cities should have fallen to so low an estate. Frederic Howe, for example, saw cities as having great potential for improving American life. "Here life is full and eager," he wrote. "Here the industrial issues, that are fast becoming dominant in political life, will first. be worked out. In the city democracy is organizing. It is becoming conscious of its powers. And as time goes on, these powers will be exercised to an increasing extent for the amelioration of those conditions that modern industrial life has created."[16] The reform creed was thus resolutely optimistic in its conviction that cities could be saved, and energetic in its pursuit of the means by which this salvation could be secured.

Within the reform movement there was widespread disagreement as to why cities had fallen upon such evil days. Some placed responsibility for municipal misgovernment upon the rapid growth of cities in the United States, and the great temptation to dishonesty that was generated by the need to develop a complex system of public works and services in urban areas within a very short space of time. Others traced the ills of urban life to the swelling tide of immigration from abroad in the decades following the Civil War and the ease with which the foreign-born population allowed itself to be exploited by corrupt political machines. And there was a strong tendency to explain the problems of cities as stemming from the failure to develop either forms of

government suitable for urban areas, or a tradition of administrative expertise in the handling of municipal affairs.

But there was also a deep conviction that the corruption of urban politics reflected a very fundamental malaise in American life, the growth of a commercial spirit and a weakening in the moral fiber of the population that was endemic in society and the economy as well as government. "The boss is not a political, he is an American institution," wrote Lincoln Steffens, and this point of view was widely shared. What was needed from the reformer's perspective was a moral regeneration of American life—a "great awakening" which would cleanse and purify not only local but national politics as well, since the movement for urban reform was only part of a much larger reform effort directed at uplifting the tone of public life in every sector of the nation's business, including the practices of private institutions where they impinged on the public interest. Symbolic of this evangelical zeal for moral improvement was the fact that a number of Protestant clergymen associated themselves with the movement for municipal reform and took a prominent part in its activities. Like abolition before it, urban reform was a moral crusade.

Moreover, in its heyday, the boss system represented an effort to govern the city through the methods of politics alone. As a result, early efforts at reform tended to place almost exclusive emphasis upon the importance of competent administration to the successful functioning of city government. In reaction against the more discreditable features of machine politics, efforts were made to "depoliticize" city government and to augment the role of the impartial expert through civil service reform, the city manager plan, and other devices. Subject as it was to simultaneous influence by doctrines of moralism and scientific management, the movement for urban reform thus sought to make city government as clean as the church and as efficient as business.

At no time did reformers lose hope that substantial improvement could be effected in the government of American cities. A great deal of this optimism was based on their knowledge of the successful operation of European cities and their conviction that American municipalities could profitably be modeled after their European counterparts. *Century Magazine* stated its belief that "we can hope for no municipal reform which shall be radical and lasting till we change our leadership to the European models." "In a score of different directions," wrote Josiah Quincy while serving as mayor of Boston, "the interests of the average citizen are better and more fully cared for, his wants more fully met, in the great city of Europe than in that of America." While recognizing the difficulty of transplanting institutions from one country to another, Richard T. Ely nevertheless argued that "what is good for Berlin is likely to be good for New York, and what answers the needs of Paris will be likely to supply a want in Chicago."[17] But there was often some discomfort attached to unfavorable comparisons of American cities with Continental cities which were political subdivisions of regimes Americans looked upon as reactionary or despotic. English cities were, therefore, the object of more unqualified admiration.

Certainly there was no doubt in the reform mind regarding the urgency of doing something to elevate urban politics, lest the corrupt city eventually corrupt the nation. Elihu Root, for example, warned his Republican colleagues that the malodorous GOP organization in Philadelphia was a source of infection in their party that could not be localized. "It is my profound conviction," he declared, "that a determined effort is necessary to save national parties from the demoralization inevitably consequent upon municipal spoliation, and, as a Republican, zealous for the welfare and reputation of my party, I advocate the foundation of a non-partisan civil movement." Unless the reform of urban politics is successful, Josiah Strong asserted, "the boss will certainly rule the city when the city rules the nation," and Strong quoted Wendell Phillips as prophesying that "the time will come when our cities will strain our institutions as slavery never did."[18]

As noted earlier, the reform perspective differed sharply from the traditional agrarian outlook inasmuch as it sought to face and solve the problems presented by the city rather than turning away in a hostile rejection of the trend toward urbanization. But it should also be remembered that much of the reform argument for the city was essentially apologetic or defensive in tone. It was conceded that the city had fallen to a very low estate politically, and the claim was simply made that the spirit and practice of urban government could —with effort—be improved. Moreover, many of the reformers were gifted publicists, and their exposures of graft and corruption in urban government, while motivated by the desire to eliminate these conditions, had also the effect of reinforcing the rural image of the city as an iniquitous environment in which the ideals of American democracy were being betrayed. In essence the reform defense of cities was based on their potentialities, not their achievements.

URBANISM AND AMERICAN DEMOCRACY

Insofar as its political reputation is concerned, the city was thus only slightly better served by reformers sympathetic to it than it was by the agrarians who looked upon it as the invariable source of political corruption. And even today, the city has still to find its philosophical protagonist, at least in the area of political thought. This is true in spite of the fact that there is an impressive amount of evidence which points to the conclusion that it is with urban America that the flowering of democracy in this country can be most clearly identified. The place of the city in the American experience has in fact been much more honorific than its position in American thought.

From a historical perspective, Arthur Schlesinger points out that it was the cities of the East which led the way in the movement for national independence which culminated in the American revolution. "Throughout the decade of controversy the seaports set the pace of resistance, supplying most of the militant leaders, conducting turbulent demonstrations at every crisis, and mobilizing farmer support when possible." In a similar vein he underlies the prominent role played by the cities in the struggle to strengthen democracy once it had been established in this country: "The first great victory for freedom of press was won by a Philadelphia lawyer defending a New York editor. . . . Faced by interstate trade restrictions, stay laws and growing social turmoil, the urban business and creditor classes feared for their future welfare and the

sanctity of property rights. The framing and ratification of the Constitution represented in considerable degree their triumph over the debtor groups and small farmers of the interior."[19]

Recent research in the general area of political behavior has also tended to refute the assumption that there is any necessary antipathy between the growth of cities and the vitality of the democratic process. In terms of some of the more obvious yardsticks that might be used to measure commitment to the norms of democracy, the urban citizen very often shows up much better than his rural counterpart. This is true, for example, with respect to two of the central attributes of democratic citizenship, an acceptance of the right of minorities to dissent from majority opinion, and an interest in the affairs of government as evidenced by participation in elections.

In a landmark study of civil liberties in the United States published in 1954, Samuel Stouffer found that rural residents were uniformly less tolerant of deviant minorities than urbanites. This rural attitude was partially explainable in terms of the operation of factors other than place of residence, especially the lower level of education which prevails in the countryside, but there nevertheless remained a residue of intolerance that was clearly associated with living in the country. As Stouffer put it:

Rural people in every region are less likely to be tolerant of non-conformists than city people, even when we compare urban and rural people with the same amount of schooling. There is something about life in a small community that makes it less hospitable to divergent opinions than is the case in our urban centers. In the anonymity of city life it is much easier for deviant behavior to flourish than in the goldfish bowl of a small community. In the large community there are sometimes so many gold-fish that nobody bothers to look at them. In the small town a lone exotic specimen can be viewed with careful critical, and occasionally devastating attention.[20]

In support of his findings, Stouffer also cites earlier studies of the degree of tolerance which prevails in various sectors of the community, including a Gallup poll conducted in 1940 which showed rural residents as being much less willing than urban dwellers to see a Catholic elected President, and a Roper study in 1947 which revealed that urbanites were far more tolerant than their rural brethren of that most unpopular minority in recent times—members of the Communist party.

Of course the fact that city people generally exhibit so much more tolerance of nonconformity than rural residents must simultaneously be weighed against the fact that cities have been quite receptive to the appeal of totalitarian ideologies, or at least have been the areas from which Communist and Fascist political groups have traditionally recruited most of their active members in this country. If the greatest threat to civil liberties is judged to come from the small ideological groups dedicated to their destruction, then the city may well be looked upon as a greater source of peril to minority rights than the country. But if the chief danger to civil liberties is rather seen as a weakening of commitment on the part of the mass of citizens to their preservation, then it is from rural America that the right to dissent has been chiefly endangered in modern times.

As far as political participation is concerned, Robert E. Lane concluded after a comprehensive survey of the literature of political behavior that residents of large cities have a much better record in this respect than citizens living in rural areas. He finds that residents of larger cities "participate in elections more than those in smaller cities" and that inhabitants of smaller cities are "more likely to vote than residents of rural areas." According to Lane, this difference in turnout mainly reflects the heightened degree of political tension in the more densely populated parts of the country. The group conflict engendered by class and ethnic rivalries in urban centers has the effect of stimulating political activity. But a variety of other factors also plays a role here, including the greater exposure of the urban citizen to stimuli from the mass media, which helps to sharpen political awareness and a sense of civic obligation in cities.

The extent to which citizens participate in politics is also related to their sense of political efficacy—the degree to which they believe such activity will have meaningful results. In this respect also Lane finds that urban citizens show up much better than rural residents: "those living in metropolitan centers have, in general, a higher sense of political efficacy than those in rural or small town areas. Perhaps because of the greater politicalization of the urbanites, their exposure to more political news and comment, their more salient class and ethnic cleavages, and their higher educational level, they are led to make politics a more significant part of their lives."[21]

It has also been suggested that urbanization has promoted the development of a two-party system in the United States, thus invigorating political discussion and activity in all parts of the country. The growth of urban population is, for example, sometimes credited with the fact that presidential elections are now closely contested in virtually all the states. However, the actual impact of urbanization upon party competition in this country is far from clear. While some studies of state politics show a correlation between the extent of urbanization and the strength of party competition, other investigations indicate that there may well be a negative relationship between the two phenomena. Certainly, there is no disputing the fact that many of the big cities in this country have become one-party enclaves.

But if such empirical evidence as exists does not always support the conclusion that democracy is inevitably strengthened by the advent of urbanization, it certainly stands in flat contradiction to the conventional agrarian assumption that rural areas are necessarily the backbone of a democratic society. Whether this evidence will seriously undermine the Jeffersonian mystique remains, however, to be seen. The force of tradition being what it is, Americans may, in the future as in the past, continue to look for the meaning of their democratic experience in the prairies rather than on the pavements. This tendency is as pronounced in the twentieth as it was in the nineteenth century: "Somewhere in our agricultural past there lie the roots of Americanism. What we are in body and spirit is not to be discovered growing embryonically in any early city; its beginnings are to be found on the homestead or in the village, and only there."[22]

NOTES

* This study was undertaken under a grant from the Rockefeller Foundation, for which the author wishes to make grateful acknowledgment.
1. A. Whitney Griswold, *Farming and Democracy* (New York, 1948), p. 19. See also Richard Hofstadter, *The Age of Reform* (New York, 1960),
pp. 23-36, and Henry Nash Smith, *Virgin Land* (New York, 1959), pp. 138-50.
2. The quotations from Jefferson are from the *Writings of Thomas Jefferson* (Washington, D.C., 1903), II, 229-30, and X, 173.
3. Morton and Lucia White, *The Intellectual versus the City* (Cambridge, Mass., 1962), pp. 17-19.
4. Madison's comment is found in *The Writings of James Madison*, ed. Gaillard Hunt (New York, 1906), VI, 96-98, while the statement by Adams appears in *The Works of John Adams* (Boston, 1852), VII, 47.
5. See Marvin Meyers, *The Jacksonian Persuasion* (New York, 1960), p. 240.
6. Arthur M. Schlesinger, Jr., *The Age of Jackson* (Boston, 1946), p. 310, n. 11.
7. George Fitzhugh, *Sociology for the South* (Richmond, Va., 1854), p. 139. However, there were southern writers who recognized that their region was greatly weakened by its failure to develop the commercial civilization associated with cities (see H. R. Helper, *The Impending Crisis of the South* [1860], esp. pp. 331-59). And Fitzhugh himself explicitly rejected the Jeffersonian prejudice in favor of an exclusively agricultural society. "Farming is the recreation of great men, the proper pursuit of dull men," he stated. "Let the ambitious South cultivate, not spurn the mechanic arts" (*op. cit.*, pp. 156, 160).
8. See Paul W. Glad, *The Trumpet Soundeth* (Lincoln, Neb., 1960), p. 112. When the returns from the election of 1896 were in, they showed the core of Bryan's electoral strength as lying in the rural Midwest and mountain regions. However, there were some states, notably in New England, where Bryan received more support in urban than he did in rural areas (see William Diamond, "Urban and Rural Voting in 1896," *American Historical Review*, XLVI (January, 1941), 281-305.
9. Peter Odegard, *Pressure Politics: The Story of the Anti-Saloon League* (New York, 1928), p. 44.
10. As quoted in Edmund A. Moore, *A Catholic Runs for President* (New York, 1956), p. 133.
11. Walter Lippmann, *Men of Destiny* (New York, 1927), p. 8.
12. Quoted in Roy V. Peel and Thomas C. Donnelly, *The 1928 Campaign: An Analysis* (New York, 1931), p. 121.
13. See Josiah Strong, *Our Country* (New York, 1885), pp. 133, 130.
14. Paul T. David and Ralph Eisenberg, *Devaluation of the Urban and Suburban Vote* (Charlottesville, Va., 1961), p. 10.
15. Richard Hofstadter, *Age of Reform* (New York, 1960), pp. 31-32.
16. Frederick C. Howe, *The City: The Hope of Democracy* (New York, 1905), pp. 7-8.
17. "An Object Lesson in Municipal Government," *Century Magazine*, XXXIX (March, 1890), 792; Josiah Quincy, "The Development of American Cities," *Arena*, XVII (March, 1897), p. 529; and Richard T. Ely, "Model Towns," *Christian Union*, November 27, 1890.

18. See Robert Treat Paine, "The Elimination of National Party Designations from Municipal Ballots," in *Proceedings* of the Fifteenth Annual Meeting of the National Municipal League, 1909, p. 292; and Josiah Strong, *The Twentieth Century City* (New York, 1898), pp. 101-2.

19. Arthur M. Schlesinger, *Paths to the Present* (New York, 1949), pp. 213, 214, 215.

20. *Communism, Conformity, and Civil Liberties* (New York, 1955), p. 130.

21. Robert E. Lane, *Political Life* (Glencoe, Ill., 1959), pp. 265, 151-52.

22. Harry J. Carman and Rexford G. Tugwell, "The Significance of American Agricultural History," *Agricultural History*, XII (April, 1938), 100.

Some Varieties of American Urban Symbolism

ANSELM L. STRAUSS

Before we examine how particular populations have expressed themselves about American urbanization, it will be useful to scrutinize some persistent antitheses in American life. Those controversies—which amount to basic ambiguities of American values—involve the conflicts of sectionalism versus national centralization, of ruralism versus urbanism, of cosmopolitanism versus specialization, and of traditionalism versus modernism. Instead of discussing those antitheses and ambiguities abstractly, we shall relate them to the whole subject of American city symbolism. . . . By seeing first some of the larger issues of American valuation as they pertain to our cities, we shall better be able to understand the predominant urban symbolism of particular regions and populations.

A host of American cities, despite all differences in size, location, or composition, continually try to validate the claims that they are typical, authentic American communities. They balance

what they are and what they feel they stand for against a tacitly accepted formula of American values and national purposes. But the facts and symbols of urban life become interchangeable in the course of argument, become confused in meeting the difficulties of expressing a city's hopes and achievements in a straightforward definitive fashion. They become confused, too, because of certain ambiguities in what may be assumed to be *the* American way of life.

This ambiguity of American urbanity and American values is significantly reflected in a lively contention over which city best deserves the title of "most American." The admirers of Chicago, New York, Kansas City, and Detroit, at least, claim honors for the city of their choice. Such claims are not new. As far back at least at 1851, a Baltimorian reassured a local audience that Baltimore "may be said to be an epitome of the nation itself";[1] and upon occasion critics of certain American values may point to

From Anselm L. Strauss, *Images of the American City* (New York: The Free Press, 1961), pp. 104-23, 270-71. Copyright © 1961 by the Free Press, a Corporation. Reprinted by permission of the publisher. Anselm L. Strauss is Professor of Sociology at the University of California, San Francisco, Medical Center.

one of these cities as a repulsive exemplar of those values. But a uniform, homogeneous American culture spread evenly throughout the nation would allow no city to claim more Americanness than was possessed by other cities; nor could any then base its claim upon a different set of values.

As long ago as 1891, de Rousiers described Chicago as the most American city, remarking that "It is here, indeed, that the American 'go ahead,' the idea of always going forward . . . attains its maximum intensity."[2] Some fifty-five years later, John Gunther writes that Chicago's "impact is overwhelmingly that of the United States, and it gives above all the sense that America and the Middle West are beating upon it from all sides."[3] In other words, he is stressing less its "striving" than its central position. A thousand miles away, the admirers of New York City stress rather different values. They assert that New York represents the nation at its most civilized and most creative; that it dominates the nation in every way; and that more different kinds of Americans, drawn from more regions, live in New York than in any other metropolis.[4] The proponents of Kansas City dwell upon still different aspects of American culture; George S. Perry who described that city for the *Saturday Evening Post*'s readers, saw it this way:

Kansas City is a kind of interior American crossroads and melting pot where the Southerner, the Northerner, the Easterner and the Westerner meet and become plain John American, with America unfolding . . . "in oceans of glory" in every direction. It got its start on the riches of Boston banks and Western lands and Northern furs. It is not only America's approximate geographical heart, but the center of gravity for her taste and emotion. The soap opera, movie or national magazine that doesn't "take" in Kansas City won't live long in the nation.[5]

Those who would give Detroit the honor of "most American," ignore the virtues of being of pioneer and dead-center America, and claim that Detroit best represents the spirit of modern twentieth-century America, exemplified in the city's superb system of mass production, in its drive, energy, purpose, and fusion of men and machines.[6] Pittsburgh's admirers claim similar industrial virtues for their city.[7] Indeed, a city need not even be among the largest to claim for itself, or to be proclaimed, the most typical of America. For instance:

It is a truism to say that Tulsa is the most American of American cities. All the forces that have gone into the making of a Republic have been intensified there. The successive stages through which the country as a whole has passed during three hundred years—Indian occupation, ranching, pioneering, industrial development . . . have been telescoped within the single lifetime of some of the older Tulsans. The result has been the quintessence of Americanism—its violence and strength, its buoyant optimism, its uncalculating generosity, its bumptious independence.[8]

The argument that one city best typifies America is couched in a standardized "logical" form: from a number of desirable attributes, certain ones are selected for emphasis while the remainder are ignored; and it is assumed or asserted that these selected attributes are possessed more abundantly by the admired city. In this way, many facets of American life are overlooked or given secondary status. The argument does not turn upon fact but upon value. Thus, if one values sheer quantity, then New York has most of everything; if one extolls the Midwest as the geographic heart of America and as the possessor of the most widespread and average national values, then he will deny priority to New York. In making such evaluations of their cities, Americans assess the nation's cultural assets and identify themselves with its history and destiny. When they represent a city as most American, they are conceiving it not only as unique and matchless but as the symbolic representative of esteemed national values.

Such great distinction can be claimed for few American cities; hence the citizens of the remaining urban centers must be content with a lesser assertion: namely, that their particular city represents at least one—and probably more —important aspects of American life. Thus, Iowa cities are conceived of as good places to live in because they appear to be friendly, peaceful, prosperous agricultural towns; and Fort Worth, Texas, surrounded by cattlemen's country, epitomizes the culture of that region. Such cities are parts of many Americas. The country is vast, its aspects staggeringly varied. Cities need not compete to share the nation's glory, they have only to point to those of their features wherein they typify some aspect, or aspects, of the entire American way of life.

Yet these aspects are not entirely congruent, in fact or in value. One of the most persistent clashes of value on the American scene has long been embodied in the sentimental preference of a rural existence to a thoroughly urban one. When Jefferson spoke of the danger of an American metropolitanism fated perhaps to destroy the sturdy virtues of a predominantly agricultural society, he was but expressing a dicotomy in American thought that persists to this day. Despite the continuous trend toward urbanization, our rural heritage remains potent, entering into American thought and action in increasingly subtle ways.

Eighteenth-century seaboard agriculture was not what farming became on the prairie a century later, nor what it is today in an era of large-scale mechanization. The men who worked the American soil and the life-styles that they evolved have varied greatly in place and time. Yet an American mythology grew up by which it was maintained that agricultural pursuits necessarily bred a certain kind of man. This agrarian mythology is and was a complex set of beliefs consisting of many elements, some of which developed from the several kinds of frontier conditions and others of which evolved after the Civil War in opposition to the dreadful urban conditions. The spirit of this agrarian ideology can be suggested by the following few sentences.

Rural life is slow and unhurried. Men lead natural, rich lives. People are friendly and their relationships are informal, yet orderly. The agricultural population is homogeneous in custom and culture, if not in racial stock. The round of existence is stable and the community is religious, moral, honest. Men are, thus, not motivated by purely individualistic impulses. If all farmers do not love one another, at least they understand each other and do not manipulate and exploit each other as do city dwellers. The very physical surroundings are healthy, home-like, restful, not dense with population. Not the least: the rural man is a sturdy democrat, his convictions nourished by his contact with nature itself and with the equalitarian discussion held around the crackerbarrel and in the meeting house.[9]

These conceptions are linked by affect rather than by logic. They evolved under considerably different historical circumstances, some during the development of the New England township, some when the prairie was settled, others while western farmers were castigating the railroad kings, and yet others at a time when rural migrants to cities became demoralized by conditions there. Although the country-city dichotomy has been with us for many generations, the content of the argument on either side has varied from decade to decade—as both cities and countrysides became transformed. Ideas die hard: in the formation of our rural mythology, old ideas accrued to new ones instead of disappearing entirely, despite their incongruence with fact and with each other. Probably no single rural community has ever stressed equally all elements of the entire ideological complex, for its very ambiguity allows its use as an effective resource. The town can use it as well as the village; and the small city can boast of home-like surroundings and friendly atmosphere, in an invidious contrast with the larger urban centers.

Sizeable cities can also be designated as outright embodiments of rural values—as when the citizens of Des Moines aver direct kinship with soil and farm; and in so doing, they may symbolically act in ways more farmlike than the equally business oriented farmer. The residents of most cities, perhaps, signify their association with sentimental rurality more obliquely, not always recognizing the nature of that feeling of kinship. Cities are referred to by their residents as "The City of Flowers," "The City of Trees," "The City of Homes." They draw upon the rich stock of rural imagery without directly stating their debt. Large cities as they grow to great size abandon such nicknames, which no longer seem to represent what the city has become, but may emphasize in cu-

riously subtle ways that their styles of urban life also partake of America's revered earlier heritage. Chicago—once called "The City of Gardens"—still boasts that it is the city of the prairie, and lays claim to a characteristic friendliness and informality that mark it off from, say, New York or Boston. (As George Perry says, "Chicago is a thousand times more relaxed, less 'mannered' than New York.")[10]

Like the smaller towns, the larger cities may stress one or more of the varied rural themes, thereby cashing in on a much wider ideological complex. The very statement that one's city is a "city of gardens" (albeit gardening is a far cry from farming), arouses connotations smacking of outdoor life, suggestions of qualities bred in close contact with the soil, of urbanities living a life of relaxation rather than of frantic pursuit of excessive monetary gain. The visitor to a city sometimes remarks, also, upon certain paradoxes because, while he notices that the place is marked only by a limited number of rural characteristics, he feels that these are among its important features. What he is really puzzling over is that all rural qualities are supposed to hang together; whereas in this particular city, surprisingly enough, they do not. The perception of such paradoxes is furthered by any obvious juxtaposition of rural and urban characteristics: a city nestled among beautiful mountains but marked by a high rate of crime and by horrendous slums, or a large urban center characterized by a noticeably leisured pace of life.[11] Thus about Portland, Oregon, Richard Neuberger remarks: "Torn between her peaceful past and a brawling future as the Pittsburgh of the West, Portland just can't make up her mind. . . . As a result of this strange ambivalence, Portland is a combination of the rustic and the metropolitan."[11] Similarly, Elsie Morrow writes of Springfield, Illinois, that, "At best, Springfield is a very typical American city, with a special flavor and pleasantness. At worst it is a town which has grown old without ever having grown up. It is something between a backward country settlement and a cosmopolis."[12]

The obverse of such pleasantly toned rural mythology, of course, is an affectively linked set of vices: cities are locales of demoralization, discomfort, standardization, artificiality, vulgar materialism, dishonesty, and so on through a richly invidious lexicon. But the rural-urban dichotomy allows black to be called white, and white, black. City dwellers have long characterized their cities as places of progress, opportunity, and excitement, the very image of civilization in contrast to countryside, small town, small city, in contrast, even, to those larger cities which appear provincial. Small cities and even villages have, in turn, affirmed that they participate in an urbane and urban civilization. Anyone who peruses popular urban histories will notice how very sensitive are their authors about the artistic, musical, and literary "culture" of their towns; they carefully list all "cultural" accomplishments and proclaim the progressiveness of their towns by example and assertion. A town which is not civilized, not progressive, not exciting would seem to have a narrow range of options; its citizens must balance its slight amount of urbanity with presumed rural virtues, or must assert disinterest in (un-American) urban characteristics; or, more subtly, must ignore their place in the backwash of American urbanization and remain content to be where they are.

Whatever else may be true of American cities, they are certainly a most varied lot, being neither all cosmopolitan nor all homespun. Nonetheless, particular cities become symbolized as embodiments of different facets of a cheerfully ambiguous rural-urban dichotomy. Thus, emerging styles of urban life receive relatively easy explanation or rationalization. It is as if people were to say: "We are a city like this because we grew up on the prairie, or because we are surrounded by farms, or because our main businesses were founded by farm boys, or because we have no great influx of alien peoples." Likewise, each different population within a single city can rationalize its differential mode of living by appealing to one mythology or another—or to elements of both. Moreover, a city seemingly fated by geographical position and history to be of a certain kind can be envisioned as another kind, and can be directed toward that image by strong interest groups which draw upon different sets of sustaining beliefs. Any city which unquestionably is undergoing change from a commercial to a manufacturing center, or from an agricultural town to a distributing mart, can likewise find ready interpretations to account for otherwise baffling changes in its social characteristics. All such explanations, whether vigorously contested or merely assumed, are answers to that important query: what is the meaning of this city, what kind of a place is it?

The rural-versus-urban conflict that marks American life is crosscut by another ambiguity which turns on a contrast between tradition and modernity. City adherents sometimes stress a lengthy history or a blessedly short one. Votaries of a city with a long history will tend to link its origins with those of the nation itself. Being old—the ideology runs—a long established city is less likely to be crude, vulgar, rough and ready; hence it will be more civilized, more civic-minded, more settled; its citizens will be more stable, have deeper personal and familial roots in the community; its population will be mostly native to it and its immigrants well assimilated; hence, fewer men will have been attracted there merely for opportunistic reasons. The older cities will have more cultivation of leisure, greater delicacy of human relations, and will pay more attention to matters which make for "taste" and "civilization."[13]

But the citizens of other American cities extoll the contrary virtues of youth and scant tradition. They regard their cities as relatively untrammeled by custom and convention. Just because their cities have not had time to settle down, they are supposed not to have developed rigid stances toward handling problems; they are therefore progressive and profoundly democratic, since men have fought their way to success there by their own honest efforts, benefiting neither from hereditary position nor from an elite upbringing. In these younger cities, it is believed that the lines between social classes have not yet grown into impermeable barriers; indeed, they may be denied to exist at all. A young city is conceived of as a place of freedom in still another sense. Its citizens have immigrated there of their own free will because they imagined it to be a place of considerable opportunity. Because the young community permits experimentation and the pursuit of opportunity, it is seen as an exciting place, at least more interesting than the stodgier older cities. Although the latter,

by reason of their earlier origins, may perhaps rightfully claim superiority in the arts of civilization—so the argument runs—the more recently founded communities will soon overtake or surpass them; indeed the cosmopolitanism of the older cities may only, in some instances, be a form of decadance.

Ardent speakers for both younger and older cities stress only certain elements in the total available vocabularies; they glory now in a town's experimental attitude, now in its famous traditional styles of cooking; they even combine the attributes of age and youth. Such symbolization occurs without strict regard for fact, since cities, as we have seen, may be represented as rather old when they are actually quite young, and cities of similar age may be conceived of in very different temporal terms.

Tradition and history are often given a peculiar reverse twist, so that certain eastern coastal cities are considered not to have important American qualities, while certain western centers are assigned crucial roles in the making of the nation. It is asserted or implied that there are histories and histories; but the basic history of the country concerns the clearing of the forests and settling of the frontier. The pioneer romance thus crowds out the colonial. Any city whose citizens did not participate in the pushing back of the frontier cannot, therefore, possibly possess the mystical qualities stemming from that glorious enterprise.

But the frontier is a series of conceptions, not merely a set of facts. These conceptions are linked with various rural and urban virtues, with different periods of our history, and with particular American regions as well. In those sections of the country where the frontier as a geographic reality has but recently disappeared, the frontier as a concept refers more to the mining camp and the railroad center than to pioneer agricultural settlements. The frontier was a rough and tough place, where men were men and the hardiest won out. Some of the same associations remain coupled in midwestern remembrances because of the region's boomtown tradition and because of the predominant romance of life on the open prairie. The Midwest is more than the geographic heart of the continent; many believe it to be at the core of what *is* America. Back east, the concept of the frontier has been sufficiently misted over by time so that it is referred to more obliquely ("the founders," "the settlers"), but these terms also carry a considerable charge of regional passion.

The frontier, as an idea, has also broken loose from any regional anchoring; it can be applied to endeavors in industrial, artistic, intellectual, and other non-geographic fields. Consequently, cities building upon the cumulative connotations of the frontier image can be thought of as commercial and industrial pioneers. A great metropolis like New York can strike its admirers as *the* "moving frontier" of the entire American economy and of the nation's civilization. The frontier concept allows some cities to be called currently progressive and others to be linked with the nation's slightly older history; while it may be used with relation to some cities so that it cuts both ways. An example is John Bowman's address to his fellow citizens of the Pittsburgh Chamber of Commerce, in which he reminded them of the city's great pioneer tradition:

But these qualities in men and women, you say, flared up generally among the pioneers of the time. . . . These qualities, however, did not flare up and stay flared up in any other community for so long a period nor did they reach so intense a glow as they did in Pittsburgh.

He goes on to claim that, "The significant fact now is that Pittsburgh through nearly a hundred years developed a new way of thinking, a new way of acting. These new ways became first nature in the people." And then, by simple transmutation, he views these ways as creative acts, and Pittsburgh's creativeness "was the application of creative ability to industry." This was its great contribution to Pittsburgh. And of course, "the old creativeness, developed here through a long period, is still in Pittsburgh."[14]

But when a city settles down, this turn of events is likely to be greeted by criticism—criticism mixed, however, with expressions of nostalgia and joy over the community's improvements. The citizens may perceive that certain civic characteristics derive from the original pioneer spirit which founded and built the town, however astonished the original settlers might be if they could witness the town's transformation.[15]

When residents identify a city with different rural or urban conceptions and with different kinds of romantic histories, they may also identify it with reference to another persistent American dichotomy: regionalism versus national integration. Since our cities are so widely scattered on such different landscapes, it is difficult not to associate a city with its region. Its domestic architecture, the clothing, speech, and action of some of its residents all proclaim it— and the people themselves sometimes proclaim it with belligerence. As is usual with cultural antinomies, men find ample room for ambiguity and for subtle argument. Two cities of the same region may vie for regional supremacy on symbolic as well as economic grounds. Each will claim to represent the region better; each will stress somewhat different areal attributes. Since no region is entirely homogeneous—if only because of its competing urban centers —there is plenty of room for dispute. In a rapidly changing region, such as the "New South," there may be even less agreement unless the resources of ambiguity are utilized in a way such that one city claims to represent the Old South, while the other is quite content to represent the New South (although a city like Charleston can claim to represent both).[16] A region is usually not exactly coterminous with a state; therefore, a city such as Biloxi, Mississippi, can affirm kinship with New Orleans and with bayou culture rather than with the rest of Mississippi.

Some cities, by virtue of the populations which founded them or immigrated to them later, are considered to be less typical of their regions than are their neighbors; these may compensate by claiming other important American values. Conversely, however, a city may receive great waves of foreign immigrants without serious impairment to its position as a regional standard bearer. A few cities are so new that they and their residents share little in common with the rest of the region, in history or in taste, and so are constrained to build some sort of urban history, however flimsy, or to engage in other ceremonial gestures to reaffirm their association with their region. An interesting case is Kingsport, Tennessee, a small city planned and founded by eastern bankers who were attracted to the site by abundant, cheap white labor.

Kingsport's historian, writing when the city was only eleven years old, nevertheless argues that had the village but known it, it "was sleeping only that it might awake into a beautiful prosperous city" for "the moral and mental fibre of the sturdy, resourceful people of the Kingsport community required two centuries in the making." While it "is true that the new city was incorporated and began its municipal life only eleven years ago . . . back of all this, unknown to many of the citizens themselves perhaps, is a setting which would be a pride to any of the oldest cities in the country."[17]

A few urban centers gladly spurn extensive regional affiliation. Their residents prefer to think of them as supra-national, even as "world cities," underline the city's role in the national economy, and flaunt its traits of national leadership, sophistication, cosmopolitanism, size, and other symbols of national and international placement. Some sense of the overwhelming impact of a world city is suggested by the breathless and inadequate ways its admirers attempt to sum it up. Thus, John Gunther, who first compares Chicago (the typical American city) with New York (the world city), writes that Chicago is "the greatest and most typically American of all cities. New York is bigger and more spectacular and can outmatch it in other superlatives, but it is a 'world' city, more European in some respects than American." Some pages later he writes that

now we come to New York City, the incomparable, the brilliant star city of cities, the forty-ninth state, a law unto itself, the Cyclopean paradox, the inferno with no out-of-bounds, the supreme expression of both the miseries and the splendors of contemporary civilization. . . . New York is at once the climactic synthesis of America, and yet the negation of America in that it has so many characteristics called un-American.[18]

Paul Crowell and A. H. Raskin merely say: "New York is not a city. It is a thousand cities, each with its own ninety-nine square miles."[19]

Many citizens of "world cities" make denigrating gestures toward more regionally inclined centers. They refer to those centers as less important, small-townish, hick towns, cow towns, and use other similar epithets. Consequently, these latter places may regard the more worldly centers with a suspicion that gains strength from the historic antagonism between countryside and city as well as from a regional passion against national centralization. However, no single city claims to be a national, or world, city in exactly the same way as any other does; and always regional traits are coupled with non-regional ones (even by residents of New York City).

Sectionalism is closely allied with economic specialization inasmuch as the various continental areas function differently in our national economy. Cities tend to become known for the industries, commercial enterprises, and services that are typical of the surrounding area. National cities, of course, have more varied functions; hence when New York City residents insist that it has "everything," this means more than that it performs all the important economic functions. The full significance of the claim is that all (the best—and possibly the worst) styles of life can be found in New York. But the Florida resort city, the Illinois farm city, or the New England manufacturing town can all be conceived of by their residents as simultaneously truly regional and truly American because what they manufacture or trade or service is necessary to the nation.

Some products or services which are limited to certain cities are of sufficient national importance that those cities come to represent some particular facet of America: Pittsburgh and Detroit come readily to mind. Although not all specializations are equally praiseworthy, or even savory, nevertheless observers of such cities as Reno and Calumet City can find ample justification for believing that sex, sin, and gambling are as much a part of American life as are automobiles or opera; and Pittsburgh residents could, until recently, declare that smoke-filled air and labor troubles were the inevitable accompaniment of heavy industrialization. As George S. Perry has phrased it:

Certainly Reno is an actual and highly special aspect of American life, as much as Monte Carlo is a part of European life. . . . Many Nevadans . . . referring both to the tourist business brought in and the large amount of tax load that gambling pays . . . remark simply: "You don't shoot Santa Claus." . . . For in the American mind, Reno remains to gambling and divorces what Pittsburgh means to steel and Hollywood to movies.[20]

Cities whose range of economic function is exceedingly narrow seem frequently to lack variety of social style and suffer from deficiencies in "culture" and other civic virtues esteemed in most towns. Hence residents from other cities may make them the butts of jibes and the objects of social criticism. In the main, the outsider misses the mark for, like physicians whose identities have grown up around the practice of specific medical skills or about the "ownership" of specific bodily areas, the specialized city tends to glorify its command over special skills and resources. Two spokesmen for a pair of our most specialized cities link special skills with the spirit of America. The first is Malcolm Bingay, writing in *Detroit Is My Home Town:*

This fluidity of life, this refusal to "jell" or ever to grow old helps to explain why everything that is right or wrong which happens to our nation seems to break here first. It is that very spirit which first conceived the idea of throwing away millions upon millions of dollars of machinery as obsolete to make way for better machinery and greater speed to meet competition. This horror of obsolescence is the "Americanism" which permitted us to triumph in two great wars. . . . Other countries remained static in the sense that while they understood our standardization of parts—to a degree—they never did catch the imponderable elements of mass production in which there is nothing permanent but change.[21]

The second spokesman is Carl Crow, who, in *The City of Flint*, writes:

The history of the interesting and dynamic city of Flint has been worth recording because it is more than the chronical of an individual city. It epitomizes the history of America . . . America is a story of the industrial development which has brought us such a high standard of living.[22]

Citizens who are intensely interested in the furtherance of the arts congregate in groups and associations that many other citizens believe are less central to the life of the community than other more vigorous business, social, and cultural institutions representing the interests of the town's more typical citizens. Sometimes cultural barrenness is excused in terms of the city's symbolic age. Given sufficient time, some say, the city will grow up, develop a rich cultural life, and take its place among the civilized cities of its size—and, one might add, among some cities a tithe of its size. The residents of Chicago sometimes use this strategy to console them-

selves or to ward off attack, and it is probably commonly used in other cities. Here is an instance from Birmingham, Alabama:

Birmingham somehow, for all her pride in the great labors which converted a cornfield into a great metropolis in little more than the span of one man's life, Birmingham is haunted by a sense of promise unfulfilled. Her more philosophic citizens are obsessed with this thought. They brood and ponder over it, and, searching their souls and the city's history, constantly seek the reason why. They come up with many answers. One is the obvious one of her youth. . . . Another answer is . . . Birmingham is a working town. . . . Painting pictures and composing music and writing books—even the widespread appreciation of those things—all rather come with time.[23]

When a specialized city becomes economically diversified, and creates or draws to it new populations with new tastes, the imagery associated with it changes radically. It remains no longer merely a steel city, a rubber town, or an agricultural community, but is represented widely as a more cosmopolitan center.

Although every city within the United States is American in a factual sense, some cities are in some other sense denied that status from time to time. Many visitors to the Southwest would agree with John Gunther that there one may feel almost as if he is leaving the United States. ("The first thing I thought was, 'Can this possibly be North America?' ")[24] But that reaction is not aroused solely by regional geography or by ethnic culture, for cities may be symbolically driven off the American landscape when they offend deeply felt standards of propriety. One critic of Pittsburgh some years ago bitterly characterized it as "A city inherited from the Middle Ages," and only partly admitted that it was one of us.[25] Reno is frequently a target for obloquy: a *Reader's Digest* article titled "Reno. Parasite on Human Weakness" is representative; its author, true to his title, could not admit that Reno is genuinely American.[26] Even Los Angeles, although it shares national characteristics conspicuously enough, seems to strike many people as odd or crazy; and, "according to its most severe critics, it is New York in purple shorts with its brains knocked out." The phrase is George S. Perry's; in less fanciful prose he sums up very well the partial denial of status to that large city when he adds that its "civilization has been declared to caricature, in one way or another, that of the entire nation."[27]

The residents of certain other cities sometimes display sensitivity to the ways in which their cities deviate from what they or outside critics conceive to be the normal national or regional urban patterns. Cincinnati has never quite recovered from Mrs. Trollope's visit nor from its reputation as a tradition-bound town located within a progressive, dynamic region.[28] When a city begins its history with a great promise but then suffers relative oblivion, it departs sufficiently from the usual regional expectations to require a set of supporting rationalizations. Thus a loyal resident of Marietta, Ohio, in 1903 mournfully took stock of a century that had passed without much progress for his town. He remarked that

a city may open the way for progress, and still not progress itself. . . . Evidently other cities . . . have excelled her [Marietta] in so many ways. . . . But at the beginning of the new century she stands young, strong, and vigorous, no longer old, except in name, with an ambition of youth and wealth of resource. . . . While it has thus taken a century of experience during which time she seems to move forward so slowly, it is well to consider that these years

were spent in laying a firm and substantial foundation whereon to build the New Marietta.[29]

In another passage, we can watch a citizen of Vincennes, Indiana, trying to puzzle out why prophesies about cities sometimes fail to materialize. Commenting on Vincennes' bustling future after "a sort of Rip Van Winkle sleep," he wrote:

This bright prospect although long delayed might have been expected from the opinions of the place and its natural advantages expressed by the missionary fathers who first visited it. . . . These men were far seeing and almost with prophetic vision foretold the future of various places they visited. . . . In no instance have their prophetic utterances failed of fruition unless it shall be in the solitary instance of Vincennes.

In urging his contemporaries on to greater civic harmony and energy, he added, "They made the same prophetic utterances with reference to Pittsburgh, Cincinnati, Louisville, Detroit, Chicago, St. Paul, St. Louis, San Francisco and many other cities. . . . And why should not their opinions with regard to Vincennes not be realized?"

The residents of most cities can escape feelings of non-typicality simply by stressing other sets of American traits, but when cities develop in astonishingly new ways, their citizens must claim, as I have already suggested, that clearly sanctioned American qualities (rurality, urbanity, sectionality) are actually present or exist in new, somewhat disguised forms.

Most curious of all is the case of New York, a city which has been passionately and repeatedly denied essential American status while its admirers have proclaimed it the greatest city in America. It is one thing to feel that this great metropolis is not the most typical of our cities, that from it foreigners receive a skewed and partial picture of the nation; but it is another matter to believe that New York as partly or wholly not American, or even "un-American." The grounds of attack and defense bring to sharp focus the ambiguity and clash of American values.[31]

In 1894 Theodore Roosevelt published an article titled, "What 'Americanism' Means" in which he argued:

There are two or three sides to the question of Americanism, and two or three senses in which the word "Americanism" can be used to express the antithesis of what is unwholesome and undesirable. In the first place we wish to be broadly American and national, as opposed to being local or sectional.[32]

In the second place, he reports, it is unwholesome for an American to become Europeanized, thus too cosmopolitan; and in the third place, the meaning pertains to those foreign immigrants who do not become quickly Americanized. These antitheses, which run through the arguments for and against New York City, can be found in another article titled "Is New York More Civilized Than Kansas?" which follows almost immediately after Roosevelt's in the same journal.[33] Kansas is defined as the more civilized (that is, as the more American) on a score of grounds, which include its homogeneity of ideal and tradition, its native population, its home life, its lack of class distinction, its religious and moral tone, and its optimal conditions for rearing children. New York is declared not to possess most of these qualities. The author even argues that Kansas is less isolated, in the civilizational as well as the geographic sense, because its greater number of railroads keep it in more intimate contact with all sections of the nation.

Through the years, New York has been accused of being too European, too suspiciously cosmopolitan, too aggressive and materialistic, too hurried and hectic, a city where family life and home life do not flourish but where— it is asserted or suspected—iniquity does. New York seems to sum up all the negative balances in the rural animus against cities, in the sectional argument against centralization and cosmopolitanism, and in the frontier bias against cities which do not share the mystic pioneer experience. No other American city is the target of such great or complete antagonism.

New York's admirers, whether they are native to the city or not, counter these arguments in two ways. They can maintain that the city is not actually deficient in these various regards. For instance, the *New York Times Magazine* makes its business the occasional publication of articles about the city which tacitly or explicitly set out to prove that New York really is a friendly place having unsuspected village-like qualities, a quiet home life, plus bits of rurality and even farming tucked away here and there. They also try to show that the large numbers of immigrants and their children, are at least as American as citizens with longer native genealogies. When New Yorkers write about themselves or about their city, their affirmation of urban identity often takes that form. (Al Smith once wrote an article titled "I Have Seven Million Neighbors.")[34]

Side by side with the outright accusation that New York fails to participate in our wholesome, rural, or village heritage runs the assertion that New York is actually our most representative city because it is our greatest. "Greatness" can be attributed on quite different grounds, for each assertion rests upon certain features of American culture judged to be of the highest importance. New York is our last frontier, the place where persons of spirit are drawn as by a magnet. It is the "moving frontier" of American culture, the most important site of progress and innovation. It is the image of America, for here the melting pot is at its most intense and here the New America—racially or culturally—is being forged rather than in the most homogeneous native American centers. Although the same theme of the urban melting pot as the epitome of American civilization is applied to other ethnically diverse cities,[35] New York is a place where all narrow local sectionalism has disappeared: because it is a great world city, as is twentieth-century America—is not this the American century! Even those who hate New York may have to admit New York's typicality on the grounds that if this is the America of today, then New York certainly best represents it. Here, for instance, is Earl Sparling's anguished summation, complete with reference to the pioneer past:

I find it an appalling place, rich for making money, poor for living. . . . But all of that is one thing. It is a different thing to shrug the whole spectacle away as something completely alien and not American. America cannot be absolved that easily. Not only is New York American, but it is the mirror in which America, after half a century of confusion, suddenly sees herself for what she is. . . . New York is the soul of America. And Americans . . . see it . . . and wonder how all this happened in a free, pioneer land.[36]

Is it any wonder that there is so much ambiguity in the symbolization of this metropolis, this New York which "is at once the climactic synthesis of America, and yet the negation of America in that it has so many characteristics called un-American?"[37] The attitude—and the bewilderment—of many Americans can be summed up in the reactions of a girl from the Midwest who, visiting New York for the first time, exclaimed that it was "just a wonderfully exciting place but so unreal; it doesn't even have trees." It is summed up also in a magnificently paradoxical set of sentences written by the editors of *Fortune* magazine, as they struggled to relate New York City to the national culture:

New York may be taken as a symbol, or it may be taken as a fact. As a symbol it is a symbol of America; its noisy, exuberant, incalculable towers rise out of the water like a man's aspirations to freedom. As a symbol it is the Gateway, the promise, the materialization of the New World. . . . But taken as a fact, New York is less Dantesque. To most Americans the fact is that "New York is not America." It is un-American in lots of ways. The concentration of power that exists among those spires is itself un-American; so are the tumultuous, vowel-twisting inhabitants who throng the sidewalks.[38]

The confusion continues. Two pages later, when the editors eloquently discuss the city's role as a great melting pot, they wrote, "In that sense New York *is* America," only to blunt the force of that assertion with "more than symbolically."

The strain between ideal and reality, or ideal and presumed fact, runs like a brilliant thread through all our antithetical thinking about America and about our cities. With a fine flair for significant ambiguities, the *Saturday Evening Post* included among more than 145 cities which it surveyed after World War II an article about "a little cow town." Its author asserted that *"The Saturday Evening Post* is running a notable series of articles about American cities. All this is well enough, but . . . if we have any truly national culture, it stems from the small town and near-by farm."[39] George S. Perry, in his book, *Cities of America* could not avoid including, either, a chapter about a town of two thousand people; and, like the editors of *Fortune*, he uses those interesting terms "fact" and "symbol"—except that he applies them to a small city. "Madison, Wisconsin," he sentimentalizes,

is both a fact and a symbol that stands for many of the finest traits in the American character. It is a place where independent people get up on their hind legs and have their say. Again, it is a seat of serious learning. Moreover, it is surrounded by that basic harmony that derives from good land that has been treated intelligently and with respect. Finally, Madison's people are almost spectacularly unapathetic. They are concerned, interested, and willing to do something about almost any public question. In many ways Madison and its environs are a miniature model of the ideal America of which many of us dream.[40]

Fact and symbol, symbol and fact: it is as if the United States had developed an urbanized economy without developing a thoroughly urbanized citizen. Americans entered a great period of city building during the nineteenth century protestingly, metaphorically walking backward; and to some extent they still do, but in exceedingly subtle ways. In the various sections of the next chapter, I shall deal both with this protest against cities, and with the regional differences between American urban cultures. In the foregoing pages, we have merely scratched the surface of American urban symbolism.

NOTES

1. John P. Kennedy, "Address. Delivered before the Maryland Institute for the Promotion of the Mechanical Arts, 21st October 1851," *Occasional* *Addresses* (New York: Putnam & Sons, 1872), p. 244.

2. Paul de Rousiers, *American Life* (New York and Paris: Firming-Didot & Co.), p. 73.

3. John Gunther, *Inside U. S. A.* (New York: Harper & Bros., 1946), p. 369.

4. Cf. The collection of articles edited by Alexander Klein, *The Empire City, A Treasury of New York* (New York: Rinehart & Co., Inc., 1955); or Paul Crowell and A. H. Raskin, "New York, 'Greatest City in the World,' " in Robert S. Allen (ed.), *Our Fair City* (New York: Vanguard Press, Inc., 1947), esp. pp. 37-39.

5. This article was reprinted in the collection titled *Cities of America* (New York: Whittlesey House, McGraw-Hill Book Co., 1947), p. 244; see also Henry Haskell and Richard Fowler, *City of the Future. A Narrative History of Kansas City* (Kansas City: F. Glenn Publishing Company, 1950), pp. 16-17; and Darrel Garwood, *Crossroads of America. The Story of Kansas City* (New York: W. W. Norton and Co., Inc., 1948), p. 327. The latter volume especially exemplifies the conception of "crossroads" as the basis for attributing more Americanism to Kansas City than to any other city.

6. Cf. "Midwestern Birthday," *Time*, LVIII (July 30, 1951), p. 14.

7. Frank C. Harper, *Pittsburgh: Forge of the Universe* (New York: Comet Press, 1957), p. 10; and *Pittsburgh and the Pittsburgh Spirit* (Pittsburgh: Chamber of Commerce, 1928), but especially the address by John Bowman, "Pittsburgh's Contribution to Civilization," pp. 1-10.

8. Angie Debo, *Tulsa: From Creek Town to Oil Capital* (Norman, Okla.: University of Oklahoma Press, 1945), p. vii.

9. For two excellent discussions of the agrarian myth see Richard Hofstadter, *The Age of Reform* (New York: Alfred A. Knopf, Inc., 1955), esp. Part I, "The Agrarian Myth and Commercial Realities," and Part II, "The Folklore of Populism"; and Henry Nash Smith, *Virgin Land. The American West as Symbol and Myth* (New York: Vintage Books, 1955, and Cambridge: Harvard University Press, 1950), esp. Book III, "The Garden of the World," pp. 138-305.

10. Cf. G. S. Perry, "Philadelphia," *Saturday Evening Post*, CCXVIII (Sept. 14, 1946), esp. p. 82.

11. "Portland, Oregon," *Saturday Evening Post*, CCXIX (March 1, 1947), 23.

12. "Springfield, Illinois," *ibid.* (Sept. 27, 1947), p. 28.

13. This theme can be readily recognized in such books on older eastern cities as Struthers Burt, *Philadelphia* (Garden City, New York: Doubleday, Doran & Co., 1945), and Cleveland Amory, *The Proper Bostonians* (New York: E. P. Dutton & Co., 1947).

14. John Bowman, in Harper, *Pittsburgh and the Pittsburgh Spirit*, *op. cit.*, pp. 5-9.

15. Dorsha Hayes, *Chicago, Crossroads of American Enterprise* (New York: Julian Messner, Inc.,

1944), p. 300; and Clara de Chambrun, *Cincinnati* (New York: Charles Scribner & Sons, 1939), p. 319.
16. Cf. Robert G. Rhett, *Charleston. An Epic of Carolina* (Richmond, Va.: Garrett and Massie, 1940).
17. Howard Long, *Kingsport, A Romance of Industry* (Kingsport, Tenn.: The Sevier Press, 1928), pp. 76, 3-4.
18. *Op. cit.*, pp. 369-70, 549.
19. *Op. cit.*, p. 37.
20. "Reno," *Saturday Evening Post,* CCXXV (July 5, 1952), 70, 72.
21. (Indianapolis: Bobbs-Merrill Co., 1946), p. 19.
22. (New York: Harper & Bros., 1945), p. 205.
23. "Birmingham, Alabama," *Saturday Evening Post,* CCXX (Sept. 6, 1947), 22.
24. *Op. cit.*, pp. 886-906, esp. p. 895.
25. F. Stother, "What Kind of Pittsburgh is Detroit?" *World's Work,* LII (Oct., 1926), 633-39.
26. Anthony Abbot in *Reader's Digest,* LX (Feb., 1952), 119-22.
27. *Op. cit.*, pp. 232, 233.
28. Alvin Harlow refers to Mrs. Trollope in *The Serene Cincinnatians* (New York: Dutton and Co., 1950).
29. Thomas J. Summers, *History of Marietta* (Marietta, Ohio: Leader Publishing Company, 1903), pp. 319-20.
30. Henry Cauthorn, *A History of the City of Vincennes, Indiana* (Cleveland: Arthur H. Clark Co., 1901), p. 220.
31. For some representative statements, pro and con, see: Mark Sullivan, "Why the West Dislikes New York. The Eternal Conflict Between City and Country," *World's Work,* LXI (1926), 406-11; "New York City," *Fortune,* XX (1939), 73-75, 83-85; Charles Merz, "The Attack on New York," *Harper's,* CLXIII (1926), 81-87; Earl Sparling, "Is New York American?" *Scribner's,* LXXX (1931), 165-73; Paul Crowell and A. H. Raskin, in R. Allen (ed.), *op. cit.,* pp. 38-39; Anonymous, "What is America?" *Nation,* CXXVIII (1921), 755; and Robert Benchley, "The Typical New Yorker," in Alexander Klein (ed.), *op. cit.,* pp. 338-42.
32. *Forum,* XVII (1894), 196-200.
33. J. W. Gleed in *ibid.,* pp. 217-34.
34. *American Magazine,* CXVI (Aug., 1933), 36-38.
35. Elsie Morrow, "South Bend," *Saturday Evening Post,* CCXXIV (June 14, 1942), 87; and "Brooklyn," *ibid.,* CCXIX (Dec. 26, 1946), 14.
36. *Op. cit.*, pp. 165-73.
37. Gunther, *op. cit.*, p. 549.
38. *Op. cit.*, p. 73.
39. E. R. Jackman, "Burns, Oregon," *Saturday Evening Post,* CCXX (Jan. 31, 1948), 2.
40. *Op. cit.*, p. 221.

Back to Nature

PETER J. SCHMITT

Some day we shall construct great pictures out-of-doors. We shall assemble the houses, control the architecture, arrange the trees and the forest, direct the roads and fences, display the slopes of the hills, lay out the farms, remove every feature that offends a sensitive eye; and persons will leave the galleries, with their limitations and limitations, to go to the country to see some of the greatest works of art that man can make . . .

Liberty Bailey, *The Outlook to Nature* (New York: MacMillan, 1905), p. 86.

Wild nature has changed almost as much as an image in American rhetoric as it has in its physical features. The first settlers once fought against "barbarism" to preserve what they knew as culture and sophistication. But after the Revolution, Americans fashioned a new identity for themselves. Fortified with European Romanticism, they took nature and not civilization as the common denominator of the new republic. Fourth

From *Back to Nature: The Arcadian Myth in Urban America* (New York: Oxford University Press, 1969), pp. xv-xxiii; 177-89. Copyright © 1969 by Oxford University Press, Inc. Reprinted by permission of the publisher. Peter J. Schmitt is Associate Professor of History at Western Michigan University.

of July orators proclaimed that American republicans were products, not victims, of the wilderness. Thomas Jefferson wrote that sturdy yeoman farmers, shielded from the artificiality of commerce and city life, lived lives of quiet simplicity as the "chosen people of god."

Jefferson's belief developed into a popular myth: one of those "attitudes" James M. Williams described as "generally prevalent ways of reacting of which people become conscious only incidentally as they try to drill them into their children or as they meet people of contrary attitudes."[1] In 1893, Frederick Jackson Turner worked the agrarian attitude into "The Significance of the Frontier in American History." But Turner spoke to the American Historical Association at a Columbian Exposition which celebrated America's urban and industrial future. Americans might still want their Presidents born on the farm in 1893, but they hardly expected a working farmer.

Turner accepted Jefferson's dichotomy between rural good and urban evil, and he noted with a touch of sadness that frontier agriculture and frontier virtue were giving way to urban complexity.[2] Later historians, most notably Richard Hofstadter and Henry Nash Smith, continued to interpret the imagery of factory and farm, of city and country, even of sophistication and simplicity, as clearly antithetical. Smith identified "nature" as a source of moral virtue, with agriculture as a way of life. He argued, however, that "the static ideas of virtue and happiness and peace drawn from the bosom of the virgin wilderness . . . proved quite irrelevant for a society committed to the ideas of civilization and progress." Leo Marx declared in *The Machine in the Garden* that America's continuing enthusiasm

for the out-of-doors represented a flight from reality into "naïve and anarchic primitivism." George Mowry called this enthusiasm a vitiating "social nostalgia" which "America's ruling economic classes" stimulated because they found "rural virtues" politically useful.[3]

But so considerable a cross section of urban intellectuals claimed to be "nature lovers" at the turn of the century that "social nostalgia" for a farmer's past may not adequately explain their commitment. Many praised their rural childhood, but few returned to farming; few seemed frustrated in the suburbs because they could not raise chickens. Urban Americans settling in suburban developments and visiting country clubs, summer camps, or national parks had little in common with their country neighbors. They looked at scenery and sportsmanship and country living, in a way, it seemed, that only "city people" could. When city dwellers began to insist on taking over suburban nature for themselves they quarreled with traditionalists who equated country living with a rural society.

Americans turning "back to nature" rather than "back to the land" responded to a philosophy only faintly related to the pattern of thought which Richard Hofstadter and others have called "agrarianism."[4] Simply put, this urban response valued nature's spiritual impact above its economic importance; it might better be called "Arcadian." Those who looked to nature for a living had categorically settled for something less than Arcadia; the man on the street, not the man on the land, might better benefit from "natural" resources. Webster's *Dictionary* cited John Burroughs in 1899 to demonstrate that "Arcadia" as a word meant little more than a "scene of simple pleasure and untroubled quiet." As a place it lay somewhere on the urban fringe, easily accessible and mildly wild, the goal of a "nature movement" led by teachers and preachers, bird-watchers, socialites, scout leaders, city-planners, and inarticulate commuters, all of whom applauded William Smythe when he offered in *City Homes on Country Lanes* "the cream of the country and the cream of the city, leaving the skim-milk for those who like that sort of thing."[5]

However ancient the Arcadian heritage, and however modern its values seem today, men trying to cope with the pressures of urbanization at the turn of the century worked hardest to define the role of nature in an industrial society. Then a whole generation of "literary commuters" took it upon themselves to translate nature into urban terms. Genteel essayists like Andrew Jackson Downing and *Harper's* editor Donald G. Mitchell had written earlier the "life of a cultivated mind in the country," as Downing put it in the 1840's.[6] They suggested urban Americans pattern themselves after the gentry they knew through English literature. From the 1880's on into the 1920's, middle-class journalists tried to combine country life and city culture in essays calculated to appeal to urban readers. These writers were scarcely gentlemen farmers. They were college professors, merchants, clerks, men of distinctly urban interests who tried to make rural America the playground of an urban society. Some, such as Ernest Thompson Seton, felt so strongly the need to reach urban readers that they embellished their writing with literary devices to attract a wider audience. Others, such as John Burroughs, argued that the message was too sacred to manipulate, and thus they began a "nature faker controversy" that em-

broiled even Theodore Roosevelt. In any event, a philosophy which seems in retrospect appropriate only to *Outing* and *Forest and Stream* blossomed in the *Ladies' Home Journal, Good Housekeeping, Atlantic Monthly,* and *Saturday Evening Post.*

Other nature enthusiasts took Arcadia out of books and tried to locate it in life, first for adults and then, more poignantly perhaps, for children. By the middle of the nineteenth century, garden suburbs, city parks, and country estates began to show the influence of landscape designers. Landscape architects like Andrew Jackson Downing and Frederick Law Olmstead tried to make American nature conform to their reading of Romantics like Uvedale Price and William Gilpin. Still relying on Price and Gilpin, Olmstead and later Charles Eliot carried down to the twentieth century the idea that nature could be made to conform to urban tastes.

Landscape designers found a lucrative field in the park movement that swept the cities in the 1880's and 1890's. But others also came to feel that city dwellers must have at least occasional contact with peaceful scenery. Psychologists, sociologists, and educators developed insights into urban behavior that suggested society could not survive without nature. Instinctivists, environmentalists, and crowd psychologists all supposed that man was not made for urban life. Many educators were impressed with G. Stanley Hall's genetic psychology. Hall argued that children must recapitulate human development from primitive rural stages to complex urban life as they matured; denial of this process in the cities bred social immaturity, crime, and chaos. Fresh Air Funds and summer camps for city children multiplied rapidly after the 1880's. The Woodcraft Indians, the Sons of Daniel Boone, the Campfire Girls, and the Boy Scouts offered outdoor exposure to city children. At the end of the nineteenth century more and more educators came to feel the schools must provide the contact with nature that city children lacked. Bluebirds and bean-sprouts had a decidedly rural savor, but "nature-study" was not designed for rural schools, and not intended to make farmers of city children.

Enthusiasts claimed the country was in the midst of a full-scale return to nature. They cited increasing state and national park statistics, the growth of commuter railways, and a variety of other sources to back their contention. Yet it always seemed that Arcadia was easier to find in literature. Twentieth-century readers found a steady stream of nature essays and suburban self-help advice in newspapers and popular magazines. Children in extraordinary numbers enjoyed the outdoor adventures of the Bobbsey Twins and the Rover Boys. Their elders put "nature romances" such as those of Gene Stratton-Porter and Harold Bell Wright on best-seller lists over and over again.

By the 1920's, however, many suburbanites began to discover urban sprawl. Some responded by joining primitivists in a retreat to wilderness areas. Under the enthusiasm of men like Benton MacKaye, others identified with the Regional Planning movement, hoping that engineering could bring about a metropolitan Arcadia. MacKaye conceived of a New England megalopolis bounded by nothing less ambitious than the Appalachian Trail. Conservative planners confined themselves to urging open-space zoning, green-belt developments, and parkway construction. Many of the regional planners reflected a growing belief that the nature movement had lost intensity, even as more and more people looked to outdoor recreation. They and men like them felt they must guard the remnants of natural environment for an urban majority not quite capable of applying Arcadian principles in day-to-day situations.

It would be idle to try to locate beginnings for the Arcadian philosophy in the influence of single individuals or even to suggest that a single individual brought change or direction to the nature movement. Some men gained more prominence than others. *Harper's* editor Donald Mitchell was better known than landscape designer Charles Eliot. Essayist John Burroughs became a legend to those who saw in him the virtues they ascribed to nature itself. But most who contributed to the Arcadian mystique were only modestly known. Just such an individual was Cornell University educator Liberty Hyde Bailey. Bailey felt himself a spokesman for the nature movement, and his writings illustrate something of the interests and fervor of the "nature-lovers." Like most nature writers, in fact like most Americans of his time, Bailey grew up in the country, but he soon decided that "horticulture" offered more than frontier farming. His reputation rests on his career as a teacher of teachers; but, convinced that city dwellers needed outdoor life, he turned in 1901 to editing Doubleday, Page's new suburban journal, *Country Life in America*. Integrating inspiration and do-it-yourself directions for the good life, he made that journal the most popular of all suburban periodicals.

Bird-watching, landscaping, and the new interest in city parks seemed proof to Bailey that urban America heard the call of the wild, but he particularly feared that city children might lose the echo of the country. In 1903 Bailey gathered together materials from his editorials and published *The Nature Study Idea,* a highwater mark in the philosophy of the nature movement. "Of late years," he wrote, "there has been a rapidly growing feeling that we must live closer to nature; and we must perforce begin with the child."[7] Correctly taught in city schools, summer camps and youth groups, in nature essays and wilderness novels, nature lore could transform first the children and then society.

Bailey hardly stood idle waiting for the gospel to trickle through formal educational channels. When the Education Committee of Boston's Twentieth Century Club invited him to lecture in 1905, he spoke on "The Outlook to Nature." The need for "landscape that is easy of access and undefiled" he found "indicated by the rapidly spreading suburban movement, by the vacationing in the country, and by the astonishing multiplication of books about nature."[8] Future Americans, rightly guided, must be neither "country-bred nor city-bred, but suburban-bred, product of neither extreme." Bailey aimed his doctrine at those who went to the country for "more room, less racket, better health, more freedom, and closer relations with sun and wind and sky" and not to take up farming.[9]

Theodore Roosevelt chose Bailey to chair his blue-ribbon "Country Life Commission" that examined agrarian ideals in 1908. The Commission collected information so disturbing that Roosevelt asked to have it printed at once, but embarrassed Congressmen forbade the Commission to continue in any capacity. Agricultural technology had outstripped the art of country living as farmers rushed pell-mell to city ways if not to city jobs. "The backbone of the rural question is at bottom a moral problem," Bailey found. We had failed to teach farmers "to hoe potatoes and to hear the birds sing at the same time."[10]

As the years went by, Bailey looked uneasily at the burgeoning nature movement. Nature-study answered increasingly to science; summer camping for all its virtues turned to institutional efficiency; popular fiction romanticized nature almost unbearably. In 1915, he published *The Holy Earth* to order Americans back to fundamentals. "Most of us live from the box and the bottle and the tin-can; we are even feeding our cattle from the factory and the bag," he wrote; "no thought of the seasons . . . comes with the trademark or the brand. And so we all live mechanically, from shop to table, without contact, and irreverently." Down through the eons of geologic time the earth was holy; but Bailey noted "how desperately soon may men reduce it all to ruin and to emptiness, and how slatternly may they violate the scenery!"[11]

Yet it seemed to Bailey that "no people should be forbidden the influence of the forest."[12] Nature writing and country-life essays might serve for dreaming, but they were not enough. Americans on the land must hold it in stewardship not only for future generations but for those already living in cities. In the public domain, wild land ought to be "held by the people to be sold in small parcels to those who desire to get out to the backgrounds but who do not want to be farmers. . . ."[13]

Bailey concluded in a later reprint of *The Holy Earth* that critics had passed him by. His essay faded in the bird and flower and forest romances dominating the nature movement. But if he could no longer believe that the nature movement would reform the whole society, Bailey still argued that the minority should impose its will on the majority as a duty to the future. However much we became a nation of cities, we could not escape our need for wild land, "and to keep this land, for ourselves and our successors," he believed, must be "the first responsibility of the race."[14]

Yet by the 1920's, Bailey acknowledged that his hopes had tarnished. The "nature movement" was active enough. Nature writers published as often as ever. Landscape architects still thought of themselves as more evangelists than engineers. Conservation was governmental policy and national park facilities already overcrowded. Nature novels and wilderness movies were immensely popular; but the great vision seemed dissipated even as its influence spread. In 1923 Bailey made his last real effort to rouse the old enthusiasm in a cryptic little volume he called *The Seven Stars*, a search through the hubbub of commerce, where men mistook "noise and tinsel and jingle for happiness."[15] Arcadia, which seemed so near at hand in *The Nature Study Idea*, evaporated as Bailey's hero moved beyond the city to suburbs where nature seemed all but lost in occasional vacant lots. Real country people appeared as indifferent as ever to their surroundings, and the quest continued into the last refuge of the backgrounds. Still, Bailey, like nature writers, landscape architects, and wilderness lovers, convinced himself that he still held the vision, however much others might have strayed, and still must point the way

even though he tailored nature worship to the problems of suburban living.

Bailey and others who made public confession of their philosophy supported parks, youth organizations, and other public causes, yet always appeared ready to withdraw to country clubs and private estates. The best-known supporters of the movement (with the exception of John Burroughs) were middle-class promoters of a genteel country life they clearly thought superior to agriculture. They made their ideas known in popular periodicals ranging from the *Atlantic Monthly* and *Saturday Review* to *The Arena* and *Cosmopolitan* and may well have provided the inspiration for a much larger group which did little more than argue that the city was no place to raise a family.

＊　　＊　　＊

The decade of the 1920's saw the rise of "The New Exploration" as Benton Mac-Kaye was to call it—an examination not of geographic resources, but of the city and the conditions that made up city life. Surveyor's transit and chain gave way to the scientific tools of psychologists, sociologists and city planners. The first reports of the new explorers gave surprising credence to nature lovers' complaints, however silly and sentimental they seemed to others. "The city of our dreams," wrote Clarence Stein, "is lost in another city which could occur to a sane mind only in a nightmare."[16] Citing evidence for New York, Stein traced successive breakdowns of the city's physical functions. Growing water and sewage problems reflected the mushrooming of residential areas around the perimeter of the old city. By 1928, 475 outlets emptied 1,100,-000,000 gallons of sewage per day into the Hudson, the East, and the Harlem

Rivers. The Passaic Valley sewer contributed another billion gallons at Robbins Reef. As one cynic remarked in 1913, beaches were areas of land washed by water, except in New York, where they were washed by garbage. Swimmers found themselves restricted to two per cent of the city's 190 mile waterfront, and oil pollution made even that area less than pleasant.

Traffic controls were frequently as primitive as sewage disposal. With the development of the skyscraper, two to six new "cities" rose from the streets of the old; massive traffic jams became a daily hazard of urban life. "Every day the congestion increases," Stein concluded, "in spite of traffic policemen, curb setbacks, one-way streets, electric traffic signals." Subways were equally crowded by 1925.[17]

Noise seemed the natural accompaniment to urban expansion. Sound proofing was in its infancy in building construction and in the transportation industry. City office workers contracted neuroses similar to shell shock as iron tires, klaxon horns, chain drives, traffic whistles, trolley bells and the thunder of elevated trains joined the air hammers and rivet guns of new construction.[18] E. E. Free, science editor for *The Forum*, found in a study of noise in New York City, which was repeated across the country, that commercial districts created a sound threshold equivalent to from one-third to one-half deafness in city workers. With the objectivity of a science fiction horror story, Free's analysis suggested that the irritation of audible sounds might well be less than the psychological assault of sounds which could only be registered by instruments.[19] New York City's Noise Abatement Commission went on to conclude that "a tiger from Siberia or Bengal could roar or snarl indefinitely" on

many streets "without attracting the auditory attention of passersby."[20] Recognizing that jangled nerves were inevitable, the Commission suggested mild controls ranging from stifling random tugboat whistles to muffling exhaust pipes on federal mail trucks. They induced the Interborough Rapid Transit Company to pad nine hundred subway turnstiles when a bank of five in Grand Central Station was rated noisier than an elevated train.

The physical transition from rural to urban life gave rise to fears of the city that sociologists further defined. Rural sociologist Charles Galpin saw city life as "immured in brick and stone, gaining its outlook, as it were, through periscopes."[21] Early urban sociologists seemed equally concerned. In 1909, Charles Cooley gave an emotion-laden vocabulary to a generation of investigators with his theories of "primary" and "secondary" relationships. He characterized primary relationships as the "intimate face-to-face association and cooperation" characteristic of rural life.[22] Cooley's followers found secondary contact typical of life in cities where men became symbols for the services they performed. The study of etiquette replaced the study of human nature, said Chicago's Robert E. Park, whenever "the individual's status is determined to a considerable degree by conventional signs—by fashion and 'front'—and the art of life is largely reduced to skating on thin surfaces and a scrupulous study of style and manners."[23]

Led by Robert Park, the University of Chicago's sociology department became a leading center for urban research. Park saw the city as "a clinic" in which human nature could be examined under stress. The "Chicago school" favored objective and heavily documented studies, but when its investigators asked such questions as "Are Modern Industry and City Life Unfavorable to the Family,"[24] with results that could only horrify most readers, it was clear that urban sociologists were deeply disturbed by their own culture.

Students of urban society responded enthusiastically to Jacob Riis' *How the Other Half Lives*. Among other things, Harvey Zorbaugh commented, "Riis did more than anyone else to make 'slumming' a popular sport."[25] By the nineteen-twenties, urban sociology was itself becoming a kind of intellectual slumming. Such studies as *The Hobo, The Social Evil in Chicago, Five Hundred Criminal Careers, Prostitution in the United States, The Unadjusted Girl*, and *The City Where Crime Is Play* indicated an almost pathological interest in human failure. In 1929, Chicago's dignified "Sociological Series" included *Suicide, Family Disorganization, Sex Freedom and Social Control, Domestic Discord, Map of Chicago's Gangland, The Ghetto* and *The Strike*. Robert Park concluded that "our great cities, as those who have studied them have learned, are full of junk, much of it human."[26]

In view of the case against the city, such scholars were hard put to account for the continued surge of population into the towns. Niles Carpenter found the "lure of the city" too great for the American people, who were being conditioned to seek the "enthralment of the urban way of life." Urbanism had reached "a point never before attained in human history." Americans, Carpenter felt, would continue to move to the cities knowing that economic opportunity was closed to them by the sheer numbers of their fellow migrants; he predicted a time when the average American might well become "so com-pletely conditioned to urban life that he simply could not conceive of living outside a city." Only Roman history offered useful parallels to modern urbanization, yet this was a most disturbing comparison, Carpenter noted, "for the end of the Roman urban society was wilderness and manorial feudalism."[27] Boston University's Ernest Groves also found urban life a "self-chosen enslavement." He reported that "the psychological causes of urban drift are socially most sinister." The individual's adjustment to city life was sociology's tormenting problem. "The mere pressing together of population, the congestion of the city, gives the impression of bigness," Groves declared, and "unless he identifies himself with this manpower, the crowd becomes an alien force and he flees from it with morbid fear."[28]

The flight from the crowd took various directions—to city parks, suburbs, country places, or to the wilderness. One of the most idealistic escapes involved the short-lived "garden city" concept. Though A. T. Stewart platted Garden City, Long Island, in 1869, Ebenezer Howard, a romantic Englishman who saw in the countryside around London "the very embodiment of Divine Love for man," did most to popularize the idea in the 1890's. In *Garden Cities of Tomorrow*, he imagined a series of carefully controlled communities which would combine selected industries with boulevards, parks and workers' cottages.[29] Howard outlined his goals much more clearly than his methods. As a result, early garden cities rarely succeeded. Perhaps the most spectacular disappointment to social reformers was the 104-acre Forest Hills Gardens on Long Island. Shortly after the turn of the century the Russell Sage Foundation Homes Company hired landscape architect Frederick

Law Olmstead, Jr., to lay out the community. Artistic public buildings absorbed so much capital that the community was soon unable to offer homes to workingmen at all. Twenty years later it was "one of the most beautiful, most artistic, most expensive and most exclusive residential parks in the world."[30]

If "garden cities" failed in their purpose, conventional suburbs multiplied with astonishing rapidity. As early as 1906, the *World Today* could truthfully announce, "suburbia is still crude, too often a hodge-podge of jerry-built atrocities, but it is the city of the future."[31] In the construction boom after World War I, as Booth Tarkington complained:

A new house would appear upon a country road; the country road would transform itself into an asphalt street with a brick drug store at the corner of a meadow . . . . What was in spring a quiet lane through fields and woods was in autumn a constantly lengthening street with trolley-cars gonging and new house-owners hurriedly putting up wooden garages in their freshly sodded "side yards."[32]

By 1925, New York had one hundred and twenty-nine incorporated satellites, Chicago fifty-seven and Boston fifty-five. These "bedroom towns," as sociologist Nels Anderson called them, dominated the landscape around all major cities; sociologists found in them the standardization, divided loyalties and disinterest that would plague them a generation later. To one angry housewife, suburban living sapped the individuality and sophistication that brought it forth. "If you have the rubber soul and cast-iron nerve necessary for social climbing," she wrote, "you will get all the bridge parties, country club life, teas, telephone gossip, and invitations your soul craves, if you 'play the game' suburban fashion, and aren't

overly particular." Narrow houses and tiny suburban yards failed to supply the nature promised in the Arcadian dream. Happiness lay further from the city, somewhere in the "real" country. "By country," she wrote, "I do not mean a farm or many acres or huge castles built in imitation of English country houses." Arcadia was instead "a simple home built along a country road, near hills or water, from a quarter of a mile to two or three miles from the railway station, and within one and one-half hours' commuting distance from the city."[33]

Such "real" country rapidly retreated before junkyards, satellite industries and real estate developments. In 1925, *Century* magazine's search for "the wildness" of New York, Boston, and Philadelphia yielded only a meager harvest of sidewalk ants, dandelions, butterflies and nighthawks.[34] All too often the feeling of vast distance and the original conditions of life were available to city dwellers only in ecological groupings at the natural history museum. Clever and exaggerated habitat settings, where painted backgrounds, waxen plants, and carefully postured animals offered "a glimpse of wild life as it is, or more often, as it has been, before man took complete possession of the land."[35] Nighthawks and painted forests could hardly recompense nature lovers for an Arcadia that seemed attainable in actuality through intelligent urban planning.

City planners had been meeting since 1909 in national conferences on the problems of simple "congestion," but now they turned to exploring the possibilities of the "metropolitan district."[36] In 1925, Lewis Mumford edited a special issue of *The Survey Graphic* which argued that regional planning was "the New Conservation," aimed at utilizing natural resources exclusively to benefit city dwellers. Mumford's contributors were members of the Regional Planning Association of America, men who had failed to remold the city to suit their fancy and had turned instead to planning a metropolitan environment "not as a temporary refuge but as a permanent seat of life and culture, urban in its advantages, permanently rural in its situation."[37]

The Russell Sage Foundation sponsored a "Regional Survey of New York and Its Environs" in 1924 to develop a master plan for New York City. Mapping out a 5,500 square mile "region" which included four hundred twenty municipalities and one-twelfth of the country's population, the survey suggested guidelines for efficient suburban expansion, traced logical traffic patterns, laid out badly needed parklands for public recreation, and in ten fat volumes surveyed the past and future prospects of the nation's largest city. "Mastering a Metropolis" on paper simply required directing its growth along the course prescribed by social scientists and city planners. Even in New York wild nature could be preserved with careful forethought. In spite of the inevitable doubling of population, "the New Yorker of 1965" would still be able to "answer the call of the wild and feel the thrill of great open spaces . . . if we plan wisely now."[38]

There was an element of urgency in the Regional Planning movement—a feeling that cities at flood tide could overrun the countryside. Benton MacKaye, in his *New Exploration, a Philosophy of Regional Planning*, borrowed his metaphors from engineering as he pleaded for legislative control of the metropolitan flood. Parkways and parks and public reserves were the tools he planned to use in halting the encroach-

ment of city on country. They would be forbidden areas legislated to channel the flow of population into practical "catch-basins"; they would be levees protecting the "indigenous environment."[39]

The new exploration moved rapidly from the old realm of what was to the realm of what could be, from mapping to planning. The explorer gave way to social scientists, economists, and engineers. If parks and open spaces were dikes against the flow of urbanization, highways, to these planners, were its channels. Older cities had followed rail and trolley lines; new developments would hinge on road construction. MacKaye and other planners designed their roadways not only to move traffic but to insure that such traffic would whisk past bits of undisturbed nature that still remained.

But MacKaye, along with his friend Walter Prichard Eaton, conceived his main defense as nothing less than a "wilderness foot-path" running the whole length of the East Coast. Such a monument to outdoor life, as Eton put it, would provide something of "the wilderness beauties, the wilderness health, the wilderness virtues, which we have so largely lost."[40] The version of such a trail that MacKaye announced in the journal of the American Institute of Architects in 1921 as "An Appalachian Trail: a Project in Regional Planning," provided for a series of public parks and open ways to cluster around the trail as a constant reminder to coastal residents that the whole world was not a city.

The nation's social planners of the 1920's left little doubt that the Arcadian mythology influenced them. Engineers hoped to remake both city and country according to its dictates. An affection for nature had become a part of the accepted way of American living. President Calvin Coolidge told delegates from 128 organizations, whom he summoned to the National Conference on Outdoor Recreation in 1924, that the right to outdoor life was as important as the right to work. Woodcraft skills should be "cultivated and cherished," he added, "like a knowledge of the humanities and the sciences."[41] Herbert Hoover explained to the Conference convened in 1926 that "the spiritual uplift, the good will, cheerfulness, and optimism that accompanies every expedition to the outdoors is the peculiar spirit that our people need in troublous times of suspicion and doubt." Believing as he did that "man and boy, the American is a fisherman," Hoover urged that unpolluted streams be preserved as wild rivers, that restorable streams be surveyed, and that only irrecoverable waters be given to industry.[42]

In high circles and in low, as Geoffrey Scott put it, "Naturalism became the aesthetic method, and the love of Nature the most genuine emotion of our age."[43] Even so astute a critic as Henry S. Canby found the "note of woods longing" a key to American thought. Bradford Torrey, John Burroughs and Stewart Edward White were not great writers, but their popularity demonstrated to Canby that "with most Americans you reach intimacy most quickly by talking about the woods."[44] Even though they dealt with a witches' brew of bats and snakes and toads, with beetles as well as bluebirds, American nature writers made "vivid and warm and sympathetic our background of nature" and touched in some not too subtle way the great American subconscious. "Say your worst of it," Canby concluded, "still the fact remains that more Americans go back to nature for one reason or another, annually, than

any civilized men before them. And more Americans, I fancy, are studying nature in clubs and public schools—or, in summer camps and the Boy Scouts . . . than even statistics could make believable."

For all their publicity and all of Canby's euphoria, however, nature lovers seemed to take themselves a bit too seriously. Whatever cause they had for bewailing the city, they were happy to earn their living there, and the country life they pictured in their essays seemed to a cosmopolitan critic like Heywood Broun, "a little too much like one of these big musical comedies—there is more beauty in it than fun."[45] John Preston noted in *The Saturday Review* that nature essayists gave to "a warbler, a hepatica, a hermit thrush, an islanded pine left from the great woods . . . a quality which is less philosophic but more immediately human" than the concerns of much greater writers. Still, suburban shelves were too often stocked with "canned fruit, canned vegetables, canned music, and canned emotions." After all, he wrote, "Campbell's Soup tastes the same in the wilderness as it does in some monstrous and neurotic apartment house." He went on to conclude with some concern:

The wilderness is still at suburban backdoors, still deep if no longer wide. But the mind has changed. We are all for analyzing now, all for groping in the minds of others. The contemplative mood has passed. It is the chemist with his test tube or the physicist with his ray who is the modern symbol of literature. We are too much interested in our neighbors' complexes, or our own inhibitions, to be concerned with expansion of soul.[46]

In spite of Preston's concern, and in spite of the insistent clamoring of social reformers, the city continued to thrive. "The notion that the world is plunging headlong into the fatal abyss of urbanism is a part of the creed of many for whom the country symbolizes all that is good in life," sociologists Noel Gist and L. A. Halbert noted in their study of "Urban Society." "While it is true that the growth of cities has been accompanied by many forms of maladjustment and social injustice," they added, "there seems to be no scientific evidence that urbanism is a pathological manifestation of a sick society. . . ."[47]

Nature worship continued in fashion in the 1920's, but the urgency with which turn-of-the-century intellectuals resisted the city had begun to evaporate. In 1900, all of the systems by which men classified experience had elevated nature. "Crowd psychology" and "instinct psychology" had turned intellectuals away from the city. "Behaviorism" and "environmentalism" had praised moral values in country life. As cities grew larger and dire catastrophes failed to materialize, sociologists like Gist and Halbert found new ways to rationalize the fact of city existence. "The Red God's Call" might echo faintly in sporting magazines, but instinct psychology, with its implicit denial of urbanization, was fast becoming obsolete. Recapitulation psychology, with its oppressive condemnation of urban childhood, was also giving way to more benign approaches to education. Even G. Stanley Hall was willing to admit that outdoor life was no longer a condition for human survival.

Gist and Halbert recognized urban life as a positive force. "Secondary relationships," the nemeses of early psychologists, suddenly ceased to be destructive. Impersonality no longer led to disintegration of rural mores but to increased freedom for individuals to choose the roles they wished to play. "Since the major portion of social contacts in the city are of the touch-and-go type, external appearance assumes a pronounced social value," they concluded; "because of the exaggerated emphasis on external form, many urban persons live behind a mask which conceals the real self." City dwellers learned to express their personalities by closely adhering to conventions and customs symbolic of their attitudes toward life. As Gist and Halbert concluded:

This masquerading, posing, playing a role, gives the outward impression of hypocrisy, and to the rural person, who deliberately avoids artificiality and who cannot understand the basis of urban relationships, the metropolite is hypocritical, untrustworthy, a "slicker." Yet withal it is a natural phenomenon, a form of social adjustment that has grown out of the exigencies of urban life.

"Social ritual," as they saw it, became "at the same time a measure of exclusiveness for the social group and a mark of prestige for the individual who accepts it as part of his pattern of behavior."

Thus nature lovers found themselves behaving according to stereotyped conventions, not because their salvation depended upon it, but because certain patterns of behavior naturally accompanied the role of country squire or suburban commuter. The nature movement lingered on in corduroy hunting coats and briar pipes, in suburban barbecues and "city homes on country lanes," but the desperate vitality that electrified it in 1900 ebbed away. Nature essays appealed to magazine editors more and more for vacation editions in May and June. Yet, no matter how much overt expression might dwindle, the myth remained as a significant part of American culture. Geoffrey Scott designated as the "Biological Fallacy" the idea that institutions and ideologies must have a birth, a growth, a decline and an end. The Arcadian view of nature did not begin with Andrew Jackson Downing or Frederick Law Olmsted. Neither did it decline with the Depression. It is as popular at midcentury, if not as well articulated, as it was when Dallas Sharp, John Burroughs, James Oliver Curwood, and Gene Stratton Porter were the writers of the hour.

As John Erskine put it in 1926, "he knows little about us who overlooks our buying up of deserted farms and converting them into a refuge from something or other."[48] If Erskine and others found it difficult to describe their feeling with great precision, they were quite convinced that it was not an extension of "agrarian" values in the twentieth century. Sportsmen condemning pot-hunters, commuters shunning "natives," landscape architects planning suburban estates, summer camp directors and city tourists, all believed that rural Americans failed to appreciate the urban response to nature. Nostalgia for some remembered agricultural past played as little part in Erskine's philosophy as it did in Theodore Roosevelt's enjoyment of "Sagamore Hill" on Long Island. If the Arcadian myth was not simply a reversion to Thomas Jefferson's agrarianism, neither was it a revival of nineteenth-century "Transcendentalism." Here again, landscape architects felt they must improve on nature with axe and hoe; they must find aesthetic, not philosophical meaning in nature. Wilderness novelists and landscape photographers composed their scenes with the techniques of English Romantic artists. Churchmen agreed that nature was a Great Book, but it yielded them only good Christian parables. Suburbanites saw no inconsistency in coming face to face with nature only in John Burroughs's essays or Ernest Thompson Seton's nature-study readers. Finally, a mythology so full of urbane illusions offered poor support for any naive primitivism. The Arcadian tradition spread most widely through the mass media, but it was hardly unsophisticated. Presidents and preachers, journalists, university professors and business executives spoke for simple outdoor values that seemed attainable only through a system of unlimited complexity.

At whatever level it appeared, from nature-study classroom to the White House, the Arcadian myth embodied an urban response to nature that seemed most appropriate for an urban age. No matter how indifferently it actually transformed city life, most Americans came to link it with status and sophistication. Many adopted the role with no understanding of its intricate philosophy. Yet in so far as they believed that country life and city culture offered more in conjunction than as opposites, they seemed to welcome the contact with "Nature."

NOTES

1. James M. Williams, *Our Rural Heritage, the Social Psychology of Rural Development* (New York: Knopf, 1925), p. 10. Permission to quote by courtesy of Appleton-Century-Crofts, Division of Merideth Publishing Company.
2. Frederick Jackson Turner, "The Significance of the Frontier in American History," in *The Frontier in American History* (New York: Henry Holt and Company, 1920); for a penetrating discussion of Turner's melancholy see William Coleman, "Science and Symbol in the Turner Frontier Hypothesis," *American Historical Review,* LXXII (October 1966), pp. 22-50.
3. Henry Nash Smith, *Virgin Land: The American West as Symbol and Myth* (New York: Vintage edition, 1957), p. 135; Leo Marx, *The Machine in the Garden: Technology and the Pastoral Ideal in America* (New York: Galaxy Book edition, 1967), p. 11; George Mowry, *The Urban Nation, 1920-1960* (New York: Hill and Wang, 1965), p. 2. See also Roderick Nash, "The American Cult of the Primitive," *American Quarterly,* XVIII (June 1966), p. 526; and Morton and Lucia White, *The Intellectual versus the City, From Thomas Jefferson to Frank Lloyd Wright* (New York: New American Library edition, 1964), p. 230.

4. The "back-to-nature" movement differed from the "back-to-the-land" program which sought to place the urban poor on garden patches in the suburbs. Social reformers such as New York lawyer Bolton Hall were sure that all men could be producers with vacant-lot gardens and rural vegetable patches. "Agriculture is unique among occupations," Hall told his audiences, "in that it can be engaged in without one's first attaining any particular experience." Any dunce, he continued, could raise a crop of onions on an acre of land. John Burroughs believed that where there were cows there was Arcadia, but to Bolton Hall the cow was merely "a ruminating machine for producing milk." The industrial metaphor was as disconcerting to nature lovers as Hall's "little lots well-tilled" were foreign to working farmers. See Bolton Hall, A Little Land and a Living (New York: Arcadia Press, 1908), pp. 40, 80; John Burroughs, Signs and Seasons, Writings of John Burroughs, VII (Boston, New York: Houghton Mifflin, 1904, 1st ed. 1886), p. 254; Bolton Hall, Three Acres and Liberty (New York: Macmillan, 1907), p. 10.

5. William Smythe, City Homes on Country Lanes (New York: Macmillan, 1922), p. 60.

6. Andrew Jackson Downing, The Architecture of Country Houses (New York: Appleton, 1850), p. 258.

7. Liberty Hyde Bailey, The Nature Study Idea (New York: Doubleday, Page, 1903), p. 14.

8. Liberty Hyde Bailey, The Outlook to Nature (New York: Macmillan, 1905), p. 8.

9. Ibid., pp. 95, 97.

10. Liberty Hyde Bailey, The Holy Earth (New York, 1943, 1st ed. 1915), pp. 26, 37.

11. Ibid., pp. 65, 114.

12. Ibid., p. 105.

13. Ibid., p. 44.

14. Liberty Hyde Bailey, Universal Service (New York: Macmillan, 1923), p. 35.

15. Liberty Hyde Bailey, The Seven Stars (New York: Macmillan, 1923), p. 7.

16. Reports of the Department of the Interior, 1925 (Washington: Government Printing Office, 1925), p. 22.

17. "Editorial," Nature-Study Review, XVII (March, 1921), 142.

18. Frank Bolles, At the North of Bearcamp Water: Chronicles of a Stroller in New England from July to December (Boston: Houghton, Mifflin, 1899, 1st ed. 1893), p. 92.

19. John Muir, Our National Parks (Boston: Houghton, Mifflin, 1901), p. 1.

20. Stewart Edward White, The Mountains (New York: McClure, Phillips, 1904), pp. 205, 206, 209; Muir, Our National Parks, p. 101.

21. Grace Seton-Thompson, Nimrod's Wife (New York: Doubleday, Page, 1907), p. 60.

22. Muir, Our National Parks, p. 56.

23. A. R. Dee, "The Story of a $2,100 House," Country Life in America, III (April, 1903), pp. 227-231; Charles V. Boyd, "The Old-Fashioned Log Cabin Is the New-Fashioned Summer Camp, with All of the Comforts of Modern Life and All of the Picturesqueness of Pioneer Days," Woman's Home Companion, XLIII (May, 1916), p. 46; Chilson Aldrich, The Real Log Cabin (New York: MacMillan, 1934, 1st ed. 1928), pp. 26-28; Frederick Brimmer, Log Cabins, Lodges and Clubhouses (New York: Appleton, 1925).

24. See Elon Jessup, Roughing It Smoothly (New York: Putnam's, 1923); Warren Miller, Camping Out (New York: George Doran, 1918); Horace Kephart's The Book of Camping and Woodcraft (New York: Outing Publishing Co., 1906) went through seven editions between 1906 and 1921.

25. "The Cabin of a Novelist," The New York Times Book Review, April 30, 1911, p. 263.

26. Stewart Edward White, The Cabin (New York: Doubleday, Page, 1911), pp. 37, 134, 135.

27. Stanton Davis Kirkman, Resources (New York: Putnam's, 1910), p. 118.

28. Kirkham, Outdoor Philosophy, the Meditations of a Naturalist (New York: Putnam's, 1912), pp. 12, 187; Kirkham, In the Open (San Francisco: Paul Elder, 1908), p. 187.

29. Joseph Knowles, Alone in the Wilderness (Boston: Small, Maynard, 1913).

30. Rockwell Kent, Wilderness, a Journal of Quiet Adventure in Alaska (New York: Modern Library Edition, 1930, 1st ed. 1920), pp. v, 135, vii, 217.

31. Clarence Stein, "Dinosaur Cities," Survey Graphic, LIV (May 1, 1925), 134.

32. Stein, "Dinosaur Cities," 136.

33. "The cacophony of a dozen loud-speakers, and of hundreds of rattling fenders and squeaking brakes, continuing with scarcely any interruption for hours at a time," sociologist Niles Carpenter wrote in 1931, "builds up a mass of noise that is as intensely nervewracking as it is peculiarly urban"; see The Sociology of City Life (New York, London, Toronto: Longmans Green, 1931), p. 238.

34. See Edward E. Free, "How Noisy Is New York," Forum, LXXV (February, 1926), pp. xxi-xxiv; Free, "Noise," ibid., LXXIX (March, 1928), pp. 382-389; "We Must Outlaw Noise," Review of Reviews, LXXXI (January, 1930), pp. 81-82.

35. New York City Department of Health, City Noise (New York: Noise Abatement Commission, 1930), p. 42.

36. Charles Galpin, Rural Life (New York: Century, 1918), p. 11.

37. Charles E. Cooley, Social Organization: A Study of the Larger Mind (New York: Scribner's, 1909), p. 23.

38. Chicago's Robert E. Park advanced this idea as early as 1915. See Park, Ernest W. Burgess, Roderick D. McKenzie, The City (Chicago: University of Chicago Press, 1925), p. 40.

39. See Charles R. Henderson, "Are Modern Industry and City Life Unfavorable to the Family," American Journal of Sociology, XIV (March, 1909), pp. 668-680.

40. Harvey Zorbaugh, *Gold Coast and Slum* (Chicago: University of Chicago, 1929), p. 255.

41. Park, Burgess, McKenzie, *The City*, p. 109.

42. Carpenter, *Sociology of City Life*, pp. 218, 468.

43. Ernest Groves, "The Urban Complex," *Sociological Review*, XII (Fall, 1920), pp. 74, 76.

44. Ebenezer Howard, *Garden Cities of Tomorrow* (London: Swan Sonnenschein, 1902, 1st ed. titled *Tomorrow*, 1898), p. 13.

45. Louis Heaton Pink, *The New Day in Housing* (New York: John Day, 1928), p. 78. Sociologist Graham Taylor found in his study of "Satellite Cities," that factory workers often failed to follow their companies into the suburbs, preferring rather to commute from the cities outward. See Taylor, *Satellite Cities: A Study of Industrial Suburbs* (New York: D. Appleton, 1915), pp. 120, *passim*.

46. Frederick W. Coburn, "The Five-Hundred-Mile City," *World Today*, XI (December, 1906), 1253.

47. Booth Tarkington, *The World Does Move* (Garden City: Doubleday, Page, 1928), p. 164.

48. Christine Frederick, "Is Suburban Living a Delusion?" *Outlook*, CXLVIII (February 22, 1928), 291, 313.

49. See, for example, Lewis S. Gannett, "The Wildness of New York," *Century*, CX (July, 1925), pp. 299-304; Samuel Scoville, Jr., "The Wildness of Philadelphia," *ibid.* (November, 1925), pp. 117-124.

50. Hermon Cary Bumpus, Jr., *Hermon Cary Bumpus, Yankee Naturalist* (Minneapolis: University of Minnesota, 1948), p. 57.

51. See "City Planning Conferences in the United States," in *Proceedings,* Second National Conference on City Planning and the Problems of Congestion (Boston, 1910), p. 3.

52. Lewis Mumford, "Regions to Live In," Regional Planning Number, *The Survey Graphic*, LIV (May 1, 1925), p. 152; see also "The Fourth Migration," *ibid.*, pp. 130-133.

53. R. L. Duffus, *Mastering a Metropolis* (New York: Harper, 1930), pp. 2, 205.

54. Benton MacKaye, *The New Exploration, a Philosophy of Regional Planning* (New York: Harcourt, Brace, 1928), p. 225.

55. Walter Prichard Eaton, *Skyline Camps . . .* (Chicago: M. A. Wilde, 1922), p. 104.

56. Calvin Coolidge, "National Recreation Opportunities," *Playground*, XVIII (July, 1924), 194; also in *Proceedings,* National Conference on Outdoor Recreation (Washington: Government Printing Office, 1924), p. 12.

57. *Proceedings,* National Conference on Outdoor Recreation (Washington: Government Printing Office, 1926), p. 164; see also Herbert Hoover, "In Praise of Izaak Walton," *Atlantic Monthly*, CXXIX (June, 1927), 812.

58. Geoffrey Scott, *The Architecture of Humanism: A Study in the History of Taste* (London: Constable, 1914, 1924), p. 76.

59. Henry S. Canby, "Back to Nature," *Yale Review*, n.s. VI (July, 1917), pp. 756, 764, 762, 755.

60. Heywood Broun, "It Seems to Heywood Broun," *Nation*, CXXVI (June 13, 1928), p. 661. Even Broun admitted to owning his own country place, however.

61. John H. Preston "Back from Nature," *Saturday Review of Literature*, III (March 12, 1927), p. 652.

62. Noel P. Gist and L. A. Halbert, *Urban Society* (New York: Thomas Crowell, 1933), pp. 48, 284, 287, 285.

63. John Erskine, "A House in the Country," *Century*, CXII (July, 1926), p. 273.

The City in Crisis

SCOTT GREER

Ours is an urban world. In a way that has never been true in the past we have given all of our hostages to the encompassing fortunes of great cities. Imperial Rome under the Augustans may have been as much as 10 per cent urban; America today is over 60 per cent urban and nearly half of the urbanites live in metropolitan areas with populations of over one million. Projecting these present tendencies into the future, an estimate made in 1960 indicates that four-fifths of the great increase in population expected by 1980 will be metropolitan, with the urban proportion of the total over 70 per cent.[1] Thus, there is little chance for most of us to escape from the city, even should we wish to; we had better begin to try to understand it.

This is a difficult assignment. It is very much as though we were studying the geography of the earth in the planet's early days, when cataclysmic change took place continually in response to pressure and heat, under cover of a nearly continuous cloud of vapor produced by the very changes we wished to observe. The nature of the city is changing, and the very rapidity of change is producing conflict and confusion in our images and our policy. Yet we must work out trial solutions; intellectual and political decisions are demanded every day and will not wait upon a final solution. Ironically and inescapably, our policy is one of the dy-

namics altering the city, and our policy rests upon our images of the city, our notions of how it works and of possible instruments for change and control.

SOME POLICY CHOICES

Our choices begin with the emerging shape of the metropolis itself. Though much is inherited, the funded energy of the past in the shape of the vast physical plant of the city does not foreclose all future choice: the projected growth for the next two decades insures that. One possibility is the retention of the general focus and structure of the city as we have inherited it. This is a more difficult job than may appear on the surface, for the original settlers, speculators, entrepreneurs, and peculators built in terms of a technology and a society that are no more. Much of the inherited city is made up of overvalued and obsolete slums, loft buildings, and nineteenth-century factories, their access barricaded by traffic. What are the possibilities of retaining such a structure for the city, what are the costs, and what are the benefits?

How should we channel new growth, and how can we do so? While urban redevelopment has resulted in a few monuments and failures dedicated to the salvage of the older parts of the city, the increasing population of the metropolis has busily built and inhabited its own version of "greenbelts" in the sub-

From Scott Greer, *The Emerging City* (New York: The Free Press, 1962), pp. 1-28. Copyright © 1962 by The Free Press of Glencoe, A Division of The Macmillan Company. Reprinted by permission of the publisher. Scott Greer is Professor of Political Science at Northwestern University.

urbs. Most of the metropolitan growth since World War II has been suburban development, and of the population growth of sixty-four million expected by 1980, over 80 per cent will be in the suburbs. Thus, the channeling of new growth competes for attention with conservation and rebuilding of older areas.[2]

A key question for consideration by either viewpoint, and one that is frequently a bone of contention between partisans of the Utopias, is traffic and transportation. What will the circulatory system of the metropolis be? Will the increasing automobile traffic force an increase in the arteries, further adjustment to the automobile as chief carrier, and thus increasing numbers of automobiles? Such a course leads public transportation into the vicious circle of fewer passengers, greater per capita cost, poor service, higher fares, fewer passengers—and a continuous encouragement to use the automobile. On the other hand, what combination of statute and the public fisc can rechannel transportation? The last war was effective, since it literally prohibited automobile traffic through rationing. Nothing else has been effective. Those committed to public transportation point out, however, that little else has been tried—while the cities subsidize the automobile drivers and the latter flourish under such subsidy.

The automobile has, as one virtue, its great ability to increase the accessibility of scattered places on the periphery of the city: suburbia is auto-borne. Suburbia is also, preponderantly, native-born and white. Those who live in the older portions of the city (and who are, in a sense, conservatives of an older urban tradition) are of a different complexion. As their numbers increase, in absolute terms, and as they become a higher proportion of the residents and voters, they increasingly make their needs felt. The growing number of ethnic residents in the limited area of the central city has often been interpreted through the classic law of gases —and many observers await, with trepidation, the day when the central city "blows its top." Struggles to break and to hold the legal and extralegal barriers used in the war of containment are continuous—they are not unrelated to the suburban movement of the white population. These struggles create continuous policy problems in the central city —and it is no wonder that mayors and race relations commissions look with some bitterness upon the suburbanites, who profit from the total work and wealth of the metropolis but refuse to share its costs.

Yet the central city also continues to produce the classic problems of urban democracy along with the wealth from which suburbia derives its income. Few of the great public parks that grace our cities are safe at night—and many are dangerous at high noon. Entire neighborhoods are the scenes of guerilla war, with *freikorps* battling for the control of the streets. The safety of person and property is not automatically assured in the greatest cities of the wealthiest nation. The battle to naturalize the immigrant and acculturate the unwashed continues, and with it the battle to civilize, through civil service and administrative law, the political and governmental organizations of the city.

These are difficult problems, for they demand solutions considering both arguments of equity and knowledge of means. Perhaps the most encompassing statement of the urban policy choice is simply: what governmental form is best suited to contain and resolve the issues that have been lightly touched on above, as well as those not mentioned and the myriads that are surely moving toward us over the horizon of history? What is the relevant constituency? What structure can both represent the interests that demand representation and, at the same time, resolve the ineluctable conflicts inherent in the contemporary metropolis?

These are only a few of the policy choices faced by the metropolis today.

THE KALEIDOSCOPE OF IMAGES

Decisions on such topics are intimately related to the guiding image, the overall theory, with which we approach the city. How shall we effectively focus this particular "booming, buzzing confusion," this complex mass of heterogeneous and transient human action moving through time? How shall we summarize patterns in a limited set of categories, so that we can relate the parts in a meaningful way?

The development of a coherent body of thought with respect to such a large and immediate subject usually begins with a metaphor. Whether it develops into a scientifically established theory or remains a metaphor, such an image provides at least a rudimentary concept, a handle for intellectual control. With respect to the metropolis, then, we may ask: What kinds of metaphors dominate our intellectual discourse? What images stand for the totality and are, for practical purposes, "theories of the city"? We shall begin by inspecting the images used by social scientists who are concerned with the city. Political scientists, economists, and sociologists have for many decades manifested a continuing interest in the urban complex.

Political scientists typically approach the city as a governmental unit with powers and duties of a specific kind. From the concern of classical theorists with the city state, from consideration of the importance of the city in the development of modern law, and from day-to-day concern with the administrative structure of urban government, they inherit a rich body of information and concepts. The city, for the political scientist, is the corporate body, the legal personality, a little prototype of the state, preceding in history the development of the nation. It rests upon a balance of power among contending interests (including the interest of the prince) and its product is the polity: order, roads, monuments, and the "authoritative allocation of values" by those with legitimate power.

Urban sociologists emphasize a geographical image of the city. Under the influence of the ecological approach, they have constructed a two dimensional theory of the city—a sprawling map of people in places. Theirs has been a metaphor emphasizing the unplanned, "blind" development of urban concentration, the regularities in the use of space that are unlegislated but enforced by mechanisms of competition for *lebensraum*. The city, for the urban ecologist, is the mass of population, heterogeneous and dense, segregated by wealth and cultural background. It is a loose congeries with a vestigial normative structure, existing like "nature's half acre" in an ecological balance. One of the competing groups is government itself—parties, patrons, officials. Although the early ecologists paid tribute to a moral order coexistent with the ecological order, the research and theory of urban sociology shows little concern for such a dimension. The equilibrium of their city rests upon an ecological balance among contending subgroups, and its product is a division of labor and rewards reflected on a map.

The economists, late comers to the study of the city, see it in two lights. First, as a matrix of locations for firms —a necessary translation of a national economy into space. Second, and more pertinent to our inquiry, some economists have been turning toward an image of the city as an economic unit— a kind of super firm, based upon relations between importers and exporters, contractors and subcontractors (with the household as the smallest firm) all involved in an import-export business. Thus, the economist sees the city as a center of production, trade, and distribution, whose basic units are economic organizations. Local government is itself a peculiar kind of firm. The economic city rests upon a division of labor among firms, competition, and cooperation within the framework of the market, with advantages and disadvantages in the form of location, multipliers, and marginal economies. The city as a whole is "in business," and its economic position may be estimated by the balance of trade.

All three of these images of the city betray the heavy hand of nineteenth-century liberalism. Although the political theorists concerned with the city sometimes misplaced their concereteness, mistaking a territorial jurisdiction for a general and universal social structure, when it came to business matters their city was rigorously limited to the constitutionally established powers and forms of city government in the United States. In the same fashion, the assumptions of laissez faire are built into the

ecological image. Competition, conflict, accommodation and assimilation take place within a framework of rules approximately the same as those advocated by Herbert Spencer—with room for social evolution, enterprise, and the survival of those most fit to survive. The economic image is simply a verbatim translation: the city becomes a small business man.

Today, all three of these approaches suffer from the same limitation: they are far too partial. Each makes assumptions basic to its explanatory power that are never defined and tested; all focus upon the city without much concern for its environment in social space and time. In order to improve explanation and prediction in particular cases, each is extended toward the bounds of the others (frequently moving past the center of the neighboring discipline, with comic results). In the process of extension the clarity of the original image, a major virtue, is lost in the confusion of "interdisciplinary" thought. The image becomes encrusted with a mass of *ad hoc* barnacles, epicycles, and hemidemisemiquavers.

Thus, the political scientist finds that his approach leads from classic political theory to the constitutioal form of municipal government with at least moderate success, but the day to day operations of government force him to look at the nongovernmental norms that determine behavior—including the folkways and mores of avoiding the law. He is led still further afield by his concern with political parties: how can one explain governmental behavior without explaining party organization? Party organization, without economic interests? And this subject is closely related to the ecologist's concern with kinds of people in space, the conflict of group interests (including the interests of firms), the accommodations that are improvised and form the basis for tradition and, perhaps, law.

When the political scientist turns to look at the city today, he finds that the corporate body is broken into dozens of separate entities: the central city is enmeshed in a web of suburbs, a tangle of villages. Yet this is still, in some sense, "one city." Now he must consider the consequences of ecological shifts in a new light: the suburbs become overwhelmingly white, higher in social class, tending toward Republican affiliation. The central city becomes an electorate of working-class and ethnic identity. Yet each is a necessary condition for the other's existence. Furthermore, the public fisc itself is affected. The "city" may be viewed as a firm, one that can prosper or go bankrupt. Public administration theory can be related to Taylorism and the theory of the firm. Yet this firm's customers are voters, and it may be forced to do business at a constant loss.

The urban ecologist has similar problems. The urban map changes, and frequently the change forces one to look at governmental action—the moral order. Urban redevelopment, zoning, governmental autonomy in the suburbs, such matters as these change the land values of the city but cannot be explained by simple competition for space. At the same time the city, as entrepreneur, struggles to control its own economic future through promotion, redevelopment, the construction of "industrial parks." The roots of these developments lie in areas of economic and political organization that are hardly amenable to exploration through census data

plotted on maps, yet they affect the maps. They represent, in some sense, an urban polity—something missing from nature's half acre.

The economist's emerging image suffers similar sea changes. He is forced to grant that zoning laws may shut off the choicest locations for industrial plants, may at an extreme impoverish a metropolitan area, while the general level of governmental services and taxes may affect the recruitment of industry to an area and hence the economic development of the city. The public fisc becomes a necessary but theoretically indigestible part of his apparatus. At the same time, if he is interested in welfare, he is forced to note that governmental services make up an area of consumption in which American urban populations frequently have static or declining products to consume. The competitive market does not produce streets, police protection, playgrounds, and parks. Here the *polity* is analagous to the market. The economist must become a student of political science in order to answer strictly economic questions.

Equally as damaging, however, as the partiality of these approaches, is the limitation in scope. A generally useful image should allow one to summarize the pertinent detail and explain cases varying widely in their surface nature; it should thus allow the interpretation of change through time. While it would be in process of continual modification and improvement, moving toward the condition of a theory, it could not be casually jettisoned. Yet Martindale, in a recent essay on Max Weber's approach to the city, indicates grave doubts as to the usefulness of the image developed by this major and influential sociologist (who was also, and originally, a political economist).

Max Weber's theory of the city, thus, leads to a rather interesting conclusion. We can grant the phenomenal increase and aggregation of modern populations as a concomitant of the industrial revolution. We should not, however, confuse physical aggregation with the growth of the city in a sociological sense. The urban community has everywhere lost its military integrity—its right to defend itself by military means. In many areas of the world it has, temporarily at least, lost its very legal and political autonomy—the same fate is possible everywhere. Meanwhile, within the city itself greater masses of residents pursue interlocal interests—as representatives of the national government, as agents in business and industries of national and international rather than of civic scope.

The modern city is losing its external and formal structure. Internally it is in a state of decay while the new community represented by the nation everywhere grows at its expense. The age of the city seems to be at an end.[3]

This statement indicates one writer's belief that the utility of the legal-social definition of the city is at an end—that the city has no separate existence and therefore no interest for the social scientist. That this is not a parochial conclusion is indicated by Albert Reiss, in an introduction to one of the most authoritative collections of readings in urban sociology.

There seems to be a decline of interest in research on cities and city life, if the research in urban demography and human ecology is excluded from consideration. This is in part due to the fact that much of the research simply considers the urban community to be a *context* within which a particular kind of theoretical problem is studied, but the context itself is not often made the object of investigation. . . . A second reason for the decline in urban research activity is the fact that there has been a shift in the problem-area division of

sociological knowledge so that certain of the problems formerly conceptualized as "urban sociology" now are viewed within another frame of reference or theory. This is true, for example, of what now are called the problem fields of industrial sociology, social stratification and mass communication. There is some reason to believe that the sociology of city life will limit itself largely to a consideration of urban structure (in the sense of community) during the next decade and that the fragmentation of the field will continue.[4]

Thus, Martindale counsels the abandonment of the city as a usable image of whatever kind, while for Reiss the city as an independent object of study becomes a study of community, from which concern with work, social class, mass communications, and other aspects of life in cities are eliminated. Surely this would also eliminate most of the sociological relevance of the metropolis. Ironically, at the point in time when the city has reached a societal dominance never before seen, it seems to elicit confessions of theoretical bankruptcy from its students.

For the economist, too, the city may cease to be a basic unit of analysis. Raymond Bernon concludes from a recent study of the New York Metropolitan Region that

we are a nation tending toward regional self-sufficiency in the production of goods. The plants in each region are developing increasingly complex ties with one another. And although they are not showing any increasing tendency to settle within the borders of metropolitan areas, nevertheless one of the major determinants of their location is the size and location of these metropolitan clusters.[5]

The overweening centralization of many economic activities in cities is, in this view, declining; in its place a considerably larger geographical area (without any of the classic characteristics of cities save economic interdependence), becomes the most useful unit for studying the problems of local economies.

THE CITY AND MASS SOCIETY

Thus, the images of the city deteriorate as the structure of the larger society alters through time: the economic city expands and diffuses, the political city loses autonomy and is merged in the national polity, the social city becomes indistinct from the larger whole, a context, a sample of modern society. This leads to another view of the city—that which identifies the city and nation, summarizing both under the rubric of "mass society." Such an image does not allow one to differentiate the city from all that is most characteristic of contemporary society nor, on the other hand, does it encourage one to investigate the internal structure of the city. It moves from vast changes in the nation to transformations of the individual.

Ortega, Spengler, Durkheim, Tonnies, these are some of the ideologues who saw the city as the summation of contemporary society, the end product of a long process transforming the ethnic groups of band and village into megalopolitan society.[6] Ortega saw the hierarchical orders crumbling beneath the waves of economic and political democracy, and prophesied the state of the masses; western culture would perish under the onslaught of the vulgar. Spengler spoke of the death of culture in the cities of the Autumn, social products of a loss of nerve that would lead, in the end, to Caesarism and the deification of massive power. Durkheim saw the city as epitomizing the social dust heap, the organic society unified by interdependence through the division of labor, but producing an unstable unity

in which consensus and solidarity are partial and problematic. Tonnies saw community give way to the urban world in which most bonds are instrumental, negotiable, contractual, while rights and duties become separated from the age-old sanctification of the community and its rewards.

Such is the image of the city as product and producer of mass society: like the magic salt mill that sank, still grinding, to the bottom of the ocean, the city processes the culture and way of life of modern man until the entire sea has been salted. It is an image particularly congruent with American folk thought; the small-town bias of American sociologists and the important rural survivals in urban American culture led many scholars to give credence to the mass image of the urban world, even before the limitations of the various partial analyses noted had become apparent. After all, Lincoln Steffens (still a revered commentator on urban life) became famous for his study, *The Shame of the Cities* and Lord Bryce spoke of American urban government as our most conspicuous failure. Carl Sandburg immortalized an earlier Chicago as "wicked," "crooked," "brutal," while Theodore Dreiser (in his novels based upon the career of Yerkes) made dramatic and credible a view of the city as a veritable jungle in which power was evil, virtue weak, and the community notable for its absence. Such an image of the city combined the view of the countryman, the frustrated reformer, and the laissez-faire liberal of Spencerian proclivities with the powerful poetry of the ideologues.[7] Ralph Borzodi raised the flat question, *Are Cities Abnormal?* and Lewis Mumford looked back in nostalgia to the communes of the thirteenth century. This pessimistic view attained academic respectability during the 1930's, particularly in the field called "Social Disorganization."[8]

The movement in American sociology to group the scattered studies of "social problems" in the more general field of social disorganization coincided roughly with the great depression. This approach referred all "problems" back to a general illness or incompetence of the social structure; pathological in its focus, it implicitly defined as the normal, healthy society the small town of an earlier America—or even the peasant community and the folk society. This use of a "rural-urban continuum" within which to organize and "explain" a heterogeneous mass of social problems resulted in a ubiquitous bias against the city—while the nation was rapidly becoming urbanized. Although such an approach usually paid lip service to processes of reorganization, the image of the city as the summation of social disorganization left precious little room for stability, order, and reconstruction.

The acceptance of such an image by urban sociologists was not unrelated to the ecological image of the city: it was nourished upon statistics indicating the concentration of crime, suicide, divorce, and other "social pathologies" in the cities as well as the various small studies of Chicago carried out under the direction and inspiration of Robert Park. Pictures of the urban extremes, the "Gold Coast," the slums, the "black belt," the "hobohemia," emphasized the dramatic variety of situations to be found in a metropolitan area.[9] Most important of all, however, was the celebrated essay of Louis Wirth, "Urbanism as a Way of Life," in which Wirth defines the city as a large, dense, permanent settlement of unlike groups and derives from these attributes certain

likely patterns of interaction and their consequences: impersonality, isolation, the decline of primary group membership, and the dominance of formal organizations.[10] These are seen as the social characteristics of the city and, by extension, of the contemporary mass society.

Upon such a basis was the "massified" image of the city formulated and built into many urban-sociology textbooks.

Such a view was probably related to the general *weltschmerz* of the deep depression: poverty, unemployment, deficit financing at home; dictatorship, purges, and, above all, the imminence of war abroad. The doctrine of the mass society and the image of the massified city corresponded to a belief in societal determinism reciprocal to the loss of *naive* faith in individual effort. The failure of men to control history in the light of their values was evident on every hand, while Marxism and other forms of historical evolutionism focused attention upon the patterns of the failure. The dissolution of consensus and the collapse of the Republic in Germany; the dramatic quality of mass persuasion used by the demagogues of the right and the left; the power of class and race as tools for organizing social power—these were some of the regular occurrences that bulked so large in the consciousness of the 1930's. Nowhere is this stated more succinctly than in Lederer's book on Hitler, *State of the Masses*, at once a technical analysis and an appreciation of that demagogue's use of the destructive forces inherent in modern, urban society.[11] Awareness of them permeated the social thought of the thirties.

The image of the massified city during the depression was one that was closely related to an image of the total society; yet the American society of the 1930's was also one in which a variety of welfare efforts were under way; the New Deal not only publicized need, it symbolized an evolving polity that tendered means toward amelioration. Pare Lorentz and Lewis Mumford made their spectacular film, "The City," emphasizing the negative judgments of contemporary urban life—but the public-works projects poured millions of man-hours into reconstruction of the city. The mass image never served an eschatological function for American thinkers; their roots in a pragmatic and ameliorative culture were too strong for this. And, once the depression and the war had passed, the image and the reality for which it stood moved very nearly 180 degrees, from moral rejection to acceptance.

In the ten years after World War II a number of influential books appeared, dealing, again, with mass society and the city—but with what a difference! In the works of David Riesman and his associates, as well as those of William Holley White, Samuel Lubell, A. C. Spectorsky, and John R. Seeley, the image of the existing mass society very closely approaches earlier utopias.[12] While the poor remain with us, they are much fewer, and a general ebullience of tone implies their eventual disappearance. While American urban life is mobile and therefore rootless in an older sense, it appears likely that shallow roots will do the trick, even roots like those of certain water plants, which allow the plants wide latitude to drift on a liquid surface. And the political apathy, the vulnerability to charisma and manipulation, the *rassenkampf*, the resentment against the social order?

They are either cured by twenty years of economic expansion, or else made orderly and predictable by the twin engines of the mass market and the mass media. (As Wallace Stevens once wrote: ". . . Oxidia, banal suburb/ One-half of all its installments paid . . . Oxidia is Olympia.")

In all of these works the mass society is practically identified with the massified city; however, there is a striking change in focus. No longer is the older central city the arena in which good and evil grapple in a dozen matches; instead, the center of the mass is now suburbia. The mass society, the crowds of the street, are located far from the warrens of revolution and crime. They are installed, more or less securely, in the ranks of the middle classes.

This image may be called that of the "mass society in an economy of plenty," as contrasted to the "mass society of deprivation." Its principle characteristics are a continuous and easy upward mobility or, as an alternative, a secure and easy access to the goods of the mass market, for all of the population—this in combination with a wide area of choice in articles of consumption, residence, "culture," social interaction itself. The rules for obtaining the abundance of this cornucopia, however, are rather limiting at the individual level as they are not clearly understood at the societal level. In general, the resident of the massified city is portrayed as committed to (and conforming to) the bureaucratic norms in his place of work, the uncodified norms of his peer group, the continuous bombardment of norms from the mass media. He is, in short, a conformist. Riesman attempts to relate these patterns to changes in the organization of the total society, and to trace the consequences in the institutional areas of work, play, politics, and the like. Whyte emphasizes the social structure of the modern corporation and its consequences for the social character and life style of its employees. The authors of *Crestwood Heights* focus upon the interlocked mechanisms of neighborhood and school as sources of conformity. It is an image of the city that has structural components very similar to those of the "mass society" predicted by the gloomy prophets of the depression, but the over-all color and tone are very different. The degree to which this is caused by a real difference in the nature of the city and the degree to which it is colored by the eyes of the observer remain to be seen.

THE CRISIS

Some forty years after urban sociologists began their intensive study of the city and political scientists became empirical students of public administration and political behavior, our image of the city is in a process of dissolution. While we are far richer in heterogeneous concepts and partial theories, as well as information of one kind and another, in crucial ways we are curiously poverty stricken. There is little order in our theories, and our data seem largely irrelevant to them. At the very point in time when we become a metropolitan society, when the problems of the metropolis excite widespread interest, study, and action, some of the scholars studying the city lean toward the notion that it has disappeared while others proffer images so disparate and discrepant that they hardly seem to refer to the same elephant.

The city is a struggle of interest groups, an administrative hierarchy working toward the perfect machine in a curious isolation from politics, or a population whose behavior may be studied as manifestations of power at least as readily as any other aggregate. Or, it is a vast piling up of people with various characteristics, literally, a social "dust heap," organized only in the myriad competing and accommodating subgroups whose arbiter is the market. Or, it is a complex of firms, whose orientation is toward supply, production, marketing, and the advantages of location. Alternatively, it is a spatially defined segment of the total society, a sample of the mass, moving toward anarchy, anomie, revolution and dictatorship—or toward conformism, simple-minded cultural uniformity, prosperity, and bureaucratic rule. Some of these images are in direct conflict, assuming polar opposites in the behavior of the urban population. Furthermore, all of them omit a consideration of most of the routine, everyday, social order that permits a daily reprieve for the dependent millions of the urban islands.

The crisis of the city is thus, in the beginning at least, an intellectual crisis. The inherited images are no longer applicable; they are partial and based upon assumptions about the total society that are unexamined and frequently outmoded. Furthermore, the action crisis of the metropolis cannot be disengaged from the intellectual crisis, for the very definition of a metropolitan problem is dependent upon one's picture of the city and the kind of life it should contain, as the choice of action to improve or revolutionize is dependent upon one's estimate of the city as an existing entity. Those who retain the image of the city as a legal person, a corporate entity, heir to the city-states of Greece, Italy, and medieval Europe, will hardly agree with those who see it chiefly as a spatial sample of a massified society. Their notions of what is, what should be, and how it may be brought about, will tend toward the poles of possibility.

The peculiar quality of this confusion, however, is the presumption of partial validity that each image of the city elicits. While the city is not "militarily autonomous," its corporate nature cannot be dismissed. Anyone who has heard the Viziers of City Hall in a great metropolis refer proudly to "The City" is disabused of the notion. No matter how the rulers are recruited, they control a polity most immediately felt by the citizen, for they rule him "where he lives." Nor can we forget the economic basis of the city and the patterns of land use that order it in space. Where, then, does the failure of urban social science lie? It would be presumptuous to answer with more than hypotheses; however, the statement of such propositions may clarify the problem of improving our image of the city. Implied or stated in the foregoing discussions, three weaknesses in the conceptualization of urban society are baldly evident: the inadequate empirical relevance of many of these images, the partial nature of the approaches, and their limited scope and special nature.

Empirical Relevance

The failure of various images of the city to be empirically relevant may not be apparent to the casual reader; our own daily observations are so persuasive as generalities that we unconsciously validate the casual empiricism of the image maker while our own values make it easy to accept the order proffered by our favorite ideologue. Yet, if the foregoing argument has virtue, arbitration among competing images is badly needed. We must cease to think like the supposed object of study, and become the student. For this purpose, the final arbiter of social science must be the empirical argument; such an argument, however, is applicable only when the image itself may be reduced to empirically relevant theory. Failure to do so has been one cause for the multiplication of images.

Some of the images are inherently untestable as stated, for they cannot possibly be falsified. Spengler, Marx, Ortega, each assumes a natural law whose unfolding can never be foretold within the limits of test: it must be inferred after the fact. Further, such ideologues appeal also to natural right, and assume that in the long run the course of history will move toward their own judgment of human behavior. We need not multiply examples of such a position. When, however, these images of the mass society are shorn of their evolutionary presuppositions and their evaluative connotations and used as working guides, they become very different. Discounting the data from the past at the same rate we use for present observations, and eliminating proleptic prediction (or prophecy) as data, we remain with a host of hypotheses as guides to the description of social behavior in the societies and cities of today.

Such description as we have available, however, suffers from sampling bias. The early studies of Gold Coast and slum, as well as very recent reports on the new suburbia, represent a selection of polar extremes and a heightening of dramatic contrasts through uncontrolled inference from limited observation. A theory that emphasizes extremes does not necessarily tell us anything at all about the excluded middle, which may, after all, include the vast majority of urban residents. The wealthy social circles of exurbia, the enclaves of the company men, are latter day equivalents of the "Taxi-Dance Hall" and the "Hobohemia": their use as ideal types of modern urban society is suspect indeed.

Nor can we accept, as clinching evidence in arbitrating among the images, the analysis of mass data provided by the census. It is limited indeed, and there are few postulates constructed to satisfactorily carry the argument from statistical aggregates to the nature óf ongoing behavior. The rhetoric of mass statistics tells us, for example, little about the nature of metropolitan government: size, number, variety of suburban municipalities, and similar data have no self-evident connection with the nature of the political process in suburbia. Nor can we infer a great deal from the information that more crime is committed in the metropolis than the middle-sized city, in the slum than in the suburb. Ingenious and skillful analysts continue to order the data provided by the census: it is a distortion of method, leading to a distortion of theory, to presume that such data will have more than a very narrow relevance to such images of the social city as we have adduced.

But the journalist, the shrewd observer, the analyst of census data, has provided most of the evidence for and against the various images of the city. None can, in the nature of his trade, supply the data for a crucial test—none of the images can be "mapped into" a model and evaluated so easily as that.

The Partially Explicated
Nature of Theory

A partially explicated theory assumes propositions in its basic explanations that are never made explicit and related to its other aspects; thus, it omits serious consideration of behavior that is crucial even to the limited aspect of things with which it deals. The advocates of scientific management in public administration focus straitly upon the formal machinery, knowing that the party structure and the various kinds of community influence constantly sway behavior away from bureaucratic norms. The urban ecologist ignores the social organization producing spatial patterns as well as that resulting from contiguity or separation. The student of public finance assumes as given, not only the economic history of his metropolis, but the mutual impact of the private enterprises and the public fisc.

To be sure, any approach must abstract; the key question, then, is the determination of criteria for exclusion or inclusion. There are two major guiding notions; first, we must include that which is necessary to the full explication of our theory (the image must be complete); second, we must move toward a closer "fit" between our theory and the delimited aspect of behavior upon which we are focused (the image must be tested). Ideally, all that is included in a given scientific approach, all that constitutes a given image of the city, must be "internal." It must make sense in the same vocabulary. An integrated approach to the urban polity does not adduce psychosomatic medicine, the technology of flood control, and the biology of fecundity into its framework *without translation*.

As the need is felt for further explanation, however, the tendency has been to add theory from every level of explanation, to mix metaphors unmercifully. Consequently, the special cases begin to outnumber the rule and social science becomes a very idiomatic language. Logically, the consequences are fatal: all can be explained after the fact, nothing can be predicted. The *ad hoc* notions from various sources become outriggers that prevent the boat from capsizing, at the cost of getting the boat in the water.

Thus, a major weakness in the various images of the city has been their lack of complete explication, and this results in a very hazy delimitation of explanatory power. The theory that is not delimited as to its application has a tendency to be continually absorbing notions at every level of generality, leaving unanswered the major question of its own internal logic, and therefore the point at which it can be profitably related to other images from other disciplines. In this light, the interdisciplinary tendency in urban studies may be a vitiating influence, for it weakens the integrity of each evolving image without uniting them in an orderly fashion.

The Limited Scope of Urban Theory

However, the images tend more and more to interpenetrate as the political scientist concerns himself with the economic growth of the city, the ecologist struggles to relate the increasingly important effects of government to the old regularities of land use, and the economist tries to deal with the corporation as a private government, the government as a public enterprise. Such shifts are not due solely to the internal dynamics of each theoretical approach; they are vitally related to the shifting relations between the great institutional areas of the society. Shrewd observers relying on personal observation note that politics may be seen as a "consumption of goods," the customer and firm as a single "organizational system," or the urban area as an "ecology of games."

They are mixing their metaphors consciously; the effort is sparked by observation of the changing relations among major areas of the culture.

At the same time, the kaleidoscope of images betrays a wavering and rapidly shifting focus—where are the key structures of the city, and what changes are definitive? Are they located in the metropolitan region as a whole? the mass society? the suburbs? the central city? The spatial abstraction (the "given" image of a congestion of human activity on the face of the earth) is evidently not defining: further and other abstraction is required.

The interpenetration of images and the shifting focus both reflect the overall dynamics of the carrying society. The analysis of the city that views it as spatially abstracted eliminates (1) the relation between the city and the larger society, and therefore (2) the key dynamics in the evolving society that largely determine the relations between institutional areas and the significant organizational unit for observation. A theory limited to "the city" is too narrow in scope to explain the changing landscape of the city itself.

THE AIM OF THIS STUDY

If the above analysis is useful, it should provide directives for the reinterpretation of contemporary urban society and the reformulation of the urban image. Such a reinterpretation must have a wider scope, a more specific empirical reference, and a greater theoretical integrity than those discussed above.

It must emphasize the study of the urban complex as a structure, but a structure intimately related to the nature of the carrying society. Thus, the image of the city must be contained within an over-all picture of urban so-ciety; "urbanization" and "urbanism," in this approach, become adjectives re-ferring to a society, not merely its pop-ulation concentrations. Furthermore, such a picture must be congruent with long-term change—in the general so-ciety, in the nature of the city, and in the relations between the two.

The approach must yield an empiri-cally relevant image, one that can be tested at many points. It must be based upon the data available, particularly those data free from the limitations of sampling bias and uncontrolled infer-ence. It must, further, yield new van-tage points from which to view old problems and create new problems with enough salience to force reconsidera-tions and improvements in the over-all image.

Finally, it must be guided by a con-cern for theoretical integrity. The focus must be delimited, the internal structure of the theory must be explicated, other-wise the image is neither clearly ap-plicable nor testable. Consequently, however, all aspects of urban life cannot be considered. Whether those empha-sized are the most useful for such an enterprise is a decision that will rest with the arbiters of improved empirical evidence and, finally, the pragmatic test of intellectual history.

NOTES

1. Philip M. Hauser, *Population Perspectives*, New Brunswick, N.J.: Rutgers University Press, 1960, "The Metropolitan Area Explosion: The Facts," Chapter 4, page 101.
2. *Ibid.*, pp. 101-106.
3. Don Martindale, "Prefatory Remarks: The The-ory of the City," in Max Weber, *The City* (trans-lated by Don Martindale and Gertrud Neuwirth), New York: The Free Press of Glencoe, 1958, p. 62.
4. Albert J. Reiss, Jr., in "Introduction: The So-ciology of Urban Life, 1946-1956," in Paul K. Hatt and Albert J. Reiss, Jr. (eds.), *Cities and Society, The Revised Reader in Urban Sociology*, New York: The Free Press of Glencoe, 1957, pp. 10-11.
5. "Urban Production and Distribution," in "The Metropolis in Ferment," *Annals of the American Academy of Political and Social Science*, 314, 20-21. Donald M. Pappenfort has made a similar observation: from a conventional ecological point of view the metropolis is not a discrete entity at all, in his opinion. See "The Ecological Field and the Metropolitan Community: Manufacturing and Management," *American Journal of Sociology*, 69, 380-385.
6. For typical works see José Ortega y Gasset, *The State of the Masses;* Oswald Spengler, *Decline of the West;* Emile Durkheim, *The Division of Labor in Society* (translated by George Simpson), New York: The Free Press of Glencoe, 1949 (especially the Preface to the Second Edition); Ferdinand Tonnies, *Gemeinschaft und Gesellschaft* (trans-lated by Charles P. Loomis as *Community and Society*), East Lansing, Mich.: Michigan State University Press, 1957.
7. For extensive and lively documentation of this melodramatic definition, see Anselm Strauss, *Im-ages of the American City*, New York: The Free Press of Glencoe, 1961, particularly Chapter 10, "Rural Aspects of Metropolitan Living." Closer to home is his "Appendix: A Note on Imagery in Urban Sociology."
8. For examples of this approach see Mable A. Elliott and Francis E. Merrill, *Social Disorganiza-tion*, New York: Harper and Brothers, 1941; and Robert E. L. Faris, *Social Disorganization*, New York: The Ronald Press, 1948.
9. Harvey W. Zorbaugh, *The Gold Coast and the Slum*, Chicago: University of Chicago Press, 1929; E. Franklin Frazier, *The Negro Family in Chi-cago*, Chicago: University of Chicago Press, 1932; Nels Anderson, *The Hobo*, Chicago: University of Chicago Press, 1923.
10. Louis Wirth, "Urbanism as a Way of Life," *American Journal of Sociology*, 44, 1-24. For a later statement more directly addressed to the mass-society hypothesis see his article on "Consen-sus and Mass Communications" in the *American Sociological Review*, 13, 1-15.
11. Emil Lederer, *State of the Masses*.
12. David Riesman, with Reuel Denny and Nathan Glazer, *The Lonely Crowd*, New Haven: Yale University Press, 1950; William H. Whyte, Jr., *The Organization Man*, New York: Simon and Schuster, 1956; Samuel Lubell, *The Future of American Politics*, Garden City, N. Y.: Doubleday and Company, Inc. (Anchor Edition), 1956 and *The Revolt of the Moderates*, New York: Harper and Brothers, 1956; A. C. Spectorsky, *The Ex-urbanites*, Philadelphia: J. B. Lippincott Company, 1955; John R. Seeley, R. Alexander Sim, and Elizabeth W. Loosly, *Crestwood Heights, A Study of the Culture of Suburban Life*, New York: Basic Books, Inc., 1955.

VIII   THE CITY IN MODERN TIMES

The city in modern times is that giant complex, the metropolis, swallowing the hinterland with its clusters of suburban communities and satellite cities. The chief characteristic of the metropolis is decentralization, which began late in the nineteenth century and reversed the trend of centralization that characterized so many of the older cities. Accelerated by the automobile, the growth of the suburbs, and the relocation of industry and manufacturing, decentralization has boomed in the twentieth century to produce the metropolis, the super-city, which in itself represents a new phase of urban growth. Between 1900 and 1950, cities with a population of one hundred thousand or more increased from 52 to 147 per cent, which meant an increase in the total U.S. population of 32 to 56 per cent. Thus, Charles Glaab and A. Theodore Brown can conclude that "the growth of the metropolis constitutes the central theme of twentieth-century American urban history."[1]

One might add that the metropolis has also become one of the central themes of American history in general for the twentieth century, and its No. 1 domestic problem. The thread of historical continuity suggests that the metropolis, rather than having created new problems, has highlighted and intensified very old ones. After all, racism, poverty, the traffic jam, and unimaginative city planning were not born with the metropolis. The extraordinary growth of the metropolis has sharpened the demands for collective responsibility, and the resistance, apathy, and failure to meet these demands have led many Americans to forget the enormous creative powers of cities and see them, as Jefferson once did, as "sores on the body politic."

This chapter seeks to isolate certainly not all but several of the critical issues bedeviling Americans in the mid-twentieth century, such as the quality of life in the metropolis, the suburb and the slum, race and poverty, racial violence, city planning and urban renewal, the dilemma of the urban police, and what they may mean for the future of urban America.

1. *A History of Urban America*, p. 270.

Hans Blumenfeld begins this chapter with an ambitious, sweeping essay. He sees the evolution of the city in terms of what went before and what may come after. By combining the approaches of an historian, an economist, an ecologist, and a city-planner, he examines three stages of "the emergence of a basically new form of human settlement," the pre-industrial city, the nineteenth-century industrial city, and the modern, sprawling metropolis of today. He attempts to answer the difficult question of what were the main forces that transformed the pre-industrial city into a modern metropolis (an urban area that "derives its identity from a single center"). To do this, he first discusses a number of crucial differences between the pre-industrial city and the metropolis and then delineates what he feels to be the major features of the metropolis—the central business area, manufacturing and related industries, housing and services, and open land—and the plans by which it may be manipulated into the city of the future.

Although he discusses the strengths and weaknesses of several schemes for the future metropolis, such as the so-called constellation, linear, and stellar metropolises, and the requirements for rational planning, he does not see the oft-accepted notion that the megalopolis is the destiny of American cities. "Megalopolis"[2]—a huge urbanized area made up of several metropolises that have expanded and grown together, such as the cities of the Ruhr in Germany or the urban strip running from Boston to Washington in the United States—is not a concept that can be applied with precision to the American scene, Blumenfeld argues, because as much as it is possible that American cities will further spill by rapid growth into one another, they will still maintain their separate identities, and, therefore, remain metropolises.

Is this too optimistic? Unlike other commentators on urban affairs, Blumenfeld is not a prophet of doom. Will the metropolis, for all its problems, be able to solve them as he suggests? Can the American city really withstand the glut of megalopolis? Can rational planning triumph over the ancient protagonists of urban sprawl—the special and vested interests of speculators, landowners, municipalities, and the free-wheeling forces of the market place?

One question that is fundamental to the nature of modern urban life is what is urbanism—that is, what are those traits that characterize the city as a special kind of human settlement? In 1938, the distinguished sociologist Louis Wirth wrote his seminal essay, "Urbanism as a Way of Life," and it became one of the most famous and influential interpretations of the modern city in our time.[3] It is also one of the most devastating critiques in the bulky literature of the city. Using the three variables of number, density, and heterogeneity as the bony skeleton of his argument, Wirth argues that urban-

2. See Jean Gottman, *Megalopolis* (New York: Twentieth Century Fund, 1961).

3. *The American Journal of Sociology*, XLIV (July 1938). For a general discussion of the quality of urban life, see Henry J. Schmandt and Warner Bloomberg, Jr. (eds.), *The Quality of Urban Life* (Beverly Hills, Calif.: Sage Publications, 1969).

ism as a way of life is a portrait of social and personal disorganization. The urbanite has lost the rich, satisfying contact with the traditional primary groups which constituted social solidarity. The weakening of kinship, the declining family, the disappearance of the neighborhood, have shifted contact to formal, impersonal, superficial, transitory secondary groups. The result: a way of life characterized by loneliness, anonymity, mental breakdown, suicide, delinquency, crime, corruption—a way of life that renders the individual helpless to manipulation by symbols and stereotypes and fosters a predatory jungle of ruthless competition, aggrandizement, and mutual exploitation. This is not the hysterics of an ambitious on-the-make politician, but the cool and seemingly dispassionate analysis of a distinguished social scientist.

Wirth may have reflected the frustrations and disenchantments of the 1930's, with its wars, depression, and insecurity. He may have seen the city with the bias of a rural or small-town American. Nevertheless, his persuasive and penetrating insights have a timeliness that would at once satisfy the ghost of Thomas Jefferson and the claims of the most recent urban critic.

Those like Herbert Gans who stress a social and behavioral rather than an ecological approach to the complexities of urbanism would not be satisfied, however. Writing twenty-four years after Wirth, Gans represents a group which is challenging the long dominance of the ecologist in urban sociology. The heart of Gans's argument is that ecology, the study of how humans adapt to their environment, and its lexicon of number, density, and heterogeneity, is simply not enough to explain *solely* the *social* characteristics of urbanism. The key determinants, then, are not ecological but those of class and what he calls the "life-cycle stage."

Gans's essay is a refutation of Wirth's thesis, and he brings to bear on that refutation a view that sees the city in its totality. The trouble with Wirth, he argues, is that he took the characteristics of one section of the city, the unstable transient area, and applied them to all sections of the city. Gans sees the city not with Wirth's preoccupation with the inner city, but in terms of three broad concentric circles: the inner city, the outer city, and the suburbs. Emphasizing the typical rather than the spectacular and exotic, he shows a multiplicity of social groups in *each* circle, discussing five that exist in the inner city alone. In effect, there is no one single way of life for the city and one single different way of life for the suburb.

The most provocative part of Gans's thesis is his analysis of the suburb which, like the central city, evokes ambivalent and contradictory attitudes. As Humphrey Carver sums them up,

Everyone likes to live in the suburbs. Everyone pokes fun at the suburbs. That's fair enough. Everyone respects those who made the suburbs. Everyone despises the suburbs. Everyone's friends live in the suburbs. Everyone hates the kind of people who live in the suburbs. Everyone wants bigger and better suburbs. Everyone thinks there is just too much suburbs. You and I live in the suburbs—it's lovely to have a nice home in the suburbs. The whole idea of the suburbs fills us with dismay, alarm, and frustration. Almost everyone's business is dedicated to making life in the suburbs more and more and more enjoyable. The suburbs are a crashing bore and desolating disappointment. The suburbs are exactly what we asked for. The suburbs are exactly what we've got.[4]

Gans attacks the "folklore" of the intellectuals and especially the theorists of the mass-society concept that has stereotyped the suburb as the faceless, numbing, debilitating refugee of conformity and homogeneity, so well characterized by Gertrude Stein's crack, "There is no there there." He destroys the notion that the move from city to suburb causes major behavior and personality changes. Above all, he shows that despite physical and demographic differences, there are more similarities than differences between the suburb and the city, especially between the suburb and the outer city.[5]

What Gans is saying is that the suburb *is* the city. Part of the folklore of the suburb is that it is a recent phenomenon, beginning particularly at the end of World War II, with the boom of low-cost housing, the subsidies of the Federal Housing Administration, and the soaring exodus from the central city. Urban historians have long argued that the suburb emerged well over a hundred years ago and was a part of such urbanization processes as transportation, economic developments, and population migrations.[6] As the most "modern" outer ring of the city, the suburb is, as Gans shows, an integral part of the metropolitan decentralization so characteristic of the modern supercity. Thus, to set up separate monolithic entities, such as "city" and "suburb," is only to confound the realities of modern urbanism.

The most confounding realities of modern urbanism, however, are the ancient plagues of poverty and discrimination, magnified by, but not generic to, the city. The most critical problem facing the city today concerns those at the end of the line—the urban poor, especially but not exclusively the American Negro, the most urbanized element of our society and the most deprived. In his essay in Chapter VI Gilbert Osofsky argued that the ghetto of today was created by the 1920's. Jeanne R. Lowe surveys the modern ghetto from World War II to the present and shows how the ghetto-making forces of the

4. *Cities in the Suburbs* (Toronto: University of Toronto Press, 1962), p. 3.
5. Confirmed suburb-baiters should pursue Gans's argument as it is expanded in his *The Levittowners: Ways of Life and Politics in a New Suburban Community* (New York: Pantheon, 1967), and his *People and Plans: Essays on Urban Problems and Solutions* (New York: Basic Books, 1968), and Scott Donaldson, *The Suburban Myth* (New York: Columbia University Press, 1969).
6. See Sam Warner, *Streetcar Suburbs: The Process of Growth in Boston* (Cambridge: M.I.T. and Harvard University Press, 1962), a first-rate scholarly performance, as is also Robert C. Wood, *Suburbia: Its People and Their Politics* (Boston: Houghton Mifflin, 1959).

early part of the century have been intensified and made even more critical, particularly by the changes in technology. Like Osofsky, she asks what makes a ghetto, and, after examining housing, employment, education, the family, and class differences among Negroes themselves, she shows that the answer lies in the unholy triumvirate of poverty, race discrimination, and blocked opportunity. Three parts of her interpretation need to be underscored: her criticism of urban education; the flaws in the stereotype of the Negro welfare recipient (which she should have developed more fully); and a point not always grasped by Americans confused by ghetto problems, especially the *white* offspring of former immigrant families, that is, there are significant differences between the Negro migrant and the earlier white migrant and foreign immigrant that account for the Negro's failure to seize a share of the American bonanza.[7]

Throughout Miss Lowe's essay there is the ring of crisis: the crises of poverty, the crisis of racial prejudice, the crisis of housing, the crisis of education, to which Edward Banfield would probably shake his gaunt head in disbelief and mutter, "Here we go again." In 1970, coming at the end of a decade when Americans were consumed by crises, Edward Banfield published his *Unheavenly City*, one of if not the most controversial books on the city in the last quarter of a century. It was a godsend for conservatives for it confirmed what they felt—and then some. For those of a liberal or radical persuasion, it was an outrage. Yet in a perverse sort of way, it was a godsend to the nonconservative because it forced him to mobilize and defend deeply held assumptions about the city. For the nonconservative, *The Unheavenly City* bristles with heresies. Banfield attacked the bastion

7. The literature about the Negro is so enormous that no attempt will be made to cite it all here, but among some of the recent books about the urban ghetto Negro, not previously cited, the following are of interest. Peter Orleans and William Russell Ellis, Jr. (eds.), *Race, Change and Urban Society* (Beverly Hills, Calif.: Sage Publications, 1971), Warner Bloomberg, Jr., and Henry J. Schmandt (eds.), *Power, Poverty, and Urban Policy* (Beverly Hills, Calif.: Sage Publications, 1968), Daniel P. Moynihan (ed.), *On Understanding Poverty: Perspectives from the Social Sciences* (New York: Basic Books, 1969), Roland L. Warren (ed.), *Politics and the Ghettos* (New York: Atherton Press, 1969), William H. Grier and Price M. Cobbs, *Black Rage* (New York: Basic Books, 1968), Henry Etzkowitz and Gerald M. Schaflander, *Ghetto Crisis: Riots or Reconciliation?* (Boston: Little, Brown, 1969), Elliot Liebow, *Tally's Corner: A Study of Negro Streetcorner Men* (Boston: Little, Brown, 1967), Constance Green, *The Secret City: A History of Race Relations in the Nation's Capitol* (Princeton: Princeton University Press, (1967); Allan H. Speer, *Black Chicago: The Making of a Negro Ghetto, 1890-1920* (Chicago: University of Chicago Press, 1967); Lee Rainwater and William L. Yancey, *The Moynihan Report and the Politics of Controversy* (Cambridge: The M.I.T. Press, 1967); August Meier and Elliott M. Rudwick, *From Plantation to Ghetto: An Interpretative History of American Negroes* (New York: Hill and Wang, 1966); Karl E. and Alma F. Taeuber, *Negroes in Cities: Residential Segregation and Neighborhood Change* (Chicago: Aldine, 1965); Charles E. Silberman, *Crisis in Black and White* (New York: Knopf, 1964); Michael Harrington, *The Other America: Poverty in the United States* (New York: Macmillan, 1962); and Kenneth Clark, *The Black Ghetto* (New York: Harper & Row, 1965).

of the Liberal Establishment with the notion that the city was not racked with a bombardment of urban crises. Indeed, if there is a crisis, Banfield argues, it is in the mind of the beholder; it is a crisis of a distorted perception, a dilemma of misguided great expectations. According to Banfield, our tolerance for adversity is alarmingly weak. What are seen as crises—poverty, racial prejudice, housing, income, education—actually are improving, but unreasonable expectations for their solution only creates an appetite of optimism that cannot be satiated. To seek and not to find creates only frustration, anxiety and ruin because the opposite result is often achieved. Prophecies of impending doom become self-fulling. Thus Banfield not only makes war on the War on Poverty and other programs, but attacks the very foundations of reform, the ethics of hope and charity. "If Banfield is right . . ." observes Richard Todd, "the noblest efforts of the past thirty years have been wrong, what progress has occurred has been accidental, and only a 180-degree shift in sensibility can begin to save us."⁸

The next selection is the heart of *The Unheavenly City*. It is at once an analysis of the American urban class structure and a new theory of the lower class. To Banfield the composition of the classes more than any other factor, sets the limits which prevent policy-makers from creating the "heavenly" city. Class structure is the crux of the city's existence. It determines its form, the quality of its life, and most of its problems. A change in the make-up of the classes, Banfield insists, changes just about everything else critical to the city, be it population density, income, housing, crime, the drop-out rate, urban services, or its race relations and political style. Always a sticky subject, class in America has usually been defined in terms of prestige symbols (income, education, family, housing, etc.). These symbols are *objective*, in the sense they can be seen and measured. Banfield presents a totally different approach. He defines class in a psychologically *subjective* framework; values, not the grandeur of one's income, determines one's class. The key value is a person's orientation toward the future, and this rests on the function of two factors: the ability to imagine a future, and the ability to discipline oneself to sacrifice present for future satisfactions. Thus, a wealthy man is not of the upper class if he does not have a powerful orientation toward the future. But Banfield does concede (and it is an interesting concession) that as it works out the wealthy usually do have a strong imagination and discipline for the future. Fortified with a method, he then proceeds to analyze the life styles of the four classes: upper, middle, working, and lower.

If Thorstein Veblen highlighted the antics of the leisure class as conspicuous consumption, Edward Banfield sees the lower class as conspicuous consumers of present-oriented pleasures and immediate gratifications (es-

8. "A Theory of the Lower Class, Edward Banfield: The Maverick of Urbanology," *The Atlantic* (September 1970), p. 52

pecially sexual and financial), unmindful of the future, except as something that cannot be controlled. Pathological, irresponsible, wallowing in squalor, relishing violence, lacking strong ties to either family, friends or community, the members of the lower class are "unable or unwilling either to control impulses or to put forth any effort at self-improvement."

Banfield writes:

The lower-class individual lives in the slum and sees little or no reason to complain. He does not care how dirty and dilapidated his housing is either inside or out, nor does he mind the inadequacy of such public facilities as schools, parks, and libraries: indeed, where such things exist he destroys them by acts of violence if he can. Features that make the slum repellent to others actually please him. He finds it satisfying in several ways. . . .

To such a statement, critics, as much in bewilderment as in indignation respond in the view of Richard Sennett: "Professor Banfield seems to live in a different country because he looks at poor people as essentially a different race of beings from you and me."[9]

Critics were also led to indict Banfield for racism, since blacks make up so, much of the urban poor. But as Richard Sennett points out: "Attacks on this book as racist miss the point: it's not blacks Banfield despises, it's poor people, whether they be white, black, or brown."[10]

It would also be a mistake to dismiss Banfield as a mindless conservative and fling his book across the room, as a student of mine did once. No intellectual Archie Bunker, he has a fine (albeit tough) mind and a distinguished career that includes ten books, a chair professorship at Harvard University, and has served as chairman of President Richard Nixon's Task Force on Model Cities. His book has been warmly received by a wide audience which includes government policy-makers. At best, Banfield's essay is the stuff exciting controversy is made of. Given a room filled with people committed to a variety of political styles—conservative, liberal, and radical —(hopefully oriented toward the past as well), armed with the weapons of Jeanne Lowe, Edward Banfield, and Morris Janowitz who follows, it would be interesting to speculate the carnage, intellectual and otherwise.

The result of ghetto life—as the fiery decade of the 1960's painfully illustrate—is the violence of riots, which seem to many Americans to be one of the main themes of contemporary urban America. Historically, urban racial conflicts are nothing new. To name just a few, there were the Detroit and Harlem riots of 1943, the Tulsa riot of 1921; the Elaine, Arkansas, riot of 1919, and the particularly vicious racial explosion in Chicago in the same

9. "Survival of the Fattest," *The New York Review of Books* (August 13, 1970), p. 23.
10. Ibid., p. 25

year. There was the East St. Louis riot of 1917, probably the worst and certainly the bloodiest in this century. There were the riots in New York, New Orleans, and Akron in 1900, and Wilmington, North Carolina in 1898, not to mention the 1863 New York draft riots, which had decided racial overtones. And one can go back further than that to the Cincinnati riots of 1841 and the Snow Hill riot in Providence, Rhode Island, in 1831. As Rap Brown says, violence is as American as "cherry pie."

The persistent, baffling question is what triggers riots? A blatant defiance of law and order? Lower-class young hoodlums running amuck? The inflexible fortress of white racism? The so-called "revolution of rising expectations"? The answer will seriously affect what is to be done with the ghetto and this in turn will affect the future of the American city.

In one of the most penetrating analyses to appear in years,[11] Morris Janowitz, combining history and sociology, not restricting his vision merely to the riots of the 1960's, but ranging far back into the early years of the twentieth century, sees three critical stages of urban racial violence. The first occurred during and immediately after World War I, such as the East St. Louis and Chicago riots. He labels these *communal* riots or "contested area" riots, because they involved "ecological warfare" directly between whites and blacks on the boundaries of the white and black communities. Usually triggered by whites, they represented the white fear of an expanding black community, and for the blacks, a desperate struggle for survival. The second stage, coming during World War II and reaching a peak in the years 1964-67, while incorporating some of the elements of the first stage, nonetheless takes on a different character. Rather than a confrontation between white and black on the edge of the ghetto, it was a war between blacks and the police, directly within the black community. Janowitz calls these *commodity* riots because they represented a protest against the larger society in the form of looting and destruction of property and retail stores. The third stage, coming after 1968, again incorporating some of the elements of the previous

---

11. The literature on urban riots is growing and will continue to grow. An important work dealing with violence in many aspects, including urban, is Hugh Davis Graham and Ted Robert Gurr, *Violence in America: Historical and Comparative Perspectives*, 2 vols. (Washington, D.C.: Superintendent of Documents, 1969). An excellent study is by Nathan S. Caplan and Jeffery M. Paige, "A Study of Ghetto Rioters," *Scientific American* (August 1968). See also National Advisory Commission on Civil Disorders, *The Report of the National Advisory Commission on Civil Disorders* (New York: Bantam Books, 1968); two articles by Robert Fogleston: "From Contention to Confrontation: The Police, the Negroes and the Riots of the 1960's," *Political Science Quarterly* (June 1968), and "White on Black: A Critique of the McCone Commission Report on the Los Angeles Riots," *Political Science Quarterly* (September 1967); John Hersey, *The Algiers Motel Incident* (New York: Knopf, 1968); the entire issue of *American Behavioral Scientist* (March-April 1968), which is devoted to urban violence and disorder; Paul Jacobs, *Prelude to Riot: A View of Urban America from the Bottom* (New York: Random House, 1967); and Jerome H. Skolnick, *Justice Without Trial: Law Enforcement in Democratic Society* (New York: John Wiley, 1966).

stages, took on the pattern of an "instrumental use of violence," whereby small, organized, armed groups of blacks, ideologues appealing to Black Power, employed calculated, selective acts of terrorism against the white community. These were people who believed that social change could be created only through violence.

As causal factors linking all three stages, Janowitz goes beyond conventional explanations, such as prejudice, poverty, income, and housing, seeing these as important but only partial answers. More important, he argues, were the agencies of social change and social control, especially the police and the mass media. He analyzes both in detail and concludes that the poor performance of both account for much of the urban racial violence in the twentieth-century. But even here, Janowitz plumbs deeper. The crux to the history of race riots is more than the patterns of communal and commodity styles of violence, more than the failure of the police and the mass media. It is in part an answer to the question raised by Ralph Ellison, the black novelist, when he asked, "But can a people live and develop for over three hundred years simply by reacting?" As Janowitz says, "The Negro outbursts have been more than a reaction to police brutality and a double standard of legal justice. In a symbolic sense, they are expressions of energies to participate in and transform the larger society. In all phases of life, the Negro is not merely reacting but acting."

If the urban police have played a critical role in most of the race riots in our history, it is surprising that historians have devoted such scant attention to the police as an urban institution.[12] Yet historically the police have

12. See Roger Lane, *Policing the City: Boston, 1822-1885* (Cambridge, Mass.: Harvard University Press, 1967), James F. Richardson, *The New York Police: Colonial Times to 1901* (New York: Oxford University Press, 1970), and Robert Fogleston, "The Police, the Negroes and the Riots of the 1960's," *Political Science Quarterly* (June 1968).

For other books written by men with a variety of backgrounds, see Orlando W. Wilson, *Police Administration*, 2nd. ed. (New York: McGraw-Hill, 1963), Michael Banton, *The Policeman and the Community* (New York: Basic Books, 1965), Wayne R. La-Fave, *Arrest* (Boston: Little, Brown, 1965), Jerome H. Skolnick, *Justice Without Trial* (New York: John Wiley and Sons, 1966), David J. Bordua, *The Police* (New York: John Wiley and Sons, 1967), Arthur Niederhoffer, *Behind the Shield: The Police in Urban Society* (New York: Doubleday, 1967), A Report by the President's Commission on Law Enforcement and Administration of Justice, *The Challenge of Crime in a Free Society* (Washington, D.C.: U.S. Government Printing Office, 1967), The President's Commission on Law Enforcement and Administration of Justice, *Task Force Report: The Police* (Washington, D.C.: U.S. Government Printing Office, 1967), Daniel Walker, as submitted to the National Commission on the Causes and Prevention of Violence, *Rights in Conflict* (New York: E. P. Dutton and Co., 1968), James Q. Wilson, *Varieties of Police Behavior* (Cambridge, Mass.: Harvard University Press, 1968), Gene Radano, *Walking the Beat* (Cleveland: World Publishing Co., 1968), William W. Turner, *The Police Establishment* (New York: G. P. Putnam's Sons, 1968), Paul Chevigny, *Police Power: Police Abuses in New York City* (New York: Pantheon Books, 1969), and "The Police and the Rest of Us," eight articles of a special supplement which appeared in *The Atlantic* (March 1967).

Two novels, written by policeman-novelist Joseph Wambaugh provide special insights into the working world of the urban police: *The New Centurions* (Boston: Little, Brown, 1970), and *The Blue Knight* (Boston: Little, Brown, 1972).

been a vital urban institution, a mirror reflecting the growth and evolution of the city, and importantly, society's attitudes toward law, crime, punishment, and authority. It has been said that a society's attitude toward justice and the mechanism of justice is an index to a society's character. Indeed, the mere existence of the police suggests the heart of urban living —the necessity for collective responsibility.

Since the 1840's, when the first police force was established, the record of the urban police has been a checkered one, for some of these reasons. First, they have had to cope with the *difficulties* of urban life, such as the impersonality of the city, urban mobility, the problems arising from the enormous diversity of the urban population itself, diversities of culture, values, attitudes, class, religion, and racial and national backgrounds. Second, society has used the police as a kind of wastebasket to dump its social failures. Yet the police are hardly trained or equipped to solve problems that have defeated the larger society. And, third, Americans have not been quite sure about what they want the police to police. As a result, the policeman has had to play a variety of roles that are both frustrating and contradictory. As one man has written, "We ask our officers to be a combination of Bat Masterson, Sherlock Holmes, Sigmund Freud, King Solomon, Hercules and Diogenes." No wonder, then, it can be said that whether you see the cop as hero or pig, his job is one of the most difficult in urban society. The question, a perennial one, is how do we get better policemen?

In the next essay, James Q. Wilson, a leading authority on law enforcement, by-passes the usual answers to this question—more salary, more training, more equipment, more guns, clearer policies. Nor is better race relations, so desperately necessary, the entire answer. Wilson finds the "answer," or at least the real beginning of an answer, in the resolution of a dilemma that has plagued the police for generations. It is the question of what actually the police are supposed to do. "The history of the American municipal police," he says, "is in great part a history of struggles to define their role in our society."

After an excellent analysis of the historical development of the urban police, Wilson shows the police have become snarled in the dilemma of playing two roles which together are contradictory and self-defeating. On the one hand, there is the glamor role of "crook catching," or law enforcement. After a discussion of the nature of crime, he demonstrates how the policeman cannot be an effective crime fighter, yet cast in that role the police face the embarrassment of *"being judged by a goal they cannot attain."* On the other hand, the bulk of policework is providing services, or maintaining order, such as dealing with quarreling families, drunks, troublesome teenagers, tavern brawls, taking the sick to a hospital, or bailing a cat out of a tree. Strengthen one role and you weaken the other. For example, the strategy for law enforcement requires centralized authority, tight surveillance of the neighborhood (with the police being seen as the adversary), precise legal codes, and clear arrest procedures. On the other hand, to maintain order and provide services requires decentralized authority, a sympathetic commitment to the neighborhood, wide discretion and tolerance, and a toning-down of arrest quotas. Wilson warns that there is no slick, magic formula to the Police Problem, but until the dilemma of role is resolved, all the money, education, and guns won't put the blue-coated Humpty-Dumpty together again.

Related but not exclusive to the dilemmas of race and poverty are two other confounding problems, old in their origins, new in their complexity— city planning and urban renewal. John L. Hancock examines the historical evolution of city planning in America from 1900 to 1940. He traces its origins as a professional art and science, its fits and starts, its emerging theoretical maturity—and its frustrations which defined the requirements for a city planner as "the wisdom of Solomon, the heart of a prophet, the patience of Job, and the hide of a rhinoceros."

Hancock's central theme is the discrepancy between the planner's goals and their fulfillment. On the one hand, the profession evolved in the Progressive Era from a motley crew ranging from landscape artists to lawyers, long on hope, short on theory. Increasing their skills, specializing their abilities, widening their vision from statistical projects and majestic but inadequate historic models, to the fusion of scientific and humanistic methods into generalized theories incorporating urban into regional planning, the planners built a profession. The consultant became the professional. On the other hand, public apathy, and special interest groups demanding the expediency of short-term "practical" goals, undermined attempts for meaningful city planning. Of the multitude of projects, few were completed. City planning became "city-mending"; patchwork replaced comprehensive planning. Thus city planning has bobbed and weaved between two legacies from the past: the goals of the Progressives of placing the group above the individual in planning for the general welfare, and the heritage of laissez faire which sacrifices over-all planning to the individual interests of commercial groups. Despite the profession's increasing sense of comprehensive planning and social responsibility, "most physical change in today's booming cities is conducted by private interests under public auspices for speculative purposes." Hancock makes it clear that the future of the American city and the quality of its life will be decided by which legacy ultimately triumphs.

The next selection concerns a critique of urban renewal, the hottest controversy of city planning.[13] Herbert Gans presents a critique with a question:

13. In the massive literature on this subject, some of the recent and outstanding books are Mel Scott, *American City Planning: Since 1890* (Berkeley: University of California Press, 1969), Ernest Erber (ed.), *Urban Planning in Transition* (New York: Grossman Publishers, 1970), Ian L. McHarg, *Design with Nature* (Garden City, N.Y.: The Natural

urban renewal for whom, the slumdwellers or the affluent white middle and upper classes? His major criticism is that most urban renewal projects have used the brawn of the federal bulldozer to tear the slums down, but have not used the federal brain to properly relocate the slumdwellers they have displaced. It is a critique built around a preposterous irony: urban renewal frequently victimizes the very people it was originally intended to benefit. Slum clearance sustains the slums. By failing to follow through with re-housing the dispossessed, urban renewal forces them into other slum areas; ergo, urban renewal often becomes slum "renewal," slums are merely shifted and made worse.

Unlike some critics of public housing, Gans does not want to burn down the barn to kill the rats. He proposes several alternative solutions, most of which hinge upon more effective federal intervention. Thus, he does not find the panacea in unrestricted private enterprise, which contributed enormously to the initial creation of the slums, nor in the simplistic doctrine that decent housing makes for the decent life. In Gans's view, there will be no fundamental improvement until a rehousing program is coupled with an effective attack upon poverty itself.

The final selection is a summation which brings us to the present and touches upon the future. Along the theme of the difference between what we wanted and what we created, Scott Greer traces the evolution of the American city from the American Revolution to the present, restating many of the political, economical, social, ideological, and technological themes that have been presented throughout this book. His thesis is that many of us indulge in a myopic nostalgia for a kind of city that no longer exists. Just as the memory

---

History Press, 1969), Victor Gruen, *The Heart of Our Cities* (New York: Simon and Schuster, 1964), Jack Tager and Park Dixon Goist (eds.), *The Urban Vision* (Homewood, Ill.: The Dorsey Press, 1970), Henry S. Churchill, *The City Is the People* (New York: W. W. Norton, 1962), John Burchard and Albert Bush-Brown, *The Architecture of America: A Social and Cultural History*, 1966), Scott Greer, *Urban Renewal and American Cities* (New York: Bobbs-Merrill, 1966), Charles Abrams, *The City Is the Frontier* (New York: Harper & Row, 1965), and Jane Jacobs, *The Death and Life of Great American Cities* (New York: Knopf, 1961). For an excellent critical review of Miss Jacobs's books, see Hans Blumenfeld, *The Modern Metropolis: Its Origins, Growth, Characteristics, and Planning* (Cambridge: The M.I.T. Press, 1967), pp. 180-89. In a class all its own is John W. Reps's magnificent *The Making of Urban America; A History of City Planning in the United States* (Princeton: Princeton University Press, 1965). See also John W. Reps, *Town Planning in Frontier America* (Princeton: Princeton University Press, 1969), and *Monumental Washington: The Planning and Development of the Capital Center* (Princeton: Princeton University Press, 1967).

There are two first-rate readers which present a comprehensive view of urban renewal: Jewel Bellush and Murray Hausknecht (eds.), *Urban Renewal: People, Politics, and Planning* (Garden City: Anchor Books, 1967), and James Q. Wilson (ed.), *Urban Renewal: The Record and the Controversy* (Cambridge: The M.I.T. Press, 1967).

Although not in the "recent" category, Martin Meyerson and Edward C. Banfield, *Politics, Planning, and the Public Interest* (New York: The Free Press, 1955), is indispensable.

of the farm and small town once preoccupied the American imagination, we are now caught up in "the imagined central city of another era," which confounds urban renewal and municipal government, particularly. According to Greer, reality begins with the realization that the metropolis constitutes a revolution in the use of space—the decentralization of urban space. To celebrate the central city at the expense of the suburb is to forget that decentralization is, like the city, here to stay. Reality is the realization that the city is not static; it is a continually changing phenomenon which must be seen in all its parts, from the inner city to the suburb. With this in mind, argues Greer, can we determine what we want and be willing to pay for it? Or: "Do we really care about our cities?"

Do we? If we do, we will have to think through and adjust old ideas about poverty, race, central planning, and the divisions of authority between federal, state, and local authority, and make them conform to the changing realities of the city.[14]

14. See also Scott Greer's collection of essays, *The Urbane View: Life and Politics in Metropolitan America* (New York: Oxford University Press, 1972). For a bleaker view of the modern city, see George Sternlieb, "The City as Sandbox," *Public Interest* (Fall 1971), and Norton E. Long, "The City as Reservation," *Public Interest* (Fall 1971).

For an interesting interpretation of the modern city from a professional philosopher's point of view, see Lawrence Haworth, *The Good City* (Bloomington, Ind.: Indiana University Press, 1963).

The Modern Metropolis

HANS BLUMENFELD

. . . We [are going to] speak of the product of . . . [the] evolution [of cities] not as the modern city" but as "the modern metropolis." The change of name reflects the fact that from its long, slow evolution the city has emerged into a revolutionary stage. It has undergone a qualitative change, so that it is no longer merely a larger version of the traditional city but a new and different form of human settlement.

There is some argument about the term. Lewis Mumford objects to "metropolis" (from the Greek words for "mother" and "city"), which historically had a very different meaning; he prefers the term "conurbation," coined by Patrick Geddes, the Scottish biologist

From *Scientific American* (September 1965), pp. 64-74. Copyright © 1965 by Scientific American, Inc. All rights reserved. Reprinted by permission. Hans Blumenfeld is a lecturer in Urban and Regional Planning at the University of Toronto.

who was a pioneer in city planning. This word, however, implies formation by the fusion of several preexisting cities; most metropolises did not originate in that way. The term "megalopolis," coined by the French geographer Jean Gottmann, is generally applied to an urbanized region that contains several metropolitan areas, such as the region extending from Boston to Washington. On the whole it seems best to retain the term "metropolis," now commonly adopted in many languages as the name for a major city center and its environs.

"Metropolitan area" can be defined in various ways; the U.S. Bureau of the Census, for instance, defines it as any area containing a nuclear city of at least 50,000 population. The new phenomenon we are considering, however, is a much bigger entity with a certain minimum critical size. In agreement with the German scholar Gerhard Isenberg, I shall define a metropolis as a concentration of at least 500,000 people living within an area in which the traveling time from the outskirts to the center is no more than about 40 minutes. Isenberg and I have both derived this definition from observations of the transformation of cities into metropolises during the first half of the 20th century. At the present time—at least in North America—the critical mass that distinguishes a metropolis from the traditional city can be considerably larger—perhaps nearing one million population.

The emergence of a basically new form of human settlement is an extremely rare event in the history of mankind. For at least 5,000 years all civilizations have been characterized predominantly by just two well-marked types of settlement: the farm village and the city. Until recently the vast majority of the population lived in villages. They produced not only their own raw materials—food, fuel and fiber —but also the manufactured goods and services they required. The cities were inhabited by only a small minority of the total population, generally less than 20 percent. These people were the ruling elite—the religious, political, military and commercial leaders—and the retinue of laborers, craftsmen and professionals who served them. The elite drew their subsistence and power from the work of the villagers by collecting tithes, taxes or rent. This system prevailed until the end of the 18th century, and its philosophy was well expressed by physiocrats of that time on both sides of the Atlantic, including Thomas Jefferson.

The industrial revolution dramatically reversed the distribution of population between village and city. A German contemporary of Jefferson's, Justus Moeser, foresaw at the very beginning of the revolution what was to come; he observed that "specialized division of labor forces workers to live in big cities." With increasing specialization there had to be increased cooperation of labor, both within and between establishments. The division of labor and increased productivity made concentration in cities possible, and the required cooperation of labor made it necessary, because the new system called for bringing together workers of many skills and diverse establishments that had to interchange goods and services.

The process fed on itself, growth inducing further growth. Many economists have noted that the rapid rise of productivity has been largely instrumental in bringing about a progressive shift of the main part of the labor force from the primary industry of raw-material production to the secondary industry of material processing and finally to the tertiary industry of services. Less attention has been paid to a related, equally important factor behind this shift, namely the "specializing out" of functions. The farmer's original functions of producing his own motive power (work animals), fuel (hay and oats), tools, building materials and consumer goods have been specialized out to secondary industries that supply him with tractors, gasoline and his other necessities. Today, in the tertiary stage, much of the work connected with secondary industry is being specialized out to purveyors of business services (accounting, control, selling, distribution). Even the functions of the household itself (personal services, housekeeping, repairs, shopping, recreation, education) are taken over by consumer-service industries.

The dual spur of specialization and cooperation of labor started a great wave of migration from country to city all over the globe. In the advanced countries the 19th-century development of long-distance transportation by steamship and railroad and of communication by the electric telegraph made it possible for cities to draw on large regions and grow to populations of millions. For a time their growth was limited by internal restrictions. Travel within the city still had to be by foot or by hoof. A New York businessman could communicate quickly with his partners in Shanghai by cablegram, but to deliver an order to an office a few blocks away he had to send a messenger. This situation limited cities to a radius of only about three miles from the center. In the absence of elevators the city was also limited in vertical expansion. The only possible growth was

interstitial, by covering every square inch of available space. Residences, factories, shops and offices all crowded close together around the center. The result was a fantastic rise in the price of city land compared with the cost of the structures that could be built on it.

This was only a transitory phase in the growth of the city, but its heritage is still with us, in structures, street patterns, institutions and concepts. We still think and talk and act in terms of "city and country" and "city and suburb," although these concepts have lost meaning in the modern metropolis and its region. The transformation was set in motion toward the end of the 19th century and early in the 20th with the invention of the telephone, the electric streetcar, the subway and the powered elevator. Even more far-reaching was the impact on the city of the automobile and the truck. With the acquisition of these aids to communication and mobility the city burst its eggshell and emerged as a metropolis. (It is worth noting that the telephone and the automobile had equally profound effects on rural life, fragmenting the old farm village and giving rise to huge, scattered farms.)

The centripetal migration from the country to the city continues unabated, but now there is an equally powerful centrifugal wave of migration from the city to the suburbs. Although on a national scale more and more of the population is becoming urban, within the urban areas there is increasing decentralization. The interaction of these two trends has produced the new form of settlement we call the metropolis. It is no longer a "city" as that institution has been understood in the past, but on the other hand it is certainly not "country" either. The fact that it is neither one nor the other has aroused nostalgic critics, who appeal for a return to "true urbanity" and to a "real countryside." But in view of the inexorable technological and economic trends that have created the metropolis these terms also require a new and different interpretation.

It has become fashionable to describe the transformation of the city into the metropolis as an "explosion." The term is misleading on two counts. The change is not destroying the city, as "explosion" implies, nor is it a sudden, unheralded event. The movement of population from the center of the city outward to an ever expanding periphery has been going on for at least a century. In the metropolitan region of New York, New Jersey and Connecticut, where the average density of population within the cities and towns of the area increased steadily up to 1860, it began to drop after that date. The outward spread of the city was nearly as strong between 1860 and 1900 as it has been since 1900. In Philadelphia the population movement away from the center of the city was actually proportionately greater in the half century between 1860 and 1910 than in the period 1900 to 1950.

Analysis of the population density in the metropolitan area of Philadelphia and that of other cities shows that the centrifugal wave of movement to the suburbs has proceeded with amazing regularity. From the center of the city out to the periphery at any one time there is a consistent decline in residential density from one zone to the next. As time has passed, the curve representing this decline has become less steep; that is, the center has lost or stood still in density while the outer areas have gained, so that the difference between them is less. Interestingly, the density gradient from the center to the periph-

ery has also become smoother (that is, less lumped around outer towns), which seems to indicate that the center is actually strengthening its influence over the outer areas. In each zone the rise in density with time eventually flattens out, as if the density has reached a "saturation" level for that zone; this level is lower for each successive zone out to the periphery. With the passage of time the crest of the wave (the zone of fastest growth) moves outward in a regular fashion. The innermost zone at the center of the city seems to show an anomaly, in that its population density is lower than that of the surrounding area, but this merely reflects the fact that the center is occupied predominantly by stores and offices. If its daytime working population were included in the census, it would have a far higher density.

One can outline a "natural history" of the modern metropolis. The metropolis is characterized first of all by a certain measure of mutual accessibility among its various parts, which determines its total size. As I have mentioned, in most cases the area embraced by the metropolis has a radius represented by a traveling time of about 40 minutes in the principal vehicle of transportation (train or auto), or about 45 minutes from door to door. With improvement in the speed of transportation the extent of the metropolis in miles can, of course, expand. In most metropolitan areas the average travel time to work for the working population as a whole is about half an hour. No more than 15 percent of the workers spend more than 45 minutes in the daily journey to work.

This may sound surprising in view of the frequent complaints of commuters about the length of their journey. The complaints are not new. A century ago a German observer declared that the distance people on the outskirts of cities had to travel to work had reached the limit of what was bearable. Probably the range of travel times to work then was wider than it is in the metropolis today. There are strong indications, however, that the half-hour average has been more or less standard. In most American small towns, although a majority of the workers are employed within the town, a sizable minority do travel long distances to work in other communities, usually because they cannot find a job in the hometown and must seek work elsewhere but do not wish to change their home.

It is one of the great advantages of the metropolis that people can change jobs without moving their homes. Breadth of choice—for workers, for employers and for consumers—is the essence of the metropolis. The worker has a choice of employers; the employer can find workers of a wide variety of skills, including professional and managerial. Even more important is the accessibility of a variety of goods and services on which any business enterprise depends. Only a metropolis can support the large inventories, transportation facilities and specialized services —particularly those of a financial, legal, technical and promotional nature—that are essential to modern business. Such services constitute the main source of economic strength of the metropolis—its true economic base. They are especially important to small, new and experimental enterprises. The metropolis, in particular its central area, therefore serves as an incubator for such enterprises. Contrary to a common impression, the big city is most suitably a home for small industries rather than large industrial complexes. The big plant, being more nearly self-sufficient, may often be as well off in a small town. This fact is

reflected in the statistics of employment: in most metropolises the number of people that are employed in manufacturing is decreasing, relatively and sometimes absolutely, while the number that are employed in services is increasing rapidly.

What is true of business services is also true of consumer services: the metropolis attracts the consumer because it offers a wide freedom of choice. Only the large population of a metropolis can support the great proliferation of special services found in the big city: large department stores, many specialty shops, opera houses, art galleries, theaters, sports stadia, special schools, large and well-equipped institutions for medical care and adult education and a host of other necessities for the full life.

To sum up, the modern metropolis differs from the traditional city in several crucial respects: (1) it combines the function of central leadership with the functions of providing the main bulk of material production and services; (2) its population is up to 10 times larger than that of the biggest preindustrial city; (3) with modern fast transportation, which has increased its commuting radius about tenfold, it is up to 100 times larger in area than the biggest city of former times; (4) it is neither city nor country but a complex of urban districts and open areas; (5) its residential and work areas are no longer combined in one place but are located in separate districts; (6) its workers have high mobility in the choice of jobs and occupations.

The feedback cycle of metropolitan growth enlarging freedom of choice and freedom of choice in turn attracting further growth has given the metropolis amazing vitality and staying power. In the premetropolis era cities laid low by war, pestilence or loss of prestige were often abandoned or reduced to weak shadows of their former glory. Even Rome became little more than a village after it lost its empire. In contrast, all the big cities destroyed in World War II have been rebuilt, most of them to beyond their prewar size. Particularly significant is the experience of Leningrad. During the Russian Revolution and again in World War II it lost about half of its population. Moreover, the revolution ended its former role as the center of government and finance and deprived it of most of its markets and sources of supply. Yet the population of Leningrad is now four million—four times what it was in 1921. This growth is especially remarkable in view of the Soviet government's policy of restricting the growth of the major cities, a policy based on Karl Marx's condemnation of big cities because of their pollution of air, water and soil. As a metropolis Leningrad is an outstanding testament to the viability of the species.

Attempts to halt the growth of the big city have been made ever since the phenomenon first appeared on the human scene. They have been singularly unsuccessful. Elizabeth I of England and after her Oliver Cromwell tried to limit the growth of London by circling it with an enforced greenbelt, but this method failed. In any case such a device, applied to a growing city, can only lead to overcrowding. To avoid big-city problems nearly all countries today have embarked on programs of industrial decentralization, often with unsatisfactory results. In the Western nations the most far-reaching attempt at decentralization is Great Britain's "new towns" plan. This program has been eminently successful in creating new centers of industry as "growth points," but it has not availed to stop the growth

of London or to limit other cities, new or old, to their planned size. Significantly, all but one of the 17 new towns built in Britain since the war are satellite towns within previously existing metropolitan regions.

The U.S.S.R., by virtue of centralized planning and ownership, has been able to carry out decentralization on a continental scale. Its program has been remarkably effective in slowing the growth of Moscow and promoting that of smaller cities. Between 1939 and 1959 the towns in the U.S.S.R. with populations of less than 200,000 grew by 84 percent; those in the 200,000-to-500,000 class grew 63 percent; those in the 500,000-to-one-million class grew 48 percent, and Moscow itself increased only 20 percent in population. Moscow has, however, gone well beyond the limit of five million that the government planned: it is now at six million, nearly four times the city's population in 1921.

In the U.S., where the forces of the market rather than central planning determine industrial locations, the growth rates in the decade 1950-1960 were 27 percent in metropolitan areas of 50,000 to 500,000 population and 35 percent in those of 500,000 to two million population. In the metropolises with a population of more than two million the average growth rate was smaller: 23 percent. This average, however, was heavily weighted by the comparatively slow-growing centers of the Northeastern sector of the nation; in Los Angeles and San Francisco, the only two metropolises of this class outside the Northeast, the growth was far above the national average for all metropolitan areas.

There is no denying that the growth of the huge metropolises has brought serious problems, chief among which are traffic congestion and the pollution of air and water by smoke, household wastes, detergents and gasoline fumes. Many cities also object that the metropolis can exist only by draining the countryside of its economic, demographic and social strength. These problems are not essentially unsolvable, however. Effective methods for control of pollution exist; they need to be applied [see "The Metabolism of Cities," by Abel Wolman, page 156]. The economic and social complaints about the metropolis seem to have little substance today. The city now repays the country in full in economic terms, as we have noted, and with the improvement in sanitation and lowering of the high 19th-century urban death rate it contributes its share of the natural population increase.

The most persistent accusation against the metropolis is that it has dissolved the family and neighborhood ties that existed in the small town and has produced anomie: the absence of any values or standards of behavior. This is questionable. A number of sociological studies in metropolises of North America and western Europe have shown that family ties remain very much alive and that a considerable amount of informal community organization can be found even in their slums.

In considering the future of the metropolis the central question is that of crowding. How much bigger can the metropolis grow? Will it eventually be "choked to death" by its own growth? Data are available for examining these questions.

It is widely believed that in a big metropolis there can only be a choice between crowding together at high densities or spending an excessive amount of time traveling to work. Actually a reasonable travel radius from a central point takes in an amazing amount of territory. At an overall travel rate of 20 miles per hour, typical for present rush-hour trips from the center to the periphery in the largest American metropolitan areas, a radius of one hour's travel describes a circle with a total area of about 1,250 square miles. No more than 312 square miles would be required to house 10 million people if they lived in single-family houses on 30-by-100-foot lots. Including streets, schools and other neighborhood facilities, the total area needed for residential use would amount to about 500 square miles. Commercial, industrial and other non-residential facilities could be accommodated amply on 150 square miles. There would be left, then, some 600 square miles, almost half of the total area within an hour's distance from the center, for parks, golf courses, forests, farms and lakes.

If the travel speed were increased to 30 miles per hour, quite feasible for both private and public transportation, the area within an hour's distance from the center could accommodate 15 million people in single-family houses on 60-by-100-foot lots, take care of all business uses and leave 1,000 square miles of open land. It may be objected that an hour is an excessive time to spend in travel to work. In practice, however, the radius from the center to the periphery would not represent the traveling distance for most workers. Relatively few would live close to the periphery, and most of these would be working at places near home rather than in the center of the city. In a metropolis of such dimensions only a small minority would have to travel more than 45 minutes to their jobs.

Evidently, then, the modern metropolis does not inherently necessitate either very high residential densities or excessively long journeys to work. The problem in planning it therefore lies in achieving a rational distribution of its components and a suitable organization of transportation facilities to connect the components.

What are the major components of the metropolis? Basically there are four: (1) the central business complex, (2) manufacturing and its allied industries, (3) housing with the attendant services and (4) open land. Let us examine each in turn.

The central area epitomizes the essence of the metropolis: mutual accessibility. It attracts particularly those functions that serve the metropolis as a whole and those that require a considerable amount of close interpersonal contact. The most conspicuous occupant of the center is diversified retail business: large department stores and specialty shops. It is surpassed in importance, however, by the closely interrelated complex of business services that occupy the giant office buildings characteristic of the central area of a metropolis: the headquarters of corporations, financial institutions and public administration and the professionals who serve them, such as lawyers, accountants and organizations engaged in promotion and public relations. Also grouped in the central area with these two categories of services are various supporting establishments, including eating and drinking places, hotels, job printers and many others.

Surprisingly, surveys show that, in spite of the recent proliferation of new office skyscrapers in the center of cities, the size of the working population in the central areas of the largest American metropolises has not actually increased over the past 30 years. Toronto, a smaller and newer metropolis, shows the same constancy in the number of central workers during the past 13 years. The explanation lies simply in the fierce competition for and the rising cost of the limited space in the center; it has caused an outward movement of those functions that can conveniently relocate farther out. Housing in the main moved out long ago; manufacturing and warehousing have tended to follow suit; so has a considerable part of the retail trade, and some of the routine business services that do not require continuous contact with their clients have also moved to less expensive locations away from the center. Modern means of communication have made this spatial separation possible. Moreover, the growth of population and purchasing power in the peripheral areas has provided bases of support there for large shopping centers, including department stores, and for many business and consumer services.

All of this indicates that the central area is undergoing a qualitative change in the direction of concentration on "higher-order" functions and at the same time is maintaining stability in quantitative terms. The forces of the market act to control overcrowding of the center. There is not much basis for the widespread fear that the metropolis will choke itself to death by uncontrolled growth.

As for manufacturing and its satellite activities, the increasing volume of production and changing technology, with a consequent requirement for more space, have made their move out to the periphery of the metropolis imperative. This is true of factories, warehouses, railroad yards, truck terminals, airports, harbor facilities and many other establishments. Three technical factors are at work: the increasing mechanization

and automation of production, which calls for more floor area per worker; a switch from the traditional multistory loft building to the one-story plant, which demands more ground area; the new practice of providing open land around the plant for parking, landscaping and plant expansion. The combined effect of these three factors has been to raise the amount of land per worker in the modern factory as much as 100 times over that occupied by the old loft building.

The next major category of land use in the metropolis—housing—accounts for the largest amount of occupied land. It also presents the greatest ills of the metropolis: slums and segregation of people by income and race.

In all metropolises the low-income families tend to be segregated in the older, high-density areas toward the center of the city. This is not by choice but because they cannot afford the prices or rents of the more spacious new homes in the outer areas. The alarming result of the centrifugal movement of new residences toward the periphery is an increasing segregation of the population by income, which in the U.S. is compounded (and partly obscured) by segregation by race. The situation is more disquieting in the metropolis than it was in the smaller city or town. There, although the poor lived in older, shabbier houses, they at least shared the schools and other public facilities with the higher-income groups. In the metropolis the people living in low-income districts, particularly the housewives and children, never even meet or come to know the rest of their fellow citizens.

Poor families are effectively prevented from moving to new housing in the suburbs not only by economic inability but also by deliberate policies of the suburban governments. Squeezed between rising expenses and inadequate tax resources, these governments have quite understandably used their power of zoning and other controls to keep out housing that does not pay its way in tax revenue. More recently the central cities have adopted policies that have much the same effect. Their programs of slum clearance and redevelopment, financed in the U.S. by the National Housing Act, have failed to replace the housing they have destroyed with sufficient new housing at rents the displaced families can afford [see "The Renewal of Cities," by Nathan Glazer, in *Cities*, Editors of *Scientific American*, eds.]. It should be obvious that housing conditions cannot be improved by decreasing the supply. Half a century ago Geddes observed: "The policy of sweeping clearance should be recognized for what I believe it is: one of the most disastrous and pernicious blunders . . . the large populations thus expelled would be . . . driven into creating worse congestion in other quarters."

Obviously the blight of slums and class segregation can be overcome only by enabling the lower-income groups to live in decent houses in desirable locations, primarily in the expanding peripheral areas, along with the middle and upper classes. The annual cost of such a program in the U.S. has been estimated at $2 billion—a modest sum compared with the amounts alloted to less constructive purposes in the national budget.

The fourth major category of metropolitan land use—open land—consists in North America at present mainly of large tracts held privately for future development. With increasing leisure there is a growing need to turn some of this land to recreational uses. In this connection we should also look at the "metropolitan region," which takes in considerably more area than the metropolis itself.

Donald J. Bogue of the University of Michigan, examining 67 metropolitan centers in the U.S., has shown that the sphere of influence of a large metropolis usually extends out to about 60 to 100 miles from the center. Typically the metropolitan region includes a number of industrial satellite towns that draw on the resources of the metropolis. The metropolis in turn looks outward to the region for various facilities, particularly recreational resorts such as large parks, lakes, summer cottages, camps, motels and lodges. In Sweden, C. F. Ahlberg, head of the Stockholm Regional Plan, has emphasized this role of the region around the capital city by naming it the "Summer Stockholm"—the widened horizon that opens up for Stockholmers when the snows have gone. Metropolises do, of course, have their winter horizons as well, typified by the ski resorts that flourish as satellites within driving distance of many an American city.

Increasingly the outer-fringe metropolitan region is becoming a popular place for retirement for people on pensions or other modest incomes who can live inexpensively in the country without being too far from the amenities of the city. This is an intriguing reversal of the ancient pattern in which the countryside was the locus of productive work and the city was the Mecca for the enjoyment of leisure.

While we are on the subject of the metropolitan region, I should like to clarify the distinction between such a region and a "conurbation" or "megalopolis." The predominant form of the metropolis is mononuclear: it derives its identity from a single center. This is the way metropolitan areas are generally organized in the U.S. and it is the only form they take in a new young settlement such as Australia, where the population is concentrated mainly in five large metropolitan areas, each centered on a single city. In the older countries of Europe, on the other hand, conurbations—metropolitan regions formed by the gradual growing together of neighboring cities—are fairly common. The outstanding examples are the cities of the Ruhr in Germany and the circle of cities that form what is known as "Randstad Holland" (including Amsterdam, Haarlem, Leiden, The Hague, Rotterdam and Utrecht). The Ruhr conurbation grew up around the coal mines. Along the French-Italian Riviera a conurbation now seems to be developing around seashore play.

There seems to be a general disposition to assume that the Boston-to-Washington axis is destined soon to become a new conurbation on a vastly larger scale than any heretofore. The available evidence does not support such a view. Each of the metropolitan areas along the seaboard remains strongly oriented to its own center. The several metropolitan regions are separated by large areas of sparse development. Conurbation can occur only when the crests of the waves of two expanding centers overlap, and except perhaps between Washington and Baltimore that is not likely to happen anywhere in North America during this century.

To get back to the problems of planning for the metropolis: How should the four main components—central business, production, residence and open land—be organized spatially? The aims here can be expressed most clearly in the form of pairs of seemingly contradictory requirements.

First, it is desirable to minimize the

need for commuting to work and at the same time maximize the ability to do so. Obviously most people would like to live close to their place of work, but to seek such an arrangement as a general proposition would be unrealistic and too restrictive. It is estimated that half of all metropolitan households contain more than one gainfully employed person, and they are not likely to be employed in the same place. Furthermore, the preferred locations for residence and work do not necessarily match up. The situation in Hudson County, N.J., across the river from Manhattan, offers a striking illustration. In 1960 the county contained 244,000 jobs and 233,000 employed residents—apparently a neat balance. On analysis, however, it turns out that 35 percent of the jobs in the county were held by people who commuted from homes elsewhere, and 32 percent of the workers who lived in the county commuted out to work. Freedom of choice, both of the place to live and of the place to work, will always depend on opportunity to travel from one place to the other.

A second ideal of planning is to provide quick access to the center of the city and also quick access to the open country. Most people have tried to achieve a compromise by moving to the suburbs. The resulting pattern of urban sprawl, however, has made this move self-defeating. The more people move out to the suburbs, the farther they have to move from the city and the farther the country moves away from them.

Third, the functions of the metropolis must be integrated, yet there are also strong reasons to separate them—for example, to separate residences from factories or offices. Isolation of the functions by rigid zoning, however, threat-

ens to break up the metropolis into barren and monotonous precincts. Evidently there is no pat answer to this problem. The optimal grain of mixture will vary with conditions.

Fourth, the social health of the metropolis requires that its people identify themselves both with their own neighborhood or group and with the metropolis as a whole. Since identification with an ingroup often leads to hostility toward outgroups, great emphasis is needed on measures that create interest and pride in the metropolis.

Fifth, the metropolis must strike a balance between continuity and receptiveness to change, between the traditions that give it identity and the flexibility necessary for growth and adaptation to new conditions.

Most of the schemes that have been proposed for shaping the future growth of the metropolis are tacitly based on these criteria, although the requirements have not generally been spelled out in precisely this form. The plans are designed to decentralize the metropolis in some way, with the dual aim of minimizing traffic congestion at the center and bringing the city closer to the countryside.

One proposal is the satellite plan I have already mentioned. In that arrangement each of the satellite towns outside the center is largely self-sufficient and more or less like the others. Another scheme somewhat similar to this is called the "constellation" plan; it would set up several widely separated units each of which would specialize in one function, such as finance, administration, cultural institutions and so on. Still another plan is the "linear" metropolis, several variants of which have been proposed. It would not be oriented toward a single center but would contain a series of them strung in a line. The advocates of this plan are attracted primarily by the possibilities it offers for easy access to open land and for unlimited expansion. Decentralization was pushed to its ultimate conclusion in the "Broadacre City" plan suggested by Frank Lloyd Wright. He proposed to disperse the activities of the city more or less evenly over the whole metropolitan region. Such a plan would be practicable only if the time and cost of travel were reduced essentially to zero. They may approach but certainly will never reach that condition.

Probably the most realistic of the many proposals is the plan called the "stellar" or "finger" metropolis. It fingers in all directions. Each finger would retain the center and thrust out would be composed of a string of towns and would be comparable to a linear city. The towns in the string would be connected to one another and to the metropolitan center by a rapid-transit line. Between the fingers would be large wedges of open country, which would thus be easily accessible both to the fingers and to the main center. The metropolis would grow by extending the fingers. This outline is the basis of current plans for the future development of Copenhagen and Stockholm and of the "Year 2000" plan for Washington, D.C.

Any plan that seeks to control the growth of the metropolis rather than leaving it to the play of market forces will require the setting up of new forms of control. Because it inevitably entails transfers of value from one piece of land to another, planning of any sort is bound to come into conflict with the existing vested interests of landowners and municipalities. It is obvious, therefore, that the implementation of rational planning would call for: (1) the creation of an overall metropolitan government for the metropolis, (2) public ownership of all or most of the land that is to be developed, (3) tax revenues sufficient to enable the metropolitan government to acquire the land and carry out the public works required for its development, (4) a national housing policy that would eliminate segregation by providing people at all income levels with freedom of choice in the location of their dwellings.

In terms of current American political folklore these are radical measures. Each of them, however, has been carried out in varying forms and to a varying degree by more than one European nation within the framework of democratic capitalism.

In the long run the development of the metropolis is likely to be influenced most powerfully by improvements in transportation and communication and by the increase in leisure time. The first may lead to an expansion of the metropolis that will embrace a whole region. The second, depending on future developments in mankind's social structure and culture, may lead to *panem et circenses* ("bread and circuses") or to *otium cum dignitate* ("leisure with dignity"). Both are possible in the metropolis.

Urbanism and Suburbanism as Ways of Life:
A Re-evaluation of Definitions*

The contemporary sociological conception of cities and of urban life is based largely on the work of the Chicago School, and its summary statement in Louis Wirth's essay, "Urbanism as a Way of Life." (40) In that paper, Wirth developed a "minimum sociological definition of the city" as "a relatively large, dense and permanent settlement of socially heterogeneous individuals." (40, p. 50) From these prerequisites, he then deduced the major outlines of the urban way of life. As he saw it, number, density, and heterogeneity created a social structure in which primary-group relationships were inevitably replaced by secondary contacts that were impersonal, segmental, superficial, transitory, and often predatory in nature. As a result, the city dweller became anonymous, isolated, secular, relativistic, rational, and sophisticated. In order to function in the urban society, he was forced to combine with others to organize corporations, voluntary associations, representative forms of government, and the impersonal mass media of communications (40, pp. 54-60). These replaced the primary groups and the integrated way of life found in rural and other pre-industrial settlements.

Wirth's paper has become a classic in urban sociology, and most texts have followed his definition and description faithfully (5). In recent years, however, a considerable number of studies and essays have questioned his formulations (1, 5, 13, 15, 17, 19, 20, 23, 24, 27, 28, 30, 35, 38, 41).[1] In addition, a number of changes have taken place in cities since the article was published in 1938, notably the exodus of white residents to low- and medium-priced houses in the suburbs, and the decentralization of industry. The evidence from these studies and the changes in American cities suggest that Wirth's statement must be revised.

There is yet another, and more important reason for such a revision. Despite its title and intent, Wirth's paper deals with urban-industrial society, rather than with the city. This is evident from his approach. Like other urban sociologists, Wirth based his analysis on a comparison of settlement types, but unlike his colleagues, who pursued urban-rural comparisons, Wirth contrasted the city to the folk society. Thus, he compared settlement types of pre-industrial and industrial society. This allowed him to include in his theory of urbanism the entire range of modern institutions which are not found in the folk society, even though many such groups (e.g., voluntary associations) are by no means exclusively urban. Moreover, Wirth's conception of the city dweller as depersonalized, atomized, and susceptible to mass movements suggests that his paper is based on, and contributes to, the theory of the mass society.

Many of Wirth's conclusions may be

* From Arnold Rose (ed.), *Human Behavior and Social Processes* (Boston: Houghton Mifflin, 1962), pp. 625-48. Copyright © 1962 by Houghton Mifflin Company. Reprinted by permission of the publisher. Herbert J. Gans is with the Center for Urban Education.

relevant to the understanding of ways of life in modern society. However, since the theory argues that all of society is now urban, *his analysis does not distinguish ways of life in the city from those in other settlements within modern society.* In Wirth's time, the comparison of urban and pre-urban settlement types was still fruitful, but today, the primary task for urban (or community) sociology seems to me to be the analysis of the similarities and differences between contemporary settlement types.

This paper is an attempt at such an analysis; it limits itself to distinguishing ways of life in the modern city and the modern suburb. A re-analysis of Wirth's conclusions from this perspective suggests that his characterization of the urban way of life applies only—and not too accurately—to the residents of the inner city. The remaining city dwellers, as well as most suburbanites, pursue a different way of life, which I shall call "quasi-primary." This proposition raises some doubt about the mutual exclusiveness of the concepts of city and suburb and leads to a yet broader question: whether settlement concepts and other ecological concepts are useful for explaining ways of life.

THE INNER CITY

Wirth argued that number, density, and heterogeneity had two social consequences which explain the major features of urban life. On the one hand, the crowding of diverse types of people into a small area led to the segregation of homogeneous types of people into separate neighborhoods (40, p. 56). On the other hand, the lack of physical distance between city dwellers resulted in social contact between them, which broke down existing social and cultural patterns and encouraged assimilation as well as acculturation—the melting pot effect (40, p. 52). Wirth implied that the melting pot effect was far more powerful than the tendency toward segregation and concluded that, sooner or later, the pressures engendered by the dominant social, economic, and political institutions of the city would destroy the remaining pockets of primary-group relationships (40, pp. 60-62). Eventually, the social system of the city would resemble Tönnies' *Gesellschaft*— a way of life which Wirth considered undesirable.

Because Wirth had come to see the city as the prototype of mass society, and because he examined the city from the distant vantage point of the folk society—from the wrong end of the telescope, so to speak—his view of urban life is not surprising. In addition, Wirth found support for this theory in the empirical work of his Chicago colleagues. As Greer and Kube (19, p. 112) and Wilensky (38, p. 121) have pointed out, the Chicago sociologists conducted their most intensive studies in the inner city.[2] At that time, these were slums recently invaded by new waves of European immigrants and rooming house and skid row districts, as well as the habitat of Bohemians and well-to-do Gold Coast apartment dwellers. Wirth himself studied the Maxwell Street Ghetto, an inner-city Jewish neighborhood then being dispersed by the acculturation and mobility of its inhabitants (39). Some of the characteristics of urbanism which Wirth stressed in his essay abounded in these areas.

Wirth's diagnosis of the city as *Gesellschaft* must be questioned on three counts. First, the conclusions derived from a study of the inner city cannot be generalized to the entire urban area. Second, there is as yet not enough evidence to prove—nor, admittedly, to deny—that number, density, and heterogeneity result in the social consequences which Wirth proposed. Finally, even if the causal relationship could be verified, it can be shown that a significant proportion of the city's inhabitants were, and are, isolated from these consequences by social structures and cultural patterns which they either brought to the city, or developed by living in it. Wirth conceived the urban population as consisting of heterogeneous individuals, torn from past social systems, unable to develop new ones, and therefore prey to social anarchy in the city. While it is true that a not insignificant proportion of the inner city population was, and still is, made up of unattached individuals (26), Wirth's formulation ignores the fact that this population consists mainly of relatively homogeneous groups, with social and cultural moorings that shield it fairly effectively from the suggested consequences of number, density, and heterogeneity. This applies even more to the residents of the outer city, who constitute a majority of the total city population.

The social and cultural moorings of the inner city population are best described by a brief analysis of the five types of inner city residents. These are:

1. the "cosmopolites";
2. the unmarried or childless;
3. the "ethnic villagers";
4. the "deprived"; and
5. the "trapped" and downward mobile.

The "cosmopolites" include students, artists, writers, musicians, and entertainers, as well as other intellectuals and professionals. They live in the city in order to be near the special "cultural" facilities that can only be located near the center of the city. Many cosmopolites are unmarried or childless. Others rear children in the city, especially if they have the income to afford the aid of servants and governesses. The less affluent ones may move to the suburbs to raise their children, continuing to live as cosmopolites under considerable handicaps, especially in the lower-middle-class suburbs. Many of the very rich and powerful are also cosmopolites, although they are likely to have at least two residences, one of which is suburban or exurban.

The unmarried or childless must be divided into two subtypes, depending on the permanence or transience of their status. The temporarily unmarried or childless live in the inner city for only a limited time. Young adults may team up to rent an apartment away from their parents and close to job or entertainment opportunities. When they marry, they may move first to an apartment in a transient neighborhood, but if they can afford to do so, they leave for the outer city or the suburbs with the arrival of the first or second child. The permanently unmarried may stay in the inner city for the remainder of their lives, their housing depending on their income.

The "ethnic villagers" are ethnic groups which are found in such inner city neighborhoods as New York's Lower East Side, living in some ways as they did when they were peasants in European or Puerto Rican villages (15). Although they reside in the city, they isolate themselves from significant contact with most city facilities, aside from workplaces. Their way of life differs sharply from Wirth's urbanism in its emphasis on kinship and the primary group, the lack of anonymity and secondary-group contacts, the weakness of formal organizations, and the suspicion of anything and anyone outside their neighborhood.

The first two types live in the inner city by choice; the third is there partly because of necessity, partly because of tradition. The final two types are in the inner city because they have no other choice. One is the "deprived" population: the very poor; the emotionally disturbed or otherwise handicapped; broken families; and, most important, the non-white population. These urban dwellers must take the dilapidated housing and blighted neighborhoods to which the housing market relegates them, although among them are some for whom the slum is a hiding place, or a temporary stop-over to save money for a house in the outer city or the suburbs (27).

The "trapped" are the people who stay behind when a neighborhood is invaded by non-residential land uses or lower-status immigrants, because they cannot afford to move, or are otherwise bound to their present location (27).[3] The "downward mobiles" are a related type; they may have started life in a higher class position, but have been forced down in the socio-economic hierarchy and in the quality of their accommodations. Many of them are old people, living out their existence on small pensions.

These five types all live in dense and heterogeneous surroundings, yet they have such diverse ways of life that it is hard to see how density and heterogeneity could exert a common influence. Moreover, all but the last two types are isolated or detached from their neighborhood and thus from the social consequences which Wirth described.

When people who live together have social ties based on criteria other than mere common occupancy, they can set up social barriers regardless of the physical closeness or the heterogeneity of their neighbors. The ethnic villagers are the best illustration. While a number of ethnic groups are usually found living together in the same neighborhood, they are able to *isolate* themselves from each other through a variety of social devices. Wirth himself recognized this when he wrote that "two groups can occupy a given area without losing their separate identity because each side is permitted to live its own inner life and each somehow fears or idealizes the other." (39, p. 283) Although it is true that the children in these areas were often oblivious to the social barriers set up by their parents, at least until adolescence, it is doubtful whether their acculturation can be traced to the melting pot effect as much as to the pervasive influence of the American culture that flowed into these areas from the outside.[4]

The cosmopolites, the unmarried, and the childless are *detached* from neighborhood life. The cosmopolites possess a distinct subculture which causes them to be disinterested in all but the most superficial contacts with their neighbors, somewhat like the ethnic villagers. The unmarried and childless are detached from neighborhood because of their life-cycle stage, which frees them from the routine family responsibilities that entail some relationship to the local area. In their choice of residence, the two types are therefore not concerned about their neighbors, or the availability and quality of local community facilities. Even the well-to-do can choose expensive apartments in or near poor neighborhoods, because if they have children, these are sent to special schools and summer camps which effectively isolate them from neighbors. In addition, both types, but especially the childless and unmarried, are transient. Therefore, they tend to live in areas marked by high population turnover, where their own mobility and that of their neighbors creates a universal detachment from the neighborhood.[5]

The deprived and the trapped do seem to be affected by some of the consequences of number, density, and heterogeneity. The deprived population suffers considerably from overcrowding, but this is a consequence of low income, racial discrimination, and other handicaps, and cannot be considered an inevitable result of the ecological make-up of the city.[6] Because the deprived have no residential choice, they are also forced to live amid neighbors not of their own choosing, with ways of life different and even contradictory to their own. If familial defenses against the neighborhood climate are weak, as is the case among broken families and downward mobile people, parents may lose their children to the culture of "the street." The trapped are the unhappy people who remain behind when their more advantaged neighbors move on; they must endure the heterogeneity which results from neighborhood change.

Wirth's description of the urban way of life fits best the transient areas of the inner city. Such areas are typically heterogeneous in population, partly because they are inhabited by transient types who do not require homogeneous neighbors or by deprived people who have no choice, or may themselves be quite mobile. Under conditions of transience and heterogeneity, people interact only in terms of the segmental roles necessary for obtaining local services.

Their social relationships thus display anonymity, impersonality, and superficiality.[7]

The social features of Wirth's concept of urbanism seem therefore to be a result of residential instability, rather than of number, density, or heterogeneity. In fact, heterogeneity is itself an effect of residential instability, resulting when the influx of transients causes landlords and realtors to stop acting as gatekeepers—that is, wardens of neighborhood homogeneity.[8] Residential instability is found in all types of settlements, and, presumably, its social consequences are everywhere similar. These consequences cannot therefore be identified with the ways of life of the city.

THE OUTER CITY AND THE SUBURBS

The second effect which Wirth ascribed to number, density, and heterogeneity was the segregation of homogeneous people into distinct neighborhoods,[9] on the basis of "place and nature of work, income, racial and ethnic characteristics, social status, custom, habit, taste, preference and prejudice." (40, p. 56) This description fits the residential districts of the *outer city*.[10] Although these districts contain the majority of the city's inhabitants, Wirth went into little detail about them. He made it clear, however, that the socio-psychological aspects of urbanism were prevalent there as well (40, p. 56).

Because existing neighborhood studies deal primarily with the exotic sections of the inner city, very little is known about the more typical residential neighborhoods of the outer city. However, it is evident that the way of life in these areas bears little resemblance to Wirth's urbanism. Both the studies which question Wirth's formulation and my own observations suggest that the common element in the ways of life of these neighborhoods is best described as *quasi-primary*. I use this term to characterize relationships between neighbors. Whatever the intensity or frequency of these relationships, the interaction is more intimate than a secondary contact, but more guarded than a primary one.[11]

There are actually few secondary relationships, because of the isolation of residential neighborhoods from economic institutions and workplaces. Even shopkeepers, store managers, and other local functionaries who live in the area are treated as acquaintances or friends, unless they are of a vastly different social status or are forced by their corporate employers to treat their customers as economic units (30). Voluntary associations attract only a minority of the population. Moreover, much of the organizational activity is of a sociable nature, and it is often difficult to accomplish the association's "business" because of the members' preference for sociability. Thus, it would appear that interactions in organizations, or between neighbors generally, do not fit the secondary-relationship model of urban life. As anyone who has lived in these neighborhoods knows, there is little anonymity, impersonality or privacy.[12] In fact, American cities have sometimes been described as collections of small towns.[13] There is some truth to this description, especially if the city is compared to the actual small town, rather than to the romantic construct of anti-urban critics (33).

Postwar suburbia represents the most contemporary version of the quasi-primary way of life. Owing to increases in real income and the encouragement of home ownership provided by the FHA, families in the lower-middle class and upper working class can now live in modern single-family homes in low-density subdivisions, an opportunity previously available only to the upper and upper-middle classes (34).

The popular literature describes the new suburbs as communities in which conformity, homogeneity, and other-direction are unusually rampant (4, 32). The implication is that the move from city to suburb initiates a new way of life which causes considerable behavior and personality change in previous urbanites. A preliminary analysis of data which I am now collecting in Levittown, New Jersey, suggests, however, that the move from the city to this predominantly lower-middle-class suburb does not result in any major behavioral changes for most people. Moreover, the changes which do occur reflect the move from the social isolation of a transient city or suburban apartment building to the quasi-primary life of a neighborhood of single-family homes. Also, many of the people whose life has changed reported that the changes were intended. They existed as aspirations before the move, or as reasons for it. In other words, the suburb itself creates few changes in ways of life. Similar conclusions have been reported by Berger in his excellent study of a working-class population newly moved to a suburban subdivision (4).

A COMPARISON OF CITY AND SUBURB

If urban and suburban areas are similar in that the way of life in both is quasi-primary, and if urban residents who move out to the suburbs do not undergo any significant changes in behavior, it would be fair to argue that the differences in ways of life between the two types of settlements have been over-estimated. Yet the fact remains that a variety of physical and demographic differences exist between the city and the suburb. However, upon closer examination, many of these differences turn out to be either spurious or of little significance for the way of life of the inhabitants (34).[14]

The differences between the residential areas of cities and suburbs which have been cited most frequently are:

1. Suburbs are more likely to be dormitories.
2. They are further away from the work and play facilities of the central business districts.
3. They are newer and more modern than city residential areas and are designed for the automobile rather than for pedestrian and mass-transit forms of movement.
4. They are built up with single-family rather than multi-family structures and are therefore less dense.
5. Their populations are more homogeneous.
6. Their populations differ demographically: they are younger; more of them are married; they have higher incomes; and they hold proportionately more white collar jobs (8, p. 131).

Most urban neighborhoods are as much dormitories as the suburbs. Only in a few older inner city areas are factories and offices still located in the middle of residential blocks, and even here many of the employees do not live in the neighborhood.

The fact that the suburbs are farther from the central business district is often true only in terms of distance, not travel time. Moreover, most people make relatively little use of downtown facilities, other than workplaces (12, 21). The downtown stores seem to hold their greatest attraction for the upper-middle class (21, pp. 91-92); the same is probably true of typically urban entertainment facilities. Teen-agers and young adults may take their dates to first-run movie theaters, but the museums, concert halls, and lecture rooms attract mainly upper-middle-class ticket-buyers, many of them suburban.[15]

The suburban reliance on the train and the automobile has given rise to an imaginative folklore about the consequences of commuting on alcohol consumption, sex life, and parental duties. Many of these conclusions are, however, drawn from selected high-income suburbs and exurbs, and reflect job tensions in such hectic occupations as advertising and show business more than the effects of residence (29). It is true that the upper-middle-class housewife must become a chauffeur in order to expose her children to the proper educational facilities, but such differences as walking to the corner drug store and driving to its suburban equivalent seem to me of little emotional, social, or cultural import.[16] In addition, the continuing shrinkage in the number of mass-transit users suggests that even in the city many younger people are now living a wholly auto-based way of life.

The fact that suburbs are smaller is primarily a function of political boundaries drawn long before the communities were suburban. This affects the kinds of political issues which develop and provides somewhat greater opportunity for citizen participation. Even so, in the suburbs as in the city, the minority who participate are the professional politicians, the economically concerned businessmen, lawyers and salesmen, and the ideologically motivated middle- and upper-middle-class people with better than average education.

The social consequences of differences in density and house type also seem overrated. Single-family houses on quiet streets facilitate the supervision of children; this is one reason why middle-class women who want to keep an eye on their children move to the suburbs. House type also has some effects on relationships between neighbors, insofar as there are more opportunities for visual contact between adjacent home-owners than between people on different floors of an apartment house. However, if occupants' characteristics are also held constant, the differences in actual social contact are less marked. Homogeneity of residents turns out to be more important as a determinant of sociability than proximity. If the population is heterogeneous, there is little social contact between neighbors, either on apartment-house floors or in single-family-house blocks; if people are homogeneous, there is likely to be considerable social contact in both house types. One need only contrast the apartment house located in a transient, heterogeneous neighborhood and exactly the same structure in a neighborhood occupied by a single ethnic group. The former is a lonely, anonymous building; the latter, a bustling micro-society. I have observed similar patterns in suburban areas: on blocks where people are homogeneous, they socialize; where they are heterogeneous, they do little more than exchange polite greetings (16).

Suburbs are usually described as being more homogeneous in house type than the city, but if they are compared to the outer city, the differences are small. Most inhabitants of the outer city, other than well-to-do homeowners, live on blocks of uniform structures as well —for example, the endless streets of rowhouses in Philadelphia and Balti-

more or of two-story duplexes and six-flat apartment houses in Chicago. They differ from the new suburbs only in that they were erected through more primitive methods of mass production. Suburbs are of course more predominantly areas of owner-occupied single homes, though in the outer districts of most American cities homeownership is also extremely high.

Demographically, suburbs as a whole are clearly more homogeneous than cities as a whole, though probably not more so than outer cities. However, people do not live in cities or suburbs as a whole, but in specific neighborhoods. An analysis of ways of life would require a determination of the degree of population homogeneity within the boundaries of areas defined as neighborhoods by resident's social contacts. Such an analysis would no doubt indicate that many neighborhoods in the city as well as the suburbs are homogeneous. Neighborhood homogeneity is actually a result of factors having little or nothing to do with the house type, density, or location of the area relative to the city limits. Brand new neighborhoods are more homogeneous than older ones, because they have not yet experienced resident turnover, which frequently results in population heterogeneity. Neighborhoods of low- and medium-priced housing are usually less homogeneous than those with expensive dwellings because they attract families who have reached the peak of occupational and residential mobility, as well as young families who are just starting their climb and will eventually move to neighborhoods of higher status. The latter, being accessible only to high-income people, are therefore more homogeneous with respect to other resident characteristics as well. Moreover, such areas have the economic and political power to slow down or prevent invasion. Finally, neighborhoods located in the path of ethnic or religious group movement are likely to be extremely homogeneous.

The demographic differences between cities and suburbs cannot be questioned, especially since the suburbs have attracted a large number of middle-class child-rearing families. The differences are, however, much reduced if suburbs are compared only to the outer city. In addition, a detailed comparison of suburban and outer city residential areas would show that neighborhoods with the same kinds of people can be found in the city as well as the suburbs. Once again, the age of the area and the cost of housing are more important determinants of demographic characteristics than the location of the area with respect to the city limits.

Characteristics, Social Organization, and Ecology

The preceding sections of the paper may be summarized in three propositions:

1. As concerns ways of life, the inner city must be distinguished from the outer city and the suburbs; and the latter two exhibit a way of life bearing little resemblance to Wirth's urbanism.
2. Even in the inner city, ways of life resemble Wirth's description only to a limited extent. Moreover, economic condition, cultural characteristics, life-cycle stage, and residential instability explain ways of life more satisfactorily than number, density, or heterogeneity.
3. Physical and other differences between city and suburb are often spurious or without much meaning for ways of life.

These propositions suggest that the concepts urban and suburban are neither mutually exclusive, nor especially relevant for understanding ways of life. They—and number, density, and heterogeneity as well—are ecological concepts which describe human adaptation to the environment. However, they are not sufficient to explain social phenomena, because these phenomena cannot be understood solely as the consequences of ecological processes. Therefore, other explanations must be considered.

Ecological explanations of social life are most applicable if the subjects under study lack the ability to *make choices*, be they plants, animals, or human beings. Thus, if there is a housing shortage, people will live almost anywhere, and under extreme conditions of no choice, as in a disaster, married and single, old and young, middle and working class, stable and transient will be found side by side in whatever accommodations are available. At that time, their ways of life represent an almost direct adaptation to the environment. If the supply of housing and of neighborhoods is such that alternatives are available, however, people will make choices, and if the housing market is responsive, they can even make and satisfy explicit *demands*.

Choices and demands do not develop independently or at random; they are functions of the roles people play in the social system. These can best be understood in terms of the *characteristics* of the people involved; that is, characteristics can be used as indices to choices and demands made in the roles that constitute ways of life. Although many characteristics affect the choices and demands people make with respect to housing and neighborhoods, the most important ones seem to be *class*—in all its economic, social and cultural ramifications—and *life-cycle stage*.[17] If people have an opportunity to choose, these two characteristics will go far in explaining the kinds of housing and neighborhoods they will occupy and the ways of life they will try to establish within them.

Many of the previous assertions about ways of life in cities and suburbs can be analyzed in terms of class and life-cycle characteristics. Thus, in the inner city, the unmarried and childless live as they do, detached from neighborhood, because of their life-cycle stage; the cosmopolites, because of a combination of life-cycle stage and a distinctive but class-based subculture. The way of life of the deprived and trapped can be explained by low socio-economic level and related handicaps. The quasi-primary way of life is associated with the family stage of the life-cycle, and the norms of child-rearing and parental role found in the upper working class, the lower-middle class, and the non-cosmopolite portions of the upper-middle and upper classes.

The attributes of the so-called suburban way of life can also be understood largely in terms of these characteristics. The new suburbia is nothing more than a highly visible showcase for the ways of life of young, upper-working-class and lower-middle-class people. Ktsanes and Reissman have aptly described it as "new homes for old values." (22) Much of the descriptive and critical writing about suburbia assumes that as long as the new suburbanites lived in the city, they behaved like upper-middle-class cosmopolites and that suburban living has mysteriously transformed them (7; 14, pp. 154-162; 25; 36). The critics fail to see that the behavior and personality patterns ascribed to suburbia are in reality those of class

and age (6). These patterns could have been found among the new suburbanites when they still lived in the city and could now be observed among their peers who still reside there—if the latter were as visible to critics and researchers as are the suburbanites.

Needless to say, the concept of "characteristics" cannot explain all aspects of ways of life, either among urban or suburban residents. Some aspects must be explained by concepts of social organization that are independent of characteristics. For example, some features of the quasi-primary way of life are independent of class and age, because they evolve from the roles and situations created by joint and adjacent occupancy of land and dwellings. Likewise, residential instability is a universal process which has a number of invariate consequences. In each case, however, the way in which people react varies with their characteristics. So it is with ecological processes. Thus, there are undoubtedly differences between ways of life in urban and suburban settlements which remain after behavior patterns based on residents' characteristics have been analyzed, and which must therefore be attributed to features of the settlement (11).

Characteristics do not explain the causes of behavior; rather, they are clues to socially created and culturally defined roles, choices, and demands. A causal analysis must trace them back to the larger social, economic, and political systems which determine the situations in which roles are played and the cultural content of choices and demands, as well as the opportunities for their achievement.[18] These systems determine income distributions, educational and occupational opportunities, and in turn, fertility patterns, child-rearing methods, as well as the entire range of consumer behavior. Thus, a complete analysis of the way of life of the deprived residents of the inner city cannot stop by indicating the influence of low income, lack of education, or family instability. These must be related to such conditions as the urban economy's "need" for low-wage workers, and the housing market practices which restrict residential choice. The urban economy is in turn shaped by national economic and social systems, as well as by local and regional ecological processes. Some phenomena can be explained exclusively by reference to these ecological processes. However, it must also be recognized that as man gains greater control over the natural environment, he has been able to free himself from many of the determining and limiting effects of that environment. Thus, changes in local transportation technology, the ability of industries to be footloose, and the relative affluence of American society have given ever larger numbers of people increasing amounts of residential choice. The greater the amount of choice available, the more important does the concept of characteristics become in understanding behavior.

Consequently, the study of ways of life in communities must begin with an analysis of characteristics. If characteristics are dealt with first and held constant, we may be able to discover which behavior patterns can be attributed to features of the settlement and its natural environment.[19] Only then will it be possible to discover to what extent city and suburb are independent—rather than dependent or intervening—variables in the explanation of ways of life.

This kind of analysis might help to reconcile the ecological point of view with the behavioral and cultural one, and possibly put an end to the conflict between conceptual positions which insist on one explanation or the other (9). Both explanations have some relevance, and future research and theory must clarify the role of each in the analysis of ways of life in various types of settlement (6, p. xxii). Another important rationale for this approach is its usefulness for applied sociology—for example, city planning. The planner can recommend changes in the spatial and physical arrangements of the city. Frequently, he seeks to achieve social goals or to change social conditions through physical solutions. He has been attracted to ecological explanations because these relate behavior to phenomena which he can affect. For example, most planners tend to agree with Wirth's formulations, because they stress number and density, over which the planner has some control. If the undesirable social conditions of the inner city could be traced to these two factors, the planner could propose large-scale clearance projects which would reduce the size of the urban population, and lower residential densities. Experience with public housing projects has, however, made it apparent that low densities, new buildings, or modern site plans do not eliminate anti-social or self-destructive behavior. The analysis of characteristics will call attention to the fact that this behavior is lodged in the deprivations of low socio-economic status and racial discrimination, and that it can be changed only through the removal of these deprivations. Conversely, if such an analysis suggests residues of behavior that can be attributed to ecological processes or physical aspects of housing and neighborhoods, the planner can recommend physical changes that can really affect behavior.

A RE-EVALUATION OF DEFINITIONS

The argument presented here has implications for the sociological definition of the city. Such a definition relates ways of life to environmental features of the city qua settlement type. But if ways of life do not coincide with settlement types, and if these ways are functions of class and life-cycle stage rather than of the ecological attributes of the settlement, a sociological definition of the city cannot be formulated.[20] Concepts such as city and suburb allow us to distinguish settlement types from each other physically and demographically, but the ecological processes and conditions which they synthesize have no direct or invariate consequences for ways of life. The sociologist cannot, therefore, speak of an urban or suburban way of life.

CONCLUSION

Many of the descriptive statements made here are as time-bound as Wirth's.[21] Twenty years ago, Wirth concluded that some form of urbanism would eventually predominate in all settlement types. He was, however, writing during a time of immigrant acculturation and at the end of a serious depression, an era of minimal choice. Today, it is apparent that high-density, heterogeneous surroundings are for most people a temporary place of residence; other than for the Park Avenue or Greenwich Village cosmopolites, they are a result of necessity rather than choice. As soon as they can afford to do so, most Americans head for the single-family house and the quasi-primary way of life of the low-density neighborhood, in the outer city or the suburbs.[22]

Changes in the national economy and in government housing policy can affect many of the variables that make up housing supply and demand. For example, urban sprawl may eventually outdistance the ability of present and proposed transportation systems to move workers into the city; further industrial decentralization can forestall it and alter the entire relationship between work and residence. The expansion of present urban renewal activities can perhaps lure a significant number of cosmopolites back from the suburbs, while a drastic change in renewal policy might begin to ameliorate the housing conditions of the deprived population. A serious depression could once again make America a nation of doubled-up tenants.

These events will affect housing supply and residential choice; they will frustrate but not suppress demands for the quasi-primary way of life. However, changes in the national economy, society, and culture can affect people's characteristics—family size, educational level, and various other concomitants of life-cycle stage and class. These in turn will stimulate changes in demands and choices. The rising number of college graduates, for example, is likely to increase the cosmopolite ranks. This might in turn create a new set of city dwellers, although it will probably do no more than encourage the development of cosmopolite facilities in some suburban areas.

The current revival of interest in urban sociology and in community studies, as well as the sociologist's increasing curiosity about city planning, suggest that data may soon be available to formulate a more adequate theory of the relationship between settlements and the ways of life within them. The speculations presented in this paper are intended to raise questions; they can only be answered by more systematic data collection and theorizing.

REFERENCES

1. Axelrod, Morris. "Urban Structure and Social Participation," *American Sociological Review*, Vol. 21 (February 1956), pp. 13–18.

2. Bell, Wendell. "Social Choice, Life Styles and Suburban Residence," in William M. Dobriner (ed.), *The Suburban Community*. New York: G. P. Putnam's Sons, 1958, pp. 225–247.

3. Bell, Wendell, and Maryanne T. Force. "Urban Neighborhood Types and Participation in Formal Associations," *American Sociological Review*, Vol. 21 (February 1956), pp. 25–34.

4. Berger, Bennett. *Working Class Suburb: A Study of Auto Workers in Suburbia*. Berkeley, Calif.: University of California Press, 1960.

5. Dewey, Richard. "The Rural–Urban Continuum: Real but Relatively Unimportant," *American Journal of Sociology*, Vol. 66 (July 1960), pp. 60–66.

6. Dobriner, William M. "Introduction: Theory and Research in the Sociology of the Suburbs," in William M. Dobriner (ed.), *The Suburban Community*. New York: G. P. Putnam's Sons, 1958, pp. xiii–xxviii.

7. Duhl, Leonard J. "Mental Health and Community Planning," in *Planning 1955*. Chicago: American Society of Planning Officials, 1956, pp. 31–39.

8. Duncan, Otis Dudley, and Albert J. Reiss, Jr. *Social Characteristics of Rural and Urban Communities, 1950*. New York: John Wiley & Sons, 1956.

9. Duncan, Otis Dudley, and Leo F. Schnore. "Cultural, Behavioral and Ecological Perspectives in the Study of Social Organization," *American Journal of Sociology*, Vol. 65 (September 1959), pp. 132–155.

10. Enders, John. *Profile of the Theater Market*. New York: Playbill, undated and unpaged.

11. Fava, Sylvia Fleis. "Contrasts in Neighboring: New York City and a Suburban Community," in William M. Dobriner (ed.), *The Suburban Community*. New York: G. P. Putnam's Sons, 1958, pp. 122–131.

12. Foley, Donald L. "The Use of Local Facilities in a Metropolis," in Paul Hatt and Albert J. Reiss, Jr. (eds.), *Cities and Society*. Glencoe, Ill.: The Free Press, 1957, pp. 237–247.

13. Form, William H., *et al.* "The Compatibility of Alternative Approaches to the Delimitation of Urban Sub-areas," *American Sociological Review*, Vol. 19 (August 1954), pp. 434–440.

14. Fromm, Erich. *The Sane Society*. New York: Rinehart & Co., Inc., 1955.

15. Gans, Herbert J. *The Urban Villagers: A Study of the Second Generation Italians in the West End of Boston*. Boston: Center for Community Studies, December 1959 (mimeographed).

16. Gans, Herbert J. "Planning and Social Life: An Evaluation of Friendship and Neighbor Relations in Suburban Communities," *Journal of the American Institute of Planners*, Vol. 27 (May 1961), pp. 134–140.

17. Greer, Scott. "Urbanism Reconsidered: A Comparative Study of Local Areas in a Metropolis," *American Sociological Review*, Vol. 21 (February 1956), pp. 19–25.

18. Greer, Scott. "The Social Structure and Political Process of Suburbia," *American Sociological Review*, Vol. 25 (August 1960), pp. 514–526.

19. Greer, Scott, and Ella Kube. "Urbanism and Social Structure: A Los Angeles Study," in Marvin B. Sussman (ed.), *Community Structure and Analysis*. New York: Thomas Y. Crowell Company, 1959, pp. 93–112.

20. Janowitz, Morris. *The Community Press in an Urban Setting*. Glencoe, Ill.: The Free Press, 1952.

21. Jonassen, Christen T. *The Shopping Center Versus Downtown*. Columbus, Ohio: Bureau of Business Research, Ohio State University, 1955.

22. Ktsanes, Thomas, and Leonard Reissmann. "Suburbia: New Homes for Old Values," *Social Problems*, Vol. 7 (Winter 1959–60), pp. 187–194.

23. Reiss, Albert J., Jr. "An Analysis of Urban Phenomena," in Robert M. Fisher (ed.), *The Metropolis in Modern Life*. Garden City, N.Y.: Doubleday & Company, Inc., 1955, pp. 41–49.

24. Reiss, Albert J., Jr. "Rural–Urban and

Status Differences in Interpersonal Contacts," *American Journal of Sociology,* Vol. 65 (September 1959), pp. 182–195.
25. Riesman, David. "The Suburban Sadness," in William M. Dobriner (ed.), *The Suburban Community.* New York: G. P. Putnam's Sons, 1958, pp. 375–408.
26. Rose, Arnold M. "Living Arrangements of Unattached Persons," *American Sociological Review,* Vol. 12 (August 1947), pp. 429–435.
27. Seeley, John R. "The Slum: Its Nature, Use and Users," *Journal of the American Institute of Planners,* Vol. 25 (February 1959), pp. 7–14.
28. Smith, Joel, William Form, and Gregory Stone. "Local Intimacy in a Middle-Sized City," *American Journal of Sociology,* Vol. 60 (November 1954), pp. 276–284.
29. Spectorsky, A. C. *The Exurbanites.* Philadelphia: J. B. Lippincott Co., 1955.
30. Stone, Gregory P. "City Shoppers and Urban Identification: Observations on the Social Psychology of City Life," *American Journal of Sociology,* Vol. 60 (July 1954), pp. 36–45.
31. Strauss, Anselm. "The Changing Imagery of American City and Suburb," *Sociological Quarterly,* Vol. 1 (January 1960), pp. 15–24.
32. Vernon, Raymond. *The Changing Economic Function of the Central City.* New York: Committee on Economic Development, Supplementary Paper No. 1, January 1959.
33. Vidich, Arthur J., and Joseph Bensman. *Small Town in Mass Society: Class, Power and Religion in a Rural Community.* Princeton, N.J.: Princeton University Press, 1958.
34. Wattell, Harold. "Levittown: A Suburban Community," in William M. Dobriner (ed.), *The Suburban Community.* New York: G. P. Putnam's Sons, 1958, pp. 287–313.
35. Whyte, William F., Jr. *Street Corner Society.* Chicago: The University of Chicago Press, 1955.
36. Whyte, William F., Jr. *The Organization Man.* New York: Simon & Schuster, 1956.
37. Wilensky, Harold L. "Life Cycle, Work, Situation and Participation in Formal Associations," in Robert W. Kleemeier, *et al.* (eds.), *Aging and Leisure: Research Perspectives on the Meaningful Use of Time.* New York: Oxford University Press, 1961, Chapter 8.
38. Wilensky, Harold L., and Charles Lebeaux. *Industrial Society and Social Welfare.* New York: Russell Sage Foundation, 1958.
39. Wirth, Louis. *The Ghetto.* Chicago: The University of Chicago Press, 1928.
40. Wirth, Louis. "Urbanism as a Way of Life," *American Journal of Sociology,* Vol. 44 (July 1938), pp. 1–24. Reprinted in Paul Hatt and Albert J. Reiss, Jr. (eds.), *Cities and Society.* Glencoe, Ill.: The Free Press, 1957, pp. 46–64. [All page references are to this reprinting of the article.]
41. Young, Michael, and Peter Willmott. *Family and Kinship in East London.* London: Routledge & Kegan Paul, Ltd., 1957.

NOTES

° I am indebted to Richard Dewey, John Dyckman, David Riesman, Melvin Webber, and Harold Wilensky for helpful comments on earlier drafts of this essay.
1. I shall not attempt to summarize these studies, for this task has already been performed by Dewey (5), Reiss (23), Wilensky (38), and others.
2. By the *inner city,* I mean the transient residential areas, the Gold Coasts and the slums that generally surround the central business district, although in some communities they may continue for miles beyond that district. The *outer city* includes the stable residential areas that house the working- and middle-class tenant and owner. The *suburbs* I conceive as the latest and most modern ring of the outer city, distinguished from it only by yet lower densities, and by the often irrelevant fact of the ring's location outside the city limits.
3. The trapped are not very visible, but I suspect that they are a significant element in what Raymond Vernon has described as the "gray areas" of the city (32).
4. If the melting pot has resulted from propinquity and high density, one would have expected second-generation Italians, Irish, Jews, Greeks, Slavs, etc. to have developed a single "pan-ethnic culture," consisting of a synthesis of the cultural patterns of the propinquitous national groups.
5. The corporation transients (36, 38), who provide a new source of residential instability to the suburb, differ from city transients. Since they are raising families, they want to integrate themselves into neighborhood life, and are usually able to do so, mainly because they tend to move into similar types of communities wherever they go.
6. The negative social consequences of overcrowding are a result of high room and floor density, not of the land coverage of population density which Wirth discussed. Park Avenue resi-

dents live under conditions of high land density, but do not seem to suffer visibly from overcrowding.

7. Whether or not these social phenomena have the psychological consequences Wirth suggested depends on the people who live in the area. Those who are detached from the neighborhood by choice are probably immune, but those who depend on the neighborhood for their social relationships—the unattached individuals, for example—may suffer greatly from loneliness.

8. Needless to say, residential instability must ultimately be traced back to the fact that, as Wirth pointed out, the city and its economy attract transient—and, depending on the sources of outmigration, heterogeneous—people. However, this is a characteristic of urban-industrial society, not of the city specifically.

9. By neighborhoods or residential districts I mean areas demarcated from others by distinctive physical boundaries or by social characteristics, some of which may be perceived only by the residents. However, these areas are not necessarily socially self-sufficient or culturally distinctive.

10. For the definition of *outer city,* see Footnote 2.

11. Because neighborly relations are not quite primary, and not quite secondary, they can also become *pseudo-primary;* that is, secondary ones disguised with false affect to make them appear primary. Critics have often described suburban life in this fashion, although the actual prevalence of pseudo-primary relationships has not been studied systematically in cities or suburbs.

12. These neighborhoods cannot, however, be considered as urban folk societies. People go out of the area for many of their friendships, and their allegiance to the neighborhood is neither intense not all-encompassing. Janowitz has aptly described the relationship between resident and neighborhood as one of "limited liability." (20, Chapter 7)

13. Were I not arguing that ecological concepts cannot double as sociological ones, this way of life might best be described as small-townish.

14. They may, of course, be significant for the welfare of the total metropolitan area.

15. A 1958 study of New York theater goers showed a median income of close to $10,000 and 35 per cent were reported as living in the suburbs (10).

16. I am thinking here of adults; teen-agers do suffer from the lack of informal meeting places within walking or bicycling distance.

17. These must be defined in dynamic terms. Thus, class includes also the process of social mobility, stage in the life-cycle, and the processes of socialization and aging.

18. This formulation may answer some of Duncan and Schnore's objections to socio-psychological and cultural explanations of community ways of life (9).

19. The ecologically oriented researchers who developed the Shevsky-Bell social area analysis scale have worked on the assumption that "social differences between the populations of urban neighborhoods can conveniently be summarized into differences of economic level, family characteristics and ethnicity." (3, p. 26) However, they have equated "urbanization" with a concept of life-cycle stage by using family characteristics to define the index of urbanization (3, 18, 19). In fact, Bell has identified suburbanism with familism (2).

20. Because of the distinctiveness of the ways of life found in the inner city, some writers propose definitions that refer only to these ways, ignoring those found in the outer city. For example, popular writers sometimes identify "urban" with "urbanity," i.e., "cosmopolitanism." However, such a definition ignores the other ways of life found in the inner city. Moreover, I have tried to show that these ways have few common elements, and that the ecological features of the inner city have little or no influence in shaping them.

21. Even more than Wirth's they are based on data and impressions gathered in the large Eastern and Midwestern cities of the United States.

22. Personal discussions with European planners and sociologists suggest that many European apartment dwellers have similar preferences, although economic conditions, high building costs, and the scarcity of land make it impossible for them to achieve their desires.

Race and Poverty in Cities: A Liberal View

JEANNE LOWE

Traditionally, Americans have regarded city slums as primarily a physical problem. The federal slum clearance legislation has been written in those terms. Largely because money to get rid of urban slums was available in such programs, cities tried to eliminate their slum areas by tearing down the buildings.

During the 1950's, however, while starting to use the new government instruments of urban redevelopment and renewal, local public officials began to discover that slum elimination entailed much more than the removal of deteriorated housing and hardware—or even the substitution of low-rent dwellings. Still, most failed to acknowledge the problems that cause people to live in slums.

By the early 1960's, the changing racial-social-economic composition of central cities had magnified and vastly complicated the traditional human problems of the slums, especially in the context of a generally prospering nation. A growing portion of the city population was unable to provide for itself, and the urban community was unable or unwilling to afford that portion adequate homes and jobs in the face of changing technology and racial discrimination. Depression-born welfare and housing programs were overwhelmed; cities' fiscal resources were depleted. Northern equal-rights laws, as well as

U.S. Supreme Court decisions, became empty promises as *de facto* segregation increased in core cities that were being strangled by the suburban middle-class white noose. Meanwhile, some renewal programs, caught in the crosscurrents of minority outcries of inequity and discrimination, civil rights demonstrations, the white backlash, and some apparently irreconcilable social issues, ground to a halt or radically changed direction.

The 1960 census exposed the facts about cities' changing composition. The older core cities in the North and northern central areas had lost population during the past decade, while suburbs grew. The drop varied from a little over one per cent in New York and Baltimore to 4.5 per cent in San Francisco and 10.7 per cent in Pittsburgh. The full extent of the loss was disguised, however, by the number of "new urbanites." The twelve largest cities experienced a combined net decrease in their white population of 2,000,000, but they gained 1,800,000 non-whites. Medium-size cities, too—Rochester, Fort Wayne, San Diego—which had had few Negroes before World War II, saw their Negro populations double even as their total populations dropped. Washington D.C. became the first of America's twenty-five big cities to have a Negro majority. By the 1960's, almost as many Negroes were living in northern, borderline and western cities as in the South, and 73

From Jeanne Lowe, *Cities in a Race with Time* (New York: Random House, 1967), pp. 278-310. Copyright © 1967, by Jeanne Lowe. Reprinted by permission of Random House, Inc. Jeanne Lowe is a writer and consultant on urban affairs.

522

per cent of all Negroes in the country lived in cities, as compared to 73 per cent on the land only half a century before.

THE WELFARE CITY

While central cities' populations fell, their budgets continued to grow, and to grow at a much faster rate than the general rise in the cost of living or the national increase in state and local spending or revenues. In the biggest cities the disproportion was worst of all.

The largest increases in expenses were for public assistance, hospitals and health services and police. More than one third of the increase in New York City's budget from $3,000,000,000 to $4,500,000,000 in the five years from 1960-61 to 1965-66 was accounted for by these three items.[1] Health and hospitals expenditures were up 72 per cent, to $337,920,221—and one third of the city's population, over 2,500,000, qualified for a projected free health-care program on the basis of their "moderate low income" in 1966. The Police Department accounted for another $364,-120,276 in the 1965-66 budget, an increase of some $141,000,000 in the past five years; but it still lacked sufficient staff to deal with growing crime. The Welfare Department's requested allocation for 1966-67 was nearly two thirds of a billion dollars, $129,000,000, over that of the previous fiscal year.

These swelling costs were directly related to the changing population composition of central cities: more relatively young low-income families reproducing more rapidly than other metropolitan core residents; more elderly and disabled people; and the striking increase in non-white and other previously rural residents. But the latter group alone received welfare outlays far out of proportion to their percentage. In New York, where Negroes comprise only 14 per cent of the city, they accounted for 45 per cent of those on welfare. Puerto Ricans, forming 8 per cent of the population, represented 30 per cent of the welfare load. The same pattern was repeated in other cities in the early 1960's.

The single biggest growth item in public welfare was Aid to Dependent Children—ADC. (Of the 600,000 persons to be aided by the New York Welfare Department in 1966, well over half were children under eighteen.) Particularly striking—and headline making—was the proportion of illegitimate children receiving such public assistance. In Washington D.C., where ADC accounted for 71 per cent of the entire welfare caseload, 40 per cent of the children were born out of wedlock.

Unfortunately, such statistics on mushrooming welfare costs, when brought to public attention by the press and public officials, provoked outcries against alleged abuses, demagoguery, and pressures for residency requirements and quick cures. The city manager of Newburgh, New York became a national figure (a hero to some) in the summer of 1961 with his sweeping plan for taking "bums" and "chiselers" off relief, which accounted for 12 per cent of his city's budget. Louis J. Lefkowitz, Republican candidate for Mayor of New York City that fall, proclaimed that if elected he would remove from public welfare the "wastrels" and "chiselers." National magazines ran apparently well-researched exposés of welfare abuses. The journalistic stereotype was the shiftless mother who had child after child at the public's expense to increase her relief payments rather than go to work.

The flight to the suburbs of middle-

and upper-income taxpayers was directly attributed to their having to pay these mounting city expenses. These fleeing city dwellers did not realize that a third of welfare costs are borne by the state government and another third or more by the federal government. One can run—but not far.

GETTING DOWN TO CASES

Why the enormously disproportionate growth in welfare and aid to dependent children? The Board of Commissioners of Cook County, Illinois, which pays Chicago's welfare bills, was so alarmed by the skyrocketing of ADC costs during the 1950's—up from $1,400,000 to $4,400,000—that in 1960 it appointed a thirty-five-member committee of specialists, civic leaders, businessmen and educators to investigate. The committee, in turn, retained the New York firm of Greenleigh Associates Inc., nationally known consultants to health and welfare organizations. Their year-long study was the most extensive and thorough ever made of a local public welfare program in the United States.

It is interesting that the publication of the findings attracted so little national attention compared to the alleged welfare abuses. Perhaps the report, as its title *Facts, Fallacies and Future* suggests, challenged many of the popular and comforting notions about who is on ADC and why. Indeed, no more than 3 per cent in the sample of 1,000 interviewed fit the popular stereotype. Nor did the report offer any panaceas.

The typical ADC mother in Chicago was a native of Mississippi, a Negro, in her thirties. She had been in Chicago fifteen years and had three children under fifteen, all born in Illinois. Her husband had lost his job as an unskilled laborer and had deserted her.[2] She had had an illegitimate child since. She had waited an average of a year and four months after that before applying for ADC. Generally, she was not free to remarry, but if she was, the new husband was unable to support the child. This was her first time on ADC; she stayed on the rolls less than three years; she did not want to have more children to boost her allotment. (In fact, it only allowed twenty-one cents per meal per person.)

Most women were found to feel great guilt and resentment about having an illegitimate child, but many did not know how to prevent conception. Almost all were anxious to be self-sustaining and to return to work. However, most had no marketable skill, and many could not leave home because their children were too young to go to school.

Moreover, that illegitimacy accounted for 50 per cent of ADC was found to reflect the general growing rate of illegitimacy in Cook County. But, as the report pointed out, of the illegitimate children who were adopted—and thus who did not go on ADC—almost 98.5 per cent were white and only 1.5 per cent Negro.

In 1962 Congress amended the Social Security Act largely on the basis of some proposals in the Greenleigh Report. It provided greater federal aid for rehabilitative and preventive services for adult recipients of ADC, including financing of day-care centers for children of working mothers, more counseling and reduced workloads for caseworkers; it gave aid for an unemployed second parent to keep families together and to encourage use of parents' earnings for their children's education (books, bus fares, shoes, etc.) without cutting their relief check.

But the Social Security Act, by its nature, is supportive and could not get at the basic root of dependency found by the Greenleigh study—"the marginal level of the families" before they applied for ADC, and a history of marginal subsistence, the end product of the social and economic effects of racial discrimination.

THE GHETTO DWELLERS

No doubt the welfare programs born in the depression dramatized certain traditional predicaments of any city newcomers' situation. The period of adjustment to complex urban life is a tension-fraught, often traumatic experience for almost all migrants, white or non-white, European, Asian, Appalachian-American, Puerto Rican or Mexican. Slum living, poverty, lack of marketable skills, low-level employment and frequent unemployment, high rates of reproduction, juvenile crime, family disorganization, ghettoization (self-imposed and socially reinforced), poor housekeeping—these have generally accompanied the first stages of life in cities, especially for rural newcomers, who comprise the majority of immigrants. But in the days of the last big urban influx, our government did not assume the burden for these problems; nor had it decided that slums were opposed to the public welfare.

Furthermore, one cannot overemphasize the special situation of the newly urban American Negro—who comprises the largest group of immigrants. He brings to the city extra-heavy baggage. He has not only the "badge of color" but also the ingrained burden of generations of cultural and economic deprivation. His move to the city makes painfully and inescapably apparent the effects of dependency and weak family organization which had their origins in slavery but were perpetuated after Reconstruction by the southern plantation system. This is the system that has shaped the mass of the "new urbanites," the people who comprise 20, 30, even 60 per cent of central cities' populations and who, during the 1970's, may be expected to increase their present number by 50 to 100 per cent.

The plantation system offered the Negro no experience with money, no incentive to save, no conception of time or progress—none of the basic experiences to prepare him for the urban money economy. Instead, it indoctrinated him to believe in his own inferiority, to be resigned, while it held him in a folk culture dominated by a spiritual, other-worldly, escapist outlook—in what sociologist E. Franklin Frazier called "the twilight of civilization."

Illegitimacy and the female-dominated household are not Negro traits. (Indeed, family instability is a characteristic by-product of male unemployment and poverty.) In the Negro's case, these traits were developed as a result of white southern culture and slavery, which deprived the Negro family of a legal base, and were perpetuated by the post-Civil War plantation system which kept the Negro male subservient, uneducated and economically insecure, usually out in the field or wandering the country looking for work, away from his family. Consequently his children were deprived of male authority and stable family life. But for the Negro man, who had almost no material possessions (he was always a tenant), his offspring were virtually the only tangible proof of his manhood, and the woman who would have him must accept this. Illegitimate children and their mothers were not rejected; instead, they were accommodated by the mothers, grandmothers and aunts who composed many lower-class southern Negro households.

But the city does not offer the mass of poor Negroes much opportunity to demonstrate the difference between what is racially and what is culturally or environmentally induced. City life tends to shatter the fragile structure of the lower-class Negro's family life and to accentuate, through differential employment opportunities, female dominance and masculine subordination. It also exposes the youngster, whose mother is probably out at work and whose father is either out of work, busy at two jobs or missing, to the worst influences of the slum.

These latest newcomers find few of the strengths of group pride in ethnic origin or the institutional supports that fortified the European immigrants. Not even the simple official process of "Americanization" which in five years is supposed to turn the foreigner into a citizen is available. The Negro's movement from one part of the country to another fails to supply that "shock of separation" which, as Oscar Handlin has written, precipitated the creation of new community organizations in cities by earlier immigrant groups. The individualized welfare services of the old city political machine have been pre-empted by impersonal government agencies, and the machine's municipal jobs for the faithful unskilled have been largely eliminated by civil service requirements or trade union restrictions. The politician does not even offer the traditional outings to the country; too often the Negro's political representative wants to keep his constituency as is.

The underworld, also, has a vested interest in preserving the minority ghetto and its hopelessness. To the despondent resident the criminal world offers "the poor man's democracy"— the chance of winning money in the numbers game. It also vends narcotics, an expensive, momentary retreat from despair, a lifetime hook that causes men to steal or kill for more and makes city streets unsafe.

The criminal world once afforded the uneducated youthful deviants in the ethnic slum illegitimate avenues to material success, but these paths are largely closed today. Crime has become as highly organized, remote and specialized as the rest of American life. Its numbers parlors are, as Richard Cloward and Lloyd Ohlin expressed it in *Delinquency and Opportunity*, like the local branch stores of a supermarket chain. The criminal hierarchy does not even provide the invisible discipline that used to hold many slum youths in line. Nor does it supply the cash that helped immigrants of earlier generations become entrepreneurs.

Even settlement houses commonly find themselves located in areas of lesser need today, because the residents whom they once served have moved away; or slum clearance and new development have altered the neighborhood. Meanwhile, vast new slum areas are neglected. Even so, settlement houses, like psychiatrically oriented social workers, are ineffective in trying to mitigate the society-induced traumas that infect the occupants of our cities' spreading black ghettos.

Meanwhile, a small group of "upper-class" Negroes, the supposed leaders and models, remain removed from and contemptuous of the masses (except for the many doctors, dentists, lawyers and businessmen who live in "golden ghettos" but enter the slum ghetto to make their living). And members of the growing middle class, who have worked their way out of the slum by dint of education and new job openings, are afraid of being dragged down by association with those still on the bottom. As the Greenleigh report noted, "upper-class Negroes are embarrassed and threatened by the public out-cry against ADC and low-income families."

This attitude, in turn, increases the alienation and frustration of the slum ghetto dweller. Speaking of the rioters at Watts in Los Angeles, a top-ranking Negro official of the federal Office of Economic Opportunity told an audience composed largely of middle-class Negroes, "Whitey isn't alone in being the object of their anger." Successful Negroes, he declared, should give the poor the benefit of their experience. But a highly placed Negro municipal employee in Los Angeles complained that he could not get other Negroes at City Hall to accompany him to the Watts area in order to persuade youngsters to get off the streets. "Why should I?" one rejoined. "I struggled for years to get out of there."

Why do middle- and upper-class Negroes fail to help their own? Primarily because the American reward system has failed to operate for them. Segregation and discrimination reinforce white stereotypes and have produced a Negro middle and upper class disproportionately small compared to the total number of Negroes, and poor compared to their white counterparts. Aside from the church, they lack the means to support their institutions. The Urban League, NAACP and CORE all rely heavily on white liberals' contributions.

His white peers have little opportunity through normal contacts and common interests to know a Negro as an individual. Practically his only civic association with white community leaders is on "interracial" committees concerned with integration or Negro rights. His isolation deprives him of the business and professional contacts and experience essential to advancing within the corporate and financial structure of American life. He does not have the extended clan that helped Europeans. Lacking entree into the American economic system, often denied credit, many Negro businessmen exploit the Negro mass as ruthlessly as do the whites. Like too many Negro doctors, lawyers, publishers and politicians, they have a vested interest in perpetuating the ghetto from which they make a living.

Ghettoization has consistently discouraged the development of a responsible elite. As Wilson wrote in *Negro Politics:* "Living in isolation from the city as a whole, . . . and desiring to differentiate himself from the [mass of disadvantaged Negroes], the middle- or upper-class Negro can see few rewards in civic leadership." Denied many of the rewards of upward mobility and the opportunity to play a serious role in American life, "the black bourgeoisie," as Frazier called them, escape into a "world of make believe," preoccupied with Negro "society" and conspicuous consumption (or else they try to earn still another Ph.D.). The Negro mass, though they may envy this elite, regards them not as models but as Uncle Toms, or as people who have been somehow "lucky in getting money"—as indeed most have been.

Who, then, is responsible for the newcomer, for easing his period of adjustment and helping him to advance?

During the late 1950's a new kind of municipal agency emerged in some cities. One of the first was Chicago's Committee on New Residents, appointed by Mayor Richard Daley as part of the city's Commission on Human Relations late in 1955 when the recent migrants' problems began to manifest themselves widely. The Committee published pamphlets and distributed thousands of simple illustrated brochures to acquaint the newcomers with the strange city and its facilities—its schools, parks, health clinics, adult educational opportunities, and even such rudimentary matters as how to use a telephone and shop at a supermarket. It organized housekeeping classes to show previously rural homemakers how to use gas stoves, incinerators and other urban novelties. It alerted other public and private agencies to the newcomers' special needs and set up field offices in "port of entry" neighborhoods.

The Committee's biggest job, however, was to find employment for the newcomers who supposedly had come in response to the siren call of industry in Chicago, traditionally a strong market for unskilled labor. The problem of finding work was twice as severe for non-white as for white newcomers.

But, as a top staff member of the Committee on New Residents commented in 1961, "In Chicago ablebodied men aren't allowed to go on relief. They assume that if you're ablebodied, you can find work. Yet there aren't jobs for the unskilled, and it's getting worse.

"In the last century, immigration was accompanied by a demand for cheap, unskilled labor. Today, you can't push a wheelbarrow or build a railroad across the country. In this highly skilled society, we can't afford to wait for the next generation. We either train them or they'll be a drag on Chicago."

One of the Committee's early acts, in 1956, had been to arrange with the city's Dunbar Vocational High School for job-training classes for newcomers. This endeavor was reported in 1959 by Ely M. Aron, chairman of the Committee, in testimony before the Board of Education calling for a larger budget.

"It seemed perfectly obvious that we only had to make known to these new residents the superb facilities . . . you had provided for trade and vocational training. Everyone—we thought—would line up to enroll in these classes, study diligently, and become a skilled worker in possibly two or three years. We sent out thousands of flyers, used every means of communication, and the result —nil.

"Now we know better. It took us a year to learn. . . . Before we can expect anyone to learn 'fine hand skills,' we must help him learn to read, understand directions, warning signals and machine dials. Today, we rejoice in the increased enrollment in the elementary school classes for adults. . . .

"It is very difficult," Aron stated, "if you're the sole head of the household, if you've moved a number of children from a rural area into a vastly complex city—it is difficult to admit that you can't read."[3]

THE BIG CHANGE

We used to have an acceptable rationalization for city slums. Fortune magazine, in a 1957 article on "The Enduring Slums," stated that they "are crowded because there are jobs to be had . . . sweepers at General Motors . . . scrap throwers at Inland Steel . . . handtruck pushers around New York's garment center." Slums were thus a sign of opportunity in cities, because newcomers are attracted to places of employment.

But these jobs have been disappearing. There is less and less heavy, unskilled and dirty work to be done—both in cities and on farms. During the 1950's, agricultural and fiber production increased by 27 per cent with 27 per cent fewer workers. This trend virtually forced migration to cities, especially from the newly mechanized plantation South.

It is now known that the high rate of unemployment during the late 1950's and early 1960's was caused not only by factory automation; a sluggish economy and consumer demand were also instrumental, and behind these, conservative government fiscal policies. But the fact remains, as Dorothy K. Norman wrote in the U.S. Department of Labor's *Monthly Labor Review* in 1965: "Production requirements in industry appear to have played a hoax on the Negro, by first expanding—especially during the war years of the 1940's and early 1950's—and enticing the Negroes from the farm into industrial jobs, often far from home, and then receding, as these same jobs have become increasingly vulnerable to technological and market changes.

"Industrial employment increased in a number of cities in 1964, but the totals did not rise much above 1960 levels. And in some of the largest centers—New York and Philadelphia—the downward trend persisted, the bulletin reported.

"Limited job opportunities in major centers of Negro concentration aggravate the already difficult situation in which Negroes find themselves when looking for employment. . . ."

The low-skill service jobs which untrained newcomers have traditionally filled in cities were even harder hit, relatively, by the switch to machines. For example, a great many immigrants who had never worked at any other non-farm job became elevator operators. Yet between 1957 and 1961 in New York City alone, 30,000 elevator operators' jobs were eliminated. It was anticipated that the unemployed operators could be transferred to bowling alleys. But the invention of the automatic pinsetter had eliminated thousands of these jobs as well. New mechanical cleaning processes used in many high-rise office buildings displaced still more low-skill people.

Municipal government itself, while a major growth sector for employment in recent years, has also increased use of machinery in activities that traditionally employed unskilled labor—general maintenance, street cleaning, street and road construction and administrative procedures.

The attrition in these jobs mirrors far-reaching structural shifts that have taken place in the economy since World War II. For while some jobs were disappearing, many others were being created. Between 1955 and 1965 the blue-collar work force grew only by 763,000; white-collar employment rose by 6,-540,000.

Within industry itself the big shift has been from production to non-production jobs (and smaller relative pay increases for the typical factory worker). The steel industry offers an extreme but vivid picture of the shifts. Between 1950 and 1961, its blue-collar employees dropped from 503,000 to 403,000—though production rose with automated equipment, and white-collar employment in its offices and laboratories climbed from 89,000 to 117,000. In 1946 there was one white-collar worker to every nine employed in steel; there was one in four by 1963. "The time may come when it will take a ton of paper to make a ton of steel," a bulletin of the Federal Reserve Bank observed.

The many new jobs in government are also skilled or professional. This does not mean that there is not a great deal of unskilled work to be done in public service. The work merely requires public financing. The 1966 Report of the National Commission on Technology, Automation and Economic Progress enumerated six different categories of potential jobs which could produce 5,300,000 new jobs which need to be filled in order to bring public services up to levels of acceptable operation.

In manpower utilization and national wealth, the country has been moving from a goods-producing to a service economy. This fact, in combination with the exodus of manufacturing plants from the crowded old rail centers,[4] has profound implications for cities and their residents. Not only is there relatively less wealth in locally taxable property; fewer jobs are left in cities for the new population. To reach plants now relocated in the suburbs, but which were accessible by urban public transportation, the Negro or Spanish-speaking worker who is barred from suburban residence (by income if not race) must drive many miles between home and work. Often he cannot afford to do so. (Meanwhile, suburban residents commute to office and professional jobs in center city.)

Since World War II, all net growth in jobs has occurred in the service sector, a 1965 study by Victor Fuchs of the National Bureau of Economic Research revealed. Moreover, Fuchs' study points out, growth within this service sector has been in jobs that make greater use of workers with higher education and relatively less use of those with only limited schooling or with physical strength. The employment increase in the field of education alone between 1950 and 1960 was found to be greater than total employment in primary metal industries in both of those years. (Most dramatic postwar advance was made by professional, technical and kindred workers. This group doubled, and by 1964 numbered 8,500,000.)

Looking ahead to the 1970's, experts foresee a continuing decline in rural manpower needs. Only 10 per cent of the nation's population will be needed to feed the country and grow fiber for it. This means continued immigration from farms and plantations, though at a somewhat slower rate than in the recent past. But the number of Negroes, Puerto Ricans and other low-income, minority residents in central cities is expected to grow and be half again as large due to the young age and high birth rate of those already there.

The number of factory jobs nationally will increase—though probably not in the old manufacturing cities, and many traditional blue-collar production jobs will be upgraded in job requirements to a white-collar or skilled level. The manufacturers remaining in cities will have less need for additional, particularly for unskilled, workers. The big proportionate increase in skilled, white-collar and professional service jobs will continue in cities (as nationally), and cities may well benefit from this trend.

The U.S. Department of Labor warned in a publication on *Manpower Needs of the 1960's* (published in 1959) that "To fill these new requirements the youth who are entering the labor market will have to have much higher skills and education." The Department's 1965 publication on *Manpower Needs in 1975* reiterated the point. It stated that "The occupational groups requiring the least educational attainment are, in general, those which are expected to show the smallest employment growth and thus provide the fewest jobs for the growing labor force. . . . The demand of employers for better trained personnel appears to be insatiable."

EDUCATION—FOR WHAT?

Yet we have been breeding a new generation that is undereducated, unemployed or unemployable—the "dropouts" who by 1965 comprised almost one third of the nation's high-school-age students. They leave school usually by tenth grade, wander the streets, form gangs and get into trouble. When this postwar generation reaches adulthood in the early 70's, when 26,000,000 young people are expected to enter the labor market, about 7,500,000 teenagers will not have completed high school. About 2,500,000 million will have failed to reach eighth grade. According to the National Urban League, "A relatively high proportion of them will be non-white." This is particularly disturbing when it is realized that 20 percent of all the new entrants into the labor force in the late 1960's will be Negro;[5] and if present trends continue, half of them will not have had a high school education.

The prospects for these undereducated boys and girls are not bright. The recent past shows that they have three times as high an unemployment rate as graduates. They earn $27 a week less, and the disparity increases as they grow older. Their decision to quit school before graduation means a lifetime of menial jobs with meager salaries or un-

employment. Indeed, many young people who dropped out of school to go to work soon found themselves out of a job and on relief. Some have recently joined the Job Corps and other new manpower training programs. Other dropouts have been adding to the urban crime wave which, during the 1960's, has seen a rise in city juvenile delinquency double the national average.

According to recent sociological studies, juvenile deviance and crime, in disproportionate amounts among the lower classes, are caused by the society that encourages certain aspirations yet withholds the possibilities of achieving these aspirations legitimately. As Cloward and Ohlin wrote in *Delinquency and Opportunity*, the cause is a discrepancy "between what lower class youth are led to want and what is actually available to them." For many young Negro males another principal cause is the early and often permanent absence of a father, as former Assistant Secretary of Labor Daniel P. Moynihan made clear in his paper on *The Negro Family*.

This combination of circumstances in ghetto areas is held to be a major cause of the recent summertime riots in Harlem, Rochester, Philadelphia, Los Angeles' Watts and other cities—circumstances to which the new government-aided anti-poverty and job training programs evidently added an extra bitter twist. The inadequately filled promise of new job opportunities and training served to exacerbate unrest in ghettos. "The Negro has gotten a much deeper sense of frustration, much deeper feelings of despair, as the gap increases between what he's actually got and what his expectations have grown to be," Dr. Philip Hauser, head of the University of Chicago's Department of Sociology, observed about the riots.

The McCone Commission, appointed by Governor Edmund Brown of California to investigate the circumstances contributing to the Watts riot, singled out inadequate schooling designed to help overcome the serious handicaps of the disadvantaged Negro child; insufficient jobs for the untrained Negro, and resentment of the police.

In a previous generation, the Italian immigrants' failure to get an education blocked their way, as they discovered too late, to economic opportunities and also led to a disproportionate rate of crime among their youth and later, among adults. For the Negro mass, moving from the twilight of civilization to cities, horizons have suddenly appeared to broaden. In cities they have achieved higher incomes and better housing conditions than in the rural South. But the newly broadened vistas of many in cities are unrealistic, considering the great obstacles.

Why should a Negro youth remain in school? Speaking primarily of the South two decades ago, the Swedish economist Gunnar Myrdal wrote in *An American Dilemma:* "Since Negroes are seldom in demand for jobs for which education is necessary, there is certainly nothing surprising in the conclusion that they, unlike whites, fail to improve their opportunities by staying in school longer." The scene has shifted more and more to northern and western city streets and their slums today.

The Negro may read in the papers about those who are succeeding. But the fact that success is news speaks for itself. What is new in today's city slum, Dr. James Conant observed in the early 1960's, is "the almost complete lack of . . . conviction" that they can ever work their way out of poverty on the part of Negro youth. "The unemployed floaters on the street are walking evidence to all youth that nothing can be accomplished by education." Conant placed a good part of the blame for the dropout problem on the discriminatory hiring practices of private companies.

Limited comfort might be derived by blaming the situation on the illiteracy and the consequent relative unemployability of the southern Negro migrant. Those who came to cities in the 1940's did have little schooling. During 1949-50 the highest migration to Chicago, for example, was of adults who had four years of education, and they subsequently bore the brunt of automation. But between 1955 and 1960, the great majority among the most mobile nonwhite migrants—men of twenty-five to twenty-nine years—had at least some high school training, and one fifth had a year or more of college.

Yet the percentage of unemployed Negroes during the recession of the early 1960's was two to three times as high as that of whites at *all* levels— unskilled, semiskilled and skilled. And even as the country neared "full employment" at the end of 1965, the Negro unemployment rate was still twice as high as whites, and it was even higher in the slums.[6] For Negro youth in 1966 it was 27 per cent, compared to 12 per cent for white youth. The President's Commission on Technology, Automation and Economic Progress warned in its 1966 report that "If non-whites continue to hold the same proportion of jobs in each occupation as in 1964, the non-white unemployment rate in 1975 will be more than five times that for the labor force as a whole."

The Negro has made the least advance in the growing sector of the economy—and not always for lack of education. In 1965, the Bureau of the

Census reported that "at all educational levels the Negro is less likely to be a white collar worker." According to a survey by the Census Bureau, among Negro men who had received some college training the proportion employed in lower-paid jobs was 41 per cent or twice the proportion of whites, while for male college graduates the proportion of Negroes in the lower-paid jobs was triple that of whites.

This survey stated, "Although advances have been made since 1950—the rate of progress has slowed and there remain large gaps between Negro and white achievement [even when years of schooling among Negroes are greater]. The political, economic and social issues affecting the Negro appear to arise not from lack of aspiration, but from high aspirations pressing against limited, and, in some places, declining opportunity. . . ." And fair employment laws don't help much.[7]

This highly demanding, specialized age affords the newcomer fewer of the jobs which he has traditionally filled and permits him a shorter period to become a self-sustaining member of the city economy. It also robs him of the realistic hope which served as an economic yeast for earlier generations.

The contrast is dramatized by the tale of a reunion, held in March 1962, of fifty men who had graduated half a century before from Brooklyn's now defunct Public School 43 in the "gray area" of Williamsburgh. "The gathering was a very satisfying experience," commented Nathan Smith, now a hardware merchant in Woodbridge, New Jersey, who initiated the reunion out of curiosity to learn how his classmates had turned out. "Not one of us failed to achieve at least modest success," he told a newspaper reporter who covered the

gathering. "We were mostly immigrants or children of immigrants. The only thing we had was hope and faith in the ideal of American opportunity."

The nature of that opportunity has changed. The era of the self-made, uneducated small businessman who could rise out of the slums is vanishing. He is no longer the backbone of the middle class; he is becoming part of the lower-middle class or the poor. More and more the American businessman has become an organization man; the former owner is now a manager; the clerk has been replaced by self-service. Although the current demand for new services is once again opening opportunities for small business concerns, the man who would be self-sustaining and advance on his own or in an organization must be educated.

THE PUT-OUTS

This suggests the third factor that limits the advance of the newcomers or the "culturally disadvantaged": educability. Much of this problem involves group values and cultural differences.

The lower class, whether white or non-white, differs from the middle class in its emphasis on immediate gratification and security, rather than on striving for individual status and achievement which necessitate thrift and postponement. There is practically no interest in academic education. Rather, learning is valued for immediate utility—filling out forms, applying for known civil service jobs, and so forth. Action is emphasized among the lower class; talk and reading are commonly regarded as unmasculine and are therefore eschewed.

Why should one break with one's group, become tomorrow-oriented and study hard in the expectation that doing well in school will lead to a better future? In today's slum areas, where the majority of dropouts live, many youths either see no reason to make the break or do not know how to make it.

From their earliest years, their deprived, circumscribed environment militates against the education necessary to succeed today. The family and immediate community often fail to provide the early life experiences, the sights, sounds, vocabularly and information which are necessary preschool preparations for learning; these the middle-class child receives almost automatically. Home life is crippled. The uneducated or undereducated parent speaks to the child in monosyllables and points at objects, and may even deride efforts to learn due to his own poor experience in school, or rude treatment by the child's teachers. The harassed mother shouts "Get out of my way" to too many children. There are no books, not even nursery rhymes, in the crowded noisy room or two called home. Study, even sleeping, is often impossible. The boy in the broken home (over one quarter of the Negro children live in families headed by women) is deprived of the essential male model.

Many lower-class parents are aware of the importance of education in this society. But many lack the money and time or the necessary knowledge to help their children. They may be reluctant to meet teachers because they speak poorly or dress badly; they lack the time and organizational sophistication to join PTA activities. Further, since equal opportunities and rewards are not generally available to educated Negroes, there is a tendency to protect children against rebuffs and disappointments. This is partly a defense; often it becomes a built-in lag.

Among the strongest detrimental influences on the Negro child is his negative self-image; he senses that society views him as inferior and expects inferior performance of him. This is attested by the limitations on his father and by the family's living environment, and in effect has been reinforced by the emphasis of many old-line organization Negroes on racial integration as the key to success.

This child is behind before he starts school. One out of every three children in the school systems of our fourteen biggest cities come from such "culturally deprived" backgrounds. In the 1970's, with the lower-class population explosion, there is expected to be one such child out of every two in big cities, and one out of four in many middle-size cities.

The school world has little relevance to the child's life. Its primers are illustrated with rosy-cheeked white children playing on grassy suburban lawns; his composition assignment is to describe "A Trip I Took." He may have left home without breakfast and be too hungry to concentrate. When he is confronted with a difficult problem, he abandons it quickly with a "who cares?" attitude. Teachers, unprepared for and demoralized by these students and their attitudes, spend so much time on discipline that they have little left for actual lessons.

"One of the reasons we have such a terrific discipline problem," an experienced Negro teacher in a New York "gray area" public school pointed out, "is that the children just don't care. School is a place where they are sent. Even children who are eleven and twelve years old have no ideas of their own as to what they want to get out of school." As a result, they get only one half to one third the exposure to learning that a student usually gets. The high residential mobility of many poor families compounds the inadequacies of the child's education. When he reaches high school, the situation is completely out of hand, the street takes over, and the gang.

The burden of blame for pupils' lower achievement also rests on the attitudes of teachers—on what Dr. Kenneth Clark, in *Dark Ghetto*, called their "cultural bias." A social worker who spent many years in East Harlem, a vast depressed community of 180,000 in upper Manhattan, observed: 'Teachers come in here with stereotypes. They feel the kids can't learn. So they don't learn."

But looking behind the statistics and the signs of "cultural deprivation," one discovers that the majority of the dropouts have average intelligence, and that 20 to 25 per cent even rank as culturally superior. Recent studies indicate that the "disadvantaged" child learns differently, more slowly, and responds to different stimuli; he apparently requires different teaching techniques or programs than those generally available. His disadvantage is not so much in natural gifts as in middle-class know-how—a lack which shows up in testing and teaching that is oriented to the middle-class culture.

Before many students drop out, they have dropped backward. Their progressive retardation may go back to third-grade level. And the boys do worse than the girls, who are more apt to have a suitable adult model in their mother, and more job opportunities at the white-collar level. Pupils who do not keep up with their grades are promoted nonetheless. By high school, the youngsters are so far behind in basic skills that many teachers find them uneducable.

"The teachers call them 'drop-outs,'" a field worker for Chicago's Committee on New Residents commented. "We call them 'put-outs.'"

As for the youngsters who move ahead at grade level, guidance counselors steer them away from jobs from which Negroes have been traditionally barred. When they cannot read well, they are shunted to vocational high schools to be trained for trades that have limited openings or are disappearing. Employers who decide to hire Negroes at higher levels or in kinds of work previously barred are not able to find enough who are qualified. College scholarships for qualified Negro students at many top institutions go begging. Attending college appears so impossible to many children from deprived communities that even preparing for it seems a fantasy. Because they live in such a separate community, Negro youths are unlikely to hear about the opportunities.

THE CITY SCHOOLS' PUBLIC

The changing nature of the urban population is dramatized by the two different school systems that exist in our metropolitan areas. These differ in budget and product as the two populations' pocketbooks and political power differ. The short-changing of cities by state legislatures compounds the fiscal disparity.

During the 1950's suburban parents put themselves and their communities into debt to build schools, raise salaries, expand curricula and improve teaching methods, to give their bumper crop of children the best education so they could get into college. Central cities also had an unexpectedly large number of pupils, but they were educating a generation of dropouts.

Dr. James Conant found that in the wealthy suburbs annual expenditures were often over $1,000 per pupil, compared to an average under $500 in slum schools; teacher pay was commensurate. (Between 1952 and 1962, nearly half the licensed teachers in New York City left the system.)

The financial issue was well put by Max Rubin, who served as chairman of the New York City Board of Education from 1961 to 1963. "Everybody wants good schools, but how far will the people go to pay for the schools?" he asked. "Politicians prefer to run on a low tax platform rather than on better schools and higher taxes. Without the priority on the part of the public, what can you expect of the school board and teachers? Until good schools become good politics, we will be struggling."

Negro organization leaders and many middle-class Negro parents have spent their energies and political leverage on integration. They have demanded that Negro children be bused into white-neighborhood schools (and the reverse), and have urged school pairing, rezoning and other expedients. They even oppose building new schools in ghettos. The Negro leaders have been reluctant to admit that the disadvantaged child (in big cities, many non-white and Spanish-speaking children test several grades below their white contemporaries) requires much more than school integration to improve his learning ability. They did not fight for the expensive special programs these children need, and they tended to ignore the uncomfortable fact that in integrated schools disadvantaged children have to attend separate classes because of their academic deficiencies.

Some significant experiments are under way on a metropolitan basis—in the Hartford, Connecticut, Boston and Los Angeles areas—to achieve greater racial balance by transferring some inner-city Negro pupils to white suburban schools. In Los Angeles the program is reported to be drawing mainly middle-class Negro children, and teachers say that poor children from Watts are upset by their exposure to Bel Air's wealth.

Perhaps the benefit of such pupil transfers is greater for the insulated suburban white children than for their Negro classmates. Associate Professor Preston Wilcox of the Columbia University School of Social Work, himself a Negro, has stated that emphasis on integration is probably harmful to the Negro child. "Psychologically, it's bad to tell a kid that he'll only make it if he sits next to a white," Wilcox comments.

In the big cities with huge and growing core ghettos, the integrationists are rapidly becoming crusaders without a feasible cause. In Philadelphia, Detroit, Chicago and New York, to cite just several big-city school systems, white pupils now form the minority, and the percentage of the white student population has been dropping a few points each year. In Washington D.C., public school enrollment in 1965 was 90 per cent Negro, compared to 85 per cent just the year before. Los Angeles was the only one of twenty-one big cities in which white enrollment did not drop that year. The trend is unlikely to level off or reverse itself, at least in the next decade.

Educational disadvantages are worsened by the unanticipated high densities in new ghetto-slum areas. Physical capacities have been overwhelmed. One old high school in East Brooklyn, built for 1,600 pupils, last year had an enrollment of 3,400, 85 per cent of them Negro and Puerto Rican. The school's wir-

ing is so antiquated that it is not possible to use modern teaching devices to
help the many students with reading
problems. The need for three sessions
means that some students start school
by seven, eat lunch at 9:30 and are free
by noon to roam the streets. Not surprisingly, the dropout rate is 40 per
cent.

Middle-class Negro parents have become so dissatisfied with the quality of
education in cities' public schools that a
number who can afford it have also removed their children. (Unlike white
families, many cannot withdraw to the
suburbs.) In the District of Columbia in
1965, over 6 per cent of the Negro students were attending private or parochial schools, often at great financial
sacrifice, and a surprising number were
the sons and daughters of public schoolteachers.

Much of the insistence by Negroes on
integration is doubtless based on a desire for quality education. (Commenting on parent attitudes, the director of
an East Harlem settlement house observed, "In most neighborhoods, the
teachers are cowed by the PTA. Here,
the parents are cowed by the teacher.")

But a dramatic reversal seems to be
coming about. In the summer of 1966,
Livingston L. Wingate, director of
Haryou-Act, the Harlem anti-poverty
agency calling for the establishment of
quality education in Negro ghettos, declared that "We must no longer pursue
the myth that integrated education is
equated with quality education." A poll
of several ghetto areas in big cities
showed that the great majority of parents are concerned with better education; only 2 per cent specifically with
school integration.

A growing self-assurance and political
awareness was evident among the par-

ents of children who were to enter a
new $5,000,000 air-conditioned East
Harlem elementary school in the fall
of 1966. At first they insisted that the
school not be opened unless it were integrated or they were given control.
Slowly they shifted to a demand for control, with appointment of a Negro or
Puerto Rican principal, and more Negro teachers.

But the problems of inadequate
funds, insufficient teachers, old overcrowded schools and outmoded curriculum still remain, and in most ghetto
areas the educational situation has been
steadily deteriorating.

THE BUSINESSMEN AND
THE EDUCATORS

Where have the big businessmen, the
"civic leaders" of cities, been in the
midst of the mounting school crisis?
Strangely silent. The big worry of the
businessman (as opposed to the father)
is that spending more on schools will
increase local taxes and scare away industry. His children do not use the public schools in central cities; few even
live in the cities. Only rarely have top
city leaders fought for central city
school improvement in recent years or
pressed state legislatures to revise school
aid formulas and local school district
taxing powers.[8]

Local business, industrial and financial leaders—the men who have been
working for downtown revitalization,
industrial redevelopment, freeway construction, metropolitan mass transit and
a "quality" urban environment in order
to stop the flight of industry, the white
middle class and the tax base—show a
strange lack of concern about the school
crisis. If the present situation is allowed
to continue, it seems obvious that their
city will be less able to attract desirable

business concerns, and the businessmen will be less able to get qualified workers for their own companies and attract white families to their redevelopments.

For at least six years, the U.S. Department of Labor has been putting up warnings. Perhaps the businessman does not perceive the implications of the inner-city school problems for his city's economic future, nor recognize that the undereducated central-city youths are likely to cause the urban manpower crisis of the 1970's. Perhaps it is hard for them to see the economic payoff in education; few even recognize the economic toll of discrimination practices.[9]

Yet the economists have been making a strong case for the return from investment in education, especially in post-industrial society. In 1960, University of Chicago economist Theodore W. Schultz, in his presidential address to the American Economic Association (and in a subsequent book on *The Economic Value of Education*), declared that "No small part of the low earnings of many Negroes, poor farm people and some older workers reflects the failure to have invested in their health and education. . . . We can ill afford to continue making the same mistake."

Schultz also observed that "If we were to treat education as pure investment, this result would suggest that the returns to education were relatively more attractive than those in non-human capital." Research has shown, he reported, that the impressive rise in real earnings per worker achieved in the past generation—the "unexplained increases" in the national income, came about "not as much through investment in capital goods, as generally assumed, but through greatly increased public and personal investment in human capital."

In 1965 the Committee for Economic Development, a national nonprofit organization of enlightened and industrial leaders, in effect endorsed his philosophy with a policy statement on *Raising Low Incomes Through Improved Education;* they urged that all possible resources, public and private, be brought to bear on adapting the educational system to the economic system, and vice versa. A CED member, William Benton, publisher of the Encyclopaedia Britannica, observed that "although education is our largest business, our factual information about the educational system, and about how best to achieve its goals, is astonishingly inadequate for the purposes of sensible planning and decision-making."

The Ford Foundation's Great Cities School Improvement Program, which in the early 1960's stimulated school systems in fourteen big cities to develop new methods and programs for teaching inner-city children, blamed the educators for public indifference. In 1963, a spokesman charged that the educators have failed to communicate the problems, and have been unwilling to evaluate the effectiveness of present methods.

"How can you expect the businessman to respond?" he asked. "He hears the Superintendent of Schools say everything is fine, and one morning he opens the paper and reads that half the students are illiterate.[10] He wonders what the schools have been doing with all the money they have.

"Educators have secured for themselves a unique isolation in American society. The majority of school systems have their own tax structure, are independent of City Hall and call themselves the answer to society's problems. The public goes along because Americans have an ingrained belief that education is the answer to everything. They tell the public what it should want and shortchange the process of planning with the people. But because the school systems refuse to evaluate themselves, they have not documented the case for what education can do, especially in central cities, and thus it becomes increasingly difficult to sell themselves. Further, their huge unwieldy administrative structure favors the status quo and penalizes the person who tries to innovate."

WHAT KIND OF EDUCATION IS THE ANSWER?

Not all educators remained oblivious to the special problems of educating inner-city children. Many were eagerly searching for new methods "to compensate for the deficiencies which hinder the disadvantaged child from taking full advantage of the conventional education program," as a 1963 bulletin of the National Education Association summarized the new movement.

New York City led the way in 1959 with its Demonstration Guidance Program, which was widely publicized as Higher Horizons. This approach offered culturally deprived children an enriched curriculum, including special counseling, more teacher attention and outings to sites of interest and cultural facilities in the larger community. Children in the pilot program responded well, and the program appealed to the general public. The new compensatory education approach was soon followed in other cities, while the program was expanded in New York schools.

There were stirrings and changes in many big-city schools, stimulated to a large extent by the millions in matching grants from the Ford Foundation. Extra personnel were added: guidance coun-selors, remedial reading teachers, assistant principals, "helping" teachers, community agents from school neighborhoods to provide a liaison with the community. Remedial programs in language skills were undertaken and class sizes were reduced; new teaching techniques were used; preschool classes prepared three- and four-year olds for learning; "alienated" parents were actively involved in school activities.

But federal money was required for a national program, and the civil rights ferment, ghetto riots and mounting concern for the urban poor pressured Congress into passing the unprecedented Elementary and Secondary Education Act of 1965. Under its Title I, over $1,-000,000,000 was made available in the first year alone for special programs for educationally deprived children in poverty areas. The recent compensatory education programs were predominant among those eligible for Title I.

This development seemed to be the most encouraging yet. Crisis had overcome local fear of federal control of education. In 1966 many cities began Higher Horizon-type programs, team teaching methods, remedial reading programs, talent development, and "preparation for work" programs. Some were also aided by the Office of Economic Opportunity. The most popular new program was for preschool children, Project Head Start, characterized as "the infant prodigy of the Great Society." President Johnson himself hailed it as "battle-tested."

In concluding this study of American cities facing their problems, it seemed necessary to document the achievements on the great new urban education frontier, and also to find out how much more federal and local money would be required to do a saturation job.

The results were disconcerting, but instructive. As of the summer of 1966, the returns from the new urban education programs generally show that "more of the same" does not have significant effect; that the "noticeable" improvements in pupils do not last under present circumstances; and that there are almost no measurable achievements to speak of.

What seemed particularly unsettling was that the U.S. Office of Education was loathe to admit to Congress or the public the ineffectiveness of most of its billion-dollar Title I program. (I later learned that the office *was* beginning to warn the educators.) HEW Secretary John W. Gardner told Congress in April that "Great educational strides can be made by specialized educational programs," and Commissioner of Education Harold Howe testified, "Our prior experience in several cities demonstrates that such special attention in and of itself will result in improved educational performance." Yet the Office of Education could not provide me with data from local schools that showed quantifiable results. It turned out that the legislative testimony was based on publications, several years old, of early efforts in the Ford Foundation Great Cities and New York's Higher Horizons.

These publications were, indeed, optimistic about the initial results. But the Ford Foundation could direct me to none of the Great Cities schools that had found significant differences between children in compensatory and conventional education programs when tested for specific achievements.[11] (Actually, these programs lacked a research component; the main concern was to get into the schools and stimulate federal action.)

Dr. Mario Fantini, formerly director of the Great Cities program in Syracuse, New York, and now a Program Associate in the Foundation's Education Program, flatly asserted that "More of the same won't have the pay-off we expect, and I doubt we'll ever have the kind of money to do the job that way. The problem with our original approach is that the schools have assumed the kids need compensation for deficiencies and that there is nothing wrong with their program. But the schools themselves are outmoded, and we have to change the process of education. There are the beginnings of a shift in this direction. But we had to start somewhere."

Pittsburgh, another of the Great Cities, has been pushing compensatory education and team teaching in slum neighborhood schools for five years and could not show measurable improvements in children's reading scores. Officials say that high pupil turnover in slum schools has made it difficult to assess the program, and the system lacks staff for more sophisticated measurements. But teachers were confident that the improved climate would eventually be reflected in achievement scores.

Coming hard on the heels of these unsettling findings, early in July a *New York Times* article reported that the city's Board of Education had quietly closed down Higher Horizons without even a press release. An independent professional evaluation of the program's first four years (grudgingly released by the Board of Education) had found virtually no measurable effect on the achievements, IQ or reading level of enrolled pupils. It was explained that budgetary limitations had made impossible the "saturation" with additional services originally envisioned. (If the original $250 per pupil had been spent on each of the 100,000 pupils involved, $250,-000,000 would have been required annually; this is almost one quarter of Congress' first-year appropriation for Title I of the Education Act.) *The New York Times'* Education Editor, Fred Hechinger, called the results shown by some pupils "the triumphs of the lucky few."

But what of Head Start, the popular and battle-tested program? In most cities it had been offered only on a summertime basis, and one could not expect a great permanent effect. But New Haven, Connecticut, has had the pre-kindergarten program as part of the regular school year for the past six years, and could provide no data of measurable change. "Through kindergarten, there is enormous noticeable improvement, but by second grade it's all gone," a school official stated. "The children come up against the same large classes, no extra aides, the old program and teachers."

This situation supported the findings of Dr. Martin Deutsch, a psychologist and director of the Institute for Developmental Studies at New York University, who pioneered the pre-kindergarten program; he claimed that a constant follow-up in later grades is necessary if early gains are not to be lost. It also seemed to support warnings to Congress by Education Commissioner Howe that "initial gains evaporate if special education programs are not maintained," and, "Only a comprehensive long-term program . . . can overcome [disadvantaged children's] deficiencies."

THE FLAWS IN THE SYSTEM

We should not belittle the great side-benefits of the new concern and funds —the greater involvement of parents and other potential leaders in inner-city neighborhoods, the expanded role of schools in local community life, health benefits for the children. (In the first summer of Head Start, 70 per cent of the children had their first medical and dental examination. In Tampa, Florida, twelve cases of tuberculosis and fifty of nutritional deficiencies were found.) Many schools are also getting adequate libraries for the first time.

Moreover, the limited effect of the initial attempts may well point the way to more effective action, and even compensatory education is better than what was happening before.

The lack of research-proven premises behind this billion-dollar educational program probably reflects the government's desperate need to do "something" about ghetto children as much as educators' unwillingness to evaluate themselves. HEW Secretary Gardner makes known his concern about the lack of educational research. (One city has had three research directors and no research results to show for it. One director, who recently resigned, gave an oral report to the Board of Education, but wished to keep the findings unwritten until used for his own professional publication purposes.)

Title III of the Educational Act is promising. This relatively unpublicized provision finances local "centers for change" to stimulate schools to a more innovative approach that relates research to practice. Known as PACE—Projects to Advance Creativity in Education—Title III also encourages higher-education institutions and local cultural organizations to provide local schools with leadership, new kinds of talents and services. Another little-known program is Title IV, which encourages educational institutions and agencies on different levels to band together on a regional basis to establish "multi-institutional laboratories" for researching and developing new ideas. One recent example of university-school affiliation is New York University's "adoption" of a school in the Bedford-Stuyvesant area, assisted by Ford Foundation funds.

It is important to take note here of the three fundamental flaws in compensatory education, the "more of same" approach. These are mostly failures of society at large, not just of the educators. Indeed, much at fault is the basic American fallacy that education is a panacea. As in public housing, we have not considered all the determining variables.

The first problem is that the schools cannot remedy the deficits of home, family and slum environment. "Remember, the children only spend nine per cent of their time in school," one educator points out. A recent study by the U.S. Office of Education found that differences in the quality of a school had very little effect on the achievement scores of children who have a strong foundation for education at home. Children from disadvantaged homes benefit relatively more from a good school, but it does not fill the gap.

Secondly, much of the present school curriculum is irrelevant for inner-city children. As Dr. Conant observed in *Slums and Suburbs,* "What can words like 'freedom,' 'liberty' and 'equality of opportunity' mean to these young people? With what kind of zeal and dedication can we expect them to withstand . . . communism?" Psychologist Dr. Kenneth Clark has repeatedly pointed out that compensatory education will not work unless the content has more meaning for children from deprived homes. A hopeful step is the publication by major publishing houses of new textbooks and readers that show Negroes, Puerto Ricans and whites as a normal part of the American scene and also include the history of the Negro in America. On the question of whether what is taught in schools is relevant, one inner-city curriculum director observes, "We're finding out how bad what we've been doing is for *both* the white and Negro child. I'd dump 90 per cent of what we teach."

Dr. Fantini asserts that "Middle class children make the schools look good. They give back what's expected of them. But what's so good about middle class know-how? We're all disadvantaged educationally. One need only examine the drop-out rate in college, the performance of most citizens in the wider social arena, the apathy towards social injustice and our inability to exercise leadership to highlight the obsolescence of current education. The deeper issue is whether the educational system is equipping people to deal with the problems of society."

Finally, there is the basic problem of motivation and discrimination. How can we persuade disadvantaged students and their parents that it is worthwhile for the youngster to remain in school and study, to defer premature employment and make the necessary personal investment of time and effort on the premise that such efforts will be rewarded? (Well over half the estimated cost of higher education in the United States comes from income deferred by students.)

As Dr. Conant concluded in *Slums and Suburbs,* "To improve the work of the slum schools requires an improvement in the lives of the families who inhabit the slums, but without a drastic change in the employment opportunities for urban Negro youth relatively little can be accomplished."

Our cities, the centers of the nation's economy, are also the end of the racial line in America. In cities we must proceed simultaneously and at full speed on two parallel fronts: improving environments *and* opportunities. There is no turning back.

NOTES

1. Making it larger than that of the State of New York.
2. As the report pointed out, ADC laws place "a premium on the absence of the father" by not giving assistance to families with employable fathers.
3. The Cook County Welfare Department established required literacy classes for such able-bodied, unemployed men.
4. Between 1960 and 1966 alone, New York City lost 80,000 manufacturing jobs; it is expected that it will lose 48,000 more by 1970, according to a study by the City Planning Commission.
5. The percentage in cities will be much higher.
6. A special Labor Department census in March 1966 of the poorest districts in the one hundred largest cities showed the overall Negro unemployment rate to be 9.4 per cent—compared to 3.8 per cent nationally. For Negro boys it was 31 per cent. Many in the prime-working-age group were not even looking for work, and thus not technically unemployed. In some "new" ghetto areas, the West Side of Chicago and Brooklyn's Bedford-Stuyvesant, unemployment ran an estimated 25 per cent in the summer of 1966, and statistics showed a sudden national increase in Negro joblessness.

7. In employment, as in housing, the effectiveness of anti-discrimination laws, including the Civil Rights Act of 1964, is hampered by inadequate enforcement powers, small budgets and weak administration, a Twentieth-Century Fund report has found. Another study reveals that extraordinary efforts, including aggressive recruiting campaigns by employers, are necessary to overcome Negroes' emotional blocks and inertia. Psychological tests have also been found to keep Negroes out of jobs.
8. One of the exceptions was Pennsylvania, led by Pittsburgh and Philadelphia and supported by Governor William Scranton. Recently, some southern states have come to spend a much higher percentage of their budgets on public education than have northern states—as part of the South's drive to attract industry from old northern cities.
9. The President's Council of Economic Advisers found that if discrimination in employment were eliminated and the Negro potential fully realized, at least $13,000,000,000 more in purchasing power would be placed in the hands of the bottom income groups, and current annual growth would double.
10. In October 1965, the New York City Board of Education released results of standardized achievement tests given to 626,148 pupils in second through tenth grade during 1964-65. These disclosed that more than half the city's pupils were behind their counterparts throughout the country in reading and arithmetic in second through eighth grade, and that sizable numbers were two, three and four years behind in reading.
11. An apparent exception has been the Banneker Schools in St. Louis, the one large-scale experiment where children are reported to be performing at grade level; but this was not one of the Ford programs and the Foundation had no evaluation of it. A part of the Banneker Schools' unusual success is believed to be the forceful personality of the principal and his use of every strategy to involve parents and students in the learning process.

Race and Class in Cities: A Conservative View

EDWARD C. BANFIELD

. . . the dominant aim of our society seems to be to middle-class-ify all of its members.

John Dollard, 1937

Much of what has happened—as well as of what is happening—in the typical city or metropolitan area can be understood in terms of three imperatives. The first is demographic: if the population of a city increases, the city must expand in one direction or another—up, down, or from the center outward. The second is technological: if it is feasible to transport large numbers of people outward (by train, bus, and automobile) but not upward or downward (by elevator), the city must expand outward. The third is economic: if the distribution of wealth and income is such that some can afford new housing and the time and money to commute considerable distances to work while others cannot, the expanding periphery of the city must be occupied by the first group (the "well-off") while the older, inner parts of the city, where most of the jobs are, must be occupied by the second group (the "not well-off").

The word "imperatives" is used to emphasize the inexorable, constraining character of the three factors that together comprise the logic of metropolitan growth. Indeed, the principal purpose of this chapter is to show that, given a rate of population growth, a transportation technology, and a dis-tribution of income, certain consequences must inevitably follow; that the city and its hinterland must develop according to a predictable pattern and that even an all-wise and all-powerful government could not change this pattern except by first changing the logic that gives rise to it. The argument is not that nothing can be done to improve matters. Rather, it is that only those things can be done which lie within the boundaries—rather narrow ones, to be sure—fixed by the logic of the growth process. Nor is it argued that the only factors influencing metropolitan development are those that relate to population, technology, and income. Countless others also influence it. . . .

The logic of growth does not explain all that needs explaining. For one thing, it does not explain why the city expanded outward as fast as it did. When they moved, the well-off were strongly impelled by economic forces to move outward—first to the outlying neighborhoods of the central city, then to inlying suburbs, and later to outlying ones. But the well-off did not have to move as soon as they did or in such numbers. If the trolley car and then the automobile were causes of their moving, they were also effects of their desire to move. (Philadelphia was the "city of homes" long before rapid transit was invented, Adna F. Weber

From *The Unheavenly City: The Nature and the Future of Our Urban Crisis* (Boston: Little, Brown, 1970), pp. 23-24; 45-66. Reprinted by the permission of the publisher. Edward C. Banfield is Henry Lee Shattuck Professor of Urban Government at Harvard University.

pointed out apropos of this in 1899.[1])
Also, the logic of growth does not explain why a considerable proportion of
the well-off failed to move at all. In
1960, for example, about 22 percent of
families in the central cities had incomes large enough to buy a new
house.[2] In fact, the median family income in the central cities was only 16
percent less than in the suburbs. Obviously, some families evaluate the advantages of central city versus suburban living differently than do others.
Furthermore, the logic of growth does
not explain the existence of slums. A
slum is not simply a district of low-
quality housing; rather, it is one in
which the style of life is squalid and
vicious.[3] The logic of growth *does* require that, in general, the lowest-in-
come people live in the oldest, highest-
density, most run-down housing, which
will be nearest to the factories, warehouses, stores, and offices of the inner, or downtown, part of the central
city; however, nothing in the logic of
growth says that such districts must be
squalid and vicious.

To account for these features of metropolitan development in the United
States, a second explanatory principle
must, so to speak, be placed over the
first one. This is the concept of class
culture. The purpose of this chapter
is to show how certain styles of life
that are learned in childhood and
passed on as a kind of collective heritage operate (within limits set by the
logic of growth) to give the city its
characteristic form and most of its
problems. It is one of the main conten-
tions of this book that the class cultures of the city, no less than its logic
of growth, set limits on what the
policymaker can accomplish.

American sociologists usually define
social class in terms of "prestige" or
"standing": an individual belongs to
one or another class (the number of
classes and the names they are given
differ from one writer to another) depending upon whether he is "looked up
to" or "looked down on" by the consensus of the community.[4] Frequently,
an index of easily measured attributes
—for example, income, education, occupation, and housing type—is treated as
an indicator of prestige or standing. It
generally turns out that the people
put in the same prestige class share the
same outlook and style of life, one that
is learned in childhood and that constitutes a "life style" for them. That is,
the prestige classes turn out to be cultures, or rather (since the outlook and
style of life of each class is a *variant* of
one common to all) subcultures.[5]

The class subcultures have been
described by many sociologists, although never with the rigor and com-
pleteness of an ethnographic report (a
fact that leaves some social scientists in
doubt as to whether they are really
subcultures).[6] There is general agreement as to their characteristics, and
what follows in the next few pages is
essentially a summary of what sociologists have reported about them. It differs from most other accounts, however, in that each class subculture is
characterized as having a distinctive
psychological orientation toward providing for a more or less distant future.

In the analysis to come, the individual's orientation toward the future
will be regarded as a function of two
factors: (1) ability to imagine a future,
and (2) ability to discipline oneself to
sacrifice present for future satisfaction.[7]
The more distant the future the individual can imagine and can discipline
himself to make sacrifices for, the
"higher" is his class. The criterion, it
should be noted, is ability, not per-

formance. Later on (in Chapter 10) it will be explained how a person may be psychologically capable of providing for the future and yet not do so. For the present, however, his time horizon may be thought of as a function of his class culture alone. The reason for defining class in terms of orientation toward the future is that this conception seems to lend itself better than any others to analysis of the kinds of problems that are of special interest to the policymaker.[8]

The class subcultures have numerous secondary characteristics associated with this primary one (the existence of a *pattern* of characteristics justifies the term *subculture*); most of these secondary characteristics are probably caused, directly or indirectly, by the primary one, but this is a question that need not be treated here. In any case, each subculture displays distinctive attitudes toward—for example—authority, self-improvement, risk, and violence, and distinctive forms of social organization, most notably of family organization. For the purposes of this book, however, the *defining* characteristic of a class subculture is—to repeat—the one primary factor; namely, psychological orientation toward providing for the future.

For present purposes it will suffice to describe four subcultures—those of the upper, middle, working, and lower classes—and to describe them schematically as ideal types.[9] In other words, what follows are generalized models of subcultures, which do not necessarily describe the cultural traits of *particular* individuals. The four subcultures should be thought of as bands (rather than points) on a continuous scale or spectrum—bands that sometimes blend and overlap so that there can exist "in-

between" positions equally characteristic of "adjoining" subcultures.

It must again be strongly emphasized that this use of the term *class* is different from the ordinary one.[10] As the term is used here, a person who is poor, unschooled, and of low status may be upper class; indeed he *is* upper class if he is psychologically capable of providing for a distant future. By the same token, one who is rich and a member of "the 400" may be lower class: he *is* lower class if he is incapable of conceptualizing the future or of controlling his impulses and is therefore obliged to live from moment to moment. In general, of course, there is at least a *rough* correspondence between being, for example, upper class in the present sense and upper class as ordinarily defined: this is because people who are capable of providing for a distant future tend by that very circumstance to get education (as distinct from schooling) and with it wealth, status, and power. Similarly, people incapable of looking ahead for more than a day or two or of controlling their impulses are likely to be poor, unskilled, and of low status for this very reason.

It should also be emphasized that behavior can rarely be explained solely in terms of class subculture. The individual belongs to other subcultures besides the class one—age group, occupational group, and ethnic group subcultures, for example. Moreover, culture is by no means the only determinant of his behavior; in many situations thorough knowledge of an individual's culture(s) would not help an observer make "interesting" predictions about his behavior.

Strong correlations have been shown to exist between IQ soore and socioeconomic status, and some investigators have claimed that these correlations are largely attributable to genetic factors.[11] These considerations suggest the possibility that one's ability to take account of the future may often depend mainly upon one's biologically inherited intelligence. The assumption being made here, however, is a contrary one—namely, that time horizon is a cultural (or subcultural) trait passed on to the individual in early childhood from his group.

THE UPPER CLASS

At the most future-oriented end of the scale, the upper-class individual expects a long life, looks forward to the future of his children, grandchildren, great-grandchildren (the family "line"), and is concerned also for the future of such abstract entities as the community, nation, or mankind. He is confident that within rather wide limits he can, if he exerts himself to do so, shape the future to accord with his purposes. He therefore has strong incentives to "invest" in the improvement of the future situation —i.e., to sacrifice some present satisfaction in the expectation of enabling someone (himself, his children, mankind, etc.) to enjoy greater satisfactions at some future time. Future-oriented culture teaches the individual that he would be cheating himself if he allowed gratification of his impulses (for example, for sex or violence) to interfere with his provision for the future.

The upper-class individual is markedly self-respecting, self-confident, and self-sufficient. He places great value on independence, curiosity, creativity, happiness, "developing one's potentialities to the full," and consideration for others. In rearing his children, he stresses these values along with the idea that one should govern one's relations with others (and, in the final analysis, with one's self) by *internal* standards rather than by conformity to an externally given code ("not because you're told to but because you take the other person into consideration").[12] The upper-class parent is not alarmed if his children remain unemployed and unmarried to the age of thirty, especially if they remain in school.[13] He does not mind being alone; indeed, he requires a good deal of privacy. He wants to express himself (he may carry self-expression to the point of eccentricity), and, in principle at least, he favors self-expression by others. He takes a tolerant, perhaps even an encouraging, view of unconventional behavior in sex, the arts, and politics. He is mindful of the rights of others and wants issues to be settled on their merits and by rational discussion. He deplores bigotry (which is not to say that he has no prejudices) and abhors violence.

It will be seen that two features of this culture—the disposition to postpone present satisfaction for the sake of improving matters in the future and the desire to "express one's personality" —are somewhat antagonistic. Upper-class (that is, future-oriented) culture permits the individual to emphasize either theme. If he thinks that his means (money, power, knowledge, and the like) are almost certainly adequate to maintain him and his "line" throughout the future he envisions, the future-oriented individual has no incentive to "invest" (that is, trade present for future satisfaction) and may therefore emphasize self-expression. If, on the other hand, he thinks that his means may *not* be adequate (he will think this, of course, no matter how large his means if his plans for the future are grand enough), he is likely to emphasize self-discipline so that he may acquire the larger stock of means that he thinks he needs. Insofar as he chooses the expressive alternative, the upper-class individual's style of life may resemble the present-oriented one of the lower class. But whereas the lower-class individual is capable *only* of present-oriented behavior, the upper-class one can choose. He may, for example, do some things that require a high degree of skill, discipline, and judgment, living the rest of the time from moment to moment. Even if he lives from moment to moment all the time, he does so by choice—it is his "thing," his mode of self-expression. By contrast, the "true" present-orientedness of the lower class is both unrelieved and involuntary.

The upper-class individual feels a strong attachment to entities (formal organizations, the neighborhood, the nation, the world) toward which he stands, or wants to stand, in a relation of fellowship. He sees the "community" (or "society") as having long-range goals and the ability to shape the future. He tends to feel that it is one's responsibility to "serve" the community by assisting in efforts for its improvement—perhaps because, his own goals being long-range ones, he has a stake in the future of the community. At any rate, he tends to be active in "public service" organizations and to feel a strong obligation (which he does not always act upon, of course) to contribute time, money, and effort to worthy causes.[14] (In the South the upper-class attitude in these matters is different. As W. J. Cash remarked, the aristocratic ideal of the planter became corrupted by frontier individualism, which, "while willing enough to ameliorate the specific instance, relentlessly laid down as its basic social postulate the doctrine that every man was completely and wholly responsible for himself."[15])

THE MIDDLE CLASS

The middle-class individual expects to be still in his prime at sixty or thereabouts; he plans ahead for his children and perhaps his grandchildren, but, less future-oriented than the ideal typical member of the upper class, he is not likely to think in terms of "line" or to be much concerned about "mankind" in the distant future. He, too, is confident of his ability to influence the future, but he does not expect to influence so distant a future as does the upper-class individual, nor is he as confident about the probable success of his efforts to influence it. The middle-class individual's self-feelings are a little less strong than those of the upper-class individual; he is also somewhat less desirous of privacy. Although he shows a good deal of independence and creativity and a certain taste for self-expression, these traits rarely lead to eccentricity. He is less likely than the upper-class individual to have means that he considers adequate to assure a satisfactory level of goal attainment throughout his anticipated future. Therefore, "getting ahead"—and the self-improvement and sacrifice of impulse gratification that it requires—will be more likely to take precedence with him over "the expression of one's personality." In the lower middle class, self-improvement is a principal theme of life, whereas in the upper middle class, self-expression is emphasized. Almost without exception, middle-class people want their children to go to college and to acquire the kind of formal training that will help them "get ahead." In matters of sex, the middle-class individual is (in principle, at least) "conventional," and in art and politics, too, he is more ready than the upper-class individual to accept the received opinion. He has regard for the rights of others; he deplores bigotry and abhors violence. He does not, however, hold these attitudes as strongly as do members of the upper class.

The middle-class individual does not feel as strong a sense of responsibility to the community as does the upper-class one, and he defines the community somewhat less inclusively. He wants (in principle, at least) to "belong" to a community and to be of "service" to it, and accordingly he joins organizations, including "service" ones. (In the lower middle class, the taste for public service and reform is relatively weak: the individual usually votes against public improvements that will not benefit him directly.) The middle-class individual, however, is less willing than the upper-class one to give time, money, and effort for public causes.

THE WORKING CLASS

The working-class individual does not "invest" as heavily in the future, nor in so distant a future, as does the middle-class one.[16] He expects to be an "old man" by the time he is fifty, and his time horizon is fixed accordingly. Also, he has less confidence than the middle-class individual in his ability to shape the future and has a stronger sense of being at the mercy of fate, a "power structure," and other uncontrollable forces. For this reason, perhaps, he attaches more importance to luck than does the middle-class individual. He is self-respecting and self-confident, but these feelings are less marked in him than in the middle-class individual and they extend to a somewhat narrower range of matters. As compared to the middle-class individual, he is little disposed toward either self-improvement or self-expression; "getting ahead" and "enlarging one's horizon" have relatively little attraction for him. In rearing his children, he emphasizes the virtues of neatness and cleanliness, honesty, obedience, and respect for external authority. (As David Riesman has observed, the problem in the working class is not, as in the upper middle class, to stimulate children; rather, it is to control them—"to teach them faith, respect, and obedience, rather than independence of mind and development of talents."[17]) If his children do not go to college, the working-class individual does not mind much. In his relations with others, he is often authoritarian and intolerant, and sometimes aggressive. He is not only a bigot but a self-righteous one. Violence and brutality are less shocking to him than to middle-class persons; indeed, he regards them—up to a point—as normal expressions of a masculine style. To the working class, the middle class appears somewhat lacking in masculinity, and the upper class—a male member of which may even weep under stress—appears decidedly feminine or "queer."

The working-class individual's deepest attachment is to his family (most of his visiting is with relatives, not friends). However, his relationship to his wife and children is not as stable or as close—for instance, does not involve as much companionship—as these relationships tend to be in the middle class.[18] Privacy is of little importance to him: he likes to have people around, and the noises and smells that they make seldom bother him (when he goes on vacation it is not to the country, which he finds too quiet and lonely, but to crowded resorts). The sense of sharing a purpose with others is not as important to him as it is to members of the upper classes, and when he joins an organization it is more likely to be for companionship and "fun" than for "service" or civic improvement. He may vote, especially if someone asks him to as a favor. His opinions on public matters are highly conventional (it does not seem to occur to him that he is entitled to form opinions of his own), and his participation in politics is motivated not by political principles but by ethnic and party loyalties, the appeal of personalities, or the hope of favors from the precinct captain.

THE LOWER CLASS

At the present-oriented end of the scale, the lower-class individual lives from moment to moment. If he has any awareness of a future, it is of something fixed, fated, beyond his control: things happen *to* him, he does not *make* them happen. Impulse governs his behavior, either because he cannot discipline himself to sacrifice a present for a future satisfaction or because he has no sense of the future. He is therefore radically improvident: whatever he cannot consume immediately he considers valueless. His bodily needs (especially for sex) and his taste for "action"[19] take precedence over everything else—and certainly over any work routine. He works only as he must to

stay alive, and drifts from one unskilled job to another, taking no interest in the work.

The lower-class individual has a feeble, attenuated sense of self; he suffers from feelings of self-contempt and inadequacy, and is often apathetic or dejected. (In her discussion of "very low-lower class" families, Eleanor Pavenstadt notes that "the saddest, and to us the outstanding characteristic of this group, with adults and children alike, was the self-devaluation."[20]) In his relations with others he is suspicious and hostile, aggressive yet dependent. He is unable to maintain a stable relationship with a mate; commonly he does not marry. He feels no attachment to community, neighbors, or friends (he has companions, not friends), resents all authority (for example, that of policemen, social workers, teachers, landlords, employers), and is apt to think that he has been "railroaded" and to want to "get even." He is a nonparticipant: he belongs to no voluntary organizations, has no political interests, and does not vote unless paid to do so.

The lower-class household is usually female-based. The woman who heads it is likely to have a succession of mates who contribute intermittently to its support but take little or no part in rearing the children. In managing the children, the mother (or aunt, or grandmother) is characteristically impulsive: once they have passed babyhood they are likely to be neglected or abused, and at best they never know what to expect next. A boy raised in a female-based household is likely at an early age to join a corner gang of other such boys and to learn from the gang the "tough" style of the lower-class man.[21]

The stress on "action," risk-taking, conquest, fighting, and "smartness" makes lower-class life extraordinarily violent. However, much of the violence is probably more an expression of mental illness than of class culture. The incidence of mental illness is greater in the lower class than in any of the others. Moreover, the nature of lower-class culture is such that much behavior that in another class would be considered bizarre seems routine.[22]

In its emphasis on "action" and its utter instability, lower-class culture seems to be more attractive to men than to women. Gans writes:

The woman tries to develop a stable routine in the midst of poverty and deprivation; the action-seeking man upsets it. In order to have any male relationships, however, the woman must participate to some extent in his episodic life style. On rare occasions, she may even pursue it herself. Even then, however, she will try to encourage her children to seek a routine way of life. Thus the woman is much closer to working class culture, at least in her aspirations, although she is not often successful in achieving them.[23]

In the chapters that follow, the term *normal* will be used to refer to class culture that is not lower class. The implication that lower-class culture is pathological seems fully warranted both because of the relatively high incidence of mental illness in the lower class and also because human nature seems loath to accept a style of life that is so radically present-oriented. This is not the main reason for using the word *normal,* however. Rather, it is that *some* word is needed to designate the sector of the class-cultural continuum that is not lower class, and no other word seems preferable on the whole.

From the beginning, the cities of the United States have had upper, middle, working, and lower classes. The relative strength of the various classes has varied greatly from time to time and place to place, although the nature of the class cultures has not. At the beginning of the nineteenth century, the free population of the United States was predominantly middle class. Most were descendants of English and American yeomen, artisans, and tradesmen, a stratum of society that had long had good opportunities to better its condition and had been confident of its ability to do so.[24] The native American inherited a culture that gave prominent place to the future-oriented virtues of self-discipline and denial, industry, thrift, and respect for law and order. He was sure that these virtues would be rewarded by success; he expected to "get on" and to "improve himself" in material and other ways. The Puritans had come to America with the intention of establishing ideal communities— "a city upon a hill"—and the millennial impulse, still powerful, took many forms in the first half of the nineteenth-century. In the towns and cities, most early Americans, especially those of English origin, were skilled craftsmen or tradesmen. Of the few in New England who were day laborers, nearly all could read and write and nearly all voted.[25]

The number of working- and lower-class people was by no means insignificant, however, especially in the cities. In every sizable city there were transient laborers—and in the seaports, sailors, and in inland cities like Cincinnati and St. Louis, boatmen, wagoners, and drifters, who, like Huckleberry Finn's father, lived from hand to mouth, worked only when they had to, drank and fought prodigiously, felt no tie to the community, and left their women and children behind to fend for themselves or to be looked after at public expense once they had moved on.[26] In every city there also were unassimilated immigrants from countries—Catholic ones—whose cultures tended to be present- rather than future-oriented. It is safe to say, however, that transients and Catholic immigrants did not comprise the whole of the working- and lower-class population. In Boston, for example, which in 1817 had only about four hundred Catholics, the native American residents must have patronized the city's two thousand prostitutes (one for every six males above the age of sixteen), hundreds of liquor shops, and the gambling houses open night and day. It must also have been the native Bostonians who denied the mayor, Josiah Quincy, reelection after he waged a vigorous war on vice.[27]

Eventually, as immigration increased, the working and lower classes—especially the latter—did come to consist disproportionately of Catholic immigrants. In 1832, for example, the South Boston Almshouse held almost twice as many immigrants as natives. "To see anything like indigence or idleness," a visitor to New England from abroad wrote a few years later, "we must penetrate into the purlieus in the seaport towns, occupied by the Irish laboring population." The districts inhabited by the Irish and the Negroes formed, he said, "a painful contrast to the general air of cleanliness and comfort."[28]

After 1840 immigration increased rapidly, the immigrants coming mainly from peasant cultures—first Irish and then, after 1885, southern Italian and eastern European—that were more present-oriented than those of New England, Great Britain, and northern Europe. Coming from places where ordinary people had never had opportunities to rise by effort and enterprise, these immigrants tended to believe that the world was ruled by fate and that only a miracle or a great piece of luck could change their situation. The idea of self-improvement—and even more that of community improvement—was unfamiliar and perhaps even unintelligible to them. They were mainly concerned about survival, not progress; how to get food, drink, and shelter for the day was what preoccupied them. Their motive in coming to this country was apparently less to improve their general condition than to escape the threat of immediate starvation. "The emigrants of this year are not like those of former ones," the *Cork Examiner* noted during the peak of the Irish emigration, "they are now actually *running away* from fever and disease and hunger. . . ."[29]

Among the native Americans it was a rare day laborer who could not read, write, and cipher; among the peasant immigrants it was a rare one who could. The immigrants from present-oriented cultures were slow to see the advantages of education and of self-improvement generally. Even to some sympathetic observers it appeared that many of them would as soon live in hovels and shanties as not. Unlike the native Americans and the more future-oriented immigrants from England and northern Europe, the peasant immigrants seldom patronized the free mechanics libraries. Very few became skilled workers. In part, perhaps, this was because employers, most of whom were native, were prejudiced against them; in part also, however, it was probably because the present-oriented outlook and style did not suit the requirements of work and organization.

It was symptomatic of these different attitudes toward self-improvement and "getting on" that compulsory school attendance laws were adopted only after large-scale peasant immigration got under way. In Massachusetts, for example, the first such law was passed in 1852 and required all children between the ages of eight and fourteen to attend for twelve weeks each year. Until then it had been taken for granted that anyone able to go to school would not fail to do so.

The Jewish immigrants were very different from the peasant peoples. Like the native Americans, they were future-oriented. They believed, as had the Puritans, who were in many ways like them, that they were under a special obligation to assist in the realization of God's plan for the future. The idea of making sacrifices in the expectation of future rewards came naturally to them. Even more than the native American, the Jewish immigrant worked to acquire the capital (not only money and other material goods but also knowledge, skill, character, attachment to family and community, etc.) that would enable him to rise. Jacob A. Riis wrote:

The poorest Hebrew knows—the poorer he is, the better he knows it—that knowledge is power, and power as the means of getting on in the world that has spurned him so long, is what his soul yearns for. He lets no opportunity slip to obtain it. Day- and night-schools are crowded with his children, who learn rapidly and with ease. Every synagogue, every second rear tenement or dark backyard, has its school and its school master, with his scourge to intercept those who might otherwise escape.[30]

The future-oriented ideal diffused rapidly throughout the population. In the latter half of the nineteenth century the whole nation seemed suddenly seized with a passion for self-improvement: in every city and in thousands of towns and villages there were lyceum discusions, Chautauquas, evening lectures, and the like. Self-improvement implied community improvement, and the native American (originally Puritan) idea that it was everyone's obligation to do what he could to bring the millennial hope to fulfillment and to create "a city on a hill" became the generally accepted doctrine of "service." To immigrants like the Jews, whose native culture was future-oriented, these tendencies were highly congenial, but to others—notably the Irish—they were alien and distasteful. Eventually, however, all the immigrant groups succumbed to the native American, future-oriented ideal. Even Negroes, whose isolation as slaves and then as Southern farmhands might, one would think, have excluded them from the culture almost altogether, were drawn toward the ideal. Although they traveled at very different rates of speed, all ethnic and racial groups were headed in the same cultural direction: from less to more future-oriented.

Movement upward along the scale of class culture tended to follow increases in income and opportunity. Those people sacrificed the present for the future who had reason to think that doing so would be in some sense profitable, and the greater the prospective rewards, the more willing they were to accept the discipline and to put forth the effort required. People generally had good grounds for believing that the future-oriented virtues would pay off. To be sure, not many rose from rags to riches, as the mythology claimed, but it was very common for the son of an unskilled laborer to become a semiskilled or a skilled one and for *his* son to emerge as a manager, teacher, or professional.[31]

It is not clear, however, whether those who moved up the occupational, income, and status ladders did so because they had absorbed a more future-oriented culture. It is possible, for example, that Patrick Kennedy, who came to this country a laborer in 1848 and was still one when he died, was present-oriented and that it was because his son, Patrick Joseph, was somehow affected by the future-oriented atmosphere of Boston that he (the son) became a leading saloon-keeper and ward politician and—*mirabile dictu*—had the foresight to send *his* son, Joseph P., to the Boston Latin School and then to Harvard College. But it is also possible that the original Patrick was just as future-oriented as his son and that he remained a laborer all his life because the circumstances of his time and place made rising too difficult for him. It makes a great difference whether one supposes that (1) the American environment instilled in the immigrant a more future-oriented view; (2) it merely gave scope to those individuals whose view was such to begin with; or (3) it produced both effects.

From every ethnic group, including, of course, the native American, some individuals were born into the lower class and others dropped into it from above. The more present-oriented a group's culture was, the larger the proportion of its members who became lower class (similarly, the more future-oriented a group's culture, the higher the proportion who entered the upper classes). The Irish, for example, contributed heavily to the lower class as compared to the Jews. From 1885 to 1890, persons born in Ireland comprised 12.6 percent of the population but accounted for 60.4 percent of the almshouse, 36.7 percent of the workhouse, and 15.5 percent of prison inmates; Jews from Russia and Austria-Hungary were 3 percent of the population but accounted for none of the almshouse, 1 percent of the workhouse, and 1 percent of the prison inmates.[32] Very likely, the present-orientedness of the Irish and the future-orientedness of the Jews had important indirect effects as well. The Anglo-Saxon Protestant elite, for example, probably discriminated against people who showed little disposition to get ahead and in favor of those who showed much.

The lower the individual was on the cultural scale, the greater the obstacles in the way of his moving up occupationally or otherwise and the less his motivation to try. At the very bottom of the scale, the desire to rise was altogether lacking—and those in the lower class rarely if ever climbed out of it. Moreover, the obstacles in the way of rising—many of which were due to the distaste future-oriented people had for the manners and morals of the extremely present-oriented—were all but insuperable. Some families doubtless remained lower class for for many generations, but most probably died out within two or three.

Each class culture implies—indeed, more or less requires—a certain sort of physical environment. It follows that a city (or district within a city) which suits one culture very well is likely to suit another very poorly or not at all.

To an upper-class individual, having a great deal of space at one's disposal is important both practically and symbolically. Being by oneself a good deal—and therefore having room enough for privacy—is essential to the development of a well-defined self; in the middle and upper classes, but not in the working class, it is thought essential that each child have a room of his or her own. The higher a family is on the class culture scale, the wider the expense of lawn (or in the case of an apartment house, the thicker the walls) that it wants between it and the neighbors. Similarly, the higher the commuter is on the scale, the more important it is to him to ride to work in solitary splendor. For the lower-middle-class person a car pool will do—it is better than the bus; the upper-middle-class person, however, finds even that distasteful.

In the middle- and upper-class cultures, one's house and grounds afford opportunities for self-improvement and self-expression.[33] To the upper-class individual, it is the latter value that is usually more important: the house is the setting for and the representation of his family line ("house"). The middle-class individual is more likely to value his house for giving scope to his impulse to improve things—not only physical things (the house and grounds) but also, and especially, his own and his family's skills, habits, feelings, and attitudes. (The do-it-yourself movement is at least in part an expression of the middle-class taste for mastering skills and "expressing one's personality.") The middle-class individual—particularly the *lower*-middle-class one—also regards the house as a means of improving his social status; having a "good address" helps one rise in the world.

In the upper- and middle-class cultures, the neighborhood and community are as important as the house and are hardly to be separated from it. It is essential to live where there are good schools, for otherwise the children might not get into good colleges. Other community facilities—parks, libraries, museums, and the like—are highly valued, as are opportunities to be of "service" by participating in civic organizations. The middle- or upper-class individual wants to feel that his local government is honest, impartial, and efficient. At the upper end of the scale, especially, he wants a sense of "belonging" to a "community"—that is, of standing in a fellowship relation to his neighbors (even though he may never see them) and thus of constituting with them a moral entity—not unlike the Puritan congregation of visible saints in the seventeenth century. This desire to belong to a community partly accounts for the exclusiveness of the "better" neighborhoods and suburbs. The exclusion of all who are not parties to the covenant (in the language of Puritanism) is a precondition of fellowship: a community, after all, consists of people who feel a sense of oneness. Where the principle of exclusion appears to be—and perhaps is—racial or ethnic, the neighbors are likely to see that in the pursuit of one of their values they have infringed upon another. Those who feel most strongly the obligation to be of "service" and to act "responsibly"—upper-middle and upper-class Jews, especially—often resolve the conflict by sponsoring a strenuous community effort to bring a certain number of Negroes (or whatever group is being discriminated against) into the neighborhood.[34]

To the working class, a different set of values to accord with its life style governs the choice of physical arrangements in the city. Space is less important to the working-class family than to the middle- or upper-class one. It prefers being "comfy" to having privacy; it is thought natural for children to sleep two or three to a room or perhaps even to a bed. Having neighbors —even noisy ones—down the hall or in a house that is adjoining or almost adjoining is taken for granted. The working-class individual has few deep friendships with his neighbors, but he likes knowing who they are and he likes seeing—and even hearing—their goings-on. (It was because the Italian working-class residents of Boston's West End took this interest in one another that Herbert J. Gans called his account of them *The Urban Villagers*.) From the working-class point of view, middle- and upper-class neighborhoods are dull and lonely. Riding to work by oneself is no fun either; the working-class person prefers a car pool but does not mind a bus or subway.

When he must choose between more and better community facilities on the one hand and lower taxes on the other, the working-class individual usually chooses the latter. He will be satisfied if his children graduate from high school, and any school that is not a blackboard jungle will do. Parks and libraries matter to him even less than schools. He has no desire to participate in community improvement projects and no wish to feel himself part of a community, except perhaps an ethnic one. If his neighbors are a mixed lot, some being hardly sane and others less than respectable, that does not concern him: he is likely to take the attitude that so long as they do not interfere with him, they can do or be what they please.

To this last statement an important qualification must be attached. The working-class individual is likely to become ugly and aggressive if members of an ethnic or racial group that he dislikes begin to "take over" his neighborhood. He is more apt to be prejudiced than are members of the middle class and much less apt to conceal his prejudice. There is no talk in working-class neighborhoods about "responsibility for reducing racial tensions."

In some areas the movement of factories to the suburban ring has led to the building of residential suburbs that are working class. Physically, these look much like middle-class ones, but in style of life the two differ sharply. The working-class suburbanite's house is not a way station on the road to something better, as is often the case with the middle class. He is also less likely than is his middle-class counterpart to forego his favorite TV program in order to collect for the Heart Fund or "serve the community" in some other way.[35]

The lower-class individual lives in the slum and sees little or no reason to complain.[36] He does not care how dirty and dilapidated his housing is either inside or out, nor does he mind the inadequacy of such public facilities as schools, parks, and libraries: indeed, where such things exist he destroys them by acts of vandalism, if he can. Features that make the slum repellent to others actually please him. He finds it satisfying in several ways. First, it is a place of excitement—"where the action is." Nothing happens there by plan and anything may happen by accident —a game, a fight, a tense confrontation with the police; feeling that something exciting is about to happen is highly congenial to people who live for the present and for whom the present is often empty. Second, it is a place of opportunity. Just as some districts of the city are specialized as a market for, say, jewelry or antiques, so the slum is specialized as one for vice and for illicit commodities generally. Dope peddlers, prostitutes, and receivers of stolen goods are all readily available there, within easy reach of each other and of their customers and victims. For "hustlers" like Malcolm Little (later Malcolm X) and the youthful Claude Brown, the slum is the natural headquarters. Third, it is a place of concealment. A criminal is less visible to the police in the slum than elsewhere, and the lower-class individual, who in some parts of the city would attract attention, is one among many there. In the slum one can beat one's children, lie drunk in the gutter, or go to jail without attracting any special notice; these are things that most of the neighbors themselves have done and that they consider quite normal.

Although it is the lower class that gives the slum its special character, lower-class people are by no means the only ones who live in it. Some blocks may be occupied only by the lower class, but in the district as a whole, the majority of residents may well be working-class and not a few middle-class. These are people whose incomes do not correspond to their class culture; in some cases they are the victims of bad luck—the death of a breadwinner, for example—but more often they are in the slum because racial discrimination, past or present, has deprived them of normal opportunities for education and employment.

For these working- and middle-class slum dwellers, life in the slum is a daily battle to preserve life, sanity and self-respect. They must send their children to schools where little or nothing is taught or learned and where the children are in constant physical and moral danger; they must endure garbage-filled alleys and rat-infested halls; if they shop in nearby stores, they must pay high prices for poor selections of inferior goods (the prices are often high only for them—for the lower class, which demands credit even though its credit rating is very poor, the same prices may actually be low); they must suffer the risk of annoyance and even of serious hardship by being mistaken for members of the lower class by policemen, teachers, landlords, and others, who either cannot discern or do not trouble to look for the clues to class differences among the poor.

To the normal people who live in the slum, the worst feature of life there is fear. Many slum dwellers, Patricia Cayo Sexton writes, "live in a generalized state of fear—of being robbed, knifed, attacked, bullied, or having their children injured. This fear colors their whole lives: their ability to learn, to work, to stay sane and healthy, to venture out of their apartments or block, to live openly and freely, to be friends with their neighbors, to trust the world, outsiders, themselves."[37]

Within the limits set by the logic of growth, the mix of class cultures more than anything else determines the city's character and the nature of its problems. Almost everything about the city —population density, per capita income, the nature and quality of housing, the crime rate, the dropout rate, the level of public services, the tenor of race relations, the style of politics— depends in some way and to some extent upon the class composition of the population. When this changes, either in a neighborhood or in the city as a whole, almost everything else changes accordingly. And except as they are compatible with the realities of class culture in the city, the most carefully contrived efforts of public and private policymakers cannot succeed, for the mix of class cultures is a constraint as real as those of income, technology, or climate. It is necessary, therefore, to form the best estimate one can of the direction that change in the class system will take.

For at least a century there has been a general movement upward on the class scale from every class except possibly the lowest. A century ago the urban population was heavily working class; now it is heavily middle class. The process of "middle-class-ification," as Dollard called it, is undoubtedly continuing at an accelerating rate and will in a few decades have reduced the working class to a very small proportion of the whole population. The upper middle class has meanwhile been increasing rapidly in its relative strength, especially since the Second World War. Eventually, the distribution of population along the class scale may be decidedly bimodal, the largest concentration being in the upper middle class and the next largest (much smaller than the first) in the lower class.

No hard data bear on these predictions. Census data on education, income, and occupation cannot be made to yield more than very approximate measures of the size of classes as defined here.[38] There are, however, many indirect indicators that are to some extent relevant. One can see evidence of the process of "middle-class-ification" in changes that have occurred in the occupational structure (in 1900, 28 percent of the work force was in skilled occupations; in 1940, 43 percent; in 1964, 58 percent); in the decline of the saloon, the poolhall, and the brothel, and the rise of the family television set (the 1880 Census counted 517 brothels in Philadelphia, and Jane Addams complained at about the same time that in some wards of Chicago, there was one saloon to every twenty-eight voters);[39] in the ever-greater sensitivity of the public to brutality such as the beating of suspects by policemen—commonplace even half a century ago—and wife and child beating ("If screams resounded through a tenement-house it was taken for granted that the child deserved all it got and more"[40]); in growing concern for civil rights (not only of Negroes but also those of women, juveniles, and persons accused of crimes); in the tendency to widen the sphere of such rights (homosexuals and hippies now receive official protection in some cities as a matter of right); in increased public support for plans to eliminate inequalities of income and opportunity (the "war on poverty" is supposed to benefit not only the poor but the old, the young, the physically disabled, the "culturally deprived," and in general the "powerless"); in the decline of the political machine and the rise of a politics of principle and ideology (in the eyes of the New Left any politics that does not allow full self-expression by all is defective); and in the growth of a mass audience for serious literature, music, and art (readers, listeners, and viewers are counted now by the millions, whereas a generation or two ago they were counted by the thousands).

The mass movement from the working into the middle class and from the lower middle into the upper middle class accounts as much as anything for the general elevation of standards that, as was contended in Chapter 1, makes most urban problems appear to be getting worse even when, *measured by a fixed standard,* they are getting better. The new standards are those of a higher class. It is because the process of "middle-class-ification" has given great numbers of people higher perspectives and standards that dissatisfaction with the city is so widespread. The city that was thought pleasant when most people were working class is thought repellent now that most are middle class, and it will be thought abhorrent when, before long, most are upper middle class.

The ascendancy of the middle and upper middle classes has increased feelings of guilt at "social failures" (that is, discrepancies between actual performance and what by the rising class standards is deemed adequate) and given rise to public rhetoric about "accepting responsibility" for ills that in some cases could not have been prevented and cannot be cured. The dropout, for example, in turning his back on education "is telling us that we never really connected with him, that in our preoccupation with others we never gave him enough time or attention."[41] This is typical. In the upper-middle-class view it is always society that is to blame. Society, according to this view, could solve all problems if it only tried hard enough; that a problem continues to exist is therefore proof positive of its guilt.

In this tendency to find society responsible for all ills, including those that are a function of rising standards, two dangers appear. One is that the allegation of social guilt may lead the individual to believe that he can do nothing to help himself. The dropout, for example, may feel himself excused from all effort once it has been established that he was never given enough time or attention, just as the juvenile delinquent may excuse himself when it has been established that he is the product of wrong social conditions. The other danger is that many people will take the talk of social guilt seriously and conclude that the society is one for which they can have no respect and in which they can place no trust. Such condemnation is mainly to be expected in those sections of society—the upper classes, especially their youth—that are most alive to moral issues, and in those other sectors —notably the poor and the minority groups—that have obvious grounds for thinking themselves victims of social injustice. To the rhetoricians, the guilty society will be "not worth saving." To those who have known all along that it is society's fault that they are at the bottom of the heap, the case will be that much clearer and their righteous anger that much hotter.[42]

NOTES

The quotation at the head of the chapter is from John Dollard, *Caste and Class in a Southern Town* (Garden City, N.Y.: Anchor Books, 1957), p. 433. The original edition was published in 1937.

Richard F. Muth, *Cities and Housing, The Spatial Pattern of Urban Residential Land Use* (Chicago: The University of Chicago Press, 1969), a technical treatise in economics, makes an important contribution to the subjects discussed in this chapter. Unfortunately, it was received too late to be mentioned in the text.

1. Adna F. Weber, *The Growth of Cities in the Nineteenth Century* (New York: Macmillan, 1899), p. 469.
2. This estimate assumes that to buy a house costing $12,500 without spending more than 20 percent of income one must have an income of at least $9,000.

3. The *Oxford English Dictionary* defines a slum as "a thickly populated neighborhood or district where the houses and conditions of life are of a squalid and wretched character." Squalor is defined as "a combination of misery and dirt." In *The Urban Villagers* (New York: The Free Press, 1962), p. 309, Herbert J. Gans says that slums are residential districts that "have been proven to be physically, socially, or emotionally *harmful* to their residents or to the larger community" (italics in the original). Robert Hunter, in *Poverty* (New York: Harper Torchbooks, 1965), p. 108, considers it a "great injustice" to use the word to refer "to working-class districts or to poverty-stricken districts relatively free from vice."

4. See the discussion of class in Gans, *The Urban Villagers*, chs. 2 and 11. See also Joseph A. Kahl, *American Class Structure* (Holt, Rinehart & Winston, 1959), especially ch. 7.

5. In many (but not all) particulars the account of class culture that follows depends heavily upon the work of Herbert J. Gans and Walter B. Miller. See especially *The Urban Villagers*, ch. 11, and Miller's articles, "Implications of Urban Lower-Class Culture for Social Work," *Social Service Review*, Vol. 33 (September 1959), and "Lower Class Culture as a Generating Milieu of Gang Delinquency," *Journal of Social Issues*, Vol. 14 (1958). See also A. B. Hollingshead, *Elmtown's Youth* (New York: Wiley, 1949); Allison Davis, "The Motivation of the Underprivileged Worker," in William Foote Whyte, ed., *Industry and Society* (New York: McGraw-Hill, 1946); William Foote Whyte, *Street Corner Society*, 2nd ed. (Chicago: University of Chicago Press, 1955); Mirra Komarovsky, *Blue-Collar Marriage* (New York: Vintage Books, 1967); A. B. Shostak and W. Gomberg, *Blue-Collar World: Studies of the American Worker* (Englewood Cliffs, N.J.: Prentice-Hall, 1965); D. G. McKinley, *Social Class and Family Life* (New York: The Free Press, 1964); Lee Rainwater, "The Lower Class: Health, Illness, and Medical Institutions" in Irwin Deutscher and Elizabeth J. Thompson, eds., *Among the People: Encounters With the Poor* (New York: Basic Books, 1968), and St. Clair Drake and Horace R. Cayton, *Black Metropolis* (New York: Harper & Row, 1945), in addition to the works cited below.

6. See Charles A. Valentine, *Culture and Poverty: Critique and Counter-Proposals* (Chicago: University of Chicago Press, 1968). Valentine complains of the use that writers on poverty make of the concept of culture; their conceptions, he says, prejudge empirical questions in the direction of policies he deplores.

Gans reassesses his views as presented in *The Urban Villagers* in *People and Plans: Essays on Urban Problems and Solutions* (New York: Basic Books, 1968), ch. 22.

7. For a critique of the claim that lower-class people cannot control their impulses ("probably the most frequently used element in discussion of lower class life") see S. M. Miller, Frank Riessman, and Arthur A. Seagull, "Poverty and Self-Indulgence: A Critique of the Non-Deferred Gratification Pattern," in Louis A. Ferman et al., *Poverty in America: A Book of Readings* (Ann Arbor: University of Michigan Press, 1965), pp. 285-302. Here, too, the argument turns largely on the implications of the concept for the content of policy. It should be noted in passing that the question of whether or not lower-class people are aware of the future is largely and perhaps wholly independent of the question of whether or not they can (or do) control their impulses. One may conceptualize the future and yet (for one reason or another) *not* be able to control an impulse.

8. Most of the statements about time horizons in what follows are empirical: they employ a somewhat special terminology to report facts that have been observed by social scientists and others. The main proposition, namely, that individuals and cultures have differing orientations toward the future, is of this character; so are many subsidiary propositions, such as that present-oriented persons tend to be in constant search of sensual gratifications. Some propositions, however, are *implications* of the main proposition; they are themselves deductive but they have been arrived at from premises that have been inductively established. No "data" support the statement that present-oriented persons are unconcerned about the welfare of their grandchildren yet unborn; such a statement follows from the *meaning* of present-orientedness.

9. An ideal type "is a freely created mental construct . . . by means of which an attempt is made to 'order' reality by isolating, accentuating, and articulating the elements of a recurrent social phenomenon . . . into an internally consistent system of relationships." Julius Gould and William L. Kolb, eds., *UNESCO Dictionary of the Social Sciences* (New York: The Free Press, 1964), p. 312.

10. The difference is greatest with respect to the class here called upper. In ordinary usage this class would probably be called upper-middle. It is not called that here because it seemed that a scale of classes running from lower to upper-middle (there being no upper class that could be placed on the same scale as the others) would be even more likely than the present terminology to cause confusion.

11. C. Burt, "Intelligence and Social Mobility," *British Journal of Statistical Psychology*, 14 (1961): 3-24. The case for the relative importance of genetic factors is argued by Arthur R. Jensen in "How Much Can We Boost IQ and Scholastic Achievement?" *Harvard Educational Review*, 39 (Winter 1969): 1-123. Rejoinders

by several other educational psychologists and by Jensen appeared in the next two issues of the *Review* (Spring and Summer 1969).

12. Melvin L. Kohn, "Social Class and Parental Values," *American Journal of Sociology,* 64 (January 1959): 340, 344, 350. See also his "Social Class and Parent-Child Relationships: An Interpretation," *American Journal of Sociology,* 68 (January 1963): 475.

13. Kenneth Keniston, *The Young Radicals* (New York: Harcourt, Brace and World, 1968), p. 265. Keniston's observation was made with respect to the upper-middle class.

14. For data on the voting behavior of various classes on local public expenditure issues, see J. Q. Wilson and E. C. Banfield, "Public-Regardingness as a Value Premise in Voting Behavior," *American Political Science Review,* 58 (December 1964): 876-887. For data on participation in organizations, see Murray Hausknecht, *The Joiners: A Sociological Description of Voluntary Association Membership* (Totowa, N.J.: Bedminster Press, 1962).

15. W. J. Cash, *The Mind of the South* (New York: Knopf, Vintage Books, 1941), p. 80.

16. Cf. Basil Bernstein's description of the British working class, "Some Sociological Determinants of Perception," *British Journal of Sociology,* Vol. 9 (1958):

The specific character of long-term goals tends to be replaced by more general notions of the future, in which chance, a friend or a relative plays a greater part than the rigorous working out of connections. Thus present, or near present, activities have greater value than the relation of the present activity to the attainment of a distant goal. The system of expectancies, or the time-span of anticipation, is shortened and this creates different sets of preferences, goals and dissatisfactions. This environment limits the perception of the developing child of and in time. Present gratifications or present deprivations become absolute gratifications or absolute deprivations for there exists no developed time continuum upon which present activity can be ranged. Relative to the middle-classes, the postponement of present pleasure for future gratifications will be found difficult. By implication a more volatile patterning of affectual and expressive behaviour will be found in the working-classes.

17. David Riesman (in collaboration with Nathan Glazer), *Faces in the Crowd,* abr. ed. (New Haven: Yale University Press, 1965), p. 254.

18. According to Lee Rainwater, in *Family Design: Marital Sexuality, Family Size, and Contraception* (Chicago: Aldine, 1965), p. 55, in the "upper-lower class" (the working class as defined here):

Though husband and wife may not go their separate ways as much as in the lower-lower class, they tend to adhere to a sharper division of labor than is true in the lower-middle class, and though they may participate together in many family activities, this seems to be more the result of default (they are thrown together in the same small home) or of a desire to keep away from unwelcome involvements outside the home than to be dictated by the values of equality and togetherness that dominate the thinking of lower-middle class men and women.

19. Erving Goffman, in "Where the Action Is" (*International Ritual* [Garden City, N.Y.: Anchor Books, 1967], p. 268), says:

Looking for where the action is, one arrives at a romatic division of the world. On the one side are the safe and silent places, the home, the well-regulated role in business, industry, and the professions; on the other are all those activities that generate expression, requiring the individual to lay himself on the line and place himself in jeopardy during a passing moment. It is from this contrast that we fashion nearly all our commercial fantasies. It is from this contrast that delinquents, criminals, hustlers, and sportsmen draw their self-respect. . . .

20. Eleanor Pavenstedt, "A Comparison of the Child Rearing Environment of Upper Lower and Very Low-Lower Class Families," *American Journal of Orthopsychiatry,* 35 (1965): 89-98.

21. On this and on the "foci" of lower-class culture, see the articles by Walter B. Miller cited earlier.

22. Jerome K. Myers and B. H. Roberts, *Family and Class Dynamics in Mental Illness* (New York: Wiley, 1959), p. 174. See also Hollingshead and Redlich, *Social Class and Mental Illness,* p. 175, and S. Minuchin et al., *Families of the Slums* (New York: Basic Books, 1968), p. 34.

23. Gans, *The Urban Villagers,* p. 246.

24. Ralph Barton Perry in *Puritanism and Democracy* (New York: Vanguard, 1944), p. 298, remarks of the English and colonial American yeomen, artisans, and tradesmen: "They were neither so unfortunate as to be imbued with a sense of helplessness, nor so privileged as to be satisfied with their present status. They possessed just enough to whet their appetites for more and to feel confident of their power to attain it."

25. Theodore Sedgwick, *Public and Private Economy* (New York: Harper and Brothers, 1836), part 1, p. 8. See also T. C. Grattan, *Civilized America* (London, Bradbury and Evans, 1859), 2: 376.

26. Cf. Richard C. Wade, *The Urban Frontier* (Chicago: University of Chicago Press, Phoenix Books, 1964), pp. 217-220.

27. J. Leslie Dunstan, *A Light to the City* (Boston: Beacon Press, 1966), pp. 41-43.

28. Grattan, *Civilized America,* 1: 98-99.

29. Quoted by Oscar Handlin in *Boston's Immigrants* (Cambridge, Mass.: Harvard University Press, 1959), p. 51. (Italics in the original.)

30. In Robert A. Woods et al., *The Poor in Great Cities* (New York: Scribner's, 1895), pp. 102-103.

31. Stephan Thernstrom, *Poverty and Progress; Social Mobility in a Nineteenth Century City* (Cambridge, Mass.: Harvard University Press, 1964), pp. 103, 107.

32. *Reports of the Industrial Commission Immigration*, Vol. XV (Washington, D.C.: U.S. Government Printing Office, 1901), p. 480. On ethnic differences relating to mobility, see Bernard C. Rosen, "Race, Ethnicity, and the Achievement Syndrome," *American Sociological Review*, 24 (1959): 47-60.

33. James Q. Wilson, in "A Guide to Reagan Country," *Commentary*, May 1967, pp. 40-41, has described vividly the care that his generation of Los Angeles boys lavished on their cars. "After marriage," he continues, "devoting energy to the improvement of a house was simply a grown-up extension of what, as a juvenile, one had done with cars."

34. Opinion polls have shown that the higher a person's socioeconomic status is, the more likely he is to favor integration of housing, transportation, and schools, as well as other forms of integration. See Paul B. Sheatsley, "White Attitudes Toward the Negro," in Talcott Parsons and Kenneth B. Clark, eds., *The Negro American* (Boston: Houghton Mifflin, 1966), p. 315. A study of social class and voting behavior in Little Rock found: "The higher the social class, the stronger was support for desegregation. Conversely, the lower the social class, the greater was support for segregation." Harlan Hahn, L. Michael Ross, and Thomas F. Pettigrew, unpublished paper, 1966.

35. Cf. Bennett M. Berger, *Working-Class Suburb: A Study of Auto Workers in Suburbia* (Berkeley: University of California Press, 1960), ch. 5.

36. Cf. John R. Seeley, "The Slum: Its Nature, Use and Users," *Journal of the American Institute of Planners*, 25 (February 1959): 10-13. 1965), p. 116.

37. Patricia Cayo Sexton, *Spanish Harlem; Anatomy of Poverty* (New York: Harper & Row, 1965) p. 116.

38. The problem of estimating the size of the classes from these and other data is discussed in the Appendix.

39. Blake McKelvey, *The Urbanization of America* (New Brunswick, N.J.: Rutgers University Press, 1963), p. 94; Jane Addams, "An Effort Toward Social Democracy," *The Forum*, October 1892, p. 228.

40. Mrs. Helen Campbell, *Darkness and Daylight; or, Lights and Shadows of New York Life* (Hartford, Conn.: Hartford Publishing Co., 1896), p. 170. On brutality in general, see Richard O'Connor, *Hell's Kitchen* (Philadelphia: Lippincott, 1958).

41. Patricia Cayo Sexton, *Education and Income* (New York: Viking, 1961), p. 200.

42. Consider, for example, the probable meaning to all concerned of the announcement (*New York Times*, July 13, 1966) by New York City's chief health officer, Dr. Howard J. Brown, that thousands of wooden benches would be burnt in "a public declaration of conscience" as symbols of dehumanized medical services in the city's clinics. That the service provided by the city to its poor was remarkably good by any standard except that of the more affluent middle class ("No hospital in the world has better professional talent," Dr. Brown admitted) was a fact obscured by the announcement ("disgraceful . . . patients . . . have to barter their dignity for their health"). That people sat on benches rather than in chairs and waited without appointments until a doctor could see them was not, until the rise of new class standards made it so, an affront; it is therefore factually incorrect to use the benches as symbols of mistreatment *in the past*. The effect of the announcement, however, must have been to make upper-middle- and upper-class people ashamed of a city which has long treated its poor so shabbily and also to tell the poor that if by any chance they thought they were fortunate in being cared for by professionals as good as any in the world they were being outrageously put upon and that they should be aggrieved and angry at not always having been given the deference and amenities that the middle class now gives to itself.

Patterns of Collective Racial Violence

MORRIS JANOWITZ

Race riots are the dramatic hallmark of the injustices of race relations in the United States. They have an explosive, destructive, and amorphous character which makes generalization very difficult. As a form of "collective behavior," their natural history is not easily recorded or analyzed. Students of race relations believe that one of the most adequate and comprehensive studies of a particular race riot still remains that prepared by the Chicago Commission on Race Relations on the Chicago rioting of 1919—the result of the careful work of the late Charles S. Johnson, which was done under the supervision of Robert E. Park of the University of Chicago.[1] Nevertheless, it is the purpose of this paper to present a sociological interpretation of changed patterns of collective racial violence in the United States over the last century. The history of race riots reflects not only the expanded aspirations of the Negro but also the techniques that have been used to maintain his inferior social position. The history of race relations in the United States has been grounded in a system of law enforcement that has denied to Negroes due process and equal protection, and that therefore has weakened the legitimacy of the agents of law enforcement, especially in the lowest Negro income areas.

The purpose of this paper is to trace the transformation in the patterns of collective racial violence in urban areas over the last 50 years through three different phases. First, the typical race riot of the period of World War I and thereafter, the communal riot, was an interracial clash, an ecologically based struggle at the boundaries of the expanding black neighborhoods. Second, during World War II, communal riots began to give way to large-scale outbursts within the black community. These riots represented a form of collective behavior against the agents and symbols of the larger society. They can be described as commodity riots because of the extensive looting that gives symbolic meaning to these outbursts. Third, the commodity-type riots that reached a high point during the period of 1964-67 have shown signs of being replaced by a new form of racial violence, a more selective, terroristic use of force with political overtones, again mainly against whites, by small organized groups of blacks.

The form and extent of collective racial violence, it is assumed, are expressions of the social structure and the agencies of social change and social control. Therefore, in particular, the role of the police and law enforcement agencies and of the mass media in fashioning patterns of collective urban violence will be explored.

A central "sociological assumption" supplies a point of departure. There

From Hugh Davis Graham and Ted Robert Gurr (eds.), *Violence in America,* Vol. 2 (Washington, D.C.: U.S. Government Printing Office, 1969). Reprinted by permission of the author. Morris Janowitz is Professor of Sociology at the University of Chicago.

is a considerable body of evidence to support this assumption, but it is best to consider it as an assumption. Social tensions generated by discrimination, prejudice, and poverty offer essential but only partial explanations of Negro mass rioting in the urban centers of the United States. Social conditions conducive for collective violence have been much more widespread than the actual selective outbursts. Allen Grimshaw, one of the most careful students of race riots, concluded in 1962 that "there is no direct relation between the level of social tension and the eruption of social violence."[2]

It is not necessary to accept all that this proposition implies because the evidence is not that solid, and more important, because significant "indirect relations" may well have operated. It is enough to reemphasize the obvious fact that, in the United States. social tensions exist where riots break out, and to accept his alternative formulation that "in every case where major rioting has occurred, the social structure of the community has been characterized by weak patterns of external control."[3] Because of the widespread potentials for racial violence, in the language of sociology, the agencies of social change and social control are crucial in accounting for actual urban racial outbreaks. Moreover, the manner in which outbursts are handled and controlled deeply influences race relations and subsequent patterns of violence. It is well to keep in mind that the supporting evidence for this basic assumption rests on the events before the mid-1960's, when a new and intensified wave of urban racial violence broke out in the United States.

On the whole, statistical studies designated to account for which cities have been struck by riots have not been highly rewarding. However, one carefully matched comparison of riot and nonriot cities by Stanley Lieberson and Arnold R. Silverman of 76 race riots between 1913 and 1963 confirms and amplifies this perspective.[4] For the period before the new wave of riots of the mid-1960's, they found (a) no support for the contention that rapid population change accompanies riots; (b) no confirmation for the hypothesis that unemployment level is a direct factor, but rather that encroachment of Negroes on the white occupational world evidently tends to increase chances of riots; and (c) no support for the notion that race riots are a consequence either of low Negro income or relatively large Negro-white discrepancies in income. Nor, for that matter, does poor Negro housing serve to distinguish riot cities from nonriot cities.

However, their evidence supports "the proposition that the functioning of local government is important in determining whether a riot will follow a precipitating incident." Thus, (a) cities with more racially integrated police forces had fewer riots; (b) cities which had more representative forms of local government (e.g., citywide election of councilmen versus district elections) had fewer riots; and (c) cities were less riot prone that had a large percentage of Negroes who were self-employed in retail trade, such as store, restaurant, or tavern owners—that is, cities that had stronger independent middle-class business groups. In short, these measures were indicators of the articulation of the Negro into the social and political fabric of the metropolitan community, reflecting stronger and more viable patterns of social control.

In addition, if one is interested in

the institutional aspects of race riots, it is necessary to focus attention on (a) the professional and organizational limitations of law enforcement agencies, and (b) the impact of the mass media. The record of law enforcement agencies over the last half century has been one of inadequate equal protection for minorities and limited capacity for dealing with urban disorders, with noteworthy exceptions and with slowly and definitely increasing levels of professionalization. Likewise, the growth of the mass media, especially television, has not been accompanied by increased standards of performance. The impact of the mass media, in its lack of a constructive role in describing problems of social change, plus its imagery of violence and its treatment of riots and law enforcement agencies, has made a positive contribution to violence.

FROM "COMMUNAL" TO "COMMODITY" RIOTS

Racial violence has a history as old as the nation itself. The institution of slavery was rooted in ready resort to violence. After the Civil War, the political control of the freed Negro was enmeshed in a variety of illegal forms of resort to violence. For the purposes of this analysis, however, the particularly devastating and explosive outbreak of collective mass racial riots can be thought of as a distinct phenomenon, although any effort at categorization is a tricky and elusive intellectual effort. The draft riots of the Civil War had clear racial overtones. But "modern" riots can be traced to the racial outbreaks that were generated during the period of World War I and again during World War II. There were, of course, riots during the interwar period, but the heaviest concentration was during wartime years. The riots of this historical era need to be distinguished from the outbursts that took place during the 1960's.

During World War I and its aftermath, the modern form of the race riot developed in Northern and border cities where the Negro was attempting to alter his position of subordination. These outbreaks had two predisposing elements. First, relatively large numbers of new migrants—both Negro and white—were living in segregated enclaves in urban centers under conditions in which older patterns of accommodation were not effective. The riots were linked to a phase in the growth and transformation of American cities. Second, the police and law enforcement agencies had a limited capacity for dealing with the outbreak of mass violence and often conspired with the white rioters against the Negro population. The historical record indicates that they did not anticipate such happenings.

The riots of this period could be called "communal" riots or "contested area" riots. They involved ecological warfare, because they were a direct struggle between the residents of white and Negro areas. The precipitating incidents would come after a period of increasing tension and minor but persistent outbursts of violence. For example, the Chicago riot of 1919 was preceded by 2 years of residential violence in which more than 27 Negro dwellings were bombed. Typically, the precipitating incident would be a small-scale struggle between white and Negro civilians—often in a public place such as a beach or in an area of unclear racial domain. In the major riots of the large cities, tension and violence would spread quickly throughout various parts of the larger community. Thus, deaths and injuries were the result of direct confrontation and fighting between whites and Negroes.

Within a few hours the riot was in full swing, and continued intermittently with decreasing intensity for a number of days. Whites invaded Negro areas and very often the riot spread to the central business district where the white population outnumbered the Negroes. Much of the violence took place on main thoroughfares and transfer points as Negroes sought to return to their homes or sought some sort of refuge. Symbolically, the riot was an expression of elements of the white community's impulse to "kick the Negro back into his place."

Despite the wide areas that were engulfed and the number of casualties inflicted, the whites involved were limited to very small groups or nuclei of activists, often encouraged by vocal bystanders to take the initiative. White youth gangs and their leaders were in the forefront in a number of cities. The Negroes fought back in time, but they seldom invaded white areas. According to available documentation, the whites were mainly armed with bricks and blunt sticks, and they fought with their fists. There were a limited number of handguns (pistols) and rifles. On occasion, Negroes were better armed because they had more of these weapons and knives as well. These riots had many incidents of direct, personal, and brutal struggle between the contestants. The personalized aspect of the violence can be inferred from reports such as that of the Chicago Commission report, which stated

that "Without the spectators, mob violence would probably have stopped short of murder in many cases."[5]

Gunshots were directed at specific and visible targets, often where one side had the overwhelming superiority. Nevertheless, deaths by beating and mauling greatly outnumber those from gunshots. Newspaper reports of snipers were exaggerated. In the East Chicago riots of 1917, there was only one case of repeated gunfire, and in Chicago in 1919, the Commission found one such serious incident and a number of more scattered occurrences, as Negroes sought to retaliate against white marauders passing by in automobiles. In fact, instead of the term "sniper" fire, the reports of the period around World War I speak of occasional "volley firing."

During these riots, rumors about specific incidents of racial strife were spread by word of mouth. Newspapers contributed to racial tension by frequently and repeatedly publishing inflammatory reports such as one that Negroes slaughtered a defenseless white child. Since the riots often lasted for several days, news reports served to recruit white activists from other parts of the city and even from out of town. Editorial efforts to calm public opinion and to demand effective law enforcement developed slowly and hardly balanced the presentation in news columns.

The restoration of civil order required the police to separate the two groups and to protect the enclaves of Negroes from whites. Frequently the police were very deficient in their duties and occasionally assisted the white rioters. In any case they were not prepared for such outbreaks. The state militia or federal troops were used repeatedly and generally displayed a higher level of professional standards. Without overlooking the casualties that were caused by the police themselves, the fundamental anatomy of these riots was a communal clash between Negroes and whites.

During World War II, the pattern of rioting underwent a transformation which took full form with outbreaks in Harlem and Brooklyn in 1964, in Watts in 1965, and in Newark and Detroit in 1967. For lack of a better term, there has been a metamorphosis from "communal" riots to "commodity" riots.[6] The Detroit riot of 1943 conformed to the communal or contested area pattern. It involved concentrations of recently arrived Negro migrants, and the precipitating incident occurred in a contested area, Belle Isle. The violence spread rapidly and produced clashes between Negroes and whites. However, the Harlem riots of 1943 contained features of the new type of rioting. The Negro population was composed of a higher concentration of long-term residents in the community. Most important, it was a riot that started within the Negro community, not at the periphery. It did not involve a confrontation between white and Negro civilians. It was an outburst against property and retail establishments, plus looting—therefore the notion of the commodity riot in the Negro community. These establishments were mainly owned by outside white proprietors. The deaths and casualties resulted mainly from the use of force against the Negro population by police and National Guard units. Some direct and active participation by white civilians may take place in

such a riot, as was the case in Detroit in 1967, but this is a minor element.

THE NATURAL HISTORY OF COMMODITY RIOTS

There have been repeated efforts to describe the various stages in the natural history of race riots, especially the commodity-type riots.[7] Two considerations need to be held in mind in pursuing this goal. The style of intervention by the law enforcement officers has deeply influenced the anatomy of race riots in the United States. During the period of the initial communal riots, the effectiveness of local police forces varied greatly, reflecting their high degree of decentralization. The increased ability of local police to seal off contested areas reduced the prospect of communal riots. Since the riots of World War I, there has been a gradual growth in the capacity of local police to prevent riots at the periphery of the Negro community, but not without conspicuous exceptions. The use of radio communications and motorized local police forces have been the essential ingredients of control. Most Northern cities have witnessed a steady and gradual expansion of the Negro residential areas, accompanied by bitter resentment and continuous minor outbreaks of violence, including bombings. But the police almost daily contain these tensions, which could explode into communal riots if there were defects in their performance. But the capacity of local enforcement agencies to deal with "border" incidents has not been matched with a capacity for controlling the resort to violence within the Negro community. The outbreak of commodity riots produced very different police responses in various communities, ranging from highly effective and professional behavior to weak and irresponsible action that exacerbated rioting and prolonged tension. Thus, the stages of a riot are not predetermined but reflect the pattern of intervention of law enforcement agencies.

Second, it is, of course, very difficult to assemble accurate documentation in order to describe the natural history of a riot and especially the behavior of rioters in a commodity riot. The riots of the 1960's have produced a number of official inquiries and a variety of private studies, but there are few adequate analyses in depth.[8]

The President's Advisory Commission on Civil Disorders (Kerner Commission) sponsored a variety of social research studies that focused mainly on the attitudes of the public and the rioters. The methodology of the sample survey was emphasized, which does not make possible a full analysis of the dynamics of the "collective behavior" of a racial riot. While teams of investigators are required to collect basic documentation, the natural history and anatomy of a riot is still best assessed by a single person who is concerned with cross-checking sources. Brig. Gen. S. L. A. Marshall has demonstrated how a single investigator can reconstruct a complex and fluid battle by after-action group interviews. This procedure has not generally been applied to race riots. Perhaps the most analytic account of a commodity riot was presented by Anthony Oberschall, a Yale University sociologist.[9]

From all sources, one conclusion emerges, namely the absence of organized conspiracy in commodity riots. However, the absence of organized conspiracy does not mean the absence of a pattern of events. Thus, Jules J. Wanderer's analysis of 75 riots during the period 1965-67 demonstrates the pattern of events in these outbursts. By means of the Guttman scale techniques, he demonstrated the consistent cumulation of a very similar configuration of violence from low to high intensity.[10] The difference from one outburst to another involved the extent to which each one proceeded through the various stages of increased and intensified collective behavior.

The motivation of contemporary commodity riots is clearly not desperation generated by the anticipation of starvation, such as in food riots in India during famine times. One is struck by the repeated reports of the carnival and happy-day spirit that pervades the early stages of a commodity riot. The new type of rioting is most likely to be set off by an incident involving the police in the ghetto where some actual or believed violation of accepted police practice has taken place. The very first phase is generally nasty and brutish: the police are stoned, crowds collect, and tension mounts. The second stage is reached with the breaking of windows. Local social control breaks down and the population recognizes that a temporary opportunity for looting is available. The atmosphere changes quickly, and this is when positive enthusiasm is released. But all too briefly. If the crowds are not dispersed and order restored, the third stage of the riot is the transformation wrought by arson, firebombs, and sniper fire and the countermeasures taken by police and uniformed soldiers.

There can be no doubt that the countermeasures employed deeply influence the course of rioting—even in some cases prolonging the period of reestablishing order. One is, of course, struck by the great variation in local response to escalated rioting and in the skill and professionalism of the forces in their counterefforts. Differences in police strategy have been partly accidental and partly the result of conscious policy, because law enforcement officials have a past record to draw on, and are continuously alerted to the possibility of riots. Thus, for example, there were wide differences in response patterns to early manifestations of disorder by local police in the 1960's. In Detroit, Ray Girardin, a former police reporter who became police commissioner, explicitly acknowledged that he followed a loose policy in the early phase of the Detroit rioting, assuming that local civilian Negro leadership would contain the disorder. He cited his previous experience in which this approach worked effectively. In his theories of riot behavior, he made frequest recourse to "sociological" terms.

By contrast, the operational code of the police in New York City under Commissioner Howard Leary and in Chicago has been to intervene with that amount of force judged to be appropriate for early stages of the confrontation. The objective was to prevent the spread of contagion. Special steps were taken to prevent routine police performance from developing into incidents which might provoke tension. However, if an incident became the focal point for tension and the collection of a crowd, the police responded early and in depth in order to prevent the second stage from actually expanding. Numerous police were sent to the scene or kept in reserve nearby. The police sought to operate by their sheer presence, not to provoke further counteraction. They sought to prevent the breaking of windows and the starting of looting that would set the stage for an escalated riot. If actual rioting threatened, one response was the early mobilization of local National Guard units and their ready reserve deployment in inner city garrisons. In part, this was designed to reduce the time required for their deployment on city streets and in part it was policy that enabled the local police to commit their reserves with the surety of having a supporting force available.

Whereas the communal riot involved a confrontation between the white and the black community, the commodity riot, especially as it entered into the third and destructive phase, represents a confrontation between the black community and law enforcement officials of the larger society. The question of the extent of the exchange of gunfire emerged as one of the most problematic dimensions. The reports in the mass media of the use of weapons during and immediately after the riots by the rioters were exaggerated, according to the investigations of the Kerner Commission.[11] In fact, the deaths inflicted by sniper fire were few. For example, it is reported that 5 of 43 deaths during the Detroit disorder were linked to sniper fire, and in Newark, 2 of 26 deaths.[12] These observations did not involve comparisons with earlier riots or an assessment that the gunfire contributed to conditions in which extensive arson developed. In fact, direct comparisons with the communal type riots underline the greater dispersal of firearms and the much more intense use of firepower. They are escalated riots because of the more extensive but still scattered use of weaponry.

A distinguishing characteristic of commodity riots is not only the widespread dispersal of small arms and rifles among the rioters, and correspondingly, the increased capacity of the local police to concentrate armed personnel in a given area. There are no adequate statistics on the distribution of weapons in the hands of participants before any particular riot started. However, there is clear evidence that, over the years, the sale and home storage of firearms has continually increased, made possible by affluence, the absence of adequate gun control legislation, and stimulated by fears of racial violence. These trends have taken place both in the white and in the Negro community. As Zimring has demonstrated in the case of personal violence, the sheer availability of weapons has tended to escalate racial conflict.[13] In addition to the already available arms, a significant stock of weapons appears to have been accumulated during the actual rioting in particular areas. Important sources of supply have been looted including sporting goods stores, general merchandise establishments, and pawnshops.

Available documentation indicates that during the third phase of the commodity riots, when sniper fire developed, it usually involved single individuals, occasionally groups of two or three persons. There is little evidence of forethought by rioters in the deployment of weapons for effectiveness or mutual fire support. Supporting fire by such snipers could render them much more destructive. In isolated cases, there is evidence of limited coordination and planning of firepower. But these cases are of minor importance in accounting for the firepower involved or its destructiveness. The crucial impact of the sniper fire derived from its interplay with arson activities. Sniper fire immobilized firefighting equipment, which permitted widespread destruction by fire, which in turn contributed to more rioting and sniper fire. In this sense, the commodity riots were escalated in intensity and sheer destruction as compared with the communal outbreaks. They were escalated also in the sense that the mass media rapidly disseminates the image and reality of mass fires and widespread looting on a scale not found in the earlier ones. The spread of fire was frequently facilitated by various incendiary bombs of a homemade nature. These firebombs have been used as antivehicle bombs, but generally with little effectiveness.

The phase of scattered sniper fire is, in some respects, a type of quasi-military situation, but the notion of an insurrection has little meaning, for snipers had no intention or capability for holding territory, nor were they part of a scheme to do so even temporarily. Frequently the sniper fire exposed police officers and National Guard units without experience to dangers with which they were not accustomed. Personal risk was clearly present. The scattered source of fire often enveloped the law enforcement units. It was this envelopment fire, especially from behind, which has led to the use of the term "guerrilla tactics," but the guerrilla concept is also not relevant since guerrillas are part of an organization, proceed with a plan, prepare paths of withdrawal, and develop sanctuaries.

Overresponse and excessive use of firepower by police and National Guard units in turn contributed to the escalation of the rioting.[14] The police were at times surrounded and, in the absence of effective command and control, were exposed to an environment that most had not previously experienced. Their behavior was conditioned by the sheer feeling of the unreality of the rioting situation and the physical disruption that takes place. They often responded with indiscriminate and uncontrolled fire. The immediate result was that they exposed numerous civilians to danger. Such fire does not suppress snipers, who can only be eliminated by carefully directed fire and counter-sniper procedures. In fact, the initial counterfire actually mobilized new rioters.

The summers of 1964 through 1967 demonstrated wide variations in the capacity of National Guard units to respond to and assist local police. On the whole, National Guard units had received little specific training in riot control and the content of any such training did not appear to have been particularly germane to actual problems. The level of National Guard effectiveness derived from their military preparedness in general. The performance of National Guard units in Newark and in Detroit has been judged by expert observers to be deficient. By contrast, the behavior of the National Guard units in Maryland and in Wisconsin (Milwaukee) has been reported to be much more in accordance with the requirements of the constabulary function; namely, the minimum use of force to restore civil law and due process. The basic question is fire control and an effective communications network. By contrast, federal troops used in Detroit were highly professional units with extensive training, who clearly displayed a higher degree of unit control and were less prone to

employ unnecessary fire. The superiority of the federal troops reflects past experience and indicates that more effective military training per se (even without additional civil disorder training), and more effective officers, produces more appropriate responses.

There is some evidence that one index to National Guard effectiveness is the extent of integration of units. Because of its fraternal spirit, most National Guard units have been able to resist Federal directives and Negroes accounted for less than 2 percent of its personnel in 1967. In those cases where integration took place, it meant that the units were seen as more legitimate by the local population. Moreover, units that were forced to integrate were more likely to be concerned with problems of conflict in the unit and developed an officer corps concerned with these issues. For example, units in Detroit and Newark were not integrated while Chicago-based units that were employed during the summer disturbances of 1965 were integrated and had Negro officers.

PARTICIPATION IN COMMODITY RIOTS

The extent of participation and the social characteristics of the riots are revealing indices of underlying factors in the social structure that condition these collective outbursts. There is every reason to believe that in the commodity riots of the 1960's, a larger number of Negroes and a greater percentage of the population of riot-torn communities actively participated in the outbursts than was the case during the older, communal-type confrontations. The commodity-type riots take place within the confines of the black ghettos, which have grown greatly in size and population since World War I. Within these massive ghettos during the hours of the most intensive outbursts, it appears as if social controls were momentarily suspended. The sheer size of the ghettos and the greater remoteness of the outer community contribute to this breakdown and to the "mobilization" of numbers. It is understandable that in the second phase of milling and looting, many residents were swept up by the sheer contagion of events, especially where law officers stood by passively while stores and shops were being entered.

It is also necessary to emphasize that the societal context had radically changed during the period of transition to commodity riots. Through the mass media, the demands of the Negro population had received widespread and favorable publicity and there was considerable sympathy in the nation for their plight. The civil-rights movements had achieved strong legitimacy. Within the black community there was strongly increased sensitivity about minority status. All these factors contributed to the intensity and participation during actual rioting.

The size of the groups rioting and their percentage of the available population, as well as their social characteristics, became matters of public debate. The Kerner Commission devoted efforts to probing these questions and refuting the claim that only a very tiny percentage—for example, less than 1 percent—of the Negro population was involved in riot-torn communities.[15] The Commission argued that the riots included a much larger active group who were generally representative of lower class slum dwellers and therefore could not be characterized as a tiny criminal

element. The size of the rioting group could be estimated from direct observation, a most hazardous approach; from extrapolations from arrest data—a technique that probably underestimated the number of the activists; or from self-reports gathered by sample surveys after the riots—an approach that grossly overstated the case. On the basis of different sources, it was estimated that between 10 to 20 percent of the potential population was involved in the riots of 1967. The lower figure of 10 percent appears to be more accurate, although even this estimate is open to serious question. Aside from the reliability of the data, the question hinges on the differing definitions of participation. To speak of even 10 percent participation is to include those persons who were caught up in the collective processes of the riot as the contagion spread.

Although there are numerous statistical and methodological weaknesses in the various analyses of the arrest data and sample surveys, the findings are relevant for describing the social characteristics of the rioters. All sources agree that women were a significant minority of the activists in the commodity riots, reflecting a broadening of the base of involvement as contrasted with the communal riots, which were mainly a men's affair. Interestingly enough, the police tended to arrest few women, either because their infractions of the law were minor or because they believed that women were not at the core of the riot.

As expected, the bulk of the rioters were young males between the ages of 15 and 34 whose skill levels were low. In a social profile of the 496 Negro males arrested in Detroit, the typical participant has been characterized as "a blue collar worker in a manufacturing plant where he earned about $120.00 a week. Although currently employed, he had experienced more than 5 weeks of unemployment in the past year. He had not participated in a government training or poverty program." In some groups of arrested Negro youths, the unemployment level reached almost 40 percent.[16] In addition, among samples of those caught up in the riots and arrested in 1967, previous arrest records comparable to the equivalent age groups in the black population at large were found. The explanation for this finding is that it is very common for young Negro males to have an arrest record—in some categories, a majority.

Clearly, these data indicate that the activists were not a tiny minority of chronic law offenders nor highly unrepresentative in terms of selected social background characteristics. The full personal and social dynamics will probably never be adequately described, for involvement relates not merely to the demographic and social characteristics but to the patterns of primary and informal group structures of the ghetto community, as well as social personality and attitude. Some clues can be drawn from the observation of various surveys that the participants over-represented single men, who frequently lived outside of family units. These were persons who were less subject to the informal group structure linked to family life and more to informal street and community life. Anthony Oberschaal is one of the few analysts who sought to probe the role of youth gangs in riots, in his case, Watts:

Another informant who has been close to some of the gangs in South Los Angeles reported, however, that gang members, in an effort to prove their claims upon leadership in a certain territory and in competition with each other, were vying for leadership over the crowds during the riots, and this meant among other things actively participating in the skirmishes against the police, breaking into the stores and setting them on fire.[17]

In other cities, especially in Chicago in 1968, gang leaders were active in seeking to dampen tensions and violent outbursts. Fogelson reports on the social difference between those arrested as disorderly persons—who tended to be younger, unemployed, and native born in the locality—and the looters, who tended to be older, less unemployed, and Southern born.[18] In other words, the looters, who joined the riots after they were under way, were more integrated into the adult occupational world.

In contrast to the criminal interpretation, the alternative formulation of the commodity riots as a form of political insurrection appears equally inadequate, if by insurrection is meant an armed social movement with an explicit set of goals. The very absence of evidence of prior planning—either rightist or leftist—would weaken such an interpretation. In 23 disorders studies by the Kerner Commission, none were "caused by, nor were they the consequence of any plan or conspiracy."[19] But more important, it is striking that during the riots of 1964 to 1967, there was a remarkable absence of visible leadership—either existing or emergent—that sought to press for collective demands. It is, of course, clear that the leadership and support of the civil-rights movement were not centrally involved in the riots. The emphasis of the civil-rights leaders on issues such as school integration, access to public accommodation, and voting rights were less directly relevant to the immediate lives of slum dwellers, who were mainly concerned with the welfare system and with immediate employment opportunities. The impact of the riots of 1967 on the civil-rights movement was drastic in that it made the movement's demands more militant. But clearly the leaders of the civil-rights movement were not activists in these outbursts. If anything, they occurred because of the inability of the civil-rights movement to accomplish sufficient social change in the slums, although the movement made a decisive contribution in intensifying aspirations and group consciousness.

Many participants, after the riots, could consciously verbalize their social and economic dilemmas and link their situation to their behavior. In interviews, they had a tendency to highlight "police brutality" as the underlying cause. Of course, many who participated merely took the events as a given fact of life and offered little explanation for their involvement.

In contrast to the communal riots, where the Negro response was a direct and primitive struggle for survival, the commodity riots had overtones which might be called parapolitical, in the sense that group consciousness pervaded this particular form of collective behavior. In balance it can be said that the commodity riot by 1967 was a form of collective action, which on occasion was large scale and included a broadly representative segment of the lower socioeconomic class of the urban community. Regardless of the amount of sympathetic interest they mobilized among middle-class Negroes, the commodity riots were a "violent lower class outburst."[20]

A final aspect of participation has been the active involvement of those in the Negro community who sought to dampen or inhibit the spread of the riot. In official reports, they have come to be described by the awkward and unfortunate term, "counterrioters." In the communal riot, such a role was not possible and, paradoxically, such behavior by Negroes during a riot was a consequence of an increase in integration of the Negro into the larger social structure as compared with the period of communal rioting. Already in the Harlem riot of 1943, more than 300 Negroes were given Civilian Defense insignias and armbands, and used as deputies. For the summer of 1967, the Kerner Commission reported that in all but 6 of 24 disorders they investigated, Negroes were actively on the streets attempting to control rioters.[21]

In some cities, political and community leaders sought to address gathering crowds. On other occasions, religious leaders and community workers walked the streets urging persons to disperse, while still other local residents assisted police and firemen in their tasks. Some of these activities were officially recognized and even sanctioned by the local authorities, but the bulk of the efforts seem to have been without official sponsorship. It is very difficult to evaluate the effectiveness of these efforts, especially in communities where extensive rioting broke out. However, it does appear that such activities had the greatest effect in communities which were on the verge of rioting and in which rioting was avoided.

SUMMER RIOTS OF 1968

It will remain for future historians to

assess whether the summer of 1968 was in fact a turning point in the era of communal riots. The trend in racial conflict from 1964 to 1967 was one of continued, and even expanded, outbreaks that appeared to reach one high point with the massive destruction of Newark and Detroit.

In the winter and spring months of 1968, the outlook for the summer of that year was bleak. Racial tensions remained high. Extremist and even moderate leaders anticipated even higher levels of violence, and a variety of analysts were thinking in the same direction. One of the writers for the Kerner Commission, assessing public opinion polls, stated "on the eve of the summer of 1968, these responses are anything but reassuring."[22] The tensions of the Vietnam crisis continued. There was no new massive national response to the social and economic needs of the black community, except in the important employment sector where industrial corporations started to abandon rigid recruitment and training procedures and to engage an increasing number of inner city personnel who would develop their qualifications on the job. Community relations were made more difficult by extremist statements by some individual police officers, who spoke of the necessity of a "tough" policy and of their plans to use heavier hardware for control purposes. The tragic assassination of Dr. Martin Luther King, Jr., served as a final element in the prelude to the summer of 1968.

However, race relations during the summer had a different character from these anticipations. In October 1968, the Department of Justice released a report by Attorney General Ramsey Clark which revealed a decline in the scope and intensity of racial riots. Quantitative measures of riots are difficult to construct, but these appear to be of relatively high validity. The definitions were carefully worked out and the same data collection procedures used to compare the months of June, July, and August, 1967, with the same months of 1968. The results showed a decline in "major" disturbances from 11 to 7, and of "serious" ones from 35 to 18, while minor outbursts increased slightly from 92 to 95. The most dramatic indicator of the decline was the drop in deaths from 87 to 19. To some degree, these data understate the full decline from 1967 to 1968, since the category "major" riots included all riots which lasted longer than 12 hours and included more than 300 persons. The very large-scale riots such as Newark and Detroit were absent in 1968. This is reflected in part in the marked decline in estimated property damage, from $56 million in 1967 for three riots in Cincinnati, Newark, and Detroit to $4 million for all damage during June, July, and August of 1968. It is, of course, very possible that no new long-term trend was at work. One hypothesis to account for the short-term and immediate pattern was the development of new tactics and new organizations that permit more effective expression of black interests and black solidarity. Another hypothesis is that improved police-community relations and higher levels of police professionalism contributed to the decline. These data seem to indicate that, while minor outbreaks continued, interaction between the police and the black community was able to reduce and contain larger and more widespread riots.

Under pressure of political and community leadership, many police took initial steps to improve communications with the Negro community through devices such as special conferences, the assigning of special officers of community relations, and improved police training. The criticism of the police in some communities and the relative success in other areas led to more professional behavior. The advocates of deescalation had more and more influence; the slogan became "manpower and not firepower." Older doctrines of riot control, which emphasized weaponry and technical characteristics, gave way to new and more flexible approaches. Police departments sought to improve their internal communications and their ability to mobilize manpower. They sought to strengthen supervision and control in the field and emphasized the need for restraint. There was a much more professional response to the problem of sniper fire, in that police were instructed not to respond with indiscriminate firepower. There was some progress toward deescalation of police response to more appropriate levels. Despite the publicity given to those few police officers who spoke about the need for tanks and Mace, the major trend in local police work was in the opposite direction.

National Guard and federal troops were deeply involved in the events of the summer of 1968. The lack of professional competence on the part of the local police to deal with problems of urban racial violence in part reflects the particular system of law enforcement that developed in the United States. Deeply influenced by British institutions, the nation did not develop a national police force that had responsibility for the control of civil disorder, in contrast to France for example. However, the United States has had extensive civil disorders throughout its history and the country found its equivalent to a gendarmerie in the state militia and later in the National Guard. The National Guard especially was organized and trained for national defense purposes, so that it seldom developed professional standards for local police support. The result has been that in both labor disputes and in race riots, federal troops have performed with high levels of effectiveness, not because of their specialized training for the task but because of generally higher organizational effectiveness.

But the division of responsibility between local, state, and federal agencies greatly complicates the conditions under which federal troops will intervene in a riot. In the Detroit riots of July 1967, federal troops were not deployed on the basis of the request of State and local authorities, but only after the Presidential representative, former Assistant Secretary of Defense Cyrus Vance, had personally inspected the city and certified the need for federal troops. There was local criticism that this procedure unduly delayed the dispatch of necessary troops. The office of the President has had to struggle to avoid premature commitment of federal troops whenever local authorities feel under pressure, but at the same time maintain the credibility of swift federal intervention if required. As a result, the Department of the Army established a Directorate for Civil Disturbance Policy and Operations to oversee such involvements. Greater use was made of federal troops in 1968 than in 1967. These troops underwent specialized training, but it was their general organizational effectiveness and command structure that enabled them to operate with the greatest restraint.

They very seldom made use of their weapons; their sheer presence was mainly responsible for limiting riot behavior. (For example, in the Washington, D.C., operation, at most 15 bullets were fired.) In fact, there were numerous occasions in which the local population welcomed the arrival of federal troops, with the clear implication that they preferred not to be policed by local personnel.

With reliance placed on the National Guard, it became abundantly clear during the summer of 1967 that racial integration in these units had to be pressed with much greater vigor. It had been federal policy to encourage such integration, and in fact all Negro units were disbanded, but the recruitment of Negroes into the National Guard lagged. Where integration of the Negro into the National Guard had taken place, it was the result of state and local political leadership. Therefore, on August 10, 1967, the President's Commission on Civil Disorders unanimously issued a set of recommendations to produce short-term improvements in riot control. These recommendations called for increased recruitment of Negro personnel into the National Guard, the establishment of standards for eliminating inferior officers, and greater reliance on specialized training. During the next year, these federal policies began to have an effect, especially in the area of improved training.

NEXT STAGE: POLITICAL VIOLENCE

Each stage in the transformation of racial violence already carries with it the elements of the next stage. In the midst of the mass rioting of 1967, there was anticipated marked decline in such outbursts and an emergence of a more selective, more delimited form of violence.[23]

The social position of the Negro in American society was changing, with an effect on patterns of racial tension. In our open society, it is necessary to underline that the commodity rioting of 1964-67 bears a parallel to one explanation of the outbursts of militancy in the trade union movement in the 1930's. The unions displayed their vigor not during the depth of the depression but during 1936 and 1937, a period of halting but increasing prosperity. It may well be that the ghetto outbursts, especially of 1965-67, were linked to the first stages—slow and incomplete—in new levels of opportunity and achievement for the Negro community. If social and economic progress were to continue, the conditions conducive to tension would then start to decline.

Although the topic is outside the scope of this paper, continued improvement of the relative socioeconomic position of the Negro in American society depends on a variety of elements of social change. Much social learning has taken place since the initial phase of the "war against poverty." The main lines of effective innovation are beginning to emerge: federal assistance in family planning, radical modification of the present welfare system including a negative income tax, special youth work training enterprises, and decentralization, plus improved quality of public education. Of special importance are the efforts to locate employment opportunities in depressed areas. Experience to date indicates that such industrial esablishments become training stations that serve to incorporate youngsters into the labor market for the first time and that, after a period of work experience, they develop incentives to seek additional training or better employment in the wider labor market. No doubt, regardless of their limited immediate impact, some of the community organizations being developed in Negro areas with foundation, trade union, and federal funds serve as a learning experience for training new leadership.

Any anticipation of a continued decline of commodity riots is also based on the assumption that a more professional police force would both extend more equal protection and would be more effective and more humane in avoiding collective outbursts. Likewise there would be a more equitable judicial system that would accord more due process to the Negro community. Thus the likelihood of destruction on the level of Newark and Detroit declines, although the escalated riot remains a possibility in any area of heavy Negro population concentration. Likewise, as Negro enclaves develop in suburban areas, forms of communal riots between Negroes and whites become a reality in these areas.

However, the essential trend was that escalated rioting and the rioting of commodity looting appeared in 1967 to be giving way to more specific, more premeditated, and more regularized uses of force. It was as if the rioters learned the lesson emphasized in the mass media, that mass destruction achieves too few tangible benefits. New outbursts appeared to be more goal directed—a diffuse goal at times, at other times a very specific one. It is almost appropriate to describe these outbursts as political violence or political terror, or even conspiratorial violence. It is not inaccurate to describe this shift as one from expressive outburst to a more instrumental use of violence. Those involved were persons who came to believe that white society cannot be changed except with violence.

The participants were likely to be persons who have taken part in previous outbursts. There was an element of organization, at least to the extent that activists are concerned with personal survival and avoidance of the police. There was an element of organization to the extent that the target seems to be selected, and the patterns repeated for a specific purpose. The local school was a particular target. The form of violence can be the harassment of a group of white schoolteachers active in union work, an assault on teacher picket lines during a strike, or a small-scale outburst at the neighborhood schoolyard and on occasion sniper fire against the police. Housing projects, especially integrated housing projects, were repeatedly subject to rifle fire and fire bombing. These incidents are created for the purpose of developing solidarity in local gangs and in paramilitary groups. The United Automobile Workers Union reported the use of terror tactics, including knifings and physical assault, against both white and black workers in the Detroit area. The union identified a group, League of Revolutionary Black Workers, in its documentation.[24]

The object seems to be to establish a vague political presence. Conspiratorial overtones are involved and the assaults spill over against social agencies and local political leaders. The line between random outbursts and these forms of political violence or political terror is difficult to draw. However, these outbursts often take place with the explicit appeal of Black Power. Traditional youth gang activities tend to resist political orientations, but signs of conscious political orientation become more visible.

Dramatic manifestations of the third phase of political violence, or conspiratorial violence, were the shootouts which occurred with police personnel during the summer of 1968 in New York City, Cleveland, Pittsburgh, Oakland, Los Angeles, and elsewhere. The amount of prior planning is difficult to ascertain, but focused selection of police personnel as specific and delimited targets is obvious. In some cases the action appears to have been a response to presumed harassment by the police. In other cases the police were responding to a call for help. In still other cases police cars were attacked without warning. For example, on September 29, 1968, a man wearing a "black cape lined with orange walked up to a police car in Harlem early yesterday and without provocation, opened fire on two patrolmen, wounding them both. . . ."[25] Other incidents developed around a police action such as the removal of a disabled vehicle. Generally these incidents seem to involve loosely and informally organized groups. It is much rarer but perhaps indicative of emerging trends that a formal organization such as the Black Panthers finds itself in repeated gun battles with the Oakland police. The shootout in Cleveland on July 26, 1968, created such community tension that Mayor Carl B. Stokes responded by the unprecedented withdrawal of white police officers and deployment of Negro officers and 500 black community leaders to maintain peace. This procedure was rapidly terminated.[26]

Such activities appear to be a new form of "defiance" politics. In the past, organized racketeers, including groups which penetrated political party organizations, made use of violence to extract a financial toll from slum communities. These traditional groups confined violent outbursts to the maintenance of their economic privilege. Practitioners of political violence and political terror are now more open in advocating violence and opposition to the larger society. They represent an effort to achieve goals much broader and vaguer than those of the racketeer. There are crude ideological overtones and especially a desire to carry violence into the white community.[27]

It is very difficult to contain terroristic eruptions of political violence. The toll is small at a given point and therefore does not produce a violent public reaction. The tactics and organizational plans are more secret and only official surveillance and covert penetration supplies an effective technique of management. The forms of organization are those of a combination of a conspiratorial and predatory gang and a paramilitary unit with overtones of a "liberation" outlook. The more secret and cohesive the group, the greater the problems of surveillance. Even though many of these paramilitary groups will break into factions, the task of control will become extremely difficult. It bodes ill when it is necessary to rely on covert operators. The control of secret operations is at best difficult; in the United States, it is very difficult.[28] The task becomes even more complex and troublesome when these surveillance agencies develop the conception, as they often do, that to collect information is not enough. They begin to believe that they must act as active agents of control, particularly in spreading distrust within these organizations. The task becomes endless and dangerous if the operators play a game without an end or develop an interest in maintaining the groups whom they are supposed to be monitoring.

The failure of the larger society to meet the needs of the black community would contribute to an environment in which conspiratorial violence will continue to flourish. However, such violence has a life of its own. Small groups of terrorists have on historical occasion been able to achieve important goals and political objectives. It is hazardous to even speculate about the conditions under which they are able to succeed. In the past, they appear to have succeeded when they were struggling against a political elite that ruled by terror and without a broad base of support. They have also succeeded when terror is merely an opening step in a broad political campaign. Neither of these conditions seems applicable. Instead it may well be the case that political violence will have counterproductive features. Only limited amounts of political violence can be employed before a point of diminishing return is reached for both the user and the social order in which it is applied.[29]

THE IMPACT OF THE MASS MEDIA

Another important institution of social control that has special relevance for collective racial violence is the mass media. A debate on this issue has raged among social scientists since the early 1930's when the Payne Foundation underwrote a group of University of Chicago social scientists in the first large-scale study of the impact of the mass-media, in this case, the consequences of movies for young people.[30]

The mass media both reflect the values of the larger society and at the same time are agents of change and devices for molding tastes and values. It is a complex task to discern their impact because they are at the same time both cause and effect. Controversies about the mass media focus particularly on the issue of their contribution to crime and delinquency and to an atmosphere of lawlessness. Among social scientists, it is generally agreed that consequences of the mass media are secondary as compared with the influence of family, technology, and the organization of modern society. But differences in the meaning and importance attributed to this "secondary factor" among social scientists are great. "Secondary" can mean still important enough to require constructive social policy, or "secondary" can mean that a factor is trivial and unimportant.

Two separate but closely linked issues require attention. First, what are the consequences of the mass media, with its high component of violence, on popular attitudes toward authority and on conditioning and acceptance of violence in social relations? Second, what have been the specific consequences of the manner in which the mass media have handled escalated rioting since the period of Watts? The managers of the mass media run their enterprises on a profit basis and one result has been that the content of channels of communication, especially television, in the United States have a distinct "violence flavor" as contrasted with other nations. This content emphasis continued to persist as of the end of 1968 despite all the public discussion about this standard of the mass media.[31] In this respect, self-regulation of the mass media has not been effective except to some extent in the comic book industry.

In my judgment, the cumulative evidence collected by social scientists over the last 30 years has pointed to a discernible, but limited, negative impact of the media on social values and on personal controls required to inhibit individual disposition into aggressive actions. Other students of the same data have concluded that their impact is so small as not to constitute a social problem.

Many studies on media impact are based on limited amounts of exposure, as contrasted to the continuous expose of real life. Other studies made use of ex post facto sample surveys that are too superficial to probe the psychological depths of these issues. More recent research employing rigorous experimental methods has strengthened the conclusion that high exposure to violence content in the mass media weakens personal and social controls.[32] These new findings are based on probing fantasy and psychological responses of young people after exposure to violence content. They have special importance for lower class groups because of the high exposure of these groups to television. These lower class groups have less involvement in printed media, which has less violence material.

The issue runs deeper than the concentration of materials on violence in the mass media. It involves as assessment of the mass media's performance in disseminating a portrayal of the Negro and social change in depth. It also involves the access that the mass media extends to the creative talent of the Negro community. The Kerner Commission emphasized the lack of effective coverage of the problems of minority groups by the mass media and the absence of minority group members, especially Negroes, in operating and supervisory positions in these enterprises. The events of the riots and the recommendations of the Kerner Commission on this aspect of the mass media produced "crash" programs to recruit and train minority group personnel. The contents of the media have become more integrated, including advertising, and a long-run impact on public opinion is likely to be felt, especially in younger persons.

It is also necessary to assess the coverage of the riots themselves by television and the impact of this coverage on social control. For example, the National Advisory Commission on Civil Disorders sought to probe the immediate impact of the mass media coverage of the riots of the summer of 1967 both on the Negro community and on the nation as a whole. They commissioned a systematic content analysis study which, despite its quantitative approach, did not effectively penetrate the issue or even satisfy the Commission itself. The content study sought to determine if "the media had sensationalized the disturbances, consistently overplaying violence and giving disproportionate amounts of time to emotional events and militant leaders."[33] The conclusion was negative because of findings that, of 837 television sequences of riot and racial news examined, 494 were classified as calm, 262 as emotional, and 81 as normal. "Only a small proportion of all scenes analyzed showed actual mob action, people looting, sniping, setting fires or being killed or injured." In addition, moderate Negro leaders were shown on television more frequently than were militant leaders. Equivalent findings were reported for the printed media.

But such a statistical balance is no indicator of the impact of the presentation. Even calm and moral presentations of the riots could have had effect on both black and white communities; more certainly, persistent presentation of "hot" messages, even though they constitute only a part of the coverage, would have an impact. Therefore, the Commission modified and in effect rejected its own statistical findings and more appropriately concluded that (1) "there were instances of gross flaws in presenting news of the 1967 riots"; and (2) the cumulative effect was important in that it "heightened reaction." "What the public saw and read last summer thus produced emotional reactions and left vivid impressions not wholly attributable to the material itself." The Commission concluded that "the main failure of the media last summer was that the totality of its coverage was not as representative as it should have been to be accurate."

The national crisis produced by escalated riots warranted massive coverage according to existing standards of mass media performance. The coverage was so extensive that there was an imbalance in presentation of the total scene in the United States, and in particular, a failure to cover successful accomplishments by community leaders and law enforcement agencies. In fact, there were overtones in the coverage of racial violence which conformed to the "crime wave" pattern of news. The result was to bring into the scope of coverage violent events that would not have been reported under "normal" circumstances.

Television has served as the main instrument for impressing the grim realities of the riots onto the mass consciousness of the nation. On-the-spot reportage of the details of the minor riots and their aftermath was extensive and was buttressed by elaborate commen-taries. If the fullest coverage of these events is deemed to be necessary as a basis for developing constructive social policy, the costs of such media coverage should not be overlooked. It is impossible to rule out the strong contention that detailed coverage of riots has had an effect on potential rioters. Such a contention does not rest on the occasional instance in which the television camera focused on the riot scene and led either rioters or police to play to the television audience. Of greater importance is the impact of pictures of the rioting on a wider audience. Again we are dealing with a process of social learning, especially for potential participants. Rioting is based on contagion, the process by which the mood and attitudes of those who are actually caught up in the riot are disseminated to a larger audience on the basis of direct contact. Television images serve to spread the contagion pattern throughout urban areas and the nation. Large audiences see the details of riots, the manner in which people participate in them, and especially the ferment associated with looting and obtaining commodities which was so much at the heart of riot behavior. Television presents detailed information about the tactics of participation and the gratifications that were derived.

A direct and realistic account of the tactical role of the mass media, in particular television, can be seen from specific case studies, such as reported in depth by Anthony Oberschall on the Watts riot. He writes:

The success of the store breakers, arsonists, and looters in eluding the police can in part be put down to the role of the mass media during the riot week. The Los Angeles riot was the first one in which rioters were able to watch their actions on television. The concentration and movements of the police in the area were well reported on the air, better than that of the rioters themselves. By listening to the continuous radio and TV coverage, it was possible to deduce that the police were moving toward or away from a particular neighborhood. Those who were active in raiding stores could choose when and where to strike, and still have ample time for retreat. The entire curfew area is a very extended one.[34]

The media disseminate the rationalizations and symbols of identification used by the rioters. The mass media serve to reenforce and spread a feeling of consciousness among those who participate or sympathize with extremist actions, regardless of the actions' origins. In particular, television offers them a mass audience far beyond their most optimistic aspirations. Knowledge of the riot would spread in any case, but immediate extensive and detailed coverage both speeds up the process and gives it a special reality. On balance, I would argue that these images serve to reenforce predispositions to participate and even to legitimate participation. To be able to generate mass media coverage, especially television coverage, becomes an element in the motivation of the rioters. The sheer ability of the rioters to command mass media attention is an ingredient in developing legitimacy. In selected highbrow intellectual circles in the United States, a language of rationalization of violence has developed. The mass media serve to disseminate a popular version of such justification. The commentaries on television were filled with pseudo-sociological interpretations and the rioters themselves given ample opportunity to offer a set of suitable rationalizations.

In the past, when rioting was of the contested area variety, the newspapers were the major mass media. In many areas they developed an operational code, informally and formally, to deal with news about rioting. The practice was to apply an embargo on news about a riot during the actual period of the riot. After the event, it would be covered. The goal was to prevent the newspapers from serving as a means for mobilizing rioters, as was the case in the riots of Chicago in 1919. With the growth of television and an intensification of competition between the press and television, this practice broke down.

It is difficult to estimate the short- and long-term effects of the mass media portrayal of riots on white and Negro opinions. However, the riots projected a new element in the mass media imagery of the Negro, if only for a limited period of time. In the past, the mass media served to reenforce the system of segregation by casting the Negro exclusively in a minority position as well as by describing and characterizing him as weak. The portrait of the Negro as weak in the mass media served to mobilize and reenforce aggressive sentiments and emotions against these groups. The extremely prejudiced person is more disposed to release his aggression if he believes that the object of his aggression is too weak to respond to his hostile feelings and emotions.[35]

Since the end of World War II, the mass media have been helping to modify the imagery of the Negro and thereby to weaken the prejudiced symbolism. The advances of the Negro in economic, social, and political life have supplied a basis by which the mass media could project a more realistic and more favorable picture of the Negro. The reasoned and moral arguments in defense of racial equality by black and white leaders provide the subject for extensive editorial commentary in the mass media. Mass media images of the Negro were enhanced by the role of Negro troops in the Korean conflict and by the increasing presentation of the Negro as policemen. Regardless of Negro leadership opinion on the war in South Vietnam, the Negro soldier's role has served to modify in a positive direction the image of the Negro in both white and Negro communities. The early phase of the civil-rights movement, with its emphasis on orderly and controlled demonstrations, served also to altar the symbolism of the Negro from that of a weak, powerless figure. The climax of this phase of change, as presented by the mass media, was the dramatic March on Washington led by the late Dr. Martin Luther King, Jr. As an event in the mass media, it was unique. The national media were focused on a predominantly black assemblage moving in an orderly and powerful fashion. In a real sense, it was a symbolic incorporation of the Negro into American society, because of the heavy emphasis on religion and the setting in the nation's capital.

In the elimination of prejudiced imagery, the Negro in the United States obviously has had to face much greater psychological barriers than any other minority group. Hostility and prejudice formed on the axis of color runs deep. Nevertheless, the secular trend in negative stereotypes toward the Negro from 1945 to 1965 has showed a dramatic decline, and the mass media have had an effect in this trend.

Even in the absence of adequate psychological studies in depth, some speculation is possible about the image projected by the riots. The view of Negroes as a group growing in strength and direction was for the moment shattered. Instead, a partial image of explosive irrationality has been dramatized. The use of sheer strength for destructive purposes rather than to achieve a goal that the white population could define as reasonable and worthwhile has served only to mobilize counter hostility and counteraggression. No doubt these images fade away as the mass media focus on reporting in depth the realities of the black community and the processes of social change that are at work.

Thus, in conclusion, the history of the race riot is more than an account of the change from communal to commodity type conflict. It is more than the history of the gross inadequacies of the system of law enforcement and the limitations in the performance of the mass media. It is in part an answer to the question posed by Ralph Ellison, the Negro novelist, "But can a people live and develop for over three hundred years simply by reacting?"[36] The Negro outbursts have been more than a reaction to police brutality and a double standard of legal justice. In a symbolic sense, they are expressions of energies to participate in and transform the larger society. In all phases of life, the Negro is not merely reacting but acting.

NOTES

1. Chicago Commission on Race Relations, *The Negro in Chicago: A Study of Race Relations and a Race Riot* (Chicago: The University of Chicago; 1922). For another riot that has been

documented in depth, see Elliott M. Rudwick, *Race Riot at East St. Louis* (Carbandale: Southern Illinois University Press, 1964).

2. Allen D. Grimshaw, "Factors Contributing to Color Violence in the United States and Great Britain," *Race*, May 1962, p. 18. See also Robin M. Williams, "Social Change and Social Conflict: Race Relations in the United States, 1944-1964," *Social Inquiry*, Apr. 1965, pp. 8-25.

3. Allen D. Grimshaw, "Actions of Police and Military in American Race Riots," *Phylon*, Fall 1963, p. 288.

4. Stanley Lieberson and Arnold R. Silverman, "Precipitants and Conditions of Race Riots," *American Sociological Review*, Dec. 1965, pp. 887-898.

5. The Chicago Commission on Race Relations, *op. cit.*, p. 23.

6. See also Allen D. Grimshaw, "Lawlessness and Violence in the United States and their Special Manifestations in Changing Negro-White Relationships." *Journal of Negro History*, Jan. 1957, pp. 52-72.

7. See for example, Hans Mattick, "The Form and Content of Recent Riots," *Midway*, Summer 1968, pp. 3-32.

8. See Allen A. Silver, "Official Interpretations of Racial Riots," *Urban Riots: Violence and Social Change, Proceedings of the Academy of Political Science*, vol. XXIX, No. 1, July 1968, pp. 146-158.

9. Anthony Oberschall, "The Los Angeles Riot of August 1965," *Social Problems*, pp. 322-334.

10. Jules J. Wanderer, "1967 Riots: A Test of the Congruity of Events," *Social Problems*, Fall 1968, pp. 193-198.

11. National Advisory Commission on Civil Disorders, *op. cit.*, p. 180.

12. Arnold Katz, "Firearms, Violence and Civil Disorders," Stanford Research Institute, July 1968, p. 10.

13. Frank Zimring, "Is Gun Control Likely to Reduce Violent Killings?" *The University of Chicago Law Review*, Summer 1968, pp. 721-737.

14. Louis C. Goldberg, "Ghetto Riots and Others: The Faces of Civil Disorder in 1967," *Journal of Peace Research*, p. 120.

15. Robert M. Fogelson and Robert B. Hill, "Who Riots? A Study of Participation in the 1967 Riots," *Supplemental Studies for the National Advisory Commission on Civil Disorders*, July 1968, pp. 221-248.

16. *The Detroit Riot: A Profile of 500 Prisoners*, Department of Labor, Mar. 1968, 28 pp.

17. Anthony Oberschall, *op. cit.*, p. 335.

18. National Advisory Commission on Civil Disorders, *Supplemental Studies*, p. 239.

19. *Ibid.*, p. 89.

20. Anthony Oberschall, *op. cit.*, p. 329.

21. The National Advisory Commission on Civil Disorders, p. 73.

22. *Ibid.*, p. 243.

23. Morris Janowitz, *The Social Control of Escalated Riots* (Chicago: The University of Chicago Press, 1967).

24. *New York Times*, Mar. 13, 1969, p. 22.

25. *New York Times*, Sept. 29, 1968.

26. For a list and analysis of 25 reported sniping incidents in July and August 1968, see *Riot Data Review* (Lemberg Center for the Study of Violence), No. 3 (Feb. 1969), pp. 1-38.

27. See Harold Cruse, *The Crisis of the Negro Intellectual* (New York: William Morrow, 1967), pp. 347-401, for an analysis of the ideologies of violence in the black community.

28. Paul Blackstock, *The Strategy of Subversion* (Chicago: Quadrangle Books, 1964).

29. Paul Blackstock, "Anarchism, Manipulated Violence and Civil Disorder," unpublished manuscript, 1968.

30. See W. W. Charter, *Motion Pictures and Youth* (New York: Macmillan, 1933).

31. See *Christian Science Monitor*, Oct. 4, 1968 for details of a survey conducted by that newspaper's staff.

32. Leonard Berkowitz, Ronald Corwin, and Mark Heironimus, "Film Violence and Subsequent Aggressive Tendencies," *Public Opinion Quarterly*, vol. XXVII (Summer 1963), pp. 217-229.

33. National Advisory Commission on Civil Disorders, p. 202.

34. Oberschall, *op. cit.*, pp. 335-336.

35. For a discussion of this psychological mechanism, see Bruno Bettelheim and Morris Janowitz, *Social Change and Prejudice* (New York: The Free Press, 1964).

36. Ralph Ellison, *Shadow and Act* (New York: Random House, 1964), p. 315.

The Dilemma of the Urban Police

Current discussions of the problems of the American police seem fraught with paradox. While everyone seems to agree about remedies, criticisms of the police arise out of radically different conceptions of the police function. Some people see the police as the chief means of ending or reducing "crime in the streets"; others see them as an agency by which white society confines and suppresses black ghettos; still others view them as an organization caught on the grinding edge of a class conflict among competing standards of order and propriety. Yes despite these utterly disparate diagnoses, the prescribed treatment tends to be quite conventional and generally endorsed—higher salaries, better training, clearer policies, more modern equipment. And a further paradox: despite this apparent agreement on what should be done, little, in fact, happens. In some places, voters and politicians appear to be universally sympathetic to the needs of the police, but they are unwilling to appropriate more money to meet those needs. In other places, the extra funds have been spent but the criticisms remain—little, apparently, has changed.

One reason for this confusion or inaction lies, I believe, in the fact that the police perform a number of quite different functions. The controversies in which the police are embroiled reveal this as various disputants empha-size crime prevention, or law enforcement, or the maintenance of order, or political power. Liberty, order, legitimacy—important and fundamental values are in conflict. The adherents of various points of view take refuge in a common (and perhaps peculiarly American) set of proposals: spend money, hire better men, buy more things. I suspect that spending more money and hiring better men *are* essential to police improvement, but I also suspect that one reason so little extra money is spent and so few men are hired is that beneath our agreement on means, we remain in deep disagreement on ends. Spend the money on *what*, and *why*? What *is* a "better" policeman, anyway?

This is not a new issue. The history of the American municipal police is in great part a history of struggles to define their role in our society. What makes the controversy so intense today is only partly that it is linked to the question of race; indeed, in the past the police have repeatedly been in conflict with new urban migrants of whatever color. The reason for the heat generated by the police question is probably the same as the reason for the emotions aroused by the crime issue: we compare present circumstances with an earlier period when we thought we had solved the problem. Police behavior, like crime, was not a major issue

From *The Atlantic*, Vol. 223, No. 3 (March 1969), pp. 129-35. Reprinted by permission of the publisher. James Q. Wilson is Professor of Government at Harvard University and a former director of the Harvard-MIT Joint Center for Urban Studies.

in the 1940s and 1950s. When the police did become an issue, it was usually because a department was found to be corrupt, and that discovery produced a standard response—bring in a reform chief, reorganize the force, and get back to work.

CROOK CATCHERS

That work was law enforcement, or so it was thought. The job of the police was to prevent crime and catch crooks. Corruption was a serious problem because it seemed to mean that crime was not being prevented and crooks were not being caught. Organized criminals were buying protection, or petty thieves were putting in a "fix," or the police themselves were stealing on the side. Reforming a department not only meant ending corruption and alliances with criminals; it also meant improving training and developing new methods—more courses on crime detection, tighter departmental discipline to prevent misconduct, better equipment to facilitate getting to the scene of a crime and analyzing clues. When the public was invited to inspect a refurbished department, it was shown the new patrol cars, the new crime laboratory, the new communications center, and perhaps the new pistol range. The policeman was portrayed as a "crime fighter," and to an important degree, of course, he was.

But that was not all or even the most important thing he was. Given the nature of the crime problem, it was impossible for him to be simply a crime fighter. Most crime is not prevented and most criminals are not caught, even in the best-run, best-manned departments. Murder, for example, is a

"private" crime, occurring chiefly off the streets and among "friends" or relatives. No police methods can prevent it, and only general domestic disarmament, an unlikely event, might reduce it. Many, if not most, assaults are similarly immune from police deterrence. Most crimes against property—burglary, auto theft, larceny—are also crimes of stealth, and though the police might, by various means, cut the rate somewhat, they cannot cut it greatly because they cannot be everywhere at once. Street crimes—robberies, muggings, purse snatches—are more susceptible to police deterrence than any other kind, though so far few, if any, departments have had the resources or the community support to carry out a really significant strategy to prevent street crime.

The result of this state of affairs is that though some police departments are regarded as "backward" and others as "modern" and "professional," neither kind seems able to bring about a substantial, enduring reduction of the crime rate. If this is true, then the characterization of the police as primarily crime fighters places them in a potentially embarrassing position, that of *being judged by a goal they cannot attain.* In the 1950s, when crime rates were either stabilized or ignored, this awkward situation and the police response to it were not apparent.

What most policemen were doing even when they were being thought of as crime fighters was not so much enforcing the law as maintaining order. In a recent study, I have tried to show what makes up the routine workload of patrolmen, the police rank which has the largest number of men. The vast majority of police actions taken in response to citizen calls involve either providing a service (getting a cat out of a tree or taking a person to a hospital) or managing real or alleged conditions of disorder (quarreling families, public drunks, bothersome teenagers, noisy cars, and tavern fights). Only a small fraction of these calls involve matters of law enforcement, such as checking on a prowler, catching a burglar in the act, or preventing a street robbery. The disorders to which the police routinely respond are not large-scale. Riots and civil commotions are, in any given city, rare occurrences, and when they happen, the police act en masse, under central leadership. Rather, the maintenance of order involves handling disputes in which only two or three people participate and which arise out of personal misconduct, not racial or class grievances.

The difference between order maintenance and law enforcement is not simply the difference between "little stuff" and "real crime" or between misdemeanors and felonies. The distinction is fundamental to the police role, for the two functions involve quite dissimilar police actions and judgments. Order maintenance arises out of a dispute among citizens who accuse each other of being at fault; law enforcement arises out of the victimization of an innocent party by a person whose guilt must be proved. Handling a disorderly situation requires the officer to make a judgment about what constitutes an appropriate standard of behavior; law enforcement requires him only to compare a person's behavior with a clear legal standard. Murder or theft is defined, unambiguously, by statutes; public peace is not. Order maintenance rarely leads to an arrest;

law enforcement (if the suspect can be found) typically does. Citizens quarreling usually want the officer to "do something," but they rarely want him to make an arrest (after all, the disputants are usually known or related to each other). Furthermore, whatever law is broken in a quarrel is usually a misdemeanor, and in most states, an officer cannot make a misdemeanor arrest unless he saw the infraction (which is rare) or unless one party or the other will swear out a formal complaint (which is even rarer).

Because an arrest cannot be made in most disorderly cases, the officer is expected to handle the situation by other means and on the spot, but the law gives him almost no guidance on how he is to do this; indeed, the law often denies him the right to do anything at all *other* than make an arrest. No judge will ever see the case, and thus no judge can decide the case for the officer. Alone, unsupervised, with no policies to guide him and little sympathy from onlookers to support him, the officer must "administer justice" on the curbstone.

EARLY PATTERNS

In the nineteenth century, it was widely recognized that the maintenance of order was the chief function of the police. Roger Lane's informative history, *Policing the City: Boston, 1822-1885* (Cambridge: Harvard University Press, 1967), recounts how that department, the oldest in the United States, was first organized as a night watch to keep the peace in the streets. Beginning in 1834, men drafted from the citizenry were required to take their turns in seeing (as the governing statute required) "that all disturbances and disorders in the night shall be prevented and suppressed." Wild creatures, human and animal alike, were to be kept off the street, and a hue and cry was to be set up should fire or riot threaten.

The job of law enforcement—that is, of apprehending criminals who had robbed or burgled the citizenry—was not among the duties of the watchmen; indeed, it was not even among the duties of the government. A victim was obliged to find the guilty party himself. Once a suspect was found, the citizen could, for a fee, hire a constable who, acting on a warrant, would take the suspect into custody. Even after detectives—that is, men charged with law enforcement rather than the maintenance of order—were added to the force in the nineteenth century, they continued to serve essentially private interests. The chief concern of the victim was restitution, and to that end, the detectives would seek to recover loot in exchange for a percentage of the take. Detectives functioned then as personal-injury lawyers operate today, on a contingency basis, hoping to get a large part, perhaps half, of the proceeds.

Since in those days there was no law against compounding a felony, the detectives were free to employ any methods they wanted to recover stolen property. And with this as their mission, it is not surprising, as Lane notes, that the best detectives were those who by background and experience were most familiar with the haunts and methods of thieves.

The emergence of a municipal police force out of its watchmen antecedents was not so much the result of mounting crime rates as of growing levels of civil disorder. In time, and with the growth of the cities to a size and heterogeneity too great to permit the operation of informal social controls, the problem of order maintenance became too severe to make reliance on part-time or volunteer watchmen feasible. The Boston Police Department was created to deal with riots, as was the Department in Philadelphia. The Boston police first acquired firearms in the aftermath of the Draft Riot of 1863, though they were not fully armed at public expense until 1884.

The Philadelphia case is illustrative of many. Like Boston, that city relied on watchmen rather than an organized, quasimilitary constabulary. But a series of riots among youthful gangs (the Rats, the Bouncers, the Schuylkill Rangers, and the Blood Tubs, among several) persuaded the city fathers that stronger measures were necessary. To a degree, the riots were under semi-official auspices, thus magnifying the embarrassment the politicians faced. It seems that volunteer fire companies were organized to handle conflagrations. The young toughs who sat about waiting for fires to happen found this boring and, worse, unrewarding, whereupon some hit upon the idea of starting a fire and racing other companies to the scene to see who could put the blaze out more quickly, and just as important, who could pick up the most loot from the building. Though this competitive zeal may have been a commendable aid to training, it led to frequent collisions between companies speeding to the same fire, with the encounter often leading to a riot. It is only a slight exaggeration to say that the Philadelphia policemen were created in part to control the Philadelphia firemen.

SOMETIMES ON SUNDAY

The growth and formal organization of the police department did not, in themselves, lead to changes in function. The maintenance of order was still the principal objective. What did lead to a change was twofold: the bureaucratization of the detectives (putting them on salary and ending the fee system), and the use of the police to enforce unpopular laws governing the sale and use of liquor. The former change led to the beginning of the popular confusion as to what the police do. The detective became the hero of the dime novel and the cynosure of the public's romantic imagination; he, and not his patrolman colleague, was the "real" police officer doing "real" police work. Enforcing liquor laws caused the police to initiate prosecutions on their own authority rather than on citizen complaint, particularly in cases where the public was deeply divided regarding the wisdom of the law. In Philadelphia, enforcing the Sunday closing laws, especially with regard to saloons, was widely resented, and when the mayor ordered the police to do it, he was, according to a contemporary account, "caricatured, ridiculed, and denounced." In Boston Mayor Jonathan Chapman was led to remark that police enforcement of temperance laws had created a situation in which "the passions of men are aroused and the community is kept in a constant state of ferment."

What kept the police from being utterly destroyed by the liquor controversy was their determination to do no more than was absolutely necessary, given whatever regime was in power. Edward Savage, the able chief of the Boston force in the 1870s and 1880s, was a man of modest but much exercised literary talents, and in one of his better-known essays, entitled "Advice to a Young Policeman," he set forth the essential rule of good police work: "In ordinary cases, if you find yourself in a position of not knowing exactly what to do, better to do too little than too much; it is easier to excuse a moderate course than an overt act."

In addition, the police provided on a large scale a number of services to citizens, especially to those who, because of drink, indolence, or circumstance, were likely to become sources of public disorder. Roger Lane calculates that in 1856 the Boston police provided "lodgings" to over nine thousand persons, not including those who had been arrested for drunkenness. By 1860 the total exceeded seventeen thousand. Perhaps because the police were the principal city agency to witness the lot of the poor, perhaps because one of the original collateral duties of the police chief was superintendent of public health, the officers provided a wide range of services in addition to lodgings—coal for needy families, soup kitchens for the hungry, and jobs as domestics for girls they thought could be lured away from a life of prostitution.

In time, this service policy, which probably did much to mitigate the hostility between police and public occasioned by the enforcement of liquor laws, was curtailed on the complaint of the leaders of the organized charities who objected, apparently, to unfair competition. The advocates of "scientific charity," it seems, did not believe the police were competent to distinguish between the deserving and the undeserving poor.

The relations between police and public even during the period of free soup were not consistently amicable. One issue was the appointment of Irish police officers. For political purposes, the Boston Whigs demanded that, as we would say today, "representatives of indigenous and culturally-deprived groups" be added to the force. Then as now, the "culturally deprived" were responsible for a disproportionate share of those arrested for crimes. Then as now, the police objected to the appointment of an Irishman on the grounds that the man selected by the politicians was not qualified and had himself been arrested for a crime a few years earlier—it seems he had participated in a riot. The police, of course, denied that they were prejudiced but claimed that appointing a person on grounds of ethnicity would be destructive of morale on the force. The mayor insisted that the appointment take place. On November 3, 1851, the new man reported for work, announcing himself loudly and proudly as "Barney McGinniskin, fresh from the bogs of Ireland!"

THE CHIEF EVIL

By the end of the nineteenth century, the groundwork had been laid for the modern municipal police force, and for the modern problems of the police. The bureaucratization of the detectives and the police enforcement of liquor laws had not as yet overshadowed the order-maintenance function of the police, but two events of the twentieth century ensured that they would—Prohibition and the Depression. The former required the police everywhere to choose between being corrupted and making a nuisance of themselves; the latter focused public attention on the escapades of bank robbers and other desperadoes such as John Dillinger, Baby Face Nelson, and Bonnie and Clyde. Police venality and rising crime rates coincided in the public mind, though in fact they had somewhat different causes. The watchman function of the police was lost sight of; their law enforcement function, and their apparent failure to exercise it, were emphasized.

President Herbert Hoover did what most Presidents do when faced with a major political issue for which the solution is neither obvious nor popular—he appointed a commission. In 1931 the National Commission on Law Observance and Law Enforcement—generally known, after its chairman, as the Wickersham Commission—made its report in a series of volumes prepared by some of the ablest academic and police experts of the day. Though many subjects were covered (especially the question of whether immigrants were more criminal than native-born Americans), the volume on the police was of special importance. On page one, the first paragraph stated a twentieth-century conception of the police function and a new standard by which policemen were to be judged:

The general failure of the police to detect and arrest criminals guilty of the many murders, spectacular bank, payroll, and other hold-ups, and sensational robberies with guns, frequently resulting in the death of the robbed victim, has caused a loss of public confidence in the police of our country. For a condition so general there must be some universal underlying causes to account for it.

Now, of course there may have been some "universal underlying causes," but the ones that come readily to mind—Prohibition, post-war readjustment, and the economic cycle—were not ones about which a presidential commission could at that time speak very candidly. Besides, it was far from clear what could be done about at least the second and third of these causes. What was necessary was to find a "universal cause" about which something could be done. Needless to say, two groups on whom we have long felt free to cast blame for everything from slums to hoof-and-mouth disease—the police and the politicians—seemed appropriate targets. Accordingly, the Commission wrote:

The chief evil, in our opinion, lies in the insecure, short term of service of the chief or executive head of the police force and in his being subject while in office to the control of politicians in the discharge of his duties.

SOME PROPOSALS

Following on this analysis, the Commission detailed a number of specific proposals—putting the police on civil service, buying modern equipment ("the wireless"), and of course, hiring better men and giving them better training. In truth, there probably was a need for some police reforms; many departments had become dumping grounds for the fat relatives of second-rate politicians, and modern bank robbers were in many cases more mobile

and efficient than the police chasing them. But the "professional" view of the police went further than merely proposing changes in equipment and manpower; it argued in addition that since the police *can* prevent crime, if the crime rate gets out of hand, it is in good measure because the police are incompetent as a result of political influence.

Now, some members of the Commission were no doubt perfectly aware that the police do not cause crime, but, like many commissions anxious to make a strong public impression and generate support for desirable changes, they inevitably overstated the case in their report. A report that said that many improvements in police practice were necessary but that these improvements, if adopted, would have only a slight effect on the crime rate would not generate many headlines. (Thirty-seven years later, the Kerner Commission had not forgotten this lesson; what made the newspapers was not its proposals for action but its charge of "white racism.")

The consequences of assigning to the police a law-enforcement, crime-prevention function to the exclusion of anything else were profound. If the job of the police is to catch crooks, then the police have a technical, ministerial responsibility in which discretion plays little part. Since no one is likely to disagree on the value of the objective, then there is little reason to expose the police to the decision-making processes of city government. *Ergo,* take the police "out of politics." So powerful (or so useful) did this slogan become that within a few decades whenever a big-city mayor tried to pick his own police chief or take charge of his department for the purpose of giving it a new direction, *the police themselves* objected on the grounds that this was an effort to exercise "political influence" over the force.

Furthermore, if the technical objective of law enforcement was primary, then non-law-enforcement duties should be taken away from the police: no more soup kitchens; no more giving lodging to drunks; no more ambulance driving. These things are not "real police work." Let the police see the public only in their role as law enforcers. Let the public, alas, see the police only as adversaries. Of course, these changes were more in the public's mind than in everyday reality. If politics was taken out of the police, the police were not taken out of politics. They continued—in fact, with the decline of party machines, they increased —their involvement in electoral politics, city hall intrigue, and legislative lobbying. And whatever professional police leadership may have said, the patrolman on the beat knew that his job was not primarily law enforcement—he was still handling as many family fights and rowdy teen-agers as ever. But lacking support in the performance of these duties, he came also to believe that his job "wasn't real police work," and accordingly that it was peripheral, if not demeaning.

But perhaps the most important consequence was the police response to the public expectation that they could prevent crime. Their response was perfectly rational and to be encountered in any organization that is judged by a standard it cannot meet— they lied. If police activity (given the level of resources and public support available) could not produce a signifi-

cant decline in crime rates, police record-keeping would be "adjusted" to keep the rates in line. Departments judged by professional standards but not controlled by professional leaders were at pains to show progress by either understating the number of crimes or overstating the number of crimes "cleared" by arrest. Often this was not the policy of the chief, but the result of judging officers by crime and arrest records.

In the public's eye, the "hero cop" was the man who made the "good pinch." For a while (until the mass media abandoned the standards of the middle-aged and the conservative in favor of the standards of the young and the radical), the ideal cop was the "G Man." FBI agents, of course, are different from municipal police forces precisely because their task *is* law enforcement, and often enforcing important laws against quite serious criminals. Few special agents need to wade into a skid-row brawl. But within city departments, the emphasis on the "good pinch" grew. This was only partly because the newspapers, and thus the public, rewarded such accomplishments; it was also because the departments rewarded it. The patrolman could look forward, in the typical case, to remaining a patrolman all his life *unless* he could get promoted or be made a detective. Promotion increasingly came to require the passing of a written examination in which college men would usually do better than less articulate but perhaps more competent "street men." Appointment as a detective, however, was in many departments available to men with a good arrest record (or a strategically placed friend in headquarters). If you want to get away from drunks, kids, and shrews, then make a pinch that will put you in line for becoming a dick. Though there is in principle nothing wrong with rewarding men for having a good arrest record, one frequent result of this system has been to take the best patrolmen off the street and put them into a headquarters unit.

POLICE REFORM: THE CHOICES AHEAD

Today, the conception of the police role underlying the foregoing arrangements is being questioned. Perhaps the landmark event was the 1967 report of the President's Commission on Law Enforcement and Administration of Justice, the executive director of which was James Vorenberg of the Harvard Law School. Unlike the Wickersham or Kerner Commission reports, this document made relatively few headlines, and the reason, I think, was that it did not provide the reporters with a catchy slogan. The nine volumes of the Vorenberg report insisted that the problems of crime and police work are complicated matters for which few, if any, easy solutions are available. There were no dramatic scandals to uncover; the police "third degree" (on which the Wickersham Commission, in the report drafted by Zechariah Chafee, lavished much attention) had declined in occurrence and significance. Most police departments had been taken out of the control of party machines (in some cases, it would appear, only to be placed under the influence of organized crime). Instead, the Commission devoted considerable attention to the order-maintenance function of the police:

A great majority of the situations in which policemen intervene are not, or are not interpreted by the police to be, criminal situations in the sense that they call for arrest. . . . A common kind of situation . . . is the matrimonial dispute, which police experts estimate consumes as much time as any other single kind of situation.

The riots in Watts and elsewhere had, by the time the report appeared, already called the attention of the public to the importance (and fragility) of public order. The rise of demands for "community control" of various public services, including the police and the schools, has placed the problem of order on the political agenda. Whether the problems of managing disorder can best be handled by turning city government over to neighborhood groups is a complicated question. (Provisionally, I would argue that war becomes more, not less, likely when a political system is balkanized.) In any case, we have come full circle in our thinking about the function of the police.

Or almost full circle. The current anxiety about crime in the streets continues to lead some to define the police task as wholly or chiefly one of crime deterrence, and thus any discussion of redefining the police role or reorganizing police departments to facilitate performing their other functions tends to get lost in the din of charges and countercharges about whether or not the police have been "hand-cuffed." This is unfortunate, not because crime in the streets is a false issue (the rates of street crime, I am convinced, *are* increasing in an alarming manner), but because handling this problem cannot be left solely or even primarily to the police; acting as if it could raises false hopes among the citizens and places unfair and distorting demands on the police. At least as much attention to the courts and correctional systems will be necessary if much progress is to be shown in reducing street crime.

The simultaneous emergence of a popular concern for both crime and order does put in focus the choices that will have to be made in the next generation of police reforms. In effect, municipal police departments are two organizations in one serving two related but not identical functions. The strategy appropriate for strengthening their ability to serve one role tends to weaken their ability to serve the other. Crime deterrence and law enforcement require, or are facilitated by, specialization, strong hierarchical authority, improved mobility and communications, clarity in legal codes and arrest procedures, close surveillance of the community, high standards of integrity, and the avoidance of entangling alliances with politicians. The maintenance of order, on the other hand, is aided by departmental procedures that include decentralization, neighborhood involvement, foot patrol, wide discretion, the provision of services, an absence of arrest quotas, and some tolerance for minor forms of favoritism and even corruption.

There is no magic formula—no pre-packaged "reform"—that can tell a community or a police chief how to organize a force to serve, with appropriate balance, these competing objectives. Just as slogans demanding "taking the police out of politics" or "putting the police in cars" have proved inadequate guides to action in the past, so also slogans demanding "foot patrolmen" or "community control" are likely to prove inadequate in the future. One would like to think that since both points of view now have ardent advocates, the debate has at last been joined. But I suspect that the two sides are talking at, or past, each other, and not *to* each other, and thus the issue, from being joined, is still lost in rhetoric.

Planners in the Changing American City, 1900-1940

JOHN L. HANCOCK

THE MODERN CHALLENGE

If *planning* in the broadest sense is man's attempt not to displace reality but to clarify it and bring all of its elements into harmony with human purpose,[1] then the urban planner's task has changed enormously in the past few hundred years. Cities have been uniquely unequal, functional concentrations of such reality since late neolithic times— the nexus of what we call "civilization." But the reality of man's traditional societies is fast disappearing as he learns nature is not just "out there" but is everywhere a constantly modifying state he can partially manipulate to free himself of life chiefly dependent upon human and animal labor. In the emerging transitional societies where growth and change are the normal condition, modern reality finds not just a small percentage of mankind urbanized but a world urbanizing so rapidly that most of the population will be drawn into its orbit in this century. This means great change: not discovery of preconditions for group life, but sustained mechanization, surplus economic growth, and social investment already bringing undreamed material comfort, intensive specialization, fragmentation and "leisure" for a third of the world; not hierarchial social division in segmented if similar containers but egalitarian, pragmatically interwoven diversity; not fatalistic acceptance of one's lot but "rising expectations."[2] It means demand for new balances of community, wealth, health, beauty, privacy, identity and so on, promoting not only cultural survival, adaptability and modification, but also human enrichment. In such fluid times a "plan" is tyranny and no planning is madness. Planning becomes an agent *for enhancing life* in an ever-changing but massing world—or it is nothing.

In this context, planning's alignment with American urban policy appropriately began with AIP's charter members in the reform decade before World War I, when the nation first confronted its "new" converging culture. The city, they said, was physically urbanized but not democratically organized. "There seems to be a sort of fatalism in American cities which compels them to follow mechanically a system once inaugurated no matter what it may be," an uncontrolled spread of cities "unusually inconvenient, insanitary, wasteful, ugly, degrading, inefficient."[3] They were not the first to say so; but in adopting reformer views of cities as dynamic *human* systems whose welfare could be partially guided and enhanced by willful public action, they were the first to propose that the means include "the new social ideal of unified and comprehensive city planning."[4] Reinforced by events to 1940, the pioneer planners were instrumental in making their ambitious proposal the very essence of modern American urban policy—in theory. In fact, however, while they had

From *Journal of the American Institute of Planners*, Vol. XXXIII, No. 5 (September 1967), pp. 290-304. Reprinted by permission of the publisher. John L. Hancock is Associate Professor of Urban Planning at the University of Washington.

found the proper focus for our times, their record in developing it through several decades of reform and change exposes still unreconciled social aims and cultural practices in urban America.

THE AMERICAN CITY SURFACE, 1800-1940

Historic American civilization is a classic example of continuing surface change. Following the initial breakdown of traditional western society, the United States prospered in material growth and suffered much societal displacement in the 15 generations separating colonial clearings from the cities of 1900. As compared to 1790, the nation was 19 times more populous, had 72 times as many urban places (doubling per decade in the period 1840-70 when manufacturing's value began exceeding agriculture's in the gross national product), covered a domain three times as large crossed in 102 hours by train or minutes by wire. It had attained the world's highest mean (not minimum) living standard, the highest population growth rate (1800-1910) and perhaps the most blurred socially mobile society.

In the profession's early years to 1940, the GNP would quadruple again; urban places and wages double; the average work week reduce a full day; cross-country travel time reduce to a day; public works spending would extend from transportation and communication to utilities, reclamation-conservation, streets-highways, and housing-community development. Urban space needs would more than double and keep changing in character as innovations like the automobile (the largest industry by 1929) helped stimulate the construction industry (next largest), and altered town form and the whole technological net.[5]

Yet amid bountiful natural, technological, and human resources, the American *manner* of settlement and the values associated with it were profoundly disruptive, especially before the 1900's. Under pragmatically developing Crown and federal encouragement of towns "Fittest for such as can trade into England" and "for a rising nation, spread over a wide and fruitful land, traversing all the seas with the rich productions of her industry . . . advancing rapidly to destinies beyond the mortal eye," urban policy was merely commercial-expansionist, permitting any local standards and practices not in conflict with mercantile contracts or democratic constitutions from which the towns derived their charters. Thus, all cities were political wards of Crown and then states, which were loathe to broaden local powers but encouraged *de facto* sources of growth. The cities all flourished according to their ability to secure external power, market, and supply. All were dominated by profit-minded oligarchies following "settle and sell, settle and sell" boom-bust practices in pursuing growth at whatever social costs. In Andrew Carnegie's words, "The American . . . need not fear the unhealthy or abnormal growth of cities. . . . The free play of economic laws is keeping all quite right. . . . Oh, these grand, immutable, all-wise laws of natural forces, how perfectly they work if human legislators would only let them alone."[6] Most did, while pursuing happiness by a reversed golden rule.

In this narrow milieu, environmental needs—civic, health, family, personal, and so forth—were subordinated to developmental ones, usually economic, in the carrying through of "city plans" too. The fact that Savannah's plan was so rigidly maintained by her philanthropist sponsors in England despite resident demands for change (they were forbidden to sell or even to profit from the land, for example) suggests in part why she was the least prosperous, least populous colonial city by the Revolution. In contrast, Philadelphia, desiccating her "greene countrie towne" plan, became the largest, most influential commercial city in the colonies and early Republic. Similarly, planning in the best of several hundred proprietor towns built between 1775 and 1906 fell apart in a generation by inability or unwillingness of the sponsors to control peripheral or later internal growth as at Lowell, whereas those paternalists who maintained planning control but failed to anticipate or permit resident desires to flourish economically and politically suffered a similar fate in town development. (As Richard Ely said of Pullman, "It is a benevolent, all-wishing feudalism which desires the happiness of the people in such a way as shall please the authorities.") Thus American developers characteristically rejected comprehensive plans altogether and used an exploitable grid core of streets and plats—in all 50 of the SMA's of 1900 and 95 per cent of today's metro cores. The common pattern in some 200 such cities by 1900 was of identical lots, 20 to 40 per cent substandard housing with dense tenantry near the center, long before the elevator and steel frame made it so dramatic. There were few permanent open spaces or neighborhood foci. There was grade-level high speed movement on main streets well before rapid transit and cars quadrupled urban travel (1890-1920), preferential location for high-paying commercial-industrial functions, permissive public controls (little municipal land ownership), sprawling peripheral growth—these were

all superimposed on unaesthetic "once-for-all" plans without adequate provision for systematic revision or extension in advance of settlement.[7] Simple to lay out, describe, convert to many uses, and extend, the stark grid of public-private origins unquestionably was yesterday's most adaptable American plan—a meritorious one for limited purposes.

Thus, the booming city did not arise from the culture floor while our backs were turned and we were tending our gardens. As an emergent development *process*, however, it bespoke the futility of rigid *a priori* and *laissez-faire* approaches or the abnegation of direction for fluid situations—and the difficulty of trying anything else.

PRESSURE FOR REORGANIZATION AND REFORM

The haphazard physical growth and social disorder accompanying American urban development, however, stimulated increasing demands for amenity, systematic physical reorganization and social reform which preceded and helped shape the modern planning movement. Physical design by the nineteenth century's new architects and landscape architects, for example, gradually assumed "comprehensive dimension, moving beyond the context of *unit* into that of *system*." Public gardens appeared about the time that Timothy Dwight urged places where "inhabitants might always find sweet air, charming walks, fountains refreshing the atmosphere, trees encircling the sun . . . objects 'found' in the country" (1821); naturalistic suburbs and *cul-de-sac* streets by the 1830's; in-city parks by the 1850's; boulevards and garden towns, idyllic leisure-class resorts and planned industrial communities by the 1870's; metropolitan park systems by the 1890's and civic centers by the 1900's. The "utopian" Mormons put 49 agricultural-industrial satellite communities around Salt Lake City using cooperative public-private methods to establish their broad streets, superblocks focused on major cultural buildings, and reclamation of a theocratic region covering the most desolate third of the nation before federal intervention. Indeed, Robert Gourlay even recommended that the Boston "district" adopt a "science of city planning" implemented by existing public powers for large-scale land reclamation, separation of major localities by green areas, and rail ties to the hub. This was a generation before Horace Bushnell (1864), urging a "new city planning profession" of specially trained men to devise "breathing spaces" without inhibiting future needs, asked why the city should "be left to the misbegotten planning of some operator totally disqualified? . . . Nothing is to be more regretted . . . than that our American nation, having a new world to make, and a clean map on which to place it, should be sacrificing our advantage so cheaply. . . ."

More characteristic of the mainstream was designer-booster collaboration on the "city beautiful" at the Chicago world's fair (1893) whose neoclassical plan, reflecting pools, greenstrips, statuary, massive buildings, macadem roads, electrification, and hidden utilities well illustrated coordinator Daniel Burnham's remark that "Beauty has always paid better than any other commodity." Convinced that physical order equalled social order, viewers went home to plan more fairs and to plant, paint, clean, and partially rebuild their cities. The

first was Washington itself which, under the McMillan Commission, secured a Park Commission (1895); District Highway Plan (1896); the first enforceable (but not enforced) building heights and zoning laws (1899); a Planning Committee under Burnham, Frederick Law Olmsted, Sr., and others (1901); and "mapped streets" (1900-06).[8] There were just a few such works before 1900, however, most of them backed by wealthy private sponsors rarely able to continue such revitalization by themselves.

The social reformers' broader search was similar in its increasing comprehensiveness and expertise. Theodore Parker advocated planned "industrial democracy" featuring low-rent housing, and improved work and health standards in the 1830's, a generation before organized civic interest in tenement reform, public health, and migrant population control (encouraging "normal distribution in town and country," reduction of urban densities, and so on—a kind of stay-on-the-land movement in contrast to the unsuccessful "back-to-the-land" resettlement efforts of the 1900-1940 period). After the Civil War a rising chorus of voices rose with those of Henry George and Edward Bellamy to promote an "economizing of social forces"; with "Golden Rule" Jones, other reform mayors and the National Municipal League (1894) to obtain more democratic local government; and with those of Richard Ely, Simon Patten, Albion Small, and others in a few universities to secure serious urban study and research on the "new America." On the grand scale perhaps, Henry D. Lloyd (lawyer, social critic, administrator, and teacher) put many of these ideas together in his proposal to raze and transform central Chicago into a permanent cultural park focus for a regional "No Mean City" of self-contained urban-rural towns built on the latest garden city, cooperative, condemnation, and electrification methods in 1899.[9]

The merger of these interests with the more prosaic, somewhat remedial, but decidedly militant national reforms of the next generation signaled the real beginning of responsible social change in modern America. The period's very name—the *progressive era*, 1906-16 (variously dated 1900-19)—indicated the demand for orderly forward transition to a world of "social justice," "social welfare," and, as John Dewey said of the era's greatest challenge, "the possibility of constructive social engineering." It demanded that these assume primacy in the quest for human progress. The ideological response to the popular demands was a clear YES.[10] The measureable results were basic change in mood and a small but crucial reorganization of mixed-enterprise democracy, which has since broadened in scale if not purpose.

THE PROFESSION EMERGES, 1907-19

The mood and means were of vital significance to the planning profession. Progressive Republicans, reform Democrats, Socialists, and nonpartisans who had led in securing state-legislated local government changes, such as home rule, new charters, reapportionment, and so forth, also brought in the first "expert planning advisors" to lecture, show slides of work elsewhere, and in several hundred cases to survey and/or replan their cities—to show people how to rebuild cities. Given the city's increasing predominance, a *laissez-faire* past more blundering than purposeful in human

terms, and faith that man must plan (though no one really knew how) in times changing more rapidly than anyone comprehended, the era's mandate for renewal fairly cried for a new profession of urban specialists. Was the mandate important? In Franklin D. Roosevelt's words on first hearing of planning (1909), "I think from that moment on I have been interested in not the mere planning of a single city but in the larger aspects of planning. It is the way of the future."[11]

Aside from a few inspiring piecemeal reports prior to 1906, there were no surveys, general planning, or professional planners as such, and as John Nolen later recalled, "no knowledge of, no interest in city planning among the people generally." Between 1907 and 1917 over 100 towns undertook "comprehensive planning"—half the 50 largest cities, 13 per cent of all with populations over 10,000. Ninety-seven municipal planning commissions and two dozen zoning codes were enabled in a few urban states. By 1917 there were dozens of municipal information clearing houses, a shelf of technical literature, and three planning-oriented magazines "to record knowledge of intelligently and earnestly and systematically planned cities" and "the history of municipal science in the making." Eleven universities offered 23 courses on planning "principles" (subordinated to other curricula); two others gave courses on the "Economics of City Planning" and "Urban Sociology." There were four annual urban conferences (one devoted specifically to planning) plus an international meeting, planning divisions in the other design professions, and an American City Planning Institute. By the war's end practically every urban interest group in the country called for an urban cabinet post or a "Federal Bureau of Municipal Information" collating and distributing "all urban information . . . instead of confining it solely to planning."[12] The art and science of planning as a force in urban reform policies was clearly underway, then, in the progressive era.

The pivotal inaugural year was 1909 when the first National Conference on City Planning and the Problems of Congestion convened at Washington with representatives from health, housing, law, social work, engineering, gardening, real estate, government, philanthrophy, conservation, architecture, landscape architecture, and so on, all calling for reform. Supported thereafter by the Russell Sage Foundation, NCCP (last part of title having been dropped in 1910) became the chief forum for bringing the movement's emergent elements together and broadcasting them in its publications (for example, *City Plan*, 1915). It met in different cities each year (in Washington once during each new administration). Most importantly for the new profession, NCCP's executive and program committees were dominated by planners who used this forum to fashion their common social commitments and systematic technical approaches into a viable pattern for urban redevelopment. "What is needed in city planning?" asked Nolen, the 1909 keynoter:

Everything . . . a wiser husbanding of our aesthetic and human as well as natural resources . . . legislation that meets more meaningfully the needs of twentieth century life . . . using to our advantage science, art, skill and experience. . . . [but above all] We should no longer be content with mere increases in population and wealth. We should insist upon asking, "How do the people live, where do they work, what do they play?"

In 1910 NCCP president Frederick Law Olmsted, Jr., called this approach "the new social ideal of unified and comprehensive city planning":

City planning, applied with common sense and with due regard for human limitations of time and place, has a breadth and ramification at once inspiring and appalling. Any mind with sufficient imagination to grasp it must be stimulated by this conception of the city as one great social organism whose welfare is in part determined by the action of the people who compose the organism today, and therefore by the collective intelligence and good will that control those actions.

By 1911 president Charles Mulford Robinson called it the "science of city planning"—a decided shift from his earlier views (see *Modern Civic Art*, 1903). Beautification was not discussed as a major NCCP topic between 1910-20 but "planning" (rather than "plan" or "plan-making"), "system," "efficient and intelligent public controls," the "ordinary citizen," and the "common welfare" became commonplace in the idiom. Remarkably free of dogma, the planners were chiefly interested in "comprehensive planning." They discussed it as a major topic in seven of the meetings between 1910-20 along with continuing discussion of its "elements": financing and administration, zoning-planning law, and official commission practices; streets, transportation, industrial, recreation and land planning; "limited dividend" (4 per cent) low-cost housing (public-private); minimum standards (some via "model" studies); the merits of particular plans and useful European practices.[13] Finally, as the war began, they created the American City Planning Institute, a professional division within NCCP whose object "shall be to study the science and advance the art of city planning." ACPI gave full membership to trained professionals and to "others who shall have special attainments in city planning," associate membership with voting privileges to related non-professionals (no more than four of whom could sit on the 21-man Board of Governors) and a few (rare) honorary memberships.[14]

The systematization of these elements was a gradual process, of course. James Sturgis Pray introduced his seminal "Principles of City Planning" class into the landscape curriculum at Harvard in 1909, the year that Patrick Abercrombie opened the School of Civic Design at Liverpool. Benjamin Marsh's textbook *Introduction to City Planning* the same year urged government responsibility ("the most important element") for the common health and welfare, stressed housing, and termed planning "the most efficient method of projecting municipal efficiency." The planners got a most vital new perspective and preplanning tool from Shelby Harrison and Paul Kellogg's *Pittsburgh Survey* (1907-09, published 1914), whiched mapped data on population, traffic, health, housing, building (location-condition-use), property values, assessments, areas served by schools, and so on. It also appended legal-fiscal suggestions for public planning from such data. On the other hand, the most famous planning report of 1909 was Daniel Burnham and Edward Bennett's magnificently rendered, vaguely regional *Plan of Chicago*, which "quite frankly takes into consideration the fact that the American city, and Chicago preeminently, is a center of industry and traffic." It merely saluted housing needs, termed planning inexpensive (not requiring large public expenditure, taxation, or public control) but stressed

(and proved) that "aroused public sentiment; and practical men of affairs" could secure new traffic, park, and building programs giving "unity and dignity" to the city.[15]

Most comprehensive reports and several texts incorporated all these elements into the planning process by 1916. The reports, for example, generally had three major parts—preplanning surveys (mapping of physical, economic, and social data), a "General Plan" with detailed parts, and appended methods of implementation. Sometimes the latter were put into the main text for emphasis. Some surveys included evidence of the city's historic "individuality" (its achievements and deficiencies in land use, for example) so that planner and public alike might "frame a concept, an ideal of what we wish the city to be" and make it a controlling factor in the plan's development. Most specific suggestions for implementation urged better employment of existing law, more home rule and degrees of municipal authority approaching those in Europe. Few suggested planning was inexpensive or short term. ("At bottom the question is whether real values are to be had from this sort of city planning, and whether the community can provide the ways and means necessary to purchase these values.") Most spoke of spending efficiently and the major reports encouraged "equitable distribution of current taxes," increased borrowing capacity, extended bonded periods, municipal condemnation "with a much larger share for the community in increasing land values," and special tax and land incentives to encourage large-scale, low-cost housing development. No two plans were alike but the basic idea was to modernize and broaden public uses by opening up and decentralizing the city where possible so as to promote environments "having a more sensitive regard for the common welfare . . . past, present and future."

Recommendations thus included differentiated building zones and street flow, overall circulatory flow, landscaped "gateways" (such as waterfronts) for public uses, park systems covering "at least 10 per cent of the city area," rerouting or elimination of grade-level transit traffic (transit systems were encouraged in larger cities), economic "zones" (blocks) but mixed income neighborhoods (new ones grouped in park-like settings around shops or schools on the city's edges to further break the grid and reduce unplanned encroachment), downtown core of facilities, and rather formal civic groupings from which major streets radiated to the various sub-centers.[16] In a more abstract, technical manner, Robinson's *City Planning* detailed thoroughfare and residential platting standards in advance of settlement; Nelson Lewis' *Planning the Modern City* concentrated on traffic circulation and control standards, drawing heavily from his experience with New York's influential "building districts" (zoning) report; NML's *Town Planning for Small Cities* by Charles Bird (manufacturer and major Progressive Party figure in Massachusetts) recommended the reorganization of several towns of 30,000 people or less into regional districts by garden city planning principles; and NML's *City Planning* (1917) by 18 authors under Nolen, brought all such "Essential Elements of a City Plan" into one text spelling out "lines of investigation, planning and control which have been found most sound in theory and most successful in practice." These texts emphasized planning's flexibility and al-

ternatives, suggesting minimums for local work but discouraging universal, textbook solutions. They simultaneously looked toward "scientific exactness." As George Ford said in his essay on the socioeconomic factors in planning:

Satisfactory methods can be arrived at only by applying modern scientific methods. It is now realized that the city is a complex organism, so complex that no doctor is safe in prescribing for it unless he has made a thorough-going and impartial diagnosis of everything that may have even the remotest bearing on the case.[17]

If there was a definite system in this work by 1917, however, there was as yet more hope than adequate empirical data for making meaningful generalizations for this inexact science.

Who were the collaborators? All were originally trained in other fields; some formed temporary teams or permanent offices for major projects (like Ford and E. P. Goodrich's Technical Advisory Corporation). Several were Europeans working extensively in North America (like Edward Bennett, Thomas Adams, and Werner Hegemann). The 18 NML authors, for example, were almost all urban-born, lectured in the universities, wrote extensively, traveled abroad regularly, and half had worked or studied (half having at least one degree from Harvard or MIT) under men whose work was largely done before ACPI was formed. By training, their breakdown into two architects, four lawyers, five landscape architects, six engineers, a realtor, a civic reform leader, and a professor of social ethics (housing specialist) parallels that of ACPI's original 75-man roster in the first two membership categories—10 architects, 12 lawyers, 18 landscape architects, 23 engineers, 6 realtors and 7 others—with leadership unevenly divided. (Beginning with Olmsted, Sr., most ACPI presidents through 1942 were originally trained in landscape architecture or engineering.) While questions of training, ethics and leadership were frequent, however, all agreed that a "planner" was defined by his experience and focus, not by special training.[18]

In 1917 when the mood was much greater than the means for planning, actual practices were very primitive, even those that were official. Judging from 250 accounts, the work usually began with a lecture or preplanning survey of needs and opportunities in which the planner sought local support —public or private (usually a civic or commercial group, occasionally a wealthy patron). If mutually agreeable, a contract was signed making the planner responsible for all plan preparations and the sponsor responsible for eventual adoption and enforcement. This step often involved forming a larger "amalgamated" citizen group to clarify goals, assist the technical staff, review detail proposals, secure an official commission with "advisory powers," and push for planning throughout the city. During the next two to three years, field representatives collected data, encouraged the movement, reported back on its pulse, and sometimes lived in the area. The home office made all basic decisions, did the final drafting, and then presented the general program for local acceptance after an appropriate publicity program. If the plan was adopted, the planner also encouraged implementation, periodic review and cooperation with other communities (particularly contiguous ones) in the urban region. His firm often performed partial services as well—having contracts for park systems, subdivisions, campuses, industrial districts, housing programs, addi-

tional surveys not followed up and so on. The Nolen office (the largest firm between 1915 and 1925), for example, had contracts in 200 cities of which 10 were for new towns and 29 for comprehensive replanning rather evenly distributed in five basic groupings from towns of 10,000 or less to metropolitan areas of 1.5 million people or more. Less than half of the plans were implemented, a third of these with any degree of fullness—a fair average in the whole period to 1940.[19]

The climax of these early activities was the federal "emergency" wartime housing-town planning program, finally combining the expertise, standards, aims, large resources *and* public powers necessary for realization. Planner-directed teams collaborated on 67 projects averaging 25 acres in size, abandoned the grid and alleys where possible, introduced the latest technical standards, sought harmonious variety (house styles and groupings, plantings, street patterns, and so forth), preserved natural features, developed the land in large pieces to avoid economic waste and to increase pedestrian convenience, and grouped major buildings to give "definite center and point to the whole design." They did such an excellent job from the resident's point of view that there was a waiting line for purchase or occupancy up to World War II, while Congress and realtors called them "too costly" for war workers and disbanded the incompleted experiment with alacrity at the war's end. As Olmsted, Jr., saw "the very valuable lesson":

We have been convinced not only theoretically but by practical experience, that the cooperation of all those who have special knowledge in the arrangement, construction and running of towns is essential to any real "town planning" and that it is per-

fectly possible to bring about the cooperation and to apply it efficiently in actual
work.

For many of the younger collaborators
too, this experience provided "a tremendous enthusiasm to build a new and
better world," as Clarence Stein said of
himself and Henry Wright.[20]

Thus, the profession had taken some
long first steps by 1919, even if they
were steps that needed more complete
public authorization and more versatile
and imaginative planner conceptualization by today's standards. There were
definite physical changes too,—a park
system, a low-cost housing program,
better circulation, an active public
agency, occasionally all of these in one
city—but, most importantly, there was a
new intent behind this work, a new
standard of measurement. As Harland
Bartholomew put it in 1917, "The welfare of the group is . . . now generally
considered to supercede the *rights of
the individual* when questions of health,
safety and general welfare arise."[21]

FLUX AND FLOW, 1920-40

But moods change, as was indicated in
the sharp tensions distinguishing urbanization's spread in the period 1920-40.
Bracketed by wars, the opening years
assumed "prosperity" and "normalcy"
obtained with minimal public direction,
while the latter ones affirmed—perhaps
conclusively—the lie in merely voluntary
subscription to modern social responsibilities and again advanced broadly empowered public-private unions to enhance, if not insure, them. Influenced
by both attitudes, the profession's markedly improved technical, legislative,
and conceptual approaches to urban,
regional, and national problems were
more theoretical than tested until the
mid-1930's.

Cities which had begun planning
earlier were quickest to resume and expand. Major reports now commonly included more sophisticated handling of
social data, zoning and land use maps
(late 1930's), capital improvement
budgets (late 1920's), and detail and
alternate plan proposals within the
"Master Plan"—the new name for general or comprehensive plans. They were
increasingly supported by empirical research in the profession (see for example the *Harvard City Planning Series,* 1931 ff.), the social sciences and
federal reports making possible more
exacting scientific generalizations. *But
the record and manner of public acceptance in the 1920's was no better or
essentially different, however "official."*
Approximately one-fifth of the thousand
city planning, zoning and housing reports made in this decade—three times
as many as in the preceding one—were
actually followed through to any degree; over 95 per cent of the general
plans made were by private firms,
though now generally under city contract. Most firms were larger. They
periodically revised survey and planning data, sometimes left a field man
as local commission head, dropped
mixed transportation recommendation
(for example, rapid transit) in favor of
automated traffic planning almost exclusively, and perhaps under pressure
to be "practical" said less about the
common welfare in adjusting to what
clients would accept. Typical of the
general case, according to several studies, the largest firm (Bartholomew Associates, after 1925) dropped housing
altogether (1923-36), obscured the
priority of community over private
rights, emphasized physical elements
alone, and fitted local situations to general standards (for example, popula-

tion, density, traffic projection) which were sometimes not flexible enough to suit rapid modern changes, although its chief remained critical of these trends (except the last) "outside the confines of his business contracts."[22]

An era affects its planners then, as everyone else. (Even Walter Lippmann wrote in 1927 that "the more or less unconscious and unplanned activities of businessmen are for once more novel, more daring and in general more revolutionary than the theories of the progressives." *Men of Destiny*. New York: Macmillan, 1927.) Consider the permissively drawn and coordinated legislative "progress." By 1935 every state had planning, zoning, plat control, or all of these written into its organic law. Public planning commissions rose from 297 in 1919 to be included in all but two of the larger cities (over 100,000 people) plus hundreds of others by 1934—95 per cent of them official, the reverse of 1919. But only a fifth had comprehensive plans, few were applying them, most were powerless advisory bodies composed of citizens often serving without pay or understanding. Massachusetts, the first state to require planning commissions (1913) had 97 by 1929, but 80 cities, including Boston, still lacked plans. Before the court approved Euclid Village's comprehensive zoning code (building and land use, height-bulk-density in "reasonable" and "substantial" relation to community safety, health, welfare, and "morals") in 1926, only 76 cities had zoning ordinances. By 1936, 1,322 or 85 per cent of the cities had them, but less than half were comprehensive, and the cities (not compelled to zone) often used them to perpetuate *status quo* discrimination and whim. Extra-territorial plat control (up to five miles, based on ACPI guidelines) permitted planning along topographical as well as jurisdictional lines in half the states by 1929, but only a few cities adopted it, almost none in conformance with master plans. Planners approved the potential significance of these legal developments but protested their loose application and the tendency to adopt zoning *in lieu of* planning. Realtors, however, were enthusiastic after some initial doubts and real estate actually emerged as "the last great individualistic American enterprise" long after industry and finance had become large-scale, mixed corporate operations. Indeed into the early depression, national administrations urged Americans to "lay plans for making plans," provided occasional models and left everything else to local good will because "at present . . . this phrase represents a social need rather than a social capacity." Thus implementation and coordination were difficult at best, apathy was common, and expediency certain. The result, in Thomas Adams' phrase, was "city-mending."[23]

Partly because of such frustrations amid growing needs, the profession did sharpen its training, roles, and theories. With programs still subordinated to other curricula in the 80 schools (1925) offering or requiring planning courses, Harvard initiated a master's degree in Landscape Architecture in City Planning, published *City Planning Quarterly* (forerunner of the *Journal*) in 1925, and, with a Rockefeller Foundation grant, inaugurated a full three-year School of City Planning under Henry Hubbard in 1929. Columbia, Cornell, and MIT also granted the MCP degree by 1940. In courses the planner's "role" was now described as analyst, creative artist, critic, and coordinator having above all . . . the social and civic welfare point of view, for the motive back of all city and regional planning is to improve the daily life and working conditions—to develop the "good life" . . . a difficult and elaborate process . . . [requiring] the wisdom of Solomon, the heart of a prophet, the patience of Job, and the hide of a rhinoceros.

In the new civil service category of "city planner" (created for the National Capitol Park and Planning Commission with ACPI help in 1926), the role demanded a man or woman (age 25-55) university graduate in landscape architecture with "at least five years of responsible and successful experience" or equivalent scholarship to head a staff preparing plans, recommendations, and regulations for an awesome number of physical "and other proper elements of city and regional planning." (Charles Eliot II received the first appointment.) The profession's growing belief that this was an increasingly specialized task may be seen in its exclusion of the new profession of public administrators from ACPI membership in 1924 and, as the renamed American Institute of Planners, its total separation from NCCP in 1934. NCCP (also keeping administrators off its executive board) then merged with ACA to become the American Planning and Civic Association, and the administrators formed under Walter Blucher (1935) into the American Society of Planning Officials. Thus, a mixed urban alliance divided into four rather specialized policy groups (including NML), with planners the only group eligible for all four memberships.[24]

The profession's most notable innovations in this period, however, had to do with broadening the concept of man's environment, its future and its planning. Adding psycho-biological to the earlier socioeconomic considerations of well-being, the enlarged views held that the search for and growth of individuality and diversity were as vital to existence in massing society as commonality of rights and opportunities. Refusing to plan from statistical projections or the noblest historic examples alone, the planners became less harsh in their blending of scientific and humanistic wisdom, perhaps less certain about future needs but certainly much concerned with the importance of the immediate, of what happens today, in getting there. Thus, Lewis Mumford urged NCCP in 1927 to develop "new social instruments and policies on a regional rather than an urban scale" which did not lead merely to more mechanized or congested cities. The planner's idiom increasingly contained such metaphors as "symbiosis," "human-scale," and "flow" (Mumford); the natural region," and "living" rather than "making a living" (Benton MacKaye); "excessive concentration [not as synonymous with congestion but] . . . as a psychological as well as economic and physical problem," and having "a more natural biological life under pleasanter and more natural conditions . . . to enjoy life itself." (Nolen)[25]

Several dozen elaborate experimental studies and abbreviated works resulted from these emphases. For example, Arthur Comey proposed "city-state" planning for three major cities joined by "interstate" freeways and arterial routes to surrounding towns, all separated by greenbelts, with population growth "automatically controlled" along the freeways until the region's "natural" limits had been reached. MacKaye preferred a smaller optimum-size (50,000 people each), "regional" city exercising conservation (natural, technical, human) and "commodity-flow" control in concert with requirements of other area foci. Several thick-volumed metropolitan, state, and regional studies by large staffs of planners, social scientists and officials defined joint public-private means for removing destructive socio-physical agents. They laid down advance guidelines according to natural or actual settlement instead of by arbitrary politics or economic expediency, clarified project priorities and area relationships, and prepared master plans as guides to the area's overall needs not as substitutes for local planning and development. All believed regions were the logical modern contexts for co-ordinating local and national priorities, although of course these reports lacked official sanction or enablement, as they generally still do. Similar principles were employed in the development of new towns and housing projects, notably those by the City Housing Corporation and Regional Planning Association of America (Stein, Wright, Mumford, MacKaye, Fritz Malcher, and others), whose superblocks, "steady-flow" traffic, greenbelts, and grouped housing arrangements sought stability, sociability, diversity, and (with proper enforcement and subsidized building methods) blight prevention. Failing to attract industry, technological interest in mass-housing, or private investors able to sustain the large initial costs and low unit profits, however, none of the period's 63 new towns (36 in the 1920's) was finished as planned. "Farm-city" and other rural resettlement proposals of the 1920's were not even constructed until the New Deal (and not really successfully then). And almost all of these "new towns" in city or country became half-finished upper-income suburbs little different in effect (not design) from ordinary ones[26]—going to people who already had more blessings, sunshine, and cultural insularity than anyone else.

The depression, however, made planning not only fashionable again but also imperative under the New Deal. Whereas Hoover pursued *recovery* using government's "reserve powers" to protect citizens against "forces beyond their control," Roosevelt also undertook programs for permanent *reform* on the broadest possible front, using these powers very pragmatically in the search for ways to renovate the whole cultural fabric. To guide them, he said in a popular explanation, "The time called for and still calls for planning." Indeed, as he told Congress that same year (1934):

I look forward to the time in the not too distant future, when annual appropriations, wholly covered by current revenue, will enable the work to proceed with a national *plan*. Such a plan will, in a generation or two, return many times the money spent on it; more important it will eliminate the use of inefficient tools, conserve and increase national resources, prevent waste, and enable millions of our people to take better advantage of the opportunities which God has given our country.[27]

Roosevelt (whose uncle Frederick Delano was a charter NCCP member) got many, if not most, such ideas directly from the profession. For example, upon entering office he canvassed a National Land Use Planning Committee (including ACPI members Alfred Bettman, Jacob Crane, Nolen, and Eliot II) "with reference to the technique of making planning effective." From their recommendations for a federal agency for national planning policy, research, and administration came the short-lived Civil Works Administration (1933-34), whose 10,000 employees made state and local surveys and plan studies, among other things. Another result was the seminal, *ex-officio* National Planning Board (renamed the National Resources Board in 1934, the National Resources Committee in 1935-36, and the National Resources Planning Board until Congress disbanded it in 1943). It unofficially reviewed all public policy on natural, industrial and human resources, served as a "permanent long-range commission" for research, planning, and coordinating of related private-public development; gathered the most complete data on American resources assembled through 1943; and lent professional talent and planning advice to whoever wanted it—41 states, 70 counties and regions, 400 towns and cities before 1940.[28]

The New Deal's pragmatic approach did not sweep away the *laissez-faire* past, but its massive planning began early, spanned the period, and seems to have made the difference between national chaos and general crisis—the century's continuing condition. Most development programs came out of the First Hundred Days legislation: NRPB, TVA (to 1937 it included town planning under Earle Draper and Tracy Augur), conservation and public works (CWA, Public Works Administration, and so forth), home financing and improvement (partly inspired by Hoover's Home Loan Bank), housing and slum clearance (PWA's Housing Division under Robert Kohn, Federal Housing Authority 1936, U.S. Housing Authority absorbing all town planning in 1937), and urban-rural resettlement (Subsistence Homesteads and the Greenbelt programs). Four of these programs originated in omnibus bills of 1933. Only NRPB and resettlement—perhaps the most revolutionary programs—failed to be made continuing works. All utilized professional services extensively as many of today's senior planners will attest. All were supported by enormous

expenditures as compared to the World War I period (247 millions spent on renewal in 1940, a third of it federal as opposed to one million spent by the federal government in 1917-18), and all emphasized planning for permanent social improvement this time not omitting that "one-third of a nation ill-housed, ill-clad, and ill-fed." As the Urbanism Committee described the "new" emphasis:

The prosperity and happiness of the teeming millions who dwell there are closely bound up with that of America, for if the city fails, America fails. The Nation cannot flourish without its urban-industrial centers, or without its countryside; or without a sound balance between them. City planning, county planning, rural planning, state planning, regional planning must be linked together in the higher strategy of American national policy, to the end that our national and local resources may best be conserved and developed for our human use.[29]

The nearly continuing state of war which has consumed so much of the nation's resources and attention since 1939 has perhaps unduly clouded our application of this comprehensive view of domestic development policy. But with its formal acceptance as the very center of such policy up through the national level, planners ceased to be merely semiofficial consultants and two generations of professional growth came to a close—in theory if not always in practice.

RETROSPECT: THE PAST AS INDEX OF PLANNING'S PLACE IN FUTURE POLICY

The contributions of any one group to the endless reorganization of American cities are both small and inseparably bound with the events to which they responded. Nevertheless, while contemporaries must draw their own conclusions knowing today's planning needs are more complex and the procedures more sophisticated and potent, one judges historical significance according to how well a people approach the fundamental problems of their own time, not necessarily by how well they also anticipate ours. But by either definition, certainly by the first, the profession's development of basic premises and relationships through 1940 seems critical to the organization of life-giving reality in this century. These might be summarized as follows:

1. In a massing democracy, communities built for social and personal well-being take precedence over mere economic-technological-physical growth.

2. The city's reorganization in these terms can be partially guided, unified, and enhanced by comprehensive planning which informs but does not inhibit the future.

3. Planning, the art and science of environmental development, is a process in which democratic choice can become meaningful, and capability can approach desire by identifying needs, amenities, minimum standards and so on and by implementing them in numerous designs for new communities in town and countryside which preserve and extend the most desirable features of each as appropriate to time and place.

4. Such planning requires collaboration of means, continuing reallocation of resources, full public empowerment and intelligent human subscription—a slow and gradual process whose success depends largely upon education to its human purposes—for layman and planner alike. The planner's role herein is as analyst, creative designer, critic, and coordinator, at the very least.

5. Planning of the "natural region" not the urban one alone seems the ideal democratic context for coordinating the flow of national and local priorities, resources, and initiative, because cities overlap in needs but are deficient in means as presently constituted.

Of course, the discovery and elaboration of these ideas was more pronounced than their implementation in the period. Hence, a good part of their significance lies in prospects for the growth of such *ideas* as a departure from the past rather than in any dramatically evident humanization of the spreading cities— which was far less than one would have hoped.

How pertinent are such views in our time? Practically every close observer since reformer Frederick Howe in 1906 finds them indispensable to a world with centers but vanishing bounds, with as much disruption as convergence, with continuing economic-technological fascinations that make any planning for liveable cities difficult to obtain, although man's psychosocial needs for contact, love, privacy, beauty, greenspace and so on are "not frills or luxuries but real biological necessities," as René Dubos says.[30] Contemporary planners can point to thousands of operative public agencies; more scientific land use, economic and demographic base studies; integration of training and research with the social, behavioral, and natural sciences; and more widespread public support. But as Melvin Webber says in his AIP policy paper on "Comprehensive Planning and Social Responsibility," none of these insures our ability "to induce those patterns that will effectively increase accessibility to the diverse opportunities for productive social intercourse that are latent in an advanced civilization." Rather "Improving capacity for rationality must be joined with improving wisdom—there is no other name. It is *here* that the road forks, the one route leading to technocratic control by elites, the other to guided expansion of individual freedom." Moreover, the early planners' legacy to the present—"an egalitarian ethic and a pragmatic orientation to betterment" which Webber states and history affirms—also implies working with the events, techniques, and potentials of one's own time in pursuing and expanding the environmental vision,[31] *without* becoming mesmerized by any of them.

Who can tell what lies ahead? Obviously the city continues its rapid surface growth while its development remains sublimated to pressures unalterable even by the best planning alone. Most physical change in today's booming cities is conducted by private interests under public auspices for speculative purposes—rebuilding business centers, transport lines and suburbs where they hope the markets are; exploiting human weaknesses and upping pressures to conform—or deceive; and relocating as fast and as far from the centers for "making a living" as incomes permit. They are not villains, but our historic attachment to *a priori* decisions covering all human possibilities in yesterday's universe and to quantitative empirical standards as the only valid proof of anything combines to fill space with cheap structures, more controlling agencies than control, and a general meanness which cuts us off from one another at home and abroad. No thriving Hometown, USA, claims to be a fast-growing democracy; it invariably claims to be the fast*est* growing population or market area in its region. Unfortunately the penalties attached to such behavior include bland acceptance of affluence by most of us, alienation or intransigence by those who cannot or will not,

probably growing public wariness, loneliness and helplessness generally. Few of us escape. All these signs of imbalance on scales unknown to traditional societies indicate our need for more mix, for new definitions of *man, living,* and *community* rather than for more distinct socioeconomic categories in a free society. If our present use-and-throw away culture is weirdly appealing, it also is a commentary, then, on our unwillingness to seek and hence our inability to begin creating handsome, balanced, *many-sided* lifeways.

So planning's future in urban policy is hardly assured despite three generations of planner pressure. Thus one comes back to the millions of individual decision-makers, perhaps most of us now indifferent, who will affect any such policy; one comes back to our mutual *desire* for life lived as freely, fully, openly, and peacefully as possible. However absurd the desire, however needing restatement today—and both are considerable—it is the profession's good fortune to have been closely identified with it since near the century's turn.

NOTES

1. Lewis Mumford, *The Culture of Cities* (New York: Harcourt, Brace, 1938), pp. 374-87, 376.
2. Ernest Weissman, "The Urban Crisis in the World," *Urban Affairs Quarterly,* I (September, 1965), pp. 65-82; V. Gordon Childe, *Man Makes Himself* (New York: Mentor Books, 1951), pp. 180-88; Gideon Sjoberg, *The Preindustrial City: Past and Present* (Glencoe: Free Press, 1960), pp. 321-44; and Walter W. Rostow, *The Stages of Economic Growth* (London: Cambridge University Press, 1960), pp. 4-11.
3. John Nolen, *Replanning Reading* (Boston: G. H. Ellis, 1910), p. 3; and "Planning Problems of Industrial Cities—Niagara Falls as an Illustration," *Proceedings of the Eleventh National Conference on City Planning* (New York: NCCP, 1919), p. 23.
4. Frederick Law Olmsted, Jr., "Basic Principles of City Planning," *Proceedings . . . Second NCCP* (Boston: NCCP, 1910), pp. 3-4.

5. Donald J. Bogue, *The Population of the United States* (Glencoe: The Free Press, 1959), pp. 4-40, 126-27, 138-39; *Historical Statistics of the United States* (Washington: Government Printing Office, 1960), *passim;* Simon Kuznets and Dorthy S. Thomas, eds., *Population Distribution and Economic Growth*, 3 vols. (Philadelphia: American Philosophical Society, 1957-63) I, pp. 2-3; II, pp. 32-38, 53, 182-83, 205-71.

6. Quoted in Walter M. Whitehill, *Boston: A Topographical History* (Cambridge: Harvard University Press, 1959), p. 1; "Thomas Jefferson, 1st Inaugural Address" (1801), Inaugural Addresses of the Presidents of the United States (Washington, D.C.: Government Printing Office, 1952), pp. 11-13; Thomas Cochran and William Miller, *The Age of Enterprise* (New York: Macmillan, 1942), pp. 3-51, 252-53, 354-58, quoted 39; Andrew Carnegie, *Triumphant Democracy* (New York: Charles Scribner's Sons, 1886), pp. 47-48.

7. Richard Ely, "Pullman: A Social Study," *Harpers Magazine*, LXX (February, 1885), pp. 405-06; Daniel J. Boorstin, *The Americans: The Colonial Experience* (New York: Random House, 1958), pp. 33-96; figures from Bogue, *Population Growth in Standard Metropolitan Areas, 1900-50* (Washington D.C.: Government Printing Office, December, 1953), pp. 10-11, checked against George Ford, ed., *City Planning Progress in the United Sates, 1917* (Washington D.C.: American Institute of Architects, 1916), pp. 5-193; Richard M. Hurd, *Principles of City Land Values* (New York: The Record and Guide, 1903), pp. 1-74, 142; Homer Hoyt, *The Structure and Growth of Residential Neighborhoods in American Cities* (Washington, D.C.: Government Printing Office, 1939), pp. 101-04, 9-122; Nolen, *New Ideals in the Planning of Cities, Towns, and Villages* (New York: American City Bureau, 1919), pp. 1-19, quoted 27; John Reps, *The Making of Urban America* (Princeton: Princeton University Press, 1965), pp. 294-438.

8. Norman J. Johnston, "A Preface to the Institute," *Journal of the American Institute of Planners*, XXXI (August, 1965), pp. 198-209, quoted 201; Timothy Dwight, *Travels in New England and New York*, 4 vols. (New Haven: np, 1821-22), I, pp. 490-91: Reps., *Making of Urban America*, pp. 263-514; Leonard J. Arrington, *Great Basin Kingdom* (Cambridge: Harvard University Press, 1958), pp. 161-94, 235-414; Gourley, *Plans for Beautifying New York and Improving the City of Boston* (Boston: Saxton Pierce, 1844), pp. 1-38; Bushnell, "City Plans," *Work and Play* (New York: Charles Scribner, 1864), p. 376. (My thanks to Prof. Joseph Smeall, UND, for this source.) Ford, ed., *City Planning Progress*, pp. 183-86. There were world's fairs in Atlanta 1895, Omaha 1898, Buffalo 1901, St. Louis 1904, Seattle 1909, and San Diego-San Francisco 1914-15.

9. Quoting Parker and Lloyd in Daniel Aaron, *Men of Good Hope* (New York: Oxford University Press, 1951), pp. 45-66, 155-56, *passim;* Roy Lubove, *The Progressive and the Slums* (Pittsburgh: University of Pittsburgh Press, 1962), pp. 1-48, 217-56; B. O. Flower, *Progressive Men, Women and the Movements of the Past Twenty-Five Years* (Boston: New Arena, 1914), *passim*.

10. Dewey, *Characters and Events*, in J. Ratner ed., (New York: Henry Holt, 1929), p. 830; Woodrow Wilson, *The New Freedom* (New York: Doubleday, 1913), quoted pp. 283, 294; George Mowrey, *The Era of Theodore Roosevelt and the Birth of Modern America, 1900-1912* (New York: Harper & Brothers, 1958), pp. 16-84, 250-95; John Ihlder, "The New Civic Spirit," *American City*, IV (March, 1911), pp. 123-27.

11. "Growing Up By Plan," *Survey*, LXVII (February, 1932), p. 506.

12. Nolen, "Twenty Years of Planning Progress in the United States, 1907-27," *Proceedings . . . Nineteenth NCCP* (Boston: NCCP, 1927), pp. 1-44 quoted; editorials, *American City*, I (September, 1909), p. 3, VIII (January, 1913), p. 95, and XX (February, 1919), pp. 127-29 quoted; Robinson, "College and University Instruction in City Planning," *City Plan*, II (April, 1916), pp. 21-23; Albion W. Small, "Fifty Years of Sociology in the United States," *American Journal of Sociology*, XXI (May, 1916), pp. 734-68; Ford, ed., *City Planning Progress*, pp. 194-99; Harlan James, "Service—the Keynote of a New Cabinet Department," *Review of Reviews*, LIX (February, 1919), pp. 187-90.

13. U.S. Congress, "Hearing . . . on the Subject of City Planning," 61st Congress, 2nd Sess., 422 Senate Documents, LIX (1910), pp. 57-105; Flavel Shurtleff, Minutes of the Conference, the General and Executive Committees, and Correspondence, NCCP, 1910-17, and "Six Years of City Planning in the United States," *Proceedings . . . Seventh NCCP* (1915) pp. 33-41; cf. *General Index of the Proceedings of the NCCP* (Boston: University Press, 1928); Nolen, "What Is Needed in City Planning?," *Hearing*, pp. 74-75; Olmsted, Jr., "Basic Principles in City Planning," *Proceedings . . . Second NCCP* (1910), pp. 3-4; Robinson, "Problems in City Planning," *Proceedings . . . Third NCCP* (1911), pp. 217-18.

14. Pamphlet, "Constitution and By-Laws of the American City Planning Institute," 1917, quoting Article II; "Resolution Adopted by the Ninth NCCP . . . on May 9, 1917," NCCP Executive Minutes.

15. Frederick J. Adams and Gerald Hodge, "City Planning Instruction in the United States: The Pioneering Days, 1900-1930," *Journal of the American Institute of Planners*, XXXI (February, 1965), pp. 43-51; Marsh, *An Introduction to City Planning* with a technical chapter by George Ford (New York: np, 1909), pp. 1-2; Kellog, ed., *The Pittsburgh Survey* (New York: Survey Associates, 1914); Richard S. Childs, "What Ails Pittsburgh? A Diagnosis and Prescription," *American City*, III (July, 1910), pp. 9-12; Charles Moore, ed., *Plan*

of Chicago . . . (Chicago: Commercial Club, 1909), pp. 1-4.
16. Ford, ed., *City Planning Progress,* pp. 5-193; W. S. Morgan and H. M. Pollack, *Modern Cities* (New York: Harper and Brothers, 1913), *passim;* Nolen, *Replanning Small Cities* (Boston: B. W. Huebsh, 1912), quoted pp. 5, 28, 58-60, 155-62, *passim;* NCCP, "Model Plan Study," special supplement in *Landscape Architecture,* III (April, 1913), and comment by Olmsted, Jr., "A City Planning Program," *Proceedings* . . . *Fifth NCCP* (1913), pp. 1-16 (see winning design by F. H. Bourse, A. C. Comey, B. A. Holdemann, and J. Nolen).
17. Robinson, *City Planning* (New York: G. P. Putnam, 1916); Lewis, *Planning the Modern City* (New York: John Wiley and Sons, 1916); Bird, *Town Planning for Small Cities,* and Nolen, ed., *City Planning,* both (New York: D. Appleton for the NML, 1917, 1916), quoting p. 353.
18. Nolen, ed., *City Planning,* pp. xiii-xxiv; "Recommended for Membership, ACPI," *ACPI Minutes,* October 25, 1917, and January 23, 1918.
19. Ford, ed., *City Planning Progress,* quoted pp. 3-4; Norman J. Johnston, "Harland Bartholomew: His Comprehensive Plans and Science of Planning," and Hancock, "John Nolen and the American City Planning Movement: A History of Culture, Change and Community Response, 1900-1940," both unpub. Ph.D. dissertations, University of Pennsylvania, 1964, pp. 1-29, 87-133, and 231-349, respectively.
20. U.S. Bureau of Industrial Housing and Transportation, *Report of the United States Housing Corporation,* James Ford and Henry Hubbard, eds., 2 vols. (Washington, D.C.: Government Printing Office, 1919-20), quoting Hubbard I, pp. 70, 77, and Olmsted, Jr., II, p. 186; U.S. Shipping Board, *Housing the Shipbuilders,* in Frederick L. Ackerman, ed. (Philadelphia: np, 1920), pp. 1-24; E. D. Litchfield, "Yorkship Village in 1917 and 1939," *American City,* LIX (November, 1939), pp. 42-43; Roy Lubove, "Homes and 'A Few Well Placed Fruit Trees': An Object Lesson in Federal Housing," *Social Research,* MV (Winter, 1960), pp. 469-74; "Town Planning Lessons to be Learned from Government Housing Operations," *Minutes* of the Third ACPI Meeting, Philadelphia, January 26-27, 1919; Stein to author, June 14, 1961.
21. *Problems of St. Louis* (St. Louis: City Plan Commission, 1917), p. xxii (Bartholomew's italics).
22. Henry and Theodora Hubbard, *Our Cities Today and Tomorrow* (Cambridge: Harvard University Press, 1929), Appendix II: Thomas Adams, *Outline of Town and City Planning* (New York: Russell Sage Foundation, 1935), pp. 5-29, *passim;* Robert Walker, *The Planning Function in Urban Government* (Chicago: University of Chicago Press, 1941), pp. 23-26, 106-220; Hancock, "Nolen," pp. 350-607; Johnston, "Bartholomew," pp. 1-29, 134-242, quoted 183.

23. Adams, *Outline,* pp. 208-309, quoted 213; Hubbards, *Our Cities,* pp. 46-76, 142-61; Massachusetts Federation of Planning Boards, "Planning Progress in Massachusetts," *Bulletin 20* (1929), pp. 1-5; Edward M. Bassett, *Zoning* (New York: Russell Sage Foundation, 1936), pp. 13-222; Euclid Village, Ohio, *v.* Ambler Realty Co., 272 *U.S. 265* and *47 Sp.Ct. 114* (1926), quoted; Charles Abrams, "Economic Changes in Real Estate," *New Architecture and City Planning,* Paul Zucker, ed. (New York: Philosophical Library, 1944), quoted p. 272; President's Commission, *Recent Social Trends,* in Wesley Mitchell, Charles Merriam *et al.,* eds., 2 vols. (New York: Macmillan, 1933), I, quoted p. xxxi.
24. Adams and Hodge, "City Planning Instruction," pp. 43-51; John Gaus, *The Graduate School of Design and the Education of Planners* (Cambridge: Harvard, 1943), pp. 3-50; "Report of a Conference on a Project for Research and Instruction in City and Regional Planning," Columbia University, May 3, 1918, mimeographed; and Nolen, "Professions Concerned in City Planning," September 29, 1933, both in Nolen Papers (Harvard folders), quoting last 2-4; U.S. Civil Service, "Planner Requirements," 1926, quoted; NCCP and ACPI *Minutes* and member correspondence, "Report of the Committee on Reorganization of the NCCP," March 2, 1934; ACPI to members, March 19, and November 7, 1924; ACPCA, memorandum, "To the Board of Directors," May 29, 1935; American Society of Planning Officials, *Newsletter* (1935), p. i. Note: the *Quarterly* became the *Planners Journal* in 1934 and the *Journal of the American Institute of Planners* in 1944.
25. Mumford, "The Next Twenty Years in City Planning," *Proceedings* . . . *Seventeenth NCCP* (1927), pp. 45-58, quoted 56, *passim;* MacKaye, *The New Exploration* (New York: Harcourt, Brace, 1928), *passim;* Nolen, "Random Notes and Reactions," 1914-20, *passim;* letter to Olmsted, Jr., October 31, 1923, and to New York *Times,* November 25, 1931, all in Nolen Papers (New York Regional Plan file); *cf.* Regional issue of *Survey,* LIV (May 1, 1925).
26. Comey, "An Answer to the Garden City Challenge," *American City,* XXIX (July, 1923), pp. 36-38; MacKaye, *New Exploration,* pp. 24-30, 56-75, quoted 26, 30; Nolen, *New Towns for Old* (Boston: Marshall Jones, 1927), pp. 133-57, *passim;* and "Regional Planning," *Encyclopedia of the Social Sciences,* XIII (1934), pp. 205-08; Russell V. Black, "County Planning Proves Its Value," *American City,* XLIV (May, 1931), pp. 116-18; National Resources Committee, *State Planning* (Washington, D.C.: Government Printing Office, 1935, 1940), and Urbanism Committee of the NRC, *Urban Planning and Land Policies* and Supplementary Report, both (Washington, D.C.: Government Printing Office, 1939), pp. 45-117, and 3-161; Roy Lubove, *Community Planning in the 1920's* (Pittsburgh: University of Pittsburgh Press, 1963), pp. 107-27; *Radburn*

Garden Homes (New York: City Housing Corporation, September, 1930), brochure; The Farm Cities Corporation (Washington: The Corporation, nd-1923) booklet; Malcher, The Steadyflow Traffic System (Cambridge: Harvard University Press, 1935); Stein, Toward New Towns for America (New York: Rheinhold, 1957).

27. Herbert Hoover, The Memoirs of . . . , 3 vols. (New York: Macmillan, 1951-52), II, p. 78; Roosevelt, On Our Way (New York: John Day, 1934), p. xii; and Public Papers and Messages, in S. I. Roseman, ed., 13 vols. (New York: Random House, 1938-45), III, p. ii.

28. Crane to Nolen and L. C. Gray, April 27, 1933, quoted ("Memorandum on the Relation of Emergency Relief Work to Planning"; "Report of the National Land Use Planning Committee," February 15-18, 1932, both Nolen Papers (NRPB folder); First Annual Report: Conference on Rural Land Utilization and Planning (Washington: USDA, July, 1933), pp. 5-16; Federal Emergency Relief Administration, Bulletin WD-3, March 2, 1934; National Resources Committee, PWA, First Through Thirteenth Circular Letters, 1933-34; and "A Plan for Planning," Report, December 1, 1934.

29. NRPB, Our Cities: Their Role in the Growth of the Nation (Washington, D.C.: Government Printing Office, 1937), quoted p. xiii; and Urban Planning and Land Policies, pp. 73-309, passim; Francis Perkins et al., The Federal Government Today (New York: American Council on Public Affairs, 1938), see individual reports; Paul Conkin, Tomorrow A New World (Ithaca: Cornell University Press for the American Historical Association, 1959), pp. 93-233, 326-31.

30. Howe, The City: The Hope of Democracy (New York: Charles Scribner's Sons, 1906), pp. 300-13; Charles Beard, "Conflicts in City Planning," Yale Review XVII (October, 1927), pp. 65-77; David Reisman et al., The Lonely Crowd (New York: Doubleday Anchor Books, 1955), p. 348, passim; John K. Galbraith, Five Speeches (Washington: Urban America, 1966), pp. 1-6; Dubos, "Man's Unchanging Biology and Evolving Psyche," Center for the Study of Democratic Institutions, Center Diary: 17 (March-April, 1967), pp. 38-44, quoted 41.

31. Webber, "Comprehensive Planning and Social Responsibility: Towards an AIP Consensus on the Profession's Roles and Purposes," Journal of the American Institute of Planners, XXIX (November, 1963), pp. 232-41, quoted 234, 236.

The Failure of Urban Renewal

HERBERT J. GANS

Suppose that the government decided that jalopies were a menace to public safety and a blight on the beauty of our highways, and therefore took them away from their drivers. Suppose, then, that to replenish the supply of automobiles, it gave these drivers a hundred dollars each to buy a good used car and also made special grants to General Motors, Ford, and Chrysler to lower the cost—although not necessarily the price—of Cadillacs, Lincolns, and Imperials by a few hundred dollars. Absurd as this may sound, change the jalopies to slum housing, and I have described, with only slight poetic license, the first fifteen years of a federal program called urban renewal.

Since 1949, this program has provided local renewal agencies with federal funds and the power of eminent domain to condemn slum neighborhoods, tear down the buildings, and resell the cleared land to private developers at a reduced price. In addition to relocating the slum dwellers in "decent, safe, and sanitary" housing, the program was intended to stimulate large-scale private rebuilding, add new tax revenues to the dwindling coffers of the cities, revitalize their downtown areas, and halt the exodus of middle-class whites to the suburbs.

For some time now, a few city planners and housing experts have been pointing out that urban renewal was not achieving its general aims, and social scientists have produced a number of critical studies of individual renewal projects. These critiques, however, have mostly appeared in academic books and journals; otherwise there has been remarkably little public discussion of the federal program. Slum-dwellers whose homes were to be torn down have indeed protested bitterly, but their outcries have been limited to particular projects; and because such outcries have rarely been supported by the local press, they have been easily brushed aside by the political power of the supporters of the projects in question. In the last few years, the civil rights movement has backed protesting slum-dwellers, though again only at the local level, while rightists have opposed the use of eminent domain to take private property from one owner in order to give it to another (especially when the new one is likely to be from out-of-town and financed by New York capital).

Slum clearance has also come under fire from several prominent architectural and social critics, led by Jane Jacobs, who have been struggling to preserve neighborhoods like Greenwich Village, with their brownstones, lofts, and small apartment houses, against the encroachment of the large high-rise projects built for luxury market and the poor alike. But these efforts have been directed mainly at private clearance outside the federal program, and their intent has been to save the city for people (intellectuals and artists, for example) who, like tourists, want jumbled diversity, antique "charm," and narrow streets for visual adventure and aesthetic pleasure. (Norman Mailer carried such thinking to its farthest point in his recent attack in the *New York Times Magazine* on the physical and social sterility of high-rise housing; Mailer's attack was also accompanied by an entirely reasonable suggestion—in fact the only viable one that could be made in this context—that the advantages of brownstone living be incorporated into skyscraper projects.)

But if criticism of the urban renewal program has in the past been spotty and sporadic, there are signs that the program as a whole is now beginning to be seriously and tellingly evaluated. At least two comprehensive studies, by Charles Abrams and Scott Greer, are nearing publication, and one highly negative analysis—by an ultra-conservative economist and often irresponsible polemicist—has already appeared: Martin Anderson's *The Federal Bulldozer*.[1] Ironically enough, Anderson's data are based largely on statistics collected by the Urban Renewal Administration. What, according to these and other data, has the program accomplished? It has cleared slums to make room for many luxury-housing and a few middle-income projects, and it has also provided inexpensive land for the expansion of colleges, hospitals, libraries, shopping areas, and other such institutions located in slum areas. As of March 1961, 126,000 dwelling units had been demolished and about 28,000 new ones built. The median monthly rental of all those erected during 1960 came to $158, and in 1962, to $192—a staggering figure for any area outside of Manhattan.

Needless to say, none of the slum-dwellers who were dispossessed in the process could afford to move into these new apartments. Local renewal agencies were supposed to relocate the dispossessed tenants in "standard" housing within their means before demolition began, but such vacant housing is scarce in most cities, and altogether unavailable in some. And since the agencies were under strong pressure to clear the land and get renewal projects going, the relocation of the tenants was impatiently, if not ruthlessly, handled. Thus, a 1961 study of renewal projects in 41 cities showed that 60 per cent of the dispossessed tenants were merely relocated in other slums; and in big cities, the proportion was even higher (over 70 per cent in Philadelphia, according to a 1958 study). Renewal sometimes even created new slums by pushing relocatees into areas and buildings which then became overcrowded and deteriorated rapidly. This has principally been the case with Negroes who, both for economic and racial reasons, have been forced to double up in other ghettos. Indeed, because almost two-thirds of the cleared slum units have been occupied by Negroes, the urban renewal program has often been characterized as Negro clearance, and in too many cities, this has been its intent.

Moreover, those dispossessed tenants who found better housing usually had to pay more rent than they could afford. In his careful study of relocation in Boston's heavily Italian West End,[2] Chester Hartman shows that 41 per cent of the West Enders lived in good housing in this so-called slum (thus suggesting that much of it should not have been torn down) and that 73 per

cent were relocated in good housing—thanks in part to the fact that the West Enders were white. This improvement was achieved at a heavy price, however, for median rents rose from $41 to $71 per month after the move.

According to renewal officials, 80 per cent of all persons relocated now live in good housing, and rent increases were justified because many had been paying unduly low rent before. Hartman's study was the first to compare these official statistics with housing realities, and his figure of 73 per cent challenges the official claim that 97 per cent of the Boston West Enders were properly re-housed. This discrepancy may arise from the fact that renewal officials collected their data after the poorest of the uprooted tenants had fled in panic to other slums, and that officials also tended toward a rather lenient evaluation of the relocation housing of those actually studied in order to make a good record for their agency. (On the other hand, when they were certifying areas for clearance, these officials often exaggerated the degree of "blight" in order to prove their case.)

As for the substandard rents paid by slum-dwellers, this is true in only a small proportion of cases, and then mostly among whites. Real-estate economists argue that families should pay at least 20 per cent of their income for housing, but what is manageable for middle-income people is a burden to those with low incomes who pay a higher share of their earnings for food and other necessities. Yet even so, Negroes generally have to devote about 30 per cent of their income to housing, and a Chicago study cited by Hartman reports that among non-white families earning less than $3,000 a year, median rent rose from 35 per cent of income before relocation to 46 per cent afterward.

To compound the failure of urban renewal to help the poor, many clearance areas (Boston's West End is an example) were chosen, as Anderson points out, not because they had the worst slums, but because they offered the best sites for luxury housing—housing which would have been built whether the urban renewal program existed or not. Since public funds were used to clear the slums and to make the land available to private builders at reduced costs, the low-income population was in effect subsidizing its own removal for the benefit of the wealthy. What was done for the slum-dwellers in return is starkly suggested by the following statistic: *only one-half of one per cent* of all federal expenditures for urban renewal between 1949 and 1964 was spent on relocation of families and individuals; and 2 per cent if payments are included.

Finally, because the policy has been to clear a district of all slums at once in order to assemble large sites to attract private developers, entire neighborhoods have frequently been destroyed, uprooting people who had lived there for decades, closing down their institutions, ruining small businesses by the hundreds, and scattering families and friends all over the city. By removing the structure of social and emotional support provided by the neighborhood, and by forcing people to rebuild their lives separately and amid strangers elsewhere, slum clearance has often come at a serious psychological as well as financial cost to its supposed beneficiaries. Marc Fried, a clinical psychologist who studied the West Enders

after relocation, reported that 46 per cent of the women and 38 per cent of the men "give evidence of a fairly severe grief reaction or worse" in response to questions about leaving their tight-knit community. Far from "adjusting" eventually to this trauma, 26 per cent of the women remained sad or depressed even two years after they had been pushed out of the West End.[3]

People like the Italians or the Puerto Ricans who live in an intensely group-centered way among three-generation "extended families" and ethnic peers have naturally suffered greatly from the clearance of entire neighborhoods. It may well be, however, that slum clearance has inflicted yet graver emotional burdens on Negroes, despite the fact that they generally live in less cohesive and often disorganized neighborhoods. In fact, I suspect that Negroes who lack a stable family life and have trouble finding neighbors, shopkeepers, and institutions they can trust may have been hurt even more by forcible removal to new areas. This suspicion is supported by another of Fried's findings—that the socially marginal West Enders were more injured by relocation than those who had been integral members of the old neighborhood. Admittedly, some Negroes move very often on their own, but then they at least do so voluntarily, and not in consequence of a public policy which is supposed to help them in the first place. Admittedly also, relocation has made it possible for social workers to help slum-dwellers whom they could not reach until renewal brought them out in the open, so to speak. But then only a few cities have so far used social workers to make relocation a more humane process.

These high financial, social, and emotional costs paid by the slum-dwellers have generally been written off as an unavoidable by-product of "progress," the price of helping cities to collect more taxes, bring back the middle class, make better use of downtown land, stimulate private investment, and restore civic pride. But as Anderson shows, urban renewal has hardly justified these claims either. For one thing, urban renewal is a slow process the average project has taken twelve years to complete. Moreover, while the few areas suitable for luxury housing were quickly rebuilt, less desirable cleared land might lie vacant for many years because developers were—and are—unwilling to risk putting up high- and middle-income housing in areas still surrounded by slums. Frequently, they can be attracted only by promises of tax write-offs, which absorb the increased revenues that renewal is supposed to create for the city. Anderson reports that, instead of the anticipated four dollars for every public dollar, private investments have only just matched the public subsidies, and even the money for luxury housing has come forth largely because of federal subsidies. Thus, all too few of the new projects have produced tax gains and returned suburbanites, or generated the magic rebuilding boom.

Anderson goes on to argue that during the fifteen years of the federal urban renewal program, the private housing market has achieved what urban renewal has failed to do. Between 1950 and 1960, twelve million new dwelling units were built, and fully six million substandard ones disappeared—all without government action. The proportion of substandard housing in the total housing supply was reduced from 37 to 19 per cent, and even among the dwelling units occupied by non-whites,

the proportion of substandard units has dropped from 72 to 44 per cent. This comparison leads Anderson to the conclusion that the private market is much more effective than government action in removing slums and supplying new housing, and that the urban renewal program ought to be repealed.

It would appear that Anderson's findings and those of the other studies I have cited make an excellent case for doing so. However, a less biased analysis of the figures and a less tendentious mode of evaluating them than Anderson's leads to a different conclusion. To begin with, Anderson's use of nationwide statistics misses the few good renewal projects, those which have helped both the slum-dwellers and the cities, or those which brought in enough new taxes to finance other city services for the poor. Such projects can be found in small cities and especially in those where high vacancy rates assured sufficent relocation housing of standard quality. More important, all the studies I have mentioned deal with projects carried out during the 1950's, and fail to take account of the improvements in urban renewal practice under the Kennedy and Johnson administrations. Although Anderson's study supposedly covers the period up to 1963, much of his data go no further than 1960. Since then, the federal bulldozer has moved into fewer neighborhoods, and the concept of rehabilitating rather than clearing blighted neighborhoods is more and more being underwritten by subsidized loans. A new housing subsidy program —known as 221(d) (3)— for families above the income ceiling for public housing has also been launched, and in 1964, Congress passed legislation for assistance to relocatees who cannot afford their new rents.

None of this is to say that Anderson would have had to revise his findings drastically if he had taken the pains to update them. These recent innovations have so far been small in scope—only 13,000 units were financed under 211-(d)(3) in the first two years—and they still do not provide subsidies sufficient to bring better housing within the price range of the slum residents. In addition, rehabilitation unaccompanied by new construction is nearly useless because it does not eliminate overcrowding. And finally, some cities are still scheduling projects to clear away the non-white poor who stand in the path of the progress of private enterprise. Unfortunately, many cities pay little attention to federal pleas to improve the program, using the local initiative granted them by urban renewal legislation to perpetuate the practices of the 1950's. Yet even with the legislation of the 1960's, the basic error in the original design of urban renewal remains: it is still a method for eliminating the slums in order to "renew" the city, rather than a program for properly rehousing slum-dwellers.

Before going into this crucial distinction, we first need to be clear that private housing is not going to solve our slum problems. In the first place, Anderson conveniently ignores the fact that if urban renewal has benefited anyone, it is private enterprise. Bending to the pressure of the real-estate lobby, the legislation that launched urban renewal in effect required that private developers do the rebuilding, and most projects could therefore get off the drawing board only if they appeared to be financially attractive to a developer. Thus, his choice of a site and his re-

building plans inevitably took priority over the needs of the slum-dwellers.

It is true that Anderson is not defending private enterprise *per se* but the free market, although he forgets that it only exists today as a concept in reactionary minds and dated economics texts. The costs of land, capital, and construction have long since made it impossible for private developers to build for anyone but the rich, and some form of subsidy is needed to house everyone else. The building boom of the 1950's which Anderson credits to the free market was subsidized by income-tax deductions to homeowners and by F.H.A. 2nd V.A. mortgage insurance, not to mention the federal highway programs that have made the suburbs possible.

To be sure, these supports enabled private builders to put up a great deal of housing for middle-class whites. This in turn permitted well-employed workers, including some non-whites, to improve their own situation by moving into the vacated neighborhoods. Anderson is quite right in arguing that if people earn good wages, they can obtain better housing more easily and cheaply in the not-quite-private market than through urban renewal. But this market is of little help to those employed at low or even factory wages, or the unemployed, or most Negroes who, whatever their earnings, cannot live in the suburbs. In consequence, 44 per cent of all housing occupied by non-whites in 1960 was still substandard, and even with present subsidies, private enterprise can do nothing for these people. As for laissez faire, it played a major role in creating the slums in the first place.

The solution, then, is not to repeal urban renewal, but to transform it from a program of slum clearance and rehabilitation into a program of urban re-housing. This means, first, building low- and moderate-cost housing on vacant land in cities, suburbs, and new towns beyond the suburbs, and also helping slum-dwellers to move into existing housing outside the slums; and then, *after* a portion of the urban low-income population has left the slums, clearing and rehabilitating them through urban renewal. This approach is common-place in many European countries, which have long since realized that pri-vate enterprise can no more house the population and eliminate slums than it can run the post office.

Of course, governments in Europe have a much easier task than ours in developing decent low-income projects. Because they take it for granted that housing is a national rather than a local responsibility, the government agencies are not hampered by the kind of real-estate and construction lobbies which can defeat or subvert American pro-grams by charges of socialism. More-over, their municipalities own a great deal of the vacant land, and have greater control over the use of private land than do American cities. But perhaps their main advantage is the lack of popular opposition to moving the poor out of the slums and into the midst of the more affluent residents. Not only is housing desperately short for all income groups, but the European class structure, even in Western socialist countries, is still rigid enough so that low- and middle-income groups can live near each other if not next to each other, and still "know their place."

In America, on the other hand, one's house and address are major signs of social status, and no one who has any say in the matter wants people of lower income or status in his neighborhood.

Middle-class homeowners use zoning as a way of keeping out cheaper or less prestigious housing, while working-class communities employ less subtle forms of exclusion. Consequently, low-income groups, whatever their creed or color, have been forced to live in slums or near-slums, and to wait until they could acquire the means to move as a group, taking over better neighborhoods when the older occupants were ready to move on themselves.

For many years now, the only source of new housing for such people, and their only hope of escaping the worst slums, has been public housing. But this is no longer a practical alternative. Initiated during the Depression, public housing has always been a politically embattled program; its opponents, among whom the real-estate lobby looms large, first saddled it with re-strictions and then effectively crippled it. Congress now permits only 35,000 units a year to be built in the entire country.

The irony is that public housing has declined because, intended only for the poor, it faithfully carried out its man-date. Originally, sites were obtained by slum clearance; after the war, however, in order to increase the supply of low-cost housing, cities sought to build pub-lic housing on vacant land. But limited as it was to low-income tenants and thus labeled and stigmatized as an institu-tion of the dependent poor, public hous-ing was kept out of vacant land in the better neighborhoods. This, plus the high cost of land and construction, left housing officials with no other choice but to build high-rise projects on what-ever vacant land they could obtain, often next to factories or along railroad yards. Because tenants of public hous-ing are ruled by a set of strict regulations—sometimes necessary, sometimes politically inspired, but always degrading—anyone who could afford housing in the private market shunned the public projects. During the early years of the program, when fewer citizens had that choice, public housing became respectable shelter for the working class and even for the unemployed middle class. After the war, federal officials decided, and rightly so, that public housing ought to be reserved for those who had no other alternative, and therefore set income limits that admitted only the really poor. Today, public housing is home for the underclass—families who earn less than $3000-$4000 annually, many with unstable jobs or none at all, and most of them non-white.

Meanwhile the enthusiasm for public housing has been steadily dwindling and with it, badly needed political support. Newspaper reports reinforce the popular image of public-housing projects as huge nests of crime and delinquency—despite clear evidence to the contrary—and as the domicile of unregenerate and undeserving families whose children urinate only in the elevators. The position of public housing, particularly among liberal intellectuals, has also been weakened by the slurs of the social and architectural aesthetes who condemn the projects' poor exterior designs as "sterile," "monotonous," and "dehumanizing," often in ignorance of the fact that the tightly restricted funds have been allocated mainly to make the apartments themselves as spacious and livable as possible, and that the waiting lists among slum-dwellers who want these apartments remain long. Be that as it may, suburban communities and urban neighborhoods with vacant land are as hostile to public housing as ever,

and their opposition is partly responsible for the program's having been cut down to its present minuscule size.

The net result is that low-income people today cannot get out of the slums, either because they cannot afford the subsidized private market, or because the project they could afford cannot be built on vacant land. There is only one way to break through this impasse, and that is to permit them equal access to new subsidized, privately built housing by adding another subsidy to make up the difference between the actual rent and what they can reasonably be expected to pay. Such a plan, giving them a chance to choose housing like all other citizens, would help to remove the stigma of poverty and inferiority placed on them by public housing. Many forms of rent subsidy have been proposed, but the best one, now being tried in New York, is to put low- and middle-income people in the same middle-income project with the former getting the same apartments at smaller rentals.

Admittedly, this approach assumes that the poor can live with the middle class and that their presence and behavior will not threaten their neighbors' security or status. No one knows whether this is really possible, but experiments in education, job training, and social-welfare programs do show that many low-income people, when once offered *genuine* opportunities to improve their lives and given help in making use of them, are able to shake off the hold of the culture of poverty. Despite the popular stereotype, the proportion of those whom Hylan Lewis calls the clinical poor, too ravaged emotionally by poverty and deprivation to adapt to new opportunities, seems to be small. As for the rest, they only reject programs offering spurious opportunities, like job-training schemes for nonexistent jobs. Further, anyone who has lived in a slum neighborhood can testify that whatever the condition of the building, most women keep their apartments clean by expenditures of time and effort inconceivable to the middle-class housewife. Moving to a better apartment would require little basic cultural change from these women, and rehousing is thus a type of new opportunity that stands a better chance of succeeding than, say, a program to inculcate new child-rearing techniques.

We have no way of telling how many slum-dwellers would be willing to participate in such a plan. However poor the condition of the flat, the slum is home, and for many it provides the support of neighboring relatives and friends, and a cultural milieu in which everyone has the same problems and is therefore willing to overlook occasional disreputable behavior. A middle-income project cannot help but have a middle-class ethos, and some lower-class people may be fearful of risking what little stability they have achieved where they are now in exchange for something new, strange, demanding, and potentially hostile. It would be hard to imagine an unwed Negro mother moving her household to a middle-income project full of married couples and far removed from the mother, sisters, and aunts who play such an important role in the female-centered life of lower-class Negroes. However, there are today a large number of stable two-parent families who live in the slums only because income and race exclude them from the better housing that is available. Families like these would surely be only too willing to leave the Harlems and Black Belts.

They would have to be helped with loans to make the move, and perhaps even with grants to buy new furniture so as not to feel ashamed in their new surroundings. They might be further encouraged by being offered income-tax relief for giving up the slums, just as we now offer such relief to people who give up being renters to become homeowners.

Undoubtedly there would be friction between the classes, and the more affluent residents would likely want to segregate themselves and their children from neighbors who did not toe the middle-class line, especially with respect to child-rearing. The new housing would therefore have to be planned to allow some voluntary social segregation for both groups, if only to make sure that enough middle-income families would move in (especially in cities where there was no shortage of housing for them). The proportion of middle- and low-income tenants would have to be regulated not only to minimize the status fears of the former, but also to give the latter enough peers to keep them from feeling socially isolated and without emotional support when problems arise. Fortunately, non-profit and limited dividend institutions, which do not have to worry about showing an immediate profit, are now being encouraged to build moderate-income housing; they can do a more careful job of planning the physical and social details of this approach than speculative private builders.

If the slums are really to be emptied and their residents properly housed elsewhere, the rehousing program will have to be extended beyond the city limits, for the simple reason that that is where most of the vacant land is located. This means admitting the low-income population to the suburbs; it also means creating new towns—self-contained communities with their own industry which would not, like the suburbs, be dependent on the city for employment opportunities, and could therefore be situated in presently rural areas. Federal support for the construction of new towns was requested as part of the 1964 Housing Act, and although Congress refused to pass it, the legislation will come up again in 1965.[4]

To be sure, white middle-class suburbanites and rural residents are not likely to welcome non-white low-income people into their communities even if the latter are no longer clearly labeled as poor. The opposition to be expected in city neighborhoods chosen for mixed-income projects would be multiplied a hundredfold in outlying areas. Being politically autonomous, and having constituencies who are not about to support measures that will threaten their security or status in the slightest, the suburbs possess the political power to keep the rehousing program out of their own vacant lots, even if they cannot stop the federal legislation that would initiate it. On the other hand, experience with the federal highway program and with urban renewal itself has demonstrated that few communities can afford to turn down large amounts of federal money. For instance, New York City is likely to build a Lower Manhattan Expressway in the teeth of considerable local opposition, if only because the federal government will pay 90 per cent of the cost and thus bring a huge sum into the city coffers. If the rehousing program were sufficiently large to put a sizable mixed-income project in every community, and if the federal government were to pick up at least 90 per cent of the tab, while also strengthening the

appeal of the program by helping to solve present transportation, school, and tax problems in the suburbs, enough political support might be generated to overcome the objections of segregationist and class-conscious whites.

Yet even if the outlying areas could be persuaded to cooperate, it is not at all certain that slum-dwellers would leave the city. Urban renewal experience has shown that for many slum-dwellers, there are more urgent needs than good housing. One is employment, and most of the opportunities for unskilled or semi-skilled work are in the city. Another is money, and some New York City slum residents recently refused to let the government inspect—much less repair—their buildings because they would lose the rent reductions they had received previously. If leaving the city meant higher rents, more limited access to job possibilities, and also separation from people and institutions which give them stability, some slum residents might very well choose overcrowding and dilapidation as the lesser of two evils.

These problems would have to be considered in planning a rehousing program beyond the city limits. The current exodus of industry from the city would of course make jobs available to the new suburbanites. The trouble is that the industries now going into the suburbs, or those that would probably be attracted to the new towns, are often precisely the ones which use the most modern machinery and the fewest unskilled workers. Thus, our rehousing plan comes up against the same obstacle—the shortage of jobs—that has frustrated other programs to help the low-income population and that will surely defeat the War on Poverty in its present form. Like so many other programs, rehousing is finally seen to depend on a step that American society is as yet unwilling to take: the deliberate creation of new jobs by government action. The building of new towns especially would have to be coordinated with measures aimed at attracting private industry to employ the prospective residents, at creating other job opportunities, and at offering intensive training for the, unskilled after they have been hired. If they are not sure of a job before they leave the city, they simply will not leave.

The same social and cultural inhibitions that make slum residents hesitant to move into a mixed-income project in the city would, of course, be even stronger when it came to moving out of the city. These inhibitions might be relaxed by moving small groups of slum residents en masse, or by getting those who move first to encourage their neighbors to follow. In any case, new social institutions and community facilities would have to be developed to help the erstwhile slum-dweller feel comfortable in his new community, yet without labeling him as poor.

Despite its many virtues, a rehousing program based on the use of vacant land on either side of the city limits would not immediately clear the slums. Given suburban opposition and the occupational and social restraints on the slum-dwellers themselves, it can be predicted that if such a program were set into motion it would be small in size, and that it would pull out only the upwardly mobile—particularly the young people with stable families and incomes —who are at best a sizable minority among the poor. What can be done now to help the rest leave the slums?

The best solution is a public effort to encourage their moving into existing neighborhoods within the city and in older suburbs just beyond the city limits. Indeed, a direct rent subsidy like that now given to relocatees could enable people to obtain decent housing in these areas. This approach has several advantages. It would allow low-income people to be close to jobs and to move in groups, and it would probably attract the unwed mother who wanted to give her children a better chance in life. It would also be cheaper than building new housing, although the subsidies would have to be large enough to discourage low-income families from overcrowding—and thus deteriorating— the units in order to save on rent.

There are, however, some obvious disadvantages as well. For one thing, because non-white low-income people would be moving into presently white or partially integrated areas, the government would in effect be encouraging racial invasion. This approach would thus have the effect of pushing the white and middle-income people further toward the outer edge of the city or into suburbs. Although some whites might decide to stay, many would surely want to move, and not all would be able to afford to do so. It would be necessary to help them with rent subsidies as well; indeed, they might become prospective middle-income tenants for rehousing projects on vacant land.

Undoubtedly, all this would bring us closer to the all-black city that has already been predicted. For this reason alone, a scheme that pushes the whites further out can only be justified when combined with a rehousing program on vacant land that would begin to integrate the suburbs. But even that could not prevent a further racial imbalance between cities and suburbs.

Yet would the predominantly non-white city really be so bad? It might be for the middle class which needs the jobs, shops, and culture that the city provides. Of course, the greater the suburban exodus, the more likely it would become that middle-class culture would also move to the suburbs. This is already happening in most American cities—obvious testimony to the fact that culture (at least of the middlebrow kind represented by tent theaters and art movie-houses) does not need the city in order to flourish; and the artists who create high culture seem not to mind living among the poor even now.

Non-white low-income people might feel more positive about a city in which they were the majority, for if they had the votes, municipal services would be more attuned to their priorities than is now the case. To be sure, if poor people (of any color) were to dominate the city, its tax revenues would decrease even further, and cities would be less able than ever to supply the high quality public services that the low-income population needs so much more urgently than the middle class. Consequently, new sources of municipal income not dependent on the property tax would have to be found; federal and state grants to cities (like those already paying half the public-school costs in several states) would probably be the principal form. Even under present conditions, in fact, new sources of municipal income must soon be located if the cities are not to collapse financially.

If non-whites were to leave the slums en masse, new ghettos would eventually form in the areas to which they would move. Although this is undesirable by conventional liberal standards, the fact is that many low-income Negroes are not yet very enthusiastic about living among white neighbors. They do not favor segregation, of course; what they want is a free choice and then the ability to select predominantly non-white areas that are in better shape than the ones they live in now. If the suburbs were opened to non-whites—to the upwardly mobile ones who want integration now—free choice would become available. If the new ghettos were decent neighborhoods with good schools, and if their occupants had jobs and other opportunities to bring stability into their lives, they would be training their children to want integration a generation hence.

In short, then, a workable rehousing scheme must provide new housing on both sides of the city limits for the upwardly mobile minority, and encouragement to move into older areas for the remainder. If, in these ways, enough slum-dwellers could be enabled and induced to leave the slums, it would then be possible to clear or rehabilitate the remaining slums. Once slum areas were less crowded, and empty apartments were going begging, their profitability and market value would be reduced, and urban renewal could take place far more cheaply, and far more quickly. Relocation would be less of a problem, and with land values down, rebuilding and rehabilitation could be carried out to fit the resources of the low-income people who needed or wanted to remain in the city. A semi-suburban style of living that would be attractive to the upper-middle class could also be provided.

At this point, it would be possible to begin to remake the inner city into what it must eventually become—the hub of a vast metropolitan complex of urban neighborhoods, suburbs, and new towns, in which those institutions and functions

that have to be at the center—the specialized business districts, the civil and
cultural facilities, and the great hospital
complexes and university campuses—
would be located.

Even in such a city, there would be
slums—for people who wanted to live
in them, for the clinical poor who would
be unable to make it elsewhere, and for
rural newcomers who would become
urbanized in them before moving on.
But it might also be possible to relocate
many of these in a new kind of public
housing in which quasi-communities
would be established to help those
whose problems were soluble and to
provide at least decent shelter for those
who cannot be helped except by letting
them live without harassment until we
learn how to cure mental illness, addiction, and other forms of self-destructive
behavior.

This massive program has much to
recommend it, but we must clearly
understand that moving the low-income
population out of the slums would not
eliminate poverty or the other problems
that stem from it. A standard dwelling
unit can make life more comfortable,
and a decent neighborhood can discourage some anti-social behavior, but by
themselves, neither can effect radical
transformations. What poor people need
most are decent incomes, proper jobs,
better schools, and freedom from racial
and class discrimination. Indeed, if the
choice were between a program solely
dedicated to rehousing, and a program
that kept the low-income population in
the city slums for another generation
but provided for these needs, the latter
would be preferable, for it would produce people who were able to leave the
slums under their own steam. Obviously, the ideal approach is one that

coordinates the elimination of slums
with the reduction of poverty.

As I have been indicating, an adequate rehousing program would be extremely costly and very difficult to carry
out. Both its complexity and expense
can be justified, however, on several
grounds. Morally, it can be argued that
no one in the Great Society should have
to live in a slum, at least not involun-
tarily.

From a political point of view, it is
urgently necessary to begin integrating
the suburbs and to improve housing
conditions in the city before the latter
becomes an ominous ghetto of poor and
increasingly angry Negroes and Puerto
Ricans, and the suburbs become enclaves of affluent whites who commute
fearfully to a downtown bastion of
stores and offices. If the visible group
tensions of recent years are allowed to
expand and sharpen, another decade
may very well see the beginning of
open and often violent class and race
warfare.

But the most persuasive argument for
a rehousing program is economic. Between 50 and 60 per cent of building
costs go into wages and create work
for the unskilled who are now increasingly unemployable elsewhere. A dwelling unit that costs $15,000 would thus
provide as much as $9000 in wages—
one-and-a-half years of respectably paid
employment for a single worker. Adding
four-and-a-half million new low-cost
housing units to rehouse half of those
in substandard units in 1960 would provide almost seven million man-years of
work, and the subsequent renewal of
these and other substandard units yet
more. Many additional jobs would also
be created by the construction and
operation of new shopping centers,
schools, and other community facilities,

as well as the highways and public transit systems that would be needed to serve the new suburbs and towns. If precedent must be cited for using a housing program to create jobs, it should be recalled that public housing was started in the Depression for precisely this reason.

The residential building industry (and the real-estate lobby) would have to be persuaded to give up their stubborn resistance to government housing programs, but the danger of future underemployment, and the opportunity of participating profitably in the rehousing scheme, should either convert present builders or attract new ones into the industry. As for the building trades unions, they have always supported government housing programs, but they have been unwilling to admit non-whites to membership. If, however, the rehousing effort were sizable enough to require many more workers than are now in the unions, the sheer demand for labor—and the enforcement of federal non-discriminatory hiring policies for public works—would probably break down the color barriers without much difficulty.

While the federal government is tooling up to change the urban renewal program into a rehousing scheme, it should also make immediate changes in current renewal practices to remove their economic and social cost from the shoulders of the slum-dwellers. Future projects should be directed at the clearance of *really harmful* slums, instead of taking units that are *run down but not demonstrably harmful* out of the supply of low-cost housing, especially for downtown revitalization and other less pressing community improvement schemes. Occupants of harmful slums, moreover, ought to be rehoused in de-

cent units they can afford. For this purpose, more public housing and 221 (d) (3) projects must be built, and relocation and rent assistance payments should be increased to eliminate the expense of moving for the slum-dweller. Indeed, the simplest way out of the relocation impasse is to give every relocatee a sizable grant, like the five-hundred dollars to one thousand dollars paid by private builders in New York City to get tenants out of existing structures quickly and painlessly. Such a grant is not only a real incentive to relocate but a means of reducing opposition to urban renewal. By itself, however, it cannot reduce the shortage of relocation housing. Where such housing now exists in plentiful supply, renewal ought to move ahead more quickly, but where there is a shortage that cannot be appreciably reduced, it would be wise to eliminate or postpone clearance and rehabilitation projects that require a large amount of relocation.

Nothing is easier than to suggest radical new programs to the overworked and relatively powerless officials of federal and local renewal agencies who must carry out the present law, badly written or not, and who are constantly pressured by influential private interests to make decisions in their favor. Many of these officials are as unhappy with what urban renewal has wrought as their armchair critics and would change the program if they could—that is, if they received encouragement from the White House, effective support in getting new legislation through Congress, and, equally important, political help at city halls to incorporate these innovations into local programs. But it should be noted that little of what I have suggested is very radical, for none of the proposals involves conflict with the entrenched American practice of subsidizing private enterprise to carry out public works at a reasonable profit. The proposals are radical only in demanding an end to our no less entrenched practice of punishing the poor. Yet they also make sure that middle-class communities are rewarded financially for whatever discomfort they may have to endure.

Nor are these suggestions very new. Indeed, only last month President Johnson sent a housing message to Congress which proposes the payment of rent subsidies as the principal method for improving housing conditions. It also requests federal financing of municipal services for tax-starved communities, and aid toward the building of new towns. These represent bold and desirable steps toward the evolution of a federal rehousing program. Unfortunately, however, the message offers little help to those who need it most. Slum-dwellers may be pleased that there will be no increase in urban renewal activity, and that relocation housing subsidies and other grants are being stepped up. But no expansion of public housing is being requested, and to make matters worse, the new rent subsidies will be available only to households above the income limits for public housing. Thus, the President's message offers no escape for the mass of the non-white low-income population from the ghetto slums; in fact it threatens to widen the gap between such people and the lower-middle-income population which will be eligible for rent subsidies.

On the other hand, as in the case of the War on Poverty, a new principle of government responsibility in housing is being established, and evidently the President's strategy is to obtain legislative approval for the principle by combining it with a minimal and a minimally controversial program for the first year. Once the principle has been accepted, however, the program must change quickly. It may have taken fifteen years for urban renewal even to begin providing some relief to the mass of slum-dwellers, but it cannot take that long again to become a rehousing scheme that will give them significant help. The evolution of federal policies can no longer proceed in the leisurely fashion to which politicians, bureaucrats, and middle-class voters have become accustomed, for unemployment, racial discrimination, and the condition of our cities are becoming ever more critical problems, and those who suffer from them are now considerably less patient than they have been in the past.

NOTES

1. M.I.T. Press, 272 pp., $5.95.
2. See the November 1964 issue of the *Journal of the American Institute of Planners.* The article also reviews all other relocation research and is a more reliable study of the consequences of renewal than Anderson's.
3. See "Grieving for a Lost Home," in *The Urban Condition,* edited by Leonard Duhl.
4. Meanwhile, several private developers are planning new towns (for example, James Rouse who is building Columbia near Baltimore, and Robert Simon who has already begun Reston, outside Washington) in which they propose to house some low-income people.

Waiting for Reality:
Birth of the Megalopolis

SCOTT GREER

The American city has always been a problem of some sort to somebody. From Jefferson's worries about the corruption of the urban masses to Johnson's concern with "renewing" our cities, there has been a presumption of failure in our urban communities. This kind of belief, however stated, has really rested upon the classical problem of social change—the dramatic disjunction between what we think we wanted, on one hand, and what we have cooperatively produced on the other.

What we have made is a society which became increasingly urban in each decade (but one) since the Revolution. We know the story but the statistics bear repeating: from less than 5 per cent urban during Washington's presidency to over 70 per cent during Johnson's. But all the time we were building an urban nation, we continued to measure it against images derived from an earlier age. The discrepancy led to moral and political efforts to reshape what was emerging in the image of that golden time.

It is conventional to attribute much of the increase in urban growth to the Civil War and its stimulation of manufacturing. However, it is important to remember that the single greatest proportionate increase of the urban population was between 1840 and 1850, when the proportion living in cities increased by nearly half. A consistent increase continued to the present, with the urban proportion rising around five per cent each decade.

The underlying cause was the increasing scale of the society. By this I mean two things: first, the increasing application of non-human energy and machines to every aspect of human work, beginning with agriculture (today our most mechanized industry); second, the increasing organization of work in large, formal structures which demand and allow spatial concentration of the factors of production and places of exchange. Increasing material wealth and increasing control over space, both resulting from the revolution in energy resources, allowed for the development of regional and national producers and markets. Around the sites of these enterprises grew the cities.

The increase of energy resources included both the development of techniques for using petrochemicals and the increase in productive lands. These latter in turn fed both national and international trade, and tended to dominate certain world markets with their produce. One result was the competitive decline in European agriculture and the movement of peasants to the cities and, in many cases, to the cities of the United States. This massive immigration shaped the basic character

From the book *The State of the Nation*, edited by David Boroff. © 1965 by The National Centennial, Inc. Published by Prentice-Hall, Inc., Englewood Cliffs, New Jersey. Reprinted by permission of the publisher.

629

of American cities—differentiating them from both the cities of other nations and the remainder of American society. All cities are polyglot and heterogeneous, but American cities had more people from further and more various origins than any in history save possibly Rome.

The cities of the latter 19th century were preeminently cities of the railroad. This major breakthrough in the use of new energies, allowing the cheap movement of heavy materials across the continental nation, increased the span of productive enterprise and of the markets. However, it did little to alleviate the problem of movement *within* the city, where animal muscles (human and equine) completed the journey of goods from distant places. Movement within the city was expensive and slow; the solution was a sharp increase in density of the increasing population. This meant crowded tenements for the poor, town houses for the rich, high-rise offices, factories, and loft buildings for work. Near the terminal stood the plants and warehouses handling the heavy goods and, near them, the dwellings of the workers.

The workers were, predominantly, poor. Over the last half of the 19th century their wages rose very slowly, while they bore the brunt of "the business cycle" in unemployment without benefit of unions. Poorly educated if at all, chained to the job, polyglot and in many cases strangers from a simpler world, they constituted a majority of the people in the rapidly growing cities. Their jerry-built neighborhoods were poorly maintained (it was a sellers' market in cheap housing, as always), and they quickly deteriorated into the generic "slums." The concentration of the poorest coincided with the concentration of the criminal, the dependent, the diseased and, as a partial consequence, the revolutionary.

The American image of these cities was ambivalent. On the one hand, those who were in revolt from the village and the isolated farms looked to the city as liberator. But many others viewed it as a pit of iniquity. Anselm Strauss (in his study, *Images of the American City*) documents the intense revulsion felt for the city among those whose basic ideal was the small town life described by Riley. The Jeffersonian myth "that the country was the source of moral integrity and vigor" survived, even as millions of country boys went to the cities to gamble their futures.

These counter-images of the city are most harshly presented in the novels of Dreiser. In his series based on the career of Yerkes, the brilliant opportunities and the terrible risks of urban existence are evoked as interwoven aspects of the same whole. More important, his naturalism illuminates the weakness of public order and the free rein of chicanery and violence. Underlying this at a deeper level is a commitment on Dreiser's part to the dominant myth of American business enterprise —that social Darwinism which saw conflict, competition and survival as the "real" facts and the moral order as a mere epiphenomenon. It was "natural" that the City Council of Chicago could be controlled through bribe, as it was natural that economic aggrandizement in the person of Yerkes should integrate the transit system and thus improve the purchasing power of the worker's nickel. It amounts to saying that whatever has resulted justifies the process from which it came.

This point of view is equally evident

in the first school of American urban studies, that of the "human ecologists." Having separated the moral order from the spatially-evident community, these scholars then ignored the former to concentrate upon a description of the latter. Implicit was a social determinism which derived the existing city from the struggle for *Lebensraum* among contending interest groups of every sort. Neither moral norms nor the structure of government exerted any real influence upon the course of life in the city.

And indeed, there was much truth in such an assumption. Lincoln Steffens and his fellow muckrakers had dug up shattering evidence of corruption and compliance in City Halls throughout the nation. Politicians were handmaidens of the highest bidders among the businessmen. Plunkitt of Tammany Hall seemed a better guide to practical politics than were professors of government; his fine distinctions between honest and dishonest graft seemed at least congruent with the real rules of the game, unlike the charters, statutes and homilies of the textbooks. Nor was there anything "unnatural" about it. The irrelevant images of a small-town and rural America were held in common by those who had drafted the democratic charters. These architects assumed the farmer, the independent producer, had both the ability and the interest to govern himself through the ballot or through taking office. The reality was the mass of new urbanites, employees, entrepreneurs, hucksters from every part of the earth, often illiterate but anxious to make their way in a frightening and promising environment.

The result was the invention of the "machines"—networks of party clubs which sold favors wholesale at the top and distributed the rewards downward at retail. When such machines coincided with ethnic groups or coalitions (and this was almost always the case), the basis was laid for a politics which succeeded in relating numbers to wealth, after a fashion. It was, however, a fashion calculated to minimize the independent effect of "the public purpose" upon the business of running the city. The public treasury, the transportation system, the use of urban lands, the administration of justice—all levers capable of controlling the development of the city—were co-opted by private enterprise. The public purpose had markedly little to do with the developing layout of American cities.

Under such circumstances the energies of reformers were focused upon the creation of integrity in government. Drawn overwhelmingly from the middle-class old Americans, civic reformers were concerned with separating public purpose and private enterprise at the level of the boss, who lined his pockets, and of the voters, who bought ethnic identity and trivial privileges. The "Good Government League" fought for the short ballot, non-partisan elections, proportional representation, initiative, referendum, recall, the city manager system, and so on through a laundry list of nostrums. Their aims were "to take government out of politics."

And there were other urban reform movements. Those who could not accept with equanimity the Spencerian dictum that the weak and ignorant should perish developed the settlement-house movement, cultural missions to the poor. Those whose eyes were shocked at the urban scene resulting from the free play of the market—the maximization of profit for those with capital to invest—began to urge the creation of the "city beautiful." So pervasive, however, was the ideological climate that reformers and unregenerate exploiters alike shared a core of basic values. For those who would take government out of politics dreamed mostly of an honest administrative government, forgetting that politics is the collective determination of the future, *demanding* the representation of divergent interests. Those who were on missions to the poor forgot that under the national credo, unemployment is part of the divine scheme of free enterprise and mass poverty certain for any city. Those who planned the city beautiful ignored the dictum that nothing capable of earning a dollar should be left to government—a rule whose practical consequence was the domination of urban patterns by the money and real estate markets.

Within such limits the achievements of reformers were limited indeed. To be sure, localized planning occurred in the centers of some cities; parks were bequeathed by the wealthy; some control over new building was instituted (becoming a new source of income for the "machines"). Meanwhile, the older urban centers were flooded with new buildings throughout the latter half of the century, with huge new systems of streets and sewers accompanying them and leading to the growth of huge new fortunes. The rapid building of the urban plant used the political machine —and fed it at the same time. Yet Seth Low, Mayor of Brooklyn, in rebuttal to Lord Bryce's condemnation of our municipal government, underscored a major point: when was so much built so rapidly for so many? The antique machinery of local government provided many opportunities to stall and stalemate; it was oiled by the flow of transactions between builders, machines and officials. The society rewarded those who "got things done"—with few questions about ultimate costs.

And indeed, as the nation moved deeper into the 20th century, a determined attack on civic government as a problem began to have some successes. As the worst abuses became rare, as voting machines began to replace political machines, the image of the local official as a trained professional became increasingly applicable. Many interlinked trends underlay the change. With cessation of immigration in the early 1920s, the population became increasingly native and acclimated to American norms and beliefs; it also became better educated, more prosperous and more highly skilled as the society increased in scale. The petty rewards of the machines shrank in value along with toleration of fraud. At the same time, the sheer growth of the cities resulted in the building of huge bureaucracies having a momentum, an order, and complex problems of their own— problems requiring a level of technical competence not to be found at random among "friends of the party." With the depression and the increasing scope of the national government these bureaucracies became intricately interdependent with the larger system: the terms of federal grants gave added leverage to the emerging cadres of professional civic bureaucrats.

Ironically, the very trends which aided in the solution of older problems produced a new and equally difficult set. The increase in scale which resulted in a wealthier and better educated citizenry on one hand, and large bureaucracies producing public goods and services on the other, also increased the average citizen's control over space. Automobiles and electronic communications decreased the dependence of the population upon the small area and dense structures of the central city.

The automobile allowed residence and workplace to be separated further in space and yet remain as close in time as before. The truck allowed enterprises to locate far from the old terminals. Increasing income decreased the marginal cost of private transportation to the citizens, while vast new areas available for development on the peripheries lowered the cost of land. Spatial freedom, along with the development of lifetime mortgages, permitted the vast bulk of the population a free choice between the old high-rise city and the horizontal neighborhoods of suburbia. Their option has been overwhelmingly for the latter.

The decentralization of urban sites was not accompanied by an expansion in the jurisdiction of the older city. For one reason or another (lack of services from the city, unwillingness to be governed and identified with it), the new settlements tended to incorporate as separate municipalities. Thus the typical American metropolis became a large central city surrounded by dozens or hundreds of small suburban towns. Today over half the total population of our metropolitan area lives outside the central city.

This situation has been defined by many as a major problem—"the metropolitan problem." There is no longer any general government for the urban area as a whole. Though it produces problems due to its interdependence—problems of transportation, housing,

race relations, drainage and sewerage, land use and so on (almost) indefinitely —there is no capability to act for the public welfare of the region. (Here the title of Robert Wood's book on metropolitan New York, *1400 Governments,* is a dramatic summary.) There is no decision-making body which has the fiscal and the police power to maintain an order referring to the interdependent population. There is no way the resident, as citizen of a *metropolis,* can have a say in the collective fate of the vast urban fabric.

The voices which have dramatized the problem have been, predominently, those who speak for the older central city. They are the ones who tell us that our cities are increasingly "blighted," increasingly inhabited by the segregated, the unemployed, the poor. They emphasize the increased public services necessary for such populations while the prosperous are leaving the city and industry and commerce locating in the industrial parks and shopping centers of the suburbs. The tax base is declining, while the demands for service increase.

And the older urban center deteriorates. The proud neighborhoods of the rich become converted into tenements for the poor and the segregated, great buildings and public monuments deteriorate and no new ones spring up to replace them, civic leaders and patrons of the arts move to the suburbs, leaching purpose and will from the city. The very cradle and core of civilization, the city, is deteriorating even as we become an urbanized society. This is another aspect of the metropolitan problem.

Major campaigns have been mounted for the purpose of re-establishing the cohesion of the city. Many efforts have been made to devise and put into being a new metropolitan government which could include the entire interdependent population of the great complexes. With only minor exceptions they have failed, sunk on the rock of the referendum. For, in our political culture inherited from an earlier era, the municipal corporation is virtually sacrosanct and can be changed only at the will of the citizens. And they, by and large, are not interested in one big government for the metropolis. The opposition, organized and led by the incumbent officials of the various sub-jurisdictions (including those of the central city) almost always has its way.

A second major effort addressed to the plight of the city is the national program of urban renewal. Growing out of the slum clearance and public housing programs of the depression, it has been expanded to a program to renew the cities—to do away with slums and replace them with new growth into the indefinite future. It is, then, a radical program—one aimed at controlling the growth and form of American cities in a way they have never been controlled before.

Unfortunately, the program is severely limited by the political culture and the legal structure. It is forced to share power with many agencies not necessarily committed to its goals. Thus, programs are initiated and guaranteed, indeed executed, by local government; the federal agency must deal with whatever interests the local political process has hoisted into office. The programs are also rigorously limited in what they can do; they can buy land and clear it, but aside from public buildings they cannot redevelop. All that must be undertaken by the private real estate industry. This means that

the urban renewal effort can be applied only where local officials want it and where the local real estate market decrees that profits can be made. These sites may or may not be the ones most in need of redevelopment and the resulting structures may contribute as much to aesthetic blight as the ones they replaced.

An equally important limit on the program is the result of governmental fragmentation. Because the program must be a municipal effort, it cannot plan and act for the metropolitan area as a whole. Yet in respect to housing markets, industrial location, transportation and retail markets, the majority of the population outside the central city is critically important to central city developments. What happens, however, is the development of a myopic, city-focused program which ignores the major wave of metropolitan growth and development, the burgeoning suburbs, in order to fixate upon the old, second-hand acres of the central city. Here the chief effects thus far have been the destruction of low-cost housing and replacement with business and public office buildings or luxury apartments. (It is not at all certain that such buildings would not have been built anyway, without public subsidy.)

Both urban renewal and metropolitan government are programs derived from another lag between what we think we want and what we have created. Now the nostalgia is not for the small town and country, but for the imagined central city of another era. People dream of the older part of the city as "hub and symbolic center" for the metropolitan area. They decry the homogeneity of the suburbs, speak of the richness of life in the urban milieu, the heterogeneity of people and cultural experiences easily available. They point then to the "decay" at the urban core. The metropolitan problem is a problem, then, of heart's desire.

But whose heart, and whose problem? Those who set up housekeeping in the suburbs were not usually refugees from the city; they were newly formed families who chose the broad, horizontal acres as most appropriate for the style of life they wanted. It is a life centered in family, home, neighborhood, local community. They do not miss the cultural opportunities of center city, for when they and their kind lived in the center they did not take advantage of them. And besides, with television and stereo they have more access to high culture than any lot of average citizens ever had before. As for tolerance of ethnic differences—segregation of the unlike even in proximity is as possible in a central city as in the South, and has long been practiced in both milieus. In truth, tolerance is most powerfully a function of formal education and it is in the middle-class suburbs that we find the most tolerant populations—not in the polyethnic slums.

As for the "decay" of the city, it is largely an optical illusion. If we insist on seeing only the older half of the metropolis, the proportion of substandard housing, poverty, dependency, *et al*, has certainly increased in recent decades. But the reason is simply the concentration of certain types of population in certain residential areas in a city whose government, not having expanded its jurisdiction, now applies only to a minority of the total population. If we take the metropolitan population as a whole, substandard housing has decreased enormously since the 1950s. The reason is precisely the rapid build-

ing of enormous stocks of new housing in the suburbs. The increase in the Negro population is similarly explained: the concentration of the oldest (therefore cheapest) housing in the center, and the proximity of lower status and unskilled jobs, makes center-city housing inevitable for most Negroes. To be sure, formal and informal segregation forces a senseless and uneconomical concentration and density; for this, however, the major remedy is likely to come through the continual increase in vacancies among the older, but still decent, housing of the middle wards— brought about in turn by the movement of white households to the suburbs.

Our slums are products of income shortage, not housing shortage. The cure lies in education, jobs and the resulting increase in the power to control one's destiny. In the same way, participation in high culture and ethnic tolerance are products of a specific kind of experience—education—and we all do not need to move into Manhattan or the Loop in order to have such experience. (In both respects, recent national policy changes seem to result in more realistic programs.) Indeed, the spatial metaphor which leads us to focus upon the hallowed ground of "the city" probably produces more confusion than anything else.

For the city as we reconstruct it from the past no longer exists. Small towns, yes; isolation from the national network and the sharp bounds of farm land leave a tangible reality in the smaller settlements. But when we reach populations large enough to support what we think of as metropolitan functions (the arts and sciences, the specialized markets) we typically find, not an urban form, but an urban texture. Megalopolis, the strip of urban development down the Middle Atlantic seaboard, is in part an artifact of spot maps. It has little unity except contiguity. Yet that is the probable pattern of our emerging regional conurbations.

Most basic to this development is the radical change in the meaning of space. Our technologies have so developed that the entire nation can participate in moments of high solemnity more easily than could be residents of a fairly small town in the recent past; television is the new public forum. At the same time for some actors in some organizations, the entire nation is one city—Megalopolis is Main Street, the airport the major crossroads. As for the average citizen, it is likely that high significance resides, for the most part, either in a realm below that of the public (i.e., the household) or above that of the city (i.e., the national Big Screen).

If we are to exert control over the shape of our cities we must begin with a candid examination of the real nature of urban civilization today. We must take into account what John Friedman has called "interactional space," rendering the metaphors derived from maps into a useful form for this United States today. We must accept the basis in value and choice of widespread decentralization, developing an aesthetic appropriate to it—a view of "the city of a thousand places, the city on wheels," as David Crane has phrased it. Most of the difficulties of our past civic policies derived from their inappropriateness to the total round and rhythm of life in a radically changing and expanding society. With a more accurate map of what is, a more adequate explanation of why it is, we may begin to approach the major question: What do we want with enough consistency and vigor to pay the price?

Or: Do we really care about our cities?

IX EPILOGUE: THE CITY AND THE HISTORIANS

It has been said that to plan for the future one must look at the past. This last chapter is a dialogue among historians concerning the past and future of the field of American urban history.[1] With his own particular emphasis, each of the four historians reviews and criticizes the work that has been done and makes suggestions of what might be done. Together they constitute an intellectual stock-taking of a field that is relatively new as a separate discipline in American history; yet, as her older sister disciplines have had to do, urban history is groping for new subject matter, new methods of research, new kinds of evidence in order to achieve her own identity.

Although the approach and ideas of each may differ, there are some binding themes that run as common threads through each essay. (1) We need more precise definitions of what we mean by "urban," "urbanism," and the "urbanization process." (2) We need a broader, more systematic conceptual framework that embraces the city in its totality. (3) We should expand to make our methodological approach more sophisticated by incorporating into our traditional historical research methods the techniques and ideas of the social scientists—the political scientists, economists, urban sociologists, urban geographers, cultural anthropologists, and quantitative analyzers.

In the first selection, Dwight Hoover surveys the diverging paths of American urban history in a broad, analytical survey of the major literature of

1. For other bibliographical essays, see Charles N. Glaab, "The Historian and the American City: A Bibliographical Survey," in Philip M. Hauser and Leo F. Schnore (eds.), *The Study of Urbanization* (New York: John Wiley, 1965), Allen F. Davis, "The American Historian vs. the City," *Social Studies*, Vol. LVI (March-April 1965), pp. 91-96, 127-35, Anne Firor Scott, "The Study of Southern Urbanization," *Urban Affairs* (March 1966), pp. 5-14; Asa Briggs, "The Study of Cities," *Australian Journal of Adult Education*, Vol. 2 (1962); and R. Richard Wohl, "Urbanism, Urbanity, and the Historian," *University of Kansas City Review* (Autumn 1955), pp. 53-61.

the field.[2] It seems more often than not that the paths twist and turn to no-where and refuse to join into a common trail. There is good reason for this. There is no consensus among historians about what actually constitutes urban history, its main organizing themes, its methodology, its scope, its impact, and, indeed, its subject matter. Should the investigator take, as it were, a double major in history and sociology, with perhaps a minor in aesthetics? Should he be a humanist or a social scientist, or both? Is the city another "frontier" or should a historian drop that red-hot generalization and stick to executing his sums in population analysis?

One path was trod by traditional historians using conventional techniques, asking the more orthodox historical questions, a trail blazed by Arthur M. Schlesinger, followed by such people as Constance Green, Bessie Pierce, Richard Wade, and Blake McKelvey. Another path was traveled by a more motley group, beginning with Robert Parks of the Chicago school of ecologists, Louis Wirth (who took a side trip), economic historians like Eric Lampard—armed to the teeth in the event he met any conventional historians—neo-ecologists like Otis D. Duncan and Leo F. Schnore. As Hoover shows, the woods are full of paths with all kind of folks—anthropologists, social psychologists, political scientists, philosophers, city planners, and dev-otees of the computer. Hoover himself suggests a few more: explorations into city boosting, expositions and fairs, popular magazines, immigrant letters, and the idea of community. Despite the inconsistencies, endemic to any new field, despite the serious if not sometimes abrasive disagreement, there is already a corpus of first-rate literature, some of which can be labeled distinguished. Urban history has come a long way since it was dominated by antiquarians, sentimentalists, and chamber-of-commerce enthusiasts who pro-duced, to paraphrase Asa Briggs, history with the brains left out.

One of the sharpest critics of urban history is Eric Lampard who, in 1961, published an article that was at once a critique of the directions taken by urban historians and a theoretical scheme for making urban history more "urban."[3] Lampard presented a critique concerning omissions: the failure to study the societal forces that created the city; the failure to construct an adequate social history by neglecting to trace urban community life; the fail-ure to construct a systematic conceptual scheme that would liberate the city

2. See also Dwight Hoover, *A Teacher's Guide to American Urban History* (Chicago: Quadrangle Books, 1971).

3. *American Historical Review* (October 1961). See also Eric Lampard, "Historical As-pects of Urbanization," *The Study of Urbanization*, edited by Philip M. Hauser and Leo F. Schnore (New York: John Wiley, 1965), pp. 519-54; and "The Evolving System of Cities in the United States," *Issues in Urban Economics*, edited by Harvey S. Perloff and Lowdon Wingo, Jr. (Baltimore: The Johns Hopkins Press, 1968), pp. 81-139; Everett S. Lee and Michael Lalli, "Population," *Growth of Seaport Cities*, edited by David T. Gilchrist (Charlottesville: University Press of Virginia, 1967), pp. 25-37; and Sidney Goldstein, *Patterns of Mobility, 1910-1950: The Norristown Study* (Phila-delphia: University of Pennsylvania Press, 1958).

from piecemeal examination; and the failure to distinguish between what *is* and what *is not* generic to the city. To fill the vacuum of omissions, Lampard proposed two related approaches: the study of the urbanization process which has moulded cities, with particular emphasis upon the causes and consequences of population concentration; the application of the techniques and insights of the ecological school of urban sociology to the comparative study of urban communities. Buttressing urbanization and demography, Lampard insisted that "urbanization is a phenomenon worth explaining in itself and one that may help in the explanation of other facets of social change."

Roy Lubove, the author of the next essay, could not agree more. The central theme of his essay is that a study of the urbanization process and all its ramifications is essential if urban history is to become a more viable and significant discipline. Reviewing three categories of urban history, Lubove is especially disenchanted with the trend of writing that loosely defines "urban" as everything that happened in cities. "If . . . we are to spare the city from becoming a kind of historical variety store—a thematic free-for-all used to explain everything, and hence nothing—it is necessary to limit or define the subject." To do this Lubove presents an approach that defines urbanization as the "city building process . . . the process of city building over time." He embraces Lampard's ideas about the ecological complex, population concentrations, and the shifting structural changes in urban communities, but goes even further. Lubove's most significant suggestion is that the objective methods of the ecologists must be balanced by the subjective approach of the behavioral school of social science. Lubove recognizes the limitations of ecology. It does not tell all. Most particularly, demographic and structural situations do not always explain why people act the way they do. The behavioralists pursue goals more elusive than and less vulnerable to the more precise and systematic analysis of the ecologists; nonetheless, their interest in attitudes, value systems, so-called cultural trait complexes, interpersonal relationships between individuals and groups is vitally important. In effect, the behavioralists tend to humanize urban studies. At present, however, there are sharp disagreements between the behavioralists and the ecologists. A reconciliation between the two schools would create a major theoretical breakthrough for all those interested in urban studies.

Another of Lubove's contributions that needs to be underscored is his development of the relationship between technology and the city. He sees it as a broad cultural phenomenon whereby technology is stitched to invention, communications, social organization, and city-building. Curiously, the vital role of technology in the urbanization process has been largely ignored by urban historians and, even more curiously, by the historians of technology themselves.

In the last essay of this book, Stephan Thernstrom, the most articulate spokesman for the so-called "new" urban history, is also dissatisfied with the general thrust of urban historical studies. He and his flock are riding the crest of a new movement that has also excited social and cultural historians. It is history from the "bottom up," the history of the inarticulate, the ordinary men and women, the "little guys," if you will, who didn't write books or hold high public office but who were nonetheless a critical force in this nation's history.[4] Thernstrom argues quite rightly that historians have skewed history in favor of the articulate, the middle and patrician classes and their formal institutions, neglecting the "grass roots," the masses at the bottom of the heap. In his pursuit of the masses, the new urban historian offers a method —quantitative analysis,[5] a machine—the computor; imaginative historical sources—city directories, local tax lists, census schedules, marriage license files, birth certificates, assessor's valuation records. He offers new directions of inquiry: internal migration from country to city, patterns of social stratification and social mobility, the social consequences of technological change, the distribution of property and power, the position of ethnic and racial groups, the evolution of the family, working-class institutions, to name a few. And the new urban historian offers a goal: "to understand how and why the complex of changes suggested by the concept 'urbanization' re-shaped society." "Society" is the key word, for it suggests an interest in historical problems that go beyond the boundaries of the cities. Thus, the new urban historian is as much a social historian as he is an urban historian.

Thernstrom represents a small but growing species of urban historians, a hard-working, determined, gritty bunch who have already made significant contributions to urban history in particular and social history in general. One of the most interesting sections of this essay, in fact, is Thernstrom's catalogue of triumphs of the new history in such areas as urban population fluidity (especially the volatile rate of urban migration), class and ethnic differentials in spatial mobility, rates and trends in social mobility, immigra-

4. See Tamara K. Hareven (ed.), *Anonymous Americans* (Englewood Cliffs, N.J.: Prentice-Hall, 1971), Jesse Lemisch, "The American Revolution Seen from the Bottom Up," in Barton J. Bernstein (ed.), *Towards a New Past: Dissenting Essays in American History* (New York: Pantheon, 1968), Rudolph Becoli, "Ethnicity: A Neglected Dimension of American History," in Herbert J. Bass (ed.), *The State of American History* (Chicago: Quadrangle Books, 1970), Samuel P. Hays, "A Systematic Social History," in George Billias and Gerald Grob (eds.), *American History: Retrospect and Prospect* (New York: Free Press, 1971), Stephan Thernstrom, *Progress and Poverty in a Nineteenth Century City* (Cambridge: Harvard University Press, 1964), Peter R. Knights, *The Plain People of Boston* (New York: Oxford University Press, 1971), Richard Sennett, *Families Against the City* (Cambridge: Harvard University Press, 1970), John Demos, *A Little Commonwealth: Family Life in Plymouth Colony* (New York: Oxford University Press, 1970), and Philip Greven, *Four Generations: Population, Land and Family in Colonial Andover* (Ithaca, N.Y., Cornell University Press, 1970).
5. For discussions on the quantitative method, see Don K. Rowney and James Q. Graham, Jr., *Quantitative History* (Homewood, Ill.: Dorsey Press, 1969), Seymour Martin Lipset and Richard Hofstadter, *Sociology and History Methods* (New York: Basic Books, 1968), and William O. Adelotte, "Quantification in History," *The American Historical Review*, 71 (April 1969), pp. 803-25.

tion and differential opportunity, comparisons between Negro migrants and European immigrants, and, to boot, the hint of a new phenomenon, "a permanent floating proletariat."

What gives this essay a particular quality is balance. Unlike some enthusiasts, Thernstrom offers neither perfection nor panacea. He acknowledges pitfalls in the quantitative method, both conceptual and mathematical (to which might be added the tendency to let the welter of statistical buckshot—the facts, figures, equations, and grafts—obscure the flesh and bones, the very *humanness* of the people being studied). Unlike other enthusiasts, he does not banish conventional historical sources (newspapers, pamphlets, magazines, manuscripts, novels, etc.) to a historical limbo with the proposition that what is really real is only that which can be counted. Mathematical tabulations are meaningful only when related to the larger context of ideology, cultural traditions, politics, religion, values, and so on. What Thernstrom offers, then, is a different path to that thorny problem of making sense out of the urbanization process.

It will be interesting to see how many recruits the new urban history wooes to its ranks in future years. It takes a special kind of personality, plus a dogged dedication, to follow hundreds of immigrants through the U.S. Census schedules, city directories, and tax rolls for a score of years. It will probably appeal to younger historians, who have the time and inclination to learn sophisticated statistical techniques in the course of their training. Older historians (good on dates, poor on math) might shutter at the prospect of "going back to school." Moreover, there is a strong conservative block in the profession who have a profound distaste for anything social "science-y."

Whether or not the differences between the historians represented here and the historians who write the more conventional urban history can be reconciled, remains to be seen. Conflict and disagreement has, however, created a boon for American urban history: pluralism, the opportunity for choice, to wit, a variety of approaches to study of the city. This is illustrated by two fairly recent books of outstanding quality: *A History of Urban America,* by Charles N. Glaab and A. Theodore Brown,[6] who incorporate the techniques of the social sciences, and *The Emergence of Metropolitan America,* by Blake McKelvey,[7] who is of the "older" school and who integrates the city into the mainstream of American history. Perhaps, then, one of the key questions for the future of American urban history is whether or not we can write history that *balances* the study of the urbanization process *and* the impact of the city upon American history. Whatever the outcome, urban history, like the city itself, will continue to be one of the most difficult, yet fascinating, challenges to the historical imagination.

6. (New York: Macmillan, 1967).
7. (New Brunswick, N.J.: Rutgers University Press, 1968).

The Diverging Paths of American Urban History

Dwight W. Hoover

The years following World War II have been characterized by an increased interest in urban themes. As succeeding census reports show growing metropolitan areas and as urban problems attract America's attention, the city looms larger and larger. Historians share in the increased awareness of the city; in the years since 1945 the number of urban histories has increased and the number of historians specializing in urban history has grown commensurately.[1] The trend at the present seems irreversible; more not less effort will be devoted to the history of the American city.

However, urban historians have not yet agreed upon an all embracing theory, one that would provide an organizing principle upon which the history of the city could be based. Several approaches have been suggested; each approach has had its disciples. No single theory has gained the universal approbation of urban historians. Each is based upon different assumptions and value systems; each has its drawbacks and its virtues. The purpose of this essay is to explore the paths that are now most heavily used by scholars of the city.

Part of the dilemma of the urban historian is the dilemma of the recent historian, whether to remain a humanist or become a social scientist, whether to turn to aesthetics or to sociology. More specifically, the problem of the urban historian begins with the subject to be studied. Is the historian to study the city or urban civilization?[2] Is urban history to attempt the formulation of a general law or urbanization, or is it to essay a comparative study of persisting institutions? Is the city itself the source of social change or is it only part of a larger source? What element in the cities is crucial to development? As scholars search for answers, the projection of Kenneth Boulding concerning the future ought to haunt us all. When 90% of the population becomes urban, Boulding says, the city will have no separate meaning. An Iowa farmer at present is an exurbanite who is part of an occupational subculture.[3] If urban culture becomes the only standard, will urban history become the only history? Perhaps the historical future belongs to the urban historian and urban interpretations.

Any consideration of a theory of urban history must start with A. M. Schlesinger. Channing's fifth volume[4] in his *A History of the United States* had hinted at the importance of the city, but the bold claims of an urban historian were initially made by Schlesinger. In 1933 he wrote *The Rise of the City* in which he attempted to place the American city in its proper perspective; and in the *Mississippi Valley Historical Review* (June 1940), his article "The City in American His-

From *American Quarterly*, xx (Summer 1968), pp. 296-317. Reprinted by permission of the author and the publisher. Dwight Hoover is Professsor of History at Ball State University.

tory" blazed a trail which many urban historians have followed. Schlesinger claimed to have found the key to social change in America in the city. For him, the city was the frontier where new ideas, revolutionary in impact, were originated, and where social practices, under pressure by problems generated by people living in close proximity, changed to fit new experiences. Innovation, hence change, in both social and intellectual spheres was a product of city life. On the basis of this assumption, Schlesinger proposed a program for historians. From colonial times to the present, the city should be the prime object of study. The major elements within the city to be investigated should be the characteristic economic institutions and social practices of the citizens. Thus, Schlesinger wished to change both the locus and the focus of American historians.

The claims of Schlesinger for an urban centered history did not go unchallenged. William Diamond the following year commented devastatingly upon some of the weaknesses of the Schlesinger thesis. His criticisms are still apropos for urban historians today. Schlesinger failed, according to Diamond, to define either the city or urbanization clearly, to take cognizance of Mumford's work which showed the city to be more than one entity, to distinguish between the cultural traits that were permanent in the city and those that were merely transitional, and to demonstrate that an urban-rural division of history was more significant than others in explaining behavior. Above all, Diamond insisted that Schlesinger's concept of the city was ambiguous, just as the Turnerian concept of the frontier had

been. All Schlesinger had done was to substitute one broad generalization for another.[5] Since neither the city nor the frontier was rigorously enough defined, no light was shed on the problem of cause in history.

Diamond's criticisms, appropriate and convincing as they appear to be, did not dim the hopes of urban historians who found the concept of the city as originator of social change appealing. Indeed, the analogy of the city with the frontier proved too compelling to discard. A decade later, W. Stull Holt explicitly thought of the city in these terms while reviewing studies done of individual cities: Bessie Pierce's *A History of Chicago*, Bayrd Still's *Milwaukee*, and Constance McLaughlin Green's *Holyoke, Massachusetts*. The histories of these specific cities, Holt said, "are like the various histories of sections of the frontier such as Roosevelt's *Winning of the West* before Turner in his famous essay saw the forest as well as the trees."[6] (One might wonder whether the comparison with Roosevelt would be considered complimentary by these historians.) Holt, however, was not completely satisfied with the generalizations of Schlesinger and tried to add to the description of the urban experience. Several consequences of living in cities were significant to Holt. These included an older population, a lowered birth rate, more freedom for women and a change in the conception of the function of the state from a negative to a positive one, necessitated by problems of public health, education and sanitation.[7] These characteristics of an urban population, both demographic and ideological, were the ones that had made the city the innovator in the American past. The quality of city populations and the necessity to regulate the environment in order to survive had produced the welfare state which is most characteristic of American life.

Two comments are in order here. Using Diamond's insight that there are trends in the city that are short rather than long range, two of Holt's city population characteristics, an older population and a lower birth rate, are temporary. Again much depends upon the definition of the city. Does the city include the suburbs? If so, the population is not noticeably older than the aging rural population. If only the inner city is used, the Negro migration to and the white flight from the center still tends to weaken the generalization. The population age is more a function of socio-economic class than residence, and the demographic features of the city reflect the social make-up of the times. Secondly, the change in political theory attributable to urban condition discounts the cries for federal regulation by farmers in the nineteenth century and the considerable federal aid to rural interests in the twentieth. One could well argue that farmers, although retaining a Jeffersonian anti-governmental ideology, were among the first to enter a planned society; and city dwellers, although not averse to aid, among the last.

Despite the demurrers, the Schlesinger thesis has persisted. Carl Bridenbaugh in *Cities in Revolt* (1955) and *Cities in the Wilderness* (1938) traced the role of cities in the American Revolution and in frontier settlement, attributing to the cities considerable credit for both these movements. Richard C. Wade has also continued the tradition in *The Urban Frontier: The Rise of Western Cities* (1959)

and *Slavery in the Cities: The Antebellum South* (1964). Despite the rural nature of both the trans-Appalachian West and the South in the pre-Civil War period, Wade portrayed cities as important transforming forces. In the South the rural institution of slavery underwent a noticeable transformation into a kind of urban segregation under the liberalizing influence of urban living conditions. In the West Wade concludes that "Cities represented the most aggressive and dynamic forces."[8] Both Bridenbaugh and Wade center the city in the middle of political, intellectual and social developments from the beginning of the Republic.

In addition to specific studies of American cities Wade has, perhaps, made the best summation of the claims for urban innovation. Among the contributions made by cities to American life Wade lists are the origin of settlement, particularly in the West; the responsibility for triggering the revolution, especially in Boston; the promotion of economic growth through city rivalry in the nineteenth century; the coming together of North and West in the Civil War because of Chicago's triumph over St. Louis as a railroad center; the degeneration of slavery in the South; the development of techniques of political manipulation such as boss rule; and the reactions to this manipulation such as progressive reform.[9] With Wade, as with Schlesinger, the cities are where social change originated.

Another urban historian, Blake McKelvey, studying the period after the Civil War, 1865-1915, made as great claims for the role of the city. McKelvey explicitly tied the city to the frontier, stating that the unexploited potential of older established cities or of hamlets near them provided a substitute for the closing of the frontier in 1890.[10] That McKelvey's book is in the Schlesinger tradition is evident in the topics he considered; economic growth, especially in banking and credit facilities; the development of regional centers with outlying tributaries; the expansion of transport facilities; and technological change. These all are cited as having been advanced by urbanization. A corollary theme was the interaction between social forces and the city, especially in education, public health, recreation and the arts. McKelvey gave much credit to the urban atmosphere for the changing of American attitudes in the social realm and economic institutions in the economic sphere.

Perhaps the most prolific woman urban historian in America is Constance McLaughlin Green, who, like McKelvey, came to consider the broader theme of the city in American development through the biography of individual cities.[11] Green's two volumes on American urban history, *American Cities in the Growth of the Nation* (1957) and *The Rise of Urban America* (1965) viewed the city as an important factor in the development of an American way of life.[12] In the earlier book Green had a series of vignettes, four involving cities of a particular type—seaboard cities of the nineteenth century, river cities, New England manufacturing cities and cities of the great plains—and four individual cities —Chicago, Seattle, Detroit and Washington. As can be seen, this division was socio-economic, reflecting an interest in unique social and economic development of particular cities. In *American Cities in the Growth of the Nation*, there was not the concerted

attempt to tie city growth in the United States together as in the later book, *The Rise of Urban America*, but Mrs. Green's second effort at a larger urban history is quite inferior to her first. *American Cities in the Growth of the Nation* has many valuable insights in it while *The Rise of Urban America* seems slim by comparison. It is essentially a conventional social and economic history placed in an urban setting, and suffers from the lack of any overall conceptual framework. While Mrs. Green assumes that cities have shaped American life, she is never as explicit as Schlesinger or Wade, making her synthesis disjointed and weak.

The kind of urban history that Wade, McKelvey and Green write is obvious. Taking the themes already extant in American history—sectionalism, the growth of public education, reform and reaction—these historians search for the roots in movements in the city. With varying degrees of sophistication, they switch the locale of historical change from the frontier to the city. Unlike Schlesinger, they are modest and less willing to make sweeping claims for the place of the city in American history, although implicitly they believe that place has been severely undervalued by earlier historians. For this group of urban historians, urban history is social history drawn from the city.

Urban history following this path does reveal a number of possibilities for further research, particularly in recent history. The role of city in civil rights movement, as Green suggests, the attraction of McCarthyism in the city, the city origins of the New Deal, isolationism in the cities, modern Republicanism in the cities, all could be studied in depth. However, the substitution of the city for the frontier as an organizing principle has pernicious as well as fruitful results. By explaining too much, the city as a cause of social change blocks other, better explanations.

Still, the use of the Schlesinger thesis gave some differentiation to urban history which biographies of individual cities or collective biographies seemed to lack. But all of the histories considered so far suffer, as Roy Lubove says, from the same difficulty: "The main point is that all the publications in this category deal with cities, or life in cities, but rarely with urban history as distinguished from social, economic or political history in the context of the city."[13] The need for a unique framework for urban history remains unmet in this approach.

Possibilities other than social history became evident in the post-World War II period. Earlier definitions of urban history by historians proved too gross and the need to be more precise was obvious. In addition, the work being done by social scientists seemed to offer a theoretical basis for a study of the city as a process of urbanization. Urban historians, like other historians, were not unaware of the prestige attached to scientific enterprises. The discipline that offered the most promising insights was sociology, which had had a continuing interest in community studies, and not political science, which had become involved elsewhere.[14]

For years the center for urban sociology was located at the University of Chicago from which sociologists fanned out to study the city. The most productive theory also came from Chicago. Robert Park, one of the pioneers of urban sociology, had derived an ecological model from biology and seemed to regard human ecology like plant and animal ecology with "social equivalents."[15] Park proposed to study population movements and land values in the aggregate and to deny the possibility of the planned urban environment. The city environment, rather, was a natural, unplanned one which determined interdependence between individuals. Park's associate, Burgess, developed an ecological map of Chicago in the 1920s which was composed of five concentric circles, each representing a different environment or natural area. The crude ecology of Park and Burgess soon came under attack as being inadequate. In the 1930s the retreat from the original ecological presumption began and the strict determinism softened, as Louis Wirth, Park's student, shifted Park's ecological emphasis somewhat in order to meet the criticisms. Starting with ideal types of cultures, urban-industrial and rural-folk, similar to the distinction between *Gemeinschaft* and *Gesellschaft* and to the urban-rural dichotomy of Schlesinger, Wirth attributed the difference between the two types to urbanization. Urbanism was:

that cumulative accentuation of the characteristics distinctive of the mode of life which is associated with the growth of cities, and finally to the changes in the direction of modes of life among people, wherever they may be, who have come under the spell of influences which the city exerts by virtue of the power of its institutions and personalities operating through the means of communication and transportation.[16]

From Wirth's statement it is apparent that while ecological considerations are still important, other influences on the creation of an urban type also must be taken into account. A theory of urbanization followed with three necessary factors: physical structure (population, technology, ecology); social organization (status groups, institutions); and collective behavior (group attitudes, ideologies). Wirth's theory has been quite fruitful; but, like many other seminal ideas, has rarely been taken whole. The diverging paths of urban history lead out from Wirth.[17] The first category, physical structure, has appealed primarily to sociologists who have emphasized ecology and population aggregates and to historians who have visualized communications as the key to the cities in naturalistic, reductionist fashion. Still others have concentrated upon the second category and traced the evolution and influence of social stratification and institutions in the growth of the city. Still others see the third as most meaningful and have written about the mutual interaction of ideas and the city. Finally, there are those historians who attempt to use all three categories in an explanation of the process of urbanization, which for these individuals, is urban history.

The first group, the ecologists, are still physically located in Chicago. The death blow to the original ecology of Park seemingly was struck by a book written by Walter Firey, *Land Use in Central Boston* (1946), which showed that community and society were inseparable and that urban land value was a function of cultural demands set by community sentiment as well as by location. Yet old ideas are hard to kill. The same year in Chicago the Chicago Community Inventory was created by a grant from the Wiebolt Foundation. In 1951, Philip M. Hauser, a sociologist interested both in studies of population and comparative urban-

ization, became director. Hauser has collaborated with Leo F. Schnore, a Wisconsin sociologist, also interested in population theory. Schnore and another sociologist, Otis D. Duncan, have attempted to revive ecology as a respectable explanation for the structure of cities, and hence are in a direct line from Robert Park. Using Amos H. Hawley's *Human Ecology* (1950) as a base, these sociologists continue to insist that population aggregates are the most important element in the study of the city and that statistical manipulation is the necessary tool. A typical ecological statement by Duncan and Schnore is contained in a 1959 issue of *American Journal of Sociology*, published by the University of Chicago. Duncan and Schnore argue that ecology offered the best insights into the perennial problems of sociologists emanating from social organization—bureaucracy and stratification. In addition the ecological approach provided a theory of social change which the cultural and behavioral schools could not do. Finally, ecology was the best base for interdisciplinary cooperation. After presenting a case for ecology, Duncan and Schnore then constructed a modified ecological complex consisting of population, environment, technology and organization.[18] The relationship between men and their environment combined with social organization and technology made up all of the necessary ingredients for urbanization. Wirth's third division was ignored and the first expanded to occupy almost the whole of urban studies.

The ecological approach has not converted a great number of sociologists. Duncan and Schnore were immediately challenged for distortion of the cultural and behavioral assumptions of sociologists and for attempting to include all of sociological endeavor under one great imperial network.[19] In addition, their belief that more orthodox methodologies were inadequate for studying social organization was not matched by a completely convincing methodology of their own. Duncan and Schnore opted for a quantitative method, deliberately incomplete (an abstract model), and for comparative analysis of aggregates.[20] For Duncan and Schnore, the greatest asset was the statistical manipulation of increased sophistication possible in the ecological approach.[21]

More recently the assumptions of the ecologists have been specifically attacked. While admitting that ecology is the "closest we have come to a systematic theory of the city,"[22] Reissman argues that ecologists are still biological determinists. The study of population aggregates and the principles that keep these aggregates operative is undertaken as analogous to animal ecology. Thus, the environment in ecological discussions assumes the causative function; adaption to the environment by man includes culture, social stratification and institutions. In finding this cause for social change the ecologists have returned to a Spencerian figure of a social organism.[23]

The rehabilitation of ecology by sociologists like Duncan and Schnore came during the 1950s when urban historians were casting about for an organizing theory. One individual in particular, Eric Lampard, has tried to promote the ecological principle as the framework for urban history.

Lampard explicitly uses the ecological ideas of Duncan and Schnore in his framework for the study of urbanization.[24] For Lampard, as for the ecologists, community structure is the result of a changing equilibrium between population and environment mediated by technology and organization. Lampard urges the adoption of the ecological complex of Amos Hawley, Otis Duncan and Leo Schnore, as well as the study of urbanization as a societal process without committing the past errors of confusing the pathological aspects of the process with the normal.

Lampard not only urges historians to be ecologists; he also dissects the failures of urban history.[25] Tracing the backgrounds of urban history, Lampard finds the difficulty in this past. Coming out of social history, urban history concentrated on social problems rather than social change, on conflicts of interest and ideas rather than social organization and social structure.[26] Because of these preoccupations, urban history lacks both a general, theoretical framework and relevant data to that framework.[27] Lampard proposes to remedy both deficiencies. "At stake in a broader view of urban history is the possibility of making the societal process of urbanization central to the study of social change. Efforts should be made to conceptualize urbanization in ways that actually *represent* social change."[28] Basic to social change is ecology—population, its changing composition and its distribution in space and time.[29] The theoretical framework for the urban historian, then, should be the study of population change. The necessary social data is to be found in migration and social mobility, which includes both occupational shifts and changes in social status.[30] Of the salient ways to advance on the city—structural, behavioral and demographical—the demographic is best, according to Lampard.[31]

Lampard represents a bridge between the neo-ecological sociologists and the urban historian. At a time when the study of population movements and ecology are out of favor with the majority of sociologists, Lampard attempts to make ecological assumptions palatable to historians and to convince historians that they must study population change. While no historian has become an avowed ecologist, certainly there is a noticeable tendency to make population studies on a quantified basis.[32]

That the study of population mobility can be instructive is illustrated by a pioneer work of Stephan Thernstrom. Thernstrom was connected with another center for studying urban and regional affairs, the Joint Center for Urban Studies of Harvard University and Massachusetts Institute of Technology. Begun in 1959, the Joint Center has been interested in basic research in a variety of disciplines including aesthetics, architectural history and urban planning. Its basic orientation was not sociological, as was Chicago's, so its studies have ranged more widely. Indeed, the ecological tradition was never strong at the Joint Center because of the considerable impact of *Land Use in Central Boston*.

Thernstrom's book, *Poverty and Progress*, did utilize criteria for studying Newburyport similar to those proposed by Lampard. Using manuscript census schedules and local records of the 1850-1880 period, Thernstrom analyzed occupational, geographic and inter-generational mobility among laborers and their sons, as well as prop-

erty accumulations and other evidence of increased affluence. All of this was designed to discover social mobility in mid-nineteenth century Newburyport. Thernstrom's conclusions were that social mobility was minimal, that occupational shifts upward were slight, and that property accumulations seldom amounted to more than a house. On the basis of these conclusions, Thernstrom hazarded an opinion that the open class system of the nineteenth century was largely mythical. As he put it, "The findings of the present study, however, when coupled with scattered evidence concerning social mobility in several twentieth-century American cities, permit a more definite verdict: to rise from the bottom of the social scale has not become increasingly difficult in modern America: If anything it appears to have become somewhat less difficult."[33]

Thernstrom's work cut in several directions. On the one hand, it opened the door for other urban historians to study further social mobility in other American cities to see if Thernstrom's results obtain. (Curiously enough, Thernstrom indicates that his findings are not too divergent from Curti's study of Trempealeau County.) In particular, those communities that had been already studied without much consideration of the time dimension by sociologists or anthropologists provide a base from which to work. Not only Yankee City, but Middletown and Elmtown, could be examined; and since some of the census data is now being programmed for computers, the possibility of machine assisted research also obtains. Thernstrom presently is engaged in just such a study of Boston under a grant from the American Council of Learned Societies. Furthermore, the study of mobility could be extended to other than the laborer category; studies of middle and upper class mobility might well be assayed. Perhaps Thernstrom, more than any other urban historian, has shown the way for further statistical attacks on the city.

On the other hand, Thernstrom's work is a devastating criticism of the ahistorical social scientist, and of W. Lloyd Warner, in particular. After giving Warner due credit for the magnitude of his efforts, Thernstrom listed his major failures: not coming to grips with social mobility, not seeing changes in population composition or in the character of institutions, and unwillingness to use objective criteria for classes. From these failures Thernstrom derives an unequivocal theorem: "The distortions of the Yankee City volumes should suggest that the student of modern society is not free to take his history or leave it alone. Interpretation of the present requires assumptions about the past."[34] The choice is between an assumed past and a studied one. Warner had been guilty of holding romantic assumptions about Newburyport's past; he had not bothered to examine that past, and, as a result, had produced a distorted study. Equally important with the critique of Warner was Thernstrom's insistence that a community study be done over a span of time. The urban historian becomes an indispensable part of a community study, not an unnecessary luxury. Because of its opening of new areas of investigation and reassertion of the value of historical methods, Thernstrom's book is a landmark in urban history.[35] But Thernstrom's position is not an ecological one; it does not operate with aggregates or mathematical models.

Another approach is to use one particular category in the study of communities as Seymour Mandlebaum has done with communications in New York in the era of Boss Tweed.[36] Rather than study population characteristics as Thernstrom did, Mandlebaum studied technology in the form of communications networks in Tweed's New York. Mandlebaum has returned to Park, who held that the key to the city is communication. However, the theoretical basis here is much more sophisticated. While Mandlebaum has not become involved in the mathematical methods of Karl W. Deutsch in *The Nerves of Government* (1963) or Richard L. Meier in *A Communications Theory of Urban Growth* (1962), he does suggest that these have promise for the future. The central theme of Mandlebaum's book is the primitive state of communication networks in New York City in Tweed's time. Basic to Tweed's ascendancy was the failure of information to be exchanged in any kind of adequate manner. Mandlebaum does effect a limited rehabilitation of Tweed, arguing that he was a product of a system of decentralized decision making and narrow, insufficient communication between decision centers. In a sense Mandlebaum suggests a theory of social change; when the price of ignorance becomes too high, citizens demand better information. When better information is had, political organizations change. When more sophistication in communications is desired, social evolution results.

There is an obvious difficulty in using communications theory as a basis for urban history. Once again a kind of naturalistic determinism permeates this theory. Communications theory shares the same real problem of neo-ecology, the use of organic analogy. Deutsch's book uses a figure that is singularly Spencerian, nerves of government; and the conception of a city hampered in social development by channels of communication can easily become the city as a biological organism. Despite this demurrer, the use of the model may be expected to increase.

Another possibility emerging from Wirth's third category this time is the study of group attitudes and ideologies regarding the city. The organizing principle in this approach might well be called, as several scholars have already done, the image of the city. The image of the city involves, not necessarily simultaneously, intellectual history, a theory of aesthetics, history of planning, perception theory and social psychology. In all cases the interest of the historian is in the concept of the city, whether that concept be a rational construct, an aesthetic reaction or a trained perception. Moreover, this approach has the virtue of being humanistic and nondeterministic.

Perhaps the most traditional way to undertake urban history in this fashion is through intellectual history, the study of the concept of urbanism and anti-urbanism. The antagonisms between rural and urban ways of life and thought have long been noted by historians as well as by those involved in popular culture. Almost every student of Jefferson has mentioned his anti-urban sentiments, and the reaction to the urbanization in the last half of the nineteenth century has been well documented.[37] However, the generalization was crude; urbanization and industrialization were sometimes used synonymously and the assumptions that anti-urbanism was a single, unchanging strand in American thought remained relatively unexamined.

An attempt to analyze some of the ideas of leading American theorists concerning the city was made, not by intellectual historians, but by a philosopher and a social worker, Morton and Lucia White. Operating from the institutional impetus of the Joint Center for Urban Studies, as well as the Center for Advanced Study in the Behavioral Sciences, the Whites gleaned selective attitudes toward the city and published them in *The Intellectual Versus the City* (1962).[38] The title gives away the plot; the opinions of the city considered are largely negative. In the individuals whose ideas were presented, from Benjamin Franklin to Frank Lloyd Wright, from the early republic to the twentieth century, anti-urbanism was a constant theme. However, the Whites were able to distinguish two varieties of anti-urbanism, one romantic and the other nonromantic. The earliest critique of the city, the romantic ones, shared by Jefferson and Emerson, held that the city was overcivilized and distorted nature. Since nature was the respository of virtue, the city was evil. The romantic view of the city is most often the one cited in anti-urban views, but it is not the most recent or persistent. Commencing after the Civil War, the second critique of the city, one shared by Robert Park and Henry James, made an opposing point, the city is undercivilized. The city had failed to achieve the kind of community necessary for human development, whether that development be intellectual as it was for Henry Adams and Henry James, or emotional as Robert Park and

Jane Addams envisaged in their hopes for improved small group relationships. The Whites professed to find anti-urbanism even in persons most intimately connected with the city in a time when the city was becoming the dominant form of American life; the concept of sophisticated anti-urbanism is perhaps their most original contribution.

While *The Intellectual Versus the City* is a compelling book, it is at the same time unsatisfactory. On the one hand, anti-urbanism is demonstrated; but, on the other, the nagging question persists as to whether the two views (or, for that matter, the many views in the book) belong in the same category, springing as they do from different premises. The romantic view could not countenance the city; the nonromantic could and did. The romantic would wish to destroy the city; the nonromantic to transform it. In addition, the growth of American cities in the period after the Civil War, the period that the Whites treat most extensively, poses the question of how this was possible without considerable intellectual energy behind it.[39] Furthermore, the twofold division of anti-urbanism is admittedly too simple; even the Whites suggest this. Hence, the investigation of anti-urban themes in American thought has continuing possibilities.

Not only could such a study be made of intellectuals, but also of leaders of popular culture. A case can be made that there is and was considerable uneasiness about urban life on the level of popular culture. One recent example of the possibility is Robert H. Walker's study of popular verse published between 1876 and 1905. After studying six thousand volumes of verse (one wonders at Walker's strength and persistence after scan-

ning some of the poems), Walker concludes that the poetical images of the city were negative, portraying the city as an ugly place where economic inequities were the rule, where crime, drunkenness, sexual excesses, amorality prevailed, where existence was characterized by craftiness, overcompetitiveness and artificiality.[40] The view of the city as immoral and threatening on a less rarefied level of abstraction does seem to support the Whites' thesis, although the poetical critique of the city is a romantic one in the nonromantic era. This, of course, does not demolish the Whites' categories; one might suppose that a poetic image would always be romantic.

A much broader approach toward the images of the city comes from Anselm Strauss, a sociologist. Recognizing Park's dictum that the city is a state of mind, Strauss tried to identify the many minds that have conceived of the city and the many cities that have been seen.[41] Strauss' book, *Images of the American City*, shows some of the possibilities in the conceptualization of the city. For richness of suggestions for further study this book must rate high in the historiography of urban studies. Strauss is impressed with the symbolic imagery of the city and treats aesthetic dimensions left out by quantifying sociologists.

Strauss began with a premise that multiplies the images of the city. He argued that the city cannot be comprehended as a whole; that, at best, only parts can be visualized. Therefore, symbolic representation of the city is necessary and such symbolism is a function of physical, social and perceptual factors. As Strauss put it:

The city, I am suggesting, can be viewed as a complex related set of symbolized areas. Any given population will be cognizant of only a small number of these areas: most areas will lie outside of effective perception; others will be conceived in such ways that will hardly ever be visited, and will indeed be avoided.[42]

For each group in each area in every age there is a city. Strauss only begins to show the possible images of the city inherent in this approach. Among those he does treat are those views of the city found in ethnic groups, in urban novels, in visiting tourists, in city boosters, in mediators between towns and cities, in planners and in suburbanites. Not that these are by any means all new views of the city; some of them were used by the Whites, Park and Wirth. The accomplishment of Strauss is to collect all of the views together as examples of the multifaceted nature of the city, to suggest the barrenness of a single image of the city, and to use literature in an imaginative way.

Strauss in the case of Chicago shows how varying images of the city, over a period of time, can coalesce into one image. However, the thrust of his work is in two other directions. One is the direction of the positive image of the city. The negative concept of the city must certainly be qualified in order to meet Strauss' suggestions. Particularly intriguing is Strauss' discussion of the image of the city held by ethnic groups and the image of the city as the country. Strauss shows how it is possible for the city to be an urban village, which leads to the question of why the city could not be also an extension of Europe or of the countryside.[43] In the second place, the insistence upon the human necessity of symbolically representing the city is thought provoking. Projected into the past, several areas for investigation become obvious. In addition to study-

ing the city in literature, the novel and the poem, why not study the city in painting? Or why not combine the two as Leo Marx did in *The Machine in the Garden* (1964), detailing the impact of technology on American imaginations? Indeed some form of middle landscape might be as typical of views of the city as views of industrialization. Or symbolic representation of a particular section of a city might be studied as Allan Trachtenberg has done for the Brooklyn Bridge, *The Brooklyn Bridge* (1965).

Basic to the theoretical underpinning of the visual concept of the city is a book from the Joint Center for Urban Studies. That book is Kevin Lynch's *The Image of the City* (1960). In *The Image of the City* Lynch holds that cities must provide an image for their inhabitants. While some are more manageable than others, having parts more easily recognized and organized into a coherent pattern, all cities are represented symbolically by their citizens.[44] To prove this thesis Lynch analyzed three rather disparate cities—Boston, Jersey City and Los Angeles—using interviews as well as field reconaissance.

In each city a form emerged; each city had the requisite identity, structure and meaning.[45] To be sure, Lynch has a message; in order to enhance the ability of Americans to learn the images of their cities a concerted attempt to operate directly on the external physical shapes of the cities must be made.[46] Lynch's book is a plea for a new kind of urban design to create the kind of a city that can be easily managed into an image. As Lynch sees the problem, the question is not whether a city has an image; it is how can designers aid the image-making process? In support of his major thesis of environmental images Lynch cites material from psychology and anthropology. Using data gathered from studies of perception and from studies of primitive tribes, Lynch holds symbolic representation of environment is found everywhere in man. At M.I.T., Lynch is striving to improve visual education through training perception for city planners.[47] Much of the image of the city approach to urban history lies in the area of design of American cities and Lynch has outlined both a method and a philosophy to come to terms with urban design.

The history of the design of American cities considered in a holistic way has been the province of Christopher Tunnard. Predating Strauss and Lynch, and yet anticipating them both, Tunnard is an ardent proponent of the city as an aesthetic whole and of city planning as a humanistic experience. Like Lynch's, Tunnard's books[48] are pleas for better civic design and for a recognition that cities do have some basic image. Tunnard asserts that American townscapes in the past, as in the present, reflect American values. As values have changed, the purposes for which cities of the past were built have become foggy or even lost. Tunnard suggests in *American Skyline* a kind of topology for American city architecture. In America there have been seven eras of city development. There are: 1609-1775, colonial; 1775-1825, young republic; 1825-1850, romantic; 1850-1880, the age of steam and iron; 1880-1910, expanding city (the city as a way of life, the city beautiful); 1910-1933, city of towers; 1933—the regional city. Each of these eras had distinctive city designs, deflecting changing values. This periodization is

as satisfactory, it seems to me, as more conventional political ones; and the study of cities as architectural entities is as viable as the study of images expressed by poets.

The impressionistic studies of Tunnard were followed by two others which were pioneering in their own ways. John Burchard and Albert Bush-Brown produced *The Architecture of America: A Social and Cultural History* (1961). Although including more than city architecture, Burchard and Bush-Brown do consider the city as occupying a central role in American art forms. Another approach to urban history through aesthetics is John W. Reps' *The Making of Urban America: A History of City Planning in the United States*.[49] In the first full-scale study of planning, Reps ranges from European backgrounds to 1910 when two-dimensional concern of width of street and spatial patterns gives way to a three-dimensional interest in design, location and mass of buildings.[50] Voluminously illustrated, *The Making of Urban America* dispels the myth that American city planning was unimaginative and undeviatingly based upon a gridiron pattern. In this, Reps and Tunnard agree. They also agree on the historic importance of the Chicago World's Fair of 1893 as a watershed for the image of the city. The arrangement of the fair made possible a visualization of architectural arrangement that was most significant in stimulating the imagination of the American public.[51] Perhaps the aesthetic history of the city could be periodized thusly, before the Chicago World's Fair and after.

The image of the city approach to urban history offers many possibilities. A history of the American concept of the city in painting, by city boosters, in immigrant letters, in school textbooks, in expositions and fairs, in popular magazines, requires more detailed exploration. The idea of community in American cities has yet to be done. These are only a few of the avenues that branch off the main path of the image of the city. However, just as the urban historians of the neo-ecological approach lean toward sociology, the core of the image of the city seems to be aesthetics, particularly city design.

Not that this approach is free of danger. Attempts to derive images must necessarily be tenuous, unless concrete plans are used, as in Reps, and the deviation could be highly subjective. The emphasis upon quantification is unlikely to intrude (although this cannot be dismissed as a possibility). Rather the necessary qualifications seem to be artistic training and sensibility, plus an ability to go behind the obvious. Urban history as a history of the images of the city will also entice another clientele, those persuaded that history is art.

Beyond those scholars who can be subsumed under one or two Wirthian categories are those who attempt a synthesis of physical structure, social organization and collective behavior. Among such urban historians are individuals such as A. Theodore Brown, Charles N. Glaab and Roy Lubove. Brown and Glaab were influenced by R. Richard Wohl who collaborated with the sociologist Anselm Strauss, and who, while teaching at the University of Chicago, was also assisting in the study of the community of Kansas City. Wohl, who had a wide-ranging mind and competencies in history, economics and sociology, did stimulate Glaab and Brown at Kansas

City.[52] Another individual prominent in the attempt to fit these categories together has been Roy Lubove. Lubove, who has done some theoretical work, prefers to call this attempt a study of "the formation of the urban environment."[53] Such a title reflects the volitional aspects of city building, which is an important part of Lubove's theory.

All three of these historians share certain assumptions. They emphasize city building as interaction between decision-making individuals and groups —holding certain ideological views and under social and economic pressures— and technological and population change. They focus attention on city planning and city promotion.[54] While these historians are sympathetic with social science and behavioral approaches, they object to the determinism of the ecological sociologists which leaves out elements of value. The human and accidental aspects of city building are emphasized, the study of rational as well as nonrational forces operating upon men and communities:

for the history of many American cities, if closely examined, demonstrates a decidedly undeterministic pattern of false starts, fundamental changes in the direction of community policy, and discernible turning points.[55]

The kind of urban studies these historians view as most promising centers upon areas and periods where technological innovation occurs, where social change is obvious and where decision-making can be found. Two works that illustrate the possibilities of this approach are Julius Rubin's *Canal or Railroad? Imitation and Innovation in the Response to the Erie Canal in Philadelphia, Baltimore, and Boston* (1961), and Sam B. Warner Jr.'s

Streetcar Suburbs: The Process of Growth in Boston, 1870-1900 (1962). In the first book, Rubin, an economist, argued that the response of three communities, Philadelphia, Baltimore and Boston to the Erie Canal was quite different and that the different responses were products not of differences in physical characteristics, nor in economic development, but rather of attitudinal differences. As Rubin put it:

> If so, the differences in behavior are to be explained by attitudinal rather than situational factors; by divergencies in the history and traditions of the three regions which produced differences in the attitudes that the decision-making groups brought to the common problem rather than by differences in the problem itself.[56]

In the second book, published by the Joint Center for Urban Studies, Warner studied suburban growth in Roxbury, West Roxbury and Dorchester, Massachusetts, through the examination of 23,000 building permits issued from 1870 to 1900. He was able to derive from this examination a process of growth which included technological change, the introduction of the streetcar; decisional factors, where to locate the lines; social mobility, the rise in occupational status of those moving to the suburbs; and an attitudinal factor, the view of the suburbs. Warner's work tied all of the Wirthian categories together into one neat package; and, since his effort was quantitative, Warner could claim to be as scientific as any ecologist. It is no surprise than that Lubove calls Warner's study one of the most satisfactory of the environmental analyses.[57]

The urban historians who operate with the definition of urbanization as the creation of a city through time

stress both planning and technology, both social organization and change. Two of Lubove's books, *The Progressives and the Slums: Tenement House Reform in New York City, 1890-1917* (1962), and *Community Planning in the 1920's: The Regional Planning Association of America* (1963), reflect his connection of the image of the city with environmental change and social reform, as does his book of readings, *The Urban Community: Housing and Planning in the Progressive Era* (1967). Lubove also emphasizes the changes in ideas from regarding the city as a product of natural forces to the view of the city as a creation of man. Lubove does not ignore technology either; his volumes add this consideration also.

Perhaps more than Lubove, A. Theodore Brown and Charles N. Glaab emphasize the connection between technology and decision-making. Brown's *Frontier Community: Kansas City to 1870* (1963) and Glaab's *Kansas City and the Railroads: Community Policy in the Growth of a Regional Metropolis* (1962) attempt to answer the question as to how Kansas City was able to become a successful regional center despite challenges from more promising sites. In both cases the answers are complex, involving city promoters, railroad and bridge development and theories of city growth. Moreover, the answers are not deterministic. Glaab and Brown also collaborated to write a general history, *A History of Urban America* (1967). In it, the authors attempt to apply the same conceptual structure which they used in their monographic studies of Kansas City. They concentrate on the process of urbanization and on the factors, physical, social and ideological, that bear on this process. They do not regard the city as a fixed environment initiating social change but treat the city as Lubove says it should be treated, as an "artifact." While *A History of Urban America* has some weaknesses, among them a tendency to overstate the role of the city in America, it is, I think, the most satisfactory urban history to date.

The younger generation of urban historians represented by Brown, Glaab and Lubove are characterized by considerable sophistication, energy and reach. They are not content to concentrate upon one part of urbanization but instead opt for a more comprehensive approach. Neither are they sympathetic with a deterministic, mechanical explanation of urbanization; they prefer humanistic explanations of city development. Because of these qualities, they are the true heirs of Louis Wirth.

For the purpose of this essay, a number of approaches to urban history have been delineated and historians have been arbitrarily placed in one or another category. The author recognizes the injustices done and admits that some urban historians belong in more than one category. McKelvey includes images of the city, Stein is very interested in the symbolic representation of communities. However, the concern has been for the major thrust of each person's ideas.

Urban history will certainly become increasingly important as people concentrate more and more in cities. The paths already laid out will be traveled, improved, widened and made more or less beautiful, but perhaps the really significant organizing principle for urban history has yet to be found. Perhaps it will come from a center for

urban or behavioral studies; perhaps it will come from another discipline; or perhaps some historian, out of his past experience or present inspiration, will hit upon a more satisfactory way of depicting the impact of the city upon American life.

NOTES

1. For bibliographical data see Allen F. Davis, "The American Historian vs. the City," *Social Studies*, LVI (Mar.-Apr. 1965), 91-96, 127-35; and Charles N. Glaab, "The Historian and the American City: A Bibliographical Survey," in Philip M. Hauser and Leo F. Schnore, eds., *The Study of Urbanization* (New York, 1965).
2. John Burchard, "Some Afterthoughts," in Oscar Handlin and John Burchard, eds., *The Historian and the City* (Cambridge, 1963), p. 254.
3. *Ibid.*, "The Death of the City," p. 143.
4. W. Stull Holt in his article, "Some Consequences of the Urban Movement in American History," *Pacific Historical Review*, XXII (Nov. 1953), 337-51, vividly recounts how he discovered that what he thought was an original idea had been anticipated by Channing.
5. "On the Danger of an Urban Interpretation of History," in Eric J. Goldman, ed., *Historiography and Urbanization* (Baltimore, 1941), pp. 67-108.
6. "Some Consequences of the Urban Movement in American History," p. 339.
7. Diamond had pointed to a lower birth rate in the city twelve years before.
8. *The Urban Frontier* (Chicago, 1964), pp. 341-42.
9. "The City in History—Some American Perspectives," in Werner Z. Hirsch, ed., *Urban Life and Form* (New York, 1963), pp. 59-77.
10. *The Urbanization of America*, 1865-1915 (New Brunswick, 1963), p. 32.
11. McKelvey studied Rochester while Green has written histories of Holyoke, Naugatuck and Washington, D.C.
12. McKelvey in his review of *The Rise of Urban America* in the *American Historical Review*, LXXI (Jan. 1966), 680, criticized Green for not emphasizing the importance of the city enough.
13. "The Urbanization Process: An Approach to Historical Research," *Journal of the American Institute of Planners*, XXXIII (Jan. 1967), 33. Lubove sees three categories in urban history: social, cultural, economic and political studies; the formation of the urban environment studies, or urban history as the process of city building

over time; and urbanization as a broad societal process. Lubove believes the second category is the most promising one, since it focuses on city building and makes possible a connection between technology and social organization.

14. R. T. Daland's "Political Science and the Study of Urbanism: A Bibliographical Essay," *American Political Science Review*, LI (June 1957), 491-509, reports on the dearth of interest in urban studies in political science in the 1950s.

15. Leonard Reissman, *The Urban Process: Cities in Industrial Society* (Glencoe, Ill., 1964), p. 98. Reissman's book contains an excellent, short description of various urban sociologists with a corresponding typology into which each is placed. Park and Burgess are called ecological empirists, Wirth and Redfield theoreticians. This should be compared to Gideon Sjoberg's chapter, "Theory and Research in Urban Sociology," in *The Study of Urbanization* where Park and Burgess are identified as the Chicago school and Wirth and Redfield as the urbanization school.

16. "Urbanism As a Way of Life," *American Journal of Sociology*, XLIV (July 1938), 1-24. Wirth's article is a landmark in the field of urbanization. Perhaps Wirth's greatest strength lay in his ability to project into the future. Reissman characterizes Wirth as a deductive theorist, a characterization that is basically sound.

17. This is not to argue that present day urban historians, or sociologists for that matter, recognize their debt to Wirth or call themselves disciples of Wirth. While his framework is a suggestive one, the fitting of individuals into that framework is an arbitrary act. Nor is the framework to be considered as a completely satisfactory one.

18. "Cultural, Behavioral and Ecological Perspectives in the Study of Social Organization," *American Journal of Sociology*, LXV (Sept. 1959), 132-46. Schnore has elaborated on this thesis in *The Urban Scene: Human Ecology and Demography* (New York, 1965).

19. Peter H. Rossi, "Comment," *American Journal of Sociology*, LXV (Sept. 1959), 146-49.

20. "Rejoinder," *American Journal of Sociology*, LXV (Sept. 1959), 149-53.

21. Otis Dudley Duncan does recognize inherent statistical problems in the theory of ecological correlations as seen in his article written with Beverly Davis, "An Alternative to Ecological Correlation," *American Sociological Review*, XVIII (Dec. 1953), 665-66.

22. *The Urban Process*, p. 93. Reissman uses the term neo-ecologists for these sociologists.

23. Roy Lubove has the same criticism in "The Urbanization Process: An Approach to Historical Research." Ecologists err in ignoring the role of values, small groups, interpersonal relations and cultural traits in shaping the city.

24. "American Historians and the Study of Urbanization," *American Historical Review*, LXVII (Oct. 1961), 49-61.

25. "Urbanization and Social Change," *The Historian and the City*.

26. *Ibid.*, pp. 226-27.

27. *Ibid.*, p. 232.

28. *Ibid.*, p. 233.

29. *Ibid.*, p. 236.

30. *Ibid.*, p. 235.

31. *Ibid.*, p. 238.

32. For bibliographical material see "The Historian and the American City: A Bibliographical Survey."

33. *Poverty and Progress* (Cambridge, 1964), p. 216.

34. *Ibid.*, p. 239.

35. *Poverty and Progress* has aroused much opposition as might be expected from its temerity in attacking a giant like Warner. Reviewers of the book had a number of qualifications both about Thernstrom's methods and conclusions.

The necessity of history in community studies is not a position solely held by historians, however, as several sociologists testify. These sociologists—John R. Seeley, Morris S. Schwartz, Kurt H. Wolff and Maurice Stein—have opted for the older tradition of humanistic, historical sociology instead of the middle range theories of Merton and the structural-functional bifurcation of the majority of sociologists of the day. For representative essays see Maurice Stein and Arthur J. Vidich, eds., *Sociology On Trial* (1963), and Arthur J. Vidich, Joseph Bensman and Maurice Stein, eds., *Reflections on Community Studies* (1964). Perhaps the most vocal and impressive individual in this group, the author, is Maurice Stein. As early as 1960, Stein's *The Eclipse of Community* traced the history of twentieth-century sociology, focusing upon the reasons for the switch of interest from community to small groups studies. His major conclusion was that the change from the study of cities to a study of peer groups was a reflection of new attitudes and tensions in sociologists themselves. Stein even spoke kindly of Park and the Lynds, at a time when such praise was quite out of fashion. To further his heresy, Stein recommended the use of some of Collingwood's insights by sociologists. (Indeed, the burden of Stein and his ilk is that the participant-observer must attain a kind of empathy with the community he is studying.) Stein, in relating how he came to a position of appreciating "how much was lost when historical contexts were abandoned in favor of historical generalizations whether these took the form of structural-functional propositions or survey reports," shows some of the characteristics of an urban historian. After learning middle range theories at Columbia from Merton, Stein had to teach urban sociology and sociology of community. In order to accomplish this Stein returned to Park, Warner and the Lynds and from them arrived at a working theory of urbanization. For Stein, sociology in the western tradition combines history, system and drama. Orthodox sociology has become interested only in system, neglecting both history and drama. To return to a wider, more vital sociology, it is necessary to turn back to history and to poetic metaphors. The polemic nature of Stein's argument from the left has stimulated much reaction, but may also serve as a corrective to sociological orthodoxy.

36. *Boss Tweed's New York* (New York, 1965).

37. From Schlesinger's *The Rise of the City* (1933) to McKelvey's *The Urbanization of America* (1963) the theme persists. Thirty years is only a short time and the step is small.

38. The thesis of *The Intellectual Versus the City* is contained in an essay by Morton White entitled "Two Stages in the Critique of the American City" in *The Historian and the City*.

39. I am indebted to Charles N. Glaab for this insight. He has proposed to do a study of pro-urban thought which is badly needed. See his "The Historian and the American Urban Tradition," *Wisconsin Magazine of History*, LXVII (Autumn 1963), 12-25, reprinted in A. S. Eisenstadt, *The Craft of American History* (Harper Torchbook, 1966), which elaborates some pro-urban sentiment. Also in opposition to the Whites is Frank Freidel, whose chapter, "Boosters, Intellectuals, and the American City," in *The Historian and the City* suggests many nonintellectuals and even some intellectuals, Benjamin Franklin for one, were procity. Boorstin's *The Americans: The National Experience* (New York, 1965), is supportive of Freidel.

40. "The Poet and the Rise of the City," *Mississippi Valley Historical Review*, XLIX (June 1962), 85-99.

41. *Images of the American City* (New York, 1961). However, Strauss' work has serious flaws in it primarily because of the lack of historical perspective. Had Strauss been more familiar with historical method, the book would have been sounder.

42. *Ibid.*, p. 59.

43. Herbert Gans, another sociologist, in his study of Italian-Americans in Boston, *The Urban Villagers* (1962), concludes that the populace did live in a symbolically bounded village. There is no logical reason why the city, contrary to Tönnies and Redfield, could not be an exten-

sion of village or folk culture. Oscar Lewis has shown that this is possible in Mexico and New York City.

44. (Cambridge, 1960), pp. 2-3.

45. *Ibid.*, p. 8.

46. *Ibid.*, p. 12.

47. Jerome Bruner in "Education as Social Invention," *Saturday Review* (Feb. 19, 1966), mentions Lynch's project with favor. Of course, the idea of underlying structure is one of Bruner's favorites, so the praise is not unexpected.

48. *The City of Man* (New York, 1953) and with Henry H. Reed, *American Skyline* (Cambridge, 1953). The first is more general, treating both European and American cities; the second is specifically oriented to the design history of American cities.

49. (Princeton, 1965).

50. *Ibid.*, p. 524.

51. The earlier views of the fair as an artistic disaster seem to be disappearing, perhaps as the proponents of Sullivan and Wright lose some of their popularity. One suspects that the denial of design that Reps, Tunnard and Lynch attack is in part a product of the rejection of nineteenth-century art and artistic values. If Victorian furniture becomes more popular (as it seems to be), this may herald further change.

52. For an article reflecting the conjunction, see R. Richard Wohl and A. Theodore Brown, "The Usable Past: A Study of Historical Traditions in Kansas City," *Huntington Library Quarterly*, XXIII (May 1960), 237-59.

53. "The Urbanization Process: An Approach to Historical Research," p. 33.

54. *Ibid.*; A. Theodore Brown and Charles N. Glaab, "Nature and Enterprise: Two Studies in the Culture of 19th Century Midwestern City Growth," *Bulletin of the Central Mississippi Valley American Studies Association*, II (Fall 1958), 1-19; Charles N. Glaab, "Visions of Metropolis: William Gilpin and Theories of City Growth in the American West," *Wisconsin Journal of History*, LXV (Autumn 1961), 21-31.

55. "Visions of Metropolis: William Gilpin and Theories of City Growth in the American West," p. 31.

56. (New York, 1961), p. 9.

57. "The Urbanization Process: An Approach to Historical Research," p. 38.

The Urbanization Process:
An Approach to Historical Research

Roy Lubove

Urban history, as understood today, is virtually synonymous with everything that happened in cities. In this urban-conscious era the city threatens to substitute for the frontier, or settlement of the West, as the key to explaining the evolution of American life. This trend is encouraged by those planners and other practitioners who seek a "usable past" to serve as a guide to current policy decisions. If, however, we are to spare the city from becoming a kind of historical variety store—a thematic free-for-all used to explain everything, and hence nothing—it is necessary to limit or define the subject. An historian once warned against an indiscriminate "urban interpretation of history." "If the city or urbanization is to be used in a causal sense," William Diamond suggested, we would have to distinguish between the "effects of urbanism, of adjustment to urbanism, and of cultural change common to city and country alike."[1] Otherwise urbanism might fallaciously be equated with broad societal trends like capitalism, industrialism, or class stratification, thus obscuring cause and effect relationships.

THE EXISTING LITERATURE

The last few years have witnessed an eruption of "urban" history, which can be divided into three broad (but not rigidly exclusive) categories.[2] Social-cultural, economic, and political studies, or some combination of them, represent one group.[3] Least satisfactory in this omnibus category are the city biographies and general accounts of urbanization. Most lack any significant conceptual framework, or fail to distinguish between urban and national history. Some are altogether episodic and trite in the antiquarian-booster tradition. The main point is that all the publications in this category deal with cities, or life in cities, but rarely with urban history as distinguished from social, economic, or political history in the context of cities.

A second group of recent publications deals with the formation of the urban environment.[4] They focus upon architecture and landscape design, housing, planning, economic development, transportation, and decisions affecting land use. Almost entirely a product of the last few years, these environmental studies provide clues to the future direction of research. A city, essentially, is an artifact, a physical container within which complex human and institutional relationships are established, and essential maintenance functions performed. This physical container or environment consists of a structure ("the spatial organization of key functional areas and essential service facilities . . . in response to certain fundamental living needs and activities of human society") and a form ("the visually perceptive features of the city which this structure produces, both the two-dimensional and three-dimen-

From the *Journal of the American Institute of Planners,* Vol. XXXIII, No. 1 (January 1967), pp. 33-39. Reprinted by permission of the publisher. Roy Lubove is Associate Professor of American History at the University of Pittsburgh.

sional forms created by surface, spaces, structures, and circulatory systems in a defined natural setting").[5] Urban history would benefit from much greater emphasis on environmental development: the specific decision by individuals or institutions which influenced urban form and structure, and with broader, social, economic, and technological trends which determined the nature of these decisions.

THE CITY BUILDING PROCESS

Apart from its intrinsic importance in the evolution of cities, environmental development suggests a more satisfactory definition of the field. Rather than viewing urban history as synonymous with everything that happened in cities, we might define it as the study of *the process of city-building over time.* The term "process" implies more attention to "observer-defined" issues (decision-making, organization, change mechanisms) in contrast to "actor-defined" problems (social pathologies and reform).[6] Reform, of course, can be viewed as a process. It is a legitimate subject of investigation, and part of the broader issue centering on the psychological-social impact of cities. Yet reform can be understood best in the context of the city-building process. Housing betterment efforts in the nineteenth and early twentieth centuries, for example, cannot be understood independently of building and sanitary technology, communications and transportation, design and subdivision practices, and a commodity conception of land and housing which allocated major decision-making responsibility to the private, speculative sector.

More generally, a focus upon the city-building process would provide a framework for analyzing social organization and change. The human personality is socially conditioned; it is the product of interpersonal relationships through which behavioral norms are transmitted and reinforced.[7] The spatial-temporal distribution of population, functions, and institutions plays a significant role in the patterning of these relationships. Depending on the aspirations and life styles of individuals or groups, differential environments might be accommodative or dysfunctional. Without subscribing to an environmental determinism, one can acknowledge that environment performs enabling and constraining functions. It provides or inhibits satisfactions throughout the life cycle and influences patterns of child rearing, family life, or peer group interaction. In this context it might be profitable to examine residential design practices in relation to social organization.[8] What is the social expression of low-rise as opposed to high-rise habitation; detached, row house or cluster development; superblock or grid subdivision? More feasible, perhaps, in terms of available historical data, would be local and sublocal studies dealing with the life styles of various population groups, and the enabling or constraining role of differential environments. An urban history addressed to the city-building process can, potentially, help clarify the elusive relationship between personality, social organization, and environment.[9] It provides a framework for examining both environmental and social change over time. Not least important this approach stimulates, if it does not necessitate, an urban history rooted in the behavioral and social sciences. It may never be possible to develop a sophisticated historical psychometrics, but it is worth trying.

An urban history addressed to the city-building process can certainly contribute to the evolution of a community typology. "Urbanization" or "city" is presently an umbrella term which encompasses a vast diversity of human experience and community types. There has never been, however, a single urban pattern. The range of American community types includes the commercial port towns, capitals and farm villages of the Colonial Era; the nineteenth century mill towns, communitarian settlements, industrial cities, and western speculative communities; and the twentieth century metropolitan centers, mass suburbs, and emergent new towns. These and other community types differed substantially according to function and scale, social homogeneity, nature of authority, and planning (or its absence). Thus community type can serve as an analytic tool for exploring the city-building process and specifically the relationship between environmental and social change. Similarly, rather than dealing with planning, housing, and other environmental variables as broad societal or administrative phenomena, it would be more accurate and realistic to trace their evolution in this community type context.

TECHNOLOGY: AN IMPORTANT
COMPONENT

Besides its value as a framework in which to explore social organization and change (implying strong links to the behavioral and social sciences), a focus upon the city-building process mandates greater emphasis upon technological development. Technology is presently ignored in much urban history, or is mentioned in passing as a sequence of invention, or is taken for granted in the sense we all know the pre-automobile city differs in form and scale from the modern day metropolis. Not only is technology a key variable associated with "distinc-

tive types of social structure," but the industrial-urban order essentially differs from the pre-industrial or feudal society in its dependence upon "inanimate sources of energy, a complex set of tools, and specialized scientific know-how in the production of goods and services."[10]

It is disappointing that such seminal works by Lewis Mumford as *Technics and Civilization* (1934) and *The Culture of Cities* (1938) have exerted so little influence in the writing of urban history (not to mention the sociological-anthropological tradition which treats technology as a cultural expression).[11] Mumford provided important clues for dealing with the relationship between invention and technology, social organization, and city-building. First and foremost, he interpreted technology as a cultural phenomenon which influenced and was influenced by "wishes, habits, ideas, goals." To put it another way, he explored the "translation of technical improvements into social processes" and the converse—the embodiment of social processes and norms in technology and the machine.[12] Mumford's account of the evolution of the "cult of the machine" from the Middle Ages to the seventeenth century provides a good example of his methodology. He examines the interaction of technics and culture in terms of the monastery-clock-measured time complex; the space-distance-movement perception of the Renaissance artist and cartographer; the impact of capitalism and commercial expansion upon space-time concepts; the changing view of nature identified with experimental science; and new patterns of social regimentation epitomized in militarism and bureaucracy.[13]

Mumford's synthesis of technology and culture, applied to the city-building process, is particularly suggestive. He is concerned not only with the shaping of urban environments through architecture, building, or transportation, but with the role of changing energy sources. City-building, Mumford recognized, is profoundly influenced by what might be termed the low-yield to high-yield energy continuum. Elaborating upon the categories and terminology devised by Patrick Geddes, Mumford divides history into a sequence of eras organized around a "technological complex." Each is rooted in distinctive resources and energy systems which, in turn, produce their representative urban types. He thus distinguishes between eotechnic civilization (tenth to eighteenth centuries: wind and water, wood and glass); paleotechnic (eighteenth to nineteenth centuries: coal and steam engine, iron); and neotechnic (1880s: electricity and dynamo, new alloys and lighter metals).[14] As William Cottrell later observed, civilization is a function of energy surpluses; the "amounts and types of energy employed condition man's way of life materially and set somewhat predictable limits on what he can do and on how society will be organized."[15] In short, the city-building process, including social organization, might be examined in relation to changes in "energy converters and fuel."

The existing body of urban history offers a surfeit of narratives about cities, and an abundance of tales about life in cities; but it largely fails to explain the city-building process in relation to technology and social organization. However, other disciplines—economics, geography, anthopology, sociology—provide insights into the nature of cities, as well as methods and concepts which might be applied to urban historical research as defined here. Space does not permit a detailed survey, but for purposes of illustration I would cite the regional studies of geographers and economists.[16] Urban history might, for example, deal with the evolution and relationship of community types, urban units, or urban-rural units over time, using the analytic tools developed by urban geographers such as "central-place" functions and "hierarchy of central places."[17] Regional economics, exemplified in the *Economic Study of the Pittsburgh Region,* suggests the use of "locational" and "economic mix" theory in tracing the history of urban development on a regional scale.[18] More specifically, it sheds light on the relationship between technology, environment, and community structure. The central theme concerns the rise and fall of an economic system superbly adapted to the coal, iron-steel, and railroad technology of the nineteenth century; and how a single locational-technological advantage—accessibility to the Connellsville coal fields—both insured Pittsburgh's industrial preeminence after 1880, and shaped the regional community pattern of metropolis, mining village, mill town, and country hamlet. Subsequently, the life of the region was affected by the emergence of by-product coke ovens, which proved more economical when situated near the furnaces rather than the mines. Pittsburgh's competitive advantage in the production of iron and steel was destroyed when access to the new, rapidly growing markets of the West became more important than access to a single source of coking coal. Other regions could compete when Connellsville coke declined in importance as the key differential in pig iron (and hence, steel) costs.

Pittsburgh's economic mix—centering on a limited number of heavy industries, and large plant organization—profoundly influenced the composition of the labor force and many other features of the regional community life. It ultimately created rigidities which have inhibited adaptation to twentieth century technological and market imperatives. Other communities have forged ahead in electronics, space, and diversity of service industries with all this implies for population growth or composition, and the nature of the community system. In short, transportation and communications technology have reduced in importance the kind of competitive-place advantage Pittsburgh enjoyed in the nineteenth century, and have enhanced the role of nontransportable, natural amenities in determining community evolution.[19]

It might be noted, in connection with electronics technology, that the relationship between communications and urbanization has not been systematically explored.[20] Richard Meier, for one, maintains that "research on urban communications systems seems to provide much greater rewards—in the form of more powerful explanations—than does research in the more traditional fields." The functioning of a city, he claims, can be studied in terms of the "origins, paths, contents, and destinations" of the communications network. From the perspective of social organization, "an increase in the communications rate is a prerequisite of socioeconomic growth, but overloading of communications channels causes distress and disorganization."[21] One might be skeptical of any tendency toward a communications reductionism, but the subject has played too vital a role in city-building to remain neglected.

I have suggested, thus far, that urban historiography can be divided into three categories. The first, indistinguishable from the history of everything that happened in cities, has produced some excellent social, cultural or political history, but not urban history as defined in this paper. The second category, embodied in the small nucleus of studies dealing with the creation of the urban environment, holds greater promise. It proposes a definition of urban history as the process of city-building over time. This implies a focus upon the city as a physical entity—an artifact—and the use of this framework to explore technological and social change. The third category is just emerging. Rooted in demography, statistics, and human ecology, it views urbanization as a broad societal process. It traces its lineage to Adna F. Weber's classic, *The Growth of Cities in the Nineteenth Century*.

THE ECOLOGIC COMPLEX

"The growth of cities," Weber wrote, "must be studied as a part of the question of the distribution of population, which is always dependent upon the economic organization of society—upon the constant striving to maintain as many people as possible upon a given area."[22] Since Weber, the distinctive feature of this approach to the study of cities has been its preoccupation with demographic phenomena. Human ecology, the branch of urban sociology developed by Park, Burgess, McKenzie, and others in the 1920's, devoted much attention to the spatial-temporal distribution of population aggregates.[23] According to a later formulation by Amos Hawley, the "focus of attention in ecology is upon the population which is either organized or in process of becoming organized." Ecology, and human ecology in particular, dealt basically with "population problems"; these included the "ways in which the develop-

ing community is affected by the size, composition, and rate of growth or decline of the population," as well as the "significance of migration for both the development of the community and the maintenance of community stability." In broadest terms, human ecology examined the "adjustment of population to the resources and other physical conditions of the habitat."[24]

Hope Tisdale, in the early 1940's, published an important theoretical statement on the demographic-ecological approach to urbanization. It was defined as a "process of population concentration," expressed in "multiplication of the points of concentration and the increase in size of individual concentrations." Cities, in this sense, were points or nodes of population concentration, and everything which influenced population change became relevant to the study of urbanization. Tisdale maintained that people were one of two requisites to urbanization—the other was technology. Urbanization was rooted in population movements, but technology determined the "form and focus" of the process. Two definitions of urbanization were objectionable from the Tisdale perspective. Urbanization viewed as a "process of radiation whereby ideas and practices spread out from the urban center" failed to "explain the appearance and growth of cities"; while city growth interpreted as an "increase in intensity of problems or traits or characteristics that are essentially urban" resulted in a "confusion of cause and effect, the presupposition of cities before urbanization." Most objectionable of all was the implicit corollary that "as problems are solved, as traits disappear, as characteristics change, deurbanization sets in."[25]

In recent years a number of sociologists, notably O. D. Duncan and Leo Schnore, have labored to establish demography and ecology as the focal points of urban research. This has led to a definition of the urbanization process in terms of an "ecological complex." This complex includes, according to Duncan and Schnore, "population, environment, technology, and organization" as the key variables.[26] Although the temporal-areal distribution of population is only one element of the complex, it sems to be favored. "The logic of ecological theory" forces the "analyst to view distinctive activities—their numbers and kinds—as *properties of aggregates of populations*."[27]

Eric Lampard has consistently (and single-handedly) urged the wholesale adaptation of ecological complex theory to urban history. "Until recently," Lampard argues, "historians have had little cause for satisfaction with their contributions to the field." American urban hisory was "largely the history of cities and their 'problems,' not the history of urbanization." Seeking relief from the variety store level of conceptualization, Lampard urged a relatively "unambiguous" definition of urbanization "in terms of population concentration." Within this framework, urbanization and community structure would be interpreted as the "outcome of a changing balance between population and environment (including habitat and other populations) moderated by technology and organization."[28] In effect, the ecological complex implied an urban historiography which dealt with the "phenomenon of population concentration and certain apparent trends in social organization, structure, and behavior." Specific cities would be studied as "an accommodation of the general movement (urbanization) to a particular set of demographic, institutional, technological, and environmental circumstances—including the contingencies of events and personalities."[29]

CITY BUILDING AND ECOLOGIC COMPLEX APPROACHES: COMPARISONS

Both the ecological complex and what I have termed the city-building process assign a major role to technology and related economic changes. Lampard describes the ecological complex as "especially suited to the analysis of those social and economic changes which are associated with industrialization."[30] He examines these changes in one study with particular emphasis upon the impact of specialization: the *"essential link between the technical and spatial conditions of economic progress."*[31] On the question of social organization, however, the theory is somewhat ambiguous. Social organization is always included as a variable, and Lampard maintains that contingencies of events and personalities are encompassed in the formulation. Just how they are encompassed, however, is clear neither in the theory nor its application. Indeed, Duncan and Schnore are critical of any behavioral, cultural analysis of social organization which focuses on the individual, on small group or interpersonal relationships, on values, or on culture "traits." They argue that the ecologist "takes the aggregate as his frame of reference and deliberately sets out to account for the forms that social organization assumes in response to varying demographic, technological, and environmental pressures." He concentrates upon "transformations of patterns of social organization" rather than "shifts in value systems or modal character structure."[32]

In favoring the analysis of aggregates

and broad societal processes, notably demography, ecological complex research has made several useful contributions. A great deal of empirical data has been synthesized (though at times one wonders if much of it is not reducible to a numbers game played with U. S. Census Reports). It has advanced our understanding of the metropolitan community—its structural, functional, and demographic differentiation, and central city-suburban relationships.[33] In minimizing the role of behavioral and subjective phenomena as change-agents, however, it limits its usefulness as a research tool. This applies to technology as well as social organization. Lewis Mumford, and more recently, Gideon Sjoberg, recognize that technology possesses a subjective dimension. Its evolution is conditioned by those very "shifts in value systems" which Schnore and Duncan relegate to the limbo of behaviorism and cultural "trait complexes." As Julius Rubin, in an important study of entrepreneurship and urban development, demonstrates, understanding of the historical process "depends as much upon the analysis of the subjective traits of groups as it does upon the analysis of the pressure of objective circumstances." Various communities, after 1825, responded differently to the challenge of the Erie Canal and emergence of the railroad, and these "differences in behavior are to be explained by attitudinal rather than situational factors; by divergences in the history and traditions of the three regions (Boston, Philadelphia, Baltimore), which produced differences in the attitudes that the decision-making groups brought to the common problem rather than by differences in the problem itself."[34]

One important contrast between the ecological complex and what I term the

city-building process centers on this issue of social organization, and the respective weight assigned to subjective,
attitudinal variables. I would maintain,
especially on the level of local and sublocal urban historiography, that social
psychology, cultural anthopology, interpersonal psychiatry, or interactionist sociology can prove useful. They can help
in explaining just how technology and
environment interact with population to
produce a structured behavioral-organi-
zational field.

The two approaches differ in another
way. The ecological complex interprets
urbanization as a broad societal process,
with singular emphasis upon the "secular phenomenon of population concentration, the multiplication of points of
concentration, or of relations among
concentrations of different size and density in various parts of the country at different times in our history."[35] I have
used the term "city-building" rather
than urbanization in order to emphasize
the weight attached to the literal process
of environmental formation. This implies
not only a concern for what geographers
call the urban "site," but for the whole
range of city-building mechanisms: architecture and landscape architecture,
housing and housing finance, the real
estate market and realty institutions,
transportation, communications, public
health and sanitation, industrial technology, and business organization. In the
most general sense, it implies an awareness of the city as an artifact whose
form and structure are greatly determined by decisions which affect land
use.[36]

The ecological complex, in practice,
frequently loses sight of the city as an
artifact. One learns about the flux of
population aggregates and their characteristics, about demographic concentra-

tions, diffusions and distributions—but
not about the specific decisions which
shaped the specific environments of specific cities, and the relationship of this
"city-building complex" to technology
and social organization. Urbanization, as
such, is an abstraction. Cities are the
entities with which one must deal, in the
final analysis, and they are created by
concrete decisions over time.

NOTES

1. William Diamond, "On the Dangers of an Urban Interpretation of History," in Eric F. Goldman (ed.), *Historiography and Urbanization: Essays in American History in Honor of W. Stull
Holt* (Baltimore: Johns Hopkins Press, 1941), pp.
96, 106, 107.
2. This paper is based primarily, though not exclusively, upon publications relating to American
urban history which have appeared since 1960.
No effort has been made to achieve complete bibliographical coverage. Previous issues of the Urban
History Group *Newsletter* (1954—), and a number
of bibliographical essays contain more complete
listings. See, Blake McKelvey, "American Urban
History Today," *American Historical Review*, LVII
(July, 1952), 919-929; Philip Dawson and Sam
B. Warner, Jr., "A Selection of Works Relating to
the History of Cities," in Oscar Handlin and John
Burchard (eds.), *The Historian and the City*
(Cambridge: MIT Press, 1963), pp. 270-290;
Allen F. Davis, "The American Historian vs. the
City," *Social Studies*, LVI (March, April, 1965),
91-96, 127-135; Charles N. Glaab, "The Historian
and the American City: A Bibliographic Survey,"
in Philip M. Hauser and Leo F. Schnore, *The
Study of Urbanization* (New York: John Wiley
and Sons, 1965), pp. 53-80.
Urbanization and historiography are examined
in the following: Arthur M. Schlesinger, Sr., "The
City in American History," *Mississippi Valley His-
torical Review*, XXVII (June, 1940), 43-66; Wil-
liam Diamond, "On the Dangers of an Urban Interpretation of History," in Eric F. Goldman (ed.),
*Historiography and Urbanization: Essays in Amer-
ican History in Honor of W. Stull Holt* (Balti-
more: Johns Hopkins Press, 1941), 67-108; David
H. Pinkney, "Urban Studies and the Histo an,"
Social Forces, XXVIII (May, 1950), 423-429;
W. Stull Holt, "Some Conseq nces of the Urban
Movement in American History," *Pacific Historical
Review*, XXII (November, 1953), 337-351; R.
Richard Wohl, "Urbanism, Urbanity, and the His-
torian," *University of Kansas City Review*, XXII
(Autumn, 1955), 53-61; Asa Briggs, The Study
of Cities," *Confluence*, VII (Summer, 1958), 107-

114; Mark D. Hirsch, "Reflections on Urban History and Urban Reform, 1856-1915," in Donald Sheehan and Harold C. Syrett (eds.), *Essays in American Historiography: Papers Presented in Honor of Allan Nevins* (New York: Columbia University Press, 1960), 109-137; Eric E. Lampard, "American Historians and the Study of Urbanization," *American Historical Review*, LXVII (October, 1961), 49-61; Charles N. Glaab, "The Historian and the American Urban Tradition," *Wisconsin Magazine of History*, XLVII (Autumn, 1963), 12-25; Oscar Handlin, "The Modern City as a Field of Historical Study," in Handlin and Burchard (eds.), *The Historian and the City*, 1-26.

3. The following publications are listed rather than evaluated. Many are excellent historical studies, irrespective of their relevance to the definition of urban history developed in this paper. Among the socio-cultural studies are: Moses Rischin, *The Promised City: New York's Jews, 1870-1914* (Cambridge, Mass.: Harvard University Press, 1962); Morton and Lucia White, *The Intellectual Versus the City: From Thomas Jefferson to Frank Lloyd Wright* (Cambridge, Mass.: Harvard University Press, 1962); Seth M. Scheiner, *Negro Mecca: A History of the Negro in New York City, 1865-1920* (New York: New York University Press, 1965); Gilbert Osofsky, *Harlem: The Making of a Ghetto: Negro New York, 1890-1930* (New York: Harper and Row, 1966); Donald B. Cole, *Immigrant City: Lawrence, Massachusetts, 1845-1921* (Chapel Hill: University of North Carolina Press, 1963); Stephan Thernstrom, *Poverty and Progress: Social Mobility in a Nineteenth Century City* (Cambridge, Mass.: Harvard University Press, 1964; Harold Kirker and James Kirker, *Bulfinch's Boston, 1787-1817* (New York: Oxford University Press, 1964); Richard C. Wade, *Slavery in the Cities: The South, 1820-1860* (New York: Oxford University Press, 1964); Alan Trachtenberg, *Brooklyn Bridge: Fact and Symbol* (New York: Oxford University Press, 1965). Also relevant are, George A. Dunlap, *The City in the American Novel, 1789-1900* (Philadelphia: Russell, 1934); Blanche H. Gelfant, *The American City Novel, 1900-1940* (Norman: University of Oklahoma Press, 1954); Robert H. Walker, "The Poet and the Rise of the City," *Mississippi Valley Historical Review*, 49 (June, 1962), 85-99; Anselm L. Strauss, *Images of the American City* (New York: Free Press, 1961). Comparative studies include, Richard C. Wade, *The Urban Frontier: The Rise of Western Cities, 1790-1830* (Cambridge, Mass.: Harvard University Press, 1959), and Asa Briggs, *Victorian Cities* (New York: Harper and Row, 1965), orig. pub., 1963. For earlier comparative works see, Carl Bridenbaugh, *Cities in the Wilderness: The First Century of Urban Life in America, 1625-1742* (New York: Ronald Press, 1938), Bridenbaugh, *Cities in Revolt, Urban Life in America, 1743-1776* (New York: Alfred A. Knopf, 1955), and Constance M.

Green, *American Cities in the Growth of the Nation* (New York: J. DeGraff, 1957).

City politics are examined in the following: Charles Garrett, *The La Guardia Years: Machine and Reform Politics in New York City* (New Brunswick: Rutgers University Press, 1961); William D. Miller, *Mr. Crump of Memphis* (Baton Rouge, Louisiana State University Press, 1964); Alex Gottfried, *Boss Cermak of Chicago: A Study of Political Leadership* (Seattle: University of Washington Press, 1962). Also political in orientation, but set apart because of its emphasis on communications networks, is Seymour J. Mandelbaum, *Boss Tweed's New York* (New York: John Wiley and Sons, 1965).

The following are economic in orientation, with particular emphasis upon entrepreneurship: Charles N. Glaab, "Business Patterns in the Growth of a Midwestern City: The Kansas City Business Community before the Civil War," *Business History Review*, XXXIII (Summer, 1959), pp. 156-174; Glaab, *Kansas City and the Railroads: Community Policy in the Growth of a Regional Metropolis* (Madison: Wisconsin State Historical Society, 1962); Julius Rubin, *Canal or Railroad? Imitation and Innovation in the Response to the Erie Canal in Philadelphia, Baltimore, and Boston* (Philadelphia: American Philosophical Society, 1961); A. Theodore Brown, *Frontier Community: Kansas City to 1870* (Columbia: University of Missouri Press, 1963). Earlier economic studies include: Vera Shlakman, *Economic History of a Factory Town: A Study of Chicopee, Massachusetts* (Northhampton, Mass., 1935); Constance M. Green, *Holyoke, Massachusetts: A Case History of the Industrial Revolution in America* (New Haven: Yale University Press, 1939); Robert G. Albion, *The Rise of New York Port, 1815-1860* (New York: The Shoe String Press, 1939); Catherine E. Reiser, *Pittsburgh's Commercial Development, 1800-1850* (Harrisburg, Pa., 1951).

Among the urban biographies are: Robert C. Reinders, *End of an Era: New Orleans, 1850-1860* (New Orleans: Pelican Pub. Co., 1965); Bayrd Still, *Milwaukee: The History of a City* (Madison: Wisconsin State Historical Society, 1948); Lawrence L. Graves (ed.), *A History of Lubbock* (Lubbock: Texas Technological College, 1962); Constance M. Green, *Washington: Village and Capital, 1800-1878* (Princeton: Princeton University Press, 1962) and Green, *Washington: Capital City, 1869-1950* (Princeton: Princeton University Press, 1963); Thomas C. Wheeler (ed.), *A Vanishing America: The Life and Times of the Small Town* (New York: Holt, Rinehart and Winston, 1964); Edward Wagenknecht, *Chicago* (Norman: University of Oklahoma Press, 1964); Sidney Glazer, *Detroit: A Study in Urban Development* (New York: Twayne Pub., 1965). The most ambitious biographies are Blake McKelvey, *Rochester, I. The Water-Power City, 1812-1854, II. The Flower City, 1855-1890, III. The Quest for Quality, 1890-1925, IV. Rochester: An Emerging Me-*

tropolis, 1925-1961 (Cambridge: James Hineman Pub. and Rochester, N.Y., 1945-1961); and Bessie L. Pierce, *A History of Chicago*, I. *The Beginning of a City, 1673-1848*, II. *From Town to City, 1848-1871*, III. *The Rise of a Modern City, 1871-1893* (New York: Alfred H. Knopf, 1937-1957). Two examples of collective biography are, James B. Allen, *The Company Town in the American West* (Norman: University of Oklahoma Press, 1966), and Page Smith, *As a City Upon a Hill: The Town in American History* (New York, Knopf, 1966). General accounts of urbanization include, Arthur M. Schlesinger, *The Rise of the City, 1878-1898* (New York: The Macmillan Co., 1933); Constance M. Green, *The Rise of Urban America* (New York: Harper and Row, 1965); Blake McKelvey, *The Urbanization of America, 1860-1915* (New Brunswick: Rutgers University Press, 1963). A comparative, structural analysis by a sociologist is, Gideon Sjoberg, *The Preindustrial City: Past and Present* (Glencoe: The Free Press, 1960). In a class by themselves are, Lewis Mumford, *The Culture of Cities* (New York: Harcourt, Brace and World, Inc., 1938) and Mumford, *The City in History: Its Origins, Its Transformations, and Its Prospects* (New York: Harcourt, Brace and World, Inc., 1961). A number of articles deal with specialized phases of urbanization: Leon S. Marshall, "The English and American Industrial City of the Nineteenth Century," *Western Pennsylvania Historical Magazine*, XX (September, 1937), 169-180; Marshall, "The Emergence of the First Industrial City: Manchester, 1780-1850," and Ralph E. Turner, "The Industrial City: Center of Cultural Change," in Caroline F. Ware (ed.), *The Cultural Approach to History* (New York: Kennikat Press, 1940), 140-161, 228-242; Bayrd Still, "Patterns of Mid-Nineteenth Century Urbanization in the Middle West," *Mississippi Valley Historical Review*, XXVIII (September, 1941), 187-206; Francis P. Weisenburger, "The Urbanization of the Middle West: Town and Village in the Pioneer Period," *Indiana Magazine of History*, XLI (March, 1945), 19-30; Oscar O. Winther, "The Rise of Metropolitan Los Angeles," *Huntington Library Quarterly*, X (August, 1947), 391-405; Frederick D. Kershner, Jr., "From Country Town to Industrial City: The Urban Pattern in Indianapolis," *Indiana Magazine of History*, XLV (December, 1949), 327-338. Bessie L. Pierce, "Changing Urban Patterns in the Mississippi Valley," *Journal of the Illinois State Historical Society*, XLIII (Spring, 1950), 46-57; R. Richard Wohl and A. Theodore Brown, "The Usable Past: A Study of Historical Traditions in Kansas City," *Huntington Library Quarterly*, XXIII (May, 1960), 237-259.

4. Sam B. Warner, Jr., *Streetcar Suburbs: The Process of Growth in Boston, 1870-1900* (Cambridge: Harvard University Press, 1962); George W. Hilton and John F. Duc, *The Electric Interurban Railways in America* (Stanford, Calif.: Stanford University Press, 1960, 1964); Roy Lu-

bove, *The Progressives and the Slums: Tenement House Reform in New York City, 1890-1917* (Pittsburgh: University of Pittsburgh Press, 1962), Lubove, *Community Planning in the 1920's: The Regional Planning Association of America* (Pittsburgh: University of Pittsburgh Press, 1963), Lubove (ed.), *H.W.S. Cleveland, Landscape Architecture as Applied to the Wants of the West* (Pittsburgh: University of Pittsburgh Press, 1965); William H. Wilson, *The City Beautiful Movement in Kansas City* (Columbia: University of Missouri Press, 1964); James E. Vance, Jr., *Geography and Urban Evolution in the San Francisco Bay Area* (Berkeley: University of California Press, 1964); Edmund H. Chapman, *Cleveland: Village to Metropolis: A Case Study of Problems of Urban Development in Nineteenth-Century America* (Cleveland: Western Reserve University Press, 1964); E. A. Gutkind, *Urban Development in Central Europe* (Glencoe: The Free Press, 1964), Vol. I., International History of City Development; Donald J. Olsen, *Town Planning in London: The Eighteenth and Nineteenth Centuries* (New Haven: Yale University Press, 1964). John W. Reps, *The Making of Urban America: A History of City Planning in the United States* (Princeton: Princeton University Press, 1965); Sumner C. Powell, *Puritan Village: The Formation of a New England Town* (Anchor edition, New York: Doubleday and Co., 1965), orig. publ., 1963; Carl W. Condit, *The Chicago School of Architecture: A History of Commercial and Public Building in the Chicago Area, 1875-1925* (Chicago: University of Chicago Press, 1964). Relevant also are; S. Giedion, *Space, Time and Architecture: The Growth of a New Tradition* (Cambridge: Harvard University Press, 1941 and subsequent editions); Lewis Mumford, *Sticks and Stones: A Study of American Architecture and Civilization*, orig. pub., 1924, *The Brown Decades: A Study of the Arts in America, 1865-1895*, orig. pub., 1931 (New York: Dover Publications Inc., 1955); John Coolidge, *Mill and Mansion: A Study of Architecture and Society in Lowell, Massachusetts, 1820-1850* (New York: Columbia University Press, 1942); David H. Pinkney, *Napoleon III and the Rebuilding of Paris* (Princeton: Princeton University Press, 1958); Nelson M. Blake, *Water for the Cities: A History of the Urban Water Supply Problem in the United States* (Syracuse: Syracuse University Press, 1956); Paul F. Conkin, *Tomorrow a New World: The New Deal Community Program* (Ithaca: Cornell University Press, 1959); Walter M. Whitchill, *Boston: A Topographical History* (Cambridge: Harvard University Press, 1959); Lloyd Rodwin, *Housing and Economic Progress: A Study of the Housing Experience of Boston's Middle-Income Families* (Cambridge: MIT Press, 1961).

Several of the volumes cited in category one (note 2) also deal, in one way or another, with the formation of the urban physical environment. The economic studies are particularly pertinent.

In terms of the definition of urban history developed in this paper, the most satisfactory of the environmental analyses are those which attempt to relate environmental and social change. A good example is Sam B. Warner's *Streetcar Suburbs*.

5. F. Stuart Chapin, "Foundations of Urban Planning," in Werner Z. Hirsch (ed.), *Urban Life and Form* (New York: Holt, Rinehart and Winston, 1963), p. 234. Also, Kevin Lynch, *The Image of the City* (Cambridge: MIT Press, 1960); and various articles in Kevin Lynch and Lloyd Rodwin (eds.), "The Future Metropolis," *Daedalus*, XC (Winter, 1961).

6. Hugh Douglas Price, *The Metropolis and its Problems* (Syracuse: Syracuse University Press, 1960), p. 25.

7. H. S. Perry and M. L. Gawel (eds.), *Harry S. Sullivan: Interpersonal Theory of Psychiatry* (New York: Norton, 1953). The sociological equivalent, interactionism, is explored in, Arnold M. Rose (ed.), *Human Behavior and Social Processes: An Interactionist Approach* (Boston: Houghton Mifflin Co., 1962). Both theories derive, in part, from social psychology. See, Anselm Strauss (ed.), *The Social Psychology of George H. Mead* (Chicago: University of Chicago Press, 1956).

8. Leon Festinger, Stanley Schachter, and Kurt Black, *Social Pressures in Informal Groups: A Study of Human Factors in Housing* (New York: Stanford, 1950), is pertinent. Also, Anthony F. C. Wallace, *Housing and Social Structure: A Preliminary Survey, with Particular Reference to Multi-Story, Low Rent, Public Housing Projects* (Philadelphia Housing Authority, 1962); Daniel M. Wilner, et al., *The Housing Environment and Family Life: A Longitudinal Study of the Effects of Housing on Morbidity and Mental Health* (Baltimore: Johns Hopkins Press, 1963); Alvin L. Schorr, *Slums and Social Insecurity* (Washington, D. C.: Social Security Administration, 1963); Herbert Gans, *The Urban Villagers: Group and Class in the Life of Italian Americans* (Glencoe, Ill.: The Free Press, 1962) and Gans, "Urbanism and Suburbanism as Ways of Life: A Re-evaluation of Definitions," in Rose (ed.), *Human Behavior and Social Processes*, pp. 625-648; Warren A. Peterson and George K. Zollschan, "Social Processes in the Metropolitan Community," *ibid.*, pp. 649-666.

9. Marc Fried and Peggy Gleicher, "Some Sources of Residential Satisfaction in an Urban Slum," *AIP Journal*, XXVII (November, 1961), 305-315, deals with Boston's West End. According to the authors, "the importance of localism in the West End, as well as in other working-class areas, can hardly be emphasized enough. This sense of a local spatial identity includes both local social relationships and local places." (p. 308.)

10. Sjoberg, *The Preindustrial City*, pp. 7, 12.

11. See also, Mumford, *Art and Technics* (New York: Columbia University Press, 1952). For the treatment of technology as a cultural phenomenon by sociologists and anthropologists see, "Social

Aspects of Technology," *The Selected Papers of Bernhard J. Stern* (New York: 1959); Otis D. Duncan (ed.), *William F. Ogburn: On Culture and Social Change* (Chicago: University of Chicago Press, 1964) and William F. Ogburn, *Social Change with Respect to Cultural and Original Nature* (New York: Dell Pub. Co., 1966) orig. publ. 1922; Melville J. Herskovits, *Economic Anthropology: The Economic Life of Primitive Peoples* (New York: W. W. Norton and Co., 1965 (orig. publ. 1940; Leslie A. White, *The Evolution of Culture: The Development of Civilizations to the Fall of Rome* (New York: McGraw-Hill, 1959); C. Daryll Forde, *Habitat, Economy and Society* (New York: E. P. Dutton and Co., 1963) orig. publ. 1949. Relevant also by an archeologist is V. Gordon Childe, *Man Makes Himself* (New York: The New American Library of World Literature, Inc., 1951) and Childe, *What Happened in History* (Baltimore: Penguin Books, Inc., 1964).

12. Lewis Mumford, *Technics and Civilization* (New York: Harcourt, Brace and World, Inc., 1934), pp. 3, 281.

13. *Ibid.*, 9-59.

14. The paleotechnic economy, according to Mumford, appeared as a mutant during the eotechnic era in the form of the blast furnace and primitive railway. The eotechnic economy persisted as a recessive until the last quarter of the nineteenth century. Writing in the late 1930's, Mumford described the eotechnic complex as a survival, the paleotechnic as a recessive, and the neotechnic as a dominant. He refers also to an emergent "biotechnic economy" in which the "biological sciences will be freely applied to technology, and in which technology itself will be oriented toward the culture of life." Generally, the biologic and social arts will take precedence over the mechanical. Mumford, *Culture of Cities*, 495-496.

15. William F. Cottrell, *Energy and Society: The Relation between Energy, Social Change, and Economic Development* (New York: McGraw-Hill, 1955), p. 32; and Joseph Mayer, "Foreword," *Ibid.*, VII.

16. This is covered in, Hauser and Schnore, *The Study of Urbanization*.

17. See, Harold M. Mayer, "A Survey of Urban Geography," *Ibid.*, 81-113. Mayer defines the central place as a "cluster of service functions located at the point most accessible to the maximum 'profit area' which can be commanded." The hierarchy of central places is defined as the "symbiotic nesting relationship of higher- and lower-order centers." (p. 89). For an example of historical urban geography see, Robert E. Dickinson, *The West European City: A Geographical Interpretation* (New York: Humanities Press, Inc., 1962). Also by Dickinson, *City, Region and Regionalism: A Geographical Contribution to Human Ecology* (New York: Humanities Press, Inc., 1947).

18. *Pittsburgh Regional Planning Association Eco-*

nomic *Study of the Pittsburgh Region: Region in Transition, Portrait of a Region,* and *Region with a Future* (Pittsburgh: Univ. of Pittsburgh Press, 1963). Along similar lines, see the eight volumes of the *New York Metropolitan Region Study* (Raymond Vernon, director). An example of regional economic analysis by an historian, suggesting the potentialities of this approach to urbanization and urban-rural relationships is, Julius Rubin, "City and Region in the Economic Growth of the American North and South before the Civil War," (unpublished, 1965).

19. Edward L. Ullman, "Amenities as a Factor in Regional Growth," *Geographical Review,* XLIV (January, 1954), 119-132; Melvin M. Webber, "Order in Diversity: Community without Propinquity," in Lowdon Wingo, Jr. (ed.), *Cities and Space: The Future Use of Urban Land* (Baltimore: Johns Hopkins Press, 1963), p. 47.

20. Mandelbaum, *Boss Tweed's New York,* is an exception.

21. Richard L. Meier, *A Communications Theory of Urban Growth* (Cambridge: 1962), Vol. 1, 2.

22. Adna F. Weber, *The Growth of Cities in the Nineteenth Century: A Study in Statistics,* orig. pub., 1899. (Ithaca: Cornell Univ. Press, 1963), p. 157.

23. The Burgess concentric zone hypothesis concerning urban growth became one of the best known and controversial contributions of the early ecologists. See, Ernest W. Burgess, "The Growth of the City: An Introduction to a Research Project," *Publications of the American Sociological Society,* XVIII (1924), 85-97; James A. Quinn, "The Burgess Zonal Hypothesis and its Critics," *American Sociological Review,* V (April, 1940), 210-218. Also by Quinn, *Human Ecology* (New York: J. B. Lippincott Co., 1950). Critical of the human ecologists as "positivistic, deterministic, mechanistic, and organismic," was Warner E. Gettys, "Human Ecology and Social Theory," *Social Forces,* XVIII (May, 1940), 469-476. Also, Mila A. Alihan, *Social Ecology: A Critical Analysis* (New York: Cooper Sq. Pub., 1938).

24. Amos H. Hawley, "Ecology and Human Ecology and Human Ecology," *Social Forces,* XXII (May, 1944), 403, 404, 405. A fuller account by Hawley, is, *Human Ecology: A Theory of Community Structure* (New York: Ronald, 1950).

25. Hope Tisdale, "The Process of Urbanization," *Social Forces,* XX (March, 1942), 311, 315.

26. Otis D. Duncan and Leo F. Schnore, "Cultural, Behavioral, and Ecological Perspectives in the Study of Social Organization," *American Journal of Sociology,* LXV (September, 1959), 135.

27. *Ibid.,* 137.

28. Lampard, "American Historians and the Study of Urbanization," pp. 49, 54, 60.

29. Eric E. Lampard, "Urbanization and Social Change: On Broadening the Scope and Relevance of Urban History," in Handlin and Burchard (eds.), *The Historian and the City,* pp. 233-234,

237. Lampard also outlines his views in "Urbanization and Urban History," *Colloquium* (Fall, 1965), pp. 12-17, 20-22.

30. Lampard, "American Historians and the Study of Urbanization," p. 60.

31. Eric E. Lampard, "The History of Cities in Economically Advanced Areas," *Economic Development and Cultural Change,* III (1954-55), 88. Specialization and the division of labor as requisites to large-scale urbanization are also stressed in, Jack P. Gibbs and Walter T. Martin, "Urbanization, Technology, and the Division of Labor: International Patterns," *American Sociological Review,* XXVII (October, 1962), 667-677. Urbanization requires that "materials be brought from great distances." Since this, in turn, depends upon specialization and technology, it follows that "the level of urbanization is contingent, at least in part, on the division of labor and technology." (p. 668.)

32. Duncan and Schnore, "Cultural, Behavioral, and Ecological Perspectives in the Study of Social Organization," pp. 144, 142. Similarly, the ecologist "is interested in the pattern of observable physical activity itself rather than the subjective expectations that individuals may entertain of their roles." (p. 137.)

33. Philip M. Hauser, "Ecological Aspects of Urban Research," in Leonard D. White (ed.), *The State of the Social Sciences* (Chicago: Univ. of Chicago Press, 1956). Along with ecological research on the metropolitan phenomenon, Hauser cites the group of studies dealing with the "specific temporal and mobility aspects of urban structure and function." (p. 237.) An example of the ecological complex approach to urbanization is, Leo F. Schnore, *The Urban Scene: Human Ecology and Demography* (New York: The Free Press, 1965).

34. Rubin, *Canal or Railroad?,* pp. 96, 9. Supporting such conclusions is, Glaab, *Kansas City and the Railroads.*

35. Lampard, "American Historians and the Study of Urbanization," p. 50.

36. William H. Form, "The Place of Social Structure in the Determination of Land Use: Some Implications for a Theory of Urban Ecology," *Social Forces,* XXXII (May, 1954), 317-323. Form argues that the "traditional ecological processes," based upon "models of eighteenth century free enterprise economics," are "no longer adequate tools to analyze changes in land use." (p. 323.) Sjoberg offers a similar criticism—"a clear account of the materialist view they espouse is definitely in order; more crucial still is the need to enumerate those premises apparently adapted from Classical Economics." Sjoberg also calls for clarification of terms, and challenges the validity of a theory of social organization and urbanism which ignores values. Gideon Sjoberg, "Theory and Research in Urban Sociology," in Hauser and Schnore, *The Study of Urbanization,* p. 66.

Reflections on the New Urban History

STEPHAN THERNSTROM

The boundaries of the modern metropolis are elusive. Once the city could be described as "a tightly settled and organized unit in which people, activities and riches are crowded into a very small area clearly separated from its nonurban surroundings," but no more.[1] Instead there is mixture, coalescence, "urban sprawl," which has blurred or erased delineations which earlier seemed meaningful.

The boundaries of the field of urban history today seem equally elusive. The label "urban" is now coming into fashion in history, as in some other disciplines. Courses in the subject have multiplied; texts and readers are being rushed into print; there are urban history newsletters published in both the United States and Britain, and an enormous, monographic literature that professes to be urban history or at least is so considered by some observers. What unites this large and disparate body of work, however, is unclear. Urban history apparently deals with cities, or with city-dwellers, or with events that transpired in cities, or with attitudes toward cities—which makes one wonder what is *not* urban history.

Nearly a decade ago Eric Lampard attempted to bring some order into the chaos by offering a penetrating critique of the existing literature and a series of suggestions for the systematic historical study not of "the city" but of "urbanization as a societal process."[2] Drawing upon recent advances in demography and human ecology, as well as upon his training in economic history, he sketched "a framework for the comparative study of the development and organization of interdependent communities in terms that embrace both westward and urban movements of population, changes in the spatial, occupational and social structures of population, and of sustenance activities." Urban history in this view was not a distinct field but a part of social history; Lampard at one point declared that his aim was to provide "a more certain and systematic foundation for the writing of American social history."

At first it seemed that this advice had fallen upon deaf ears. A discussion of Lampard's manifesto was held at the 1961 American Historical Association meetings; the questioning of the author, according to one observer, "revealed limited understanding of his position and less sympathy for it."[3] Even today we lack much in the way of research that seems to be a direct outcome of Lampard's plea. The broad framework he proposed has not yet been the source of a major book on "urbanization as a societal process."

Lampard's insistence on the relevance of demographic and ecological perspectives, however, prefigured a development that took place in the

From *Daedalus*, Vol. 100 (Spring 1971), pp. 359-75. Reprinted by permission of the publisher. Stephan Thernstrom is Professor of History at the University of California, Los Angeles.

United States in the 1960's—the emergence of an intellectual tendency that I have called, for want of a better term, "the new urban history."[4]

The label "the new urban history" may have been somewhat misleading in three respects. First, the image it conveyed of a monolithic "old" history was obviously oversimplified. Earlier work by a number of well-established scholars pointed in the direction in which the new urban historians were to move; Oscar Handlin's studies of immigration and assimilation, for instance, were important models.

It did, however, seem that most historical writing about cities and city-dwellers was deficient, not only because it lacked the breadth and analytical rigor which Lampard called for but because it dealt with only a small segment of the population—the visible, articulate elements of the community rather than the masses of ordinary people. The existing literature was based largely upon traditional literary sources, sources which were socially skewed. They revealed relatively little of the social experience of ordinary people, and when they did treat ordinary people they spoke with the accent of a particular class, and too often indicated more about the perceptions of that class than about life at the lower rungs of the social ladder.

This complaint, and consequent appeals for a new "grassroots" history, a history "from the bottom up," had often been heard before.[5] What was somewhat new in this instance was the awareness of readily available and largely unexploited historical sources which could be used for these purposes. The discovery of the parish register as a source of demographic information permitted and stimulated the rich outpouring of work in English and French historical demography in recent years; in similar fashion, the discovery of surviving manuscript schedules of the United States Census, and then of a host of similar materials—city directories, local tax lists, and so forth —provided the base for the new urban history in the United States.

Not that these sources were entirely unknown to previous investigators, any more than the English and French parish registers were.[6] The problem was how to use them to full advantage. The sheer quantity and complexity of the information they contained was bewildering; simply reading the material and turning it over in one's mind would not do at all. It was this pressing need, I think, more than any prior conviction about the desirability of importing the methods of other social sciences into history that made us look to other disciplines for useful concepts, analytical techniques, and data-processing methods. The desire to explore new territory forced the selective borrowing of new methods; we did not make forays across disciplinary boundaries for the sheer joy of seeing what was on the other side.

A second possibly misleading feature of the phrase, "the new urban history," lies with the term "urban," which seems to imply that this is a distinctive specialized field of historical inquiry. I am doubtful about that. The city is a distinctive legal entity, and there are certain phenomena peculiar to it. But the decisive features of urban life in modern times are not spatially distributed in a way that justifies urban history, or for that matter urban sociology, as a special field.[7] The delineation of fields is, of course, largely a matter of convenience, and I do not call for a moratorium on the use of "urban" in course descriptions and the like. It is important, however, to recognize that most of the subjects that have preoccupied the new urban historians—the flow of population from country to city, patterns of social stratification and social mobility, the social consequences of technological change, the distribution of property and power, the position of ethnic and racial groups, and so on—are not confined to the city, and should not be approached as if they were. They involve the workings of the society as a whole, though of course they have different manifestations in communities of varying sizes and types. It is not paradoxical, therefore, that the volume which in a sense marked the beginning of the new urban history—Merle Curti's 1959 study, *The Making of an American Community*—dealt not with a city at all, but with a rural county in Wisconsin.[8] The modern city is so intimately linked to the society around it, and is so important a part of the entire social order that few of its aspects can safely be examined in isolation. The term "urban" in the label "the new urban history" is thus not to be taken as a disavowal of interest in what happens outside cities, nor as a claim that here is a new historical field with a turf of its own from which trespassers should be warned. The ultimate aim of the new urban historian, in my view at least, is to understand how and why the complex of changes suggested by the concept "urbanization" reshaped society. Urban history, in this formulation, lies squarely within the domain of social history, and for the student of modern society it is indeed nearly coterminous with social history.

A final comment on the label "the new urban history" is that although it consciously echoes "the new economic history," the analogy should not be pressed too far. Quantitative evidence plays a greater role in both types of literature than in their traditional counterparts. In both there is less sheer description, and more use of theory. But the differences are important.

The new economic historians are equipped with a theory that purports to represent the workings of a total system and which can be employed to resolve questions about the past as well as the present. The relationship of the new urban historians to theory is quite different. There can be debate over the applicability of modern economic theory to particular historical problems, but there is little question that it is a very powerful tool for dealing with certain kinds of issues. A comparably powerful general social theory which bears upon the matters of prime concern to the urban historian simply does not exist as yet.

There is some reason, indeed, to doubt that it ever will, given the nature of human society. This is not the place to argue the case at length, but there are good grounds for denying the relevance of the universalist model of explanation to historical analysis, and for believing that it is more profitable to strive for theoretical generalizations of a more modest scope, limited in space and time, restricted to certain contexts.[9] I would be the last to argue that it is the business of the historian to concentrate on the ineffable uniqueness of his subject and to refrain from generalization at all. The historian, I think, should generalize as widely as he can, and should strive to "make his conceptualization more explicit, his use of theory more deliberate, his effort to derive further hypotheses for testing bolder and more systematic."[10] But when the desire to abstract, schematize, and universalize leads to the neglect of *essential* features of the historical context, as can be said about a number of efforts to apply imported social science theories to historical problems, we have not advanced knowledge. One principal function of historical research informed by social science concerns is precisely to edit, refine, and enrich theory by identifying and exploring important historical developments which cannot be neatly explained by existing theory.

The relationship of the new urban historian to social science theory, therefore, is critical and eclectic. Instead of applying *a* theory, like the new economic historian, he must draw upon a variety of social sciences, as well as his own historical sense, to identify elements of the historical situation that may have been important and to gain clues as to how these might be measured and analyzed. Perhaps it will some day be possible to develop a model of the process of urbanization which applies equally well to ancient Athens and contemporary Chicago, though I doubt it, but it seems in any event clear that to search for such regularities today, given both the state of existing social science theory and the level of present understanding of the social systems of those two communities, would be unrewarding.

For the present, high priority must go to the careful description and analysis of particular communities and the processes which formed them, for little is known about even some of the most elementary aspects of these matters. As J. A. Banks sensibly observes, "no useful purpose is served by putting forward plausible hypotheses to explain the 'facts' when we do not know what the facts are."[11] There are, of course, facts in abundance in the massive existing literature of American urban history, but they are of little value for two reasons. For the most part, as previously noted, these works focused upon formal institutions and the articulate elements of the community, to the neglect of underlying social processes and mass behavior. Second, earlier investigators typically assumed the uniqueness of the community with which they dealt, and arranged their evidence in categories that precluded systematic comparison with other cities; "the usual shelf of urban history books," Sam B. Warner remarks, "looks like a line of disconnected local histories."[12]

A good many scholars now at work are conscious of both of these failings and are attempting to remedy them. There is growing agreement on the dimensions of past urban life that are most in need of study, and a new awareness of the need to employ categories that will facilitate systematic comparison and contrast. There are, however, important practical difficulties to be overcome. These stem from the character of the available evidence. The United States Bureau of the Census and a host of other governmental and private bodies regularly produce information about the social and economic characteristics of city-dwellers. In some instances the published aggregated data can readily be used to illuminate an important issue, as in a recent study which computed indexes of dissimilarity for nineteenth-century immigrant groups from census data on their distribution by ward and challenged common assumptions about "the ghetto."[13]

Most of the published evidence, however, is not sufficiently rich to supply the details which are analytically strategic. Thus the occupational distribution of Irish immigrants living in American cities in 1870 can be discovered, but not that of the Negroes with whom one would like to compare them. Separate tabulations for blacks were made in subsequent censuses, but never any which distinguished black migrants from the rural South from Negroes born in the North and long familiar with urban culture, information essential to any attempt to determine the extent to which the occupational handicaps of black city-dwellers were attributable to the rural origins of much of the group.

Furthermore, even the most detailed census material provides only a snapshot at one moment in time, when what is needed is an understanding of the dynamics of a process occurring over time.[14] The population registration systems of a few favored European countries supply longitudinal evidence concerning a few basic characteristics; elsewhere the urban historian has to *create* it by painstakingly tracing people over a span of years. Only by following him through subsequent manuscript census schedules, tax records, city directories, and the like can we discover whether the Michael O'Reilly who had fled the Irish potato famine only to find little more to eat for himself and his family as a day laborer in the slums of Boston in 1850 later found a better job, became a homeowner, lived in a better neighborhood, became a pillar of his church and the Democratic party, and was able to educate his children. Only by tracing the experiences of hundreds of Michael O'Reillys and his contemporaries from other backgrounds can one develop systematic knowledge of the dynamics of urban social stratification in the past.

Even in the age of the computer this is a difficult task. The development of electronic data-processing methods has been of crucial significance to historians working in this field, but not because the computer makes it possible to treat dozens of cities simultaneously rather than only one. The computer rather allows the investigator to do in one setting kinds of microscopic social analyses that were previously impossible, except in communities with a very small population.[15] To treat any large city in this fashion entails the manipulation of enormous quantities of data. In my current Boston research I have dozens of items of information about each of nearly 8,000 individual sample members, close to half a million facts to be made sense of. Other ongoing studies of Buffalo and Philadelphia in the nineteenth century treat the total population rather than selected samples, and involve several million items.[16] To collect this mass of evidence is itself a gigantic task, and then there are hard intellectual choices to be made as to coding schemes and analytical procedures. No wonder, then, that at this point one can make only highly provisional generalizations about the process of urbanization in the American past, generalizations based on a scattering of cases that may not be representative. When we possess rather detailed knowledge about the common laborers of Newburyport, Massachusetts, in the late nineteenth century but lack comparable observations about the laborers of New York City, it is risky to generalize about the urban working class of the period.

There is a further important limitation upon what is known at present. Most investigators have done their probing in one brief period, 1850-1880, because the richest source for such studies—the manuscript schedules of the United States Census—are available for only those years. Prior to 1850 the census provided little social data; most of the 1890 schedules were destroyed by fire; and the 1900 and subsequent censuses are still closed to investigators. In fact there are other sources which are nearly as satisfactory for these purposes; for the post-1880 period in Boston I have employed marriage license files, birth certificates, city directories, and assessor's valuation records, for instance, and in states like New York and New Jersey there are manuscript schedules from excellent state censuses which extend into the twentieth century.[17] A number of new demographic studies of colonial New England communities suggest that it may be possible to treat the pre-1850 as well as the post-1880 period satisfactorily.[18] But the first research in the new urban history was stimulated by discovery of the uses of the U. S. Census manuscript schedules, and most of the work published so far is limited in its chronological focus by the availability of those materials.

To emphasize these practical limitations is not, of course, to call for a twenty-year moratorium on generalization and speculation until all the facts are in. As the following examples illustrate, a number of studies already done have corrected significant distortions in our understanding of the past and have shed new light on important issues.[19]

1. *Urban population fluidity.* Nineteenth-century Americans assumed that the supply of free land in the West assured free movement, and that the city was a closed, confining, static en-

vironment. Frederick Jackson Turner gave eloquent expression to this view, and it later found seeming confirmation in several studies which disclosed extremely high rates of population turnover on the frontier. Recent research, however, places the matter in a very different perspective, for it appears that the urban population was if anything *more* volatile than the rural population.[20] The burgeoning cities drew into them many more newcomers than rural areas long before the closing of the frontier at the end of the century. What is more, migration to the city was a more complex and dynamic process than has been understood, for only a minority of newcomers permanently settled in the community they first entered. Cities grew rapidly from the heavy volume of net in-migration, but gross in-migration was several times higher than that, for there was massive out-migration at the same time. Boston, for example, then a city of less than half a million, gained some 65,000 new residents from net migration between 1880 and 1890, but more than a million people moved through the city in those years to produce that net gain! The typical urban migrant moved through three or more communities before he settled down around middle age. We have long been aware that cities grew by attracting outsiders into them, but the magnitude of the incessant flow of people into and out of them has never been suspected.

This holds for small communities in the late-nineteenth century—Newburyport, Poughkeepsie—as well as for large ones like Boston, Chicago, Omaha, and Philadelphia, and it applies to southern cities like Birmingham and Atlanta as much as to northern communities. Small cities, indeed, appear to have had somewhat less stable populations than large ones, contrary to stereotype, probably because residents of the metropolis could move a considerable distance (socially as well as physically) and still remain within its boundaries. Despite the automobile, improved national communications, and other developments which have generally been thought to have facilitated the flow of people from place to place, the fragmentary data on the period since 1890 suggest the opposite trend—toward a less volatile population.

2. *Class and ethnic differentials in spatial mobility.* Poor people, immigrants, and blacks were trapped in "slums" and "ghettos," while the middle class was free to move on when opportunity beckoned: such is the prevailing stereotype of the American city of the past. Today there is some grain of truth in this view, for well-educated professionals and managers do indeed move from place to place more often than other occupational groups, and it appears that spatial mobility and economic success are positively correlated. In the nineteenth- and early-twentieth-century city, however, the situation was radically different.[21] Groups low on the social scale were spatially much more volatile than their social betters. There were indeed certain ecological clusters of poor people in particular neighborhoods, though the prevalence of ghettos in even this sense has been exaggerated. More important, though, is the recent discovery that few of these individuals lived in any one neighborhood for very long. If there was anything like "a culture of poverty" in the American city, it lacked deep local roots, for most of the people exposed to it were incessantly on the move from place to place. In the

one community for which information is available over a span of a full century—Boston—it was not until the 1930's that the contemporary pattern began to appear.

Two implications follow from this. One is that, while contemporary migration differentials may plausibly be interpreted in terms of an economic model in which labor mobility yields higher returns, the older pattern hints at the existence of a quite different phenomenon—a permanent floating proletariat, ever on the move physically but rarely winning economic gains as a result of movement. This is speculative, for no one has yet devised a convenient method of systematically tracing past out-migrants and assessing how they fared in other communities,[22] but at least one may note that backward extrapolations from current labor mobility studies seem entirely unjustified. No single issue raised thus far by research in the new urban history is in more need of clarification than this one.

A second conclusion of importance may be drawn from this finding: the extreme volatility of the urban masses severely limited the possibilities of mobilizing them politically and socially, and facilitated control by other more stable elements of the population. It is suggestive, for example, that less than a quarter of the working-class residents of Los Angeles in 1900 were still to be found there two decades later, but more than 80 per cent of the members of the six middle-class Protestant sects that dominated the city politically and economically.[23] In these sharp class differentials in out-migration rates lies a clue, perhaps, to the neglect of ordinary working people in the newspapers, local histories, and so on.

The bulk of the citizens who had lived for long in one place and had a wide circle of acquaintances were in fact part of the middle class; they were "the community," while the masses of ordinary workers were transients who could easily be ignored.

3. *Rates and trends in social mobility.* No aspect of urban life in the past is more important than the class structure, and none has received so little serious attention. Implicit assumptions about the functioning of the class system abound in conventional historical accounts, but empirical research into the dynamics of social stratification is rare. Particularly lacking are careful accounts of class as it shapes the life cycle of individuals and their children. The meaning of one's class position depends not only on the advantages or disadvantages it entails today but upon how it affects one's prospects in the future. The study of social mobility, therefore, occupies a central role in the work of the new urban historians.

It is difficult as yet to generalize broadly on the basis of the scattered findings available, for local and temporal variations in opportunity levels were considerable, but it does seem clear that some of my own earlier work—on the laborers of Newburyport—was misleading in its emphasis upon the barriers to working-class occupational achievement. The exceptional sluggishness of the local economy and the large concentration of recent Irish immigrants in the city yielded unduly low estimates of blue collar occupational mobility in general, though even in Newburyport there was impressive social mobility of another kind—advance to home ownership. In other communities, however, the occupational horizon was notably more open.[24] Career mobility a notch or two up the occupational ladder was common, and intergenerational mobility more common still. Four in ten of the sons of the unskilled and semi-skilled workers of Boston attained a middle-class job (though only a minor clerical or sales position in most cases), and another 15 to 20 per cent became skilled craftsmen. Analysis by categories more refined than "skilled," "low white collar," "unskilled," and so on discloses that a great deal of this occupational movement involved only slight changes in status,[25] but the over-all impression of fluidity and openness remains. It is also noteworthy that, despite the old tradition of social criticism which sees the class system becoming more rigid as a result of the spread of factory production, the close of the frontier, the shrinking of class differentials in birth rates, and various other causes, there seems to have been astonishing uniformity in mobility rates over a long span of time.

4. *Immigration and differential opportunity.* Though the social system was impressively fluid, there was enormous variation in the opportunities open to particular ethnic groups.[26] Native Americans of native parentage were generally in a much more advantageous situation than second-generation immigrants of similar class origins, who were in turn better able to advance themselves than their immigrant fathers. As important as these broad differences were variations within these general categories. Poor white rural migrants to Birmingham and Atlanta remained more heavily proletarian than migrants to Boston from rural New England. Particular European groups— the British, the Germans, the Jews—

rose quickly, while others like the Irish and the Italians found the environment far more constricted. It may have been the extreme diversity of the experience of particular groups more than general satisfaction with the social system that accounted for the relative absence of militant working-class protest aimed at fundamental social change.[27] With all of the major immigrant groups, however, there was general upward movement with increased length of residence in America.

5. *Negro migrants and European immigrants.* In recent years the clustering of black city-dwellers on the lowest rungs of the social ladder has often been attributed to the continuing influx of uneducated, unskilled migrants from backward rural areas. Earlier European immigrant groups entered American society at the bottom too, the argument runs, because they were unfamiliar with and ill-adapted to urban industrial ways. It took generations for them to rise; Negroes in general have not yet done so because so many are still first-generation newcomers from the southern countryside. A test of the "last of the immigrants" theory in late-nineteenth-century Boston, however, suggests that few of the economic disabilities of black people were attributable to their lack of acquaintance with urban culture.[28] There were some similarities between black newcomers from the South and Irish immigrants; both groups were overwhelmingly concentrated in menial jobs. But the second-generation Irish moved ahead impressively, though more slowly than their counterparts of British or German background, while northern-born blacks were only a shade better off than the rawest black newcomer. Still more

striking, Negro males whose *fathers* had been born in the North, and who thus had deep family roots in the free black community of antebellum Boston, were in the same dismal position. Even in what was widely regarded as the most advanced and progressive northern city with respect to race relations, and even by comparison with the European immigrant group which was slowest to rise, the situation of blacks was *sui generis*.

This brief review of some of the findings of recent research in the new urban history is meant to be illustrative, not exhaustive. Fascinating work is now under way on black family structure in nineteenth- and early-twentieth-century cities, work which promises to shatter the conventional wisdom on that subject and to force the rewriting of a major portion of American social history.[29] The family structure of other groups and its relationship to other phenomena is just beginning to receive the scrutiny it so clearly deserves.[30] The texture of neighborhood life, and the flow of people between socially distinct sections of the city is coming into focus as another major area for investigation.[31] Institutions like schools, churches, and voluntary associations are coming to be approached in terms of function as well as formal arrangements.[32] The interaction between urban environments and the social organization of work too is beginning to receive serious study.[33]

All this is heartening, but it would be well to conclude on a cautionary note. The emphasis of research in the new urban history thus far has been heavily quantitative. The sources which had been most neglected by previous investigators were peculiarly well-suited to quantitative treatment and seemed to offer a quick pay-off to those willing to attempt it. This was salutary on the whole, I think, because there was a great deal to be learned from even the most simple-minded efforts to measure phenomena which in the past had been discussed on the basis of colorful examples and casual impressions. Andrew Carnegie was a poor boy. Q.E.D.: the typical millionaire of the Gilded Age came from humble origins. (Or, worse yet, Q.E.D.: many poor boys of the era became millionaires.) Some of this work has been superficial, to be sure, or positively misleading. An inadequate formulation of the research problem; the use of categories which blur significant distinctions; employing mathematical techniques ill-suited to the problem at hand: any of these can lead the investigator badly astray. But there are comparable pitfalls for the unwary in every branch of history, and an abundant supply of researchers who will stumble upon them. And it seems to me that the blunders of quantifiers are at least a little more open to exposure and future correction, since the procedure itself forces an investigator to make explicit assumptions which are left implicit in other kinds of work.

There are, however, abuses that eager quantifiers are especially likely to commit, and a word of warning about these is in order. Some enthusiasts appear to assume that the hard evidence that can be gleaned from census schedules, city directories, and the like is the only reliable source of knowledge about past social behavior, and that more traditional sources—newspapers, sermons, manuscripts, novels, and so forth—are so socially skewed as to be quite worthless. What can be counted is real; what cannot is to be left to the storytellers and mythmakers.

This is dangerously obtuse. The descriptive material available in such sources serves several indispensable functions.[34] First, it can provide information essential to arranging harder data in meaningful categories; for instance, instead of imposing an occupational classification scheme derived from research by contemporary sociologists, one may gain clues as to the extent to which division of labor and skill dilution had taken place in particular trades in a given community and develop a scheme more appropriate to the context. Second, such evidence may yield hints of patterns whose existence can be confirmed and explored through statistical analysis; the complaint of a social worker that Irish laborers withdrew their children from school and sacrificed their education in order to accumulate funds to purchase homes suggests a hypothesis worth careful testing. Conversely, descriptive material can assist in the interpretation of relationships that appear in the statistical data by indicating what underlying mechanism produced the observed relationship.

Most important, it is only through such evidence that the investigator may begin to understand the perceptions and emotions of the people he is dealing with. The austerely objective facts uncovered by empirical social research influence the course of history as they are filtered through the consciousness of obstinately subjective human beings. Religion, ideology, cultural traditions—these affected human behavior in the past and shaped the meaning of the demographic and eco-logical patterns which can be neatly plotted on a map or graph. If we fail to grapple with these dimensions of the past and make no effort to examine them in the light of what we know from harder data, we will have shirked the most difficult but also the most re-warding of challenges.

NOTES

For valuable criticisms of an earlier draft of this essay I am indebted to those scholars who attended the Rome Conference, and to Stanley Coben of UCLA, Clyde Griffen of Vassar College, and Herbert Gutman of the University of Rochester.

1. Jean Gottmann, *Megalopolis: The Urban-ized Northeastern Seaboard of the United States* (Cambridge, Mass.: M.I.T. Press, 1961), p. 5.
2. Eric E. Lampard, "American Historians and the Study of Urbanization," *American Historical Review*, 67 (October 1961), 49-61. The argu-ment is further extended in two subsequent papers, "Urbanization and Social Change: On Broadening the Scope and Relevance of Urban History," in Oscar Handlin and John Burchard, eds., *The Historian and the City* (Cambridge, Mass.: M.I.T. Press and Harvard University Press, 1963), pp. 225-247, and "The Dimensions of Urban History: A Footnote to the 'Urban Crisis,'" *Pacific Historical Review*, 39 (August 1970), 261-278.
3. Charles N. Glaab, "The Historian and the American City: A Bibliographic Survey," in Philip M. Hauser and Leo Schnore, eds., *The Study of Urbanization* (New York: Wiley, 1965), pp. 53-80.
4. For examples of such work, see Stephan Thernstrom and Richard Sennett, eds., *Nine-teenth-Century Cities: Essays in the New Urban History* (New Haven: Yale University Press, 1969), and other specimens cited below. For related developments in Britain, see H. J. Dyos, ed., *The Study of Urban History* (London: Edward Arnold Ltd., 1968), chiefly the papers by Dyos, Armstrong, Dyos and Baker, and Foster, and a forthcoming publication of the Cambridge Group for the History of Population and Social Structure, E. A. Wrigley, ed., *The Study of Nineteenth-Century Society*. Work along somewhat similar lines is going on in France, Sweden, and doubtless other countries as well; on Sweden see Sune Åkerman, "Projects and Re-search Priorities," in *Särtryck ur Historisk Tid-skrift* (1970). My limited knowledge, however,

forces me to concentrate on research in American urban history in this paper. In the near future, however, it may be possible to make useful comparative studies of urbanizing communities across national boundaries.
5. See, for instance, the papers by Caroline Ware and Constance M. Green in Caroline Ware, ed., *The Cultural Approach to History* (New York: Columbia University Press, 1940). For that matter, one aim of the New History of the Pro-gressive Era was to "emphasize the experience of the ordinary men and women of the past": Oscar and Mary Handlin, "The New History and the Ethnic Factor in American Life," *Per-spectives in Amerian History*, 4 (1970), 5.
6. Manuscript census schedules were utilized by Oscar Handlin in *Boston's Immigrants: A Study in Acculturation* (Cambridge, Mass.: Harvard University Press, 1941), and extensively by F. L. Owsley and his students in their investigations of the antebellum South; see *Plain Folk of the Old South* (Baton Rouge: Louisiana State Uni-versity Press, 1949) and the monographs upon which that synthesis was based. In neither case, however, was there an attempt to use the sched-ules to trace the changing situation of in-dividuals over time, which has been one of the chief aims of the new urban historians.
7. For a thoughtful appraisal of the state of urban sociology as a field which reaches a similar conclusion, see Robert Gutman and David Popenoe's introduction to *Neighborhood, City and Metropolis: An Integrated Reader in Urban Sociology* (New York: Random House, 1970), pp. 3-23.
8. Curti's work was the first effort to write social history by tracing every resident of a community from census to census for as long as he remained there, and the first to employ mechanical data-processing methods—in this case a counter-sorter rather than a computer—for such purposes. The book was unfortunately conceived as an effort to test Turner's frontier thesis, which was not the most fruitful frame for the data, but the fundamental issues with which it dealt— migration and population turnover, economic and social mobility, the distribution of political power—were precisely the matters the new urban historians sought to explore in other settings.
9. For good statements of this position see Samuel H. Beer, "Political Science and History," in Melvin Richter, ed., *Essays in Theory and History: An Approach to the Social Sciences* (Cambridge, Mass.: Harvard University Press, 1970), pp. 41-73, and William O. Aydelotte, "Notes on the Problem of Historical Generaliza-tion," in Louis Gottschalk, ed., *Generalization in the Writing of History* (Chicago: University of Chicago Press, 1963), pp. 163-172.
10. Beer, "Political Science and History," p. 45.
11. J. A. Banks, "Historical Sociology and the Study of Population," *Dædalus* (Spring 1968), p. 399.

12. Sam B. Warner, "If All the World Were Philadelphia: A Scaffolding for Urban History, 1774-1930," *Amerian Historical Review*, 74 (October 1968), 26-43.

13. Sam B. Warner and Colin B. Burke, "Cultural Change and the Ghetto," *Journal of Contemporary History*, 4 (October 1969), 173-187. See also Stanley Lieberson, *Ethnic Patterns in American Cities* (Glencoe, Ill.: Free Press, 1963), and Karl and Alma Taeuber, *Negroes in Cities: Residential Segregation and Neighborhood Change* (Chicago: Aldine Publishing Company, 1965) for further demonstrations of what can be done with aggregated data.

14. For elaboration, see Stephan Thernstrom, *Poverty and Progress: Social Mobility in a Nineteenth-Century City* (Cambridge, Mass.: Harvard University Press, 1964), passim; Thernstrom, "Notes on the Historical Study of Social Mobility," *Comparative Studies in Society and History*, 10 (January 1968), 162-172.

15. The statistical analysis in *Poverty and Progress* was done by hand tabulation; the drudgery and potential errors were at about the limit of tolerance with even that small city. Five of the nine primarily quantitative projects reported on in *Nineteenth-Century Cities* employed a computer, and in the other four computer analysis is projected for a later stage.

16. The Buffalo study is under the direction of Herbert Gutman of the University of Rochester and Laurence Glasco of the University of Pittsburgh; the Philadelphia project is being done by Theodore Hershberg of the University of Pennsylvania.

17. For a useful guide to these, see Henry J. Dubester, *State Censuses: An Annotated Bibliography of Censuses of Population Taken After the Year 1790 by States and Territories of the United States* (Washington: Library of Congress, 1948).

18. John Demos, *A Little Commonwealth: Family Life in Plymouth Colony* (New York: Oxford University Press, 1970); Philip Greven, *Four Generations: Population, Land, and Family in Colonial Andover, Massachusetts* (Ithaca: Cornell University Press, 1970); Kenneth Lockridge, *A New England Town: The First Hundred Years* (New York: Norton, 1970). Robert Doherty of the University of Pittsburgh will soon be completing a related study, a comparative analysis of urbanization, industrialization, and social change in five New England towns, 1800-1860.

19. Much of what follows is drawn from unpublished sections of my forthcoming study of migration and social mobility in Boston, 1880-1968; unless otherwise indicated, documentation will be found there.

20. For further discussion of population turnover, see Thernstrom and Peter R. Knights, "Men in Motion: Some Data and Speculations on Urban Population Mobility in Nineteenth-Century Amer-ica," *Journal of Interdisciplinary History*, 1 (Fall 1970), and the literature cited there. Additional confirming details may be found in Paul Worthman, "Working Class Mobility in Birmingham, Alabama, 1880-1914," in Tamara K. Hareven, ed., *Anonymous Americans: Explorations in Nineteenth Century Social History* (Englewood Cliffs, N. J.: Prentice-Hall, 1971); Howard P. Chudacoff, "Men in Motion: Residential and Occupational Mobility in Omaha, 1880-1920," Ph.D. diss., University of Chicago, 1969.

21. Thernstrom and Knights, "Men in Motion."

22. For discussion of one rather inconclusive attempt and its difficulties, see *ibid.*

23. Unpublished research in progress by Gregory Singleton of Northwestern University and Michael Hanson of UCLA.

24. Worthman, "Working Class Mobility"; Chudacoff, "Men in Motion"; Richard J. Hopkins, "Occupational and Geographic Mobility in Atlanta, 1870-1896," *Journal of Southern History*, 34 (May 1968), 200-213.

25. Clyde Griffen, "Problems in the Study of Social Mobility," to appear in the *Journal of Social History* in 1971.

26. Stephan Thernstrom, "Immigrants and WASPS: Ethnic Differences in Occupation Mobility in Boston, 1880-1940," in Thernstrom and Sennett, eds., *Nineteenth-Century Cities;* Clyde Griffen, "Making It in America: Social Mobility in Mid-Nineteenth Century Poughkeepsie," *New York History*, 51 (October 1970); Marc Raphael, "The European Immigrant in Los Angeles, 1910-1928," unpublished seminar paper, University of California, Los Angeles, 1970.

27. As suggested by Norman Birnbaum in his afterword to Thernstrom and Sennett, eds., *Nineteenth-Century Cities*, pp. 421-430.

28. Stephan Thernstrom and Elizabeth H. Pleck, "The Last of the Immigrants? A Comparative Analysis of Black and Immigrant Social Mobility in Late-Nineteenth Century Boston," unpublished paper for the 1970 meetings of the Organization of American Historians.

29. A major study by Herbert Gutman is nearing completion.

30. See, for example, the essays by Richard Sennett and Lynn Lees in Thernstrom and Sennett, eds., *Nineteenth-Century Cities;* Sennett's book, *Families Against the City: Middle-Class Homes of Industrial Chicago, 1872-1890* (Cambridge, Mass.: Harvard University Press, 1970); and the forthcoming study of immigrant working-class families by Virginia McLaughlin of Princeton University.

31. See the Griffen and Blumin essays in Thernstrom and Sennett, eds., *Nineteenth-Century Cities;* Chudacoff, "Men in Motion"; Sam B. Warner, *The Private City: Philadelphia in Three Periods of Its Growth* (Philadelphia: University of Pennsylvania Press, 1968); Warner, *Streetcar Suburbs: The Process of Growth in*

Boston, 1870-1900 (Cambridge, Mass.: Harvard University Press, 1962).

32. On education, see Michael B. Katz, *The Irony of Early School Reform: Educational Innovation in Mid-Nineteenth Century Massachusetts* (Cambridge, Mass.: Harvard University Press, 1968); on religion, Gregory Singleton, "Religion and Social Change in Los Angeles, 1850-1930," Ph.D. diss. in progress, University of California, Los Angeles.

33. Warner, *The Private City.*

34. For fuller discussion of some of these, see M. Anderson's chapter on "The Study of Family Structure in Nineteenth-Century Britain," in Wrigley, ed., *Nineteenth-Century Society.*